The USS Arizona Men
75th Anniversary

By

T.J. Cooper

2nd Edition

Dedication

This book is dedicated to all the men of the USS Arizona at Pearl Harbor, Hawaii. I would like to thank Ray Emory who has helped verify many of the details, the USS Arizona Survivor's Association, the many family members of the men who served for their support and contributions, the many VFW and American Legion Posts that have contributed many photos and put me in touch with families and the many State and County Historical Societies. I would also like to thank Nick Soley for all of his help and encouragement with this book. Without the many eyewitness reports and the family stories about these men, this book would not be nearly as interesting.

Much has been written about the Pearl Harbor attack and the loss of ships, but very little has been written about the men that experienced these events first hand. It is my hope that this book will provide a better understanding of the terrible loss we suffered at the hands of the Japanese on that day and create a lasting memory to all the men of the USS Arizona. Some of these men's contributions to this country were lost forever on that day and others would go on to help make this great country what it is today.

Let us never forget the sacrifices made for our freedom and how very important it is that we ensure that these brave men will live on in our hearts and continue to be a symbol of the freedom we all cherish today.

TABLE OF CONTENTS

USS Arizona shipmates May 16, 1937, Bremerton, Washington.
All of these men had served 10 years or more.[1]

_____

[1] Photo of USS Arizona shipmates, May 16, 1937 provided by the granddaughter of Walter Charles Ebel, Diane Moore.

CHAPTER ONE: The Arizona's Last Minutes

The Arizona returned to Pearl Harbor on Friday, December 5, 1941 after spending a week at sea performing training exercises. The men were excited to return to port. Many were planning their shore leave and thinking about presents they would send home for Christmas. To the men, the Arizona was their home. Their shipmates were family. But, on Sunday, December 7th all of that changed.

At 7:57 am sixteen Japanese torpedo planes attacked the northwest side of Ford Island. They were hoping to find American aircraft carriers in port and this was where they normally moored. Instead they found the USS Utah a target ship and the cruiser USS Raleigh. Utah was sunk first.

Meanwhile on board the USS Arizona, men were preparing for Sunday morning services usually held on the quarterdeck. Others were planning their shore leave, or had just returned. Still others were engaged in writing letters home, taking their morning showers or just visiting with other sailors on board. Most of the men were wearing shorts and t-shirts, the uniform of the day.

Corporal, Michael Soley was high in the mainmast, watching the Nevada's band and color guard when his attention was drawn to an aircraft diving. As it roared overhead, he could see red circles on the wings and fuselage. He watched as the Nevada's formation scattered as machine gun blasts hit the deck.

Coxswain, Edward Janikowski had stood the Sunday morning watch for less than a half hour when the warplanes swooped across his ship so low that he could clearly see the faces of the pilots behind their canopies, the wing markings positively identifying them as Japanese. The officer in charge ordered "general quarters" and dispatched Edward to summon key personnel to organize a defense.

Seaman, First Class, Donald Stratton had gotten up early and went for breakfast at 7 am. And then down to sick bay to visit with a friend. He had just stepped out of the mess area near the casemate on the bow of the ship when he could hear sailors yelling and hollering. Looking out at Ford Island he could see all sorts of planes. They would peel off and he could see the Rising Sun insignia on their wings and bombs exploding. He headed for his battle station and arrived at the sky control platform just when "general quarters" sounded.

When "General Quarters" was sounded, those on board, scrambled to their duty stations. Because the power had been knocked out early, the "General Quarters" was in many cases, passed along verbally. The members of the Arizona Band made their way to their battle station, the Black Powder Room. Contrary to what was reported by other sources, the members of the band were not sleeping, they had all headed for the black powder room where they were incinerated instantly when the bomb crashed through 3 levels and exploded in the black powder room.

In a matter of minutes, Arizona was firing back at the bombers. They fired on the high altitude bombers but could not reach them. The shells were bursting before reaching the altitude of the Japanese bombers. A small group of men on the Number II turret remained at their stations firing back while fires and explosions surrounded them. They gave their lives fighting back. In the No. 3 turret, the men were confronted by smoke, darkness and fumes from the sea water reaching the batteries. Water was coming in and was knee deep by the time they were ordered out.

Shortly after 8 a.m., Arizona was hit aft on top of the No. 3 turret and bounced over the side. Another bomb went through the after deck but it didn't explode. The third bomb glanced off the face plate of Turret II and penetrated the deck to explode in the black powder magazine, which in turn, set off adjacent smokeless powder magazines. The explosion shook the ship like an earthquake. There was a huge explosion, raising the ship out of the water followed by a ball of flame that went 500 to 600 feet in the air and through the ship. It engulfed the whole foremast and bow of the ship. Debris showered down on Ford Island. Many of the men on board ship at the time were incinerated. Those that were not incinerated immediately were burned beyond recognition. Many had their clothes burned off and their shoes blown off. A massive effort was underway to get the injured into launches taking them to the USS Solace (Hospital Ship) or to Ford Island where they were taken to first aid stations and later to the Hospital. Many of these injured did not survive their massive injuries. Because of the extreme burns many of these men received, they were unable to identify them. The fires burned for two days. This made recovery or identification of any remains, impossible.

Eighty-seven Marines were attached to the USS Arizona, five officers, eighteen non-commissioned officers and sixty-four nonrated men. One of their battle stations was on the mainmast. When "General Quarters" was sounded they began scurrying up the mainmast only to be cut down by machine gun fire. The explosion in the black powder room sent a fire ball that engulfed the ship. In their attempts to exit the mainmast, the rungs on the ladder were red hot, making it difficult to climb down, many were burned. Once they reached the deck, they were again faced with fires and the strafing from the Japanese planes. The other marine battle station was on gun crews. These men were killed instantly when the bomb hit the black powder room, causing a huge explosion and fire. The whole port compartment, A-704, from the quarter deck on was a flaming inferno. Bodies and fires were everywhere. Of the Eighty-Seven Marines, only fifteen survived.

The injured and badly burned were taken to the Naval Hospital at Pearl. Many of these men died within the first days after the attack. Identified, they were buried initially in the naval cemetery. Later they were moved and the initial identification records were misplaced and they were buried in the Punchbowl as crewmembers of the Arizona "unidentified". Others were transported to the mainland where they spent months recovering from their injuries.

Survivors made their way to the quarterdeck to abandon ship. Those that were able to abandon ship were faced with oil and fires on the water. The men on the launches were faced with the continual strafing from Japanese planes as they attempted to rescue men in the water. Of the compliment of 1,514 officers and men, only 337 survived. Many of those that survived were not on board at the time.

Upon reaching shore, unable to fight back, they were taken to various officers' homes where the wives were handing out clean clothes. Those that had to swim were covered in oil.

Nearly 2 days after the attack, the survivors were marched to the post office, given post cards to fill out stating "I'm Ok will write later". This was the first information family members received.

In the days and weeks to follow, the survivors were put on work crews. Some worked attempting to rescue men still trapped in other ships. Some worked collecting the bodies that were floating on the water. Others were on burial detail.

An attempt to recover bodies from the ship was made. Divers negotiated the oil filled murky waters but the dangers of becoming trapped and injuries to the men made this task too hazardous. The recovery was abandoned.

Unlike the movie "Pearl Harbor" there was no lining up of caskets for people to walk amongst and say their good bye's to. First of all, many of the recovered bodies were unidentifiable. Secondly, because of the danger of disease, they were buried right away. Thirdly, a great majority of the men's bodies were never recovered; they remain on board ship to this day.

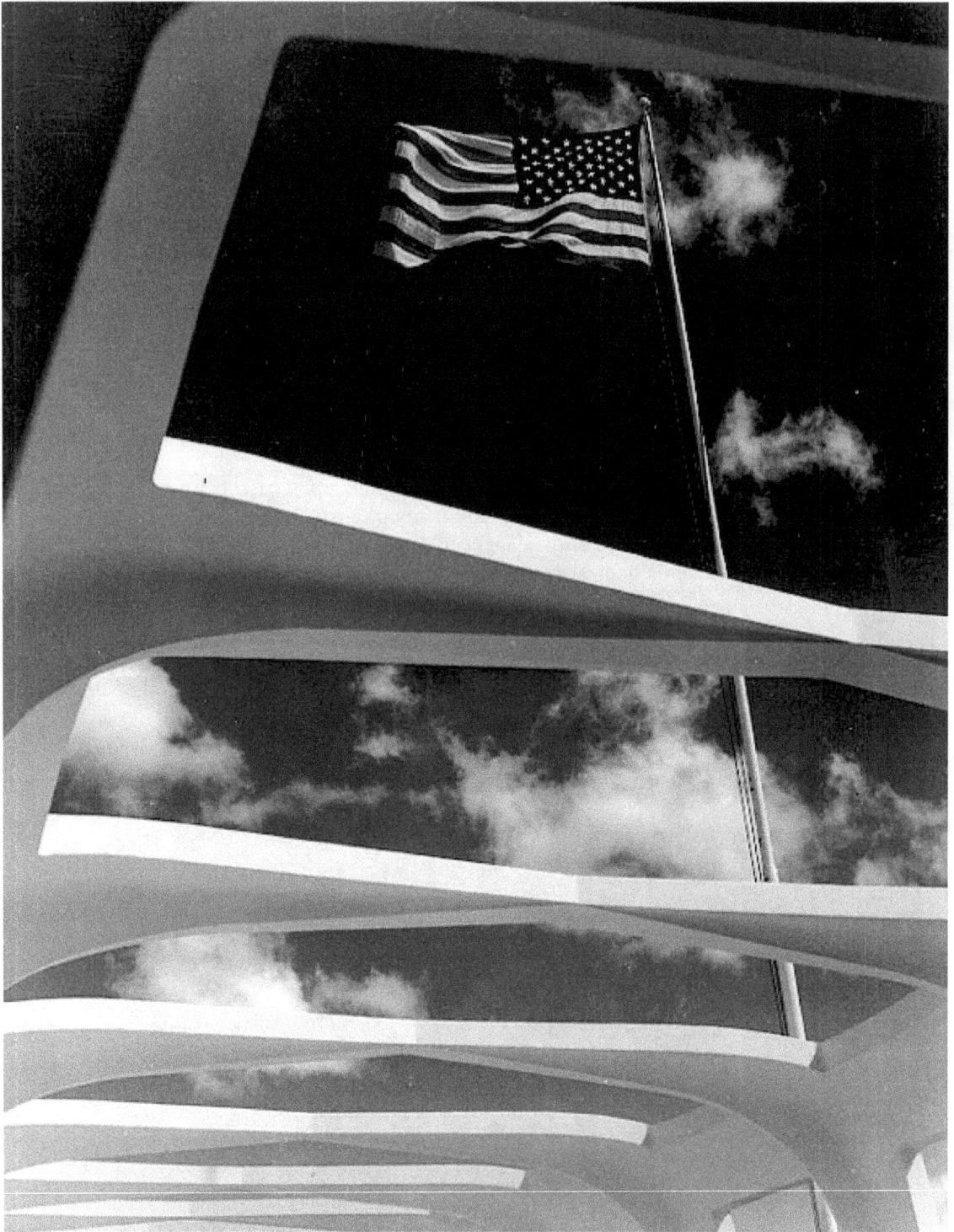

Photo # USN 1072409 Flag of the USS Arizona Memorial at Pearl Harbor, July 1962

CHAPTER TWO: FDR's "Day of Infamy" Speech to the Congress of the United States:

Yesterday, December 7, 1941 -- a date which will live in infamy -- the United States of America was suddenly and deliberately attacked by naval and air forces of the Empire of Japan.

The United States was at peace with that Nation and, at the solicitation of Japan, was still in conversation with its Government and its Emperor looking toward the maintenance of peace in the Pacific. Indeed, one hour after Japanese air squadrons had commenced bombing in Oahu, the Japanese Ambassador to the United States and his colleague delivered to the Secretary of State of form reply to a recent American message. While this reply stated that it seemed useless to continue the existing diplomatic negotiations, it contained no threat or hint of war or armed attack.

It will be recorded that the distance of Hawaii from Japan makes it obvious that the attack was deliberately planned many days or even weeks ago. During the intervening time the Japanese Government had deliberately sought to deceive the United States by false statements and expressions of hope for continued peace.

The attack yesterday on the Hawaiian Islands has caused severe damage to American naval and military forces. Very many American lives have been lost. In addition American ships have been reported torpedoed on the high seas between San Francisco and Honolulu.

Yesterday the Japanese Government also launched an attack against Malaya.

Last night Japanese forces attacked Hong Kong.

Last night Japanese forces attacked Guam.

Last night Japanese forces attacked the Philippine Islands.

Last night the Japanese attacked Midway Island.

Japan has, therefore, undertaken a surprise offensive extending throughout the Pacific area. The facts of yesterday speak for themselves. The people of the United States have already formed their opinions and well understand the implications to the very life and safety of our Nation.

As Commander-in-Chief of the Army and Navy I have directed that all measures be taken for our defense. Always will we remember the character of the onslaught against us.

No matter how long it may take us to overcome this premeditated invasion, the American people in their righteous might will win through to absolute victory.

I believe I interpret the will of the Congress and of the people when I assert that we will not only defend ourselves to the uttermost but will make very certain that this form of treachery shall never endanger us again.

Hostilities exist. There is no blinking at the fact that our people, our territory, and our interests are in grave danger.

With confidence in our armed forces -- with the unbounded determination of our people -- we will gain the inevitable triumph -- so help us God.

I ask that the Congress declare that since the unprovoked and dastardly attack by Japan on Sunday, December seventh, a state of war has existed between the United States and the Japanese Empire.

Franklin D. Roosevelt

CHAPTER THREE: The DANFS History of the USS Arizona (BB-39)

Photo # NH 94785 USS Arizona in the East River, New York City, circa mid-1916

The USS Arizona (BB-39) was laid down on March 16, 1914 at the New York Navy Yard. Launched on June 19, 1915, she was sponsored by Miss Esther Ross, daughter of a prominent Arizona pioneer citizen, Mr. W. W. Ross of Prescott, Arizona. Arizona was commissioned at her builder's yard on October 17, 1916 with Captain John D. McDonald in command.

Arizona departed New York on November 16, 1916 for shakedown training off the Virginia capes and Newport, proceeding thence to Guantanamo Bay, Cuba. She returned to Norfolk on December 16th, and later test fired her battery and conducted torpedo-defense exercises in Tangier Sound. The battleship returned to her builder's yard the day before Christmas of 1916 for post-shakedown overhaul. Completing these repairs and alterations on April 3, 1917, she cleared the yard on that date for Norfolk, arriving there on the following day to join Battleship Division 8.

Within days, the United States entered World War I. Arizona operated out of Norfolk throughout the war, serving as a gunnery training ship and patrolling the waters of the eastern seaboard from the Virginia capes to New York. An oil-burner, she had not been deployed to European waters owing to a scarcity of fuel oil in the British Isles—the base of other American battleships sent to reinforce the Grand Fleet.

A week after the armistice of November 11, 1918 stilled the guns on the western front, Arizona stood out of Hampton Roads for Portland, England, and reached her destination on November 30, 1918, putting to sea with her division on December 12th to rendezvous with the transport George Washington, the ship carrying President Woodrow Wilson to the Paris Peace

Conference. Arizona, one of the newest and most powerful American dreadnoughts, served as part of the honor escort convoying the President to Brest, France, on December 13, 1918.

Embarking 238 homeward-bound veterans in the precursor of a "Magic Carpet" operation of a later war, Arizona sailed from Brest for New York on December 14th, and arrived off Ambrose Light on the afternoon of Christmas Day, 1918. The next day, she passed in review before Secretary of the Navy Josephus Daniels, who was embarked in the yacht Mayflower off the Statue of Liberty, before entering New York Harbor in a great homecoming celebration. The battleship then sailed for Hampton Roads on January 22, 1919, returning to her base at Norfolk on the following day.

Arizona sailed for Guantanamo Bay with the fleet on February 4, 1919, and arrived on the 8th. After engaging in battle practices and maneuvers there, the battleship sailed for Trinidad on March 17th, arriving there five days later for a three-day port visit. She then returned to Guantanamo Bay on March 29th for a brief period, sailing for Hampton Roads on April 9th. Arriving at her destination on the morning of the 12th, she got underway late that afternoon for Brest, France, ultimately making arrival there on April 21, 1919.

The battleship stood out of Brest Harbor on May 3rd, bound for Asia Minor, and arrived at the port of Smyrna eight days later to protect American lives there during the Greek occupation of that port—an occupation resisted by gunfire from Turkish nationals. Arizona provided temporary shelter on board for a party of Greek nationals, while the battleship's marine detachment guarded the American consulate; a number of American citizens also remained on board Arizona until conditions permitted them to return ashore. Departing Smyrna on June 9th for Constantinople, Turkey, the battleship carried the United States consul-at-large, Leland E. Morris, to that port before sailing for New York on June 15th. Proceeding via Gibraltar, Arizona reached her destination on June 30th.

Entering the New York Navy Yard for upkeep soon thereafter, the battleship cleared that port on January 6, 1920 to join Battleship Division 7 for winter and spring maneuvers in the Caribbean. She operated out of Guantanamo Bay during this period, and also visited Bridgetown, Barbados, in the British West Indies, and Colon, in the Panama Canal Zone, before she sailed north for New York, arriving there on May 1, 1920. Departing New York on May 17th, Arizona operated on the Southern Drill Grounds, and then visited Norfolk and Annapolis, before returning to New York on June 25th. Over the next six months, the ship operated locally out of New York. During this time she was given the alphanumeric hull designation, BB-39, on July 17, 1920, and, on August 23rd, she became flagship for Commander Battleship Division 7, Rear Admiral Edward W. Eberle.

Photo # NH 57651 USS Arizona at Guantanamo Bay, Cuba, January 1920

Sailing from New York on January 4, 1921, Arizona joined the fleet as it sailed for Guantanamo Bay and the Panama Canal Zone. Arriving at Colon, on the Atlantic side of the isthmian waterway. On January 19th, Arizona transited the Panama Canal for the first time on that day, arriving at Panama Bay on the 20th. Underway for Callao, Peru, on the 22d, the fleet arrived there nine days later, on the 31st, for a six-day visit. While she was there, Arizona hosted a visit from the President of Peru. Underway for Balboa on February 5, 1921, Arizona arrived at her destination on the 14th; transiting the canal again the day after Washington's Birthday, the battleship reached Guantanamo Bay on the 26th. She operated thence until April 24, 1921, when she sailed for New York, steaming via Hampton Roads.

Arizona reached New York on April 29th, and remained under overhaul there until June 15th. She steamed thence for Hampton Roads on the latter date, and on the 21st operated off Cape Charles with Army and Navy observers to witness the experimental bombings of the ex-German submarine U-117. Returning to New York, the battleship there broke the flag of Vice Admiral John D. McDonald (who, as a captain, had been Arizona's first commanding officer) on July 1st. and sailed for Panama and Peru on July 9th. She arrived at the port of Callao on July 22nd as flagship for the Battle Force, Atlantic Fleet, to observe the celebrations accompanying the centennial year of Peruvian independence. On July 27th, Vice Admiral McDonald went ashore and represented the United States at the unveiling of a monument commemorating the accomplishments of San Martin, who had liberated Peru from the Spanish yoke a century before.

Sailing for Panama Bay on August 3rd, Arizona became flagship for Battleship Division 7 when Vice Admiral McDonald transferred his flag to Wyoming (BB-33) and Rear Admiral Josiah S. McKean broke his flag on board as commander of the division on August 10th at Balboa. The following day, the battleship sailed for San Diego, arriving there on August 21, 1921.

Over the next 14 years, Arizona alternately served as flagship for Battleship Divisions 2, 3 or 4. Based at San Pedro during this period, Arizona operated with the fleet in the operating areas off the coast of southern California or in the Caribbean during fleet concentrations there. She participated in a succession of fleet problems (the annual maneuvers of the fleet that served as the culmination of the training year), ranging from the Caribbean to the waters off the west coast of central America and the Canal Zone; from the West Indies to the waters between Hawaii and the west coast.

Following her participation in Fleet Problem IX (January 1929), Arizona transited the Panama Canal on February 7th for Guantanamo Bay, whence she operated through April. She then proceeded to Norfolk Navy Yard, entering it on May 4, 1929 to prepare for modernization. Placed in reduced commission on July 15, 1929, Arizona remained in yard hands for the next 20 months; tripod masts, surmounted by three-tiered fire control tops, replaced the old cage masts; 5-inch, 25-caliber antiaircraft guns replaced the 3-inch 50-caliber weapons with which she had been equipped. She also received additional armor to protect her vitals from the fall of shot and blisters to protect her from torpedo or near-miss damage from bombs. In addition, she received new boilers as well as new main and cruising turbines. Ultimately, she was placed in full commission on 1 March 1931.

A little over two weeks later, on March 19, 1931, President Herbert C. Hoover embarked on board the recently modernized battleship, and sailed for Puerto Rico and the Virgin Islands, standing out to sea from Hampton Roads that day. Returning on March 29th, Arizona disembarked the Chief Executive and his party at Hampton Roads, and then proceeded north to Rockland, Maine, to run her post-modernization standardization trials. After a visit to Boston, the battleship dropped down to Norfolk, whence she sailed for San Pedro on August 1, 1931, stationed on Battleship Division 3, Battle Force.

Over the next decade, Arizona continued to operate with the Battle Fleet, and took part in the succession of fleet problems that took the fleet from the waters of the northern pacific and Alaska to those surrounding the West Indies, and into the waters east of the Lesser Antilles.

On September 17, 1938, Arizona became the flagship for Battleship Division 1, when Rear Admiral Chester W. Nimitz broke his flag. Detached on May 27, 1939 to become Chief of the Bureau of Navigation, Nimitz was relieved on that day by Rear Admiral Russell Willson.

Arizona's last fleet problem was XXI. At its conclusion, the United States Fleet was retained in Hawaiian waters, based at Pearl Harbor. She operated in the Hawaiian Operating Area until late that summer, when she returned to Long Beach on September 30, 1940. She was then overhauled at the Puget Sound Navy Yard, Bremerton, Wash., into the following year. Her last flag change-of-on command occurred January 23, 1941, when Rear Admiral Isaac C. Kidd relieved Rear Admiral Willson as Commander, Battleship Division 1.

The battleship returned to Pearl Harbor on February 3, 1941 to resume the intensive training maintained by the Pacific Fleet. She made one last visit to the west coast, clearing "Pearl" on June 11, 1941 for Long Beach, ultimately returning to her Hawaiian base on July 8th. Over the next five months, she continued exercises and battle problems of various kinds on type training and tactical exercises in the Hawaiian operating area. She underwent a brief overhaul at the Pearl Harbor Navy Yard commencing on October 27, 1941, receiving the foundation for search radar atop her foremast. She conducted her last training in company with her division mates Nevada (BB-36) and Oklahoma (BB-37), conducting a night firing exercise on the night of December 4, 1941. All three ships moored at quays ("keys") along Ford Island on the 5th, with Arizona mooring at berth F-7.

Scheduled to receive a tender availability, Arizona took the repair ship Vestal (AR-1) alongside her port side on Saturday, December 6th. The two ships thus lay moored together on the morning of December 7th; among the men on board Arizona that morning were Rear Admiral Kidd and the battleship's captain, Capt. Franklin Van Valkenburgh, and Lt. Col. Daniel R. Fox, USMC, the division marine officer.

Shortly before 0800, Japanese aircraft from six fleet carriers struck the Pacific Fleet as it lay in port at Pearl Harbor, and in the ensuing two attack waves, wreaked devastation on the Battle Line and on air and military facilities defending Pearl Harbor.

On board Arizona, the ship's air raid alarm went off about 0755, and the ship went to general quarters soon thereafter. Insofar as it could be determined soon after the attack, the ship sustained eight bomb hits. The one that most likely caused the ship's destruction came from the 800-kilogram bomb dropped by the Nakajima B5N2 Type 97 carrier attack plane commanded by

Lt. Comdr. Kasumi Tadashi, of the carrier Hiryu's air unit, that glanced off the face plate of Turret II and penetrated the deck to explode in the black powder magazine, which in turn set off adjacent smokeless powder magazines. A cataclysmic explosion ripped through the forward part of the ship, touching off fierce fires that burned for two days; debris showered down on Ford Island in the vicinity. Many of the men on board ship at the time were incinerated leaving recovery or identification of any remains, impossible.

Acts of heroism on the part of Arizona's officers and men, sailors and marines, were many, headed by those of Lt. Comdr. Samuel G. Fuqua, the ship's first lieutenant and senior surviving officer on board, whose coolness in attempting to quell the fires and get survivors off the ship earned him the Medal of Honor. Fuqua's "calmness," Sgt. John M. Baker, USMC, a survivor of the battleship's marine detachment, later recounted, "gave me courage, and I looked around to see if I could help." Posthumous awards of the Medal of Honor also went to Rear Admiral Kidd, the first flag officer to be killed in the Pacific war, and to Capt. Van Valkenburgh, who reached the bridge and was attempting to fight his ship when the bomb hit on the magazines destroyed her. Twenty-three ships (destroyers, destroyer escorts and high speed transports) honored men from Arizona's ship's company who perished that morning.

The blast that destroyed Arizona and sank her at her berth alongside of Ford Island consumed the lives of 1,177 of the 1,512 men on board at the time—over half of the casualties suffered by the entire fleet on the "Day of Infamy."

Photo # 80-G-19942 USS Arizona burning at Pearl Harbor, 7 December 1941

Placed "in ordinary" at Pearl Harbor on December 29, 1941, Arizona was struck from the Naval Vessel Register on December 1, 1942. Her wreck was cut down so that very little of the superstructure lay above water; her after main battery turrets and guns were removed to be emplaced as coast defense guns. Arizona's wreck remains at Pearl Harbor, a memorial to the men of her crew lost that December morn in 1941. On March 7, 1950, Admiral Arthur W. Radford, Commander in Chief of the Pacific Fleet, instituted the raising of colors over Arizona's remains, and legislation during the administrations of Presidents Dwight D. Eisenhower and John F. Kennedy designated the wreck a national shrine. A memorial was built spanning the ship; it was dedicated on May 30, 1962.

Arizona (BB-39) was awarded one battle star for her service in World War II.[2]

---

[2] Dictionary of American Naval Fighting Ships.

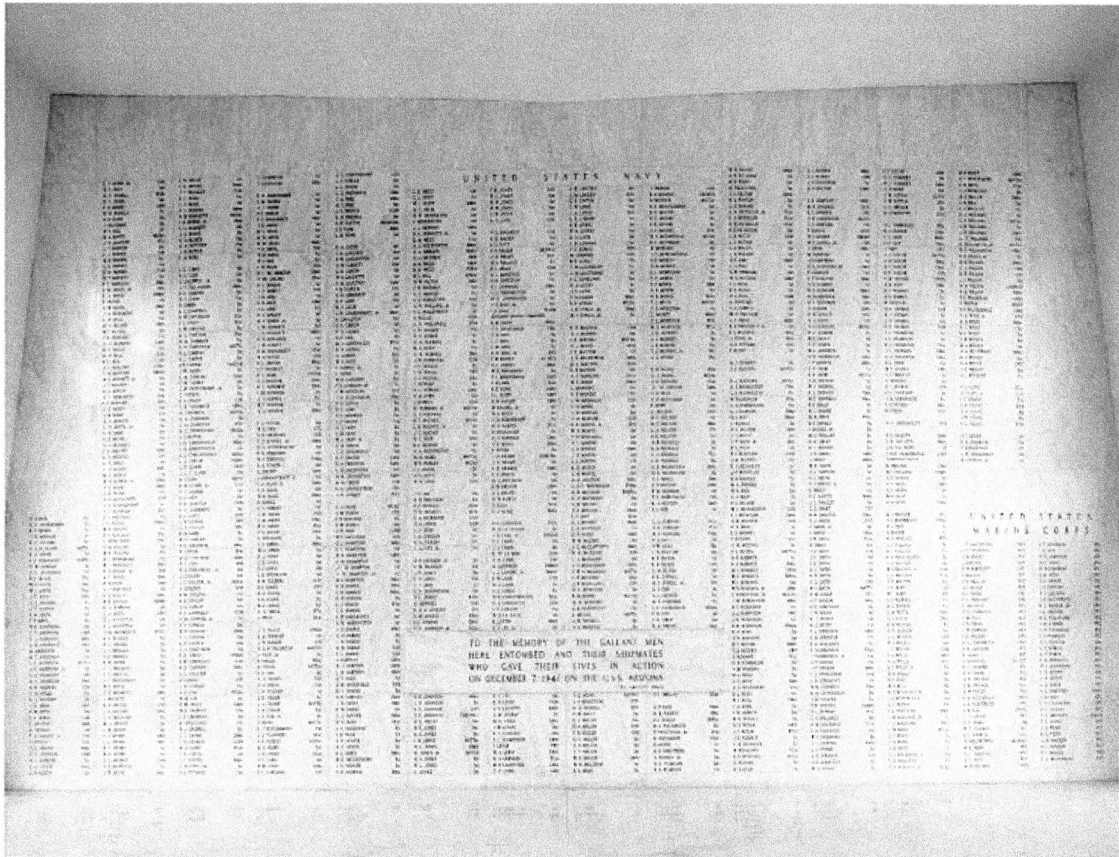

Photo # USN 1067058 Interior of the USS Arizona Memorial at Pearl Harbor, January 1963

Photo # NH 97326-KN USS Arizona Memorial, Pearl Harbor, Hawaii, June 1987

13

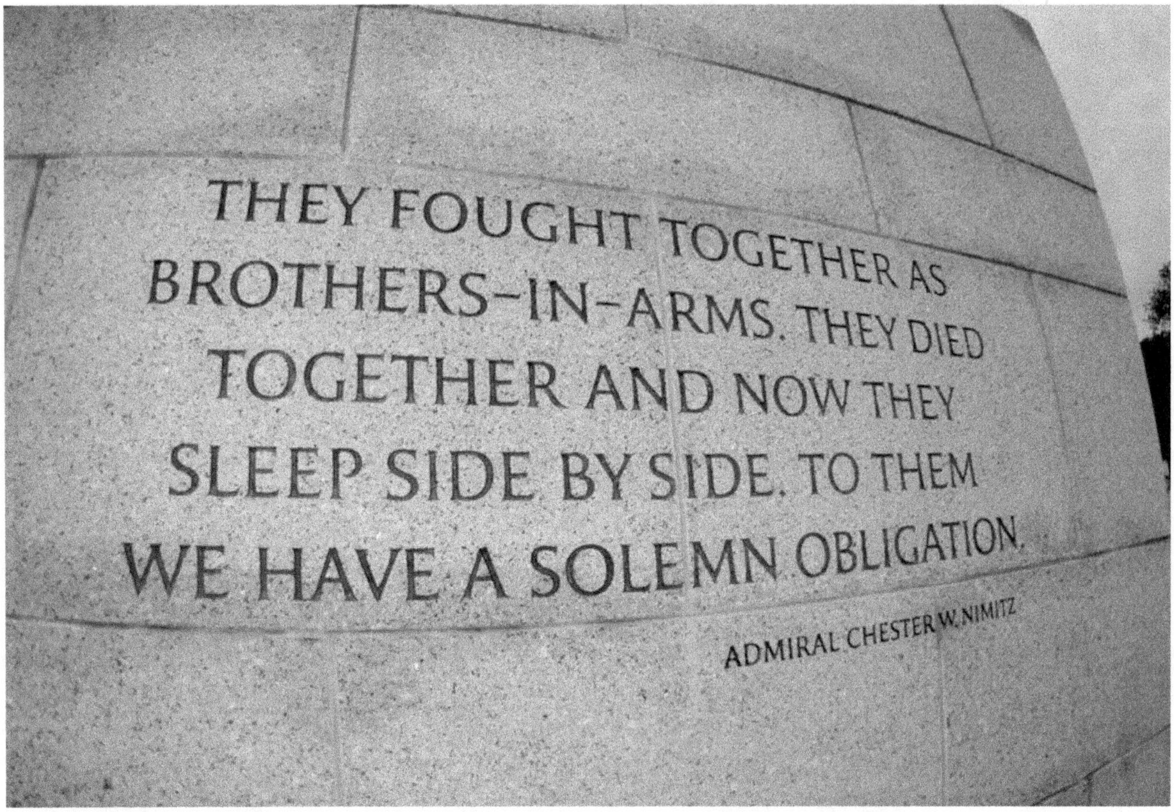

THEY FOUGHT TOGETHER AS
BROTHERS-IN-ARMS. THEY DIED
TOGETHER AND NOW THEY
SLEEP SIDE BY SIDE. TO THEM
WE HAVE A SOLEMN OBLIGATION.

ADMIRAL CHESTER W. NIMITZ

CHAPTER 4: The Navy Crew

Photo # 80-G-19942 USS Arizona burning at Pearl Harbor, 7 December 1941

There were 35 sets of brothers, one father and son and numerous sets of cousins serving on the USS Arizona at the time of the attack on December 7, 1941. 1177 men were lost on that day. Of that number, 126 men from the USS Arizona remain unidentified and are buried in mass graves in the "Punch bowl" cemetery.

There were 647 remains recovered at Pearl Harbor and they were initially buried by the Navy with white crosses that marked their ship, date of death and "Unidentified". The remains of these 647 men were re-interred by the Army in 1949 and mingled in 252 gravesites in the National Memorial Cemetery of the Pacific in Honolulu. Their gravesites, in the crater of a dormant volcano were simply marked as "Unknown". Lorraine Marks-Haislip, historian and congressional lobbyist for the USS Arizona spent thousands of hours and more than a decade fighting to correct this treatment of these men. Years of research by Ray Emory has established and located identification of the ship they were on and in some cases, their duty stations. A bill was passed H.R. 3806, requiring the Secretary of Veterans Affairs to add certain identifying information to the inscriptions on the markers on certain graves in the National Memorial Cemetery of the Pacific containing the remains of unknowns who died in the Japanese attack on Pearl Harbor. The name of ship, death place and date, now identifies them as casualties of the attack on Pearl Harbor.

Aaron, Hubert Charles Titus Fireman, Second Class, Serial No: 346 86 21, US Navy. Hubert was born October 22, 1919 in Garland, Arkansas the youngest son of Alfred Alonzo and Jemima (Davis) Aaron. He enlisted in the US Navy on October 14, 1940 in Little Rock, Arkansas and reported for duty on the USS Arizona on January 4, 1941. Hubert was killed in action on December 7, 1941 in Pearl Harbor, Hawaii. He was awarded the American Defense Service Medal, World War II Victory Medal and Purple Heart Medal posthumously. Hubert remains on duty on the USS Arizona. He is commemorated on the USS Arizona Memorial and the Memorial Tablets of the Missing, National Memorial Cemetery of the Pacific, Honolulu, Hawaii. Hubert was survived by his Father, Mr. Alfred Alonzo Aaron, Route 1, Box 153, Texarkana, Arkansas.[3]

Abercrombie, Samuel Adolphus Seaman, First Class, Serial No: 360 19 81, US Navy. Samuel was born May 18, 1919 in Leggett, Texas, the child of John Thomas Abercrombie and Maudie Rice Abercrombie. His mother died less than three months later. His father died by the time he was 11. Samuel had ten older half siblings. He was living with an older brother when he enlisted in the US Navy on August 2, 1940 in Houston, Texas and completed his basic training at the Naval Training Station in San Diego, California. Samuel reported for duty on the USS Arizona on October 14, 1940. He was killed in action on December 7, 1941, in Pearl Harbor, Hawaii. Samuel was awarded the American Defense Service Medal, World War II Victory Medal and Purple Heart Medal posthumously. He remains on duty on the USS Arizona. Samuel is commemorated on the USS Arizona Memorial and the Memorial Tablets of the Missing, National Memorial Cemetery of the Pacific, Honolulu, Hawaii. He was survived by his Brother, Mr. Richard Edwards Abercrombie of Leggett, Texas.[4]

Adams, Robert Franklin Seaman, First Class, Serial No: 272 41 83, US Navy. Robert was born in 1922 in Waterloo, Alabama, son of Jim Lucas and Connie Mary (Poole) Adams. His father died when he was 6 years old. Robert graduated from a Waterloo High School in 1940 and enlisted in the US Navy on October 5, 1940 in Birmingham, Alabama. Robert completed his basic training at the Naval Training Station in Norfolk, Virginia and reported for duty on the USS Arizona on December 4, 1940. He was killed in action on December 7, 1941, in Pearl Harbor, Hawaii. Robert was awarded the American Defense Service Medal, World War II Victory Medal and Purple Heart Medal posthumously. He remains on duty on the USS Arizona. Robert is commemorated on the USS Arizona Memorial and the Memorial Tablets of the Missing, National Memorial Cemetery of the Pacific, Honolulu, Hawaii. He was survived by his Mother, Mrs. Connie Mary Adams, General Delivery, Waterloo, Alabama.[5]

---

[3] Hubert Charles Titus Aaron, Photo and information provided by family member, Susan Higginbotham.
[4] Samuel Adolphus Abercrombie, information provided by the National Archives and records Administration, Photo provided by Wilson Clement.
[5] Robert Franklin Adams, Photo from the Courier Journal, Florence, AL, In Memorian, Robert Franklin Adams, December 2, 1992.

Adkison, James Dillion   Seaman, First Class, Serial No: 356 26 31, US Navy. James was born April 17, 1920 in Elbert, Texas, the son of Edward Washington and Rosa Lee (Selvage) Adkison. He enlisted in the US Navy on March 14, 1940 in Dallas, Texas and completed his basic training at the Naval Training Station in San Diego, California. He reported for duty on the USS Arizona on August 25, 1940. James was killed in action on December 7, 1941 in Pearl Harbor, Hawaii. He was awarded the American Defense Service Medal, World War II Victory Medal and Purple Heart Medal posthumously. James remains on duty on the USS Arizona. He is commemorated on the USS Arizona Memorial and the Memorial Tablets of the Missing, National Memorial Cemetery of the Pacific, Honolulu, Hawaii. James was survived by his Father, Mr. Edward Washington Adkison, 1914 18th Street, Lubbock, Texas.[6]

Aguirre, Reyner Aceves   Seaman, Second Class, Serial No: 382 46 97, US Navy. Reyner was born on July 30, 1918 in San Gabriel, California the son of Francisco Aguirre and Rosa Aceves Aguirre. He attended Alhambra City High School, Alhambra, California. Reyner enlisted in the US Navy on June 6, 1941 in Los Angeles, California and completed his basic training at the Naval Training Station in San Diego, California. Reyner reported for duty on the USS Arizona on August 13, 1941. He was killed in action on December 7, 1941 in Pearl Harbor, Hawaii. Reyner was awarded the American Defense Service Medal, World War II Victory Medal and Purple Heart Medal posthumously. He remains on duty on the USS Arizona. Reyner is commemorated on the USS Arizona Memorial and the Memorial Tablets of the Missing, National Memorial Cemetery of the Pacific, Honolulu, Hawaii. He was survived by his Mother, Mrs. Rose Aguirre, 2014 Teagarden Lane, Alhambra, California. The Reyner A. Aguirre American Legion Post 748 in San Gabriel, California was named in his honor.[7]

Aguon, Gregorio San Nicholas   Steward's Mate, First Class, Serial No: 421 03 48, US Navy. Gregorio was born in 1921 in Agana, Guam the son of Juan T. and Joaquina S. M. Aguon. He enlisted in the US Navy on December 2, 1938 at the Naval Station in Guam. Gregorio reported for duty on the USS Arizona on April 3, 1939. He was killed in action on December 7, 1941 in Pearl Harbor, Hawaii. Gregorio was awarded the American Defense Service Medal, World War II Victory Medal and Purple Heart Medal posthumously. He remains on duty on the USS Arizona. Gregorio is commemorated on the USS Arizona Memorial and the Memorial Tablets of the Missing, National Memorial Cemetery of the Pacific, Honolulu, Hawaii and the Sons of Guam Pearl Harbor Memorial, Guam. He was survived by his Father, Mr. Juan Torres Aguon, Lot 1158 San Nicholas Street, Agana, Guam.

---

[6] James Dillion Adkison, Jr., Photo courtesy of the USS Arizona Obituaries Community.
[7] Reyner Aceves Aguirre, photo courtesy of the Reyner A. Aguirre American Legion Post 748, San Gabriel, California.

Ahern, Richard James Fireman, First Class, Serial No: 382 12 14, US Navy. Richard was born on October 2, 1921 in Gurley, Cheyenne, Nebraska the son of James Daniel and Sadie Catherine (Penry) Ahern. He enlisted in the US Navy on October 10, 1939 in Los Angeles, California and completed his basic training at the Naval Training Station in San Diego, California. Richard reported for duty on the USS Arizona on December 20, 1939. He was killed in action on December 7, 1941 in Pearl Harbor, Hawaii. Richard was awarded the American Defense Service Medal, World War II Victory Medal and Purple Heart Medal posthumously. He remains on duty on the USS Arizona. Richard is commemorated on the USS Arizona Memorial and the Memorial Tablets of the Missing, National Memorial Cemetery of the Pacific, Honolulu, Hawaii. He was survived by his Father, Mr. James Daniel Ahern, 6617 Vesper Avenue, Van Nuys, California.[8]

Alberovsky, Francis Severin Boilermaker, First Class, Serial No: 299 79 29, US Navy. Francis was born May 7, 1916 in Batavia, Illinois, the son of Severin Alberovsky and Barbara Weinzetti Painsipp Alberovsky. His mother died when he was 12 years old. Francis enlisted in the US Navy on November 5, 1935 in Chicago, Illinois and completed his basic training at the Naval Training Station in Great Lakes, Illinois. Francis reported for duty on the USS Arizona April 20, 1936. He was killed in action on December 7, 1941 in Pearl Harbor, Hawaii. Francis was awarded the American Defense Service Medal, World War II Victory Medal and Purple Heart Medal posthumously. He remains on duty on the USS Arizona. Francis is commemorated on the USS Arizona Memorial and the Memorial Tablets of the Missing, National Memorial Cemetery of the Pacific, Honolulu, Hawaii. He was survived by his Wife, Mrs. Marie Donna Alberovsky, 285 Orizaba Avenue, Long Beach, California.[9]

Albright, Galen Winston Seaman, First Class, Serial No: 291 65 75, US Navy. Galen was born January 3, 1922 in Francesville, Indiana, the son of Calvin Denton and Amy Ellen (Funk) Albright. He enlisted in the US Navy on October 8, 1940 in Indianapolis, Indiana and completed his training at the Naval Training Station in Great Lakes, Illinois. Galen reported for duty on the USS Arizona on December 9, 1940. He was killed in action on December 7, 1941 in Pearl Harbor, Hawaii. Galen was awarded the American Defense Service Medal, World War II Victory Medal and Purple Heart Medal posthumously. He remains on duty on the USS Arizona. Galen is commemorated on the USS Arizona Memorial and the Memorial Tablets of the Missing, National Memorial Cemetery of the Pacific, Honolulu, Hawaii. He was survived by his Father, Mr. Calvin Albright, Brook, Indiana.[10]

---

[8] Richard James Ahern, Information provided by family member, Thomas Penry.

[9] Francis Severin Alberovsky, Photo from "Lost and Presumed Dead" by Matt Hanley, The Beacon-News, Chicago, IL, December 6, 2011.

[10] Galen Winston Albright, Photo provided by family member, Tiffany L. Heinisch.

Alexander, Elvis Author   Seaman, Second Class, Serial No: 368 64 98, US Navy. Elvis was born in April 1917 in Beebe, Arkansas, the son of Charles E. and Lillie Alma (Edwards) Alexander. He enlisted in the US Navy on April 21, 1941 in Salt Lake City, Utah and completed his basic training at the Naval Training Station in San Diego, California. Elvis reported for duty on the USS Arizona on July 13, 1941. He was killed in action on December 7, 1941 in Pearl Harbor, Hawaii. Elvis was awarded the American Defense Service Medal, World War II Victory Medal and the Purple Heart Medal posthumously. He remains on duty on the USS Arizona. Elvis is commemorated on the USS Arizona Memorial and the Memorial Tablets of the Missing, National Memorial Cemetery of the Pacific, Honolulu, Hawaii. He was survived by his Father, Mr. Charles Edward Alexander, Leslie, Arkansas.[11]

Allen, Robert Lee   Ship fitter, Third Class, Serial No: 346 76 58, US Navy. Robert was born in about 1918 in Texas the son of Jake Curby and Bertha Farrar Allen. He enlisted in the US Navy on December 12, 1939 in Little Rock, Arkansas and completed his basic training at the Naval Training Station in Great Lakes, Illinois. He reported for duty on the USS Arizona March 9, 1940. Robert was killed in action on December 7, 1941 in Pearl Harbor, Hawaii. He was awarded the American Defense Service Medal, World War II Victory Medal and Purple Heart Medal posthumously. Robert remains on duty on the USS Arizona. He is commemorated on USS Arizona Memorial and the Memorial Tablets of the Missing, National Memorial Cemetery of the Pacific, Honolulu, Hawaii. Robert was survived by his Father, Mr. Jacob Curby Allen, General Delivery, Roseburg, Oregon.

Allen, William Clayborn   Electrician's Mate, First Class, Serial No: 381 19 83, US Navy. William was born October 30, 1910 in Kansas City, Missouri son of William C. and Mallie (Coffman) Allen. He enlisted in the US Navy on June 18, 1935 in San Diego, California and completed his basic training at the Naval Training Station in San Diego, California. William served on the USS Arizona from February 18, 1936 until he was killed in action on December 7, 1941 in Pearl Harbor, Hawaii. He was awarded the American Defense Service Medal, World War II Victory Medal and Purple Heart Medal posthumously. William remains on duty on the USS Arizona. He is commemorated on the USS Arizona Memorial and the Memorial Tablets of the Missing, National Memorial Cemetery of the Pacific, Honolulu, Hawaii. He was survived by his Wife, Mrs. Margaret Frances Allen, 1240 Magnolia, Long Beach, California.[12]

Allen, William Lewis   Storekeeper, Second Class, V-6, Serial No: 624 06 00, US Navy Reserve. William was born September 30, 1896 in Washington County, Indiana. He re-enlisted in the US Navy on September 15, 1941 in Houston, Texas and completed his basic training at the

---

[11] Elvis Author Alexander, Information provided by the National Archives and Records Administration. Photo provided by family member, Bennie Smith.

[12] William Clayborn Allen, Photo and information provided by family member, Doris Jones.

Naval Training Station in San Diego, California. He reported for duty on the USS Arizona on November 3, 1941. William was killed in action on December 7, 1941 in Pearl Harbor, Hawaii. He was awarded the American Defense Service Medal, World War II Victory Medal and Purple Heart Medal posthumously. William remains on duty on the USS Arizona. He is commemorated on the USS Arizona Memorial and the Memorial Tablets of the Missing, National Memorial Cemetery of the Pacific, Honolulu, Hawaii. William was survived by his Wife, Mrs. William Lewis Allen, 501 Western Union Building, Houston, Texas.

Alley, Jay Edgar Gunner's Mate, First Class, Serial No: 261 87 66, US Navy. Jay was born February 1, 1916 in Iredell County, North Carolina the son of Lonnie Alley and Patsy (Hager) Alley. He enlisted in the US Navy on September 18, 1935 in Raleigh, North Carolina and completed his basic training at the Naval Training Station in Norfolk, Virginia. He reported for duty on the USS Arizona on February 24, 1936. Jay was killed in action on December 7, 1941 in Pearl Harbor, Hawaii. *Jay was at his post, manning a gun turret, fighting back when the explosion occurred.* He was awarded the American Defense Service Medal, World War II Victory Medal and Purple Heart Medal posthumously. Jay remains on duty on the USS Arizona. He is commemorated on the USS Arizona Memorial and the Memorial Tablets of the Missing, National Memorial Cemetery of the Pacific, Honolulu, Hawaii and the Iredell County, North Carolina World War II Memorial. Jay was survived by his Parents, Mr. and Mrs. Lonnie E. Alley, Mooresville, North Carolina.[13]

Allison, Andrew K. Fireman, First Class, Serial No: 295 30 27, US Navy. Andrew was born August 16, 1915 in Hardin County, Tennessee to Arthur D. and Icey (Bain) Allison. He enlisted in the US Navy on February 12, 1936 in Nashville, Tennessee and completed his basic training at the Naval Training Station in Great Lakes, Illinois. He reported for duty on the USS Arizona on June 17, 1936. Andrew was killed in action on December 7, 1941 in Pearl Harbor, Hawaii. He was awarded the American Defense Service Medal, World War II Victory Medal and Purple Heart Medal posthumously. Andrew remains on duty on the USS Arizona. He is commemorated on the USS Arizona Memorial and the Memorial Tablets of the Missing, National Memorial Cemetery of the Pacific, Honolulu, Hawaii and Neill Cemetery, Savannah, Tennessee. Andrew was survived by his Parents, Mr. and Mrs. Arthur Leroy Allison, Route 2, Trenton, Tennessee. (Later address: Steele, Missouri.) His brother, John T. was also killed on board the USS Arizona during the Japanese Attack.

Allison, J. T. Fireman, First Class, Serial No: 295 53 43, US Navy. John was born December 28, 1920 in Hardin, Tennessee, the son of Arthur and Icie Allison. He enlisted in the US Navy on December 5, 1939 in Nashville, Tennessee and completed his basic training at the Naval Training Station in Great Lakes, Illinois. John reported for duty on the USS Arizona on March 29, 1939. He was killed in action on December 7, 1941 in Pearl Harbor, Hawaii. John was awarded the American Defense Service Medal, World War II Victory Medal and Purple Heart Medal posthumously. He remains on duty on the USS Arizona. John is commemorated on the USS Arizona Memorial and the Memorial Tablets of the Missing, National Memorial Cemetery of the Pacific, Honolulu, Hawaii and Neill Cemetery, Savannah, Tennessee. He was

---

[13] Jay Edgar Alley, Information and photo provided by his sister, Mary Gibson.

survived by his Father, Mr. Arthur Leroy Allison, Steele, Missouri. His brother, Andrew K. Allison was also killed on board the USS Arizona during the Japanese attack.

Alten, Ernest Mathew, Jr Seaman, Second Class, Serial No: 376 30 81, US Navy. Ernest was born March 20, 1924 in Alameda County, California to Ernest Mathew and Bernice Mary (Fehley) Alten. He enlisted in the US Navy on April 18, 1941 in San Francisco, California and completed his basic training at the Naval Training Station in San Diego, California. He reported for duty on the USS Arizona on July 13, 1941. Ernest was killed in action on December 7, 1941 in Pearl Harbor, Hawaii. He was awarded the American Defense Service Medal, World War II Victory Medal and Purple Heart Medal posthumously. Ernest remains on duty on the USS Arizona. He is commemorated on the USS Arizona Memorial and the Memorial Tablets of the Missing, National Memorial Cemetery of the Pacific, Honolulu, Hawaii. Ernest was survived by his Mother, Mrs. Bernice Alten, 2755 Vallecito Place, Oakland, California.

Amacher, Charles Andrew Seaman, First Class, Serial No. 385 95 85, US Navy. Charles was born on January 12, 1920 in Wallapa, Washington the son of Edward and Margaret A. (Walker) Amacher. He graduated from Valley High School in Raymond, Washington in 1938. Charles enlisted in the US Navy January 17, 1941 in Seattle, Washington and completed his basic training at the Naval Training Station in San Diego, California. He reported for duty on the USS Arizona, where he was serving on December 7, 1941 when the Japanese attacked Pearl Harbor. He later served on the submarine, USS Albacore serving until 1947 and achieving the rank of Chief Electrician's Mate. Charles worked as an electrician and in nuclear refueling at Puget Sound Naval Shipyard for 29 years. He retired in 1978. Charles died on August 29, 2003 in Allyn, Washington. He was survived by his wife of 59 years, Lucille Raisoni Amacher, a son, Mike Amacher of Allyn; a daughter, Vicki Betsinger of Allyn; a brother, Ernie Amacher of Raymond; two sisters, Hanna Wheaton of South Bend, Washington and Dorothy Moore of Canyonville, Oregon; and three grandchildren, Nickolas Biskeborn and Abbey and Andrew Amacher.[14]

Amon, Frederick Purdy Seaman, First Class, Serial No: 311 51 54, US Navy. Frederick was born January 9, 1921 in Niles, Michigan, the oldest of ten children born to Frederick H. and Nola Dale (Purdy) Amon. His parents divorced in 1938. He enlisted in the US Navy on October 8, 1940 in Detroit, Michigan and completed his basic training at the Naval Training Station in Great Lakes, Illinois. Frederick reported for duty on the USS Arizona December 9, 1940 where he was a Radio Operator. He was killed in action on December 7, 1941 in Pearl Harbor, Hawaii. Frederick was awarded the American Defense Service Medal, World War II Victory Medal and Purple Heart Medal posthumously. He remains on duty on the USS Arizona. Frederick is commemorated on the USS Arizona Memorial and the Memorial Tablets of the Missing, National Memorial Cemetery of the Pacific, Honolulu, Hawaii. He was survived by his Mother, Mrs. Nola Dale Amon, 36 North State, Niles, Michigan. The VFW post in Niles, Michigan was named in his and his brother's honor.[15]

---

[14] Charles Andrew Amacher, Information from the Kitsap Sun newspaper September 5, 2003.
[15] Frederick Purdy Amon, Photo and information provided by his sister, Margaret Treesh.

Anderson, Charles Titus Carpenter's Mate, Second Class, Serial No: 382 11 74, US Navy. Charles was born March 23, 1921 in Evansville, Indiana to Charles S. and Coraetta (Trent) Anderson. He enlisted in the US Navy on October 10, 1939 in Los Angeles, California and completed his basic training at the Naval Training Station in San Diego, California. Charles reported for duty on the USS Arizona December 20, 1939. He was killed in action on December 7, 1941 in Pearl Harbor, Hawaii. Charles was awarded the American Defense Service Medal, World War II Victory Medal and Purple Heart Medal posthumously. He remains on duty on the USS Arizona. Charles is commemorated on the USS Arizona Memorial and the Memorial Tablets of the Missing, National Memorial Cemetery of the Pacific, Honolulu, Hawaii. He was survived by his Parents, Mr. and Mrs. Charles S. Anderson, 625 North Main Street, Elsinore, California.[16]

Anderson, Delbert Jake Boatswain's Mate, Second Class, Serial No: 328 47 13, US Navy. Delbert was born August 26, 1917 in Verona, North Dakota, the son of John and Bessie Anderson. He enlisted in the US Navy on March 16, 1937 in Minneapolis, Minnesota and completed his basic training at the Naval Training Station in Great Lakes, Illinois. Delbert reported for duty on the USS Arizona September 19, 1937. He was killed in action on December 7, 1941 in Pearl Harbor, Hawaii, struck by machine gun bullets. Delbert was awarded the American Defense Service Medal, World War II Victory Medal and Purple Heart Medal posthumously. He remains on duty on the USS Arizona. Delbert is commemorated on USS Arizona Memorial and the Memorial Tablets of the Missing, National Memorial Cemetery of the Pacific, Honolulu, Hawaii. He was survived by his Father, Mr. Edwin Sigfried Anderson, Dilworth, Minnesota. Delbert's twin brother, John Delmer Anderson was also serving on the USS Arizona and was among those who survived.[17]

Anderson, Donald William Signalman, Third Class, Serial No: 393 27 18, US Navy. Donald was born October 16, 1920 in Oregon, the son of William H. and Esther Anderson. He enlisted in the US Navy on July 13, 1938 in Portland, Oregon and completed his basic training at the Naval Training Station in San Diego, California. Donald reported for duty on the USS Arizona on January 2, 1939. He was killed in action on December 7, 1941 in Pearl Harbor, Hawaii. Donald was awarded the American Defense Service Medal, World War II Victory Medal and Purple Heart Medal posthumously. He remains on duty on the USS Arizona. Donald is commemorated on the USS Arizona Memorial and the Memorial Tablets of the Missing, National Memorial Cemetery of the Pacific, Honolulu, Hawaii. He was survived by his Father, Mr. William H. Anderson, 319 Pittock Block, Portland, Oregon.[18]

---

[16] Charles Titus Anderson, Photo and information provided by his nephew, drofkahr on Ancestry.com
[17] Delbert Jake Anderson, Photo Pat Shannahan, The Arizona Republic.
[18] Donald William Anderson, Photo provided by family member, Janice Stensrude.

Anderson, Harry   Seaman, First Class, Serial No: 382 23 14, US Navy. Harry was born July 25, 1920 in Brooklyn, New York the son of Douglas J. and Mary A. Chamberlain. He enlisted in the US Navy on July 25, 1940 in Los Angeles, California and completed his basic training at the Naval Training Station in San Diego, California. He reported for duty on the USS Arizona on October 14, 1940. Harry was killed in action on December 7, 1941 in Pearl Harbor, Hawaii. He was awarded the American Defense Service Medal, World War II Victory Medal and Purple Heart Medal posthumously. Harry remains on duty on the USS Arizona. He is commemorated on the USS Arizona Memorial and the Memorial Tablets of the Missing, National Memorial Cemetery of the Pacific, Honolulu, Hawaii. Harry was survived by his Mother, Mrs. Mary Chamberlain, 11209 Pope Avenue, Lynwood, California.

Anderson, Howard Taisey   Fireman, First Class, Serial No: 328 75 66, US Navy. Howard was born February 7, 1921 in Sharon, North Dakota. He enlisted in the US Navy on October 8, 1940 in Minneapolis, Minnesota and completed his basic training at the Naval Training Station in Great Lakes, Illinois. He reported for duty on the USS Arizona on December 9, 1940. Howard was killed in action on December 7, 1941 in Pearl Harbor, Hawaii. He was awarded the American Defense Service Medal, World War II Victory Medal and Purple Heart Medal posthumously. Howard remains on duty on the USS Arizona. He is commemorated on the USS Arizona Memorial and the Memorial Tablets of the Missing, National Memorial Cemetery of the Pacific, Honolulu, Hawaii. Howard was survived by his Mother, Mrs. Hanna Knute Amundson, 316 North 8th Street, Grand Forks, North Dakota.[19]

Anderson, Irwin Corinthis   Steward's Mate, First Class, Serial No: 265 69 79, US Navy. Irwin was born in about 1916 in Virginia to Jonas M. and Jessie G. Anderson. He graduated from Booker T. Washington High School in Norfolk, Virginia and studied printing for two years at Hampton Institute, now called Hampton University. He didn't have money to continue. Irwin enlisted in the US Navy on January 2, 1936 in Norfolk, Virginia and reported for duty on the USS Arizona on April 22, 1936. Irwin was killed in action on December 7, 1941 in Pearl Harbor, Hawaii. He was awarded the American Defense Service Medal, World War II Victory Medal and Purple Heart Medal posthumously. Irwin remains on duty on the USS Arizona. He is commemorated on the USS Arizona Memorial and the Memorial Tablets of the Missing, National Memorial Cemetery of the Pacific, Honolulu, Hawaii. Irwin was survived by his Father, Mr. Jonas M. Anderson, 2431 Hale Street, Norfolk, Virginia.

Anderson, James Pickins, Jr.   Seaman, First Class, Serial No: 376 15 27, US Navy. James was born June 7, 1917 in Rome, Oregon the son of James Pickens and Ella Elizabeth Anderson. He enlisted in the US Navy on November 4, 1940 in San Francisco, California and completed his basic training at the Naval Training Station in San Diego, California. James reported for duty on the USS Arizona January 11, 1941. He was killed in action on December 7, 1941 in Pearl Harbor, Hawaii. James was awarded the American Defense Service Medal, World War II Victory Medal and Purple Heart Medal posthumously. He remains on duty on the USS Arizona. James is commemorated on the USS Arizona Memorial and the Memorial Tablets of the Missing, National Memorial Cemetery of the Pacific, Honolulu, Hawaii. He was survived by his Father, Mr. James Pickens Anderson, Sr., Jordan Valley, Oregon.

---

[19] Howard Taisey Anderson, photo provided by David Dunnavant.

Anderson, John Delmar Boatswain's Mate, Second Class, Division 1 & 4, Serial No. 328 46 30, US Navy. John and his twin brother, Jake were born on August 26, 1917 in Verona, North Dakota. He was the son of John and Bessie Anderson. *The family later moved to Dilworth, Minnesota where they grew up and graduated from high school.* John and his twin brother Jake, enlisted in the US Navy March 16, 1937 in Minneapolis, Minnesota and completed their basic training at the Naval Training Station in Great Lakes, Illinois. He was transferred from the USS Ellet (DD-398) to the USS Arizona on December 6, 1940. John was serving on December 7, 1941 when the Japanese attacked Pearl Harbor. *He remembers rowing into the burning water around the USS Arizona, searching in vain for his twin brother later found among the battleship's nearly 1200 dead.* He later was assigned duty on the USS Mac Donough. John served as a meteorologist in Roswell, New Mexico, KSWS TV from 1953 to 1968. John passed away November 13, 2015 in New Mexico. His twin brother, Delbert was killed in action while serving on the USS Arizona.[20]

Anderson, Lawrence Donald Lieutenant, Junior Grade, Serial No: 0-120159, US Navy Reserve. Lawrence was born August 21, 1918 in Galesburg, Illinois to August R. and Mabel L. (Guider) Anderson. He attended junior college and then Iowa State University, where he joined the Naval Reserves. In December 1940 he attended the Naval Reserve Midshipmen's School at Northwestern University. He was commissioned Ensign on March 14, 1941 and was serving as Junior Watch and Division 4 Officer on the USS Arizona. His battle station was Turret IV. Lawrence died on December 8, 1941 on board the USS Solace. He was assigned body #29 and was buried in Mount Olive Cemetery, Waukon, Iowa. Hawaii. He was awarded the American Defense Service Medal, World War II Victory Medal and Purple Heart Medal posthumously. He is commemorated on the USS Arizona Memorial and the Memorial Tablets of the Missing, National Memorial Cemetery of the Pacific, Honolulu, Hawaii. Lawrence was survived by his Father, Mr. August R. Anderson, 27 West Liberty Street, Waukon, Iowa.[21]

Anderson, Robert Adair Gunner's Mate, Third Class, Serial No: 342 10 20, US Navy. Robert was born October 12, 1920 in Missouri to James Clark and Josephine Mary Agnes (Lombard) Anderson. He enlisted in the US Navy on January 17, 1939 in Kansas City, Missouri and completed his basic training at the Naval Training Station in Great Lakes, Illinois. Robert reported for duty on the USS Arizona July 8, 1939. In a letter written home on November 29th he said "everything is so mixed up" that he did not know whether the ship would soon head to the west coast. "We don't even know what the next thing we will do when we get out to sea for a little practice. It is better this way because it might fall into the wrong hands and that may cause a little trouble." He was killed in action on December 7, 1941 in Pearl Harbor, Hawaii. Robert was awarded the American Defense Service Medal, World War II Victory Medal and Purple Heart Medal posthumously. He remains on duty on the USS Arizona. Robert is commemorated on the USS Arizona Memorial and the Memorial Tablets of the Missing, National Memorial Cemetery of the Pacific, Honolulu, Hawaii. He was

---

[20] John Delmar Anderson, Information and photo, Pat Shannahan, The Arizona Republic.
[21] Lawrence Donald Anderson, information from the Dubuque Telegraph Herald, Dubuque, Iowa.

survived by his Parents, Mr. and Mrs. James C. Anderson, 4232 Prospect Avenue, Kansas City, Missouri.[22]

 **Andrews, Brainerd Wells** Chief Carpenter's Mate, Serial No: 212 25 76, US Navy. Brainerd was the second of four boys born August 31, 1910 in Roxbury, Vermont to Homer G. Andrews and Eva (Bell) Andrews. He was born in Roxbury, Vermont on August 31, 1910. Brainerd enlisted in the US Navy on August 31, 1937 and reported for duty on the USS Arizona on November 17, 1939. He was killed in action on December 7, 1941 in Pearl Harbor, Hawaii. Brainerd was awarded the American Defense Service Medal, World War II Victory Medal and Purple Heart Medal posthumously. He remains on duty on the USS Arizona. Brainerd is commemorated on the USS Arizona Memorial and the Memorial Tablets of the Missing, National Memorial Cemetery of the Pacific, Honolulu, Hawaii. He was survived by his Father, Mr. Homer G. Andrews, 162 South Main Street, St. Albans, Vermont.[23]

Angle, Earnest Hersea Fireman, Second Class, Serial No: 266 21 93, US Navy. Earnest was born February 13, 1922 in Wyoming, West Virginia to Vessie E. and Dana (Church) Angle. He enlisted in the US Navy on October 7, 1940 in Richmond, Virginia and completed his basic training at the Naval Training Station in Norfolk, Virginia. Earnest reported for duty on the USS Arizona December 11, 1940. He was killed in action on December 7, 1941 in Pearl Harbor, Hawaii. Earnest was awarded the American Defense Service Medal, World War II Victory Medal and Purple Heart Medal posthumously. He remains on duty on the USS Arizona. Earnest is commemorated on the USS Arizona Memorial and the Memorial Tablets of the Missing, National Memorial Cemetery of the Pacific, Honolulu, Hawaii. He was survived by his Father, Mr. Vessie E. Angle, Quinwood, West Virginia.

Anthony, Glenn Samuel Seaman, First Class, Serial No: 250 41 03, US Navy. Glenn was born August 6, 1918 in Armstrong County, Pennsylvania, son of Edward Anthony and Irene (Lankerd) Anthony. He enlisted in the US Navy on February 4, 1936 and reported for duty on the USS Arizona on June 17, 1936. Glenn was killed in action on December 7, 1941 in Pearl Harbor, Hawaii. He was awarded the American Defense Service Medal, World War II Victory Medal and Purple Heart Medal posthumously. Glenn remains on duty on the USS Arizona. He is commemorated on the USS Arizona Memorial and the Memorial Tablets of the Missing, National Memorial Cemetery of the Pacific, Honolulu, Hawaii. Glenn was survived by his Wife, Mrs. G. S. Anthony, 2313 East 11th Street, Long Beach, California.

---

[22] Robert Adair Anderson, Photo from "A USS Arizona Crewman Longs to be Home for the Holidays", HistoryNet.com, October 5, 2011.
[23] Brainerd Wells Andrews, information provided by his Nephew, Bing Andrews.

Aplin, James Raymond Chief Water Tender, Serial No: 201 13 73, US Navy. James was born in about 1905 in Massachusetts. He was called back into service in the US Navy on October 18, 1940 in San Diego, California and reported for duty on the USS Arizona January 27, 1941. He was killed in action on December 7, 1941 in Pearl Harbor, Hawaii. James was awarded the American Defense Service Medal, World War II Victory Medal and Purple Heart Medal posthumously. He remains on duty on the USS Arizona. James is commemorated on the USS Arizona Memorial and the Memorial Tablets of the Missing, National Memorial Cemetery of the Pacific, Honolulu, Hawaii. He was survived by his Wife, Mrs. Mary Margaret Aplin, 3711 47th Street, San Diego, California.[24]

Apple, Robert William Fireman, First Class, Serial No: 299 84 50, US Navy. Robert was born in 1918 in Illinois, the son of Frank and Rose Apple. His father, a veteran of the Spanish-American War, died when Robert was about six. He enlisted in the US Navy on February 9, 1937 in Chicago, Illinois and reported for duty on the USS Arizona on June 19, 1937. Robert was killed in action on December 7, 1941 in Pearl Harbor, Hawaii. He was awarded the American Defense Service Medal, World War II Victory Medal and Purple Heart Medal posthumously. Robert remains on duty on the USS Arizona. He is commemorated on USS Arizona Memorial and the Memorial Tablets of the Missing, National Memorial Cemetery of the Pacific, Honolulu, Hawaii. Robert was survived by his Mother, Mrs. Rose Marie Apple, 411 11th Avenue, Sterling, Illinois.

His brother, James was serving on board the USS West Virginia and survived the attack at Pearl Harbor on December 7th.[25]

Aprea, Frank Anthony Coxswain, Serial No: 223 58 16, US Navy. Frank was born April 6, 1921 in New York the oldest of four children to Genaro and Michelina Aprea. *He grew up in Brooklyn, New York and attended Eastern District High School. Frank was a member of the Civilian Conservation Corps repairing roads before he enlisted in the US Navy on October 23, 1939 in New York, New York and reported for duty on the USS Arizona on January 4, 1941. Assigned death #526, Frank died from burns received in action on December 7, 1941 in Pearl Harbor, Hawaii. His remains were identified by the name on his waist band.*[26] Frank was awarded the American Defense Service Medal, World War II Victory Medal and Purple Heart Medal posthumously. Frank was buried in St. John's Cemetery, Middle Village, Queens, New York. He is commemorated on the USS Arizona Memorial and the Memorial Tablets of the Missing, National

---

[24] James Raymon Aplin, Information and photo from "Remembering 2 who never came home" by Kathie Neff, Staff writer, The Eagle-Tribune, Windham, NH, Saturday, December 7, 1991.

[25] Robert William Apple, Information and photo provided by family member, Joseph A. Meslovich, Jr., 9/8/2008.

[26] Frank Anthony Aprea, Report of Changes, USS Arizona for the month ending 31st day of December, 1941, page 35, line 2.

Memorial Cemetery of the Pacific, Honolulu, Hawaii. The US Navy sent an empty coffin with a flag and they are buried in St. John's Cemetery. Frank was survived by his Father, Mr. and Mrs. Joseph Aprea, 753 Grand Street, Brooklyn, New York, two sisters, Jenny and Lucy and brother, Michael.[27]

Arledge, Eston Signalman, Second Class, Serial No: 359 97 73, US Navy. Eston was born on November 11, 1917 in Nibletts Bluff, Calcasieu Parish, Louisiana. He was the son of John Thomas Arledge and Edna Estelle Lyons Arledge. Eston served in the CCC before joining the Navy. He enlisted in the US Navy on January 7, 1938 in Houston, Texas and reported for duty on the USS Arizona on April 28, 1938. Eston was killed in action on December 7, 1941 in Pearl Harbor. He was awarded the American Defense Service Medal, World War II Victory Medal and Purple Heart Medal posthumously. Eston remains on duty on the USS Arizona. He is commemorated on the USS Arizona Memorial and the Memorial Tablets of the Missing, National Memorial Cemetery of the Pacific, Honolulu, Hawaii. Eston was survived by his Father, Mr. John Thomas Arledge, Route 1, Box 29, Vinton, Louisiana. [28]

Arnaud, Achilles "Archie" Fireman, Third Class, Serial No: 274 62 43, US Navy. Achilles was born March 16, 1923 in Arnaudville, Saint Landry, Louisiana the son of Jean Cantwell Arnaud and Marie Cornelia Taylor. He was 17 when he enlisted in the US Navy. Archie enlisted in the US Navy on April 22, 1941 in New Orleans, Louisiana and reported for duty on the USS Arizona on November 18, 1941. He was killed in action on December 7, 1941 in Pearl Harbor, Hawaii. Achilles was awarded the American Defense Service Medal, World War II Victory Medal and Purple Heart Medal posthumously. He remains on duty on the USS Arizona. Achilles is commemorated on the USS Arizona Memorial and the Memorial Tablets of the Missing, National Memorial Cemetery of the Pacific, Honolulu, Hawaii. Achilles was survived by his Father, Mr. Cantwell J. Arnaud, Route 1, Arnaudville, Louisiana.[29]

Arnold, Thell Clerk, First Class, Serial No: 346 69 59, US Navy. Thell was born August 21, 1919 in Oklahoma City, Oklahoma, the son of Christopher Columbus Arnold and Mattie Jane Ellis (Pollock) Arnold. He enlisted in the US Navy on March 11, 1938 in Little Rock, Arkansas and reported for duty on the USS Arizona on August 6, 1938. Thell was killed in action on December 7, 1941 in Pearl Harbor, Hawaii. He was awarded the American Defense Service Medal, World War II Victory Medal and Purple Heart Medal posthumously. Thell remains on duty on the USS Arizona. He is commemorated on the USS Arizona Memorial and the Memorial Tablets of the Missing, National Memorial Cemetery of the Pacific, Honolulu, Hawaii. Thell was survived by his Brother, Mr. Charley McClendon Arnold, Route 1, Alma, Arkansas.

---

[27] Frank Anthony Aprea, Photo and information provided by his Sister, Lucy (Aprea) Peters and her son, Len Peters.
[28] Eston Arledge, Photo provided by his niece, Joy D. Moore.
[29] Achilles "Archie" Arnaud, information and picture provided by family members, Seola Arnaud Edwards Author of Chez Les Arnaud (Antoine Arnaud et Odiede Robin)

Arrant, John Anderson Machinist's Mate, First Class, Serial No: 268 20 03, US Navy. John was born September 27, 1917 in Seale, Alabama to John Canty and Mary E. (Thigpen) Arrant. *He quit school in the 10th grade to help with the family farm and work as a clerk for Better Food Stores. Being underage, his father gave written consent for him to enlisted in the US Navy on January 20, 1936 in Macon, Georgia and reported for duty on the USS Arizona on June 17, 1936.* He was killed in action on December 7, 1941 in Pearl Harbor, Hawaii. John was awarded the American Defense Service Medal, World War II Victory Medal and Purple Heart Medal posthumously. He remains on duty on the USS Arizona. John is commemorated on the USS Arizona Memorial and the Memorial Tablets of the Missing, National Memorial Cemetery of the Pacific, Honolulu, Hawaii. He was survived by his Parents, Mr. and Mrs. John Canty Arrant of Homestead, Florida; Brothers, James F of Miami, Florida and Cpl Jesse T. Arrant of the Marine Barracks, New River, North Carolina and Sisters; Robert Arrant Bussey and Betty L. Arrant both from Homestead, Florida. The Arrant-Smith VFW Post #4127 in Homestead, Florida was named in his honor.[30]

Arvidson, Carl Harry Chief Machinist's Mate, Serial No: 299 20 54, US Navy. Carl was born on March 31, 1899 in Karlstad, Sweden the son of Charles T. and Hildur Arvidson. He enlisted in the US Navy on December 3, 1937 in Brooklyn, New York and reported for duty on the USS Arizona on July 9, 1940. He was killed in action on December 7, 1941 in Pearl Harbor, Hawaii. Carl was awarded the American Defense Service Medal, World War II Victory Medal and Purple Heart Medal posthumously. He remains on duty on the USS Arizona. Carl is commemorated on the USS Arizona Memorial and the Memorial Tablets of the Missing, National Memorial Cemetery of the Pacific, Honolulu, Hawaii. He was survived by his Wife, Mrs. Corinne Berniece Arvidson, 1921 Gregory Way, Bremerton, Washington.

Ashmore, Wilburn James Seaman, Second Class, Serial No: 274 65 13, US Navy. Wilburn was born in about 1917 in Allen, Louisiana the son of William Alfred and Louella Ashmore. He enlisted in the US Navy on June 17, 1941 in New Orleans, Louisiana and completed his basic training at the Naval Training Station in San Diego, California. He reported for duty on the USS Arizona on August 13, 1941. Wilburn was killed in action on December 7, 1941 in Pearl Harbor, Hawaii. Wilburn was working in the boiler room of the ship at the time the ship was bombed. He was awarded the American Defense Service Medal, World War II Victory Medal and Purple Heart Medal posthumously. Wilburn remains on duty on the USS Arizona. He is commemorated on the USS Arizona Memorial and the Memorial Tablets of the Missing, National Memorial Cemetery of the Pacific, Honolulu, Hawaii. Wilburn was survived by his Parents, Mr. and Mrs. William Alfred Ashmore, P.O. Box 77, Elizabeth, Louisiana and four sisters, Edna, Helen, Evie and Bertie; and two brothers, Millard and LaVerne.[31]

Atkins, Gerald Arthur Hospital Apprentice, First Class, Serial No: 316 64 41, US Navy. Gerald was born October 17, 1919 in Nebraska the only son of Bernard B. Atkins, a policeman and Lola Kelly Atkins. His mother died when he was about ten years old and he was raised by his father. Gerald attended Gothenburg High School where he played several sports, including track. As of 2018 Gerald was still one of the best 100 yard dash runners in Gothenburg's history. He enlisted in the US Navy on April 30, 1940 in Omaha, Nebraska and

---

[30] John Anderson Arrant, Photo and information provided by his Niece, Liz Arrant.
[31] Wilburn James Ashmore, information from The Times, Shreveport, Louisiana.

reported for duty on the USS Arizona on August 22, 1941. Gerald was killed in action on December 7, 1941 in Pearl Harbor, Hawaii. He was awarded the American Defense Service Medal, World War II Victory Medal and Purple Heart Medal posthumously. Gerald remains on duty on the USS Arizona. He is commemorated on the USS Arizona Memorial and the Memorial Tablets of the Missing, National Memorial Cemetery of the Pacific, Honolulu, Hawaii. Gerald was survived by his Father, Mr. Bernard Beals Atkins, Gothenburg, Nebraska.[32]

Austin, Laverne Alfred Seaman, First Class, Aviation Unit VO-1, Serial No: 238 71 27, US Navy. Laverne was born July 25, 1923 in New York, son of Alfred C. and Jessie C. Austin. *He grew up in Madison County, New York. When he was young his mother and father divorced. Laverne spent his younger years with his father and returned to live with his mother in High School. When he was 17, in his senior year of high school he wanted to enlist in the Navy, so his mother signed a waiver.* He enlisted in the US Navy on December 5, 1940 in Albany, New York and reported for duty on the USS Arizona on September 8, 1941.[33] Laverne was killed in action on December 7, 1941 in Pearl Harbor, Hawaii. He was awarded the American Defense Service Medal, World War II Victory Medal and Purple Heart Medal posthumously. Laverne remains on duty on the USS Arizona. He is commemorated on the USS Arizona Memorial and the Memorial Tablets of the Missing, National Memorial Cemetery of the Pacific, Honolulu, Hawaii. His body was later recovered and sent home for burial in the Peterboro Cemetery, Perryville, New York. Laverne was survived by his Father, Mr. Alfred C. Austin, Perryville, New York.[34]

Autry, Eligah T., Jr. Coxswain, Serial No: 356 11 54, US Navy. Eligah was born in 1919 in Oklahoma son of Elijah T. Autrey and Carrie Lee (Lanham) Autry. He enlisted in the US Navy on August 9, 1939 in Dallas, Texas and completed his basic training at the Naval Training Station in San Diego, California. Eligah reported for duty on the USS Arizona October 20, 1939. He was killed in action on December 7, 1941 in Pearl Harbor, Hawaii. Eligah was awarded the American Defense Service Medal, World War II Victory Medal and Purple Heart Medal posthumously. He remains on duty on the USS Arizona. Eligah is commemorated on the USS Arizona Memorial and the Memorial Tablets of the Missing, National Memorial Cemetery of the Pacific, Honolulu, Hawaii. He was survived by his Father, Mr. Eligah T. Autry, Broadview Hotel, Pampa, Texas.[35]

---

[32] Gerald Arthur Atkins, Information from The Lincoln Star, Lincoln, Nebraska and the Gothenburg High School.

[33] Laverne Alfred Austin, Photo taken from the Syracuse Herald Journal, Syracuse, New York, November 26, 1940. Photo is of Laverne, age 17, being examined at the Navy recruiting station.

[34] Laverne Alfred Austin, Information provided by his cousin, Joyce and her daughter, Laura Hastings.

[35] Eligah T. Autry, Jr., Information and Photo provided by family member, Elaine Oakes, 9/8/2008.

Aves, Willard "Bill" Charles Fireman, Second Class, Serial No: 300 19 18, US Navy. Willard was born on June 28, 1921 in Kingston, DeKalb County, Illinois, son of Charles John Aves and Mamie Melvina (Glidden) Aves of Kingston, Illinois. *He was the youngest of three children, two older sisters, Mildred "Millie" and Irene. He had a younger sibling that died during child birth along with his mother when he was 4 years old. Willard was always known as Bill. Bill spent a lot of time building model airplanes. The frames were made of balsa wood and covered with colored tissue paper. He was a member of a drum and bugle corps in Kingston. Bill attended and graduated from the Kingston Village Schools in Illinois.* After graduation he enlisted in the US Navy on October 8, 1940 in Chicago, Illinois and completed his basic training at the Naval Training Station in Great Lakes, Illinois. Bill reported for duty on the USS Arizona on December 9, 1940. His family never saw him again. Bill was killed in action on December 7, 1941 in Pearl Harbor, Hawaii. He was on duty that day. Bill was awarded the American Defense Service Medal, World War II Victory Medal and Purple Heart Medal posthumously. He remains on duty on the USS Arizona. Bill is commemorated on the USS Arizona Memorial and the Memorial Tablets of the Missing, National Memorial Cemetery of the Pacific, Honolulu, Hawaii. Willard (Bill's) family received a telegram from the Navy Department on Christmas Eve 1941 telling them that Bill was missing and presumed dead. That was the family's Christmas that year and ever since then there is a special star shining for Bill. He was survived by his Father, Mr. Charles Aves of Kingston, Illinois and his two sisters, Mildred and Irene. The American Legion Post 1010 was named in his honor.[36]

Aydell, Miller Xavier Watertender, Second Class, Serial No: 274 31 17, US Navy. Miller was born October 2, 1919 in Livingston Parish, Louisiana to Austin Xavier and Theresa (Vicknair) Aydell. He enlisted in the US Navy on October 8, 1937 in New Orleans, Louisiana and reported for duty on the USS Arizona on January 25, 1938. Miller was killed in action on December 7, 1941 in Pearl Harbor, Hawaii. He was awarded the American Defense Service Medal, World War II Victory Medal and Purple Heart Medal posthumously. Miller remains on duty on the USS Arizona. He is commemorated on the USS Arizona Memorial and the Memorial Tablets of the Missing, National Memorial Cemetery of the Pacific, Honolulu, Hawaii. Miller was survived by his Father, Mr. Austin Xavier Aydell, French Settlement, Louisiana.

Ayers, Dee Cumpie Seaman, Second Class, Serial No: 356 53 76, US Navy. Dee was born January 11, 1917 in Elmo, Texas son of Durward Cumpie Ayers and Nannie (Johnston) Ayers. His father, also named Dee Cumpie was a farmer and died in 1937. His mother remarried to a widower, Robert Burton Wood. He was the father of Horace Van Wood, making him his stepbrother. He enlisted in the US Navy on March 7, 1941 in Dallas, Texas and completed his basic training at the Naval Training Station in San Diego, California. Dee reported for duty on the USS Arizona June 7, 1941. *Assigned death #388, Dee died from drowning on December 7, 1941 in Pearl Harbor, Hawaii. He was*

---

[36] Willard "Bill" Charles Aves, Information and Photo provided by family member Ginger Glass, 9/13/2008.

identified by the name "AYERS" on his shorts.[37] He was awarded the American Defense Service Medal, World War II Victory Medal and Purple Heart Medal posthumously. His remains were identified by his name on his shorts. His remains were sent home to Texas and were buried in the White Rose Cemetery, Wills Point, Texas. He is commemorated on the USS Arizona Memorial and the Memorial Tablets of the Missing, National Memorial Cemetery of the Pacific, Honolulu, Hawaii. Dee was survived by his Mother, Mrs. Nannie Wood, Box 58, Terrell, Texas. His step-brother, Horace Van Wood was also killed in action on board the USS Arizona that fateful day. His cousin, Brooxey J. Johnston, Jr. was serving on board the USS Arizona and survived.

Badilla, Manuel Dominic   Fireman, First Class, Serial No: 382 11 60, US Navy. Manuel was born May 16, 1921 in Santa Barbara, California to Manuel and Sallie Cush (Olivas) Badilla. *Manuel's father, a truck driver, died of a sudden heart attack, June 18, 1930 in Santa Barbara. Manuel was 9 years old at the time. His mother Sallie worked in the Canneries as a machine operator. These were hard times. When the 1933 earthquake struck, their apartment wall facing the street collapsed and they had an open view of downtown Long Beach. The depression was at an all time low, and his mother was having a hard time making ends meet. By the time he turned 17, Manuel had dropped out of High School to work full time.* He enlisted in the US Navy on October 10, 1939 in Los Angeles, California and completed his basic training at the Naval Training Station in San Diego, California. Manuel reported for duty on the USS Arizona December 20, 1939. *The night before the Pearl Harbor attack, Manuel had attended the battle of the bands with his best friend, Greg and was planning to attend Mass on the Arizona in the morning then go to Honolulu for the day.* He was killed in action on December 7, 1941 in Pearl Harbor, Hawaii. *Initially his remains were believed to have been recovered and buried in the Punchbowl. His family petitioned the government to exhume the remains. The dental records identified the remains as another man.* Manuel was awarded the American Defense Service Medal, World War II Victory Medal and Purple Heart Medal posthumously. He remains on duty on the USS Arizona. Manuel is commemorated on the USS Arizona Memorial and the Memorial Tablets of the Missing, National Memorial Cemetery of the Pacific, Honolulu, Hawaii. He was survived by his Mother, Mrs. Sally Cush Johnson, 1217 Ohio Street, Long Beach, California.[38]

Bagby, Walter Franklin   Shipfitter, Third Class, Serial No. 342 20 85, US Navy. Walter was born in about 1916 in Missouri the son of Noah Franklin and Lyda Fern (Page) Bagby. He enlisted in the US Navy March 25, 1940 in Kansas City, Missouri and completed his basic training at the Naval Training Station in Great Lakes, Illinois. Walter reported for duty on the USS Arizona July 12, 1940 where he was serving on December 7, 1941 when the Japanese attacked Pearl Harbor. His Official Statement:
    "I was at my battle station in D-504 when the first explosion came, and then the smoke got so bad that I couldn't breathe, then I

---

[37] Dee Cumpie Ayers, Report of Changes of the USS Arizona for the month ending 31st day of December, 1941, page 35 line 14. Photo and additional family information from a nephew of Horace Van Wood, Terry W. Wood and Larry Turner of Wills Point, who has spent considerable time researching the local men on the Arizona.

[38] Manuel Dominic Badilla, Photo provided by family member, Phelicia Gardner. Family story taken from: "Manuel Dominic Badilla – A Life Not Forgotten" by Harold Fowler, Nephew.

went down into D-311 to try and get a gas mask, but I couldn't get in. Then I came up to top side through the warrant officers hatch on the port side. Then I swam over to the key and the Solace rescue party picked me up[39]

Walter was missing in action on November 30, 1942, during the Battle of Tassafaronga, Guadalcanal while serving on board the USS New Orleans (CA-32). He was declared dead December 1, 1943. He is commemorated on the Memorial Tablets of the Missing, Fort William McKinley, Manila, Philippines. He was awarded the Purple Heart Medal posthumously. Walter was survived by his Father, Mr. Noah F. Bagby, Route 4, Adrian, Missouri.[40]

Baird, Billy Byron Seaman, First Class, Serial No: 291 65 70, US Navy. Billy was born in 1922 in Indiana. He enlisted in the US Navy on October 8, 1940 in Indianapolis, Indiana and completed his basic training at the Naval Training Station in Great Lakes, Illinois. He reported for duty on the USS Arizona on December 9, 1940. Billy was killed in action on December 7, 1941 in Pearl Harbor, Hawaii. He was awarded the American Defense Service Medal, World War II Victory Medal and Purple Heart Medal posthumously. Billy remains on duty on the USS Arizona. He is commemorated on the USS Arizona Memorial and the Memorial Tablets of the Missing, National Memorial Cemetery of the Pacific, Honolulu, Hawaii. Billy was survived by his Mother, Mrs. Verne Baird, 111 Main Street, Monticello, Indiana.[41]

Bajorims (Bajorinas), Joseph Seaman, First Class, Serial No: 300 20 53, US Navy. Joseph was born May 5, 1918 In Chicago Heights, Illinois, the son of Joseph and Rose (Bukowska) Bajorinas. He enlisted in the US Navy on October 8, 1940 in Chicago, Illinois and completed his basic training at the Naval Training Station in Great Lakes, Illinois. Joseph reported for duty on the USS Arizona on December 9, 1940. He was killed in action on December 7, 1941 in Pearl Harbor, Hawaii. Joseph was awarded the American Defense Service Medal, World War II Victory Medal and Purple Heart Medal posthumously. He remains on duty on the USS Arizona. Joseph is commemorated on the USS Arizona Memorial and the Memorial Tablets of the Missing, National Memorial Cemetery of the Pacific, Honolulu, Hawaii. He was survived by his Father, Mr. Joseph Bajorinas, 309 East 14th Street, Chicago, Illinois.[42]

---

[39] Statement Regarding Attack on U.S.S. ARIZONA, December 7, 1941 by BAGBY, Walter Franklin, SF3c, U.S. Navy, "R" Division, to his Commanding Officer, U.S.S. ARIZONA, December 17, 1941, Pearl Harbor, T.H.

[40] Walter Franklin Bagby, Information and picture provided by family member, Joyce Stewart.

[41] Billy Byron Baird, Photo courtesy of the Carroll County, Indiana Museum.

[42] Joseph Bajorims (Bajorinas), Information and photo provided by the Bajorinas family through the Bloom High School, Chicago, Illinois.

Baker, Robert Dewey Chief Machinist's Mate, Serial No: 324 92 86, US Navy. Robert was born May 18, 1902 in Marion, Illinois. He enlisted in the US Navy on February 18, 1938 in San Pedro, California. Robert transferred from the USS Oklahoma to the USS Arizona on March 29, 1940. He was killed in action on December 7, 1941 in Pearl Harbor, Hawaii. Robert was awarded the American Defense Service Medal, World War II Victory Medal and Purple Heart Medal posthumously. He remains on duty on the USS Arizona. Robert is commemorated on the USS Arizona Memorial and the Memorial Tablets of the Missing, National Memorial Cemetery of the Pacific, Honolulu, Hawaii. He was survived by his Wife, Mrs. Garnette Lucille Baker, 3038-A East 3rd Street, Long Beach, California.

Ball, Masten A. Fireman, First Class, Serial No. 321 22 70, US Navy. Masten was born May 1, 1919 in Linn Grove, Iowa. He was the son of Wiley W. and Rebecca Ball. Masten enlisted in the US Navy December 21, 1937 in Des Moines, Iowa and completed his basic training at the Naval Training Station in Great Lakes, Illinois. He reported for duty on the USS Arizona July 9, 1938. Masten was serving on board the USS Arizona on December 7, 1941, when the Japanese attacked Pearl Harbor. *He was on deck and was blown off in the water during the attack. His brother, William V. Ball was killed in action on board the USS Arizona during the Japanese attack.* He was transferred to Bishops Point for duty after the attack. His brother William was killed in action on the USS Arizona. Maston served in the Navy until December 1957 with 20 years service. He died August 4, 1985 in New London, Connecticut.

Ball, William V. Seaman, First Class, Serial No: 321 21 91, US Navy. William was born July 15, 1920 in Len Grove, Iowa. He enlisted in the US Navy on October 11, 1938 in Des Moines, Iowa and completed his basic training at the Naval Training Station in Great Lakes, Illinois. He reported for duty on the USS Arizona on January 1, 1939. William was killed in action on December 7, 1941 in Pearl Harbor, Hawaii. He was awarded the American Defense Service Medal, World War II Victory Medal and Purple Heart Medal posthumously. William remains on duty on the USS Arizona. He is commemorated on the USS Arizona Memorial and the Memorial Tablets of the Missing, National Memorial Cemetery of the Pacific, Honolulu, Hawaii. William was survived by his Father, Mr. W. W. Ball, Fredericksburg, Iowa. His brother, Masten A. Ball was also serving on board the USS Arizona and survived. The five Sullivan brothers enlisted to avenge the loss of their friend, William.[43]

Ballard, Galen Owen Fireman, First Class, B Division, Serial No. 311 14 62, US Navy. Galen was born on February 24, 1916 in Cedar Springs, Michigan. He enlisted in the US Navy November 18, 1935 in Detroit, Michigan and completed his basic training at the Naval Training Station in Great Lakes, Illinois. Galen reported for duty on the USS Arizona March 14, 1936 where he was serving on December 7, 1941, when the Japanese attacked Pearl Harbor. *He was on liberty when the attack began. By the time he was able to report for duty, the Arizona was already burning. Galen was due for discharge on December 31, 1941 but there were no more discharges after Pearl Harbor so he served thru the end of the war. Galen was transferred to a*

---

[43] William V. Ball, Photo from WCF Courier, Waterloo, IA, "Victims of 1941 Pearl Harbor attack remembered" by Pat Kinney, December 7, 2011.

salvage party to help divers retrieve safes with records from the Arizona. He did this for about two weeks. He later saw duty in the Marshalls, Majurao, Kwajalen, Eniwetok, Palau Islands, Ulithi and other atolls and islands during World War II. Galen went on to serve in the Korean War. He retired from the Navy after 22 years of service in 1957. Married to Dotty Cramer, with 2 young sons, he moved his family to Spooner, Wisconsin where he earned a teaching degree and taught school, earned a Master's and kept on teaching until he retired in 1975. In December of 1991, Galen wrote a letter to the Tampa Bay Times regarding the 50th Anniversary of the Attack at Pearl Harbor:

"It was no 'celebration' I believe I understand the intent of a Dec. 20 letter to the editor, and it is not entirely without merit. However, as a survivor of the USS Arizona, I deeply resent her reference to the 50th Anniversary of the Japanese attack on Pearl Harbor and the accompanying activities and services as a "Celebration". None of my fellow survivors or I were in a mood to celebrate as we attended the ceremonies aboard the USS Arizona Memorial the morning of Dec. 7, 1991. I am also sure that the relatives of those who died were not celebrating as they attended the ceremonies honoring those men and then tossed flowers upon the watery grave of their loved ones! Neither did I note any mood of celebration when I attended ceremonies at the Punchbowl Cemetery where the remains of servicemen of all branches of the military services are interred. To me, the 50th anniversary commemoration served a duel purpose. The primary purpose was to afford an opportunity to express our respect in honoring those who gave their lives in that disastrous sneak attack of the Japanese on Dec. 7, 1941. The other purpose was to remind our nation to remain alert and vigilant so that we never again invite attack by an aggressor nation by being unprepared and complacent. If that lesson is learned, then those courageous men who gave their lives that infamous Dec. 7 will not have died in vain".[44]

Galen died on October 24, 1995 in Dunedin, Pinellas, Florida from a massive heart attack and is buried in Section 59, Row 15, Site 70, Bay Pines National Cemetery, Bay Pines, Florida.

Bandy, Wayne Lynn Musician, Second Class, Serial No: 337 41 33, US Navy. Wayne was born on October 14, 1920 in Waynesville, Missouri the son of Reverend John Livingston Bandy and Martha May (Davis) Bandy. His home was Waynesville, Missouri. Wayne enlisted in the US Navy on October 9, 1940 and attended the Navy School of Music in Washington, DC graduating on May 23, 1941 as a member of the USS Arizona Band. He reported for duty on the USS Arizona on June 17, 1941. Wayne was killed in action on December 7, 1941 in Pearl Harbor, Hawaii. *His battle station was in the black powder room passing ammunition to the Arizona's gunners during the attack. None of the band members survived the explosion.* He was awarded the American Defense Service Medal, World War II Victory Medal and Purple Heart Medal posthumously. Wayne remains on duty on the USS Arizona. He is commemorated on the USS Arizona Memorial and the Memorial Tablets of the Missing, National Memorial Cemetery of the Pacific, Honolulu, Hawaii. Wayne was survived by his Father, Rev. John L. Bandy, Waynesville, Missouri and his Brother, Paul Bandy.[45]

---

[44] Galen Owen Ballard, letter to the editor, Tampa Bay Times, St. Petersburg, Florida, December 29, 1991, Page 47.

[45] Wayne Lynn Bandy, Photo from USS Arizona's Last Band by Molly Kent. By permission of the author. For more information about this book, go to www.USSARIZONASLASTBAND.com.

Bangert, John Henry, Jr. Fire Controlman, First Class, F Division, Serial No: 243 50 77, US Navy. John was born on August 1, 1916 In Pennsylvania. He enlisted in the Navy on January 27, 1936 in Philadelphia, Pennsylvania and reported for duty on the USS Arizona on June 17, 1936. He had just signed on for another three years when he was killed in action on December 7, 1941 in Pearl Harbor, Hawaii. John's battle station was the port antiaircraft director station. He was awarded the American Defense Service Medal, World War II Victory Medal and Purple Heart Medal posthumously. John's remains were recovered and he was buried in Plot O Row 0 Grave 189, National Memorial Cemetery of the Pacific, Honolulu, Hawaii. He is commemorated on the USS Arizona Memorial. John was survived by his Father, Mr. John Henry Bangert, Sr., 4358 North Franklin Street, Philadelphia, Pennsylvania.[46]

Bardon, Charles Thomas Seaman, Second Class, Serial No: 356 59 04, US Navy. Charles was born May 27, 1924 in Tulsa, Oklahoma the son of Charles Douglas Bardon and Eula Mae Bardon. He enlisted in the US Navy on May 29, 1941 in Dallas, Texas and completed his basic training at the Naval Training Station in San Diego, California. Charles reported for duty on the USS Arizona on August 13, 1941. He was killed in action on December 7, 1941 in Pearl Harbor, Hawaii. Charles was awarded the American Defense Service Medal, World War II Victory Medal and Purple Heart Medal posthumously. He remains on duty on the USS Arizona. Charles is commemorated on the USS Arizona Memorial and the Memorial Tablets of the Missing, National Memorial Cemetery of the Pacific, Honolulu, Hawaii. He was survived by his Mother, Mrs. Eula Mae Bardon, Box 345, Bixby, Oklahoma.

Barker, Loren Joe Coxswain, Serial No: 321 39 46, US Navy. Loren was born on August 23, 1921 to Joseph M. Barker and Eva B. (Keck) Barker. *He graduated from the Keosauqua High School in 1938 and was the youngest member of the class. Loren enlisted in the Navy on March 6, 1940 at the age of 18 and on March 5th was sent to the Great Lakes Naval training station near Chicago. He returned home for his first furlough in May and during this period he was married. Joe, as he was called, was secretly married on May 23, 1940 to Miss Susan Elizabeth Tharp of Keosauqua. The ceremony was performed by the Rev. T. E. Clark at the Baptist church in Monticello, Missouri and was attended by the groom's mother. Two months later he sailed for Hawaii, where he was assigned to the USS Arizona. He reported for duty on July 12, 1940. Loren was given a second furlough in November 1940; this was to be his last visit home. In January, 1941, he returned to Hawaii. His last message to his parents was a cabled Thanksgiving greeting dated November 20, 1941.* Loren was killed in action on December 7, 1941 in Pearl Harbor, Hawaii. He was awarded the American Defense Service Medal, World War II Victory Medal and Purple Heart Medal posthumously. Loren remains on duty on the USS Arizona. He is commemorated on the USS Arizona Memorial and the Memorial Tablets of the Missing, National Memorial Cemetery of the Pacific, Honolulu, Hawaii. Loren was survived by his Parents, Mr. Joseph M. Barker and Mrs. Iva B. (Keck) Barker, Keosauqua, Iowa, his wife, Susan Elizabeth (Tharp) Barker; a sister, Mrs. Bruce Davis of Keosauqua; a grandmother, Mrs. Jennie Keck of Keosauqua and three nieces.[47]

---

[46] John Henry Bangert, Jr., Photo and information provided by family members, Carolyn Brascetta and John R. and Linda Bangert.

[47] Loren Joe Barker, Information and Photo provided by family member, Mark Tunnell, 9/16/2008.

Barner, Walter Ray Seaman, Second Class, Serial No: 360 25 73, US Navy. Walter was born November 13, 1921 in Wichita Falls, Texas son of Robert and Frances Barner. He enlisted in the US Navy on November 12, 1940 in Houston, Texas and completed his basic training at the Naval Training Station in San Diego, California. Walter reported for duty on the USS Arizona on January 11, 1941. He was killed in action on December 7, 1941 in Pearl Harbor, Hawaii. Walter was awarded the American Defense Service Medal, World War II Victory Medal and Purple Heart Medal posthumously. He remains on duty on the USS Arizona. Walter is commemorated on the USS Arizona Memorial and the Memorial Tablets of the Missing, National Memorial Cemetery of the Pacific, Honolulu, Hawaii. He was survived by his Father, Mr. Robert S. Barner, 1707 Magnolia, Wichita Falls, Texas.

Barnes, Charles Edward Yeoman, Third Class, Serial No: 337 41 46, US Navy. Charles was born September 26, 1922 in Kansas the son of Carter Barnes. He enlisted in the US Navy on October 15, 1940 in St. Louis, Missouri and completed his basic training at the Naval Training Station in Great Lakes, Illinois. He reported for duty on the USS Arizona on December 9, 1940. Charles was killed in action on December 7, 1941 in Pearl Harbor, Hawaii. He was awarded the American Defense Service Medal, World War II Victory Medal and Purple Heart Medal posthumously. Charles remains on duty on the USS Arizona. He is commemorated on the USS Arizona Memorial and the Memorial Tablets of the Missing, National Memorial Cemetery of the Pacific, Honolulu, Hawaii. Charles was survived by his Father, Mr. Carter Barnes, Box 192 Senath, Missouri.

Barnes, Delmar Hayes Lieutenant, Junior Grade, Serial No: 0-059940, US Navy Reserve. Delmar was born in Chicago, Illinois on November 21, 1900. He was adopted by Lloyd J. Barnes and Lotta J. Barnes (purported to be his mother's sister). *His home state was California but he grew up in Roseburg, Oregon. In the mid to late 1920's Del was posted to Shanghai, China with his first wife, Avie. He and his wife were popular among the officers and their wives and the civilians in the American colony of Shanghai. A great deal of socializing went on within this tight enclave, much of it characterized by heavy drinking and a huge strain on his relationship with his wife. His marriage did not survive the Shanghai posting.* Delmar was posted to the USS Arizona in 1938. He was killed in action on December 7, 1941 in Pearl Harbor, Hawaii. *His battle station was Station #35 which was next to the magazine that held the 14" ammunition and the black powder room.* Delmar was awarded the American Defense Service Medal, World War II Victory Medal and Purple Heart Medal posthumously. He remains on duty on the USS Arizona. Delmar is commemorated on the USS Arizona Memorial and the Memorial Tablets of the Missing, National Memorial Cemetery of the Pacific, Honolulu, Hawaii. He was survived by his Wife, Mrs. Delmar H. Barnes, 800 Aileen Street, Oakland, California and his adoptive parents, Lloyd J. and Lotta J. Barnes.[48]

---

[48] Delmar Hayes Barnes, Information and Picture provided by family member, Nephew, Howard S. Cox.

Barnett, William Thermon Fireman, Third Class, Serial No: 346 92 39, US Navy. William was born May 30, 1920 in Fort Scott, Kansas to William and Emma Marie (Ewing) Barnett. He enlisted in the US Navy on March 28, 1941 in Little Rock, Arkansas and completed his basic training at the Naval Training Station in San Diego, California. He reported for duty on the USS Arizona on July 13, 1941. William was killed in action on December 7, 1941 in Pearl Harbor, Hawaii. He was awarded the American Defense Service Medal, World War II Victory Medal and Purple Heart Medal posthumously. William remains on duty on the USS Arizona. He is commemorated on the USS Arizona Memorial and the Memorial Tablets of the Missing, National Memorial Cemetery of the Pacific, Honolulu, Hawaii. William was survived by his Father, Mr. William Albert Barnett, El Paso, Arkansas.[49]

Barth, DeWayne Boatswain's Mate, First Class, Serial No. 321 07 89, US Navy. DeWayne was born on August 3, 1916 in Ellington Township, Iowa. In 1930 he was living with his Aunt and Uncle: Lewie and Hattie E. Barth of Ellington, Iowa. He enlisted in the US Navy August 14, 1936 in Mason City, Iowa and completed his basic training at the Naval Training Station in Great Lakes, Illinois. DeWayne reported for duty on the USS Arizona December 2, 1936 where he was serving on December 7, 1941, when the Japanese attacked Pearl Harbor. His official statement:

"On the morning of the raid, December 7, 1941, I was in the fourth division part of the ship, when Haerling, Boatswain's mate first class, passed the word that the Japs were raiding. All the men in the compartment closed the air and battle ports and then went to their battle stations in turret four.

My station is in the pointer's group, so I went in the turret from the topside and manned the sound powered phones to the booth. After the first bomb hit the main power went off in the turret. We tried the auxiliary power, but it did not work. About that time the lower handling room crew came up in the pits from below, as water was coming in fast. When we left the turret the water and gas, of some kind, was in the turret, so the entire crew went outside.

Lieutenant Commander S. G. Fuqua was giving orders to pick up the wounded and abandon ship, to Ford Island. I then manned No. 2 motor launch and Lieutenant Commander Fuqua gave us orders to pick up men from the water which was covered with oil so thick they could hardly swim. We took one boat load of men to Ford Island and then went in close to the Arizona to see if there were any more men on deck. All the time the Japs were strafing the boats and men in the water. We then made for magazine island and loaded the wounded men in a truck and took them to the hospital.

Through the calmness and presence of mind of Lieutenant Commander Fuqua, a number of men was picked up in the oil and water and saved from drowning or burning to death.

During the entire attack, all hands were calm and gave no sign of terror."[50]

DeWayne was assigned duty on Salvage Crane Mary Anne after the attack. He retired from the Navy in 1958. During his service he received the Bronze Star and Purple Heart and achieved a rank of Chief Warrant Officer, Grade 4. He also served in the Korean War. DeWayne died on February 6, 2004 in Houston, Texas and is buried in Section N1, Site 625, Houston National Cemetery, Houston, Texas. DeWayne was survived by his Wife, Mrs. Maggie Barth and two daughters.

---

[49] William Thermon Barnett, Photo provided by family member, Nancy L. Barnett.
[50] Confidential Statement of DeWayne Barth, Boatswain's Mate First Class, U.S. Navy, January 5, 1942.

Bartlett, Paul Clement   Machinist's Mate, First Class, Serial No: 359 96 11, US Navy. Paul was born April 18, 1918 in Rockdale, Texas, son of Jesse J. Bartlett and Lucile J. Bartlett. He enlisted in the US Navy on September 10, 1937 in Houston, Texas and reported for duty on the USS Arizona on January 7, 1938. Paul was killed in action on December 7, 1941 in Pearl Harbor, Hawaii. He was awarded the American Defense Service Medal, World War II Victory Medal and Purple Heart Medal posthumously. Paul remains on duty on the USS Arizona. He is commemorated on the USS Arizona Memorial and the Memorial Tablets of the Missing, National Memorial Cemetery of the Pacific, Honolulu, Hawaii. Paul was survived by his Father, Mr. Jesse James Bartlett, Route 3, Rockdale, Texas.

Bass, Edward Forester   Fireman, Second Class, V-6, Serial No. 413 21 73, US Navy. Edward was born on November 4, 1911 in Washington, Ohio, the son of William and Daisy (Curtis) Bass. He enlisted in the US Navy December 7, 1937 in San Francisco, California and completed his basic training at the Naval Training Station in San Diego, California. Edward reported for duty on the USS Arizona February 18, 1940. He was serving on board the USS Arizona on December 7, 1941 when the Japanese attacked Pearl Harbor. Edward was taken aboard the USS Tennessee after the attack. On January 4, 1942 he was assigned to 14th Naval District, Section Base, Bishop's Point, Oahu, Hawaii. He later went on to serve on board the USS Hunter Liggett, USS Fuller, USS Shelikof and later the Amphibious Force Pacific Fleet. Edward died on December 27, 1988 in Norwich, Connecticut.

Bates, Edward Monroe, Jr.   Ensign, Serial No: 0-095313, US Navy Reserve. Edward was born on September 19, 1919 in Philadelphia, Pennsylvania. He enlisted in the Naval Reserve on July 12, 1940 as an apprentice seaman. Following active duty training on board the USS Wyoming (BB-32), Edward received an appointment as a midshipman on August 10, 1940. He was commissioned an Ensign on November 14, 1940 and reported for duty on December 1, 1940. Edward served as a junior watch and division officer in the ship's F Division. He was killed in action on December 7, 1941, Pearl Harbor, Hawaii. Edward was awarded the American Defense Service Medal, World War II Victory Medal and Purple Heart Medal posthumously. He remains on duty on the USS Arizona. Edward is commemorated on the USS Arizona Memorial and the Memorial Tablets of the Missing, National Memorial Cemetery of the Pacific, Honolulu, Hawaii. He was survived by his Mother, Mrs. Elizabeth N. Bates, 4 Gilchrist Road, Great Neck, New York. The USS Bates (DE-68) was named after him. On May 25, 1945, while patrolling two miles south of Ie Shima, the USS Bates came under attack by three Japanese planes and was sunk, suffering 23 crew losses.

Bates, Robert Alvin   Pharmacist's Mate, Third Class, Serial No: 356 18 86, US Navy. Robert was born on January 26, 1919 in Black, Texas, son of John Alvin Bates and Lonella (Edwards) Bates. He enlisted in the US Navy on January 10, 1940 in Dallas, Texas and completed his basic training at the Naval Training Station in San Diego, California. Robert reported for duty on the USS Arizona on May 27, 1941. He was killed in action on December 7, 1941 in Pearl Harbor, Hawaii. Robert was awarded the American Defense Service Medal, World War II Victory Medal and Purple Heart Medal posthumously. He remains on duty on the USS Arizona. Robert is commemorated on the USS Arizona Memorial and the Memorial Tablets of the Missing, National Memorial Cemetery of the Pacific, Honolulu, Hawaii. He was survived by his Parents, Mr. and Mrs. L. Griffin, General Delivery, Kamay, Texas.[51]

Bator, Edward Fireman, First Class, Serial No: 238 63 76, US Navy. Edward was born on March 15, 1915 in New York Mills, New York to Stanley Bator and Julianna (Kantor) Bator. He enlisted in the US Navy on January 22, 1940 in Albany, New York and reported for duty on the USS Arizona January 4, 1941. Edward was killed in action on December 7, 1941 in Pearl Harbor, Hawaii. He was awarded the American Defense Service Medal, World War II Victory Medal and Purple Heart Medal posthumously. Edward remains on duty on the USS Arizona. He is commemorated on the USS Arizona Memorial and the Memorial Tablets of the Missing, National Memorial Cemetery of the Pacific, Honolulu, Hawaii. Edward was survived by his Father, Mr. Stanley Bator, 6 Maple Street, New York Mills, New York. The Edward Bator – USS Arizona Pearl Harbor Memorial Monument in New York Mills, New York was named in his honor.[52]

Bauer, Harold Walter Radioman, Third Class, Serial No: 410 14 26, US Navy. Harold was born March 4, 1914 in Kansas. He enlisted in the US Navy on November 13, 1940 and reported for duty on the USS Arizona on January 25, 1941. Harold was killed in action on December 7, 1941 in Pearl Harbor, Hawaii. He was awarded the American Defense Service Medal, World War II Victory Medal and Purple Heart Medal posthumously. Harold remains on duty on the USS Arizona. He is commemorated on the USS Arizona Memorial and the Memorial Tablets of the Missing, National Memorial Cemetery of the Pacific, Honolulu, Hawaii. Harold was survived by his Wife, Mrs. Beatrice Rose Bauer, 1337 Betting Street, Wichita, Kansas.[53]

Baumeister, William Nicolas Aviation Chief Machinist's Mate, VP-11, Serial No. 110 93 01, US Navy. William was born on October 4, 1894 in New York, New York. He enlisted in the US Navy December 13, 1917 and was listed in the US Navy Reserve in 1930 at Pearl Harbor. William reported for duty on the USS Arizona May 13, 1937. He extended his enlistment for three years on February 6, 1941. William was serving on board the USS Arizona on December 7, 1941 when the Japanese attacked Pearl Harbor. He was wounded in action later in the war and his wife, Mrs. Helen Baumeister, 64 South Pine Street, Albany, New York was notified. William died March 26, 1982 in Alameda County, California.

---

[51] Robert Alvin Bates, Information provided by his First Cousin, Wayne Witt Bates.

[52] Edward Bator, Photo provided by family member, Susan Harvey.

[53] Harold Walter Bauer, hand painted picture painted by his sister, Francis Sayer.

Beaumont, James Ammon   Seaman, Second Class, Serial No: 356 56 63, US Navy. James was born in about 1921 in Texas. He enlisted in the US Navy on April 18, 1941 in Dallas, Texas and completed his basic training at the Naval Training Station in San Diego, California. He reported for duty on the USS Arizona on July 13, 1941. James was killed in action on December 7, 1941 in Pearl Harbor, Hawaii. He was awarded the American Defense Service Medal, World War II Victory Medal and Purple Heart Medal posthumously. James remains on duty on the USS Arizona. He is commemorated on the USS Arizona Memorial and the Memorial Tablets of the Missing, National Memorial Cemetery of the Pacific, Honolulu, Hawaii. James was survived by his Father, Mr. John Oscar Beaumont, 1935 Burbank, Dallas, Texas.[54]

Beck, George Richard   Seaman, First Class, Serial No: 382 30 19, US Navy. George was born March 31, 1918, the 10th child of 11 children born to John and Miranda Jane (Stafford) Beck. He enlisted in the US Navy on November 6, 1940 in Los Angeles, California and completed his basic training at the Naval Training Station in San Diego, California. George reported for duty on the USS Arizona on January 11, 1941. He died on December 10, 1941 from the burns he sustained in the attack on December 7, 1941 in Pearl Harbor, Hawaii. He was assigned death #115.[55] George was awarded the American Defense Service Medal, World War II Victory Medal and Purple Heart Medal posthumously. He was buried in Plot B, Row 0, Grave 324, National Memorial Cemetery of the Pacific, Honolulu, Hawaii. He is commemorated on the USS Arizona Memorial. George was survived by his Father, Mr. John Beck, 2635 Rich Street, Los Angeles, California.[56]

Becker, Harvey Herman   Gunner's Mate, Second Class, Serial No. 342 07 81, US Navy. Harvey was born September 28, 1916, the son of Willie F. and Freda Becker. He enlisted in the US Navy July 12, 1938 in Kansas City, Missouri and completed his basic training at the Naval Training Station in Great Lakes, Illinois. He reported for duty on the USS Arizona October 23, 1938 where he was serving on December 7, 1941, when the Japanese attacked Pearl Harbor. After the attack, Harvey was transferred to the USS Tennessee for duty. His two brothers, Marvin Otto and Wesley Paulson were both killed in action on board the USS Arizona. Harvey's father, Mr. William Becker, Nekoma, Kansas was notified. Harvey died October 4, 1979 and is buried in the Forest Lawn Memorial Park, Covina, California.[57]

---

[54] James Ammon Beaumont, photo curtsey LCDR G. Dale McKissick, USNR, Memorial, Dallas Convention Center, Dallas, Texas.
[55] George Richard Beck, Report of Changes, USS Arizona for the month ending 31st day of December, 1941, page 37, line 6.
[56] George Richard Beck, Information and Photo provided by family member, Joyce King Banks.
[57] Harvey Herman Becker, Photo and information provided by family member, Sharon Hays.

Becker, Marvin Otto   Gunner's Mate, Third Class, Serial No: 342 16 74, US Navy. Marvin was born in 1919 in Union, Kansas, son of William F Becker and Freda Becker. He enlisted in the US Navy on December 19, 1939 in Kansas City, Missouri and completed his basic training at the Naval Training Station in Great Lakes, Illinois. Marvin reported for duty on the USS Arizona on March 15, 1940. He was killed in action on December 7, 1941 in Pearl Harbor, Hawaii. Marvin was awarded the American Defense Service Medal, World War II Victory Medal and Purple Heart Medal posthumously. He remains on duty on the USS Arizona. Marvin is commemorated on the USS Arizona Memorial and the Memorial Tablets of the Missing, National Memorial Cemetery of the Pacific, Honolulu, Hawaii. He was survived by his Father, Mr. William F. Becker, Nekoma, Kansas. His brother, Wesley Paulson was serving on board the USS Arizona and was lost. Marvin's other Brother; Harvey Herman was serving on the Arizona and was among the survivors.[58]

Becker, Wesley Paulson   Seaman, First Class, Serial No: 342 38 97, US Navy. Wesley was born in about 1923 in Kansas. He enlisted in the US Navy on January 28, 1941 in Kansas City, Missouri and completed his basic training at the Naval Training Station in Great Lakes, Illinois. He reported for duty on the USS Arizona on April 27, 1941. Wesley was killed in action on December 7, 1941 in Pearl Harbor, Hawaii. He was awarded the American Defense Service Medal, World War II Victory Medal and Purple Heart Medal posthumously. Wesley remains on duty on the USS Arizona. He is commemorated on the USS Arizona Memorial and the Memorial Tablets of the Missing, National Memorial Cemetery of the Pacific, Honolulu, Hawaii. Wesley was survived by his Father, Mr. William F. Becker, Nekoma, Kansas. His brother, Marvin was also serving on board the USS Arizona and was killed in action. His other Brother, Harvey Herman, was serving on the Arizona and was among the survivors.[59]

Bedford, Purdy Renaker   Fireman, First Class, Serial No: 279 53 07, US Navy. Purdy was born October 23, 1919 in Harrison, Kentucky to Henry Clay Bedford and Norma B. (Jouett) Bedford. He enlisted in the US Navy on November 1, 1937 in Cincinnati, Ohio and reported for duty on the USS Arizona on March 12, 1938. Purdy was killed in action on December 7, 1941 in Pearl Harbor, Hawaii. He was awarded the American Defense Service Medal, World War II Victory Medal and Purple Heart Medal posthumously. Purdy remains on duty on the USS Arizona. He is commemorated on the USS Arizona Memorial and the Memorial Tablets of the Missing, National Memorial Cemetery of the Pacific, Honolulu, Hawaii and the Pythian Grove Cemetery, Berry,

---

[58] Marvin Otto Becker, Information and picture provided by the Pottawatomie County, Kansas genealogy database.

[59] Wesley Paulson Becker, Information and picture provided by the Pottawatomie County, Kansas Genealogy database.

Kentucky. Purdy was survived by his Father, Mr. Henry Clay Bedford, Rural Route 5, Cynthiana, Kentucky.[60]

Beerman, Henry Carl Carpenter's Mate Third Class, Serial No: 385 82 44, US Navy. Henry was born in 1920 in Washington State to William H. Beerman and Hattie Beerman. He enlisted in the US Navy on October 5, 1939 in Seattle, Washington and completed his basic training at the Naval Training Station in San Diego, California. Henry reported for duty on the USS Arizona on December 20, 1939. He was killed in action on December 7, 1941 in Pearl Harbor, Hawaii. Henry was awarded the American Defense Service Medal, World War II Victory Medal and Purple Heart Medal posthumously. He remains on duty on the USS Arizona. Henry is commemorated on the USS Arizona Memorial and the Memorial Tablets of the Missing, National Memorial Cemetery of the Pacific, Honolulu, Hawaii. He was survived by his Father, Mr. William Henry Beerman, Route 1, Tieton, Washington.

Beggs, Harold Eugene Fireman, First Class, Serial No: 337 21 11, US Navy. Harold was born on December 15, 1920 in Pleasant Grove, Illinois the son of Claude Beggs and Opha Beggs. He enlisted in the US Navy on October 9, 1939 in St. Louis, Missouri and completed his basic training at the Naval Training Station in San Diego, California. Harold reported for duty on the USS Arizona on December 20, 1939. He was killed in action on December 7, 1941 at Pearl Harbor, Hawaii. Harold was awarded the American Defense Service Medal, World War II Victory Medal and Purple Heart Medal posthumously. Harold remains on duty on the USS Arizona. He is commemorated on the USS Arizona Memorial and the Memorial Tablets of the Missing, National Memorial Cemetery of the Pacific, Honolulu, Hawaii. Harold was survived by his Wife, Mrs. Letis Elladee (Grant) Beggs, Bessville, Missouri. The VFW Post 5222 in Vienna, Illinois is named for him and his best friend Jesse Herbert Gurley.[61]

Bell, Hershel Homer Fire Controlman, Second Class, Serial No: 337 08 39, US Navy. Hershel was born December 30, 1919 to Ira Newton Bell and Ona B. Bell of Decatur, Illinois. He enlisted in the US Navy on August 12, 1938 in St. Louis, Missouri and reported for duty on the USS Arizona on April 15, 1939. Hershel was killed in action on December 7, 1941 in Pearl Harbor, Hawaii. He was awarded the American Defense Service Medal, World War II Victory Medal and Purple Heart Medal posthumously. Hershel remains on duty on the USS Arizona. He is commemorated on the USS Arizona Memorial and the Memorial Tablets of the Missing, National Memorial Cemetery of the Pacific, Honolulu, Hawaii. Hershel was survived by his Father, Mr. Ira Newton Bell, 128 Ruth Street, Decatur, Illinois.

Bell, Richard Leroy Seaman, Second Class, Serial No: 382 51 25, US Navy. Richard was born January 25, 1923 to Wayne L. Bell and Amelia O. Bell of Los Angeles, California. He enlisted in the US Navy on July 28, 1941 in Los Angeles, California and completed his basic training at the Naval Training Station in San Diego, California. Richard reported for duty on the USS Arizona on October 10, 1941. He was killed in action on December 7, 1941 in Pearl Harbor,

---

[60] Purdy Renaker Bedford, Photo courtesy of Sharon Benefiel Palmer.
[61] Harold Eugene Beggs, Photo courtesy of Virginia Beggs Karaker.

Hawaii. Richard was awarded the American Defense Service Medal, World War II Victory Medal and Purple Heart Medal posthumously. He remains on duty on the USS Arizona. Richard is commemorated on the USS Arizona Memorial and the Memorial Tablets of the Missing, National Memorial Cemetery of the Pacific, Honolulu, Hawaii. He was survived by his Father, Mr. Wayne LeRoy Bell, 6137 Carpenter Avenue, North Hollywood, California.

Bellamy, James Curtis Officer's Steward, Serial No: 261 90 49, US Navy. James was born in about 1912 in North Carolina. He enlisted in the US Navy on February 4, 1936 in Raleigh, North Carolina and reported for duty on the USS Arizona on June 17, 1936. He was killed in action on December 7, 1941 in Pearl Harbor, Hawaii. James was awarded the American Defense Service Medal, World War II Victory Medal and Purple Heart Medal posthumously. He remains on duty on the USS Arizona. James is commemorated on the USS Arizona Memorial and the Memorial Tablets of the Missing, National Memorial Cemetery of the Pacific, Honolulu, Hawaii. He was survived by his Wife, Mrs. Velma Bellamy, 1430 Myrtle Avenue, Long Beach, California.

Bemis, Edwin Wallace Seaman, First Class, Aviation Unit (VO-1), Serial No. 328 69 21, US Navy. Edwin was born on June 13, 1920 in North Dakota to Charles E. Bemis and Viola Bemis. He enlisted in the US Navy May 21, 1940 in Minneapolis, Minnesota and completed his basic training at the Naval Training Station in Great Lakes, Illinois. Edwin transferred from the USS Medusa Aviation Repair Unit to the USS Arizona on August 4, 1941. He was serving on the USS Arizona on December 7, 1941 when the Japanese attacked Pearl Harbor. Edwin served in the US Navy until May 28, 1946. He died on May 22, 1976 in Los Angeles, California.

Benford, Sam Austin Baker, Second Class, Serial No: 328 51 37, US Navy. Sam was born August 1, 1917. He enlisted in the US Navy on February 2, 1938 in Minneapolis, Minnesota and completed his basic training at the Naval Training Station in Great Lakes, Illinois. He reported for duty on the USS Arizona on July 9, 1938. Sam was killed in action on December 7, 1941 in Pearl Harbor, Hawaii. He was awarded the American Defense Service Medal, World War II Victory Medal and Purple Heart Medal posthumously. Sam remains on duty on the USS Arizona. He is commemorated on the USS Arizona Memorial and the Memorial Tablets of the Missing, National Memorial Cemetery of the Pacific, Honolulu, Hawaii. Sam was survived by his Wife, Mrs. Bernice Clara Benford, 605 Magnolia Avenue, Long Beach, California.

Bennett, Earl Dean Gunner's Mate, Third Class, Serial No. 337 21 12, US Navy. Earl was born on June 1, 1923 in Shattuck, Oklahoma. He enlisted in the US Navy October 9, 1939 in St. Louis, Missouri and completed his training at the Naval Training Station in San Diego, California. Earl reported for duty on the USS Arizona December 20, 1939 where he was serving on December 7, 1941 when the Japanese attacked Pearl Harbor. He was transferred to the USS Tennessee for duty after the attack. After the war he earned a bachelor of science degree from John Brown University, a master's in business administration from Harvard Business School and a doctorate from the University of Michigan. Earl taught at Louisiana Tech, Harvard Business School, the University of Michigan, The University of Texas and Texas A&M University before retiring in 1990. He died on January 31, 2005 in Texas and is buried in College Station Cemetery, College Station, Texas. Earl was preceded in death by his Parents: Fred J. and Bertha M. Bennett; Grandfather, Samuel Bennett and son David Bennett. Survived by his Wife, Agnes Bennett of College Station; a daughter and son-in-law, Elaine and Steve Gartrell of Houston; a daughter-in-law and her husband, Lisa and Rod Robinson of College Station; and three grandchildren.[62]

Bennett, William Edmond, Jr. Yeoman, Third Class, Serial No: 336 95 99, US Navy. William was born in 1924 to William E. Bennett and Nora A. Bennett of Paris, Illinois. He enlisted in the US Navy on February 9, 1937 in St. Louis, Missouri and reported for duty on the USS Arizona on June 19, 1937. William was killed in action on December 7, 1941 in Pearl Harbor, Hawaii. He was awarded the American Defense Service Medal, World War II Victory Medal and Purple Heart Medal posthumously. William remains on duty on the USS Arizona. He is commemorated on the USS Arizona Memorial and the Memorial Tablets of the Missing, National Memorial Cemetery of the Pacific, Honolulu, Hawaii. William was survived by his Father, Mr. William Edmond Bennett, 202 West Jefferson, Anna, Illinois.

Benson, James Thomas Seaman, First Class, Serial No: 272 40 40, US Navy. James was born in about 1920 in Texas. He enlisted in the US Navy on September 28, 1940 in Birmingham, Alabama and completed his basic training at the Naval Training Station in Norfolk, Virginia. He reported for duty on the USS Arizona on December 4, 1940. James was killed in action on December 7, 1941 in Pearl Harbor, Hawaii. He was awarded the American Defense Service Medal, World War II Victory Medal and Purple Heart Medal posthumously. James remains on duty on the USS Arizona. He is commemorated on the USS Arizona Memorial and the Memorial Tablets of the Missing, National Memorial Cemetery of the Pacific, Honolulu, Hawaii. James is survived by his Father, Mr. John Benson, Post Office, New Castle, Alabama.

Berdollt, George Anthony, Jr. Fire Controlman, Third Class, Serial No. 337 20 67, US Navy. George was born on August 7, 1918 in Missouri the son of George A. and Gladys Berdollt, Sr. He enlisted in the US Navy October 3, 1939 in St. Louis, Missouri and completed his training at the Naval Training Station in San Diego, California. George reported for duty on the USS Arizona December 20, 1939 where he was serving on December 7, 1941 when the Japanese attacked Pearl Harbor. He later served on the USS Dunlap. George died on February 11, 1961 in Denver, Colorado and is buried in Section L, Site 513, Fort Logan National Cemetery, Denver, Colorado.

Bergin, Roger Joseph Fireman, Second Class, Serial No: 311 51 65, US Navy. Roger was born August 16, 1916 in Goodrich, North Dakota the son of Austin Frederick and Marian Irene "Birdie" (Bickel) Bergin. He enlisted in the US Navy on October 8, 1940 in Detroit, Michigan and completed his basic training at the Naval Training Station in Great Lakes, Illinois. He reported for duty on the USS Arizona on December 9, 1940. Roger was killed in action on December 7, 1941 in Pearl Harbor, Hawaii. He was awarded the American Defense Service Medal, World War II Victory Medal and Purple Heart Medal posthumously. Roger remains on duty on the USS Arizona. He is commemorated on the USS Arizona Memorial and the Memorial Tablets of the Missing, National Memorial Cemetery of the Pacific, Honolulu, Hawaii. Roger was survived by his Father, Mr. Austin Frederick Bergin, Moose Jaw, Saskatchewan, Canada.[63]

---

[62] Earl Dean Bennett, Photo from Harvard Business School Yearbook, Boston, Massachusetts, 1947, Page 103.
[63] Roger Joseph Bergin, Information provided by his brother, Charles Bergin.

Berkanski, Albert Charles   Coxswain, Serial No: 266 05 02, US Navy. Albert was born September 27, 1923 in Shenandoah, Pennsylvania, son of Michal and Anna (Dragowski) Berkanski. He worked for the Civilian Conservation Corps before enlisting in the US Navy on January 22, 1940 in Richmond, Virginia. Albert "Seggie" completed his basic training at the Naval Training Station in Norfolk, Virginia. He reported for duty on the USS Arizona on September 30, 1940. Albert was killed in action on December 7, 1941 in Pearl Harbor, Hawaii. He was awarded the American Defense Service Medal, World War II Victory Medal and Purple Heart Medal posthumously. Albert remains on duty on the USS Arizona. He is commemorated on the USS Arizona Memorial and the Memorial Tablets of the Missing, National Memorial Cemetery of the Pacific, Honolulu, Hawaii. Albert was survived by his Parents, Mr. and Mrs. Michael Berkanski, 49 South Pine Street, Mount Carmel, Pennsylvania.[64]

Bernard, Frank Peter   Shipfitter, Second Class, Serial No: 328 39 68, US Navy. Frank was born July 24, 1915 in Grafton, North Dakota to Henry and Josephine Bernard. *He was in most all accounts, a devil-may-care kid. Frank did not graduate from high school; he had the ability but lacked the motivation.* He enlisted in the US Navy on September 4, 1935 in Minneapolis, Minnesota and reported for duty on the USS Arizona on January 11, 1936. *In his last letter to his older brother, he wrote "I think that I will get hitched to that little girl up in Washington, she is a honey and she will join the church to marry me. What do you think of that? Is it all right to do that.."* He was killed in action on December 7, 1941 in Pearl Harbor, Hawaii. Frank was awarded the American Defense Service Medal, World War II Victory Medal and Purple Heart Medal posthumously. He remains on duty on the USS Arizona. Frank is commemorated on the USS Arizona Memorial and the Memorial Tablets of the Missing, National Memorial Cemetery of the Pacific, Honolulu, Hawaii. He was survived by his Father, Mr. Henry Louis Bernard, 103 Wakeman Avenue, Grafton, North Dakota.[65]

Berry, Gordon Eugene   Fireman, Second Class, Serial No: 372 20 45, US Navy. Gordon was born in 1922 to Clem C. Berry and Edith Berry of Southside, Kansas. His father, Clem died when he was just 10 years old and he went to live with an older brother, Charles. He enlisted in the US Navy on November 7, 1940 in Denver, Colorado and completed his basic training at the Naval Training Station in San Diego, California. Gordon reported for duty on the USS Arizona on January 11, 1941. He was killed in action on December 7, 1941 in Pearl Harbor, Hawaii. Gordon was awarded the American Defense Service Medal, World War II Victory Medal and Purple Heart Medal posthumously. He remains on duty on the USS Arizona. Gordon is commemorated on the USS Arizona Memorial and the Memorial Tablets of the Missing, National Memorial Cemetery of the Pacific, Honolulu, Hawaii. He was survived by his Mother, Mrs. Edith Boulden, Bayfield, Colorado.[66]

---

[64] Albert Charles Berkanski, Photo from the Mount Carmel Item Newspaper, Mount Carmel, Pennsylvania, Wednesday, January 21, 1942, Page 1

[65] Frank Peter Bernard, information and photo provided by his nephew, Dick Bernard.

[66] Gordon Eugene Berry, Photo courtesy of the Pine River Valley Heritage Museum.

45

Berry, James Winford Fireman, Second Class, Serial No: 279 73 70, US Navy. James was born on November 17, 1915 in Creek, Michigan to George Berry and Nellie A. (Garvison) Berry. He enlisted in the US Navy on October 7, 1940 in Cincinnati, Ohio and completed his basic training at the Naval Training Station in Great Lakes, Illinois. James reported for duty on the USS Arizona on December 9, 1940. He was killed in action on December 7, 1941 in Pearl Harbor, Hawaii. James was awarded the American Defense Service Medal, World War II Victory Medal and Purple Heart Medal posthumously. He remains on duty on the USS Arizona. James is commemorated on the USS Arizona Memorial and the Memorial Tablets of the Missing, National Memorial Cemetery of the Pacific, Honolulu, Hawaii. He was survived by his Parents, Mr. and Mrs. George C. Berry, Box 73A, Route 1, Sylvania, Ohio.[67]

Bersch, Arthur Anthony Seaman, First Class, Serial No: 321 48 95, US Navy. Arthur was born August 16, 1920 in Muscatine, Iowa to Edward and Nellie Bersch. He attended St. Mathias School where he was a member of the high school basketball team. He enlisted in the US Navy on October 15, 1940 in Des Moines, Iowa and completed his basic training at the Naval Training Station in Great Lakes, Illinois. Arthur reported for duty on the USS Arizona on December 9, 1940. He was killed in action on December 7, 1941 in Pearl Harbor, Hawaii. Arthur was awarded the American Defense Service Medal, World War II Victory Medal and Purple Heart Medal posthumously. He remains on duty on the USS Arizona. Arthur is commemorated on the USS Arizona Memorial and the Memorial Tablets of the Missing, National Memorial Cemetery of the Pacific, Honolulu, Hawaii. He was survived by his Parents, Mr. and Mrs. Edward C. Bersch, 314 Cedar Street, Muscatine, Iowa; Sister, Mrs. Jack Scheard of Indianapolis, Indiana; one brother, Gene Bersch and his grandfather, Anton Bersch of Muscatine, Iowa.[68]

Bertie, George Allan Seaman, Second Class, Serial No: 381 42 61, US Navy. George was born in about 1923 in Pennsylvania. He enlisted in the US Navy on June 2, 1941 in San Diego, California and completed his basic training at the Naval Training Station in San Diego, California. He reported for duty on the USS Arizona on October 2, 1941. George was killed in action on December 7, 1941 in Pearl Harbor, Hawaii. He was awarded the American Defense Service Medal, World War II Victory Medal and Purple Heart Medal posthumously. George remains on duty on the USS Arizona. He is commemorated on the USS Arizona Memorial and the Memorial Tablets of the Missing, National Memorial Cemetery of the Pacific, Honolulu, Hawaii. George was survived by his Father, Mr. G. A. Bertie, 721-1/2 East Portland Street, Phoenix, Arizona.

---

[67] James Winford Berry, Information and Photo provided by family member, Mary Taylor.

[68] Arthur Anthony Bersch, information from the Muscatine Journal and News Tribune, December 30, 1943, photo from the Quad-City Times, Davenport, Iowa, May 5, 1942, page 3.

Bibby, Charles Henry Fireman, Second Class, Serial No: 272 41 40, US Navy. Charles was born in 1919 to Henry and Geneveive Bibby of Jefferson, Alabama. He enlisted in the US Navy on October 4, 1940 in Birmingham, Alabama and completed his basic training at the Naval Training Station in Norfolk, Virginia. Charles reported for duty on the USS Arizona on December 4, 1940. He was killed in action on December 7, 1941 in Pearl Harbor, Hawaii. Charles was awarded the American Defense Service Medal, World War II Victory Medal and Purple Heart Medal posthumously. He remains on duty on the USS Arizona. Charles is commemorated on the USS Arizona Memorial and the Memorial Tablets of the Missing, National Memorial Cemetery of the Pacific, Honolulu, Hawaii. He was survived by his Father, Mr. Henry Bibby, Littleton, Alabama.[69]

Bickel, Kenneth Robert Fireman, First Class, Serial No: 372 06 28, US Navy. Kenneth was born April 25, 1914 in Kimball, Nebraska. He enlisted in the US Navy on July 9, 1938 in Denver, Colorado and reported for duty on the USS Arizona on October 23, 1938. He was killed in action on December 7, 1941 in Pearl Harbor, Hawaii. Kenneth was awarded the American Defense Service Medal, World War II Victory Medal and Purple Heart Medal posthumously. He remains on duty on the USS Arizona. Kenneth is commemorated on the USS Arizona Memorial and the Memorial Tablets of the Missing, National Memorial Cemetery of the Pacific, Honolulu, Hawaii. He was survived by his Daughter, Miss Sherry Lee Bickel, c/o Mrs. Mary E. Bickel, Potter, Nebraska.

Bicknell, Dale Deen Seaman, First Class, Serial No: 385 87 13, US Navy. Dale was born in 1922 to Bert B. and Mabel Bicknell of Independence, Washington. He enlisted in the US Navy on May 15, 1940 in Seattle, Washington and completed his basic training at the Naval Training Station in San Diego, California. Dale reported for duty on the USS Arizona on October 28, 1940. He was killed in action on December 7, 1941 in Pearl Harbor, Hawaii. Dale was awarded the American Defense Service Medal, World War II Victory Medal and Purple Heart Medal posthumously. He remains on duty on the USS Arizona. Dale is commemorated on the USS Arizona Memorial and the Memorial Tablets of the Missing, National Memorial Cemetery of the Pacific, Honolulu, Hawaii. He was survived by his Father, Mr. Bert B. Bicknell, Route 2, Box 288, Rochester, Washington.

Bircher, Frederick Robert Radioman, Third Class, Serial No: 405 10 62, US Navy. Frederick was born in 1918 to George and Irene Bircher of Philadelphia, Pennsylvania. He enlisted in the US Navy on October 3, 1940 in Philadelphia, Pennsylvania and reported for duty on the USS Arizona on April 4, 1941. Frederick was killed in action on December 7, 1941 in Pearl Harbor, Hawaii. He was awarded the American Defense Service Medal, World War II Victory Medal and Purple Heart Medal posthumously. Frederick remains on duty on the USS Arizona. He is commemorated on the USS Arizona Memorial and the Memorial Tablets of the Missing, National Memorial Cemetery of the Pacific, Honolulu, Hawaii. Frederick was survived by his Father, Mr. George Bircher, 221 Olney Avenue, Philadelphia, Pennsylvania.[70]

---

[69] Charles Henry Bibby, photo provided by his nephew, Bill and JoDell Bibby.
[70] Frederick Robert Bircher, Photo from "Philadelphia Naval Heroes Who Gave Lives for their Country" The Philadelphia Inquirer, Tuesday Morning, May 5, 1942.

Bird, Leroy Alexander   Chief Turret Captain, Serial No. 261 74 37, US Navy. Leroy was born December 9, 1911 in South Carolina the son of Leonard and Rena Milton Bird. He enlisted in the US Navy July 2, 1930 and completed his basic training at the Naval Training Station in San Diego, California. Leroy reported for duty on the USS Arizona on November 25, 1936. He was serving on the USS Arizona on December 7, 1941 when the Japanese attacked Pearl Harbor. After the attack, Leroy served on the USS Enterprise (CV-6) for temporary duty. He was later transferred to the Receiving Station in Washington, DC. Leroy served in the US Navy until August 31, 1960 having attained the rank of Commander, serving as the Gunnery Officer on board the USS Midway in 1955. He died July 24, 1985 in Alleghany County, North Carolina and is buried in the Mount Zion Cemetery, Piney Creek, North Carolina.[71]

Birdsell, Estelle   Machinist's Mate, First Class, Serial No. 336 76 80, US Navy. Estelle was born April 22, 1912 in Arkansas the son of Roy and Lillie Birdsell. He enlisted in the US Navy December 11, 1933 in St. Louis, Missouri and completed his basic training at the Naval Training Station in Great Lakes, Illinois. Estelle reported for duty on the USS Arizona March 17, 1934. He was not on board on December 7, 1941, when the Japanese attacked Pearl Harbor. Estelle lived in an apartment complex off base. Another shipmate, Galen Ballard banged on his door and the two headed off for Pearl Harbor. By the time they reached the main Navy landing, hoping to catch a launch out to their ship, the Arizona had already sunk and was on fire. After the attack, he was transferred to the USS Dale (DD-353) for duty. His brother, Rayon Delois Birdsell was killed in action on board the USS Arizona. Father, Mr. Roy Birdsell, Holcomb, Missouri. Estelle died June 28, 1989 in Pahrump, Nevada and was buried in the Chief Tecopa Cemetery, Pahrump, Nevada.

Birdsell, Rayon Delois   Fireman, Second Class, Serial No: 337 51 58, US Navy. Rayon was born October 16, 1922. He enlisted in the US Navy on January 21, 1941 in St. Louis, Missouri and completed his basic training at the Naval Training Station in Great Lakes, Illinois. He reported for duty on the USS Arizona on May 23, 1941. Rayon was killed in action on December 7, 1941 in Pearl Harbor, Hawaii. He was awarded the American Defense Service Medal, World War II Victory Medal and Purple Heart Medal posthumously. Rayon remains on duty on the USS Arizona. He is commemorated on the USS Arizona Memorial and the Memorial Tablets of the Missing, National Memorial Cemetery of the Pacific, Honolulu, Hawaii and Greene County Memorial Gardens Cemetery, Paragould, Arkansas. Rayon was survived by his Father, Mr. Roy Birdsell, Holcomb, Missouri and his brother, Estelle Birdsell who was also serving on board the USS Arizona.[72]

Birge, George Albert   Seaman, First Class, Serial No: 234 18 45, US Navy. George was born February 19 1919 to Albert and Mary Birge of Buffalo, New York. He enlisted in the US Navy on May 11, 1938 in Buffalo, New York and reported for duty on the USS Arizona on

---

[71] Leroy Alexander Bird, Photo from USS Midway CV-41, World Cruise Book, 1955.
[72] Rayon Delois Birdsell, Photo provided by Rick Jamison.

August 3, 1941, transferring from Sub Base, Pearl Harbor. George was killed in action on December 7, 1941 in Pearl Harbor, Hawaii. He was awarded the American Defense Service Medal, World War II Victory Medal and Purple Heart Medal posthumously. George remains on duty on the USS Arizona. He is commemorated on the USS Arizona Memorial and the Memorial Tablets of the Missing, National Memorial Cemetery of the Pacific, Honolulu, Hawaii. George was survived by his Father, Mr. Albert Benjamin Birge, 1266 East Ferry Street, Buffalo, New York.

Birtwell, Daniel Thomas Jr. Lieutenant Commander, Serial No. 0-03022, US Navy. Daniel was born on October 29, 1903 in Washington, DC. He was the son of Daniel T. and Nellie L. Birtwell. He was commissioned May 13, 1941 in the US Navy. Daniel was serving on the USS Arizona as Engineer Officer on December 7, 1941 when the Japanese attacked Pearl Harbor. His battle station was Main Engineering Control. Daniel commanded the USS Longshaw (DD-559) from December 4, 1943 thru 1944. He died on August 1, 1971 in Santa Clara, California. Daniel was survived by his wife, Eleanor, two sons, Daniel of Shingle Springs and Charles of San Mateo, and a daughter, Mrs. Robert McCoy of Los Altos, California. He was buried in the Alta Mesa Memorial Park, Palo Alto, California.[73]

Bishop, Grover Barron Machinist's Mate, First Class, Serial No: 355 95 79, US Navy. Grover was born on August 30, 1916 in Ladonia, Texas to Grover Bishop and Anna (Barron) Bishop. He enlisted in the US Navy on January 11, 1936 in Dallas, Texas and reported for duty on the USS Arizona on June 6, 1936. Grover was killed in action on December 7, 1941 in Pearl Harbor, Hawaii. He was awarded the American Defense Service Medal, World War II Victory Medal and Purple Heart Medal posthumously. Grover remains on duty on the USS Arizona. He is commemorated on the USS Arizona Memorial and the Memorial Tablets of the Missing, National Memorial Cemetery of the Pacific, Honolulu, Hawaii. Grover was survived by his Wife, Mrs. Johnnie Earl Bishop, Ladonia, Texas.[74]

Bishop, Millard Charles Fireman, Third Class, Serial No: 272 41 22, US Navy. Millard was born in 1922 to John W. and Carrie Bishop of Albertville, Alabama. He enlisted in the US Navy on October 4, 1940 in Birmingham, Alabama and completed his basic training at the Naval Training Station in Norfolk, Virginia. Millard reported for duty on the USS Arizona on December 4, 1940. He was killed in action on December 7, 1941 in Pearl Harbor, Hawaii. Millard was awarded the American Defense Service Medal, World War II Victory Medal and Purple Heart Medal posthumously. He remains on duty on the USS Arizona. Millard is commemorated on the USS Arizona Memorial and the Memorial Tablets of the Missing, National Memorial Cemetery of the Pacific, Honolulu, Hawaii. He is survived by his Father, Mr. John Wesley Bishop, Route 3, Albertville, Alabama.

---

[73] Daniel Thomas Birtwell, Jr., Photo from Lucky Bag Yearbook, United States Naval Academy, Annapolis, MD.
[74] Grover Barron Bishop, Photo provided by family member, Dennis Deel.

Bishop, Wesley Horner, Jr. Radioman, Third Class, V-3, Serial No: 405 09 03, US Navy Reserve. Wesley was born October 4, 1920 in Moorestown, New Jersey to Wesley Horner and Margaret F. Bishop. He enlisted in the US Navy on October 14, 1940 and reported for duty on the USS Arizona on April 3, 1941. He was killed in action on December 7, 1941 in Pearl Harbor. Wesley was awarded the American Defense Service Medal, World War II Victory Medal and Purple Heart Medal posthumously. He remains on duty on the USS Arizona. Wesley is commemorated on the USS Arizona Memorial and the Memorial Tablets of the Missing, National Memorial Cemetery of the Pacific, Honolulu, Hawaii. He was survived by his Mother, Mrs. Margaret F. Bishop, 308 Linden Street, Moorestown, New Jersey.[75]

Blais, Albert Edward Radioman, Third Class, Serial No: 403 48 30, US Navy Reserve. Albert was born on November 1, 1922 in Fall River, Massachusetts the son of William H and Florence Blais. He enlisted in the US Navy on December 11, 1939 in New York City, New York and reported for duty on the USS Arizona on April 4, 1941. He was killed in action on December 7, 1941 in Pearl Harbor, Hawaii. Albert was awarded the American Defense Service Medal, World War II Victory Medal and Purple Heart Medal posthumously. He remains on duty on the USS Arizona. Albert is commemorated on the USS Arizona Memorial and the Memorial Tablets of the Missing, National Memorial Cemetery of the Pacific, Honolulu, Hawaii. He was survived by his Father, Mr. William H. Blais, 2052 Harrison Avenue, Bronx, New York.[76]

Blake, James Monroe Fireman, Second Class, Serial No: 337 41 36, US Navy. James was born November 7, 1921 in Phelps County, Rolla, Missouri to Harmon M. Blake and Rebecca B. Blake of Rolla, Missouri. He enlisted in the US Navy on October 15, 1940 in St. Louis, Missouri and completed his basic training at the Naval Training Station in Great Lakes, Illinois. James reported for duty on the USS Arizona on December 9, 1940. He was killed in action on December 7, 1941 in Pearl Harbor, Hawaii. James was awarded the American Defense Service Medal, World War II Victory Medal and Purple Heart Medal posthumously. He remains on duty on the USS Arizona. James is commemorated on the USS Arizona Memorial and the Memorial Tablets of the Missing, National Memorial Cemetery of the Pacific, Honolulu, Hawaii. He was survived by his Father, Mr. Harmon M. Blake, Route 2, Rolla, Missouri.

---

[75] Wesley Horner Bishop, Jr., Photo from New Jersey Honor States.
[76] Albert Edward Blais, Photo from New York Honor States.

Blanchard, Albert Richard Coxswain, Serial No: 328 61 88, US Navy. Albert was born February 11, 1918 in St. Paul, Minnesota. He enlisted in the US Navy on November 14, 1939 in Minneapolis, Minnesota and completed his basic training at the Naval Training Station in Great Lakes, Illinois. He reported for duty on the USS Arizona on January 27, 1940. Albert was killed in action on December 7, 1941 in Pearl Harbor, Hawaii. He was awarded the Purple Heart Medal posthumously. Albert remains on duty on the USS Arizona. He is commemorated on the USS Arizona Memorial and the Memorial Tablets of the Missing, National Memorial Cemetery of the Pacific, Honolulu, Hawaii. Albert was survived by his Mother, Mrs. Anna B. Spock, 739 Margaret Street, St. Paul, Minnesota.

Blankenship, Theron Andrew Seaman, First Class, Serial No: 272 41 52, US Navy. Theron was born March 20, 1922 to William Matthew and Leona Josephine (Chaney) Blankenship. He enlisted in the US Navy on October 5, 1940 in Birmingham, Alabama and completed his basic training at the Naval Training Station in Norfolk, Virginia. He reported for duty on the USS Arizona on December 4, 1940. Theron was killed in action on December 7, 1941 in Pearl Harbor, Hawaii. He was awarded the American Defense Service Medal, World War II Victory Medal and Purple Heart Medal posthumously. Theron remains on duty on the USS Arizona. He is commemorated on the USS Arizona Memorial and the Memorial Tablets of the Missing, National Memorial Cemetery of the Pacific, Honolulu, Hawaii. Theron was survived by his Father, Mr. William M. Blankenship, Route 3, Hartselle, Alabama.

Blanton, Atticus "Snooky" Lee Shipfitter, Third Class, Serial No: 268 54 51, US Navy. Atticus was born December 29, 1920 to Frank Marvin and Annie Lottie (Kennedy) Blanton of Lady Lake, Florida. He enlisted in the US Navy on September 30, 1940 in Macon, Georgia and completed his basic training at the Naval Training Station in Norfolk, Virginia. Atticus reported for duty on the USS Arizona on December 4, 1940. He was killed in action on December 7, 1941 at Pearl Harbor, Hawaii. Atticus was awarded the American Defense Service Medal, World War II Victory Medal and Purple Heart Medal posthumously. He remains on duty on the USS Arizona. Atticus is commemorated on the USS Arizona Memorial and the Memorial Tablets of the Missing, National Memorial Cemetery of the Pacific, Honolulu, Hawaii. He was survived by his Mother, Mrs. Annie Lottie Blanton, Lady Lake, Florida.

Blieffert, Richmond Frederick Seaman, First Class, Serial No: 385 86 31, US Navy. Richmond was born March 4, 1919 to Carl F. and Gertrude H. Blieffert of Port Orchard, Washington. He enlisted in the US Navy on April 8, 1940 in Seattle, Washington and completed his basic training at the Naval Training Station in San Diego, California. Richmond reported for duty on the USS Arizona on July 2, 1940. He was killed in action on December 7, 1941 in Pearl Harbor, Hawaii. Richmond was awarded the American Defense Service Medal, World War II Victory Medal and Purple Heart Medal posthumously. He remains on duty on the USS Arizona. Richmond is commemorated on the USS Arizona Memorial and the Memorial Tablets of the Missing, National Memorial Cemetery of the Pacific, Honolulu, Hawaii. He was survived by his Father, Mr. Carl Blieffert, Route 2, Port Orchard, Washington.

Block, Ivan Lee Pharmacist's Mate, Second Class, Serial No: 372 06 32, US Navy. Ivan was born on May 29, 1918 to Verne Gibbons Block and Sarah Viola (Buckelew) Block. He enlisted in the US Navy on July 9, 1938 and reported for duty on the USS Arizona on July 19, 1941. Ivan was killed in action on December 7, 1941 in Pearl Harbor, Hawaii. He was awarded the American Defense Service Medal, World War II Victory Medal and Purple Heart Medal posthumously. Ivan remains on duty on the USS Arizona. He is commemorated on the USS Arizona Memorial and the Memorial Tablets of the Missing, National Memorial Cemetery of the Pacific, Honolulu, Hawaii. Ivan was survived by his Father, Mr. Vern Gibbons Block, Glorieta, New Mexico.[77]

Blount, Wayman Boney Seaman, First Class, Serial No: 360 25 59, US Navy. Wayman was born March 26, 1920 in Keith, Texas, the son of Robert Orear and Lillia Dale (Burns) Blount. He enlisted in the US Navy on November 8, 1940 in Houston, Texas and completed his basic training at the Naval Training Station at San Diego, California. He reported for duty on the USS Arizona on January 11, 1941. Wayman was killed in action on December 7, 1941 in Pearl Harbor, Hawaii. He was awarded the American Defense Service Medal, World War II Victory Medal and Purple Heart Medal posthumously. Wayman remains on duty on the USS Arizona. He is commemorated on the USS Arizona Memorial and the Memorial Tablets of the Missing, National Memorial Cemetery of the Pacific, Honolulu, Hawaii. Wayman was survived by his Father, Mr. Robert Blount, Iola, Texas.

Bodey, Edward Raymond Boatswain's Mate, Second Class, Serial No. 272 10 71, US Navy. Edward was born on August 3, 1916 in Birmingham, Alabama the son of Edward Thomas and Juanita (Spann) Bodey. He enlisted in the US Navy October 8, 1935 in Birmingham, Alabama and completed his basic training at the Naval Training Station in Norfolk, Virginia. He reported for duty on the USS Arizona November 23, 1938. Edward was serving on December 7, 1941 when the Japanese attacked Pearl Harbor. He died on January 19, 1950 in Santa Maria, California and is buried in Section N, Site 2353, Golden Gate National Cemetery, San Bruno, California.

Boggess, Roy Eugene Shipfitter, Second Class, Serial No: 337 01 26, US Navy. Roy was born on September 3, 1919 in Ridgefarm, Illinois to Thomas Elsworth Boggess and Roxaline R. (Richards) Boggess. He enlisted in the US Navy on October 11, 1937 in St. Louis, Missouri and completed his basic training at the Naval Training Station in Great Lakes, Illinois. Roy reported for duty on the USS Arizona on October 15, 1938. He was killed in action on December 7, 1941 in Pearl Harbor, Hawaii. Roy was awarded the American Defense Service Medal, World War II Victory Medal and Purple Heart Medal posthumously. He remains on duty on the USS Arizona. Roy is commemorated on the USS Arizona Memorial and the Memorial Tablets of the Missing, National Memorial Cemetery of the Pacific, Honolulu, Hawaii. He was survived by his Wife, Mrs. Naomi Jane Boggess, 2016 Lewis Avenue, Long Beach, California.[78]

---

[77] Ivan Lee Block, Photo from the Albuquerque Journal, Albuquerque, New Mexico, Friday, December 26, 1941, Page 5.
[78] Roy Eugene Boggess, Photo provided by Leanna Alexander.

Bohlender, Sam Gunner's Mate, Second Class, Serial No: 372 06 70, US Navy. Sam was born October 11, 1919 in Greeley, Colorado to Phillip T. and Elizabeth Bohlender of Beebe Draw, Colorado. He enlisted in the US Navy on September 9, 1938 in Denver, Colorado and completed his basic training at the Naval Training Station in San Diego, California. Sam reported for duty on the USS Arizona on March 11, 1939. He was killed in action on December 7, 1941 in Pearl Harbor, Hawaii. Sam was awarded the American Defense Service Medal, World War II Victory Medal and Purple Heart Medal posthumously. He remains on duty on the USS Arizona. Sam is commemorated on the USS Arizona Memorial and the Memorial Tablets of the Missing, National Memorial Cemetery of the Pacific, Honolulu, Hawaii. He was survived by his Father, Mr. Philip T. Bohlender, Box No. 83, La Salle, Colorado.[79]

Bolling, Gerald Revese Seaman, First Class, Serial No: 346 83 13, US Navy. Gerald was born September 15, 1922 in Van Buren, Arkansas to Charles Jason Bolling and Mary Julia (Flowers) Bolling. He enlisted in the US Navy on August 2, 1940 in Little Rock, Arkansas and completed his basic training at the Naval Training Station in San Diego, California. Gerald reported for duty on the USS Arizona on October 14, 1940. He was killed in action on December 7, 1941 in Pearl Harbor, Hawaii. Gerald was awarded the American Defense Service Medal, World War II Victory Medal and Purple Heart Medal posthumously. He remains on duty on the USS Arizona. Gerald is commemorated on the USS Arizona Memorial and the Memorial Tablets of the Missing, National Memorial Cemetery of the Pacific, Honolulu, Hawaii and Fort Smith National Cemetery, Fort Smith, Arkansas. He was survived by his Father, Mr. Charles Jason Bolling, 219 North 15th Street, Van Buren, Arkansas.

Bolling, Walter Karr Fireman, Third Class, Serial No: 287 45 86, US Navy. Walter was born March 22, 1922 in Floyd County, Kentucky to Walter Karr and Frances (O'Dell) Bolling, Sr. He enlisted in the USS Navy on October 15, 1940 in Louisville, Kentucky and completed his basic training at the Naval Training Station in Great Lakes, Illinois. He reported for duty on the USS Arizona on December 9, 1940. Walter was killed in action on December 7, 1941 in Pearl Harbor, Hawaii. He was awarded the American Defense Service Medal, World War II Victory Medal and Purple Heart Medal posthumously. Walter remains on duty on the USS Arizona. He is commemorated on the USS Arizona Memorial and the Memorial Tablets of the Missing, National Memorial Cemetery of the Pacific, Honolulu, Hawaii. Walter was survived by his Mother, Mrs. Francis Bolling, West Prestonsburg, Kentucky.[80]

---

[79] Sam Bohlender, Information and photo provided by family member, Sharon J. Monroe.
[80] Walter Karr Bolling, Photo and information from family member, C. Faulk, the Boling Family Tree.

Bonebrake, Buford Earl Fireman, Second Class, Serial No: 342 30 56, US Navy. Buford was born October 8, 1922 in Concordia, Kansas to Charles E. and Mabel Bonebrake of Concordia, Kansas. He enlisted in the US Navy on October 11, 1940 in Kansas City, Missouri and completed his basic training at the Naval Training Station in Great Lakes, Illinois. Buford reported for duty on the USS Arizona on December 9, 1940. He was killed in action on December 7, 1941 in Pearl Harbor, Hawaii. Buford was awarded the American Defense Service Medal, World War II Victory Medal and Purple Heart Medal posthumously. He remains on duty on the USS Arizona. Buford is commemorated on the USS Arizona Memorial and the Memorial Tablets of the Missing, National Memorial Cemetery of the Pacific, Honolulu, Hawaii. He was survived by his Mother, Mrs. Mabel Bonebrake, 1009 Broadway, Concordia, Kansas.[81]

Bonfiglio, William John Electrician's Mate, First Class, Serial No: 299 71 74, US Navy. William was born June 23, 1910 in Elkhart, Indiana. He enlisted in the US Navy on August 5, 1936 in San Diego, California. He transferred from the USS Pensacola to the USS Arizona on April 29, 1940. William was killed in action on December 7, 1941 In Pearl Harbor, Hawaii. He was awarded the American Defense Service Medal, World War II Victory Medal and Purple Heart Medal posthumously. William remains on duty on the USS Arizona. He is commemorated on the USS Arizona Memorial and the Memorial Tablets of the Missing, National Memorial Cemetery of the Pacific, Honolulu, Hawaii. William was survived by his Wife, Mrs. Dorothy Roberta Bonfiglio, 118 Cooper Street, Brooklyn, New York.

Booth, Robert Sinclair, Jr. Ensign, Serial No: 0-095322, US Navy Reserve. Robert was born on January 25, 1915 in Hickory, North Carolina to Robert Sinclair Booth Sr. and Annie L. Booth. He attended the University of Maryland, College Park, Md., for three years, majoring in electrical engineering, and among his civilian jobs, worked as an ordinary seaman on ships of the Baltimore Mail and Isthmian Lines that visited ports in France, Germany, Egypt, Arabia, India, Malaya and South Africa. He enlisted in the naval reserve as an apprentice seaman at Washington, D.C., on 9 July 1940, and received training in the auxiliary (ex-battleship) Wyoming (AG-17) (15 July-9 August 1940), receiving an honorable discharge on 9 August 1940. The following day, Booth received an appointment as a midshipman in the naval reserve and reported for training duty at the Naval Reserve Midshipman's School at New York quartered on board Illinois (IX-15). He completed his training on 13 November 1940 and received his commission as an ensign in the naval reserve on the 14th. On December 1, 1940, Ens. Booth reported for duty on the USS Arizona (BB-39). One year later, he was still serving on the battleship in her E [Engineering] Division, with his battle station in the after distribution room on the first platform deck. He was among the 1,177 killed on board when Japanese bombs sank Arizona during the surprise attack on Pearl Harbor on 7 December 1941. He was awarded the American Defense Service Medal, World War II Victory Medal and Purple Heart Medal posthumously. Robert remains on duty on the USS Arizona. He is commemorated on the USS Arizona Memorial and the Memorial Tablets of the Missing, National Memorial Cemetery of the Pacific, Honolulu, Hawaii and Arlington National Cemetery, Arlington, Virginia. Robert was survived by his Father, Mr. R. Sinclair

---

[81] Buford Earl Bonebrake, Information and photo provided by family member Rita Snyder, Petty Family Tree.

Booth, 2301 Cathedral Avenue NW, Washington, DC. The USS Booth (DE-170) was named in his honor.[82]

Booze, Asbury Legare Boatswain's Mate, First Class, Serial No: 267 94 89, US Navy. Asbury was born September 10, 1908 in Georgia to Clarence George and Pauline Booze. He enlisted in the US Navy on August 2, 1938 in Chefoo, China and reported for duty on the USS Arizona on April 26, 1940. He was killed in action on December 7, 1941 in Pearl Harbor, Hawaii. Asbury was awarded the American Defense Service Medal, World War II Victory Medal and Purple Heart Medal posthumously. He remains on duty on the USS Arizona. Asbury is commemorated on the USS Arizona Memorial and the Memorial Tablets of the Missing, National Memorial Cemetery of the Pacific, Honolulu, Hawaii. He was survived by his Father, Mr. Clarence George Booze, 211 Ellis Street, Augusta, Georgia.

Borger, Richard Chief Machinist's Mate, Serial No: 304 97 10, US Navy. Richard was born June 10, 1903 in Chicago, Illinois the son of Hendrick D. and Grace (Bass) Borger. His mother died when he was 4 years old and he was sent to live with aunts and uncles. He enlisted in the US Navy on March 25, 1935 in San Diego, California and reported for duty on the USS Arizona on December 9, 1937. He was killed in action on December 7, 1941 in Pearl Harbor, Hawaii. Richard was awarded the American Defense Service Medal, World War II Victory Medal and Purple Heart Medal posthumously. He remains on duty on the USS Arizona. Richard is commemorated on the USS Arizona Memorial and the Memorial Tablets of the Missing, National Memorial Cemetery of the Pacific, Honolulu, Hawaii. He was survived by his Wife, Mrs. Evelyn Mae Borger, 1026 West 20th Street, San Pedro, California.[83]

Borovich, Joseph John Seaman, First Class, Serial No: 376 08 95, US Navy. Joseph was born December 31, 1919 to George and Katie Borovich of Hollister, California. Joseph worked on farms around Hollister, California. Once while spraying pear trees he got pesticide mist in his face. His vision became blurry and when he tried to enlist in the Navy, he was rejected. Even so, he stopped at the recruiting depot every time he drove a load of pears to San Jose. One day as he was leaving the recruiting office, after having failed the eye test yet again, the recruiter called out, "Any man who wants to get into the Navy as badly as you do will get right in!" He enlisted in the US Navy on July 24, 1940 in San Francisco, California and completed his basic training at the Naval Training Station in San Diego, California. Joseph reported for duty on the USS Arizona on October 8, 1940. He was killed in action on December 7, 1941 in Pearl Harbor, Hawaii. Joseph was awarded the American Defense Service Medal, World War II Victory Medal and Purple Heart Medal posthumously. He remains on duty on the USS Arizona. Joseph is commemorated on the USS Arizona Memorial and the Memorial Tablets of the Missing, National Memorial Cemetery

---

[82] Robert Sinclair Booth, Jr., Photo and information from Dictionary of American Naval Fighting Ships, USS Booth (DE-170) History.
[83] Richard Borger, Photo provided by family member, Rich Borger.

of the Pacific, Honolulu, Hawaii. He was survived by his Father, Mr. George Borovich, 823 7th Street, Hollister, California.[84]

Bosley, Kenneth Leroy Electrician's Mate, Third Class, Serial No: 321 48 87, US Navy. Kenneth was born in 1922 to Clarence and Mildred Bosley of Sioux City, Iowa. He enlisted in the US Navy on October 15, 1940 in Des Moines, Iowa and completed his basic training at the Naval Training Station in Great Lakes, Illinois. Kenneth reported for duty on the USS Arizona on December 9, 1940. He was killed in action on December 7, 1941 in Pearl Harbor, Hawaii. Kenneth was awarded the American Defense Service Medal, World War II Victory Medal and Purple Heart Medal posthumously. He remains on duty on the USS Arizona. Kenneth is commemorated on the USS Arizona Memorial and the Memorial Tablets of the Missing, National Memorial Cemetery of the Pacific, Honolulu, Hawaii. He was survived by his Father, Mr. Clarence A. Bosley, 1124 22nd Street, Sioux City, Iowa.[85]

Boviall, Walter Robert Aviation Machinist's Mate, Second Class, Aviation Unit (VO-1), Serial No: 299 88 04, US Navy. Walter was born August 22, 1918 in Wisconsin the son of Robert and Le Anna Boviall. He enlisted in the US Navy on December 2, 1937 in Chicago, Illinois and completed his basic training at the Naval Training Station in Great Lakes, Illinois. He reported for duty on the USS Arizona on March 12, 1938. Walter was killed in action on December 7, 1941 in Pearl Harbor, Hawaii. He was awarded the American Defense Service Medal, World War II Victory Medal and Purple Heart Medal posthumously. Walter remains on duty on the USS Arizona. He is commemorated on the USS Arizona Memorial and the Memorial Tablets of the Missing, National Memorial Cemetery of the Pacific, Honolulu, Hawaii. Walter was survived by his Father, Mr. James Boviall, Route 2, Walworth, Wisconsin. The Rutledge-Boviall-Schauf-Madison American Legion Post 95 in Delavan, Wisconsin was named in his honor.[86]

Bowen, Andrew Jackson, Jr. Chief Machinist's Mate, Serial No. 359 73 89, US Navy. Andrew was born on September 29, 1911 in Kansas the son of Andrew Jackson and Birdie M. (Hubbard) Bowen. He enlisted in the US Navy October 10, 1932 in Houston, Texas and completed his basic training at the Naval Training Station in San Diego, California. Andrew reported for duty on the USS Arizona October 26, 1932 where he was serving on December 7, 1941 when the Japanese attacked Pearl Harbor. After the attack, Andrew was transferred to the USS Salt Lake City for duty. Andrew died January 19, 1969 in Los Angeles, California.

---

[84] Joseph John Borovich, Photo provided by David Dunnavant, story from the Gilroy Dispatch.
[85] Kenneth Leroy Bosley, Photo from 1939 Yearbook, Central High School, Sioux City, Iowa, Page 46
[86] Walter Robert Boviall, Photo curtsey of Lawrence Malsch, Commander, Rutledge-Boviall-Schauf-Madison American Legion Post 95, Delavan, Wisconsin.

Bowman, Howard "Howdie" Alton Seaman, Second Class, Serial No: 321 49 00, US Navy. Howard was born September 29, 1919 in Lang, Saskatchewan, Canada to Dennis and Florence Bowman. His family moved to Coon Rapids, Iowa in the fall of 1921. *Howdie attended the local schools and took an active part in school activities. He was a member of the glee club, the mixed chorus, the boy's quartet, played football and baseball, and graduated in 1939.* Howdie enlisted in the US Navy on October 15, 1940 in Des Moines, Iowa and completed his basic training at the Naval Training Station in Great Lakes, Illinois. He reported for duty on the USS Arizona on December 9, 1940. Howard was killed in action on December 7, 1941 in Pearl Harbor, Hawaii. Howard was awarded the American Defense Service Medal, World War II Victory Medal and Purple Heart Medal posthumously. He remains on duty on the USS Arizona. Howard is commemorated on the USS Arizona Memorial and the Memorial Tablets of the Missing, National Memorial Cemetery of the Pacific, Honolulu, Hawaii. He was survived by his Father, Mr. Dennis Bowman, 1020 7th Avenue, Coon Rapids, Iowa.[87]

Boyd, Charles Andrew Carpenter's Mate, Third Class, Serial No: 272 30 48, US Navy. Charles was born February 16, 1919 in Alabama to Charles H and Hattie Lou (Miller) Boyd. He enlisted in the US Navy on April 17, 1940 in Birmingham, Alabama. He transferred from the USS Kilty to the USS Arizona on March 22, 1941. Charles was killed in action on December 7, 1941 in Pearl Harbor, Hawaii. He was awarded the American Defense Service Medal, World War II Victory Medal and Purple Heart Medal posthumously. Charles remains on duty on the USS Arizona. He is commemorated on the USS Arizona Memorial and the Memorial Tablets of the Missing, National Memorial Cemetery of the Pacific, Honolulu, Hawaii. Charles was survived by his Father, Mr. Charles Hendrix Boyd, Route 4, Dothan, Alabama.

Boydstun, Don Jasper Seaman, Second Class, Serial No: 356 59 12, US Navy. Don was born June 7, 1922 in Fort Worth, Texas to James Jasper Boydstun and Ivy I. (Ward) Boydstun of Fort Worth, Texas. He enlisted in the US Navy on June 3, 1941 in Dallas, Texas and completed his basic training at the Naval Training Station in San Diego, California. Don reported for duty on the USS Arizona on August 13, 1941. He was killed in action on December 7, 1941 in Pearl Harbor, Hawaii. Don was awarded the American Defense Service Medal, World War II Victory Medal and Purple Heart Medal posthumously. He remains on duty on the USS Arizona. Don is commemorated on the USS Arizona Memorial and the Memorial Tablets of the Missing,

---

[87] Howard Alton Bowman, Photo and information from Local Boys "Missing In Action In Performance of His Duty And In Service of His Country", Coon Rapids Enterprise Newspaper, Coon Rapids, Carrol County, Iowa, Friday, December 26, 1941.

National Memorial Cemetery of the Pacific, Honolulu, Hawaii. He was survived by his Parents, Mr. and Mrs. James Jasper Boydstun, 3059 Hale Street, Fort Worth, Texas. (Cousin of R.L. Boydstun)[88]

Boydstun, R. L. Seaman, Second Class, Serial No: 356 59 28, US Navy. R.L. was born June 14, 1923 in Fort Worth, Texas. He enlisted in the US Navy on June 3, 1941 in Dallas, Texas and completed his basic training at the Naval Training Station in San Diego, California. He reported for duty on the USS Arizona on August 13, 1941. R.L. was killed in action on December 7, 1941 in Pearl Harbor, Hawaii. He was awarded the American Defense Service Medal, World War II Victory Medal and Purple Heart Medal posthumously. R.L. remains on duty on the USS Arizona. He is commemorated on the USS Arizona Memorial and the Memorial Tablets of the Missing, National Memorial Cemetery of the Pacific, Honolulu, Hawaii. Seaman Boydstun was survived by his Parents, Mr. and Mrs. Edgar Boydstun, 2803 Lula, Fort Worth, Texas. (Cousin of Don Boydstun)

Brabbzson, Oran "Buttercup" Merrill Musician, Second Class, Serial No: 223 81 96, US Navy. Oran was born July 14, 1922 to Oran Brabbzson and Violet (Knudsen) Brabbzson of Queens, New York. He enlisted in the US Navy on September 5, 1940 and attended the Navy School of Music in Washington DC graduating on May 23, 1941. Oran reported for duty on the USS Arizona June 17, 1941. He was killed in action on December 7, 1941 in Pearl Harbor, Hawaii. *The battle station for all of the band members was in the black powder room passing ammunition to the Arizona's gunners during the attack. None of the band members survived the explosion.* He was awarded the American Defense Service Medal, World War II Victory Medal and Purple Heart Medal posthumously. Oran remains on duty on the USS Arizona. He is commemorated on the USS Arizona Memorial and the Memorial Tablets of the Missing, National Memorial Cemetery of the Pacific, Honolulu, Hawaii. Oran was survived by his Father, Mr. Oran Milton Brabbzson, Lancaster Street, East Meadow, Hempstead, New York.[89]

Bradley, Bruce Dean Seaman, Second Class, Serial No: 300 19 36, US Navy. Bruce was born January 29, 1922 in Illinois the son of Daniel and Luella Marie Bradley. He enlisted in the US Navy on October 8, 1940 in Chicago, Illinois and completed his basic training at the Naval Training Station in Great Lakes, Illinois. He reported for duty on the USS Arizona on December 9, 1940. Bruce was killed in action on December 7, 1941 in Pearl Harbor, Hawaii. He was awarded the American Defense Service Medal, World War II Victory Medal and Purple Heart Medal posthumously. Bruce remains on duty on the USS Arizona. He is commemorated on the USS Arizona Memorial and the Memorial Tablets of the Missing, National Memorial Cemetery of the Pacific, Honolulu, Hawaii and Wyoming Cemetery, Paw Paw, Illinois. Bruce was survived

---

[88] Don Jasper Boydstun, Photo provided by family member, Craig Hansen.
[89] Oran Merrill Brabbzson, Photo from USS Arizona's Last Band by Molly Kent. By permission of the author. For more information about this book, go to www.USSARIZONASLASTBAND.com.

by his Father, Mr. Daniel Bradley, Paw Paw, Illinois.

Bradshaw, Harry Frederick Seaman, First Class, Serial No 321 36 41, US Navy. Harry was born October 15, 1921 in Charles City, Iowa to Ray and Macie (Cahal) Bradshaw. He enlisted in the US Navy November 15, 1939 in Des Moines, Iowa and completed his training at the Naval Training Station in Great Lakes, Illinois. He reported for duty on the USS Arizona January 27, 1940. Harry was serving on the Arizona December 7, 1941 when the Japanese attacked Pearl Harbor. He was later killed in action while serving on board the USS Neosho (AO-23) during the Battle of the Coral Sea on May 7, 1942. Buried at sea, he is commemorated on the Memorial Tablets of the Missing, Fort William McKinley, Manila, Philippines and Oak Hill Cemetery, Belle Plaine, Iowa. Harry was awarded the Purple Heart Medal posthumously.
He was survived by his Wife, Mrs. Jeanette S. Bradshaw, c/o S. B. Bellamy Lumber Company, Nashua, Iowa, son, Dennis Conrad Bradshaw and parents, Mr. and Mrs. Ray Bradshaw of Belle Plaine, Iowa. The American Legion Hall in Belle Plaine was renamed Jennings-Bradshaw Post #39 in his honor.[90]

Brakke, Kenneth Gay Fireman, Third Class, Serial No: 385 92 39, US Navy. Kenneth was born December 4, 1920 to Andrew T. and Inga Kjarstad (Stockton) Brakke of Seattle, Washington. He enlisted in the US Navy on November 5, 1940 in Seattle, Washington and completed his basic training at the Naval Training Station in San Diego, California. Kenneth reported for duty on the USS Arizona on January 11, 1941. He was killed in action on December 7, 1941 in Pearl Harbor, Hawaii. Kenneth was awarded the American Defense Service Medal, World War II Victory Medal and Purple Heart Medal posthumously. He remains on duty on the USS Arizona. Kenneth is commemorated on the USS Arizona Memorial and the Memorial Tablets of the Missing, National Memorial Cemetery of the Pacific, Honolulu, Hawaii. He was survived by his Father, Mr. Andrew Brakke, 5528 Wallingford Avenue, Seattle, Washington.[91]

Braydis, John Seaman, First Class, Serial No. 228 21 09, US Navy. John was born on December 4, 1908 in New Jersey. He enlisted in the US Navy October 5, 1939 in Los Angeles, California and completed his basic training at the Naval Training Station in San Diego, California. He transferred from the USS Argonne to the USS Arizona on May 27, 1941. He was serving on the Arizona December 7, 1941 when the Japanese attacked Pearl Harbor. He went on to serve on board the USS Monterey (CV-26) during the war. John died on January 2, 1972 in Calaveras, California.

---

[90] Harry Frederick Bradshaw, Photo from Belle Plaine High School yearbook 1939.
[91] Kenneth Gay Brakke, Photo provided by family member, Karen Clawson.

Bridges, James Leon Seaman, First Class, Serial No: 295 76 69, US Navy. James was born November 18, 1916 in Harrison, Kentucky to Ulysses Alfred and Ella Gertrude (Raley) Bridges. He enlisted in the US Navy on October 4, 1940 in Nashville, Tennessee and completed his basic training at the Naval Training Station in Norfolk, Virginia. He reported for duty on the USS Arizona on December 4, 1940. James was killed in action on December 7, 1941 in Pearl Harbor, Hawaii. He was awarded the American Defense Service Medal, World War II Victory Medal and Purple Heart Medal posthumously. James remains on duty on the USS Arizona. He is commemorated on the USS Utah Memorial and the Memorial Tablets of the Missing, National Memorial Cemetery of the Pacific, Honolulu, Hawaii. James was survived by his Father, Mr. Ulysses A. Bridges, 512 East 3rd Avenue, Fountain City, Knoxville, Tennessee. His cousin, Paul Hyatt Bridges was also killed in action aboard the USS Arizona.[92]

Bridges, Paul Hyatt Seaman, First Class, Serial No: 295 76 85, US Navy. Paul was born in 1923 to Robert E. and Cora Bridges of Breckenridge, Arkansas. He enlisted in the US Navy on October 4, 1940 in Nashville, Tennessee and completed his basic training at the Naval Training Station in Norfolk, Virginia. Paul reported for duty on the USS Arizona on December 4, 1940. He was killed in action on December 7, 1941 in Pearl Harbor, Hawaii. Paul was awarded the American Defense Service Medal, World War II Victory Medal and Purple Heart Medal posthumously. He remains on duty on the USS Arizona. Paul is commemorated on the USS Arizona Memorial and the Memorial Tablets of the Missing, National Memorial Cemetery of the Pacific, Honolulu, Hawaii. He was survived by his Father, Mr. Robert E. Bridges, 303 North Pruett Street, Paragould, Arkansas. His cousin, James Leon Bridges also was killed in action aboard the USS Arizona.

Bridie, Robert Maurice Fireman, First Class, Serial No: 321 49 14, US Navy. Robert was born in 1916 to David and Jennie (McCurnin) Bridie of Washington, Iowa. He enlisted in the US Navy on October 15, 1940 in Des Moines, Iowa and completed his basic training at the Naval Training Station in Great Lakes, Illinois. Robert reported for duty on the USS Arizona on December 9, 1940. He was killed in action on December 7, 1941 in Pearl Harbor, Hawaii. Robert was awarded the American Defense Service Medal, World War II Victory Medal and Purple Heart Medal posthumously. He remains on duty on the USS Arizona. Robert is commemorated on the USS Arizona Memorial and the Memorial Tablets of the Missing, National Memorial Cemetery of the Pacific, Honolulu, Hawaii. He was survived by his Wife, Mrs. Robert Maurice Bridie, 1955 Atlantic, Long Beach, California.[93]

Brignole, Erminio Joseph Seaman, Second Class, Serial No: 376 35 43, US Navy. Erminio was born April 20, 1923 in Alameda, California. He enlisted in the US Navy on June 26, 1941 in San Francisco, California and completed his basic training at the Naval Training Station in San Diego, California. He reported for duty on the USS Arizona on August 29, 1941. Erminio was killed in action on December 7, 1941 in Pearl Harbor, Hawaii. He was awarded the American Defense Service Medal, World War II Victory Medal and Purple Heart Medal

---

[92] James Leon Bridges, Photo Log Cabin 1938, Bethel College, McKenzie, Tennessee.
[93] Robert Maurice Bridie, Photo from California Honor States.

posthumously. Erminio remains on duty on the USS Arizona. He is commemorated on the USS Arizona Memorial and the Memorial Tablets of the Missing, National Memorial Cemetery of the Pacific, Honolulu, Hawaii. Erminio was survived by his Mother, Mrs. Angela Cervetto, 127 Romie Lane, Salinas, California.

Brittan, Charles Edward Seaman, Second Class, Serial No: 376 30 80, US Navy. Charles was born on March 2, 1924 in Chico, California to Laura Hamilton Brittan and Charles R. Brittan. He had two younger sisters Ellean May Brittan Farfan and Lois Colleen Brittan Carlson. Charles enlisted in the US Navy on April 18, 1941 in San Francisco, California and completed his basic training at the Naval Training Station in San Diego, California. At 17 years old, he was the youngest sailor on board the Arizona when he reported for duty on July 13, 1941. Charles was killed in action on December 7, 1941 in Pearl Harbor, Hawaii. *He was burned all over his body so severely that he died before he could be put aboard the motor launch from the hospital ship Solace. Charles was recognized by a shipmate by a tattoo he had on his shoulder.* The disposition of his remains is unclear. He may have been buried in the "Punchbowl" in a grave marked "unknown". Charles was awarded the American Defense Service Medal, World War II Victory Medal and Purple Heart Medal posthumously. He is commemorated on the USS Arizona Memorial and the Memorial Tablets of the Missing, National Memorial Cemetery of the Pacific, Honolulu, Hawaii. Charles was survived by his Mother, Mrs. Laura Brittan, 724 Franklin Street, San Francisco, California.[94]

Broadhead, Johnnie Cecil Fireman, Second Class, Serial No: 272 41 16, US Navy. Johnnie was born February 6, 1922 to William Walter and May L. Broadhead of Kincheon, Alabama. He was the youngest of three children. Johnnie was only 19 years old when he was killed. His family was from the southern part of Chilton County, Alabama where they were peach farmers. Making a living on the farm at that time was difficult so he enlisted in the US Navy on October 4, 1940 in Birmingham, Alabama and completed his basic training at the Naval Training Station in Norfolk, Virginia. Johnnie reported for duty on the USS Arizona on December 4, 1940. He was killed in action on December 7, 1941 in Pearl Harbor, Hawaii. *The story goes that 3 days prior to Pearl Harbor, his mother saw and heard a mocking bird chirping at her window each morning leading up to the 7th. She considered this a bad omen. She didn't see it after the 7th and soon learned of Johnnie's death. After his death, their mother would never turn her calendar to the month of December.* Johnnie was awarded the American Defense Service Medal, World War II Victory Medal and Purple Heart Medal posthumously. He remains on duty on the USS Arizona. Johnnie is commemorated on the USS Arizona Memorial and the Memorial Tablets of the Missing, National Memorial Cemetery of the Pacific, Honolulu, Hawaii. He was survived by his Father, Mr. William Walter Broadhead and his Mother, Mrs. Lena Mae Broadhead, Route 1, Billingsley, Alabama.[95]

---

[94] Charles Edward Brittan, Information and photo provided by his niece, Catherine Farfan Crnkovich.
[95] Johnnie Cecil Broadhead, Photo and story provided by family member, Kim Gillespie.

Brock, Walter Pershing Seaman, First Class, Serial No: 287 45 91, US Navy. Walter was born September 30, 1921 in Kentucky to Foster C. and Julia Brock. *He was bright, funny and well liked. Walter was engaged at the time of his death to a girl from London, KY.* He enlisted in the US Navy on October 15, 1940 in Louisville, Kentucky and completed his basic training at the Naval Training Station in Great Lakes, Illinois. He reported for duty on the USS Arizona on December 9, 1940. Walter was killed in action on December 7, 1941 in Pearl Harbor, Hawaii. He was awarded the American Defense Service Medal, World War II Victory Medal and Purple Heart Medal posthumously. Walter remains on duty on the USS Arizona. He is commemorated on the USS Arizona Memorial and the Memorial Tablets of the Missing, National Memorial Cemetery of the Pacific, Honolulu, Hawaii and A.R. Dyche Memorial Park, London, Kentucky. Walter was survived by his Father, Mr. Foster C. Brock, Rural Route 1, London, Kentucky.[96]

Bromley, George Edward Signalman, Third Class, Serial No: 385 78 30, US Navy. George was born February 24, 1921 to Walter D. and Ruby P. Bromley of Tacoma, Washington. He enlisted in the US Navy on July 12, 1938 in Seattle, Washington and reported for duty on the USS Arizona on March 7, 1939. George was killed in action on December 7, 1941 in Pearl Harbor, Hawaii. He was awarded the American Defense Service Medal, World War II Victory Medal and Purple Heart Medal posthumously. George's remains were recovered and he was buried in Plot A, Row 0, Grave 514, National Memorial Cemetery of the Pacific, Honolulu, Hawaii. He is commemorated on the USS Arizona Memorial. George was survived by his Father, Mr. Walter David Bromley, Route 6, Box 381, Tacoma, Washington. His brother Jimmie was also lost on the USS Arizona that day.[97]

Bromley, Jimmie Seaman, First Class, Serial No: 385 84 78, US Navy. Jimmie was born in 1918 to Walter D. and Ruby P. Bromley of Tacoma, Washington. He enlisted in the US Navy on January 8, 1940 in Seattle, Washington and completed his basic training at the Naval Training Station in San Diego, California. Jimmie reported for duty on the USS Arizona on March 26, 1940. He was killed in action on December 7, 1941 in Pearl Harbor, Hawaii. Jimmie was awarded the American Defense Service Medal, World War II Victory Medal and Purple Heart Medal posthumously. He remains on duty on the USS Arizona. Jimmie is commemorated on the USS Arizona Memorial and the Memorial Tablets of the Missing, National Memorial Cemetery of the Pacific, Honolulu, Hawaii. He was survived by his Father, Mr. Walter David Bromley, Route 6, Box 381, Tacoma, Washington. His brother, George was killed in action on the USS Arizona that day.[98]

---

[96] Walter Pershing Brock, Photo and information provided by his nephew, I. Brock.
[97] George Edward Bromley, Photo and information provided by family member, Paula Mazurek.
[98] Jimmy Bromley, Photo and information provided by family member, Paula Mazurek.

Brooks, Robert Neal Ensign, Serial No: O-098042, US Navy Reserve. Robert was born in 1920 to John M. Brooks and Pearl Marie (Morford) Brooks of Poulsbo, Washington. He was commissioned on May 15, 1941. Robert was the Assistant Communications Officer on the USS Arizona. He was killed in action on December 7, 1941 in Pearl Harbor, Hawaii. Robert was awarded the American Defense Service Medal, World War II Victory Medal and Purple Heart Medal posthumously. He remains on duty on the USS Arizona. Robert is commemorated on the USS Arizona Memorial and the Memorial Tablets of the Missing, National Memorial Cemetery of the Pacific, Honolulu, Hawaii. He was survived by his Father, Mr. John M. Brooks, 7545 12th Northwest, Seattle, Washington.[99]

Broome, Loy Raymond Signalman, Third Class, Serial No: 359 97 80, US Navy. Loy was born July 4, 1916 in Oklahoma. He enlisted in the US Navy on January 7, 1938 in Houston, Texas and completed his basic training at the Naval Training Station in San Diego, California. Loy reported for duty on the USS Arizona on April 28, 1938. He was killed in action on December 7, 1941 in Pearl Harbor, Hawaii. Loy was awarded the American Defense Service Medal, World War II Victory Medal and Purple Heart Medal posthumously. He remains on duty on the USS Arizona. Loy is commemorated on the USS Arizona Memorial and the Memorial Tablets of the Missing, National Memorial Cemetery of the Pacific, Honolulu, Hawaii. He was survived by his Mother, Mrs. Lula Mae Brown, 4010 South Yukon Street, Tulsa, Oklahoma.

Brooner, Allen Ottis Seaman, First Class, Serial No: 291 65 46, US Navy. Allen was born on June 11, 1922 in Dale, Indiana the youngest son of Ottis Irvin Brooner and Mary Thompson (Painter) Brooner. He enlisted in the US Navy on September 25, 1940 in Indianapolis, Indiana and completed his basic training at the Naval Training Station in Great Lakes, Illinois. Allen reported for duty on the USS Arizona on December 9, 1940. He was killed in action on December 7, 1941 in Pearl Harbor, Hawaii. Allen was awarded the American Defense Service Medal, World War II Victory Medal and Purple Heart Medal posthumously. He remains on duty on the USS Arizona. Allen is commemorated on the USS Arizona Memorial and the Memorial Tablets of the Missing, National Memorial Cemetery of the Pacific, Honolulu, Hawaii. He was survived by his Father, Mr. Ottis I. Brooner, Dale, Indiana.[100]

---

[99] Robert Neal Brooks, Photo from the Tyee Yearbook, University of Washington, Seattle, Washington, Class of 1939.
[100] Allen Ottis Brooner, Photo from Indiana State Museum, Heroes from the Heartland, Submitted by Daryl Lovell.

Brophy, Myron Alonzo   Fireman, Second Class, Serial No: 212 54 40, US Navy. Myron was born on November 1, 1919 in East Dorset, Vermont to Myron Alonzo Brophy and Mary E. (Sheller) Brophy. He was eight when his father died and 13 when his mother died, both from cancer. Myron enlisted in the US Navy on January 23, 1940 in Springfield, Massachusetts and reported for duty on the USS Arizona on January 4, 1941. Myron was killed in action on December 7, 1941 in Pearl Harbor, Hawaii. He was awarded the American Defense Service Medal, World War II Victory Medal and Purple Heart Medal posthumously. Myron remains buried on the USS Arizona. He is commemorated on the USS Arizona Memorial and the Memorial Tablets of the Missing, National Memorial Cemetery of the Pacific, Honolulu, Hawaii and East Dorset Cemetery, East Dorset, Vermont. Myron was survived by his Sister, Mrs. Pernas Jacobs, 22 West Street, Rutland, Vermont.[101]

Brown, Charles Martin   Seaman, Second Class, Serial No: 382 29 42, US Navy. Charles enlisted in the US Navy on October 30, 1940 in Los Angeles, California and completed his basic training at the Naval Training Station in San Diego, California. He reported for duty on the USS Arizona on January 11, 1941. Charles was killed in action on December 7, 1941 in Pearl Harbor, Hawaii. He was awarded the American Defense Service Medal, World War II Victory Medal and Purple Heart Medal posthumously. Charles remains on duty on the USS Arizona. He is commemorated on the USS Arizona Memorial and the Memorial Tablets of the Missing, National Memorial Cemetery of the Pacific, Honolulu, Hawaii. Charles was survived by his Mother, Mrs. Clyde M. Van Duesen, 3822 York Boulevard, Los Angeles, California.

Brown, Elwyn LeRoy   Electrician's Mate, Third Class, Serial No: 342 30 12, US Navy. Elwyn was born on July 19, 1919 in Kansas City, Kansas to Minor Loren Brown and Lydia M. (Bodenhausen) Brown of Kentucky, Kansas. He enlisted in the US Navy on October 14, 1940 in Kansas City, Missouri and completed his basic training at the Naval Training Station in Great Lakes, Illinois. Elwyn reported for duty on the USS Arizona December 9, 1940. He was killed in action on December 7, 1941 in Pearl Harbor, Hawaii. Elwyn was awarded the American Defense Service Medal, World War II Victory Medal and Purple Heart Medal posthumously. He remains on duty on the USS Arizona. Elwyn is commemorated on the USS Arizona Memorial and the Memorial Tablets of the Missing, National Memorial Cemetery of the Pacific, Honolulu, Hawaii. He was survived by his Father, Mr. Minor Loren Brown, Route 1, Richland, Kansas.

---

[101] Myron Alonzo Brophy, Photo and information provided by family member, Cameron Bryant.

Brown, Frank George Quartermaster, Third Class, Serial No: 393 32 60, US Navy. Frank was born November 9, 1922 in Baker City, Oregon. *He was the youngest child of Fred and Grace Elizabeth Humphreys Brown. He grew up on the family farm in Keating, Oregon. In 1934, when Frank was 12 years old, his mother committed suicide.* Frank enlisted in the US Navy on December 8, 1939 in Portland, Oregon and completed his basic training at the Naval Training Station in San Diego, California. He reported for duty on the USS Arizona on February 24, 1940. Frank was killed in action on December 7, 1941 in Pearl Harbor, Hawaii. He was awarded the American Defense Service Medal, World War II Victory Medal and Purple Heart Medal posthumously. Frank remains on duty on the USS Arizona. He is commemorated on the USS Arizona Memorial and the Memorial Tablets of the Missing, National Memorial Cemetery of the Pacific, Honolulu, Hawaii. Frank was survived by his Father, Mr. Fred Brown, 1407 Ninth Street, Baker, Oregon.[102]

Brown, Gene Richard Seaman, First Class, Serial No. 291 65 66, US Navy. Gene was born December 21, 1920. He enlisted in the US Navy October 6, 1940 in Indianapolis, Indiana and completed his training at the Naval Training Station at Great Lakes, Illinois. He reported for duty on the USS Arizona December 9, 1940. He was serving on the Arizona December 7, 1941, when the Japanese attacked Pearl Harbor. Gene was killed in action on April 7, 1945 while serving on board the YMS-427 in Nakagusuku Bay, Okinawa as a result of shrapnel wounds received by direct hit on his ship from enemy shore battery. He was buried at sea on April 8, 1945 and is memorialized on the Tablets of the Missing at the National Memorial Cemetery of the Pacific in Honolulu, Hawaii. He was awarded the Purple Heart Medal posthumously. Gene was survived by his Parents, Mr. and Mrs. Loren C. Brown, 328 West Lewis Street, Fort Wayne, Indiana.

Brown, Richard Corbett Seaman, First Class, Serial No: 376 16 92, US Navy. Richard was born September 17, 1918 in Fresno, California to Clifford Charles and Anna Brown. *His cousin, Jack M. Jensen and he were bosom buddies growing up in Chowchilla, CA in the 1920's and 30's. They went to the enlistment office together in late 1940 and Richard was sworn in on November 27, 1940 in San Francisco, California.* He completed his basic training at the Naval Training Station in San Diego, California. Richard reported for duty on the USS Arizona on January 25, 1941. He was killed in action on December 7, 1941 in Pearl Harbor, Hawaii. Richard was awarded the American Defense Service Medal, World War II Victory Medal and Purple Heart Medal posthumously. Assigned death #498, his body was recovered on December 16, 1941. He was identified by his name on his skivvies. [103] Richard's remains were sent home and he was buried at the Chowchilla District Cemetery, Chowchilla, California. Richard is commemorated on the USS Arizona Memorial and the Memorial Tablets of the Missing, National Memorial Cemetery of the Pacific, Honolulu, Hawaii. He was survived by his Mother, Mrs. Annie Kendall, Route 2, Box 128, Chowchilla, California. The VFW Post #9896 in Chowchilla, California is named in his honor.[104]

---

[102] Frank George Brown, Information and photo provided by researcher, Lolita Cunningham.

[103] Richard Corbett Brown, Report of Changes, USS Arizona for the month ending 31st day of December, 1942, page 42, line 23.

[104] Richard Corbett Brown, information and picture provided by his cousin, John Jensen.

Brown, William "Buzz" Howard   Seaman, Second Class, (V-6), Serial No: 654 00 83, US Navy. William was born in about 1923 to William Franklyn and Evelyn (Brazzeal) Brown. He enlisted in the US Navy on June 24, 1941 in Portland, Oregon and completed his basic training at the Naval Training Station in San Diego, California. He reported for duty on the USS Arizona on August 29, 1941. William was killed in action on December 7, 1941 in Pearl Harbor, Hawaii. He was awarded the American Defense Service Medal, World War II Victory Medal and Purple Heart Medal posthumously. William remains on duty on the USS Arizona. He is commemorated on the USS Arizona Memorial and the Memorial Tablets of the Missing, National Memorial Cemetery of the Pacific, Honolulu, Hawaii. William was survived by his Parents, Mr. and Mrs. William F. Brown, 218 North B Street, Forest Grove, Oregon.

Browne, Harry Lamont   Chief Machinist's Mate, Serial No: 316 06 78, US Navy. Harry was born February 24, 1905 in Nebraska. He was recalled to active duty in the US Navy on January 23, 1939 at the Naval Recruiting Station in Omaha, Nebraska and reported for duty on the USS Arizona on February 24, 1939. He was killed in action on December 7, 1941 in Pearl Harbor, Hawaii. Harry was awarded the American Defense Service Medal, World War II Victory Medal and Purple Heart Medal posthumously. He remains on duty on the USS Arizona. Harry is commemorated on the USS Arizona Memorial and the Memorial Tablets of the Missing, National Memorial Cemetery of the Pacific, Honolulu, Hawaii. He was survived by his Wife, Mrs. Louise Roseann Browne, 202 West 91st Street, Los Angeles, California.

Browning, Robert James   Seaman, Second Class, Serial No. 360 41 25, US Navy. Robert enlisted in the US Navy June 23, 1941 in Houston, Texas and completed his training at the Naval Training Station in San Diego, California. He reported for duty on the USS Arizona August 29, 1941. He was serving on December 7, 1941, when the Japanese attacked Pearl Harbor. He was assigned duty on the USS Patterson (DD-392) and reported for duty December 9, 1941.

Browning, Tilmon David   Seaman, First Class, Serial No: 266 28 46, US Navy. Tilmon was born in about 1924 in Logan, West Virginia to Dewey Tilmon Browning and Eula M. (Conley) Browning. He enlisted in the US Navy on December 21, 1940 in Richmond, Virginia and reported for duty on the USS Arizona on April 4, 1941. Tilmon was killed in action on December 7, 1941 in Pearl Harbor, Hawaii. He was awarded the American Defense Service Medal, World War II Victory Medal and Purple Heart Medal posthumously. Tilmon remains on duty on the USS Arizona. He is commemorated on the USS Arizona Memorial and the Memorial Tablets of the Missing, National Memorial Cemetery of the Pacific, Honolulu, Hawaii. Tilmon was survived by his Father, Mr. Dewey Tilmon Browning, Omar, West Virginia.

Bruce, John Franklin   Gunner's Mate, Third Class, Serial No. 287 37 86, US Navy. John was born March 18, 1917 in Nebo, Kentucky to Benjamin Newt and Grace (Williams) Bruce. He enlisted in the US Navy March 12, 1940 in Louisville, Kentucky and completed his training at the Naval Training Station in Great Lakes, Illinois. He reported for duty on the USS Arizona July 12, 1940. He was serving on the Arizona December 7, 1941, when the Japanese attacked Pearl Harbor. He later served on the USS Stephen Potter (DD-538), USS Los Angeles (CA-135), USS Marshall (DD-676) and Fleet activities, Yokosuka, Japan. John was awarded the Navy Good Conduct Medal, American Campaign Medal, American Defense Service Medal, Asiatic-Pacific Campaign Medal, WWII Victory Medal, Navy Occupation Service Medal and Armed Forces Expeditionary Medal. He was a career Navy man, retiring on May 31, 1970 with the rank of Senior Chief Gunner's Mate. John died December 6, 1984 in Orlando, Florida and is buried in Section 44, Row 1, Site 13 of Bay Pines National Cemetery, Bay Pines Florida.[105]

Brune, James William Radioman, Third Class, (V-3), Serial No: 411 04 44, US Navy Reserve. James was born in about 1918 in Missouri to Henry and Amelia Brune. He enlisted in the US Navy on September 7, 1940 in St. Louis, Missouri and attended US Naval Reserve Radio School in Indianapolis, Indiana. He reported for duty on the USS Arizona on January 25, 1941. He was killed in action on December 7, 1941 in Pearl Harbor, Hawaii. James was awarded the American Defense Service Medal, World War II Victory Medal and Purple Heart Medal posthumously. He remains on duty on the USS Arizona. James is commemorated on the USS Arizona Memorial and the Memorial Tablets of the Missing, National Memorial Cemetery of the Pacific, Honolulu, Hawaii. He was survived by his Mother, Mrs. Amelia Thekla Brune, 3621-A Tennessee Avenue, St. Louis, Missouri.[106]

Bruner, Lauren Fay Fire Controlman, Third Class, Serial No. 385 79 49, US Navy. Lauren was born in 1920 in Washington. He enlisted in the US Navy November 15, 1938 at Seattle, Washington. He reported for duty on the USS Arizona February 11, 1939 after completion of training at the Naval Training Station in San Diego, California. Lauren was serving on December 7, 1941 when the Japanese attacked Pearl Harbor. Lauren was wounded in action during the attack and his Mother, Mrs. Lucille Iowa Kellerman, Box 38, McCleary, Washington, was notified. He spent from December 7, 1941 until December 30, 1941 on the hospital ship USS Solace. On the 30th of December he was transferred to the Naval Hospital in Pearl Harbor. Lauren was transferred to a hospital on the mainland on January 11, 1942. After recovery from his wounds he was assigned duty on the USS Coghlan (DD-606) and participated in eight major engagements (Aleutian Islands and seven South Pacific operations enroute to the Philippines). His ship was decommissioned at Charleston, South Carolina in late 1945. Lauren was transferred to Subic Bay in the Philippines to await passage to Shanghai, China where he boarded the USS Duluth (CL-87). He served on that ship until late 1946. Lauren left the Navy in February 1947 having attained Chief Fire Controlman rank.[107]

---

[105] John Franklin Bruce, Photo provided by family member, J. M. Bruce.

[106] James William Brune, Photo from Missouri Honor States.

[107] Lauren Fay Bruner, Photo from, "Survivor with Local Ties featured in USS Arizona documentary" by Tommi Halvorsen Gatlin, The News Tribune, Tacoma, WA, July 3, 2013.

Bruns, Martin Benjamin Yeoman, Second Class, Aviation Unit (VO-1), Serial No. 360 00 72, US Navy. Martin was the youngest of three brothers born on January 24, 1919 to William Bruns and Laura (Ludwig) Bruns. Martin was a farm boy from rural Fredericksburg Texas. He joined the navy for $36 a month and three meals a day. "It was the Depression," he said. "And I was sick and tired of making $2.50 a week as an itinerant farmhand. He enlisted in the US Navy September 9, 1938. After boot camp he reported for duty on the USS Arizona June 7, 1940. For the next two years, he served on its deck force, scrubbing and polishing the brass fittings and teakwood decks. He learned to sleep in a hammock, to cook for the 20-man mess, to pull boat-crew duty and to fire the ship's massive 14-inch guns. The peacetime navy was woefully understaffed, Martin said. On the Arizona, there weren't even enough sailors to service all the gun turrets at one time. By the summer of 1940, however, distant rumblings in the Far East brought the possibility of war with Japan, laughable as it was to most American military leaders, into sharper focus. Martin said nobody seemed to take seriously the possibility of an attack on the powerful complex of the U.S. Air and Sea might mass at Pearl.

It was Friday night, December 5th when the Arizona slid into Pearl Harbor's Battleship Row after two weeks of sea maneuvers. The USS Nevada was anchored astern. Tennessee, West Virginia, Maryland and Oklahoma were lined up, like ducks in a shooting gallery, in the oily water ahead. Ford Island's quays and rocky shore lay only a few hundred yards off their starboard side.

"There wasn't a bit of static in the air," Martin said of his unsuspecting mates. "Saturday night was calm weather, a beautiful sunset." Most of my shipmates spent Saturday night on shore at a Navy-run nightclub called the Blue Moon. I stayed on the Arizona, reading.

Sunday morning, I was up early, to sell newspapers for a friend who had gone ashore to be with his just-arrived wife. As I climbed the layers of sweeping, wide decks, I found many of my customers still in their hammocks. Messes had been set up for late breakfast. Shortly before 8 a.m., I went aft to write up my collection report. The Marine guard was readying for its daily flag-raising ritual. Moments later, the first bomb hit. I felt a rumble, and then the ship wobbled and shook a little bit. There wasn't much noise. But the lights went out and I heard the bugler play AIR DEFENSE. Next thing I saw was the fires. Arizona's forward two-thirds disappeared in a massive fireball that climbed more than 400 feet over the churning harbor. I barely felt the explosion. But I saw the ship's towering foremast buckle and begin to fall. I watched men with their shoes blown off and blood pouring out of their ears and noses straggle from the doomed ship's hatches to stand dazed in the morning light.

The flames and smoke were vicious. By the time we began to evacuate the ship, there were dying men everywhere. Four or five times I swam from the Arizona to Ford Island with soot-blackened, nearly exhausted men. I remember begging them to keep kicking to make it to shore.[108]

Martin received a commendation for his actions on that day: "He assisted in fighting fires ... while the decks were being strafed and bombed by enemy aircraft and later assisted badly burned men over to the life lines. On orders to abandon ship, he rescued injured men who were faltering in the water and swam them to a nearby quay. He then assisted in loading wounded men in a 50-foot motor launch and proceeded with the launch toward a boat landing, assisting in the rescue of men in the water on the way. After discharging the wounded men at the landing, he manned an abandoned 50-foot motor launch as engineer and returned to his ship to pick up the remaining survivors on board and men at the quay. On the way back to the landing more

---

[108] "Day of Infamy" by Andy Lindstrom 12/7/1991, Tallahassee Democrat, Tallahassee, Florida.

survivors were picked up from the water. He then returned for a final trip to the Arizona making certain no more survivors were left stranded, and then passed the remaining battleship moorings looking for survivors. During the period he was making these boat trips, Japanese aircraft were continuing with heavy bombing and strafing attacks in the area. His initiative and devotion to duty under heavy enemy fire were in keeping with the highest traditions of the United States Naval Service." E. H. Geiselman, Captain, US Navy.

At day's end, Martin was reassigned to a Navy aircraft squadron and spent the rest of the war on carrier duty. "We saw combat," he said, "But never again like on the Arizona."

Martin retired from the Navy in 1968 with 30 years of service with a rank of Lieutenant. After several state-government jobs, he worked part time at Buck Lake Animal Hospital. He died on May 9, 2004 in Tallahassee, Florida and is buried in Culley's Meadowwood Memorial Park, Tallahassee, Florida.[109]

Bryan, Leland Howard   Seaman, First Class, Serial No: 356 26 94, US Navy. Leland was born March 10, 1923 in Gorman, Texas to William H. and Zesta A. (Hampton) Bryan. He enlisted in the US Navy on April 10, 1940 in Dallas, Texas and completed his basic training at the Naval Training Station in San Diego, California. He reported for duty on the USS Arizona on July 2, 1940. Leland was killed in action on December 7, 1941 in Pearl Harbor, Hawaii. He was awarded the American Defense Service Medal, World War II Victory Medal and Purple Heart Medal posthumously. Leland remains on duty on the USS Arizona. He is commemorated on the USS Arizona Memorial and the Memorial Tablets of the Missing, National Memorial Cemetery of the Pacific, Honolulu, Hawaii.

Leland was survived by his Mother, Mrs. Ersta Pittman, Gorman, Texas. His brother, Jimmy was serving on board the USS Nevada and watched as his brother was killed.[110]

Bryant, Lloyd Glenn   Boatswain's Mate, Second Class, Serial No: 337 20 43, US Navy. Lloyd was born November 15, 1919 in Greene County, Illinois to Harvey W. and Rachel J. (Beasley) Bryant. He enlisted with his best friend, Vincent Thomas on October 4, 1939 in St. Louis, Missouri and they completed their basic training at the Naval Training Station in Great Lakes, Illinois. He reported for duty on the USS Arizona on December 31, 1939. A few months before he died, he wrote his mother who had been concerned about the possibility of war, "Don't worry mother, the only thing that could sink us would be a direct hit from a bomb." That is exactly what happened. Lloyd was killed in action on December 7, 1941 in Pearl Harbor, Hawaii. He was awarded the American Defense Service Medal, World War II Victory Medal and Purple Heart Medal posthumously. Lloyd remains on duty on the USS Arizona. He is commemorated on the USS Arizona Memorial and the Memorial Tablets of the Missing, National Memorial Cemetery of the Pacific, Honolulu, Hawaii. Lloyd was survived by his wife, Mrs. Helen Margaret Bryant, 831 3rd Avenue, Los Angeles, California. The American Legion Hall in Hillview, Illinois was named in memory of Lloyd Bryant and his best friend, Vincent Thomas.[111]

---

[109] Information, story and photo of Martin Benjamin Bruns provided by family member, Tracy Cleaton.
[110] Leland Howard Bryan, Information and photo provided by family member, Darren Bryan.
[111] Lloyd Glenn Bryant, Information and photo provided by family member, Rosella Thien.

Buckley, Jack C. Fire Controlman, Third Class, Serial No: 287 45 85, US Navy. Jack was born August 25, 1922 in Pike County, Kentucky to John Kenner and Lydia Margaret (Adkins) Buckley. He enlisted in the US Navy on October 15, 1940 in Louisville, Kentucky and completed his basic training at the Naval Training Station in Great Lakes, Illinois. Jack reported for duty on the USS Arizona on December 9, 1940. He was killed in action on December 7, 1941 in Pearl Harbor, Hawaii. Jack was awarded the American Defense Service Medal, World War II Victory Medal and Purple Heart Medal posthumously. He remains on duty on the USS Arizona. Jack is commemorated on the USS Arizona Memorial and the Memorial Tablets of the Missing, National Memorial Cemetery of the Pacific, Honolulu, Hawaii. He was survived by his Mother, Mrs. Lydia Buckley, Box 173, Pikeville, Kentucky

Budd, Robert Emile Fireman, Second Class, Serial No: 311 51 52, US Navy. Robert was born in 1923 to David B. and Bertha Budd of Ira, Michigan. He enlisted in the US Navy on October 8, 1940 in Detroit, Michigan and completed his basic training at the Naval Training Station in Great Lakes, Illinois. Robert reported for duty on the USS Arizona on December 9, 1940. He was killed in action on December 7, 1941 in Pearl Harbor, Hawaii. Robert was awarded the American Defense Service Medal, World War II Victory Medal and Purple Heart Medal posthumously. He remains on duty on the USS Arizona. Robert is commemorated on the USS Arizona Memorial and the Memorial Tablets of the Missing, National Memorial Cemetery of the Pacific, Honolulu, Hawaii. He was survived by his Father, Mr. David Benjamin Budd, 15745 Winthrop Avenue, Detroit, Michigan.

Buehl, Herbert Vincent Fireman, Third Class, E Division, Serial No. 300 19 34, US Navy. Herbert was born on January 20, 1922 in Monroe, Wisconsin, Son of George and Frieda Buehl. He enlisted in the US Navy October 8, 1940 in Chicago, Illinois and completed his training at the Naval Training Station in Great Lakes, Illinois. Herbert reported for duty on the USS Arizona December 9, 1940. He was serving on the Arizona December 7, 1941 when the Japanese attacked Pearl Harbor. When the powder magazines exploded, he was about to go down a ladder to the handling room. He didn't remember going down, but in one second, he was on the floor of the turret. Electricity was out and in total darkness, smoke and fumes began filling the air and in a joint effort with others, Herb opened a door to enable them to breathe. There were three officers and four men in his group with no communication, when one officer climbed to the top and called down to them to come out, "The whole ship is on fire." Unable to successfully lower a boat, it was every man individually into the oily water. Herb managed to swim to a key where others had made it and they pulled him half out of the water and he was told to make it on his own, there were others to pull in. A motor launch came by but had no time to stop; you jumped into it as it passed. "There was so much oil on our bodies; we almost slid off the other side of the boat." After surviving the ordeal on the Arizona, he was assigned duty on the USS Farragut (DD-348) and reported for duty on December 14, 1941. He was awarded the Navy Good Conduct Medal, American Defense Service Medal, Asiatic Pacific Campaign Medal with Bronze Star and the World War II Victory Medal. Herbert died on March 4, 2002 in Beloit, Illinois after a brief battle with cancer. He was buried in Floral Lawns Memorial Gardens, Beloit, Illinois. Herbert was survived by his wife, Helen; sons, Thomm Buehl of Madison, WI and David (Mary) Buehl of Leeds, NY; daughter Brenda (Ben) Harris of Louisville.[112]

---

[112] Herbert Vincent Buehl, Photo provided by family member, Joy Frost.

Buhr, Clarence Edward   Seaman, First Class, Serial No: 372 16 86, US Navy. Clarence was born March 31, 1922 in Cheyenne, Wyoming to Otto E. and Ann M. (McGraw) Buhr. He enlisted in the US Navy on August 10, 1940 in Denver, Colorado and completed his basic training at the Naval Training Station in San Diego, California. Clarence reported for duty on the USS Arizona on December 14, 1940. He was killed in action on December 7, 1941 in Pearl Harbor, Hawaii. Clarence was awarded the American Defense Service Medal, World War II Victory Medal and Purple Heart Medal posthumously. He remains on duty on the USS Arizona. Clarence is commemorated on the USS Arizona Memorial and the Memorial Tablets of the Missing, National Memorial Cemetery of the Pacific, Honolulu, Hawaii. He was survived by his Father, Mr. Otto Edward Buhr, 820 North 1st Street, Raton, New Mexico.

Burcham, Jimmie Charles   Seaman, First Class, Serial No. 274 45 62, US Navy. Jimmie was born on June 27, 1920 in Louisiana to James Henry and Effie Ellen (Walker) Burcham. He enlisted in the US Navy June 5, 1940 in New Orleans, Louisiana and completed his training at the Naval Training Station in San Diego, California. Jimmie reported for duty on the USS Arizona September 8, 1940. He was serving on the Arizona December 7, 1941 when the Japanese attacked Pearl Harbor. On the 13th of December 1941 he was taken on board the USS Lexington (CV-2) where he served until March 1942. Jimmie he served in the US Navy until January 16, 1956. He died from cancer on April 9, 1997 in Portales, New Mexico and is buried in Portales Cemetery, Portales, New Mexico.

Burden, Ralph Leon   Radioman, Third Class, Serial No: 279 74 11, US Navy. Ralph was born December 28, 1916 in Wapakoneta, Ohio to Robert W. and Leona L. (Hunnaman) Burden. Both of his parents had passed. His Mother died in 1917 and his Father died in 1933. He enlisted in the US Navy on October 15, 1940 in Cincinnati, Ohio and completed his basic training at the Naval Training Station in Great Lakes, Illinois. Ralph reported for duty on the USS Arizona on December 9, 1940. He was killed in action on December 7, 1941 in Pearl Harbor, Hawaii. On December 22nd relatives and friends received Christmas Greetings from him. The cards had been mailed on December 7th. Ralph was awarded the American Defense Service Medal, World War II Victory Medal and Purple Heart Medal posthumously. He remains on duty on the USS Arizona. Ralph is commemorated on the USS Arizona Memorial and the Memorial Tablets of the Missing, National Memorial Cemetery of the Pacific, Honolulu, Hawaii. He was survived by his Guardian, Mr. Samuel Arthur Bobb, 703 Murray Street, Wapakoneta, Ohio.

Burdette, Ralph Warren   Musician, Second Class, Serial No: 224 09 35, US Navy. Ralph was born in 1921 to Harry S. and Mable Burdette of Plainfield, New Jersey. He enlisted in the US Navy on February 4, 1941 and attended the Navy School of Music in Washington, DC graduating on May 23, 1941. Ralph reported for duty on the USS Arizona on June 17, 1941. He was killed in action on December 7, 1941 in Pearl Harbor, Hawaii. *The battle station for all of the band members was in the black powder room passing ammunition to the Arizona's gunners during the attack. None of the band members survived the explosion.* Ralph was awarded the American Defense Service Medal, World War II Victory Medal and Purple Heart Medal posthumously. He remains on duty on the USS Arizona. Ralph is commemorated on the USS Arizona Memorial, the Memorial Tablets of the Missing, National Memorial Cemetery of the Pacific, Honolulu, Hawaii and Rural Hill Cemetery, Whitehouse, New Jersey. He was survived by his Father, Mr. Harry S. Burdette, 305 Clinton Avenue, Plainfield, New Jersey.[113]

Burk, Leland Howard Gunner's Mate, Third Class, Turret III, Serial No. 337 41 56, US Navy. Leland was born on July 29, 1915 in Callao, Missouri. He enlisted in the US Navy October 15, 1940 in St. Louis, Missouri and completed his training at the Naval Training Station in Great Lakes, Illinois. Leland reported for duty on the USS Arizona December 9, 1940. He was serving on the Arizona December 7, 1941 when the Japanese attacked Pearl Harbor. His story follows:

"As I recall, on December 7, 1941, most of the men had just finished chow when the Air Defense Alarm sounded the top gunners to their stations at about 7:45 a.m. Shortly after that, General Quarters sounded all the crew to their battle stations.

It was about 755 when the first Japanese planes came in. It caught us by surprise. We had suspected something was up a few days before the attack. When our ship had been out on maneuvers, there had been contact with submarines. The Captain had also given permission to shoot back if any planes started diving. We had returned to Pearl Harbor on Friday night.

The bombing started at about 8:00 a.m. I was in the lower handling room. I was a 3rd Class Gunners Mate and my battle station was on the fourteen inch guns. When they sounded General Quarters, I was at my battle station holding onto the tray that we pulled to ram the shell into the gun. When the bomb hit, it was all we could do to hold on; it shook the ship so you could hardly stand up.

We were immediately ordered out of the turret to fight fire. When I came out, I crawled through an overhang onto the quarter deck and there were guys laying all around moaning and groaning for help. Most of their clothes were either blown or burned off. I helped move some of the injured and their flesh would stick to your hands when you handled them. We got them on some boats that were picking up the injured. The ship was on fire and we started a bucket brigade. The ship was starting to go down. Lt. Commander Fuqua was the Senior Officer aboard the ship. I remember saying to him, "Commander, there's no use in fighting it anymore," and he gave us orders to abandon ship. We threw a life raft overboard and got on it. The ship was so low at this time that we could just step on the life raft. We realized that there were no paddles, so we started swimming ashore for Ford Island. The oil was thick on the water and some of it was on fire. There wasn't any fire where we went in. While swimming toward shore I heard some guys hollering. They were giving up and going down. As I turned around to see them, a big wave of water hit me in the face and oil and water got into my mouth and I swallowed some. Another sailor and I were staying so far apart and swimming together.

When we swam past a dredging line, we realized we could wade on in from there. When we got on shore we got under a palm tree and used the leaves to wipe the oil from our faces and eyes. At that time I was also sick at my stomach from the oil I had swallowed. The first wave of bombing had stopped. A truck drove by and picked us up and took us to a dispensary on Ford Island so we could clean up.

The dispensary was just being built and did not have a roof on it yet. It just had walls and a concrete floor. The second wave of the attack was starting. While standing there in the dispensary, a bombshell landed about 15 feet away from me and it went through the concrete

---

[113] Ralph Warren Burdette, Photo from USS Arizona's Last Band by Molly Kent. By permission of the author. For more information about this book, go to www.USSARIZONASLASTBAND.com.

floor forcing white sand back out of the hole. I was lucky again as it did not explode—it was a dud. I think it may have been an armor piercing shell and was meant for a steel deck of a ship. We started to run outside but the guys said the planes were machine gunning the area. Anyway, I had survived a second time in about a half-hour.

The only clothes I had on was a pair of white shorts, a skivvy shirt, and shoes. The Marines had opened their barracks to us and we went in and got some Marine Khaki's from their lockers to put on. They didn't have any shore big enough to fit me so I had to wipe the oil out of my own.

Later, the survivors of the Arizona were taken over to a receiving ship and we were issued dungarees and blue shirts. I was temporarily assigned to the USS Tennessee. Two days later, I was assigned to the USS Pennsylvania Battleship which was in dry dock.

It was here I met up with my good friend Paul Terry whom I entered the Navy and went through boot camp with. We were so glad to see each other. He thought I had gone down with the Arizona. He could not do enough for me. He gave me cigarettes, money, and a blanket. At this time, this was all I had. My records, money, and everything I had went down on the Arizona.

After about a week in dry dock, we headed the Pennsylvania back for the states. The ship was are-armed with 5-inch dual purpose 38 guns and quad 40 millimeter guns and 20 millimeter guns at Hunters Point in San Francisco. We then headed for the Midway battle but by the time we got there the battle was over. All we saw was debris and oil from sunken ships.

From there we went to the Marshall and Gilbert Islands. Next, we headed to the Aleutian Islands—Attu and some others I don't remember. We took them but got the bow blown up and had to go back for repairs. We stopped at Kodiak, Alaska but had to go on to Bremerton, Washington, to get the repairs.

Afterwards, we went to the Kiska Islands to take them from the Japs; however, when we got there they were gone. We then went south to the Heberdine Islands to rendezvous to take the Philippines.

I didn't make it to the Philippines as I was ordered to Washington, D.C. for Advanced Gunnery and Hydraulic School for six weeks and became First Class Gunners Mate. After schooling, I was sent back to San Francisco to help put the APA 206 Sibley into Commission which was a troop carrier. The first raid we made was to take the 4th Division Marines into Iwo Jima. After we unloaded the troops we served as a hospital ship. We had six doctors aboard. We buried several men at sea each morning.

The next raid was at Okinawa, where the 1st Division Marines were to serve as a back-up. We made a false run on the lower side of the island. A lot of the ships were hit by suicide planes. We didn't unload our troops.

I was promoted to Chief Petty Officer and transferred to Northwestern University as a ROTC and V-12 instructor. I was there for about one year and after my six year term was up I was discharged in September, 1946, at Great Lakes, Illinois."[114]

Leland died on January 14, 2003 at the Veteran's Hospital in Columbia, Missouri. and is buried in Hillcrest Memorial Gardens, Macon, Missouri. He was preceded in death by his wife, Ileene Lenora (Christopher) Burk. Leland was survived by his only daughter, Pat Marie; and his son, Mike Burk.

Burke, Frank Edmond, Jr. Storekeeper, Second Class, Serial No: 359 99 95, US Navy. Frank enlisted in the US Navy on July 12, 1938 in Houston, Texas and completed his basic training at the Naval Training station in San Diego, California. He reported for duty on the USS Arizona on March 12, 1939. Frank was killed in action on December 7, 1941 in Pearl Harbor, Hawaii. He was awarded the American Defense Service Medal, World War II Victory

---

[114] Statement of Leland Howard Burk, Survivor of the USS Arizona, http://www.ussarizonafacts.org/honor.htm

Medal and Purple Heart Medal posthumously. Frank remains on duty on the USS Arizona. He is commemorated on the USS Arizona Memorial and the Memorial Tablets of the Missing, National Memorial Cemetery of the Pacific, Honolulu, Hawaii. Frank was survived by his Wife, Mrs. Elizabeth Jessie Burke, P. O. Box 390, Pasadena, Texas.

Burnett, Charlie Leroy   Seaman, Second Class, Serial No: 295 76 90, US Navy. Charlie was born in about 1919 to Joseph M. and Effie E. Burnett of Tennessee. He enlisted in the US Navy on October 4, 1940 in Nashville, Tennessee and completed his basic training at the Naval Training Station in Norfolk, Virginia. Charlie reported for duty on the USS Arizona December 4, 1940. He was killed in action on December 7, 1941 in Pearl Harbor, Hawaii. Charlie was awarded the American Defense Service Medal, World War II Victory Medal and Purple Heart Medal posthumously. He remains on duty on the USS Arizona. Charlie is commemorated on the USS Arizona Memorial and the Memorial Tablets of the Missing, National Memorial Cemetery of the Pacific, Honolulu, Hawaii. He was survived by his Father, Mr. Joseph Marshall Burnett, Route 3, Seymour, Tennessee.

Burns, John Edward   Fireman, First Class, Serial No: 243 78 22, US Navy. John was born in about 1916 in Pennsylvania to John F. and Louise A. (Mauger) Burns. He enlisted in the US Navy on October 9, 1940 in Philadelphia, Pennsylvania and completed his basic training at the Naval Training Station in Newport, Rhode Island. He reported for duty on the USS Arizona on December 10, 1940. John was killed in action on December 7, 1941 in Pearl Harbor, Hawaii. He was awarded the American Defense Service Medal, World War II Victory Medal and Purple Heart Medal posthumously. John remains on duty on the USS Arizona. He is commemorated on the USS Arizona Memorial and the Memorial Tablets of the Missing, National Memorial Cemetery of the Pacific, Honolulu, Hawaii. John was survived by his Father, Mr. John Francis Burns, 75 Corclear Street, Wilkes-Barre, Pennsylvania.[115]

Bush, William Jack   Ensign, US Navy. William was born on September 10, 1915 in Skagit County, Washington. He enlisted in the US Navy and reported for duty on the USS Arizona where he was serving on December 7, 1941 when the Japanese attacked Pearl Harbor. [116] Official statement:

"At about two or three minutes before 0800 Sunday, I was asleep in my room when I faintly heard a siren. Shortly thereafter I distinctly heard G.Q. I put some clothes on and went up from lower wardroom country to the second deck. Lt. C.T. Janz was sending everyone in the vicinity to shelter below the armored deck. I went down with Lt. Janz and about forty enlisted men. Before we could close the hatch, there were three violent blasts with flame and powder fumes entering the compartment. I then told all personnel in the vicinity to get out and go topside to avoid the gas. About twenty (20) enlisted personnel and I went topside. I saw the entire ship forward of #3 turret to be a raging fire. I asked Ensign Davison about fighting the fire and he told me there was no water in the fire main. Shortly thereafter, Ensign Davison and I got three boats

---

[115] John Edward Burns, Photo from the Wilkes-Barre Times Leader, The Evening News, December 22, 1941, Page 3.
[116] William Jack Bush, photo Lucky Bag Yearbook, United States Naval Academy, Annapolis, MD, Class of 1938.

clear of the oil fire on the water and picked up the men in the water who had jumped to get clear of the fire. We took several boatloads of badly burned and injured men to Ford Island landing and continued picking up men in the water between the ship and the shore. I took one boat alongside the quarter of the Arizona and waited until everyone gathered on the stern had been taken off. Ensign Lenning, Ensign Miller and Lt. Comdr. Fuqua made sure no one could be rescued from the after end of the ship before they left. We then picked the men up out of the water and put everyone ashore at Ford Island landing. Lt. Comdr. Fuqua took one boat and left to search the water for injured men. After sending all injured men to the dispensary, we took the remainder to the air raid shelter below Admiral Bellinger's quarters. Ensign Davison assisted me in directing the rescue work even though he was badly burned himself."[117]

He served his country through out World War II and later the Korean War attaining the rank of Captain. William died on April 14, 1999 in Medford, Oregon and is buried in Section 21, Site 1177, Eagle Point National Cemetery, Eagle Point, Oregon.

Busick, Dewey Olney Fireman, Third Class, Serial No: 279 73 72, US Navy. Dewey was born in June of 1918 in Franklin County, Ohio to Clarence Lewis and Zelda (Thompson) Busick of Norwich, Ohio. He enlisted in the US Navy on October 7, 1940 in Cincinnati, Ohio and completed his basic training at the Naval Training Station in Great Lakes, Illinois. Dewey reported for duty on the USS Arizona on December 9, 1940. He was killed in action on December 7, 1941 in Pearl Harbor, Hawaii. Dewey was awarded the American Defense Service Medal, World War II Victory Medal and Purple Heart Medal posthumously. He remains on duty on the USS Arizona. Dewey is commemorated on the USS Arizona Memorial and the Memorial Tablets of the Missing, National Memorial Cemetery of the Pacific, Honolulu, Hawaii. He was survived by his Father, Mr. Clarence Lewis Busick, Route 1, Calloway, Ohio.

Butcher, David Adrian Fireman, Second Class, Serial No: 311 51 25, US Navy. David was born April 27, 1919 in Knoxville, Tennessee to Marion Lee and Lillie Mae (Lawhorn) Butcher. He enlisted in the US Navy on October 1, 1940 in Detroit, Michigan and completed his basic training at the Naval Training Station in Great Lakes, Illinois. He reported for duty on the USS Arizona on December 9, 1940. David was killed in action on December 7, 1941 in Pearl Harbor, Hawaii. He was awarded the American Defense Service Medal, World War II Victory Medal and Purple Heart Medal posthumously. David remains on duty on the USS Arizona. He is commemorated on the USS Arizona Memorial and the Memorial Tablets of the Missing, National Memorial Cemetery of the Pacific, Honolulu, Hawaii and Oakview Cemetery, Royal Oak, Michigan. David was survived by his Mother, Mrs. Lillie May Curtice, Route 4, Box 136, Snohomish, Washington.

---

[117] Statement of Ensign W. J. Bush, U.S.S. Arizona, Last Action Report.

Butler, John Dabney Fireman, First Class, Serial No: 359 99 96, US Navy. John was born to James Roscoe Butler and Eva E. (Brandenburg) Butler of Texas. He enlisted in the US Navy on July 12, 1938 in Houston, Texas and completed his basic training at the Naval Training Station in San Diego, California. John reported for duty on the USS Arizona on October 23, 1938. He was killed in action on December 7, 1941 in Pearl Harbor, Hawaii. John was awarded the American Defense Service Medal, World War II Victory Medal and Purple Heart Medal posthumously. He remains on duty on the USS Arizona. John is commemorated on the USS Arizona Memorial and the Memorial Tablets of the Missing, National Memorial Cemetery of the Pacific, Honolulu, Hawaii. He was survived by his Father, Mr. James Roscoe Butler, 746 Arkansas Avenue, San Antonio, Texas.

Byard, Ralph Duncan Chief Commissary Steward, Serial No. 291 38 24, US Navy. Ralph was born on January 31, 1914 in Indiana, the son of Newman and Clara Elizabeth (Duncan) Byard. He enlisted in the US Navy March 2, 1932. Ralph reported for duty on the USS Arizona on July 24, 1932 where he served until December 7, 1941 when the Japanese attacked Pearl Harbor. After the attack, Ralph was transferred to the Submarine Base at Pearl Harbor. Ralph retired from the Navy attaining a rank of Commander. He died on August 8, 1990 in Bridgeport, Connecticut.[118]

Byrd, Charles Dewitt Seaman, First Class, Serial No: 295 75 98, US Navy. Charles was born in about 1922 in Tennessee to Arthur B. and Mallie Byrd. He enlisted in the US Navy on October 3, 1940 in Nashville, Tennessee and completed his basic training at the Naval Training Station in Norfolk, Virginia. He reported for duty on the USS Arizona on December 9, 1940. Charles was killed in action on December 7, 1941 in Pearl Harbor, Hawaii. He was awarded the American Defense Service Medal, World War II Victory Medal and Purple Heart Medal posthumously. Charles remains on duty on the USS Arizona. He is commemorated on the USS Arizona Memorial and the Memorial Tablets of the Missing, National Memorial Cemetery of the Pacific, Honolulu, Hawaii. Charles was survived by his Father, Mr. Arthur B. Byrd, Box 742, Kingsport, Tennessee.[119]

---

[118] Ralph Duncan Byard, from the Recensio Yearbook, Miami University, Oxford, OH, Class of 1949.

[119] Charles DeWitt Byrd, Photo from the Kingsport Times, Kingsport, Tennessee, May 29, 1942, Page 1.

Cabay, Louis Clarence Seaman, First Class, Serial No: 300 19 37, US Navy. Louis was born in about 1923 in Illinois. He enlisted in the US Navy on October 8, 1940 in Chicago, Illinois and completed his basic training at the Naval Training Station in Great Lakes, Illinois. He reported for duty on the USS Arizona on December 9, 1940. Louis was killed in action on December 7, 1941 in Pearl Harbor, Hawaii. He was awarded the American Defense Service Medal, World War II Victory Medal and Purple Heart Medal posthumously. Louis remains on duty on the USS Arizona. He is commemorated on the USS Arizona Memorial and the Memorial Tablets of the Missing, National Memorial Cemetery of the Pacific, Honolulu, Hawaii. Louis was survived by his Father, Mr. Frank Cabay, 512 Henderson Avenue, Joliet, Illinois.[119]

Cade, Richard Esh Seaman, Second Class, Serial No: 385 99 81, US Navy. Richard was born in 1924 in Bellingham, Washington. He was the son of Richard and Madeline Cade. Richard enlisted in the US Navy on April 19, 1941 in Seattle, Washington and completed his basic training at the Naval Training Station in San Diego, California. He reported for duty on the USS Arizona on July 13, 1941. Richard was killed in action on December 7, 1941 in Pearl Harbor, Hawaii. He was awarded the American Defense Service Medal, World War II Victory Medal and Purple Heart Medal posthumously. Richard remains on duty on the USS Arizona. He is commemorated on the USS Arizona Memorial and the Memorial Tablets of the Missing, National Memorial Cemetery of the Pacific, Honolulu, Hawaii. Richard was survived by his Father, Mr. Richard Esh Cade, Sr., 2727 Grove Street, Bellingham, Washington.

Caldwell, Charles, Jr. Seaman, Second Class, Serial No: 342 30 62, US Navy. Charles was born on April 21, 1921 to Charles Caldwell and Ramah (Simpson) Caldwell. He enlisted in the US Navy on October 15, 1940 in Kansas City, Missouri and completed his basic training at the Naval Training Station in Great Lakes, Illinois. Charles reported for duty on the USS Arizona on December 9, 1940. He was killed in action on December 7, 1941 in Pearl Harbor, Hawaii. Charles was awarded the American Defense Service Medal, World War II Victory Medal and Purple Heart Medal posthumously. He remains on duty on the USS Arizona. Charles is commemorated on the USS Arizona Memorial and the Memorial Tablets of the Missing, National Memorial Cemetery of the Pacific, Honolulu, Hawaii. He was survived by his Father, Mr. Charles Caldwell, Sr., Grand Avenue, Milan, Missouri.

Callaghan, James "Jimmy" Thomas Boatswain's Mate, Second Class, Serial No: 371 99 94, US Navy. James was born on May 11, 1916 in Denver, Colorado to Cornelius Martin Callaghan and Catherine Ann (Munday) Callaghan of Denver, Colorado. *Both parents preceded him in death. His father, Police Sgt. Cornelius Callaghan died in 1936. His mother, Catherine died in 1922.* He enlisted in the US Navy on December 11, 1936 in Denver, Colorado and reported for duty on the USS Arizona April 15, 1937. James was killed in action on December 7, 1941 in Pearl Harbor, Hawaii. He was awarded the American Defense Service Medal, World War II Victory Medal and Purple Heart Medal posthumously. James remains on duty on the USS Arizona. He is commemorated on the USS Arizona Memorial and the Memorial Tablets of the Missing, National Memorial Cemetery of the Pacific, Honolulu, Hawaii. James was survived by his four Sisters, Mrs. Cornelia Marie (Callaghan) Catlett, 3333 Gaylord Street, Denver, Colorado, Mrs.

---

[119] Louis Clarence Cabay, Photo from the Chicago Tribune, Chicago, Illinois, May 5, 1942, Page 10.

Marguerite (Callaghan) Davis, Mrs. Dorothy (Callaghan) Miroslavich and Rosemary (Callaghan) Kalcevic, and brother Daniel all of Denver, Colorado. His brother, John M. Callaghan, Gunner's Mate, 2nd class had been serving with him on the USS Arizona until he was transferred November 20, 1941 to an Asiatic Station for duty on board the USS Chaumont. Once war broke out, his brother, John went on to serve on the USS Chaumont. Another brother, Frank J. Callaghan, Sgt. was killed in action on December 24, 1944. He was a top turret Gunner on a B-17 in the Eighth Army Air Force serving in England, and flying missions over Germany when he was lost.[120]

Camden, Raymond Edward   Seaman, Second Class, Serial No: 356 42 45, US Navy. Raymond was born in 1922 to Benjamin C. Camden and Bessie (Bridgewater) Camden of Drumright, Oklahoma. He enlisted in the US Navy on November 13, 1940 in Dallas, Texas and completed his basic training at the Naval Training Station in San Diego, California. Raymond reported for duty on the USS Arizona January 11, 1941. He was killed in action on December 7, 1941 in Pearl Harbor, Hawaii. Raymond was awarded the American Defense Service Medal, World War II Victory Medal and Purple Heart Medal posthumously. He remains on duty on the USS Arizona. Raymond is commemorated on the USS Arizona Memorial and the Memorial Tablets of the Missing, National Memorial Cemetery of the Pacific, Honolulu, Hawaii. He was survived by his Father, Mr. Benjamin C. Camden, 408 East 1st Street, Dumright, Oklahoma.[121]

Camm, William Fielden   Yeoman, Second Class, Serial No: 346 70 98, US Navy. William was born July 30, 1921 in Prairie County, Arkansas to Ernest Clayton Camm and Nona Blanche (Streight) Camm. He enlisted in the US Navy on October 1, 1938 in Little Rock, Arkansas and completed his basic training at the Naval Training Station in San Diego, California. William reported for duty on the USS Arizona on January 2, 1939. He was killed in action on December 7, 1941 in Pearl Harbor, Hawaii. William was awarded the American Defense Service Medal, World War II Victory Medal and Purple Heart Medal posthumously. He remains on duty on the USS Arizona. William is commemorated on the USS Arizona Memorial and the Memorial Tablets of the Missing, National Memorial Cemetery of the Pacific, Honolulu, Hawaii. He was survived by his Father, Mr. Ernest Clayton Camm, Hazen, Arkansas.

Campa, Ralph   Seaman, First Class, Serial No: 360 31 10, US Navy. Ralph was born November 17, 1920 in Alameda County, California. He enlisted in the US Navy on January 23, 1941 in San Diego, California and completed his basic training at the Naval Training Station in San Diego, California. Ralph reported for duty on the USS Arizona on April 26, 1941. He was killed in action on December 7, 1941 in Pearl Harbor, Hawaii. Ralph was awarded the American Defense Service Medal, World War II Victory Medal and Purple Heart Medal posthumously. He remains on duty on the USS Arizona. Ralph is commemorated on the USS Arizona Memorial and the Memorial Tablets of the Missing, National Memorial Cemetery of the Pacific, Honolulu, Hawaii. He was survived by his Mother, Mrs. Maria Campa, 520 East 24th Street, National City, California.

---

[120] James Thomas Callaghan, Information and photo provided by family member, Michael Reger.
[121] Raymond Edward Camden, Photo provided by family member Michael A. Copeland.

Campbell, Burdette Charles Seaman, First Class, Serial No: 382 36 88, US Navy. Burdette was born about 1924 in Nebraska the son of Ezra and Emma Campbell. He enlisted in the US Navy on January 23, 1941 in Los Angeles, California and completed his basic training at the Naval Training Station in San Diego, California. Burdette reported for duty on the USS Arizona on April 26, 1941. He was killed in action on December 7, 1941 in Pearl Harbor, Hawaii. Burdette was awarded the American Defense Service Medal, World War II Victory Medal and Purple Heart Medal posthumously. Burdette remains on duty on the USS Arizona. He is commemorated on the USS Arizona Memorial and the Memorial Tablets of the Missing, National Memorial Cemetery of the Pacific, Honolulu, Hawaii. Burdette was survived by his Father, Mr. Ezra Arthur Campbell, 4488 Lovett Street, Los Angeles, California.[122]

Campbell, Frank Monroe Ensign, US Navy. Frank was born November 9, 1918 in California to Frank M. and Ada D. (Tompkins) Campbell. He was commissioned an Ensign on March 14, 1941. Frank reported for duty on the USS Arizona, as Junior Watch and Division 5 Officer assigned as the starboard Anti-Aircraft battery officer. He was serving on December 7, 1941 when the Japanese attacked Pearl Harbor. Frank was getting into the motor launch to head for church services ashore when the attack began. He labored to help save his shipmates. Frank died March 30, 1994 in Ocala, Florida at the age of 76. His ashes were interred on the USS Arizona December 7, 1996.

Campbell, George Kilgore Chief Turret Captain, Serial No. 261 31 81, US Navy. George was born December 19, 1903 in Chatham County, North Carolina, the son of Joseph Moore and Martha (Fowler) Campbell. He re-enlisted in the US Navy on November 3, 1932 in Bremerton, Washington. He reported for duty on the USS Arizona on May 26, 1934 and was serving on the Arizona December 7, 1941, when the Japanese attacked Pearl Harbor. His official report:

"I was in the CPO quarters when I first heard machine gun firing and I knew something was up. I started for my general quarter's station, which is #4 turret. As is my usual habit, I went down to the third deck and proceeded aft to the lower handling room of #4 turret. When I arrived there I found most of the fourth division already present. I remained in the lower handling room approximately three minutes when the lights went off and everything was pitch dark. I ordered everybody from the lower room up into the turret. My division officer was not there, so I had to take immediate charge. About that time E. H. Pecotte, GM2c, showed up with a flashlight and we got up into the turret chamber. Gas then began to become evident in the turret, and the men couldn't breathe very well. This gas was apparently from the storage batteries, and was leaking through around the sprung water-tight door. Pecotte discovered the source of this odor and immediately pulled off his dungaree shirt and trousers and stuffed them around the edges of the door where the odor was coming from. This did not clear the turret of gases, but it did stop the supply, and helped considerably. Water was rising rapidly and it was already up to the pointer group. I then sent Pecotte outside on deck to see if it was safe to leave the turret and have the men all leave.

When Pecotte came back into the turret he reported that he had asked Lt. Comdr. S. G. Fuqua if the ship was being abandoned, and was told that it was, so I ordered all hands out on

---

[122] Burdette Charles Campbell, photo from California Honor States.

deck. We stayed under the overhang of the turret for about fifteen minutes. In the meantime I ordered three men to cut life rafts down and put them over the side aft and secure them to the lifeline. Pecotte then took a flashlight and said he was going back in the turret to make sure that everyone was out of the turret. Under the overhang, just as he started back in the turret, he met Peil, W. J., BM2c, coming out of the turret. Peil stated that he had been crawling around and feeling for anyone left in the turret, and that he did not believe anyone was left. However, Pecotte completed his inspection of the turret and returned stating that he had found no one inside the turret. Pecotte and Peil then began picking up wounded men and removing them to the overhang of the turrets and later to the boats for transportation to the hospital and Solace. This they were doing under the supervision of Lt. Comdr. Fuqua, who had complete charge of the quarterdeck.

A man on deck of the Vestal called for someone to throw off their lines. I ordered Graham, AMM1c to throw the Vestal's lines off, but noted that he was already doing so. From there, I ordered everyone aft on the quarterdeck and we boarded a motor boat and proceeded to Ford Island. That is about all that I know about the attack."[123]

After the attack, George was transferred to the USS Hancock (CV-19) for duty. He retired from the US Navy after 30 years of service and was awarded the Marine Corps Good Conduct Medal with 3 Bronze Stars, American Defense Service with Fleet Clasp, American Campaign Medal, Asiatic Pacific Campaign Medal with Bronze Star, European-African-Middle Eastern Campaign Medal, National Defense Service Medal, Korean Service Medal, United Nations Service Medal, Combat Action Ribbon, Pearl Harbor Commemorative Medal, Republic of Korea War Service Medal and the Republic of Korea Presidential Unit Citation. George died March 2, 1973 in Albemarle, Stanly, North Carolina.[124]

Caplinger, Donald William Ship's Cook, Third Class, Serial No: 279 73 73, US Navy. Donald was born January 18, 1918 to Homer Lawrence Caplinger and Eva Inez (Moberly) Caplinger of Hillsboro, Ohio. He enlisted in the US Navy on October 7, 1940 in Cincinnati, Ohio and completed his basic training at the Naval Training Station in Great Lakes, Illinois. Donald reported for duty on the USS Arizona on December 9, 1940. He was killed in action on December 7, 1941 in Pearl Harbor, Hawaii. Donald was awarded the American Defense Service Medal, World War II Victory Medal and Purple Heart Medal posthumously. He remains on duty on the USS Arizona. Donald is commemorated on the USS Arizona Memorial and the Memorial Tablets of the Missing, National Memorial Cemetery of the Pacific, Honolulu, Hawaii. He was survived by his Mother, Mrs. Eva Inez Caplinger, Route 7, Hillsboro, Ohio.[125]

---

[123] Confidential Statement of George Kilgore Campbell, CTC, U.S. Navy regarding the attack on Pearl Harbor, T. H. December 7, 1941.

[124] George Kilgore Campbell, Picture provided by family member, Clarence Campbell.

[125] Donald William Caplinger, Information and photo provided by family member, Bob Freda Proctor.

Carey, Francis Lloyd   Storekeeper, Third Class, Serial No: 223 60 99, US Navy. Francis was born August 5, 1919 in Jersey City, New Jersey to Francis D. and Geraldine M. (Stroub) Carey. He enlisted in the US Navy on December 5, 1939 in New York, New York and reported for duty on the USS Arizona on January 4, 1941. He was killed in action on December 7, 1941 in Pearl Harbor, Hawaii. Francis was awarded the American Defense Service Medal, World War II Victory Medal and Purple Heart Medal posthumously. He remains on duty on the USS Arizona. Francis is commemorated on the USS Arizona Memorial and the Memorial Tablets of the Missing, National Memorial Cemetery of the Pacific, Honolulu, Hawaii. He was survived by his Grandmother, Mrs. Mary Carey, 124 Allers Boulevard, Roosevelt, New York.[126]

Carlisle, Robert Wayne   Seaman, First Class, Serial No: 356 43 60, US Navy Reserve. Robert was born October 24, 1923 in Cleburne, Texas to John Byron and Maude Alma (Flatt) Carlisle. He enlisted in the US Navy on November 27, 1940 in Dallas, Texas and completed his basic training at the Naval Training Station in San Diego, California. He reported for duty on the USS Arizona on January 25, 1941. Robert was killed in action on December 7, 1941 in Pearl Harbor, Hawaii. He was awarded the American Defense Service Medal, World War II Victory Medal and Purple Heart Medal posthumously. Robert remains on duty on the USS Arizona. He is commemorated on the USS Arizona Memorial and the Memorial Tablets of the Missing, National Memorial Cemetery of the Pacific, Honolulu, Hawaii. Robert was survived by his Father, Mr. John Byron Carlisle, 218 West Brooklyn Street, Dallas, Texas.[127]

Carlson, Harry "Bud" Ludwig   Storekeeper, Third Class, Serial No: 207 24 34, US Navy. Harry was born May 23, 1921 in Norwich, Connecticut to Cornelius Eskil and Agnes Helen (Myesky) Carlson. He enlisted in the US Navy on October 16, 1939 in New Haven, Connecticut and reported for duty on the USS Arizona on December 30, 1940. Harry was killed in action on December 7, 1941 in Pearl Harbor, Hawaii. *After Pearl Harbor, Bud was reported "Missing in Action" for months. His brother, Ray Carlson reported of how Bud's picture would be facedown on the floor, and the one on a table, would be facedown every single morning. There would be knocks on the door and when someone would answer the door, no one was there. It about drove his Mother crazy. Once he was reported "Killed in Action" all of this stopped.* He was awarded the American Defense Service Medal, World War II Victory Medal and Purple Heart Medal posthumously. Harry remains on duty on the USS Arizona. He is commemorated on the USS Arizona Memorial and the Memorial Tablets of the Missing, National Memorial Cemetery of the Pacific, Honolulu, Hawaii. Harry was survived by his Father, Mr. Raymond Eskil Carlson, 16 St. Regis Avenue, Norwich, Connecticut. Carlson Street, Norwich, Connecticut was named in his honor.[128]

---

[126] Francis Lloyd Carey, Information and photo provided by family member, Patti Durant.

[127] Robert Wayne Carlisle, Photo curtsey of LCDR G. Dale McKissick, USNR, Memorial, Dallas Convention Center, Dallas, Texas.

[128] Harry Ludwig Carlson, Information and photo provided by his Niece, Rosalyn (Carlson) Lachapelle.

Carlson, Ray Christian   Seaman, Second Class, Serial No. 385 92 23, US Navy. Ray was born May 14, 1921. He enlisted in the US Navy October 31, 1940 in Seattle, Washington and completed his training at the Naval Training Station in San Diego, California. He reported for duty on the USS Arizona December 30, 1940. He was serving on the Arizona December 7, 1941, when the Japanese attacked Pearl Harbor. After the attack, Ray was transferred to the USS Mc Donough (DD-351) for duty. He served until July 3, 1944. Ray died July 12, 1980 and is buried in the Crown Hill Cemetery, Seattle, Washington.

Carmack, Harold Milton   Fireman, Second Class, Serial No: 372 20 36, US Navy. Harold was born in about 1922 in Colorado to Oscar Walter and Lena Carmack of Los Pinos, Colorado. He enlisted in the US Navy on November 5, 1940 in Denver, Colorado and completed his basic training at the Naval Training Station in San Diego, California. Harold reported for duty on the USS Arizona on January 11, 1941. He was killed in action on December 7, 1941 in Pearl Harbor, Hawaii. Harold was awarded the American Defense Service Medal, World War II Victory Medal and Purple Heart Medal posthumously. He remains on duty on the USS Arizona. Harold is commemorated on the USS Arizona Memorial and the Memorial Tablets of the Missing, National Memorial Cemetery of the Pacific, Honolulu, Hawaii. He was survived by his Father, Mr. Oscar Walter Carmack, Bayfield, Colorado.

Carpenter, Robert Nelson   Steward's Mate, First Class, Serial No: 250 40 00, US Navy. Robert was born August 11, 1915 in Pittsburgh, Pennsylvania. He enlisted in the US Navy on October 1, 1935 and reported for duty on the USS Arizona on April 28, 1941. He was killed in action on December 7, 1941 in Pearl Harbor, Hawaii. Robert was awarded the American Defense Service Medal, World War II Victory Medal and Purple Heart Medal posthumously. He remains on duty on the USS Arizona. Robert is commemorated on the USS Arizona Memorial and the Memorial Tablets of the Missing, National Memorial Cemetery of the Pacific, Honolulu, Hawaii. He was survived by his Wife, Mrs. Dorothy Bright Carpenter, Route 1, Box 179, Hickory, Virginia.[129]

Carroll, Robert Lewis   Seaman, First Class, Serial No: 262 43 27, US Navy. Robert was born October 19, 1921 in Bladen County, North Carolina to Patrick Caviness and Nannie C. (Johnson) Carroll. He enlisted in the US Navy on November 13, 1939 in Raleigh, North Carolina and reported for duty on the USS Arizona on December 30, 1940. He was killed in action on December 7, 1941 in Pearl Harbor, Hawaii. Robert was awarded the American Defense Service Medal, World War II Victory Medal and Purple Heart Medal posthumously. He remains on duty on the USS Arizona. Robert is commemorated on the USS Arizona Memorial and the Memorial Tablets of the Missing, National Memorial Cemetery of the Pacific, Honolulu, Hawaii. He was survived by his Father, Mr. Pat Calvin Carroll, Route 1, St. Pauls, North Carolina.[130]

---

[129] Robert Nelson Carpenter, Photo from Virginia Honor States.
[130] Robert Lewis Carroll, Photo from North Carolina Honor States.

Carson, Carl Malvin   Seaman, First Class, Serial No. 342 81 03, US Navy. Carl was born on July 26, 1921 in Cherryvale, Kansas to Melvin and Cora Nancy Elizabeth (King) Carson. He enlisted in the US Navy March 27, 1940 in Kansas City, Missouri and completed his training at the Naval Training Station in Great Lakes, Illinois. Carl reported for duty on the USS Arizona July 12, 1940. He was serving on the Arizona December 7, 1941 when the Japanese attacked Pearl Harbor. Carl was out on deck doing the morning chores, all of a sudden, a plane came along, I didn't much attention to it because planes were landing a Ford Island all the time. Suddenly the chips started flying all around me, the plane was strafing. I looked up and could see the meatball on the wings. The plane was so close I could see the pilot looking at me. I ran forward and tried to get under cover. The Officer of the Deck ordered be back to close the hatches. While working to close the hatches another plane began strafing. I went forward and went inside the ship and then started back to my battle station when a bomb went off. I learned later it was near turret number 4, right about where I had been working. The blast from the bomb knocked me out and ruptured both my lungs. When I woke up it was dark, I picked up a flashlight and started down to my battle station. They wouldn't let me in; the water-tight door was sealed. After about 20 minutes I finally outlasted the guy on the other side and gained entry. The turret was filled with smoke and the water was knee deep. The senior division officer told us to all come out on deck and help fight fires but there was nothing we could do. The ship was a total loss. We were told to abandon ship. Before I did, I ran into a friend of mine, he was crying and asking for help. I looked at him in horror; the skin on his face and arms was just hanging like a mask or something. I took hold of his arm and the skin came off in my hand. There was nothing I could do for him. We just practically stepped off on the quarter deck into the water. I didn't know how bad I was hurt. I got out there about 10 feet and I guess I must have passed out. I went down in the water and everything was just as peaceful and nice, that it would have been so easy to just let go. I saw this bright light and something made me come to. I got back up to the surface and the oil was a fire all around. The fire was approaching me; it wasn't more than two feet away. Someone reached down and pulled me up out of the water. That man saved my life. A motor launch took me over to Ford Island. I walked down to the barracks with the rest of the crew. I must have passed out because I was taken over to the sick bay at Ford Island. Later a dead shell hit right in the center of the sick bay and it kind of brought me to and I looked over and saw another shipmate lying across from me. He was holding his intestines with his hands. He looked up at me and said, "war sure is hell isn't it, shipmate." I said, "yah it is." Since I wasn't bleeding anywhere, I got up and walked out of there. After spending several weeks in the hospital, he was returned to duty and spent the rest of the war in the Pacific Theatre. Carl was awarded the Purple Heart, 6 Navy Good Conduct Medals, The Asiatic-Pacific Campaign Medal with 3 Stars, Navy Occupation Service Medal (Asia) and the Pearl Harbor Commemorative Medal. He retired from the Navy in 1961. Carl died from cancer on January 13, 2001 in Bolivar, Kansas and was buried in Barren Creek Cemetery, Bolivar, Kansas. He was survived by his wife of 45 years, Mrs. Anna (Reynolds) Carson and two brothers and their wives, Robert and Ilona Carlson, who live on a farm adjoining that of Carl and Anna, and Jerry Lee and Kitty Carson of Dearing, Kansas; a sister Joan Robinett of Coffeyville, Kansas.[131]

---

[131] Carl Malvin Carson, Photo and information provided by himself.

Carter, Burton Lowell Seaman, Second Class, Serial No: 381 38 76, US Navy. Burton was born on August 16, 1923 in Long Beach, California to Fred Eugene Carter and Rosadele (McClure) Carter. *He dropped out of high school to follow his best friend into the Navy. Burton got his father drunk to sign his enlistment papers.* He enlisted in the US Navy on December 19, 1940 in San Diego, California and completed his basic training at the Naval Training Station in San Diego, California. Burton reported for duty on the USS Arizona on August 24, 1941. *Burton wanted to join his best friend, Delbert Wueste on liberty from the Arizona on December 6, 1941. He forged a pass with an officer's signature. The two friends went to a dance and had a few drinks. At the end of the night, out of money and worried he would get caught, Burton returned to the ship. The next morning he was dead.* He was killed in action on December 7, 1941 in Pearl Harbor, Hawaii. Burton was awarded the American Defense Service Medal, World War II Victory Medal and Purple Heart Medal posthumously. He remains on duty on the USS Arizona. Burton is commemorated on the USS Arizona Memorial and the Memorial Tablets of the Missing, National Memorial Cemetery of the Pacific, Honolulu, Hawaii. He was survived by his Father, Mr. Fred Eugene Carter, 1636 Fern Street, San Diego, California.[132]

Carter, Paxton Turner Chief Petty Officer, Acting Pay Clerk, Serial No: 0-105890, US Navy. Paxton was born in 1913 in Hattiesburg, Mississippi to John Dickerson "Tobias Cornelius" and Carrie Lee (Shedd) Carter. He enlisted in the US Navy on September 18, 1934 and reported for duty on the USS Arizona on December 18, 1934. *Paxton had had premonitions. On his last leave home in the summer of 1941, he told his father-in-law, "If you ever see me again, we'll be at war – but I don't think I'll ever be back."* Paxton was killed in action on December 7, 1941 in Pearl Harbor, Hawaii. His battle station was the First Division, manning the forward turret of 14 inch guns. Paxton was awarded the American Defense Service Medal, World War II Victory Medal and Purple Heart Medal posthumously. He remains on duty on the USS Arizona. Paxton is commemorated on the USS Arizona Memorial and the Memorial Tablets of the Missing, National Memorial Cemetery of the Pacific, Honolulu, Hawaii. He was survived by his Wife, Mrs. Edyth Carter, 4507 Elizabeth Street, Bell, California.[133]

---

[132] Burton Carter, Story from Corvallis Gazette-Times, December 7, 1999 "Finally, answers for one lost sailor's family" by Chelsea J. Carter.

[133] Paxton Turner Carter, information and picture provided by family member, Melissa Newcomer.

Casey, James Warren Seaman, First Class, Serial No: 385 86 19, US Navy. James was born in 1917 in Washington State to George Washington and Roberta Maime (Daniel) Casey. He enlisted in the US Navy on March 13, 1940 in Seattle, Washington and completed his basic training at the Naval Training Station in San Diego, California. He reported for duty on the USS Arizona on June 14, 1940. James was killed in action on December 7, 1941 in Pearl Harbor, Hawaii. He was awarded the American Defense Service Medal, World War II Victory Medal and Purple Heart Medal posthumously. James remains on duty on the USS Arizona. He is commemorated on the USS Arizona Memorial and the Memorial Tablets of the Missing, National Memorial Cemetery of the Pacific, Honolulu, Hawaii. James was survived by his Father, Mr. George Washington Casey, 7810 5th Northeast, Seattle, Washington.[134]

Casilan, Epifanio Miranda Steward's Mate, Third Class, Serial No: 497 94 62, US Navy. Epifanio was born October 7, 1906 in Tanawan, Leyte, Philippine Islands. *He emigrated to the U.S on February 9, 1929 on board the US Army Transport "Grant". Epifanio enlisted in the US Navy on August 7, 1934 and applied for citizenship while serving on board the USS Colorado in 1938.* He transferred from the USS Pennsylvania to the USS Arizona on February 3, 1941. Epifanio was killed in action on December 7, 1941 in Pearl Harbor, Hawaii. He was awarded the American Defense Service Medal, World War II Victory Medal and Purple Heart Medal posthumously. Epifanio remains on duty on the USS Arizona. He is commemorated on the USS Arizona Memorial and the Memorial Tablets of the Missing, National Memorial Cemetery of the Pacific, Honolulu, Hawaii. Epifanio was survived by his Wife, Mrs. Alice Balard Casilan, 264 West 22nd, New York, New York.

Caskey, Clarence Merton Seaman, First Class, Serial No: 385 82 94, US Navy. Clarence was born September 18, 1922 in Carlsberg, Washington, the eldest son of Earl L. and Rellie M. Caskey. *He ran away from home to join the Navy as his parents did not want him to join.* Clarence enlisted in the US Navy on October 10, 1939 in Seattle, Washington and completed his basic training at the Naval Training Station in San Diego, California. He reported for duty on the USS Arizona on December 20, 1939. Clarence was killed in action on December 7, 1941 in Pearl Harbor, Hawaii. He was awarded the American Defense Service Medal, World War II Victory Medal and Purple Heart Medal posthumously. Clarence remains on duty on the USS Arizona. He is commemorated on the USS Arizona Memorial and the Memorial Tablets of the Missing, National Memorial Cemetery of the Pacific, Honolulu, Hawaii. Clarence was survived by his Parents, Mr. and Mrs. Earl Leonard Caskey, 1321 West 5th Street, Port Angeles, Washington. Within a month of the attack, Clarence's father joined the Army Engineers, his mother joined the motor pool at Ft. Lawton driving jeeps, his younger brother joined the Navy and his younger sister went into nurses training. The Port Angeles, Washington Chapter No. 9 of the Disabled American Veterans (DAV) is named in honor of Clarence.[135]

---

[134] James Warren Casey, Photo from Washington Honor States.
[135] Clarence Merton Caskey, Information and picture provided by family member, Bettelu Caskey McDaniel.

Castleberry, Claude William, Jr. Seaman, First Class, Serial No: 356 33 58, US Navy. Claude was born December 3, 1916 to Claude William, Sr. and Isla Martha (Williams) Castleberry of Denton, Texas. He enlisted in the US Navy on July 31, 1940 in Dallas, Texas and completed his basic training at the Naval Training Station in San Diego, California. Claude reported for duty on the USS Arizona on October 14, 1940. He was killed in action on December 7, 1941 in Pearl Harbor, Hawaii. Claude was awarded the American Defense Service Medal, World War II Victory Medal and Purple Heart Medal posthumously. He remains on duty on the USS Arizona. Claude is commemorated on the USS Arizona Memorial and the Memorial Tablets of the Missing, National Memorial Cemetery of the Pacific, Honolulu, Hawaii and the IOOF Cemetery, Denton, Texas. He was survived by his Father, Mr. Claude William Castleberry, Sr., 212 Highland, Denton, Texas.[136]

Catsos, George Fireman, First Class, Serial No: 257 81 81, US Navy. George was born September 3, 1906 in Linn, Massachusetts. He enlisted in the US Navy on September 18, 1939 in New York, New York and reported for duty on the USS Arizona on January 4, 1941. George was killed in action on December 7, 1941 in Pearl Harbor, Hawaii. He was awarded the American Defense Service Medal, World War II Victory Medal and Purple Heart Medal posthumously. George remains on duty on the USS Arizona. He is commemorated on the USS Arizona Memorial and the Memorial Tablets of the Missing, National Memorial Cemetery of the Pacific, Honolulu, Hawaii. George was survived by his Wife, Mrs. Irene Catsos, 3123 Pierce Street, San Francisco, California.[137]

Chace, Raymond Vincent Chief Storekeeper, (PA), Serial No: 206 25 83, US Navy. Raymond was born January 25, 1901 in New York to George Paul Chace and Elizabeth Gertrude (Coughlin) Chace. He re-enlisted in the US Navy on July 1, 1937 and again on May 24, 1941. He began serving on the USS Arizona on October 21, 1935. Raymond was killed in action on December 7, 1941 in Pearl Harbor, Hawaii. He was awarded the American Defense Service Medal, World War II Victory Medal and Purple Heart Medal posthumously. Raymond remains on duty on the USS Arizona. He is commemorated on the USS Arizona Memorial and the Memorial Tablets of the Missing, National Memorial Cemetery of the Pacific, Honolulu, Hawaii. Raymond was survived by his Wife, Mrs. Eleanor Vuccino Chace, 737 Gaviota Avenue, Long Beach, California.[138]

Chadwick, Charles Bruce Machinist's Mate, Second Class, Serial No: 274 34 53, US Navy. Charles was born in about 1917 in Mississippi to Charles Wright and Estelle Chadwick. He enlisted in the US Navy on July 13, 1938 in New Orleans, Louisiana and reported for duty on the USS Arizona November 10, 1938. Charles was killed in action on December 7, 1941 in Pearl Harbor, Hawaii. He was awarded the American Defense Service Medal, World War II Victory Medal and Purple Heart Medal posthumously. Charles remains on duty on the USS Arizona. He

---

[136] Claude William Castleberry, Jr., Photo from the 1934 Denton High School Yearbook, Denton, Texas.
[137] George Catsos, Photo from California Honor States.
[138] Raymond Vincent Chace, Photo from California Honor States.

is commemorated on the USS Arizona Memorial and the Memorial Tablets of the Missing, National Memorial Cemetery of the Pacific, Honolulu, Hawaii. Charles was survived by his Father, Mr. Charles Wright Chadwick, Rena Lara, Mississippi.

Chadwick, Harold Steward's Mate, First Class, Serial No: 337 00 76, US Navy. Harold was born in about 1916 in Louisiana. He enlisted in the US Navy on October 5, 1937 in St. Louis, Missouri and reported for duty on the USS Arizona on May 3, 1938. He was killed in action on December 7, 1941 in Pearl Harbor, Hawaii. Harold was awarded the American Defense Service Medal, World War II Victory Medal and Purple Heart Medal posthumously. He remains on duty on the USS Arizona. Harold is commemorated on the USS Arizona Memorial and the Memorial Tablets of the Missing, National Memorial Cemetery of the Pacific, Honolulu, Hawaii. He was survived by his Mother, Mrs. Elizabeth Chadwick, 4023 Morgan Avenue, Los Angeles, California.

Chandler, Edwin Ray Seaman, First Class, Serial No. 385 80 41, US Navy. Edwin was born April 23, 1916 in Millport, Lamar County, Alabama, the son of John Carlisle and Maude Pearl (Johnson) Chandler. He was the oldest of 8 siblings. Edwin enlisted in the US Navy March 13, 1939 in Seattle, Washington and completed his basic training at the Naval Training Station in San Diego, California. He married Mary Louise McCary on July 29, 1939 in Los Angeles, California. He reported for duty on the USS Arizona May 14, 1939. He was on shore leave from the Arizona on December 7, 1941, when the Japanese attacked Pearl Harbor. After the attack, Edwin was transferred to the US Sub Base for duty. His Brother, Donald Ross Chandler was killed in action on board the USS Arizona. Edwin served in the US Navy for 18 years, retiring in 1957. He died June 25, 1982 in Clairmont, California. He was survived by his Wife, Mary Louise and three daughters, Sharon, Karen and Lorie Beth. His wife, Mary Louise was murdered in Clairmont on October 13, 1994.[139]

Chapman, Naaman N. Seaman, First Class, Serial No: 372 21 22, US Navy. Naaman was born in about 1918 in Mitchell, Nebraska to Henry N. Chapman and Inez L. Chapman. He enlisted in the US Navy on November 23, 1940 in Denver, Colorado and completed his basic training at the Naval Training Station in San Diego, California. Naaman reported for duty on the USS Arizona on June 7, 1941. He was killed in action on December 7, 1941 in Pearl Harbor, Hawaii. Naaman was awarded the American Defense Service Medal, World War II Victory Medal and Purple Heart Medal posthumously. He remains on duty on the USS Arizona. Naaman is commemorated on the USS Arizona Memorial and the Memorial Tablets of the Missing, National Memorial Cemetery of the Pacific, Honolulu, Hawaii. He was survived by his Father, Mr. Henry Naaman Chapman, Mitchell, Nebraska and his brother, Noel B. Chapman who was also serving on board the USS Arizona and survived the Japanese attack.[140]

---

[139] Edwin Ray Chandler, Information and Photo provided by his 1st Cousin, David Johnson.

[140] Naaman N. Chapman, Photo from the Nebraska, Iowa War Dead, World-Herald, Omaha, Nebraska, Sunday, July 4, 1943.

Chapman, Noel B. Seaman, Second Class, Serial No. 372 29 00, US Navy. Noel was born on May 22, 1920 in Branson, Colorado. He enlisted in the US Navy March 20, 1941 in Denver, Colorado and completed his basic training at the Naval Training Station in San Diego, California. He reported for duty on the USS Arizona September 18, 1941 where he was serving on December 7, 1941 when the Japanese attacked Pearl Harbor. He went on to serve on the USS Chester. Noel died on February 29, 2004 in Mitchell, Nebraska. The following is his obituary:

MITCHELL — Memorial funeral services for Noel B. Chapman, 83, of Mitchell, who died Sunday, Feb. 29, 2004, at his home, will be held at 10:30 a.m., Wednesday, March 3, at Jones Mortuary in Mitchell with Reverend Ron Nuss-Warren officiating. Masonic Rites will be provided by Masonic Lodge #263. At Noel's request, his remains were cremated, and internment will be at the Mitchell Cemetery. Jones Mortuary in Mitchell is in charge of arrangements. Memorials have been established to Prairie Haven Hospice and the Nebraska Children's Home. He was born May 22, 1920, in Atwell, Colo., to Henry N. and Inez L. (Moody) Chapman. He grew up in Branson, Colo., and Farley, N.M., before moving with his family to Mitchell, where he graduated from Mitchell High School in 1938. He then attended Doane College and later Peru State College. He served his country with the United States Navy from 1941 until 1946. He was a survivor of the Pearl Harbor attack and was stationed on the ship U.S.S. Arizona. He married Illene Elizabeth Turpin on July 8, 1946, in Mitchell. He had worked in the dry bean business all of his life. He owned and operated H.N. Chapman and Sons Dry Bean Elevator, which later became the Chapman-Cawley Elevator. At that time, he also worked for Harpstrieth and Company. In 1978, he went to work for Kelley Bean until 1986. He then worked part-time for Kelley Bean during harvest until he retired in 1996. He married Beatrice Strauch on Jan. 8, 1993, in Mitchell.

He was a member of Masonic Lodge #263 in Mitchell, the American Legion and the Chapman-Whipple V.F.W. He is survived by his wife Beatrice Chapman of Mitchell; daughter Beth Chapman of Scottsbluff; son and daughter-in-law Jeff and Marge Chapman of Lyman; stepchildren, Manuel and Jean Strauch, and Harold and Peg Strauch, all of Mitchell, and Carol and Steve Miller of Cheyenne, Wyo.; grandchildren, Noelle and Jacob Chapman; and Jason, Michael and Dirk Strauch; and sister Pauline Martin of Fort Collins, Colo. He was preceded in death by his parents; his first wife; two brothers and one brother-in-law. His brother, Naaman Chapman was killed in action on board the USS Arizona. Noel's ashes were interred on the USS Arizona December 7, 2004.[141]

Chappell, William Robert Seaman, First Class, Serial No. 279 73 52, US Navy. William was born in Ohio. He enlisted in the US Navy on October 7, 1940 in Cincinnati, Ohio and completed his training at the Naval Training Station in Great Lakes, Illinois. William reported for duty on the USS Arizona December 9, 1940. He was serving on the Arizona December 7, 1941 when the Japanese attacked Pearl Harbor. He went on to serve on the USS Alywin (DD-355). William was missing in action February 1, 1943 while serving on board the USS DeHaven (DD-469) at Salvo Sound, Lunga Point, Guadalcanal. Friends of Chappell also stationed aboard the DeHaven, reported to his wife that he was killed when on duty in a gun turret, fighting off Japanese bombers attacking his ship. Chappell, who is credited with shooting down at least six enemy planes, participated in the battles of the Solomon Islands, Midway, Pearl

---

[141] Noel B. Chapman, Photo from The Honolulu Star Bulletin Newspaper, Honolulu, Hawaii, December 5, 2004.

Harbor and the Coral Sea.[142] William is listed on the Tablets of the Missing at Fort William McKinley Cemetery, Manila, Philippines. He received the Purple Heart Medal. William was survived by his Wife, Mrs. Margaret Jane Chappell, 7216 Maryland Avenue, Deer Park, Cincinnati, Ohio.

Charlton, Charles Nicholas Watertender, First Class, Serial No: 385 57 39, US Navy Reserve. Charles was born April 27, 1911 in Sitka, Alaska to John Charles and Pelegria Polly (Simanoff) Charlton. He re-enlisted in the US Navy on February 15, 1936 in Bremerton, Washington. Charles had been serving on board the USS Arizona from April 20, 1935 until he was killed in action on December 7, 1941 in Pearl Harbor, Hawaii. He was awarded the American Defense Service Medal, World War II Victory Medal and Purple Heart Medal posthumously. Charles remains on duty on the USS Arizona. He is commemorated on the USS Arizona Memorial and the Memorial Tablets of the Missing, National Memorial Cemetery of the Pacific, Honolulu, Hawaii. Charles was survived by his Wife, Mrs. Lillian Ester Charlton, 587 22nd Street, San Pedro, California.

Chernucha, Harry Gregory Musician, Second Class, Serial No: 223 91 08, US Navy. Harry was born September 25, 1922. His parents were White Russians that escaped Russia during the Russian Revolution. *Harry played saxophone and played in his High School Band and a dance band called the Jolly Rogers.* He enlisted in the US Navy on October 24, 1940 and attended the Navy School of Music in Washington, DC graduating on May 23, 1941. He reported for duty on the USS Arizona on June 17, 1941 as a member of the USS Arizona Band. Harry was killed in action on December 7, 1941 in Pearl Harbor, Hawaii. *The battle station for all of the band members was in the black powder room passing ammunition to the Arizona's gunners during the attack. None of the band members survived the explosion.* He was awarded the American Defense Service Medal, World War II Victory Medal and Purple Heart Medal posthumously. Harry remains on duty on the USS Arizona. He is commemorated on the USS Arizona Memorial and the Memorial Tablets of the Missing, National Memorial Cemetery of the Pacific, Honolulu, Hawaii. Harry was survived by his Father, Mr. Harasim Chernucha, 60 Northridge Avenue, North Merrick, New York.[143]

Chester, Edward Seaman, First Class, Serial No: 411 15 83, US Navy. Edward was born in about 1923 in Kansas the only child of Kenneth Joseph and Pauline Chester. He enlisted in the US Navy on September 30, 1940 in Kansas City, Missouri and completed his basic training at the Naval Training Station in Great Lakes, Illinois. He reported for duty on the USS Arizona on January 17, 1941. Edward was killed in action on December 7, 1941 in Pearl Harbor, Hawaii. He was awarded the American Defense Service Medal, World War II Victory Medal and Purple Heart Medal posthumously. Edward remains on duty on the USS Arizona. He is commemorated on the USS Arizona Memorial and the Memorial Tablets of the Missing, National Memorial Cemetery of the Pacific, Honolulu, Hawaii. Edward was survived by his Father, Mr. Kenneth Joseph Chester, 3510 Wyandotte Avenue, Kansas City, Kansas.

---

[142] William Robert Chappell, information from The Cincinnati Enquirer, Cincinnati, Ohio, April 29, 1943, "Seaman Killed in Action after Downing Six Japs" Page 6
[143] Harry Gregory Chernucha, Photo and information from the The Mepham 1942 yearbook, Treasure Chest, dedication page, "Mepham's Sons… Uncle Sam's Servants", Merrick, New York.

Christensen, Elmer Emil Machinist's Mate, Second Class, Serial No: 268 42 39, US Navy. Elmer was born about 1917 in Illinois to Ole N. and Anna Christensen. He enlisted in the US Navy on November 14, 1938 in Salt Lake City, Utah and completed his basic training at the Naval Training Station in San Diego, California. He reported for duty on the USS Arizona on March 11, 1939. Elmer was killed in action on December 7, 1941 in Pearl Harbor, Hawaii. He was awarded the American Defense Service Medal, World War II Victory Medal and Purple Heart Medal posthumously. Elmer remains on duty on the USS Arizona. He is commemorated on the USS Arizona Memorial and the Memorial Tablets of the Missing, National Memorial Cemetery of the Pacific, Honolulu, Hawaii. Elmer was survived by his Father, Mr. Olaf Nelson Christensen, Buffalo, Wyoming.[144]

Christensen, Lloyd Raymond Fireman, First Class, Serial No: 316 62 66, US Navy. Lloyd was born May 21, 1921 in Nebraska to Carl Martin and Marie Emmaline (Killham) Christensen. He enlisted in the US Navy on January 10, 1940 in Omaha, Nebraska and completed his basic training at the Naval Training Station in Great Lakes, Illinois. He reported for duty on the USS Arizona on March 26, 1940. Lloyd was killed in action on December 7, 1941 in Pearl Harbor, Hawaii. He was awarded the American Defense Service Medal, World War II Victory Medal and Purple Heart Medal posthumously. Lloyd remains on duty on the USS Arizona. He is commemorated on the USS Arizona Memorial and the Memorial Tablets of the Missing, National Memorial Cemetery of the Pacific, Honolulu, Hawaii and the Central City Cemetery, Central City, Nebraska. Lloyd was survived by his Father, Mr. Carl Martin Christensen, Route 1, Alda, Nebraska.[145]

Christiansen, Edward "Sonny" Lee Baker, Third Class, Serial No: 342 18 28, US Navy. Edward was born June 24, 1921 in Kansas to Carl Edward and Winona Marie (Canny) Christiansen. He enlisted in the US Navy on January 17, 1940 in Kansas City, Missouri and completed his basic training at the Naval Training Station in Great Lakes, Illinois. He reported for duty on the USS Arizona on March 26, 1940. Edward was killed in action on December 7, 1941 in Pearl Harbor, Hawaii. *With his brother, Harlan, Edward was going ashore to have a photograph taken to send home to their mother. Edward noticed that his cover (hat) was soiled and returned to his quarters to get a clean one and was never seen again.* He was awarded the American Defense Service Medal, World War II Victory Medal and Purple Heart Medal posthumously. Edward remains buried on the USS Arizona. He is commemorated on the USS Arizona Memorial and the Memorial Tablets of the Missing, National Memorial Cemetery of the Pacific, Honolulu, Hawaii and Park Cemetery, Columbus, Kansas. Edward was survived by his Father, Mr. Carl N. Christiansen, 318 North Sycamore Street, Columbus, Kansas and his brother, Harlan Carl, also serving on the Arizona.[146]

---

[144] Elmer Emil Christensen, Photo from Wyoming Honor States.

[145] Lloyd Raymond Christensen, Photo from Nebraska Honor States.

[146] Edward Lee Christiansen, Photo and information provided by Jerry Lee Wigington.

Christiansen, Harlan Carl Seaman, Second Class, Serial No. 342 51 69, US Navy. Harlan was born on September 14, 1922 in Jewell County, Western Kansas the son of Carl Edward and Winona Marie (Canny) Christiansen. He enlisted in the US Navy August 19, 1941 at Kansas City, Missouri and completed his basic training at the Naval Training Station in Great Lakes, Illinois. He reported for duty on the USS Arizona November 3, 1941 where he was serving on December 7, 1941 when the Japanese attacked Pearl Harbor. Carl and his brother had planned to go ashore and have their picture taken together to send to their parents back home in Columbus, Kansas. While waiting on the quarterdeck for his brother, he observed his brother stop halfway down the hatch and called out that he had forgotten something and would be right back. He never saw his brother again. His brother, Edward Lee Christiansen was killed in action on board the USS Arizona. General quarters sounded and he went to his assigned battle station in No. 4 powder magazine. When the No. 2 magazine exploded there was total darkness and gasses coming in. He located a doorway into No. 3 magazine and from there struggled to topside and on to Ford Island. Next of Kin: Father, Mr. Carl N. Christiansen, 318 North Sycamore Street, Columbus, Kansas. After the war, Harlan returned home to Columbus, Kansas and served as Chief of Police for 36 years. He died on July 14, 2002 in Columbus, Kansas and is buried in Park Cemetery, Columbus, Kansas.[147]

Chung-Hoon, Gordon Paiea Lieutenant, Serial No. 0-05170, US Navy. Gordon was born on July 25, 1910 in Honolulu Hawaii. He was commissioned in the US Navy August 1, 1941 and was serving on the USS Arizona as 2nd Batt. Cont. W&D. Gordon was serving on December 7, 1941 when the Japanese attacked Pearl Harbor. His battle station was Secondary Forward. After the attack, Gordon was the CO on the USS John W. Thomason (DD-760) and then served on the USS Norton Sound (AVM-1). Gordon also served in the Korean War retiring from the service on October 1959 as a Rear Admiral. During his career, he was awarded the Navy Cross, Silver Star, American Defense Service Medal, Asiatic-Pacific Campaign Medal and World War II Victory Medal. He died on July 24, 1979 and is buried in Section M, Site 454-A, National Memorial Cemetery of the Pacific, Honolulu, Hawaii. The USS Chung-Hoon (DDG-93) was named in honor of Rear Admiral, Gordon Paiea Chung-Hoon.[148]

Cihlar, Lawrence John Pharmacist's Mate, Third Class, Serial No: 328 60 66, US Navy. Lawrence was born in 1920 to John Albert Cihlar and Mildred Elizabeth "Millie" (Prchal) Cihlar. He enlisted in the US Navy on September 13, 1939 in Minneapolis, Minnesota and reported for duty on the USS Arizona December 6, 1940. Lawrence was killed in action on December 7, 1941 in Pearl Harbor, Hawaii. He was awarded the American Defense Service Medal, World War II Victory Medal and Purple Heart Medal posthumously. Lawrence remains on duty on the USS Arizona. He is commemorated on the USS Arizona Memorial and the Memorial Tablets of the Missing, National Memorial Cemetery of

---

[147] Harlan Carl Christiansen, Photo and information provided by Jerry Lee Wigington.
[148] Gordon Paiea Chung-Hoon, Portrait from the USS Chung-Hoon website.

the Pacific, Honolulu, Hawaii. Lawrence was survived by his Father, Mr. John Albert Cihlar, New Prague, Minnesota.[149]

Clark, George Francis Gunner's Mate, Third Class, Serial No: 337 26 19, US Navy. George was born March 31, 1921 in Paris, Illinois to Clarence A. and Flossie Pearl (Kees) Clark. He enlisted in the US Navy on January 16, 1940 in St. Louis, Missouri and completed his basic training at the Naval Training Station in Great Lakes, Illinois. He reported for duty on the USS Arizona on March 26, 1940. George was killed in action on December 7, 1941 in Pearl Harbor, Hawaii. He was awarded the American Defense Service Medal, World War II Victory Medal and Purple Heart Medal posthumously. George remains on duty on the USS Arizona. He is commemorated on the USS Arizona Memorial and the Memorial Tablets of the Missing, National Memorial Cemetery of the Pacific, Honolulu, Hawaii. George was survived by his Father, Mr. Clarence Clark, 1208 South Marshall Street, Paris, Illinois.

Clark, John Crawford Todd Fireman, Third Class, Serial No: 376 15 30, US Navy. John was born in about 1923 in California to Joseph and Ellen Clark. He enlisted in the US Navy on November 5, 1940 in San Francisco, California and completed his basic training at the Naval Training Station in San Diego, California. He reported for duty on the USS Arizona on January 11, 1941. John was killed in action on December 7, 1941 in Pearl Harbor, Hawaii. He was awarded the American Defense Service Medal, World War II Victory Medal and Purple Heart Medal posthumously. John remains on duty on the USS Arizona. He is commemorated on the USS Arizona Memorial and the Memorial Tablets of the Missing, National Memorial Cemetery of the Pacific, Honolulu, Hawaii. John was survived by his Father, Mr. Joe Clark, Route 2, Box 193, Selma, California.

Clark, Malcolm Baker, Third Class, Serial No: 274 49 17, US Navy. Malcolm was born July 27, 1917 in Pollock, Louisiana to John C. and Ollie Clark. He enlisted in the US Navy on August 9, 1940 in New Orleans, Louisiana and completed his basic training at the Naval Training Station in San Diego, California. He reported for duty on the USS Arizona on October 10, 1940. Malcolm was killed in action on December 7, 1941 in Pearl Harbor, Hawaii. He was awarded the American Defense Service Medal, World War II Victory Medal and Purple Heart Medal posthumously. Malcolm remains on duty on the USS Arizona. He is commemorated on the USS Arizona Memorial and the Memorial Tablets of the Missing, National Memorial Cemetery of the Pacific, Honolulu, Hawaii, Pollock Cemetery, Pollock, Louisiana and the Pearl Harbor Memorial in Pollock, Louisiana. Malcolm was survived by his Mother, Mrs. Ollie Clark, Pollock, Louisiana, a brother, Bernard, also in the Navy at Newport, R.I. and two sisters, Mrs. C. W. Howard of Labadieville and Helene Clark of Pollock..[150]

Clark, Robert William, Jr. Fire Controlman, Third Class, Serial No: 234 28 21, US Navy. Robert was born October 1, 1917 in Eagle Rock, Pennsylvania to Robert William Clark, Sr., and Jennie Bell (Twombly) Clark. He enlisted in the US Navy on October 9, 1940 in Buffalo, New York and completed his basic training at the Naval Training Station in Newport, Rhode Island. Robert reported for duty on the USS Arizona on December 10, 1940. He was killed in action on December 7, 1941 in Pearl Harbor, Hawaii. Robert was awarded the American Defense Service Medal, World War II Victory Medal and Purple Heart Medal posthumously. He

---

[149] Lawrence John Cihlar, Photo and information provided by family member, Faith Padgett.

[150] Clark, Malcolm, information and photo from the Times of Shreveport, Louisiana, May 5, 1942 page 16.

remains on duty on the USS Arizona. Robert is commemorated on the USS Arizona Memorial and the Memorial Tablets of the Missing, National Memorial Cemetery of the Pacific, Honolulu, Hawaii. He was survived by his Parents, Mr. and Mrs. Robert William Clark, Sr., General Delivery, Pleasantville, Pennsylvania. The Robert Clark High School, Pleasantville, Pennsylvania was named in his honor.

Clarke, Robert Eugene Seaman, First Class, Serial No: 342 18 59, US Navy. Robert was born on October 9, 1920 in Pittsburg, Kansas to George Henry Clarke and Mae Irene (McCoy) Clarke. He enlisted in the US Navy on January 22, 1940 in Kansas City, Missouri and completed his basic training at the Naval Training Station in Great Lakes, Illinois. Robert reported for duty on the USS Arizona on March 26, 1940. He was killed in action on December 7, 1941 in Pearl Harbor, Hawaii. Robert was awarded the American Defense Service Medal, World War II Victory Medal and Purple Heart Medal posthumously. He remains on duty on the USS Arizona. Robert is commemorated on the USS Arizona Memorial and the Memorial Tablets of the Missing, National Memorial Cemetery of the Pacific, Honolulu, Hawaii. He was survived by his Father, Mr. George Henry Clarke, 1221 Murphy Street, Great Bend, Kansas.

Clash, Donald Fireman, Second Class, Serial No: 300 19 56, US Navy. Donald was born January 24, 1919 in Brown County, Minnesota to Daniel and Viola Clash. He enlisted in the US Navy on October 8, 1940 in Chicago, Illinois and completed his basic training at the Naval Training Station in Great Lakes, Illinois. Donald reported for duty on the USS Arizona on December 9, 1940. He was killed in action on December 7, 1941 in Pearl Harbor, Hawaii. Donald was awarded the American Defense Service Medal, World War II Victory Medal and Purple Heart Medal posthumously. He remains on duty on the USS Arizona. Donald is commemorated on the USS Arizona Memorial and the Memorial Tablets of the Missing, National Memorial Cemetery of the Pacific, Honolulu, Hawaii. He was survived by his Father, Mr. Daniel Clash, 820 West B Street, Iron Mountain, Michigan.

Clayton, Robert Roland Coxswain, Serial No: 382 11 69, US Navy. Robert was born August 26, 1920 in Los Angeles, California to Raymond S. and Nan N. (Case) Clayton. He enlisted in the US Navy on October 10, 1939 in Los Angeles, California and completed his basic training at the Naval Training Station in San Diego, California. He reported for duty on the USS Arizona on December 20, 1939. Robert was killed in action on December 7, 1941 in Pearl Harbor, Hawaii. He was awarded the American Defense Service Medal, World War II Victory Medal and Purple Heart Medal posthumously. Robert remains on duty on the USS Arizona. He is commemorated on the USS Arizona Memorial and the Memorial Tablets of the Missing, National Memorial Cemetery of the Pacific, Honolulu, Hawaii. Robert was survived by his Father, Mr. Raymond Samuel Clayton, 2415 T. 2nd Street, Long Beach, California. His brother, Gerald Lee Clayton was killed on board the USS Oklahoma on December 7, 1941. Pictured, Robert is on the right and his brother, Gerald Lee is on the left.[151]

Clemmens, Claude Albert Seaman, First Class, Serial No: 356 27 00, US Navy. Claude was born February 15, 1919 in Oklahoma, the youngest son of George and Molly Clemmens. He enlisted in the US Navy on April 12, 1940 in Dallas, Texas and completed his

---

[151] Robert Roland Clayton, Photo from the Nebraska, Iowa War Dead, World-Herald, Omaha, Nebraska, Sunday, July 4, 1943.

basic training at the Naval Training Station in San Diego, California. Claude reported for duty on the USS Arizona on June 16, 1940. He was killed in action on December 7, 1941 in Pearl Harbor, Hawaii. Claude was awarded the American Defense Service Medal, World War II Victory Medal and Purple Heart Medal posthumously. His remains were recovered on December 23, 1941, badly decomposed. The disposition of his body is unclear; it is possible he was buried in one of the unknown graves at the Punchbowl.[152] He is commemorated on the USS Arizona Memorial and the Memorial Tablets of the Missing, National Memorial Cemetery of the Pacific, Honolulu, Hawaii. Claude was survived by his Sister, Mrs. Ella Hendricks, Route 1, Talala, Oklahoma.

Clift, Ray Emerson Coxswain, Serial No: 342 18 01, US Navy. Ray was born on January 10, 1921 to Cornelius D. and Golda Irene (Bell) Clift in Bridgeport, Illinois. He enlisted in the US Navy on January 10, 1940 in Kansas City, Missouri and completed his basic training at the Naval Training Station in Great Lakes, Illinois. Ray reported for duty on the USS Arizona March 26, 1940. He was killed in action on December 7, 1941 in Pearl Harbor, Hawaii. Ray was awarded the American Defense Service Medal, World War II Victory Medal and Purple Heart Medal posthumously. He remains on duty on the USS Arizona. Ray is commemorated on the USS Arizona Memorial and the Memorial Tablets of the Missing, National Memorial Cemetery of the Pacific, Honolulu, Hawaii. He was survived by his Mother, Mrs. Golda I. Clift, 3522 Nicholson Street, Kansas City, Missouri.

Cloues, Edward "Eddie" Blanchard Ensign, Serial No: 0-085051, US Navy. Edward was born on December 26, 1917 at Warner, New Hampshire to Alfred S. Cloues and Hattie B. Cloues. He graduated from the Naval Academy on June 6, 1940 and reported for duty on the USS Arizona on June 29, 1940 where he served as Junior Watch and Division 2 Officer. Edward was killed in action on December 7, 1941 in Pearl Harbor, Hawaii. His battle station was Turret II. Edward was awarded the American Defense Service Medal, World War II Victory Medal and Purple Heart Medal posthumously. He remains on duty on the USS Arizona. Edward is commemorated on the USS Arizona Memorial and the Memorial Tablets of the Missing, National Memorial Cemetery of the Pacific, Honolulu, Hawaii. He was survived by his Mother, Mrs. Hattie B. Cloues, Warner, New Hampshire. The USS Cloues (DE-265) was named after him. It served from 1943 in the Pacific until decommissioned in December, 1945, earning three battle stars. The Wilkins-Cloues-Bigelow-Pearson American Legion Post 39 in Warner, New Hampshire was named in his honor.[153]

---

[152] Report of Changes of the USS Arizona for the month ending 31st day of December, 1941, page 47, line 3, Claude Albert Clemmens.
[153] Edward Blanchard Cloues, Photo from The Lucky Bag Yearbook, United States Naval Academy, Annapolis, MD, Class of 1940.

Clough, Edward Jay   Gunner's Mate, First Class, Serial No: 316 36 05, US Navy.   Edward was born in 1914 in Nebraska to Caleb Gardner and Ida May Clough. He enlisted in the US Navy prior to 1934 in and reported for duty on the USS Arizona on March 17, 1934. He was killed in action on December 7, 1941 in Pearl Harbor, Hawaii. Edward was awarded the American Defense Service Medal, World War II Victory Medal and Purple Heart Medal posthumously. He remains on duty on the USS Arizona. Edward is commemorated on the USS Arizona Memorial and the Memorial Tablets of the Missing, National Memorial Cemetery of the Pacific, Honolulu, Hawaii. He was survived by his Sister, Miss Helen Clough, 2958 Dudley Street, Lincoln, Nebraska.[154]

Clouser, Marion Howard   Gunner's Mate, First Class, Serial No. 291 38 33, US Navy. Marion was born on October 13, 1913 in Montgomery County, Indiana, son of Marion E. and Nancy Agnes (Maguire) Clouser. He re-enlisted in the US Navy March 3, 1938. He began serving on the USS Arizona July 24, 1932. Marion was serving on the Arizona December 7, 1941 when the Japanese attacked Pearl Harbor. Howard tells of swimming through burning oil on the water and watching his buddy die from his burns. He went on to serve on the USS Phelps. Marion died on July 3, 1974 in Bolivar, Missouri and is buried in the Greenwood Cemetery, Bolivar, Missouri.[155]

Cobb, Ballard "Buck" Burgher   Seaman, First Class, Serial No: 356 33 03, US Navy. Ballard was born on January 2, 1920 in Ladonia, Fannin County, Texas to William Harvey Cobb and Josephine (McCracken) Cobb of Dallas, Texas. He enlisted in the US Navy on August 6, 1940 in Dallas, Texas and completed his basic training at the Naval Training Station in San Diego, California. Ballard reported for duty on the USS Arizona on October 8, 1940. He was killed in action on December 7, 1941 in Pearl Harbor, Hawaii. Ballard was awarded the American Defense Service Medal, World War II Victory Medal and Purple Heart Medal posthumously. He remains on duty on the USS Arizona. Ballard is commemorated on the USS Arizona Memorial and the Memorial Tablets of the Missing, National Memorial Cemetery of the Pacific, Honolulu, Hawaii. He was survived by his Brother, Mr. Johnny J. Cobb, 4703 Bryan Street, Dallas, Texas.[156]

Coburn, George Wesley   Seaman, First Class, Serial No. 393 40 03, US Navy. George was born May 16, 1918 in Montgomery, Alabama the son of Charles Overton and Frances Charlene (Brown) Coburn. He enlisted in the US Navy September 25, 1940 in Portland, Oregon and completed his basic training at the Naval Training Station in San Diego, California. He

---

[154] Edward Jay Clough, Photo from Nebraska, Iowa War Dead, World Herald Newspaper, Omaha, Nebraska, Sunday, July 4, 1943.
[155] Marion Howard Clouser, Photo and information provided by his Niece, Deanna Flinn.
[156] Ballard Burger Cobb, photo curtsey LCDR G. Dale McKissick, USNR, Memorial, Dallas Convention Center, Dallas, Texas.

reported for duty on the USS Arizona January 25, 1941. He was serving on the Arizona December 7, 1941, when the Japanese attacked Pearl Harbor. After the attack, George was transferred to the Submarine Base at Pearl Harbor. He served in both World War II and the Korean War in the US Navy until February 19, 1953 having achieved the rank of Chief Gunner's Mate. George died February 26, 2001 and is buried in the Williamette National Cemetery, Portland, Oregon.

Coburn, Walter Overton   Seaman, First Class, Serial No: 337 26 33, US Navy. Walter was born September 16, 1920 in St. Louis, Missouri to Charles O. and Frances Charlene (Brown) Coburn. He enlisted in the US Navy on January 23, 1940 in St. Louis, Missouri and completed his basic training at the Naval Training Station in Great Lakes, Illinois. Walter reported for duty on the USS Arizona on March 26, 1940. He was killed in action on December 7, 1941 in Pearl Harbor, Hawaii. Walter was awarded the American Defense Service Medal, World War II Victory Medal and Purple Heart Medal posthumously. He remains on duty on the USS Arizona. Walter is commemorated on the USS Arizona Memorial and the Memorial Tablets of the Missing, National Memorial Cemetery of the Pacific, Honolulu, Hawaii. He was survived by his Mother, Mrs. Frances Coburn, Route 8, Box 525, Tulsa, Oklahoma.

Cockrum, Kenneth Earl   Machinist's Mate, First Class, Serial No: 291 45 47, US Navy. Kenneth was born May 16, 1916 in Brownstown, Indiana to Charles Thomas Cochrane and Anna Bell (Lucas) Cochrane of Seymour, Indiana. He enlisted in the US Navy on August 8, 1935 in Indianapolis, Indiana and completed his training at the Naval Training Station in Great Lakes, Illinois. Kenneth reported for duty on the USS Arizona on December 11, 1936. His enlistment had expired and he was waiting for the Arizona to return to the mainland at the time he was killed in action on December 7, 1941 in Pearl Harbor, Hawaii. Kenneth was awarded the American Defense Service Medal, World War II Victory Medal and Purple Heart Medal posthumously. He remains on duty on the USS Arizona. Kenneth is commemorated on the USS Arizona Memorial and the Memorial Tablets of the Missing, National Memorial Cemetery of the Pacific, Honolulu, Hawaii. He was survived by his Father, Mr. Charles Tom Cockrum, 512 East 2nd Street, Seymour, Indiana.[157]

Coffin, Robert   Shipfitter, Third Class, Serial No: 385 82 96, US Navy. Robert was born in March 1917 in Wenatchee, Washington to Daniel Jonathan and Lillian May (Peters) Coffin. He enlisted in the US Navy on October 10, 1939 in Seattle, Washington and completed his basic training at the Naval Training Station in San Diego, California. Robert reported for duty on the USS Arizona December 20, 1939. He was killed in action on December 7, 1941 in Pearl Harbor, Hawaii. Robert was awarded the American Defense Service Medal, World War II Victory Medal and Purple Heart Medal posthumously. He remains on duty on the USS Arizona. Robert is commemorated on the USS Arizona Memorial and the Memorial Tablets of the Missing, National Memorial Cemetery of the Pacific, Honolulu, Hawaii. He was survived by his Father, Mr. Daniel Jonathan Coffin, 405 South 10th Street, Yakima, Washington.

Coffman, Marshal Herman   Gunner's Mate, Third Class, Serial No: 291 56 75, US Navy. Marshal enlisted in the US Navy on November 2, 1938 in Indianapolis, Indiana and completed his basic training at the Naval Training Station in Great Lakes, Illinois. He reported for duty on the USS Arizona on March 25, 1939. Marshal was killed in action on December 7, 1941 in Pearl Harbor, Hawaii. He was awarded the American Defense Service Medal, World

---

[157] Kenneth Earl Cockrum, Photo from the 1931 Patriot Yearbook, Shields High School, Seymour, Indiana.

War II Victory Medal and Purple Heart Medal posthumously. Marshal remains on duty on the USS Arizona. He is commemorated on the USS Arizona Memorial and the Memorial Tablets of the Missing, National Memorial Cemetery of the Pacific, Honolulu, Hawaii. Marshal was survived by his Mother, Mrs. Callie Wynema Boals, 531 East Lewis Street, Fort Wayne, Indiana.

Coker, Charles Walter   Lieutenant, Serial No. 0-05860, US Navy. Charles was born August 31, 1914 in Mississippi to Walter Bernard and Lorine (Robbins) Coker. He was commissioned June 3, 1940 in the US Navy and was serving on the USS Arizona as Watch and Division Officer. He was serving on December 7, 1941, when the Japanese attacked Pearl Harbor. His battle station was Spot L. Charles attained the rank of Commander and was the Commanding Officer of the USS Mattaponi (AO-41) from December 12, 1956 to September 30, 1957. He died May 31, 1987 in San Mateo, California.[158]

Cole, David Lester   Ensign, Serial No: 0-095348, US Naval Reserve. David was born May 30, 1919 in Sacramento, California to David Vincent and Lillian Sarah (Curl) Cole. He was commissioned on November 14, 1940 in the US Navy Reserve. David was serving on the Arizona as the Junior Watch and Division 5 Officer. His battle station was Starboard, AA RKO. David was killed in action on December 7, 1941 in Pearl Harbor, Hawaii. He was awarded the American Defense Service Medal, World War II Victory Medal and Purple Heart Medal posthumously. David remains on duty on the USS Arizona. He is commemorated on the USS Arizona Memorial and the Memorial Tablets of the Missing, National Memorial Cemetery of the Pacific, Honolulu, Hawaii. David was survived by his Father, Mr. David V. Cole, 2674 Franklin Boulevard, Sacramento, California. An American Legion Post in Sacramento, California was named in his honor.[159]

Colegrove, Willett Stillman, Jr.   Seaman, Second Class, Serial No: 385 99 85, US Navy. Willett was born on October 29, 1923 in Los Angeles, California to Willett Stillman and Bertha Lucille (Victor) Colegrove. He enlisted in the US Navy on April 21, 1941 in Seattle, Washington and completed his basic training at the Naval Training Station in San Diego, California. Willett reported for duty on the USS Arizona on December 5, 1941, two days before the attack. He was killed in action on December 7, 1941 in Pearl Harbor, Hawaii. Willett was awarded the American Defense Service Medal, World War II Victory Medal and Purple Heart Medal posthumously. He is commemorated on the USS Arizona Memorial and is buried in Section Mb, Site 92, National Memorial Cemetery of the Pacific, Honolulu, Hawaii. Willett was survived by his Father, Lt. Willett S. Colegrove, Sr., Naval Torpedo Station, Keyport, Washington.

---

[158] Charles Walter Coker, Photo from Lucky Bag Yearbook, United States Naval Academy, Annapolis, MD, Class of 1937.
[159] David Lester Cole, Photo from California Honor States and information provided by family member Ivy Marie McLaury.

Collier, John   Fireman, Second Class, Serial No: 393 42 57, US Navy. John enlisted in the US Navy on November 4, 1940 in Portland, Oregon and completed his basic training at the Naval Training Station in San Diego, California. He reported for duty on the USS Arizona on January 11, 1941. John was killed in action on December 7, 1941 in Pearl Harbor, Hawaii. He was awarded the American Defense Service Medal, World War II Victory Medal and Purple Heart Medal posthumously. John remains on duty on the USS Arizona. He is commemorated on the USS Arizona Memorial and the Memorial Tablets of the Missing, National Memorial Cemetery of the Pacific, Honolulu, Hawaii. John was survived by his Brother, Edward Collier, Cloverdale, Oregon.

Collier, Linald Long, Jr.   Baker, Third Class, Serial No: 360 01 70, US Navy. Linald was born November 22, 1916 to Linald and Alma M. Collier of Galveston, Texas. He enlisted in the US Navy on November 14, 1938 in Houston, Texas and completed his basic training at the Naval Training Station in San Diego, California. Linald reported for duty on the USS Arizona on March 11, 1939. He was killed in action on December 7, 1941 in Pearl Harbor, Hawaii. Linald was awarded the American Defense Service Medal, World War II Victory Medal and Purple Heart Medal posthumously. He remains on duty on the USS Arizona. Linald is commemorated on the USS Arizona Memorial and the Memorial Tablets of the Missing, National Memorial Cemetery of the Pacific, Honolulu, Hawaii. He was survived by his Father, Mr. Linald Lodinger Collier, 214 13th Street, Galveston, Texas.

Collins, Austin   Shipfitter, Third Class, Serial No: 291 61 61, US Navy. Austin was born July 26, 1919 in Webster, Kentucky to Lon and Dellar (Griffith) Collins. He enlisted in the US Navy on January 11, 1940 in Indianapolis, Indiana and completed his basic training at the Naval Training Station in Great Lakes, Illinois. He reported for duty on the USS Arizona on March 26, 1940. Austin was killed in action on December 7, 1941 in Pearl Harbor, Hawaii. He was awarded the American Defense Service Medal, World War II Victory Medal and Purple Heart Medal posthumously. Austin remains on duty on the USS Arizona. He is commemorated on the USS Arizona Memorial and the Memorial Tablets of the Missing, National Memorial Cemetery of the Pacific, Honolulu, Hawaii. Austin was survived by his Father, Mr. Lon Collins, Route 3, Sebre, Kentucky.[160]

Collins, Billy Murl   Seaman, First Class, Serial No: 382 11 75, US Navy. Billy was born September 4, 1922 in Arizona to Oscar Myers and Loma Collins. He enlisted in the US Navy on October 10, 1939 in Los Angeles, California and completed his basic training at the Naval Training Station in San Diego, California. He reported for duty on the USS Arizona on December 20, 1939. Billy was killed in action on December 7, 1941 in Pearl Harbor. Hawaii. He was awarded the American Defense Service Medal, World War II Victory Medal and Purple Heart Medal posthumously. Billy remains on duty on the USS Arizona. He is commemorated on the USS Arizona Memorial and the Memorial Tablets of the Missing, National Memorial Cemetery of the Pacific, Honolulu, Hawaii. Billy was survived by his Father, Mr. Oscar Myers Collins, 233 Williams Street, Barstow, California.[161]

---

[160] Austin Collins, Photo from Kentucky Honor States.
[161] Billy Murl Collins, Photo from the Barstow High Memorial.

Combs, Clyde Jefferson   Seaman, First Class, Serial No. 291 65 63, US Navy. Clyde was born on December 11, 1921 in Maumee, Indiana. He was raised on a farm with three sisters and two brothers. After high school graduation, he enlisted in the US Navy October 8, 1940 in Indianapolis, Indiana and completed his basic training at the Naval Training Station in Great Lakes, Illinois. He reported for duty on the USS Arizona December 9, 1940 where he was serving on December 7, 1941, when the Japanese attacked Pearl Harbor. The following is his story as told on March 25, 2004:

"On the morning of December 7, 1941, I was in the Chief's Quarters way up forward folding my laundry. One of the Chiefs yelled, "Hey, the California is on fire." I looked up to see a Jap plane shooting out at Ford Island. I recognized the "Rising Sun" on his wing. I didn't have to think. I knew we were being attacked so I did a hundred yard dash aft to my battle station, which was in Turret 3. I passed the O.D. (officer of the deck) who at that time sounded G.Q. which meant, "Report to your battle stations." (Those few seconds head start were one of the reasons I survived.) I made it almost to Deck 7 when a bomb exploded nearby. We who were there, couldn't breathe, but finally made it into the lower powder handling room of Turret 3. We didn't know of the damage at the time except we could feel we were listing to port and suspected we were sinking. It was impossible to perform our battle station duties in Turret 3 because the powder was wet and the hoist had no electrical power. All we could do was go up in the gun room as the rising water dictated. We stayed there until around 9:30 am and finally went out on deck and were shocked beyond belief at what had happened to our home. The deck was riddled with bullet holes, and body parts were scattered everywhere. The body of one of my friends was hanging from the mast. We couldn't do anything to help anyone so four or five of us removed some of our clothing and shoes and jumped overboard into the burning water in order to swim to Ford Island, which was approximately 100 years away. Bad Idea! It was impossible to swim so we made our way back to the quay and to the ladder leading back to the ship's deck. Luckily, that part of the ship had not sustained much damage. Minutes later a sailor walked out of a burning compartment and said, "Help me Combs." I didn't know who he was since he was burned beyond recognition. In the meantime our Division Officer had gotten the Captain's gig going and was picking up casualties, so we got the burned sailor down into the boat. He died on the way to the beach. I later learned that his name was Criswell, one of my best friends from Indiana.

Once on Ford Island we found a bunker where sailors and families were collecting. Finally, the sailors were moved to a location at the base where we reported in, giving our names, ships and other information. From there we were sent to a sunken, open air theater where we stayed until we were reassigned to a new duty station. I chose to be transferred to the USS Selfridge (DDE-357). This duty lasted until the war was over and was mostly in the Pacific Theater, which was full of more war.

It was very sad losing 1,077 of my shipmates and difficult to understand why I survived and they didn't. Yet, I can say that the Navy prepared me well, especially in the areas of plane recognition and discipline duty. These things, along with the fact that my battle station was one of only 2 safe places on the ship, and my advance sprint to that location, were probably what saved me that day."

With the loss of the Arizona, Clyde was assigned to the USS Selfridge (DD-357). Throughout the bulk of the war, the destroyer remained in the Pacific, involved primarily with screening transport operations. On October 6, 1943, the Selfridge and two other destroyers intercepted a Japanese destroyer barge force of six destroyers and three transports that were attempting to rescue stranded Japanese soldiers on Vella Lavella Island in the Solomons. Fighting was heavy and one American destroyer was sunk and the USS Selfridge was heavily damaged by a Japanese torpedo. The Selfridge received temporary repairs before heading to San Diego for overhaul. Following repairs, the destroyer was ordered to the Western pacific where the USS Selfridge participated in the invasion of the Marianas and the Liberation of Guam as well as participation in the Battle of the Philippine Sea. In September of 1944, the Selfridge was ordered to the Atlantic where the destroyer supported transatlantic escort duty until the surrender of Germany in May of 1945. On May 12, 1946, SK1c Clyde Combs was honorably discharged from the Navy, but recalled to active duty during the Korean Conflict. He remained in the Navy, serving in the U.S. Navy Reserve and retired as Chief Store Keeper in October of 1979.

Clyde married Margaret Jeanette Riddle on July 6, 1946. They had a daughter, Linda, who has lived in Ouray County, Colorado since 1981. To be closer to their daughter, Clyde and Margaret moved to Montrose, Colorado in August of 2002. The couple moved from Pompano Beach, Florida, where they had lived for twenty years.

Clyde loved sports, mostly auto racing, pro basketball and was a fan of the Indiana University Hoosiers basketball team. Clyde was active with the Senior Center at the Pavilion in Montrose. He was also active in his community and a good neighbor. He was a devoted and loving husband of 58 years, as well as a loving and special father.

Clyde passed away at his home on Saturday, February 26, 2005. He is survived by his wife, Margaret; his daughter, Linda Hoeksema and her husband, Ron; three sisters and two brothers. On May 17, 2005 a Memorial Ceremony and Internment was held at Pearl Harbor, Hawaii for Clyde as he rejoined his brothers on the USS Arizona. [162]

Condon, Daniel Jerome   Lieutenant, Junior Grade, US Navy Reserve. Daniel was born on November 29, 1914 in Omaha, Nebraska. He was commissioned November 30, 1940 in the US Navy and was serving on the USS Arizona as Junior Medical Officer. His battle station was Amid Dressing Station on December 7, 1941 when the Japanese attacked Pearl Harbor. He retired from the service in March 1946 having achieved the rank of Commander. Daniel served as the Medical Examiner for Maricopa County, Arizona for many years. Daniel died on September 10, 1992 in Phoenix, Arizona and is buried in Section 18D, Site 1775, National Memorial Cemetery of Arizona, Phoenix, Arizona.

Conlin, Bernard Eugene   Seaman, Second Class, Serial No: 337 63 25, US Navy. Bernard was born November 22, 1923 in Illinois to Henry Edward and Rosa (Adkins) Conlin. He enlisted in the US Navy on June 18, 1941 in St. Louis, Missouri and reported for duty on the USS Arizona on October 11, 1941. He was killed in action on December 7, 1941 in Pearl Harbor, Hawaii. Bernard was awarded the American Defense Service Medal, World War II Victory Medal and Purple Heart Medal posthumously. He remains on duty on the USS Arizona. Bernard is commemorated on the USS Arizona Memorial and the Memorial Tablets of the Missing, National Memorial Cemetery of the Pacific, Honolulu, Hawaii. He was survived by his Mother, Mrs. Rosa Conlin, 516 East Grand Avenue, Decatur, Illinois. His brother, James was serving on the USS Arizona and was killed in action. [163]

---

[162] Clyde Jefferson Combs, Information, story and picture provided by his daughter, Linda Hoeksema.
[163] Bernard Eugene Conlin, Information and photo provided by Niece, Rose Mary Gossman.

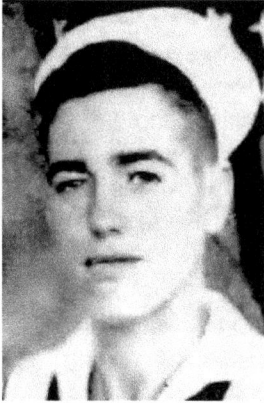

Conlin, James Leo Fireman, Second Class, Serial No: 337 32 00, US Navy. James was born June 8, 1922 in Illinois to Henry Edward and Rosa (Adkins) Conlin. He enlisted in the US Navy on June 11, 1940 in St. Louis, Missouri and completed his basic training at the Naval Training Station in Great Lakes, Illinois. He reported for duty on the USS Arizona on October 12, 1940. James was killed in action on December 7, 1941 in Pearl Harbor, Hawaii. He was awarded the American Defense Service Medal, World War II Victory Medal and Purple Heart Medal posthumously. James remains on duty on the USS Arizona. He is commemorated on the USS Arizona Memorial and the Memorial Tablets of the Missing, National Memorial Cemetery of the Pacific, Honolulu, Hawaii. James was survived by his Mother, Mrs. Rosa Conlin, 516 East Grand Avenue, Decatur, Illinois. His brother, Bernard was also serving on the USS Arizona and was killed in action.[164]

Connelly, Richard Earl Chief Quartermaster, Serial No: 242 81 03, US Navy. Richard was born June 5, 1906 the son of Ralph Raymond and Martha O. (Weidman) Connelly. He re-enlisted in the US Navy on August 19, 1938 in San Pedro, California and reported for duty on the USS Arizona on June 16, 1939 transferring from the USS Algorma. He was killed in action on December 7, 1941 in Pearl Harbor, Hawaii. Richard was awarded the American Defense Service Medal, World War II Victory Medal and Purple Heart Medal posthumously. He remains on duty on the USS Arizona. Richard is commemorated on the USS Arizona Memorial and the Memorial Tablets of the Missing, National Memorial Cemetery of the Pacific, Honolulu, Hawaii. He was survived by his Wife, Mrs. Geraldine Connelly, 1239 East 4th Street, Long Beach, California.

Conrad, Homer Milton, Jr. Seaman, First Class, Serial No: 283 29 10, US Navy. Homer was born March 15, 1921 in Wayne County, Indiana to Homer M. and Lola May Conrad of Canton, Ohio. He enlisted in the US Navy on September 20, 1939 in Cleveland, Ohio and completed his basic training at the Naval Training Station in Great Lakes, Illinois. Homer reported for duty on the USS Arizona on May 7, 1940. He was killed in action on December 7, 1941 in Pearl Harbor, Hawaii. Homer was awarded the American Defense Service Medal, World War II Victory Medal and Purple Heart Medal posthumously. He remains on duty on the USS Arizona. Homer is commemorated on the USS Arizona Memorial and the Memorial Tablets of the Missing, National Memorial Cemetery of the Pacific, Honolulu, Hawaii and Crown Hill Cemetery, Orrville, Ohio. He was survived by his Father, Mr. Homer Milton Conrad, Sr., 1147 Bedford Avenue Southwest, Canton, Ohio. His brother, Walter Ralph was also lost on the Arizona.[165]

---

[164] James Leo Conlin, Information and Photo provided by Niece, Rose Mary Gossman.
[165] Homer Milton Conrad, Jr., Photo from McKinley High School, Canton, Ohio 1939.

Conrad, Robert Frank Seaman, Second Class, Serial No: 382 38 23, US Navy. Robert was born on July 26, 1922 to Clarence and Georgana Conrad of Tulare, California. He enlisted in the US Navy on February 3, 1941 in Los Angeles, California and completed his basic training at the Naval Training Station in San Diego, California. Robert reported for duty on the USS Arizona on August 24, 1941. He was killed in action on December 7, 1941 in Pearl Harbor, Hawaii. Robert was awarded the American Defense Service Medal, World War II Victory Medal and Purple Heart Medal posthumously. He remains on duty on the USS Arizona. Robert is commemorated on the USS Arizona Memorial and the Memorial Tablets of the Missing, National Memorial Cemetery of the Pacific, Honolulu, Hawaii. He was survived by his Father, Mr. Clarence William Conrad, 3910 Moore Street, Venice, California.

Conrad, Walter Ralph Quartermaster, Second Class, Serial No: 283 18 21, US Navy. Walter was born September 29, 1917 to Homer Milton and Lola May Conrad of Canton, Ohio. He enlisted in the US Navy on July 7, 1936 in Cleveland, Ohio and completed his basic training at the Naval Training Station in Great Lakes, Illinois. Walter reported for duty on the USS Arizona on June 6, 1937. He was killed in action on December 7, 1941 in Pearl Harbor, Hawaii. Walter was awarded the American Defense Service Medal, World War II Victory Medal and Purple Heart Medal posthumously. He remains on duty on the USS Arizona. Walter is commemorated on the USS Arizona Memorial and the Memorial Tablets of the Missing, National Memorial Cemetery of the Pacific, Honolulu, Hawaii. He was survived by his Wife, Mrs. Irene Marie Conrad, 1036 Stockton, Lynwood, California. His brother, Homer was also killed in action on the Arizona.[166]

Conter, Louis Anthony Quartermaster, Third Class, Serial No. 372 11 63, US Navy. Louis was born September 13, 1921 in Ojibwa, Wisconsin. He enlisted in the US Navy November 15, 1939 in Denver, Colorado and completed his basic training at the Naval Training Station in San Diego, California. He reported for duty on the USS Arizona January 24, 1940. Louis was serving on the Arizona December 7, 1941, when the Japanese attacked Pearl Harbor. Louis was on watch the morning of the attacks. He remembered standing at his quarterdeck station, between the ship's third turret and main deck, when sirens began to sound at 7:55 a.m. as Japanese planes started bombing the harbor. His most vivid memory came at 8:05 a.m. when a bomb hit an ammunition magazine located between turrets one and two, causing a massive explosion famously captured on media news reels. The blast knocked him to the deck while other sailors were thrown off the side of the ship. Everything forward of the ship blew up with the magazine, Guys started coming out of the fire and we would lay them down on the deck because we didn't want them jumping over the sides. There was fire all around the ship and we knew if they jumped over, they would be killed anyway.

On the quarterdeck, we were knee-deep in water. Men from other ships threw lines over to our ship so they could come aboard and help with the fire. About five of them came across before the lines burned up and the rest fell into the burning water. We were able to get some of

---

[166] Walter Ralph Conrad, Photo from "Navy's War Dead Include 14 in Canton District", The Canton Repository, Canton, Ohio, Tuesday, May 5, 1942, Page 12.

them out, but they were badly burned. When captain said "abandon ship" we went into life boars and started picking men out of the water and fire. When the second attack hit, we fought from the water. After both waves of attacks, he and surviving sailors spent more than 10 days helping put out fires and retrieving bodies on their ship. He later served in Rabaul, New Guinea and Europe. Louis was recalled to service in 1950 and participated in the Korean War serving on the USS Bon Homme Richard (CV/CVA-31). He retired from the Navy after having served 23 years in December 1967 with a rank of Lieutenant Commander.[167]

Cook, Lonnie David   Seaman, First Class, No. 3 Turret Crew, Serial No. 346 79 37, US Navy. Lonnie was born on November 19, 1920 in Morris, Oklahoma. He enlisted in the US Navy April 3, 1940 in Little Rock, Arkansas and completed his basic training at the Naval Training Station in San Diego, California. He reported for duty on the USS Arizona July 2, 1940. He was to go to Honolulu on liberty on December 7, 1941, when the Japanese attacked Pearl Harbor. Up early, he took a shower in the bow of the ship and returned to lower handling room of turret #3. I was changing clothes in front of my locker when the bombs began to drop. Chief Turret Captain came in the turret and said Jap's were bombing us. We started up in the turret to our battle stations. I was on the shell deck when the bow of the ship blew up. The turret crew gathered up in the gun room and it was very smoky. It was thought by our leader that we were being gassed. They had us pull off our "T" shirts and stuff them in the sight ports. We soon found the smoke was inside the turret. We were told to go out on the starboard quarter deck and get life rafts in the water. We took off all the burned and wounded men we could find. When we were told to abandon ship, the ship had sunk far enough so I could step off the deck into a motor launch. He later served on the USS Patterson and after 2 months, he transferred to the USS Aylwin (DD-355) where he saw action in Rabul, The Coral Sea Battle and The Battle of Midway. He later served on the USS Pringle and saw action in the Marshall Islands, Guam, Saipan, Tinian and the Philippines. He then served on the USS Hall (DD-583) returning to the Pacific to land troops on Iwo Jima and Okinawa. Lonnie was discharged on April 9, 1948 and returned home to Morris, Oklahoma.[168]

Coole, Lloyd Edward   Seaman, First Class, Serial No. 300 19 33, US Navy. Lloyd was born September 27, 1918 in Giles, Wisconsin the son of John James and Ellen Amanda (Nelson) Coole. He enlisted in the US Navy October 8, 1940 in Chicago, Illinois and completed his basic training at the Naval Training Station in Great Lakes, Illinois. He reported for duty on the USS Arizona December 9, 1940. Lloyd was serving on the Arizona December 7, 1941 when the Japanese attacked Pearl Harbor. When the bomb hit the ship, Lloyd was in the No. 3 gun turret. He survived by jumping overboard and swimming through burning oil to Ford Island. After the attack, Lloyd was transferred to the USS Mac Donough (DD-351) for duty. Lloyd died June 26, 1982 in Eugene, Oregon and is buried in Garden of the Apostles, Lane Memorial Gardens, Eugene, Oregon.

Cooper, Clarence Eugene   Fireman, Second Class, Serial No: 382 29 78, US Navy. Clarence was born June 15, 1918 in Kalispell, Montana to Ralph Charles and Eva Cordelia (Terry) Cooper. He enlisted in the US Navy on November 1, 1940 in Los Angeles, California and completed his basic training at the Naval Training Station in San Diego, California. Clarence reported for duty on the USS Arizona on December 30, 1940. He was killed in action on

[167] Louis Anthony Conter, Information, story and picture provided by himself.
[168] Lonnie David Cook, Information and picture provided by himself.

December 7, 1941 in Pearl Harbor, Hawaii. Clarence was awarded the American Defense Service Medal, World War II Victory Medal and Purple Heart Medal posthumously. He remains on duty on the USS Arizona. Clarence is commemorated on the USS Arizona Memorial and the Memorial Tablets of the Missing, National Memorial Cemetery of the Pacific, Honolulu, Hawaii. He was survived by his Mother, Mrs. F. C. Firanzo, Box 6, Casmalia, California. His Brother, Kenneth was also killed in action while serving on board the USS Arizona.

Cooper, Kenneth Erven   Fireman, Second Class, Serial No: 382 29 81, US Navy. Kenneth was born February 20, 1920 in Kalispell, Montana to Ralph Charles and Eva Cordelia (Terry) Cooper of Santa Barbara, California. He enlisted in the US Navy on November 1, 1940 with his brother Clarence in Los Angeles, California and completed his basic training at the Naval Training Station in San Diego, California. Kenneth reported for duty on the USS Arizona on December 30, 1940. He was killed in action on December 7, 1941 in Pearl Harbor, Hawaii. Kenneth was awarded the American Defense Service Medal, World War II Victory Medal and Purple Heart Medal posthumously. He remains on duty on the USS Arizona. Kenneth is commemorated on the USS Arizona Memorial and the Memorial Tablets of the Missing, National Memorial Cemetery of the Pacific, Honolulu, Hawaii. He was survived by his Mother, Mrs. F. C. Firanzo, Box 6, Casmalia, California. His brother, Clarence was also killed in action while serving on board the USS Arizona.

Coplin, Norman Walter   Seaman, First Class, 6th Division, Serial No. 372 10 36, US Navy. Norman was born on November 25, 1919 in Scottsbluff, Nebraska. He was almost 20 when he enlisted in the US Navy on October 4, 1939 in Denver, Colorado and completed his basic training at the Naval Training Station in San Diego, California. He reported for duty on the USS Arizona December 20, 1939. Norman was serving on the Arizona December 7, 1941 when the Japanese attacked Pearl Harbor. He manned his battle station, until ordered to abandon ship. Then, he provided aid to the injured and helped get them to Ford Island Hospital. Norman also survived the sinking of the USS Lexington during the Battle of the Coral Sea and was on the USS Thompson (DE-203) at Leyte Gulf. He was honorably discharged in 1945 as a Chief Boatswain's Mate and joined the Miami, Florida police department. He rose to the rank of Lieutenant and spent several years as a U.S. Customs Agent at the Port of Miami. Norman died on August 2, 1996 in Hollywood, Florida. His ashes were interred on the USS Arizona December 7, 1996.

Corbin, Ralph Victor Leon   Seaman, First Class, Serial No. 342 30 58, US Navy. Ralph was born on November 9, 1918 in Putnam County, Missouri, son of Alfred Herman and Kettie Klyde (Kincad) Corbin. He enlisted in the US Navy October 11, 1940 in Kansas City, Missouri and completed his basic training at the Naval Training Station in Great Lakes, Illinois. He reported for duty on the USS Arizona December 9, 1940. Ralph was serving on the Arizona December 7, 1941 when the Japanese attacked Pearl Harbor. He went on to serve on the USS Chester. Ralph died on October 25, 2007 in Nevada, Iowa.

Corcoran, Gerard John   Seaman, First Class, Serial No: 223 64 58, US Navy. Gerard was born in about 1922 in New York to John J. and Katherine Corcoran. He enlisted in the US Navy on January 23, 1940 in New York, New York and completed his basic training at the Naval Training Station in Newport, Rhode Island. Gerard reported for duty on the USS Arizona on January 8, 1941. He was killed in action on December 7, 1941 in Pearl Harbor, Hawaii. Gerard was awarded the American Defense Service Medal, World War II Victory Medal and Purple Heart Medal posthumously. He remains on duty on the USS Arizona. Gerard is commemorated on the USS Arizona Memorial and the Memorial Tablets of the Missing, National Memorial Cemetery of the Pacific, Honolulu, Hawaii. He was survived by his Father, Mr. John Corcoran, 4063 97th Street, Corona, Flushing, New York.

Corey, Ernest Eugene Pharmacist's Mate, Third Class, Serial No: 393 30 92, US Navy. Ernest was born September 8, 1920 in Spokane, Washington to Ernest R. and Bertha Caroline (Mader) Corey. He enlisted in the US Navy on September 16, 1939 in Portland, Oregon and completed his basic training at the Naval Training Station in San Diego, California. He reported for duty on the USS Arizona on December 6, 1940. Ernest was killed in action on December 7, 1941 in Pearl Harbor, Hawaii. He was awarded the American Defense Service Medal, World War II Victory Medal and Purple Heart Medal posthumously. Ernest remains on duty on the USS Arizona. He is commemorated on the USS Arizona Memorial and the Memorial Tablets of the Missing, National Memorial Cemetery of the Pacific, Honolulu, Hawaii. Ernest was survived by his Wife, Mrs. Silvia Irma Corey, 2058 15th Avenue West, Seattle, Washington.[169]

Cornelius, Lyle Richard Seaman, Second Class, Serial No. 376 35 42, US Navy. Lyle was born on February 8, 1924. He enlisted in the US Navy June 26, 1941 in San Francisco, California and completed his basic training at the Naval Training Station in San Diego, California. Lyle reported for duty on the USS Arizona August 29, 1941. He was serving on December 7, 1941 when the Japanese attacked Pearl Harbor. After the attack, Lyle was transferred to the USS Dale (DD-353) for duty where he served until September of 1944 when he was transferred to the Pacific Fleet Radar Center, Camp Catlin, Pearl Harbor for advanced courses in Radar Operations. Lyle died on February 14, 1992. His ashes were interred on the USS Arizona on July 11, 1992.

Cornelius, Phillip Wayne Ship's Cook, Third Class, Serial No: 360 26 35, US Navy. Phillip was born in 1914 in Collingsworth County, Texas to Fred N. Cornelius and Myrtle Alice (Driskill) Cornelius of Olton, Texas. His mother died in childbirth in 1920. He enlisted in the US Navy on November 16, 1940 in Houston, Texas and completed his basic training at the Naval Training Station in San Diego, California. P.W. reported for duty on the USS Arizona on June 9, 1941. He was killed in action on December 7, 1941 in Pearl Harbor, Hawaii. Phillip was awarded the American Defense Service Medal, World War II Victory Medal and Purple Heart Medal posthumously. He remains on duty on the USS Arizona. Phillip is commemorated on the USS Arizona Memorial and the Memorial Tablets of the Missing, National Memorial Cemetery of the Pacific, Honolulu, Hawaii. He was survived by his Father, Mr. Fred Nuton Cornelius, Lubbock, Texas.

Corning, Russel Dale Radioman, Third Class, Y-3, Serial No: 413 52 53, US Navy. Russell was born in 1921 to Hadley L. and Maggie R. Corning. He enlisted in the US Navy on October 2, 1940 and reported for duty on the USS Arizona on April 27, 1941. Russell was killed in action on December 7, 1941 in Pearl Harbor, Hawaii. He was awarded the American Defense Service Medal, World War II Victory Medal and Purple Heart Medal posthumously. Russell remains on duty on the USS Arizona. He is commemorated on the USS Arizona Memorial and the Memorial Tablets of the Missing, National Memorial Cemetery of the Pacific, Honolulu, Hawaii. Russell was survived by his Mother, Mrs. Roberta Corning, 1275 Columbine Street, Denver, Colorado.[170]

---

[169] Ernest Eugene Corey, photo and information provided by daughter, Delores Corey-Johnson.
[170] Russel Dale Corning, Photo from the 1939 East High School Yearbook, Denver, Colorado.

Cosby, Ray Charles Seaman, First Class, Serial No. 300 19 38, US Navy. Ray was born September 9, 1920. He enlisted in the US Navy October 8, 1940 in Chicago, Illinois and completed his basic training at the Naval Training Station in Great Lakes, Illinois. He reported for duty on the USS Arizona December 9, 1940. He was serving on the Arizona December 7, 1941 when the Japanese attacked Pearl Harbor. He went on to serve on the USS Chester, the USS Massachusetts (BB-59), USS Deneobla (AD-12) and the USS Piedmont (AD-17). Ray died July 8, 2011 in Chelsea, Massachusetts and is buried in Holy Cross Cemetery, Malden, Massachusetts.[171]

Coulter, Arthur Lee Seaman, First Class, Serial No: 356 42 05, US Navy. Arthur was born on October 29, 1916 in Jefferson, Oklahoma, the son of Thomas Leon Coulter and Mabel Larue (Tedford) Coulter. He enlisted in the US Navy on November 9, 1940 in Dallas, Texas and completed his basic training at the Naval Training Station in San Diego, California. Arthur reported for duty on the USS Arizona on January 11, 1941. He was killed in action on December 7, 1941 in Pearl Harbor, Hawaii. Arthur was awarded the American Defense Service Medal, World War II Victory Medal and Purple Heart Medal posthumously. He remains on duty on the USS Arizona. Arthur is commemorated on the USS Arizona Memorial and the Memorial Tablets of the Missing, National Memorial Cemetery of the Pacific, Honolulu, Hawaii. He was survived by his Father, Mr. Thomas Leon Coulter, Jefferson, Oklahoma.[172]

Cowan, William Coxswain, Serial No: 342 10 37, US Navy. William was born in 1919 to William Price Cowan and Barbara Gertrude (Hillen) Cowan of Kansas City, Missouri. He enlisted in the US Navy on January 24, 1939 in Kansas City, Missouri and completed his basic training at the Naval Training Station in Great Lakes, Illinois. William reported for duty on the USS Arizona on July 8, 1939. He was killed in action on December 7, 1941 in Pearl Harbor, Hawaii. William was awarded the American Defense Service Medal, World War II Victory Medal and Purple Heart Medal posthumously. He remains on duty on the USS Arizona. William is commemorated on the USS Arizona Memorial and the Memorial Tablets of the Missing, National Memorial Cemetery of the Pacific, Honolulu, Hawaii. He was survived by his Father, Mr. William P. Cowan, 2708 Olive Street, Kansas City, Missouri.

Cowden, Joel Beman Seaman, Second Class, Serial No: 393 44 62, US Navy. Joel was born in 1917 in Oregon to Joel B. and Alma S. (Schnetzky) Cowden. He enlisted in the US Navy on December 3, 1940 and completed his basic training at the Naval Training Station in San Diego, California. Joel reported for duty on the USS Arizona on June 26, 1941. He was killed in action on December 7, 1941 in Pearl Harbor, Hawaii. Joel was awarded the American Defense Service Medal, World War II Victory Medal and Purple Heart Medal posthumously. He remains on duty on the USS Arizona. Joel is commemorated on the USS Arizona Memorial and the Memorial Tablets of the Missing, National Memorial Cemetery of the Pacific, Honolulu, Hawaii. He was survived by his Mother, Mrs. Alma Cowden Jepson, 574 East 14th

---

[171] Ray Charles Cosby, Photo from the Obituary of Ray Charles Cosby in the Boston Globe, July 10, 2011.
[172] Arthur Lee Coulter, Information provided by family member, Jim Coulter.

Street, Eugene, Oregon. [173]

Cox, Gerald Clinton   Musician, Second Class, Serial No: 300 38 24, US Navy. Gerald was born on August 17, 1922 in Veroqua, Wisconsin to Nat T. Cox and Amy Estella (Walling) Cox. He enlisted in the US Navy on February 27, 1941 and completed his basic training at the Naval Training Station in Great Lakes, Illinois. Gerald attended the Navy School of Music in Washington, DC graduating on May 23, 1941 as a member of the USS Arizona Band. He was an accomplished musician who played both the clarinet and the guitar. Gerald reported for duty on the USS Arizona on June 17, 1941. He was killed in action on December 7, 1941 in Pearl Harbor, Hawaii at the young age of 19. Gerald was awarded the American Defense Service Medal, World War II Victory Medal and Purple Heart Medal posthumously. His remains were recovered and he was buried in Plot M, Row 1, Grave 27, National Memorial Cemetery of the Pacific, Honolulu, Hawaii. Gerald is commemorated on the USS Arizona Memorial. He was survived by his Father, Mr. Nat Cox, 417 15th Avenue, East Moline, Illinois.[174]

Cox, John Madison, Jr.   Lieutenant Commander, Serial No. 57510, US Navy Reserve. John was born November 24, 1898 in Waycross, Georgia to John Madison and Willella (Lockhart) Cox. He was commissioned in the US Navy and reported for duty on the USS Arizona where he was serving as Assistant Gunnery and Air Defense Officer on December 7, 1941 when the Japanese attacked Pearl Harbor. His battle station was Sky Control. After the attack, John was transferred to the USS Neosho for duty. He later served as Commander on board the USS Beaumont (PG-60). He died August 18, 1968 In Los Angeles, California.[175]

   Cox, William Milford   Seaman, First Class, Serial No: 287 38 37, US Navy. William was born December 9, 1919 in Harlan County, Kentucky to William M. and Leona L. (Maze) Cox. He enlisted in the US Navy on March 26, 1940 in Louisville, Kentucky and completed his basic training at the Naval Training Station in Great Lakes, Illinois. William reported for duty on the USS Arizona on July 12, 1940. He was killed in action on December 7, 1941 in Pearl Harbor, Hawaii. William was awarded the American Defense Service Medal, World War II Victory Medal and Purple Heart Medal posthumously. He remains on duty on the USS Arizona. William is commemorated on the USS Arizona Memorial and the Memorial Tablets of the Missing, National Memorial Cemetery of the Pacific, Honolulu, Hawaii. He was survived by his Mother, Mrs. Leona Cox, Harlan, Kentucky.

---

[173] Joel Beman Cowden, Photo taken from "Purple Heart to Late Joel Cowden", Eugene Register/Guard, August 22, 1943.
[174] Gerald Clinton Cox, Photo from USS Arizona's Last Band by Molly Kent. By permission of the author. For more information about this book, go to www.USSARIZONASLASTBAND.com.
[175] John Madison Cox, Jr., Photo from the 1922 Lucky Bag Yearbook, US Naval Academy, Annapolis, Maryland, Page 282.

Cozad, Francis Burnard G. Seaman, Second Class, Serial No. 368 50 23, US Navy. Francis was born on May 12, 1922 in Montana, the son of Albert Elmer and Alma B. (Harris) Cozad. He enlisted in the US Navy August 6, 1940 in Salt Lake City, Utah and completed his basic training at the Naval Training Station in San Diego, California. Francis reported for duty on the USS Arizona October 14, 1940. On temporary duty with the Fleet Camera Party, Francis was serving on the Arizona December 7, 1941 when the Japanese attacked Pearl Harbor. Francis died on July 31, 1995 in Sacramento, California.

Craft, Harley Wade Carpenter's Mate Third Class, Serial No: 393 26 76, US Navy. Harley was born on November 13, 1918 in Oregon to Lee Wade Craft and Rita May (Carney) Craft. He enlisted in the US Navy on May 18, 1938 in Portland, Oregon and completed his basic training at the Naval Training Station in San Diego, California. Harley reported for duty on the USS Arizona on January 2, 1939. He was killed in action on December 7, 1941 in Pearl Harbor, Hawaii. Harley was awarded the American Defense Service Medal, World War II Victory Medal and Purple Heart Medal posthumously. He remains on duty on the USS Arizona. Harley is commemorated on the USS Arizona Memorial and the Memorial Tablets of the Missing, National Memorial Cemetery of the Pacific, Honolulu, Hawaii. He was survived by his Mother, Mrs. May Soule, General Delivery, Hoskins, Oregon.

Crawley, Wallace Dewight Coxswain, Serial No: 291 61 69, US Navy. Wallace was born in 1922 to James and Mamie Crawley of Posey, Indiana. He enlisted in the US Navy on January 18, 1940 in Indianapolis, Indiana and completed his basic training at the Naval Training Station in Great Lakes, Illinois. Wallace reported for duty on the USS Arizona on March 26, 1940. He was killed in action on December 7, 1941 in Pearl Harbor, Hawaii. Wallace was awarded the American Defense Service Medal, World War II Victory Medal and Purple Heart Medal posthumously. He remains on duty on the USS Arizona. Wallace is commemorated on the USS Arizona Memorial and the Memorial Tablets of the Missing, National Memorial Cemetery of the Pacific, Honolulu, Hawaii. He was survived by his Mother, Mrs. Mamie Croddy, Clarksburg, Indiana.[176]

Cremeens, Louis Edward Seaman, First Class, Serial No: 381 34 13, US Navy. Louis was born in about 1918 in New Madrid County, Missouri to Steven I. and Pearl Cremeens. He enlisted in the US Navy on June 6, 1940 in San Diego, California and completed his basic training at the Naval Training Station in San Diego, California. He reported for duty on the USS Arizona on September 8, 1940. Louis was killed in action on December 7, 1941 in Pearl Harbor, Hawaii. He was awarded the American Defense Service Medal, World War II Victory Medal and Purple Heart Medal posthumously. Louis remains on duty on the USS Arizona. He is commemorated on the USS Arizona Memorial and the Memorial Tablets of the Missing, National Memorial Cemetery of the Pacific, Honolulu, Hawaii. Louis was survived by his Father, Mr. Stephen Ishmeal Cremeens, 1st Street and 19th Avenue, Yuma, Arizona.

---

[176] Wallace Dewight Crawley, Photo posted on Fold3 by his 1st cousin 1x removed.

Criscuolo, Michael Yeoman, Second Class, Serial No: 375 94 94, US Navy. Michael was born August 5, 1921 in Pacific Grove, California the son of Antonio and Lucia (Pappacoda) Criscuolo. He enlisted in the US Navy on June 13, 1939 in San Francisco, California and completed his basic training at the Naval Training Station in San Diego, California. He reported for duty on the USS Arizona on September 11, 1939. On November 16, 1941, Michael wrote the following to his local paper, the Monterey Herald:

USS ARIZONA

November 16, 1941

MONTEREY HERALD

Gentlemen:

I have written an article" In Defense of the Uniform", and would appreciate it greatly if you would find room in my home town paper to print it. There are a lot of service men there now.

IN DEFENSE OF THE UNIFORM

Records from 1930 to 1939 show that out of every ten men that applied for enlistment in the Navy, only one was accepted. The percentage indeed speaks for itself.

I have often wondered how many civilians have stopped and thought of what the service men go through; the sailor's weeks at sea, watches day and night out in the cold drenched with salt spray, undergoing tedious hours of gunnery drills in order to be able to shoot fast and straight, and hours in fire rooms at 120 degrees, or the soldier's long hours of marching whether it is warm, cold, or raining, mile after mile of dust with no alternative but to plunge on through; or of the extended periods both must spend away from home.

During the long hears between times of National Emergency there are men who enlist in the service simply because they cannot find work on the outside, or because their parents have given them up as incorrigibles and send them to the Army or Navy to get them straightened out. Actually the percentage of enlisted men in this category is small even in peace time, but civilians have a tendency to think of all enlisted men in this light, especially if they have no friends or close relatives who have enlisted, and do not understand the motives behind a man's enlistment. But, regardless of what our motives have been when we enlisted, we feel that we have a job to do and we are in for a specific purpose. This is particularly true of the men who have come in since the emergency. The parents of these men understand their motives and are trying in every way to give them backing and support, but letters and cookies from home, which may be 5,000 miles away, cannot completely fill the need which men feel for warm personal contacts and understanding from the people he meets where he is stationed at the time.

Every individual should remember that the men who are serving in the Armed Forces of our fine country came from a home like his own. Service men were doing the same things that you are doing, going on dates with the girls in the community, and enjoying other pleasant pastimes. Donning a uniform does not make him forget the things he liked to do at home. It puts him in a class that all can be proud of. At the same time it puts him in a class where acquaintances are difficult to obtain.

Service men can sense whether or not you regard them as inferior or whether you regard them as lonely men seeking recreation, who are deserving of your respect and friendship as defenders of the flag.

Please remember that we are human and enjoy good company.
Very truly yours,

109

Michael Criscuolo, Yeoman Second Class, US Navy[177]

Michael was killed in action on December 7, 1941 in Pearl Harbor, Hawaii. He was awarded the American Defense Service Medal, World War II Victory Medal and Purple Heart Medal posthumously. Michael remains on duty on the USS Arizona. He is commemorated on the USS Arizona Memorial and the Memorial Tablets of the Missing, National Memorial Cemetery of the Pacific, Honolulu, Hawaii. Michael was survived by his Father, Mr. Antonia Criscuolo, 1179 5th Street, Monterey, California.[178]

Criswell, Wilfred John Seaman, First Class, Serial No: 291 65 74, US Navy. Wilfred was born June 20, 1919 in Indiana to Carris Lee and Daisy Mae (Mansfield) Criswell. He enlisted in the US Navy on October 8, 1940 in Indianapolis, Indiana and reported for duty on the USS Arizona December 9, 1940. *He was burned beyond recognition during the attack on December 7, 1940 in Pearl Harbor. His best friend, Clyde Combs helped him down into a boat. Wilfred died on the way to the beach.* He was awarded the American Defense Service Medal, World War II Victory Medal and Purple Heart Medal posthumously. Wilfred's remains were sent home for burial in the Riverside Cemetery in Brook, Indiana. He is commemorated on the USS Arizona Memorial and the Memorial Tablets of the Missing, National Memorial Cemetery of the Pacific, Honolulu, Hawaii. Wilfred was survived by his Father, Mr. Carris Criswell, Brook, Indiana.[179]

Crothers, Lee Raymond Boatswain's Mate, First Class, Serial No. 328 10 95, US Navy. Lee was born on September 8, 1907 the son of Francis Albert and Della E. Crothers of Powell, Michigan. He enlisted in the US Navy April 20, 1933 in Los Angeles, California. Lee served on the USS Arizona from May 6, 1933 until December 7, 1941 when the Japanese attacked Pearl Harbor. After the attack, Lee was transferred to salvage duty on the USS Utah (AG-16). Lee was shot to death by guerillas in Leyte, Philippine Islands on July 16, 1946. His remains were sent stateside and he is buried in Section B, Site 380, Golden Gate National Cemetery, San Bruno, California.

Crowe, Cecil Thomas Gunner's Mate, Second Class, Serial No: 287 15 47, US Navy. Cecil was born September 5, 1915 in Powell County, Kentucky to Lonnie and Lila (Chaney) Crowe. He enlisted in the US Navy on December 17, 1935 in Louisville, Kentucky and reported for duty on the USS Arizona on April 20, 1936. He was killed in action on December 7, 1941 in Pearl Harbor, Hawaii. Cecil was awarded the American Defense Service Medal, World War II Victory Medal and Purple Heart Medal posthumously. He remains on duty on the USS Arizona. Cecil is commemorated on the USS Arizona Memorial and the Memorial Tablets of the Missing, National Memorial Cemetery of the Pacific, Honolulu, Hawaii. He was survived by his Sister,

---

[177] Letter to Monterey Herald, November 16, 1941 from Michael Criscuolo on board the USS Arizona provided by family member, Jason Jenson.
[178] Michael Criscuolo, Photo and information provided by family member, Jason Jenson.
[179] Wilfred John Crisell, Photo provided by family member, Sandy Duncan.

Miss Juanita May Crowe, Masonic Widows & Orphans Home, St. Matthews, Kentucky. Both of his parents died before he was 15 years old.

Crowley, Thomas Ewing Lieutenant Commander, Serial No: 0-063012, US Navy. Thomas was born on April 18, 1902 in Madison, Illinois to James and Helen S. (Feuerstein) Crowley. He enlisted in the US Navy on March 6, 1919 and was discharged on January 31, 1923. A member of the Naval Reserve, he was commissioned assistant dental surgeon on December 23 1929 and served at naval stations at Great Lakes, Illinois, San Diego, California, Guantanamo Bay, Cuba and Lakehurst, New Jersey, as well as at sea. Thomas reported for duty on the USS Arizona on May 23, 1941. His battle station was Amid Dressing Station. Thomas was killed in action on December 7, 1941 in Pearl Harbor, Hawaii. He was awarded the American Defense Service Medal, World War II Victory Medal and Purple Heart Medal posthumously. Thomas remains on duty on the USS Arizona. He is commemorated on the USS Arizona Memorial and the Memorial Tablets of the Missing, National Memorial Cemetery of the Pacific, Honolulu, Hawaii. He was survived by his Wife, Mrs. Thomas Ewing Crowley, 1109 South Citrus, Los Angeles, California. The USS Crowley (DE-303) was named in his honor. The USS Crowley received five battle stars for her World War II service.[180]

Cruz, Henry Mesa Mess Attendant, First Class, Serial No. 421 03 83, US Navy. Henry was born December 24, 1920 in Agana Guam the eldest of twelve children born to Jose C. and Andrea M. Cruz. He enlisted in the US Navy February 1, 1939 in Guam and reported for duty on the USS Argonne in May 1939 where he served until he was transferred to the USS Arizona on February 2, 1940. Henry was serving on the Arizona December 7, 1941 when the Japanese attacked Pearl Harbor. After the attack, Henry was transferred to the USS Dobbin (AD-3) for duty. Henry died on March 12, 2012 in Chula Vista, California and is buried at the Miramar National Cemetery in San Diego, California.

Culp, Donald Arthur Seaman, Second Class, Serial No. 393 56 21, US Navy. Donald was born October 5, 1922 in Richland, Washington to Charles Frederick and Gladys Juanita (Rahier) Culp. He enlisted in the US Navy June 19, 1941 in Portland, Oregon and completed his basic training at the Naval Training Station in San Diego, California. He reported for duty on the USS Arizona August 29, 1941. He was serving on the Arizona December 7, 1941 when the Japanese attacked Pearl Harbor. Donald died on December 18, 1944 while serving on board the USS Monaghan (DD-354) when his ship was caught up in typhoon "Cobra", rolled to starboard and sunk. There were only six survivors. Donald was among one of the missing, and was declared dead. He was lost at sea and is commemorated on the Memorial Tablets of the Missing, Fort William McKinley, Manila, Philippines. Donald was survived by his Wife, Mrs. Ruth Marie K. Culp of Grandview, Washington.

Curry, William Joseph Watertender, Second Class, Serial No: 341 95 61, US Navy. William was born in about 1910 to Johnson and Martha Belle (Carson) Curry. He enlisted in the US Navy on January 10, 1936 in Kansas City, Missouri. He transferred from the USS Henderson to the USS Arizona on March 20, 1941. William was killed in action on December 7, 1941 in Pearl Harbor, Hawaii. He was awarded the American Defense Service Medal, World War II Victory Medal and Purple Heart Medal posthumously. William remains on duty on the USS Arizona. He is commemorated on the USS Arizona Memorial and the Memorial Tablets of the

---

[180] Thomas Ewing Crowley, Photo from California Honor States.

Missing, National Memorial Cemetery of the Pacific, Honolulu, Hawaii. William was survived by his Wife, Mrs. Aletha Mae Curry, 133 NW 18th Avenue, Portland, Oregon.

Curtis, Lloyd B. Seaman, First Class, Serial No: 382 29 64, US Navy. Lloyd was born December 10, 1919 to Maurice B. Curtis and Hattie Pearl (Choplin) Curtis of Elk Fork, Missouri. He enlisted in the US Navy on November 1, 1940 in Los Angeles, California and completed his basic training at the Naval Training Station in San Diego, California. Lloyd reported for duty on the USS Arizona on December 30, 1940. He was killed in action on December 7, 1941 in Pearl Harbor, Hawaii. Lloyd was awarded the American Defense Service Medal, World War II Victory Medal and Purple Heart Medal posthumously. He remains on duty on the USS Arizona. Lloyd is commemorated on the USS Arizona Memorial and the Memorial Tablets of the Missing, National Memorial Cemetery of the Pacific, Honolulu, Hawaii. He was survived by his Father, Mr. Maurice B. Curtis, Route 2, Green Ridge, Missouri.[181]

Curtis, Lyle Carl Radioman, Second Class, Serial No: 328 48 60, US Navy. Lyle was born in October 1918 in Blenker, Wisconsin to Ralph George and Lilian Ethelyn (Andress) Curtis. He enlisted in the US Navy on September 14, 1937 in Minneapolis, Minnesota and completed his basic training at the Naval Training Station in Great Lakes, Illinois. Lyle transferred from the USS California to the USS Arizona on August 26, 1941. He was killed in action on December 7, 1941 in Pearl Harbor, Hawaii. Lyle was awarded the American Defense Service Medal, World War II Victory Medal and Purple Heart Medal posthumously. He remains on duty on the USS Arizona. Lyle is commemorated on the USS Arizona Memorial and the Memorial Tablets of the Missing, National Memorial Cemetery of the Pacific, Honolulu, Hawaii. He was survived by his Father, Mr. Ralph George Curtis, Glidden, Wisconsin.[182]

Cybulski, Harold Bernard Seaman, First Class, Serial No: 382 10 05, US Navy. Harold was born January 10, 1921 in Alameda County, California to Max Joseph Cybulski and Josephine Dorothy (Buczynsk) Cybulski. He enlisted in the US Navy on June 15, 1939 in Los Angeles, California and completed his basic training at the Naval Training Station in San Diego, California. He reported for duty on the USS Arizona on September 11, 1939. Harold was killed in action on December 7, 1941 in Pearl Harbor, Hawaii. He was awarded the American Defense Service Medal, World War II Victory Medal and Purple Heart Medal posthumously. Harold remains on duty on the USS Arizona. He is commemorated on the USS Arizona Memorial and the Memorial Tablets of the Missing, National Memorial Cemetery of the Pacific, Honolulu, Hawaii. Harold was survived by his Mother, Mrs. Josephine Dorothy Stamas, 1537 Yale Street, Santa Monica, California.[183]

---

[181] Lloyd B. Curtis, Information provided by family member, Thomas Crump.
[182] Lyle Carl Curtis, Photo provided by family member, Linda Curtis
[183] Harold Bernard Cybulski, Photo from the 1937 University High School Yearbook, Los Angeles, California.

Cychosz, Francis Anton Seaman, First Class, Serial No: 300 19 57, US Navy. Francis was born July 2, 1923 in Bessemer, Michigan to Henry and Josephine M. (Strelcheck) Cychosz. *His father was killed at the age of 27 on August 22, 1923 when Francis was just six weeks old when the truck he was driving was struck by a Soo Line freight train.* He enlisted in the US Navy on October 8, 1940 in Chicago, Illinois and completed his basic training at the Naval Training Station in Great Lakes, Illinois. Francis reported for duty on the USS Arizona on December 9, 1940. He was killed in action on December 7, 1941 in Pearl Harbor, Hawaii. Francis was awarded the American Defense Service Medal, World War II Victory Medal and Purple Heart Medal posthumously. He remains on duty on the USS Arizona. Francis is commemorated on the USS Arizona Memorial and the Memorial Tablets of the Missing, National Memorial Cemetery of the Pacific, Honolulu, Hawaii. He was survived by his Mother, Mrs. Josephine Cychosz, 217 West Iron Street, Bessemer, Michigan.[184]

Czarnecki, Anthony Francis Machinist's Mate, First Class, Serial No. 311 14 02, US Navy. Anthony was born on February 7, 1915 in Roger City, Michigan, son of Martin Czarnecki. He enlisted in the US Navy October 14, 1935 in Detroit, Michigan and completed his basic training at the Naval Training Station in Great Lakes, Illinois. He reported for duty on the USS Arizona February 8, 1936. He was serving on December 7, 1941 when the Japanese attacked Pearl Harbor. He went on to serve on the USS Bagley. His brother, Stanley Czarnecki, also serving on the USS Arizona was killed in action during the attack. Stanley died on January 2, 2004 in Michigan and is commemorated at Woodland Cemetery, Jackson, Michigan. Anthony joined his brother on the Arizona. His ashes were interred on the USS Arizona December 7, 2004.

Czarnecki, Stanley Fireman, First Class, Serial No: 311 38 90, US Navy. Stanley was born in 1919 to Martin Czarnecki and Vasonaca Czarnecki of Blackman, Michigan. He enlisted in the US Navy on December 18, 1939 in Detroit, Michigan and reported for duty on the USS Arizona on May 21, 1940. Stanley was killed in action on December 7, 1941 in Pearl Harbor, Hawaii. He was awarded the American Defense Service Medal, World War II Victory Medal and Purple Heart Medal posthumously. Stanley remains on duty on the USS Arizona. He is commemorated on the USS Arizona Memorial and the Memorial Tablets of the Missing, National Memorial Cemetery of the Pacific, Honolulu, Hawaii. Stanley was survived by his Father, Mr. Martin Czarnecki, 2353 Clark Drive, Jackson, Michigan and his brother, Anthony Francis Czarnecki who was also serving on boar the USS Arizona and survived.[185]

---

[184] Francis Anton Cychosz, Photo and information provided by his first-cousin, Christine R. Shaw.
[185] Stanley Czarnecki, Photo from Michigan Honor States.

Czekajski, Theophil "Phil" Signalman, Third Class, Serial No: 411 09 48, US Navy Reserve. Theophil was born in about 1922 in Windber, Pennsylvania to Marcin and Zofia (Popek) Czekajski. He enlisted in the US Navy on October 5, 1940 in Detroit, Michigan and completed his basic training at the Naval Training Station in Great Lakes, Illinois. He reported for duty on the USS Arizona on March 6, 1941. Theophil was killed in action on December 7, 1941 in Pearl Harbor, Hawaii. He was awarded the American Defense Service Medal, World War II Victory Medal and Purple Heart Medal posthumously. Theophil remains on duty on the USS Arizona. He is commemorated on the USS Arizona Memorial and the Memorial Tablets of the Missing, National Memorial Cemetery of the Pacific, Honolulu, Hawaii. Thoephil was survived by his Mother, Mrs. Sophia Czekajski, 6479 Debuel Street, Detroit, Michigan.

Dahlheimer, Richard Norbert Seaman, First Class, Serial No: 328 64 65, US Navy. Richard was born on December 29, 1921 in Minnesota to William Joseph and Alice Mary (Anfang) Dahlheimer. He enlisted in the US Navy on January 16, 1940 in Minneapolis, Minnesota and completed his basic training at the Naval Training Station in Great Lakes, Illinois. Richard reported for duty on the USS Arizona on March 26, 1940. He was killed in action on December 7, 1941 in Pearl Harbor, Hawaii. Richard was awarded the American Defense Service Medal, World War II Victory Medal and Purple Heart Medal posthumously. He remains on duty on the USS Arizona. Richard is commemorated on the USS Arizona Memorial and the Memorial Tablets of the Missing, National Memorial Cemetery of the Pacific, Honolulu, Hawaii. He was survived by his Father, Mr. William Dahlheimer, Rogers, Minnesota.

Daniel, Alfred Eugene Gunner's Mate, First Class, Serial No. 336 85 25, US Navy. Alfred was born October 28, 1912 in Murphysboro, Illinois to William R. and Catherine Mary (Katzmark) Daniel. He enlisted in the US Navy October 15, 1935 in St. Louis, Missouri and completed his basic training at the Naval Training Station in Great Lakes, Illinois. He reported for duty on the USS Arizona February 8, 1936. Alfred survived the attack by being on Christmas leave and on the way home on December 7, 1941 when the Japanese attacked Pearl Harbor. Alfred was transferred to salvage work on the USS Utah and received the Navy and Marine Corps medal for his actions:

"The President of the United States of America Takes Pleasure in presenting the Navy and Marine Corps Medal to Chief Gunner's Mate Alfred Eugene Daniel, United States Navy, for meritorious conduct and outstanding performance of duty while voluntarily engaged in diving operations incident to the salvage of vessels damaged by enemy action at Pearl Harbor on 7 December 1941. During the extraordinarily hazardous conditions inside submerged vessels totaling well over 100 hours of successful under water work, his individual efforts contributed in a large measure to the success of the diving phase of these operations and were in keeping with the highest traditions of the United States Naval Service."

On May 13, 1944 he was appointed Ensign while serving on board the USS Takanis Bay (CVE-89). Alfred served 20 years in the US Navy and was a veteran of World War II and the Korean War. He died September 25, 1990 in Murphysboro, Illinois and is buried in Saint Andrews Cemetery, Murphysboro, Illinois.[186]

---

[186] Alfred Eugene Daniel, Photo provided by C. Ann Carruthers.

Daniel, Lloyd Maxton   Yeoman, First Class, Serial No: 368 29 27, US Navy. Lloyd was born March 21, 1916 in Murray, Iowa to Lloyd L. and Ruby Daniel. He enlisted in the US Navy on January 17, 1935 in Salt Lake City, Utah and reported for duty on the USS Arizona December 19, 1938. He was killed in action on December 7, 1941 in Pearl Harbor, Hawaii. Lloyd was awarded the American Defense Service Medal, World War II Victory Medal and Purple Heart Medal posthumously. He remains on duty on the USS Arizona. Lloyd is commemorated on the USS Arizona Memorial and the Memorial Tablets of the Missing, National Memorial Cemetery of the Pacific, Honolulu, Hawaii and Mountain View Cemetery, Big Timber, Montana. He was survived by his Wife, Mrs. Hazel Lilian Daniel, 108 East Lewis Street, Livingston, Montana.[187]

Danik, Andrew Joseph   Seaman, Second Class, Serial No: 283 41 79, US Navy. Andrew was born in 1921 in Pennsylvania to John and Magdolin "Maggie" (Lazor) Danik. He enlisted in the US Navy on October 16, 1940 in Cleveland, Ohio and completed his basic training at the Naval Training Station in Great Lakes, Illinois. He reported for duty on the USS Arizona on December 9, 1940. Andrew was killed in action on December 7, 1941 in Pearl Harbor, Hawaii. He was awarded the American Defense Service Medal, World War II Victory Medal and Purple Heart Medal posthumously. Andrew remains on duty on the USS Arizona. He is commemorated on the USS Arizona Memorial and the Memorial Tablets of the Missing, National Memorial Cemetery of the Pacific, Honolulu, Hawaii. Andrew was survived by his Father, Mr. John Danik, 704 Amherest Street, Akron, Ohio.[188]

Darch, Phillip Zane   Seaman, First Class, Serial No: 201 72 85, US Navy. Phillip was born in October 27, 1921 in Watertown, Massachusetts to Phillip James and Lucy Myrtle (Robinson) Darch of Watertown, Massachusetts. He enlisted in the US Navy on April 23, 1940 in Boston, Massachusetts and completed his basic training at the Naval Training Station in Norfolk, Virginia. Phillip reported for duty on the USS Arizona on September 30, 1940. He was killed in action on December 7, 1941 in Pearl Harbor, Hawaii. Phillip was awarded the American Defense Service Medal, World War II Victory Medal and Purple Heart Medal posthumously. He remains on duty on the USS Arizona. Phillip is commemorated on the USS Arizona Memorial and the Memorial Tablets of the Missing, National Memorial Cemetery of the Pacific, Honolulu, Hawaii. He was survived by his Father, Mr. Phillip J. Darch, 43 Irving Street, Watertown, Boston, Massachusetts and two sisters.[189]

---

[187] Lloyd Maxton Daniel, Photo from Montana Honor Sites., information Great Falls Tribune of Great Falls, Montana
[188] Andrew Joseph Danik, Photo from The Akron Beacon Journal, Akron, Ohio, July 16, 1942, Page 15.
[189] Phillip Zane Darch, Photo provided by his great-nephew, Barry Brown.

Dare, James Ashton Ensign, Serial No. 0-06310, US Navy. James was born December 5, 1915 in Washington State. He was commissioned in the US Navy June 1, 1939 and was serving as Watch and Division Officer on the USS Arizona where he was serving on December 7, 1941 when the Japanese attacked Pearl Harbor. His battle station was Turret II. He later served on board the USS Maryland during World War II. James served as commander of the USS Douglas H. Fox (DD-779 during the Korean War and was awarded the Bronze Star Medal with Combat "V" for meritorious service. He also served on board the USS Compass Island (EAG-153). During the Dominican Crisis he was serving as Commander Amphibious Squadron TEN and commanded the Caribbean Ready Group which landed at Santo Domingo, Dominican Republic and was awarded the Legion of Merit with Combat "V" for exceptionally meritorious service. James attained the rank of Rear Admiral in 1967. He died June 1, 1988 in San Diego, California.[190]

Daugherty, Paul Eugene Electrician's Mate, Third Class, Serial No: 279 65 51, US Navy. Paul was born August 7, 1918 in Congo, Ohio. He was a graduate of St. Wendelin High School, where he played football, baseball and basketball. Paul also participated in the Senior Class Play where he played the leading role. He attended Assumption College in Ontario for two years. Paul enlisted in the US Navy on January 23, 1940 in Cincinnati, Ohio and completed his basic training at the Naval Training Station in Great Lakes, Illinois. He reported for duty on the USS Arizona on March 26, 1940. Paul was killed in action on December 7, 1941 in Pearl Harbor, Hawaii. He was awarded the American Defense Service Medal, World War II Victory Medal and Purple Heart Medal posthumously. Paul remains on duty on the USS Arizona. He is commemorated on the USS Arizona Memorial and the Memorial Tablets of the Missing, National Memorial Cemetery of the Pacific, Honolulu, Hawaii. Paul was survived by his Father, Mr. Lawrence Daugherty, 411 East Tiffin Street, Fostoria, Ohio. Lake Daugherty was named in honor of Paul. The Daugherty Lake is a reservoir in Hancock County, Ohio.[191]

Davis, Carl Everette Gunner's Mate, Third Class, Serial No. 287 36 27, US Navy. Carl enlisted in the US Navy January 17, 1940 in Louisville, Kentucky and completed his basic training at the Naval Training Station in Great Lakes, Illinois. He reported for duty on the USS Arizona March 26, 1940. He was serving on the Arizona December 7, 1941 when the Japanese attacked Pearl Harbor. After the attack, Carl was transferred to the Fleet Machine-gun School for duty.

---

[190] James Ashton Dare, Photo Lucky Bag Yearbook, United States Naval Academy, Annapolis, MD, class of 1939.

[191] Paul Eugene Daugherty, Photo from The Froslin Yearbook, Saint Wendelin High School, Fostoria, Ohio, 1936.

Davis, Elvin Clay   Seaman, First Class, Serial No. 382 41 43, US Navy. Elvin was born on January 16, 1918 in Tennessee to Willie Dillard and Blanche (Nixon) Davis. He enlisted in the US Navy October 4, 1940 in Nashville, Tennessee and completed his basic training at the Naval Training Station in Norfolk, Virginia. He reported for duty on the USS Arizona December 4, 1940. Elvin was serving on the Arizona December 7, 1941 when the Japanese attacked Pearl Harbor. He was shooting craps the night before the bombing and had won a few dollars. The money was somewhere close by his bunk. When the bomb went off, he scooped up what he could and stuffed the money down his pants. The family still has one of the two dollar bills, stained with diesel fuel. He later went on to serve on the USS Lexington (CV-2), USS Thomas Stone, US Naval Station in Oran, Africa, the Naval Air Station, Patuxent River, Maryland and the USS Oberon. Elvin served over 30 years until February of 1961 having served in the Korean and the Vietnam wars in addition to World War II. He was awarded the American Defense Medal, American Theater Medal, Good Conduct Medal, Asiatic Pacific Campaign Medal with two stars, European African Middle Eastern Medal with one star, World War II Victory Medal, Navy Occupation European and the National Defense Medal. Elvin died on April 14, 1985 in Lafayette, Tennessee and is buried in the Smith Chapel Cemetery, Red Boiling Springs, Tennessee.[192]

Davis, John Quitman   Seaman, First Class, Serial No: 274 48 43, US Navy. John was born September 15, 1921 in Tangipahoa, Louisiana to Perry Quitman and Lady Velma (Varnado) Davis. He enlisted in the US Navy on July 30, 1940 in New Orleans, Louisiana and completed his basic training at the Naval Training Station in San Diego, California. He reported for duty on the USS Arizona on October 14, 1940. John was killed in action on December 7, 1941 in Pearl Harbor, Hawaii. He was awarded the American Defense Service Medal, World War II Victory Medal and Purple Heart Medal posthumously. John remains on duty on the USS Arizona. He is commemorated on the USS Arizona Memorial and the Memorial Tablets of the Missing, National Memorial Cemetery of the Pacific, Honolulu, Hawaii. John was survived by his Father, Mr. Perry Quitman Davis, Tangipahoa, Louisiana.[193]

Davis, Milton Henry   Seaman, First Class, Serial No: 342 15 11, US Navy. Milton was born on March 4, 1920 in Hanover, Kansas to John Franklin and Martha Lucinda (Alkire) Hidy. He graduated from Holton High School, Jackson Co., Kansas in 1939. Milton enlisted in the US Navy on November 7, 1939 in Kansas City, Missouri and completed his basic training at the Naval Training Station in Great Lakes, Illinois. He reported for duty on the USS Arizona on February 10, 1940. Milton was killed in action on December 7, 1941 in Pearl Harbor, Hawaii. He was awarded the American Defense Service Medal, World War II Victory Medal and Purple Heart Medal posthumously. Milton remains on duty on the USS Arizona. He is commemorated on the USS Arizona Memorial and the Memorial Tablets of the Missing, National Memorial Cemetery of the Pacific, Honolulu, Hawaii and Holton Cemetery, Jackson County, Kansas.

---

[192] Elvin Clay Davis, Information and photo provided by his son, Chuck Davis.

[193] John Quitman Davis, Photo from Louisiana Honor States and information provided by family member, Brian Davis.

Milton was survived by his Foster-father, Mr. Walter F. Davis, 100 Lincoln Street, Holton, Kansas.

Davis, Murle Melvin Radioman, Second Class, Serial No: 283 23 66, US Navy Reserve. Murle was born in about 1917 in Ohio to Raymond Thomas and Louisa Davis. He enlisted in the US Navy on May 3, 1938 in Cleveland, Ohio. He transferred from the USS Maryland to the USS Arizona on March 29, 1940. Murle was killed in action on December 7, 1941 in Pearl Harbor, Hawaii. He was awarded the American Defense Service Medal, World War II Victory Medal and Purple Heart Medal posthumously. Murle remains on duty on the USS Arizona. He is commemorated on the USS Arizona Memorial and the Memorial Tablets of the Missing, National Memorial Cemetery of the Pacific, Honolulu, Hawaii. Murle was survived by his Father, Mr. Raymond Thomas Davis, 537 Wherle Avenue, Newark, Ohio.[194]

Davis, Myrle Clarence Fireman, Third Class, Serial No: 321 49 13, US Navy. Myrle was born November 20, 1920 in Boyer Valley Township, Sac County, Iowa to Harold Elwood and Ida Gladys (Maxson) Davis. He enlisted in the US Navy on October 15, 1940 in Des Moines, Iowa and completed his basic training at the Naval Training Station in Great Lakes, Illinois. He reported for duty on the USS Arizona on December 9, 1940. Myrle was killed in action on December 7, 1941 in Pearl Harbor, Hawaii. He was awarded the American Defense Service Medal, World War II Victory Medal and Purple Heart Medal posthumously. Myrtle remains on duty on the USS Arizona. He is commemorated on the USS Arizona Memorial and the Memorial Tablets of the Missing, National Memorial Cemetery of the Pacific, Honolulu, Hawaii. Myrle was survived by his Father, Mr. Harold E. Davis, 1104 Duncombe Street, Sac City, Iowa.[195]

Davis, Thomas Ray Shipfitter, First Class, Serial No: 261 25 70, US Navy. Thomas was born November 17, 1904 in Davie, North Carolina to William Absolom and Jennie Eucracia (Miller) Davis. He enlisted in the US Navy on September 13, 1932 in San Pedro, California. He re-enlisted in the US Navy on September 13, 1939. Thomas served on the Arizona from September 18, 1937 until he was killed in action on December 7, 1941 in Pearl Harbor, Hawaii. He was awarded the American Defense Service Medal, World War II Victory Medal and Purple Heart Medal posthumously. Thomas remains on duty on the USS Arizona. He is commemorated on the USS Arizona Memorial and the Memorial Tablets of the Missing, National Memorial Cemetery of the Pacific, Honolulu, Hawaii. Thomas was survived by his Wife, Mrs. Gertrude Mary Davis, 2190 Maine Avenue, Long Beach, California.[196]

---

[194] Murle Melvin Davis, Photo taken from The Reveille, Newark High School, Newark, Ohio, 1937.
[195] Myrle Clarence Davis, Photo provided by family member, Edna Rolston.
[196] Thomas Ray Davis, Photo provided by family member, Judy Hildebrand.

Davis, Walter Mindred Fireman, Second Class, Serial No: 337 41 37, US Navy. Walter was born in about 1920 in Missouri to Clarence R. and Irene Davis. He enlisted in the US Navy on October 15, 1940 in St. Louis, Missouri and completed his basic training at the Naval Training Station in Great Lakes, Illinois. He reported for duty on the USS Arizona on December 9, 1940. Walter was killed in action on December 7, 1941 in Pearl Harbor, Hawaii. He was awarded the American Defense Service Medal, World War II Victory Medal and Purple Heart Medal posthumously. Walter remains on duty on the USS Arizona. He is commemorated on the USS Arizona Memorial and the Memorial Tablets of the Missing, National Memorial Cemetery of the Pacific, Honolulu, Hawaii. Walter was survived by his Father, Mr. Clarence R. Davis, Route 5, Fulton, Missouri.

Davison, Henry "Hank" Donald Ensign, Serial No. 0-06956, US Navy. Henry was born on April 5, 1916 in Arkansas. He was commissioned officer in the US Navy serving on the USS Arizona as Watch and Junior Division 3 Officer on December 7, 1941 when the Japanese attacked Pearl Harbor. Henry had the 8-12 deck watch on that fateful morning.

"It was just before colors, in fact, I had already sent the messenger down to make the 8 o'clock reports to the Captain. Then I heard a dive bomber attack from overhead. I looked through my spyglass and saw the red dots on the wings. That made me wonder, but I still couldn't believe it until I saw some bombs falling. The first one hit up by the air station. I sounded the air raid alarm and notified the Captain. The Captain and Lt. Comdr. Fuqua came on deck, and the Captain went on up to the bridge. Mr. Fuqua told me to sound General Quarters. About that time we took a bomb hit on the starboard side of the quarterdeck, just about abreast of No. 4 turret. We grabbed the men available and started dropping the deck hatches and leading out hoses on the quarterdeck. About this time, the planes that had made the initial dive bomb attack strafed the ship. Mr. Fuqua and I told all hands to get in the marine compartment. It was reported to us that we had a bomb in the executive officers' office. Mr. Fuqua told me to call the center engine room and get pressure on the fire mains. Then he went up to the boat deck. I told the Boatswain's mate of the watch to do that. Then I went into the O.D.'s booth to do it myself. Just after I stepped in the booth we took another hit which seemed to be on the starboard side of the quarterdeck just about frame 88. The Boatswain's mate and I were trapped in the booth by the flames. We started out of the booth, trying to run through the flames aft on the quarterdeck. We couldn't get through so we went over the lifeline into the water. I was conscious of a sweetish, sickening smell to the flame. After I got in the water, my first intention was to go to the key and then onto the quarterdeck or swim to the gangway and get aboard. But after I took one look at the ship, I decided that it was useless, she had settled down by the bow, and appeared broken in two. The foremast was toppled over; she was a mass of flames from the forecastle to just forward of turret 3. I was helped into a motor launch by Ensign Bush and another man. Then we in turn took the motor launch and picked up as many survivors as we could find in the water. We took them over to the landing at Ford Island. There we were met by Air Station Marines, who helped us get the wounded ashore. After we had unloaded the motor launch Ensign Bush and I took the barge, which had come up and took it back over alongside the quarterdeck where we gathered another load of injured. On our return to Ford Island, we noticed three more boats alongside the Arizona, so we proceeded to the air raid shelter. Then I went up to the dispensary for first aid treatment."[197]

Henry was badly burned during the attack and was hospitalized for about three weeks. His father, Mr. William E. Davison, 2110 North Palm Street, Little Rock, Arkansas was notified.

---

[197] Statement of Ensign H.D. Davison, U.S.S. Arizona, Last Action Report.

Henry went on to serve on the USS Craven. He was awarded the Silver Star for his actions in the Battle of Vella Gulf:

"The President of the United States of America takes pleasure in presenting the Silver Star to Lieutenant Henry Donald Davison (NSN: 0-85052), United States Navy, for conspicuous gallantry and intrepidity in action as Executive Officer of the Destroyer U.S.S. Craven (DD-382), in combat against enemy Japanese naval forces during an engagement in Vella Gulf, Solomon Islands, on the night of 6-7 August 1943. Fearlessly and relentlessly tracking hostile surface vessels, Lieutenant Davison supplied vital information to his Commanding Officer and the Gunnery Division with such speed and accuracy that his ship was able to deliver a devastating attack which contributed to the success of our Task Force in sinking one Japanese cruiser and three destroyers during this hazardous engagement. His courage, outstanding efficiency, and untiring devotion to duty were an inspiration to his officers and men and were in keeping with the highest traditions of the United States Naval Service."

Henry retired from the Navy in 1963 with a rank of Commander. He spent the next 21 ½ years as faculty member, Department of Engineering Technology, St. Petersburg Junior College, teaching mathematics, physics, mechanical design, circuit theory, engineering graphics and computer programming. He died on February 19, 1999 in St. Petersburg, Florida and is buried in Memorial Park Cemetery, St. Petersburg, Florida.[198]

Day, William John   Seaman, Second Class, Serial No: 385 89 17, US Navy. William was born September 30, 1920 in Kirkland, Washington to William Franklin and Elizabeth Catherine (McGinnis) Day. He enlisted in the US Navy on August 8, 1940 in Seattle, Washington and completed his basic training at the Naval Training Station in San Diego, California. He reported for duty on the USS Arizona on January 4, 1941. William was killed in action from wounds he received on December 8, 1941 in Honolulu, Hawaii. He was assigned death #232 when his body was recovered on December 10, 1941.[199] He was awarded the American Defense Service Medal, World War II Victory Medal and Purple Heart Medal posthumously. William was buried in Plot A, Row 0, Grave 515, National Memorial Cemetery of the Pacific, Honolulu, Hawaii. He is commemorated on the USS Arizona Memorial. William was survived by his Father, Mr. William Franklin Day, 4100 Aurora Avenue, Seattle, Washington.

---

[198] Henry Donald Davison, Photo from 1940 Lucky Bag Yearbook, United States Naval Academy, Annapolis, Maryland, page 320.
[199] Report of Changes of the USS Arizona for the month ending 31st day of December, 1941, page 51, line 11, William John Day.

De Armoun, Donald Edwin Gunner's Mate, Third Class, Serial No: 375 94 65, US Navy. Donald was born on March 31, 1921 in Fresno, California to William Homer and Rose Minnie (Shubert) DeArmoun. *Donald and his cousin Howard (Sandy) Ibbotson were raised together near Bass Lake, California and were very close. Sandy quit high school just before graduation and joined the Navy in May of 1939.* Donald joined shortly after on June 13, 1939 in San Francisco, California and completed his basic training at the Naval Training Station in San Diego, California. They were both assigned to the USS Arizona. Donald reported for duty on the USS Arizona on September 11, 1939. He was killed in action on December 7, 1941 in Pearl Harbor, Hawaii. Donald was awarded the American Defense Service Medal, World War II Victory Medal and Purple Heart Medal posthumously. He remains on duty on the USS Arizona. Donald is commemorated on the USS Arizona Memorial and the Memorial Tablets of the Missing, National Memorial Cemetery of the Pacific, Honolulu, Hawaii. He was survived by his Mother, Mrs. Rose Minnie DeArmoun, 3043 Washington Avenue, Fresno, California and one brother. *Donald's mother was a widow when her son was killed. She never could talk about her son and never really recovered from losing him.* His cousin, Howard Burt Ibbotson was also killed in action on board the USS Arizona. [200]

De Castro, Vicente Officer's Steward, Serial No: 497 94 69, US Navy. Vicente was born in April 2, 1904 in the Philippine Islands. He re-enlisted in the US Navy on September 3, 1938 in San Pedro, California. He served on board the USS West Virginia (BB-48) from February 17, 1938 until he was transferred to the USS Arizona on June 24, 1940. Vicente was killed in action on December 7, 1941 in Pearl Harbor, Hawaii. He was awarded the American Defense Service Medal, World War II Victory Medal and Purple Heart Medal posthumously. Vicente remains on duty on the USS Arizona. He is commemorated on the USS Arizona Memorial and the Memorial Tablets of the Missing, National Memorial Cemetery of the Pacific, Honolulu, Hawaii. Vicente was survived by his Mother, Mrs. Juana Guitterz, Batangas, Batangas, Philippine Islands.

Dean, Lyle Bernard Coxswain, Serial No: 342 17 16, US Navy. Lyle was born on September 10, 1920 in Kingman, Kansas to William Almon and Effie May (Walck) Dean. He enlisted in the US Navy on December 27, 1939 in Kansas City, Missouri and completed his basic training at the Naval Training Station in Great Lakes, Illinois. Lyle reported for duty on the USS Arizona on March 23, 1940. He was killed in action on December 7, 1941 in Pearl Harbor, Hawaii. Lyle was awarded the American Defense Service Medal, World War II Victory Medal and Purple Heart Medal posthumously. He remains on duty on the USS Arizona. Lyle is commemorated on the USS Arizona Memorial and the Memorial Tablets of the Missing, National Memorial Cemetery of the Pacific, Honolulu, Hawaii. He was survived by his Mother, Mrs. Effie Dean, 132 Pine Street, Kingman, Kansas.[201]

---

[200] Information and Photo on Donald Edwin DeArmoun provided by family member, Betty McPherson.
[201] Lyle Bernard Dean, Family information provided by family member, David Dillman.

Dean, William Ernest Boatswain's Mate, First Class, 6th and 1st Division, Serial No. 385 62 60, US Navy. William was born August 5, 1917 in Hoquiam, Grays Harbor, Washington to Joseph Carl and Mildred Ester (Wimer) Dean. He enlisted in the US Navy August 2, 1940 and reported for duty on the USS Arizona January 23, 1941. He was serving on the Arizona December 7, 1941 when the Japanese attacked Pearl Harbor. He was on liberty the morning of the 7th. William had spent the night of the 6th at the YMCA. He was awakened early on the 7th to the drone of low-flying planes, exploding shells and plaster falling from the overhead. From the YMCA, he and other sailors crammed into cabs and were sped to the Navy Exchange Building. Here, an Emergency Survivor Office had been set up. William was given duty on a motor launch for that day, to relay messages between locations on the harbor to the ships; to pull bodies from the water and anything else that needed doing. Temporarily stationed on the USS Tennessee, he applied for duty on the USS J. Franklin Bell and was transferred. William retired from the Navy in 1956 achieving a rank of Commander. He died on January 14, 1996 in Tacoma, Washington.

Dearing, John "Jack" Davis Watertender, Second Class, Serial No. 282 93 18, US Navy. John was born April 20, 1911 to John and Edna Pearl (Arter) Dearing. He enlisted in the US Navy in 1928 at age 17. According to his sister, Jack was quite spirited and it was either the service or reform school. He had been serving on the USS Arizona from August 12, 1932 until December 7, 1941 when the Japanese attacked and sunk the Arizona at Pearl Harbor. On the morning of the 7th Jack was on a weekend pass with his wife. He went on to serve on the USS Honolulu (CL-48) until November of 1943. John also served on board the USS Sitkoh Bay (CVE-86) from March of 1944 until June of 1945. He died April 16, 2003 in Walnut Creek, California.[202]

Decker, Deward Coxswain, Serial No. 287 36 24, US Navy. Deward was born on January 12, 1919 in Grayson County, Kentucky the son of Bertie Decker and Icy Woodcock Decker. He enlisted in the US Navy January 16, 1940 in Louisville, Kentucky and completed his basic training at the Naval Training Station in Great Lakes, Illinois. He reported for duty on the USS Arizona March 26, 1940. Deward was serving on the Arizona December 7, 1941 when the Japanese attacked Pearl Harbor. After the attack, Deward was transferred to Bishops Point for duty. Deward died on May 12, 1977 in Caneyville, Kentucky.[203]

Deritis, Russell Edwin Seaman, First Class, Serial No: 385 86 62, US Navy. Russell was born in about 1923 in Pennsylvania to Anthony and Elvira DeRitis. He enlisted in the US Navy on April 10, 1940 in Seattle, Washington and completed his basic training at the Naval

---

[202] John "Jack" Davis Dearing, Photo provided by family member, Alan Gould, story provided by family member, Betty Dovenbarger.
[203] Deward Decker, information and photo provided by family member, Sharon Garwood.

Training Station in San Diego, California. He reported for duty on the USS Arizona on July 2, 1940. Russell was killed in action on December 7, 1941 in Pearl Harbor, Hawaii. He was awarded the American Defense Service Medal, World War II Victory Medal and Purple Heart Medal posthumously. Russell remains on duty on the USS Arizona. He is commemorated on the USS Arizona Memorial and the Memorial Tablets of the Missing, National Memorial Cemetery of the Pacific, Honolulu, Hawaii. Russell was survived by his Guardian, Mr. Aldon Deritis, 8048 East C Street, Tacoma, Washington. The DeRitis Playground in Philadelphia, Pennsylvania is named in his honor.

Deserano, Joseph Charles   Molder, First Class, Serial No. 392 93 74, US Navy. Joseph was born on May 12, 1910. He enlisted in the US Navy July 1, 1935 and reported for duty on the USS Arizona February 11, 1938. Joseph was serving on the Arizona December 7, 1941 when the Japanese attacked Pearl Harbor. He was transferred to the USS Argonne (AG-31) after the attack. He went on to serve on board the USS Essex (CV-9) until June of 1944. Joseph died on April 9, 1969 in Bremerton, Oregon and is buried in Section S, Site 3000, Willamette National Cemetery, Portland, Oregon

De Witt, John James   Coxswain, Serial No: 346 80 81, US Navy. John was born on February 19, 1920 in Hilleman, Arkansas to Onley and Louella (Doss) Dewitt. He enlisted in the US Navy on June 7, 1940 in Little Rock, Arkansas and completed his basic training at the Naval Training Station in San Diego, California. John reported for duty on the USS Arizona on October 8, 1940. He was killed in action on December 7, 1941 in Pearl Harbor, Hawaii. John was awarded the American Defense Service Medal, World War II Victory Medal and Purple Heart Medal posthumously. He remains on duty on the USS Arizona. John is commemorated on the USS Arizona Memorial and the Memorial Tablets of the Missing, National Memorial Cemetery of the Pacific, Honolulu, Hawaii. He was survived by his Father, Mr. Onley DeWitt, Hilleman, Arkansas.

Dial, John Buchanan   Seaman, First Class, Serial No: 274 49 13, US Navy. John was born in about 1921 in Mississippi to Christopher Columbus and Rachel K. (Butler) Dial. He enlisted in the US Navy on August 9, 1940 in New Orleans, Louisiana and completed his basic training at the Naval Training Station in San Diego, California. He reported for duty on the USS Arizona on October 8, 1940. John was killed in action on December 7, 1941 in Pearl Harbor, Hawaii. He was awarded the American Defense Service Medal, World War II Victory Medal and Purple Heart Medal posthumously. John remains on duty on the USS Arizona. He is commemorated on the USS Arizona Memorial and the Memorial Tablets of the Missing, National Memorial Cemetery of the Pacific, Honolulu, Hawaii. John was survived by his Father, Mr. Christopher C. Dial, 1403 River Avenue, Hattiesburg, Mississippi.

Dick, Ralph R. Gunner's Mate, First Class, Serial No: 271 82 62, US Navy. Ralph was born April 15, 1904 in Midland City, Alabama to Charlie Harrison and Lila E (Clements) Dick. He enlisted in the US Navy December 11, 1935 in San Pedro, California. He re-enlisted December 9, 1939. Ralph served on the USS Arizona from August 26, 1938 until he was killed in action on December 7, 1941 in Pearl Harbor, Hawaii. He was awarded the American Defense Service Medal, World War II Victory Medal and Purple Heart Medal posthumously. Ralph remains on duty on the USS Arizona. He is commemorated on the USS Arizona Memorial and Memorial Tablets of the Missing, National Memorial Cemetery of the Pacific, Honolulu, Hawaii. Ralph was survived by his Wife, Mrs. Charlotte Gregory Dick, 236 East 12th Street, Long Beach, California.

Dickerson, William Charles A. Radioman, Second Class, Aviation Unit (VO-1), Serial No. 337 06 28, US Navy. William was born in 1915 in Tennessee. He enlisted in the US Navy April 12, 1938 in Springfield, Illinois and reported for duty on the USS Arizona December 13, 1938. William was serving on the USS Arizona on December 7, 1941 when the Japanese attacked Pearl Harbor. After the attack, he was taken on board the USS Tennessee and then later transferred to the Naval Station, Pearl Harbor for further assignment. In June 1942 he was transferred to Scouting Squad One. In May 1944, he was being transferred from Navy 129 to the Naval Hospital, West Coast, for treatment.

Dickinson, Merle Edward Gunner's Mate, Third Class, Serial No. 321 39 44, US Navy. Merle was born March 9, 1919 in Brighton, Iowa the son of Cy B. and Ethel B. Dickinson. He enlisted in the US Navy March 6, 1940 in Des Moines, Iowa and reported for duty on the USS Arizona July 12, 1940. Merle was serving on the Arizona December 7, 1941 when the Japanese attacked Pearl Harbor. He went through a port hole and swam to Ford Island. Merle didn't talk about it much except to say that the water was on fire and there were dead bodies everywhere. This affected him all his life. After the attack, Merle was transferred to the USS Tennessee for duty. He served until March 13, 1946. Merle died July 23, 1973 in Brighton, Iowa and was buried at the Hillcrest Cemetery, Brighton, Iowa.

Dine, John George Fireman, Second Class, Serial No: 376 14 91, US Navy. John was born October 30, 1922 in Fresno, California to Henry and Maggie (Nickle) Dine. He enlisted in the US Navy on October 31, 1940 in San Francisco, California and completed his basic training at the Naval Training Station in San Diego, California. John reported for duty on the USS Arizona on December 30, 1940. He was killed in action on December 7, 1941 in Pearl Harbor, Hawaii. John was awarded the American Defense Service Medal, World War II Victory Medal and Purple Heart Medal posthumously. He remains on duty on the USS Arizona. John is commemorated on the USS Arizona Memorial and the Memorial Tablets of the Missing, National Memorial Cemetery of the Pacific, Honolulu, Hawaii. He was survived by his Father, Mr. Henry Dine, 2251 Cherry Street, Fresno, California.[204]

---

[204] John George Dine, Photo provided by David Dunnavant.

Dineen, Robert Joseph   Seaman, First Class, Serial No: 234 24 63, US Navy. Robert was born October 3, 1919 in Susquehanna, Pennsylvania to John Joseph and Loretta (Kane) Dineen. His mother died just before his 7th birthday. He enlisted in the US Navy on April 24, 1940 in Buffalo, New York and completed his basic training at the Naval Training Station in Newport, Rhode Island. Robert reported for duty on the USS Arizona on January 4, 1941. He was killed in action on December 7, 1941 in Pearl Harbor, Hawaii. Robert was awarded the American Defense Service Medal, World War II Victory Medal and Purple Heart Medal posthumously. He remains on duty on the USS Arizona. Robert is commemorated on the USS Arizona Memorial and the Memorial Tablets of the Missing, National Memorial Cemetery of the Pacific, Honolulu, Hawaii. He was survived by his Father, Mr. John Joseph Dineen, 106 Willow Street, Susquehanna, Pennsylvania. A memorial to Robert hangs in the American Legion Post 440 at Hornell, New York.[205]

Dobey, Milton Paul, Jr.   Seaman, First Class, Serial No: 360 27 19, US Navy. Milton was born December 25, 1921 to Milton Paul and Harriett Dobey of Houston, Texas. He enlisted in the US Navy on November 26, 1940 in Houston, Texas and completed his basic training at the Naval Training Station in San Diego, California. Milton reported for duty on the USS Arizona on January 25, 1941. He was killed in action on December 7, 1941 in Pearl Harbor, Hawaii. Milton was awarded the American Defense Service Medal, World War II Victory Medal and Purple Heart Medal posthumously. He remains on duty on the USS Arizona. Milton is commemorated on the USS Arizona Memorial and the Memorial Tablets of the Missing, National Memorial Cemetery of the Pacific, Honolulu, Hawaii. He was survived by his Father, Mr. Milton Paul Dobey, Sr., 1340 Witter Street, Houston, Texas.

Dobson, Clarence Junior   Gunner's Mate, Third Class, Serial No. 342 17 96, US Navy. Clarence was born on August 21, 1920 in Kansas the Son of Clarence W. and Olive V. Dobson. He enlisted in the US Navy January 9, 1940 in Kansas City, Missouri and completed his basic training at the Naval Training Station in Great Lakes, Illinois. He reported for duty on the USS Arizona March 26, 1940. Clarence was serving on the Arizona December 7, 1941 when the Japanese attacked Pearl Harbor. He was badly burned during the attack and was transferred to the US Naval Hospital at Mare Island, California. Clarence died on March 6, 1990 in Bakersfield, California.

Doherty, George Walter   Seaman, Second Class, Serial No: 376 36 75, US Navy. George was born on April 13, 1921 in Saskatoon, Saskatchewan, Canada. He was the son of George Clarence and Ethel Leola (Cox) Doherty. George enlisted in the US Navy on July 15, 1941 in San Francisco, California and completed his basic training at the Naval Training Station in San Diego, California. He reported for duty on the USS Arizona on September 18, 1941. George was killed in action on December 7, 1941 in Pearl Harbor, Hawaii. He was awarded the American Defense Service Medal, World War II Victory Medal and Purple Heart Medal posthumously. George remains on duty on the USS Arizona. He is commemorated on the USS Arizona Memorial and the Memorial Tablets of the Missing, National Memorial Cemetery of the Pacific, Honolulu, Hawaii. George was survived by his Mother, Mrs. Ethel Lee Doherty Brewer, Ramona Avenue, Route 1, Box 489-C, Monterey, California. His Brother, John Albert was also

---

[205] Robert Joseph Dineen, Photo provided by the Arthur H. Cunningham American Legion Post 440, Hornell, NY.

killed in action on board the USS Arizona. His other Brother John Andrew was among the survivors of the Arizona.

Doherty, John Albert Machinist's Mate, Second Class, Serial No: 368 41 33, US Navy. John was born on March 8, 1919 in Saskatoon, Saskatchewan, Canada. He was the son of George Clarence and Ethel Leola (Cox) Doherty. John enlisted in the US Navy on July 11, 1938 in Salt Lake City, Utah and completed his basic training at the Naval Training Station in San Diego, California. He reported for duty on the USS Arizona on October 23, 1938. John was killed in action on December 7, 1941 in Pearl Harbor, Hawaii. He was awarded the American Defense Service Medal, World War II Victory Medal and Purple Heart Medal posthumously. John remains on duty on the USS Arizona. He is commemorated on the USS Arizona Memorial and the Memorial Tablets of the Missing, National Memorial Cemetery of the Pacific, Honolulu, Hawaii. John was survived by his Mother, Mrs. Ethel Lee Doherty Brewer, Ramona Avenue, Route 1, Box 489-C, Monterey, California. His Brother, George Walter was killed in action on the Arizona. His other Brother, John Andrew, was among the survivors of the Arizona.

Doherty, John Andrew Chief Gunner's Mate, Serial No. 212 08 24, US Navy. John enlisted in the US Navy July 11, 1938 in Salt Lake City, Utah. He served on the USS Arizona from November 4, 1938 until he was wounded in action on December 7, 1941, during the Japanese attack on Pearl Harbor. His official report:

"I was in the chief's quarters when the air raid alarm sounded. At the same time he heard something hit. I went immediately to my battle station which was the A.A. Battery. When I arrived on the boat deck, I saw the forecastle waving up and down and fire and smoke coming up through seams of the deck.

I went to the port side to see if the ammunition hoists were rigged and they were ok. I then went to the starboard side and the crew was rigging no. 1-3 hoist for hoisting ammunition.

I noticed that the no. 3 gun wasn't firing due to safety bearing when the foot firing mechanism cut out. I was then shocked and suddenly surrounded by smoke and flames. I was backing away from the smoke and I can't remember much from then on.

I was in the water and being helped in a boat and from there to a hospital.

Only man dead and I'm not sure was Anderson, BM2c. I think was hit by machine gun bullets."[206]

He went on to serve on the USS Reid. His brothers, George Walter and John Albert were killed in action on board the USS Arizona. John's mother, Mrs. Ethel Doherty Brewer, Ramona Avenue, Route 1, Box 438-C, Monterey, California was notified.

---

[206] Statement of J.A. Doherty, CGM, U.S.S. Arizona, Last Action Report.

Donegan, Timothy Albert Printer, First Class, Serial No. 204 32 90, US Navy. Timothy was born on September 20, 1901 in Wakefield, Massachusetts to William J. and Catherine (Kelleher) Donegan of Massachusetts. He re-enlisted in the US Navy April 8, 1937 and reported for duty on the USS Arizona October 31, 1930. where he was serving on December 7, 1941 when the Japanese attacked Pearl Harbor. Tim received commendations for his actions following the attack, pulling many sailors from the wreckage and the burning water surrounding his ship. He never forgot the horrors of that day. He was transferred to the USS Argonne (AG-31) after the attack. Timothy died on April 14, 1957 in San Francisco, California and is buried in Section V, Site 3156, Golden Gate National Cemetery, San Bruno, California.

Donohue, Ned Burton Fireman, First Class, Serial No: 368 42 92, US Navy. Ned was born on July 2, 1921 in Tallmadge, Utah to Murl Burton and Myrtle Mae (Redford) Donohue. He enlisted in the US Navy on January 10, 1939 in Salt Lake City, Utah at age 17. After completing his training at the Naval Training Station in San Diego on April 4, 1939, he reported for duty on the USS Arizona on April 29, 1939. On the morning of December 7, 1941, Ned left his cousin May's home and returned to his ship. May wanted Ned to delay returning to the ship so he could attend church with her and her husband that morning. But Ned insisted that he return in time for his 8:00 a.m. duty. Ned probably arrived at his duty station the Engineering Department in the boiler room of the ship shortly before the explosion. Ned was killed in action on December 7, 1941 in Pearl Harbor, Hawaii. He was awarded the American Defense Service Medal, World War II Victory Medal and Purple Heart Medal posthumously. Ned remains on duty on the USS Arizona. He is commemorated on the USS Arizona Memorial and the Memorial Tablets of the Missing, National Memorial Cemetery of the Pacific, Honolulu, Hawaii. Ned was survived by his Parents, Mr. and Mrs. Murl Burton Donohue, Rains, Utah.[207]

Dority, John Monroe Seaman, First Class, Serial No: 382 23 21, US Navy. John was born October 14, 1917 in Salt Lake City, Utah to Milton Henry and Loretta Marine (Payne) Dority. He enlisted in the US Navy on July 26, 1940 in Los Angeles, California and completed his basic training at the Naval Training Station in San Diego, California. He reported for duty on the USS Arizona October 14, 1940. John was killed in action on December 7, 1941 in Pearl Harbor, Hawaii. He was awarded the American Defense Service Medal, World War II Victory Medal and Purple Heart Medal posthumously. John remains on duty on the USS Arizona. He is commemorated on the USS Arizona Memorial and the Memorial Tablets of the Missing, National Memorial Cemetery of the Pacific, Honolulu, Hawaii. John was survived by his Mother, Mrs. Loretta Marie Heintz, 1003 Telegraph Road, Santa Fe Springs, California.

Doucett, John Walter Gunner's Mate, Third Class, Serial No. 385 86 63, US Navy. John was born on January 11, 1921 in Washington the son of William J. and Elizabeth (Reid) Doucett. He enlisted in the US Navy April 10, 1940 in Seattle, Washington and completed his basic training at the Naval Training Station in San Diego, California. He reported for duty on the USS Arizona July 2, 1940. John was serving on the Arizona December 7, 1941 when the

---

[207] Information and Photo on Ned Burton Donohue provided by family member, Bob Cameron.

Japanese attacked Pearl Harbor. After the attack, John was transferred to the USS Jarvis (DD-393) for duty. He went on to serve on the USS Enterprise. John died on February 11, 2007 in Monroe, Washington.

Dougherty, Ralph Mc Clearn Fire Controlman, First Class, Serial No: 131 61 29, US Navy. Ralph was born in October 3, 1898 in Pope County, Minnesota to William F. Collins and Martha Louise (Park) Dougherty. He enlisted in the US Navy prior to 1920 and was shown as serving on board the USS Idaho. Ralph served on the USS Arizona from March 23, 1931 until he was killed in action on December 7, 1941 in Pearl Harbor, Hawaii. He was awarded the American Defense Service Medal, World War II Victory Medal and Purple Heart Medal posthumously. Ralph remains on duty on the USS Arizona. He is commemorated on the USS Arizona Memorial and the Memorial Tablets of the Missing, National Memorial Cemetery of the Pacific, Honolulu, Hawaii. Ralph was survived by his Sister, Mrs. Edward Weeks Cross, 62 Randolph Street, Springfield, Massachusetts.

Doyle, Wand B. Coxswain, Serial No: 287 35 98, US Navy. Wand was born on August 10, 1918 in Edmonson, Kentucky to Hardin and Bessie (Gross) Doyle. He enlisted in the US Navy on January 10, 1940 in Louisville, Kentucky and completed his basic training at the Naval Training Station in Great Lakes, Illinois. Wand reported for duty on the USS Arizona on March 26, 1940. He was killed in action on December 7, 1941 in Pearl Harbor, Hawaii. Wand was awarded the American Defense Service Medal, World War II Victory Medal and Purple Heart Medal posthumously. He remains on duty on the USS Arizona. Wand is commemorated on the USS Arizona Memorial and the Memorial Tablets of the Missing, National Memorial Cemetery of the Pacific, Honolulu, Hawaii. He was survived by his Father, Mr. Hardin Doyle, Kyrock, Kentucky.[208]

Driver, Bill Lester Radioman, Third Class, Serial No: 356 11 42, US Navy. Bill was born July 2, 1917 in Texas to Edgar E. and Hulda T. (Frosch) Driver. He enlisted in the US Navy on January 16, 1939 in Dallas, Texas and completed his basic training at the Naval Training Station in San Diego, California. Bill reported for duty on the USS West Virginia (BB-48) on August 17, 1939. He was transferred from the USS West Virginia to the USS Arizona on August 2, 1941. Bill was killed in action on December 7, 1941 in Pearl Harbor, Hawaii. He was awarded the American Defense Service Medal, World War II Victory Medal and Purple Heart Medal posthumously. Bill remains on duty on the USS Arizona. He is commemorated on the USS Arizona Memorial and the Memorial Tablets of the Missing, National Memorial Cemetery of the Pacific, Honolulu, Hawaii. Bill was survived by his Parents, Mr. and Mrs. Edgar E. Driver, General Delivery, Sentinel, Oklahoma.

---

[208] Wand B. Doyle, Photo from Kentucky Honor States.

Ducrest, Louis Felix Seaman, First Class, Serial No: 274 48 59, US Navy. Louis was born April 4, 1920 in Broussard, Louisiana. *He was the eighth of eleven children born to Thomas Lucien Ducrest and Regina St. Julien. His father was a pharmacist and also served as Postmaster. Louis graduated from St. Cecelia School in May 1937 and entered Southwestern Louisiana Institute. He was not fond of studying and preferred to have a good time with his friends. His outgoing personality and easy ways made him a "happy-go-lucky" guy. He loved people. After completing a year as SLI, he hitch-hiked to California to visit friends and find a job. After a few months, he returned to Broussard and went to work at the Billeaud Sugar Factory.* He enlisted in the US Navy on July 31, 1940 in New Orleans, Louisiana and completed his basic training at the Naval Training Station in San Diego, California. *His father had to sign for him as he was not old enough, and this decision would later cause regret to his parent.* He reported for duty on the USS Arizona on October 14, 1940. Louis was killed in action on December 7, 1941 in Pearl Harbor, Hawaii. He was awarded the American Defense Service Medal, World War II Victory Medal and Purple Heart Medal posthumously. Louis remains on duty on the USS Arizona. He is commemorated on the USS Arizona Memorial and the Memorial Tablets of the Missing, National Memorial Cemetery of the Pacific, Honolulu, Hawaii. Louis was survived by his Father, Mr. Thomas Lucien Ducrest, Broussard, Louisiana. The American Legion Post 69, Lafayette, LA, is named after Felix Ducrest and Stanley Martin.[209]

Duke, Robert Edward Chief Commissary Steward, Serial No: 261 42 31, US Navy. Robert was born in 1904 in North Carolina. He enlisted in the US Navy on August 26, 1939 at the Norfolk Naval Yard in Portsmouth, Virginia and reported for duty on the USS Arizona on July 6, 1940. Robert was killed in action on December 7, 1941 in Pearl Harbor, Hawaii. He was awarded the American Defense Service Medal, World War II Victory Medal and Purple Heart Medal posthumously. Robert remains on duty on the USS Arizona. He is commemorated on the USS Arizona Memorial and the Memorial Tablets of the Missing, National Memorial Cemetery of the Pacific, Honolulu, Hawaii. Robert was survived by his Wife, Mrs. Nellie Irene Duke, 4363 Voltaire Street, Ocean Beach, California.

Dullum, Jerald Fraser Electrician's Mate, Third Class, Serial No: 368 47 41, US Navy. Jerald was born July 23, 1921 in East Helena, Montana to Eugene H. and Eva Collena Bradley (Fraser) Dullum. He enlisted in the US Navy on February 7, 1940 in Salt Lake City, Utah and completed his basic training at the Naval Training Station in San Diego, California. He reported for duty on the USS Arizona on May 30, 1940. Jerald was killed in action on December 7, 1941 in Pearl Harbor, Hawaii. He was awarded the American Defense Service Medal, World War II Victory Medal and Purple Heart Medal posthumously. Jerald remains on duty on the USS Arizona. He is commemorated on the USS Arizona Memorial and the Memorial Tablets of the Missing, National Memorial Cemetery of the Pacific,

---

[209] Louis Felix Ducrest, Information provided by Mr. Willis Ducrest, Mrs. Irene D. Updike and The Daily Advertiser, by Billie Dejean Landry. Photo provided by the Stanley Martin, Felix Ducrest American Legion Post 69, Lafayette, LA.

Honolulu, Hawaii. Jerald was survived by his Father, Mr. Eugene H. Dullum, 513 East Clark Street, East Helena, Montana. The Cory-Dullum VFW post in East Helena was named in part, in his honor.[210]

Dunaway, Kenneth Leroy Electrician's Mate, Third Class, Serial No: 376 12 94, US Navy. Kenneth was born August 26, 1923, the son of John Wesley and Bessie Louisa (Cobb) Dunaway. He enlisted in the US Navy on October 10, 1940 in San Francisco, California and completed his basic training at the Naval Training Station in San Diego, California. Kenneth reported for duty on the USS Arizona on January 11, 1941. He was killed in action on December 7, 1941 in Pearl Harbor, Hawaii. Kenneth was awarded the American Defense Service Medal, World War II Victory Medal and Purple Heart Medal posthumously. He remains buried on the USS Arizona. Kenneth is commemorated on the USS Arizona Memorial and the Memorial Tablets of the Missing, National Memorial Cemetery of the Pacific, Honolulu, Hawaii. He was survived by his Father, Mr. John Wesley Dunaway, Box 442, Blackwell, Oklahoma.[211]

Duncan, Henry Barnett Fire Controlman, Third Class, Serial No. 372 16 72, US Navy. Henry was born June 15, 1918 in Oklahoma the son of Jessie Carroll and Samye Jane (Warren) Duncan. He enlisted in the US Navy August 5, 1940 in Denver, Colorado and completed his basic training at the Naval Training Station in San Diego, California. He reported for duty on the USS Arizona October 8, 1940. He was serving on the Arizona December 7, 1941 when the Japanese attacked Pearl Harbor. After the attack, Henry was transferred to the USS Maryland (BB-46) for duty. Henry served through the end of the war. He was recalled and served during the Korean War. Henry died August 12, 1974 and is buried in Section Z, Site 333, Santa Fe National Cemetery, Santa Fe, New Mexico.

Duncan, Tommie Wilson Boatswain's Mate, Second Class, Serial No. 265 71 87, US Navy. Tommie was born on September 3, 1914, in Currituck County, North Carolina, the son of Ruben Acklin and Emma Jane (Forbes) Duncan. He enlisted in the US Navy on June 17, 1936 in Norfolk, Virginia and reported for duty on the USS Arizona on April 29, 1940. Tommie was serving on the Arizona December 7, 1941 when the Japanese attacked Pearl Harbor. After the attack, Tommie was transferred to the USS Aylwin (DD-355) for duty. Tommie died on April 5, 2000 in Currituck, North Carolina and is buried in Morre's Cemetery, Currituck, North Carolina.

---

[210]Jerald Fraser Dullum, Photo from "Fraser – A Short History of the Fraser Clan and our own Branch of Frasers in Canada and the United States" compiled by L. A. Milne, published 1944.
[211] Kenneth Leroy Dunaway, Photo from Oklahoma Honor States.

Dunham, Elmer Marvin Seaman, First Class, Serial No: 376 09 01, US Navy. Elmer was born on March 7, 1920 in Fresno, California to Robert Sumner and Alma Matilda (Harper) Dunham. *He was the fourth child and oldest son born of eleven children born to Robert and Alma. Memories are scarce of Marvin but the family remembers him working on his car, both mechanically and doing maintenance. He was either washing and polishing or repairing his car. Just before joining the service, he gave his life to God and witnessed to whoever would listen. He had his Bible with him at all times and his mother was told that he was dressing and getting ready to leave the ship for church with the ship was attacked. As a child, Marvin felt the responsibility of helping the family financially and sold newspapers and magazines, many times walking miles to try and sell in areas where he thought there were some workers with some extra change that might buy his reading materials. This was the depression, when very few people had jobs and very little money.* He enlisted in the US Navy on July 24, 1940 in San Francisco, California and completed his basic training at the Naval Training Station in San Diego, California. Elmer reported for duty on the USS Arizona on October 14, 1940. He was killed in action on December 7, 1941 in Pearl Harbor, Hawaii. Elmer was awarded the American Defense Service Medal, World War II Victory Medal and Purple Heart Medal posthumously. He remains on duty on the USS Arizona. Elmer is commemorated on the USS Arizona Memorial and the Memorial Tablets of the Missing, National Memorial Cemetery of the Pacific, Honolulu, Hawaii. He was survived by his Father, Mr. Robert Dunham, 607 Bond Street, Fresno, California.[212]

Dupree, Arthur Joseph Fireman, Second Class, Serial No: 342 30 50, US Navy. Arthur was born on May 7, 1918 in St. Joseph, Missouri to Joseph David and Mabel Gertrude (Sanders) Dupree. *Arthur was named after his uncle who died in World War I on the last day and last hour of the war. After Arthur's death, the family stopped using that first and middle name in combination.* He enlisted in the US Navy on October 10, 1940 in Kansas City, Missouri and completed his basic training at the Naval Training Station in Great Lakes, Illinois. Arthur reported for duty on the USS Arizona on December 9, 1940. He was killed in action on December 7, 1941 in Pearl Harbor, Hawaii. Arthur was awarded the American Defense Service Medal, World War II Victory Medal and Purple Heart Medal posthumously. He remains on duty on the USS Arizona. Arthur is commemorated on the USS Arizona Memorial and the Memorial Tablets of the Missing, National Memorial Cemetery of the Pacific, Honolulu, Hawaii. He was survived by his Father, Mr. Joseph David Dupree, Route 2, St. Joseph, Missouri.[213]

---

[212] Elmer Marvin Dunham, Photo and information provided by his sister, Doris Eckhardt.
[213] Arthur Joseph DuPree, photo and information provided by family member, J. Donley.

Durham, William Teasdale Seaman, First Class, Serial No: 262 51 86, US Navy. William was born April 25, 1919 in Chatham, North Carolina to Edward Watson and Jennie F. Durham. He enlisted in the US Navy on March 5, 1940 in Raleigh, North Carolina and reported for duty on the USS Arizona on September 30, 1940. William was killed in action on December 7, 1941 in Pearl Harbor, Hawaii. He was awarded the American Defense Service Medal, World War II Victory Medal and Purple Heart Medal posthumously. William remains on duty on the USS Arizona. He is commemorated on the USS Arizona Memorial and the Memorial Tablets of the Missing, National Memorial Cemetery of the Pacific, Honolulu, Hawaii. William was survived by his Father, Mr. Edward Watson Durham, Route 1, Pittsboro, North Carolina.[214]

Dvorak, Alvin Albert Boatswain's Mate, Second Class, Serial No: 328 51 60, US Navy. Alvin was born April 3, 1918 in Tripp County, South Dakota the son of Joseph T. and Emma (Mach) Dvorak. His father Joseph, died on January 13, 1919 and his mother, Emma, Died 4 days later on January 17th, both of the Spanish Flu when he was only 9 months old. He went to live with his mother's sister and her husband in Pine County, Minnesota. Sometime later he was sent to live with his grandparents, living in Park Township, Minnesota. It is not known how long he stayed with his grandparents, but in 1937 he was living in Stillwater, Minnesota when he enlisted in the US Navy on March 2, 1938 in Minneapolis, Minnesota, his brother in law signed for him. Alvin completed his basic training at the Naval Training Station in Great Lakes, Illinois. He reported for duty on the USS Arizona on July 9, 1938. *Alvin was badly burned during the attack on Pearl Harbor on December 7, 1941. He escaped the inferno of the Arizona by crossing over from the Arizona on a line to the USS Vestal. He was being transferred to the Naval Hospital, Mare Island, California on board the USAT Coolidge. While on board, Alvin died from his wounds on December 24, 1941.* He was awarded the American Defense Service Medal, World War II Victory Medal and Purple Heart Medal posthumously. Alvin was buried in Section A-7, Site 923, Fort Snelling National Cemetery, Minneapolis, Minnesota. He is commemorated on the USS Arizona Memorial. Alvin was survived by his Sister Harriet (Dvorak) Heaser and her husband, Mr. Casper Heaser, 721 15th Avenue SE, Minneapolis, Minnesota and a brother, Arthur A. Dvorak.[215]

---

[214] William Teasdale Durham, photo and information provided by family member, Ruth Thomas.

[215] Alvin Albert Dvorak, Photo and information from Al Johnson, member of the Pine County Geneological Society.

Eaton, Emory Lowell Fireman, Third Class, Serial No: 356 36 72, US Navy. Emory was born September 27, 1918 in Kansas to James Leslie and Minta Belle (Whaley) Eaton. He enlisted in the US Navy on November 4, 1940 in Dallas, Texas and completed his basic training at the Naval Training Station in San Diego, California. He reported for duty on the USS Arizona on January 11, 1941. Emory was killed in action on December 7, 1941 in Pearl Harbor, Hawaii. He was awarded the American Defense Service Medal, World War II Victory Medal and Purple Heart Medal posthumously. Emory remains on duty on the USS Arizona. He is commemorated on the USS Arizona Memorial and the Memorial Tablets of the Missing, National Memorial Cemetery of the Pacific, Honolulu, Hawaii. Emory was survived by his Father, Mr. James Leslie Eaton, 409-1/2 West 3rd Street, Bartlesville, Oklahoma.

Ebel, Walter Charles Chief Turret Captain, Serial No: 140 06 89, US Navy. Walter was born March 22, 1895 in Genesee, Idaho the only child to Charles Frank and Frieda Clara (Mattausch) Ebel. He was a career Navy man enlisting from about 1915 and had served on board the USS Arizona from December 16, 1926 until he was killed in action on December 7, 1941 in Pearl Harbor, Hawaii. *In the Crossing the Line Ceremony on July 24, 1940, Walter was Neptunus Rex, Ruler of the Raging Main.* He had spent 15 years aboard the Arizona. Walter was awarded the American Defense Service Medal, World War II Victory Medal and Purple Heart Medal posthumously. He remains on duty on the USS Arizona. Walter is commemorated on the USS Arizona Memorial and the Memorial Tablets of the Missing, National Memorial Cemetery of the Pacific, Honolulu, Hawaii. He was survived by his Wife, Mrs. Florence Ethel Ebel and his son, 115-1/2 13th Street, Long Beach, California.[216]

Eberhart, Vincent Henry Coxswain, Serial No: 328 64 89, US Navy. Vincent was born April 11, 1921 in Minnesota to George and Clara (Malzahn) Eberhart. He enlisted in the US Navy on January 23, 1940 in Minneapolis, Minnesota and completed his basic training at the Naval Training Station in Great Lakes, Illinois. Vincent reported for duty on the USS Arizona on March 26, 1940. He was killed in action on December 7, 1941 in Pearl Harbor, Hawaii. Vincent was awarded the American Defense Service Medal, World War II Victory Medal and Purple Heart Medal posthumously. He remains on duty on the USS Arizona. Vincent is commemorated on the USS Arizona Memorial and the Memorial Tablets of the Missing, National Memorial Cemetery of the Pacific, Honolulu, Hawaii. He was survived by his Mother, Mrs. Clara Eberhart, 528-1/2 South Front Street, Mankato, Minnesota.[217]

Echols, Charles Louis, Jr. Electrician's Mate, Third Class, Serial No: 287 36 32, US Navy. Charles was born in about 1918 in Alabama to Charles L. and Stella L. Echols. He enlisted in the US Navy on January 17, 1940 in Louisville, Kentucky and completed his basic training at the Naval Training Station in Great Lakes, Illinois. He reported for duty on the USS Arizona on March 26, 1940. Charles was killed in action on December 7, 1941 in Pearl Harbor,

---

[216] Walter Charles Ebel, Information and photo provided by his granddaughter, Diane Moore.
[217] Vincent Henry Eberhart, Photo from Minnesota Honor States.

Hawaii. He was awarded the American Defense Service Medal, World War II Victory Medal and Purple Heart Medal posthumously. Charles remains on duty on the USS Arizona. He is commemorated on the USS Arizona Memorial and the Memorial Tablets of the Missing, National Memorial Cemetery of the Pacific, Honolulu, Hawaii. Charles was survived by his Father, Mr. Charles Louie Echols, Sr., Marion, Tennessee.

Echternkamp, Henry Clarence Seaman, First Class, Serial No: 385 91 30, US Navy. Henry was born on March 26, 1917 in Sequim, Clallam County, Washington to William and Grace Ellen (Cays) Echternkamp. He enlisted in the US Navy on October 11, 1940 in Seattle, Washington and completed his basic training at the Naval Training Station in San Diego, California. Henry reported for duty on the USS Arizona January 8, 1941. He died on December 12, 1941 from 3rd degree burns received during the attack on Pearl Harbor, Honolulu, Hawaii. He was assigned death #461.[218] Henry was awarded the American Defense Service Medal, World War II Victory Medal and Purple Heart Medal. He was buried initially in Nuuanu Cemetery, Honolulu, Hawaii but was later interred in Plot A, Row 0, Grave 525, National Memorial Cemetery of the Pacific, Honolulu, Hawaii. Henry is commemorated on the USS Arizona Memorial. He was survived by his Parents, Mr. and Mrs. William F. Echternkamp, Sequim, Washington, four brothers, Elmer, Arthur, Floyd and Billy and four sisters Mrs. Ellen Barton, Mrs. Mary Jane Loucks and Anna and Tillie Echternkamp. The Henry Clarence Echternkamp VFW Post 4760 in Sequim, Washington was named in Henry's honor.[219]

Edmonson, Kenneth Eugene Coxswain, Serial No. 382 11 77, US Navy. Kenneth was born February 21, 1921, the son of D.C. Edmondson and Floy Edmonson. He enlisted in the US Navy October 10, 1939 in Los Angeles, California and completed his training at the Naval Training Station, San Diego, California. Kenneth reported for duty on the USS Arizona December 20, 1939. He was serving on the Arizona December 7, 1941 when the Japanese attacked Pearl Harbor. Kenneth died October 1, 2005 and his ashes were interred in the well of turret four of the USS Arizona.

Edmunds, Bruce Roosevelt Yeoman, Second Class, Serial No: 381 03 61, US Navy. Bruce was born November 10, 1907 in New Hampshire to Horace W. and Sadie R. (Bruce) Edmunds. His mother died in 1931 and his father died in 1935. He enlisted in the US Navy on December 10, 1937 and reported for duty on the USS Arizona on December 12, 1937. Bruce was killed in action on December 7, 1941 in Pearl Harbor, Hawaii. He was awarded the American Defense Service Medal, World War II Victory Medal and Purple Heart Medal posthumously. Bruce remains on duty on the USS Arizona. He is commemorated on the USS Arizona Memorial and the Memorial Tablets of the Missing, National Memorial Cemetery of the Pacific, Honolulu, Hawaii. Bruce was survived by his Aunt, Mrs. B. B. Wing, 3 South Spring Street, Concord, New Hampshire.[220]

---

[218] Report of Changes of the USS Arizona for the month ending 31st day of December, 1941, page 54, line 21, Henry Clarence Echternkamp.

[219] Henry Clarence Echternkamp, Information and photo provided by Anna Hardgrove and the Clallam County Genealogical Society, Washington.

[220] Bruce Roosevelt Edmunds, Photo from New Hampshire Honor States.

Eernisse, William Frederick Painter, First Class, Serial No: 316 16 63, US Navy. William was born July 27, 1909 in South Dakota to John L. and Maude (Stott) Eernisse. He enlisted in the US Navy on March 24, 1937 in San Diego, California. William served on the USS Arizona from December 20, 1939 until he was killed in action on December 7, 1941 in Pearl Harbor, Hawaii. He was awarded the American Defense Service Medal, World War II Victory Medal and Purple Heart Medal posthumously. William remains on duty on the USS Arizona. He is commemorated on the USS Arizona Memorial and the Memorial Tablets of the Missing, National Memorial Cemetery of the Pacific, Honolulu, Hawaii. William was survived by his Wife, Mrs. Dorothy Virginia Eernisse, 460 South Kern Avenue, East Los Angeles, California.[221]

Egan, Paul Howard Fire Controlman, Third Class, Serial No. 382 11 45, US Navy. Paul was born on December 24, 1920 in Watseka, IL, the son of Joseph John Egan and Gladys Egan. He enlisted in the US Navy on September 16, 1939 in Los Angeles, California at age 18. Paul completed his training at the Naval Training Station at San Diego, California and reported for duty on the USS Arizona on November 10, 1939. He was serving on board the Arizona on December 7, 1941 when the Japanese attacked Pearl Harbor. Paul's battle station on the Arizona was a "range six," the range finder located on the lower platform of the mainmast.

"I was on the main deck by a turret barbette changing clothes to go to church on the Nevada when someone ran through the compartment yelling for everyone to get up to the third deck. The Japanese are attacking! The Japanese are attacking!

I couldn't believe what I heard. I looked out of a port and saw everyone running to battle stations on the Vestal, which was tied up alongside. I looked forward just as a torpedo hit the battleship West Virginia. It sent a geyser of water as high as her masts. I could see other planes coming in over the liberty landing and heading directly toward us.

When I started to my station, general quarters sounded. Sailors and Marines jammed the ladders trying to get to their stations. I finally got out on deck and was climbing up a ladder on the starboard strut of the mainmast behind Lt. Sanderson of the Marines. When he fell over, I realized for the first time we were being strafed by planes.

I was hooking up the intercommunication phones at my station when the Arizona blew up. She seemed to buck and shake for ages before things became quiet. No words of mine can describe the wreckage of the Arizona in those next few moments. The foremast began to topple forward. Flames and smoke seemed to cover the ship.

I ran to the quarterdeck and asked the junior officer of the deck if it was all right to leave the ship. He was standing there with his long glass under his arm as though nothing had happened. He didn't seem to hear what I was saying, so I jumped into the water and swam toward Ford Island. The rest of that day is still like a nightmare. He helped treat severely burned survivors on Ford Island.[222]

Paul was transferred to the USS Tennessee for a short time after the attack and then on to the destroyer USS Dunlap. He spent the rest of the war on a succession of ships in the Pacific campaigns. He was discharged from the Navy on October 11, 1947 and returned to the Navy in

---

[221] William Frederick Eernisse, Information and photo provided by family member, Kelly Freitag.
[222] Arizona Survivor 'Sees' Flaming End, Evening Tribune, San Diego, California, Tuesday, December 9, 1958.

1950 to serve in the Korean War. Paul died on November 26, 1992 and is buried in Section MB, Site 5, National Memorial Cemetery of the Pacific, Honolulu, Hawaii. His ashes were entombed in turret four of the USS Arizona in the waters of Pearl Harbor, January 12, 1993. Paul was survived by his loving wife, Mary Parrot Egan, five children, Michael, Paul, John, Christine, and Anne Marie. Three brothers, Joseph John, Jr., Robert and Charles.

Egnew, Robert "Buddy" Ross Seaman, First Class, Serial No: 337 41 66, US Navy. Robert was born May 21, 1920 in Illinois to Roscoe Hayes and Inez Renee (Brill) Egnew of Catlin, Illinois. His mother, Inez, died when he was 16 years old. He enlisted in the US Navy on October 15, 1940 in St. Louis, Missouri and completed his basic training at the Naval Training Station in Great Lakes, Illinois. Robert reported for duty on the USS Arizona on December 9, 1940. He was killed in action on December 7, 1941 in Pearl Harbor, Hawaii. Robert was awarded the American Defense Service Medal, World War II Victory Medal and Purple Heart Medal posthumously. He remains on duty on the USS Arizona. Robert is commemorated on the USS Arizona Memorial and the Memorial Tablets of the Missing, National Memorial Cemetery of the Pacific, Honolulu, Hawaii. He was survived by his Father, Mr. Roscoe Hayes Egnew, 404 East Washington Street, Hoopeston, Illinois. The Buddy Egnew VFW Post #4828 in Hoopeston, Illinois was named in his honor.[223]

Ehlert, Charles Casper Signalman, Third Class, Serial No: 299 89 64, US Navy. Casper was born February 8, 1918 in Wisconsin to Jasper and Anna (Horst) Ehlert. He enlisted in the US Navy on March 9, 1936 in Chicago, Illinois and completed his basic training at the Naval Training Station in Great Lakes, Illinois. Casper reported for duty on the USS Arizona on July 9, 1938. He was killed in action on December 7, 1941 in Pearl Harbor, Hawaii. Casper was awarded the American Defense Service Medal, World War II Victory Medal and Purple Heart Medal posthumously. He remains buried on the USS Arizona. Casper is commemorated on the USS Arizona Memorial and the Memorial Tablets of the Missing, National Memorial Cemetery of the Pacific, Honolulu, Hawaii. He was survived by his Parents, Mr. and Mrs. Casper Ehlert, 1635 Indiana Avenue, Sheboygan, Wisconsin.[224]

Ehrmantraut, Frank, Jr. Seaman, First Class, Serial No: 291 61 58, US Navy. Frank was born October 17, 1921 in Indianapolis, Indiana to Frank and Etalee L. Ehrmantraut. He enlisted in the US Navy on January 11, 1940 in Indianapolis, Indiana and completed his basic training at the Naval Training Station in Great Lakes, Illinois. He reported for duty on the USS Arizona on March 26, 1940. Frank was killed in action on December 7, 1941 in Pearl Harbor, Hawaii. He was awarded the American Defense Service Medal, World War II Victory Medal and Purple Heart Medal posthumously. Frank remains on duty on the USS Arizona. He is commemorated on the USS Arizona Memorial and the Memorial Tablets of the Missing, National Memorial Cemetery of the Pacific, Honolulu, Hawaii.

---

[223] Robert Ross Egnew, Photo provided by the Buddy Egnew VFW Post 4828, Hoopeston, Illinois.
[224] Charles Casper Ehlert, Photo and information provided by family member, Molly Baumann.

Frank was survived by his Father, Mr. Frank Ehrmantraut, 21 North Randolph Street, Indianapolis, Indiana.[225]

Elkins, Merle Seaman, First Class, Serial No. 295 76 87, US Navy. Merle was born September 22, 1919 in Arkansas. He enlisted in the US Navy on October 4, 1940 in Nashville, Tennessee and completed his training at the Naval Training Station in Norfolk, Virginia. He reported for duty on the USS Arizona on December 4, 1940. Merle was serving on the Arizona on December 7, 1941 when the Japanese attacked Pearl Harbor. After the attack, Merle was sent to the Receiving Station at Pearl Harbor for general detail duty and then on to work at the Naval Yard at Pearl Harbor. He served until November 7, 1944. Merle died November 22, 1982 in Colbert, Spokane, Washington.

Elliott, Lawrence Emitt Machinist's Mate, First Class, Serial No. 295 09 47, US Navy. Lawrence was born on June 13, 1909 in Hiram, Georgia, the son of Oliver Cicero and Lydia E. (Wilson) Elliott. He enlisted in the US Navy in 1928. Lawrence served on the USS Arizona from January 5, 1929 until December 7, 1941 when the Japanese attacked Pearl Harbor. He was on shore leave that morning. The attack started while he was walking across the grounds of the YMCA on the way to a friend's home. Hearing that Pearl Harbor was being attacked he caught a ride with an officer. By the time he arrived at the port, the USS Arizona had already been sunk. He spent the following months working with the salvage crew. Lawrence died on May 16, 1997 and is buried in Forest Lawn Memory Gardens, Meridian, Mississippi.

Ellis, Francis Arnold, Jr. Electrician's Mate, Third Class, Serial No: 328 60 62, US Navy. Francis was born March 11, 1920 in Chicago the son of Francis Arnold and Isabelle (Smith) Ellis. He enlisted in the US Navy on September 13, 1939 in Minneapolis, Minnesota and completed his basic training at the Naval Training Station in San Diego, California. He reported for duty on the USS Arizona on March 27, 1940. Francis was killed in action on December 7, 1941 in Pearl Harbor, Hawaii. He was awarded the American Defense Service Medal, World War II Victory Medal and Purple Heart Medal posthumously. Francis remains on duty on the USS Arizona. He is commemorated on the USS Arizona Memorial and the Memorial Tablets of the Missing, National Memorial Cemetery of the Pacific, Honolulu, Hawaii. Francis was survived by his Father, Mr. Francis Arnold Ellis, Sr., 15 Chelsea Court, Winnipeg, Manitoba, Canada.

---

[225] Frank Ehrmantraut, Jr, Photo from The Indianapolis News, Indianapolis, Indiana, May 5, 1942, Page 13.

Ellis, George William   Ship's Cook, First Class, Serial No. 311 53 56, US Navy.   George was born on August 31, 1920 in Omaha, Nebraska, the son of George Harrison Ellis and Nina Suphonia (Davis) Ellis.   He enlisted in the US Navy on February 2, 1938 in Omaha, Nebraska and reported for duty on the USS Arizona June 4, 1938.   George was serving on the Arizona December 7, 1941 when the Japanese attacked Pearl Harbor.   His brother, Richard Everett Ellis was also serving on board the USS Arizona and was killed in action on December 7, 1941.   George died February 1, 2002 in Huntington Beach, California.[226]

Ellis, Richard Everrett   Seaman, Second Class, Serial No: 316 74 38, US Navy.   Richard was born on May 8, 1922 in Omaha, Nebraska to George Harrison Ellis and Nina Suphonia (Davis) Ellis.   He enlisted in the US Navy on January 16, 1941 in Omaha, Nebraska and reported for duty on the USS Arizona on April 27, 1941.   Richard was killed in action on December 7, 1941 in Pearl Harbor, Hawaii.   He was awarded the American Defense Service Medal, World War II Victory Medal and Purple Heart Medal posthumously.   Richard remains on duty on the USS Arizona.   He is commemorated on the USS Arizona Memorial and the Memorial Tablets of the Missing, National Memorial Cemetery of the Pacific, Honolulu, Hawaii.   Richard was survived by his Father, Mr. George Harrison Ellis, 3608 Ohio Street, Omaha, Nebraska.   His brother, George William Ellis was also serving on board the USS Arizona and survived the attack.[227]

Ellis, Wilbur Danner   Radioman, Second Class, Serial No: 328 51 48, US Navy.   Wilbur was born in about 1916 in Missouri and was adopted by Wilfred Sylvester and Flora (Royce) Ellis.   He enlisted in the US Navy on February 15, 1938 in Minneapolis, Minnesota and completed his basic training at the Naval Training Station in Great Lakes, Illinois.   He reported for duty on the USS Arizona on December 6, 1940, transferring from the USS Mississippi.   Wilbur was killed in action on December 7, 1941 in Pearl Harbor, Hawaii. He was awarded the American Defense Service Medal, World War II Victory Medal and Purple Heart Medal posthumously.   Wilbur remains on duty on the USS Arizona.   He is commemorated on the USS Arizona Memorial and the Memorial Tablets of the Missing, National Memorial Cemetery of the Pacific, Honolulu, Hawaii.   Wilbur was survived by his Wife, Mrs. Genevieve Barbara Ellis, 1904 Bermuda, Long Beach, California.[228]

[226] George William Ellis, Photo provided by his niece, Linda R. Hewitt-Mundt.
[227] Richard Everrett Ellis, Photo from Nebraska Honor States.
[228] Wilbur Danner Ellis, Photo from California Honor States.

Elwell, Royal   Seaman, First Class, Serial No: 356 40 94, US Navy. Royal was born May 21, 1920 in Upshur, Texas to Oscar Wilde and Sarah Annie (Davis) Elwell. He enlisted in the US Navy on November 2, 1940 in Dallas, Texas and completed his basic training at the Naval Training Station in San Diego, California. Royal reported for duty on the USS Arizona on December 30, 1940. He died on December 10, 1941 from 2nd degree burns received in action on December 7, 1941 in Pearl Harbor, Hawaii. He was assigned death #130, identified by his tag.[229] Royal was awarded the American Defense Service Medal, World War II Victory Medal and Purple Heart Medal posthumously. He was buried in Plot C, Row 0, Grave 940, National Memorial Cemetery of the Pacific, Honolulu, Hawaii. Royal is commemorated on the USS Arizona Memorial. He was survived by his Father, Mr. Oscar Wilde Elwell, 305 North Avenue, Pittsburg, Texas and a twin brother. His cousin, Weldon Harvey Milligan was also killed on board the USS Arizona.

Embrey, Bill Eugene   Fireman, Third Class, Serial No: 376 15 78, US Navy. Bill was born December 7, 1922 in Colorado to Stephen Lee and Sallie Dickenson (Johnson) Embrey. He enlisted in the US Navy on November 9, 1940 in San Francisco, California and completed his basic training at the Naval Training Station in San Diego, California. He reported for duty on the USS Arizona on January 11, 1941. Bill was killed in action on December 7, 1941 in Pearl Harbor, Hawaii. He was awarded the American Defense Service Medal, World War II Victory Medal and Purple Heart Medal posthumously. Bill remains on duty on the USS Arizona. He is commemorated on the USS Arizona Memorial and the Memorial Tablets of the Missing, National Memorial Cemetery of the Pacific, Honolulu, Hawaii. Bill was survived by his Father, Mr. Stephen Lee Embrey, 1116 Delmonte Avenue, Salinas, California.[230]

Emery, Jack Mandeville   Ensign, Serial No: 0-082845, US Navy Reserve. Jack was born on October 9, 1916 in Los Angeles, California to Ralph De Votie and Katherine Frances (Kelly) Emery. He was appointed Ensign in the US Naval Reserve on May 20, 1939 and reported for active duty on the USS Arizona on November 13, 1939 serving as Signal Officer. Jack was killed in action on December 7, 1941 in Pearl Harbor, Hawaii. His battle station was Battle Signal Station. Jack was awarded the American Defense Service Medal, World War II Victory Medal and Purple Heart Medal posthumously. He remains on duty on the USS Arizona. Jack is commemorated on the USS Arizona Memorial and the Memorial Tablets of the Missing, National Memorial Cemetery of the Pacific, Honolulu, Hawaii. He was survived by his Mother, Mrs. Kathryn F. Emery, 3811 Howe Street, Oakland, California and brothers, Ralph D., Joseph, Henry G. and sister, Ellen Emery. The USS Emery (DE-28) was named in his honor.[231]

---

[229] Report of Changes of the USS Arizona for the month ending 31st day of December, 1941, page 54, line 30, Royal Elwell.
[230] Bill Eugene Embrey, Information provided by family member, Greg Bahl.
[231] Jack Mandeville Emery, Photo and information provided by family member, Martha Williams.

Emery, John "Jack" Marvin Gunner's Mate, Third Class, Serial No: 328 62 82, US Navy. John was born April 26, 1919 in Gardner, North Dakota to Carl C. and Freida A. (Sandberg) Emery. He enlisted in the US Navy on December 12, 1939 in Minneapolis, Minnesota and completed his basic training at the Naval Training Station in Great Lakes, Illinois. John reported for duty on the USS Arizona on March 26, 1940. He was killed in action on December 7, 1941 in Pearl Harbor, Hawaii. *Jack's death came at the start of the war. His brother, Bob, was killed in action during the Normandy Campaign on June 23, 1944. And their family was changed forever. "It's something they never got over, you can't help but think how the family dynamics changed with those deaths and how different things might have been had they not been killed. After their deaths, the health of their mother, Freida, failed and within years she was in a wheelchair and needed constant care. Their father, Carl refused to talk about his sons' deaths or the war that caused them." Betty Halverson, Jack's sister, recalls her mother utter through tears her wish that her boys had been conscious's objectors, because their jail terms wouldn't last forever. 50 years later, Betty said, "The worst part is not knowing, The worst part is not having a body to bury, The worst part is that it just keeps going on, even after all these years. I still miss Jack."*[232] John was awarded the American Defense Service Medal, World War II Victory Medal and Purple Heart Medal posthumously. He remains on duty on the USS Arizona. John is commemorated on the USS Arizona Memorial and the Memorial Tablets of the Missing, National Memorial Cemetery of the Pacific, Honolulu, Hawaii and Nora Lutheran Church Cemetery, Gardner, North Dakota. He was survived by his Father, Mr. Carl C. Emery, Route 2, Gardner, North Dakota.[233]

Emery, Wesley Vernon Storekeeper, Second Class, Serial No: 291 55 63, US Navy. Wesley was born in about 1921 in Bedford, Indiana the eldest son of Ira Benton and Texie (Kelly) Emery. He enlisted in the US Navy on July 12, 1938 in Indianapolis, Indiana and completed his basic training at the Naval Training Station in Great Lakes, Illinois. Wesley reported for duty on the USS Arizona on April 15, 1939. He was killed in action on December 7, 1941 in Pearl Harbor, Hawaii. Wesley was awarded the American Defense Service Medal, World War II Victory Medal and Purple Heart Medal posthumously. He remains on duty on USS Arizona. Wesley is commemorated on the USS Arizona Memorial and the Memorial Tablets of the Missing, National Memorial Cemetery of the Pacific, Honolulu, Hawaii. Wesley was survived by his Father, Mr. Ira Benton Emery, Route 2, Bedford, Indiana his Mother, Mrs. Texie Emery, Brother Dale Ellen and sister Mary Emery.

---

[232] John "Jack" Marvin Emery, Information taken from The Forum Newspaper, Fargo, North Dakota, "50 years haven't erased pain of war for local family" by Lifestyle columnist, Cathy Mauk, Sunday, December 8, 1991.
[233] John "Jack" Marvin Emery, Photo provided by family member, Jarrett Emery Halverson.

Enger, Stanley Gordon Gunner's Mate, Third Class, Serial No: 328 61 16, US Navy. Stanley was born February 4, 1920 in Hennepin County, Minnesota to Carl Siguard and Hattie (Lundquist) Enger. His family called him Shadow because he had wanderlust and ran away a few times when he was a boy, his sister Katharine recalled years later. He enlisted in the US Navy on October 3, 1939 in Minneapolis, Minnesota and completed his basic training at the Naval Training Station in Great Lakes, Illinois. He reported for duty on the USS Arizona on December 31, 1939. Stanley was killed in action on December 7, 1941 in Pearl Harbor, Hawaii. He was awarded the American Defense Service Medal, World War II Victory Medal and Purple Heart Medal posthumously. Stanley remains on duty on the USS Arizona. He is commemorated on the USS Arizona Memorial and the Memorial Tablets of the Missing, National Memorial Cemetery of the Pacific, Honolulu, Hawaii. Stanley was survived by his Father, Mr. Carl S. Enger, 8101 Lyndale Avenue South, Minneapolis, Minnesota.[234]

Enos, James Robert Seaman, Second Class, Serial No. 382 46 81, US Navy. James was born on June 2, 1924 in Los Angeles, California the son of John A. and Olive G. (Whitacre) Enos. He enlisted in the US Navy June 4, 1941 in Los Angeles, California and completed his basic training at the Naval Training Station in San Diego, California. James reported for duty on the USS Arizona August 13, 1941. He had been sent back to the states for Signalman Training at San Diego and was there when his ship, USS Arizona, was sunk by the Japanese on December 7, 1941. Afterwards, he was assigned to the USS Pennsylvania. James later served in the Korean War and the Vietnam War. James died on March 31, 1994 and is buried in Section A, Site 700, Riverside National Cemetery, Riverside, California.[235]

Erickson, Robert Seaman, First Class, Serial No: 385 91 80, US Navy. Robert was born in 1923 in Wisconsin to Sam and Ida Erickson. He enlisted in the US Navy on October 22, 1940 in Seattle, Washington and completed his basic training at the Naval Training Station in San Diego, California. He reported for duty on the USS Arizona on December 30, 1940. Robert was killed in action on December 7, 1941 in Pearl Harbor, Hawaii. He was awarded the American Defense Service Medal, World War II Victory Medal and Purple Heart Medal posthumously. Robert remains on duty on the USS Arizona. He is commemorated on the USS Arizona Memorial and the Memorial Tablets of the Missing, National Memorial Cemetery of the Pacific, Honolulu, Hawaii. Robert was survived by his Father, Mr. Sam Erickson, Route 4, Snohomish, Washington.

---

[234] Stanley Gordon Enger, Photo from the Minneapolis Star, Minneapolis, Minnesota, May 8, 1942, page 12.
[235] James Robert Enos, Photo provided by family member.

Erwin, Stanley Joe   Machinist's Mate, First Class, Serial No: 359 97 85, US Navy. Stanley was born February 13, 1919 in Missouri to Joseph Marion and Lois Belle (Henderson) Erwin. He enlisted in the US Navy on January 8, 1938 in Houston, Texas and completed his basic training at the Naval Training Station in San Diego, California. He reported for duty on the USS Arizona on April 28, 1938. Stanley was killed in action on December 7, 1941 in Pearl Harbor, Hawaii. He was awarded the American Defense Service Medal, World War II Victory Medal and Purple Heart Medal posthumously. Stanley remains on duty on the USS Arizona. He is commemorated on the USS Arizona Memorial and the Memorial Tablets of the Missing, National Memorial Cemetery of the Pacific, Honolulu, Hawaii. Stanley was survived by his Mother, Mrs. Lois Belle Erwin, 150 North Milam Street, San Benito, Texas.[236]

Erwin, Walton Aluard   Seaman, First Class, Serial No: 356 43 36, US Navy. Walton was born on June 27, 1921 in Texas to George Rushing and Bertha (Darden) Erwin. He enlisted in the US Navy on November 26, 1940 in Dallas, Texas and completed his basic training at the Naval Training Station in San Diego, California. Walton reported for duty on the USS Arizona on January 25, 1941. He was killed in action on December 7, 1941 in Pearl Harbor, Hawaii. Walton was awarded the American Defense Service Medal, World War II Victory Medal and Purple Heart Medal posthumously. He remains on duty on the USS Arizona. Walton is commemorated on the USS Arizona Memorial and the Memorial Tablets of the Missing, National Memorial Cemetery of the Pacific, Honolulu, Hawaii. He was survived by his Father, Mr. George Rushing Erwin, 1008 Orient Street, San Angelo, Texas.

Eskew, Weldon Virgil L.   Machinist's Mate, First Class, A Division, Serial No. 291 48 96, US Navy. Weldon was born October 12, 1918 in Arlington, Indiana the son of James Thomas and Edith Marie Eskew. He went to Arsenal Technical High School in Indianapolis, Indiana, where the family moved when he was about 9 years old. Weldon enlisted in the US Navy on November 18, 1936 and reported for duty on the USS Arizona April 3, 1937. Weldon was serving on the Arizona December 7, 1941 when the Japanese attacked Pearl Harbor. His station was in the Ice Machines, which furnished refrigeration for the food supplies. He would have slept on a cot in the A Division, which was on the second deck, in the central part of the ship, on the Port side. His wife, Evelyn arrived from the mainland on December 6, 1941. Weldon traded duties with someone who was on punishment and therefore couldn't go ashore. After the attack on Pearl, Weldon was assigned to the USS Salt Lake City where he served from December 18, 1941 until November 6, 1942. He served on the USS Arneb as part of Operation Deepfreeze. While aboard, he was pinned against a bulkhead when the ship was holed by an iceberg. Weldon served 19-1/2 years in the Navy. He passed away in August 1971 in Tucson, Arizona. He was in a car wreck caused by a heart attack while he was driving.

---

[236] Stanley Joe Erwin, Photo taken from the San Benio, Texas Historical Society.

Estep, Carl James   Seaman, First Class, Serial No: 356 31 39, US Navy. Carl was born in about 1921 to Parris E. and Alice Estep of Anna, Texas. He enlisted in the US Navy on July 30, 1940 in Dallas, Texas and completed his basic training at the Naval Training Station in San Diego, California. Carl reported for duty on the USS Arizona on October 14, 1940. He was killed in action on December 7, 1941 in Pearl Harbor, Hawaii. Carl was awarded the American Defense Service Medal, World War II Victory Medal and Purple Heart Medal posthumously. He remains on duty on the USS Arizona. Carl is commemorated on the USS Arizona Memorial and the Memorial Tablets of the Missing, National Memorial Cemetery of the Pacific, Honolulu, Hawaii. He was survived by his Father, Mr. Parris E. Estep, Anna, Texas.

Estes, Carl Edwen   Seaman, First Class, Serial No: 360 20 20, US Navy. Carl was born in about 1921 in Kansas to Glen Whitson and Myrtle Estes. He enlisted in the US Navy on August 6, 1940 in Houston, Texas and completed his basic training at the Naval Training Station in San Diego, California. He reported for duty on the USS Arizona on October 8, 1940. Carl was killed in action on December 7, 1941 in Pearl Harbor, Hawaii. He was awarded the American Defense Service Medal, World War II Victory Medal and Purple Heart Medal posthumously. Carl remains on duty on the USS Arizona. He is commemorated on the USS Arizona Memorial and the Memorial Tablets of the Missing, National Memorial Cemetery of the Pacific, Honolulu, Hawaii. Carl was survived by his Father, Mr. Glen Whitson Estes, General Delivery, Freer, Texas.

Estes, Forrest Jesse   Fireman, First Class, Serial No: 375 94 60, US Navy. Forrest was born in 1918 in Montana, son of Jessie M. and Elizabeth Estes. He enlisted in the US Navy on June 9, 1939 in San Francisco, California and completed his basic training at the Naval Training Station in San Diego, California. Forrest reported for duty on the USS Arizona on September 11, 1939. He was killed in action on December 7, 1941 in Pearl Harbor, Hawaii. Forrest was awarded the American Defense Service Medal, World War II Victory Medal and Purple Heart Medal posthumously. He remains on duty on the USS Arizona. Forrest is commemorated on the USS Arizona Memorial and the Memorial Tablets of the Missing, National Memorial Cemetery of the Pacific, Honolulu, Hawaii. He was survived by his Mother, Mrs. Elizabeth Dailey, 4460 X Street, Sacramento, California.[237]

---

[237] Forrest Jesse Estes, Photo and information provided by family member, Mary Klinefelter.

Etchason, Leslie Edgar   Seaman, First Class, Serial No: 337 41 61, US Navy. Leslie was born November 18, 1918 in Clay County, Illinois to Isaac "Ike" Walter and Maude Lola (Smith) Etchason. He enlisted in the US Navy on October 15, 1940 in St. Louis, Missouri and completed his basic training at the Naval Training Station in Great Lakes, Illinois. He reported for duty on the USS Arizona on December 9, 1940. Leslie was killed in action on December 7, 1941 in Pearl Harbor, Hawaii. He was awarded the American Defense Service Medal, World War II Victory Medal and Purple Heart Medal posthumously. Leslie remains on duty on the USS Arizona. He is commemorated on the USS Arizona Memorial and the Memorial Tablets of the Missing, National Memorial Cemetery of the Pacific, Honolulu, Hawaii. Leslie was survived by his Father, Mr. Isaac Walter Etchason, Box 46, Sycamore Street, Flora, Illinois.[238]

Eulberg, Richard Henry   Fire Controlman, Second Class, Serial No: 321 23 77, US Navy. Richard was born on February 28, 1917 in Iowa to Henry J. and Elsie M. (Bittner) Eulberg. He enlisted in the US Navy on March 9, 1938 in Des Moines, Iowa and completed his basic training at the Naval Training Station in Great Lakes, Illinois. Richard reported for duty on the USS Arizona on July 9, 1938. He was killed in action on December 7, 1941 in Pearl Harbor, Hawaii. Richard was awarded the American Defense Service Medal, World War II Victory Medal and Purple Heart Medal posthumously. He remains on duty on the USS Arizona. Richard is commemorated on the USS Arizona Memorial and the Memorial Tablets of the Missing, National Memorial Cemetery of the Pacific, Honolulu, Hawaii. He was survived by his Father, Mr. Henry J. Eulberg, Garnavillo, Iowa.

Evans, Evan Frederick   Ensign, Serial No: 0-095377, US Naval Reserve. Evan was born December 6, 1916 in San Francisco County, California to Lieutenant Commander Frederick and Catherine Belle Evans. He was commissioned November 14, 1940 and served as the Junior Watch and Division 6 officer. His battle station was Port AA Battery Officer. Evan was killed in action on December 7, 1941 in Pearl Harbor, Hawaii. He was awarded the American Defense Service Medal, World War II Victory Medal and Purple Heart Medal posthumously. Evan remains on duty on the USS Arizona. He is commemorated on the USS Arizona Memorial and the Memorial Tablets of the Missing, National Memorial Cemetery of the Pacific, Honolulu, Hawaii. Evan was survived by his Wife, Mrs. Gretta G. Evans, 4122 Lakeshore Avenue, Oakland, California.

Evans, John Willard   Seaman, First Class, Serial No. 272 41 88, US Navy. John was born on January 1, 1922 in Waterloo, Alabama. He enlisted in the US Navy on October 4, 1940 in Birmingham, Alabama and completed his basic training at the Naval Training Station in Norfolk, Virginia. John reported for duty on the USS Arizona on December 3, 1940. He was serving on the Arizona on December 7, 1941 when the Japanese attacked Pearl Harbor. On the morning of the attack, John was setting out chairs for a Sunday service aboard the Arizona. He went to his battle station when the attack started but soon realized the ship was doomed. He smelled

---

[238] Leslie Edgar Etchason, Photo taken from Leslie Etchason, U.S. Family Photo Collection, 1941.

something and knew it was going to blow up. John eventually swam to safety through the oily, burning harbor water. After the attack, John was transferred to the USS Mac Donough for duty. He continued his service during the war on other ships and received: Presidential Unit Citation, American Defense Service Medal with four bronze stars, Philippine Liberation Medal, European African Middle Eastern Campaign Medal, World War II Victory Medal and Good Conduct Medal. John died on September 19, 2005 in Dallas, Texas and is buried in Section 76, Site 432, Dallas Fort Worth National Cemetery, Dallas, Texas.[239]

Evans, Mickey Edward   Seaman, First Class, Serial No: 337 46 54, US Navy. Mickey was born in 1922 in Springfield, Missouri to James Silas Evans. He enlisted in the US Navy on November 29, 1940 in St. Louis, Missouri and completed his basic training at the Naval Training Station in Great Lakes, Illinois. He reported for duty on the USS Arizona on January 18, 1941. Mickey was killed in action on December 7, 1941 in Pearl Harbor, Hawaii. He was awarded the American Defense Service Medal, World War II Victory Medal and Purple Heart Medal posthumously. Mickey remains on duty on the USS Arizona. He is commemorated on the USS Arizona Memorial and the Memorial Tablets of the Missing, National Memorial Cemetery of the Pacific, Honolulu, Hawaii. Mickey was survived by his Father, Mr. James S. Evans, 745 North Delaware Avenue, Springfield, Missouri.

Evans, Paul Anthony   Seaman, First Class, Serial No: 337 25 04, US Navy. Paul was born on August 22, 1919 in Fillmore, Illinois to Morgan and Lydia Louise (Understall) Evans. He enlisted in the US Navy on December 27, 1939 in St. Louis, Missouri and completed his training at the Naval Training Station in Great Lakes, Illinois. Paul reported for duty on the USS Arizona on March 23, 1940. He was killed in action on December 7, 1941 in Pearl Harbor, Hawaii. Paul was awarded the American Defense Service Medal, World War II Victory Medal and Purple Heart Medal posthumously. He remains on duty on the USS Arizona. Paul is commemorated on the USS Arizona Memorial and the Memorial Tablets of the Missing, National Memorial Cemetery of the Pacific, Honolulu, Hawaii. He was survived by his Father, Mr. Morgan Evans, Fillmore, Illinois.[240]

Evans, William Orville   Seaman, Second Class, Serial No: 368 53 27, US Navy. William was born February 6, 1913 in Geneva, Idaho to William Rufus Rogers and Eliza (Bischoff) Evans. He enlisted in the US Navy on November 5, 1940 in Salt Lake City, Utah and completed his basic training at the Naval Training Station in San Diego, California. He reported for duty on the USS Arizona on January 11, 1941. William was killed in action on December 7, 1941 in Pearl Harbor, Hawaii. He was awarded the American Defense Service Medal, World War II Victory Medal and Purple Heart Medal posthumously. William remains on duty on the USS Arizona. He is commemorated on the USS Arizona Memorial and the Memorial Tablets of the Missing, National Memorial Cemetery of the Pacific, Honolulu, Hawaii. William was survived by his Mother, Mrs. Eliza Evans Nourland, Geneva, Idaho.

---

[239] John Willard Evans, photo curtsey LCDR G. Dale McKissick, USNR, Memorial, Dallas Convention Center, Dallas, Texas.
[240] Paul Anthony Evans, Photo and information provided by family member, Michael Stephen "Steve" Jackson.

Eversole, Elmer Everett Seaman, First Class, Serial No. 287 45 89, US Navy. Elmer was born May 12, 1921 in Kentucky to Arthur and Bonnie B. Eversole. He enlisted in the US Navy October 15, 1940 in Louisville, Kentucky and completed his basic training at the Naval Training Station in Great Lakes, Illinois. Elmer reported for duty on the USS Arizona December 9, 1940. He was serving on the Arizona December 7, 1941 when the Japanese attacked Pearl Harbor. After the attack, Elmer was transferred to the USS Dale for duty. Elmer died on November 9, 1982 in Renton, Washington.

Ewell, Alfred Adam Watertender, First Class, Serial No: 380 72 42, US Navy. Alfred was born on August 25, 1911 in Idaho to Quarles Denton and May (Luxton) Ewell. He enlisted in the US Navy in Washington State and re-enlisted on October 23, 1935 in San Pedro, California. Alfred served on the USS Arizona from April 3, 1931 until he was killed in action on December 7, 1941 in Pearl Harbor, Hawaii. He was awarded the American Defense Service Medal, World War II Victory Medal and Purple Heart Medal posthumously. Alfred remains on duty on the USS Arizona. He is commemorated on the USS Arizona Memorial and the Memorial Tablets of the Missing, National Memorial Cemetery of the Pacific, Honolulu, Hawaii. Alfred was survived by his Wife, Mrs. Evelyn Elizabeth Ewell, 9709 Maie Avenue, Los Angeles, California.

Eyed, George Storekeeper, Third Class, Serial No: 291 51 97, US Navy. George was September 18, 1918 in Indianapolis, Indiana to Walt and Mannine Eyed. His father died in a traffic accident when George was just six years old. Then his mother died just before his 16th birthday. His only sister, Helen, died of tuberculosis the next year. He enlisted in the US Navy on October 5, 1937 and reported for duty on the USS Arizona on June 4, 1938. George was killed in action on December 7, 1941 in Pearl Harbor, Hawaii. He was awarded the American Defense Service Medal, World War II Victory Medal and Purple Heart Medal posthumously. George remains on duty on the USS Arizona. He is commemorated on the USS Arizona Memorial and the Memorial Tablets of the Missing, National Memorial Cemetery of the Pacific, Honolulu, Hawaii. George was survived by his Guardian, Mr. Joe D. Avid, 623 North New Jersey, Indianapolis, Indiana.[241]

Eyman, Lawrence Oliver Seaman, First Class, Serial No. 356 33 95, US Navy. Lawrence was born on September 17, 1921 in Drumright, Oklahoma, the son of David Earl and Helen Reba (West) Eyman. He enlisted in the US Navy August 6, 1940 in Dallas, Texas and completed his basic training at the Naval Training Station in San Diego, California. Lawrence reported for duty on the USS Arizona October 8, 1940. He was serving on the Arizona December 7, 1941 when the Japanese attacked Pearl Harbor. After the attack, Lawrence was transferred to the USS Chester for duty. Lawrence died on May 5, 1968 in Oklahoma City, Oklahoma and is buried in Section 10, Site 2294, Fort Gibson National Cemetery, Fort Gibson, Oklahoma.

---

[241] George Eyed, Photo provided by history teacher, Thomas Clark, Lake Central High School, St. John, Indiana.

Falge, Francis "Frank" Marion Lieutenant, US Navy. Francis was born on October 11, 1903 in Manitowoc, Wisconsin. He enlisted in the US Navy in 1919 and graduated from the Naval Academy in 1924. In February of 1941 he was recalled to active service and reported for duty on the USS Arizona where he was serving as Assistant Damage Control Officer and Assistant 1st Lieutenant on December 7, 1941 when the Japanese attacked Pearl Harbor. He was on shore leave attending mass at the time of the attack. He quickly went to the harbor and helped in rescue efforts for the next several days. Francis died on January 1, 2000 in Carmel, Monterey, California and was interred on the USS Arizona on April 26, 2000.[242]

Fallis, Alvin Eustance Jr. Pharmacist's Mate, Second Class, Serial No: 346 67 53, US Navy. Alvin was born in about 1915 in Arkansas to Alvin Eustance and Lillian (Jones) Fallis. He enlisted in the US Navy on August 17, 1937 in Little Rock, Arkansas and reported for duty on the USS Arizona on January 19, 1940. He was killed in action on December 7, 1941 in Pearl Harbor, Hawaii. Alvin was awarded the American Defense Service Medal, World War II Victory Medal and Purple Heart Medal posthumously. He remains on duty on the USS Arizona. Alvin is commemorated on the USS Arizona Memorial and the Memorial Tablets of the Missing, National Memorial Cemetery of the Pacific, Honolulu, Hawaii. He was survived by his Wife, Mrs. Louise Lester Fallis, 2859 F Street, San Diego, California.

Fansler, Edgar Arthur Seaman, First Class, Serial No: 337 25 05, US Navy. Edgar was born April 5, 1920 in Welch, Oklahoma to Edgar Arthur and Mary Edna (Pendergraft) Fansler. He enlisted in the US Navy on December 27, 1939 in St. Louis, Missouri and completed his basic training at the Naval Training Station in Great Lakes, Illinois. Edgar reported for duty on the USS Arizona on March 23, 1940. He was killed in action on December 7, 1941 in Pearl Harbor, Hawaii. Edgar was awarded the American Defense Service Medal, World War II Victory Medal and Purple Heart Medal posthumously. He remains on duty on the USS Arizona. Edgar is commemorated on the USS Arizona Memorial and the Memorial Tablets of the Missing, National Memorial Cemetery of the Pacific, Honolulu, Hawaii and the Miami Cemetery, Miami, Oklahoma. He was survived by his Mother, Mrs. Mary Fansler, Route 1, Welch, Oklahoma.

Farmer, John "Bill" Wilson Coxswain, Serial No: 287 35 56, US Navy. John was born in 1921 in Tennessee to John and Artie Farmer. He enlisted in the US Navy on December 27, 1939 in Louisville, Kentucky and completed his basic training at the Naval Training Station in Great Lakes, Illinois. He reported for duty on the USS Arizona on March 23, 1940. John was killed in action on December 7, 1941 in Pearl Harbor, Hawaii. He was awarded the American Defense Service Medal, World War II Victory Medal and Purple Heart Medal posthumously. John remains on duty on the USS Arizona. He is commemorated on the USS Arizona Memorial and the Memorial Tablets of the Missing, National Memorial Cemetery of the Pacific, Honolulu, Hawaii. John was survived by his Mother, Mrs. Artie Farmer, 2517 O'Cole Street, East Chattanooga, Tennessee.[243]

---

[242] Francis "Frank" Marion Falge, Photo from Lucky Bag Yearbook, United States Naval Academy, Annapolis, MD, class of 1924.

[243] John "Bill" Wilson Farmer, Photo taken from the Chattanooga, Tennessee Newspaper, Sunday, December 4, 1966.

Farquhar, Lawrence Albert Fire Controlman, Second Class, Serial No. 385 78 99, US Navy. Lawrence was born on March 16, 1921 in Treasure, Montana the son of George Archibald and Ina May (Briggs) Farquhar. He enlisted in the US Navy September 13, 1938 and reported for duty on the USS Arizona January 2, 1939. Lawrence was serving on the Arizona December 7, 1941 when the Japanese attacked Pearl Harbor. He was wounded in action during the attack and he was transferred to the Naval Hospital at Mare Island, California. Lawrence died on May 24, 1986 in Orange County, California.

Faulkner, Paul Harding Seaman, First Class, Serial No. 266 01 80, US Navy. Paul was born on June 25, 1921 in Roanoke, Virginia. He enlisted in the US Navy December 21, 1939 in Richmond, Virginia and completed his basic training at the Naval Training Station in Norfolk, Virginia. Paul reported for duty on the USS Arizona March 8, 1940. He was serving on the Arizona December 7, 1941 when the Japanese attacked Pearl Harbor. After the attack, Paul was transferred to the USS Mac Donough for duty. He retired from the Navy in April 1971. Paul died on April 3, 2006 and is buried in Blue Ridge Memorial Gardens, Roanoke, Virginia.

Fay, Lawrence Edward Gunner's Mate, Third Class, Serial No. 360 09 46, US Navy. Lawrence enlisted in the US Navy December 7, 1939 in Houston, Texas and completed his basic training at the Naval Training Station in San Diego, California. He reported for duty on the USS Arizona February 24, 1940. Lawrence was serving on the Arizona December 7, 1941 when the Japanese attacked Pearl Harbor. His official statement:

"On the morning of December 7, 1941, I had just returned to the turret when the air raid alarm was sounded. It was only a minute or so until General Quarters was sounded and I went up to the gun to man my station. We had been hit by that time and all lights were out in the turret. No telephone in the turrets would work.

The division officer ordered all men out on deck to fight fires. I tried the fire plug just aft of turret III, and there was no water, so I found a fire extinguisher on deck, but it only lasted a second or so. Keener said, "There is a man", so we got him out and then helped a couple more. Mr. Fuqua and Mr. Miller were taking charge of fire fighting and cutting the Vestal's lines so they could get underway. We opened the hatches to the officers' quarters, so that they could escape and then I got a light and went back into turret III, to see if anyone was still there. No one was found, so I went back out on deck and helped get a life raft over the side, but it was of no use, as the raft was drifting into the burning oil and we had to swim. A boat came alongside with Otterman, Bruns, Mr. Fuqua and Mr. Miller in it and picked several men out of the water. They carried us to the landing and Mr. Fuqua returned to the ship to see if any one else had been left."[244]

After the attack, Lawrence was transferred to the USS Bagley for duty. He later served on the USS Randolph (CV-15).

Fegurgur, Nicholas San Nicolas Mess Attendant, Second Class, Serial No: 421 05 68, US Navy. Nicholas was born in about 1921 in Guam to Enrique Fegurgur and Maria Antoigue San Nicolas. He enlisted in the US Navy on February 1, 1940 at the Naval Station in Guam and reported for duty on the USS Arizona on June 24, 1940. He was killed in action on December 7,

---

[244] Confidential Statement of Lawrence Edward Fay, GM3c, U.S. Navy, U.S.S. Arizona, Concerning Action Against Enemy on December 7, 1941.

1941 in Pearl Harbor, Hawaii. Nicholas was awarded the American Defense Service Medal, World War II Victory Medal and Purple Heart Medal posthumously. He remains on duty on the USS Arizona. Nicholas is commemorated on the USS Arizona Memorial and the Memorial Tablets of the Missing, National Memorial Cemetery of the Pacific, Honolulu, Hawaii and the Sons of Guam Pearl Harbor Memorial, Guam. He was survived by his Father, Mr. Enrique Fegurgur Fegurgur, Lot 3027, Sinajana, Guam.

Felton, Nathaniel   Mess Attendant, First Class, Serial No. 272 23 21, US Navy. Nathaniel was born on January 15, 1920. He enlisted in the US Navy on October 20, 1939 in Birmingham, Alabama and completed his basic training at the Naval Training Station in Norfolk, Virginia. Nathaniel reported for duty on the USS Arizona January 19, 1940 and was serving on the Arizona on December 7, 1941 when the Japanese attacked Pearl Harbor. After the attack, Nathaniel was transferred to the USS Drayton for duty. Nathaniel died on December 24, 1978 and is buried in Section 6, Site 3575, Calverton National Cemetery, Calverton, New York.

Fess, John Junior   Fireman, First Class, Serial No: 382 09 68, US Navy. John was born September 14, 1920 to John H. and Persis K. (Shugg) Fess. He enlisted in the US Navy on June 13, 1939 in Los Angeles, California and completed his basic training at the Naval Training Station in San Diego, California. John reported for duty on the USS Arizona on September 11, 1939. He was killed in action on December 7, 1941 in Pearl Harbor, Hawaii. John was awarded the American Defense Service Medal, World War II Victory Medal and Purple Heart Medal posthumously. He remains on duty on the USS Arizona. John is commemorated on the USS Arizona Memorial and the Memorial Tablets of the Missing, National Memorial Cemetery of the Pacific, Honolulu, Hawaii. He was survived by his Mother, Mrs. John H. Fess, 1729 Arlington Avenue, Los Angeles, California.[245]

Field, Jennings Pemble   Ensign, US Navy Reserve. Jennings was born December 29, 1920 in Merigold, Mississippi, the son of Jennings Pemble Field and Matilda Catherine "Kate" Byrne Field. He was commissioned Ensign in the US Navy on March 14, 1941 and was serving as Junior Watch and Division 3 Officer on the USS Arizona. His battle station was Turret III on December 7, 1941 when the Japanese attacked Pearl Harbor. After the attack, Jennings was taken on board the USS Solace Hospital Ship to care for his injuries. Jennings retired from the Navy in June 1954 as a Captain. He died April 17, 1986 in Germantown, Shelby, Tennessee and was buried at the Crigger Cemetery, Munford, Tipton, Tennessee.

Fields, Bernard   Radioman, Second Class, Serial No: 411 02 46, US Naval Reserve. Bernard was born in about 1916 in Cleveland to Bernard and Sylvia Feigenbaum. He changed his name from Feigenbaum to Fields when he enlisted. Bernard enlisted in the US Navy on August 27, 1940 and reported for duty on the USS Arizona January 25, 1941. Bernard was killed in action on December 7, 1941 in Pearl Harbor, Hawaii. He was awarded the American Defense Service Medal, World War II Victory Medal and Purple Heart Medal posthumously. Bernard remains on duty on the USS Arizona. He is commemorated on the USS Arizona Memorial and the Memorial Tablets of the Missing, National Memorial Cemetery of the Pacific,

---

[245] John Junior Fess, Photo from the 1937 Torrance High School Yearbook, Torrance, California.

Honolulu, Hawaii. Bernard was survived by his Mother, Mrs. Bernard Feigenbaum, 1301 East Boulevard, Cleveland, Ohio.

Fields, Reliford Mess Attendant, Second Class, Serial No: 272 22 87, US Navy. Reliford was born in about 1917 in Florida the son of Jessie and Mary Fields. He enlisted in the US Navy on October 12, 1939 in Birmingham, Alabama and reported for duty on the USS Arizona on February 20, 1940. He was killed in action on December 7, 1941 in Pearl Harbor, Hawaii. Reliford was awarded the American Defense Service Medal, World War II Victory Medal and Purple Heart Medal posthumously. He remains on duty on the USS Arizona. Reliford is commemorated on the USS Arizona Memorial and the Memorial Tablets of the Missing, National Memorial Cemetery of the Pacific, Honolulu, Hawaii. He was survived by his Mother, Mrs. Mary Watkins Fields, P.O. Box 492, Quincy, Florida.

Fife, Ralph Elmer Seaman, First Class, Serial No: 382 23 42, US Navy. Ralph was born January 23, 1920 to Raymond Ralph and Elsie Bell (Cain) Fife. He enlisted in the US Navy on July 26, 1940 in Los Angeles, California and completed his basic training at the Naval Training Station in San Diego, California. He reported for duty on the USS Arizona on October 14, 1940. Ralph was killed in action on December 7, 1941 in Pearl Harbor, Hawaii. He was awarded the American Defense Service Medal, World War II Victory Medal and Purple Heart Medal posthumously. Ralph remains on duty on the USS Arizona. He is commemorated on the USS Arizona Memorial and the Memorial Tablets of the Missing, National Memorial Cemetery of the Pacific, Honolulu, Hawaii. Ralph was survived by his Father, Mr. Raymond R. Fife, 102 Brotherton Street, Corona, California.[246]

Filkins, George Arthur Coxswain, Serial No: 328 65 25, US Navy. George was born January 6, 1922 at Fort Snelling, Minnesota to Sgt.William Henry and Lydia Elizabeth (Chapin) Filkins. He enlisted in the US Navy on January 24, 1940 in Minneapolis, Minnesota and completed his basic training at the Naval Training Station in Great Lakes, Illinois. George reported for duty on the USS Arizona on March 26, 1940. He was killed in action on December 7, 1941 in Pearl Harbor, Hawaii. George was awarded the American Defense Service Medal, World War II Victory Medal and Purple Heart Medal posthumously. He remains on duty on the USS Arizona. George is commemorated on the USS Arizona Memorial and the Memorial Tablets of the Missing, National Memorial Cemetery of the Pacific, Honolulu, Hawaii and Fort Snelling National Cemetery, Minneapolis, Minnesota. He was survived by his Mother, Mrs. Lydia Elizabeth Filkins, 2350 West Seventh Street, St. Paul, Minnesota and one sister, Blanche.

Finger, William Ralph Signalman, First Class, Serial No. 283 14 90, US Navy. William was born June 1, 1915 in Akron, Ohio the son of Alfred C. and Olive M. (Cramer) Finger. He enlisted in the US Navy September 17, 1935 in Cleveland, Ohio and reported for duty on the USS Arizona July 10, 1941. William was serving on the Arizona December 7, 1941 when the Japanese attacked Pearl Harbor. After the attack, William was transferred to the Section Base, Bishop's Point, Oahu, Hawaii for duty. In September 1943 he achieved the rank of Ensign while serving on board the USS Hammondsport (APV-2). Less than a year later, August 31, 1944 he was appointed the rank of Lieutenant while serving on board the USS LST-592. William died October 22, 2006 in Lake, California.

---

[246] Ralph Elmer Fife, Photo from the 1937 Corona High School Yearbook, Corona, California.

150

Firth, Henry Amis Fireman, Third Class, Serial No: 381 37 80, US Navy. Henry was born May 12, 1919 in Kentucky to Frank and Edith Firth. He enlisted in the US Navy on November 7, 1940 in San Diego, California and completed his basic training at the Naval Training Station in San Diego, California. He reported for duty on the USS Arizona on January 11, 1941. Henry was killed in action on December 7, 1941 in Pearl Harbor, Hawaii. He was awarded the American Defense Service Medal, World War II Victory Medal and Purple Heart Medal posthumously. Henry remains on duty on the USS Arizona. He is commemorated on the USS Arizona Memorial and the Memorial Tablets of the Missing, National Memorial Cemetery of the Pacific, Honolulu, Hawaii. Henry was survived by his Mother, Mrs. Edith M. Shrope, 1247 Columbia Street, San Diego, California.

Fischer, Leslie Henry Seaman, First Class, Serial No: 328 79 93, US Navy. Leslie was born November 17, 1923 in Sioux City, Iowa to Edward and Rose Emilie (Otto) Fischer. He enlisted in the US Navy on November 27, 1940 in Minneapolis, Minnesota and completed his basic training at the Naval Training Station in San Diego, California. Leslie reported for duty on the USS Arizona on January 18, 1941. He was killed in action on December 7, 1941 in Pearl Harbor, Hawaii. Leslie was awarded the American Defense Service Medal, World War II Victory Medal and Purple Heart Medal posthumously. He remains on duty on the USS Arizona. Leslie is commemorated on the USS Arizona Memorial and the Memorial Tablets of the Missing, National Memorial Cemetery of the Pacific, Honolulu, Hawaii. He was survived by his Father, Mr. Edward Fischer, 1537 North Cass Street, Milwaukee, Wisconsin.[247]

Fisher, Delbert Ray Seaman, First Class, Serial No: 372 16 36, US Navy. Delbert was born in 1920 in Wyoming to Floyd Delbert and Bessie J. (Tull) Fisher. He enlisted in the US Navy on August 3, 1940 in Denver, Colorado and completed his basic training at the Naval Training Station in San Diego, California. He reported for duty on the USS Arizona on October 14, 1940. Delbert was killed in action on December 7, 1941 in Pearl Harbor, Hawaii. He was awarded the American Defense Service Medal, World War II Victory Medal and Purple Heart Medal posthumously. Delbert remains on duty on the USS Arizona. He is commemorated on the USS Arizona Memorial and the Memorial Tablets of the Missing, National Memorial Cemetery of the Pacific, Honolulu, Hawaii. Delbert was survived by his Father, Mr. Floyd Delbert Fisher, Laramie, Wyoming.

Fisher, James Anderson Mess Attendant, First Class, Serial No: 265 99 61, US Navy. James was born June 29, 1921 in Virginia to Anderson Perry and Pearl Fisher. He enlisted in the US Navy on October 17, 1939 in Richmond, Virginia and reported for duty on the USS Arizona on January 19, 1940. He was killed in action on December 7, 1941 in Pearl Harbor, Hawaii. James was awarded the American Defense Service Medal, World War II Victory Medal and Purple Heart Medal posthumously. He remains on duty on the USS Arizona. James is commemorated on the USS Arizona Memorial and the Memorial Tablets of the Missing, National Memorial Cemetery of the Pacific, Honolulu, Hawaii and the Andrew's & Brown Cemetery, Greenville, County, Virginia. He was survived by his Father, Mr. Anderson Perry Fisher, Emporia, Virginia.

---

[247] Leslie Henry Fischer, photo from the Chicago Tribune, Chicago, Illinois, May 5, 1942, Page 9.

Fisher, Robert Ray Seaman, Second Class, Serial No: 376 23 26, US Navy. Robert was born in about 1923 in Oregon. He quit high school to join the Navy he was sworn in January 28, 1941 in San Francisco, California. Robert completed his training at the US Naval Training Station in San Diego, California on April 10, 1941. He was transferred to sea, assigned duty on the USS Arizona (BB-39) and boarded the ship April 27, 1941. Robert was killed in action on December 7, 1941 in Pearl Harbor, Hawaii. He was awarded the American Defense Service Medal, World War II Victory Medal and Purple Heart Medal posthumously. Robert remains on duty on the USS Arizona. He is commemorated on the USS Arizona Memorial and the Memorial Tablets of the Missing, National Memorial Cemetery of the Pacific, Honolulu, Hawaii. Robert was survived by his Father, Mr. Ray Sterling Fisher, 3210 Filbert Street, Oakland, California.[248]

Fisk, Charles Porter, III Yeoman, First Class, Aviation Unit (VO-1), Serial No: 368 18 92, US Navy. Charles was born October 25, 1911 in Montana, the only son of Charles Porter and Agnes Adora (Eaman) Fisk. He enlisted in the US Navy August 8, 1937 in San Francisco, California and reported for duty on the USS Arizona on August 7, 1937. Charles was killed in action on December 7, 1941 in Pearl Harbor, Hawaii. He was awarded the American Defense Service Medal, World War II Victory Medal and Purple Heart Medal posthumously. Charles remains on duty on the USS Arizona. He is commemorated on the USS Arizona Memorial and the Memorial Tablets of the Missing, National Memorial Cemetery of the Pacific, Honolulu, Hawaii and Forsyth Cemetery, Forsyth, Montana. Charles was survived by his Parents, Mr. Charles Porter Fisk, Jr. and Mrs. Agnes Adora (Eaman) Fisk, 821 West 4th Street, Long Beach, California and three sisters, Mrs. Bessie E Fisk Clark, Mary and Jean Fisk.

Fitch, Harry Lionel Ensign, US Navy Reserve. Harry was born on September 24, 1914 in Luther, Michigan the son of Harry Russel Fitch and Minnie (Frisbie) Fitch. He was commissioned Ensign in the US Navy in June 1941 and was serving as Junior Watch and Division R Officer. His battle station was Repair IV on the USS Arizona December 7, 1941 when the Japanese attacked Pearl Harbor. Harry was on liberty at the time of the attack. As his taxi came to the boat landing that morning he could see the smoke rising from burning oil floating around the ships. "The smoke was so thick we could not identify which ships were burning. I spied the Arizona boat making a bow wave as it approached the landing and the boat's crew leaped onto the dock to secure the boat; men in grimy dirty white uniforms began leaping onto the dock. I edged close to the boat to jump aboard when Ensign Greasy Glenn jumped off the boat onto the dock. He yelled "It's no use, Fitch. The ship's been abandoned." I couldn't believe it. Then I began hearing snatches of talk, a bomb going down the stack and blowing up. At first I was stunned. The sense of tragedy has taken a while to develop." Harry went on to serve on the USS South Dakota the remaining of the War. He was also the commanding officer of the USS Murray (DD-576) from August 22, 1953 to August 1955. Harry died on June 3, 2005 in Port Townsend, Washington and was interred with full military honors on the USS Arizona on December 7, 2005.

Fitch, Simon Mess Attendant, First Class, Serial No: 360 07 29, US Navy. Simon was born in about 1920 in Houston, Texas to Arthur and Carrie Mae (Chandler) Fitch. He enlisted in the US Navy on October 14, 1939 in Houston, Texas and reported for duty on the USS Arizona on January 19, 1940. Simon was killed in action on December 7, 1941 in Pearl Harbor, Hawaii.

---

[248] Robert Ray Fisher, Information and Photo provided by family members, Kathy and Phillip Fisher.

He was awarded the American Defense Service Medal, World War II Victory Medal and Purple Heart Medal posthumously. Simon remains on duty on the USS Arizona. He is commemorated on the USS Arizona Memorial and the Memorial Tablets of the Missing, National Memorial Cemetery of the Pacific, Honolulu, Hawaii. Simon was survived by his Father, Mr. Arthur Fitch, 4522 Inker Street, Houston, Texas.

Fitzsimmons, Eugene James Fireman, Third Class, Serial No: 300 19 41, US Navy. Eugene was born in 1921 in Aurora, Illinois to Richard Francis and Gertrude Eileen (Lannen) Fitzsimmons. He enlisted in the US Navy on October 8, 1940 in Chicago, Illinois and completed his basic training at the Naval Training Station in Great Lakes, Illinois. He reported for duty on the USS Arizona on December 9, 1940. Eugene was killed in action on December 7, 1941 in Pearl Harbor, Hawaii. He was awarded the American Defense Service Medal, World War II Victory Medal and Purple Heart Medal posthumously. Eugene remains on duty on the USS Arizona. He is commemorated on the USS Arizona Memorial and the Memorial Tablets of the Missing, National Memorial Cemetery of the Pacific, Honolulu, Hawaii. Eugene was survived by his Father, Mr. Richard Francis Fitzsimmons, 713 Gates Street, Aurora, Illinois.[249]

Flanagan, Guy Spalding, Jr. Ensign, US Navy Reserve. Guy was born on September 9, 1918 in Illinois. He was commissioned Ensign June 12, 1941 and was serving as Junior Watch and Division 3 Officer. His battle station was Turret III. Guy was wounded in action on board the USS Arizona on December 7, 1941 when the Japanese attacked Pearl Harbor.

"I was in the bunk room that morning and everyone there thought it was a joke to have an air raid on Sunday. Then I heard the explosion. Undressed, I climbed into some kaki clothes and shoes. Then the General Alarm went off. "I made for my GQ station. I don't remember any word passed over the speaker system. My station was the lower room of turret 3. Just as the men and I got down the ladder leading to the passageway between the lower rooms of turret 3 and 5, a bomb exploded. The lights went out. It seemed to be on the third deck, starboard side between turrets 3 and 4. When that bomb hit, it made a whish with a gust of hot air and sparks flew. There followed a very nauseating gas and smoke immediately afterwards. Before this time, "Condition Red" had been set in the lower room of turret 3 and the men in the passage and I was unable to get out of the passageway. I beat on the door for some minutes before someone inside the turret opened the door. We got all the men we could find in the passage way into the lower room, and then dogged down the passageway door. We were unable to dog down the door of the port passageway between turrets 3 and 4 because it had been sprung by an explosion. The air in the turret was fairly clear for awhile, but finally gas or smoke started coming in. The men made quite a bit of confusion at first but they were very obedient when Ensign Field and I ordered them to keep quiet. About this time we got a flashlight and saw the turret was very misty with smoke. Just after this, we heard a hissing noise which was later discovered to be air leaking from holes in the forward transverse bulkhead of the lower room. Ensign Field tried to get Central Station on the ship's service phone, but the phones were out. We also tried the sound powered phones which were also out. Conditions from smoke were getting

---

[249] Eugene James Fitzsimmons, Photo and information provided by family member, Michalene Lannen Hauser.

worse and worse. It was then that we decided that we would have to leave the lower room. We sent men up the ladder to open the hatches to the electric deck, shell room and pits. The men had difficulty opening the first hatch. Men were coughing badly when it was finally opened. We went up to the pits on the double. There were two men and Ensign Field and I left in the lower room when water began to enter the room. It was about 8 inches deep when Ensign Field and I finally left. We were the last two up. We climbed the ladder closing all the hatches behind us. I took charge of the men in the pits and Ensign Field went out on deck to help Lt. Cmdr. Fuqua. We saw smoke entering the pits through the pointers and trainers telescope slots. I urged the men to take off their shirts, and we closed the openings with clothes. After a short time, we got word from Ensign Field to come out on deck; the ship seemed to be ablaze from the boat deck forward. We then unlashed the life raft on the starboard side of turret 3, and threw it into the water. I sent the men aboard the raft and shoved it off. I was then called aft, and helped men who were wounded into the barge, leaving for Ford Island. I went in the barge for Ford Island and helped men to the front of the air-raid shelter and into trucks taking them to medical aid. By this time, the ship was ablaze from forward of turret 3 to the bow. There were no boats to make another trip when I returned to the Landing. I went to the air-raid shelter."[250]

His mother, Mrs. Guy S. Flanagan, Sr., 812 South Broad Street, Mankato, Minnesota was notified. Guy retired from the Navy in 1959 achieving the rank of Lieutenant Commander. He died on November 17, 1991 in Roseville, Minnesota and is commemorated in Section MB, Site 39, Fort Snelling National Cemetery, Minneapolis, Minnesota. His ashes were interred on the USS Arizona May 13, 1992.

Flannery, James Lowell Storekeeper, Third Class, Serial No: 279 73 78, US Navy. James was born in about 1919 in Kentucky to Rev. James H. and Martha E. (Creech) Flannery. He enlisted in the US Navy on October 7, 1940 in Cincinnati, Ohio and completed his basic training at the Naval Training Station in Great Lakes, Illinois. James reported for duty on the USS Arizona on December 9, 1940. He was killed in action on December 7, 1941 in Pearl Harbor, Hawaii. James was awarded the American Defense Service Medal, World War II Victory Medal and Purple Heart Medal posthumously. He remains on duty on the USS Arizona. James is commemorated on the USS Arizona Memorial and the Memorial Tablets of the Missing, National Memorial Cemetery of the Pacific, Honolulu, Hawaii. He was survived by his Father, Rev. James Harvey Flannery, 1806 Jackson Avenue, Portsmouth, Ohio and his brother, Wendell Lee Flannery who was also serving on board the USS Arizona and survived the Japanese attack. The James L. Flannery American Legion Post #276 of South Shore, Kentucky was named in his honor.[251]

Flannery, Wendell Lee Coxswain, Serial No. 279 72 82, US Navy. Wendell was born on March 22, 1921 in Kentucky to James H. and Martha E. (Creech) Flannery. He enlisted in the US Navy on September 9, 1940 in Cincinnati, Ohio and completed his basic training at the Naval Training Station in Norfolk, Virginia. Wendell reported for duty on the USS Arizona December 4, 1940. He was serving on the Arizona December 7, 1941 when the Japanese attacked Pearl Harbor. His brother, James Lowell Flannery was killed in action on board the USS Arizona during the Japanese attack. Wendell died on July 17, 1999 and is buried in Bellefonte Memorial Gardens, Flatwoods, Kentucky.

---

[250] Official statement of G. S. Flannigan, Ensign, D-V(G), U.S.S. Arizona after the attack at Pearl Harbor.
[251] James Lowell Flannery, Photo provided by the James L. Flannery American Legion Post #276, South Shore, Kentucky.

Floege, Frank Norman   Musician, Second Class, Serial No: 300 38 73, US Navy. Frank was born on November 20, 1921 in Chicago, Illinois to Frank Floege, Sr. and Agnes (Frisk) Floege. *His younger brother Warren Floege was born Sept 22, 1923. Frank's father left the family before Warren was born. His grandmother only heard from him once when he wanted to take Frank to live with him and offered Agnes a sum of $500. Frank's grandmother told him that Agnes was not interested as there was another son now. Frank Senior was never heard from again. His mother, Agnes died when both sons were fairly young. Probably when they were 6 & 8 years of age. Both boys were placed in an orphanage called "Illinois Soldiers and Sailors Home" (ISSCS) of Normal, Illinois. Over the years, they lived in foster homes after the orphanage.* Frank graduated from Thornton Township High School in 1939 and enlisted is the US Navy on March 28, 1941 and completed his basic training at the Naval Training Station in Great Lakes, Illinois. He reported for duty on the USS Arizona on June 17, 1941. Frank was a member of the band and Orchestra while in high school. After graduating he decided to go into the Navy. He entered the U.S. Navy School of Music in April 1941. Frank was an Apprentice Seaman when he graduated from the School of Music. He was hoisting up gun powder bags under gun turret number 2 when the bomb entered through the upper deck and exploded, killing all the band members. He was awarded the American Defense Service Medal, World War II Victory Medal and Purple Heart Medal posthumously. Frank remains on duty on the USS Arizona. He is commemorated on the USS Arizona Memorial and the Memorial Tablets of the Missing, National Memorial Cemetery of the Pacific, Honolulu, Hawaii. Frank was survived by his Guardian, Mr. John Howard Russell, 1120 East Grove Street, Bloomington, Illinois.[252]

Flory, Dale Frederick   Watertender, Second Class, Serial No. 336 99 69, US Navy. Dale was born on November 17, 1918 in Greene County, Indiana. He was the son of Elmer David Flory and Clara A. (Killinger) Flory. Dale enlisted in the US Navy on August 24, 1937 in St. Louis, Missouri and reported for duty on the USS Arizona June 14, 1940. Dale was serving on the Arizona December 7, 1941 when the Japanese attacked Pearl Harbor. He had missed being aboard the Arizona by 15 minutes having landed on the Island just that much too late to board ship. After the attack, Dale was transferred to the USS Neosho for duty. He was killed in action while serving on board the USS Neosho (AO-23) on May 7, 1942 during the Battle of the Coral Sea. He is commemorated on the Memorial Tablets of the Missing, Fort William McKinley, Manila, Philippines. Dale was survived by his Wife, Mrs. Lola Garmette Florey, Box 442, Ocean Park, California and his Father, Mr. Elmer David Flory, Route 1, Bloomfield, Indiana. His brother, Max Edward Flory was killed in action on board the USS Arizona on December 7, 1941.[253]

---

[252] Frank Norman Floege, Information and picture provided by family member, Gusti Williams.
[253] Dale Frederick Flory, Photo provided by the Greene County Historical Society, Bloomfield, Illinois.

Flory, Max Edward Seaman, Second Class, Serial No: 337 56 12, US Navy. Max was born on October 6, 1922 in Greene County, Indiana to Elmer David and Clara Alice (Killinger) Flory. He enlisted in the US Navy on March 6, 1941 in St. Louis, Missouri and reported for duty on the USS Arizona on July 8, 1941. Max was killed in action on December 7, 1941 in Pearl Harbor, Hawaii. *His family received word on Sunday, December 21, 1941 that he had been killed in action.* He was awarded the American Defense Service Medal, World War II Victory Medal and Purple Heart Medal posthumously. Max remains on duty on the USS Arizona. He is commemorated on the USS Arizona Memorial and the Memorial Tablets of the Missing, National Memorial Cemetery of the Pacific, Honolulu, Hawaii and Grandview Cemetery, Bloomfield, Indiana. Max was survived by his Father, Mr. Elmer David Flory, Route 1, Bloomfield, Indiana. His brother, Dale Frederick, was serving on the Arizona and was among the survivors.[254]

Fones, George Everett Fire Controlman, Third Class, Serial No: 256 32 38, US Navy. George was born in November of 1920 in the District of Columbia to Arthur Melvin and Maida Corine (Weaver) Fones. He enlisted in the US Navy on July 11, 1938 in Washington, DC and reported for duty on the USS Arizona on March 31, 1940. George was killed in action on December 7, 1941 in Pearl Harbor, Hawaii. He was awarded the American Defense Service Medal, World War II Victory Medal and Purple Heart Medal posthumously. George remains on duty on the USS Arizona. He is commemorated on the USS Arizona Memorial and the Memorial Tablets of the Missing, National Memorial Cemetery of the Pacific, Honolulu, Hawaii. George was survived by his Mother, Mrs. Maida Corine Fones, 1620 Massachusetts Avenue SE, Washington, DC.

Forbis, James Leamon Coxswain, Serial No. 287 36 07, US Navy. James was born January 25, 1920 in Monroe, Kentucky, the son of James Coleman and Rose Frances (Adams) Forbis. He enlisted in the US Navy on January 16, 1940 in Louisville, Kentucky and completed his basic training at the Naval Training Station in Great Lakes, Illinois. He reported for duty on the USS Arizona March 26, 1940. James was serving on the Arizona December 7, 1941 when the Japanese attacked Pearl Harbor. After the attack, James was transferred to the USS Craven (DD-382) for duty. James passed away May 3, 2000 and is buried in the Horse Cave Municipal Cemetery in Horse Cave, Kentucky.

Ford, Jack Crosby Seaman, First Class, Serial No: 382 23 39, US Navy. Jack was born in 1920 in Colorado to Alfred James and Catherine Kate (Crosby) Ford. He enlisted in the US Navy on July 26, 1940 in Los Angeles, California and completed his basic training at the Naval Training Station in San Diego, California. Jack reported for duty on the USS Arizona on October 14, 1940. He was killed in action on December 7, 1941 in Pearl Harbor, Hawaii. Jack was awarded the American Defense Service Medal, World War II Victory Medal and Purple Heart Medal posthumously. He remains on duty on the USS Arizona. Jack is commemorated on the USS Arizona Memorial and the Memorial Tablets of the Missing, National Memorial Cemetery of the Pacific, Honolulu, Hawaii. He was survived by his Father, Mr. Alfred J. Ford, 11550 11th Street, Santa Monica, California.[255]

---

[254] Max Edward Flory, Photo provided by the Greene County Historical Society, Bloomfield, Illinois.

Ford, William Walker   Electrician's Mate, Third Class, Serial No: 279 72 62, US Navy. William was born on April 2, 1922 in Covington, Kentucky to Walker M. and Eula Mae (Kite) Ford. He enlisted in the US Navy on September 5, 1940 in Cincinnati, Ohio and completed his basic training at the Naval Training Station in Norfolk, Virginia. William reported for duty on the USS Arizona on December 4, 1940. He was killed in action on December 7, 1941 in Pearl Harbor, Hawaii. William was awarded the American Defense Service Medal, World War II Victory Medal and Purple Heart Medal posthumously. He remains on duty on the USS Arizona. William is commemorated on the USS Arizona Memorial and the Memorial Tablets of the Missing, National Memorial Cemetery of the Pacific, Honolulu, Hawaii. He was survived by his Mother, Mrs. Eula May Evans, 3204 Roger Street, Covington, Kentucky.[256]

Foreman, Elmer Lee   Fireman, Second Class, Serial No: 291 65 73, US Navy. Elmer was born in about 1916 in Indiana. He enlisted in the US Navy on October 8, 1940 in Indianapolis, Indiana and completed his basic training at the Naval Training Station in Great Lakes, Illinois. He reported for duty on the USS Arizona on December 9, 1940. Elmer was killed in action on December 7, 1941 in Pearl Harbor, Hawaii. He was awarded the American Defense Service Medal, World War II Victory Medal and Purple Heart Medal posthumously. Elmer remains on duty on the USS Arizona. He is commemorated on the USS Arizona Memorial and the Memorial Tablets of the Missing, National Memorial Cemetery of the Pacific, Honolulu, Hawaii. Elmer was survived by his Mother, Mrs. Sarah Foreman, Route 2, Delphi, Indiana.

Fortenberry, Alvie Charles   Coxswain, Serial No: 274 41 93, US Navy. Alvie was born on February 7, 1921 in Magnolia, Mississippi to Archie Arthur and Isabelle (Simmons) Fortenberry. Soon after his graduation from the Progress High School, he enlisted in the US Navy on December 16, 1939 in New Orleans, Louisiana and completed his basic training at the Naval Training Station in Norfolk, Virginia. Alvie reported for duty on the USS Arizona March 29, 1940. He was killed in action on December 7, 1941 in Pearl Harbor, Hawaii. Alvie was awarded the American Defense Service Medal, World War II Victory Medal and Purple Heart Medal posthumously. He remains on duty on the USS Arizona. Alvie is commemorated on the USS Arizona Memorial, the Memorial Tablets of the Missing, National Memorial Cemetery of the Pacific, Honolulu, Hawaii and Mount Zion Cemetery. He was survived by his Parents, Mr. and Mrs. Archie Arthur Fortenberry, Magnolia, Mississippi and six brothers and one sister. The Allen-Fortenberry VFW Post in Magnolia was named in his honor.[257]

---

[255] Jack Crosby Ford, Photo from Artisan Winter Yearbook, Manual Arts High School, Los Angeles California, 1935 Page 25.

[256] William Walker Ford, Photo provided by David Dunnavant, Find A Grave.

[257] Alvie Charles Fortenberry, Photo from the Clarion-Ledger, Jackson, Mississippi, December 28, 1941, Page 17.

Foster, James Park, Jr. Seaman, First Class, Serial No. 260 07 15, US Navy. James was born on June 19, 1920 in Hoxie, Arkansas. He enlisted in the US Navy on October 12, 1939 in Houston, Texas and completed his basic training at the Naval Training Station in San Diego, California. James reported for duty on the USS Arizona December 20, 1939. He was serving on the Arizona December 7, 1941 when the Japanese attacked Pearl Harbor.

I was sitting in the head that morning, in the foc'sle, when all the men started running down from the topside. No one was saying a word. After I fought my way up the ladder, I did a hundred yard dash to the boat deck. There I met Admiral Kidd and the Captain running for the bridge. I think Admiral Kidd gave me his last order, "Man your Battle Station," I said "yes, Sir!" Then I met McCarron and Lightfoot. We made a feeble attempt to fire the gun, but it ended in failure. These four men were all I saw and had any contact with. Then, the big BANG! We all three landed on a hatch. Broke my nose. I was burned, but did not know it at the time. Lightfoot was really burned and later died. McCarron was okay. We got up and looked at each other. Then, another explosion and we all dispersed. Me to the oily waters of Pearl Harbor and Ford Island.

James was wounded in action during the attack. His father, Mr. James Park Foster, Sr., 111 Ventura Street, Santa Paula, California was notified. After the attack, James was transferred to USS Salt Lake City for duty. James passed away May 10, 1997 in Cold Springs, Texas. He was survived by his wife, Robbie J. Foster.

Fowler, George Parten Seaman, Second Class, Serial No: 356 38 99, US Navy. George was born September 28, 1922 in Texas to Hansel George and Mildred Lucille (Parten) Fowler. *He was the second Boy Scout in Mart, TX to attain the rank of Eagle Scout and was a member of the local Hi-Y organization. According to scoutmaster, George Wheeler, he was one of the finest boys ever to come under his supervision and was a great influence to the boys with whom he worked and played.* George enlisted in the US Navy on October 19, 1940 in Dallas, Texas and completed his basic training at the Naval Training Station in San Diego, California. He reported for duty on the USS Arizona on January 11, 1941. George was killed in action on December 7, 1941 in Pearl Harbor, Hawaii. *His family was notified on Saturday, December 20, 1941 that he was missing in action.* He was awarded the American Defense Service Medal, World War II Victory Medal and Purple Heart Medal posthumously. George remains on duty on the USS Arizona. He is commemorated on the USS Arizona Memorial and the Memorial Tablets of the Missing, National Memorial Cemetery of the Pacific, Honolulu, Hawaii. George was survived by his Father, Mr. Hance George Fowler, 213 North Crisswell, Mart, Texas. The Hillman-Fowler American Legion Post #153, Mart, Texas was named in his honor.[258]

---

[258] George Parten Fowler, Photo and information provided by Patricia Williams Curry, Directory, Nancy Nail Memorial Library, Mart, TX.

Fowler, Ralph Edward Boatswain's Mate, First Class, Serial No. 381 19 08, US Navy. Ralph was born July 22, 1915 in Kansas to William Owen and Olive May "Ollie" (Bradshaw) Fowler. He enlisted in the US Navy on February 13, 1935 in San Diego, California. He served on the USS Arizona from June 10, 1935 until December 7, 1941 when the Japanese attacked Pearl Harbor. After the attack, Ralph was transferred to salvage work on the USS Utah. He served in the US Navy until May 1960. Ralph died October 5, 1972 in Marin, California; he was only 57 years old.

Fowler, Robert Dale Seaman, Second Class, Serial No. 321 52 50, US Navy. Robert enlisted in the US Navy on November 27, 1940 in Des Moines, Iowa and completed his basic training at the Naval Training Station in Great Lakes, Illinois. He reported for duty on the USS Arizona January 18, 1941. Robert was serving on the Arizona December 7, 1941 when the Japanese attacked Pearl Harbor. After the attack, Robert was transferred to the USS Maury for duty.

Frank, Leroy George Seaman, First Class, Serial No: 295 55 47, US Navy. Leroy was born on April 24, 1917 in First View, Colorado to Roy Elton and Laura Frances (Skinner) Frank. He enlisted in the US Navy on December 16, 1939 in Nashville, Tennessee and reported for duty on the USS Arizona on March 29, 1940. Leroy was killed in action on December 7, 1941 in Pearl Harbor, Hawaii. He was awarded the American Defense Service Medal, World War II Victory Medal and Purple Heart Medal posthumously. Leroy remains on duty on the USS Arizona. He is commemorated on the USS Arizona Memorial and the Memorial Tablets of the Missing, National Memorial Cemetery of the Pacific, Honolulu, Hawaii. Leroy was survived by his Father, Mr. Roy Elton Frank, Harrisburg, Arkansas.

Frazier, Glen Chief Gunner's Mate, Serial No. 346 26 24, US Navy. Glen was born on July 9, 1901. He enlisted in the US Navy on April 9, 1934 in Raleigh, North Carolina. Glen served on the USS Arizona from July 23, 1938 until December 7, 1941 when the Japanese attacked Pearl Harbor. After the attack, Glen was assigned salvage work on the USS Utah. Glen died on January 31, 1996 in Arkansas and is buried in Frazier Cemetery, Magnolia, Arkansas.

Frederick, Charles Donald Electrician's Mate, Second Class, Serial No: 368 44 09, US Navy. Charles was born in about 1920 in Louisiana to Severin Ursin and Alice (Mouton) Frederick. He enlisted in the US Navy on July 11, 1939 in Salt Lake City, Utah and completed his basic training at the Naval Training Station in San Diego, California. He reported for duty on the USS Arizona on March 27, 1940. Charles was killed in action on December 7, 1941 in Pearl Harbor, Hawaii. He was awarded the American Defense Service Medal, World War II Victory Medal and Purple Heart Medal posthumously. Charles remains on duty on the USS Arizona. He is commemorated on the USS Arizona Memorial and the Memorial Tablets of the Missing, National Memorial Cemetery of the Pacific, Honolulu, Hawaii. Charles was survived by his Father, Mr. Severin Ursin Frederick, 312 South Saint Valie Street, Abbeville, Louisiana. Donald Frederick Boulevard in Abbeville, Louisiana is named in honor of Charles Donald Frederick.[259]

---

[259] Charles Donald Frederick, Photo and information from family member, Courtney Bourque Frederick.

Free, Thomas Augusta   Machinist's Mate, First Class, Serial No: 151 54 85, US Navy. Thomas was born on February 2, 1891 in Union Springs, Alabama to William Alson and Mary Jane (Arrington) Free. He enlisted in the US Navy on December 12, 1917 in Houston, Texas. Thomas was a career Navy man, serving on: USS Langley, USS Litchfield, USS Borie, USS Ramapo, USS Wharton and finally the USS Arizona. He reported for duty on the USS Arizona on October 10, 1941, joining his son, William. Thomas was killed in action on December 7, 1941 in Pearl Harbor, Hawaii. He was awarded the American Defense Service Medal, World War II Victory Medal and Purple Heart Medal posthumously. Thomas remains on duty on the USS Arizona with his son. He is commemorated on the USS Arizona Memorial and the Memorial Tablets of the Missing, National Memorial Cemetery of the Pacific, Honolulu, Hawaii. Thomas was survived by his Daughter, Miss Myrtle Free, Navasota, Texas. His son, William was killed in action on the Arizona.[260]

Free, William Thomas   Seaman, Second Class, Serial No: 381 40 04, US Navy. William was born January 19, 1923 in Portsmouth, Virginia son of Thomas Augusta and Myrtle Alvin (Bice) Free. He enlisted in the US Navy on January 30, 1941 in San Diego, California and completed his basic training at the Naval Training Station in San Diego, California. William reported for duty on the USS Arizona on April 27, 1941. He was killed in action on December 7, 1941 in Pearl Harbor, Hawaii. William was awarded the American Defense Service Medal, World War II Victory Medal and Purple Heart Medal posthumously. He remains on duty on the USS Arizona with his father. William is commemorated on the USS Arizona Memorial and the Memorial Tablets of the Missing, National Memorial Cemetery of the Pacific, Honolulu, Hawaii. He was survived by his Mother, Mrs. Myrtle Free Waterman, Route 9, Box 1106, c/o Otto Adams, Houston, Texas. His Father, Thomas was killed in action on the Arizona.

French, John Edmund   Lieutenant Commander, Serial No: O-57562, US Navy. John was born on March 6, 1900 in Maine. Appointed from Maine, he graduated from the United States Naval Academy in 1922. John's battle station was the Conning Tower. John was killed in action on December 7, 1941 in Pearl Harbor, Hawaii. He was awarded the American Defense Service Medal, World War II Victory Medal and Purple Heart Medal posthumously. John's remains were recovered and he was buried in Section 12, Site 3060, Arlington National Cemetery, Arlington, Virginia. He is commemorated on the USS Arizona Memorial. John was survived by his Wife, Mrs. John Edmund French, 121 South La Peer Drive, Beverly Hills, California.[261]

---

[260] Thomas Augusta Free, Photo and information provided by David Dunnavant, Find a Grave Memorial.
[261] John Edmund French, Photo from The Lucky Bag Yearbook, United States Naval Academy, Annapolis, MD, Class of 1922.

160

Frizzell, Robert Niven   Seaman, Second Class, Serial No: 376 35 03, US Navy. Robert was born in 1923 in Utah to Francis and Alma Frizzell. He enlisted in the US Navy on June 21, 1941 in San Francisco, California and completed his basic training at the Naval Training Station in San Diego, California. He reported for duty on the USS Arizona August 29, 1941. Robert was killed in action on December 7, 1941 in Pearl Harbor, Hawaii. He was awarded the American Defense Service Medal, World War II Victory Medal and Purple Heart Medal posthumously. Robert remains on duty on the USS Arizona. He is commemorated on the USS Arizona Memorial and the Memorial Tablets of the Missing, National Memorial Cemetery of the Pacific, Honolulu, Hawaii. Robert was survived by his Father, Mr. Francis Niven Frizzell, Route 2, Box 283, Orland, California.

Frye, Everett Ellsworth   Seaman, First Class, Serial No. 342 30 64, US Navy. Everett was born on April 24, 1925. He enlisted in the US Navy October 15, 1940 in Kansas City, Missouri and completed his basic training at the Naval Training Station in Great Lakes, Illinois. He reported for duty on the USS Arizona December 9, 1940. Everett was serving on December 7, 1941 when the Japanese attacked Pearl Harbor. After the attack, Everett was transferred to the USS Phoenix for duty. Everett died on November 20, 2005 and is buried in Lawn Memorial Gardens, Dumas, Texas.

Fulton, Robert Wilson   Aviation Metalsmith, First Class, Aviation Unit (VO-1), Serial No: 272 13 68, US Navy. Robert was born July 22, 1915 in Alabama, son of John Calvin and Margaret (Seals) Fulton. He enlisted in the US Navy on July 14, 1936 in Birmingham, Alabama and reported for duty on the USS Arizona on December 28, 1936. Robert was killed in action on December 7, 1941 in Pearl Harbor, Hawaii. He was awarded the American Defense Service Medal, World War II Victory Medal and Purple Heart Medal posthumously. Robert remains on duty on the USS Arizona. He is commemorated on the USS Arizona Memorial and the Memorial Tablets of the Missing, National Memorial Cemetery of the Pacific, Honolulu, Hawaii. Robert was survived by his Mother, Mrs. Maggie Fulton, Akron, Alabama.

Funk, Frank Francis   Boatswain's Mate, Second Class, Serial No: 336 94 43, US Navy. Frank was born in about 1917 in Missouri to Heinrich and Rosena Funk. *By 1930, both of his parents had died and he was living in an orphanage.* He enlisted in the US Navy on November 24, 1936 in St. Louis, Missouri and reported for duty on the USS Arizona on April 3, 1937. Frank was killed in action on December 7, 1941 in Pearl Harbor, Hawaii. He was awarded the American Defense Service Medal, World War II Victory Medal and Purple Heart Medal posthumously. Frank remains on duty on the USS Arizona. He is commemorated on the USS Arizona Memorial and the Memorial Tablets of the Missing, National Memorial Cemetery of the Pacific, Honolulu, Hawaii. Frank was survived by his Guardian, Mr. Con Kelleher, 7600 St. Charles Rock Road, St. Louis County, Missouri and brother of Nick Funk, 1819 South Tenth Street, St. Louis, Missouri.[262]

---

[262] Frank Francis Funk, Photo from Missouri Honor States.

Funk, Lawrence Henry Seaman, First Class, Serial No: 300 18 19, US Navy. Lawrence was born on March 5, 1922 in Roscoe, Illinois to Oscar Andrew and Mary Anna (Zimmerman) Funk. He enlisted in the US Navy on October 8, 1940 in Chicago, Illinois and completed his basic training at the Naval Training Station in Great Lakes, Illinois. Lawrence reported for duty on the USS Arizona on December 9, 1940. He was killed in action on December 7, 1941 in Pearl Harbor, Hawaii. Lawrence was awarded the American Defense Service Medal, World War II Victory Medal and Purple Heart Medal posthumously. He remains on duty on the USS Arizona. Lawrence is commemorated on the USS Arizona Memorial and the Memorial Tablets of the Missing, National Memorial Cemetery of the Pacific, Honolulu, Hawaii and the Adeline Cemetery, Adeline, Illinois. He was survived by his Parents, Mr. Oscar Funk and Mrs. Mary Ann (Zimmerman) Funk, 422 Union Street, Rockton, Illinois.[263]

Fuqua, Samuel Glenn Commander, Serial No. 0-01781, US Navy. Samuel was born on October 15, 1899 in Laddonia, Missouri. He was commissioned in the US Navy on June 23, 1938 and reported for duty on the USS Arizona where he was serving as Damage Control Officer, 1st Lieutenant on December 7, 1941 when the Japanese attacked Pearl Harbor. Last Action Report:

"I was in the ward room eating breakfast about 0755 when a short signal on the ship's air raid alarm was made, I Immediately went to the phone and called the officer of the deck to sound general quarters and then shortly thereafter ran up to the starboard side of the quarter deck to see if he had received word. On coming out of the ward room hatch on the port side, I saw a Japanese plane go by, the machine guns firing, at an altitude of about 100 feet. As I was running forward on the starboard side of the quarter deck, approximately by the starboard gangway, I was apparently knocked out by the blast of a bomb, which I learned later had struck the face plate of No. 4 turret on the starboard side and had glanced off and gone through the deck just forward on the captain's hatch, penetrating the decks and exploding on the third deck. When I came to and got up off the deck the ship was a mass of flames amidships on the boat deck and the deck aft was awash to about frame 90. The anti-aircraft battery and machine guns apparently were still firing at this time. Some of the Arizona boats had pulled clear of the oil and were lying off the stern.

At this time I attempted, with the assistance of the crews of No. 3 and No. 4 turrets to put out the fire which was coming from the boat deck, and which had extended to the quarter deck. There was no water on the fire mains. However, about 14 CO_2's were obtained that were stowed on the port side and held the flames back from the quarter deck in order to pick up wounded who were running down the boat deck out of the flames. I placed about 70 wounded and injured in the boats, which had been picked up off the deck aft and landed them at the Ford Island landing. This was completed about 0900 or 0930. Not knowing whether the Captain or the Admiral had ever reached the bridge, I had the Captain's hatch opened up, immediately after I came to, and sent Officers Ensign G. B. Lenning, U.S.N.R. and Ensign J.D. Miller, U.S.N, down to search the Captain's and Admiral's cabins to see if they were there. By that time the Captain's Cabin and Admiral's Cabin were about waist deep in water. A search of the two cabins revealed that the Admiral and Captain were not there. Knowing that they were on board I assumed that they had proceeded to the bridge. All personnel, but 3 or 4 men from turrets No. 3 and No. 4 were saved.

---

[263] Lawrence Henry Funk, Photo from the Morning Star, Rockford, IL, "Rockford Sailors In Pacific Battle Zones" Sunday, December 7, 1941, Page 3.

About 0900, seeing that all guns of the anti-aircraft and secondary battery were out of action and that the ship could not possibly be saved, I ordered all hands to abandon Ship.

From information received from other personnel on board, a bomb had struck the forecastle, just about the time the air raid siren, at 0755. A short interval thereafter, there was a terrific explosion on the forecastle, apparently from the bomb penetrating the magazine. Approximately 30 seconds later a bomb hit the boat deck, apparently just forward of the stack and one went down the stack and one hit the face plate of No. 4 turret. It is not known whether a torpedo hit the ship, but I have heard indirectly that the Commanding Officer of the U.S.S. Vestal stated that 2 torpedoes passed under his vessel which was secured alongside the Arizona, and struck the Arizona.

The first attack occurred about 0755. I saw approximately 15 torpedo planes, which had come in to the attack from the direction of the Navy Yard. These planes also strafed the ship after releasing their torpedoes. Shortly thereafter there was a dive bomber and strafing attack of about thirty planes. This attack was very determined, planes diving within 500 feet before releasing bombs. I believe there was a third attack of horizontal bombers about 0900, these planes came in from ahead at a height of about 10, 000 feet. There were about twelve planes in the flight that I saw.

The personnel of the anti-aircraft and machine gun batteries on the Arizona lived up to the best traditions of the Navy. I could hear guns firing on the ship long after the boat deck was a mass of flames. I can not single out any one individual who stood out in acts of heroism above the others, as all of the personnel under my supervision conducted themselves with the greatest heroism and bravery."[264]

Samuel died on January 27, 1987 in Decatur, Georgia and is buried in Section 59, Arlington National Cemetery, Arlington, Virginia. He was awarded the Congressional Medal of Honor, Legion of Merit, American Defense Service Medal, American Campaign Medal and World War II Victory Medal.

Medal of Honor Citation: For distinguished conduct in action, outstanding heroism, and utter disregard of his own safety, above and beyond the call of duty during the attack on the Fleet in Pearl Harbor, by Japanese forces on 7 December 1941. Upon the commencement of the attack, Lieutenant Commander Fuqua rushed to the quarterdeck of the U.S.S. Arizona to which he was attached where he was stunned and knocked down by the explosion of a large bomb which hit the quarterdeck, penetrated several decks, and started a severe fire. Upon regaining consciousness, he began to direct the fighting of the fire and the rescue of wounded and injured personnel. Almost immediately there was a tremendous explosion forward, which made the ship appear to rise out of the water, shudder and settle down by the bow rapidly. The whole forward part of the ship was enveloped in flames which were spreading rapidly, and wounded and burned men were pouring out of the ship to the quarterdeck. Despite these conditions, his harrowing experience, and severe enemy bombing and strafing, at the time, Lieutenant Commander Fuqua continued to direct the fighting of fires in order to check them while the wounded and burned could be taken from the ship, and supervised the rescue of these men in such an amazingly calm and cool manner and with such excellent judgment, that it inspired everyone who saw him and undoubtedly resulted in the saving of many lives. After realizing that the ship could not be saved and that he was the senior surviving officer aboard, he directed that it be abandoned, but continued to remain on the quarterdeck and directed abandoning ship and rescue of personnel until satisfied that all personnel that could be had been saved, after which he left the ship with the (last) boatload. The conduct of Lieutenant Commander Fuqua was not only in keeping with the

---

[264] Statement of Lt. Comdr. S. G. Fuqua, U.S.N. of the attack on the U.S.S. Arizona, 7 December 1941.

highest traditions of the Naval Service but characterizes him as an outstanding leader of men.

Samuel also served in the Army in World War I. In 1942 he was stationed on the cruiser Tuscaloosa (CA-37) escorting convoys to Murmansk. He was promoted to Rear Admiral by a "tombstone" promotion that advanced officers below admiral one permanent grade upon retirement if they had been specifically commended for performance in combat.

Gager, Roy Arthur   Seaman, Second Class, Serial No: 342 30 61, US Navy. Roy was born August 13, 1922 in Amarillo, Texas, the youngest son of Herman Noah and Winnie (Cox) Gager. He enlisted in the US Navy on October 14, 1940 in Kansas City, Missouri and completed his basic training at the Naval Training Station in Great Lakes, Illinois. Roy reported for duty on the USS Arizona on December 9, 1940. He was killed in action on December 7, 1941 in Pearl Harbor, Hawaii; he was barely 19 years old. Roy was awarded the American Defense Service Medal, World War II Victory Medal and Purple Heart Medal posthumously. He remains on duty on the USS Arizona. Roy is commemorated on the USS Arizona Memorial and the Memorial Tablets of the Missing, National Memorial Cemetery of the Pacific, Honolulu, Hawaii. Roy was survived by his Parents, Mr. and Mrs. Herman Noah Gager, 1304 Polk Street, Topeka, Kansas. They received a missing person notice three days before Christmas 1941.

Gallagher, William Fred   Chief Electrician's Mate, Serial No. 213 94 68, US Navy. William was born August 25, 1901. He enlisted in the US Navy on June 18, 1940 in San Diego, California and reported for duty on the USS Arizona July 2, 1940. William was serving on the Arizona December 7, 1941 when the Japanese attacked Pearl Harbor. After the attack, William was transferred to the USS Salt Lake City for duty. William died on March 22, 1985 in San Diego, California.

Garfield, Jerome Harold   Ensign, US Navy. Jerome was born on October 31, 1915 in Salt Lake City, Utah to Jack and Dorothy Garfield. He was commissioned Ensign in the US Navy February 28, 1941 and was serving as Communication Watch Officer on the USS Arizona on December 7, 1941 when the Japanese attacked Pearl Harbor. After the attack, Jerome was assigned temporary duty on the USS Tennessee. Shortly thereafter he was ordered to COM 14 for duty. Jerome died on January 1, 2004 in Menlo Park, California. His ashes were interred on the USS Arizona March 26, 2004.

Gargaro, Ernest Russell   Seaman, Second Class, Serial No: 368 64 96, US Navy. Ernest was born May 21, 1919 in Murray, Utah. He enlisted in the US Navy on April 18, 1941 in Salt Lake City, Utah and completed his basic training at the Naval Training Station in San Diego, California. He reported for duty on the USS Arizona on July 13, 1941. Ernest was killed in action on December 7, 1941 in Pearl Harbor, Hawaii. He was awarded the American Defense Service Medal, World War II Victory Medal and Purple Heart Medal posthumously. Ernest remains on duty on the USS Arizona. He is commemorated on the USS Arizona Memorial and the Memorial Tablets of the Missing, National Memorial Cemetery of the Pacific, Honolulu, Hawaii. Ernest was survived by his Mother, Mrs. Christina Gargaro, 152-1/2 South State Street, Salt Lake City, Utah.[265]

---

[265] Ernest Russell Gargaro, Photo from Utah Honor States.

Garlington, Raymond Wesley   Seaman, First Class, Serial No: 356 43 54, US Navy. Raymond was born April 9, 1920 in Big Spring, Texas to George Waltern and Alma C. (Jurdinski) Garlington. He enlisted in the US Navy on November 27, 1940 in Dallas, Texas and completed his basic training at the Naval Training Station in San Diego, California. Raymond reported for duty on the USS Arizona on January 25, 1941. He was killed in action on December 7, 1941 in Pearl Harbor, Hawaii. Raymond was awarded the American Defense Service Medal, World War II Victory Medal and Purple Heart Medal posthumously. He remains on duty on the USS Arizona. Raymond is commemorated on the USS Arizona Memorial and the Memorial Tablets of the Missing, National Memorial Cemetery of the Pacific, Honolulu, Hawaii. He was survived by his Father, Mr. George W. Garlington, 534 Kains Avenue, Albany, California and a brother, Thomas of Albany, California.

Garrett, Orville "Bill" Wilmer   Shipfitter, Second Class, Serial No: 342 11 44, US Navy. Orville was born March 16, 1917 in Saline County, Missouri to Marion Francis and Kathryn Lydia (Narron) Garrett. *His mother died in 1920 when Bill was almost three. Bill and his younger sister, Cecil Mae went to live with their grandparents, Charles Henry and Cizzier Jane Tumlinson Narron near Miami. His grandfather, Charles, died 5 years later, and his grandmother, Cizzier died in 1932. At that time, they then moved in with their older sister, Nettie and her husband, Jack. Bill worked with Jack on the farm, learning the skills needed for a horse and mule based farming. He enjoyed the outdoors, hunting and fishing with the other neighbor boys and playing cards in the evening.* He enlisted in the US Navy on May 9, 1939 in Kansas City, Missouri and completed his basic training at the Naval Training Station in San Diego, California. Orville reported for duty on the USS Arizona on October 20, 1939. He was killed in action on December 7, 1941 in Pearl Harbor, Hawaii. Orville was awarded the American Defense Service Medal, World War II Victory Medal and Purple Heart Medal posthumously. He remains on duty on the USS Arizona. Orville is commemorated on the USS Arizona Memorial and the Memorial Tablets of the Missing, National Memorial Cemetery of the Pacific, Honolulu, Hawaii and High Hill Cemetery, Slater, Missouri. He was survived by his Father, Mr. Marion Francis Garrett, 552 West Washington Street, Marshall, Missouri, step mother and Aunt, Lydia Narron Garrett, and four sisters, Loraine Bahr, Nettie Crane, Hazel Pauley and Cecil Mae Fletcher. He was also survived by nine half siblings and cousins.[266]

Gartin, Gerald Ernest   Seaman, First Class, Serial No: 376 16 85, US Navy. Gerald was born in about 1921 in Nevada to Vic C. and Virginia D. Gartin. He enlisted in the US Navy on November 27, 1940 in San Francisco, California and completed his basic training at the Naval Training Station in San Diego, California. Gerald reported for duty on the USS Arizona on January 25, 1941. He was killed in action on December 7, 1941 in Pearl Harbor, Hawaii. Gerald was awarded the American Defense Service Medal, World War II Victory Medal and Purple Heart Medal posthumously. He remains on duty on the USS Arizona. Gerald is commemorated on the USS Arizona Memorial and the Memorial Tablets of the Missing, National Memorial Cemetery of the Pacific, Honolulu, Hawaii. He was survived by his Mother, Mrs. Virginia Lulu Sanguinetti, 1127 Clay Street, San Francisco, California.

---

[266] Orville Wilmer Garrett, Information from the Memorial/dedication Service on March 12, 2011 at High Hill Cemetery, Slater, Missouri provided by family member, Beverly Harris. Photo from the Central Junior High School Yearbook, Kansas City, Missouri, 1927.

Gaskins, Walter James   Seaman, First Class, Serial No. 268 53 04, US Navy.   Walter was born June 22, 1922 in Georgia the son of Henry and Nattie M. Gaskins.   He enlisted in the US Navy September 19, 1940 in Macon, Georgia and completed his basic training at the Naval Training Station in Norfolk, Virginia.   Walter reported for duty on the USS Arizona December 4, 1940.   He was serving on the Arizona December 7, 1941 when the Japanese attacked Pearl Harbor.   After the attack, Walter was transferred to the USS MacDonough for duty.   He died July 27, 1989 and is buried at Gaskins Cemetery, Nashville, Georgia.

Gaudette, William Frank   Seaman, First Class, Serial No: 393 43 01, US Navy.   William was born in 1921 in Washington.   He enlisted in the US Navy on November 12, 1940 in Portland, Oregon and completed his basic training at the Naval Training Station in San Diego, California.   He reported for duty on the USS Arizona on June 7, 1941.   William was killed in action on December 7, 1941 in Pearl Harbor, Hawaii.   He was awarded the American Defense Service Medal, World War II Victory Medal and Purple Heart Medal posthumously.   William remains on duty on the USS Arizona.   He is commemorated on the USS Arizona Memorial and the Memorial Tablets of the Missing, National Memorial Cemetery of the Pacific, Honolulu, Hawaii.   William was survived by his Mother, Mrs. Vine Jones, 356 17th Avenue, Longview, Washington.[267]

Gaultney, Ralph Martin   Electrician's Mate, Third Class, Serial No: 300 03 00, US Navy.   Ralph was born September 23, 1910 in Illinois, the eldest son of William M. and Nellie A. (Kent) Gaultney.   He enlisted in the US Navy on January 16, 1940 in Chicago, Illinois and completed his basic training at the Naval Training Station in Great Lakes, Illinois.   Ralph reported for duty on the USS Arizona on March 26, 1940.   On December 7th he was blown overboard into the burning oil.   Assigned death # 523, Ralph died December 24, 1941 in the Naval Hospital at Pearl Harbor from 2nd and 3rd burns received on December 7, 1941.[268]   He was awarded the American Defense Service Medal, World War II Victory Medal and Purple Heart Medal posthumously.   Ralph was interred in a Navy Plot in the Halawa Cemetery, Honolulu, Hawaii.   Ralph is commemorated on the USS Arizona Memorial and the Memorial Tablets of the Missing, National Memorial Cemetery of the Pacific, Honolulu, Hawaii.   He was survived by his Parents, Mr. and Mrs. William Gaultney, North Buck Street, LeRoy, Illinois.   His brother Leonard Gaultney, MM1c was lost on the heavy cruiser, USS Vincennes near the Philippine Islands and his younger brother, David Gaultney, Jr. died fighting on Iwo Jima.

Gaut, Harold Woodson   Seaman, First Class, Serial No. 272 40 24, US Navy.   Harold was born on January 15, 1920 in Brilliant, Alabama, the son of Adron Clayton Gaut and Maude Lee (Dickey) Gaut.   He enlisted in the US Navy on September 28, 1940 in Birmingham, Alabama and completed his basic training at the Naval Training Station in Norfolk, Virginia.   Harold reported for duty on the USS Arizona December 4, 1940.   He was serving on the Arizona December 7, 1941 when the Japanese attacked Pearl Harbor.   Harold's battle station was inside the Arizona's turret four.   After the ship sank, he made his way through interior passageways to turret three and escaped.   After the attack, Harold was transferred to the USS Chester for duty.   Harold died on January 27, 1995 in Santa Rosa, California and was interred on the Arizona June 9, 1995.

---

[267] William Frank Gaudette, Photo from the 1940 Chinook Yearbook, Swim Team, Pullman, Washington.
[268] Report of Changes of the USS Arizona for the month ending 31st day of December, 1941, page 59, line 11, Ralph Martin Gaultney.

Gazecki, Philip Robert Ensign, Serial No: 0-106988, US Navy Reserve. Philip was born April 15, 1920 in Neenah, Wisconsin to Philip J. and Leona M. Gazecki. He attended Harvard College, Cambridge, Massachusetts and was commissioned Ensign on May 24, 1941 and was serving on the Arizona as Junior Watch and Division M Officer. His battle station was Starboard Engine Room. Philip was killed in action on December 7, 1941 in Pearl Harbor, Hawaii. He was awarded the American Defense Service Medal, World War II Victory Medal and Purple Heart Medal posthumously. Philip remains on duty on the USS Arizona. He is commemorated on the USS Arizona Memorial and the Memorial Tablets of the Missing, National Memorial Cemetery of the Pacific, Honolulu, Hawaii. Philip was survived by his Father, Mr. Philip John Gazecki, 547 1st Street, Menasha, Wisconsin.[269]

Gebhardt, Kenneth Edward Seaman, First Class, Serial No: 328 75 63, US Navy. Kenneth was born on July 16, 1917 in Annmouse, North Dakota to Anthony Edward and Ethel Marie (Cole) Gebhardt. He enlisted in the US Navy on October 8, 1940 in Minneapolis, Minnesota and completed his basic training at the Naval Training Station in Great Lakes, Illinois. Kenneth reported for duty on the USS Arizona on December 9, 1940. He was killed in action on December 7, 1941 in Pearl Harbor, Hawaii. Kenneth was awarded the American Defense Service Medal, World War II Victory Medal and Purple Heart Medal posthumously. He remains on duty on the USS Arizona. Kenneth is commemorated on the USS Arizona Memorial and the Memorial Tablets of the Missing, National Memorial Cemetery of the Pacific, Honolulu, Hawaii. He was survived by his Father, Mr. Anthony Edward Gebhardt, Balta, North Dakota. His brother, Garland enlisted in the Navy to avenge the death of his brother, Kenneth.

Geer, Kenneth Floyd Seaman, Second Class, Serial No: 382 31 71, US Navy. Kenneth was born in 1923 in Colorado to Ray Vinta and Edith May (Kennedy) Geer. He enlisted in the US Navy on November 26, 1940 in Los Angeles, California and completed his basic training at the Naval Training Station in San Diego, California. Kenneth reported for duty on the USS Arizona on January 25, 1941. He was killed in action on December 7, 1941 in Pearl Harbor, Hawaii. Kenneth was awarded the American Defense Service Medal, World War II Victory Medal and Purple Heart Medal posthumously. He remains on duty on the USS Arizona. Kenneth is commemorated on the USS Arizona Memorial and the Memorial Tablets of the Missing, National Memorial Cemetery of the Pacific, Honolulu, Hawaii. He was survived by his Father, Mr. Ray Vinta Geer, 1618 Richfield Avenue, Downey, California.

---

[269] Philip Robert Gazecki, Photo from the Harvard Album Yearbook, Harvard College, Cambridge, Massachusetts, Class of 1941.

Geise, Marvin Frederick   Seaman, First Class, Serial No: 300 17 98, US Navy. Marvin was born August 15, 1920 in Beloit, Wisconsin to Walter Sands and Ruth (Moran) Geise. He enlisted in the US Navy on October 8, 1940 in Chicago, Illinois and completed his basic training at the Naval Training Station in Great Lakes, Illinois. Marvin reported for duty on the USS Arizona on December 9, 1940. He was killed in action on December 7, 1941 in Pearl Harbor, Hawaii. Marvin was awarded the American Defense Service Medal, World War II Victory Medal and Purple Heart Medal posthumously. He remains on duty on the USS Arizona. Marvin is commemorated on the USS Arizona Memorial and the Memorial Tablets of the Missing, National Memorial Cemetery of the Pacific, Honolulu, Hawaii. He was survived by his Mother, Mrs. Ruth Cox, Branigan Hotel, Beloit, Wisconsin.[270]

Geiselman, Ellis Hugh   Commander, Serial No. 0-00780, US Navy. Ellis was born October 8, 1895 in Hanover, Pennsylvania the son of Elder John Geiselman and Anna Margaret (Bollinger) Geiselman. Commissioned June 23, 1938, he was serving as the Executive Officer. Ellis was serving on board the USS Arizona on December 7, 1941 when the Japanese attacked Pearl Harbor. He died on October 24, 1970 in Toledo, Ohio. His obituary follows:

Capt. Ellis H. Geiselman, 75, who served 31 years in the Navy before retiring as Commanding Officer of the battleship USS Mississippi, died Saturday in the Cherry Hill Nursing Home after a long illness. He lived at 2357 Scottwood Ave. A 1917 graduate of the U.S. Naval Academy, Captain Geiselman was assigned to the USS Arizona when it was sunk by the Japanese at Pearl Harbor on December 7, 1941, escaping probable death because he was not on board at the time. Captain Geiselman was born in Hanover, Pennsylvania and lived in Toledo 22 years after retiring from the Navy. He was employed in the government division of the old Kaiser Jeep Corporation, retiring in 1960. Surviving are his son, Michael J., of Cambridge, Massachusetts and brother, Ralph, of Pittsburgh. Services will be Tuesday at 3 p.m. in the Walker-Feilbach Mortuary, Talmadge Road, with burial in Woodlawn Cemetery.[271]

Gemienhardt, Samuel Henry, Jr.   Machinist's Mate, Second Class, Serial No: 279 48 08, US Navy. Samuel was born in 1914 in Ohio to Samuel Henry Gemienhardt, Sr. and Cora Elizabeth (Moore) Gemienhardt. He enlisted in the US Navy on November 5, 1935 in Cincinnati, Ohio and reported for duty on the USS Arizona on April 20, 1936. Samuel was killed in action on December 7, 1941 in Pearl Harbor, Hawaii. He was awarded the American Defense Service Medal, World War II Victory Medal and Purple Heart Medal posthumously. Samuel remains on duty on the USS Arizona. He is commemorated on the USS Arizona Memorial and the Memorial Tablets of the Missing, National Memorial Cemetery of the Pacific, Honolulu, Hawaii. Samuel was survived by his Father, Mr. Samuel Henry Gemienhardt, Sr., 190 Brehl Avenue, Columbus, Ohio.

---

[270] Marvin Frederick Geise, Photo and information provided by family member, Ron Geise.
[271] Ellis Hugh Geiselman, Photo from the Lucky Bag Yearbook, United States Naval Academy, Annapolis, MD, Class of 1918.

Genest, Dayton Merrill Seaman, First Class, Serial No 382 35 99, US Navy. Dayton was born September 4, 1922 in Los Angeles, California, the son of Dayton M. and Alina (Henson) Genest. He enlisted in the US Navy on January 23, 1941 in Los Angeles, California and completed his basic training at the Naval Training Station in San Diego, California. He reported for duty on the USS Arizona April 27, 1941. Dayton was serving on the Arizona December 7, 1941 when the Japanese attacked Pearl Harbor. He was later Lost at Sea on December 18, 1944 while serving on the USS Monaghan (DD-354). The Monahan was caught up in "Typhoon "Cobra" in the Philippine Sea and was sunk. He survived Typhoon Cobra on December 18, 1944, one of thirteen to make it to a raft. All other hands were lost. According to the last living survivor, Evan Fenn, Dayton clung to the raft as long as he could. Space in the raft had been reserved for those who had been seriously injured. There were only 6 survivors. Dayton was among the missing. He is commemorated on the Memorial Tablets of the Missing, Fort William McKinley, Manila, Philippines. He was survived by his wife, Mrs. Loraine Carnell Genest, 2650 Prospect Avenue, La Crescenta, California.[272]

Gholston, Roscoe "Rocky" Yeoman, Second Class, Serial No: 356 13 37, US Navy. Roscoe was born September 9, 1920 in Van Zandt County, Texas to Lemuel Roscoe and Beulah Opal Gholston. He enlisted in the US Navy on June 13, 1939 in Dallas, Texas and completed his basic training at the Naval Training Station in San Diego, California. He reported for duty on the USS Arizona on September 11, 1939. Roscoe died on board the USS Solace hospital ship from wounds received in action on December 7, 1941 at Pearl Harbor, Hawaii. He was awarded the American Defense Service Medal, World War II Victory Medal and Purple Heart Medal posthumously. The disposition of his body is unclear; it is possible he was buried in one of the unknown graves in the Punchbowl.[273] He is commemorated on the USS Arizona Memorial and the Memorial Tablets of the Missing, National Memorial Cemetery of the Pacific, Honolulu, Hawaii. Roscoe was survived by his Mother, Mrs. Beulah Opal Gholston, c/o F. Patterson, Jericho Heights, Clarendon, Texas.[274]

Gibson, Billy Edwin Seaman, First Class, Serial No: 342 33 54, US Navy. Billy was born on June 1, 1921 in Farmington, Kansas to Walter Samuel and Clara Cynthia (Thomas) Gibson. Billy was a former Effingham High School Student and Locomotive Finished Material Co. employee, the first Atchison County youth to give his life during WWII. He enlisted in the US Navy on November 27, 1940 in Kansas City, Missouri and completed his basic training at the Naval Training Station in Great Lakes, Illinois. Billy reported for duty on the USS Arizona on January 18, 1941. He was killed in action on December 7, 1941 at Pearl Harbor, Hawaii. *On Christmas Eve, 1941, Clara Gibson of Atchison was notified by the Department of the Navy that her son, Seaman 1st Class Billy Edwin Gibson, was MIA in the attack. It was not until some time*

---

[272] Dayton Merrill Genest, Photo and information provided by his son, Dave Jenest. (pictured Dayton Merrill Genest and wife, Loraine Bowers Jenest)

[273] Report of Changes of the USS Arizona for the month ending 31st day of December, 1941, page 60, line 18, Roscoe Gholston.

[274] Roscoe Gholston, Photo provided by Laura Blaylock.

in 1942 that they received official notice that he had gone down on the USS Arizona. Billy was awarded the American Defense Service Medal, World War II Victory Medal and Purple Heart Medal posthumously. He remains on duty on the USS Arizona. Billy is commemorated on the USS Arizona Memorial and the Memorial Tablets of the Missing, National Memorial Cemetery of the Pacific, Honolulu, Hawaii. He was survived by his Mother, Mrs. Clara C. Gibson, 619 Atchison Street, Atchison, Kansas.[275]

Gibson, Claude Clenton Seaman, First Class, Serial No. 272 41 68, US Navy. Claude was born March 3, 1920 the son of Claude B and Donna Mae (Freeman) Gibson. He enlisted in the US Navy October 5, 1940 in Birmingham, Alabama and completed his basic training at the Naval Training Station in Norfolk, Virginia. He reported for duty on the USS Arizona December 4, 1940. Claude was serving on the Arizona December 7, 1941 when the Japanese attacked Pearl Harbor. After the attack, Claude was transferred to the USS Patterson for duty. Claude died December 14, 1986 in Jefferson County, Alabama and is buried in Shepherd Cemetery, Fayette County, Alabama.

Giesen, Karl Anthony Yeoman, Second Class, Serial No: 321 23 75, US Navy. Karl was born on September 3, 1917 to Henry J. and Nellie M. Giesen. He lost his father when he was only 14. Karl enlisted in the US Navy on March 9, 1938 in Des Moines, Iowa and completed his basic training at the Naval Training Station in Great Lakes, Illinois. He served in the Philippines before he reported for duty on the USS Arizona on July 9, 1938. He was killed in action on December 7, 1941 at Pearl Harbor, Hawaii. Karl was awarded the Purple Heart Medal posthumously. He remains on duty on the USS Arizona. Karl is commemorated on the USS Arizona Memorial, the Memorial Tablets of the Missing, National Memorial Cemetery of the Pacific, Honolulu, Hawaii and St. Aloysius Catholic Cemetery, Calmar, Iowa. He was survived by his Wife, Mrs. Helen Lucille Giesen, 503 Winneshiek Avenue, Decorah, Iowa, Mother, Nellie M. Giesen and Daughter, Barbara Ann Giesen. The Halverson-Giesen American Legion Post No. 266 in Decorah, Iowa was named in his honor.[276]

Gilbert, Arthur Barnes Seaman, First Class, Serial No. 262 67 94, US Navy. Arthur was born February 28, 1922. He enlisted in the US Navy September 23, 1940 in Raleigh, North Carolina and completed his basic training at the Naval Training Station in Norfolk, Virginia. Arthur reported for duty on the USS Arizona December 4, 1940. He was serving on the Arizona on December 7, 1941 when the Japanese attacked Pearl Harbor. After the attack, A

Gill, Richard Eugene Seaman, First Class, Aviation Unit (VO-1), Serial No: 376 07 08, US Navy. Richard was born on October 20, 1921 in Wells, Nevada son of Harry and Blanche (Jeffrey) Gill. He enlisted in the US Navy on June 13, 1940 in San Francisco, California and reported for duty on the USS Arizona on February 5, 1941. Richard was killed in action on December 7, 1941 at Pearl Harbor, Hawaii. *His parents received word from the Navy Department on January 31, 1942.* He was awarded the American Defense Service Medal, World War II Victory Medal and Purple Heart Medal posthumously. Richard remains on duty on the USS Arizona. He is commemorated on the USS Arizona Memorial and the Memorial Tablets of

[275] Billy Edwin Gibson, Information from "The Story of Billy Gibson" by Patty Moore, Reporter, Atchison Daily Globe, Monday, November 16, 2009.
[276] Karl Anthony Giesen, Photo and family information provided by Stacey Gossling, Decorah Genealogy Association.

the Missing, National Memorial Cemetery of the Pacific, Honolulu, Hawaii. Richard was survived by his Parents, Mr. and Mrs. Harry Eugene Gill, Box 41, Beowawe, Nevada.

Gillem, Charles M. Seaman, First Class, Serial No. 287 47 94, US Navy. Charles was born January 25, 1915. He enlisted in the US Navy November 27, 1940 in Louisville, Kentucky and completed his basic training at the Naval Training Station in Great Lakes, Illinois. He reported for duty on the USS Arizona January 18, 1941. Charles was serving on the Arizona on December 7, 1941 when the Japanese attacked Pearl Harbor. After the attack, Charles was transferred to the USS Lexington for duty. The USS Lexington (CV-2) was sunk May 7, 1942 during the Battle of Coral Sea. Charles died March 28, 1979.

Gillenwater, Charles Ervin Seaman, First Class, Serial No. 295 76 75, US Navy. Charles was born on April 21, 1922 in Greenville, Texas, the son of Mack Edd and Valda Romie (Steele) Gillenwater. He enlisted in the US Navy October 4, 1940 in Nashville, Tennessee and completed his basic training at the Naval Training Station in Norfolk, Virginia. Charles reported for duty on the USS Arizona December 4, 1940. He was serving on the Arizona on December 7, 1941 when the Japanese attacked Pearl Harbor. After the attack, Charles was transferred to the USS Patterson for duty. Charles died on December 4, 1987 in Metairie, Louisiana.

Gillespie, David William Seaman, First Class, Serial No. 372 16 92, US Navy. David was born on November 13, 1920 in Colfax, New Mexico, the son of Edward Thomas and Nelle Opal (Taylor) Gillespie. He enlisted in the US Navy August 12, 1940 in Denver, Colorado and completed his basic training at the Naval Training Station in San Diego, California. He reported for duty on the USS Arizona October 14, 1940. David was serving on the Arizona on December 7, 1941 when the Japanese attacked Pearl Harbor. After the attack, David was transferred to the USS Aylwin for duty. David died on January 11, 1992 in Rogue River, Oregon.

Giovenazzo, Michael James Watertender, Second Class, Serial No: 299 91 23, US Navy. Michael was born on January 4, 1920 in Moline, Illinois. He enlisted in the US Navy on August 2, 1938 in Chicago, Illinois and completed his basic training at the Naval Training Station in Great Lakes, Illinois. Michael reported for duty on the USS Arizona December 4, 1938. *He was on shore leave on Saturday with a friend, they returned to the ship on Saturday night.* Michael was killed in action on December 7, 1941 at Pearl Harbor, Hawaii. *He was engaged to be married in January 1942.* Michael was awarded the American Defense Service Medal, World War II Victory Medal and Purple Heart Medal posthumously. He remains on duty on the USS Arizona. Michael is commemorated on the USS Arizona Memorial and the Memorial Tablets of the Missing, National Memorial Cemetery of the Pacific, Honolulu, Hawaii. He was survived by his Father, Mr. George Giovenazzo, 415 15th Street, Silvis, Illinois and his brother, Sam Giovenazzo who joined the Navy on December 31, 1941 and was sent to Pearl shortly after his enlistment. (His other brother, was serving on the USS Vestal, the repair ship moored along side the Arizona on December 7th)[277]

---

[277] Michael James Giovenazzo, Photo and information provided by family member, Jon Orendorff.

Givens, Harold Reuben Yeoman, Second Class, Serial No: 393 35 28, US Navy. Harold was born October 21, 1920 in Missouri to Ruben Rolla and Mayme Givens. He enlisted in the US Navy on April 10, 1940 in Portland, Oregon and completed his basic training at the Naval Training Station in San Diego, California. He reported for duty on the USS Arizona on July 2, 1940. Harold was killed in action on December 7, 1941 at Pearl Harbor, Hawaii. He was awarded the American Defense Service Medal, World War II Victory Medal and Purple Heart Medal posthumously. Harold remains on duty on the USS Arizona. He is commemorated on the USS Arizona Memorial and the Memorial Tablets of the Missing, National Memorial Cemetery of the Pacific, Honolulu, Hawaii. Harold was survived by his Parents, Mr. and Mrs. Reuben Rollo Givens, Morehouse, Missouri, one sister, Mrs. Hunter Black and two brothers, Russel Givens of Brownsville, Tennessee, and Ralph Givens of Morehouse.[278]

Glenn, Richard Clyde Ensign, Serial No. O-100121, US Navy. Richard was born May 28, 1918 in Perry, Kansas the son of William Clyde Glenn and Belle Hatch. He was commissioned Ensign in the US Navy February 7, 1941 and was serving on the USS Arizona as Junior Watch and Division 7 Officer on December 7, 1941 when the Japanese attacked Pearl Harbor. His battle station was Sec. Battalion. Officer 2 & 4. Richard was killed in action on board the USS Juneau on November 13, 1942 during the battle of Guadalcanal. He was awarded the American Campaign Medal, Asiatic Pacific Campaign Medal and the Purple Heart Medal posthumously. Richard is commemorated on the Memorial Tablets of the Missing, Fort William McKinley, Manila, Philippines. He was survived by his Mother, Mrs. W. C. Glenn, 1821 West Fairchild, Manhattan, Kansas.[279]

Gobbin, Angelo Ship's Cook, First Class, Serial No: 250 18 50, US Navy. Angelo was born on July 26, 1889 in Italy. He re-enlisted in the US Navy on January 28, 1938 in San Pedro, California and again on October 29, 1941 in Pearl Harbor. Angelo served on the USS Arizona from December 28, 1931 until he died of wounds received on December 7, 1941 at Pearl Harbor, Hawaii.[280] He was awarded the American Defense Service Medal, World War II Victory Medal and Purple Heart Medal posthumously. Angelo's remains were recovered and he was buried in Plot A, Row 0, Grave 482, National Memorial Cemetery of the Pacific, Honolulu, Hawaii. He is commemorated on the USS Arizona Memorial. Angelo was survived by his Wife, Mrs. Marguerite Lou Gobbin, 4120 East 15th Street, Long Beach, California.

Goff, Wiley Coy Seaman, Second Class, Serial No: 356 55 14, US Navy. Wiley was born March 27, 1917 in Oklahoma, the son of William F. and Martha Elizabeth (Caughey) Goff. He enlisted in the US Navy on March 22, 1941 in Dallas, Texas and completed his basic training at the Naval Training Station in San Diego, California. Wiley reported for duty on the USS Arizona on July 16, 1941. He was killed in action on December 7, 1941 at Pearl Harbor, Hawaii.

---

[278] Harold Reuben Givens, Photo and information from The Siskeston Herald, Sikeston, Missouri, December 25, 1941, Page 1.

[279] Richard Clyde Glenn, Photo from Lucky Bag Yearbook, United States Naval Academy, Annapolis, MD, Class of 1941.

[280] Angelo Gobbin, Report of Changes of the USS Arizona for the month ending 31st day of December, 1941, page 60, line 28, Angelo Gobbin.

Wiley was awarded the American Defense Service Medal, World War II Victory Medal and Purple Heart Medal posthumously. He remains on duty on the USS Arizona. Wiley is commemorated on the USS Arizona Memorial and the Memorial Tablets of the Missing, National Memorial Cemetery of the Pacific, Honolulu, Hawaii. He was survived by his Father, Mr. William Finest Goff, Lamont, Oklahoma.

Goldsberry, William Joseph   Seaman, First Class, Serial No. 316 71 77, US Navy. William was born September 4, 1923, the son of William A. and Lillian Goldsberry. He enlisted in the US Navy November 27, 1940 in Omaha, Nebraska and completed his basic training at the Naval Training Station in Great Lakes, Illinois. William reported for duty on the USS Arizona January 18, 1941. He was wounded in action while serving on the Arizona on December 7, 1941 when the Japanese attacked Pearl Harbor. William was transferred to the US Naval Hospital at Pearl Harbor. In May 1944 he was wounded in action again while serving on board the USS Nehenta Bay (CVE-74). His father, Mr. William Arzi Goldsberry, 1328 Avenue F, Council Bluffs, Iowa was notified. He served in the US Navy until June of 1962. William died November 4, 1980.

Gomez, Edward, Jr.   Seaman, First Class, Serial No: 372 16 16, US Navy. Edward was born in 1921 to Edward and Josephine Gomez. He enlisted in the US Navy on July 11, 1940 in Denver, Colorado and completed his basic training at the Naval Training Station in San Diego, California. Edward reported for duty on the USS Arizona on October 14, 1940. He was killed in action on December 7, 1941 at Pearl Harbor, Hawaii. Edward was awarded the American Defense Service Medal, World War II Victory Medal and Purple Heart Medal posthumously. He remains on duty on the USS Arizona. Edward is commemorated on the USS Arizona Memorial and the Memorial Tablets of the Missing, National Memorial Cemetery of the Pacific, Honolulu, Hawaii. He was survived by his Father, Mr. Edward Gomez, Sr., 1990 South Huron Street, Denver, Colorado. *In September 1945 his parents filed suit asking $100,000 in damages from the Imperial Japanese government for the death of their son on grounds that the attack on Pearl Harbor was an "illegal act". According to the parents, he was "murdered in peace-time".*

Good, Leland "Bud"   Seaman, Second Class, Serial No: 337 41 65, US Navy. Leland was born October 8, 1918 in Wayne City, Illinois to Almon and Adda (Smith) Good. He enlisted in the US Navy on October 15, 1940 in St. Louis, Missouri and completed his basic training at the Naval Training Station in Great Lakes, Illinois. Leland reported for duty on the USS Arizona on December 9, 1940. He was killed in action on December 7, 1941 at Pearl Harbor, Hawaii. Leland was awarded the American Defense Service Medal, World War II Victory Medal and Purple Heart Medal posthumously. He remains on duty on the USS Arizona. Leland is commemorated on the USS Arizona Memorial and the Memorial Tablets of the Missing, National Memorial Cemetery of the Pacific, Honolulu, Hawaii. He was survived by his Father, Mr. Almon Good, Wayne City, Illinois.[281]

---

[281] Leland Good, Photo provided by the Wayne County, Illinois Historical Society.

Goodwin, William Arthur   Seaman, Second Class, Serial No: 372 16 96, US Navy. William was born January 6, 1921 in Lincoln County, Oklahoma to Isaac Claude and Nellie (Vanderpool) Goodwin. *At the age of 2-1/2 he and his brother, Joseph were placed in St. Vincent's Orphan Asylum in Denver due to the illness of their mother. Later, they were in Mullen's Home for Boys in Fort Logan, Colorado. Both parents died in their 20's. When William left the Home for Boys, he went to Colorado Springs and joined the CCCs.* He enlisted in the US Navy on August 12, 1940 in Denver, Colorado and completed his basic training at the Naval Training Station in San Diego, California. William reported for duty on the USS Arizona on October 14, 1940. He was killed in action on December 7, 1941 at Pearl Harbor. William was in Division 4 and assigned to Turret #4 as his battle station. He was awarded the American Defense Service Medal, World War II Victory Medal and Purple Heart Medal posthumously. William is believed to have been buried in one of the unknown graves in the Punchbowl and the remains were exhumed by military forensics in 2001 to be tested. He is commemorated on the USS Arizona Memorial and the Memorial Tablets of the Missing, National Memorial Cemetery of the Pacific, Honolulu, Hawaii and the National Memorial Cemetery of Arizona, Phoenix, Arizona. William was survived by his Grandmother, Mrs. Mary Ann Campbell, 4475 West 30th Street, Denver, Colorado and his older brother, Joseph Campbell, serving on a minesweeper.[282]

Gordon, Donald Eugene   Gunner's Mate, Second Class, Serial No. 381 27 90, US Navy. Donald was born June 23, 1920 in Los Angeles, California. He enlisted in the US Navy June 9, 1939 from Lemon Grove, California where he lived with his parents. He reported for duty on the USS Arizona September 11, 1939 when it was in port at Long Beach, California. From there the Arizona went to Bremerton, Washington and then on to Pearl Harbor. He was serving on December 7, 1941 when the Japanese attacked Pearl Harbor.

"On the morning of the 7th, I was in the 4th Division Compartment on the Arizona when he heard the first bomb hit the ship. I went down to the handling room of the 4th turret and changed into his dungarees. General Quarters sounded and he went to his battle station which was gun captain of the center gun in #4 turrets.

As we started to get the guns ready for firing while being tossed around by bombs hitting the ship, there was a big explosion and the ship rose up and settled down.

The last man to leave the handling room was knee deep in water; I climbed straight up three decks to the gun pits and was still knee deep in water. We then got word from the turret officer to evacuate the turret and assemble outside the turret under the overhang. The ship was afire from the #3 turret forward. By this time, the quarter deck was even with the water and the division officer gave the order to abandon ship. Whenever the enemy planes would strafe the deck, we waited until they passed over and 3 or 4 men would run out and jump over the side between strafing. The oil was burning about 50 feet to our left from where we jumped in and then swam ashore to Ford Island and went to an air raid shelter.

In the afternoon, I took a boat to the Naval Station at Pearl Harbor and stayed at Block Recreation Center that night. The next day, December 8th I was assigned to a burial working party. On Tuesday, December 9th I was assigned to the USS McDonough (DD-351). On the following day we went out to sea. My parents got word that he was OK on Christmas Day 1941."

---

[282] William Arthur Goodwin, Photo and information provided by his brother, Joseph & Ruth Campbell.

Donald remained in the Navy until he retired in 1960. Settling in San Diego, he worked for the City of San Diego for twenty years until he retired in 1980. Donald met his wife at a baseball game in Fenway Park, Boston. They just celebrated their 63rd Anniversary. They have six lovely children, all doing well. After retiring from the City of San Diego, they traveled a great deal. Donald passed away peacefully at home on March 27, 2012.[283]

Gordon, Peter Charles, Jr. Fireman, First Class, Serial No: 372 12 22, US Navy. Peter was born March 31, 1920 in Primera, Colorado to Peter Charles and Antonia (Cermak) Gordon. *His father was a coal miner and he was born in a mining camp near Trinidad, Colorado. After graduating from Trinidad High School, he joined the Navy in hopes of gaining the skills for a trade.* He enlisted in the US Navy on December 13, 1939 in Denver, Colorado and completed his basic training at the Naval Training Station in San Diego, California. He reported for duty on the USS Arizona on February 24, 1940. Peter was killed in action on December 7, 1941 at Pearl Harbor, Hawaii. He was awarded the American Defense Service Medal, World War II Victory Medal and Purple Heart Medal posthumously. Peter remains on duty on the USS Arizona. He is commemorated on the USS Arizona Memorial and the Memorial Tablets of the Missing, National Memorial Cemetery of the Pacific, Honolulu, Hawaii. Peter was survived by his Father, Mr. Pete Gordon, Morley, Colorado.[284]

Goshen, William "Gene" Eugene Seaman, First Class, 5th Division, Serial No. 287 38 50, US Navy. William was born April 22, 1919 in Harlan County, Kentucky to Jesse and Lillie (Wyatt) Goshen. He enlisted in the US Navy on March 27, 1940 at Louisville, Kentucky and completed his basic training at the Naval Training Station in Great Lakes, Illinois. He reported for duty on the USS Arizona July 12, 1940. William was serving on December 7, 1941 when the Japanese attacked Pearl Harbor. On the morning of the 7th, Gene was on the aft deck taking a smoke, before going ashore for liberty. He wasn't paying attention to what was going on and suddenly heard the GQ Alarm. He ran to his Battle Station at the #5 Gun where he placed the headphones on his head and waited for the other crew to get there. Gene was standing in the hatchway, looking out at what was happening. No other crewmen assigned to the No. 5 Gun ever made it there. They all died on the Arizona. The next thing he new was he was bushing off from the bottom of the harbor. He got to the surface and started swimming back to the Arizona until he realized that she was on fire from bow to stern and decided to swim to Ford Island. Once there, he collapsed and started throwing up oil and salt water. There was another sailor near him. The other sailor mentioned that they should seek shelter somewhere. Gene agreed and went to stand up. However, when this happened, the skin on his forehead came down over his eyes. He asked the other sailor to lead him. It wasn't until they got to shelter, that someone pushed the skin from his eyes, back to his forehead.[285] He was burned over much of his body during the attack but survived. William was taken to the Naval Hospital, Pearl Harbor for initial treatment. Later he was transported to the Mare Island Naval Hospital in California for treatment. At the Mare Island Hospital he called out to another

---

[283] Donald Eugene Gordon, Information, story and photo provided by himself in a letter in 2008.

[284] Peter Charles Gordon, Jr., Photo provided by family member Rebecca Gillis.

[285] William "Gene" Eugene Goshen, excerpts from his survival story told by his son, William E. Goshen, Jr., Pearl Harbor Survivors Project.

wounded Arizona sailor in the burn ward (Edward Janikowski) who did not recognize him due to his burns. On May 28, 1942 he was transferred to the USS Fletcher (DD-445). Later he was transferred to the USS Brown (DD-546). William left the Navy on December 2, 1947 and was employed by Chrysler. He retired in 1980. His obituary follows:

William E. Goshen, Sr., 86 died Thursday, July 21, 2005, in Spring City Health Care. He was born on April 22, 1919 in Kentucky, Son of Jesse Goshen and Lillie Wyatt Goshen. He was a resident of Rhea County for three years, moved from Florida and was of the Christian faith. He was a member of the Oakland Masonic Lodge in Oaklandon, Ind., a veteran of the U.S. Navy and served in WWII on the USS Arizona, the USS Fletcher and the USS Brown. He was preceded in death by his wife Billie R. Goshen; a son, David A. Goshen; parents Jesse and Lillie Wyatt Goshen, and four sisters. Survivors include his son, William "Bill" Goshen of Dayton; one grandchild David A. Goshen, II of Dayton; and several nieces and nephews. [286]

Gosselin, Edward Webb Ensign, Serial No: 0-097031, US Navy Reserve. Edward was born on May 1, 1917 in Hamden, Connecticut to Edward Napoleon and Florilla Helena (Webb) Gosselin. He was educated at Yale University and graduated class of 1939. Edward enlisted as an Apprentice Seaman in the Navy on September 30, 1940. His first duty station was the USS Arizona where he reported for duty on May 3, 1941. Edward was commissioned an Ensign on March 14, 1941 and served as Junior Watch and Engineer Division B Officer. His battle station was Boiler Control. Edward was killed in action on December 7, 1941 at Pearl Harbor, Hawaii. He was awarded the American Defense Service Medal, World War II Victory Medal and Purple Heart Medal posthumously. Edward remains on duty on the USS Arizona. He is commemorated on the USS Arizona Memorial and the Memorial Tablets of the Missing, National Memorial Cemetery of the Pacific, Honolulu, Hawaii and Mount Olivet Cemetery, Joliet, Illinois. Edward was survived by his Father, Mr. Edward N. Gosselin, 200 Richards Street, Joliet, Illinois. The USS Gosselin (APD-126) was named in his honor. USS Gosselin received one battle star for her World War II service.[287]

Gosselin, Joseph Adjutor Alfred Radioman, First Class, Serial No: 212 43 57, US Navy. Joseph was born July 7, 1914 in Chicopee, Massachusetts to one of eleven children born to Adolph and Hermine Gosselin. He enlisted in the US Navy on March 24, 1936 in Springfield, Massachusetts. He served on board the USS Saratoga before serving on the USS Arizona. Joseph reported for duty on the USS Arizona on December 17, 1936. He was killed in action on December 7, 1941 at Pearl Harbor, Hawaii. Joseph was awarded the American Defense Service Medal, World War II Victory Medal and Purple Heart Medal posthumously. He remains on duty on the USS Arizona. Joseph is commemorated on the USS Arizona Memorial and the Memorial Tablets of the Missing, National Memorial Cemetery of the Pacific, Honolulu, Hawaii. He was survived by his Father, Mr. Adolphe Gosselin, 65 Maple Street, Chicopee Falls, Massachusetts.

---

[286] William Eugene Goshen, Obituary, the Herald News, Dayton, TN, July 22, 2005.
[287] Edward Webb Gosselin, Information from the Dictionary of American Naval Fighting Ships.

Gould, Harry Lee Seaman, First Class, Serial No: 337 48 47, US Navy. Harry was born September 28, 1918 in Springfield, Illinois to Harry A. and Katie Gould. He enlisted in the US Navy on December 16, 1940 in St. Louis, Missouri and completed his basic training at the Naval Training Station in Great Lakes, Illinois. Harry reported for duty on the USS Arizona on May 23, 1941. He was killed in action on December 7, 1941 at Pearl Harbor, Hawaii. Harry was awarded the American Defense Service Medal, World War II Victory Medal and Purple Heart Medal posthumously. He remains on duty on the USS Arizona. Harry is commemorated on the USS Arizona Memorial and the Memorial Tablets of the Missing, National Memorial Cemetery of the Pacific, Honolulu, Hawaii. He was survived by his Father, Mr. Harry Gould, 1221 North 8th Street, Springfield, Illinois.[288]

Gove, Rupert "Bert" Clair Seaman, First Class, Serial No: 376 09 26, US Navy. Rupert was born September 27, 1920 in Humboldt, California to Romaldo Levi and Laura (Adrian) Gove. He enlisted in the US Navy on July 30, 1940 in San Francisco, California and completed his basic training at the Naval Training Station in San Diego, California. Rupert reported for duty on the USS Arizona on October 14, 1940. He was killed in action on December 7, 1941 at Pearl Harbor, Hawaii. Rupert was awarded the American Defense Service Medal, World War II Victory Medal and Purple Heart Medal posthumously. He remains on duty on the USS Arizona. Rupert is commemorated on the USS Arizona Memorial and the Memorial Tablets of the Missing, National Memorial Cemetery of the Pacific, Honolulu, Hawaii. He was survived by his Father, Mr. Romaldo Levi Gove, 6932 Lockwood Street, Oakland, California.

Grabowsky, Leon Ensign, US Navy. Leon was born on September 18, 1917 in Paris, France. He graduated from the Naval Academy in 1941. Leon reported for duty on the USS Arizona where he was serving on December 7, 1941 as Engineer Junior Watch and Division A Officer. His battle station was the Plotting Room. When the Japanese attacked Pearl Harbor, Leon was ashore. He went on to serve on the USS Leutze during the battle of Iwo Jima and took over the vessel when the commanding officer was wounded. Under his command, the Leutze took part in the battle of Okinawa and was almost sunk in a kamikaze attack. He also served in the Korean War. During the Vietnam War, he was awarded the Navy Cross and Bronze Star. He was later an executive officer at the China Lake base, where he helped develop the Sidewinder air-to-air missile. His final assignment was commander of the Concord Naval Weapons Station. Leon retired in 1971. He died on July 28, 2000 and is buried in Section 66, Site 5556, Arlington National Cemetery, Arlington, Virginia. He was survived by his wife, Joanne, two sons and three daughters.[289]

---

[288] Harry Lee Gould, Photo from the Capitoline Yearbook, Springfield High School, Springfield, Illinois, 1936.

[289] Leon Grabowsky, Photo taken from the Lucky Bag Yearbook, United States Naval Academy, Annapolis, MD, Class of 1941.

Graham, Donald Alexander Aviation Machinist's Mate, First Class, Aviation Unit (VO-1), Serial No. 161 55 64, US Navy. Donald was born on June 17, 1900 in Pennsylvania the son of James and Mary Ellen (Gilroy) Graham. He re-enlisted in the US Navy August 18, 1937 at San Pedro, California. Donald served on the USS Arizona from February 27, 1936 until December 7, 1941 when the Japanese attacked Pearl Harbor. His official statement:

"On the morning of December 7, 1941, I was aboard the U.S.S. Arizona, being attached to the "V" Division on the ship. When the attack started I was in the aviation workshop which is located forward of the quarterdeck, starboard side, frame 84 to 88.

On hearing the explosions and gun reports, Wentzlaff, E., AOM2c, came in saying we were being attacked and bombed by Jap planes. The air raid siren sounded, followed by the General Quarters alarm. I stepped outside the shop and started to my general quarters station, on the quarterdeck, shouting "let's go". A bomb hit the after end of #4 turret, glancing off onto the quarterdeck, at the Captain's hatch, starboard side. As I stepped on the quarterdeck, Lieutenant commander Fuqua, USN., said in a steady voice, "Put that fire out back aft", which the bomb had started. I called to Wentzlaff, AOM2c, Hurst, AMM3c, Burns, Yeo2c, and Lane, RM3c to rig the fire hose aft, as they were going to our General Quarters Station with me. Me and Hurst grabbed the fire hose off its stowage on the fumigation box and assisted by Wentzlaff took it to the fire plug at #4 turret, frame #110. Bruns and Lane got another fire hose from the rack in compartment A-704, starboard side and proceeded to hook it up at #3 turret amidships. Mr. Fuqua said in a calm, cool voice, "Turn it on", when he saw that we had hooked up the hose. Wentzlaff, leading the end of the hose to the bomb hole where the deck was afire. I said to Mr. Fuqua, when the valve was opened, "There is no water pressure on". He then told me to see if I could get pressure turned on. I rushed to the Officer-of-the-Deck's booth to call up for pressure, but the phones were all knocked off the hooks and out of commission, as while this was taking place there had been bomb hits up forward, shuddering the ship violently and planes strafing the decks. It seemed as though the magazines forward blew up while we were hooking up the fire hose, as the noise was followed by an awful "Swish" and hot air blew out of the compartments. There had been bomb hits at the first start and yellowish smoke was pouring out of the hatches from below decks. There were lots of the men coming out on the quarterdeck with every stitch of clothing and shoes blown off, painfully burned and shocked. Mr. Fuqua was the senior officer on deck and set an example for the men in being unperturbed, calm, cool, and collective, exemplifying the courage and traditions of an officer under fire. It seemed like the men painfully burned, shocked and dazed, became inspired and took things in stride, seeing Mr. Fuqua, so unconcerned about the bombing and strafing, standing on the quarterdeck. As there was no "going to Pieces" or "growing panicky", noticeable, and he directed the moving of the wounded and burned men who were on the quarterdeck to the motor launches and boats, he gave orders to get the life rafts on #3 barbette down, supervised the loading of the wounded and burned casualties, assisted by Ensign J.D. Miller, who set a very good example for a younger officer in being cool, calm and collective. The crew from #3 and #4 turrets had to come out on deck as the turrets were flooded and proceeded to help with the casualties and getting the life rafts over the side.

The signal gang, quartermasters, and all hands on the bridge went up as the signal men were trying to put out a fire in the signal rack and grabbing signal flags out to hoist a signal, the whole bridge went up, flames enveloping and obscuring them from view as the flames shot upward twice as high as the tops. A bomb hit on the starboard side of the after 5-inch guns and antiaircraft gun, and got most of the marine crew and antiaircraft crews. It seemed as though one bomb hit the port after antiaircraft crew and came down through the casemate and Executive Officer's Office. The whole port compartment, A-704, from the quarter deck on was a flaming

178

inferno and the ship settled rapidly from forward aft. The wardroom, portside, was flooded even with the bottom of the deck coamings and yellowish gaseous smoke continued to pour out of the ventilators and machine shop hatch, amidships.

After the big explosion and "Swish", the men painfully burned and wounded, dazed beyond comprehension, came out on the quarter deck and I had to stop some of them from entering into the flames later on, and directed them over to the starboard side of the deck to the gangway for embarking and encouraging them to be calm.

The Vestal, tied up alongside the port side, did not seem to get hit hard and started to get underway, so I stood by to cast off lines on the quarter deck portside and cast off their bow lines as the Lieutenant Commander on her wanted to save the line to tie up to one of the buoys, and assisted by a seaman from #4 turret, we rendered the bow line around and cast her off. Then getting the small life raft on # turret barbette port side off and over the port stern, the water and oil being on deck and the ship settling fastly we got orders to embark in the motor boat at the starboard stern quarter. Lieutenant Commander Fuqua and a few others still being aboard. We landed at B.O.Q. landing, Ford Island. Smith, BM2c, USN, boat coxswain making many trips for wounded and burned men, being delivered by Lieutenant Commander Fuqua, still on board.

Courage and performance of all hands was of the highest order imaginable, especially being handicapped by adverse conditions and shipmates being blown up alongside them, there was no disorder or tendency to run around in confusion. Thanks to the coolness and calm manner Lieutenant Commander Fuqua and Ensign J. D. Miller installed confidence in the crew surviving."[290]

Donald was awarded the Navy Cross for his actions that day:

The Navy Cross is presented to Donald A. Graham, Aviation Machinist's Mate First Class, U.S. Navy, for exceptional courage, presence of mind, and devotion to duty and disregard for his personal safety while serving on board the U.S.S. ARIZONA (BB-39) during the Japanese attack on the United States Pacific Fleet in Pearl Harbor, Territory of Hawaii, 7 December 1941. Although his shipmates were leaving the blazing U.S.S. ARIZONA, on his own initiative Aviation Machinist Mate First Class Graham faced the intense fire on the deck, severe bombing and withering machine gun fire of enemy strafing planes to release lines connecting the battleship with a repair vessel, U.S.S. VESTAL, thus aiding the latter in getting underway. The conduct of Aviation Machinist's Mate First Class Graham throughout this action reflects great credit upon himself, and was in keeping with the highest traditions of the United States Naval Service.

After the attack, Donald was transferred to the Receiving Station at Pearl Harbor for temporary duty and then on to Observation Squadron One at Pearl Harbor. Donald died on February 11, 1976 and is buried in Mt Hope Cemetery, San Diego, California.

---

[290] Confidential Statement of Donald A. Graham, Aviation Machinist's Mate First Class, U.S. Navy- U.S.S. Arizona, Pearl Harbor, T.H., December 15, 1941.

Granger, Raymond Edward Fireman, Third Class, Serial No: 321 49 16, US Navy. Raymond was born April 2, 1921 in Des Moines, Iowa, the eldest son of Lloyd and Georgia (Reeve) Granger. His mother died when he was just two years old. *He graduated from East High School in the spring of 1940. Tall and athletic, Raymond was an expert swimmer and diver. He applied for entrance into the Navy immediately after his graduation, but was not accepted until October 15, 1940 in Des Moines, Iowa. Raymond was just 18 then.* Following his basic training at the Naval Training Station in Great Lakes, Illinois, Raymond took special instruction in electricity. He reported for duty on the USS Arizona on December 9, 1940. One of his responsibilities was attending to lights and other electrical equipment aboard the Arizona. He was on duty in the engine room of the Arizona at the time of the Japanese attack. A bomb exploded near him and his engine-room crew-mates. It is believed he was killed instantly. He was awarded the American Defense Service Medal, World War II Victory Medal and Purple Heart Medal posthumously. Raymond remains on duty on the USS Arizona. He is commemorated on the USS Arizona Memorial and the Memorial Tablets of the Missing, National Memorial Cemetery of the Pacific, Honolulu, Hawaii. Raymond was survived by his Step-Mother, Mrs. Hazel Granger, 2304 Dean Avenue, Des Moines, Iowa and a brother, Robert. His father preceded him in death in 1929.[291]

Grant, Lawrence Everett Yeoman, Third Class, Serial No: 337 25 52, US Navy. Lawrence was born in 1922 to Harry C. and Hazel A. Grant. He enlisted in the US Navy on January 3, 1940 in St. Louis, Missouri and completed his basic training at the Naval Training Station in Great Lakes, Illinois. Lawrence reported for duty on the USS Arizona on March 26, 1940. He was killed in action on December 7, 1941 at Pearl Harbor, Hawaii. Lawrence was awarded the American Defense Service Medal, World War II Victory Medal and Purple Heart Medal posthumously. He remains on duty on the USS Arizona. Lawrence is commemorated on the USS Arizona Memorial and the Memorial Tablets of the Missing, National Memorial Cemetery of the Pacific, Honolulu, Hawaii. He was survived by his Father, Mr. Harry C. Grant, 2333 Tennessee Avenue, St. Louis, Missouri.[292]

Gray, Albert "Jimmy" James Seaman, First Class, Serial No: 414 46 38, US Navy Reserve. Albert was born June 27, 1923 in Montana the son of Albert and Florence Elizabeth Gray. He enlisted in the US Navy Reserve Radio School on October 9, 1940 in Seattle, Washington and completed his basic training at the Naval Training Station in San Diego, California. He reported for duty on the USS Arizona on April 27, 1941. Albert was killed in action on December 7, 1941 at Pearl Harbor, Hawaii. He was awarded the American Defense Service Medal, World War II Victory Medal and Purple Heart Medal posthumously. Albert remains on duty on the USS Arizona. He is commemorated on the USS Arizona Memorial and the Memorial

---

[291] Raymond Edward Granger, Photo and information provided by family members from These Honored Dead, That We May Take Increased Devotion 'I Have No Regrets,' Says Mother of Raymond E. Granger, Des Moines Newspaper, Des Moines, Iowa.
[292] Lawrence Everett Grant, Photo from Missouri Honor States.

Tablets of the Missing, National Memorial Cemetery of the Pacific, Honolulu, Hawaii and Eden Cemetery, Guemes, Washington. Albert was survived by his Mother, Mrs. Florence Elizabeth Gray, Route 1, Anacortes, Washington.[293]

Gray, James Victor Seaman, First Class, Serial No. 272 52 22, US Navy. James enlisted in the US Navy October 7, 1940 in New Orleans, Louisiana and completed his basic training at the Naval Training Station in San Diego, California. He reported for duty on the USS Arizona January 8, 1941. James was serving on the Arizona on December 7, 1941 when the Japanese attacked Pearl Harbor. After the attack, James was transferred to the USS Mac Donough for duty.

Gray, Lawrence Moore Fireman, First Class, Serial No: 342 18 31, US Navy. Lawrence was born on June 29, 1921 to Edward E. and Bessie Anna (Moore) Gray. He enlisted in the US Navy on January 17, 1940 in Kansas City, Missouri and completed his basic training at the Naval Training Station in Great Lakes, Illinois. Lawrence reported for duty on the USS Arizona on March 26, 1940. He was killed in action on December 7, 1941 at Pearl Harbor, Hawaii. Lawrence was awarded the American Defense Service Medal, World War II Victory Medal and Purple Heart Medal posthumously. He remains on duty on the USS Arizona. Lawrence is commemorated on the USS Arizona Memorial and the Memorial Tablets of the Missing, National Memorial Cemetery of the Pacific, Honolulu, Hawaii. He was survived by his Father, Mr. Edward E. Gray, Wheeling, Missouri.

Gray, William James Seaman, First Class, Serial No: 382 29 70, US Navy. William was born in 1915 in California to William James and Mary E. Gray. He enlisted in the US Navy on November 1, 1940 in Los Angeles, California and completed his basic training at the Naval Training Station in San Diego, California. He reported for duty on the USS Arizona on December 30, 1940. William was killed in action on December 7, 1941 at Pearl Harbor, Hawaii. He was awarded the American Defense Service Medal, World War II Victory Medal and Purple Heart Medal posthumously. William remains on duty on the USS Arizona. He is commemorated on the USS Arizona Memorial and the Memorial Tablets of the Missing, National Memorial Cemetery of the Pacific, Honolulu, Hawaii. William was survived by his Father, Mr. William James Gray, Sr., 1237 East 19th Street, Long Beach, California.[294]

---

[293] Albert James Gray, photo provided by family member, Wendy Willis.
[294] William James Gray photo provided by family member, Jim Gray

Green, Clay Douglas, Jr. Gunner's Mate, First Class, Serial No. 295 75 40, US Navy. Clay was born on July 8, 1922 in Dayton, Rhea County, Tennessee. His parents were Colonel Clay Douglas Green, US Army and Barbara Marie Green. Clay enlisted in the US Navy on September 27, 1940 in Nashville, Tennessee and completed his basic training at the Naval Training Station in Norfolk, Virginia. He reported for duty on the USS Arizona December 4, 1940. Clay was serving on the Arizona on December 7, 1941 when the Japanese attacked Pearl Harbor. He remembered leaving the USS Arizona to look up and see the planes of the Japanese coming and he re-entered the ship to get the men on board out. He remembered wading in water up to his knees trying to get men to shore that had jumped overboard into the water. Clay was also injured, and stayed in the Naval Hospital in Virginia for a year. He returned to active duty and received the American Area Campaign ribbon, World War II Victory Ribbon, Asiatic-Pacific Campaign ribbon with nine (9) bronze stars, Philippine Liberation Campaign Ribbon, and the American Defense Ribbon with bronze. Clay was discharged from the Navy on March 15, 1946. After the war Clay settled down in Chattanooga, Tennessee and went into the Construction business. He worked in the construction business until he retired in 2000 at the age of 78. Clay died on December 24, 2007 at the VA Hospital, in Decatur, Georgia. He was survived by his wife, Mrs. Hazel V. Green.[295]

Green, Glen Hubert Seaman, First Class, Serial No: 376 16 22, US Navy. Glen was born on July 12, 1917 in Jasper, Mississippi to Barry Walker and Mary Lulu (Sims) Green. He enlisted in the US Navy on November 15, 1940 and reported for duty on the USS Arizona on January 11, 1941. Glen was killed in action on December 7, 1941 at Pearl Harbor, Hawaii. He was awarded the American Defense Service Medal, World War II Victory Medal and Purple Heart Medal posthumously. Glen remains on duty on the USS Arizona. He is commemorated on the USS Arizona Memorial and the Memorial Tablets of the Missing, National Memorial Cemetery of the Pacific, Honolulu, Hawaii and Enon Cemetery, Waldrup, Mississippi. Glen was survived by his Father, Mr. Barry Walker Green, Route 1, Paulding, Mississippi.

Green, James William Gunner's Mate, Third Class, Serial No. 311 42 73, US Navy. James was born March 20, 1922 in Detroit Michigan. He joined the US Navy March 20, 1940 in Detroit, Michigan at age 18, and after completing basic training at the Naval Training Station in Great Lakes, Illinois, he reported for duty on the USS Arizona on July 12, 1940. James was serving on the Arizona on December 7, 1941 when the Japanese attacked Pearl Harbor. He had the early magazine watch on the morning of December 7th and survived the attack. After the Arizona exploded and sank, he helped get wounded into lifeboats, and then swam to Ford Island. Days later he worked on the burial detail. Later, he became a diver and worked salvage details on the Arizona, Oglala and West Virginia. He served aboard several other ships and left the Navy in April of 1946. James died February 22, 1996, less than a month shy of turning 74. His ashes were interred in the 4th barbette of the USS Arizona on December 7, 1996.

---

[295] Clay Douglas Green, Jr., Information and photo provided by his wife, Mrs. Hazel V. Green.

Greenfield, Carroll Gale   Seaman, First Class, Serial No: 393 41 84, US Navy. Carroll was born in about 1919 in Nebraska to Hansford and Alice Greenfield. He enlisted in the US Navy on October 23, 1940 in Portland, Oregon and completed his basic training at the Naval Training Station in San Diego, California. He reported for duty on the USS Arizona on December 30, 1940. Carroll was killed in action on December 7, 1941 at Pearl Harbor, Hawaii. He was awarded the American Defense Service Medal, World War II Victory Medal and Purple Heart Medal posthumously. Carroll remains on duty on the USS Arizona. He is commemorated on the USS Arizona Memorial and the Memorial Tablets of the Missing, National Memorial Cemetery of the Pacific, Honolulu, Hawaii. Carroll was survived by his Father, Mr. Hansford Greenfield, 604 1st Street, Silverton, Ohio.[296]

Griffin, Reese Olin   Electrician's Mate, Third Class, Serial No: 360 25 60, US Navy. Reese was born in July 1917 in Texas to John Reese and Anna O. Griffin. He enlisted in the US Navy on November 8, 1940 in Houston, Texas and completed his basic training at the Naval Training Station in San Diego, California. Reese reported for duty on the USS Arizona on January 11, 1941. He was killed in action on December 7, 1941 at Pearl Harbor, Hawaii. Reese was awarded the American Defense Service Medal, World War II Victory Medal and Purple Heart Medal posthumously. He remains on duty on the USS Arizona. Reese is commemorated on the USS Arizona Memorial and the Memorial Tablets of the Missing, National Memorial Cemetery of the Pacific, Honolulu, Hawaii. He was survived by his Father, Mr. John Reese Griffin, Route 1, Dickinson, Texas.

Griffiths, Robert Alfred   Electrician's Mate, Third Class, Serial No: 381 28 85, US Navy. Robert was born August 12, 1921 in San Diego, California to Robert Colcord and Mabel (Scovell) Griffiths. He enlisted in the US Navy on September 9, 1939 in San Diego, California and completed his basic training at the Naval Training Station in San Diego, California. Robert reported for duty on the USS Arizona on November 10, 1939. He was killed in action on December 7, 1941 at Pearl Harbor, Hawaii. Robert was awarded the American Defense Service Medal, World War II Victory Medal and Purple Heart Medal posthumously. He remains on duty on the USS Arizona. Robert is commemorated on the USS Arizona Memorial and the Memorial Tablets of the Missing, National Memorial Cemetery of the Pacific, Honolulu, Hawaii. He was survived by his Father, Mr. Robert C. Griffiths, 4068 Iowa Street, San Diego, California.

Grim, George Edwin   Gunner's Mate, First Class, Serial No. 371 88 04, US Navy. George was born June 20, 1911 in McGrew, Nebraska, the son of John C. and Agnes M. Grim. He enlisted in the US Navy on February 10, 1934 in Denver, Colorado and reported for duty on the Arizona on July 12, 1934. George was serving on the USS Arizona on December 7, 1941 when the Japanese attacked Pearl Harbor. After the attack, George was transferred to the USS Tennessee for duty. George served 22 years in the Navy, retiring in April 1956. He died October 7, 1989 in Lyman, Nebraska.

Grissinger, Robert Beryle   Seaman, Second Class, Serial No: 368 64 90, US Navy. Robert was born in 1923 to Harry B. and Pauline Grissinger. He enlisted in the US Navy on April 18, 1941 in Salt Lake City, Utah and completed his basic training at the Naval Training Station in San Diego, California. Robert reported for duty on the USS Arizona on July 13, 1941.

---

[296] Carroll Gale Greenfield, Photo from Oregon Honor States and The Statesman Journal of Salem, Oregon.

He was killed in action on December 7, 1941 at Pearl Harbor, Hawaii. Robert was awarded the American Defense Service Medal, World War II Victory Medal and Purple Heart Medal posthumously. He remains on duty on the USS Arizona. Robert is commemorated on the USS Arizona Memorial and the Memorial Tablets of the Missing, National Memorial Cemetery of the Pacific, Honolulu, Hawaii. He was survived by his Father, Mr. Harry B. Grissinger, 837 Chicago Avenue, Savanna, Illinois.

Grosnickle, Warren Wilbert Electrician's Mate, Second Class, Serial No: 321 23 55, US Navy. Warren was born November 5, 1920 in Boone, Iowa to Arthur and Amy (Lark) Grosnickle. He enlisted in the US Navy on January 26, 1938 in Des Moines, Iowa and completed his basic training at the Naval Training Station in Great Lakes, Illinois. Warren reported for duty on the USS Arizona on June 4, 1938. He was killed in action on December 7, 1941 at Pearl Harbor, Hawaii. Warren was awarded the American Defense Service Medal, World War II Victory Medal and Purple Heart Medal posthumously. He remains on duty on the USS Arizona. Warren is commemorated on the USS Arizona Memorial and the Memorial Tablets of the Missing, National Memorial Cemetery of the Pacific, Honolulu, Hawaii. He was survived by his Wife, Mrs. Edith Eleanor Grosnickle , two children, 611 West 5th Street, Boone, Iowa, his Parents, Mr. and Mrs. Arthur Grosnickle.

Gross, Milton "Hungry" Henry Chief Storekeeper, Serial No: 320 69 42, US Navy. Milton was born March 18, 1906 in Iowa to William Henry and Jennie Florence (Wickersham) Gross. He enlisted in the US Navy on June 6, 1935 in San Diego, California and reported for duty on the USS Arizona on July 27, 1937. Milton was killed in action on December 7, 1941 at Pearl Harbor, Hawaii. He was awarded the American Defense Service Medal, World War II Victory Medal and Purple Heart Medal posthumously. Milton remains on duty on the USS Arizona. He is commemorated on the USS Arizona Memorial and the Memorial Tablets of the Missing, National Memorial Cemetery of the Pacific, Honolulu, Hawaii. Milton was survived by his Son, Mr. Rodney Jerome Gross, 792 26th Street, San Pedro, California.[297]

Grundstrom, Richard Gunner Seaman, Second Class, Serial No: 382 36 95, US Navy. Richard was born September 3, 1923 in Los Angeles, California the only son born to Gunner Chris and Thelma A. (Sachs) Grundstrom. He enlisted in the US Navy on January 23, 1941 in Los Angeles, California and completed his basic training at the Naval Training Station in San Diego, California. He reported for duty on the USS Arizona on April 26, 1941. Richard was killed in action on December 7, 1941 at Pearl Harbor. He was awarded the American Defense Service Medal, World War II Victory Medal and Purple Heart Medal posthumously. Richard remains on duty on the USS Arizona. He is commemorated on the USS Arizona Memorial and the Memorial Tablets of the Missing, National Memorial Cemetery of the Pacific, Honolulu, Hawaii. Richard was survived by his Father, Mr. Gunner Chris Grundstrom, 6313 Bakman Avenue, North Hollywood, California. *Richard's father Gunner, enlisted after Pearl Harbor telling the Los Angeles Times in March 1942 that he wanted to take his son's place and whip the Japanese.*

---

[297] Milton Henry Gross, Picture and information provided by family member Joey C. Rickabaugh.

Guerin, Charles William, Jr. Seaman, First Class, Serial No. 385 91 06, US Navy. Charles was born in 1923 in Seattle, Washington, the son of Charles W. and Zola J. Guerin. He enlisted in the US Navy October 1, 1940 in Seattle, Washington and reported for duty on the USS Arizona January 8, 1941. Charles was serving on the Arizona on December 7, 1941 when the Japanese attacked Pearl Harbor. After the attack, Charles was transferred to the USS Mac Donough (DD-351) for duty. He died on December 22, 2007 and his ashes were placed in the well of Turret Number 4, his battle station, on the USS Arizona on December 7, 2008.

Guna, Andrew Boatswain's Mate, First Class, Serial No. 283 15 50, US Navy. Andrew was born on September 23, 1915 in Blaine, Ohio the sun of an immigrant coal miner. He enlisted to help feed his seven brothers and sisters. He lost his mother and a brother to the flu epidemic of 1918. He enlisted in the US Navy October 15, 1935 in Cleveland, Ohio and reported for duty on the USS Arizona February 8, 1936. Andrew left the USS Arizona on December 5, 1941 for re-enlistment leave in the CONUS. On completion, he was to meet the ship at the Puget Sound Navy Yard. On arrival at San Francisco on December 11th, he was ordered to return to Pearl Harbor to assist in the salvage and other duties. He went on to command two amphibious ships, participated in three beach landings and served on a distant Aleutian Islands outpost during the cold war before retiring as a Lieutenant Commander in March 1958, having spent 23 years in the Navy. He died on March 1, 2006 in Wilmington, California. His ashes were placed on the USS Arizona on December 7, 2006. Andrew was survived by his wife, Cozette Guna.[298]

Gurley, Jesse Herbert Storekeeper, Third Class, Serial No: 337 21 18, US Navy. Jesse was born November 22, 1919 in Vienna, Illinois to Jessie G. and Chattye M. (Dunn) Gurley. He enlisted in the US Navy on October 9, 1939 in St. Louis, Missouri and completed his basic training at the Naval Training Station in San Diego, California. He reported for duty on the USS Arizona on December 20, 1939. Jesse was killed in action on December 7, 1941 at Pearl Harbor, Hawaii. He was awarded the American Defense Service Medal, World War II Victory Medal and Purple Heart Medal posthumously. Jesse remains on duty on the USS Arizona. He is commemorated on the USS Arizona Memorial and the Memorial Tablets of the Missing, National Memorial Cemetery of the Pacific, Honolulu, Hawaii. Jesse was survived by his Wife, Mrs. Anna Isabella Gurley, Karnak, Illinois. The VFW Post 5222 in Vienna, Illinois is named after him and his best friend, Eugene Beggs.

---

[298] Andrew Guna, Photo provided by Will Stein.

Navy Whaleboat Rowing Team:[299]

Adrian, Missouri.[300]

Haas, Curtis "Curt" Junior Musician, Second Class, Serial No: 316 70 82, US Navy. Curtis was born March 26, 1919 in Missouri. He enlisted in the US Navy on November 12, 1940 and attended the Navy School of Music in Washington, DC graduating on May 23, 1941 as a member of the USS Arizona Band. He reported for duty on the USS Arizona on June 17, 1941. Curtis was killed in action on December 7, 1941 at Pearl Harbor, Hawaii. The battle station for all of the band members was in the black powder room passing ammunition to the Arizona's gunners during the attack. None of the band members survived the explosion. He was awarded the American Defense Service Medal, World War II Victory Medal and Purple Heart Medal posthumously. Curtis remains on duty on the USS Arizona. He is commemorated on the USS Arizona Memorial and the Memorial Tablets of the Missing, National Memorial Cemetery of the Pacific, Honolulu, Hawaii. Curtis was survived by his Uncle, Mr. Earl J. Haas,

---

[299] Navy Whale Boat Crew Picture, provided by Nancy Maack, niece of Walter Hamilton Simon.
[300] Curtis Junior Haas, Photo from USS Arizona's Last Band by Molly Kent by permission of the author. For more information about this book, go to www.USSARIZONASLASTBAND.com

Haden, Samuel William   Coxswain, Serial No: 342 18 74, US Navy. Samuel was born on February 4, 1916 in Clay County, Kansas to Joseph Grant and Laura Lula (Poots) Haden. He enlisted in the US Navy on January 23, 1940 in Kansas City, Missouri and completed his basic training at the Naval Training Station in Great Lakes, Illinois. Samuel reported for duty on the USS Arizona on March 26, 1940. He was killed in action on December 7, 1941 at Pearl Harbor, Hawaii. Samuel was awarded the American Defense Service Medal, World War II Victory Medal and Purple Heart Medal posthumously. He remains buried on the USS Arizona. Samuel is commemorated on the USS Arizona Memorial and the Memorial Tablets of the Missing, National Memorial Cemetery of the Pacific, Honolulu, Hawaii. He was survived by his Father, Mr. Joseph Grant Haden of Kansas.

Haerling, Howard Gustave   Boatswain's Mate, First Class, Serial No. 170 06 45, US Navy. Howard was born April 4, 1899 in LaMars, Iowa the son of Frank and Emma H. Haerling. He enlisted in the US Navy February 10, 1932 in Des Moines, Iowa. Howard served on the USS Arizona from September 17, 1938 until December 7, 1941 when the Japanese attacked Pearl Harbor. His official statement:

"At approximately four to eight (0756) on December 7, 1941, I was on the Quarter-Deck talking to the Boatswain, when the Quartermaster of the Vestal yelled over to us that Jap planes were raiding across on the other side of the channel.

I jumped up and took a look and then notified the Officer-of-the-Deck and then proceeded in through the Marine Compartment and passed the word, and went on into my division compartment and passed the word, "Japs are Raiding", and had my division close all doors and then go to the third deck to give the A. A. (Anti-Aircraft) Battery a hand in handling A. A. ammunition on the third deck.

The first bomb hit the quarterdeck, as near as I remember, about 0758, abreast the Captain's hatch, forward of the Admiral's hatch. At that time they sounded General Quarters. The fourth division proceeded to try to man No. Four turret, through the handling room. Shortly after getting down there, there was a severe concussion and all the power went off. ZED fittings had been set and we could not get up through turret Four, so we broke ZED fittings and came out through turret Three. We were in the chambers of turret three for a matter of about fifteen minutes and we got word to come out, following one another, and abandon ship, across the quarterdeck, to Ford Island.

Upon reaching the quarterdeck, I found Lieutenant Commander S. G. Fuqua, standing on the Starboard side of the quarterdeck, abreast of the quarter starboard boom, giving directions to the crew and telling them to take it easy, not get excited and abandon ship for Ford Island. During all this time, Lieutenant Commander Fuqua stood there paying no attention to his own safety and making sure that all men that were on the ship at the time, so far as he knew, were safely in the water and headed toward Ford Island. He was picking up wounded men and having them removed to boats and men who were able to do so were left to swim to the Island. Through his orders and physical assistance, some thirty or forty wounded men were removed from the quarterdeck and carried to safety, thereby saving them from being burned to death on board ship. During all this time Lieutenant Commander Fuqua was standing there, there was a continual hail of machine gun bullets and shrapnel around him. He was still on the quarterdeck looking for wounded men when I left the ship.

That is about all I can recall of the attack."[301]

After the attack, Howard was transferred to duty at Bishops Point Section Base. He died from a cerebral hemorrhage on February 13, 1956 in Raymond, Washington.

---

[301] Confidential Statement of Howard Gustave Haerling, Boatswain Mate First Class, U. S. Navy, January 5, 1942, Pearl Harbor, T.H.

Haerry, Raymond John Coxswain, Serial No. 201 71 97, US Navy. Raymond was born in January 28, 1922 in Patterson, New Jersey. He enlisted in the US Navy March 11, 1940 in Boston, Massachusetts and completed his basic training at the Naval Training Station in Norfolk, Virginia. Raymond reported for duty on the USS Arizona September 30, 1940. He was serving on the Arizona on December 7, 1941 when the Japanese attacked Pearl Harbor. Fortunately, he was topside when the nearly one ton armor piercing bomb penetrated the deck and caused a massive internal explosion that ripped the great ship apart. He was manning an anti-aircraft gun when he was suddenly blown into the waters of Pearl Harbor. The water was literally on fire from the fuel oil that was spilling from the ship's ruptured tanks. He managed to swim to nearby Ford Island by swimming underwater and surfacing to push the flaming oil aside with his arms in front of him. He still remembers the horror of swimming past burning corpses and body parts as he struggled to swim to the relative safety of Ford Island. After the attack, Raymond went on to serve on the USS Opportune (ARS-41), USS Allagash (AO-97, USS Luiseno (ATF-156) and the USS Muna Kea (AAE-22). He was awarded the Navy Good Conduct Medal with one Star, American Defense Service Medal with Fleet Clasp, Asiatic Pacific Campaign Medal, World War II Victory Medal and National Defense Service Medal. Raymond served in the Navy for 24 years, retiring in November 1964.

Haffner, Floyd Bates Fireman, First Class, Serial No: 337 11 69, US Navy. Floyd was born on June 22, 1915 in Browning, Schuyler, Illinois, son of Charles E. and Ida Jane (Bates) Haffner. He enlisted in the US Navy on January 17, 1939 in St. Louis, Missouri and completed his basic training at the Naval Training Station in Great Lakes, Illinois. Floyd reported for duty on the USS Arizona on July 8, 1939. He was killed in action on December 7, 1941 at Pearl Harbor, Hawaii. Floyd was awarded the American Defense Service Medal, World War II Victory Medal and Purple Heart Medal posthumously. He remains on duty on the USS Arizona. Floyd is commemorated on the USS Arizona Memorial and the Memorial Tablets of the Missing, National Memorial Cemetery of the Pacific, Honolulu, Hawaii. He was survived by his Parents, Mr. and Mrs. Charles Haffner, General Delivery, Browning, Illinois; three sisters, Mrs. Marvin McMullen and Mrs. Geneva Busby of Canton, Illinois and Mrs. Eva Mathis of Browning, Illinois; two brothers, Robert of Galesburg, Illinois and Harold of Canton, Illinois.[302]

Haines, Robert Wesley Seaman, Second Class, Serial No: 372 29 02, US Navy. Robert was born February 28, 1924 in Denver, Colorado to Fred J. and Anna M. Haines. He enlisted in the US Navy on March 20, 1941 in Denver, Colorado and completed his basic training at the Naval Training Station in San Diego, California. Robert reported for duty on the USS Arizona on August 13, 1941. He was killed in action on December 7, 1941 at Pearl Harbor, Hawaii. Robert was awarded the American Defense Service Medal, World War II Victory Medal and Purple Heart Medal posthumously. He remains on duty on the USS Arizona. Robert is commemorated on the USS Arizona Memorial and the Memorial Tablets of the Missing, National

---

[302] Floyd Bates Haffner, Photo and information provided by the Schuyler County Historical Museum, Illinois.

Memorial Cemetery of the Pacific, Honolulu, Hawaii. He was survived by his Mother, Mrs. Anna M. Haines, 4023 Delta, San Diego, California.

Hall, John Rudolph Chief Boatswain's Mate, Serial No: 346 39 95, US Navy. John was born January 18, 1907 in Arkansas to Bruce and Ida Hall. He enlisted in the US Navy on September 17, 1938 in San Pedro, California and reported for duty on the USS Arizona on July 11, 1940 transferring from the USS Colorado. John was killed in action on December 7, 1941 at Pearl Harbor, Hawaii. He was awarded the American Defense Service Medal, World War II Victory Medal and Purple Heart Medal posthumously. John remains on duty on the USS Arizona. John is commemorated on the USS Arizona Memorial and Memorial Tablets of the Missing, National Memorial Cemetery of the Pacific, Honolulu, Hawaii. He was survived by his Parents, Mr. and Mrs. Bruce Henry Hall, Roland, Arkansas.

Halloran, William Ignatius Ensign, Serial No: 0-101711, US Navy Reserve. William was born on July 23, 1915 in Cleveland, Ohio, son of Lawrence James and Stella Rose (McGuire) Halloran. *He graduated from Cathedral Latin School in 1933. William worked as editor of the Shopping News Junior while attending John Carroll University. He transferred to Ohio State University, graduating with a B.S. in journalism in 1938. In campus affairs there, he was president of the Newman Club, president of the Interracial Council and an important member of the Lantern staff. He immediately began work as a United Press International reporter with the Columbus Citizen. In early 1940, UPI transferred him to Cleveland, where he worked as the UPI representative in the Cleveland Press building. With a deteriorating world situation, he left the Cleveland Press to volunteer for active duty in the US. Naval Reserve as an apprentice seaman on August 14, 1940.* William was commissioned as an Ensign on June 12, 1941 and was assigned to the Naval Air Station, San Pedro California and later to the USS Arizona as Chief Warrant Officer, Asst. Ship Secretary. His battle station was the Communications Office. William was killed in action on December 7, 1941 at Pearl Harbor, Hawaii. He was posthumously awarded the Purple Heart Medal, American Defense Fleet Medal, Asiatic Pacific Campaign Medal and the World War II Freedom Medal. William remains on duty on the USS Arizona. He is commemorated on the USS Arizona Memorial and the Memorial Tablets of the Missing, National Memorial Cemetery of the Pacific, Honolulu, Hawaii. William was survived by his Parents, Mr. and Mrs. Lawrence James Halloran, 3311 West 100th Street, Cleveland, Ohio. The USS Halloran (DE-305) was named in his honor. In 1945 a Cleveland city park was named in Halloran's honor and Halloran Hall at Ohio State University is named in honor of William.[303]

---

[303] William Ignatius Halloran, Photo and information provided by his brother, Lawrence Halloran.

Hamilton, Clarence James   Machinist's Mate, First Class, Serial No: 385 71 88, US Navy. Clarence was born August 13, 1919 in Henderson County, North Carolina. He enlisted in the US Navy on January 11, 1937 in Seattle, Washington and completed his basic training at the Naval Training Station in San Diego, California. Clarence reported for duty on the USS Arizona on April 15, 1937. He was killed in action on December 7, 1941 at Pearl Harbor, Hawaii. Clarence was awarded the American Defense Service Medal, World War II Victory Medal and Purple Heart Medal posthumously. He remains on duty on the USS Arizona. Clarence is commemorated on the USS Arizona Memorial and the Memorial Tablets of the Missing, National Memorial Cemetery of the Pacific, Honolulu, Hawaii. He was survived by his Wife, Mrs. Margaret Marion Hamilton, 502 Olympia Avenue, Bremerton, Washington.

Hamilton, Edwin Carrell   Seaman, First Class, Serial No: 372 26 23, US Navy. Edwin was born in about 1922 in Colorado to Charles Carrell and Ethel Hamilton. He enlisted in the US Navy on January 27, 1941 in Denver, Colorado and completed his basic training at the Naval Training Station in San Diego, California. He reported for duty on the USS Arizona on March 27, 1941. Edwin was killed in action on December 7, 1941 at Pearl Harbor, Hawaii. He was awarded the American Defense Service Medal, World War II Victory Medal and Purple Heart Medal posthumously. Edwin remains on duty on the USS Arizona. He is commemorated on the USS Arizona Memorial and the Memorial Tablets of the Missing, National Memorial Cemetery of the Pacific, Honolulu, Hawaii. Edwin was survived by his Parents, Mr. and Mrs. Charles Carrell Hamilton, 1221 Sherman Street, Denver, Colorado.

Hamilton, Elsworth Fonzo   Aviation Chief Machinist's Mate, Aviation Unit (VO-1), Serial No. 170 40 15, US Navy. Elsworth was born on July 11, 1894 in Ritchie, West Virginia to William and Laura Hamilton. He enlisted in the US Navy on December 1, 1917, served during World War I, re-enlisted in the Navy July 22, 1937 in Pensacola, Florida and reported for duty on the USS Arizona August 3, 1940. He was serving on the USS Arizona on December 7, 1941 when the Japanese attacked Pearl Harbor. After the attack, he was transferred to Observation Squadron One. Elsworth died on December 9, 1969 and is buried in Section W, Site 892, National Memorial Cemetery of the Pacific, Honolulu, Hawaii.

Hamilton, James Edward   Seaman, First Class, Serial No. 291 68 00, US Navy. James was born on August 27, 1920. He enlisted in the US Navy December 30, 1940 in Indianapolis, Indiana and reported for duty on the USS Arizona June 26, 1941. James was serving on the USS Arizona on December 7, 1941 when the Japanese attacked Pearl Harbor. After the attack, James was transferred to the USS Mac Donough (DD-351) for duty. James died on November 25, 2004 in Michigan and was buried in the Allied Veteran's Cemetery, Port Huron, Michigan.

Hamilton, William Holman Gunner's Mate, Third Class, Serial No: 346 71 00, US Navy. William was born in 1921 in Arkansas, son of Eugene Alexander and Voda Lee (Holman) Hamilton. He enlisted in the US Navy on October 1, 1938 in Little Rock, Arkansas and completed his basic training at the Naval Training Station in San Diego, California. William reported for duty on the USS Arizona on March 11, 1939. He was killed in action on December 7, 1941 at Pearl Harbor, Hawaii. William was awarded the American Defense Service Medal, World War II Victory Medal and Purple Heart Medal posthumously. He remains on duty on the USS Arizona. William is commemorated on the USS Arizona Memorial and the Memorial Tablets of the Missing, National Memorial Cemetery of the Pacific, Honolulu, Hawaii. He was survived by his Father, Mr. Eugene Alexander Hamilton, 2327 South Central Street, Oklahoma City, Oklahoma.[304]

Hammerud, George Winston Seaman, First Class, Serial No: 368 50 14, US Navy. George was born in 1915 in North Dakota to George H. and Rachel (Munch) Hammerud. He enlisted in the US Navy on August 6, 1940 in Salt Lake City, Utah and completed his basic training at the Naval Training Station in San Diego, California. He reported for duty on the USS Arizona on March 20, 1941. George was killed in action on December 7, 1941 at Pearl Harbor, Hawaii. He was awarded the American Defense Service Medal, World War II Victory Medal and Purple Heart Medal posthumously. George remains on duty on the USS Arizona. He is commemorated on the USS Arizona Memorial and the Memorial Tablets of the Missing, National Memorial Cemetery of the Pacific, Honolulu, Hawaii. George was survived by his Father, Mr. George H. Hammerud, Box 267, Valley City, North Dakota.[305]

Hampton, J. C. Fireman, First Class, Serial No: 342 18 09, US Navy. JC was born on July 17, 1917 in White, Tennessee, son of Willie Riley and Vallie Annah (Ballard) Hampton. He enlisted in the US Navy on January 16, 1940 in Kansas City, Missouri and completed his basic training at the Naval Training Station in Great Lakes, Illinois. JC reported for duty on the USS Arizona on March 26, 1940. He was killed in action on December 7, 1941 at Pearl Harbor, Hawaii. JC was awarded the American Defense Service Medal, World War II Victory Medal and Purple Heart Medal posthumously. He remains on duty on the USS Arizona. JC is commemorated on the USS Arizona Memorial and the Memorial Tablets of the Missing, National Memorial Cemetery of the Pacific, Honolulu, Hawaii. He was survived by his Father, Mr. Willie Hampton, Meade, Kansas.[306]

---

[304] William Holman Hamilton, Photo provided by family member FCC(SW) W. L. George, US Navy.

[305] George Winston Hammerud, Photo from North Dakota Honor States.

[306] J.C. Hampton, Photo from Kansas Honor States.

Hampton, Ted W, Jr. Seaman, First Class, Serial No: 356 34 41, US Navy. Ted was born April 27, 1922 in Oklahoma. He enlisted in the US Navy on August 6, 1940 in Dallas, Texas and completed his basic training at the Naval Training Station in San Diego, California. Ted reported for duty on the USS Arizona on October 8, 1940. He was killed in action on December 7, 1941 at Pearl Harbor, Hawaii. Ted was awarded the American Defense Service Medal, World War II Victory Medal and Purple Heart Medal posthumously. He remains on duty on the USS Arizona. Ted is commemorated on the USS Arizona Memorial and the Memorial Tablets of the Missing, National Memorial Cemetery of the Pacific, Honolulu, Hawaii. He was survived by his Father, Mr. Ted W. Hampton, Sr., 811 East Broadway, Seminole, Oklahoma.

Hampton, Walter Lewis Boatswain's Mate, Second Class, Serial No: 328 16 43, US Navy. Walter was born on January 2, 1907 in Barnesville, Minnesota, son of Pearley H. and Mary Sophia (Bredemeier) Hampton. He enlisted in the US Navy on September 15, 1939 in Philadelphia, Pennsylvania and reported for duty on the USS Arizona on December 30, 1940. Walter was killed in action on December 7, 1941 at Pearl Harbor, Hawaii. He was awarded the American Defense Service Medal, World War II Victory Medal and Purple Heart Medal posthumously. Walter remains on duty on the USS Arizona. He is commemorated on the USS Arizona Memorial and the Memorial Tablets of the Missing, National Memorial Cemetery of the Pacific, Honolulu, Hawaii. Walter was survived by his Wife, Mrs. Jane Hampton, 614 East Clementine Street, Philadelphia, Pennsylvania and his Parents, Mr. and Mrs. Pearley H. Hampton of Barnesville, Minnesota.[307]

Hand, Vernon Seaman, First Class, Serial No. 268 54 43, US Navy. Vernon was born March 21, 1919 in Douglas, Georgia the son of Austin and Annie Jane (Blanton) Hand. He enlisted in the US Navy September 30, 1940 in Macon, Georgia and completed his basic training at the Naval Training Station in Norfolk, Virginia. He reported for duty on the USS Arizona December 4, 1940. Vernon was serving on the Arizona on December 7, 1941 when the Japanese attacked Pearl Harbor.

Shortly before 8 a.m. he was on the stern deck cleaning the turrets' three massive barrels when the sailors noticed a swarm of oncoming planes. He saw the first Japanese planes come in with the Rising Sun on their sides, and he saw the first explosions. As the battle stations alert sounded, he descended deep into the bowels of the turret to his station.

Japanese bombs pounded the Arizona as it sat moored off Pearl Harbor. The ship took four direct hits and three near misses. The final blow came at 8:10 a.m., just 10 minutes into the battle. A 1,750 pound armor-piercing bomb dropped from a high-altitude Kate bomber, slammed through the deck in from of the No. 2 turret and exploded the ship's forward magazine.

The blast broke the forward hull in half and caused the bridge and the rest of the foredeck to collapse to fill the void. In the back of the ship, he stayed at his station until forced out by the onrushing seawater. He would stay at one level until forced out by the water. Eventually, he found himself on deck. He stayed with the ship until the water was at the side of the ship and then he just walked out into the water. Soon after, he was towed to the safety of Ford Island by an overcrowded rescue boat. He volunteered for the first ship he could get on. After the attack, Vernon was transferred to the USS Chester for duty and later served on board the USS Indiana (BB-58). Vernon continued to serve in the Navy until he retired in 1959.[308]

---

[307] Walter Lewis Hampton, Photo from Pennsylvania Honor States.
[308] Vernon Hand, story from the Marietta, GA Daily Journal Newspaper, April 7, 2003.

He died April 5, 2003 in Mableton, Georgia and is buried at Crest Lawn Cemetery, Atlanta, Georgia.

Hanna, David "Buster" Darling Electrician's Mate, Third Class, Serial No: 356 26 17, US Navy. David was born on October 13, 1920 in Limestone County, Texas, the only son of Robert Marcus and Stella (Crockett) Hanna. His father died when he was nine years old. He enlisted in the US Navy on April 5, 1940 in Dallas, Texas and completed his basic training at the Naval Training Station in San Diego, California. David reported for duty on the USS Arizona on June 16, 1940. He was killed in action on December 7, 1941 at Pearl Harbor, Hawaii. David was awarded the American Defense Service Medal, World War II Victory Medal and Purple Heart Medal posthumously. He remains on duty on the USS Arizona. David is commemorated on the USS Arizona Memorial and the Memorial Tablets of the Missing, National Memorial Cemetery of the Pacific, Honolulu, Hawaii. He was survived by his Mother, Mrs. Stella Hanna, General Delivery, Groesbeck, Texas. The Ashburn Hanna American Legion Post 288 in Groesbeck, Texas was named in his honor.[309]

Hansen, Carlye B. Machinist's Mate, Second Class, Serial No: 368 42 86, US Navy. Carlyle was born September 25, 1920 in Salt Lake City, Utah. He enlisted in the Navy on January 10, 1939 in Salt Lake City, Utah and completed his basic training at the Naval Training Station in San Diego, California. He reported for duty on the USS Arizona on April 29, 1939. Carlye was killed in action on December 7, 1941 at Pearl Harbor, Hawaii. He was awarded the American Defense Service Medal, World War II Victory Medal and Purple Heart Medal posthumously. Carlye remains on duty on the USS Arizona. He is commemorated on the USS Arizona Memorial and the Memorial Tablets of the Missing, National Memorial Cemetery of the Pacific, Honolulu, Hawaii. Carlyle was survived by his Father, Mr. Hyrum Hansen, 834 Windsor Street, Salt Lake City, Utah.[310]

Hansen, Harvey Ralph Seaman, First Class, Serial No: 300 11 25, US Navy. Harvey was born April 16, 1922 in Racine, Wisconsin the son of Hartwig Marinius and Louise S. Hansen both were immigrants from Norway. *He enlisted in the Navy on July 9, 1940 at Chicago fresh out of Horlick High School. The only job he could find was part time, pumping gas at a Milwaukee service station. He wanted to go to college, but neither he nor his family could afford it. So, he decided to enlist, with the money he earned earmarked for a college education. His brother, Clarence had also enlisted and Harvey met with his brother less than two weeks before the attack. His brother was stationed on the USS Enterprise which was not in port the day of the attack.* Harvey enlisted in the US Navy on July 9, 1940 in

---

[309] David "Buster" Darling Hanna, Information and Photo provided by family member, Sammie Loupet.
[310] Carlyle B. Hansen, Photo provided by family member of Ned Burton Donohue, Bob Cameron.

Chicago, Illinois and completed his basic training at the Naval Training Station in Great Lakes, Illinois. He reported for duty on the USS Arizona on August 3, 1941, transferring from the Sub Base, Pearl Harbor. Harvey died of wounds received in action on December 7, 1941 at Pearl Harbor, Hawaii. He was awarded the American Defense Service Medal, World War II Victory Medal and Purple Heart Medal posthumously. Harvey's remains were identified by his name on his skivvy shirt and he was buried in Plot C, Row 0, Grave 999, National Memorial Cemetery of the Pacific, Honolulu, Hawaii.[311] He is commemorated on the USS Arizona Memorial. Harvey was survived by his Father, Mr. Hartvig Hansen, 1921 Prospect Street, Racine, Wisconsin. His brother was killed in the fall of 1942 in the South Pacific. The Harvey R. Hansen American Legion Post 310 in Racine, Wisconsin was named in his honor.[312]

Hanzel, Edward Joseph Watertender, First Class, Serial No: 328 39 85, US Navy. Edward was born on October 6, 1915 in Minnesota the son of John and Sophie (Rynda) Hanzel. He enlisted in the US Navy on September 10, 1935 and reported for duty on the USS Arizona on January 11, 1936. Edward was killed in action on December 7, 1941 at Pearl Harbor. He was awarded the American Defense Service Medal, World War II Victory Medal and Purple Heart Medal posthumously. Edward's remains were recovered and he was buried in Plot C, Row 0, Grave 753, National Memorial Cemetery of the Pacific, Honolulu, Hawaii. He is commemorated on the USS Arizona Memorial. Edward was survived by his Father, Mr. John Hanzel, New Prague, Minnesota.[313]

Hardin, Charles Eugene Seaman, First Class, Serial No: 346 87 74, US Navy. Charles was born August 31, 1922 in Turkey Run, Arkansas to Charles E. and Lola Fay (Goss) Hardin. He graduated from Monette High in the spring of 1940. Charles was elected the most popular, best all-around, friendliest, and wittiest boy in the class. He was also elected vice-president of the junior class, served as reporter for his senior class and played very good roles in both the senior and junior class plays. Charles enlisted in the US Navy on November 15, 1940 in Little Rock, Arkansas and completed his basic training at the Naval Training Station in San Diego, California. He reported for duty on the USS Arizona on January 11, 1941. Charles was killed in action on December 7, 1941 at Pearl Harbor, Hawaii. He was awarded the American Defense Service Medal, World War II Victory Medal and Purple Heart Medal posthumously. Charles remains on duty on the USS Arizona. He is commemorated on the USS Arizona Memorial and the Memorial Tablets of the Missing, National Memorial Cemetery of the Pacific, Honolulu, Hawaii. Charles was survived by his Father, Mr. Charles E. Hardin, 311 Whittier Street, St. Louis, Missouri.[314]

---

[311] Report of Changes of the USS Arizona for the month ending 31st day of December, 1941, Page 64, line 17, Harvey Ralph Hansen.

[312] Harvey Ralph Hansen, Information and photo provided by Marion Hansen (sister) and Peg Anderson, Journal Times article, Friday, December 6, 1991.

[313] Edward Joseph Hanzel, Photo from Minnesota Honor States.

[314] Charles Eugene Hardin, Information and photo provided by family member, Carol Matlock.

Hargis, Paul Eugene   Yeoman, Third Class, Serial No. 266 03 99, US Navy. Paul was born on May 31, 1921 in Exmore, Northampton County, Virginia. He enlisted in the US Navy December 15, 1939 in Richmond, Virginia and completed his basic training at the Naval Training Station in Norfolk, Virginia. He reported for duty on the USS Arizona March 29, 1940 where he was serving on December 7, 1941 when the Japanese attacked Pearl Harbor. He went on to serve on board the Destroyer Escort, USS Edwin A. Howard (DE-346). Paul died on March 21, 2000 in Exmore, Virginia.

Hargraves, Kenneth William   Seaman, Second Class, Serial No: 386 01 53, US Navy. Kenneth was born on March 27, 1922 in Missoula, Montana, the son of John Samuel and Minnie Jane (Reynolds) Hargraves. He enlisted in the US Navy on June 19, 1941 in Seattle, Washington and completed his basic training at the Naval Training Station in San Diego, California. Kenneth reported for duty on the USS Arizona on August 29, 1941. He was killed in action on December 7, 1941 at Pearl Harbor, Hawaii. Kenneth was awarded the American Defense Service Medal, World War II Victory Medal and Purple Heart Medal posthumously. He remains on duty on the USS Arizona. Kenneth is commemorated on the USS Arizona Memorial and the Memorial Tablets of the Missing, National Memorial Cemetery of the Pacific, Honolulu, Hawaii. He was survived by his Father, Mr. John Samuel Hargraves, Box 334, Wapato, Washington.

Harr, Oliver Virgil   Machinist's Mate, First Class, Serial No. 328 45 19, US Navy. Oliver was born on January 7, 1918 in Anamoose, North Dakota the son of Karl and Dorothea (Diede) Harr. He enlisted in the US Navy November 17, 1936 in Minneapolis, Minnesota and completed his basic training at the Naval Training Station in Great Lakes, Illinois. Oliver reported for duty on the USS Arizona April 10, 1937. He was serving on the Arizona on December 7, 1941 when the Japanese attacked Pearl Harbor. After the attack, Oliver was transferred to the USS Dale (DD-353) for duty. Oliver died on July 8, 1983 in Kalispell, Montana and is buried in the Conrad Memorial Cemetery, Kalispell, Montana.

Harrell, Allen Boyd "Choc"   Seaman, First Class, Serial No. 346 87 33, US Navy. Allen was born July 2, 1917 in Whitefield, Oklahoma, the son of James Marion and Lelah Ethel (Holmes) Harrell. He enlisted in the US Navy November 4, 1940 in Little Rock, Arkansas and completed his basic training at the Naval Training Station in San Diego, California. Allen reported for duty on the USS Arizona January 11, 1941. He was wounded in action on the USS Arizona December 7, 1941 when the Japanese attacked Pearl Harbor. He spent 10 days in the Naval Hospital at Pearl Harbor before being transferred to the USS Salt Lake City for duty. Allen died December 15, 1997 in Borger, Texas.[315]

---

[315] Allen Boyd Harrell, Photo and information provided by family member, Bryan Cross.

Harrington, Keith Homer Seaman, First Class, Serial No: 337 25 15, US Navy. Keith was born in about 1922 in Missouri to Homer R. and Tillie Rose Harrington. He enlisted in the US Navy on December 27, 1939 in St. Louis, Missouri and completed his basic training at the Naval Training Station in Great Lakes, Illinois. He reported for duty on the USS Arizona on March 23, 1940. Keith was killed in action on December 7, 1941 at Pearl Harbor, Hawaii. He was awarded the American Defense Service Medal, World War II Victory Medal and Purple Heart Medal posthumously. Keith remains on duty on the USS Arizona. He is commemorated on the USS Arizona Memorial and the Memorial Tablets of the Missing, National Memorial Cemetery of the Pacific, Honolulu, Hawaii. Keith was survived by his Mother, Mrs. Rose Williams, 1900-A Louisiana, St. Louis, Missouri.[316]

Harris, George Ellsworth Machinist's Mate, First Class, Serial No: 336 68 81, US Navy. George was born on June 17, 1909 in Illinois to James D. and Nora J. Harris. He enlisted in the US Navy on June 19, 1936 in San Pedro, California and reported for duty on the USS Arizona on January 11, 1937. George was killed in action on December 7, 1941 at Pearl Harbor, Hawaii. He was awarded the American Defense Service Medal, World War II Victory Medal and Purple Heart Medal posthumously. George remains on duty on the USS Arizona. He is commemorated on the USS Arizona Memorial and the Memorial Tablets of the Missing, National Memorial Cemetery of the Pacific, Honolulu, Hawaii. George was survived by his Mother, Mrs. Nora Josephine Rendleman, Route 3, Box 79, Carterville, Illinois.[317]

Harris, Henry Sherman Seaman, First Class, Serial No. 272 41 77, US Navy. Henry was born March 15, 1921. He enlisted in the US Navy October 5, 1940 in Birmingham, Alabama and completed his basic training at the Naval Training Station in Norfolk, Virginia. Henry reported for duty on the USS Arizona December 4, 1940. He was assigned the duty of gunners, operating the elevation and firing of the gun.

On the morning of December 7th, having finished breakfast, he and other members of the crew were at the ship's boat deck where his quarters were when he heard "general quarters". He immediately made his way to his battle station where he and five others began firing. Then a bomb hit the bow, forcing him to leave his battle station. As he ran, he tripped over something and was knocked out. When he awoke, he was laying on his stomach with his head on his arm. Seeing the deck had been torn up, he realized what was happening. Henry found a way off of the ship by jumping one story below to the Galley deck. As he got there, flames from another bomb hit him on the left side of his body. He fell into the water 30 feet below. Looking around he sighted a motor launch about 100 feet away. He swam for it and climbed aboard. It was then that he realized he had suffered injuries. Skin was hanging about four or five inches off of his body. Eighty percent of his body had been burned. On Ford Island they spent a couple of hours in a bomb shelter until a truck picked him up and took him to a dispensary. The next day he was moved to the Naval Hospital at Honolulu where he remained until December 19. He was then transferred to the Naval Hospital at Mare Island, California. After five months Henry tried to walk for the first time since the attack. Once he started feeling better, he was given a 30 day

---

[316] Keith Homer Harrington, Photo from Missouri Honor States.
[317] George Ellsworth Harris, Photo provided by his great great Nephew, Daniel R. Brown.

leave, but in May of 1943 he was sent to Seattle for five months. He was then sent to the Aviation Cadet Selection Board in Kansas City, MO for limited duty. After three months there, he suffered a relapse and was sent to Great Lakes, Illinois for more treatment. It was at Great Lakes that he received the Purple Heart and a medical discharge from the Navy. Since then he has also received the Congressional Medal of Survival.

Henry passed away on Sunday, February 15, 2009 in Phil Campbell, Alabama and was buried at the Mimosa Cemetery with full military honors. He was survived by one son, Larry Harris of Alabama, one daughter, Sharon Cole of Columbia, one brother, Charles Harris of California and 4 grandchildren, 10 great grandchildren and 4 great, great grandchildren.

Harris, Hiram Dennis   Seaman, First Class, Serial No: 393 37 71, US Navy. Hiram and his twin brother, Wallace Drew were born on July 7, 1920 in Coweta, Georgia, the sons of James Render and Bessie Mae (Couch) Harris. Hiram had 11 brothers and 2 sisters. He enlisted in the US Navy on July 23, 1940 in Portland, Oregon and completed his basic training at the Naval Training Station in San Diego, California. Hiram reported for duty on the USS Arizona on October 8, 1940. He was killed in action on December 7, 1941 at Pearl Harbor, Hawaii. Hiram was awarded the American Defense Service Medal, World War II Victory Medal and Purple Heart Medal posthumously. He remains on duty on the USS Arizona. Hiram is commemorated on the USS Arizona Memorial and the Memorial Tablets of the Missing, National Memorial Cemetery of the Pacific, Honolulu, Hawaii. He was survived by his Father, Mr. James Render Harris, Route C, Griffin, Georgia.

Harris, James William   Fireman, First Class, Serial No: 295 55 36, US Navy. James was born November 21, 1921 in Holland, Missouri to Porter Kirby and Frances Evaline (Martin) Harris. He enlisted in the US Navy on December 16, 1939 in Nashville, Tennessee and reported for duty on the USS Arizona on March 29, 1940. *His brother, Markus Harris was serving on board the USS Vega at Pearl Harbor at the time. The two brothers had plans to meet ashore on the morning of the 7th. As his brother was leaving the ship to go ashore, the general alarm sounded.* He was killed in action on December 7, 1941 at Pearl Harbor, Hawaii. *After the attack, his brother, Marcus wanted to go in search of his brother but the enlisted men were not allowed off the ship so he got an officer to look and was informed that he was missing.* James was awarded the American Defense Service Medal, World War II Victory Medal and Purple Heart Medal posthumously. He remains on duty on the USS Arizona. James is commemorated on the USS Arizona Memorial and the Memorial Tablets of the Missing, National Memorial Cemetery of the Pacific, Honolulu, Hawaii. He was survived by his Parents, Mr. and Mrs. Porter Kirby Harris, Holland, Missouri.

Harris, John David   Seaman, First Class, Serial No. 346 83 49, US Navy. John was born June 25, 1920 in Linden, Texas. He enlisted in the US Navy August 7, 1940 in Little Rock, Arkansas and completed his basic training at the Naval Training Station in San Diego, California. John reported for duty on the USS Arizona October 14, 1940. He was serving on the Arizona on December 7, 1941 when the Japanese attacked Pearl Harbor. John was trapped in the bottom of No. 4 Turret. Fire and smoke prevented the ammunition handlers their normal way out. With smoke and fumes coming in from the bomb explosion an ensign knew a passageway into No. 3 turret. On the way out they took off their clothes (except skivvies) and stuffed them in bulkhead holes where they could feel the hot fumes and smoke coming in. When he saw daylight, a man on the deck jerked him out of the turret. Water was on the quarterdeck and was black with oil. John jumped over the side where the fire had not yet reached. Covered with oil, he was pulled into the boat. Once they reached Ford Island officers wives were handing out sheets and blankets. Assigned to the USS Patterson, a mini task force was sent to reinforce the defenders of Wake Island. Before they could reach them, they received news of their surrender. John remained on the Patterson for the remainder of the war, fighting for every island from Honolulu to Japan. He retired after 20 years service in May 1960. John passed away August 11, 2001 after a long illness and was buried beside his wife Trudy in Cave Springs Cemetery near Linden, Texas. He is survived by sons Dean Harris of Scotts Valley, California and Jeff Harris of Linden; daughters Devonna Blair of Bossier City, Louisiana and Susan Baxley of Ft. Myers, Florida.

Harris, Noble Burnice Coxswain, Serial No: 337 25 79, US Navy. Noble was born July 9, 1918, the son of George Lewis and Golda E. Harris. He enlisted in the US Navy on January 9, 1940 in St. Louis, Missouri and completed his basic training at the Naval Training Station in Great Lakes, Illinois. Noble reported for duty on the USS Arizona on March 26, 1940. He was killed in action on December 7, 1941 at Pearl Harbor, Hawaii. Noble was awarded the American Defense Service Medal, World War II Victory Medal and Purple Heart Medal posthumously. He remains on duty on the USS Arizona. Noble is commemorated on the USS Arizona Memorial and the Memorial Tablets of the Missing, National Memorial Cemetery of the Pacific, Honolulu, Hawaii. He was survived by his Father, Mr. George Lewis Harris, P.O. Box 169, St. Charles, Missouri.

Harris, Peter John Coxswain, Serial No: 316 62 91, US Navy. Peter was born September 17, 1918 in Lincoln, Nebraska, the son of Peter and Elizabeth Harris. He enlisted in the US Navy on January 24, 1940 in Omaha, Nebraska and completed his basic training at the Naval Training Station in Great Lakes, Illinois. Peter reported for duty on the USS Arizona on March 26, 1940. He was killed in action on December 7, 1941 at Pearl Harbor, Hawaii. Peter was awarded the American Defense Service Medal, World War II Victory Medal and Purple Heart Medal posthumously. He remains on duty on the USS Arizona. Peter is commemorated on the USS Arizona Memorial and the Memorial Tablets of the Missing, National Memorial Cemetery of the Pacific, Honolulu, Hawaii. He was survived by his Parents, Mr. and Mrs. Peter Harris, 305 H Street, Lincoln, Nebraska, a brother, John Harris serving in the U.S. Army and a sister, Pauline.[318]

Hart, James Willard Fireman, First Class, Serial No. 287 35 01, US Navy. James was born October 17, 1921 in Corbin, Kentucky the son of James Emby Hart and Ida Pearl Lawson Hart. He enlisted in the US Navy December 12, 1939 in Louisville, Kentucky and completed his basic training at the Naval Training Station in Great Lakes, Illinois. He reported for duty on the USS Arizona March 9, 1940. James was serving on the Arizona on December 7, 1941 when the Japanese attacked Pearl Harbor. *He was on liberty that fateful day. Pete's family was originally told that Pete was missing and presumed dead in the attack on the Arizona. They did not find out otherwise for several months when Pete sent a letter home detailing what happened. He never spoke to his family about what happened at Pearl Harbor. Based on the account from one*

---

[318] Peter John Harris, Photo and information from The Lincoln Star, Lincoln, Nebraska, January 26, 1942, Page 1.

survivor, after the attack, James may have reported to the USS Tennessee. He may have also taken part in salvage and recovery of his shipmates' remains. After the attack, James was transferred to Bishops Point, Oahu, Hawaii for duty. He died at his home at the age of 89 on February 11, 2010 in San Diego, California. His ashes were scattered at sea off the coast of San Diego by the U.S. Navy. [319]

Hartland, Alfred Jack   Seaman, First Class, Serial No. 385 76 30, US Navy. Alfred was born August 14, 1920 in Seattle, Washington the son of Alfred J. and Amanda H. (Johnson) Hartland. He enlisted in the US Navy January 10, 1938 in Seattle, Washington and reported for duty on the USS Arizona April 28, 1938. Alfred was serving on the USS Arizona on December 7, 1941 when the Japanese attacked Pearl Harbor. After the attack, Alfred was transferred to the USS Monaghan for duty and served until August 19, 1946. He later served in the Korean War. Alfred died on February 27, 1988 in Seattle, Washington.

Hartley, Alvin   Gunner's Mate, Third Class, Serial No: 372 17 13, US Navy. Alvin was born May 10, 1922 in Oklahoma, the son of Evy Hartley. He enlisted in the US Navy on August 12, 1940 in Denver, Colorado and completed his basic training at the Naval Training Station in San Diego, California. Alvin reported for duty on the USS Arizona on October 8, 1940. He was killed in action on December 7, 1941 at Pearl Harbor, Hawaii. Alvin was awarded the American Defense Service Medal, World War II Victory Medal and Purple Heart Medal posthumously. He remains on duty on the USS Arizona. Alvin is commemorated on the USS Arizona Memorial and the Memorial Tablets of the Missing, National Memorial Cemetery of the Pacific, Honolulu, Hawaii. He was survived by his Mother, Mrs. Evy Hartley, Woodville, Oklahoma.

Hartsoe, Max June   Gunner's Mate, Third Class, Serial No: 337 17 56, US Navy. Max was born on April 16, 1921 in Cardwell, Missouri, the son of Otho H. and Bertha Mae (Underwood) Hartsoe. He enlisted in the US Navy on September 5, 1939 in St. Louis, Missouri and completed his basic training at the Naval Training Station in San Diego, California. Max reported for duty on the USS Arizona on November 10, 1939. He was killed in action on December 7, 1941 at Pearl Harbor. Max was awarded the American Defense Service Medal, World War II Victory Medal and Purple Heart Medal posthumously. He remains on duty on the USS Arizona. Max is commemorated on the USS Arizona Memorial and the Memorial Tablets of the Missing, National Memorial Cemetery of the Pacific, Honolulu, Hawaii. He was survived by his Parents, Mr. and Mrs. Otho H. Hartsoe, Box 21, Cardwell, Missouri; twin brother, Vernon and two sisters, Peggy J. and Carlyon M. Hartsoe.

Hartson, Lonnie Moss   Signalman, Third Class, Serial No: 407 38 56, US Navy. Lonnie was born February 1, 1923 in Dallas, Texas to Hugh Milner and Velma I. (Moss) Hartson. His father had given his written permission to join the Navy after he graduated from Forest Avenue High School in June 1940. He was just 17 years old when he enlisted in the US Navy on June 11, 1940 in Dallas, Texas and completed his basic training at the Naval Training Station in San Diego, California. Lonnie reported for duty on the USS Arizona on July 9, 1941. He was killed in action on December 7, 1941 at Pearl Harbor, Hawaii. Lonnie was awarded the American Defense Service Medal, World War II Victory Medal and Purple Heart Medal posthumously. He remains on duty on the USS Arizona. Lonnie is

---

[319] James Willard Hart, Information taken from his obituary.

commemorated on the USS Arizona Memorial and the Memorial Tablets of the Missing, National Memorial Cemetery of the Pacific, Honolulu, Hawaii. He was survived by his Father, Mr. Hugh Milner Hartson, 1435 Glenn Street, Dallas, Texas.[320]

Hasl, James Thomas Fireman, First Class, Serial No: 316 52 89, US Navy. James was born in about 1918 in Nebraska. He enlisted in the US Navy on December 2, 1937 in Omaha, Nebraska and reported for duty on the USS Arizona on March 12, 1938. James was killed in action on December 7, 1941 at Pearl Harbor, Hawaii. He was awarded the American Defense Service Medal, World War II Victory Medal and Purple Heart Medal posthumously. James remains on duty on the USS Arizona. He is commemorated on the USS Arizona Memorial and the Memorial Tablets of the Missing, National Memorial Cemetery of the Pacific, Honolulu, Hawaii. James was survived by his Parents, Mr. and Mrs. John Hasl, 1472 Pinkney Street, Omaha, Nebraska.[321]

Hauff, Richard Gunner's Mate, Third Class, Serial No. 328 61 63, US Navy. Richard was born February 28, 1920 in North Dakota, the son of Andreas and Mathilda Hauff. He enlisted in the US Navy November 7, 1939 in Minneapolis, Minnesota and completed his basic training at the Naval Training Station in Great Lakes, Illinois. Richard reported for duty on the USS Arizona February 10, 1940. He was serving on the USS Arizona on December 7, 1941 when the Japanese attacked Pearl Harbor. He was thrown clear of the wreckage, and had no idea of how he got off the ship, because his last remembrance was that he was below the ship when the Arizona was bombed. After the attack, Richard was transferred to the USS Tucker for duty. Richard died August 9, 1989 in Ellendale, North Dakota.

Haverfield, James Wallace Ensign, Serial No: 0-101721, US Navy Reserve. James was born on April 11, 1917 in Uhrichsville, Ohio, the son of Dr. George Tracy and Bessie E. (Long) Haverfield. After receiving his B.A. from Ohio State University in 1939, he enlisted in the Naval Reserve as an apprentice seaman on September 11, 1940. After completing his training at Northwestern University, he was commissioned an Ensign on June 12, 1941 and reported for duty on the USS Arizona on June 28, 1941. James was serving on the USS Arizona as Junior Watch and Division 6 Officer. His battle station was Assistant Anti-Aircraft Battery Officer. James was killed in action on December 7, 1941 at Pearl Harbor, Hawaii. He was awarded the American Defense Service Medal, World War II Victory Medal and Purple Heart Medal posthumously. James remains on duty on the USS Arizona. He is commemorated on the USS Arizona Memorial and the Memorial Tablets of the Missing, National Memorial Cemetery of the Pacific, Honolulu, Hawaii. James was survived by his Father, Dr. Tracy Haverfield, 6118 North Water Street,

[320] Lonnie Moss Hartson, photo curtsey LCDR G. Dale McKissick, USNR, Memorial, Dallas Convention Center, Dallas, Texas.
[321] James Thomas Hasl, Photo from the Nebraska, Iowa War Dead, World-Herald, Omaha, Nebraska, Sunday, July 4, 1943, Page 103.

Uhrichsville, Ohio. The Navy destroyer escort vessel, USS Haverfield (DE-393) was named in his honor as well as Haverfield Hall, a dormitory on the Ohio State University Campus.[322]

Havins, Harvey Linfille Seaman, First Class, Serial No: 375 99 17, US Navy. Harvey was born in May 5, 1914 in Wills Point, Texas to William Alexander and Permelia E. (Wright) Havins. He enlisted in the US Navy on December 6, 1939 in San Francisco, California and completed his basic training at the Naval Training Station in San Diego, California. Harvey reported for duty on the USS Arizona on February 24, 1940. He was killed in action on December 7, 1941 at Pearl Harbor, Hawaii. Harvey was awarded the American Defense Service Medal, World War II Victory Medal and Purple Heart Medal posthumously. He remains on duty on the USS Arizona. Harvey is commemorated on the USS Arizona Memorial and the Memorial Tablets of the Missing, National Memorial Cemetery of the Pacific, Honolulu, Hawaii. He was survived by his Father, Mr. William Alexander Havins, P.O. Box 477, Shafter, California.[323]

Hawkins, Russell Dean Signalman, Third Class, Serial No: 337 28 13, US Navy. Russell was born January 10, 1922 in Sac County, Iowa to Archie Earl and Rose Agnes (Batton) Hawkins. He enlisted in the US Navy on March 12, 1940 in St. Louis, Missouri and completed his basic training at the Naval Training Station in Great Lakes, Illinois. He reported for duty on the USS Arizona on July 12, 1940. Russell was seen to have been killed in action on December 7, 1941 at Pearl Harbor, Hawaii. Assigned death No. 541 by the US Naval Hospital at Pearl.[324] He was awarded the American Defense Service Medal, World War II Victory Medal and Purple Heart Medal posthumously. Russell remains on duty on the USS Arizona. He is commemorated on the USS Arizona Memorial and the Memorial Tablets of the Missing, National Memorial Cemetery of the Pacific, Honolulu, Hawaii. His remains were returned home and he is buried in Oak Hill Cemetery, Taylorville, Illinois. Russell was survived by his Father, Mr. Archie Earl Hawkins, Route 1, Taylorville, Illinois.[325]

Hayes, John Doran Boatswain's Mate, First Class, Serial No: 320 93 88, US Navy. John was born December 3, 1914 in Charles City, Iowa, the son of Cleveland and Blanche Minervia (Doran) Hayes. He enlisted in the US Navy on August 14, 1934 in Des Moines, Iowa and completed his basic training at the Naval Training Station in Great Lakes, Illinois. John served on the USS Arizona from December 4 1934 until he was killed in action on December 7, 1941 at Pearl Harbor, Hawaii. He was awarded the American Defense Service Medal, World War II Victory Medal and Purple Heart Medal posthumously. John remains on duty on the USS Arizona. He is commemorated on the USS Arizona Memorial and the Memorial Tablets of the Missing, National Memorial Cemetery

---

[322] James Wallace Haverfield, Photo and information provided by Ohio State University.

[323] Harvey Linfille Havins, Photo and information provided by his nephew, William Mitchell.

[324] Report of Changes of the USS Arizona Flag Allowance (CBD-1) Commander Battleship Division ONE for the period ending 7th day of December, 1941, page 1, line 13, Russell Dean Hawkins.

[325] Russell Dean Hawkins, Photo from Illinois Honor States.

of the Pacific, Honolulu, Hawaii. John was survived by his Wife, Mrs. Virginia Geraldine Hayes, 117 West 53rd Street, Long Beach, California and a daughter, Sharon Virginia Hayes.[326]

Hayes, Kenneth Merle Fireman, First Class, Serial No: 375 90 28, US Navy. Kenneth was born July 22, 1918 in Lassen, California. He enlisted in the US Navy on July 6, 1938 in San Francisco, California and completed his basic training at the Naval Training Station in San Diego, California. He reported for duty on the USS Arizona on October 21, 1938. Kenneth was killed in action on December 7, 1941 at Pearl Harbor, Hawaii. He was awarded the American Defense Service Medal, World War II Victory Medal and Purple Heart Medal posthumously. Kenneth remains on duty on the USS Arizona. He is commemorated on the USS Arizona Memorial and the Memorial Tablets of the Missing, National Memorial Cemetery of the Pacific, Honolulu, Hawaii. Kenneth was survived by his Wife, Mrs. Kenneth M. Hayes, 829-1/2 North Soto Street, Los Angeles, California. The VFW Post in Quincy, California was named in his honor.

Haynes, Curtis James Quartermaster, Second Class, Serial No: 368 34 50, US Navy. Curtis was born in 1918 the son of James E. and Evelyn Haynes. He enlisted in the US Navy on June 16, 1936 in Salt Lake City, Utah and completed his basic training at the Naval Training Station in San Diego, California. Curtis reported for duty on the USS Arizona on September 28, 1936. He was killed in action on December 7, 1941 at Pearl Harbor, Hawaii. Curtis was awarded the American Defense Service Medal, World War II Victory Medal and Purple Heart Medal posthumously. He remains on duty on the USS Arizona. Curtis is commemorated on the USS Arizona Memorial and the Memorial Tablets of the Missing, National Memorial Cemetery of the Pacific, Honolulu, Hawaii. He was survived by his Father, Mr. James Emmery Haynes, 202 South 7th Street, Boise, Idaho.

Hays, William Henry Storekeeper, Third Class, Serial No: 342 17 62, US Navy. William was born on February 6, 1919 in Oregon County, Missouri to Maud William and Gertrude Lilas (Fry) Hays. He enlisted in the US Navy on January 8, 1940 in Kansas City, Missouri and completed his basic training at the Naval Training Station in Great Lakes, Illinois. William reported for duty on the USS Arizona on March 26, 1940. He was killed in action on December 7, 1941 at Pearl Harbor, Hawaii. William was awarded the American Defense Service Medal, World War II Victory Medal and Purple Heart Medal posthumously. He remains on duty on the USS Arizona. William is commemorated on the USS Arizona Memorial and the Memorial Tablets of the Missing, National Memorial Cemetery of the Pacific, Honolulu, Hawaii. He was survived by his Father, Mr. Maud William Hays, Hugoton, Kansas.[327]

---

[326] John Doran Hayes, Photo and information taken from the Huntingdon Daily News, Huntingdon, PA, February 2, 1942, Page 5
[327] William Henry Hays, photo and information provided by his great niece, Cassie Cairns.

Hazdovac, Jack Claudius   Seaman, First Class, Serial No: 376 09 60, US Navy. Jack was born in April of 1920 to Peter and Mamie Rashimina (Nielsen) Hazdovac. He enlisted in the US Navy on August 6, 1940 in San Francisco, California and completed his basic training at the Naval Training Station in San Diego, California. He reported for duty on the USS Arizona on November 11, 1940. Jack was killed in action on December 7, 1941 at Pearl Harbor, Hawaii. He was awarded the American Defense Service Medal, World War II Victory Medal and Purple Heart Medal posthumously. Jack remains on duty on the USS Arizona. He is commemorated on the USS Arizona Memorial and the Memorial Tablets of the Missing, National Memorial Cemetery of the Pacific, Honolulu, Hawaii. Jack was survived by his Father, Mr. Peter Givo Hazdovac, 1240 1st Street, Monterey, California.[328]

Head, Frank Bernard   Chief Yeoman, Serial No: 371 73 17, US Navy. Frank was born December 21, 1909 in Colorado to Paul Bernard and Grace M. (Carter) Head. He enlisted in the US Navy on November 8, 1935 in Mare Island, California and was transferred from the USS Tennessee to the USS Arizona on November 10, 1939, reporting for duty on November 17, 1939. He was killed in action on December 7, 1941 at Pearl Harbor, Hawaii. Frank was awarded the American Defense Service Medal, World War II Victory Medal and Purple Heart Medal posthumously. He remains on duty on the USS Arizona. Frank is commemorated on the USS Arizona Memorial and the Memorial Tablets of the Missing, National Memorial Cemetery of the Pacific, Honolulu, Hawaii. He was survived by his Wife, Mrs. Adella Carlson Head, 636 Lime Avenue, Long Beach, California.

Heater, Verrell Roy   Seaman, First Class, Serial No: 393 43 09, US Navy. Verrell was born on June 24, 1918 in Oregon the son of Asa Raymond and Hallie E. (Knecht) Heater. He enlisted in the US Navy on November 12, 1940 in Portland, Oregon and completed his basic training at the Naval Training Station in San Diego, California. Verrell reported for duty on the USS Arizona on January 11, 1941. He was killed in action on December 7, 1941 at Pearl Harbor, Hawaii. Verrell was awarded the American Defense Service Medal, World War II Victory Medal and Purple Heart Medal posthumously. He remains on duty on the USS Arizona. Verrell is commemorated on the USS Arizona Memorial and the Memorial Tablets of the Missing, National Memorial Cemetery of the Pacific, Honolulu, Hawaii. He was survived by his Father, Mr. Ray Heater, P.O. Box 112, Sherwood, Oregon.

---

[328] Jack Claudius Hazdovac, Photo from El Susurro Yearbook, Monterey Union High School, Monterey California, 1938.

Heath, Alfred Grant Seaman, First Class, Serial No: 372 13 78, US Navy. Alfred was born March 15, 1916 in Spencer, Wisconsin to Grant and Ella Heath. He enlisted in the US Navy on *By the time Alfred was 3 years old, his mother was gone and he was raised by his father.* March 13, 1940 in Denver, Colorado and completed his basic training at the Naval Training Station in San Diego, California. He reported for duty on the USS Arizona on July 14, 1940. Alfred was killed in action on December 7, 1941 at Pearl Harbor, Hawaii. He was awarded the American Defense Service Medal, World War II Victory Medal and Purple Heart Medal posthumously. Alfred's remains were recovered and he was buried in Plot C, Row 0, Grave 924, National Memorial Cemetery of the Pacific, Honolulu, Hawaii. He is commemorated on the USS Arizona Memorial. Alfred was survived by his Father, Mr. Grant Heath, Spencer, Wisconsin.[329]

Hebel, Robert Lee Signalman, Third Class, Serial No: 411 02 91, US Naval Reserve. Robert was born on January 1, 1922 in Chicago, Illinois, the son of Cyril E. and Alice L. (Voss) Hebel. He enlisted in the US Navy on August 27, 1940 in Chicago, Illinois and completed his basic training at the Naval Training Station in Great Lakes, Illinois. Robert reported for duty on the USS Arizona on June 23, 1941. He was killed in action on December 7, 1941 at Pearl Harbor, Hawaii. Robert was awarded the American Defense Service Medal, World War II Victory Medal and Purple Heart Medal posthumously. He remains on duty on the USS Arizona. Robert is commemorated on the USS Arizona Memorial and the Memorial Tablets of the Missing, National Memorial Cemetery of the Pacific, Honolulu, Hawaii. He was survived by his Grandparents, Paul and Cora Voss, Sr., 3652 South Hamilton Avenue, Chicago, Illinois; brothers Don and James Hebel and sister Jean Hebel.[330]

Heckendorn, Warren Guy Seaman, First Class, Serial No: 360 27 05, US Navy. Warren was born January 4, 1917 in Trinity, Texas to John Robert and Julia Elizabeth (Hennessey) Heckendorn. He enlisted in the US Navy on November 25, 1940 in Houston, Texas and completed his basic training at the Naval Training Station in San Diego, California. He reported for duty on the USS Arizona on January 25, 1941. Warren was killed in action on December 7, 1941 at Pearl Harbor, Hawaii. He was awarded the American Defense Service Medal, World War II Victory Medal and Purple Heart Medal posthumously. Warren remains on duty on the USS Arizona. He is commemorated on the USS Arizona Memorial and the Memorial Tablets of the Missing, National Memorial Cemetery of the Pacific, Honolulu, Hawaii. Warren was survived by his Father, Mr. John Robert Heckendorn, Route 1, Box 212, Dickinson, Texas.[331]

---

[329] Alfred Grant Heath, Photo and information from the Marshfield News-Herald, Marshfield, Wisconsin, December 24, 1941, Page 1.
[330] Robert Lee Hebel, Photo and information provided by family member, Bob Hebel.
[331] Warren Guy Heckendorn, Photo from Texas Honor States.

Hedger, Jess Laxton   Seaman, First Class, Serial No: 300 19 42, US Navy. Jess was born in about 1920 in Springfield, Illinois. He enlisted in the US Navy on October 8, 1940 in Chicago, Illinois and completed his basic training at the Naval Training Station in Great Lakes, Illinois. He reported for duty on the USS Arizona on December 9, 1940. Jess was killed in action on December 7, 1941 at Pearl Harbor, Hawaii. He was awarded the American Defense Service Medal, World War II Victory Medal and Purple Heart Medal posthumously. Jess remains on duty on the USS Arizona. He is commemorated on the USS Arizona Memorial and the Memorial Tablets of the Missing, National Memorial Cemetery of the Pacific, Honolulu, Hawaii. Jess was survived by his Mother, Mrs. Maggie Hedger, 3804 Pershing Avenue, San Diego, California.

Hedrick, Paul Henry   Boatswain's Mate, First Class, Serial No: 261 74 48, US Navy. Paul was born May 12, 1913 in North Carolina, the son of O.H. Hedrick and Eine L. Hedrick. He re-enlisted in the US Navy April 21, 1936. Paul served on the USS Arizona from November 25, 1930 until he was killed in action on December 7, 1941 at Pearl Harbor, Hawaii. He was awarded the American Defense Service Medal, World War II Victory Medal and Purple Heart Medal posthumously. Paul remains on duty on the USS Arizona. He is commemorated on the USS Arizona Memorial and the Memorial Tablets of the Missing, National Memorial Cemetery of the Pacific, Honolulu, Hawaii. Paul was survived by his Wife, Mrs. Frances Jeanne Hedrick and daughter, Judith Hedrick, 2987 Sunny Nook Drive, Los Angeles, California. The Hedrick-Rhodes VFW Post 5206 in Hendersonville, North Carolina was named in his honor.[332]

Heely, Leo Shinn   Seaman, Second Class, Serial No: 372 30 44, US Navy. Leo was born January 8, 1918 in Mesa, Colorado, the son of Charles Eugene and Cora Jane (Stringer) Heely. He enlisted in the US Navy on April 19, 1941 in Denver, Colorado and completed his basic training at the Naval Training Station in San Diego, California. Leo reported for duty on the USS Arizona on July 22, 1941. He was killed in action on December 7, 1941 at Pearl Harbor, Hawaii. Leo was awarded the American Defense Service Medal, World War II Victory Medal and Purple Heart Medal posthumously. He remains on duty on the USS Arizona. Leo is commemorated on the USS Arizona Memorial and the Memorial Tablets of the Missing, National Memorial Cemetery of the Pacific, Honolulu, Hawaii. He was survived by his Father, Mr. Charles Eugene Heely, Mesa, Colorado.

Heidt, Edward Joseph   Fireman, First Class, Serial No: 382 10 90, US Navy. Edward was born June 19, 1916 in Los Angeles, California, the son of George Edward and Genevieve Heidt. He enlisted in the US Navy on September 13, 1939 in Los Angeles, California and completed his basic training at the Naval Training Station in San Diego, California. Edward reported for duty on the USS Arizona on November 10, 1939. He was killed in action on December 7, 1941 at Pearl Harbor, Hawaii. Edward was awarded the American Defense Service Medal, World War II Victory Medal and Purple Heart Medal posthumously. He remains on duty on the USS Arizona with his brother. Edward is commemorated on the USS Arizona Memorial and the Memorial Tablets of the Missing, National

---

[332] Paul Henry Hedrick, Photo and information from the Asheville Citizen-Times, Asheville, North Carolina, January 30, 1942, Page 15.

Memorial Cemetery of the Pacific, Honolulu, Hawaii. He was survived by his Mother, Mrs. Genevieve Dunlap, 3545 Linda Vista Terrace, Los Angeles, California. His Brother, Wesley was killed in action on board the USS Arizona.[333]

Heidt, Wesley John Machinist's Mate, Second Class, Serial No: 382 10 89, US Navy. Wesley was born May 17, 1917 in Los Angeles, California, the son of George Edward and Genevieve Heidt. He enlisted in the US Navy on September 13, 1939 in Los Angeles, California and completed his basic training at the Naval Training Station in San Diego, California. Wesley reported for duty on the USS Arizona on February 16, 1940. He was killed in action on December 7, 1941 at Pearl Harbor, Hawaii. Wesley was awarded the American Defense Service Medal, World War II Victory Medal and Purple Heart Medal posthumously. He remains on duty on the USS Arizona with his brother. Wesley is commemorated on the USS Arizona Memorial and the Memorial Tablets of the Missing, National Memorial Cemetery of the Pacific, Honolulu, Hawaii. He was survived by his Mother, Mrs. Genevieve Dunlap, 3545 Linda Vista Terrace, Los Angeles, California. His Brother, Edward was killed in action on board the USS Arizona.[334]

Hein, Douglas Ensign, Serial No. O-100120, US Navy. Douglas was born in California. He was commissioned Ensign February 7, 1941 in the US Navy. Douglas was serving on the USS Arizona on December 7, 1941 as Communications Watch Officer when the Japanese attacked Pearl Harbor. His official report:

"I left the J.O. [junior officers] Mess at General Quarters. As I went to the boat deck, I noticed that some of starboard A.A. guns were firing. I think they were the forward ones. Then I went up to the signal bridge. I looked around and saw that there was nothing that I could do. I saw the admiral on the signal bridge. Then I went up to the nav bridge. The only people up there were the captain, the quartermaster and myself. The quartermaster asked the captain if he wanted to go into the conning tower but the captain did not want to, making phone calls. Suddenly the whole bridge shook like it was in an earthquake, flame came through the bridge windows which had been broken by gunfire. We three were trying to get out the port door at the after end of the bridge during all this shaking, but could not. We staggered to the starboard side and fell on the deck just forward of the wheel. Finally I raised my head and turned it and saw that the port door was open. I got up and ran to it, and ran down the port ladders, passing through flames and smoke. Then I climbed half way down the signal bridge ladder and had to jump to the boat deck as it was bent way under. Then I climbed down a handrail to the galley deck. The flames and smoke on the boat deck and galley deck were decreasing in intensity; I believe they were powder flames. I walked aft and down the ladder to the port quarterdeck. Then I walked to the other side and down the officer's ladder to the barge."[335] He was wounded in action during the attack.

[333] Edward Joseph Heidt, Photo taken from the Pylon Yearbook, Leuzinger High School, Lawndale, California, Class of 1936.
[334] Wesley John Heidt, Photo taken from the Pylon Yearbook, Leuzinger High School, Lawndale, California, Class of 1936.
[335] Statement of Ensign D. Hein, U.S.S. Arizona, Last Action Report

Douglas was later killed in action on June 4, 1945 while serving on board the USS Antietam. Douglas was survived by his Parents, Captain and Mrs. H. R. Hein, USN, 2265 Broadway, San Francisco, California.[336]

Heinz, Robert Henry   Seaman, First Class, Serial No. 372 26 24, US Navy. Robert was born July 15, 1923 In Denver, Colorado the son of Henry Edward Heinz and Lydia Tribelhorn. He enlisted in the US Navy January 27, 1941 in Denver, Colorado and completed his basic training at the Naval Training Station in San Diego, California. Robert reported for duty on the USS Arizona April 27, 1941. He was serving on the USS Arizona on December 7, 1941 when the Japanese attacked Pearl Harbor. After the attack, Robert was transferred to the USS Chester for duty. Robert died November 29, 1999 in Denver, Colorado.

Helm, Merritt Cameron   Seaman, First Class, Serial No: 328 62 63, US Navy. Merritt was born November 1, 1921 in Tower, Minnesota, the son of Lucian Merritt and Inez I. (Wiseman) Helm. He enlisted in the US Navy on December 5, 1939 in Minneapolis, Minnesota and completed his basic training at the Naval Training Station in Great Lakes, Illinois. Merritt reported for duty on the USS Arizona on March 9, 1940. He was killed in action on December 7, 1941 at Pearl Harbor, Hawaii. Merritt was awarded the American Defense Service Medal, World War II Victory Medal and Purple Heart Medal posthumously. He remains buried on the USS Arizona. Merritt is commemorated on the USS Arizona Memorial and the Memorial Tablets of the Missing, National Memorial Cemetery of the Pacific, Honolulu, Hawaii. He was survived by his Father, Lucian Merritt Helm, North Third Street, Tower, Minnesota.

Henderson, William Walter   Seaman, Second Class, Serial No: 381 37 37, US Navy. William was born on October 6, 1920 in Bondurant, Iowa, the son of Walter Lin and Iva Henderson. He enlisted in the US Navy on October 11, 1940 and completed his basic training at the Naval Training Station in San Diego, California. William reported for duty on the USS Arizona on June 25, 1941. He was killed in action on December 7, 1941 at Pearl Harbor, Hawaii. William was awarded the American Defense Service Medal, World War II Victory Medal and Purple Heart Medal posthumously. He remains on duty on the USS Arizona. William is commemorated on the USS Arizona Memorial and the Memorial Tablets of the Missing, National Memorial Cemetery of the Pacific, Honolulu, Hawaii. He was survived by his Father, Mr. Walter L. Henderson, 425 East 5th Street North, Newton, Iowa.[337]

Hendon, Robert Marvin   Chief Gunner's Mate, Serial No. 295 17 88, US Navy. Robert was born on April 25, 1912 in Choctaw County, Mississippi. He enlisted in the US Navy April 8, 1930. Robert served on the USS Arizona from March 23, 1931 until on December 7, 1941 when the Japanese attacked Pearl Harbor. After the attack, Robert was assigned salvage duty on the USS Utah. He served in the Navy until June 30, 1956 attaining the rank of Lieutenant Commander. Robert died on May 24, 1984 and is buried in Section 5, Site 2251, Riverside National Cemetery, Riverside, California.

---

[336] Douglas Hein, Photo from Lucky Bag Yearbook, United States Naval Academy, Annapolis, MD, class of 1941.
[337] William Walter Henderson, Photo from California Honor States.

Hendricksen, Frank Fireman, Second Class, Serial No: 311 51 59, US Navy. Frank was born in 1921 in Michigan, he was the adopted son of Garritt and Minnie Bessie Klein (Meulekamp) Hendricksen. He enlisted in the US Navy on October 8, 1940 in Detroit, Michigan and completed his basic training at the Naval Training Station in Great Lakes, Illinois. Frank reported for duty on the USS Arizona on December 9, 1940. He was killed in action on December 7, 1941 at Pearl Harbor, Hawaii. Frank was awarded the American Defense Service Medal, World War II Victory Medal and Purple Heart Medal posthumously. He remains buried on the USS Arizona. Frank is commemorated on the USS Arizona Memorial and the Memorial Tablets of the Missing, National Memorial Cemetery of the Pacific, Honolulu, Hawaii. He was survived by his Father, Mr. Gerrit Hendriksen, 724 West South Street, Kalamazoo, Michigan.[338]

Henry, John William Ensign, Serial No. 0-06951, US Navy. John was born on August 29, 1917. He was commissioned June 6, 1940 in the US Navy serving on the USS Arizona as Watch and Junior Division F Officer and Aide to the Executive officer on December 7, 1941 when the Japanese attacked Pearl Harbor. His battle station was the Plot Room. John later served in the Korean War. He retired from the Navy in 1966 achieving a rank of Captain. John died on January 24, 1985 of a Heart Attack. He was buried in Section 66, Site 4792, Arlington National Cemetery, Arlington, Virginia. John was survived by his wife, Mrs. Ruth W. Henry, two sons, Michael and Peter and three daughters, Sheila, Norah and Eileen.

Herring, James Junior Signalman, Third Class, Serial No: 321 29 52, US Navy. James was born in 1921 in Iowa City, Iowa to James Henry and Ruth Henrietta (Rees) Herring. He enlisted in the US Navy on January 25, 1939 in Des Moines, Iowa and completed his basic training at the Naval Training Station in Great Lakes, Illinois. James reported for duty on the USS Arizona on July 8, 1939. He was killed in action on December 7, 1941 at Pearl Harbor, Hawaii. James was awarded the American Defense Service Medal, World War II Victory Medal and Purple Heart Medal posthumously. He remains on duty on the USS Arizona. James is commemorated on the USS Arizona Memorial and the Memorial Tablets of the Missing, National Memorial Cemetery of the Pacific, Honolulu, Hawaii and Oakland Cemetery, Iowa City, Iowa. He was survived by his Father, Mr. James H. Herring, 430 South Van Buren Street, Iowa City, Iowa.[339]

---

[338] Frank Hendricksen, Photo from Michigan Honor States.
[339] James Junior Herring, Photo from the Quad-City Times, Davenport, Iowa, May 5, 1942, page 3.

Herriott, Robert Asher, Jr. Seaman, First Class, Serial No: 356 49 02, US Navy. Robert was born on March 27, 1923, the son of Robert Asher and Elizabeth F. (Ward) Herriott. He enlisted in the US Navy on January 22, 1941 in Dallas, Texas and completed his basic training at the Naval Training Station in San Diego, California. Robert reported for duty on the USS Arizona on April 27, 1941. He was killed in action on December 7, 1941 at Pearl Harbor, Hawaii. Robert was awarded the American Defense Service Medal, World War II Victory Medal and Purple Heart Medal posthumously. He remains on duty on the USS Arizona. Robert is commemorated on the USS Arizona Memorial and the Memorial Tablets of the Missing, National Memorial Cemetery of the Pacific, Honolulu, Hawaii. He was survived by his Father, Mr. Robert Asher Herriott, Sr., 1006 Dale Street, Dallas, Texas.[340]

Hess, Darrell Miller Fire Controlman, First Class, Serial No: 299 77 96, US Navy. Darrell was born January 8, 1916 in Homer, Winona, Minnesota to Franklin Almar and Zoe Ida (Bell) Hess. He enlisted in the US Navy on July 30, 1935 in Chicago, Illinois and completed his basic training at the Naval Training Station in Great Lakes, Illinois. He reported for duty on the USS Arizona on November 23, 1935. Darrell was killed in action on December 7, 1941 at Pearl Harbor, Hawaii. He was awarded the American Defense Service Medal, World War II Victory Medal and Purple Heart Medal posthumously. Darrell was identified by a ring of keys in his pocket. The disposition of his body is unclear; it is possible he was buried in one of the unknown graves in the Punchbowl.[341] He is commemorated on the USS Arizona Memorial and the Memorial Tablets of the Missing, National Memorial Cemetery of the Pacific, Honolulu, Hawaii. Darrell was survived by his Wife, Mrs. Estella Marie Hess, 243 East 7th South, Salt Lake City, Utah.[342]

Hessdorfer, Anthony Joseph Machinist's Mate, Second Class, Serial No: 385 75 33, US Navy. Anthony was born in 1918 in Cuthbart, Saskatoon, Canada, the son of George Conrad and Elizabeth (Miller) Hessdorfer. He enlisted in the US Navy on October 13, 1937 in Seattle, Washington and completed his basic training at the Naval Training Station in San Diego, California. Anthony reported for duty on the USS Arizona on January 25, 1938. He was killed in action on December 7, 1941 at Pearl Harbor, Hawaii. Anthony was awarded the American Defense Service Medal, World War II Victory Medal and Purple Heart Medal posthumously. He remains on duty on the USS Arizona. Anthony is commemorated on the USS Arizona Memorial and the Memorial Tablets of the Missing, National Memorial Cemetery of the Pacific, Honolulu, Hawaii. He was survived by his Father, Mr. George Conrad Hessdorfer, 611 North 4th Street, Yakima, Washington.

---

[340] Robert Asher Herriott, Jr., photo curtsey LCDR G. Dale McKissick, USNR, Memorial, Dallas Convention Center, Dallas, Texas.
[341] Report of Changes of the USS Arizona for the month ending 31st day of December, 1941, page 66, line 29, Darrell Miller Hess.
[342] Darrell Miller Hess, Photo from Utah Honor States.

Hetrick, Clarendon Robert Seaman, First Class, Serial No. 381 38 37, US Navy. Clarendon was born to Elmer E. Hetrick and Hazel E. Hetrick on May 26, 1923 in Cheyenne, Wyoming. He was number six of an even dozen children, three boys older and two sisters older, two boys younger and four younger sisters. The family moved to Lemon Grove, California some time in 1926. I attended school in California until the 10th grade, at this time I dropped out and joined the US Navy at San Diego, California November 28, 1940. I took my training at San Diego Naval Training Center. After completion of my training I was assigned to the USS Arizona and reported for duty January 25, 1941. Needless to say this was my home on December 7, 1941 when the Japanese attacked Pearl Harbor.

On this day I was getting ready for Liberty. When the bombing started, I was in the forward head getting ready to shower. At the sound of guns firing I looked out to the port side of the ship and all I could see was a Jap plane. At this time I knew what was happening and I ran down to my battle station which was on the 3rd deck. I was a hoist operator there. We set up the conveyor belt and then were requested to help in the 5 inch magazine, which was one deck lower. After getting there and starting to pass ammo up the elevator, there was an explosion which knocked us to the deck and we lost all power which put us in the dark. We then started to smell smoke and when you smell smoke in a magazine, it is NO PLACE to be!!

I started to abandon ship by going thru the hatch and found someone blocking my way so I told him to move and he said "I can't". So I pushed him thru and didn't see him again. As I left the ship all I could see was fire. I jumped off the starboard side and swam to Ford Island. Later in the day I was put aboard the USS Tennessee for the night.

On December 8th, I went to the receiving station where I was able to shower and get some clean clothes. Later that same day I was assigned to the USS Lexington where I stayed for about three weeks. Early in 1942, I was assigned to North Island, San Diego, California for aircraft training, then to Kaneohe to form Torpedo Squadron 10. From there I was assigned to the USS Saratoga where I was wounded in action during the invasion of Iwo Jima. (His parents, Mr. and Mrs. Elmer Emery Hetrick, Lemon Grove, California were notified.) I served on the USS Saratoga until after the war ended.

I returned to San Diego for leave and hoping to stay there, I married the greatest person in the world, Myrtle Jeanne Sessum. Unfortunately, to my disliking, I was sent right back to Pearl Harbor. I was discharged in 1946 and within 30 days I joined the Naval Reserve on active duty at North Island. Later I served at Los Alamitos Naval Air station.

In 1949 I left the Navy and joined the US Air Force at Long Beach, California. From there I was sent to Korea, back to the USA, Langley Field, Virginia then to Hill Field, Utah. From there I went to Loan France, back to New Mexico and in January 1961 I retired to the Modesto, California area. I have three sons, one in Modesto, California, one in Arizona and one in Las Vegas, Nevada. [343]

Hibbard, Robert Arnold Baker, Second Class, Serial No: 287 15 42, US Navy. Robert was born on October 14, 1917 in Clay County, Kentucky, the son of Joseph Burchil and Addie (Wolfe) Hibbard. He enlisted in the US Navy on December 16, 1935 in Louisville, Kentucky and reported for duty on the USS Arizona on April 20, 1936. Robert was killed in action on December 7, 1941 at Pearl Harbor, Hawaii. He was awarded the American Defense Service Medal, World War II Victory Medal and Purple Heart Medal posthumously. Robert remains on duty on the USS Arizona. He is commemorated on the USS Arizona Memorial and the Memorial

---

[343] Information and photo provided by Clarendon Hetrick, August 26, 2008.

Tablets of the Missing, National Memorial Cemetery of the Pacific, Honolulu, Hawaii. Robert was survived by his Father, Mr. Joe Burchil Hibbard, Route 1, Corbin, Kentucky.

Hickman, Arthur Lee Signalman, Third Class, Serial No: 321 20 94, US Navy. Arthur was born August 2, 1920 in Coin, Iowa to Arthur Stanley and Anna America (Haynes) Hickman. He enlisted in the US Navy on October 19, 1937 in Des Moines, Iowa and completed his basic training at the Naval Training Station in Great Lakes, Illinois. Arthur reported for duty on the USS Arizona on February 26, 1938. He was killed in action on December 7, 1941 at Pearl Harbor, Hawaii. Arthur was awarded the American Defense Service Medal, World War II Victory Medal and Purple Heart Medal posthumously. He remains on duty on the USS Arizona. Arthur is commemorated on the USS Arizona Memorial and the Memorial Tablets of the Missing, National Memorial Cemetery of the Pacific, Honolulu, Hawaii. He was survived by his Father, Mr. Arthur S. Hickman, Route 2, Box 739-A, Bremerton, Washington.

Hicks, Elmer Orville Gunner's Mate, Third Class, Serial No: 393 30 19, US Navy. Elmer was born January 8, 1920 in Valier, Montana to Elwood Booker and Ethel V. (Graff) Hicks. He graduated from the Potlatch High School in Potlatch, Idaho. Elmer enlisted in the US Navy on August 14, 1939 in Portland, Oregon and completed his basic training at the Naval Training Station in San Diego, California. He reported for duty on the USS Arizona on October 20, 1939. Elmer was killed in action on December 7, 1941 at Pearl Harbor, Hawaii. He was awarded the American Defense Service Medal, World War II Victory Medal and Purple Heart Medal posthumously. Elmer remains on duty on the USS Arizona. He is commemorated on the USS Arizona Memorial and the Memorial Tablets of the Missing, National Memorial Cemetery of the Pacific, Honolulu, Hawaii. Elmer was survived by his Father, Mr. Elwood Booker Hicks, Route 3, Garfield, Washington.[344]

Hicks, Ralph Dueard Painter, Second Class, Serial No: 336 84 55, US Navy Reserve. Ralph was born on April 17, 1915 in Walnut Grove, Missouri. *He was the fourth of five children born to James Isom and Nelle Ellen (Butcher) Hicks. His family lived on a 100 acre farm where they raised chicks, horses, cows, mules and crops of corn and grain. Ralph was blond and had fluffy hair, so everyone called him "Fluffy". His father died when he was six in 1921 and the family moved into a two-room house that his mother had inherited from her grandfather. Ralph's mother died while he was still in school in 1932. He then went to live with his grandmother. While attending Walnut Grove High School, he played football and was on the "Little Ten" football team that won the championship that year.* He enlisted in the US Navy on September 10, 1935 in St. Louis, Missouri and reported for duty on the USS Arizona January 11, 1936. Ralph had just completed his second tour of duty and was awaiting transport home when he was killed in action on December 7, 1941 at Pearl Harbor, Hawaii. He was awarded the American Defense Service

---

[344] Elmer Orville Hicks, Photo provided by the Potlatch High School, Potlatch, Idaho.

211

Medal, World War II Victory Medal and Purple Heart Medal posthumously. Ralph remains on duty on the USS Arizona. He is commemorated on the USS Arizona Memorial and the Memorial Tablets of the Missing, National Memorial Cemetery of the Pacific, Honolulu, Hawaii. Ralph was survived by his Guardian, Mr. Everal Hicks, Santa Paul, California; brother, Lt. Aubrey T. Hicks (later Captain) was a Marine on Midway Island; brother, Stg. James L. Hicks (Army, in the Philippine and died in a Japanese Prison Camp, having participated in the Bataan Death March in 1942 and sister, Wilma Hicks Jones of Los Angeles.[345]

Hill, Bartley Taylor Aviation Ordnanceman, Third Class, Aviation Unit (VO-1), Serial No: 265 71 24, US Navy. Bartley was born October 29, 1915 in Craven County, North Carolina to Orem Howard and Catherine Elizabeth (Taylor) Hill. He enlisted in the US Navy on February 10, 1940 San Pedro, California and reported for duty on the USS Arizona on November 18, 1940. Bartley was killed in action on December 7, 1941 at Pearl Harbor, Hawaii. He was awarded the American Defense Service Medal, World War II Victory Medal and Purple Heart Medal posthumously. Bartley remains on duty on the USS Arizona. He is commemorated on the USS Arizona Memorial and the Memorial Tablets of the Missing, National Memorial Cemetery of the Pacific, Honolulu, Hawaii. Bartley was survived by his Wife, Mrs. Nonie Louise Hill, 41 Ontario Street, Long Beach, California.

Hill, Richard Howe Yeoman, Second Class, Serial No. 382 07 41, US Navy. Richard was born October 16, 1918 in Ashton, New Hampshire, the son of Howard Harris and Hanna Augusta (Libbey) Hill. He enlisted in the US Navy September 14, 1938 in Los Angeles, California and completed his basic training at the Naval Training Station in San Diego, California. He reported for duty on the USS Arizona March 11, 1939. Due to a bad tooth, Richard was resting up from dental surgery. He stayed with a friend the night of December 6, 1941 and was not on board the USS Arizona on the morning of December 7, 1941 when the Japanese attacked Pearl Harbor. Richard died March 17, 2004 in Zephyrhills, Florida.

Hilton, Wilson Woodrow Gunner's Mate, First Class, Serial No: 261 85 55, US Navy. Wilson was born on November 10, 1913 in Catawba County, North Carolina, the son of Amos Wilbern and Lillie Elizabeth (Rudisill) Hilton. He enlisted in the US Navy on December 12, 1934 in Raleigh, North Carolina. Wilson served on the USS Arizona from June 10, 1935 until he was killed in action on December 7, 1941 at Pearl Harbor, Hawaii. He was awarded the American Defense Service Medal, World War II Victory Medal and Purple Heart Medal posthumously. Wilson's remains were identified when he was removed from the ship and he was returned home for burial in Section B, Site 657, Salisbury National Cemetery, Salisbury, North Carolina.[346] He is commemorated on the USS Arizona Memorial. Wilson was survived by his Father, Mr. Amos W. Hilton, Route 4, Vale, North Carolina.[347]

---

[345] Ralph Dueard Hicks, Information, story and picture provided by his Niece, Terry Vaughn.
[346] Report of Changes of the USS Arizona for the month ending 31st day of December, 1941, page 67, line 6, Wilson Woodrow Hilton.
[347] Wilson Woodrow Hilton, Photo from North Carolina Honor States.

Hindman, Frank Weaver   Seaman, First Class, Serial No: 272 41 89, US Navy. Frank was born on December 9, 1921 in Blue Mountain, Alabama, the son of Jessie Wood and Minnie Dora (Walker) Hindman. He enlisted in the US Navy on October 5, 1940 in Birmingham, Alabama and completed his basic training at the Naval Training Station in Norfolk, Virginia. Frank reported for duty on the USS Arizona on December 4, 1940. Frank and a friend from Alabama stationed at Schofield Barracks had spent the previous Saturday night out on the town. They had swapped uniforms for some unknown reason and had changed back into their correct uniforms in a building at Pearl Harbor. The friend told his parents that Frank had started walking to his ship and had probably been onboard just a short time before the Japanese attack started. He was killed in action on December 7, 1941 at Pearl Harbor, Hawaii. Frank was awarded the American Defense Service Medal, World War II Victory Medal and Purple Heart Medal posthumously. He remains buried on the USS Arizona. Frank is commemorated on the USS Arizona Memorial and the Memorial Tablets of the Missing, National Memorial Cemetery of the Pacific, Honolulu, Hawaii. He was survived by his Father, Mr. Jessie Wood Hindman, 504 North Center Avenue, Piedmont, Alabama.[348]

Hinton, John Harold   Chief Signalman (AA), Serial No. 233 45 76, US Navy. John was born January 14, 1900 in Wentworth, Ontario, Canada the son of Francis and Lucy(Brown) Hinton. He enlisted in the US Navy on March 19, 1919 in Niagara, New York. John served on the USS Arizona from June 3, 1933 until December 7, 1941 when the Japanese attacked Pearl Harbor. He was taken on board the USS Tennessee during the attack and later sent to the Pooling Officer at Pearl for assignment. In February 1942 he was transferred to the USS Astoria for duty. John was discharged from the service on January 22, 1947 at the rank of Chief Boatswain. He died February 18, 1960 in New York and is buried in Lakeview Cemetery, Sweden, New York.

Hjelle, Clarence Otto   Seaman, Second Class, Serial No. 385 92 65, US Navy. Clarence was born on November 12, 1922 in Tacoma, Washington, the son of Robert and Jennie Hjelle. He enlisted in the US Navy November 12, 1940 in Seattle, Washington and completed his basic training at the Naval Training Station in San Diego, California. He reported for duty on the USS Arizona January 11, 1941. He was serving on the Arizona December 7, 1941 when the Japanese attacked Pearl Harbor. After the attack, Clarence was transferred to the Submarine Base, Pearl Harbor. He died on October 23, 1972 in Mountlake Terrace, Washington.

Hodges, Garris Vada   Fireman, Second Class, Serial No: 356 41 24, US Navy. Garris was born October 14, 1923 in Texas, the son of Franklin and Laurine Hodges. *They were share-croppers in Texas and spent most of their time planting and harvesting in the Texas Panhandle between Lubbock, Texas and Portales, New Mexico. Garris had never seen an ocean until he joined the Navy.* He enlisted in the US Navy on November 4, 1940 in Dallas, Texas and completed his basic training at the Naval Training Station in San Diego, California. Garris reported for duty on the USS Arizona on January 11, 1941. He was killed in action on December 7, 1941 at Pearl Harbor, Hawaii. Garris was awarded the American Defense Service Medal, World War II Victory Medal and Purple Heart Medal

---

[348] Frank Weaver Hindman, Photo and information provided by his nephew, Frank W. Hindman II.

213

posthumously. He remains on duty on the USS Arizona. Garris is commemorated on the USS Arizona Memorial and the Memorial Tablets of the Missing, National Memorial Cemetery of the Pacific, Honolulu, Hawaii. He was survived by his Father, Mr. Ben Frank Hodges, Flynn, Texas. Garris was specifically remembered at the 66th Pearl Harbor Ceremony on December 7, 2007. The theme of the ceremony was "Past, Present and Future". This was very fitting because his great-niece, Bailey Sharbrough, re-enlisted during the ceremony with Admiral Willard at her side.[349]

Hoelscher, Lester John Hospital Apprentice, First Class, Serial No: 316 66 46, US Navy. Lester was born in 1923 in Nebraska, the son of Frank Peter and Mary S. (Cook) Hoelscher. He enlisted in the US Navy on July 17, 1940 in Omaha, Nebraska and reported for duty on the USS Arizona on November 3, 1941. Lester was killed in action on December 7, 1941 at Pearl Harbor, Hawaii. He was awarded the American Defense Service Medal, World War II Victory Medal and Purple Heart Medal posthumously. Lester remains on duty on the USS Arizona. He is commemorated on the USS Arizona Memorial and the Memorial Tablets of the Missing, National Memorial Cemetery of the Pacific, Honolulu, Hawaii. Lester was survived by his Father, Mr. Frank Peter Hoelscher, Madison, Nebraska.[350]

Holland, Claude Herbert, Jr. Seaman, Second Class, Serial No: 272 41 59, US Navy. Claude was born May 31, 1922, the son of Claude H. and W. Emeline Holland. He enlisted in the US Navy on October 5, 1940 in Birmingham, Alabama and completed his basic training at the Naval Training Station in Norfolk, Virginia. Claude reported for duty on the USS Arizona on December 4, 1940. He was killed in action on December 7, 1941 at Pearl Harbor, Hawaii. Claude was awarded the American Defense Service Medal, World War II Victory Medal and Purple Heart Medal posthumously. He remains on duty on the USS Arizona. Claude is commemorated on the USS Arizona Memorial and the Memorial Tablets of the Missing, National Memorial Cemetery of the Pacific, Honolulu, Hawaii. He was survived by his Father, Mr. Claude Herbert Holland, Sr., Route 1, West Blocton, Alabama.

Holland, Fred McKenzie Seaman, First Class, Serial No. 360 25 70, US Navy. Fred was born February 4, 1918 in Texas, the son of Fredrick R. and Cora (McKenzie) Holland. He enlisted in the US Navy November 12, 1940 in Houston, Texas and completed his basic training at the Naval Training Station in San Diego, California. He reported for duty on the USS Arizona January 11, 1941. Fred was serving on the USS Arizona on December 7, 1941 when the Japanese attacked Pearl Harbor. After the attack, Fred was transferred to the USS Maury for duty. He died July 15, 1977 and is buried in Section F, Site 96, Houston National Cemetery, Houston, Texas.

---

[349] Garris Vada Hodges, Information and photo provided by his Nephew, Tim Hodges.
[350] Lester John Hoelscher, Photo provided by family member, Sharon Stout.

214

Hollenbach, Paul Zepp Seaman, First Class, Serial No: 223 96 21, US Navy. Paul was born in 1920, the son of Elsie Hollenbach. He enlisted in the US Navy on December 3, 1940 in New York, New York and completed his basic training at the Naval Training Station in San Diego, California. Paul reported for duty on the USS Arizona on July 8, 1941. He was killed in action on December 7, 1941 at Pearl Harbor, Hawaii. Paul was awarded the American Defense Service Medal, World War II Victory Medal and Purple Heart Medal posthumously. He remains on duty on the USS Arizona. Paul is commemorated on the USS Arizona Memorial and the Memorial Tablets of the Missing, National Memorial Cemetery of the Pacific, Honolulu, Hawaii. He was survived by his Mother, Mrs. Elsie Hollenbach Wornberger, 100-39 205th Street, Hollis, New York.[351]

Hollis, Ralph "Red" Lieutenant, Junior Grade, Serial No: 0-073936, US Navy Reserve. Ralph was the Communications Watch Officer on the USS Arizona. He was born on September 10, 1906 in Crawfordsville, Georgia. Ralph graduated valedictorian from high school in 1923. He enlisted in the Navy as apprentice seaman the fall of 1923 and was discharged in March 1926. He got a job with the Palm Beach Fire Department but was recalled to active duty on May 6, 1941. Ralph was appointed Ensign in the Naval Reserve on November 21, 1934 and was called to active duty in May 1941. He reported for duty on the USS Arizona in September 1941. In a letter to his mother dated December 1, 1941 he wrote "Within a week we will be at war with Japan." He did not elaborate. The letter arrived after his death. Ralph was killed in action on December 7, 1941 at Pearl Harbor, Hawaii. He was awarded the Purple Heart Medal, American Defense Service Medal, Asiatic Pacific Area Campaign Medal and World War II Victory Medal posthumously. Ralph remains on duty on the USS Arizona. He is commemorated on the USS Arizona Memorial and the Memorial Tablets of the Missing, National Memorial Cemetery of the Pacific, Honolulu, Hawaii. Ralph was survived by his Wife, Mrs. Ralph Hollis, 111 Corona, Long Beach, California. The USS Hollis (DE-794) was named in his honor. USS Hollis received one battle star for her World War II Service.[352]

Hollowell, George Sanford Coxswain, Serial No: 381 28 11, US Navy. George was born July 9, 1920 in Phoenix, Arizona to George Arthur Hollowell and Loreana Hattie Bowen. He enlisted in the US Navy on June 9, 1939 in San Diego, California and completed his basic training at the Naval Training Station in San Diego, California. He reported for duty on the USS Arizona on September 11, 1939. George was seriously burned and taken to the hospital ship Solace where he died on December 7, 1941 at Pearl Harbor, Hawaii. He was awarded the American Defense Service Medal, World War II Victory Medal and Purple Heart Medal posthumously. The disposition of his body is unclear; he was identified when his body was removed from the ship. It is possible he was buried in

---

[351] Paul Zepp Hollenbach, Photo from Jamaica High School Yearbook, Jamaica, New York, 1920.
[352] Ralph Hollis, Photo from the Destroyer Escort Photo Indes for the USS Hollis (DE-794).

one of the unknown graves in the Punchbowl.[353] George is commemorated on the USS Arizona Memorial and the Memorial Tablets of the Missing, National Memorial Cemetery of the Pacific, Honolulu, Hawaii. He was survived by his Mother, Mrs. Wilburn McMillen, Route 9, Box 645, Phoenix, Arizona.[354]

Holmes, Lowell D. Fireman, Third Class, Serial No: 272 40 05, US Navy. Lowell was born August 27, 1920 in Alabama to Harvey Washington and Eunice (Pennington) Holmes. He enlisted in the US Navy on September 23, 1940 in Birmingham, Alabama and completed his basic training at the Naval Training Station in Norfolk, Virginia. Lowell reported for duty on the USS Arizona on December 4, 1940. He was killed in action on December 7, 1941 at Pearl Harbor, Hawaii. Lowell was awarded the American Defense Service Medal, World War II Victory Medal and Purple Heart Medal posthumously. He remains on duty on the USS Arizona. Lowell is commemorated on the USS Arizona Memorial and the Memorial Tablets of the Missing, National Memorial Cemetery of the Pacific, Honolulu, Hawaii. He was survived by his Father, Mr. Harvey Washington Holmes, Rockcastle, Alabama.

Holmes, Roy Willard Seaman, First Class, Serial No. 311 51 38, US Navy. Roy was born February 18, 1922 in Novi, Michigan, the son of William Lacey and Florance Rosina (Woodworth) Holmes. He enlisted in the US Navy October 1, 1940 in Detroit, Michigan and completed his basic training at the Naval Training Station in Great Lakes, Illinois. He reported for duty on the USS Arizona December 9, 1940. Roy was serving on the USS Arizona on December 7, 1941 when the Japanese attacked Pearl Harbor. After the attack, Roy was transferred to the USS Patterson for duty. Roy died August 14, 2006 in Redford, Michigan.

Homann, Alfred James Lieutenant, Serial No. 0-02816, US Navy. Alfred was born on May 18, 1899 in Nevada City, California, the son of Alfred John and Florence (Kirkman) Homann. He was commissioned an officer in the US Navy June 5, 1930 and was serving on the USS Arizona as Senior Assistant Engineering Officer on the USS Arizona on December 7, 1941 when the Japanese attacked Pearl Harbor. His battle station was Fuel Oil Control. During the Battle of Leyte Gulf, Alfred was the Commander of the USS Lackawanna. Commander Alfred J. Homann, USN was commended for outstanding seamanship which made possible the rescue of all aboard the minesweeper, USS Wasmuth, when that vessel was so badly battered by storm and exploding depth charges that it was abandoned in the Aleutian Area on December 27, 1942. The Wasmuth was escorting a convoy in a raging gale 30 miles off the Aleutians when two depth charges were wrenched from their racks by the waves. The depth charges exploded under the Wasmuth's fantail and carried away a portion of the ship's after section. With the damaged Wasmuth slowly, but surely sinking, Commander Homann skillfully brought the Ramapo, a tanker, alongside after a three and a half hour battle with the raging sea and took off everyone aboard the minesweeper. Alfred died October 10, 1985 in Santa Clara, California.[355]

---

[353] Report of Changes of the USS Arizona for the month ending 31st day of December, 1941, page 67, line 13, George Sanford Hollowell.

[354] George Sanford Hollowell, Photo taken from a newspaper article on July 9, 1973, provided by friend, Norma Cook.

[355] Alfred James Homann, Photo from the Lucky Bag Yearbook, United States Naval Academy, Annapolis, MD, Class of 1922.

Homer, Henry Vernon   Seaman, First Class, Serial No: 337 25 65, US Navy. Henry was born in 1922, the son of Harry and Kathryn M. (Graves) Homer. He enlisted in the US Navy on January 9, 1940 in St. Louis, Missouri and completed his basic training at the Naval Training Station in Great Lakes, Illinois. Henry reported for duty on the USS Arizona on March 26, 1940. He was killed in action on December 7, 1941 at Pearl Harbor, Hawaii. Henry was awarded the American Defense Service Medal, World War II Victory Medal and Purple Heart Medal posthumously. He remains on duty on the USS Arizona. Henry is commemorated on the USS Arizona Memorial and the Memorial Tablets of the Missing, National Memorial Cemetery of the Pacific, Honolulu, Hawaii. He was survived by his Father, Mr. Harry Homer, 900-1/2 East Adams Street, Springfield, Illinois.[356]

Hooks, Woodrow Robert   Seaman, Second Class, Serial No. 624 01 39, US Navy. Woodrow was born August 1, 1918 in Crockett, Texas, the son of James Warren and Louisa Alice Elizabeth (Jones) Hooks. He enlisted in the US Navy June 23, 1941 in Houston, Texas and completed his basic training at the Naval Training Station in San Diego, California. Woodrow reported for duty on the USS Arizona August 29, 1941. He was serving on December 7, 1941 when the Japanese attacked Pearl Harbor. After the attack, Woodrow was transferred to the Submarine Base, Pearl Harbor. On October 5, 1942 he was transferred to the USS Grayling (SS-209). Woodrow died August 12, 1997 in San Diego, California.

Hooper, Clifford Charles   Radioman, Second Class, V3, Serial No. 413 25 68, US Navy. Clifford was born on January 9, 1907 in Mangum, Oklahoma to Charles H. and Katie A. (Word) Hooper. He enlisted in the US Navy August 26, 1934 and reported for duty on the USS Arizona January 23, 1941. Clifford was serving on the USS Arizona on December 7, 1941 when the Japanese attacked Pearl Harbor. After the attack, Clifford was transferred to the USS Louisville for duty. He served until September 7, 1945. Clifford died on June 19, 1981 in Colorado and is buried in Section S, Site 4247, Fort Logan National Cemetery, Denver, Colorado.

Hopkins, Homer David   Seaman, First Class, Serial No: 311 49 88, US Navy. Homer was born in 1921 in Muskegon, Michigan to David Thomas and Alma Hopkins. He enlisted in the US Navy on September 9, 1940 in Detroit, Michigan and completed his basic training at the Naval Training Station in Norfolk, Virginia. Homer reported for duty on the USS Arizona on December 4, 1940. He was killed in action on December 7, 1941 at Pearl Harbor, Hawaii. Homer was awarded the American Defense Service Medal, World War II Victory Medal and Purple Heart Medal posthumously. He remains on duty on the USS Arizona. Homer is commemorated on the USS Arizona Memorial and the Memorial Tablets of the Missing, National Memorial Cemetery of the Pacific, Honolulu, Hawaii. He was survived by his Father, Mr. David Thomas Hopkins, 1294 Marquette Avenue, Muskegon, Michigan.[357]

---

[356] Henry Vernon Homer, Photo and information provided by family member, J. V. Graves.
[357] Homer David Hopkins, Photo provided by the Muskegon County World War II Veteran Project.

Horn, Melvin Freeland Fireman, Third Class, Serial No: 279 73 68, US Navy. Melvin was born March 31, 1916 in Delaware County, Ohio to William and Daisy Leona (Evans) Horn. He graduated from Sunbury High School in 1934 and enlisted in the US Navy on October 7, 1940 in Cincinnati, Ohio and completed his basic training at the Naval Training Station in Great Lakes, Illinois. Melvin reported for duty on the USS Arizona on December 9, 1940. He was killed in action on December 7, 1941 at Pearl Harbor, Hawaii. Melvin was awarded the American Defense Service Medal, World War II Victory Medal and Purple Heart Medal posthumously. His remains were recovered and he was buried in Plot A, Row 0, Grave 483, National Memorial Cemetery of the Pacific, Honolulu, Hawaii. Melvin is commemorated on the USS Arizona Memorial. He was survived by his Sister, Mrs. Pearl Nichols, RFD, Croton, Ohio and four brothers, Bert of Galena, Jim of Mt. Vernon, Ed of Ft. Bragg, NC and Alvin of Los Angeles, CA.[358]

Horrell, Harvey Howard Signalman, First Class, Serial No: 261 65 16, US Navy. Harvey was born on June 6, 1911 in Pender County, North Carolina to Jasper Ann and Maggie Jane (Horne) Horrell. He enlisted in the US Navy in 1928 and reported for duty on the USS Arizona on June 7, 1941. Harvey was killed in action on December 7, 1941 at Pearl Harbor, Hawaii. He was awarded the American Defense Service Medal, World War II Victory Medal and Purple Heart Medal posthumously. Harvey remains on duty on the USS Arizona. He is commemorated on the USS Arizona Memorial and the Memorial Tablets of the Missing, National Memorial Cemetery of the Pacific, Honolulu, Hawaii and the Haw Bluff Baptist Church Cemetery, Kelly, North Carolina. Harvey was survived by his Mother, Mrs. Maggie J. Horrell, 914 North 4th Street, Wilmington, North Carolina and two brothers.

Horrocks, James William Chief Gunner's Mate, Serial No: 256 15 24, US Navy. James was born in 1911 in Missouri the son of Samuel and Claire Horrocks. He re-enlisted in the US Navy on December 4, 1936. James served on the USS Arizona from May 8, 1933 until he was killed in action on December 7, 1941 at Pearl Harbor, Hawaii. He had served in the Navy for 19 years. He was awarded the American Defense Service Medal, World War II Victory Medal and Purple Heart Medal posthumously. James remains on duty on the USS Arizona. He is commemorated on the USS Arizona Memorial and the Memorial Tablets of the Missing, National Memorial Cemetery of the Pacific, Honolulu, Hawaii. James was survived by his Wife, Mrs. Virginia Mary Ellen Horrocks, 536 Elm Street, Nogales, Arizona.

Hosler, John Emmet Seaman, First Class, Serial No: 279 73 71, US Navy. John was born July 3, 1922 in Fairfield County, Ohio, the son of Harry E. and Lota May Hosler. He enlisted in the US Navy on October 7, 1940 in Cincinnati, Ohio and completed his basic training at the Naval Training Station in Great Lakes, Illinois. John reported for duty on the USS Arizona on December 9, 1940. He was killed in action on December 7, 1941 at Pearl Harbor, Hawaii. John was awarded the American Defense Service Medal, World War II Victory Medal and Purple Heart Medal posthumously. He remains on duty on the USS Arizona. John is commemorated on the USS Arizona Memorial and the Memorial Tablets of the Missing, National Memorial Cemetery of the Pacific, Honolulu, Hawaii. He was survived by his Mother, Mrs. Lota May Hosler, 209 South Grand Avenue, Columbus, Ohio.

---

[358] Melvin Freeland Horn, Photo provided by family member, James Payne.

House, Clem Raymond Chief Water Tender (PA), Serial No: 336 15 27, US Navy. Clem was born August 14, 1902 in Missouri to John H. and Frances A. House. He served on the USS Arizona from June 16, 1925 until he was killed in action on December 7, 1941 at Pearl Harbor, Hawaii. He was awarded the American Defense Service Medal, World War II Victory Medal and Purple Heart Medal posthumously. Clem remains on duty on the USS Arizona. He is commemorated on the USS Arizona Memorial and the Memorial Tablets of the Missing, National Memorial Cemetery of the Pacific, Honolulu, Hawaii. Clem was survived by his Wife, Mrs. Audry House, 1541 East 67th Street, Long Beach, California.

Housel, John James Storekeeper, First Class, Serial No: 336 72 62, US Navy. John was born January 9, 1911 in Missouri, the son of Eddie and Maude Housel. He enlisted in the Navy on March 16, 1932 and completed his basic training at the Naval Training Station in Great Lakes, Illinois. John served on the USS Arizona from July 28, 1932 until he was killed in action on December 7, 1941 at Pearl Harbor, Hawaii. He was awarded the American Defense Service Medal, World War II Victory Medal and Purple Heart Medal posthumously. John remains on duty on the USS Arizona. He is commemorated on the USS Arizona Memorial and the Memorial Tablets of the Missing, National Memorial Cemetery of the Pacific, Honolulu, Hawaii. John was survived by his Mother, Mrs. Maude Housel, 215 West 3rd Street, Sedalia, Missouri.[359]

Howard, Elmo Seaman, First Class, Serial No: 287 44 17, US Navy. Elmo was born in March 20, 1921 in Woodford County, Kentucky, the son of John and Lena Howard. *His family farmed not only their own farm, but two adjacent farms. Elmo got heat stroke working one summer and missed a year of school. He graduated from Versailles High School on June 4, 1940. Elmo delayed his enlistment in order to help on the farm that summer after graduation. He told his mother that when he got out of the Navy he would go to college.* Elmo enlisted in the US Navy on September 4, 1940 in Louisville, Kentucky and completed his basic training at the Naval Training Station in Great Lakes, Illinois. He reported for duty on the USS Arizona on November 10, 1940. Elmo was killed in action on December 7, 1941 at Pearl Harbor, Hawaii. He was awarded the American Defense Service Medal, World War II Victory Medal and Purple Heart Medal posthumously. Elmo remains on duty on the USS Arizona. He is commemorated on the USS Arizona Memorial and the Memorial Tablets of the Missing, National Memorial Cemetery of the Pacific, Honolulu, Hawaii. *When Elmo's parents heard the news about Pearl Harbor they knew they had two sons serving there. Elmo was on the Arizona and the other son had applied for a transfer to the Arizona, but they didn't know if the transfer had gone through. It wasn't until January that they heard from the surviving son. They received a telegram on December 20, 1941 telling them that Elmo was Missing in Action. On January 26, 1942, they received a telegram declaring him officially dead.* He was survived by his Parents, Mr. and Mrs. John Wallace Howard, Route 1, Wilmore, Kentucky and 2 sisters and 6 brothers. *After the attack, Elmo's brother, John Allen Howard was assigned to a diving group. After two dives on the Arizona, John refused to go back down stating*

---

[359] John James Housel, Photo and information provided by the Smith Cotton's World War II Memorial.

that he did not want to find his brother down there. He was assigned to another ship and they left Pearl Harbor. To this day, he never speaks about Elmo or the attack on Pearl Harbor.[360]

Howard, Rolan George Gunner's Mate, Third Class, Serial No: 321 38 50, US Navy. Rolan was born March 16, 1914 in Austin, Minnesota. He enlisted in the US Navy on January 24, 1940 in Mason City, Iowa and completed his basic training at the Naval Training Station in Great Lakes, Illinois. He reported for duty on the USS Arizona on March 26, 1940. Rolan was killed in action on December 7, 1941 at Pearl Harbor, Hawaii. He was awarded the American Defense Service Medal, World War II Victory Medal and Purple Heart Medal posthumously. Rolan remains on duty on the USS Arizona. He is commemorated on the USS Arizona Memorial and the Memorial Tablets of the Missing, National Memorial Cemetery of the Pacific, Honolulu, Hawaii. Rolan was survived by his Father, Mr. Harry Rhoads Howard, 605 North Kenwood Avenue, Austin, Minnesota.[361]

Howatt, John Paul Ensign, Serial No. 0-06869, US Navy. John was born on August 25, 1917 in Beijing, China. He was commissioned officer in the US Navy June 6, 1940 serving on the USS Arizona as Radio Officer, Division C on December 7, 1941 when the Japanese attacked Pearl Harbor. His battle station was the Communication Office. He later served on board the USS California, USS Thompson, USS Winslow, USS Jeffers and the USS Dashell. He retired from the Navy in 1958. John died on January 11, 1987 in St. Petersburg, Florida of Lung Cancer and his ashes were scattered in the Gulf of Mexico.[362]

Howe, Darrell Robert Seaman, Second Class, Serial No: 393 54 07, US Navy. Darrell was born in 1921, son of Albert M. and Laura Howe. He enlisted in the US Navy on April 22, 1941 in Portland, Oregon and completed his basic training at the Naval Training Station in San Diego, California. Darrell reported for duty on the USS Arizona on July 13, 1941. He was killed in action on December 7, 1941 at Pearl Harbor. Darrell was awarded the American Defense Service Medal, World War II Victory Medal and Purple Heart Medal posthumously. He remains on duty on the USS Arizona. Darrell is commemorated on the USS Arizona Memorial and the Memorial Tablets of the Missing, National Memorial Cemetery of the Pacific, Honolulu, Hawaii. He was survived by his Father, Mr. Albert M. Howe, Box 663, Sweet Home, Oregon.

---

[360] Elmo Howard, Photo and information provided by family member, Cathy Giles.
[361] Rolan George Howard, Photo from the Globe Gazette, Mason City, Cerro Gordo County, Iowa, Friday, March 6, 1942, Page 14.
[362] John Paul Howatt, Photo from the Lucky Bag Yearbook, United States Naval Academy, Annapolis, MD, Class of 1940.

Howell, Leroy (Edgar Leroyce)   Coxswain, Serial No: 291 62 34, US Navy. Leroy was born November 19, 1921, the son of Frederick M. and Elizabeth Howell. *He attended the Gas City schools but did not graduate from high school. He spent a year with his uncle at Pontiac, IL where he was learning electrical work. When the work became too heavy, he returned to Gas City and stayed with his sister, Mrs. Lester Kellogg. He was a member of the National Guard while in Illinois, and his father obtained his discharge from the Guard so that he could enlist in the navy, which had always been his ambition. He tried three times before he was accepted by the navy, as at that time they had more applicants than they could accept. In the meantime, he spent three months in the CCC camp near Fort Wayne.* He finally was accepted by the navy on March 26, 1940 in Indianapolis, Indiana and completed his basic training at the Naval Training Station in Great Lakes, Illinois. Leroy reported for duty on the USS Arizona on July 12, 1940. Assigned Death #37, Leroy died on December 10, 1941 from 3rd degree burns received on December 7, 1941 at Pearl Harbor, Hawaii.[363] Leroy was awarded the American Defense Service Medal, World War II Victory Medal and Purple Heart Medal posthumously. Leroy's remains were sent home and he was buried in the Riverside Cemetery in Gas City, Indiana. He is commemorated on the USS Arizona Memorial and the Memorial Tablets of the Missing, National Memorial Cemetery of the Pacific, Honolulu, Hawaii. Leroy was survived by his Father, Mr. Frederick M. Howell, 107 South F Street, Gas City, Indiana, two brothers and four sisters. The Leroyce Howell VFW Post 6728 in Gas City, IN was named in his honor.[364]

Hubbard, Haywood, Jr.   Mess Attendant, Second Class, Serial No: 266 16 86, US Navy. Haywood was born November 29, 1921 in Virginia, the son of Haywood and Mary A. Hubbard. He enlisted in the US Navy on August 6, 1940 in Richmond, Virginia and completed his basic training at the Naval Training Station in Great Lakes, Illinois. Haywood reported for duty on the USS Arizona on November 10, 1940. He was killed in action on December 7, 1941 at Pearl Harbor, Hawaii. Haywood was awarded the American Defense Service Medal, World War II Victory Medal and Purple Heart Medal posthumously. He remains on duty on the USS Arizona. Haywood is commemorated on the USS Arizona Memorial and the Memorial Tablets of the Missing, National Memorial Cemetery of the Pacific, Honolulu, Hawaii. He was survived by his Father, Mr. Haywood Hubbard, Sr., Route 3, Lynchburg, Virginia.

Huffman, Clyde Franklin   Fireman, First Class, Serial No: 279 72 56, US Navy. Clyde was born September 4, 1918 in Hocking County, Ohio to Lorn Delno and Ella Jane Huffman. He enlisted in the US Navy on September 3, 1940 in Cincinnati, Ohio and completed his basic training at the Naval Training Station in Norfolk, Virginia. Clyde reported for duty on the USS Arizona on December 4, 1940. He was killed in action on December 7, 1941 at Pearl Harbor, Hawaii. Clyde was awarded the American Defense Service Medal, World War II Victory Medal and Purple Heart Medal posthumously. He remains on duty on the USS Arizona. Clyde is commemorated on the USS Arizona Memorial and the Memorial Tablets of the Missing, National Memorial Cemetery of the

---

[363] Leroy Howell, Report of Changes of the USS Arizona for the month ending 31st day of December, 1941, page 68, line 28.
[364] Leroy Howell, Photo and information provided by Jerry L. Long, Leroyce Howell VFW Post 6728 in Gas City, IN.

Pacific, Honolulu, Hawaii. He was survived by his Father, Mr. Lorn Delno Huffman, South Bloomingville, Ohio.[365]

Hughes, Bernard Thomas Musician, Second Class, Serial No: 243 88 64, US Navy. Bernard was born October 1, 1922, the son of Thomas Philip and Gertrude G. Hughes. He enlisted in the US Navy on February 26, 1941 and attended the Navy School of Music in Washington, DC graduating on May 23, 1941 as a member of the USS Arizona Band. Bernard reported for duty on the USS Arizona on June 17, 1941. He was killed in action on December 7, 1941 at Pearl Harbor, Hawaii. Bernard's battle station for all of the band members was in the black powder room passing ammunition to the Arizona's gunners during the attack. None of the band members survived the explosion. He was awarded the American Defense Service Medal, World War II Victory Medal and Purple Heart Medal posthumously. Bernard remains on duty on the USS Arizona. He is commemorated on the USS Arizona Memorial and the Memorial Tablets of the Missing, National Memorial Cemetery of the Pacific, Honolulu, Hawaii. Bernard was survived by his Father, Mr. Thomas Philip Hughes, 103 Cooper Street, Athens, Pennsylvania.[366]

Hughes, James Curtis Seaman, First Class, Serial No. 295 55 29, US Navy. James was born on August 23, 1917 in Alabama to James Nelson and Beulah Mae (Rice) Hughes. He enlisted in the US Navy December 16, 1939 in Nashville, Tennessee and reported for duty on the USS Arizona March 29, 1940. James was serving on the USS Arizona on December 7, 1941 when the Japanese attacked Pearl Harbor. After the attack, James was transferred to the USS Patterson (DD-392) for duty. James died on March 10, 1995 and is buried in Green Haven Memorial Gardens, Henagar, Alabama.

Hughes, Lewis Burton, Jr. Seaman, First Class, Serial No: 272 41 63, US Navy. Lewis was born in 1921 in Northport, Alabama to Lewis B. and Alabama J. Hughes. He enlisted in the US Navy on October 5, 1940 in Birmingham, Alabama and completed his basic training at the Naval Training Station in Norfolk, Virginia. He reported for duty on the USS Arizona on December 4, 1940. Lewis was killed in action on December 7, 1941 at Pearl Harbor, Hawaii. He was awarded the American Defense Service Medal, World War II Victory Medal and Purple Heart Medal posthumously. Lewis remains on duty on the USS Arizona. He is commemorated on the USS Arizona Memorial and the Memorial Tablets of the Missing, National Memorial Cemetery of the Pacific, Honolulu, Hawaii. Lewis was survived by his Father, Mr. Lewis Burton Hughes, Sr., P.O. Box 932, Tuscaloosa, Alabama.

Hughey, James Clynton Seaman, First Class, Serial No: 272 41 82, US Navy. James was born July 30, 1922 in Tennessee. He enlisted in the US Navy on October 5, 1940 in Birmingham, Alabama and completed his basic training at the Naval Training Station in Norfolk, Virginia. James reported for duty on the USS Arizona December 4, 1940. Assigned death #424, James died on December 10, 1941 from 3rd degree burns he received on December 7, 1941 at

---

[365] Clyde Franklin Huffman, Photo from The Logan Daily News, Logan, Ohio, Wedensday, December 31, 1941, Page 1.

[366] Bernard Thomas Hughes, Photo from USS Arizona's Last Band by Molly Kent. By permission of the author. For more information about this book, go to www.USSARIZONASLASTBAND.com.

Pearl Harbor, Hawaii.[367] He was awarded the American Defense Service Medal, World War II Victory Medal and Purple Heart Medal posthumously. His remains were interred in Nuuanu Cemetery, Honolulu, Hawaii. He is commemorated on the USS Arizona Memorial and the Memorial Tablets of the Missing, National Memorial Cemetery of the Pacific, Honolulu, Hawaii. James was survived by his Father, Mr. James Samuel Hughey, General Delivery, Waverly, Tennessee.

Huie, Doyne Conley Hospital Apprentice, First Class, Serial No: 337 32 73, US Navy. Doyne was born on October 24, 1921 in Gideon, Missouri to Walter McKinley and Nancy Bramlet (Moore) Huie. He enlisted in the US Navy on July 2, 1940 in St. Louis, Missouri and reported for duty on the USS Arizona on November 3, 1941. Doyne was killed in action on December 7, 1941 at Pearl Harbor, Hawaii. He was awarded the American Defense Service Medal, World War II Victory Medal and Purple Heart Medal posthumously. Doyne's remains were recovered and he was returned home for burial in Section 31, Site 2284, Springfield National Cemetery, Springfield, Missouri. He is commemorated on the USS Arizona Memorial. Doyne was survived by his Father, Mr. Walter McKinley Huie, Box 458, Gideon, Missouri.

Hull, Lester De Lance Seaman, First Class, Serial No. 356 34 82, US Navy. Lester was born on May 23, 1921 in Yale, Oklahoma the son of Isaac Solomon and Nora D. (Gumm) Hull. He enlisted in the US Navy August 9, 1940 in Dallas, Texas and completed his basic training at the Naval Training Station in San Diego, California. He reported for duty on the USS Arizona October 14, 1940. Lester was serving on the USS Arizona on December 7, 1941 when the Japanese attacked Pearl Harbor. After the attack, Lester was transferred to the USS Chester for duty. Lester died on May 10, 1991 in Arlington, Texas.

Hunter, Robert Fredrick Seaman, First Class, Serial No: 283 45 34, US Navy. Robert was born in about 1922 in Ohio. He enlisted in the US Navy on November 27, 1940 in Cleveland, Ohio and reported for duty on the USS Arizona on January 18, 1941. He was killed in action on December 7, 1941 at Pearl Harbor, Hawaii. Robert was awarded the American Defense Service Medal, World War II Victory Medal and Purple Heart Medal posthumously. He remains on duty on the USS Arizona. Robert is commemorated on the USS Arizona Memorial and the Memorial Tablets of the Missing, National Memorial Cemetery of the Pacific, Honolulu, Hawaii. He was survived by his Mother, Mrs. Florence Faith Smith, 2106 Washington Street, Toledo, Ohio.

Huntington, Henry Louis Seaman, Second Class, Serial No: 382 37 63, US Navy. Henry was born in about 1923 in Idaho, the son of Frank Myron and Cora Belle (Heard) Huntington. He enlisted in the US Navy on January 27, 1941 in Los Angeles, California and completed his basic training at the Naval Training Station in San Diego, California. Henry reported for duty on the USS Arizona on April 27, 1941. He was killed in action on December 7, 1941 at Pearl Harbor, Hawaii. Henry was awarded the American Defense Service Medal, World War II Victory Medal and Purple Heart Medal posthumously. He remains on duty on the USS Arizona. Henry is commemorated on the USS Arizona Memorial and the Memorial Tablets of the Missing, National

[367] Report of Changes of the USS Arizona for the month ending 31st day of December, 1941, page 69, line 4, James Clynton Hughey.

223

Memorial Cemetery of the Pacific, Honolulu, Hawaii. He was survived by his Father, Mr. Frank Huntington, 9th and Sterling, Route 2, San Bernardino, California.[368]

Hurd, Willard Hardy   Mess Attendant, Second Class, Serial No: 295 73 23. US Navy. Willard was born August 7, 1922 in Tennessee, the son of Charles and Beulah Mae (Duckett) Hurd. He enlisted in the US Navy on August 20, 1940 in Nashville, Tennessee and completed his basic training at the Naval Training Station in Norfolk, Virginia. Willard reported for duty on the USS Arizona on November 28, 1940. He was killed in action on December 7, 1941 at Pearl Harbor, Hawaii. Willard was awarded the American Defense Service Medal, World War II Victory Medal and Purple Heart Medal posthumously. He remains on duty on the USS Arizona. Willard is commemorated on the USS Arizona Memorial and the Memorial Tablets of the Missing, National Memorial Cemetery of the Pacific, Honolulu, Hawaii. He was survived by his Mother, Mrs. Beulah Mae Hurd, Collierville, Tennessee.

Hurley, Wendell Ray   Musician, Second Class, Serial No: 291 66 49, US Navy. Wendell was born September 12, 1919 in Indiana to Raymond and Edna Hazel (Landrum) Hurley. He enlisted in the US Navy on November 14, 1940 and attended the Navy School of Music in Washington, DC graduating on May 23, 1941 as a member of the USS Arizona Band. He reported for duty on the USS Arizona June 17, 1941. Wendell was killed in action on December 7, 1941 at Pearl Harbor, Hawaii. The battle station for all of the band members was in the black powder room passing ammunition to the Arizona's gunners during the attack. None of the band members survived the explosion. He was awarded the American Defense Service Medal, World War II Victory Medal and Purple Heart Medal posthumously. Wendell remains on duty on the USS Arizona. He is commemorated on the USS Arizona Memorial and the Memorial Tablets of the Missing, National Memorial Cemetery of the Pacific, Honolulu, Hawaii. Wendell was survived by his Father, Mr. Raymond Hurley, 3636 South Gallatin Street, Marion, Indiana.[369]

Hurst, Milton Thomas   Aviation Machinist's Mate, Third Class, Serial No. 234 22 44, US Navy. Milton was born September 10, 1920 in North East, Pennsylvania, the eldest son of Arthur and Florence Hurst. He enlisted in the US Navy December 13, 1940 in Buffalo, New York and reported for duty on the USS Arizona October 1, 1940. He was serving on the Arizona December 7, 1941 when the Japanese attacked Pearl Harbor. His official statement:

"When the attack on Pearl Harbor began on December 7, 1941, I was on the quarter deck smoking a cigarette. The first bit of excitement I noticed was the Officer-of-the-Deck and Junior O.D. was standing near the Admiral's gangway; they were pointing and looking west toward Ford Island.

Out of curiosity, I went over to the life line to see what everyone was looking at. I saw a large column of smoke going up into the air.

At this time the Officer of the Deck told the boatswain's mate of the watch to sound general alarm, which he did on the double. At the time I thought there was a fire on one of the ships or on the Air Station so I went up into #5 casemate to see what was going on.

---

[368] Henry Louis Huntington, Photo from The San Bernardino County Sun, San Bernardino, California, Thursday, December 25, 1941, Page 13.
[369] Wendell Ray Hurley, Photo from USS Arizona's Last Band by Molly Kent. By permission of the author. For more information about this book, go to www.USSARIZONASLASTBAND.com.

It was now that the first word was said about an air attack and then everyone seemed to think it was the Army having a mock attack. I watched several planes sweep over Ford Island and one went over our fantail and I saw the red spot on the wing.

Our guns then opened up and it first struck me we were being attacked. I then went back on the quarter deck and the ward was passed to go below. Everyone in the vicinity started below and just as I reached the armor deck general quarters was sounded.

My general quarters station was not down there so I started back up the ladder which was made a little difficult because a marine officer was fighting his way below. When I reached the main deck there was a fire in the Executive Officers office.

Lane, an aviation radioman, and Burns our yeoman and I started to get a hose to fight the fire. At this time a fire broke out on the quarter deck and we dragged the hose out there. Lane screwed the nozzle on while I went to turn on the water at the plug forward of #3 turret.

A bomb then hit somewhere forward of me and knocked me down. I finished turning on the water and started out where Lane was to help him but he was no longer there.

I noticed there was no water coming out of the nozzle so I started to go forward and saw many marines and sailors laying about the deck badly burned. One I tried to help but he was pretty well blown up.

Someone yelled "get out of here" so I picked up someone and started to carry him off. Someone said to let him go, he was dead. It was pretty hot then and several men were running around badly burned so with a couple of other fellows, one of whom was Burns, I helped to get these men over to the life line and told them to go over the side.

I then went over to the blister and jumped into the water. I was near a mooring key so I went under it and took off my pants and socks. My shoes got separated some place back.

From there I swam to the motor launch tied up along side of the key. Someone helped me out onto the key, then we were all busy for sometime helping other ones out and putting the injured into the launch. The launch was going to the Solace, so when it started pulling away I dove over the side and started to swim to Ford Island. It was the furthest and fastest swim I ever made.

Upon reaching land we were directed to the bomb shelter where I remained until taken over to the Receiving Barracks where I stayed until coming to Ford Island."[370]

After the attack, Milton was transferred to the Naval Air Station at Pearl Harbor and later served aboard the naval carriers, USS Ticonderoga, USS Valley Forge and the USS America. Milton retired from the Navy after 31 years service in 1970 as a Lieutenant Commander. He passed away on October 16, 2010 after a brief illness and was buried at the Riverside Memorial Park in Jacksonville, Florida with full military honors.

---

[370] Confidential Statement of Milton Thomas Hurst, Aviation Machinist's Mate, Third Class, U.S. Navy, USS Arizona regarding the attack on Pearl Harbor, T. H., December 7, 1941.

Hutchins, Edward Francis Lieutenant, Serial No. 0-04009, US Navy Edward was Born July 1, 1907 in Albany, New York the son of Walter Luce Hutchins and Clara H. (Barmore) Hutchins. He commissioned in the US Navy on June 2, 1937 and reported for duty on the USS Arizona where he was serving as Aide & Flag Secretary on December 7, 1941 when the Japanese attacked Pearl Harbor. He retired from the Navy as a Captain in 1955. Edward died May 17, 1979 in Santa Monica, California.[371]

Huval, Ivan Joseph Seaman, First Class, Serial No: 274 48 56, US Navy. Ivan was born in 1922 in Louisiana, the son of Alfred and Stella Marie (Guidry) Huval. He enlisted in the US Navy on July 31, 1940 in New Orleans, Louisiana and completed his basic training at the Naval Training Station in San Diego, California. Ivan reported for duty on the USS Arizona on October 8, 1940. He was killed in action on December 7, 1941 at Pearl Harbor, Hawaii. Ivan was awarded the American Defense Service Medal, World War II Victory Medal and Purple Heart Medal posthumously. He remains on duty on the USS Arizona. Ivan is commemorated on the USS Arizona Memorial and the Memorial Tablets of the Missing, National Memorial Cemetery of the Pacific, Honolulu, Hawaii. He was survived by his Father, Mr. Alfred Huval, Route 1, Folsom, Louisiana.

Huys, Arthur Albert Seaman, First Class, Serial No: 291 65 67, US Navy. Arthur was born December 3, 1916 in Mishawaka, Indiana the only son of Hector Huys and Margaret Barbara DeVlieger. *His parents divorced when he was quite young and his mother and grandmother helped to raise him. Arthur lost a portion of his right pinkie finger while working at the Ball Factory in Mishawaka. He was also employed by the General Tire and Rubber Company and at the American Rock Wool plant before he enlisted in the US Navy on October 8, 1940 in Indianapolis, Indiana.* Arthur completed his basic training at the Naval Training Station in Great Lakes, Illinois. He reported for duty on the USS Arizona on December 9, 1940. Assigned death #125, Arthur died on December 10, 1941 from wounds received in action on December 7, 1941 at Pearl Harbor, Hawaii.[372] *His mother, Margaret was completely devastated by his death and spent much of her life in mourning.* He was awarded the American Defense Service Medal, World War II Victory Medal and Purple Heart Medal posthumously. Arthur's remains were shipped home and buried in the Oakridge Cemetery, Goshen, Indiana. Arthur is commemorated on the USS Arizona Memorial and the Memorial Tablets of the Missing, National Memorial Cemetery of the Pacific, Honolulu, Hawaii. He was survived by his Mother, Mrs. Margaret Barbara DeVlieger, Box 54, Wabash, Indiana. The Lumaree – Huys VFW Post 286 in Wabash, Indiana was named in his honor.[373]

---

[371] Edward Francis Hutchins, Photo from Lucky Bag Yearbook, United States Naval Academy, Annapolis, MD, Class of 1937

[372] Arthur Albert Huys, Report of Changes of the USS Arizona for the month ending 31st day of December, 1941, page 69, line 13.

[373] Arthur Albert Huys, Photo and information provided by the Lumaree – Huys VFW Post 286, Wabash, Indiana.

Huzar, Peter Water Tender, First Class, Serial No. 207 18 69, US Navy. Peter was born in about 1915 in New York to Nickolas and Martha Huzar. He enlisted in the US Navy August 25, 1936 in New Haven, Connecticut and reported for duty on the USS Arizona February 3, 1937. Peter was serving on the USS Arizona on December 7, 1941 when the Japanese attacked Pearl Harbor. After the attack, Peter was transferred to the USS Nevada (BB-36) for duty where he served until 1945.

Hyde, William Hughes Coxswain, Serial No: 337 15 29, US Navy. William was born April 1, 1922 to George Albert and Elna Hughes. He enlisted in the US Navy on June 12, 1939 in St. Louis, Missouri and completed his basic training at the Naval Training Station in San Diego, California. He reported for duty on the USS Arizona on September 11, 1939. William was killed in action on December 7, 1941 at Pearl Harbor, Hawaii. He was awarded the American Defense Service Medal, World War II Victory Medal and Purple Heart Medal posthumously. William remains on duty on the USS Arizona. He is commemorated on the USS Arizona Memorial and the Memorial Tablets of the Missing, National Memorial Cemetery of the Pacific, Honolulu, Hawaii and Quitman Methodist Church Cemetery, Cleburne County, Arkansas. William was survived by his Father, Mr. George Albert Hyde, 6521 Michigan Avenue, St. Louis, Missouri.[374]

Hyslope, Charles Edward Fireman, First Class, Serial No. 321 23 57, US Navy. Charles was born June 11, 1919 in Indiana, Iowa, the son of Wilbur H. and Bessie F. (Talbott) Hyslope. He enlisted in the US Navy on February 2, 1938 in Des Moines, Iowa and completed his basic training at the Naval Training Station in Great Lakes, Illinois. Charles reported for duty on the USS Arizona June 4, 1938. He was serving on December 7, 1941 when the Japanese attacked Pearl Harbor. After the attack, Charles was transferred to salvage duty on the USS Utah. He was later transferred to the USS Argonne. On February 24, 1942, Charles was tried by Summary Court Martial on board the USS Argonne (AG-31). In August 1942, Charles was transferred to the USS Wharton for transport to the West Coast for assignment. He died June 21, 1955 and is buried in the Glendale Cemetery, Des Moines, Iowa.

Iak, Joseph Claude Yeoman, Third Class, Serial No: 223 61 68, US Navy. Joseph was born in May of 1919 in Brooklyn, New York to Harold Joseph and Margaret Bessie (Smith) Iak. He and his older brother enlisted together. Joseph enlisted in the US Navy on December 13, 1939 in New York, New York and reported for duty on the USS Arizona on March 1, 1940. His older brother enlisted in the US Army, serving on the east coast. Joseph was killed in action on December 7, 1941 at Pearl Harbor, Hawaii. *When his older brother found out that his little brother went down with the Arizona, he asked for and got a transfer to a unit assigned to fight in the Pacific against the Japanese.* He was awarded the American Defense Service Medal, World War II Victory Medal and Purple Heart Medal posthumously. Joseph remains on duty on the USS Arizona. He is commemorated on the USS Arizona Memorial and the Memorial Tablets of the Missing, National Memorial

---

[374] William Hughes Hyde, Photo from St. Louis Post-Dispatch, St. Louis, Missouri, Reported Missing, William H. Hyde, Friday, December 26, 1941, Page 8A.

Cemetery of the Pacific, Honolulu, Hawaii. Joseph was survived by his Father, Mr. Harold Joseph Iak, 316-1/4 West 47th Street, Los Angeles, California.[375]

Ibbotson, Howard "Sandy" Burt Fireman, First Class, Serial No: 382 07 98, US Navy. Howard was born March 8, 1921 at Fullerton, California the only son of Burton J. and Jessie (De Armoun) Ibbotson. Sandy quit high school just before graduation and joined the Navy on November 16, 1938 in Los Angeles, California. He completed his basic training at the Naval Training Station in San Diego, California. Sandy reported for duty on the USS Arizona on June 10, 1939. *His cousin, Donald De Armoun joined shortly after. Sandy and his cousin, Donald were both serving on the USS Arizona and were killed in action on December 7, 1941 at Pearl Harbor, Hawaii.* He was awarded the American Defense Service Medal, World War II Victory Medal and Purple Heart Medal posthumously. Sandy remains on duty on the USS Arizona. He is commemorated on the USS Arizona Memorial and the Memorial Tablets of the Missing, National Memorial Cemetery of the Pacific, Honolulu, Hawaii. Sandy was survived by his Parents, Mr. Burton J. Ibbotson and Mrs. Jessie (De Armoun) Ibbotson, Bass Lake, California. His cousin, Donald DeArmoun was killed in action on board the USS Arizona.[376]

Ingalls, Richard Fitch Ship's Cook, Third Class, Serial No: 238 68 27, US Navy. Richard was born October 2, 1918, the son of Raymond and Verna (Wood) Ingalls. He enlisted in the US Navy on September 17, 1940 in Albany, New York and completed his basic training at the Naval Training Station in Norfolk, Virginia. Richard reported for duty on the USS Arizona on January 4, 1941. He was killed in action on December 7, 1941 at Pearl Harbor, Hawaii. Richard was awarded the American Defense Service Medal, World War II Victory Medal and Purple Heart Medal posthumously. He remains on duty on the USS Arizona. Richard is commemorated on the USS Arizona Memorial and the Memorial Tablets of the Missing, National Memorial Cemetery of the Pacific, Honolulu, Hawaii. He was survived by his Father, Mr. Raymond F. Ingalls, 19 Franklin Avenue, Clinton, New York. His brother, Theodore was also killed in action on the Arizona. The Helmuth-Ingalls American Legion Post 232 in Clinton, New York was named in both the brothers' names.[377]

---

[375] Joseph Claude Iak, Information provided by family member, Jim Iak, Photo from the 1937 Washington High School Yearbook, Washington, New Jersey.

[376] Howard "Sandy" Burt Ibbotson, Photo and information provided by family member, Betty McPherson.

[377] Richard Fitch Ingalls, Photo courtesy of the Helmuth-Ingalls American Legion Post 232, Clinton, New York.

Ingalls, Theodore A. Ship's Cook, Third Class, Serial No: 238 63 06, US Navy. Theodore was born December 7, 1921, the son of Raymond and Verna (Wood) Ingalls. He enlisted in the US Navy on December 11, 1939 in Albany, New York and reported for duty on the USS Arizona on March 1, 1940. Theodore was killed in action on December 7, 1941 at Pearl Harbor, Hawaii. He was awarded the American Defense Service Medal, World War II Victory Medal and Purple Heart Medal posthumously. Theodore remains on duty on the USS Arizona. He is commemorated on the USS Arizona Memorial and the Memorial Tablets of the Missing, National Memorial Cemetery of the Pacific, Honolulu, Hawaii. Theodore was survived by his Father, Mr. Raymond F. Ingalls, 19 Franklin Avenue, Clinton, New York. His Brother, Richard was serving on the Arizona and was lost. The Helmuth-Ingalls American Legion Post 232 in Clinton, New York was named in both the brothers' names.[378]

Ingraham, David Archie Fire Controlman, Third Class, Serial No: 342 19 02, US Navy. David was born February 1, 1922 in Topeka, Kansas to Earl Eugene and Ruth A. Ingraham. F*or his sister, Dorothy, David remains "King David" the family daredevil, the youngster who wanted to contribute to the family income and the brother, forever young, who never got a shot at life. Dorothy and David were the youngest of eight brothers and sisters.* He quit high school to enlist in the US Navy on February 2, 1940 in Kansas City, Missouri and completed his basic training at the Naval Training Station in Great Lakes, Illinois. David reported for duty on the USS Arizona on July 12, 1940. He was killed in action on December 7, 1941 at Pearl Harbor, Hawaii. David was awarded the American Defense Service Medal, World War II Victory Medal and Purple Heart Medal posthumously. He remains on duty on the USS Arizona. David is commemorated on the USS Arizona Memorial and the Memorial Tablets of the Missing, National Memorial Cemetery of the Pacific, Honolulu, Hawaii. He was survived by his Father, Mr. Earl Eugene Ingraham, 1210 Harrison Street, Topeka, Kansas.[379]

Inselman, Donald Seaman, First Class, 4th Division, Serial No. 372 14 39, US Navy. Donald was born on December 24, 1915 in Litchfield, Minnesota, the son of Ellis Kelly and Emma (Hunt) Inselman. He enlisted in the US Navy April 10, 1940 in Denver, Colorado and completed his basic training at the Naval Training Station in San Diego, California. He reported for duty on the USS Arizona July 2, 1940. Donald was serving on the USS Arizona on December 7, 1941 when the Japanese attacked Pearl Harbor. He survived the sinking by escaping through a darkened turret and finding his way to a nearby repair ship. After the attack, Donald was transferred to the USS Chester for duty. He served until April 10, 1946. Donald died on January 12, 1999 in Commerce City, Colorado.[380]

---

[378] Theodore A. Ingalls, Photo courtesy of the Helmuth-Ingalls American Legion Post 232, Clinton, New York.

[379] David Archie Ingraham, Story from "A Sister Still Grieves, Attack: Topekan who lost brother in attack doesn't believe in closure" by Steve Fry, The Topeka Capital-Journal, Topeka, Kansas, Friday, December 7, 2001.

[380] Donald Inselman, survival story from the History Colorado, WWII Manuscript Collection.

Isham, Orville Adalbert   Chief Gunner's Mate, Serial No: 393 06 30, US Navy. Orville was born on November 11, 1911 in Oklahoma, the son of John and Mary Alice (Beck) Isham. He re-enlisted in the US Navy on July 19, 1938. Orville served on the USS Arizona from December 19, 1936 until he was killed in action on December 7, 1941 at Pearl Harbor, Hawaii. He was awarded the American Defense Service Medal, World War II Victory Medal and Purple Heart Medal posthumously. Orville remains on duty on the USS Arizona. He is commemorated on the USS Arizona Memorial and the Memorial Tablets of the Missing, National Memorial Cemetery of the Pacific, Honolulu, Hawaii. Orville was survived by his Wife, Mrs. Alice Agnes (Wickenberg) Isham, 1122 McCulley Street, Honolulu, Hawaii and son, James Isham.[381]

Isom, Luther James   Seaman, First Class, Serial No: 272 41 53, US Navy. Luther was born February 24, 1921 in Madison County, Alabama to John Claborn and Pearl Leona (Butner) Isom. He enlisted in the US Navy on October 5, 1940 in Birmingham, Alabama and completed his basic training at the Naval Training Station in Norfolk, Virginia. Luther reported for duty on the USS Arizona on December 4, 1940. Assigned death #59, Luther died on December 10, 1941 from wounds received in action on December 7, 1941 at Pearl Harbor, Hawaii.[382] He was awarded the American Defense Service Medal, World War II Victory Medal and Purple Heart Medal posthumously. Luther's remains were recovered and he was shipped home for burial in Block 33, Row 1, Maple Hill Cemetery, Huntsville, Alabama. He is commemorated on the USS Arizona Memorial and the Memorial Tablets of the Missing, National Memorial Cemetery of the Pacific, Honolulu, Hawaii. Luther was survived by his Mother, Mrs. Pearl Isom, 16 New Row, West Huntsville, Alabama. The Gentry-Isom VFW Post 2702 in Huntsville, Alabama was named in his honor and another.[383]

Iversen, Earl Henry   Seaman, Second Class, Serial No: 376 23 74, US Navy. Earl was born on April 21, 1920 in Mendocino County, California to Iver Henry and Erma Eileen (Ferguson) Iversen. He enlisted in the US Navy with his brother Norman on January 30, 1941 in San Francisco, California and completed his basic training at the Naval Training Station in San Diego, California. Earl reported for duty on the USS Arizona on April 27, 1941. He was killed in action on December 7, 1941 at Pearl Harbor, Hawaii. Earl was awarded the American Defense Service Medal, World War II Victory Medal and Purple Heart Medal posthumously. He remains on duty on the USS Arizona with his brother. Earl is commemorated on the USS Arizona Memorial and the Memorial Tablets of the Missing, National Memorial Cemetery of the Pacific, Honolulu, Hawaii and the Golden Gate National Cemetery, San Bruno, California. He was survived by his Father, Mr. Iver Henry Iversen, Route 2, Box 1355, Salinas, California. His Brother, Norman was also killed in action on board the USS Arizona.

---

[381] Orville Adalbert Isham, Photo provided by his ex-wife, Barbara Hargrove.
[382] Luther James Isom, Report of Changes of the USS Arizona for the month ending 31st day of December, 1941, Page 70, line 23.
[383] Luther James Isom, Photo provided by family member, Rejeana (Turner) Broderick.

Iversen, Norman Kenneth   Seaman, Second Class, Serial No: 376 23 73, US Navy. Norman was born on December 4, 1923 in Mendocino County, California to Iver Henry and Erma Eileen (Ferguson) Iversen. He enlisted in the US Navy with his brother Earl on January 30, 1941 in San Francisco, California and completed his basic training at the Naval Training Station in San Diego, California. Norman reported for duty on the USS Arizona on April 27, 1941. He was killed in action on December 7, 1941 at Pearl Harbor, Hawaii. Norman was awarded the American Defense Service Medal, World War II Victory Medal and Purple Heart Medal posthumously. He remains on duty on the USS Arizona with his brother. Norman is commemorated on the USS Arizona Memorial and the Memorial Tablets of the Missing, National Memorial Cemetery of the Pacific, Honolulu, Hawaii and the Golden Gate National Cemetery, San Bruno, California. He was survived by his Father, Mr. Iver Henry Iversen, Route 2, Box 1355, Salinas, California. His Brother, Earl was killed in action on board the USS Arizona.

Ivey, Charles Andrew, Jr.   Seaman, Second Class, Serial No: 382 29 39, US Navy. Charles was the son of Charles Andrew Ivey and Maggie (Mahaffey) Ivey. He enlisted in the US Navy on October 30, 1940 in Los Angeles, California and completed his basic training at the Naval Training Station in San Diego, California. He reported for duty on the USS Arizona on December 30, 1940. Charles was killed in action on December 7, 1941 at Pearl Harbor, Hawaii. He was awarded the American Defense Service Medal, World War II Victory Medal and Purple Heart Medal posthumously. Charles remains on duty on the USS Arizona. He is commemorated on the USS Arizona Memorial and the Memorial Tablets of the Missing, National Memorial Cemetery of the Pacific, Honolulu, Hawaii. Charles was survived by his Father, Mr. Charles A. Ivey, Sr., 151 West 126th Street, Los Angeles, California.

Jackson, David Paul, Jr.   Seaman, First Class, Serial No: 356 36 84, US Navy. David was born June 24, 1923 in Gainesville, Texas to David Paul Jackson, Sr. and May (Greene) Jackson. He enlisted in the US Navy on December 31, 1940 in Dallas, Texas and completed his basic training at the Naval Training Station in San Diego, California. He reported for duty on the USS Arizona on April 26, 1941. Assigned death #306, David died on December 10, 1941 from wounds received in action on December 7, 1941 at Pearl Harbor, Hawaii. He was awarded the American Defense Service Medal, World War II Victory Medal and Purple Heart Medal posthumously. The disposition of his body is unclear, it is possible he was buried in one of the unknown graves at the Punchbowl.[384] In 1947, his remains were identified and he was returned to Krum, Texas for burial. David is commemorated on the USS Arizona Memorial and the Memorial Tablets of the Missing, National Memorial Cemetery of the Pacific, Honolulu, Hawaii and the Jackson Cemetery, Krum, Texas. He was survived by his Parents, Mr. and Mrs. David Paul Jackson, Sr., Krum, Texas, two brothers, Gary L. and Jerry Jackson and one sister, Dionita Jackson.[385]

[384] Report of Changes of the USS Arizona for the month ending 31st day of December, 1941, page 70, line 27, David Paul Jackson, Jr.
[385] David Paul Jackson, Jr., Photo and information provided by family member, Paulette Kincade. Photo is his 1939-1940 High School photo, Krum High School, Krum, Texas.

Jackson, Robert Woods   Yeoman, Third Class, Serial No: 316 62 42, US Navy. Robert was born on December 21, 1921 in Iowa, the son of Marion Dean and Eula Frances (Woods) Jackson. He enlisted in the US Navy on December 27, 1939 in Omaha, Nebraska and completed his basic training at the Naval Training Station in Great Lakes, Illinois. Robert reported for duty on the USS Arizona on March 26, 1940. *Robert was serving as the ship's librarian and supervisor of telephone service.* He was killed in action on December 7, 1941 at Pearl Harbor, Hawaii. *On Sunday, December 21, 1941 exactly two weeks after the attack and the very day Robert would have celebrated his 20th birthday, his father was notified through a telegram from the Navy Department that his son "is missing following action in the performance of his duty and in service to his country." On January 28, 1942, they received another telegram from the Navy Department stating that he had been declared to have lost his life.* Robert was awarded the American Defense Service Medal, World War II Victory Medal and Purple Heart Medal posthumously. He remains on duty on the USS Arizona. Robert is commemorated on the USS Arizona Memorial and the Memorial Tablets of the Missing, National Memorial Cemetery of the Pacific, Honolulu, Hawaii. He was survived by his Father, Mr. Marion Dean Jackson, Glenwood, Iowa.[386]

James, John Burditt   Seaman, First Class, Serial No: 360 27 22, US Navy. John was born on January 5, 1923 in Real County, Texas, the son of Doc Trubles and Nell A. (Burditt) James. He enlisted in the US Navy on November 27, 1940 in Houston, Texas and completed his basic training at the Naval Training Station in San Diego, California. John reported for duty on the USS Arizona on January 25, 1941. He was killed in action on December 7, 1941 at Pearl Harbor, Hawaii. John was awarded the American Defense Service Medal, World War II Victory Medal and Purple Heart Medal posthumously. He remains on duty on the USS Arizona. John is commemorated on the USS Arizona Memorial and the Memorial Tablets of the Missing, National Memorial Cemetery of the Pacific, Honolulu, Hawaii. He was survived by his Mother, Mrs. Nell Burditt James, c/o J. J. Burditt, Leakey, Texas.

Janikowski, Edward Joseph   Coxswain, Serial No. 328 64 12, US Navy. Edward was born on February 2, 1920 in Winona, Minnesota. He was the son of Felix Janikowski and Julia (Cierzan) Janikowski. He came from a family of three brothers: Lawrence, John and Felix, Jr. and three sisters: Alice, Bernadine and Josephine. He attended St. Stanislaus Grade School and Cotter High School. Edward enlisted in the Navy January 9, 1940 in Minneapolis, Minnesota and completed his basic training at the Naval Training Station in Great Lakes, Illinois. After completing basic training, he reported for duty on the USS Arizona March 26, 1940. Edward was serving on December 7, 1941 when the Japanese attacked Pearl Harbor.

Edward had stood the Sunday morning watch for less than a half hour when the war planes swooped across his ship so low he could clearly see the faces of the pilots behind their canopies, the wing markings positively identifying them as Japanese. The officer in charge

---

[386] Robert Woods Jackson, Photo & Information from "Pearl Harbor Attack Touched Glenwood" by Joe Foreman, Editor, Glenwood Opinion-Tribune, Tuesday, December 6, 2011.

ordered general quarters sounded and dispatched Janikowski to summon key personnel to organize a defense.

As Edward raced along the deck, a bomb struck the ship's forward magazine touching off a series of explosions that tore the bow off the Arizona. Almost simultaneously another bomb struck, exploding deep within the crippled battlewagon just as Edward opened the door to the ship's wardroom. The force of the explosion blew him backwards twenty fee, over the ship's rail and into the water.

Fuel from bomb-ruptured tanks was blazing on the surface. Hampered by a shrapnel wound in his right foot, but still conscious, Edward gamely began the ten block swim to shore. Sailors aboard a launch fished him from the sea and flames. Japanese navy planes machine gunned the launch carrying the wounded, but miraculously, only one man was injured. He was taken with the injured to the hospital ship USS Solace where he was treated for shock, burns to his hands, head, face and legs and shrapnel wounds to his foot and chest.

Stripped of all identification and belongings in the attack, Edward recuperated aboard the USS Solace until he could be shipped to a hospital in Vallejo, California. He arrived there on Christmas Day and was able to call his parents to reassure them that he would be alright.

He spent three months stateside recuperating from his wounds. Edward returned to duty at Pearl Harbor in March, 1942 and served 38 months aboard the admiral's launch.

The navy became a career for Edward. He returned to Winona Minnesota in 1945, to marry Genevieve Salaski at St. Stanislaus Church. They had two children: Mary and David. Genevieve died in 1981. In 1985, he married Marion Legreid and had three step-children: Beverly, Marita, and Ralph. Edward had the distinct honor of being the first Winona serviceman to be wounded in World War II. He received the Purple Heart Medal, the Naval Combat Medal, the Asiatic-Pacific Defense Medal and a special commendation for his involvement in the Pearl Harbor attack.

In 1991, he returned to Pearl for the 50th Anniversary and had the pleasure of personally meeting President George Bush and his wife, Barbara. Edward served in the Navy for 21 years and retired as a Chief Boatswain's Mate. After retiring he spent 18 years working in the Bremerton, Washington shipyards, retiring in 1976. After retirement, he returned to his beloved Winona, Minnesota and was a member of the Eagles Club, V.F.W., American Legion and the Red Men Club.

Edward passed away on August 19, 2004 in Winona, Minnesota and was buried with full military honors in St. Mary's Cemetery, Winona, Minnesota. Edward was survived by his daughter, Mary Riley; son, David Janikowski of Port Orchard, Washington; his wife, Marion; three stepchildren, Beverly Engel, Marita Legreid and Ralph Legreid, Jr.; seven grandchildren; four great-grandchildren; two brothers, Lawrence and John and one sister, Bernadine Modjeski.[387]

Jante, Edwin Earl Yeoman, Third Class, Serial No: 321 38 51, US Navy. Edwin was born on February 18, 1920 in Garner, Iowa, the son of Edward Henry and Freda Emma Marie (Dietz) Jante. His twin sister, Edna Jante died at birth. Edwin enlisted in the US Navy on January 24, 1940 in Des Moines, Iowa and completed his basic training at the Naval Training Station in Great Lakes, Illinois. He reported for duty on the USS Arizona on March 26, 1940. Edwin was killed in action on December 7, 1941 at Pearl Harbor, Hawaii. He was awarded the American Defense Service Medal, World War II Victory Medal and Purple Heart Medal posthumously. Edwin remains on duty on the USS Arizona. He is commemorated on the USS Arizona Memorial and the Memorial Tablets of the Missing,

---

[387] Edward Joseph Janikowski information and picture provided by his wife, Marion Janikowski.

National Memorial Cemetery of the Pacific, Honolulu, Hawaii. Edwin was survived by his Father, Mr. Edward Jante, Route 3, Garner, Iowa. The Edwin Jante VFW Post 5515 in Garner, Iowa was named in his honor.[388]

Janz, Clifford Thurston Lieutenant, Serial No: 0-070304, US Navy, Division E. Clifford was born on February 19, 1910 in New York, the son of Joseph T. and Edna Janz. On June 21, 1927 he was admitted to the US Naval Academy and US Navy Hospital, Anne Arundel, Maryland. On June 4, 1931 he was commissioned as Ensign, serving in Engineer W & D, Radar Officer on board the USS Arizona. Clifford was killed in action on December 7, 1941 at Pearl Harbor, Hawaii. His battle station was the Forward Dist. Room. He was awarded the American Defense Service Medal, World War II Victory Medal and Purple Heart Medal posthumously. Clifford remains on duty on the USS Arizona. He is commemorated on the USS Arizona Memorial and the Memorial Tablets of the Missing, National Memorial Cemetery of the Pacific, Honolulu, Hawaii. Clifford was survived by his Wife, Mrs. Clifford Thurston Janz, 3637 Arizona Street, San Diego, California.[389]

Jastrzemski, Edwin Charles Seaman, First Class, Serial No: 311 38 43, US Navy. Edwin was born January 16, 1919 in Connecticut to Stephen T. and Bennie H. Jastrzemski. Unable to find work, he enlisted in the US Navy on December 11, 1939 in Detroit, Michigan and completed his basic training at the Naval Training Station in Great Lakes, Illinois. Edwin reported for duty on the USS Arizona on March 1, 1940. *Edwin was an altar boy aboard the Arizona and Mass was typically held at 8 a.m. on Sundays. Since the attack began about 7:55 a.m., Edwin was likely in the center of the bombing. His mother always took some comfort believing that Edwin was on deck with the priest when the attack occurred.* He was killed in action on December 7, 1941 at Pearl Harbor, Hawaii. Edwin was awarded the American Defense Service Medal, World War II Victory Medal and Purple Heart Medal posthumously. He remains on duty on the USS Arizona. Edwin is commemorated on the USS Arizona Memorial and the Memorial Tablets of the Missing, National Memorial Cemetery of the Pacific, Honolulu, Hawaii. He was survived by his Father, Mr. Stephen Jastrzemski, 1503 Annesley Street, Saginaw, Michigan. The Jastrzemski-Lelo American Legion Post 439 in Saginaw Township, Michigan was named in his honor.[390]

---

[388] Information and Photo of Edwin Earl Jante provided by family member, Sally Jante Prohaska, 10/16/2008.
[389] Clifford Thurston Janz, Photo from Lucky Bag Yearbook, United States Naval Academy, Annapolis, MD, Class of 1931.
[390] Edwin Charles Jastrzemski, Photo and information provided by his great-nephew, Cole Waterman.

Jeans, Victor "Larry" Lawrence   Watertender, Second Class, Serial No: 393 26 47, US Navy. Larry was born on August 23, 1918 in Eugene, Oregon, the son of James Darwin and Edith Viola (Dodd) Jeans. *All the men in the Jeans family went by their middle names. So Victor went by "Larry".* He enlisted in the US Navy on April 11, 1938 in Portland, Oregon and completed his basic training at the Naval Training Station in San Diego, California. *Larry transferred for duty to the USS Arizona on August 6, 1938 to join his older brother, Lee who was serving on the Arizona at the time. Shortly before the attack, Larry's brother, Lee transferred to PT boat training and was stationed on the east coast.* Larry was killed in action on December 7, 1941 at Pearl Harbor, Hawaii. He was awarded the American Defense Service Medal, World War II Victory Medal and Purple Heart Medal posthumously. Larry remains on duty on the USS Arizona. He is commemorated on the USS Arizona Memorial and the Memorial Tablets of the Missing, National Memorial Cemetery of the Pacific, Honolulu, Hawaii. Larry was survived by his Parents, Mr. James "Darwin" Jeans, Mrs. Edith Viola Jeans, General Delivery, Eugene, Oregon and brothers, Elza "Rodney", James "Lee" (Also serving in the US Navy) and sister, Ella Vivian Jeans.[391]

Jeffers, Warren Edwin   Seaman, First Class, Serial No. 311 38 36, US Navy. Warren was born on March 29, 1921 in Michigan to Linden and Bertha Jeffers. He enlisted in the US Navy December 11, 1939 in Detroit, Michigan and reported for duty on the USS Arizona March 1, 1940. Warren was serving on the USS Arizona on December 7, 1941 when the Japanese attacked Pearl Harbor. After the attack, Warren was transferred to the USS Monaghan (DD-354) for duty. Warren died on July 26, 2002 in Mesa, Arizona. His ashes were interred on the USS Arizona in 2003.

Jeffries, Keith   Coxswain, Serial No: 223 61 66, US Navy. Keith was born March 29, 1918 in Alden, Pennsylvania, the son of James Glidden and Pauline Jeffries. His mother died in 1935. He enlisted in the US Navy on December 12, 1939 in New York, New York and reported for duty on the USS Arizona on March 1, 1940. Keith was killed in action on December 7, 1941 while engaged as a gunner on the forward deck of the USS Arizona at Pearl Harbor, Hawaii. He was awarded the American Defense Service Medal, World War II Victory Medal and Purple Heart Medal posthumously. Keith remains on duty on the USS Arizona. He is commemorated on the USS Arizona Memorial and the Memorial Tablets of the Missing, National Memorial Cemetery of the Pacific, Honolulu, Hawaii. Keith was survived by his Father, Mr. James Glidden Jeffries, 162 Sharpe Street, Alden, Nanticoke, Pennsylvania.[392]

---

[391] Victor Lawrence Jeans, Photo provided by family member, Dave Jeans.
[392] Keith Jeffries, Photo provided by the Newport township Community Organization, Luzerne County, PA.

Jenkins, Robert Henry Dawson   Seaman, Second Class, Serial No: 356 44 26, US Navy. Robert was born on September 26, 1921 in Dallas, Texas, the son of William W. and Sallie (Vandeman) Jenkins. He enlisted in the US Navy on December 4, 1940 in Dallas, Texas and completed his basic training at the Naval Training Station in San Diego, California. Robert reported for duty on the USS Arizona on February 25, 1941. He was killed in action on December 7, 1941 at Pearl Harbor, Hawaii. Robert was awarded the American Defense Service Medal, World War II Victory Medal and Purple Heart Medal posthumously. He remains on duty on the USS Arizona. Robert is commemorated on the USS Arizona Memorial and the Memorial Tablets of the Missing, National Memorial Cemetery of the Pacific, Honolulu, Hawaii. He was survived by his Father, Mr. William W. Jenkins, 608 3rd Avenue, Dallas, Texas.[393]

Jensen, Keith Marlow   Electrician's Mate, Third Class, Serial No: 368 45 05, US Navy. Keith was born May 19, 1918 in Sandy, Utah to Evan Orlando and Edith (Brown) Jensen. He enlisted in the US Navy on September 11, 1939 in Salt Lake City, Utah and completed his basic training at the Naval Training Station in San Diego, California. He reported for duty on the USS Arizona on November 10, 1939. Keith was killed in action on December 7, 1941 at Pearl Harbor, Hawaii. He was awarded the American Defense Service Medal, World War II Victory Medal and Purple Heart Medal posthumously. Keith remains on duty on the USS Arizona. He is commemorated on the USS Arizona Memorial and the Memorial Tablets of the Missing, National Memorial Cemetery of the Pacific, Honolulu, Hawaii. Keith was survived by his Father, Mr. Evan Orlando Jensen, 988 East 2nd South, Sandy, Utah.[394]

Johann, Paul Frederick   Gunner's Mate, Third Class, Serial No: 321 38 94, US Navy. Paul was born on December 7, 1919 in Alta Vista, Iowa, the son of Peter and Melinda Wilhelmina Mary (Joachim) Johann. He enlisted in the US Navy on February 14, 1940 in Des Moines, Iowa and completed his basic training at the Naval Training Station in Great Lakes, Illinois. Paul reported for duty on the USS Arizona on July 12, 1940. He was killed in action on December 7, 1941 at Pearl Harbor, Hawaii *while manning his battle station in the magazine room (storage of weapons) below decks.* Paul was awarded the American Defense Service Medal, World War II Victory Medal and Purple Heart Medal posthumously. He remains on duty on the USS Arizona. Paul is commemorated on the USS Arizona Memorial and the Memorial Tablets of the Missing, National Memorial Cemetery of the Pacific, Honolulu, Hawaii. He was survived by his Parents, Mr. and Mrs. Peter Johann, Box 277, AltaVista, Iowa; 2 brothers, Norbert and Robert and a sister, Norma. The Paul Johann VFW Post 4069 in Alta Vista, Iowa was named in his honor.[395]

---

[393] Robert Henry Dawson Jenkins, photo courtesy of LCDR G. Dale McKissick, USNR, Memorial, Dallas Convention Center, Dallas, Texas.

[394] Keith Marlow Jensen, Photo from the Jordan High School Yearbook, Sandy, Utah, 1935.

[395] Paul Frederick Johann, Information and photo provided by his brother, Robert Johann.

Johnson, David Andrew Jr.   Officer's Cook, Second Class, Serial No: 223 26 80, US Navy. David was born in about 1909 in Virginia. He enlisted in the US Navy on December 3, 1935 in Brooklyn, New York and reported for duty on the USS Arizona on March 24, 1936. He was killed in action on December 7, 1941 at Pearl Harbor. David was awarded the American Defense Service Medal, World War II Victory Medal and Purple Heart Medal posthumously. He remains on duty on the USS Arizona. David is commemorated on the USS Arizona Memorial and the Memorial Tablets of the Missing, National Memorial Cemetery of the Pacific, Honolulu, Hawaii. He was survived by his Father, Mr. David A. Johnson, Sr., Box 100, Route 4, Norfolk, Virginia.

Johnson, Donald R.   Seaman, First Class, Serial No. 321 48 46, US Navy. Donald enlisted in the US Navy October 8, 1940 in Des Moines, Iowa and completed his basic training at the Naval Training Station in Great Lakes, Illinois. He reported for duty on the USS Arizona December 9, 1940. Donald was transferred to Flight Signal School in San Diego on October 17, 1941. He was in San Diego when the Japanese attacked Pearl Harbor.

Johnson, Edmund Russell Paul   Machinist's Mate, First Class, Serial No: 375 77 92, US Navy. Edmund was born on May 29, 1918 in Boston, Massachusetts, the son of Edmund Augustus and Sophie Agnes (Buczkowski) Johnson. He enlisted in the US Navy on June 10, 1936 in San Francisco, California and completed his basic training at the Naval Training Station in San Diego, California. Edmund reported for duty on the USS Arizona on April 29, 1940 transferring from the USS Pensacola. He was killed in action on December 7, 1941 at Pearl Harbor, Hawaii. Edmund was awarded the American Defense Service Medal, World War II Victory Medal and Purple Heart Medal posthumously. He remains on duty on the USS Arizona. Edmund is commemorated on the USS Arizona Memorial and the Memorial Tablets of the Missing, National Memorial Cemetery of the Pacific, Honolulu, Hawaii. He was survived by his Wife, Mrs. Martha Eva Johnson, 529 Golden Avenue, Long Beach, California.

Johnson, John Russell   Radioman, Third Class, Serial No: 201 60 38, US Navy. John was born in 1918 in Brockton, Massachusetts. He enlisted in the US Navy on October 20, 1937 in Boston, Massachusetts and reported for duty on the USS Arizona on March 8, 1938. He was killed in action on December 7, 1941 at Pearl Harbor, Hawaii. John was awarded the American Defense Service Medal, World War II Victory Medal and Purple Heart Medal posthumously. He remains on duty on the USS Arizona. John is commemorated on the USS Arizona Memorial and the Memorial Tablets of the Missing, National Memorial Cemetery of the Pacific, Honolulu, Hawaii. He was survived by his Wife, Mrs. Eleanor Louise Johnson, 799 Belmont Street, Brockton, Massachusetts.[396]

Johnson, Neil Francis   Coxswain Serial No. 316 60 06 US Navy   Neil enlisted in the US Navy September 19, 1939 in Omaha, Nebraska and completed his basic training at the Naval Training Station in Great Lakes, Illinois. He reported for duty on the USS Arizona February 10, 1940. Neil was serving on the USS Arizona on December 7, 1941 when the Japanese attacked Pearl Harbor. After the attack, Neil was transferred to Bishops Point for duty.

---

[396] John Russell Johnson, Photo from Massachusetts Honor States.

Johnson, Samuel Earle   Commander, Medical Corps, Serial No: 0-014934, US Navy. Samuel was born on June 11, 1889 in Chilton County, Alabama, the son of Joseph Samuel and Sarah Elizabeth (Strock) Johnson. He graduated from Vanderbilt Medical School, Nashville Tennessee in 1915 as a physician. Samuel served as a Sergeant in the Hospital Corps National Guard for three years. He was commissioned June 23, 1938 and was serving on the USS Arizona as Senior Medical Officer. Samuel was killed in action on December 7, 1941 at Pearl Harbor, Hawaii. His battle station was the forward Dressing Station. He was awarded the American Defense Service Medal, World War II Victory Medal and Purple Heart Medal posthumously. Samuel remains on duty on the USS Arizona. He is commemorated on the USS Arizona Memorial and the Memorial Tablets of the Missing, National Memorial Cemetery of the Pacific, Honolulu, Hawaii. Samuel is survived by his Wife, Mrs. Matalie (Harper) Johnson, Clanton, Alabama.[397]

Johnson, Sterling Conrad   Coxswain, Serial No: 385 86 65, US Navy. Sterling was born November 7, 1919 in Tacoma, Washington the third child of Carl Gerhart and Lyda Elisa (Osness) Johnson. *He was a former student at Lincoln High School in Tacoma and had been in the Navy for a year and a half. Sterling excelled in sports, especially baseball and swimming.* He enlisted in the US Navy on April 10, 1940 in Seattle, Washington and completed his basic training at the Naval Training Station in San Diego, California. He reported for duty on the USS Arizona on July 2, 1940. *Sterling gave swim lessons on the ship. He loved the Navy. Times were tough at home during those times. His father was disabled with a bad heart. Consequently, the family couldn't afford much but Sterling always made sure that his baby sister, Janice would get a doll at Christmas.* Sterling was killed in action on December 7, 1941 at Pearl Harbor, Hawaii. Sterling was awarded the American Defense Service Medal, World War II Victory Medal and Purple Heart Medal posthumously. He remains on duty on the USS Arizona. Sterling is commemorated on the USS Arizona Memorial and the Memorial Tablets of the Missing, National Memorial Cemetery of the Pacific, Honolulu, Hawaii. He was survived by his Parents, Mr. and Mrs. Carl Garhart Johnson, 3702 South Wilkeson Street, Tacoma, Washington three brothers, Robert, Allen and Kermit and two sisters, Genevieve and Janice.[398]

Johnston, Brooxey Johnny, Jr.   Gunner's Mate, Third Class Serial No. 356 34 83 US Navy   Brooxey was born on August 24, 1920 in Tomball, Texas to Brooxey J. and Willie B. (Shaw) Johnston. He enlisted in the US Navy August 9, 1940 in Dallas, Texas and completed his basic training at the Naval Training Station in San Diego, California. Brooxey reported for duty on the USS Arizona October 14, 1940. He was serving on the USS Arizona on December 7, 1941 when the Japanese attacked Pearl Harbor. After the attack, Brooxey was transferred to the USS MacDonough (DD-351) for duty. He went on to serve in the Korean War retiring with the rank of Lieutenant Commander. Brooxey died on July 22, 1988 in Tomball, Texas and is buried in the Houston National Cemetery, Houston, Texas.

---

[397] Samuel Earle Johnson, Photo and information provided by family member, John (Jack) Kane.
[398] Sterling Conrad Johnson, Photo and information provided by his nephew, Chris Nighswonger.

Jolley, Berry Stanley Seaman, Second Class, Serial No: 660 00 16, US Navy Reserve. Berry was born May 13, 1923 in Yale, Utah to Nephi Williamson and Zelpha (Huber) Jolley. He enlisted in the US Navy on May 28, 1941 in Salt Lake City, Utah and completed his basic training at the Naval Training Station in San Diego, California. Berry reported for duty on the USS Arizona on August 13, 1941. He was killed in action on December 7, 1941 at Pearl Harbor, Hawaii. Berry was awarded the American Defense Service Medal, World War II Victory Medal and Purple Heart Medal posthumously. He remains on duty on the USS Arizona. Berry is commemorated on the USS Arizona Memorial and the Memorial Tablets of the Missing, National Memorial Cemetery of the Pacific, Honolulu, Hawaii and Pleasant View Cemetery, Burley, Idaho. He was survived by his Uncle, Mr. William E. Tinsley, 421 North Almo Street, Burley, Idaho.

Jones, Daniel Pugh Seaman, Second Class, Serial No: 272 41 66, US Navy. Daniel was born April 21, 1922, the son of William Franklin and Mary Frances Molly (Hallman) Jones. *He was born into a farming family located off Clemmons Road, a dusty red dirt, one lane road nicknamed the "Pea Vine Highway", with 2 older brothers and 7 sisters. Daniel was blond, short and always smiling, caring and personable. Daniel and his brother, Woodrow were inseparable. When you saw one, the other would be in his shadow. They were full of fun, joking, playing tricks on each other or teamed up on others. A story the boys were know for was: On a neighboring farm, the ole farmer had a prized Model "T" Ford, which he shined and drove only on Sundays. It was Halloween, and the boys were refused a treat, so they disassembled and reassembled the Model "T" on top of the farmer's barn. Still, that trick was better than the previous year's trick. They put the farmer's outhouse on top of his barn.* Daniel enlisted in the US Navy on October 5, 1940 in Birmingham, Alabama and completed his basic training at the Naval Training Station in Norfolk, Virginia. Daniel reported for duty on the USS Arizona on December 4, 1940. He was killed in action on December 7, 1941 at Pearl Harbor, Hawaii. Daniel was awarded the American Defense Service Medal, World War II Victory Medal and Purple Heart Medal posthumously. He remains on duty on the USS Arizona with his brother, Woodrow. Daniel is commemorated on the USS Arizona Memorial and the Memorial Tablets of the Missing, National Memorial Cemetery of the Pacific, Honolulu, Hawaii and Coaling Cemetery, Coaling, Alabama. He was survived by his Father, Mr. William Franklin Jones, Route 1, Cottondale, Alabama. His brother, Woodrow was also killed in action on the Arizona.[399]

Jones, Edmon Ethmer Seaman, First Class, Serial No: 372 20 32, US Navy. Edmon was born in about 1923 in Oklahoma the son of Ambus Otto and Corsey Jones. He enlisted in the US Navy with his brother, Homer on November 5, 1940 in Denver, Colorado and completed his basic training at the Naval Training Station in San Diego, California. Edmon reported for duty on the USS Arizona on January 11, 1941. He was killed in action on December 7, 1941 at Pearl Harbor, Hawaii. Edmon was awarded the American Defense Service Medal, World War II Victory Medal and Purple Heart Medal posthumously. He remains on duty on the USS Arizona. Edmon is commemorated on the USS Arizona Memorial and the Memorial Tablets of the Missing, National Memorial Cemetery of the Pacific, Honolulu, Hawaii. Edmon was survived by his Parents, Mr. and Mrs. Ambus Otto Jones, Box 244, Montrose, Colorado. His brother, Homer was also killed in action on the Arizona.

---

[399] Daniel Pugh Jones, Information, stories and photo provided by his Niece, Patricia J. Jones.

Jones, Floyd Baxter Mess Attendant, Second Class, Serial No: 274 35 59, US Navy. Floyd was born December 15, 1920 in Shreveport, Louisiana, the son of Willie and Corene Jones. He enlisted in the US Navy on October 5, 1938 in New Orleans, Louisiana and completed his basic training at the Naval Training Station in San Diego, California. Floyd reported for duty on the USS Arizona on April 3, 1939. He was killed in action on December 7, 1941 at Pearl Harbor, Hawaii. He was the only military member from Shreveport, Louisiana killed in the attack but as he was black no mention of his service was noted in the papers until a recapitulation of war dead after the Japanese surrender in late 1945. Floyd was awarded the American Defense Service Medal, World War II Victory Medal and Purple Heart Medal posthumously. He remains on duty on the USS Arizona. Floyd is commemorated on the USS Arizona Memorial and the Memorial Tablets of the Missing, National Memorial Cemetery of the Pacific, Honolulu, Hawaii. He was survived by his Father, Mr. Willie Jones, 1947 Logan Street, Shreveport, Louisiana. The American Legion Post 525 was named in memory of Floyd and another African-American man who died in the war. [400]

Jones, Harry Cecil Gunner's Mate, Third Class, Serial No: 393 35 91, US Navy. Harry was born on January 1, 1915 on the family farm 8 miles southwest of Bucklin, Kansas, the son of Charley B. and Alma Jones. He enlisted in the US Navy on May 20, 1940 in Portland, Oregon. After basic training at the Naval Training Station in San Diego, California, he reported for duty on the USS Arizona on August 25, 1940. Harry was killed in action on December 7, 1941 at Pearl Harbor, Hawaii. He was awarded the American Defense Service Medal, World War II Victory Medal and Purple Heart Medal posthumously. Harry remains on duty on the USS Arizona. He is commemorated on the USS Arizona Memorial and the Memorial Tablets of the Missing, National Memorial Cemetery of the Pacific, Honolulu, Hawaii. Harry was survived by his Parents, Mr. and Mrs. Charles B. Jones, General Delivery, Bucklin, Kansas and his two sisters, Mildred Lee and Betty Olson. [401]

Jones, Henry, Jr. Mess Attendant, First Class, Serial No: 274 36 02, US Navy. Henry enlisted in the US Navy on November 5, 1938 in New Orleans, Louisiana and completed his basic training at the Naval Training Station in San Diego, California. He reported for duty on the USS Arizona on April 3, 1939. Henry was killed in action on December 7, 1941 at Pearl Harbor, Hawaii. He was awarded the American Defense Service Medal, World War II Victory Medal and Purple Heart Medal posthumously. Henry remains on duty on the USS Arizona. He is commemorated on the USS Arizona Memorial and the Memorial Tablets of the Missing, National Memorial Cemetery of the Pacific, Honolulu, Hawaii. Henry was survived by his Wife, Mrs. Mae Ethel Jones, 1434 Myrtle Avenue, Long Beach, California.

Jones, Homer Lloyd Seaman, First Class, Serial No: 372 22 31, US Navy. Homer was born in about 1915 in Texas the son of Ambus Otto and Corsey Jones. He enlisted with his brother, Edmun in the US Navy on November 5, 1940 in Denver, Colorado and completed his

---

[400] Floyd Baxter Jones, Information and photo provided by researcher, John Andrew Prime. The photo was provided by his brother Harry to the Shreveport Times.
[401] Harry Cecil Jones, Photo and information provided by his sister, Betty Olson.

basic training at the Naval Training Station in San Diego, California. He reported for duty on the USS Arizona on January 11, 1941. Homer was killed in action on December 7, 1941 at Pearl Harbor, Hawaii. He was awarded the American Defense Service Medal, World War II Victory Medal and Purple Heart Medal posthumously. Homer remains on duty on the USS Arizona with his brother, Edmon. He is commemorated on the USS Arizona Memorial and the Memorial Tablets of the Missing, National Memorial Cemetery of the Pacific, Honolulu, Hawaii. Homer was survived by his Parents, Mr. and Mrs. Ambus Otto Jones, Box 244, Montrose, Colorado. His brother, Edmon was also killed in action on the USS Arizona.

Jones, Hubert Hayes Chief Watertender (PA), Serial No. 507 85 26, US Navy. Hubert was born January 6, 1901 in Cumberland County, Kentucky to Joseph Andrew Jackson and Mary Elizabeth (Willis) Jones. He enlisted in the US Navy on April 29, 1933. He served on the USS Arizona from December 4, 1937 until December 7, 1941 when the Japanese attacked Pearl Harbor. Hubert was wounded during the attack and he was treated initially at Tripler General Hospital in Honolulu and then was taken to the US Naval Hospital at Pearl Harbor for further treatment. He was later transferred to the Naval Hospital on the Mainland. His wife, Mrs. Grace Lee Jones, Route 1, Box 370, Huntington Beach, California was notified of his wounds. Hubert died on November 5, 1956 in Corona, California at age 55.

Jones, Hugh Ivory, Jr. Seaman, Second Class, Serial No: 382 37 88, US Navy. Hugh was born on June 29, 1923 in Shawnee, Oklahoma, the son of Hugh Ivory and Vera Alice (McGuire) Jones. He enlisted in the US Navy on January 30, 1941 in Los Angeles, California and completed his basic training at the Naval Training Station in San Diego, California. Hugh reported for duty on the USS Arizona on April 27, 1941. He was killed in action on December 7, 1941 at Pearl Harbor, Hawaii. Hugh was awarded the American Defense Service Medal, World War II Victory Medal and Purple Heart Medal posthumously. He remains on duty on the USS Arizona. Hugh is commemorated on the USS Arizona Memorial and the Memorial Tablets of the Missing, National Memorial Cemetery of the Pacific, Honolulu, Hawaii. He was survived by his Father, Mr. Hugh Ivory Jones, 1656 2nd Street, Manhattan Beach, California.[402]

Jones, Leland Seaman, First Class, Serial No: 346 76 94, US Navy. Leland enlisted in the US Navy on December 19, 1939 in Little Rock, Arkansas and completed his basic training at the Naval Training Station in Great Lakes, Illinois. He reported for duty on the USS Arizona on March 26, 1940. Leland was killed in action on December 7, 1941 at Pearl Harbor, Hawaii. He was awarded the American Defense Service Medal, World War II Victory Medal and Purple Heart Medal posthumously. Leland remains on duty on the USS Arizona. He is commemorated on the USS Arizona Memorial and the Memorial Tablets of the Missing, National Memorial Cemetery of the Pacific, Honolulu, Hawaii. Leland was survived by his Father, Mr. Hobert Sam Jones, Route 1, Jacksonville, Arkansas.[403]

---

[402] Information and Photo of Hugh Ivory Jones Jr provided by family member, Linda Craig.
[403] Leland Jones, Photo from Tennessee Honor States.

Jones, Thomas Raymond   Ensign, Serial No: 0-096268, US Navy Reserve. Thomas was commissioned Ensign in the US Navy on February 28, 1941 and served on the USS Arizona as Junior Watch and Division L Officer. His battle station was the Forward Battle Lookout. Thomas was killed in action on December 7, 1941 at Pearl Harbor, Hawaii. He was awarded the American Defense Service Medal, World War II Victory Medal and Purple Heart Medal posthumously. Thomas remains on duty on the USS Arizona. He is commemorated on the USS Arizona Memorial and the Memorial Tablets of the Missing, National Memorial Cemetery of the Pacific, Honolulu, Hawaii. Thomas was survived by his Mother, Mrs. Susie B. Jones, Elm Street, Tallulah, Louisiana.[404]

Jones, Warren Allen   Yeoman, Third Class, Serial No: 316 51 74, US Navy. Warren was born on October 27, 1917 in Edgar, Nebraska, the son of Robert Turner and Martha Caroline (Rempp) Jones. He graduated from Kearney High School in 1936. Warren enlisted in the US Navy on September 14, 1937 in Omaha, Nebraska and reported for duty on the USS Arizona on May 17, 1939. He was killed in action on December 7, 1941 at Pearl Harbor, Hawaii. His four year enlistment had expired in September 1941 but was not discharged because the possibility of war loomed in the Pacific. Warren was awarded the American Defense Service Medal, World War II Victory Medal and Purple Heart Medal posthumously. He remains on duty on the USS Arizona. Warren is commemorated on the USS Arizona Memorial and the Memorial Tablets of the Missing, National Memorial Cemetery of the Pacific, Honolulu, Hawaii. He was survived by his Wife, Mrs. Helen Josephine Jones, 510 East 26th Street, Kearney, Nebraska and a seventeen-month old son. [405]

Jones, Willard Worth   Seaman, First Class, Serial No: 295 76 77, US Navy. Willard was born on September 29, 1917 in Hardin County, Tennessee. He enlisted in the US Navy on October 4, 1940 in Nashville, Tennessee and completed his basic training at the Naval Training Station in Norfolk, Virginia. Willard reported for duty on the USS Arizona on December 4, 1940. He was killed in action on December 7, 1941 at Pearl Harbor, Hawaii. Willard was awarded the American Defense Service Medal, World War II Victory Medal and Purple Heart Medal posthumously. He remains on duty on the USS Arizona. Willard is commemorated on the USS Arizona Memorial and the Memorial Tablets of the Missing, National Memorial Cemetery of the Pacific, Honolulu, Hawaii. He was survived by his Father, Mr. Victor Worth Jones, Route 2,

---

[404] Thomas Raymond Jones, Photo from The Gumbo Yearbook, Louisiana State University, Baton Rouge, Louisiana, 1937.
[405] Warren Allen Jones, Photo from Nebraska Honor States.

Hornbeak, Tennessee. The Veterans of Foreign Wars (VFW) Jones-Walker Post #4862 is named in honor of Willard Worth Jones and Harry E. Walker.[406]

Jones, Woodrow Wilson Seaman, Second Class, Serial No: 272 53 36, US Navy. Woodrow was born August 14, 1919, the son of William Franklin and Mary F. Jones. *He was taller than his brother, Daniel, more serious, blunt and honest. He was born into a farming family located off Clemmons Road, a dusty red dirt, one lane road nicknamed the "Pea Vine Highway", with 2 older brothers and 7 sisters. Woodrow and his brother, Daniel were inseparable. When you saw one, the other would be in his shadow. They were full of fun, joking, playing tricks on each other or teamed up on others. A story the boys were known for was; on a neighboring farm, the ole farmer had a prized Model "T" Ford, which he shined and drove only on Sundays. It was Halloween, and the boys were refused a treat, so they disassembled and reassembled the Model "T" on top of the farmer's barn. Still, that trick was better than the previous year's trick. They put the farmer's outhouse on top of his barn.* Woodrow enlisted in the US Navy on January 21, 1941 in Birmingham, Alabama and reported for duty on the USS Arizona on July 8, 1941. Woodrow was killed in action on December 7, 1941 at Pearl Harbor, Hawaii. He was awarded the American Defense Service Medal, World War II Victory Medal and Purple Heart Medal posthumously. Woodrow remains on duty on the USS Arizona. He is commemorated on the USS Arizona Memorial and the Memorial Tablets of the Missing, National Memorial Cemetery of the Pacific, Honolulu, Hawaii. Woodrow was survived by his Father, Mr. William Franklin Jones, Route 1, Cottondale, Alabama. His brother, Daniel Pugh Jones was also killed in action on the Arizona.[407]

Joyce, Calvin Wilbur Fireman, Second Class, Serial No: 279 56 02, US Navy. Calvin was born in May of 1919 in Hamilton, Ohio to Clinton Benjamin and Mary Myrtle Joyce. He enlisted in the US Navy on June 21, 1938 in Cincinnati, Ohio and reported for duty on the USS Arizona on November 10, 1938. He was killed in action on December 7, 1941 at Pearl Harbor, Hawaii. Calvin was awarded the American Defense Service Medal, World War II Victory Medal and Purple Heart Medal posthumously. He remains on duty on the USS Arizona. Calvin is commemorated on the USS Arizona Memorial and the Memorial Tablets of the Missing, National Memorial Cemetery of the Pacific, Honolulu, Hawaii. He was survived by his Mother, Mrs. Mary Myrtle Joyce, 419 Patterson Boulevard, Dayton, Ohio.

Judd, Albert John Coxswain, Serial No: 311 20 63, US Navy. Albert was born in 1919 in Tennessee to David D. and Edna M. Judd. He enlisted in the US Navy on February 9, 1937 in Detroit, Michigan and reported for duty on the USS Arizona July 19, 1937. He was killed in action on December 7, 1941 at Pearl Harbor, Hawaii. Albert was awarded the American Defense Service Medal, World War II Victory Medal and Purple Heart Medal posthumously. He remains on duty on the USS Arizona. Albert is commemorated on the USS Arizona Memorial and the Memorial Tablets of the Missing, National Memorial Cemetery of the Pacific,

---

[406] Willard Worth Jones, Photo provided by the people at the Veterans of Foreign Wars Jones-Walker Post #4862.

[407] Woodrow Wilson Jones, Information, stories and photo provided by his Niece, Patricia J. Jones.

Honolulu, Hawaii. He was survived by his Mother, Mrs. Edna May Schilke, 15877 Evanston Avenue, Detroit, Michigan.[408]

Kagarice, Harold Lee Chief Storekeeper, Serial No: 355 54 65, US Navy. Harold was born on March 24, 1906 in Hutchinson, Kansas, the son of Isaac and Grace Verena (Smith) Kagarice. He enlisted in the US Navy on January 11, 1936 in San Pedro, California and reported for duty on the USS Arizona on April 26, 1939. Harold was killed in action on December 7, 1941 at Pearl Harbor, Hawaii. He was only days away from retiring when he was killed. He was awarded the American Defense Service Medal, World War II Victory Medal and Purple Heart Medal posthumously. Harold remains on duty on the USS Arizona. He is commemorated on the USS Arizona Memorial and the Memorial Tablets of the Missing, National Memorial Cemetery of the Pacific, Honolulu, Hawaii. Harold was survived by his Wife, Mrs. Edith Clara (Ohler) Kagarice, 1300 Blake Street, Berkeley, California and daughter, Shirley Grace Kagarice.[409]

Kaiser, Robert Oscar Fireman, First Class, Serial No: 337 17 03, US Navy. Robert was born in about 1921 in Germany, the son of Oscar Emil and Elizabeth (Berger) Kaiser. *Robert and his mother came to America from Germany alone and she eventually married Oscar Emil Kaiser who then adopted Robert as his son. Robert played the Saxophone in his Senior High School Band, Normandy High School, Normandy, Missouri.* He enlisted in the US Navy on August 11, 1939 in St. Louis, Missouri and completed his basic training at the Naval Training Station in San Diego, California. Robert reported for duty on the USS Arizona on October 20, 1939. He was killed in action on December 7, 1941 at Pearl Harbor, Hawaii. Robert was awarded the American Defense Service Medal, World War II Victory Medal and Purple Heart Medal posthumously. He remains on duty on the USS Arizona. Robert is commemorated on the USS Arizona Memorial and the Memorial Tablets of the Missing, National Memorial Cemetery of the Pacific, Honolulu, Hawaii. He was survived by his Father, Mr. Oscar E. Kaiser, 6653 Enright Street, University City, St. Louis, Missouri.[410]

---

[408] Albert John Judd, Photo from Michigan Honor States.
[409] Harold Lee Kagarice, Photo provided by his Niece, Dixie Kagarice Nordyke.
[410] Robert Oscar Kaiser, Photo from the St. Louis Post-Dispatch, St. Louis, Missouri, December 28, 1941, Page 30.

Karb, Joseph Frank Chief Watertender, Serial No. 383 38 08, US Navy. Joe was born October 4, 1907 in Port Washington, Wisconsin to Joanna Karb who very soon became a single mother. He enlisted in the US Navy November 24, 1924 at the very young age of 17 and served on the USS Enterprise, serving in the South Pacific going to places such as Samoa, New Zealand and Australia. On December 30, 1933 he married Marie Latapie in Yuma, Arizona. He reported for duty on the USS Arizona on June 14, 1940, assigned to the Engineering Department, B Division. He was returning from shore leave on December 7, 1941 when the Japanese attacked Pearl Harbor. Joe had just come thru the main gate to go on duty when he heard a big explosion. Nobody knew what it was at first, but as he scanned the harbor, he realized it was the Arizona. As he got closer he couldn't even see the ship, it was completely engulfed in smoke. He grabbed a patrol boat, escaping strafing runs by the Japanese, and with others, helped pick up the wounded and dying from the ship and the harbor's blood-and-oil-soaked waters. After the attack, he was assigned duty repairing the USS Nevada. Renovating and giving the Nevada a complete overhaul, was the hardest work Joe ever did while serving in the Navy. After the Japanese invaded the Aleutian Islands in 1942, Joe and his shipmates were sent to assist in dislodging the Japanese from the Islands of Kiska and Attu. He later returned to Pearl Harbor where he served until 1944, when he was sent to France for D-Day, the 6th of June. His ship was in the water near Normandy. In early 1946, after the war ended, Joe was stationed in San Francisco where he worked for the 12th Naval District at Treasure Island as a Chief Petty Officer until he retired from active duty in December, 1946. In 1954, after completing eight years in the Reserves, Joe retired from the United States Navy after serving his beloved country for 30 years. This very special unassuming man is one of America's truly "unsung" heroes. Joseph passed away November 25, 2002. He was preceded in death by his wife of 57years, Marie. Joseph was survived by his daughter, Joan Gillette, and a son-in-law Leonard Gillette, who live in Palo Cedro, California; grandson, Gregory Jeffries, a grand daughter, Sherry Henry and a grand-son-in-law Zane Henry; three great-grandchildren: twin boys, Austin and Chase Henry and Allison Henry.[411]

Katt, Eugene Louis Seaman, Second Class, Serial No: 376 22 75, US Navy. Eugene was born November 17, 1916 in Picher, Oklahoma to Louis and Ruth J. (Gamble) Katt. He enlisted in the US Navy on January 24, 1941 in San Francisco, California and completed his basic training at the Naval Training Station in San Diego, California. He reported for duty on the USS Arizona on August 24, 1941. Eugene was killed in action on December 7, 1941 at Pearl Harbor, Hawaii. He was awarded the American Defense Service Medal, World War II Victory Medal and Purple Heart Medal posthumously. Eugene remains on duty on the USS Arizona. He is commemorated on the USS Arizona Memorial and the Memorial Tablets of the Missing, National Memorial Cemetery of the Pacific, Honolulu, Hawaii. Eugene was survived by his Father, Mr. Louis Katt, P.O. Box 136, Los Gatos, California.

Keener, C. H. Gunner's Mate, Third Class, Serial No. 295 38 75, US Navy. CH enlisted in the US Navy September 22, 1937 in Nashville, Tennessee and reported for duty on the USS Arizona March 8, 1938. He was serving on the USS Arizona on December 7, 1941 when the Japanese attacked Pearl Harbor. After the attack, he was transferred to the USS Dale (DD-353) for duty.

---

[411] Joseph Frank Karb, Photo and information provided by his daughter, Joan Gillette.

Keffer, Carl Emerson   Seaman, First Class, Serial No. 279 72 86, US Navy. Carl was born April 22, 1921 in Ironton, Ohio, the son of Hiram and Lucinda (Colvin) Keffer. He enlisted in the US Navy September 9, 1940 in Cincinnati, Ohio and completed his basic training at the Naval Training Station in Norfolk, Virginia. He reported for duty on the USS Arizona December 4, 1940. He was serving on the USS Arizona on December 7, 1941 when the Japanese attacked Pearl Harbor. After the attack, Carl was transferred to the USS Craven for duty. He later served on board the USS Prometheus and was an Advanced Gunner's Mate. He received the following citations, American Defense with One Gold Star, Asiatic-Pacific Medal, America Aria, Victory Medal and Good Conduct. Carl died April 28, 1997 in Elyria, Ohio.[412]

Keller, Paul Daniel   Molder, First Class, Serial No: 311 39 77, US Navy. Paul was born April 19, 1918 in Michigan to John D. and Nettie R. Keller. He enlisted in the US Navy on January 3, 1940 in Detroit, Michigan and completed his basic training at the Naval Training Station in Great Lakes, Illinois. Paul reported for duty on the USS Arizona on March 22, 1940. Paul was killed in action on December 7, 1941 at Pearl Harbor, Hawaii. He was awarded the American Defense Service Medal, World War II Victory Medal and Purple Heart Medal posthumously. Paul remains on duty on the USS Arizona. He is commemorated on the USS Arizona Memorial and the Memorial Tablets of the Missing, National Memorial Cemetery of the Pacific, Honolulu, Hawaii. Paul was survived by his Mother, Mrs. Nettie Johnson Smith, 142 Jackson Street, Coldwater, Michigan.[413]

Kelley, Bruce Draper   Lieutenant Commander, Serial No. 0-02431, US Navy. Bruce was born January 21, 1902 in Tacoma, Washington, the son of Frank Harrison and Jean Leslie (Richardson) Kelley. He was commissioned an officer in the US Navy August 1, 1939 serving on the USS Arizona as the Gunnery Officer, Athletic Officer. On December 7, 1941 when the Japanese attacked Pearl Harbor, his battle station was F. C. Tower. He was assigned temporary duty on the USS Tennessee after the attack and on December 10, 1941 he was assigned to the USS Maryland. Bruce later became the commanding officer of the U.S. Naval Torpedo Station in Keyport, Washington. He retired from the US Navy in June 1956 as a Captain. Bruce died January 7, 1988.[414]

---

[412] Carl Emerson Keffer, Photo provided by his son-in-law, Jerry Snyder.

[413] Paul Daniel Keller, Photo from Michigan Honor States.

[414] Bruce Draper Kelley, Photo from Lucky Bag Yearbook, United States Naval Academy, Annapolis, MD, Class of 1925.

Kelley, James Dennis Shipfitter, Third Class, Serial No: 356 15 54, US Navy. James was born on April 7, 1921 in San Diego, California son of James Frank and Mary Annette (Cole) Kelley. While in high school, James lettered in football and was a member of the staff on the school paper. He graduated from Bowlegs High School in Bowlegs, Oklahoma in May 1939. James enlisted in the US Navy on August 9, 1939 in Dallas, Texas and completed his basic training at the Naval Training Station in San Diego, California. He reported for duty on the USS Arizona on October 20, 1939. James was killed in action on December 7, 1941 at Pearl Harbor, Hawaii. He was awarded the American Defense Service Medal, World War II Victory Medal and Purple Heart Medal posthumously. James remains on duty on the USS Arizona. He is commemorated on the USS Arizona Memorial and the Memorial Tablets of the Missing, National Memorial Cemetery of the Pacific, Honolulu, Hawaii. James was survived by his Wife, Mrs. James Dennis Kelley, 602 West Elk Avenue, Glendale, California.[415]

Kellogg, Wilbur Leroy Fireman, First Class, Serial No: 372 14 26, US Navy. Wilbur was born in 1918 in Colorado, the son of Walter Leroy and Dora Anabelle (Davis) Kellogg. *He was eight years old when his mother died. Wilbur and his brothers then went to live with his maternal grandparents on a farm in Colorado.* Wilbur enlisted in the US Navy on April 3, 1940 in Denver, Colorado and completed his basic training at the Naval Training Station in San Diego, California. He reported for duty on the USS Arizona on July 8, 1940. Wilbur was killed in action on December 7, 1941 at Pearl Harbor, Hawaii. He was awarded the American Defense Service Medal, World War II Victory Medal and Purple Heart Medal posthumously. Wilbur remains on duty on the USS Arizona. He is commemorated on the USS Arizona Memorial and the Memorial Tablets of the Missing, National Memorial Cemetery of the Pacific, Honolulu, Hawaii. Wilbur was survived by his Father, Mr. Walter Leroy Kellogg, Shenandoah, Iowa.[416]

Kelly, Robert Lee Chief Electrician's Mate, Serial No: 267 22 16, US Navy. Robert was born July 28, 1902 in Georgia to William Jordan and Julia Etta (Newsome) Kelley. He re-enlisted in the US Navy on October 12, 1935 in San Pedro, California and reported for duty on the USS Arizona on April 29, 1940 transferring from the USS Pensacola. He was killed in action on December 7, 1941 at Pearl Harbor, Hawaii. Robert was awarded the American Defense Service Medal, World War II Victory Medal and Purple Heart Medal posthumously. He remains on duty on the USS Arizona. Robert is commemorated on the USS Arizona Memorial and the Memorial Tablets of the Missing, National Memorial Cemetery of the Pacific, Honolulu, Hawaii. He was survived by his Wife, Mrs. Dorothy Augusta Kelly, 619 East 7th Street, Long Beach, California.

---

[415] James Dennis Kelley, Photo taken from the Daily Oklahoman Newspaper, January 1942.
[416] Wilbur Leroy Kellogg, Family information provided by Gary Branum.

Keniston, Donald Lee   Seaman, Second Class, Serial No: 279 83 35, US Navy. Donald was born April 26, 1924 in Ohio. He enlisted in the US Navy on June 23, 1941 in Cincinnati, Ohio and completed his basic training at the Naval Training Station in Great Lakes, Illinois. Donald reported for duty on the USS Arizona October 11, 1941, joining his brother Kenneth. He was killed in action on December 7, 1941 at Pearl Harbor, Hawaii. Donald was awarded the American Defense Service Medal, World War II Victory Medal and Purple Heart Medal posthumously. He remains on duty on the USS Arizona with his brother. Donald is commemorated on the USS Arizona Memorial and the Memorial Tablets of the Missing, National Memorial Cemetery of the Pacific, Honolulu, Hawaii and Mount Washington Cemetery, Mount Washington, Ohio. He was survived by his Mother, Mrs. Burnette Sharpe, 4150 Kirby Avenue, Cincinnati, Ohio. His brother, Kenneth was killed in action on the Arizona.[417]

Keniston, Kenneth Howard   Fireman, Third Class, Serial No: 279 75 69, US Navy. Kenneth was born December 14, 1922 in Ohio. He enlisted in the US Navy on November 27, 1940 in Cincinnati, Ohio and completed his basic training at the Naval Training Station in Great Lakes, Illinois. Kenneth reported for duty on the USS Arizona on January 18, 1940. He was killed in action on December 7, 1941 at Pearl Harbor, Hawaii. *"Kenny" was by his clothes locker waiting for a call over the loud speaker telling the ship's crew that the launch to take the Catholic men to their church service was along side. It was then a chief came running down the passageway shouting, "The Japs are attacking. Man your battle stations." Kenny's battle station was the No. 2 gun as an electrician. An armor-piercing bomb went through the decks next to that gun turret and exploded in their ammunition locker.* He was awarded the American Defense Service Medal, World War II Victory Medal and Purple Heart Medal posthumously. Kenneth remains on duty on the USS Arizona. He is commemorated on the USS Arizona Memorial and the Memorial Tablets of the Missing, National Memorial Cemetery of the Pacific, Honolulu, Hawaii. Kenneth was survived by his Mother, Mrs. Burnette Sharpe, 4150 Kirby Avenue, Cincinnati, Ohio. His brother, Donald was killed in action on the Arizona.[418]

Kennard, Kenneth Frank   Gunner's Mate, Third Class, Serial No: 393 30 46, US Navy. Kenneth was born on January 7, 1918 in Missouri to Charles William and Maggie (Pickett) Kennard. He enlisted in the US Navy on August 16, 1939 in Portland, Oregon and completed his basic training at the Naval Training Station in San Diego, California. Kenneth reported for duty on the USS Arizona on October 20, 1939. He was killed in action on December 7, 1941 at Pearl Harbor, Hawaii. Kenneth was awarded the American Defense Service Medal, World War II Victory Medal and Purple Heart Medal posthumously. He remains on duty on the USS Arizona. Kenneth is commemorated on the USS Arizona Memorial and the Memorial Tablets of the Missing, National Memorial Cemetery of the Pacific,

---

[417] Donald Lee Keniston, Photo and information provided by family member, Jackie Townes.
[418] Kenneth Howard Keniston, Photo and information provided by family member, Jackie Townes.

Honolulu, Hawaii. He was survived by his Father, Mr. Charles W. Kennard, Payette, Idaho.[419]

Kennington, Charles Cecil Seaman, First Class, Serial No: 295 53 51, US Navy. Charles was born in 1920 in Tennessee. He enlisted in the US Navy on December 5, 1939 in Nashville, Tennessee and completed his basic training at the Naval Training Station in Great Lakes, Illinois. Charles reported for duty on the USS Arizona on March 29, 1940. He was killed in action on December 7, 1941 at Pearl Harbor, Hawaii. Charles was awarded the American Defense Service Medal, World War II Victory Medal and Purple Heart Medal posthumously. He remains on duty on the USS Arizona with his brother, Milton. Charles is commemorated on the USS Arizona Memorial and the Memorial Tablets of the Missing, National Memorial Cemetery of the Pacific, Honolulu, Hawaii. He was survived by his Parents, Mr. and Mrs. Van Arthur Kennington, 1021 North 18th Avenue, Humboldt, Tennessee four brothers and six sisters. His brother, Milton was killed in action on the Arizona and another brother, Lt. Lloyd D. was killed in action against the Germans in the First World War.[420]

Kennington, Milton Homer Seaman, First Class, Serial No: 295 60 56, US Navy. Milton was born in 1921 in Tennessee. He enlisted in the US Navy on March 5, 1940 in Nashville, Tennessee and completed his basic training at the Naval Training Station in Great Lakes, Illinois. Milton reported for duty on the USS Arizona on July 12, 1940. He was killed in action on December 7, 1941 at Pearl Harbor, Hawaii. Milton was awarded the American Defense Service Medal, World War II Victory Medal and Purple Heart Medal posthumously. He remains on duty on the USS Arizona with his brother, Charles. Milton is commemorated on the USS Arizona Memorial and the Memorial Tablets of the Missing, National Memorial Cemetery of the Pacific, Honolulu, Hawaii. He was survived by his Father, Mr. Van Arthur Kennington, 1021 North 18th Avenue, Humboldt, Tennessee, four brothers and six sisters. His brother, Charles was killed in action on the Arizona and another brother, Lt. Lloyd D. was killed in action against the Germans in the First World War.[421]

Kent, Texas Thomas, Jr. Seaman, Second Class, Serial No: 386 01 77, US Navy. Texas was born on October 25, 1920, the youngest of 10 children to Texas Thomas and Maude M. (Wiseman) Kent of Newburg, Arkansas. He enlisted in the US Navy on June 25, 1941 in Seattle, Washington and completed his basic training at the Naval Training Station in San Diego, California. Texas reported for duty on the USS Arizona on August 29, 1941. He was killed in action on December 7, 1941 at Pearl Harbor, Hawaii. Texas was awarded the American Defense Service Medal, World War II Victory Medal and Purple Heart Medal posthumously. He remains on duty on the USS Arizona. Texas is commemorated on the USS Arizona Memorial and the Memorial Tablets of the Missing, National Memorial Cemetery of the Pacific, Honolulu, Hawaii

---

[419] Kenneth Frank Kennard, Photo from Idaho Honor States.

[420] Charles Cecil Kennington, Photo provided by his Nephew, Charles Allison, Treasurer, Humboldt Historical Society, Humboldt, TN.

[421] Milton Homer Kennington, Photo provided by his Nephew, Charles Allison, Treasurer, Humboldt Historical Society, Humboldt, TN.

and the Izard County War Memorial, Melbourne, Arkansas. He was survived by his Father, Mr. Texas Thomas Kent, Sr., Brockwell, Arkansas.

Kidd, Isaac Campbell Rear Admiral, Serial No: 0-005715, US Navy. Isaac was born on March 26, 1884 in Cleveland, Ohio to Isaac and Jemina Campbell Kidd. On appointment from his native state, he then entered the U.S. Naval Academy, from which he graduated as a Passed Midshipman on February 12, 1906. He first served on the USS Columbia, which carried the Marine Expeditionary Force to the Canal Zone and participated in the round-the-world cruise of the "Great White Fleet." On May 17, 1907, he reported to the USS New Jersey. During this tour, he completed the two years at sea then required before commissioning and was commissioned an Ensign of the US Navy on February 13, 1908. He transferred on May 2, 1910 to the USS North Dakota, where he served until June 1913. He then joined the USS Pittsburgh on June 30, 1913, and during the Mexican trouble of 1914-16 he served as First lieutenant. Following this tour, he served as Aide and Flag Secretary on the staff of Commander-in-Chief, Pacific Fleet, aboard the flagships USS Pittsburgh and USS San Diego. He returned to the Naval Academy in August 1916 and was serving as an instructor on the Academic Staff when the United States entered World War I.

In 1918, he joined the USS New Mexico, serving on that battleship during her fitting out, during her service in the last months of the war, and until July 1919. His next tours were as Aide and Flag Lieutenant to Commander-in-Chief, Atlantic Fleet, and in 1921 as Aide in Charge of Buildings and Grounds for the Superintendent of the Naval Academy. Cdr. Kidd then served as Executive Officer on the USS Utah from May 1925 until November 1926. He then assumed his first command on the USS Vega, which he held until June 1927.

There followed a long period of shore duty first as Captain of the Port at Cristobal, Canal Zone and then from June 1930 as Chief of Staff to Commander Fleet Base Force. For three years, he was in charge of the Officer Detail Section of the Bureau of Navigation in Washington, DC. He returned to sea duty from February 25, 1935 to June 7, 1936 as Commander Destroyer Squadron One, Scouting Force. He then completed the Senior and Advanced Courses at the Naval War College in Newport, Rhode Island, remaining there to serve on the staff for several months.

In September 1938, Captain Kidd assumed command of the battleship USS Arizona, serving until February 1940. He was then designated Commander Battleship Division One and Chief of Staff and Aide to Commander Battleships, Battle Force, with the accompanying rank of Rear Admiral. RADM Kidd was killed in action on December 7, 1941 at Pearl Harbor, Hawaii. He became the first flag officer to lose his life in World War II and the first in the U.S. Navy to meet death in action against any foreign enemy. Isaac remains on duty on the USS Arizona; he died on the signal bridge. He is commemorated on the USS Arizona Memorial and the Memorial Tablets of the Missing, National Memorial Cemetery of the Pacific, Honolulu, Hawaii. Isaac was survived by his Wife, Mrs. Inez Nellie (Gilmore) Kidd, Carvel Hall, Annapolis, Maryland and by a son, Isaac C. Kidd, Jr. U.S. Naval Academy Class of 1942. Isaac was awarded the Congressional Medal of Honor:

Medal of Honor Citation: For conspicuous devotion to duty, extraordinary courage and complete disregard of his own life, during the attack on the Fleet in Pearl Harbor, by Japanese forces on 7 Dec 1941. Rear Adm. Kidd immediately went to the bridge and, as Commander Battleship Division One, courageously discharged his duties as Senior Officer Present Afloat until the USS Arizona, his Flagship, blew up from magazine explosions and a direct bomb hit on the bridge which resulted in the loss of his life.

In addition to the Medal of Honor, RADM Kidd was posthumously awarded the Purple Heart Medal. He previously had won the Cuban Pacification Medal while on the USS Columbia; the Mexican Service Medal while aboard the USS Pittsburgh; and the World War I Victory Medal, Atlantic Fleet Clasp while aboard the USS New Mexico. He was also entitled to the American Defense Service Medal, Fleet Clasp, Asiatic-Pacific Campaign Medal with one engagement star, and the World War II Victory Medal. The destroyer, USS Kidd (DD-661) was named in his honor.

The first thing that we must know about him is that the Admiral did not like his name. In fact, he was usually known as "Cap" to family and friends. This was apparently derived from his days at the Academy when classmates dubbed him with the moniker after Captain William Kidd of pirate lore. In fact, according to son "Ike" Kidd, Jr., "one of his first letters to me when I first attended the Academy was of him apologizing for naming me after him. I never minded the name, but apparently he did."

"Cap" was a boxer during his time at the Academy. He maintained a daily regimen of exercise throughout his life, both at sea and while in port. Whenever the Arizona was in port at Pearl Harbor, he could be seen taking walks every day on Ford Island. According to many of the survivors of the Arizona, Kidd was also a father figure to many in his crew. He held their respect, being described as "fair" and "a working admiral." He would have little biographical note cards that he stuck to the mirror in his bathroom that kept him apprised of his men's lives, families, rent, conditions of their children. One story tells of a young Marine assigned to the Admiral who announced that he was getting married. Kidd delayed the ship's departure from San Francisco so that the young man could get his home and marriage started and in order before leaving. The first person to arrive with a housewarming gift was RADM Kidd.

The destroyer, USS Kidd (DD-661) was named in his honor 3 years after his death. In 1979, a second ship, USS Kidd (DDG-993) was named in his honor. The USS Kidd (DDG-993) was decommissioned in March of 1998. On January 22, 2005, the destroyer, USS Kidd (DDG-100) became the third vessel to bear the name of RADM Kidd.[422]

Kiehn, Ronald William Machinist's Mate, Second Class, Serial No: 321 21 88, US Navy. Ronald was born December 2, 1919 in Benson, Minnesota the son of Frederick Wilhelm Kiehn and Irene (Schafer) Kiehn. He enlisted in the US Navy on December 7, 1937 in Des Moines, Iowa and completed his basic training at the Naval Training Station in Great Lakes, Illinois. He reported for duty on the USS Arizona on March 12, 1938. *Ronald was discharged from the Navy on December 6, 1941 but because the Arizona was to deploy back to Long Beach Naval Station the following Saturday, he decided to stay on board with his buddies for the trip back.* Ronald was killed in action on December 7, 1941 at Pearl Harbor, Hawaii. He was awarded the American Defense Service Medal, World War II Victory Medal and Purple Heart Medal posthumously. Ronald remains on duty on the USS Arizona. He is commemorated on the USS Arizona Memorial and the Memorial Tablets of the Missing, National Memorial Cemetery of the Pacific, Honolulu, Hawaii. Ronald was survived by his Wife, Mrs. Margaret Berenice (Barfield) Kiehn, Route 1, Box 91, Hemet, California and a three month old son, Ronald William Kiehn, Jr.

---

[422] Biography of Rear Admiral Isaac Campbell Kidd, Sr. (1884-1941) USS Kidd & Veterans Memorial, Baton Rouge, LA http://www.usskidd.com/ Living History.

Kieselbach, Charles Ermin Carpenter's Mate, First Class, Serial No: 336 84 58, US Navy. Charles was born January 14, 1916 in Jefferson City, Missouri to Charles Ernest and Emma Louise (Schwartz) Kieselbach. He enlisted in the US Navy on September 10, 1935 in St. Louis, Missouri. He served on the USS Arizona from January 11, 1936 until he was killed in action on December 7, 1941 at Pearl Harbor, Hawaii. Charles was awarded the American Defense Service Medal, World War II Victory Medal and Purple Heart Medal posthumously. He remains on duty on the USS Arizona. Charles is commemorated on the USS Arizona Memorial and the Memorial Tablets of the Missing, National Memorial Cemetery of the Pacific, Honolulu, Hawaii. He was survived by his Wife, Mrs. June Kieselbach, 2224 Canal Street, Long Beach, California.

King, Gordon Blane Seaman, First Class, Serial No: 295 76 65, US Navy. Gordon was born February 20, 1920 in Tennessee, the son of William Thomas and Alice Daisy (Bohannon) King. He enlisted in the US Navy on October 4, 1940 in Nashville, Tennessee and completed his basic training at the Naval Training Station in Norfolk, Virginia. Gordon reported for duty on the USS Arizona on December 4, 1940. He was killed in action on December 7, 1941 at Pearl Harbor, Hawaii. Gordon was awarded the American Defense Service Medal, World War II Victory Medal and Purple Heart Medal posthumously. He remains on duty on the USS Arizona. Gordon is commemorated on the USS Arizona Memorial and the Memorial Tablets of the Missing, National Memorial Cemetery of the Pacific, Honolulu, Hawaii. He was survived by his Parents, Mr. and Mrs. William Thomas King, Davis Avenue, Knoxville, Tennessee and siblings: Hazel, Blanche, Ruth, Helen, Charles, Marion and Clyde King.[423]

King, Leander Cleaveland Seaman, First Class, Serial No: 356 28 86, US Navy. Leander enlisted in the US Navy on May 17, 1940 in Dallas, Texas and completed his basic training at the Naval Training Station in San Diego, California. He reported for duty on the USS Arizona on August 25, 1940. Leander was killed in action on December 7, 1941 at Pearl Harbor, Hawaii. He was awarded the American Defense Service Medal, World War II Victory Medal and Purple Heart Medal posthumously. Leander remains on duty on the USS Arizona. He is commemorated on the USS Arizona Memorial and the Memorial Tablets of the Missing, National Memorial Cemetery of the Pacific, Honolulu, Hawaii. Leander was survived by his Mother, Mrs. Bonnie Jewel King, 1609 Pine Street, Dallas, Texas.[424]

---

[423] Gordon Blane King, photo and information provided by family member, Cheryl Ryan.
[424] Leander Cleveland King, photo curtsey LCDR G. Dale McKissick, USNR, Memorial, Dallas Convention Center, Dallas, Texas.

King, Lewis Meyer Fireman, First Class, Serial No: 262 37 78, US Navy. Lewis was born April 29, 1921 in North Carolina. He enlisted in the US Navy on September 12, 1939 in Raleigh, North Carolina and reported for duty on the USS Arizona on January 8, 1941. Lewis was killed in action on December 7, 1941 at Pearl Harbor, Hawaii. He was awarded the American Defense Service Medal, World War II Victory Medal and Purple Heart Medal posthumously. Lewis remains on duty on the USS Arizona. He is commemorated on the USS Arizona Memorial and the Memorial Tablets of the Missing, National Memorial Cemetery of the Pacific, Honolulu, Hawaii. Lewis was survived by his Parents, Mr. and Mrs. Arthur Lee King, Knightdale, North Carolina. On December 21, 2010, the Knightdale American Legion Post 529 was renamed the Lewis Meyer King Post 529, Knightdale, North Carolina in honor of Lewis.[425]

King, Robert Nicholas, Jr. Ensign, Serial No: 0-096609, US Navy Reserve. Robert was born in about 1914 in New York to Robert Nicholas Sr., and Evelyn E. King. He attended Columbia University and was commissioned Ensign on March 14, 1941. Robert was serving as Junior Watch and Division 1 Officer. His battle station was Turret 1. Robert was killed in action on December 7, 1941 at Pearl Harbor, Hawaii. He was awarded the American Defense Service Medal, World War II Victory Medal and Purple Heart Medal posthumously. Robert remains on duty on the USS Arizona. He is commemorated on the USS Arizona Memorial and the Memorial Tablets of the Missing, National Memorial Cemetery of the Pacific, Honolulu, Hawaii. Robert was survived by his Father, Mr. Robert N. King, Sr., 112 East 74th Street, New York, New York.[426]

Kinney, Frederick William Musician, First Class, Bandmaster, Serial No: 279 25 26, US Navy. Frederick was born on July 31, 1909 in Robinson Creek, Kentucky, the son of George Washington and Mary E. (Johnson) Kinney. He enlisted in the US Navy on November 3, 1926. Frederick graduated from the Musician's School on January 12, 1928. Assigned duty on the USS West Virginia on September 30, 1931 and served on the West Virginia until June 5, 1934. Later he served on the USS New Mexico, USS Pennsylvania, USS Argonne and finally on the USS Arizona. He was recommended for advancement to Bandmaster on the USS Arizona on July 22, 1941. He was killed in action on December 7, 1941 at Pearl Harbor, Hawaii. *Frederick's battle station, as a band member, was in the black powder room passing ammunition to the Arizona's gunners during the attack. None of the band members survived the explosion.* He was awarded the American Defense Service Medal, World War II Victory Medal and Purple Heart Medal posthumously. Frederick remains on duty on the USS Arizona. He is commemorated on the USS Arizona Memorial and the Memorial Tablets of the Missing, National Memorial

---

[425] Lewis Meyer King, Information provided by the Lewis Meyer King American Legion Post 529, Knightdale, North Carolina.
[426] Robert Nicholas King, Jr., Photo from New York Honor States.

Cemetery of the Pacific, Honolulu, Hawaii. Frederick was survived by his Wife, Mrs. Elizabeth M. (Von Babo) Kinney, 2307 8ᵗʰ Street, Bremerton, Washington.[427]

Kinney, Gilbert Livingston Quartermaster, Second Class, Serial No: 382 09 35, US Navy. Gilbert was born June 15, 1921 in Los Angeles, California to Harold Sheldon and Gladys (Hoard) Kinney. He enlisted in the US Navy on May 16, 1939 in Los Angeles, California and completed his basic training at the Naval Training Station in San Diego, California. Gilbert reported for duty on the USS Arizona on September 8, 1939. He was killed in action on December 7, 1941 at Pearl Harbor, Hawaii. Gilbert was awarded the American Defense Service Medal, World War II Victory Medal and Purple Heart Medal posthumously. He remains on duty on the USS Arizona. Gilbert is commemorated on the USS Arizona Memorial and the Memorial Tablets of the Missing, National Memorial Cemetery of the Pacific, Honolulu, Hawaii and the Mountain View Cemetery and Mausoleum, Altadena, California. He was survived by his Father, Mr. Harold Sheldon Kinney, 661 South Los Robles Avenue, Pasadena, California.

Kirchoff, Wilbur Albert Seaman, First Class, Serial No: 337 42 10, US Navy. Wilbur was born May 20, 1915 In St. Louis County, Missouri, the son of Albert and Ester Kirchoff. He enlisted in the US Navy on October 22, 1940 in St. Louis, Missouri and completed his basic training at the Naval Training Station in Great Lakes, Illinois. Wilbur reported for duty on the USS Arizona on January 18, 1941. He was killed in action on December 7, 1941 at Pearl Harbor, Hawaii. Wilbur was awarded the American Defense Service Medal, World War II Victory Medal and Purple Heart Medal posthumously. He remains on duty on the USS Arizona. Wilbur is commemorated on the USS Arizona Memorial and the Memorial Tablets of the Missing, National Memorial Cemetery of the Pacific, Honolulu, Hawaii. He was survived by his Father, Mr. Albert F. Kirchhoff, Route 1, Box 67, Rosebud, Missouri.[428]

Kirk, Guy Duane Seaman, First Class, Serial No. 385 91 16, US Navy. Guy was born February 14, 1917 in Douglas, Washington, son of Guy Elsworth Kirk and Oliva Marie (Hagen) Kirk. He enlisted in the US Navy on October 4, 1940 in Seattle, Washington and reported for duty on the USS Enterprise. He was transferred to the USS Arizona, reporting for duty on January 8, 1941. Guy was serving on the Arizona on December 7, 1941 when the Japanese attacked Pearl Harbor. After the attack, Guy was transferred to the USS Patterson for duty. On February 1, 1945 he was promoted to Chief Gunner's Mate. Guy was killed in action on May 19, 1945 and is buried in the Forest Home Cemetery, Ponoka, Alberta, Canada.

---

[427] Frederick William Kinney, Photo from USS Arizona's Last Band by Molly Kent. By permission of the author. For more information about this book, go to www.USSARIZONASLASTBAND.com.
[428] Wilbur Albert Kirchoff, Photo from St. Louis Post-Dispatch, St. Louis, Missouri, December 27, 1941, Page 5

Kirkpatrick, Thomas Leroy Captain, Chaplain Corps, Serial No: 0-928860, US Navy. Thomas was born on July 5, 1887 in Cozad, Nebraska. He was appointed Acting Chaplain, U.S. Navy, February 19, 1918. After serving as chaplain to stations in the United States and abroad, Chaplain Kirkpatrick was assigned to the USS North Dakota on June 24, 1919. For the next 20 years he served on the USS Utah, USS Pittsburgh and USS Saratoga in addition to duty at Samoa from 1935 to 1937. Commander Thomas Kirkpatrick, Chaplain, reported for duty on the USS Arizona on September 13, 1940 and was promoted to Captain on July 1, 1941. Kirkpatrick represented the Protestant faith. *On Sunday morning, Thomas was in the wardroom of the Arizona with some of his fellow officers enjoying a cup of coffee. The wardroom mess was across from the admiral's cabin on the left side of the second deck. When general quarters were sounded, Thomas rushed to his battle station in sickbay to minister to any casualties. The location of sickbay was on the same deck just forward of gun turret number one. Most of the men in that area of the ship were gone in an instant from the massive explosions of the forward magazines.* Thomas was killed in action on December 7, 1941 at Pearl Harbor, Hawaii. He was awarded the American Defense Service Medal, World War II Victory Medal and Purple Heart Medal posthumously. Thomas remains on duty on the USS Arizona. He is commemorated on the USS Arizona Memorial and the Memorial Tablets of the Missing, National Memorial Cemetery of the Pacific, Honolulu, Hawaii. Thomas was survived by his Wife, Mrs. Thomas Leroy Kirkpatrick, 330 West Lockwood Avenue, Webster Groves, Missouri. The USS Kirkpatrick (DE-318) was named after Thomas in 1943 and remained in service until 1960.[429]

Kissinger, Walter Marlond Machinist's Mate, First Class, Serial No. 243 54 52, US Navy, M Division, Machinery. Walter was born June 6, 1918, son of John Kissinger and Mary (Loose) Kissinger. His father died at a young age from tuberculosis when Walter was only nine years old. Walter enlisted in the US Navy September 16, 1936 in Philadelphia, Pennsylvania and reported for duty on the USS Arizona September 10, 1937. On September 15, 1940, Walter extended his enlistment 2 years. He was serving on the USS Arizona on December 7, 1941 when the Japanese attacked Pearl Harbor. On that morning, he was down in the bottom of the ship doing maintenance when he heard all the noise above. The first bomb struck and that's when things started to happen. Fires broke out, and he tried to save several of his friends as the water was filling up inside. He and a friend made it topside and were told to abandon ship. They jumped into the water which was on fire from the burning fuel. They had to swim hand in hand, because his friend was hurt, swimming under water as to not get burned. They would come up for a breath of air when they could see an opening from the fire. Walter was burned around his mouth, and carried those scars with him always. A big piece of the ship came down and hit his friend on the head knocking him away from Walt. He couldn't go after him because of the chaos. Walt never saw his friend again and carried the guilt of his loss the rest of his life. After the attack, Walter was transferred to the USS Whitney for duty. When Walt got out of the Navy, he married Reba Behmer. They had two children, Jenny Kissinger and Mark B. Kissinger. Walt worked as a plumber, owning his own business until his health failed him. He loved to go fishing and was seen often wearing his sailor

---

[429] Thomas Leroy Kirkpatrick, Photo #NH 68504 Capt. Thomas L. Kirkpatrick, USN (ChC) Naval History Center.

hat, walking with a fishing pole in one hand and his tackle box in the other. Walter died a very sick and lonely man. He was divorced, but his ex-wife took him in near the end helping him because he had no-one else. Walt died on June 17, 1988 from emphysema.[430]

Klann, Edward Ship's Cook, First Class, Serial No: 375 34 62, US Navy. Edward was born October 10, 1907 in Detroit, Michigan, the son of August and Marie Klann. *The Klanns were German Lutherans who immigrated to America in 1879 and settled in the Detroit area of Michigan.* He enlisted in the US Navy on October 11, 1938 and reported for duty on the USS Arizona on February 18, 1941. Edward was killed in action on December 7, 1941 at Pearl Harbor, Hawaii. He was awarded the American Defense Service Medal, World War II Victory Medal and Purple Heart Medal posthumously. Edward remains on duty on the USS Arizona. He is commemorated on the USS Arizona Memorial and the Memorial Tablets of the Missing, National Memorial Cemetery of the Pacific, Honolulu, Hawaii. Edward was survived by his Parents, Mr. and Mrs. August Klann, 3897 Gilbert Street, Detroit, Michigan. *Edward was a loving son, brother and uncle. His descendents honor his memory and sacrifice to this day.* Two great nephews served in the Navy. One's reenlistment took place aboard the USS Arizona Memorial. A great, great nephew graduated from the US Naval Academy in May 2012, has seen and touched Edward's Purple Heart and visited the USS Arizona Memorial.[431]

Kline, Robert Edwin Gunner's Mate, Second Class, Serial No: 234 16 98, US Navy. Robert was born October 28, 1919 in New York to Arthur Lowery and Lura Susan (Holcomb) Kline. He enlisted in the US Navy on October 13, 1937 in Buffalo, New York and reported for duty on the USS Arizona on March 8, 1938. *After the attack, many of Roberts papers were found floating in the water and were recovered.* Robert was killed in action on December 7, 1941 at Pearl Harbor, Hawaii. He was awarded the American Defense Service Medal, World War II Victory Medal and Purple Heart Medal posthumously. Robert remains on duty on the USS Arizona. He is commemorated on the USS Arizona Memorial and the Memorial Tablets of the Missing, National Memorial Cemetery of the Pacific, Honolulu, Hawaii and Arlington National Cemetery, Arlington, Virginia. *On Memorial Day 2006, while taking their children through Arlington Cemetery, they found that there were memorial headstones for men who were lost at sea or, for whatever reason, were not able to have a burial because the remains were lost. Upon inquiring at the main office, they found that Robert had never had a funeral and was entitled to one, along with a memorial headstone. Since they were the next of kin, they were able to choose the memorial stone and any veteran's cemetery, they choose Arlington. In October of 2006, the entire family arrived at Arlington and Robert was given a full military service with the family being presented with a folded flag.* Robert was survived by his Parents, Mr. and Mrs. Arthur Lowell Kline, 563 South Park Avenue, Buffalo, New York; Sister, Anna Ruth Kline and

---

[430] Information and photos provided by Joni Kissinger Martines, 9/1/2008.
[431] Edward Klann, Photo provided by family members, Gale and Suzanne Hunt as passed down to them from Edward's parents, August and Marie Klann.

Brothers, Arthur "Artie" Lowry, Jr., Grant "Klinie" Holcomb, Eugene "Gene" Lowell and Gerald Lamont Kline.[432]

Klopp, Francis Lawrence   Gunner's Mate, Third Class, Serial No: 379 55 99, US Navy. Francis was born on December 3, 1914 in Tiffin, Ohio to John Joseph and Theresa Eleanora (Houk) Klopp. He enlisted in the US Navy on June 21, 1938 in Cincinnati, Ohio and reported for duty on the USS Arizona on November 10, 1938. Francis was killed in action on December 7, 1941 at Pearl Harbor, Hawaii. He was awarded the American Defense Service Medal, World War II Victory Medal and Purple Heart Medal posthumously. Francis remains on duty on the USS Arizona. He is commemorated on the USS Arizona Memorial and the Memorial Tablets of the Missing, National Memorial Cemetery of the Pacific, Honolulu, Hawaii. Francis was survived by his Father, Mr. John Joseph Klopp, 208 Walker Street, Tiffin, Ohio.

Knight, Robert Wagner   Electrician's Mate, Third Class, Serial No: 279 72 81, US Navy. Robert was born on May 1, 1922 in Fairfield County, Ohio, the son of James Adrian and Cora Blanche (Wagner) Knight. He enlisted in the US Navy on September 9, 1940 in Cincinnati, Ohio and completed his basic training at the Naval Training Station in Norfolk, Virginia. Robert reported for duty on the USS Arizona on December 4, 1940. He was killed in action on December 7, 1941 at Pearl Harbor, Hawaii. Robert was awarded the American Defense Service Medal, World War II Victory Medal and Purple Heart Medal posthumously. He remains on duty on the USS Arizona. Robert is commemorated on the USS Arizona Memorial and the Memorial Tablets of the Missing, National Memorial Cemetery of the Pacific, Honolulu, Hawaii and the Obetz Cemetery, Obetz, Ohio. He was survived by his Father, Mr. James Adrian Knight, Route 1, Lancaster, Ohio.[433]

Knubel, William, Jr.   Seaman, First Class, Serial No: 342 32 51, US Navy. William enlisted in the US Navy on November 12, 1940 in Kansas City, Missouri and completed his basic training at the Naval Training Station in Great Lakes, Illinois. He reported for duty on the USS Arizona on January 18, 1941. William was killed in action on December 7, 1941 at Pearl Harbor, Hawaii. He was awarded the American Defense Service Medal, World War II Victory Medal and Purple Heart Medal posthumously. William remains on duty on the USS Arizona. He is commemorated on the USS Arizona Memorial and the Memorial Tablets of the Missing, National Memorial Cemetery of the Pacific, Honolulu, Hawaii. William was survived by his Father, Mr. William Knubel, Sr., Route 3, Summit, Missouri.

Koch, Walter Ernest   Seaman, First Class, Serial No: 328 62 81, US Navy. Walter was born February 2, 1919 in Iowa to Louis J. and Anna B. Koch. He enlisted in the US Navy on December 12, 1939 in Minneapolis, Minnesota and completed his basic training at the Naval Training Station in Great Lakes, Illinois. He reported for duty on the USS Arizona on March 9, 1940. *On December 20th his brother received a message that Walter was missing in action. On the 23rd of December he received another telegram informing him that Walter had been killed in action, but Christmas day a third telegram said Walter was alive and well.[434] Assigned death*

---

[432] Robert Edwin Kline, Information and photo provided by his Niece, Carol A. (Kline) DeGraba.

[433] Robert Wagner Knight, Photo from Ohio Honor States.

[434] Walter Ernest Koch, information from The Bismarck Tribune, Bismarck, North Dakota, December 26, 1941, Page 1.

#399, Walter died on December 11, 1941 from shrapnel wounds received in action on December 7, 1941 at Pearl Harbor, Hawaii. He was awarded the American Defense Service Medal, World War II Victory Medal and Purple Heart Medal posthumously. His body was sent home for burial in the G.A.R. Cemetery, Devil's Lake, North Dakota. He is commemorated on the USS Arizona Memorial and the Memorial Tablets of the Missing, National Memorial Cemetery of the Pacific, Honolulu, Hawaii. Walter was survived by his Brother, Mr. Adam W. Koch, 424 4th Street South, Moorhead, Minnesota.

Koenekamp, Clarence Dietrich Fireman, First Class, Serial No: 385 79 73, US Navy. Clarence was born February 15, 1918 to Herman John Dietrich and Elise M. (Johanssen) Koenekamp. He enlisted in the US Navy on December 13, 1938 in Seattle, Washington and completed his basic training at the Naval Training Station in San Diego, California. Clarence reported for duty on the USS Arizona on April 29, 1939. *He was serving with his brother, Emil on board the Arizona until November 11, 1941 when his brother was transferred to the West Coast.* He was killed in action on December 7, 1941 at Pearl Harbor, Hawaii. Because of the confusion and utter chaos, the family received a MIA for both brothers. Clarence was awarded the American Defense Service Medal, World War II Victory Medal and Purple Heart Medal posthumously. He remains on duty on the USS Arizona. Clarence is commemorated on the USS Arizona Memorial and the Memorial Tablets of the Missing, National Memorial Cemetery of the Pacific, Honolulu, Hawaii. He was survived by his Parents, Mr. and Mrs. Herman J. D. Koenekamp, 802 Seeley Street, Raymond, Washington.[435]

Koeppe, Herman Oliver Ship's Cook, Third Class, Serial No: 300 19 46, US Navy. Herman was born on July 10, 1922 in Ottawa, Illinois, the son of Oscar Hermann and Martha Rose (Seward) Koeppe. He enlisted in the US Navy on October 8, 1940 in Chicago, Illinois and completed his basic training at the Naval Training Station in Great Lakes, Illinois. Herman reported for duty on the USS Arizona on December 9, 1940. He was killed in action on December 7, 1941 at Pearl Harbor, Hawaii. Herman was awarded the American Defense Service Medal, World War II Victory Medal and Purple Heart Medal posthumously. He remains on duty on the USS Arizona. Herman is commemorated on the USS Arizona Memorial, the Memorial Tablets of the Missing, National Memorial Cemetery of the Pacific, Honolulu, Hawaii and Abraham Lincoln National Cemetery, Elwood, Illinois. He was survived by his Mother, Mrs. Martha Sherman, R. F. D. 4, Ottawa, Illinois. The Veterans of Foreign Wars Post 2470, Ottawa, Illinois was named in his honor along with shipmate, James McCarrens and Robert Halterman killed on board the USS Oklahoma.[436]

Kolajajck, Brosig Seaman, First Class, Serial No: 360 25 65, US Navy. Brosig was born on December 4, 1915 in Texas, the son of Frank and Maggie (Dobwinski) Kolajajck. He enlisted in the US Navy on November 8, 1940 in Houston, Texas and completed his basic training at the Naval Training Station in San Diego, California. Brosig reported for duty on the USS Arizona on January 11, 1941. Assigned death # 168, Brosig died on December 10, 1941 from burns received in action on December 7, 1941 at Pearl Harbor, Hawaii.[437] He was awarded the

---

[435] Clarence D. Koenekamp, Information provided by family member, Skip Brown.
[436] Herman Oliver Koeppe, Photo provided by the James McCarrens, nephew of James F. McCarrens and the VFW Post 2470, Ottawa, IL
[437] Report of Changes of the USS Arizona for the month ending 31st day of December, 1941, page 74, line 30, Brosig Kolajajck.

American Defense Service Medal, World War II Victory Medal and Purple Heart Medal posthumously. Brosig's remains were recovered and he was buried in Plot A, Row 0, Grave 521, National Memorial Cemetery of the Pacific, Honolulu, Hawaii. He is commemorated on the USS Arizona Memorial. Brosig was survived by his Father, Mr. Frank Kolajajck, Route 1, Anderson, Texas.

Konnick, Albert Joseph   Carpenter's Mate, Third Class, Serial No: 243 50 67, US Navy. Albert was born September 14, 1916 in Wilkes-Barre, Pennsylvania, the son of George and Pauline Konnick. He re-enlisted in the US Navy on January 14, 1936. *Albert and his best friend, Brinley Varchol both played on the USS Arizona's baseball team. Al was a 1ˢᵗ baseman and Brinley played 2ⁿᵈ base. Both were being scouted by the National Baseball League to play once their enlistments ran out. Unfortunately, they were both killed at Pearl Harbor.* Albert served on the USS Arizona from December 28, 1936 until he was killed in action on December 7, 1941 at Pearl Harbor, Hawaii. He was awarded the American Defense Service Medal, World War II Victory Medal and Purple Heart Medal posthumously. Albert remains on duty on the USS Arizona. He is commemorated on the USS Arizona Memorial and the Memorial Tablets of the Missing, National Memorial Cemetery of the Pacific, Honolulu, Hawaii. Albert was survived by his Father, Mr. George Konnick, 11 Auburn Street, Wilkes-Barre, Pennsylvania.[438]

Kosec, John Anthony   Boatswain's Mate, Second Class, Serial No: 283 19 79, US Navy. John was the son of Thomas and Mary Kosec. He enlisted in the US Navy on February 9, 1937 in Cleveland, Ohio and reported for duty on the USS Arizona on June 19, 1937. He was killed in action on December 7, 1941 at Pearl Harbor, Hawaii. John was awarded the American Defense Service Medal, World War II Victory Medal and Purple Heart Medal posthumously. He remains on duty on the USS Arizona. John is commemorated on the USS Arizona Memorial and the Memorial Tablets of the Missing, National Memorial Cemetery of the Pacific, Honolulu, Hawaii. John was survived by his Wife, Mrs. Katherine Therese Kosec, 106 Magnolia Avenue, Long Beach, California.

Kovar, Robert   Seaman, First Class, Serial No: 311 49 80, US Navy. Robert was born in 1921, the son of Stefan and Mary (William) Kovar. He enlisted in the US Navy on September 9, 1940 in Detroit, Michigan and completed his basic training at the Naval Training Station in Norfolk, Virginia. Robert reported for duty on the USS Arizona on December 4, 1940. He was killed in action on December 7, 1941 at Pearl Harbor, Hawaii. Robert was awarded the American Defense Service Medal, World War II Victory Medal and Purple Heart Medal posthumously. He remains on duty on the USS Arizona. Robert is commemorated on the USS Arizona Memorial and the Memorial Tablets of the Missing, National Memorial Cemetery of the Pacific, Honolulu, Hawaii. He was survived by his Father, Mr. Stefan Kovar, 5254 South Winchester Street, Chicago, Illinois.

---

[438] Albert Joseph Konnick, Photo from Pennsylvania Honor States.

Kramb, James Henry   Seaman, First Class, Serial No: 234 17 15, US Navy. James was born in about 1921 in New York, the son of Charles H. and Ruth Kramb. He enlisted in the US Navy on November 3, 1937 in Buffalo, New York and reported for duty on the USS Arizona on March 8, 1938. James was killed in action on December 7, 1941 at Pearl Harbor, Hawaii. He was awarded the American Defense Service Medal, World War II Victory Medal and Purple Heart Medal posthumously. James remains on duty on the USS Arizona with his brother, John. He is commemorated on the USS Arizona Memorial and the Memorial Tablets of the Missing, National Memorial Cemetery of the Pacific, Honolulu, Hawaii. James was survived by his Father, Mr. Charles H. Kramb, Sr., 35 Fairholm Road, Rochester, New York. His brother, John was killed in action on the Arizona. His other brother, Charles was killed in action on February 8, 1942 while serving on board the USS Canopus during the attempted defense of Bataan.[439]

Kramb, John David   Metalsmith, First Class, Serial No: 243 18 16, US Navy. John was born in about 1917 in New York, the son of Charles H. and Ruth Kramb. He was just 13 years old when his mother died in 1930. John enlisted in the US Navy on March 23, 1938 in Buffalo, New York and reported for duty on the USS Arizona on January 23, 1939. John was killed in action on December 7, 1941 at Pearl Harbor, Hawaii. He was awarded the American Defense Service Medal, World War II Victory Medal and Purple Heart Medal posthumously. John remains on duty on the USS Arizona with his brother, James. He is commemorated on the USS Arizona Memorial and the Memorial Tablets of the Missing, National Memorial Cemetery of the Pacific, Honolulu, Hawaii. John was survived by his Father, Mr. Charles H. Kramb, Sr., 35 Fairholm Road, Rochester, New York. His brother, James was killed in action on the Arizona. His other brother, Charles was killed in action on February 8, 1942 while serving on board the USS Canopus during the attempted defense of Bataan.[440]

Kramer, Robert Rudolph   Gunner's Mate, Second Class, Serial No: 291 55 25, US Navy. Robert was born June 27, 1920 in Indiana to Rudolph Charles and Frances Kramer. He enlisted in the US Navy June 3, 1938 in Indianapolis, Indiana and completed his basic training at the Naval Training Station in Great Lakes, Illinois. He reported for duty on the USS Arizona March 11, 1939. Robert was killed in action on December 7, 1941 at Pearl Harbor, Hawaii. He was awarded the American Defense Service Medal, World War II Victory Medal and Purple Heart Medal posthumously. Robert's remains were recovered and he was buried in Plot A, Row 0, Grave 520, National Memorial Cemetery of the Pacific, Honolulu, Hawaii. His parents received a package from the Navy department which contained some of their son's

---

[439] James Henry Kramb, Photo from "Remembering the fallen, Brothers Killed in infamous attack" by Sean Lahman, June 9, 2012 posted in Journalism.
[440] John David Kramb, Photo from "Remembering the fallen, Brothers Killed in Infamous Attack" by Sean Lahman, June 9, 2012 posted in Journalism.

personal belongings, including an oil-soaked $10 bill, two fifty-cent pieces, a high school graduation ring and other belongings on June 11th 1942.[441] He is commemorated on the USS Arizona Memorial. Robert was survived by his Father, Mr. Rudolph Charles Kramer, New Point, Indiana.[442]

Krause, Fred Joseph Seaman, First Class, Serial No: 328 61 83, US Navy. Fred was born September 4, 1920 in Le Sueur, Minnesota to Earnest Robert and Mary Martha (Morgenthaler) Krause. He enlisted in the US Navy on November 14, 1939 in Minneapolis, Minnesota and completed his basic training at the Naval Training Station in Great Lakes, Illinois. He reported for duty on the USS Arizona on January 27, 1940. Fred was killed in action on December 7, 1941 at Pearl Harbor, Hawaii. He was awarded the American Defense Service Medal, World War II Victory Medal and Purple Heart Medal posthumously. Fred remains on duty on the USS Arizona. He is commemorated on the USS Arizona Memorial and the Memorial Tablets of the Missing, National Memorial Cemetery of the Pacific, Honolulu, Hawaii. Fred was survived by his Father, Mr. Ernest Robert Krause, 129 3rd Street, Le Sueur, Minnesota.[443]

Krissman, Max Sam Seaman, Second Class, Serial No: 382 47 96, US Navy. Max was born February 12, 1924 in Illinois. He enlisted in the US Navy on June 24, 1941 in Los Angeles, California and completed his basic training at the Naval Training Station in San Diego, California. He reported for duty on the USS Arizona on August 29, 1941. Assigned death #307, Max died on December 10, 1941 from burns received in action on December 7, 1941 at Pearl Harbor, Hawaii. He was awarded the American Defense Service Medal, World War II Victory Medal and Purple Heart Medal posthumously. His remains were sent home for burial in Home of Peace Cemetery, Los Angeles, California. Max is commemorated on the USS Arizona Memorial and the Memorial Tablets of the Missing, National Memorial Cemetery of the Pacific, Honolulu, Hawaii. He was survived by his Mother, Mrs. Anna Krissman, 217 North Bailey Street, Los Angeles, California.

Kruger, Richard Warren Quartermaster, Second Class, Serial No: 375 91 49, US Navy. Richard was born December 19, 1919 in California to Henry and Helena Kruger. He enlisted in the US Navy on September 12, 1938 in San Francisco, California and completed his basic training at the Naval Training Station in San Diego, California. He reported for duty on the USS Arizona on January 2, 1939. Richard was killed in action on December 7, 1941 at Pearl Harbor, Hawaii. He was awarded the American Defense Service Medal, World War II Victory Medal and Purple Heart Medal posthumously. Richard remains on duty on the USS Arizona. He is commemorated on the USS Arizona Memorial and the Memorial Tablets of the Missing, National Memorial Cemetery of the Pacific, Honolulu, Hawaii. Richard was survived by his Father, Mr. Herman Henry Kruger, 830 45th Avenue, San Francisco, California.

Kruppa, Adolph Louis Seaman, First Class, Serial No: 360 32 41, US Navy. Adolph was born June 15, 1921 in Texas, the son of Emile Joseph and Rosa (Valigura) Kruppa. He enlisted in the US Navy on January 24, 1941 in Houston, Texas and completed his basic training at the Naval Training Station in San Diego, California. Adolph reported for duty on the USS

---

[441] Robert Rudolph Kramer, information from The Tribune, Seymour, Indiana, June 11, 1942, Page 1.
[442] Robert Rudolph Kramer, Photo provided by the Town of New Point, IN. New Point High School, 1938 graduating class.
[443] Fred Joseph Krause, Photo provided by the Le Sueur Museum, Le Sueur, Minnesota.

Arizona on April 27, 1941. He was killed in action on December 7, 1941 at Pearl Harbor, Hawaii. Adolph was awarded the American Defense Service Medal, World War II Victory Medal and Purple Heart Medal posthumously. He remains on duty on the USS Arizona. Adolph is commemorated on the USS Arizona Memorial and the Memorial Tablets of the Missing, National Memorial Cemetery of the Pacific, Honolulu, Hawaii. He was survived by his Father, Mr. Emil Joe Kruppa, Placedo Junction, Texas.

Kuhn, Harold Joseph   Seaman, First Class, Serial No. 393 37 67, US Navy. Harold was born on June 9, 1922 in the Bronx, New York City, New York the son of John Alfred and Katherine Kuhn. He had six siblings. His mother passed away in about 1939. He enlisted in the US Navy July 23, 1940 in Portland, Oregon and completed his basic training at the Naval Training Station in San Diego, California. He reported for duty on the USS Arizona October 1, 1940. Harold was serving on the USS Arizona on December 7, 1941 when the Japanese attacked Pearl Harbor. Harold was among a group of six men trapped in the Port Anti-Aircraft Director. He had the fewest injuries and was the first to go across the escape rope to the USS Vestal. After the attack, Harold was transferred to the USS Patterson for duty. Harold died on August 5, 1999 in North Fort Lauderdale, Florida.

Kukuk, Howard Helgi   Seaman, First Class, Serial No: 328 79 95, US Navy. Howard was born on June 18, 1922 in North Dakota, the son of Elmer Edward and Thruda Kukuk. He enlisted in the US Navy on November 27, 1940 in Minneapolis, Minnesota and completed his basic training at the Naval Training Station in Great Lakes, Illinois. Howard reported for duty on the USS Arizona on January 18, 1941. He was killed in action on December 7, 1941 at Pearl Harbor, Hawaii. Howard was awarded the American Defense Service Medal, World War II Victory Medal and Purple Heart Medal posthumously. He remains on duty on the USS Arizona. Howard is commemorated on the USS Arizona Memorial, the Memorial Tablets of the Missing, National Memorial Cemetery of the Pacific, Honolulu, Hawaii and Cavalier Cemetery, Cavalier, North Dakota. He was survived by his Father, Mr. Elmer Edward Kukuk, Cavalier, North Dakota.

Kula, Stanley   Ship's Cook, Third Class, Serial No: 316 69 08, US Navy. Stanley was born in 1922, the son of Joseph and Antonie Kula. He enlisted in the US Navy on October 7, 1940 in Omaha, Nebraska and completed his basic training at the Naval Training Station in Great Lakes, Illinois. Stanley reported for duty on the USS Arizona on December 9, 1940. He was killed in action on December 7, 1941 at Pearl Harbor, Hawaii. Stanley was awarded the American Defense Service Medal, World War II Victory Medal and Purple Heart Medal posthumously. He remains on duty on the USS Arizona. Stanley is commemorated on the USS Arizona Memorial and the Memorial Tablets of the Missing, National Memorial Cemetery of the Pacific, Honolulu, Hawaii and Saint Johns Cemetery, Bellevue, Nebraska. He was survived by his Parents, Mr. and Mrs. Joseph F. Kula, 4152 K Street, Omaha, Nebraska.

Kurtz, Stanley Robert   Seaman, First Class, Serial No. 393 38 11, US Navy. Stanley was born on August 19, 1921, son of Elias G. Kurtz and Sena I. Kurtz of Dayton, Oregon. He enlisted in the US Navy August 7, 1940 in Portland, Oregon and completed his basic training at the Naval Training Station in San Diego, California. He reported for duty on the USS Arizona October 8, 1940. Stanley was injured while serving on the USS Arizona December 7, 1941 when the Japanese attacked Pearl Harbor. During the attack, he was taken on board the USS

Tennessee. Because of his wounds, he was taken to the Naval Hospital at Pearl for treatment and later transferred to the Naval Hospital on the mainland. Stanley was killed in action while serving on board the USS Maddox when it was sunk by air attack off Gela, Sicily on July 10, 1943. He is commemorated on the Tablets of the Missing, Sicily-Rome American Cemetery, Nettuno, Italy. He was survived by his Mother, Mrs. Sena I. Davis, 3207 NE 71st Avenue, Portland, Oregon.

Kusie, Donald Joseph Radioman, Third Class, Aviation Unit (VO-1), Serial No: 328 69 17, US Navy. Donald was born January 1, 1919 in Dickinson, North Dakota, the son of Anton and Mary Kusie. *After graduating from Dickinson High School, he spent 4-1/2 years in the Civilian Conservation Corps, serving in Garrison & Thompson, Minnesota and Palos Verdes and Upland, California.* Donald enlisted in the US Navy on May 21, 1940 in Minneapolis, Minnesota and completed his basic training at the Naval Aviation Station in San Diego, California. Donald reported for duty on the USS Arizona on March 19, 1941. He was killed in action on December 7, 1941 at Pearl Harbor, Hawaii. Donald was awarded the American Defense Service Medal, World War II Victory Medal and Purple Heart Medal posthumously. He remains on duty on the USS Arizona. Donald is commemorated on the USS Arizona Memorial and the Memorial Tablets of the Missing, National Memorial Cemetery of the Pacific, Honolulu, Hawaii and the Dickinson Cemetery, Dickinson, North Dakota. He was survived by his Parents, Mr. and Mrs. Anton Joseph Kusie, 561 2nd Street East, Dickinson, North Dakota; Brother, Floyd of Chicago, IL; Twin brother and sister, Myron and Margaret of Dickinson.[444]

La France, William Richard Seaman, First Class, Serial No: 311 49 67, US Navy. William was born July 22, 1921 in Saginaw, Michigan to William Philip and Esther May (Mason) La France. He enlisted in the US Navy on September 9, 1940 in Detroit, Michigan and completed his basic training at the Naval Training Station in Norfolk, Virginia. William reported for duty on the USS Arizona on December 4, 1940. He was killed in action on December 7, 1941 at Pearl Harbor, Hawaii. William was awarded the American Defense Service Medal, World War II Victory Medal and Purple Heart Medal posthumously. He remains on duty on the USS Arizona. William is commemorated on the USS Arizona Memorial and the Memorial Tablets of the Missing, National Memorial Cemetery of the Pacific, Honolulu, Hawaii. He was survived by his Father, Mr. William Phillip LaFrance, 1213 Monroe Street, Saginaw, Michigan.[445]

---

[444] Donald Joseph Kusie, Photo and information provided by his Sister-In-Law, Katherine Kusie.
[445] William Richard La France, Photo from the freepages.genealogy.rootsweb.ancestry.com.

La Mar, Ralph B. Fire Controlman, Third Class, Serial No: 382 08 44, US Navy. Ralph was born in 1921 in Iowa, the son of Floyd Ival and Gennie La Mar. He enlisted in the US Navy on January 11, 1939 in Los Angeles, California and completed his basic training at the Naval Training Station in San Diego, California. Ralph reported for duty on the USS Arizona on July 1, 1939. He was killed in action on December 7, 1941 at Pearl Harbor, Hawaii. Ralph was awarded the American Defense Service Medal, World War II Victory Medal and Purple Heart Medal posthumously. He remains on duty on the USS Arizona. Ralph is commemorated on the USS Arizona Memorial and the Memorial Tablets of the Missing, National Memorial Cemetery of the Pacific, Honolulu, Hawaii. He was survived by his Father, Mr. Floyd Ival LaMar, 2222 Kelton Avenue, West Los Angeles, California.[446]

La Salle, Willard Dale Seaman, First Class, Serial No: 393 38 07, US Navy. Willard was born October 27, 1919 in Moores Hollow, Oregon, the son of Emerson Andrew and Blanche Eva (Rowe) La Salle. He enlisted in the US Navy on August 7, 1940 in Portland, Oregon and completed his basic training at the Naval Training Station in San Diego, California. Willard reported for duty on the USS Arizona on October 8, 1940. He was killed in action on December 7, 1941 at Pearl Harbor, Hawaii. Willard was awarded the American Defense Service Medal, World War II Victory Medal and Purple Heart Medal posthumously. He remains on duty on the USS Arizona. Willard is commemorated on the USS Arizona Memorial and the Memorial Tablets of the Missing, National Memorial Cemetery of the Pacific, Honolulu, Hawaii. He was survived by his Mother, Mrs. Blanche LaSalle, Dixie, Washington.

Laderach, Robert Paul Fire Controlman, Second Class, Serial No: 258 18 30, US Navy. Robert was born on May 8, 1917 in Beverly, West Virginia, the son of Earnest and Mary Agnes (Adams) Laderach. He enlisted in the US Navy on October 5, 1937 in Baltimore, Maryland and reported for duty on the USS Arizona on March 8, 1938. Robert was killed in action on December 7, 1941 at Pearl Harbor, Hawaii. He was awarded the American Defense Service Medal, World War II Victory Medal and Purple Heart Medal posthumously. Robert remains on duty on the USS Arizona. He is commemorated on the USS Arizona Memorial, the Memorial Tablets of the Missing, National Memorial Cemetery of the Pacific, Honolulu, Hawaii and Hazelwood Cemetery, Elkins, West Virginia. Robert was survived by his Father, Mr. Ernest Laderach, Beverly, West Virginia.[447]

---

[446] Ralph B. La Mar, Photo from 1937 University High School Yearbook, Los Angeles, California.
[447] Robert Paul Laderach, Photo from World War II Young American Patriots, Randolph County, West Virginia 1941-1945.

Lake, John Ervin   Acting Pay Clerk, Serial No: 87160, US Navy. John was born on October 22, 1910 in Chicago, Illinois to John Ervin and Clara Belle Ervin (Barjoni) Lake. He enlisted in the Navy on April 13, 1928. After service on several ships and stations ashore, John was warranted Acting Pay Clerk on September 16, 1940 and assigned to the heavy cruiser, USS Salt Lake City (CA-25). He reported for duty on the USS Arizona on September 20, 1940 where he was serving as Assistant to Supply Officer. His battle station was Coding Board. John was killed in action on December 7, 1941 at Pearl Harbor, Hawaii. He was awarded the American Defense Service Medal, World War II Victory Medal and Purple Heart Medal posthumously. Ervin remains on duty on the USS Arizona. He is commemorated on the USS Arizona Memorial and the Memorial Tablets of the Missing, National Memorial Cemetery of the Pacific, Honolulu, Hawaii. John was survived by his Wife, Mrs. Dorothy Lake, Jr., 853 West 22nd Street, San Pedro, California and two sons, John and Martin. The destroyer escort USS Lake (DE-301) was named in his honor.[448]

Lakin, Donald Lapier, Jr.   Seaman, First Class, Serial No: 382 30 11, US Navy. Donald was born June 7, 1917, the son of Joseph Jordan and Blanche M. Lakin of Marion, Kansas. His mother, Blanche died in 1935. He enlisted in the US Navy on November 5, 1940 in Los Angeles, California and completed his basic training at the Naval Training Station in San Diego, California. Donald reported for duty on the USS Arizona on December 30, 1940. *On the morning of the 7th of December, Donald was with his brother, Joseph on the No. 2 motor boat shining the bright work when the attack began. They heard a loud explosion on Ford Island and a plane came over, very low so they headed for their battle stations. Assigned death #127, Donald was extensively covered in oil and died from burns received during the action on December 7, 1941 at Pearl Harbor, Hawaii.*[449] He was awarded the American Defense Service Medal, World War II Victory Medal and Purple Heart Medal posthumously. Donald's remains were recovered and he was buried in Plot D, Row 0, Grave 10, National Memorial Cemetery of the Pacific, Honolulu, Hawaii. He is commemorated on the USS Arizona Memorial. Donald was survived by his Father, Mr. Joseph Jordan Lakin, 512 East 4th Street, Ontario, California. His brother, Joseph was also killed in action on board the USS Arizona.[450]

Lakin, Joseph Jordon   Seaman, First Class, Serial No: 382 29 92, US Navy. Joseph was born October 17, 1919, the son of Joseph Jordan and Blanche M. Lakin. His mother, Blanche died in 1935. He enlisted in the US Navy on November 2, 1940 in Los Angeles, California and completed his basic training at the Naval Training Station in San Diego, California. Joseph reported for duty on the USS Arizona on December 30, 1940. *On the morning of the 7th of December, Joseph was with his brother, Donald on the No. 2 motor boat shining the bright work when the attack began. They heard a loud explosion on Ford Island and a plane came over, very low so they headed for their battle stations. Joseph died on December 10, 1941 as a result of wounds received in*

[J]ohn Ervin Lake, Jr. Photo from California Honor States.

[449] Report of Changes of the USS Arizona for the month ending 31st day of December, 1941, page 76, line 16, Donald Lapier Lakin, Jr.

[450] Donald Lapier Lakin, Jr., Photo provided by family members, Marianne & Jim Reynolds.

action on December 7, 1941 at Pearl Harbor, Hawaii[451] He was awarded the American Defense Service Medal, World War II Victory Medal and Purple Heart Medal posthumously. His remains were recovered and he was buried in Plot D, Row 0, Grave 32, National Memorial Cemetery of the Pacific, Honolulu, Hawaii. Joseph is commemorated on the USS Arizona Memorial. He was survived by his Father, Mr. Joseph Jordan Lakin, 512 East 4th Street, Ontario, California. His brother, Donald was also killed in action on board the USS Arizona.[452]

Lamb, George Samuel Chief Shipfitter, Serial No: 276 85 86, US Navy. George was born December 12, 1907 in Florida. He enlisted in the US Navy on November 14, 1936 in San Pedro, California and reported for duty on the USS Arizona on January 23, 1937. George was killed in action on December 7, 1941 at Pearl Harbor, Hawaii. He was awarded the American Defense Service Medal, World War II Victory Medal and Purple Heart Medal posthumously. George remains on duty on the USS Arizona. He is commemorated on the USS Arizona Memorial and the Memorial Tablets of the Missing, National Memorial Cemetery of the Pacific, Honolulu, Hawaii. George was survived by his Wife, Mrs. Almeda Marie Lamb, 1931 West Willard Street, Long Beach, California and son, Curtis.

Lancaster, James Daniel Seaman, First Class, Serial No. 262 47 53, US Navy. James was born November 6, 1919 near Smithfield, North Carolina the son of Rev. W. H. and Lena Lancaster. He enlisted in the US Navy December 19, 1939 in Raleigh, North Carolina and completed his basic training at the Naval Training Station in Norfolk, Virginia. James reported for duty on the USS Arizona March 29, 1940. He was serving on the USS Arizona on December 7, 1941 when the Japanese attacked Pearl Harbor. While James was heading for his battle station, he was thrown into the water from the explosion amidships. The water was on fire so he dove under the burning oil and made it to the captain's boat and began to pull men in. He rescued nearly 17 men taking them to Ford Island. James was seriously injured himself and was taken to an air raid shelter where he was cleaned up and given clothes. James spent six days as a volunteer aboard the USS West Virginia. He was injured on the 10th of January 1942 while working on the Arizona Salvage Party and was sent to the Pearl Harbor Naval Hospital for treatment spending 15 days there. He later served on the USS George Clymer (AP-57) and USS Takanis Bay (CVE-89). He died June 25, 2010 in Lillington, North Carolina and is buried in the Pinecrest Memorial Park, Clayton, North Carolina.[453]

---

[451] Report of Changes of the USS Arizona for the month ending 31st day of December, 1941, page 76, line 17, Joseph Jordon Lakin.

[452] Joseph Jordon Lakin, Photo provided by family members, Marianne & Jim Reynolds.

[453] James Daniel Lancaster, Photo and story provided by his daughter, Carol L. Lancaster.

Landman, Henry Aviation Metalsmith, Second Class, Aviation Unit (VO-1), Serial No: 311 23 60, US Navy. Henry was born in 1917 in Michigan, the son of Casper and Sophia Landman. He enlisted in the US Navy on November 3, 1937 in Detroit, Michigan and reported for duty on the USS Arizona on December 19, 1938. *He was due to be discharged from the Navy in November Henry was last seen helping to man a hose on the deck of the Arizona.* He was killed in action on December 7, 1941 at Pearl Harbor. He was awarded the American Defense Service Medal, World War II Victory Medal and Purple Heart Medal posthumously. Henry remains on duty on the USS Arizona. He is commemorated on the USS Arizona Memorial and the Memorial Tablets of the Missing, National Memorial Cemetery of the Pacific, Honolulu, Hawaii. Henry was survived by his Father, Mr. Casper Landman, 411 Moore Street, Saginaw, Michigan. *One of Henry's best friends was his cousin, Otto Nikolai. Upon Henry's death, Otto was determined to honor Henry's memory by joining the Navy. He did so against the wishes of most of his family. The decision cost him his life, as he died aboard the USS Plymouth in 1943.*[454]

Landreth, Ralph William Gunner's Mate, Second Class, Serial No. 382 10 94, US Navy. Ralph was born on January 17, 1921 in Carthage, Missouri. He enlisted in the US Navy September 14, 1939 in Los Angeles, California and completed his basic training at the Naval Training Station in San Diego, California. Ralph reported for his first duty on the USS Arizona November 10, 1939. He was serving on the USS Arizona on December 7, 1941 when the Japanese attacked Pearl Harbor. Ralph had just bought the Sunday paper and was headed down to his living quarters in turret 4 when he saw the low flying planes. When general quarters sounded, he headed to his battle station in the gun pits. Shortly after he reached the gun turret, he was knocked off his feet by a huge explosion. Men were coming up from the lower handling room, escaping the fires. He followed them up to the quarterdeck. The admiral's barge was tied alongside and he and several others stepped into it to ride to Ford Island. Ralph spent the rest of the day pulling bodies from the oil slicked water. Following the attack he was assigned duty on the USS Pennsylvania for a few months. He later served on a sub chaser, the USS SC-670 in the Aleutian Islands for two years. He also served on the aircraft carrier USS Tarawa. Ralph was honorably discharged from the Navy in 1947. He lived the remainder of his life in Florida. Ralph died on March 26, 2008 in Rockledge, Florida and is buried in Section 1F, Row 4A, Site 13, Florida National Cemetery, Bushnell, Florida.

---

[454] Henry Landman, Photo and information provided by family member, Michelle Roy.

Landry, James Joseph, Jr. Baker, Second Class, Serial No: 201 60 42, US Navy. James was born in January 19, 1920 in Amesbury, Massachusetts, the son of James and Helen Landry. *His father, James was a French Canadian and served in France during World War I, where he met his wife, Helen. His parents, James and Helen are believed to have married in France and immigrated to America, becoming citizens in 1917.* James enlisted in the US Navy on October 27, 1937 in Boston, Massachusetts and reported for duty on the USS Arizona on March 8, 1938. James was killed in action on December 7, 1941 at Pearl Harbor, Hawaii. *After his mother, Helen got the news of her only son's death; she never seemed to have recovered. Reportedly, she died of sorrow.* He was awarded the American Defense Service Medal, World War II Victory Medal and Purple Heart Medal posthumously. James remains on duty on the USS Arizona. He is commemorated on the USS Arizona Memorial and the Memorial Tablets of the Missing, National Memorial Cemetery of the Pacific, Honolulu, Hawaii and Union Cemetery, Amesbury, Massachusetts. James was survived by his Father, Mr. James Joseph Landry, Sr., 22 Market Street, Amesbury, Massachusetts. The High School football stadium in Amesbury, Massachusetts is named after him.[455]

Lane, Edward Wallace Coxswain, Serial No: 372 11 56, US Navy. Edward enlisted in the US Navy on November 15, 1939 in Denver, Colorado and completed his basic training at the Naval Training Station in San Diego, California. He reported for duty on the USS Arizona on January 24, 1940. Edward was killed in action on December 7, 1941 at Pearl Harbor, Hawaii. He was awarded the American Defense Service Medal, World War II Victory Medal and Purple Heart Medal posthumously. Edward remains on duty on the USS Arizona. He is commemorated on the USS Arizona Memorial and the Memorial Tablets of the Missing, National Memorial Cemetery of the Pacific, Honolulu, Hawaii. Edward was survived by his Mother, Mrs. Lillian Louise Robertson, 115 West 3rd Avenue, Cheyenne, Wyoming.[456]

Lane, Glenn Harvey Radioman, Third Class, Aviation Unit (VO-1), Serial No. 328 66 25, US Navy. Glenn was born on January 29, 1918 on a farm near Williams, Iowa. As a young man he spent 2 years in the CCC Camps becoming a crew leader. He left CCC in 1939 after war was declared in Europe, and knowing there was no way the war would not be coming to the US. He had an uncle that had told him if he was going to be drafted; he may as well join the Navy where he would have regular meals and dry clothes and bunk. In the Army or Marines you could spend days in trenches with rain and rats. So he enlisted in the Navy on February 25, 1940 at age 22. He spent his boot camp at Great Lakes. He was in company 13-40 (a summer company) where they gave them summer underwear. It was the coldest he had ever been. On graduation day, May 1, 1940 it was snowing so hard, their white hats filled up with snow while marching on the parade grounds. Glen excelled in the scholastic exams

---

[455] James Joseph Landry, Jr., Photo and information provided by family member, Paul H. Landry.
[456] Edward Wallace Lane, Photo from the 1934 Wyo Yearbook, University of Wyoming, Laramie, Wyoming.

graduating at the top of his class. He was given a choice as to what specialization school he wanted. He asked for aviation (pilot) school but was given Aviation Radio School instead. He had to wait until July to get into this school and spent July to October in that school. He graduated and was assigned to Observation Squadron One on the Arizona but had to wait for the Arizona to come into port in December 1940. They shipped out for Pearl Harbor in January 1941 and spent six months at Pearl returning stateside in June and then back to Pearl. By August 1941 Glenn had worked up to Petty Officer, 3rd Class.

While in Pearl we would go out to sea for a week, come back and the other force would go out. During this time, Japanese subs were shadowing them. They would see their periscope, and then they would surface to charge their batteries. We would illuminate them and they would submerge immediately. They would not answer or identify themselves during this time.

Friday, December 5th we flew our 3 planes back into Pearl and landed on Ford Island. They were returning the slow moving battleships to Pearl where they could be protected. They had set up and anticipated a submarine attack.

Saturday the 6th, was the regular routine, I had shore leave. There were so many sailors and marines on shore and little to do, so we bought Christmas cards and returned to the ship.

Sunday, December 7th we were up at 6 am, had breakfast and decided to stay on board. We wanted to save our money because we were to return stateside on the 13th. So I went down to the storage room (aviation) to address my Christmas cards. I was getting ready to take a shower when I heard explosions on Ford Island so I went up to the forecastle where we could see the fires burning. The crew all thought it was a mock attack by the Army. Then I saw a plane that had a fish on it. (The Army didn't have torpedoes.) I saw the rising sun insignia under their wings, attacking ships ahead of us. I yelled "Wake up! This is an Air Raid! The Japs are attacking!" General alarm was then sounded and we were all told to seek cover. I went aft to the aviation workshop and helped wake men who were still sleeping there and closed battle ports in the optical shop. The order came for all hands not assigned to anti-aircraft batteries to go to the third deck. I started for the third deck but just then, General Quarters was sounded. I came back and started for my General Quarters station, which is a repair station (patrol five). We were hit aft and also in one or two other places on the ship. Word came, "Fire in the Executive Officer's Office." Hurst, Bruns, Wentzlaff and I manned a fire hose and went on the quarterdeck to connect it and fight the fire aft on the quarterdeck where the bomb had hit us.

While waiting for water pressure I heard coughing coming from a hatch where smoke was billowing up. I went down the ladder and felt with my feet until I located the man that was coughing. It was CDR Fuqua. I tried to carry him but he was too heavy. Finally I said "Climb up that ladder you SOB or die here!" I finally got him up to our station. We propped him up out of the way and continued trying to fight the fires. While fighting the fires the officer got up and wandered off. He survived. I was on the nozzle end of the hose and told Hurst and Bruns to turn on the water. They did, but no water came. I turned around to see if the hose had any kinks in it and at that time there was an explosion which knocked me off the ship.

I awoke in the water, covered in oil. Swimming was difficult, I had two choices, try to swim for Ford Island, which looked miles away or try for the Nevada. I swam to the Nevada and climbed aboard. Everything was so white and every time I touched anything it would be black from the oil I had on me. I went to the 1st casemate battery and they would not let me in saying "you're filthy! we live here" I finally went to the 3rd casemate battery and they let me in. As I was sitting there, they called sickbay, thinking I was hurt and reported that they had a "messman" they thought was injured. I spoke up and said "I am not a messman!" So they took me to a mirror and showed me that I was so covered in oil that I looked like a black man. I removed the towel from my neck and they saw that my skin was white. They gave me some seawater and I washed my head and face. I tried to wash my arms but the skin was coming off so I stopped. While on the Nevada, a bomb hit her forward and blew through the 1st casemate battery. If they had not turned me away I could have been killed there with them.

After that I helped fight fires until I was so tired I went to the blacksmith shop and went to sleep. A guy came up to me and woke me up asking if I was ok. I told him to leave me alone I was sleeping. But upon inspection it was discovered that I had suffered shrapnel wounds and burns. I was sent over to the hospital ship Solace where I was put to bed, my cuts and bruises treated. I couldn't see either until my eyes were washed out and treated. I was released from the Solace after 13 days and was sent to Receiving Barracks where Mr. Fuqua told me to rejoin the aviation unit at Ford Island.

My first flight was on December 24th we went on an early morning air sweep looking for submarines. I spent several weeks at this then I was assigned to a dive bomber squadron, Air group Five on the USS Yorktown. We flew sorties during the Battle of the Coral Sea. Then I was transferred to Airgroup 3 and participated in the Battle of Midway. Yorktown was sunk during the Battle of Midway so we were instructed to fly northwest and try to meet up with the two other carriers. We ended up ditching in the water having run out of fuel, and my pilot would not change direction to look for the carriers. I grabbed my survival gear, side pistol, canteen, 1st aid kit, emergency rations, parachute and the raft. We got into the raft, soaking wet, and dropped the anchor to prevent our raft from drifting to the Marshall Islands which was held by the Japanese.

The first night was cold. We used the parachute to cover us but everything was water soaked. The next morning we broke open some brown bread and had a sip of water from my canteen. We then spent the rest of the day watching for planes. At about 2 pm I saw a plane and took my mirror, flashing light at the plane. Just when I was about to give up (the plane just kept going and it did not seem we had been seen) the plane turned. The pilot later told us that he saw a flash on his side window, turned and saw us. It was a PBY. They landed on the water and pulled us in. We were flown into Midway.

After the battle of Midway, the cold storage lockers were knocked out and they were full of meat that was spoiling. I was assigned duty to remove the rotten meat from the lockers, and then take out to sea beyond the coral reefs and feed to the sharks. I was filthy by the time we completed the first run. I decided I was not going to continue in this, so on the way back I slid off the back of the truck and found some empty barracks. I found a bunk, stripped off my clothes, found some clean underwear in one locker a canteen with some water, which I poured over my head and cleaned up. I found more clothes in another locker and went to bed.

The next day I had hard tack and cold coffee. Then I walked down to the beach and saw sea planes. There was a Chief there that I recognized from the Arizona, Bob Slaughter, and I worked with him for a couple of days. They were heading back to Pearl on the USS Pensacola, a cruiser. So I asked if I could return to Pearl with them. The officer said he couldn't legally authorize my transfer. So I got on the Pensacola and hid out. I was discovered after a few days and taken to the skipper. We talked and the skipper requested that I be reassigned to the Pensacola. When we got to Pearl, the skipper was told I was needed on an aircraft carrier.

I was returned stateside for a survivor leave, which was supposed to be 6 months. I had called my fiancée before heading stateside and asked her to meet me at Alameda California. She arrived 2 days before me. The Chaplain arranged for an apartment for her and when I arrived he picked me up and took me to her. We were married and I spent about 30 days on leave when I was ordered to report to the USS Long Island. Later I was assigned to Airgroup Ten on the USS Hornet until she was sunk in the Battle of Santa Cruz. I then was assigned to Airgroup Six on the USS Enterprise where I made Aviation Radioman, first class. I then received orders to go to Airgroup Twelve on the Saratoga. The commanding officer from the Arizona learned I was aboard and I put in to go to school, I had enough time. I made Chief but had to give up my chief hat for my first class rating in order to go to school.

I had spent July of 1942 to January 1944 in the pacific. I then went to school and was assigned to convoy duty in the Atlantic until the war ended in Europe. At about that time I learned my mother was dying and I requested leave to go home to Minnesota. They were just getting ready to invade Japan and I was told I was needed in the Pacific theatre. I had just gotten money to go to home when they dropped the "A" bomb and the war came to an end.

I spent 30 years in the Navy. I served in a transport outfit in the Korean War and served in a patrol squadron doing recon work in the Vietnam War. After that, I was in a training squadron A-3 on a carrier. I retired from the Navy in 1969. Bought an old rundown trailer park and my wife opened a shop. I dabbled in real estate over the years. Bought the place I now live in and sold off the remaining real estate I owned. Glen passed away December 10, 2011.[457]

Lane, Mancel Curtis Seaman, First Class, Serial No: 356 34 52, US Navy. Mancel was born in 1922 in Newton, Harvey, Kansas, the son of Roscoe Conklin and Mary Jane Lane. He enlisted in the US Navy on August 9, 1940 in Dallas, Texas and completed his basic training at the Naval Training Station in San Diego, California. Mancel reported for duty on the USS Arizona on November 8, 1940. He was killed in action on December 7, 1941 at Pearl Harbor, Hawaii. Mancel was awarded the American Defense Service Medal, World War II Victory Medal and Purple Heart Medal posthumously. He remains buried on the USS Arizona. Mancel is commemorated on the USS Arizona Memorial and the Memorial Tablets of the Missing, National Memorial Cemetery of the Pacific, Honolulu, Hawaii. He was survived by his Father, Mr. Roscoe Conklin Lane, Elm Street, Newkirk, Oklahoma.[458]

Langdell, Joseph Kopcho Ensign, US Navy Reserve. Joseph was born on October 12, 1914 in Wilton, New Hampshire. He was the first of three sons born to Luther Mark and Annie Kopcho Langdell. He became an Eagle Scout in 1931 and met Mrs. Eleanor Roosevelt while a delegate to the 1932 National 4-H Encampment in Washington, DC. Graduating from Boston University in 1938 with a Bachelor of Science degree in Business Administration, Joseph joined the Boston firm of Elliott Davis and Company, Certified Public Accountants as a Junior Accountant. At 26, he joined the V-7 Naval Reserve program, which offered a Commission to college graduates. After a 30-day cruise aboard the USS New York, as an apprentice seaman, he was appointed a Midshipman at the US Naval Reserve's Midshipmen's School, Tower Hall, Northwestern University, Chicago. He was among the first one thousand officers of some 20,000 who were commissioned at Northwestern before the program ended in 1945. Commissioned Ensign D-V(G), US Naval Reserve on March 14, 1941, he was ordered to the USS Arizona, Pearl Harbor. On December 7, 1941 when the Japanese attacked Pearl Harbor, Joseph was suddenly awakened in Bachelor Officers Quarters by the sounds of the Japanese surprise attack. Rushing outside, he witnessed the Arizona sink in just nine minutes. Joseph remained in Pearl Harbor until June of 1942 when he was ordered to the destroyer USS Fraizer (DD-607), then under construction in San Francisco. During his brief time there, he married Elizabeth Hamilton McGauhy, whom he had met as a Midshipman in Chicago. Commissioned July 30, 1942, the USS Frazier headed across the Pacific to Noumea, New Caledonia and then north to Guadalcanal where she escorted damaged ships away from the battle of Iron Bottom Bay. While blockading Japanese held Point Sirius at Kiska, Alaska, the Fraizer sank the Japanese submarine I-31. Joseph reported to the Naval Amphibious Training Command in September 1943. In 1944 he reported to the Commander,

---

[457] Lane, Glen Harvey, story, picture and information provided by Glen Harvey Lane.
[458] Mancel Curtis Lane, Photo and information provided by the Mancel Lane Family.

Seventh Fleet for duty with the Advance Bases Division, which was building up for the invasion of Japan. Lt. Langdell then reported to the Commander, Philippine Sea Frontier in Manila, where he organized recreation activities with the Welfare and Recreation Division until the war ended. In October 1945 he was commissioned a Lieutenant Commander, US Naval Reserve. He retired with the rank of Lieutenant Commander to Yuba City, California. Joseph died February 4, 2014 at age 100 years, three months and 24 days old. His ashes will be entombed inside the USS Arizona, rejoining his shipmates on December 7, 2016, the 75th Anniversary of the attack.[459]

Lange, Richard Charles Seaman, First Class, Serial No: 376 09 45, US Navy. Richard was born in 1919, the son of Charles Bruno and Edith Mae (Joslin) Lange. *He graduated from Vallejo Senior High School, Vallejo, California in 1937. While there he played football and baseball (catcher). He was a student at Berkeley, after graduating from high school and before entering the navy where he was a member of the rowing team at Berkeley.* He enlisted in the US Navy on August 6, 1940 in San Francisco, California and completed his basic training at the Naval Training Station in San Diego, California. Richard reported for duty on the US Arizona on October 14, 1940. He was killed in action on December 7, 1941 at Pearl Harbor, Hawaii. Richard was awarded the American Defense Service Medal, World War II Victory Medal and Purple Heart Medal posthumously. He remains on duty on the USS Arizona. Richard is commemorated on the USS Arizona Memorial and the Memorial Tablets of the Missing, National Memorial Cemetery of the Pacific, Honolulu, Hawaii. He was survived by his Parents, Mr. and Mrs. Charles Bruno Lange, 1411 Gordon Street, Vallejo, California.[460]

Langenwalter, Orville John Storekeeper, Second Class, Serial No: 321 23 43, US Navy. Orville was born October 31, 1917 in Troy, Illinois, the son of John Samuel and Emma Salone (Bress) Langenwalter. *The family moved to Iowa when Orville was three years old. He attended a one-room country school and worked on the family farm. The farming operation ended due to the great depression in 1937.* Orville worked at several jobs during the next year and enlisted in the US Navy on January 26, 1938 in Des Moines, Iowa. After boot camp at Great Lakes, Illinois he reported for duty on the USS Arizona on June 4, 1938. Orville was killed in action on December 7, 1941 at Pearl Harbor, Hawaii. He was awarded the Purple Heart Medal, American Defense Service Medal, World War II Victory Medal posthumously. Orville remains on duty on the USS Arizona. He is commemorated on the USS Arizona Memorial and the Memorial Tablets of the Missing, National Memorial Cemetery of the Pacific, Honolulu, Hawaii. Orville was survived by his Parents, Mr. John S. Langenwalter and Mrs. Emma S. Langenwalter, Toledo, Iowa and 4 brothers, Wilbur, Vernon, Earl and Neil and 3 sisters, Leona, Ruth and Mildred.[461]

---

[459] Joseph Langdell, Information and photo provided by himself.
[460] Richard Charles Lange, Information and photo provided by family member, Sharon Murray.
[461] Orville John Langenwalter, Information and photo provided by his brother, Earl Langenwalter.

Lanouette, Henry John Coxswain, Serial No: 207 21 10, US Navy. Henry was born in 1919 in Wallingford, New Haven, Connecticut the son of Henry and Edda Lanouette. He enlisted in the US Navy on October 19, 1937 in New Haven, Connecticut and completed his basic training at the Naval Training Station in Newport, Rhode Island. He reported for duty on the USS Arizona on March 8, 1938. Henry was killed in action on December 7, 1941 at Pearl Harbor, Hawaii. *After having received a telegram stating that their son was dead, they received a second telegram on December 28th stating "Your son John B. is Alive".* He was awarded the American Defense Service Medal, World War II Victory Medal and Purple Heart Medal posthumously. Henry remains on duty on the USS Arizona. He is commemorated on the USS Arizona Memorial and the Memorial Tablets of the Missing, National Memorial Cemetery of the Pacific, Honolulu, Hawaii. Henry was survived by his Father, Mr. Henry Lanouette, 135 Prince Street, Wallingford, Connecticut.

Larson, Leonard Carl Fireman, Third Class, Serial No: 385 92 67, US Navy. Leonard was born in about 1922 in Minnesota. He enlisted in the US Navy on November 12, 1940 in Seattle, Washington and completed his basic training at the Naval Training Station in San Diego, California. He reported for duty on the USS Arizona on January 11, 1941. Leonard was killed in action on December 7, 1941 at Pearl Harbor, Hawaii. He was awarded the American Defense Service Medal, World War II Victory Medal and Purple Heart Medal posthumously. Leonard remains on duty on the USS Arizona. He is commemorated on the USS Arizona Memorial and the Memorial Tablets of the Missing, National Memorial Cemetery of the Pacific, Honolulu, Hawaii. Leonard was survived by his Father, Mr. Carl Oscar Larson, Outlook, Washington.[462]

Lattin, Bleecker Radioman, Third Class, Serial No: 223 65 65, US Navy. He was born with the last name of Arrighi but later took the last name of his stepfather, Howard Lattin. Bleecker enlisted in the US Navy on February 13, 1940 in New York, New York and completed his basic training at the Naval Training Station in Norfolk, Virginia. He reported for duty on the USS Arizona on September 30, 1940. Bleecker was killed in action on December 7, 1941 at Pearl Harbor. He was awarded the American Defense Service Medal, World War II Victory Medal and Purple Heart Medal posthumously. Bleecker remains on duty on the USS Arizona. He is commemorated on the USS Arizona Memorial and the Memorial Tablets of the Missing, National Memorial Cemetery of the Pacific, Honolulu, Hawaii. Bleecker was survived by his Mother, Mrs. Ruth J. Lattin, 54 Warren Avenue, Chelsea, Boston, Massachusetts. The Jayne-Lattin VFW Post 2913, Patchogue, New York was named in Bleecker's honor and Kenneth L. Jayne who died on board the USS Oklahoma.[463]

---

[462] Leonard Carl Larson, Photo from Washington Honor States.
[463] Bleecker Lattin, Photo provided by Bob Parente, Ret. US Army, Past Commander, Jayne-Lattin VFW Post 2913, Patchogue, NY.

Lawrence, Thomas "Gunner" Hurshel Seaman, First Class, Serial No. 356 37 19, US Navy. Thomas was born September 5, 1920 in Dallas, Texas to Salas and Leona (Adcock) Lawrence. He enlisted in the US Navy October 7, 1940 in Dallas, Texas and completed his basic training at the Naval Training Station in San Diego, California. He reported for duty on the USS Arizona January 8, 1941. Thomas was serving on the USS Arizona on December 7, 1941 when the Japanese attacked Pearl Harbor. He was able to swim to shore through all of the fire. After the attack, Thomas was transferred to the USS Patterson (DD-392) for duty. Thomas married Delores Ann Meyer in 1944 and had five children, two of whom were boys who went on to serve in the Navy. He was a Navy career man. Thomas died of a heart attack on November 6, 1966 while serving at the Naval Station in Rota, Spain.[464]

Lawson, James Lenox Gunner's Mate, Third Class, Serial No. 360 11 89, US Navy. James was born on February 1, 1922. He enlisted in the US Navy February 13, 1940 in Houston, Texas and completed his basic training at the Naval Training Station in San Diego, California. James reported for duty on the USS Arizona May 30, 1940. His battle station was Turret 4 where he was serving on the USS Arizona on December 7, 1941 when the Japanese attacked Pearl Harbor. He went on to serve on the USS Mugford (DD-389) in which he was engaged in battles from Guadalcanal throughout the South Pacific. James died on June 15, 2001 and his ashes were interred on the USS Arizona, December 7, 2001. He was survived by his son, Bruce and daughters, Deb, Patti, Peggy and Beth.

Lawson, Leonard George Seaman, First Class, Serial No. 274 52 27. US Navy. Leonard was born January 14, 1922 in Chickasha, Oklahoma to Thomas Leonard and Katie May (Fletcher) Lawson. He enlisted in the US Navy October 7, 1940 in New Orleans, Louisiana and completed his basic training at the Naval Training Station in San Diego, California. Leonard reported for duty on the USS Arizona January 8, 1941. He was serving on the USS Arizona on December 7, 1941 when the Japanese attacked Pearl Harbor. After the attack, Leonard was transferred to the USS Chester for duty. He later served on board the USS Indiana (BB-58) and the USS Casco (AVP-12). Leonard died on January 3, 1990 in Riverton, Wyoming.

Lee, Carroll Volney, Jr. Seaman, First Class, Serial No: 372 17 05, US Navy. Carroll was born on October 19, 1920 in Long Beach, California, the son of Carroll Volney and Rosella "Ella" (Watkins) Lee. He enlisted in the US Navy on August 12, 1940 in Denver, Colorado and completed his basic training at the Naval Training Station in San Diego, California. Carroll reported for duty on the USS Arizona on October 8, 1940. He was killed in action on December 7, 1941 at Pearl Harbor, Hawaii. Carroll was awarded the Bronze Star Medal, American Defense Service Medal, World War II Victory Medal and the Purple Heart Medal posthumously. He remains on duty on the USS Arizona. Carroll is commemorated on the USS Arizona Memorial and the Memorial Tablets of the Missing, National Memorial Cemetery of the Pacific, Honolulu, Hawaii and the Hill Crest Cemetery, Morris Rancy, Gillespie County, Texas. He was survived by his Father, Mr. Carroll Volney Lee, Sr., Quemado, Texas.

---

[464] Thomas Hurshel Lawrence, picture provided by family member, Brandy Rivers.

Lee, Henry Lloyd   Seaman, First Class, Serial No: 262 45 17, US Navy. Henry was born on August 23, 1921 in Horry, South Carolina, the son of John Henry and Agnes P. (Gerald) Lee. He enlisted in the US Navy on November 29, 1939 in Raleigh, North Carolina and reported for duty on the USS Arizona on March 8, 1940. Henry was killed in action on December 7, 1941 at Pearl Harbor, Hawaii. He was awarded the American Defense Service Medal, World War II Victory Medal and Purple Heart Medal posthumously. Henry remains on duty on the USS Arizona. He is commemorated on the USS Arizona Memorial and the Memorial Tablets of the Missing, National Memorial Cemetery of the Pacific, Honolulu, Hawaii and the Good Hope Baptist Church Cemetery, Horry County, South Carolina. Henry was survived by his Mother, Mrs. Aggie Lee, Route 1, Box 89, Conway, South Carolina.[465]

Leedy, David Alonzo   Fire Controlman, Second Class, Serial No: 321 18 85, US Navy. David was born on October 30, 1919 in Rapid City, South Dakota, the son of Harry Glen and Mabel Grace (Wood) Leedy. *His family moved to the Muscatine, Iowa area in 1927. David attended Muscatine high school where he was a member of the high school track and cross country teams and graduated in 1937.* He enlisted in the US Navy on August 10, 1937 in Des Moines, Iowa and reported for duty on the USS Arizona on April 29, 1940. David was killed in action on December 7, 1941 at Pearl Harbor, Hawaii. *His parents were notified by telegram on Sunday, December 21, 1941 that David was missing in action.* He was awarded the American Defense Service Medal, World War II Victory Medal and Purple Heart Medal posthumously. David remains on duty on the USS Arizona. He is commemorated on the USS Arizona Memorial and the Memorial Tablets of the Missing, National Memorial Cemetery of the Pacific, Honolulu, Hawaii. David was survived by his Father, Mr. Harry G. Leedy, 109 East Fulliam Avenue, Muscatine, Iowa.[466]

Leggett, John Goldie   Boatswain's Mate, Second Class, Serial No: 262 21 57, US Navy. John was born in 1916 in Poplar Point, Martin, North Carolina the youngest of 10 children born to Jesse Augustus and Goldie Pierce Leggett. *His mother died in 1916, possibly in childbirth and his father died in 1932.* John enlisted in the US Navy on July 22, 1937 in Raleigh, North Carolina and reported for duty on the USS Arizona on March 8, 1938. He was killed in action on December 7, 1941 at Pearl Harbor, Hawaii. John was awarded the American Defense Service Medal, World War II Victory Medal and Purple Heart Medal posthumously. He remains on duty on the USS Arizona. John is commemorated on the USS Arizona Memorial and the Memorial Tablets of the Missing, National Memorial Cemetery of the Pacific, Honolulu, Hawaii. He was survived by his Wife, Mrs. Helen Irene Leggett, 3112 East 65th Street, Seattle, Washington.

---

[465] Henry Lloyd Lee, Photo and information from Young American Patriots, The Youth of South Carolina in World War II, Volume II, Horry County, Page 282, National Publishing Company, Richmond, VA, 1950.
[466] David Alonzo Leedy, Photo from the Quad-City Times, Davenport, Iowa, May 5, 1942, page 3.

Legros, Joseph "McNeil" McNeil   Seaman, First Class, Serial No: 274 52 53, US Navy. Joseph was born in 1919 in Louisiana, the son of O'Neil and Lesa (Henry) Legros. *Mac played basketball in high school. He rode a horse six miles to and from school for practice.* He enlisted in the US Navy on October 11, 1940 in New Orleans, Louisiana and completed his basic training at the Naval Training Station in San Diego, California. Joseph reported for duty on the USS Arizona on January 8, 1941. *Joseph signed up for the service life insurance. He wrote his mother about it and said he would forward the information in his next letter which he sent later. Unable to locate the letter, the government told his parents that his father made too much money and was not dependant on him so they did not receive any compensation.* He was killed in action on December 7, 1941 at Pearl Harbor, Hawaii. Joseph was awarded the American Defense Service Medal, World War II Victory Medal and Purple Heart Medal posthumously. He remains on duty on the USS Arizona. Joseph is commemorated on the USS Arizona Memorial and the Memorial Tablets of the Missing, National Memorial Cemetery of the Pacific, Honolulu, Hawaii. He was survived by his Parents, Mr. and Mrs. O'Neal Legros, Route 1, Box 29, Morse, Louisiana and nine siblings.[467]

Leigh, Malcolm Hedrick   Gunner's Mate, Third Class, Serial No: 262 45 02, US Navy. Malcolm was born March 31, 1920 in North Carolina, the son of Otie Vesper and Daisy Leigh. He enlisted in the US Navy on November 28, 1939 in Raleigh, North Carolina and reported for duty on the USS Arizona on March 8, 1940. Assigned death # 141, Malcolm died on December 10, 1941 from 2nd degree burns received in action on December 7, 1941 at Pearl Harbor, Hawaii.[468] He was awarded the American Defense Service Medal, World War II Victory Medal and Purple Heart Medal posthumously. His remains were sent home and he was buried in the Oak Lawn Municipal Cemetery, Louisburg, North Carolina. Malcolm is commemorated on the USS Arizona Memorial and the Memorial Tablets of the Missing, National Memorial Cemetery of the Pacific, Honolulu, Hawaii. He was survived by his Father, Mr. Otie Vesper Leigh, Main Street, Bunn, North Carolina.

Leight, James Webster   Seaman, Second Class, Serial No: 382 44 50, US Navy. James was born June 18, 1923 in Los Angeles, California, the son of William J. Leight. James attended the Garfield High School, Los Angeles, California. He enlisted in the US Navy on April 22, 1941 in Los Angeles, California and completed his basic training at the Naval Training Station in San Diego, California. James reported for duty on the USS Arizona on July 13, 1941. He was killed in action on December 7, 1941 at Pearl Harbor, Hawaii. James was awarded the American Defense Service Medal, World War II Victory Medal and Purple Heart Medal posthumously. He remains on duty on the USS Arizona. James is commemorated on the USS Arizona Memorial and the Memorial Tablets of the Missing, National Memorial Cemetery of

---

[467] Joseph Legros, Photo provided by family member, Patricia Blanchard. Information from his brother, James R. LeGros.

[468] Report of Changes of the USS Arizona for the month ending 31st day of December, 1941, page 77, line 7, Malcolm Hedrick Leigh.

the Pacific, Honolulu, Hawaii. He was survived by his Father, Mr. William Jonathan Leight, 2835 Olive Street, Huntington Park, California.[469]

Leighton, Lindsay Ray Watertender, First Class, Serial No. 341 81 40, US Navy. Lindsay was born November 30, 1910 in Effingham, Kansas the son of Ray Horace and Pearl (Lindsey) Leighton. He enlisted in the US Navy in 1932 and was serving on the USS Arizona from January 7, 1933 until December 7, 1941 when the Japanese attacked Pearl Harbor. Lindsay had been given shore leave one hour before Japanese planes bombed and sank the Arizona. He later served on the USS Tennessee and then on the USS Enterprise at the Battle of Midway. He was later assigned to the USS Franklin which was engaged in the Battle of the Philippines and last served on the USS Boxer. Lindsey was discharged from the Navy in 1946 having attained the rank of Lieutenant, Junior Grade. Lindsey died on December 18, 2004 in Pittsfield, Massachusetts. He was survived by his Wife of 59 years, Georgianna St. Lawrence Leighton, a son, Lindsey R. Leighton Jr. of San Diego; a daughter, Linda S. Leighton of Pleasantville, New York; a sister, Marcia McGill of Arizona and two grandchildren.[470]

Lencses, Louis Gunner's Mate, Third Class, Serial No. 337 21 20, US Navy. Louis was born in about 1917. He enlisted in the US Navy October 9, 1939 in St. Louis, Missouri and completed his basic training at the Naval Training Station in San Diego, California. He reported for duty on the USS Arizona December 20, 1939. Louis was serving on the USS Arizona on December 7, 1941 when the Japanese attacked Pearl Harbor. After the attack, Louis was assigned duty in the Pearl Harbor Naval Shipyard. In February 1943 he was transferred to the West Coast for assignment to New Construction. He later served on board the USS Le Hardy (DE-20) and the John C. Butler (DE-339). Louis died at the age of 43 on January 27, 1960 in the Hines Veterans Hospital after a lengthy illness and was buried in the Harrison Cemetery, Carbondale, Illinois.

Lenning, George Birmingham Ensign, US Navy Reserve. George was commissioned in the US Navy August 20, 1938 and was serving as W Y D Assistant Navigator on the USS Arizona. He was serving on December 7, 1941 when the Japanese attacked Pearl Harbor. His battle station was Central Station. His report follows:

"I was asleep in my room located in the Lower Ward Room about eight frames aft of the athwartships armored bulkhead on the third deck. I awakened upon the passing of the word, "All hands man you're General Quarters Stations!!" and had commenced dressing when I heard a violent explosion somewhere forward. The lights went out on both the normal lighting circuit and the battle circuit. I completed dressing and started forward and up the ladder to the second deck when a very close and violent explosion sent flame and burning debris down the ladder. After falling back for a moment, I ascended to the second deck and found the smoke and fire, caused by a bomb hit outside the Captain's Cabin, too dense to pass through. I went to the foot of the ladder and connected the fire hose, bur there was no pressure. This failing, I soaked a towel in the waste water bucket under the basin in my room and proceeded up and forward to find that the oil covered water was not rushing into the second deck from what appeared to be forward. I attempted to drop the hatch to the Lower Ward Room Country but was

---

[469] James Webster Leight, Photo from the War Memorial Book, Garfield High School, Los Angeles, California, Winter 1944.
[470] Lindsey Leighton Obituary, December 21, 2004, The Berkshire Eagle, Pittsfield, Massachusetts.

able to loosen only one supporting bar. By this time, the water was waist deep on the second deck with the Lower Ward Room Country filling rapidly.

I heard an intermittent screaming from the Captain's Cabin and swam in there and brought out a mess attendant who had been badly injured. Another mess attendant joined me from someplace and with the water almost reaching the overhead, I emerged with the wounded mess attendant to the quarterdeck where I met Lieutenant Commander Fuqua, USN., who gave the command, "All hands abandon ship!!", after all wounded men were put into the boats that were alongside the starboard quarterdeck. An oil fire was burning from about frame 110 forward in flames forty to fifty feet in height.

The boats were transporting the wounded men to Ford Island. I dove over the stern and was later picked up well clear of the ship by a boat that was picking up survivors in the water. On orders of the senior officer, Lieutenant Commander Fuqua, USN, I proceeded with the boat and survivors to the Aiea Landing where I stayed during the remainder of the attack." [471]

After the attack George was transferred to Com 11 for temporary duty.

Leopard, Curtis James Boatswain's Mate, First Class, Serial No. 267 49 50, US Navy. Curtis was born April 17, 1904 in Newberry, South Carolina the son of Alfred Solomon and Sallie E. (Bouknight) Leopard. He enlisted in the US Navy November 19, 1930 and reported for duty on the USS Arizona December 6, 1930. Curtis was serving on the USS Arizona on December 7, 1941 when the Japanese attacked Pearl Harbor. After the attack, Curtis was transferred to the USS Sacramento (PG-19) for duty. He died December 1, 1982 in Oceanside, California and is buried in the Newberry Memorial Gardens, Southeast Newberry, South Carolina.

Leopold, Robert Lawrence Ensign, Serial No: 0-095884, US Navy Reserve. Robert was born on November 11, 1916 in Louisville, Kentucky, the son of Lawrence S. and Irma (Swabacher) Leopold. He enlisted in the Naval Reserve on July 10, 1940. Following training in the gunnery training ship USS Wyoming (AG-17), he was appointed midshipman September 16, 1940 and commissioned Ensign on December 12, 1940. Robert reported for duty on the USS Arizona two weeks later serving as Communications Watch Officer. His battle station was the Communications Office. Robert was killed in action on December 7, 1941 at Pearl Harbor, Hawaii. He was awarded the American Defense Service Medal, World War II Victory Medal and Purple Heart Medal posthumously. Robert remains on duty on the USS Arizona. He is commemorated on the USS Arizona Memorial and the Memorial Tablets of the Missing, National Memorial Cemetery of the Pacific, Honolulu, Hawaii. Robert was survived by his Father, Mr. Lawrence S. Leopold, 2325 Longest Avenue, Louisville, Kentucky. The destroyer escort USS Leopold (DE-319) was named in his honor. The USS Leopold was torpedoed and sunk by the German U-boat, U-255 south of Iceland on March 9, 1944. 171 of her crew were lost with the ship and remain on duty [472]

---

[471] Confidential Statement of Ensign George B. Lennig, D-V(G), USNR., In connection with the destruction of the U.S.S. Arizona on December 7, 1941. as imparted on December 20, 1941

[472] Robert Lawrence Leopold, Dictionary of American Naval Fighting Ships, Naval Historical Center, USS Leopold (DE-319).

Lesmeister, Steve Louie Electrician's Mate, Third Class, Serial No: 328 75 62, US Navy. Steve was born December 21, 1919 in North Dakota, the son of Ludwig F. and Teresa M. (Dillman) Lesmeister. He enlisted in the US Navy on October 8, 1940 in Minneapolis, Minnesota and completed his basic training at the Naval Training Station in Great Lakes, Illinois. Steve reported for duty on the USS Arizona on December 9, 1940. He was killed in action on December 7, 1941 at Pearl Harbor, Hawaii. Steve was awarded the American Defense Service Medal, World War II Victory Medal and Purple Heart Medal posthumously. He remains on duty on the USS Arizona. Steve is commemorated on the USS Arizona Memorial and the Memorial Tablets of the Missing, National Memorial Cemetery of the Pacific, Honolulu, Hawaii. He was survived by his Father, Mr. Ludwig F. Lesmeister, Selz, North Dakota.

Levar, Frank Chief Water Tender, Serial No: 304 99 35, US Navy Reserve. Frank was born January 5, 1904 in Washington State to George and Josephine Levar. He was serving on board the USS Mallard in the Panama Canal Zone in 1930. Frank served on the USS Arizona from September 3, 1935 until he was killed in action on December 7, 1941 at Pearl Harbor, Hawaii. Frank was awarded the American Defense Service Medal, World War II Victory Medal and Purple Heart Medal posthumously. He remains on duty on the USS Arizona. Frank is commemorated on the USS Arizona Memorial and the Memorial Tablets of the Missing, National Memorial Cemetery of the Pacific, Honolulu, Hawaii. He was survived by his Wife, Mrs. Patricia Ann Levar, 4840 East 58th Street, Maywood, California.[473]

Lewis, Wayne Alman Carpenter's Mate Third Class, Serial No: 262 45 44, US Navy. Wayne was born February 29, 1920, the son of William Jasper and Lura S. (Crow) Lewis. *He was the youngest child and only son. His mother died when he was about 16 years old. Before enlisting, he was a member of the Order of DeMolay and Boy Scouts of America.* Wayne enlisted in the US Navy on November 29, 1939 in Raleigh, North Carolina and reported for duty on the USS Arizona on March 8, 1940. He was killed in action on December 7, 1941 at Pearl Harbor, Hawaii. Wayne was awarded the American Defense Service Medal, World War II Victory Medal and Purple Heart Medal posthumously. He remains on duty on the USS Arizona. Wayne is commemorated on the USS Arizona Memorial and the Memorial Tablets of the Missing, National Memorial Cemetery of the Pacific, Honolulu, Hawaii. He was survived by his Father, Mr. William Jaspar Lewis, 107 Railroad Street, Arcadia, South Carolina.[474]

---

[473] Frank Levar, Photo taken from Duwamish 1924, Renton High School Yearbook, Renton, Washington.
[474] Wayne Alman Lewis, Information and photo provided by family members, Delores Brawley, Nellie Crowe and Curt & Ellen Faulkenberry.

Lewis, William E. Lieutenant, Junior Grade, US Navy. William was born on November 9, 1908 in Pueblo, Colorado. He was the son of Mr. and Mrs. D. J. Lewis, 35 Carlisle Place, Pueblo, Colorado. William attended Rush Medical School at Chicago and was a physician at Tacoma, Washington when he was called into service in May 1941 and reported for duty on the USS Arizona. He was serving on the USS Arizona as Junior Medical Officer on December 7, 1941 when the Japanese attacked Pearl Harbor. His battle station was Aft Dressing Station. William served in the Navy until November 11, 1968 when he retired as a Captain.[475]

Lewison, Neil Stanley Fire Controlman, Third Class, Serial No: 299 78 63, US Navy. Neil was born May 15, 1916 in Melrose, Wisconsin the son of Nels Luthro and Wilhelmina Emelia Anna (Affeldt) Lewison. He enlisted in the US Navy on September 10, 1935 in Chicago, Illinois and completed his basic training at the Naval Training Station in Great Lakes, Illinois. Neil reported for duty on the USS Arizona on January 11, 1936. He was killed in action on December 7, 1941 at Pearl Harbor, Hawaii. Neil was awarded the American Defense Service Medal, World War II Victory Medal and Purple Heart Medal posthumously. He remains on duty on the USS Arizona. Neil is commemorated on the USS Arizona Memorial and the Memorial Tablets of the Missing, National Memorial Cemetery of the Pacific, Honolulu, Hawaii and the Melrose Cemetery, Melrose, Wisconsin. He was survived by his Mother, Mrs. Nels Lewison, Melrose, Wisconsin.

Lightfoot, Worth "Tommy" Ross Gunner's Mate, Third Class, Serial No: 356 20 37, US Navy. Worth was born May 13, 1919 the son of William Worth Lightfoot, a former state prohibition law enforcement officer who died in 1938 and Mittielbell (Ross) Lightfoot. His grandfather was the late Capt. William Lightfoot, a Texas Ranger and Mittiebell (Ross) Lightfoot. Worth was a graduate of Pachal High School and Allen Military Academy. He enlisted in the US Navy on November 15, 1939 in Dallas, Texas and completed his basic training at the Naval Training Station in San Diego, California. Worth reported for duty on the USS Arizona on January 24, 1940. He died on February 1, 1942 from burns received on December 7, 1941 at Pearl Harbor, Hawaii. Worth was awarded the American Defense Service Medal, World War II Victory Medal and Purple Heart Medal posthumously. He was *"Commended by Commanding Officer, USS ARIZONA for distinguished conduct during the Japanese attack on Pearl Harbor, T.H., on 7 December 1941 in which attack that vessel was destroyed and in which he was wounded in action. His heroism in fighting his ship was in keeping with the highest traditions of the Naval Service. He is recommended for the award of the Purple Heart medal. He is entitled to the Asiatic-Pacific Campaign Medal with bronze star. Authorized to wear Asiatic-Pacific Service Ribbon with bronze star. E.H. Geiselman, Captain, U.S. Navy."* He was buried in Plot C, Row 0, Grave 1006, National Memorial Cemetery of the Pacific, Honolulu, Hawaii. Worth is commemorated on the USS Arizona Memorial. He was survived by his Mother, Mrs. Mittielbell Lightfoot, 603-B West 3rd Street, Fort Worth, Texas and two sisters, Mrs. Buck Baker of Fort Worth and Lt Opal Lightfoot of the Army Nursing Corps, Camp Bowie.

---

[475] William E. Lewis, Information and Photo provided by his son, David Lewis.

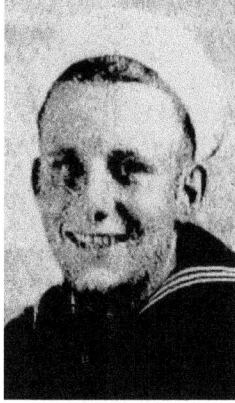

Linbo, Gordon Ellsworth Gunner's Mate, First Class, Serial No: 393 13 00, US Navy. Gordon was born in 1915 in North Dakota, the son of Richard N. and Clara Barnes (Palmer) Linbo. He re-enlisted in the US Navy on May 28, 1938 in Bremerton, Washington. Gordon served on the USS Arizona from July 14, 1934 until he was killed in action on December 7, 1941 at Pearl Harbor, Hawaii. He was awarded the American Defense Service Medal, World War II Victory Medal and Purple Heart Medal posthumously. Gordon remains on duty on the USS Arizona. He is commemorated on the USS Arizona Memorial and the Memorial Tablets of the Missing, National Memorial Cemetery of the Pacific, Honolulu, Hawaii. Gordon was survived by his Wife, Mrs. Doris Harstad Linbo, 3720 South L, Tacoma, Washington.[476]

Lincoln, John "Jack" William Fireman, First Class, Serial No: 321 48 43, US Navy. John was born February 23, 1922 in Dysart, Iowa to Abraham William and Lois Marion (Hoebel) Lincoln. He enlisted in the US Navy on October 8, 1940 in Des Moines, Iowa and completed his basic training at the Naval Training Station in Great Lakes, Illinois. John reported for duty on the USS Arizona on December 9, 1940. He was killed in action on December 7, 1941 at Pearl Harbor, Hawaii. John was awarded the American Defense Service Medal, World War II Victory Medal and Purple Heart Medal posthumously. He remains on duty on the USS Arizona. John is commemorated on the USS Arizona Memorial and the Memorial Tablets of the Missing, National Memorial Cemetery of the Pacific, Honolulu, Hawaii and Pleasant Hill Cemetery, Blairstown, Iowa. He was survived by his Parents, Mr. and Mrs. Abe W. Lincoln, Norway, Iowa, sister, Mary and a brother, Richard Lincoln.

Lindsay, James Mitchell Shipfitter, Second Class, Serial No: 272 16 22, US Navy. James was born in 1919 in Alabama to John Mitchell and Carrie S. (Drummond) Lindsay. He enlisted in the US Navy on September 21, 1937 in Birmingham, Alabama and completed his basic training at the Naval Training Station in Norfolk, Virginia. He reported for duty on the USS Arizona on March 8, 1938. James was killed in action on December 7, 1941 at Pearl Harbor, Hawaii. He was awarded the American Defense Service Medal, World War II Victory Medal and Purple Heart Medal posthumously. James remains on duty on the USS Arizona. He is commemorated on the USS Arizona Memorial and the Memorial Tablets of the Missing, National Memorial Cemetery of the Pacific, Honolulu, Hawaii. James was survived by his Wife, Mrs. Winifred Ana-Martha Lindsay, Holyoke, Colorado and son, Terril Lindsay. The James Mitchell Lindsay American Legion Post #164 in Citronelle, Alabama and the Zeiler-Owens-Lindsay VFW Post 6482 in his wife's hometown of Holyoke, Colorado were named in his honor.

Lindsey, Jack Lawton Seaman, First Class, Serial No. 295 38 73, US Navy. Jack was born on October 5, 1918. He enlisted in the US Navy September 22, 1937 in Nashville, Tennessee and reported for duty on the USS Arizona March 8, 1938. Jack was serving on the USS Arizona on December 7, 1941 when the Japanese attacked Pearl Harbor. After the attack, Jack was transferred to the USS Flusser (DD-368) for duty. Jack died on June 6, 1982 in Arkansas and is buried in Section 20, Site 311, Fayetteville National Cemetery, Fayetteville, Arkansas.

---

[476] Gordon Ellsworth Linbo, Photo from The Daily Chronicle, Centralia, Washington, May 7, 1945.

Linton, George Edward Fireman, Second Class, Serial No: 372 14 15, US Navy. George was born May 11, 1919 in Wyoming to Harry Graves and Hattie (Petty) Linton. *His mother's parents were early pioneers of Laramie County, Wyoming.* He enlisted in the US Navy on April 3, 1940 in Denver, Colorado and completed his basic training at the Naval Training Station in San Diego, California. George reported for duty on the USS Arizona on July 2, 1940. He was killed in action on December 7, 1941 at Pearl Harbor, Hawaii. George was awarded the American Defense Service Medal, World War II Victory Medal and Purple Heart Medal posthumously. He remains on duty on the USS Arizona. George is commemorated on the USS Arizona Memorial and the Memorial Tablets of the Missing, National Memorial Cemetery of the Pacific, Honolulu, Hawaii and the Wheatland Cemetery, Wheatland, Wyoming. He was survived by his Parents, Mr. and Mrs. Harry Graves Linton, Wheatland, Wyoming; three brothers and one sister: Billy Linton of the US Air Corps at Victorville, California, Everett Charles who enlisted in the US Navy February 6, 1942 and is stationed at Great Lakes, Illinois, Raymond Joe and Mrs. Cora Bowman of Wheatland.[477]

Lipke, Clarence William Fireman, Second Class, Serial No: 311 55 87, US Navy. Clarence was born in 1923, the son of Charles Frederick and Margaret Lipke. He was very young and needed his parent's permission to enlist. Clarence enlisted in the US Navy on November 27, 1940 in Detroit, Michigan and completed his basic training at the Naval Training Station in Great Lakes, Illinois. He reported for duty on the USS Arizona on January 18, 1941. He had just transferred to Fireman, Second Class to be with his best friend, Chester John Miller who also died that day. Clarence was killed in action on December 7, 1941 at Pearl Harbor, Hawaii. He was awarded the Purple Heart Medal posthumously. Clarence remains on duty on the USS Arizona. He is commemorated on the USS Arizona Memorial and the Memorial Tablets of the Missing, National Memorial Cemetery of the Pacific, Honolulu, Hawaii. Clarence was survived by his Parents, Mr. and Mrs. Charles Frederick Lipke, 4 brothers and 2 sisters, 7588 East Grixdale, Detroit, Michigan. The Lipke Park in Detroit, Michigan was named after hem and his Brother, Nicholas who also died in World War II.[478]

Lipple, John Anthony Shipfitter, First Class, Serial No: 250 41 44, US Navy. John was born October 9, 1916 in Altoona, Pennsylvania, the son of Anthony and Caroline Lipple. *His brother, Joe, will remember him as a driven, likable young man who often hitchhiked to Altoona to peddle berry bushels for a quarter during the Great Depression. He recalled John hunting through the woods for ginseng. He'd dry it out and sell the roots. In the summer, he'd pick blackberries and haul them down to Altoona. Just to get a few cents to get by. Opportunity, as much or more than Uncle Sam steered John into the Navy.* He re-enlisted in the US Navy on June 28, 1940 in San Francisco, California and completed his basic training at the Naval Training Station in San Diego, California.

---

[477] George Edward Linton, Photo and information provided by family members, Sister, Cora (Linton) Bowman, Nephew, Carl Bowman and Gary L. Griswold.
[478] Clarence William Lipke, Photo and information provided by family member, Dawn Lipke.

John reported for duty on the USS Arizona on August 30, 1940. He was killed in action on December 7, 1941 at Pearl Harbor, Hawaii. John was awarded the American Defense Service Medal, World War II Victory Medal and Purple Heart Medal posthumously. He remains on duty on the USS Arizona. John is commemorated on the USS Arizona Memorial and the Memorial Tablets of the Missing, National Memorial Cemetery of the Pacific, Honolulu, Hawaii. He was survived by his Mother, Mrs. Caroline C. Lipple, Box 103, Ashville, Pennsylvania. The John Lipple VFW Post #4315, Ashville, Pennsylvania was named in his honor.[479]

Lisenby, Daniel Edward   Seaman, First Class, Serial No: 272 25 34, US Navy. Daniel was born in 1921 in Dothan, Alabama the son of Smitson Derzial M. and Cassey Lisenby. He enlisted in the US Navy on December 12, 1939 in Birmingham, Alabama and completed his basic training at the Naval Training Station in Norfolk, Virginia. He reported for duty on the USS Arizona on September 30, 1940. Daniel was killed in action on December 7, 1941 at Pearl Harbor, Hawaii. He was awarded the American Defense Service Medal, World War II Victory Medal and Purple Heart Medal posthumously. Daniel remains on duty on the USS Arizona. He is commemorated on the USS Arizona Memorial and the Memorial Tablets of the Missing, National Memorial Cemetery of the Pacific, Honolulu, Hawaii. Daniel is survived by his Father, Mr. Daniel Smitson Lisenby, Route 2, Dothan, Alabama.

Livers, Raymond Edward   Seaman, First Class, Serial No: 372 20 00, US Navy. Raymond was born in about 1920 in Federal, Colorado, the son of Ira E. and Effie M. (Irby) Livers. He enlisted in the US Navy on October 29, 1940 in Denver, Colorado and completed his basic training at the Naval Training Station in San Diego, California. Raymond reported for duty on the USS Arizona on December 30, 1940. He was killed in action on December 7, 1941 at Pearl Harbor, Hawaii. *When the family was notified of his death, his mother had a stroke and was never the same again.* Raymond was awarded the American Defense Service Medal, World War II Victory Medal and Purple Heart Medal posthumously. He remains on duty on the USS Arizona with his brother Wayne. Raymond is commemorated on the USS Arizona Memorial and the Memorial Tablets of the Missing, National Memorial Cemetery of the Pacific, Honolulu, Hawaii. He was survived by his Parents, Mr. and Mrs. Ira Edward Livers, Box 26, Belen, New Mexico; two brothers, Ira E, Jr. and James W. of Los Angeles, California and two sisters, Mrs. George Tomberlin of Huntington Park, California and Mrs. Don Vermuelon, of Burton, Washington. His brother, Wayne was also killed in action on the USS Arizona.[480]

Livers, Wayne Nicholas   Fireman, First Class, Serial No: 372 15 13, US Navy. Wayne was born in about 1922 in Santa Rita, New Mexico, the son of Ira E. and Effie M. (Irby) Livers. *Wayne played high school football as a center for the Albuquerque Eagles.* He enlisted in the US Navy on June 5, 1940 and reported for duty on the USS Arizona on March 20, 1941. Wayne was killed in action on December 7, 1941 at Pearl Harbor, Hawaii. *When the family was notified of his death, his mother had a stroke and was never the same again.* He was awarded the American Defense Service Medal, World War II Victory Medal and Purple Heart Medal posthumously. Wayne remains on duty on the USS Arizona with his brother Raymond. He is commemorated on the USS

---

[479] John Anthony Lipple, Photo and information provided by family member, Edward Callahan.
[480] Raymond Livers, Photo provided by family member, Bernice Livers.

Arizona Memorial and the Memorial Tablets of the Missing, National Memorial Cemetery of the Pacific, Honolulu, Hawaii. Wayne was survived by his Parents, Mr. and Mrs. Ira Edward Livers, Box 26, Belen, New Mexico; two brothers, Ira E, Jr. and James W. of Los Angeles, California and two sisters, Mrs. George Tomberlin of Huntington Park, California and Mrs. Don Vermuelon, of Burton, Washington. His brother, Raymond was also killed in action on the USS Arizona.[481]

Lock, Douglas A. Seaman, First Class, Serial No: 234 29 57, US Navy. Douglas was born in 1924 in Connecticut, the son of Stanley Onease and Eva Marie (Stone) Lock. *His father, Chief Quartermaster Stanley O. Lock was a naval reservist that was recalled for recruiting duty and was serving at the Buffalo, New York Office.* Douglas enlisted in the US Navy on November 22, 1940 in Buffalo, New York and reported for duty on the USS Arizona on July 8, 1941. Douglas was killed in action on December 7, 1941 at Pearl Harbor, Hawaii. He was awarded the American Defense Service Medal, World War II Victory Medal and Purple Heart Medal posthumously. Douglas remains on duty on the USS Arizona. He is commemorated on the USS Arizona Memorial and the Memorial Tablets of the Missing, National Memorial Cemetery of the Pacific, Honolulu, Hawaii. Douglas was survived by his Father, Mr. Stanley Onease Lock, Route 2, Forestville, New York.[482]

Lohman, Earl Wynne Seaman, First Class, Serial No: 311 55 44, US Navy. Earl was born February 23, 1922 in Hamilton, Michigan to Henry Edward and Gertrude Jeanette (Kolvoord) Lohman. He enlisted in the US Navy on November 22, 1940 in Detroit, Michigan and completed his basic training at the Naval Training Station in Great Lakes, Illinois. Earl reported for duty on the USS Arizona on January 18, 1941. He was killed in action on December 7, 1941 at Pearl Harbor, Hawaii. Earl was awarded the American Defense Service Medal, World War II Victory Medal and Purple Heart Medal posthumously. *His mother, Mrs. John Smidt of Hamilton received the Purple Heart Medal awarded posthumously to her son, Earl Wynne Lohman 17 years later.* He remains on duty on the USS Arizona. Earl is commemorated on the USS Arizona Memorial and the Memorial Tablets of the Missing, National Memorial Cemetery of the Pacific, Honolulu, Hawaii and Riverside Cemetery, Hamilton, Michigan. He was survived by his Mother, Mrs. Gertrude Janet Smidt, Route 2, Hamilton, Michigan.

Lomax, Frank Stuart Ensign, Serial No: 0-085055, US Navy. Frank was born in April 24, 1918 in Broken Bow, Nebraska, the son of James Conrad and Lyle (Young) Lomax. He graduated from the Naval Academy and was commissioned June 6, 1940. Frank was the officer in charge of the port antiaircraft director station. He left to check out a problem with ammunition and was not seen again. Frank was killed in action on December 7, 1941 at Pearl Harbor, Hawaii. He was awarded the American Defense Service Medal, World War II Victory Medal and Purple Heart Medal posthumously. Frank remains on duty on the USS Arizona. He is commemorated on the USS Arizona Memorial and the Memorial Tablets of the Missing, National Memorial Cemetery of the Pacific, Honolulu, Hawaii. Frank was survived by his Father, Mr. James C. Lomax, Route 4, Broken Bow, Nebraska.[483]

---

[481] Wayne Livers, Photo provided by family member, Bernice Livers.

[482] Douglas A. Lock, Information from newspaper article, "Arkwright Man's Son is Listed Missing in Pacific Action", Dunkirk (N.Y.) Evening Observer, Wednesday, December 24, 1941, Page 7.

[483] Frank Stuart Lomax, Photo from the Lucky Bag Yearbook, US Naval Academy, Annapolis, MD, Class of 1940.

Lomibao, Marciano   Officer's Steward, Serial No: 497 80 62, US Navy. Marciano was born October 24, 1901 in Buenlag, Binmaley, Philippine Islands. He enlisted in the US Navy on June 26, 1921. Marciano served on the USS Arizona from December 31, 1937 until he was killed in action on December 7, 1941 at Pearl Harbor, Hawaii. He was awarded the American Defense Service Medal, World War II Victory Medal and Purple Heart Medal posthumously. Marciano remains on duty on the USS Arizona. He is commemorated on the USS Arizona Memorial and the Memorial Tablets of the Missing, National Memorial Cemetery of the Pacific, Honolulu, Hawaii. Marciano was survived by his Mother, Mrs. Ana Bautista, Buenlag Bimmaley, Pangasinan, Philippine Islands.[484]

Long, Benjamin Franklin   Chief Yeoman (AA), Serial No: 261 21 51, US Navy. Benjamin was born on January 29, 1904 in Edgecombe, North Carolina to Richard Denson and Maggie Ellen (Weaver) Long. He enlisted in the US Navy on December 24, 1936 in San Pedro, California. Benjamin served on the USS Arizona from May 1, 1940 until he was killed in action on December 7, 1941 at Pearl Harbor, Hawaii. He was awarded the American Defense Service Medal, World War II Victory Medal and Purple Heart Medal posthumously. Benjamin remains on duty on the USS Arizona. He is commemorated on the USS Arizona Memorial and the Memorial Tablets of the Missing, National Memorial Cemetery of the Pacific, Honolulu, Hawaii and the Pineview Cemetery, South Rocky Mount, North Carolina. Benjamin was survived by his Wife, Mrs. Emilia Portusach Long, 526 Lisbon Street, San Francisco, California.

Lott, Russell Ardell   Seaman, First Class, Serial No. 321 23 45, US Navy. Russell was born on January 19, 1920 in Kingsley, Iowa. He enlisted in the US Navy January 26, 1938 in Des Moines, Iowa and completed his basic training at the Naval Training Station in Great Lakes, Illinois. He reported for duty on the USS Arizona June 4, 1938. Russell was serving on the USS Arizona on December 7, 1941 when the Japanese attacked Pearl Harbor. During the attack, he was knocked unconscious by explosions that rocked the ship. When he awoke, he ripped the burned flesh from his arms and sought escape. Dangling from a 60 for long line stretched four stories above a cauldron of fire; he made his way hand over hand to safety. After the attack, Russell was transferred to the USS Whitney temporarily. Shortly thereafter, Russell was transferred to the USS Phelps (DD-360) for duty. He was awarded the Purple Heart, Philippine Defense Medal, Philippine Liberation Ribbon and the Asiatic-Pacific Campaign Medal. Russell died on May 22, 2003 in Fort Dodge, Iowa. His ashes were interred on the USS Arizona in 2003.

---

[484] Marciano Lomibao, Photo and information taken from Declaration of Intention to become US Citizen, January 19, 1937.

Lounsbury, Thomas William Seaman, Second Class, Serial No: 300 19 03, US Navy. Thomas was born in 1923, the son of Robert J. and Florence H. Lounsbury. He enlisted in the US Navy on October 8, 1940 in Chicago, Illinois and completed his basic training at the Naval Training Station in Great Lakes, Illinois. Thomas reported for duty on the USS Arizona on December 9, 1940. He was killed in action on December 7, 1941 at Pearl Harbor, Hawaii. Thomas was awarded the American Defense Service Medal, World War II Victory Medal and Purple Heart Medal posthumously. He remains on duty on the USS Arizona. Thomas is commemorated on the USS Arizona Memorial and the Memorial Tablets of the Missing, National Memorial Cemetery of the Pacific, Honolulu, Hawaii. He was survived by his Father, Mr. Robert Lounsburg, 409 Austin Avenue, Woodstock, Illinois.[485]

Loustanau, Charles "Charley" Bernard Seaman, First Class, Serial No: 321 52 57, US Navy. Charles was born May 29, 1915 in Dedham, Iowa to John E. and Katherine (Johannsen) Loustaunau. *He was an all round athlete, and outstanding baseball player and a crack swimmer.* Charley enlisted in the US Navy on November 27, 1940 in Des Moines, Iowa using his own name, Charles Bernard Loustanau, *although he used and was always known by his step-father's name, Johansen.* He completed his basic training at the Naval Training Station in Great Lakes, Illinois. He reported for duty on the USS Arizona on January 18, 1941. Charles was killed in action on December 7, 1941 at Pearl Harbor, Hawaii. He was awarded the American Defense Service Medal, World War II Victory Medal and Purple Heart Medal posthumously. Charles remains on duty on the USS Arizona. He is commemorated on the USS Arizona Memorial and the Memorial Tablets of the Missing, National Memorial Cemetery of the Pacific, Honolulu, Hawaii. Charles was survived by his Mother, Mrs. Katherine Johansen, Route 1, Gray, Iowa. The DeWitt Loustanau American Legion Post 20 in Dedham, Iowa was named in his honor.[486]

Loveland, Frank Crook Seaman, Second Class, Serial No: 368 59 34, US Navy. Frank was born April 15, 1922 in Bloomington, Idaho, the son of Harlon Acel and Orilla Alzada (Crook) Loveland. He enlisted in the US Navy on January 24, 1941 in Salt Lake City, Utah and completed his basic training at the Naval Training Station in San Diego, California. Frank reported for duty on the USS Arizona on August 24, 1941. He was killed in action on December 7, 1941 at Pearl Harbor, Hawaii. Frank was awarded the American Defense Service Medal, World War II Victory Medal and Purple Heart Medal posthumously. He remains on duty on the USS Arizona. Frank is commemorated on the USS Arizona Memorial and the Memorial Tablets of the Missing, National Memorial Cemetery of the Pacific,

---

[485] Thomas William Lounsbury, Photo from Chicago Tribune, Chicago, Illinois, May 5, 1942, Page 9.
[486] Charles Bernard Loustanau, Information and photo provided by Gene Derner, DeWitt-Loustanau American Legion Post 20, Dedham, Iowa. Additional info from the Coon Rapids Enterprise newspaper, Coon Rapids, Iowa, Friday December 26, 1941.

Honolulu, Hawaii. He was survived by his Mother, Mrs. Orilla Loveland Malone, 280 10th Street, Idaho Falls, Idaho.[487]

Lucey, Neil Jermiah Seaman, First Class, Serial No: 223 67 53, US Navy. Neil was born in 1924 in Jersey City, New Jersey the son of Timothy and Margaret (Scannell) Lucey. He enlisted in the US Navy on March 12, 1940 in New York, New York and completed his basic training at the Naval Training Station in Norfolk, Virginia. He reported for duty on the USS Arizona on October 11, 1940. Neil was killed in action on December 7, 1941 at Pearl Harbor, Hawaii. He was awarded the American Defense Service Medal, World War II Victory Medal and Purple Heart Medal posthumously. Neil remains on duty on the USS Arizona. He is commemorated on the USS Arizona Memorial and the Memorial Tablets of the Missing, National Memorial Cemetery of the Pacific, Honolulu, Hawaii. Neil was survived by his Father, Mr. Timothy Lucey, 54 Monticello Avenue, Jersey City, New Jersey.[488]

Lukasavitz, Steven Jerome Seaman, First Class, Serial No. 311 49 68, US Navy. Steven was born on September 2, 1918 in Michigan to John and Pearl Lukasavitz. He enlisted in the US Navy September 9, 1940 in Detroit, Michigan and completed his basic training at the Naval Training Station in Norfolk, Virginia. He reported for duty on the USS Arizona December 4, 1940. Steven was serving on the USS Arizona on December 7, 1941 when the Japanese attacked Pearl Harbor. His official Statement:

"When air raid was sounded at approximately 0800 I went up to the boat deck to gun II, took my station on the fuse setters seat. The gun crew was all present. While waiting for further orders I watched as the planes swooped down torpedoing other ships. The Gun Captain was standing by the ready box. We hollered to open and see if any ammunition was in the box. There wasn't any in it. He told me to report down to the five inch AA magazine and handling room and if I saw anyone from the magazines to tell them to follow me and send up the ammunition as soon as possible. Several of the magazine crew met me on the way to the third deck. We had enough men to man the magazine and handling room. We dogged down the magazine watertight door, and broke open the hoist. The magazine keeper was present. He phoned to ask what type of shells to send up and to turn on the power on the hoist. When first explosion went off we were given orders to try and send up ammunition by means of the hand crank. We tried but could not budge the hoist. A second explosion went off at this time knocking all of us back against the bulkhead. Water was up to our ankles. Someone hollered to get out, so we scrambled up the hand ladder. The ship was all full of fumes and hot. When I got to the top I was by number three turret. I vomited and felt better. We tried to get down the life rafts. The large ones were difficult, but the small ones came down quite easy. Turk, 1st class aviation machinist hollered to me to help unmoor the USS Vestal, moored to our port side. The Captain on the bridge gave us orders not to cut the mooring lines. It was difficult for Turk and me to handle this but we managed to get the lines off the bits. The water and oil was flooding the marine compartment on the main deck. A motor boat came along side. I was told to get aboard and was taken to the Air Station and received dry clothing and food."[489]

---

[487] Frank Crook Loveland, Photo from Idaho Honor States.

[488] Neil Jermiah Lucey, Photo from the 1944 St. Mary's High School Yearbook, Perth Amboy, New Jersey.

[489] Confidential statement of S. J. Lukasavitz, Seaman First Class, U.S. Navy, Pearl Harbor, T.H. December 15, 1941.

He was wounded during the attack and was transferred to the US Naval Hospital at Pearl Harbor for treatment. In January 1943, Steven was transferred via the USS Solace to the US Mobile Naval Hospital No. 4. Steven died on November 11, 1978 in Saginaw, Michigan.

Luna, James Edward   Seaman, Second Class, Serial No: 272 41 81, US Navy. James was born January 7, 1922 in Alabama, the son of Joe Walker and Mary Luna. He enlisted in the US Navy on October 5, 1940 in Birmingham, Alabama and completed his basic training at the Naval Training Station in Norfolk, Virginia. James reported for duty on the USS Arizona on December 4, 1940. He was killed in action on December 7, 1941 at Pearl Harbor, Hawaii. James was awarded the American Defense Service Medal, World War II Victory Medal and Purple Heart Medal posthumously. He remains on duty on the USS Arizona. James is commemorated on the USS Arizona Memorial and the Memorial Tablets of the Missing, National Memorial Cemetery of the Pacific, Honolulu, Hawaii. He was survived by his Father, Mr. Joe Walker Luna, 116 South 8th Street, Seminole, Oklahoma.

Luzier, Ernest Burton   Machinist's Mate, Second Class, Serial No: 382 08 19, US Navy. Ernest was born January 4, 1920 in Los Angeles, California to Ernest B. and Susie (Williams) Luzier. He enlisted in the US Navy on December 14, 1938 in Los Angeles, California and completed his basic training at the Naval Training Station in San Diego, California. He reported for duty on the USS Arizona on June 2, 1939. Ernest was killed in action on December 7, 1941 at Pearl Harbor, Hawaii. He was awarded the American Defense Service Medal, World War II Victory Medal and Purple Heart Medal posthumously. Ernest remains on duty on the USS Arizona. He is commemorated on the USS Arizona Memorial and the Memorial Tablets of the Missing, National Memorial Cemetery of the Pacific, Honolulu, Hawaii. Ernest was survived by his Mother, Mrs. I. J. Sullivan, 241 East Meyer Road, Norwalk, California.[490]

Lynch, Emmett "Rusty" Isaac   Musician, Second Class, Serial No: 287 39 39, US Navy. Emmett was born in about 1916 in Tennessee. *He was a 1939 graduate of Georgetown College. Emmett was orphaned at an early age and grew up in a Louisville Children's Home.* He enlisted in the US Navy on April 29, 1940 in Kentucky and attended the Navy School of Music in Washington, DC graduating on May 23, 1941 as a member of the USS Arizona Band. He reported for duty on the USS Arizona on June 17, 1941. *As member of the band, Emmett was at his battle station in the black powder room passing ammunition to the Arizona's gunners during the attack.* Emmett was killed in action on December 7, 1941 at Pearl Harbor, Hawaii. He was awarded the American Defense Service Medal, World War II Victory Medal and Purple Heart Medal posthumously. Emmett remains on duty on the USS Arizona. He is commemorated on the USS Arizona Memorial and the Memorial Tablets of the Missing, National Memorial Cemetery of the Pacific, Honolulu, Hawaii and Georgetown University, Washington, DC. Emmett was survived by his Wife, Mrs.

---

[490] Ernest Burton Luzier, Photo from Continental Yearbook, George Washington High School, Los Angeles, CA, Class of 1938, Page 30.

Lorraine Lynch, 3219 M Street SE, Washington, DC. A Music Scholarship was established in his honor at Georgetown College, Washington, D.C.[491]

Lynch, James Robert, Jr. Gunner's Mate, Third Class, Serial No: 356 34 29, US Navy. James was born on October 25, 1917 in Comanche, Texas, the son of James Robert Lynch, Sr. and Celeste (Small) Lynch. He enlisted in the US Navy on August 9, 1940 in Dallas, Texas and completed his basic training at the Naval Training Station in San Diego, California. James reported for duty on the USS Arizona on October 14, 1940. He was killed in action on December 7, 1941 at Pearl Harbor, Hawaii. James was awarded the American Defense Service Medal, World War II Victory Medal and Purple Heart Medal posthumously. He remains on duty on the USS Arizona. James is commemorated on the USS Arizona Memorial and the Memorial Tablets of the Missing, National Memorial Cemetery of the Pacific, Honolulu, Hawaii and Blanket Cemetery, Blanket, Texas. He was survived by his Father, Mr. James Robert Lynch, Sr., Blanket, Texas.[492]

Lynch, William Joseph, Jr. Seaman, First Class, Serial No: 356 41 89, US Navy. William was born in 1922 in Kaufman County, Texas, the son of William Joseph and Mary Marie (Wyatt) Lynch. He enlisted in the US Navy on November 7, 1940 in Dallas, Texas and completed his basic training at the Naval Training Station in San Diego, California. William reported for duty on the USS Arizona on January 11, 1941. He was killed in action on December 7, 1941 at Pearl Harbor, Hawaii. William was awarded the American Defense Service Medal, World War II Victory Medal and Purple Heart Medal posthumously. He remains on duty on the USS Arizona. William is commemorated on the USS Arizona Memorial and the Memorial Tablets of the Missing, National Memorial Cemetery of the Pacific, Honolulu, Hawaii. He was survived by his Father, Mr. William Joseph Lynch, General Delivery, Greenville, Texas.[493]

MacQueen, Donald Elmer Ensign, US Navy. Donald was born on December 13, 1915 in New Jersey to Alexander Hamilton and Harriet Lethea (Robertson) MacQueen. He was commissioned Ensign in the US Navy December 12, 1940 and was serving on the USS Arizona as Ship's Secretary, Chief Warrant Officer, Division C. He was not on board on December 7, 1941 when the Japanese attacked Pearl Harbor. Donald had swapped duty with a fellow officer. At home with his wife, a neighbor came to the door to tell him that Pearl Harbor was being attacked. He left his breakfast on the table and started driving to Pearl Harbor with a friend in his Buick. Japanese planes strafed the car. They exited the car and got out and crawled. They left the car where it was and went on foot. The Arizona was aflame when they got there. His battle station was the Coding Room. Donald was assigned to Naval Intelligence after the attack. He died on June 20, 1988 in Northborough, Massachusetts and is buried in the Howard Street Cemetery, Northborough, Massachusetts.

---

[491] Emmett Isaac Lynch, Information from Georgetown University, Washington, DC.
[492] James Robert Lynch, Photo from the Find A Grave memorial provided by Harlon.
[493] William Joseph Lynch, Jr., Information and picture provided by family member, Lynda Lehman.

Maddox, Raymond Dudley   Chief Electrician's Mate, Serial No: 286 97 98, US Navy. Raymond was born July 28, 1910 in Kentucky. He enlisted in the US Navy on May 26, 1937 in Pearl Harbor, Territory of Hawaii and completed his basic training at the Naval Training Station in San Diego, California. He reported for duty on the USS Tennessee (BB-43) on January 1, 1939. Raymond was transferred to the USS Neches on April 25, 1939 and finally to the USS Arizona on December 19, 1940. He was killed in action on December 7, 1941 at Pearl Harbor, Hawaii. Raymond was awarded the American Defense Service Medal, World War II Victory Medal and Purple Heart Medal posthumously. He remains on duty on the USS Arizona. Raymond is commemorated on the USS Arizona Memorial and the Memorial Tablets of the Missing, National Memorial Cemetery of the Pacific, Honolulu, Hawaii. He was survived by his Wife, Mrs. Margaret Rose Maddox, 401 West 71st Street, Los Angeles, California.[494]

Madrid, Arthur John   Seaman, Second Class, Serial No: 382 39 69, US Navy. Arthur was born in 1922 in Arizona the son of Manuel B. and Mary Madrid. He enlisted in the US Navy on February 15, 1941 in Los Angeles, California and completed his basic training at the Naval Training Station in San Diego, California. Arthur reported for duty on the USS Arizona on September 16, 1941. He was killed in action on December 7, 1941 at Pearl Harbor, Hawaii. Arthur was awarded the American Defense Service Medal, World War II Victory Medal and Purple Heart Medal posthumously. He remains on duty on the USS Arizona. Arthur is commemorated on the USS Arizona Memorial and the Memorial Tablets of the Missing, National Memorial Cemetery of the Pacific, Honolulu, Hawaii. He was survived by his Father, Mr. Manuel B. Madrid, 430 Savoy Street, Los Angeles, California.[495]

Mafnas, Francisco Reyes   Mess Attendant, Second Class, Serial No: 421 05 64, US Navy. Francisco was born June 4, 1919 in Guam, son of Jose Cruz and Filomenia Laguana (Reyes) Mafnas. He enlisted in the US Navy on January 3, 1940 at the Naval Station in Guam and reported for duty on the USS Arizona on March 14, 1940. Assigned death #312, Francisco died from a penetrating wound to his head received in action on December 7, 1941 at Pearl Harbor, Hawaii.[496] He was awarded the American Defense Service Medal, World War II Victory Medal and Purple Heart Medal posthumously. Francisco's remains were recovered and he was buried in Plot B, Row 0, Grave 837, National Memorial Cemetery of the Pacific, Honolulu, Hawaii. He is commemorated on the USS Arizona Memorial and the Sons of Guam Pearl Harbor Memorial, Guam. Francisco was survived by his Mother, Mrs. Filomenia Reyes Mafnas, Lot 710, Agana, Guam.

---

[494] Raymond Dudley Maddox, Photo provided by his son, Victor E. Maddox.
[495] Arthur John Madrid, Photo from the 1940 Abraham Lincoln High School Yearbook, Ontario, California.
[496] Report of Changes of the USS Arizona for the month ending 31st day of December, 1941, Page 79, line 14, Francisco Reyes Mafnas.

Magee, Gerald James Storekeeper, Third Class, Serial No: 238 63 59, US Navy. Gerald was born in 1922, the son of Thomas F. and Mary A. Magee. He enlisted in the US Navy on January 8, 1940 in Albany, New York and reported for duty on the USS Arizona on March 29, 1940. He was killed in action on December 7, 1941 at Pearl Harbor, Hawaii. He was awarded the American Defense Service Medal, World War II Victory Medal and Purple Heart Medal posthumously. Gerald remains on duty on the USS Arizona. He is commemorated on the USS Arizona Memorial and the Memorial Tablets of the Missing, National Memorial Cemetery of the Pacific, Honolulu, Hawaii. Gerald was survived by his Father, Mr. Thomas F. Magee, 1135 Steuben Street, Utica, New York.[497]

Mainwaring, Billy Braun Fireman, Third Class, Serial No. 356 41 26, US Navy. Billy was born on October 21, 1921 in Oklahoma to William H. and Elsie J. Mainwaring. He enlisted in the US Navy November 4, 1940 in Dallas, Texas and completed his basic training at the Naval Training Station in San Diego, California. He reported for duty on the USS Arizona January 11, 1941. Billy was serving on the USS Arizona on December 7, 1941 when the Japanese attacked Pearl Harbor. After the attack, Billy was transferred to the US Naval Shipyard, Pearl Harbor for duty. Billy died on October 10, 1972 in Pinellas, Florida.

Malaski, John Seaman, First Class, Serial No. 376 09 27, US Navy. John was born December 6, 1916 to Joe and Anastasia (Mazejka) Malaski. He enlisted in the US Navy July 30, 1940 in San Francisco, California and completed his basic training at the Naval Training Station in San Diego, California. He reported for duty on the USS Arizona October 8, 1940. John was serving on the USS Arizona on December 7, 1941 when the Japanese attacked Pearl Harbor. After the attack, John was transferred to the USS Northampton (Sunk December 1, 1942 during the battle of Tassafaronga.) John died July 22, 2006 in Benold, Illinois.

Malcolm, Everett Allen Ensign, US Navy. Everett was born April 18, 1916 in Maxwell, New Mexico. He was commissioned Ensign in the US Navy February 7, 1941 and was serving as Junior Watch and Division 2 Officer on the USS Arizona on December 7, 1941 when the Japanese attacked Pearl Harbor. His battle station was Turret II. After the attack he was assigned temporary duty on the USS Tennessee. On December 18, 1941 he was ordered to Pac Fleet Pooling Officer, Receiving Station, Pearl. Everett died September 2, 2005 in San Jose, California.[498]

---

[497] Gerald James Magee, Photo from New York Honor States.
[498] Everett Allen Malcolm, Photo from Lucky Bag Yearbook, United States Naval Academy, Annapolis, MD, 1941.

Malecki, Frank Edward   Chief Yeoman, Serial No: 328 01 72, US Navy. Frank was born January 1, 1899 in Minnesota, son of Joseph Malecki and Francisco Malecki. *He was a career serviceman and had enlisted prior to 1930.* Frank served on the USS Arizona from October 31, 1936 until he was killed in action on December 7, 1941 at Pearl Harbor, Hawaii. He was awarded the American Defense Service Medal, World War II Victory Medal and Purple Heart Medal posthumously. Frank remains on duty on the USS Arizona. He is commemorated on the USS Arizona Memorial and the Memorial Tablets of the Missing, National Memorial Cemetery of the Pacific, Honolulu, Hawaii. Frank was survived by his Wife, Mrs. Minnie Louise Malecki, 2132 Monitor, Long Beach, California.[499]

Malinowski, John Stanley   Signalman, Third Class, Serial No: 410 75 26, US Navy Reserve. *John came from a desperately poor family, born in 1914 to Stanley and Rose Malinowski. He left school and enlisted in the US Navy on October 7, 1940 in Muskegon, Michigan at the age of sixteen by claiming to be older. His purpose was to provide some income for his family.* John completed his basic training at the Naval Training Station in Great Lakes, Illinois. He reported for duty on the USS Arizona on March 6, 1941. He was killed in action on December 7, 1941 at Pearl Harbor, Hawaii, at the age of seventeen, one of the youngest people on board. John was awarded the American Defense Service Medal, World War II Victory Medal and Purple Heart Medal posthumously. He remains on duty on the USS Arizona. John is commemorated on the USS Arizona Memorial and the Memorial Tablets of the Missing, National Memorial Cemetery of the Pacific, Honolulu, Hawaii. He was survived by his Father, Mr. Stanley Malinowski, 1864 Crawley, Muskegon, Michigan.[500]

Malson, Harry Lynn   Storekeeper, Third Class, Serial No: 291 46 64, US Navy. Harry was born in 1919 in Illinois, the son of William "Harry" and Ruth Malson. His father died suddenly when Harry was 11 months old. He enlisted in the US Navy on December 3, 1935 in Indianapolis, Indiana and reported for duty on the USS Arizona on April 20, 1936. Harry was killed in action on December 7, 1941 at Pearl Harbor, Hawaii. He was awarded the American Defense Service Medal, World War II Victory Medal and Purple Heart Medal posthumously. Harry remains on duty on the USS Arizona. He is commemorated on the USS Arizona Memorial and the Memorial Tablets of the Missing, National Memorial Cemetery of the Pacific, Honolulu, Hawaii. Harry was survived by his Wife, Mrs. Frances Alwilda Malson, 424 North Randolph, Indianapolis, Indiana.[501]

---

[499] Frank Edward Malecki, Photo from the Star Tribune, Minneapolis, Minnesota, January 9, 1942, Page 9.
[500] John Stanley Malinowski, Information and photo provided by the Muskegon County World War II Veterans Project.
[501] Harry Lynn Malson, Information and photo provided by family member, Jan Lunn.

Mancuso, Joseph   Seaman, First Class, Serial No. 250 51 26, US Navy. Joseph was born October 12, 1917. He enlisted in the US Navy September 11, 1939 in Pittsburgh, Pennsylvania and reported for duty on the USS Rigel January 25, 1939. He transferred to the USS Arizona January 8, 1941. He was serving on December 7, 1941 when the Japanese attacked Pearl Harbor. Joseph was wounded and was taken to the US Naval Hospital in Pearl Harbor. He was transferred to the US Naval Hospital on the Mainland on February 20, 1942. Joseph died August 24, 1985. and was buried in Section 20A, Site 2865 in Riverside National Cemetery, Riverside, California.

Manion, Edward Paul   Seaman, Second Class, Serial No: 300 26 83, US Navy. Edward was born on November 14, 1922 in Decatur, Illinois. He was the son of Mr. & Mrs. Richard Manion of Campbell's Island. Edward enlisted in the US Navy on November 28, 1940 in Chicago, Illinois and completed his basic training at the Naval Training Station in Great Lakes, Illinois. He reported for duty on the USS Arizona on January 18, 1941. Edward was killed in action on December 7, 1941 at Pearl Harbor, Hawaii. He was awarded the American Defense Service Medal, World War II Victory Medal and Purple Heart Medal posthumously. Edward remains on duty on the USS Arizona. He is commemorated on the USS Arizona Memorial and the Memorial Tablets of the Missing, National Memorial Cemetery of the Pacific, Honolulu, Hawaii. Edward was survived by his Father, Mr. Richard Newell Manion, Campbell's Island, East Moline, Illinois.[502]

Manlove, Arthur Cleon   Electrician's Mate, Serial No: 75731, US Navy. Arthur was born on March 19, 1901 in Tipton, Indiana, the son of Thomas A. and Emma Josephine (Pearce) Manlove. He enlisted in the US Navy on August 28, 1923 and was appointed a warrant officer Electrician while assigned to the cruiser USS Augusta in December 1936. He later served on the USS Colorado. Arthur reported for duty on the USS Arizona on November 3, 1941. He was serving on the Arizona as Assistant to Engineering Officer. Arthur was killed in action on December 7, 1941 at Pearl Harbor, Hawaii. He was awarded the American Defense Service Medal, World War II Victory Medal and Purple Heart Medal posthumously. Arthur remains on duty on the USS Arizona. He is commemorated on the USS Arizona Memorial and the Memorial Tablets of the Missing, National Memorial Cemetery of the Pacific, Honolulu, Hawaii. Arthur was survived by his Wife, Mrs. Glenola M. Manlove, 152 South Pine Street, Orange, California. The escort ship USS Manlove (DE-36), 1943-1947, was named in honor of Electrician Manlove. The USS Manlove received five battle stars for her World War II service.[503]

---

[502] Edward Paul Manion, Information and photo provided by family member, Michael T. Manion, Ph.D..
[503] Arthur Cleon Manlove, Information and photo, Dictionary of American Naval Fighting Ships, Naval Historical Center, USS Manlove (DE-36).

Mann, Charles Clark Lieutenant, Serial No. 0-01965, US Navy. Charles was born in 1914 in Illinois to Goldie Mann. He received an appointment to the US Naval Academy at Annapolis May 31, 1934 and was commissioned May 31, 1937 in the US Navy and reported for duty on the USS Arizona where he was serving as the Division Radio Officer on December 7, 1941 when the Japanese attacked Pearl Harbor. He was the Commanding Officer of the USS Dennis J. Buckley (DD-808) from June 1947 to June 20, 1948. He later attained the rank of Rear Admiral.[504]

Mann, William "Bill" Edward Gunner's Mate, Third Class, Serial No: 385 80 07, US Navy. William was born on April 20, 1920 in Satsop, Grays Harbor, Washington, the eldest of 13 children born to Arthur Carl Helvey and Charlotte E. I. (Borden) Mann. *"He was the ideal big brother." He used to babysit the younger brothers and sisters while his parents went into town to do the shopping. While he babysat, he would play the guitar and sing to them. His sister, Virginia, cut her foot and had to have stitches, so Bill would carry her back and forth to school until her foot healed. When Bill joined the Track team in High School he won a big trophy. He loved to run and would run back and forth to school. It was quite a ways since they lived in the country. When he was a senior in High School he built himself a car, he then took his mom's knitting needles and took the string that was used to tie the groceries together and knit curtains for his car. His mother asked him why he joined the Navy. His answer was, "If there is going to be a war, I want to sleep in a clean bed."* He enlisted in the US Navy on January 10, 1939 in Seattle, Washington and completed his basic training at the Naval Training Station in San Diego, California. William reported for duty on the USS Arizona on April 29, 1939. He was killed in action on December 7, 1941 at Pearl Harbor, Hawaii. *The family received notice that he was missing in action a couple of days before Christmas. They were not notified of his death until the middle of January 1942. The family got a call from a shipmate telling them that Bill had just gone below to get dressed to go ashore to attend church when the attack began. He was not seen again.* William was awarded the American Defense Service Medal, World War II Victory Medal and Purple Heart Medal posthumously. He remains on duty on the USS Arizona. William is commemorated on the USS Arizona Memorial and the Memorial Tablets of the Missing, National Memorial Cemetery of the Pacific, Honolulu, Hawaii. He was survived by his Parents, Mr. and Mrs. Arthur Carl Mann, Route 1, Box 212, Elma, Washington. The VFW Post 1948 in Elma, Washington was named after Bill Mann.[505]

Manning, LeRoy Seaman, Second Class, Serial No: 287 48 07, US Navy. LeRoy was born August 21, 1923 in Harlan, Kentucky, the son of Roy and Lucy (Smith) Manning. He enlisted in the US Navy on November 27, 1940 in Louisville, Kentucky and completed his basic training at the Naval Training Station in Great Lakes, Illinois. LeRoy reported for duty on the USS Arizona on January 18, 1941. He was killed in action on December 7, 1941 at Pearl Harbor,

---

[504] Charles Clark Mann, Photo from Lucky Bag Yearbook, United States Naval Academy, Annapolis, MD, Class of 1934.
[505] William Edward Mann, information, picture and family stories provided by his sister, Virginia Heppe, and family member, Rhoda Tolle.

Hawaii. LeRoy was awarded the American Defense Service Medal, World War II Victory Medal and Purple Heart Medal posthumously. He remains on duty on the USS Arizona. LeRoy is commemorated on the USS Arizona Memorial and the Memorial Tablets of the Missing, National Memorial Cemetery of the Pacific, Honolulu, Hawaii. He was survived by his Parents, Mr. and Mrs. Roy Manning, Box 1245, Lynch, Kentucky.

Manske, Robert Francis Yeoman, Second Class, Serial No: 321 23 60, US Navy. Robert was born April 14, 1919 in Waterloo, Iowa, the son of Frank Walter and Katherine (Burger) Manske. He enlisted in the US Navy on February 2, 1938 in Des Moines, Iowa and reported for duty on the USS Arizona on July 9, 1938. *On the morning of the attack, Robert was sick and had gone to Sick Bay. He had gone to high school with the Sullivan Brothers. It was because of his death that the Sullivan Brothers enlisted.* Robert was killed in action on December 7, 1941 at Pearl Harbor, Hawaii. He was awarded the American Defense Service Medal, World War II Victory Medal and Purple Heart Medal posthumously. Robert remains on duty on the USS Arizona. He is commemorated on the USS Arizona Memorial and the Memorial Tablets of the Missing, National Memorial Cemetery of the Pacific, Honolulu, Hawaii. Robert was survived by his Mother, Mrs. Katherine Manske, Grant Highway, Waterloo, Iowa.[506]

Marcum, Harry Bedford Chief Electrician's Mate, Serial No. 268 00 47, US Navy. Harry was born April 4, 1910 in Tennessee to Claiborne Shelby and Selina (Byrd) Marcum. He enlisted in the US Navy on November 6, 1929. He served on the USS Arizona from September 12, 1930 until December 7, 1941 when the Japanese attacked Pearl Harbor. After the attack, Harry was transferred to the USS Whitney for duty. Shortly thereafter, he was transferred to the USS Hull (DD-350) for duty. In January 1942, Harry was transferred to the USS Solace for medical treatment. In November 1942, Harry was assigned duty at the Naval Air Station in Pearl Harbor. Harry re-enlisted for four years in January 1943. He died January 21, 1974 in Los Angeles, California.

Marinich, Steve Matt Coxswain, Serial No: 368 48 84, US Navy. Steve was born August 6, 1920 in Yugoslavia and came to the United States with his parents on March 6, 1935, residing in Park City, Utah until his enlistment. *At the time of his enlistment, Steve was a junior in high school. He was active in high school sports, with two years of experience as a first string football player.* He enlisted in the US Navy May 31, 1940 in Salt Lake City, Utah and completed his basic training at the Naval Training Station in San Diego, California. He reported for duty on the USS Arizona on September 8, 1940. Steve was killed in action on December 7, 1941 at Pearl Harbor, Hawaii. He was awarded the American Defense Service Medal, World War II Victory Medal and Purple Heart Medal posthumously. Steve remains on duty on the USS Arizona. He is commemorated on the USS Arizona Memorial and the Memorial Tablets of the Missing, National Memorial Cemetery of the Pacific, Honolulu, Hawaii. Steve was survived by his Father, Mr. Vick Marinich, 313 Empire Canyon, Park City, Utah.[507]

---

[506] Robert Francis Manske, Photo provided by family member, Jean Bergsma Maddux.
[507] Steve Matt Marinich, Information and picture taken from "Navy Reveals Death of Utah Sailor", Salt Lake Tribune, January 7, 1942, Page 14.

Maris, Elwood Henry   Seaman, First Class, Serial No: 360 15 39, US Navy. Elwood was born March 24, 1922 in Texas, the only son of Earl Louis and Vera D. Maris. He enlisted in the US Navy on June 7, 1940 in Houston, Texas and completed his basic training at the Naval Training Station in San Diego, California. Elwood reported for duty on the USS Arizona on November 28, 1940. He was killed in action on December 7, 1941 at Pearl Harbor, Hawaii. Elwood was awarded the American Defense Service Medal, World War II Victory Medal and Purple Heart Medal posthumously. He was identified as having been killed in action on the 7th with no other information available.[508]   Elwood is commemorated on the USS Arizona Memorial and the Memorial Tablets of the Missing, National Memorial Cemetery of the Pacific, Honolulu, Hawaii and the Holland Cemetery, Village Mills, Texas. He was survived by his Father, Mr. Earl Louis Maris, General Delivery, Rosharon, Texas.[509]

Marks, Edward Joseph   Coxswain, Serial No. 250 45 23, US Navy. Edward was born October 16, 1919 in Bruceton, Pennsylvania. He enlisted in the US Navy October 19, 1937 in Pittsburgh, Pennsylvania and reported for duty on the USS Arizona March 8, 1938. He was on leave the morning of December 7, 1941 when the Japanese attacked Pearl Harbor. Edward died July 1, 1986 in Sacramento, California.

Marling, Joseph Henry   Seaman, Second Class, Serial No: 368 61 56, US Navy. Joseph was born in about 1924 in Montana, son of Henry R. Marling and Hazel Irene (Fourman) Marling Flansburg. *His father died in 1939 at age 45. Joseph's mother remarried.* He enlisted in the US Navy on February 18, 1941 in Salt Lake City, Utah and completed his basic training at the Naval Training Station in San Diego, California. Joseph reported for duty on the USS Arizona on September 18, 1941. He was killed in action on December 7, 1941 at Pearl Harbor, Hawaii. Joseph was awarded the American Defense Service Medal, World War II Victory Medal and Purple Heart Medal posthumously. He remains on duty on the USS Arizona. Joseph is commemorated on the USS Arizona Memorial and the Memorial Tablets of the Missing, National Memorial Cemetery of the Pacific, Honolulu, Hawaii. He was survived by his Mother, Mrs. Hazel Marling Flansburg, Box 563, Philipsburg, Montana.

---

[508] Elwood Henry Maris, Report of Changes of the USS Arizona for the month ending 31st day of December, 1941, page 80, line 26.
[509] Elwood Henry Maris, Photo provided by family member Toni Casteel.

Marlow, Urban Herschel Coxswain, Serial No: 336 84 57, US Navy. Urban was born June 7, 1915 in Collins, Missouri, the son of William Harrison Marlow and Minnie Catherine (Bear) Marlow. He enlisted in the US Navy September 10, 1935 in St. Louis, Missouri and reported for duty on the USS Arizona on January 11, 1936. During the attack on December 7, 1941 at Pearl Harbor, he was blown off the ship, badly burned and died in the hospital two days later.[510] Urban was awarded the American Defense Service Medal, World War II Victory Medal and Purple Heart Medal posthumously. Assigned death #204, the disposition of his body is unclear; it is possible he was buried in one of the unknown graves at the Punchbowl. He is commemorated on the USS Arizona Memorial and the Memorial Tablets of the Missing, National Memorial Cemetery of the Pacific, Honolulu, Hawaii. Urban was survived by his Mother, Mrs. Minnie Catherine Marlow, Humansville, Missouri.[511]

Marsh, Benjamin Raymond, Jr. Ensign, Serial No: 0-097865, US Navy Reserve. Benjamin was born on October 11, 1916 in Lansing, Michigan, the son of Benjamin Raymond Marsh, Sr. and Marjorie Marsh. He enlisted in the Naval Reserve on August 17, 1940 at Detroit, Michigan. His enlistment terminated on February 13, 1941 and he was appointed midshipman in the Naval Reserve the following day, receiving his commission as Ensign on May 16, 1941. Benjamin was initially assigned to the USS Tangier, but was transferred to the USS Arizona on November 4, 1941. He was serving on the USS Arizona as Engineer Jr. Watch and Division M Officer. His battle station was the Port Engine room. Benjamin was killed in action on December 7, 1941 at Pearl Harbor, Hawaii. He was awarded the American Defense Service Medal, World War II Victory Medal and Purple Heart Medal posthumously. Benjamin remains on duty on the USS Arizona. He is commemorated on the USS Arizona Memorial and the Memorial Tablets of the Missing, National Memorial Cemetery of the Pacific, Honolulu, Hawaii. Benjamin was survived by his Father, Mr. Benjamin R. Marsh, Sr., 525 Rivard Boulevard, Grosse Pointe, Detroit, Michigan. The destroyer escort USS Marsh (DE-699) was named in his honor. The USS Marsh received one battle star for her World War II service and four battle stars for her Korean service.[512]

Marsh, William Arthur Seaman, First Class, Serial No: 368 52 75, US Navy. William was born on May 20, 1918 in Cold Spring, Missouri, the son of Henry Isaac and Nettie Pearl (Jones) Marsh. He enlisted in the US Navy on October 21, 1940 in Salt Lake City, Utah and completed his basic training at the Naval Training Station in San Diego, California. William reported for duty on the USS Arizona on December 30, 1940. Assigned death #453, William died December 12, 1941 from 3rd degree burns received during the action on December 7, 1941 at Honolulu, Hawaii.[513] William was initially interred in a Navy Plot, in Nuuanu Cemetery,

---

[510] Report of Changes of the USS Arizona for the month ending 31st day of December, 1941, Page 80, line 30, Urban Herschel Marlow.

[511] Urban Herschel Marlow, Photo provided by Jan Lunn, family member of Harry Malson.

[512] Benjamin Raymond Marsh, Jr., Photo and information from US Naval History, Destroyer Escort Photo Index for the USS Marsh (DE-699).

[513] William Arthur Marsh, Report of Changes of the USS Arizona for the month ending 31st day of December, 1941, Page 81, line 1.

Honolulu, Hawaii. He was later buried in Plot E, Row 0, Grave 134, National Memorial Cemetery of the Pacific, Honolulu, Hawaii. William was awarded the American Defense Service Medal, World War II Victory Medal and Purple Heart Medal posthumously. He is commemorated on the USS Arizona Memorial. William was survived by his Father, Mr. Henry Isaacs Marsh, Route 3, Twin Falls, Idaho.

Marshall, Thomas Donald   Seaman, Second Class, Serial No: 376 23 55, US Navy. Thomas was born January 20, 1924 in San Francisco the only child of Mr. and Mrs. Thomas Levis Marshall. He was 17 years old at the time of his enlistment in the US Navy on January 29, 1941. Thomas completed his basic training at the Naval Training Station in San Diego, California. He reported for duty on the USS Arizona on April 17, 1941. Thomas was killed in action on December 7, 1941 at Pearl Harbor, Hawaii. He was awarded the American Defense Service Medal, World War II Victory Medal and Purple Heart Medal posthumously. Thomas remains on duty on the USS Arizona. He is commemorated on the USS Arizona Memorial and the Memorial Tablets of the Missing, National Memorial Cemetery of the Pacific, Honolulu, Hawaii. Thomas was survived by his Parents, Mr. and Mrs. Thomas Levis Marshall, 462 Niagara Avenue, San Francisco, California His cousin, Gordon W. Marshall was serving on board the USS Utah and had just been approved to transfer to the USS Arizona, but before the transfer came in, Pearl Harbor was attacked. His cousin survived the attack on the USS Utah.[514]

Martin, Hugh Lee   Yeoman, Third Class, Serial No: 368 44 43, US Navy. Hugh was born January 1, 1921 in Chesterfield, Idaho to Victor Robiou and Elva Lora (Merrick) Martin. He enlisted in the US Navy on August 15, 1939 in Salt Lake City, Utah and completed his basic training at the Naval Training Station in San Diego, California. Hugh reported for duty on the USS Arizona on October 19, 1939. He was killed in action on December 7, 1941 at Pearl Harbor, Hawaii. Hugh was awarded the American Defense Service Medal, World War II Victory Medal and Purple Heart Medal posthumously. He remains on duty on the USS Arizona. Hugh is commemorated on the USS Arizona Memorial and the Memorial Tablets of the Missing, National Memorial Cemetery of the Pacific, Honolulu, Hawaii. He was survived by his Father, Mr. Victor Martin, 3838 South State Street, Salt Lake City, Utah.[515]

Martin, James Albert   Gunner's Mate, First Class, Serial No: 355 82 93, US Navy. James was born in about 1912 in Texas the son of James Espie Martin and Margaret Gillian (Simpson) Martin. He enlisted in the US Navy in 1933 in Dallas, Texas and completed his basic training at the Naval Training Station in San Diego, California. He served on the USS Arizona from June 7, 1933 until he was killed in action on December 7, 1941 at Pearl Harbor, Hawaii. James was awarded the American Defense Service Medal, World War II Victory Medal and Purple Heart Medal posthumously. He remains on duty on the USS Arizona. James is commemorated on the USS Arizona Memorial and the Memorial Tablets of the Missing, National Memorial Cemetery of the Pacific, Honolulu, Hawaii. He was survived by his Mother, Mrs. James Espie Martin, 618 Pulliam Street, San Angelo, Texas.

---

[514] Thomas Donald Marshall, Photo and information provided by family member, Eugenia Fletcher.
[515] Hugh Lee Martin, Photo from 1938 Blackfoot High School Yearbook, Blackfoot, Idaho.

Martin, James Orrwell Seaman, Second Class, Serial No: 376 22 65, US Navy. James was born in about 1922 in Minnesota to David and Leta Martin. He enlisted in the US Navy on January 23, 1941 in San Francisco, California and completed his basic training at the Naval Training Station in San Diego, California. He reported for duty on the USS Arizona on April 27, 1941. James was killed in action on December 7, 1941 at Pearl Harbor, Hawaii. He was awarded the American Defense Service Medal, World War II Victory Medal and Purple Heart Medal posthumously. James remains on duty on the USS Arizona. He is commemorated on the USS Arizona Memorial and the Memorial Tablets of the Missing, National Memorial Cemetery of the Pacific, Honolulu, Hawaii. James was survived by his Father, Mr. David Martin, Route 1, Box 61, Oakley, California.

Martin, Luster "Bug" Lee Fireman, Third Class, Serial No: 356 42 20, US Navy. Luster was born March 10, 1916 in Oklahoma to George and Rella V. Martin. His father passed away in 1918. He enlisted in the US Navy November 9, 1940 in Dallas, Texas and completed his basic training at the Naval Training Station in San Diego, California. He reported for duty on the USS Arizona January 11, 1941. Luster was killed in action on December 7, 1941 at Pearl Harbor, Hawaii. He was awarded the American Defense Service Medal, World War II Victory Medal and Purple Heart Medal posthumously. Luster remains buried on the USS Arizona. He is commemorated on the USS Arizona Memorial and the Memorial Tablets of the Missing, National Memorial Cemetery of the Pacific, Honolulu, Hawaii. Luster was survived by his Mother, Mrs. Rella V. Whittington, Fort Smith, Arkansas.[516]

Mason, Byron Dalley Seaman, Second Class, Serial No: 368 54 42, US Navy. Byron was born on June 3, 1912 in Milo, Idaho, the son of Joseph Henry and Eleanor (Armstrong) Mason. He was a one time welterweight boxing champion in Idaho. He also sang Bass in the Mason Quartet and was active in Music and Drama in High School. Byron enlisted in the Navy on November 26, 1940 in Salt Lake City, Utah and served on the USS West Virginia for a time before he reported for duty on the USS Arizona on August 25, 1941. Byron was killed in action on December 7, 1941 at Pearl Harbor, Hawaii. He was awarded the American Defense Service Medal, World War II Victory Medal and Purple Heart Medal posthumously. Byron remains on duty on the USS Arizona. He is commemorated on the USS Arizona Memorial and the Memorial Tablets of the Missing, National Memorial Cemetery of the Pacific, Honolulu, Hawaii. Byron was survived by his Parents, Mr. and Mrs. Joseph Henry Mason, Ririe, Idaho.[517]

Mastel, Clyde "Buddy" Harold Seaman, Second Class, Serial No: 376 26 73, US Navy. Clyde was born October 23, 1923 in Parshall, North Dakota, the son of Peter Junior and Iva Lorena (McDermott) Mastel. He enlisted in the US Navy on February 25, 1941 in San Francisco, California and completed his basic training at the Naval Training Station in San Diego, California. Clyde reported for duty on the USS Arizona on September 18, 1941. He was killed in action on December 7, 1941 at Pearl Harbor, Hawaii. Clyde was awarded the American Defense Service Medal, World War II Victory Medal and Purple Heart Medal posthumously. He remains on duty on the USS Arizona. Clyde is commemorated on the USS Arizona Memorial

---

[516] Luster Lee Martin, Photo provided by family member, David L. Sorenson.

[517] Byron Dalley Mason, Information and photo provided by his brother, Sterling Mason.

and the Memorial Tablets of the Missing, National Memorial Cemetery of the Pacific, Honolulu, Hawaii. He was survived by his Father, Mr. Peter Junior Mastel, Route 7, Box 4852, Sacramento, California.

Masters, Dayton Monroe   Gunner's Mate, Third Class, Serial No: 356 18 49, US Navy. Dayton was born on October 19, 1919 in Granbury, Texas, the youngest of four sons born to Archie Norten and Willena (Wright) Masters. He enlisted in the US Navy on November 8, 1939 in Dallas, Texas and completed his basic training at the Naval Training Station in San Diego, California. Dayton reported for duty on the USS Arizona on January 24, 1940. He died from wounds received on December 7, 1941 at Pearl Harbor. Dayton was awarded the American Defense Service Medal, World War II Victory Medal and Purple Heart Medal posthumously. He remains on duty on the USS Arizona. Dayton is commemorated on the USS Arizona Memorial and the Memorial Tablets of the Missing, National Memorial Cemetery of the Pacific, Honolulu, Hawaii. He was survived by his Parents, Mr. and Mrs. Archie Norton Masters, Route 2, Avoca, Texas.

Masterson, Cleburne Earl Carl   Pharmacist's Mate, First Class, Serial No: 371 51 87, US Navy. Cleburne was born March 16, 1902 in Kansas, the only son of Henry E. and Eva J. Masterson. He enlisted in the US Navy on June 7, 1939 in Washington, D.C. and reported for duty on the USS Arizona on March 1, 1940. Assigned death #452, Cleburne died from drowning during the action on December 7, 1941 at Pearl Harbor [518]. He was awarded the American Defense Service Medal, World War II Victory Medal and Purple Heart Medal posthumously. Cleburne's remains were recovered and he was buried in Nuuanu Cemetery. He was later moved to Plot M, Row 0, Grave 1034, National Memorial Cemetery of the Pacific, Honolulu, Hawaii. He is commemorated on the USS Arizona Memorial. Cleburne was survived by his Wife, Mrs. Helen Juanita Masterson, 2525 East 10th Street, Long Beach, California.

Masterson, Kleber Sandlin   Lieutenant, Serial No. 0-03745, US Navy. Kleber was born on July 12, 1908 in San Jon, New Mexico. He was commissioned in the US Navy June 30, 1937 and was serving as Assistant Main Battery, W&D, Senior Watch Officer on the USS Arizona on December 7, 1941 when the Japanese attacked Pearl Harbor. His battle station was the Plotting Room. During his time in the service, Kleber was awarded 2 Navy Distinguished Service Medals, Legion of Merit, Navy Commendation Medal, American Defense Service Medal and the World War II Victory Medal. In January 1960 Kleber attained the rank of Rear Admiral. Kleber died on May 3, 1998 and is buried in Section 46, Site 4, Arlington National Cemetery, Arlington, Virginia.

Mathein, Harold Richard   Boilermaker, Second Class, Serial No: 336 96 02, US Navy. Harold was born October 20, 1919 in Lincoln, Illinois the son of George Henry Mathein and Harriette Hattie (Britton) Mathein. He enlisted in the US Navy on February 9, 1937 in St. Louis, Missouri and reported for duty on the USS Arizona June 19, 1937. Harold was killed in action on December 7, 1941 at Pearl Harbor, Hawaii. He was awarded the American Defense Service Medal, World War II Victory Medal and Purple Heart Medal posthumously. Harold remains buried on the USS Arizona. He is commemorated on the USS Arizona Memorial and the Memorial Tablets of the Missing, National Memorial Cemetery of the Pacific, Honolulu, Hawaii.

---

[518] Report of Changes of the USS Arizona for the month ending 31st day of December, 1941, Page 81, line 9, Cleburne Earl Carl Masterson.

Harold was survived by his Father, Mr. George Henry Mathein, 2155 South 13th Street, Springfield, Illinois.

Mathison, Charles Harris   Seaman, First Class, Serial No: 382 23 89, US Navy. Charles was born in 1922 in Wisconsin the son of Oscar Mathison and Emily (Kerr) Mathison. He enlisted in the US Navy on August 6, 1940 in Los Angeles, California and completed his basic training at the Naval Training Station in San Diego, California. Charles reported for duty on the USS Arizona on October 14, 1940. He was killed in action on December 7, 1941 at Pearl Harbor, Hawaii. Charles was awarded the American Defense Service Medal, World War II Victory Medal and Purple Heart Medal posthumously. He remains on duty on the USS Arizona. Charles is commemorated on the USS Arizona Memorial and the Memorial Tablets of the Missing, National Memorial Cemetery of the Pacific, Honolulu, Hawaii. He was survived by his Mother, Mrs. Emily Sampson, 1132 White Rock Avenue, Waukesha, Wisconsin.

Matney, Vernon Merferd   Fireman, First Class, Serial No: 356 15 96, US Navy. Vernon was born on January 6, 1921 in Coleman, Oklahoma, the son of Claude Harrison and Bertie Lee (Millican) Matney. *Vernon joined the Navy to "See the world and all the pretty foreign girls."* He enlisted in the US Navy on September 12, 1939 in Dallas, Texas and completed his basic training at the Naval Training Station in San Diego, California. Vernon reported for duty on the USS Arizona on March 1, 1940. He was killed in action on December 7, 1941 at Pearl Harbor, Hawaii. *Randle Dean Smart, GM1c visited the family after being released from the hospital. According to Smart, Vernon had been working as a third class gunner with him during the attack. The last he saw of him before loosing consciousness, Vernon was continuing his work at the gun.* Vernon was awarded the American Defense Service Medal, World War II Victory Medal and Purple Heart Medal posthumously. He remains on duty on the USS Arizona. Vernon is commemorated on the USS Arizona Memorial and the Memorial Tablets of the Missing, National Memorial Cemetery of the Pacific, Honolulu, Hawaii and the Garden of Memories, Paducah, Texas. He was survived by his Parents, Mr. and Mrs. Claude H. Matney, Guthrie Route, Box 25, Paducah, Texas. The VFW Post in Paducah, Texas was named in his honor. It took his sister, Ms. Mildred Shavor 63 years to obtain a monument for Vernon in the local cemetery.[519]

Mattlage, Herbert   Ensign, US Navy. Herbert born January 23, 1917 in Bayside, Borough of Queens, New York, New York. He was the youngest son of William F. Mattlage and Margaret (Kolmar) Mattlage. Herbert was a graduate of Pawling School in Pawling, New York and Dartmouth College, class of 1939 in Hanover. Herbert joined the Navy in September 10, 1940. He was commissioned Ensign in the US Navy June 6, 1941 and was serving on the USS Arizona as Engineer Jr. Watch & Division E Officer. His battle station was the After Dist. Board on December 7, 1941 when the Japanese attacked Pearl Harbor. After the attack Herbert served in the Pacific on the USS Nevada, USS Franklin and the USS West Virginia. He was present in Tokyo Bay for the signing of the peace treaty with Japan. He then taught at Pawling School for one year where he coached an undefeated football team. Herbert moved to a teaching position at Belmont Hill School and attended Harvard

---

[519] Vernon Merferd Matney, Photo and information provided by his sister, Mrs. Mildred Shavor.

Graduate School of Education and earned a master's degree. He taught, coached and was a dorm master for 37 years before retiring in 1982. Herbert then lived in Moultonboro and Hanover until moving to Concord in July of 2002. He loved tennis, squash, coaching and watching sports. Herbert was most happy at his home on the shores of Lake Winnipesaukee. Herbert died August 16, 2005 at Harris Hill Center, Concord, New Hampshire.

Mattox, James Durant Aviation Metalsmith, Third Class, Aviation Unit (VO-1), Serial No: 272 24 33, US Navy. James was born on June 16, 1919 in Pensacola, Florida, the son of Lonnie James and Lavada Bell (Hinote) Mattox. He enlisted in the US Navy on November 21, 1939 in Birmingham, Alabama and reported for duty on the USS Arizona on October 1, 1940. James was killed in action on December 7, 1941 at Pearl Harbor, Hawaii. He was awarded the American Defense Service Medal, World War II Victory Medal and Purple Heart Medal posthumously. James remains on duty on the USS Arizona. He is commemorated on the USS Arizona Memorial and the Memorial Tablets of the Missing, National Memorial Cemetery of the Pacific, Honolulu, Hawaii and the Bayview Cemetery, Pensacola, Florida. James was survived by his Father, Mr. Lonnie James Mattox, 802 East Patten Street, Pensacola, Florida.[520]

May, Louis Eugene Ship's Cook, Second Class, Serial No: 342 01 09, US Navy. Louis was born March 29, 1916 in Hepler, Kansas to William Edward and Lula Mary (Hoefle) May. He enlisted in the US Navy on March 16, 1937 in Kansas City, Missouri and reported for duty on the USS Arizona July 24, 1937. Louis was killed in action on December 7, 1941 at Pearl Harbor, Hawaii. He was awarded the American Defense Service Medal, World War II Victory Medal and Purple Heart Medal posthumously. Louis remains on duty on the USS Arizona. He is commemorated on the USS Arizona Memorial and the Memorial Tablets of the Missing, National Memorial Cemetery of the Pacific, Honolulu, Hawaii. Louis was survived by his Parents, Mr. and Mrs. William Edward May, 524 West Beach Street, Chanute, Kansas, three brothers, Lee and Everett, serving in the Navy and John who was recently discharged from a cavalry detachement.

Maybee, George Frederick Radioman, Second Class, Serial No: 413 24 47, US Naval Reserve. George was born on November 17, 1912 in Santa Rosa, California, the son of Arthur Alma and Edna Gertrude (Karman) Maybee. *"Both George and his brother John were involved with radio at a very early age, starting with crystal sets and progressing to Ham Radio in the early 30's and the building of commercial transmission systems in the late 30's. George and his brother, John were members of the Navy Reserves prior to the war due to their interest in radio technology. When the war was eminent they were both called up. His brother John was let go due to a slight heart murmur."[521]* He enlisted in the US Navy on January 11, 1938 and reported for duty on the USS Arizona on January 23, 1941. George was killed in action on December 7, 1941 at Pearl Harbor, Hawaii. He was awarded the American Defense Service Medal, World War II Victory Medal and Purple Heart Medal posthumously. George remains on duty on the USS Arizona. He is commemorated on the USS Arizona Memorial and the Memorial Tablets of the Missing, National Memorial Cemetery of the Pacific, Honolulu, Hawaii. George

---

[520] James Durant Mattox, photo from the Arizona State Library, Archives and Public Records
[521] George Frederick Maybee, Information provided by his nephew, George K. Maybee.

was survived by his Mother, Mrs. Edna Gertrude Maybee, 713 South Davis Street, Santa Rosa, California. A small park across the street from his home was dedicated in George's name.

Mayfield, Lester Ellsworth Fireman, First Class, Serial No: 372 09 41, US Navy. Lester was born in 1918 in Stone City, Colorado the son of James William and Mattie May (Wands) Mayfield. He enlisted in the US Navy on August 12, 1939 in Denver, Colorado and completed his basic training at the Naval Training Station in San Diego, California. Lester reported for duty on the USS Arizona on October 20, 1939. He was killed in action on December 7, 1941 at Pearl Harbor, Hawaii. Lester was awarded the American Defense Service Medal, World War II Victory Medal and Purple Heart Medal posthumously. He remains on duty on the USS Arizona. Lester is commemorated on the USS Arizona Memorial and the Memorial Tablets of the Missing, National Memorial Cemetery of the Pacific, Honolulu, Hawaii. He was survived by his Father, Mr. James William Mayfield, Stone City, Colorado.

Mayo, Rex Haywood Electrician's Mate, Second Class, Serial No: 272 16 08, US Navy. Rex was born in about 1916 in Florida, the son of Felix M. and Lovie Mayo. He enlisted in the US Navy on September 8, 1937 in Birmingham, Alabama and completed his basic training at the Naval Training Station in Norfolk, Virginia. Rex reported for duty on the USS Arizona on March 8, 1938. He was killed in action on December 7, 1941 at Pearl Harbor, Hawaii. Rex was awarded the American Defense Service Medal, World War II Victory Medal and Purple Heart Medal posthumously. He remains on duty on the USS Arizona. Rex is commemorated on the USS Arizona Memorial and the Memorial Tablets of the Missing, National Memorial Cemetery of the Pacific, Honolulu, Hawaii. He was survived by his Grandmother, Mrs. Addie Melvin, Kynesville, Florida.

McCarron, John Harry Gunner's Mate, Second Class, Serial No. 400 47 05, US Navy. John was born on March 11, 1919 in Tewksbury, Massachusetts. He enlisted in the US Navy Reserve in 1936 and enlisted full time in the Navy September 8, 1937. John reported for duty on the USS Arizona March 8, 1938 it was his first ship and his first real home. He was serving as a gun captain on December 7, 1941 when the Japanese attacked Pearl Harbor. Although John was wounded, he survived the attack. He later served on board the USS Lamberto, USS Manchester, USS Missouri, USS Yosemite and USS Bennington. Additionally he served in the Korean War and the Vietnam War. John served 32 years in the Navy and was awarded the Purple Heart, Navy Good Conduct Medal, American Theater Medal, Asiatic Pacific Campaign Medal and the Korean Service Medal. John died on June 22, 2007 in San Diego, California.

McCary, William Moore Musician, Second Class, Serial No: 272 49 25, US Navy. William was born in 1925 in Alabama the son of William Nabers and Nell M. (Moore) McCary. He enlisted in the US Navy December 9, 1940 in Birmingham, Alabama and attended the Navy School of Music in Washington, DC, graduating on May 23, 1941. He and reported for duty on the USS Arizona on June 17, 1941. William was killed in action on December 7, 1941 at Pearl Harbor, Hawaii. *William was a member of the USS Arizona's Band. The battle station for all of the band members was in the black powder room passing ammunition to the Arizona's gunners during the attack. None of the band members survived the explosion.* He was awarded the American Defense Service Medal, World War II Victory Medal and Purple Heart Medal posthumously. William remains on duty on the USS Arizona. He is commemorated on the USS Arizona Memorial and the Memorial Tablets of the Missing, National Memorial Cemetery of the Pacific, Honolulu, Hawaii. William was survived by his Father, Mr. William Nabers McCary, Route 2, Birmingham, Alabama.[522]

McClafferty, John Charles   Boatswain's Mate, Second Class, Serial No: 283 08 35, US Navy. John was born July 13, 1915 in Ohio, the son of Fred and Ethel McClafferty. He re-enlisted in the US Navy on July 3, 1936 and again on February 28, 1941 in Cleveland, Ohio. John served on the USS Arizona from August 11, 1933 until he was killed in action on December 7, 1941 at Pearl Harbor, Hawaii. He was awarded the American Defense Service Medal, World War II Victory Medal and Purple Heart Medal posthumously. John's remains were recovered and he was buried in I-15, 382, Oahu Cemetery, Nuuanu (US Naval Cemetery) Nuuanu, Hawaii. He is commemorated on the USS Arizona Memorial. John was survived by his Father, Mr. Fred McClafferty, 45 Linden Avenue, Youngstown, Ohio.

McClung, Harvey Manford   Ensign, Serial No: 0-101797, US Navy Reserve. Harvey was born February 17, 1918 in Mundale, New York, the son of Rev. Nathan B. and Anna M. McClung. He graduated from the New Florence High School, Geneva College and the Midshipman's Training School of Northwestern University. Commissioned on June 12, 1941, he was the Assistant Communications Officer. His battle station was Flag Radar Plot. Harvey was killed in action on December 7, 1941 at Pearl Harbor, Hawaii. He was awarded the American Defense Service Medal, World War II Victory Medal and Purple Heart Medal posthumously. Harvey remains on duty on the USS Arizona. He is commemorated on the USS Arizona Memorial and the Memorial Tablets of the Missing, National Memorial Cemetery of the Pacific, Honolulu, Hawaii. Harvey was survived by his Mother, Mrs. Anna McClung, New Florence, Pennsylvania.[523]

McDonald, Don Erwin   Seaman, First Class, Serial No. 393 27 85, US Navy. Don was born October 13, 1920 in Portland, Oregon, the son of Aurelius Miner and Lydia (Falkner) McDonald. He enlisted in the US Navy November 15, 1938 in Portland, Oregon and reported for duty on the USS Arizona March 11, 1939. Don was serving on the USS Arizona on December 7, 1941 when the Japanese attacked Pearl Harbor. After the attack, Don was transferred to the USS Flusser for duty. He died March 11, 2003 and is buried in Section III, Avery Stoddard Cemetery, Ledyard, Connecticut.

---

[522] William Moore McCary, Photo from USS Arizona's Last Band by Molly Kent. By permission of the author. For more information about this book, go to www.USSARIZONASLASTBAND.com.
[523] Harvey Manford McClung, Photo from the Geneva College Class of 1939 yearbook, provided by the Geneva College, Beaver Falls, PA.

McFaddin, Lawrence James Yeoman, Second Class, Serial No: 321 23 94, US Navy. Lawrence was born June 27, 1919 in Chicago, Illinois. He enlisted in the US Navy on March 9, 1938 in Des Moines, Iowa and completed his basic training at the Naval Training Station in Great Lakes, Illinois. He reported for duty on the USS Arizona on July 9, 1938. Lawrence was killed in action on December 7, 1941 at Pearl Harbor, Hawaii. He was awarded the American Defense Service Medal, World War II Victory Medal and Purple Heart Medal posthumously. Lawrence remains on duty on the USS Arizona. He is commemorated on the USS Arizona Memorial and the Memorial Tablets of the Missing, National Memorial Cemetery of the Pacific, Honolulu, Hawaii. Lawrence was survived by his Wife, Mrs. Betty Imogene McFaddin, 1357 Lagoon Avenue, Wilmington, California.[524]

McFall, Charles William Gunner's Mate, First Class, Serial No. 371 73 63, US Navy. Charles was born September 22, 1906. He enlisted in the US Navy on November 2, 1928. Charles served on the USS Arizona from March 23, 1931 until December 7, 1941 when the Japanese attacked Pearl Harbor. He died June 23, 1984 and is buried at Plot OS-A 137, Fort Rosencrans National Cemetery, San Diego, California.

McGlasson, Joe Otis Gunner's Mate, Third Class, Serial No: 337 21 28, US Navy. Joe was born May 11, 1917 in White Hall, Illinois, the son of Thomas A. and Stella May (Mason) McGlasson. His mother died when he was just 5 years old. Joe left school in the 8th grade to work and help his family. He and an older brother, Russell served in the Civilian Conservation Corps during the Depression. He enlisted in the US Navy on October 9, 1939 in St. Louis, Missouri and reported for duty on the USS Arizona on December 20, 1939. Joe was killed in action on December 7, 1941 at Pearl Harbor, Hawaii. He was awarded the American Defense Service Medal, World War II Victory Medal and Purple Heart Medal posthumously. Joe remains on duty on the USS Arizona. He is commemorated on the USS Arizona Memorial and the Memorial Tablets of the Missing, National Memorial Cemetery of the Pacific, Honolulu, Hawaii. Joe was survived by his Father, Mr. Tom McGlasson, 361 Fulton Street, White Hall, Illinois.[525]

McGrady, Samme Willie Genes Steward's Mate, First Class, Serial No: 272 25 22, US Navy. Samme was born in about 1919 in Alabama to Willie and Mary McGrady. He enlisted in the US Navy on December 21, 1939 in Birmingham, Alabama and reported for duty on the USS Arizona on March 29, 1940. Samme was killed in action on December 7, 1941 at Pearl Harbor, Hawaii. He was awarded the American Defense Service Medal, World War II Victory Medal and Purple Heart Medal posthumously. Samme remains on duty on the USS Arizona. He is commemorated on the USS Arizona Memorial and the Memorial Tablets of the Missing, National Memorial Cemetery of the Pacific, Honolulu, Hawaii. Samme was survived by his Father, Mr. Willie McGrady, Route 3, Troy, Alabama.

---

[524] Lawrence James McFaddin, Photo from California Honor States.
[525] Joe Otis McGlasson, Information and photo provided by family member, Autumn L. Martinage.

McGuire, Francis Raymond Storekeeper, Second Class, Serial No: 299 88 87, US Navy. Francis was born in 1916 in Illinois, the son of John R. and Minnie K. McGuire. He enlisted in the US Navy on January 19, 1938 in Chicago, Illinois and reported for duty on the USS Arizona on June 4, 1938. Francis was killed in action on December 7, 1941 at Pearl Harbor, Hawaii. He was awarded the American Defense Service Medal, World War II Victory Medal and Purple Heart Medal posthumously. Francis remains on duty on the USS Arizona. He is commemorated on the USS Arizona Memorial and the Memorial Tablets of the Missing, National Memorial Cemetery of the Pacific, Honolulu, Hawaii. Francis was survived by his Father, Mr. John Robert McGuire, Wallace, Michigan.[526]

McHughes, John Breckenridge Chief Water Tender, Serial No: 294 83 51, US Navy. John was born July 20, 1902 in Hardeman County, Tennessee the son of James Carroll and Dollie M. (Moss) McHughes. He enlisted in the US Navy on May 13, 1938 in San Pedro, California and reported for duty on the USS Arizona on November 25, 1938. John was killed in action on December 7, 1941 at Pearl Harbor, Hawaii. He was awarded the American Defense Service Medal, World War II Victory Medal and Purple Heart Medal posthumously. John remains on duty on the USS Arizona. He is commemorated on the USS Arizona Memorial and the Memorial Tablets of the Missing, National Memorial Cemetery of the Pacific, Honolulu, Hawaii. John was survived by his Wife, Mrs. Thelma Courter McHughes, Route 3, Box 670, Everett, Washington.

McIntosh, Harry George Seaman, First Class, Serial No: 376 14 90, US Navy. Harry was born in about 1921 in Lincoln, Nebraska to George W. and Anne Louise (Letterman) McIntosh. He enlisted in the US Navy on October 31, 1940 in San Francisco, California and completed his basic training at the Naval Training Station in San Diego, California. Harry reported for duty on the USS Arizona on December 30, 1940. He was killed in action on December 7, 1941 at Pearl Harbor, Hawaii. Harry was awarded the American Defense Service Medal, World War II Victory Medal and Purple Heart Medal posthumously. He remains on duty on the USS Arizona. Harry is commemorated on the USS Arizona Memorial and the Memorial Tablets of the Missing, National Memorial Cemetery of the Pacific, Honolulu, Hawaii. He was survived by his Sister, Miss Corda Robinson, 223 NW 3rd Street, Visalia, California.[527]

McKenna, Kenneth Kermit Signalman, First Class, Flag Division, Serial No. 310 82 94, US Navy. Kenneth was born on May 24, 1909 in Ohio, the son of Henry N. and Pearl (Culbertson) McKenna. He enlisted in the US Navy December 1, 1926 and reported for duty on the USS Tennessee in 1939. He transferred to the USS Arizona on June 1, 1941. He was serving on December 7, 1941 when the Japanese attacked Pearl Harbor. Kenneth died on December 5, 1993 after a long battle with cancer. He is buried in Section C, Site 66, Biloxi National Cemetery, Biloxi, Mississippi. He was survived by his wife, Norma McKenna and a son, Tim Halloran.

---

[526] Francis Raymond McGuire, Photo provided by family member, J. Mulenburg.
[527] Harry George McIntosh, Photo and information provided by his niece, Darlene Davis.

306

McKinnie, Russell Lee   Steward's Mate, Second Class, Serial No: 295 55 52, US Navy. Russell was born in 1923, the son of Willie and Leathy McKinnie. He enlisted in the US Navy on December 18, 1939 in Nashville, Tennessee and reported for duty on the USS Arizona on March 8, 1940. Russell was killed in action on December 7, 1941 at Pearl Harbor, Hawaii. He was awarded the American Defense Service Medal, World War II Victory Medal and Purple Heart Medal posthumously. Russell remains on duty on the USS Arizona. He is commemorated on the USS Arizona Memorial and the Memorial Tablets of the Missing, National Memorial Cemetery of the Pacific, Honolulu, Hawaii. Russell was survived by his Father, Mr. Willie McKinnie, Box 74, Hughes, Arkansas.

McKosky, Michael Martin   Seaman, First Class, Serial No: 355 43 34, US Navy. Michael was born June 12, 1922. He enlisted in the US Navy on November 27, 1940 in Dallas, Texas and completed his basic training at the Naval Training Station in San Diego, California. Michael reported for duty on the USS Arizona on January 25, 1941. He was killed in action on December 7, 1941 at Pearl Harbor, Hawaii. Michael was awarded the American Defense Service Medal, World War II Victory Medal and Purple Heart Medal posthumously. He remains on duty on the USS Arizona. Michael is commemorated on the USS Arizona Memorial and the Memorial Tablets of the Missing, National Memorial Cemetery of the Pacific, Honolulu, Hawaii. He was survived by his Mother, Mrs. Ethel McKosky, Box 66, Talihina, Oklahoma.

McPherson, John Blair "JB"   Seaman, First Class, Serial No: 295 76 68, US Navy. John was born January 11, 1920 in Lenoir City, Tennessee, the son of Charlie and Linnie P. (McDaniel) McPherson. He enlisted in the US Navy on October 4, 1940 in Nashville, Tennessee and completed his basic training at the Naval Training Station in Norfolk, Virginia. John reported for duty on the USS Arizona on December 4, 1940. He was killed in action on December 7, 1941 at Pearl Harbor, Hawaii. John was awarded the American Defense Service Medal, World War II Victory Medal and Purple Heart Medal posthumously. He remains on duty on the USS Arizona. John is commemorated on the USS Arizona Memorial and the Memorial Tablets of the Missing, National Memorial Cemetery of the Pacific, Honolulu, Hawaii. He was survived by his Father, Mr. Charlie McPherson, 201 Atkin Street, Knoxville, Tennessee.[528]

Means, Louis   Steward's Mate, First Class, Serial No: 360 06 12, US Navy. Louis was born in about 1922 in Texas. He enlisted in the US Navy on September 16, 1939 in Houston, Texas and completed his basic training at the Naval Training Station in Norfolk, Virginia. He reported for duty on the USS Arizona on January 2, 1940. Louis was killed in action on December 7, 1941 at Pearl Harbor. Hawaii. He was awarded the American Defense Service Medal, World War II Victory Medal and Purple Heart Medal posthumously. Louis remains on duty on the USS Arizona. He is commemorated on the USS Arizona Memorial and the Memorial Tablets of the Missing, National Memorial Cemetery of the Pacific, Honolulu, Hawaii. Louis was survived by his Father, Mr. Eddie Means, 3022 Drew Street, Houston, Texas.

Meares, John "Jack" Morgan   Seaman, Second Class, Serial No: 311 50 32, US Navy. John was born on January 6, 1916 in Anderson County, South Carolina, the son of Thomas Capers and Sara Wiseford (Reynolds) Meares. He enlisted in the US Navy on September 17, 1940 in Detroit, Michigan and completed his basic training at the Naval Training Station in Great

---

[528] John Blair McPherson, Photo provided by his great nephew, Nicholas Brown.

Lakes, Illinois. John reported for duty on the USS Arizona on August 24, 1941. He was killed in action on December 7, 1941 at Pearl Harbor, Hawaii. John was awarded the American Defense Service Medal, World War II Victory Medal and Purple Heart Medal posthumously. He remains on duty on the USS Arizona. John is commemorated on the USS Arizona Memorial and the Memorial Tablets of the Missing, National Memorial Cemetery of the Pacific, Honolulu, Hawaii and the Williamston Memorial Park, Williamston, South Carolina. He was survived by his Mother, Mrs. Sarah Reynolds Meares, 301 East North Street, Greenville, South Carolina.

Melvin, Earle Thomas Chief Fire Controlman, Serial No. 335 84 59, US Navy. Earle was born October 15, 1901 in Tamaroa, Illinois, the son of Walter Miles and Altha Mae (George) Melvin. He re-enlisted in the US Navy December 3, 1938. Earl served on the USS Arizona from March 31, 1931 until December 7, 1941 when the Japanese attacked Pearl Harbor. After the attack, Earle was transferred to the USS Blue for duty. He then went on to serve on board the USS Pennsylvania (BB-38). Earle died February 7, 1947 in California.

Menefee, James Austin Seaman, First Class, Serial No: 295 55 34, US Navy. James was born in about 1917 in Hinds County, Mississippi the son of Cecil Lafayette and Helen (Johnson) Menefee. He enlisted in the US Navy on December 16, 1939 in Nashville, Tennessee and reported for duty on the USS Arizona on June 6, 1940. James was killed in action on December 7, 1941 at Pearl Harbor, Hawaii. He was awarded the American Defense Service Medal, World War II Victory Medal and Purple Heart Medal posthumously. James remains on duty on the USS Arizona. He is commemorated on the USS Arizona Memorial and the Memorial Tablets of the Missing, National Memorial Cemetery of the Pacific, Honolulu, Hawaii. James was survived by his Father, Mr. Cecil Lafayette Menefee, 221 Erie Street, Jackson, Mississippi.

Meno, Vicente Gogue Mess Attendant, Second Class, Serial No: 421 05 15, US Navy. Vicente was born in 1921 in Agana, Guam the son of Maria Glardo Meno. He enlisted in the US Navy on October 2, 1939 at the US Naval Station in Guam and reported for duty on the USS Arizona on June 9, 1941. He was killed in action on December 7, 1941 at Pearl Harbor, Hawaii. Vicente was awarded the American Defense Service Medal, World War II Victory Medal and Purple Heart Medal posthumously. He remains on duty on the USS Arizona. Vicente is commemorated on the USS Arizona Memorial and the Memorial Tablets of the Missing, National Memorial Cemetery of the Pacific, Honolulu, Hawaii and the Sons of Guam Pearl Harbor Memorial, Guam. He was survived by his Father, Mr. Quintin Delgado Meno, Lot 2037-13, Padre Palomo Street, Agana, Guam.

Menzenski, Stanley Paul Coxswain, Serial No: 223 59 94, US Navy. Stanley was born in 1923 in New York, the son of Vincent and Sophia (Nowicki) Menzenski. He enlisted in the US Navy on November 22, 1939 in New York, New York and reported for duty on the USS Arizona on September 30, 1940. Stanley was killed in action on December 7, 1941 at Pearl Harbor, Hawaii. He was awarded the American Defense Service Medal, World War II Victory Medal and Purple Heart Medal posthumously. Stanley remains on duty on the USS Arizona. He is commemorated on the USS Arizona Memorial and the Memorial Tablets of the Missing, National Memorial Cemetery of the Pacific, Honolulu, Hawaii. Stanley was survived by his Father, Mr. Vincent Menzenski, 10 Croton Terrace, Yonkers, New York.

Merrill, Howard Deal   Ensign, Serial No: 0-085057, US Navy. Howard was born on December 16, 1917 in Provo, Utah, the son of Leslie Shepard and Stella Elvira (Petersen) Merrill. He was appointed midshipman at the Naval Academy on June 25, 1936. Howard was commissioned Ensign on June 6, 1940 and reported for duty on the USS Arizona on July 2, 1940 serving as Engineer W & D Officer, Division M. His battle station was the Central Engine Room. Howard was killed in action on December 7, 1941 at Pearl Harbor, Hawaii. He was awarded the American Defense Service Medal, World War II Victory Medal and Purple Heart Medal posthumously. Howard remains on duty on the USS Arizona. He is commemorated on the USS Arizona Memorial and the Memorial Tablets of the Missing, National Memorial Cemetery of the Pacific, Honolulu, Hawaii. Howard was survived by his Father, Mr. Leslie S. Merrill, 2761 Harrison Avenue, Ogden, Utah. The destroyer escort, USS Merrill (DE-392) was named in his honor. The American Legion Post 9 in Ogden, Utah was named Baker-Merrill in honor of him and another local man, Herman Baker who died in World War I.[529]

Metcalf, John Howard   Seaman, Second Class, Serial No. 328 75 64, US Navy. John was born May 8, 1921 in East Grand Forks, Minnesota to Frederick Howard and Mabel (Meyers) Metcalf. He enlisted in the US Navy October 8, 1940 in Minneapolis, Minnesota and completed his basic training at the Naval Training Station in Great Lakes, Illinois. He reported for duty on the USS Arizona December 9, 1940. He was serving on the USS Arizona on December 7, 1941 when the Japanese attacked Pearl Harbor. After the attack, John was transferred to the USS Patterson (DD-392) for duty. John died March 2, 1986 in Ironton, Ohio.

Migliaccio, Thomas William   Seaman, Second Class, Serial No. 207 24 48, US Navy. Thomas was born January 16, 1917 in Groton, Connecticut. He enlisted in the US Navy November 1, 1939 in New Haven, Connecticut and reported for duty on the USS Arizona March 20, 1941. He was serving on the USS Arizona on December 7, 1941 when the Japanese attacked Pearl Harbor. He later served on the USS Ranger (CV-4) and the USS Henderson (AP-1). During his service, Thomas was awarded the American Defense Service Medal, American Campaign Medal, Asiatic Pacific Campaign Medal and the World War II Victory Medal.

Miles, Oscar Wright   Seaman, First Class, Serial No: 346 83 21, US Navy. Oscar was born May 15, 1919, the third child and first son of David E. and Mabel E. Miles in Saline, Arkansas. *While Oscar was still very young, his father died of complications due to a brain tumor. His mother later married William Haney of the Green Hill community. The Haneys had five children and Oscar grew up surrounded by a large and loving family. He graduated from Drew Central High School in 1939 and enrolled in the Monticello Civilian Conservation Corps (CCC).* Oscar enlisted in the U.S. Navy on August 2, 1940 in Little Rock, Arkansas and completed his basic training at the Naval Training Station in San Diego, California. He

---

[529] Howard Deal Merrill, Photo and information from the Dictionary of American Naval Fighting Ships, Naval Historical Center, USS Merrill (DE-392).

reported for duty on the USS Arizona on October 14, 1940. Oscar was killed in action on December 7, 1941 at Pearl Harbor, Hawaii. *His family was notified on December 21, 1941 that he was "missing in action". A telegram dated January 31, 1942, said all efforts to locate Oscar had failed and that he was therefore "been officially declared to have lost his life in the service of his country".* He was awarded the American Defense Service Medal, World War II Victory Medal and Purple Heart Medal, American Defense Medal, Asiatic Pacific Campaign Medal, WWII medal and the American Medal posthumously. Oscar remains buried on the USS Arizona. He is commemorated on the USS Arizona Memorial and the Memorial Tablets of the Missing, National Memorial Cemetery of the Pacific, Honolulu, Hawaii. Oscar was survived by his Mother, Mrs. Mabel Haney, Route 1, Wilmar, Arkansas. The Miles-Foss VFW/American Legion Hut was built chiefly by returning veterans and named in honor of Oscar Miles and Rodney Foss both of whom died on that terrible day.[530]

Milhorn, Harvey Hollis Gunner's Mate, Third Class, 5th and 6th Divisions, Serial No. 295 55 11, US Navy. Harvey was born on November 21, 1921 in Harlan, Kentucky to Fred Oliver and Grace Kate (Miller) Milhorn. He enlisted in the US Navy December 13, 1939 in Nashville, Tennessee and reported for duty on the USS Arizona March 29, 1940. He was serving on the USS Arizona on December 7, 1941 when the Japanese attacked Pearl Harbor. His battle station was on the mainmast. His official statement regarding bravery in action:

"Sunday morning, December 7, 1941, I went to my General Quarters Station when air raid was sounded, but did not have any ammunition and as I was coming down the mainmast I noted that two men were firing Anti-aircraft Gun No. One. They were PARKER, W. W., S1c, USN, and MOORE, F. K., S1c, USN.

Parker was taking the shells out of the fuse pot, placing them in the tray and in turn ramming them home, then going around the gun and firing them. I saw him fire two rounds. MOORE, F. K., S1c, USN, was standing by the fuse pot with another shell.

There was an explosion up forward and the ship was on fire on the boat deck and up forward and it was so hot I went back up on the mast, and when I saw a chance, I ran down the mast again and down on the quarterdeck and down the ship's side. I swam to Ford Island, where I saw PARKER. He said the explosion blew him over the side and that it killed MOORE. They were the only men I saw around the gun."[531]

After the attack, Harvey was transferred to the USS Keosanqua (AT-38) for duty. Harvey died on October 2, 2002 in Virginia Beach, Virginia.

Miller, Chester John Fireman, Second Class, Serial No: 311 55 80, US Navy. Chester enlisted in the US Navy on November 27, 1940 in Detroit, Michigan and completed his basic training at the Naval Training Station in Great Lakes, Illinois. He reported for duty on the USS Arizona on January 18, 1941. Chester was killed in action on December 7, 1941 at Pearl Harbor, Hawaii. He was awarded the American Defense Service Medal, World War II Victory Medal and Purple Heart Medal posthumously. Chester remains on duty on the USS Arizona. He is commemorated on the USS Arizona Memorial and the Memorial Tablets of the Missing, National Memorial Cemetery of the Pacific, Honolulu, Hawaii. Chester was

---

[530] Oscar Wright Miles, From the Museum by Sheilla Lampkin, Advance Correspondent, Advance Monticellonian, Wednesday, March 14, 2007, Page 3B. Additional information provided by his nephew, Merle Scogin Melancon.
[531] Confidential Statement from MILHORN, H.H., G.M.3c., USN, USS Arizona to Commanding Officer of U.S.S. Arizona regarding Bravery in Action. Pearl Harbor, T.H., December 18, 1941.

survived by his Father, Mr. John William Miller, 7607 East Hildale, Detroit, Michigan.[532]

Miller, Doyle Allen   Coxswain, Serial No: 342 13 97, US Navy. Doyle was born in about 1920 in Arkansas, the son of George Francis and Eva L. Miller. He enlisted in the US Navy on October 4, 1939 in Kansas City, Missouri and completed his basic training at the Naval Training Station in Great Lakes, Illinois. Doyle reported for duty on the USS Arizona on December 31, 1939. He was killed in action on December 7, 1941 at Pearl Harbor, Hawaii. Doyle was awarded the American Defense Service Medal, World War II Victory Medal and Purple Heart Medal posthumously. He remains on duty on the USS Arizona. Doyle is commemorated on the USS Arizona Memorial and the Memorial Tablets of the Missing, National Memorial Cemetery of the Pacific, Honolulu, Hawaii. He was survived by his Father, Mr. George Francis Miller, Rural Route 1, Adona, Arkansas.

Miller, Forrest Newton   Chief Electrician's Mate, Serial No: 341 48 14, US Navy. Forrest was born July 30, 1901 in Garfield, Kansas to George Lincoln and Luverne (Breeden) Miller. He enlisted in the US Navy on August 12, 1937 in Bremerton, Washington. He reported for duty on the USS Arizona on September 6, 1940, transferring from the USS Chaumont. Forrest was killed in action on December 7, 1941 at Pearl Harbor, Hawaii. He was awarded the American Defense Service Medal, World War II Victory Medal and Purple Heart Medal posthumously. Forrest remains on duty on the USS Arizona. He is commemorated on the USS Arizona Memorial and the Memorial Tablets of the Missing, National Memorial Cemetery of the Pacific, Honolulu, Hawaii. Forrest was survived by his Wife, Mrs. Vivian Dorothy Miller, 528 West 21st Street, San Pedro, California.[533]

Miller, George Stanley   Seaman, First Class, Serial No: 279 73 69, US Navy. George was born September 2, 1920 in Logan, Ohio to George Harley and Mary Elizabeth (Vandeveer) Miller. He enlisted in the US Navy with his brother, Jessie, on October 7, 1940 in Cincinnati, Ohio and completed his basic training at the Naval Training Station in Great Lakes, Illinois. George reported for duty on the USS Arizona on December 9, 1940. He was killed in action on December 7, 1941 at Pearl Harbor, Hawaii. *The day of the attack was the 37th wedding anniversary of the Miller brother's parents, Harley and Mary Miller, and the family was celebrating with a special Sunday dinner at their farm near the village of Ostrander. No one ever turned on the radio so they did not hear about the attack until later.* He was awarded the American Defense Service Medal, World War II Victory Medal and Purple Heart Medal posthumously. George remains on duty on the USS Arizona. He is commemorated on the USS Arizona Memorial and the Memorial Tablets of the Missing, National Memorial Cemetery of the Pacific, Honolulu, Hawaii and the Fairview Cemetery, Ostrander, Delaware County, Ohio. George was survived by his Father, Mr. George Harley Miller, Route 2, Marysville, Ohio. His brother, Jessie was killed in action on the Arizona.[534]

---

[532] Chester John Miller, Photo from Michigan Honor States.

[533] Forrest Newton Miller, Information and photo provided by family member, Kellie Paxton.

[534] George Stanley Miller, Information and Photo from The Columbus Dispatch, "Recalling the Miller boys/Union County brothers lost in war" by Holly Zachariah, Saturday, November 12, 2011.

Miller, Jessie Zimmer   Seaman, First Class, Serial No: 279 73 75, US Navy. Jessie was born in 1914 in Logan, Ohio to George Harley and Mary Elizabeth (Vadeveer) Miller. He enlisted in the US Navy with his brother, George on October 7, 1940 in Cincinnati, Ohio and completed his basic training at the Naval Training Station in Great Lakes, Illinois. He reported for duty on the USS Arizona on December 9, 1940. Jessie was killed in action on December 7, 1941 at Pearl Harbor, Hawaii. *The day of the attack was the 37ᵗʰ wedding anniversary of the Miller brother's parents, Harley and Mary Miller, and the family was celebrating with a special Sunday dinner at their farm near the village of Ostrander. No one ever turned on the radio so they did not hear about the attack until later.* He was awarded the American Defense Service Medal, World War II Victory Medal and Purple Heart Medal posthumously. Jessie remains on duty on the USS Arizona. He is commemorated on the USS Arizona Memorial and the Memorial Tablets of the Missing, National Memorial Cemetery of the Pacific, Honolulu, Hawaii. Jesse was survived by his Father, Mr. George Harley Miller, Route 2, Marysville, Ohio. His brother, George was killed in action on the Arizona.[535]

Miller, Jim Dick   Ensign, Serial No. 0-06335, US Navy. Jim was born on July 2, 1917 in Van Buren, Arkansas. He attended Amarillo Junior College before entering the US Naval Academy in 1935. Jim graduated the Academy in 1939 and was deployed to the USS Arizona where he was serving as Watch & Division 3 Officer on December 7, 1941 when the Japanese attacked Pearl Harbor. His official report:

"I had gotten up at about 0745, and had started to dress when a short air raid alarm sounded. The Arizona's air raid alarm consisted of the sounding for three blasts of a warning howler over the general announcing system. What I heard was only one short blast as though some one had accidently touched the switch. I felt one explosion near the ship which seemed to me like a no-load shot on No. 2 Catapult. However it was followed by two more explosions, and I decided it was not a no-load shot, but of course had no idea just what the explosions were. Then the word was passed to set Condition ZED below the third deck. I slipped on a uniform and started to go down to the third deck to check up on my water tight doors and hatches. I still did not realize that there was actually an air raid. As soon as I came up to the second deck from the lower wardroom, I met a gunner's mate who said he was trying to find the magazine keys. I went into the Captain's Cabin to call him and get the keys if possible. The Captain was not there. I then looked in the Gunnery Officer's stateroom to see if I could get the keys from him, but he was not in either. By that time the gunner's mate had left me, and I went on down to the third deck.

General Quarters was sounded. I went into Turret III through the lower handling room to the booth, took the turret officer's station and manned the 2JE phones to Plot. Communications to Plot were OK. However, Turret III was the only turret I heard on the line. Shortly after I had reached the booth the turret was shaken by a bomb explosion of not very great intensity. After a minute or two a much more terrific explosion shoot the turret. Smoke poured in through the overhang hatch, and I could see nothing but reddish flame outside. The 2JE phones went dead, all power went off the turret, and all lights went out. From all reports that I could get from inside the turret, the turret was not even half manned. I believe that it was at about this time that a bomb hit on the starboard side of the quarterdeck next to Turret IV, penetrated down to the third deck

---

[535] Jessie Zimmer Miller, Information and photo from the Columbus Dispatch, "Recalling the Miller boys/Union County brothers lost in war" by Holly Zachariah, Saturday, November 12, 2011.

and exploded. From later examination I found that this bomb had glanced off the side of Turret IV and then had penetrated the decks. My lower handling room crew was shaken up, and water began coming into the lower handling room. Explosion gases were filling the turret from the overhang hatch and from openings into the lower room. I stepped outside the turret to see what the condition was on the quarterdeck. There were several small Fires on the deck and awnings. I noticed several badly burned men lying on deck and saw Ensign Anderson, who had been Junior Officer of the Deck, lying on deck with a bad cut on his head.

I figured that with the turret not completely manned, with all power off, and with the turret full of suffocating gas, we could do nothing toward repelling the attack. I sent the word into the turret for all hands to come outside and fight fires. All hands came out.

Ensign Field and Ensign Flanagan were at their battle stations in the lower handling room. They were the last to come out of the turret and reported to me that everybody had gotten out and that all hatches in the turret had been closed behind them. I found all fire hoses already connected to plugs on the quarterdeck, but there was no water on the fire mains. An attempt to call the center engine room on the ship's service telephone was unsuccessful because the ship's service telephones were out of commission. It was also impossible to reach the engine room because of fire, smoke and gas. The First Lieutenant was on the quarterdeck and in charge. About all we could do was to try to put out fires and drag some of the wounded men under the protection of the overhangs of the turrets. We put out several of the small fires – papers and awnings on deck – with buckets of water. Fuel oil was coming up from some place on the port side and was catching on fire. The ship was down by the bow, and the quarterdeck began to become awash starting at the break of the deck at frame 88. The main and forecastle decks forward of frame 88 were ablaze. Oil on top of the water was feeding the fire. At one time the First Lieutenant asked me if I had seen the Captain or the Admiral. I told him I had been in the Captain's cabin and had not seen him. He wanted me to go down into the cabin and check again. White, T.A., BM2c, and I went down into the cabin, looked around, felt in the Captain's bed, but could find no trace of him. However, it was dark and the smoke was bad, and it is possible that we could have missed him. Nevertheless, I am sure he was not there. We did not go into the Admiral's cabin. We came back up to the quarterdeck.

Our boats, which were tied up to the quays and booms, were manned by some of the men who had swum to them from the side of the ship. One of the first boats which came alongside was a motor launch from the Solace with a medical rescue party. This boat took all our stretcher cases off the quarterdeck. Of these men the only ones that I recognized were Ensign Schubert, Ensign Anderson, Stephenson, H.D., S1c, and a ship's cook, name unknown. Most of the men who were burned were unrecognizable. Shortly after the stretcher cases had been removed to the solace motor launch, the First Lieutenant ordered abandon ship. All of our guns had ceased firing, the main, forecastle, and boat decks were burning; smoke obstructed a view of the foremast and the forward part of the ship. All Officers' quarters aft were flooded and the quarterdeck forward was awash. Our life rafts were cut down and put into the water and all hands ordered to go over the side. Men found the rafts difficult to paddle, and most of them crawled aboard motor launches or started swimming toward Ford Island. The First Lieutenant, Ensign Field, and about half a dozen men and I were the last to leave in one of our fifty-foot motor launches. We picked up quite a few more men who were swimming toward to island. We made the officers' landing at Ford Island, and all hands went ashore except the boat crew, Ensign Field, and the First Lieutenant. The latter said that he was going back out and try to pick up any more men he could find. I was told to remain in charge of the men on Ford Island. We went to the air raid shelter at the northeastern corner of the island. All injured men were sent to the air station hospital as fast as possible. The rest remained in the air raid shelter until the raid was clear." [536]

---

[536] Bombing of U.S.S. Arizona, Report of Ensign Jim D. Miller while on board the U.S.S. Tennessee after the attack on December 7, 1941.

He received the Navy Cross for his actions that day:

> *The Navy Cross is presented to Jim Dick Miller, Lieutenant (jig.), U.S. Navy, for exceptional courage, presence of mind, and devotion to duty and disregard for his personal safety while serving on board the U.S.S. ARIZONA (BB-39) during the Japanese attack on the United States Pacific Fleet in Pearl Harbor, Territory of Hawaii, 7 December 1941. Upon Turret III of the U.S.S. ARIZONA becoming untenable due to gas from a bomb hit on the quarterdeck penetrating several decks and starting a fire, Lieutenant (jig.) Miller ordered his turret crew out to fight fires. Almost immediately, a tremendous explosion forward made the ship appear to rise out of the water, shudder and settle rapidly down by the bow. The whole forward part of the ship was enveloped in flames spreading rapidly; wounded and burned men poured onto the quarterdeck. Despite these conditions plus severe enemy bombing and strafing, Lieutenant (jig.) Miller assisted in directing firefighting to check them while wounded and burned could be taken from the ship. He supervised their rescue in such an amazingly clam, cool manner and with such excellent judgment, it inspired everyone who saw him and undoubtedly resulted in saving many lives. After the abandon ship order he remained on the quarterdeck assisting in directing abandon ship and rescue of personnel, until satisfied that all personnel who could be, had been saved, after which he left his ship with the last boatload. Furthermore, after leaving his ship, on his own initiative he engineered a motor launch that proceeded to the quays and picked up personnel seeking protection from the severe fires, and rescued many men from the water. The conduct of Lieutenant (jig.) Miller throughout this action reflects great credit upon himself, and was in keeping with the highest traditions of the United States Naval Service.*

Jim conducted wartime patrols in the Pacific on the USS Spearfish. His other wartime honors include the Silver Star and Bronze Star. He earned the Legion of Merit and the Gold Star during his 30 year career. He also served in the Korean War and the Vietnam War. Jim died on January 19, 2000 in Coronado, California and is buried in Section CBE, Row 3, Site 111, Fort Rosencrans National Cemetery, Point Loma, San Diego, California. He was preceded in death by his wife, Mary Jane Sullivan.

Miller, John David Seaman, First Class, Aviation Unit (VO-1), Serial No: 356 44 02, US Navy. John was born in about 1919 in Texas to John O. and Texas Anna Miller. *John married, Sybil J. Windham. His young wife died before John enlisted in October 1940.* He enlisted in the US Navy on December 3, 1940 in Dallas, Texas and completed his training at the Naval Aviation Station in San Diego, California. He reported for duty on the USS Arizona on July 14, 1941 transferring from the USS California Aviation Unit (VO-2). John was killed in action on December 7, 1941 at Pearl Harbor, Hawaii. He was awarded the American Defense Service Medal, World War II Victory Medal and Purple Heart Medal posthumously. John remains on duty on the USS Arizona. He is commemorated on the USS Arizona Memorial and the Memorial Tablets of the Missing, National Memorial Cemetery of the Pacific, Honolulu, Hawaii. John was survived by his Father, Mr. John Oren Miller, Box 505, Post, Texas. The VFW Post 6797 in Post, Garza County, Texas was named the John Miller/Luman Post 6797 in his honor.[537]

---

[537] John David Miller, Photo provided by the Miller/Luman VFW Post 6797, Post Texas.

Miller, William Oscar Signalman, Third Class, Serial No: 337 28 07, US Navy. William was born October 1, 1919 in Todds Point Township, Findlay, Illinois to Lewis Ezra and Nannie J. (Tuttle) Miller. He enlisted in the US Navy on March 12, 1940 in St. Louis, Missouri and completed his basic training at the Naval Training Station in Great Lakes, Illinois. He reported for duty on the USS Arizona on July 12, 1940. William was killed in action on December 7, 1941 at Pearl Harbor, Hawaii. He was awarded the American Defense Service Medal, World War II Victory Medal and Purple Heart Medal posthumously. William remains on duty on the USS Arizona. He is commemorated on the USS Arizona Memorial and the Memorial Tablets of the Missing, National Memorial Cemetery of the Pacific, Honolulu, Hawaii and the Antioch Cemetery, Brunswick, Illinois. William was survived by his Mother, Mrs. Nannie Miller Brummitt, General Delivery, Findlay, Illinois.

Milligan, Weldon Harvey Seaman, First Class, Serial No: 346 85 42, US Navy. Weldon was born January 6, 1919 in Pittsburg, Texas the only son of James Harvey and Ida Davis Milligan. *Weldon was a tease. He had a great sense of humor and loved playing jokes on everyone. He also loved to dance. He and his sister would sneak out of the house and go dancing at night. His mother did not approve of dancing.*[538] Weldon enlisted in the US Navy on October 4, 1940 in Little Rock, Arkansas with his cousin, Royal Elwell. He transferred from the USS Brazos for duty on the USS Arizona on January 4, 1941. Weldon was killed in action on December 7, 1941 at Pearl Harbor, Hawaii. He was awarded the American Defense Service Medal, World War II Victory Medal and Purple Heart Medal posthumously. Weldon remains on duty on the USS Arizona. He is commemorated on the USS Arizona Memorial and the Memorial Tablets of the Missing, National Memorial Cemetery of the Pacific, Honolulu, Hawaii. Weldon was survived by his Father, Mr. James Harvey Milligan, Pittsburg, Texas. His Foster Brother, Robert Hudnall and his cousin, Royal Elwell were also killed on board the USS Arizona.

Millikin, Donald Hugh Seaman, Second Class, Serial No. 356 18 54, US Navy. Donald was born October 9, 1920 in Eudora, Arkansas, the son of James Moton and Helen Sophia (Johnson) Millikin. He enlisted in the US Navy November 8, 1939 in Dallas, Texas and reported for duty on the USS Vestal (AR-4) January 21, 1940. USS Arizona August 3, 1941. Donald was serving on the USS Arizona on December 7, 1941 when the Japanese attacked Pearl Harbor. In 1982, he gave his statement of his experiences that day:

"I was a Seaman at the time, a 1st Class Seaman. I was 21 years of age. The fact that I was there meant that I was in the Navy previous to the war starting. I didn't join the Navy to fight. I needed a job like most of us did. It ended up with a fight, and it all started right there at Pearl Harbor. In 1939 when I joined the Navy, I went aboard the USS Vestal, which was a converted collier (bulk cargo ship designed to carry coal). It had been converted into a repair ship, and they took us into Long Beach. In 1940, we went to Hawaii. I was transferred from there to the sub base and from the sub base to the Arizona. On the morning of the attack, it happened that the USS Vestal was alongside the Arizona. I didn't even know it.

I was a mess cook. That's the fella that cleans up the dishes and brings the food in. In any case, on this particular morning, we had cleaned up, had the dishes up, and the tables up. On

---

[538] Weldon Harvey Milligan, Information provided by his neice, Suzanne Asaff Blankenship.

the old Arizona where we were, the 3rd division, we just had tables and benches that came down off the ceiling, the "overhead" we called it. Then when we were finished, we stuck them back up and fastened them, and then we swung our hammocks from that. It was customary in Hawaii that we all had our uniforms on while we served the food. When we were cleaning up, we stripped down to our shorts. It kept us cool.

When I had finished with the clean up, I walked over to the porthole and stuck my head out to get a little fresh air. I saw a plane diving down out of the sky. I thought it was one of ours. Another one was behind that, and I thought at the time that it was rather early for them to be practicing. But when he pulled out, something left him. It wasn't close enough for me to even see what plane it was; I didn't even know the Japanese were attacking anybody. I thought they were still building little funny toys out of matchsticks and things. I thought it was the Germans. So, I went to my battle station, which was down in the lower powder handling room. I ran by the quarter deck. This is the place where the officer of the day is, messengers and all that. Everybody comes aboard there and leaves the ship there, and it was close to where I worked, which was the 3rd division. It was on the fantail and so was the 4th division. These two divisions were the only two that really got anybody off the ship to any degree simply because we were not on fire, and we weren't blown to smithereens.

Well, the quarter deck was on the opposite side of the ship this time because the side of the ship I was on, the 3rd division, was tied up to the key, so the "spokes" all came in from the opposite side. As a result, the port side had the quarterdeck on it. As I ran out to my battle station, I was yelling to sound General Quarters. Nobody did, by the way. It was unlikely that anybody would. Anyway, going to my battle station saved my life, which has lasted now for 62 years, so I'm not doing too shabby. But I am getting old enough that I think that I probably should tell this story because somebody will be interested.

In any case, the lower powder handling room is just that. It's way down in the bowels of the ship, and we were the ones that put the powder on the elevators that went up to the big guns. We had turret number 3 that coincided with our division, the 3rd division. The powders and the shells all came from down below and were elevated. They were all jammed into the big guns, and then they were fired. There were two of us that made it down there. The first thing you do when you get there (and I wasn't a talker or a telephone man", but whoever got there first was to pick up the phone and make contact until the talker got there. So, I was the first man down, and I tried to talk to somebody with no answer on the other end.

On the way down, I noticed the bumping and banging of the ship. I thought that the rest of the guns were in action fighting back with whoever it was. It turned out that I was wrong. It was their bombs and their torpedoes and the explosions of them hitting our ship and our magazine blowing up that I was feeling rather than us fighting back. As a matter of fact, we never did fight back. We stayed down there for quite some time, and never did get in contact with anybody up in the Gun Captain's station or any place else. Finally, a bomb landed close to where we were, and all the lights went out. Smoke started coming in there with us, so we battened down all the hatches and got out the battle lanterns, and there we were trying to get everything ready to fight.

We finally decided that we better find out where everybody else was. So we started up through the turret. Now this was a long way crawling up through there. It was dark with many twists and turns. We banged into a few things on the way up, but the other fella and I finally made it to the top. We never met anybody in the turret except the two of us. And when we got to the tho, there was a hole that went back to the back end of the turret. We grabbed a bar and swung down from the little hatch that was underneath onto the deck, and I was in front. This was Sunday morning as you'll remember. I was told later by this young fella (and I don't remember his name unfortunately or what he looked like because it's been quite a while) after we got over on the beach, that I had stuck my head out and looked around. The entire ship almost, except where we were, was on fire and sunk. He told me that I said, "This is a hell of a day to air bedding." Strangely enough, it was Sunday, and this was the day that we always took our bedding out and put it on the side of the ship and wherever else we could to air it out. I haven't the foggiest notion why a thing like that would come to my mind, but he swore that that's what I said.

Well, we swung down, and there were a few people back there. They were coming out of holes, bomb holes and whatnot. There were two of the life rafts that were on turret number four that were gone. They must have taken those to the beach already. The two that were on our turret were still there. We went over and cut one of them down and put it in the water. People jumped over the side until it was full. They were all standing about knee deep in the water. Well, I was in there too. It was pretty oily, and I got out of the water. There was only possibly a foot of ship above the water there at the time. I crawled back on the ship and went for the other life raft. There was a Filipino and a Black mess attendant that crawled out of a bomb hole at the same time and went over the railing. They jumped in the water, and both swam ashore not even waiting for that life raft. Well, we put the other life raft in, and the same thing happened to that. I came back aboard, and to the best of my recollection there were about five or six of us left on the ship. I never did see anybody else. The reason I didn't go in the life raft was because if the wind had changed just slightly, the fire with the ship totally on fire all around us would have engulfed me, and I figured that it was safer to stay where I was and head for the Tennessee. Which was directly astern of us. It was quite a swim, but it didn't have any oil to amount to anything back there. So I and four or five others stayed on the ship and were waiting for a boat or something to come by. It was a holocaust all over the place.

During the time we were on the ship, a couple of things happened that were of interest I suppose. One of them is rather gruesome. On the port side of the ship there was a doorway, same as the one that was on the starboard side, where you went from what was the main deck. The fantail back there was the main deck on the ship. It went all the way forward, and anything above that was superstructure and below it was below decks. Well, because of the fact that they had the quarterdeck back there, they always had one or two marines back there guarding on whichever side of the ship that the quarterdeck was on, and it was on the port side that time. They always had the gun rack just inside the door, and about five feet in there so nobody would stumble over it. A marine came out of nowhere, and I was standing with another fella looking around for a boat or anything to get to the beach. All of a sudden, here was the Marine walking towards that door. His gun was in there, his rifle. He very calmly walked into the door and into the fire, and we never saw him again. That's what training will do for you. It was quite impressive. It was gruesome too.

By the way, the war was over for the most part. There was some shooting, but the big attack was over. They'd quit shooting us pretty much. There were still panes around, but they weren't really bothering us very much. Somebody had put up the colors. I don't know whether this was when they were doing colors that morning or not, and I don't think they ever finished it. But somebody had put up the flag back on the stern of the ship. It was up in any case, and one of the people that was back there with us declared that if we struck the flag, that is pulled it down, that the Japanese would quit attacking us, that is, our ship. It was an idea that, just like any other stupid idea that comes into your head under circumstances like that, is a crazy idea. So he went to pull the flag down, and the rest of us were just as crazy. We went over and fought him to keep him from doing it because we thought it was important that it stayed up. I can't see where it makes any difference one way or the other now, but at the time, it seemed like it was a terribly important thing for us to keep it up there. As a matter of fact, one of the guys got knocked in the water during the little shoving match, but it was just another silly thing that happened to us.

Then along came a Captain's barge from nowhere and came and picked us up and took us over to Ford Island. None of us were very well dressed. Most of us were in our underwear and all greasy and oily. And from over there by an Admiral's house, we watched the ship burn and the rest of the mess. I never did see anybody else come off of the ship. There were, according to what people tell me, 1400 people on the ship, and that 1200 of them roughly were killed that day.

317

There have been a lot of things that have been said about this day, that Washington knew and that sort of thing. I don't know; they probably did. But the thing that impressed me more about this was the shame of the fact that we who were being trusted and paid to defend our ships and our nation, for the most part didn't fire a shot in our own defense. Now I know that there wasn't the collusion that people seem to think there was because a lot of the people, including some mighty able Captains and Admirals, died there. Certainly they didn't know. They wouldn't have volunteered to die I don't think. I haven't run into anybody Japanese that would do that. None of us did. But, die they did.

Most of us that were left, volunteered to go on destroyers, which was about the only think that came back in there for a while. We spent, at least I did, the rest of the war on a destroyer. A lot of people were killed later during the war from the group that got off of the Arizona. All of us have to be old because I was young when it happened. Hence, the reason I'm telling this story. I guess it's worthwhile to put it down. Somebody will probably really want to know what happened from someone who was there. So, I bid you farewell. Thanks for your attention, and for God's sake, don't let it happen again."

After the attack, Donald was transferred to the USS Patterson for duty. Donald passed away February 23, 1984 in Otis, Oregon and his ashes were interred on the USS Arizona on March 19, 1984.[539]

Mims, Robert Lang   Seaman, First Class, Serial No: 268 40 00, US Navy. Robert was born November 2, 1921 in Baker, Georgia. He enlisted in the US Navy on November 28, 1939 in Macon, Georgia and reported for duty on the USS Arizona on March 8, 1940. He was killed in action on December 7, 1941 at Pearl Harbor, Hawaii. Robert was awarded the American Defense Service Medal, World War II Victory Medal and Purple Heart Medal posthumously. He remains on duty on the USS Arizona. Robert is commemorated on the USS Arizona Memorial and the Memorial Tablets of the Missing, National Memorial Cemetery of the Pacific, Honolulu, Hawaii and Colquitt City Cemetery, Colquitt, Georgia. He was survived by his Mother, Mrs. Beatrice Irene Mims Kidd, Newton, Florida.

Mini, James Haile   Lieutenant, Junior Grade, Serial No. 0-05421, US Navy. James was born on February 6, 1913 in California. He was commissioned June 6, 1938 in the US Navy and was serving as Senior Aviator, W & D Officer on the USS Arizona. He was serving on December 7, 1941 when the Japanese attacked Pearl Harbor. His battle station was a Plane. James died on December 7, 1963 in California and is buried in Section OFF, Site 62-A, Fort Rosencrans National Cemetery, San Diego, California.[540]

Mlinar, Joseph   Coxswain, Serial No: 250 54 29, US Navy. Joseph was born on October 5, 1920 in Johnstown, Pennsylvania. He enlisted in the US Navy on February 5, 1940 in Pittsburgh, Pennsylvania and completed his basic training at the Naval Training Station in Norfolk, Virginia. He reported for duty on the USS Arizona on September 30, 1940. Joseph was killed in action on December 7, 1941 at Pearl Harbor, Hawaii. He was awarded the American

---

[539] Donald Hugh Millikin, Photo, information and story provided by family member, Terry Jenson.
[540] James Haile Mini, Photo from Lucky Bag Yearbook, United States Naval Academy, Annapolis, Maryland, Class of 1935.

Defense Service Medal, World War II Victory Medal and Purple Heart Medal posthumously. Joseph remains on duty on the USS Arizona. He is commemorated on the USS Arizona Memorial and the Memorial Tablets of the Missing, National Memorial Cemetery of the Pacific, Honolulu, Hawaii. Joseph was survived by his Father, Mr. Michel Mlinar, 103 Elisabeth Street, Johnstown, Pennsylvania.

Mode, Stanley Robert Electrician's Mate, First Class, Serial No. 393 24 66, US Navy. Stanley was born December 28, 1918 in Portland, Oregon, the son of Henry and Clara (Schrieber) Mode. He moved to Clark County Washington in 1940. Stanley enlisted in the US Navy October 13, 1937 in Portland, Oregon and reported for duty on the USS Arizona January 25, 1938. He was serving on the USS Arizona on December 7, 1941 when the Japanese attacked Pearl Harbor. After the attack, Stanley was transferred to the USS Louisville for duty. He was a letter carrier for 20 years. Stanley died October 24, 1998 of leukemia at 79 years. Survived by wife Jeanne; daughter Theresa Auste; sons Michael and Patrick, two brothers and three grandchildren. Burial was with military honors in St. John's Catholic Cemetery.

Molpus, Richard Preston Chief Metalsmith, Serial No: 276 63 49, US Navy. Richard was born August 14, 1908 in Lauderdale County, Mississippi to Lewis Harvey and Mattie (Walker) Molpus. He enlisted in the US Navy on November 14, 1936 in Louisville, Kentucky and completed his basic training at the Naval Training Station in Great Lakes, Illinois. Richard served on the USS Arizona from September 17, 1938 until he was killed in action on December 7, 1941 at Pearl Harbor, Hawaii. He was awarded the American Defense Service Medal, World War II Victory Medal and Purple Heart Medal posthumously. Richard remains on duty on the USS Arizona. He is commemorated on the USS Arizona Memorial and the Memorial Tablets of the Missing, National Memorial Cemetery of the Pacific, Honolulu, Hawaii. Richard was survived by his Wife, Mrs. Bertha Francis Molpus, 1655 Ronan Avenue, Wilmington, California and two children.

Mommer, Rolland Earl Boatswain's Mate, Second Class, Turret 1, Serial No. 291 52 34, US Navy. Rolland was born on May 21, 1918 in Fort Wayne, Indiana, son of Malcolm Mommer and Bernadette (Blee) Mommer. He graduated from South Side High School. Shortly after, November 4, 1937, he and seven of his buddies went down to the Post Office in Indianapolis and enlisted in the US Navy. After a 6 weeks course at Great Lakes Training Center, he was sent to San Pedro, California and on March 12, 1938 he reported for duty on the USS Arizona. Rolland went on Re-Enlisted leave in November 1941 and was not on board the ship when the Japanese attacked Pearl Harbor. Rolland was immediately called back from leave and was aboard a destroyer and then he was sent to Naval Mine Warfare School in Yorktown, Virginia. He graduated as a Boatswain's Mate, Second Class in July 8, 1944 and was sent to Bainbridge Island in the State of Washington. He was then assigned duty on the USS Goyety, a minesweeper that was commissioned in September 23, 1944. He spent the remainder of the war in the South Pacific sweeping mines. After the war Rolland worked at International Harvester for 30 years. "He was a man who believed in his country, a good husband, father, grandfather and a good Christian man" Helen Mommer. Rolland died on June 13, 2003 in Fort Wayne, Indiana.

Monroe, Donald Steward's Mate, Second Class, Serial No: 37 19 39, US Navy. Donald was born in 1920. His father, Guy, died in 1933 in North Webster Groves, Missouri, and his mother, Lucille, died a short time later. *Donald was one of several orphans adopted and raised during the Depression by Nannie Stewart, a truant officer.* He enlisted in the US Navy on September 19, 1939 in St. Louis, Missouri and completed his basic training at the Naval Training Station in Norfolk, Virginia. He reported for duty on the USS Arizona on January 2, 1940. Donald was killed in action on December 7, 1941 at Pearl Harbor, Hawaii. After his death, an ensign on the battleship, John Paul Howatt, wrote to Father Flanagan stating *"he was a fine example of what a young American should be, and in every sense more than lived up to the very highest standards set by our Navy and our country. Donald was proud of Boys Town; I know that Boys Town is proud of him. If he is an example of the average boy from Boys Town, then I can easily see why our whole country is proud of Boys Town."* He was awarded the American Defense Service Medal, World War II Victory Medal and Purple Heart Medal posthumously. Donald remains on duty on the USS Arizona. He is commemorated on the USS Arizona Memorial and the Memorial Tablets of the Missing, National Memorial Cemetery of the Pacific, Honolulu, Hawaii. Donald was survived by his Aunt, Mrs. Nannie Steward, 700 Wellington Avenue, Webster Groves, Missouri. The American Legion Post #375 in North Webster, Missouri was named in his honor.[541]

Montgomery, Robert Eugene Seaman, Second Class, Serial No: 376 26 36, US Navy. Robert was born in about 1923 in Michigan to Elmer E. and Naomi Montgomery. He enlisted in the US Navy on February 20, 1941 in San Francisco, California and completed his basic training at the Naval Training Station in San Diego, California. He reported for duty on the USS Arizona on September 18, 1941. Robert was killed in action on December 7, 1941 at Pearl Harbor, Hawaii. He was awarded the American Defense Service Medal, World War II Victory Medal and Purple Heart Medal posthumously. Robert remains on duty on the USS Arizona. He is commemorated on the USS Arizona Memorial and the Memorial Tablets of the Missing, National Memorial Cemetery of the Pacific, Honolulu, Hawaii. Robert was survived by his Father, Mr. Elmer Ellsworth Montgomery, 269 Vernon Street, Oakland, California.

Moody, Robert Edward Seaman, First Class, Serial No: 295 76 82, US Navy. Robert was born on February 25, 1919 in Carpenter, Mississippi. *He was the fourth of ten children born to Robert Alexander and Irene (Landers) Moody. He attended elementary school and went through the 11th grade of Utica High School before enlisting in the Civilian Conservation Corps, working in North Carolina. Returning to Utica, he farmed with his father for a year before enlisting in the US Navy on October 4, 1940 in Nashville, Tennessee and completed his basic training at the Naval Training Station in Norfolk, Virginia.* Robert reported for duty on the USS Arizona on December 4, 1940. He was killed in action on December 7, 1941 at Pearl Harbor, Hawaii. Robert was awarded the American Defense Service Medal, World War II Victory Medal and Purple Heart Medal posthumously. He remains on duty on the USS Arizona. Robert is commemorated on the USS Arizona Memorial and the Memorial Tablets of the Missing, National Memorial Cemetery of the Pacific, Honolulu, Hawaii. He was survived by his Parents, Mr. and Mrs. Robert Alexander Moody, Route 3, Utica,

---

[541] Donald Monroe, Photo and information provided by the Girls and Boys Town, Boys Town, Nebraska.

Mississippi. On December 12, 1945, the American Legion Post in Utica honored Robert Moody and Lloyd Davis, the first two Utica men killed in World War II, by naming the post the Moody-Davis American Legion Post.[542]

Moore, Douglas Carlton Seaman, First Class, Serial No: 262 45 24, US Navy. Douglas was born in 1922 in South Carolina, the son of Garnett Carlton and Pearl Blair Moore. He enlisted in the US Navy on November 28, 1939 in Raleigh, North Carolina and reported for duty on the USS Arizona on March 8, 1940. Douglas was killed in action on December 7, 1941 at Pearl Harbor, Hawaii. He was awarded the American Defense Service Medal, World War II Victory Medal and Purple Heart Medal posthumously. Douglas remains on duty on the USS Arizona. He is commemorated on the USS Arizona Memorial and the Memorial Tablets of the Missing, National Memorial Cemetery of the Pacific, Honolulu, Hawaii. Douglas was survived by his Father, Mr. Garnett Carlton Moore, 253 Nixton Street, Anderson, South Carolina. His Uncle, James Carlton Moore was also killed in action on board the USS Arizona on December 7th.[543]

Moore, Fred Kenneth Seaman, First Class, Serial No: 356 35 02, US Navy. Fred was born on December 17, 1921 in Campbell, Texas to Rev. Fred K. and Frances Luella (Gray) Moore. He enlisted in the US Navy on July 31, 1940 in Dallas, Texas and completed his basic training at the Naval Training Station in Norfolk, Virginia. He was killed in action on December 7, 1941 at Pearl Harbor, Hawaii. Fred was awarded the Navy Cross Medal, American Defense Service Medal, World War II Victory Medal and Purple Heart Medal posthumously.

The Navy Cross is presented to Fred Kenneth Moore, Seaman First Class, U.S. Navy, for exceptional courage, presence of mind, and devotion to duty and disregard for his personal safety while serving on board the U.S.S. ARIZONA (BB-39) during the Japanese attack on the United States Pacific Fleet in Pearl Harbor, Territory of Hawaii, 7 December 1941. Despite orders from his gun captain to take cover, Seaman First Class Fred Kenneth Moore remained at his undermanned station with two other members of his antiaircraft gun crew under heavy enemy strafing. He assisted in keeping the gun in operation until he was killed at his station by an explosion. The conduct of Seaman First Class Moore throughout this action reflects great credit upon himself, and was in keeping with the highest traditions of the United States Naval Service. He gallantly gave his life for his country.

Fred remains on duty on the USS Arizona. He is commemorated on the USS Arizona Memorial and the Memorial Tablets of the Missing, National Memorial Cemetery of the Pacific, Honolulu, Hawaii and Forest Park Cemetery, Greenville, Texas. Fred was survived by his Father,

---

[542] Robert Edward Moody, Information from, The Masons and the Methodists in Utica, Mississippi, compiled by James E. Price, 1998.
[543] Douglas Carlton Moore, Photo and information from The Greenville News, Greenville, South Carolina, January 18, 1942, Page 8.

Rev. Fred Moore, 2317 Church Street, Greenville, Texas. The destroyer escort, USS Moore (DE-240) was named in his honor.[544]

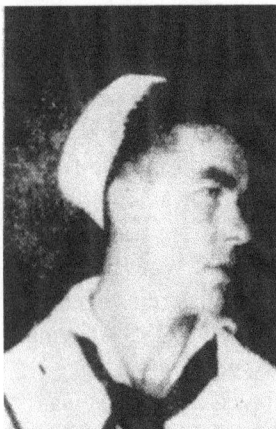

Moore, James Carlton Shipfitter, Third Class, Serial No: 262 45 25, US Navy. James was born in about 1919 in Georgia to James Carlton and Dorsie (Johnson) Moore. He enlisted in the US Navy on November 28, 1939 in Raleigh, North Carolina and reported for duty on the USS Arizona on March 8, 1940. James was killed in action on December 7, 1941 at Pearl Harbor, Hawaii. He was awarded the American Defense Service Medal, World War II Victory Medal and Purple Heart Medal posthumously. James remains on duty on the USS Arizona. He is commemorated on the USS Arizona Memorial and the Memorial Tablets of the Missing, National Memorial Cemetery of the Pacific, Honolulu, Hawaii. James was survived by his Mother, Mrs. Dorsie Moore, 5 E Street, Anderson, South Carolina. His nephew, Douglas Carlton Moore was also killed in action on board the USS Arizona December 7th.[545]

Moorhouse, William Starks Musician, Second Class, Serial No: 342 29 10, US Navy. William was born August 14, 1922 in Wichita, Kansas. He enlisted in the US Navy on September 23, 1940 and attended the Navy School of Music in Washington, DC graduating on May 23, 1941 as a member of the USS Arizona Band. He reported for duty on the USS Arizona on June 17, 1941. The battle station for all of the band members was in the black powder room passing ammunition to the Arizona's gunners during the attack. None of the band members survived the explosion. He was killed in action on December 7, 1941 at Pearl Harbor, Hawaii. William was awarded the Purple Heart Medal posthumously. He remains on duty on the USS Arizona. William is commemorated on the USS Arizona Memorial and the Memorial Tablets of the Missing, National Memorial Cemetery of the Pacific, Honolulu, Hawaii. He was survived by his Father, Mr. Harold Mack Moorhouse, 905 West 12th Street, Wichita, Kansas.[546]

Moorman, Russell Lee Seaman, Second Class, Serial No: 382 37 93, US Navy. Russell was born January 3, 1923 in Kansas. He enlisted in the US Navy on January 31, 1941 and completed his basic training at the Naval Training Station in San Diego, California. He reported for duty on the USS Arizona on April 27, 1941. Assigned death #341, Russell died on December 9, 1941 from 3rd degree burns received during the December 7, 1941 attack at Pearl Harbor, Hawaii.[547] He was awarded the American Defense Service Medal, World War II Victory Medal and Purple Heart Medal posthumously. Russell was interred in a Navy Plot, Nuuanu Cemetery, Honolulu, Hawaii. He is commemorated on the USS Arizona Memorial and the Memorial Tablets of the Missing, National Memorial Cemetery of the Pacific, Honolulu, Hawaii.

---

[544] Fred Carlton Moore, Information from the Dictionary of American Naval Fighting Ships, (1969) Vol. 4, p. 433.

[545] James Carlton Moore, Information and Photo from The Greenville News, Greenville, South Carolina, January 18, 1942, Page 8.

[546] William Starks Moorhouse, Photo from USS Arizona's Last Band by Molly Kent. By permission of the author. For more information about this book, go to www.USSARIZONASLASTBAND.com.

[547] Russell Lee Moorman, Report of Changes of the USS Arizona for the month ending 31st day of December, 1941, Page 84, line 30.

Lee was survived by his Father, Mr. Russell Steenrod Moorman, 353 West Myrtle Street, Glendale, California.

Morgan, Wayne Seaman, First Class, Serial No: 376 03 59, US Navy. Wayne was born February 14, 1919 in Bakersfield, California to Elmer Minor and Angelica (Barcellos) Morgan. He enlisted in the US Navy on March 12, 1940 in San Francisco, California and completed his basic training at the Naval Training Station in San Diego, California. Wayne reported for duty on the USS Arizona on June 16, 1940. He was killed in action on December 7, 1941 at Pearl Harbor, Hawaii. Wayne was awarded the American Defense Service Medal, World War II Victory Medal and Purple Heart Medal posthumously. He remains on duty on the USS Arizona. Wayne is commemorated on the USS Arizona Memorial and the Memorial Tablets of the Missing, National Memorial Cemetery of the Pacific, Honolulu, Hawaii. He was survived by his Father, Mr. Elmer Minor Morgan, 135 Hyde Street, San Francisco, California.

Morgareidge, James Orries Fireman, Second Class, Serial No: 372 20 38, US Navy. James was born August 19, 1919 in Lovell, Wyoming, the son of Charles Benjamin and Fannie Mae (Tibbits) Morgareidge. He enlisted in the US Navy on November 4, 1940 in Denver, Colorado and completed his basic training at the Naval Training Station in San Diego, California. James reported for duty on the USS Arizona on January 11, 1941. He was killed in action on December 7, 1941 at Pearl Harbor, Hawaii. James was awarded the American Defense Service Medal, World War II Victory Medal and Purple Heart Medal posthumously. He remains on duty on the USS Arizona. James is commemorated on the USS Arizona Memorial and the Memorial Tablets of the Missing, National Memorial Cemetery of the Pacific, Honolulu, Hawaii. He was survived by his Parents, Mr. and Mrs. Charles Ben Morgareidge, Ten Sleep, Wyoming. In 1945, his parents filed a claim against the Japanese government for the death of their son.[548]

Morley, Eugene Elvis Fireman, Second Class, Serial No: 337 39 83, US Navy. Eugene was born in about 1922 in Arkansas, the son of Claude W. and Stella Morley. He enlisted in the US Navy on September 26, 1940 in St. Louis, Missouri and completed his basic training at the Naval Training Station in Great Lakes, Illinois. Eugene reported for duty on the USS Arizona on January 18, 1941. He was killed in action on December 7, 1941 at Pearl Harbor, Hawaii. Eugene was awarded the American Defense Service Medal, World War II Victory Medal and Purple Heart Medal posthumously. He remains on duty on the USS Arizona. Eugene is commemorated on the USS Arizona Memorial and the Memorial Tablets of the Missing, National Memorial Cemetery of the Pacific, Honolulu, Hawaii. He was survived by his Father, Mr. Claude W. Morley, 2004 Beckwith Street, Madison, Illinois.[549]

Morris, Owen Newton Seaman, First Class, Serial No: 272 40 39, US Navy. Owen was born in 1922 in Alabama the son of Samuel Green and Anna Lou Della (Hollis) Morris. He enlisted in the US Navy on September 28, 1940 in Birmingham, Alabama and completed his basic training at the Naval Training Station in Norfolk, Virginia. He reported for duty on the

---

[548] James Orries Morgareidge, Photo from Wyoming Honor States.
[549] Eugene Elvis Morley, Photo from The St. Louis Star and Times, St Louis, Missouri, December 22, 1941, Page 7.

USS Arizona on December 4, 1940. Owen was killed in action on December 7, 1941 at Pearl Harbor, Hawaii. He was awarded the American Defense Service Medal, World War II Victory Medal and Purple Heart Medal posthumously. Owen remains on duty on the USS Arizona. He is commemorated on the USS Arizona Memorial and the Memorial Tablets of the Missing, National Memorial Cemetery of the Pacific, Honolulu, Hawaii. Owen was survived by his Father, Mr. Green Morris, 1600 North 16th Street, Bessemer, Alabama.

Morrison, Earl Leroy Seaman, First Class, Serial No: 368 48 32, US Navy. Earl was born June 5, 1922 in Richland, Montana to Hugh Earl and Anna Morgarete (Jorgensen) Morrison. He enlisted in the US Navy on April 26, 1940 in Salt Lake City, Utah and completed his basic training at the Naval Training Station in San Diego, California. *He had hoped to join his older brother Leon, who had been serving on board the Arizona. But by the time he finished basic, his brother had been transferred to duty on the USS Gwen.* Earl reported for duty on the USS Arizona on January 4, 1941. Assigned death #543, Earl was killed in action on December 7, 1941 at Pearl Harbor, Hawaii. He was identified by his initials on his cigarette case "ELM".[550] He was awarded the American Defense Service Medal, World War II Victory Medal and Purple Heart Medal posthumously. *Earl's remains at the time of burial were listed on Navy papers as "Unknown X-50" and were placed in grave number 543 at the Halawa Naval Cemetery in Oahu. When his remains were moved to the "Punchbowl" cemetery, he was placed in Plot Q-1147 and the letters "E.L.M" were etched by someone in the headstone. At one point, all the headstones were replaced and his headstone just reads as "unknown" USS Arizona December 7, 1941.* Earl is commemorated on the USS Arizona Memorial and the Memorial Tablets of the Missing, National Memorial Cemetery of the Pacific, Honolulu, Hawaii. He was survived by his Mother, Mrs. Anna Morrison Peterson, Box 275, Sidney, Montana.[551]

Morse, Edward "Bud" Charles Seaman, Second Class, Serial No: 311 51 50, US Navy. Edward was born August 25, 1919 in Battle Creek, Michigan son of County Clerk Mr. Edward J. Morse and Mrs. Dorothy E. Morse. He enlisted in the US Navy on October 8, 1940 in Detroit, Michigan and completed his basic training at the Naval Training Station in Great Lakes, Illinois. Edward reported for duty on the USS Arizona on December 9, 1940. He was killed in action on December 7, 1941 at Pearl Harbor, Hawaii. Edward was awarded the American Defense Service Medal, World War II Victory Medal and Purple Heart Medal posthumously. His remains were recovered and he was sent home for burial in Hicks Cemetery, Battle Creek, Michigan. Edward is commemorated on the USS Arizona Memorial. He was survived by his Father, Mr. Edward Jack Morse, 57 Bluff Street, Battle Creek, Michigan.[552]

---

[550] Report of Changes of the USS Arizona for the month ending 31st day of December, 1941, Page 85, line 5, Earl Leroy Morrison.

[551] Earl Leroy Morrison, Information and picture provided by his great nephew, Christopher Fritz.

[552] Edward "Bud" Charles Morse, Photo from The Detroit Free Press, Detroit, Michigan, August 23, 1942, Page 75.

Morse, Francis Jerome Boatswain's Mate, First Class, Serial No: 371 99 93, US Navy. Francis was born November 22, 1919 in Lamar, Colorado, the son of Roy B. and Clara May (Dyer) Morse. His father, Roy died in an accident in 1930. Francis enlisted in the US Navy on December 11, 1936 in Denver, Colorado and reported for duty on the USS Arizona April 15, 1937. He was killed in action on December 7, 1941 at Pearl Harbor, Hawaii. Francis was awarded the American Defense Service Medal, World War II Victory Medal and Purple Heart Medal posthumously. He remains on duty on the USS Arizona. Francis is commemorated on the USS Arizona Memorial and the Memorial Tablets of the Missing, National Memorial Cemetery of the Pacific, Honolulu, Hawaii and the Memorial Section ME, marker 129, Arlington National Cemetery, Arlington, Virginia. He was survived by his Wife, Mrs. Dorothy Marjorie Morse, 914 Loma Vista Drive, Long Beach, California. His brother, Norman Roi Morse was also killed in action on the USS Arizona.[553]

Morse, George Robert Seaman, Second Class, Serial No: 368 55 45, US Navy. George was born in about 1923 in Montana to George B. and Lulu May Morse. He enlisted in the US Navy on December 7, 1940 in Salt Lake City, Utah and completed his basic training at the Naval Training Station in San Diego, California. George reported for duty on the USS Arizona on April 27, 1941. He was killed in action on December 7, 1941 at Pearl Harbor, Hawaii. George was awarded the American Defense Service Medal, World War II Victory Medal and Purple Heart Medal posthumously. He remains on duty on the USS Arizona. George is commemorated on the USS Arizona Memorial and the Memorial Tablets of the Missing, National Memorial Cemetery of the Pacific, Honolulu, Hawaii. He was survived by his Father, Mr. George B. Morse, 730 Cherry Street, Missoula, Montana.[554]

Morse, Norman Roi Watertender, Second Class, Serial No: 372 06 60, US Navy. Norman was born July 19, 1921 in Lamar, Colorado, the son of Roy B. and Clara May (Dyer) Morse. His father, Roy died in an accident in 1930. Norman enlisted in the US Navy on August 13, 1938 in Denver, Colorado and completed his basic training at the Naval Training Station in San Diego, California. He reported for duty on the USS Arizona on December 2, 1938. Norman was killed in action on December 7, 1941 at Pearl Harbor, Hawaii. He was awarded the American Defense Service Medal, World War II Victory Medal and Purple Heart Medal posthumously. Norman remains on duty on the USS Arizona with his brother Francis. He is commemorated on the USS Arizona Memorial and the Memorial Tablets of the Missing, National Memorial Cemetery of the Pacific, Honolulu, Hawaii and the Memorial Section ME, marker 130, Arlington National Cemetery, Arlington, Virginia. Norman was survived by his Mother, Mrs. May Morse, 108 Ash Avenue, Newport News, Virginia. His brother, Francis Jerome Morse was also killed in action on the USS Arizona.[555]

---

[553] Francis Jerome Morse, Photo courtesy, History Colorado (Clara May Morse Collection, Scan #10025422).

[554] George Robert Morse, Photo provided by his nephew, Bruce M. Larsen.

[555] Norman Roi Morse, Photo courtesy, History Colorado (Clara May Morse Collection, Scan #10025422).

Moss, Tommy Lee Steward's Mate, Second Class, Serial No: 291 60 91, US Navy. Tommy was born April 19, 1915 in Christian County, Kentucky, the son of Buck and Lucy (Carr) Moss. He enlisted in the US Navy on November 22, 1939 in Indianapolis, Indiana and reported for duty on the USS Arizona on February 16, 1940. Tommy was killed in action on December 7, 1941 at Pearl Harbor, Hawaii. He was awarded the American Defense Service Medal, World War II Victory Medal and Purple Heart Medal posthumously. Tommy remains on duty on the USS Arizona. He is commemorated on the USS Arizona Memorial and the Memorial Tablets of the Missing, National Memorial Cemetery of the Pacific, Honolulu, Hawaii. Tommy was survived by his Father, Mr. Buck Moss, Route 1, Herndon, Kentucky.

Moulton, Gordon Eddy Fireman, First Class, Serial No: 375 92 03, US Navy. Gordon was born in about 1922 in California to Eddy S. and Larissa Alice Moulton. He enlisted in the US Navy on November 9, 1938 in San Francisco, California and reported for duty on the USS Arizona on March 11, 1939. He was killed in action on December 7, 1941 at Pearl Harbor, Hawaii. Gordon was awarded the American Defense Service Medal, World War II Victory Medal and Purple Heart Medal posthumously. He remains on duty on the USS Arizona. Gordon is commemorated on the USS Arizona Memorial and the Memorial Tablets of the Missing, National Memorial Cemetery of the Pacific, Honolulu, Hawaii. He was survived by his Foster brother, Mr. Harold Aubrey Moulton, 64 South 19th Street, San Jose, California.

Muncy, Claude Machinist's Mate, Second Class, Serial No: 382 07 37, US Navy. Claude was born in 1922, the son of Claude H. Muncy and Essie (Tudor) Muncy. He enlisted in the US Navy on September 13, 1938 in Los Angeles, California and completed his basic training at the Naval Training Station in San Diego, California. Claude reported for duty on the USS Arizona on March 11, 1939. He was killed in action on December 7, 1941 at Pearl Harbor, Hawaii. Claude was awarded the American Defense Service Medal, World War II Victory Medal and Purple Heart Medal posthumously. He remains on duty on the USS Arizona. Claude is commemorated on the USS Arizona Memorial and the Memorial Tablets of the Missing, National Memorial Cemetery of the Pacific, Honolulu, Hawaii. He was survived by his Mother, Mrs. Essie Catherine Jordon, 1024 Myrtle Avenue, Long Beach, California.[556]

Murdock, Charles Luther Watertender, First Class, Serial No: 272 08 41, US Navy. Charles was born July 10, 1916, the son of Charles J. W. Murdock and Sleety (Rains) Murdock. He enlisted in the US Navy on December 17, 1934 in Birmingham, Alabama. Charles served on the USS Arizona from April 17, 1935 until he was killed in action on December 7, 1941 at Pearl Harbor, Hawaii. He was awarded the American Defense Service Medal, World War II Victory Medal and Purple Heart Medal posthumously. Charles remains on duty on the USS Arizona. He is commemorated on the USS Arizona Memorial and the Memorial Tablets of the Missing, National Memorial Cemetery of the Pacific, Honolulu, Hawaii. Charles was survived by his Parents,

---

[556] Claude Muncy, Photo provided by family member, Carolyn Graham-Lopez from the San Diego Union Newspaper, Wednesday, February 4, 1942, Page 8.

Mr. and Mrs. Charles W. Murdock, Route 3, Henagar, Alabama; Brothers, DeWayne, Thomas and Verlon; Sisters, Lysonia Ladd and Vera Slaton. His brother Melvin was also killed in action on board the USS Arizona. His other brother, Thomas was serving on the Arizona and was among the survivors.[557]

Murdock, Melvin Elijah Watertender, Second Class, Serial No: 295 41 74, US Navy. Melvin was born October 19, 1918, son of Charles J. W. Murdock and Sleety (Rains) Murdock. He enlisted in the US Navy on April 25, 1938 in Nashville, Tennessee and reported for duty on the USS Arizona on August 12, 1938. Melvin was killed in action on December 7, 1941 at Pearl Harbor, Hawaii. He was awarded the American Defense Service Medal, World War II Victory Medal and Purple Heart Medal posthumously. Melvin remains on duty on the USS Arizona. He is commemorated on the USS Arizona Memorial and the Memorial Tablets of the Missing, National Memorial Cemetery of the Pacific, Honolulu, Hawaii. Melvin was survived by his Parents, Mr. and Mrs. Charles J. W. Murdock, Route 3, Henagar, Alabama, brothers: DeWayne, Thomas and Verlon; Sisters, Lysonia Ladd and Vera Slaton. His brother Charles was also killed in action on board the USS Arizona. His other brother, Thomas was serving on the Arizona and was among the survivors.[558]

Murdock, Thomas Daniel Chief Yeoman, Serial No. 271 98 91, US Navy. Thomas was born September 21, 1908, son of Charles Wesley Murdock and Mary Sleety (Rains) Murdock. Thomas enlisted in the US Navy March 5, 1930. He served on the USS Arizona from June 4, 1931 until December 7, 1941 when the Japanese attacked Pearl Harbor. Thomas was married and lived offshore. His brothers, Charles Luther and Melvin Elijah Murdock were killed in action on board the USS Arizona. After the attack, navy divers swam into the submerged wreckage of the Arizona searching for any identifiable belongings of the sailors that they could pass on to their families. Unable to find anything on his brothers, Thomas donned a diving suit and swam through the sunken battleship to find his brothers' lockers. He retrieved a bowling ball, pocketknife, shaving mug and a pair of scissors for his parents. He died August 25, 1979 in Long Beach, California.

Murphy, James Joseph Seaman, First Class, Serial No: 381 40 15, US Navy. James was born on August 18, 1920 in Cleator Moor, England the son of Richard Murphy and Mary (Jackson) Murphy. *He traveled with his parents to the USA on the ship Laviathan in 1923. The family immigrated onward to Bisbee, Arizona where their relatives were living.* James enlisted in the US Navy on January 30, 1941 in San Diego, California and completed his basic training at the Naval Training Station in San Diego, California. James served briefly on the USS Enterprise before reporting for duty on the USS Arizona on April 27, 1941. He was killed in action on December 7, 1941 at Pearl Harbor, Hawaii. His parents received a telegram on December 20, 1941 informing them of their son's death. James was awarded the American Defense Service

---

[557] Charles Luther Murdock, Information and photo provided by family member, Patti Hays.
[558] Melvin Elijah Murdock, information and photo provided by family member, Patti Hays.

Medal, World War II Victory Medal and Purple Heart Medal posthumously. He remains on duty on the USS Arizona. James is commemorated on the USS Arizona Memorial and the Memorial Tablets of the Missing, National Memorial Cemetery of the Pacific, Honolulu, Hawaii. He was survived by his Father, Mr. Richard Murphy, Box 2144, Bisbee, Arizona. The VFW Post 836 in Bisbee, Arizona was named in his honor.[559]

Murphy, James Palmer Fireman, Third Class, Serial No: 279 75 70, US Navy. James was the son of John Murphy and Pauline (Arwood) Murphy. He enlisted in the US Navy on November 27, 1940 in Cincinnati, Ohio and completed his basic training at the Naval Training Station in Great Lakes, Illinois. James reported for duty on the USS Arizona January 19, 1941. He was killed in action on December 7, 1941 at Pearl Harbor, Hawaii. James was awarded the American Defense Service Medal, World War II Victory Medal and Purple Heart Medal posthumously. He remains on duty on the USS Arizona. James is commemorated on the USS Arizona Memorial and the Memorial Tablets of the Missing, National Memorial Cemetery of the Pacific, Honolulu, Hawaii. He was survived by his Father, Mr. John Murphy, 1743 William Howard Taft Road, Cincinnati, Ohio.[560]

Murphy, Jessie Huell Seaman, First Class, Serial No: 274 41 84, US Navy. Jessie was born November 29, 1918 in Louisiana. He enlisted in the US Navy on December 13, 1939 in New Orleans, Louisiana and reported for duty on the USS Arizona on March 29, 1940. Assigned death #510, Jessie died of wounds received in action on December 7, 1941 at Pearl Harbor, Hawaii. His remains were identified by the waist band markings "Murphy, JH".[561] He was awarded the American Defense Service Medal, World War II Victory Medal and Purple Heart Medal posthumously. Jessie's remains were sent home and he was buried in the Thigpen Cemetery, in Picayune, Mississippi. He is commemorated on the USS Arizona Memorial and the Memorial Tablets of the Missing, National Memorial Cemetery of the Pacific, Honolulu, Hawaii. Jessie was survived by his Mother, Mrs. Irene Jane Murphy, 1247 North Claiborne Street, New Orleans, Louisiana.

Murphy, Thomas Joseph, Jr. Storekeeper, First Class, Serial No: 265 62 32, US Navy. Thomas was born July 12, 1913. He enlisted in the US Navy on November 15, 1933 in Richmond, Virginia and reported for duty on the USS Arizona on August 7, 1939. He was killed in action on December 7, 1941 at Pearl Harbor, Hawaii. Thomas was awarded the American Defense Service Medal, World War II Victory Medal and Purple Heart Medal posthumously. He remains on duty on the USS Arizona. Thomas is commemorated on the USS Arizona Memorial and the Memorial Tablets of the Missing, National Memorial Cemetery of the Pacific, Honolulu, Hawaii. He was survived by his Mother, Mrs. Thomas Joseph Murphy, 345 Grosvenor Street, Douglaston, Flushing, New York. (Father serving with the US Navy).

Musick, Clay Henry Seaman, First Class, Serial No. 360 25 45, US Navy. Clay was born on August 2, 1917 in Texas. He enlisted in the US Navy November 6, 1940 in Houston, Texas and completed his basic training at the Naval Training Station in San Diego, California.

---

[559] James Joseph Murphy, Photo from The Bisbee Daily Review Newspaper.
[560] James Palmer Murphy, Photo from the1935 Lawlor Professionals School yearbook.
[561] Report of Changes of the USS Arizona for the month ending 31st day of December, 1941, Page 86, line 17, Jessie Huell Murphy.

He reported for duty on the USS Arizona on January 25, 1941. He was serving on December 7, 1941 when the Japanese attacked Pearl Harbor. Clay was a bow hook in the No. 2 motor boat.

On the morning of the 7th, he and the Lakin brothers were shining bright work. They heard a loud explosion on Ford Island and a plane came over, very low so they headed for their battle stations. Clay's station was AA magazine second platform below third deck. Clay helped rig a conveyor on the third deck to receive ammunition from the magazine. Since he was a hoistman he started a roundup when the ship took its first hit. The explosion knocked the ship's lights out except the blue battle lights and sent him reeling. As he reached for the crank to crank up the ammo, the second explosion came. That sent him against the bulkhead and then on the apron of the hoist. He picked himself up again after another explosion; the metal was very, very hot and he had difficulty breathing. Someone said "Let's get out of here!" He was helped up the ladder on the bulkhead. When they got to the third deck, Clay was asked if he could make it. He took the first step on the ladder and does not remember anything until he stepped out on the port quarterdeck. Clarendon Hetrick helped him through the hatch. He went through officer's country enroute. The Japanese were machine-gunning the quarterdeck; a lot of men were under the turrets for protection. Others were on fire and were rolling on the deck to try and put the fire out. Dazed from the explosions, Clay went to the starboard side of the ship. A tug was alongside trying to put out the fire but could not get up enough water pressure so they started picking up survivors. They made their way to a boat deck where he was pulled on board the tug.

Clay was wounded in action during the attack. He was taken to one of the several Naval Hospital huts, and later to the Naval Hospital. His right shoulder and right hip were busted up and he had an injury to his knee and right ankle. He also suffered burns to his hands, legs and face. Clay was transferred on December 18, 1941 to the USAT Coolidge, arriving in the states on Christmas Day. He was taken to the Naval Hospital on the mainland for further treatment. Clay received a medical discharge seven months later on July 8, 1942. His father, Mr. William Henry Musick, 720 Indiana Street, Weslaco, Texas was notified of his condition. Clay died on May 25, 2004 in Temple, Texas and is buried at Bellwood Memorial Park.

Myers, James Gernie (Gernie Tharp Myers) Storekeeper, First Class, Serial No: 341 62 69, US Navy. James was born May 2, 1906 in Browning, Missouri the second son of three sons born to Andrew Washington and Mary Susan (Hoskins) Myers. *His older brother, Claude was killed in the First World War. His younger brother, Bernie was killed by lightning at age 15 in 1914.* James enlisted in the US Navy on May 3, 1928 in Missouri and reported for duty on the USS Arizona on June 22, 1939. He was killed in action on December 7, 1941 at Pearl Harbor, Hawaii. James was awarded the American Defense Service Medal, World War II Victory Medal and Purple Heart Medal posthumously. He remains on duty on the USS Arizona. James is commemorated on the USS Arizona Memorial and the Memorial Tablets of the Missing, National Memorial Cemetery of the Pacific, Honolulu, Hawaii. He was survived by his Sons, James Gernie Myers, Jr. age 9, and Gordon Myers age 5, 3332 Russell Avenue, Seattle, Washington. His wife had died in 1940 and the sons were living with their grandmother in Seattle.[562]

---

[562] James Gernie Myers (Gernie Tharp Myers), Information and photo from "First Gold Star Mother in her town of both World Wars", Kansas City Star Newspaper, Kansas City, Missouri, Sunday, October 18, 1942, Page 32.

Mylan, Jack Clement   Signalman, Second Class, Serial No. 385 75 37, US Navy. Jack was born on July 29, 1917 in Mitchell, South Dakota. He enlisted in the US Navy October 13, 1937 in Seattle, Washington and reported for duty on the USS Arizona January 25, 1938. Jack was serving on the USS Arizona on December 7, 1941 when the Japanese attacked Pearl Harbor. After the attack, Jack was transferred to the USS Neosho for duty. Jack retired from the US Navy after nearly 22 years service in July 1959. He died on September 25, 1987 in Buena, Washington.

Naasz, Erwin H.   Shipfitter, Second Class, Serial No: 342 07 64, US Navy. Erwin was born January 4, 1916 in Kingman, Kansas, the son of John and Minnie Naasz. He enlisted in the US Navy on July 5, 1938 in Kansas City, Missouri and completed his basic training at the Naval Training Station in Great Lakes, Illinois. He reported for duty on the USS Arizona on October 23, 1938. Erwin was killed in action on December 7, 1941 at Pearl Harbor, Hawaii. He was awarded the American Defense Service Medal, World War II Victory Medal and Purple Heart Medal posthumously. Erwin remains on duty on the USS Arizona. He is commemorated on the USS Arizona Memorial and the Memorial Tablets of the Missing, National Memorial Cemetery of the Pacific, Honolulu, Hawaii and the Walnut Hill Cemetery, Kingman, Kansas. Erwin was survived by his Mother, Mrs. Minnie Crumley, Route 1, Rego, Kansas.

Nadel, Alexander Joseph   Musician, Second Class, Serial No: 224 14 64, US Navy. Alexander was born April 14, 1921 in New York to Gegnard and Amelia Nadel. He enlisted in the US Navy February 27, 1941 and attended the Navy School of Music in Washington, DC graduating on May 23, 1941 as a member of the USS Arizona Band. Alex reported for duty on the USS Arizona on June 17, 1941. He was killed in action on December 7, 1941 at Pearl Harbor, Hawaii. *The battle station for all of the band members was in the black powder room passing ammunition to the Arizona's gunners during the attack. None of the band members survived the explosion.* Alex was awarded the American Defense Service Medal, World War II Victory Medal and Purple Heart Medal posthumously. He remains on duty on the USS Arizona. Alex is commemorated on the USS Arizona Memorial and the Memorial Tablets of the Missing, National Memorial Cemetery of the Pacific, Honolulu, Hawaii. He was survived by his Mother, Mrs. Amelia Nadel, 24-17 26th Street, Astoria, Long Island City, New York.[563]

---

[563] Alexander Joseph Nadel, Photo from USS Arizona's Last Bank by Molly Kent by permission of the author. For more information about this book, go to www.USSARIZONASLASTBAND.com.

Nations, James Garland Fire Controlman, Second Class, Serial No: 262 28 76, US Navy. James was born July 22, 1918 in Pickens, South Carolina, the son of Blansco Ila and Floy (Rampey) Nations. He enlisted in the US Navy on May 18, 1938 in Raleigh, North Carolina and reported for duty on the USS Arizona on November 10, 1938. James was killed in action on December 7, 1941 at Pearl Harbor, Hawaii. He was awarded the American Defense Service Medal, World War II Victory Medal and Purple Heart Medal posthumously. James remains on duty on the USS Arizona. He is commemorated on the USS Arizona Memorial and the Memorial Tablets of the Missing, National Memorial Cemetery of the Pacific, Honolulu, Hawaii and the Nations Cemetery, Wilmot, North Carolina. James was survived by his Father, Mr. Blansco Ila Nations, Route 2, Pickens, South Carolina.[564]

Naylor, J. D. Signalman, Second Class, Serial No: 360 00 88, US Navy. James was born December 25, 1920 in Louisiana, the son of Carl Welch and Celeste (Harvey) Naylor. He enlisted in the US Navy on September 10, 1938 in Houston, Texas and completed his basic training at the Naval Training Station in San Diego, California. James reported for duty on the USS Arizona on January 2, 1939. He was killed in action on December 7, 1941 at Pearl Harbor, Hawaii. James was awarded the American Defense Service Medal, World War II Victory Medal and Purple Heart Medal posthumously. He remains on duty on the USS Arizona. James is commemorated on the USS Arizona Memorial and the Memorial Tablets of the Missing, National Memorial Cemetery of the Pacific, Honolulu, Hawaii. He was survived by his Parents, Mr. and Mrs. Carl Welch Naylor, 311 Bishop Street, DeRitter, Louisiana, two brothers, James, in the army stationed in South Carolina and Harvey Jean Naylor; two sisters, Mrs. Lois McCullough and Joyce Naylor, all of De Ridder, Louisiana.

Neal, Tom Dick Seaman, First Class, Serial No: 356 26 10, US Navy. Tom was born in 1919 the son of J. W. and Bell Neal. He enlisted in the US Navy on July 17, 1940 in Dallas, Texas and completed his basic training at the Naval Training Station in San Diego, California. Tom reported for duty on the USS Arizona on October 8, 1940. He was killed in action on December 7, 1941 at Pearl Harbor, Hawaii. Tom was awarded the American Defense Service Medal, World War II Victory Medal and Purple Heart Medal posthumously. He remains on duty on the USS Arizona. Tom is commemorated on the USS Arizona Memorial and the Memorial Tablets of the Missing, National Memorial Cemetery of the Pacific, Honolulu, Hawaii. He was survived by his Mother, Mrs. Bell B. Neal, 231 Page Street, Dallas, Texas.[565]

---

[564] James Garland Nations, photo from HonorStates.org.
[565] Tom Dick Neal, photo provided by his Niece, Tamara Miller.

Necessary, Charles Raymond   Seaman, First Class, Serial No: 342 33 47, US Navy. Charles was born in about 1924, the son of Bryan and Ella L. Necessary. *He attended the William Chrisman High School in Independence, Missouri where he was an excellent musician and a member of the ROTC.* Charles left during his senior year to enlist in the US Navy on November 27, 1940 in Kansas City, Missouri and completed his basic training at the Naval Training Station in Great Lakes, Illinois. He reported for duty on the USS Arizona on January 18, 1941. Charles was killed in action on December 7, 1941 at Pearl Harbor, Hawaii. He was awarded the American Defense Service Medal, World War II Victory Medal and Purple Heart Medal posthumously. Charles remains on duty on the USS Arizona. He is commemorated on the USS Arizona Memorial and the Memorial Tablets of the Missing, National Memorial Cemetery of the Pacific, Honolulu, Hawaii. Charles was survived by his Father, Mr. Bryan Necessary, 307-1/2 Pleasant, Independence, Missouri.[566]

Neipp, Paul   Seaman, Second Class, Serial No: 382 46 35, US Navy. Paul was born May 13, 1922 in California, the son of William A. and Margaret Neipp. He enlisted in the US Navy on May 23, 1941 in Los Angeles, California and completed his basic training at the Naval Training Station in San Diego, California. Paul reported for duty on the USS Arizona on August 13, 1941. He was killed in action on December 7, 1941 at Pearl Harbor, Hawaii. Paul was awarded the American Defense Service Medal, World War II Victory Medal and Purple Heart Medal posthumously. He remains on duty on the USS Arizona. Paul is commemorated on the USS Arizona Memorial and the Memorial Tablets of the Missing, National Memorial Cemetery of the Pacific, Honolulu, Hawaii. He was survived by his Father, Mr. William A. Neipp, 858 25th Street, San Pedro, California.[567]

Nelsen, George   Ship's Cook, Second Class, Serial No: 385 79 46, US Navy. George was born July 22, 1918 in Washington, the son of George and Maria Nelsen. He enlisted in the US Navy on November 14, 1938 in Seattle, Washington and completed his basic training at the Naval Training Station in San Diego, California. George reported for duty on the USS Arizona on March 11, 1939. Assigned death #331, George died from 3rd degree burns on December 9, 1941 at Honolulu, Hawaii.[568] He was buried in Plot C, Row 0, Grave 144, National Memorial Cemetery of the Pacific, Honolulu, Hawaii. He was awarded the American Defense Service Medal, World War II Victory Medal and Purple Heart Medal posthumously. George is commemorated on the USS Arizona Memorial. He was survived by his Father, Mr. George Nelsen, Sr., Route 1, Box 328, Enumclaw, Washington.

---

[566] Charles Raymond Necessary, Information and photo provided by Jason Stacy, Staff Advisor, The William Chrisman Envoy, William Chrisman High School, Independence, Missouri.

[567] Paul Neipp, Photo provided by his nephew, John Jensen.

[568] Report of Changes of the USS Arizona for the month ending 31st day of December, 1941, Page 86, line 28, George Nelsen.

Nelson, Grady Lee, Jr. Seaman, Second Class, Serial No. 356 57 42, US Navy. Grady was born November 16, 1922 in Coleman, Texas. His uncle, Chief Turret Captain, Lawrence Adolphus Nelson persuaded him to join the navy. He enlisted in the US Navy May 5, 1941 in Dallas, Texas and completed his basic training at the Naval Training Station in San Diego, California. Grady reported for duty on the USS Arizona September 18, 1941. He was serving with his Uncle on the USS Arizona on December 7, 1941 when the Japanese attacked Pearl Harbor. After the attack, Grady was transferred to the USS Dale (DD-353) for duty. Grady's Uncle Lawrence Adolphus Nelson was also serving on the USS Arizona but he was killed in the attack on Pearl Harbor. He served 30 years in the Navy. Grady passed away June 14, 1993 at age 69. His ashes were placed inside the number 4 turret Barbette beneath the USS Arizona Memorial December 7, 1993 at a private afternoon service. He was survived by his wife Loralee of Houston.

Nelson, Harl Coplin Seaman, First Class, Serial No: 346 87 57, US Navy. Harl was born October 11, 1917 in Union, Arkansas to Joseph Frank and Verna Beatrice (Franklin) Nelson. He enlisted in the US Navy on November 9, 1940 in Little Rock, Arkansas and completed his basic training at the Naval Training Station in San Diego, California. He reported for duty on the USS Arizona on January 11, 1941. *Harl had jaundice and was in sickbay the morning of the seventh.* He was killed in action on December 7, 1941 at Pearl Harbor, Hawaii. Harl was awarded the American Defense Service Medal, World War II Victory Medal and Purple Heart Medal posthumously. He remains on duty on the USS Arizona. Harl is commemorated on the USS Arizona Memorial and the Memorial Tablets of the Missing, National Memorial Cemetery of the Pacific, Honolulu, Hawaii and Ebenezer Cemetery, Bluff City, Arkansas. He was survived by his Father, Mr. Joseph Frank Nelson, Route 4, Rosston, Arkansas.

Nelson, Henry Clarence Boatswain's Mate, First Class, Serial No: 328 34 03, US Navy. Henry was born November 1, 1909 in Grand Meadow, Minnesota to John M. and Helena Bertha (Springer) Nelson. *He graduated from the Wahkon High School in 1928. While in school he was active in basketball and other activities.* Henry enlisted in the US Navy on November 16, 1933 in Minneapolis, Minnesota and completed his basic training at the Naval Training Station in Great Lakes, Illinois. He reported for duty on the USS Arizona on February 25, 1934. Henry was killed in action on December 7, 1941 at Pearl Harbor, Hawaii. He was awarded the American Defense Service Medal, World War II Victory Medal and Purple Heart Medal posthumously. Henry remains on duty on the USS Arizona. He is commemorated on the USS Arizona Memorial and the Memorial Tablets of the Missing, National Memorial Cemetery of the Pacific, Honolulu, Hawaii. Henry was survived by his Parents, Mr. and Mrs. John M. Nelson, Wahkon, Minnesota; three sisters, Mrs. James Carrington of Foxboro, Wisconsin, Mrs. Ole Olson of Duluth, Minnesota and Mrs. Herbert Garberg of Brainerd, Minnesota; and three brothers, Ernest of Redtop, Minnesota, George and Clifford of Wahkon, Minnesota.[569]

---

[569] Henry Clarence Nelson, Information and photo from "Best of the Mess" May 21, 1942 – Henry Clarence Nelson Obituary, Mille Lacs Messenger, Mille Lacs, Minnesota.

Nelson, Lawrence "Jack" Adolphus Chief Turret Captain (PA), Serial No: 355 45 56, US Navy. Lawrence was born April 11, 1898 in Hill, Texas to Mrs. Gippie Lee Nelson. He enlisted in the US Navy on December 30, 1922 in Dallas, Texas and reported for duty on the USS Arizona on December 6, 1937. He was killed in action on December 7, 1941 at Pearl Harbor, Hawaii. Lawrence was awarded the American Defense Service Medal, World War II Victory Medal and Purple Heart Medal posthumously. He remains on duty on the USS Arizona. Lawrence is commemorated on the USS Arizona Memorial and the Memorial Tablets of the Missing, National Memorial Cemetery of the Pacific, Honolulu, Hawaii. He was survived by his Wife, Mrs. Gippie Lee Nelson, 1038 Stanley Avenue, Long Beach, California and his nephew, Grady Lee Nelson, Jr. who was also serving on the Arizona and survived the attack.

Nelson, Richard Eugene Fireman, Third Class, Serial No: 328 75 77, US Navy. Richard was born June 30, 1921 in Harwood, North Dakota, the eldest son of Axel W. and Ester S. Nelson. He enlisted in the US Navy on October 8, 1940 in Minneapolis, Minnesota and completed his basic training at the Naval Training Station in Great Lakes, Illinois. Richard reported for duty on the USS Arizona on December 9, 1940. He was killed in action on December 7, 1941 at Pearl Harbor, Hawaii. Richard was awarded the American Defense Service Medal, World War II Victory Medal and Purple Heart Medal posthumously. He remains on duty on the USS Arizona. Richard is commemorated on the USS Arizona Memorial and the Memorial Tablets of the Missing, National Memorial Cemetery of the Pacific, Honolulu, Hawaii. He was survived by his Father, Mr. Axel W. Nelson, RFD, Harwood, North Dakota. The American Legion Post #297 in Harwood, North Dakota was named in his honor.

Newell, Bobby Earl Seaman, Second Class, Serial No. 342 46 57, US Navy. Bobby enlisted in the US Navy May 27, 1941 in Kansas City, Missouri and completed his basic training at the Naval Training Station in San Diego, California. He reported for duty on the USS Arizona August 13, 1941. He was serving on the USS Arizona on December 7, 1941 when the Japanese attacked Pearl Harbor. After the attack, Bobby was transferred to the Submarine Base at Pearl Harbor for duty. He later served on board the USS Plunger (SS-179) and the USS Sea Poacher (SS-406).

Nichols, Alfred Rose Seaman, First Class, Serial No: 272 41 60, US Navy. Alfred was born May 9, 1923 in Fayette, Alabama, the son of Louis Gustus and Mary Ella (Willingham) Nichols. He enlisted in the US Navy on October 5, 1940 in Birmingham, Alabama and completed his basic training at the Naval Training Station in Norfolk, Virginia. Alfred reported for duty on the USS Arizona on December 4, 1940. He was killed in action on December 7, 1941 at Pearl Harbor, Hawaii. Alfred was awarded the American Defense Service Medal, World War II Victory Medal and Purple Heart Medal posthumously. He remains on duty on the USS Arizona. Alfred is commemorated on the USS Arizona Memorial and the Memorial Tablets of the Missing, National Memorial Cemetery of the Pacific, Honolulu, Hawaii. He was survived by his Sister, Mrs. Carrie Mac Dockery, Fayette, Alabama. His brother, Louis was also killed in action on board the USS Arizona. The James Black-Nichols Brothers VFW Post 5406 in Fayette, Alabama was named in his honor.

Nichols, Bethel Allan Seaman, First Class, Serial No: 385 89 48, US Navy. Bethel was born November 23, 1921, the son of George Dewey and Esther Elizabeth (Mead) Nichols. He enlisted in the US Navy on August 15, 1940 in Seattle, Washington and completed his basic training at the Naval Training Station in San Diego, California. Bethel reported for duty on the

USS Arizona on November 11, 1940. He was killed in action on December 7, 1941 at Pearl Harbor, Hawaii. Bethel was awarded the American Defense Service Medal, World War II Victory Medal and Purple Heart Medal posthumously. He remains on duty on the USS Arizona. Bethel is commemorated on the USS Arizona Memorial and the Memorial Tablets of the Missing, National Memorial Cemetery of the Pacific, Honolulu, Hawaii and the Fern Hill Cemetery, Menlo, Washington. He was survived by his Father, Mr. George Dewey Nichols, Route 1, Box 306, Raymond, Washington.

Nichols, Clifford Leroy Turret Captain, First Class, Serial No: 355 81 20, US Navy. Clifford was born June 8, 1911 in New York, the son of Arthur and Mable Nichols. He re-enlisted in the US Navy January 14, 1938. He served on the USS Arizona from March 31, 1932 until he was killed in action on December 7, 1941 at Pearl Harbor, Hawaii. He was awarded the American Defense Service Medal, World War II Victory Medal and Purple Heart Medal posthumously. Clifford remains on duty on the USS Arizona. He is commemorated on the USS Arizona Memorial and the Memorial Tablets of the Missing, National Memorial Cemetery of the Pacific, Honolulu, Hawaii. Clifford was survived by his Wife, Mrs. Cecelia Marie Nichols, 156 East Neece Street, Long Beach, California.

Nichols, John Edward Radioman, First Class, Serial No. 320 98 43, US Navy. John was born August 17, 1916 in Knoxville, Iowa. He enlisted in the US Navy July 15, 1935 in Des Moines, Iowa and reported for duty on the USS Arizona December 2, 1936. He was serving on December 7, 1941 when the Japanese attacked Pearl Harbor. John was the only radioman to survive the attack. After the attack, John was transferred to Cincpac Flag, Submarine Base at Pearl Harbor for duty. He retired after 25 years in the Navy as a Commander. He was instrumental, along with others, in raising money to build the USS Arizona Memorial in Pearl Harbor. After retiring from the Navy he spent 13 years with Data Graphics in San Diego, California. He died at age 77 on July 28, 1995 in San Diego, California and was survived by his wife, Lileth, a daughter and grandchildren.

Nichols, Louis Duffie Seaman, Second Class, Serial No: 272 55 33, US Navy. Louis was born June 19, 1919 in Alabama to Louis Gustus and Mary Ella (Willingham) Nichols. He enlisted in the US Navy on February 7, 1941 and reported for duty on the USS Arizona August 13, 1941. Louis was killed in action on December 7, 1941 at Pearl Harbor, Hawaii. He was awarded the American Defense Service Medal, World War II Victory Medal and Purple Heart Medal posthumously. Louis remains on duty on the USS Arizona. He is commemorated on the USS Arizona Memorial and the Memorial Tablets of the Missing, National Memorial Cemetery of the Pacific, Honolulu, Hawaii. Louis was survived by his Sister, Mrs. Carrie Mac Dockery, Fayette, Alabama. His brother, Seaman, First Class, Alfred Rose Nichols was also killed in action on board the USS Arizona. The James Black-Nichols Brothers VFW Post 5406 in Fayette, Alabama was named in his honor.

Nicholson, Glen Eldon Electrician's Mate, Third Class, Serial No: 328 76 34, US Navy. Glen was born in about 1917 in North Dakota to James Hugh and Hazel Nicholson. He enlisted in the US Navy October 15, 1940 in Minneapolis, Minnesota and completed his basic training at the Naval Training Station in Great Lakes, Illinois. He reported for duty on the USS Arizona September 18, 1941. Glen was killed in action on December 7, 1941 at Pearl Harbor, Hawaii. He was awarded the American Defense Service Medal, World War II Victory Medal and Purple Heart Medal posthumously. Glen remains on duty on the USS Arizona. He is commemorated on the USS Arizona Memorial and the Memorial Tablets of the Missing, National Memorial Cemetery of the Pacific, Honolulu, Hawaii. Glen was survived by his Father, Mr. James Hugh Nicholson, Bowesmont, North Dakota.

Nicholson, Hancel Grant   Seaman, First Class, Serial No: 372 26 39, US Navy. Hancel was born July 11, 1924 in Lucas, Iowa the son of Thomas L. and Helen Dorothy (Norman) Nicholson. He enlisted in the US Navy January 29, 1941 in Denver, Colorado and completed his basic training at the Naval Training Station in San Diego, California. Hancel reported for duty on the USS Arizona April 27, 1941. He had been in the Navy for 11 months when he was killed in action on December 7, 1941 at Pearl Harbor, Hawaii. He was awarded the American Defense Service Medal, World War II Victory Medal and Purple Heart Medal posthumously. Hancel remains on duty on the USS Arizona. He is commemorated on the USS Arizona Memorial and the Memorial Tablets of the Missing, National Memorial Cemetery of the Pacific, Honolulu, Hawaii. Hancel was survived by his Parents, Mr. and Mrs. Thomas L. Nicholson, 1236 Champa Street, Denver, Colorado. *The Waterloo Daily Courier, Waterloo Iowa, September 28, 1945 shows an article stating that Mrs. Nicholson was asking $100,000 in damages from the Imperial Japanese government for the death of her son on grounds that the attack on Pearl Harbor was an "illegal act".*

Nides, Thomas "Tommy" James   Electrician's Mate, First Class, Serial No: 274 00 96, US Navy. Thomas was born October 8, 1909 in New Orleans, Louisiana, the son of Thomas James and Ophelia (Rapp) Nides of New Orleans, Louisiana. He re-enlisted in the US Navy July 16, 1938. Thomas served on the USS Arizona from September 15, 1932 until he was killed in action on December 7, 1941 at Pearl Harbor, Hawaii. *On Saturday night, December 6th, he was invited for dinner and as an overnight guest. Due to the battle of the bands at Bloch Arena, he elected to decline the invitation and remained to support the Arizona's band. The decision cost him his life.* He was awarded the American Defense Service Medal, World War II Victory Medal and Purple Heart Medal posthumously. Thomas remains on duty on the USS Arizona. He is commemorated on the USS Arizona Memorial and the Memorial Tablets of the Missing, National Memorial Cemetery of the Pacific, Honolulu, Hawaii. Thomas was survived by his Wife, Mrs. Frances Opal (Lee) Nides and daughter Elaine Nides, 2040 Constitution Lane, Long Beach, California.[570]

Nielsen, Floyd Theadore   Carpenter's Mate Third Class, Serial No: 368 48 77, US Navy. Floyd was born July 24, 1918 in Ferron, Utah, the son of Christian Theadore Nielsen and Ethel Lugene (Crawford) Neilsen. He enlisted in the US Navy May 31, 1940 in Salt Lake City, Utah and reported for duty on the USS Arizona September 8, 1940. Floyd was killed in action on December 7, 1941 at Pearl Harbor, Hawaii. He was awarded the American Defense Service Medal, World War II Victory Medal and Purple Heart Medal posthumously. Floyd remains on duty on the USS Arizona. He is commemorated on the USS Arizona Memorial and the Memorial Tablets of the Missing, National Memorial Cemetery of the Pacific, Honolulu, Hawaii and the Ferron City Cemetery, Ferron, Utah. Floyd was survived by his Father, Mr. Christian Theadore Nielsen, Ferron, Utah.

Niemara, Stanley Joseph   Seaman, First Class, Serial No. 311 51 26, US Navy. Stanley was born October 19, 1921 in West Rutland, Vermont the son of Joseph and Julia (Wozniak) Niemara. He enlisted in the US Navy October 1, 1940 in Detroit, Michigan and completed his basic training at the Naval Training Station in Great Lakes, Illinois. Stanley reported for duty on the USS Arizona December 9, 1940. He was serving on the USS Arizona on December 7, 1941 when the Japanese attacked Pearl Harbor. After the attack, Stanley was sent to Bishop's Point for duty. Stanley suffered with cancer and was in and out of the hospital most of the year. He passed away December 25, 1992 in Dearborn Heights, Michigan. Stanley was survived by his wife, Alice.

---

[570] Thomas James Nides, Information provided by close family friend, CDR Arthur R. Lee USN (ret).

Noonan, Robert Harold   Seaman, First Class, Serial No: 311 49 69, US Navy. Robert was born in 1920 in Michigan, the son of Wesley Johnson and Rena Bell (Curtis) Noonan. He enlisted in the US Navy September 9, 1940 in Detroit, Michigan and completed his basic training at the Naval Training Station in Norfolk, Virginia. He reported for duty on the USS Arizona December 4, 1940. Robert was killed in action on December 7, 1941 at Pearl Harbor, Hawaii. He was awarded the American Defense Service Medal, World War II Victory Medal and Purple Heart Medal posthumously. Robert remains on duty on the USS Arizona. He is commemorated on the USS Arizona Memorial, the Memorial Tablets of the Missing, National Memorial Cemetery of the Pacific, Honolulu, Hawaii and Pine Tree Cemetery, Corunna, Michigan. Robert was survived by his Mother, Mrs. Rena Bell Murdock, North Brady Street, Corunna, Michigan.

Nowosacki, Theodore Lucian   Ensign, Serial No: 0-098290, US Navy Reserve. Theodore was born in about 1915 in New York, New York to Wotciech and Jadwiga Nowosacki. He was commissioned Ensign June 6, 1941 and was serving on the USS Arizona as Engineer Jr. Watch and Division A Officer. His battle station was Repair II. Theodore was killed in action on December 7, 1941 at Pearl Harbor, Hawaii. He was awarded the American Defense Service Medal, World War II Victory Medal and Purple Heart Medal posthumously. Theodore remains on duty on the USS Arizona. He is commemorated on the USS Arizona Memorial and the Memorial Tablets of the Missing, National Memorial Cemetery of the Pacific, Honolulu, Hawaii. Theodore was survived by his Father, Mr. John Nowosacki, 619 East 9th Street, New York, New York.[571]

Nusser, Raymond Alfred   Gunner's Mate, Third Class, Serial No: 299 78 04, US Navy. Raymond was born in 1917 in Wisconsin, the son of William and Marie (Ripple) Nusser. He enlisted in the US Navy July 30, 1935 in Chicago, Illinois and reported for duty on the USS Arizona July 8, 1938. He was killed in action on December 7, 1941 at Pearl Harbor, Hawaii. Raymond was awarded the American Defense Service Medal, World War II Victory Medal and Purple Heart Medal posthumously. He remains on duty on the USS Arizona. Raymond is commemorated on the USS Arizona Memorial and the Memorial Tablets of the Missing, National Memorial Cemetery of the Pacific, Honolulu, Hawaii. Raymond was survived by his Father, Mr. William George Nusser, 18 Main Street, Oshkosh, Wisconsin.[572]

[571] Theodore Lucian Nowosacki, Photo from New York Honor States.
[572] Raymond Alfred Nusser, Photo and information from the Wisconsin Rapids Daily Tribune, Tuesday, December 30, 1941.

Nye, Frank Erskine Seaman, First Class, Serial No: 376 16 89, US Navy. Frank was born May 20, 1921 in California, the son of Jesse Morrison and Agnes (Davidson) Nye. He enlisted in the US Navy November 27, 1940 in San Francisco, California and completed his basic training at the Naval Training Station in San Diego, California. Frank reported for duty on the USS Arizona January 25, 1941. He was killed in action on December 7, 1941 at Pearl Harbor, Hawaii. Frank was awarded the American Defense Service Medal, World War II Victory Medal and Purple Heart Medal posthumously. He remains on duty on the USS Arizona. Frank is commemorated on the USS Arizona Memorial and the Memorial Tablets of the Missing, National Memorial Cemetery of the Pacific, Honolulu, Hawaii. He was survived by his Mother, Mrs. Agnes Logsdon, 1735 Parker Street, Berkeley, California.[573]

O'Brion, Edward Francis Joseph Seaman, First Class, Serial No. 400 15 44, US Navy. Edward enlisted in the US Navy June 29, 1939 in Portland, Maine and reported for duty on the USS Arizona December 30, 1940. He was serving on the USS Arizona on December 7, 1941 when the Japanese attacked Pearl Harbor. After the attack, Edward was transferred to the USS Patterson (DD-392) for duty.

O'Bryan, George "David" David Fire Controlman, Third Class, Serial No: 287 33 85, US Navy. George was born August 11, 1920 in Kentucky, the son of John Raymond and Mary Lucy (Smith) O'Bryan. *He came from a large family of nine boys and two girls. Eight of the men and one of the women served in the military.* George enlisted in the US Navy November 20, 1939 in Louisville, Kentucky and completed his basic training at the Naval Training Station in Great Lakes, Illinois. He reported for duty on the USS Arizona January 11, 1941. George was killed in action on December 7, 1941 at Pearl Harbor, Hawaii. He was awarded the American Defense Service Medal, World War II Victory Medal and Purple Heart Medal posthumously. George remains on duty on the USS Arizona with his brother, Joseph. He is commemorated on the USS Arizona Memorial and the Memorial Tablets of the Missing, National Memorial Cemetery of the Pacific, Honolulu, Hawaii. George was survived by his Parents, Mr. and Mrs. John Raymond O'Bryan, Brothers: Paul Harold, Aloysius, Raymond, Samuel, Earl, John and Vincent and sisters, Elizabeth and Mabel O'Bryan, New Hope, Kentucky. His brother, Joseph was also killed in action on the USS Arizona.[574]

---

[573] Frank Erskine Nye, Photo from the 1938 Berkeley High School Yearbook, Berkeley, California.
[574] George David O'Bryan, Information and Photo provided by his nephew, David O'Bryan.

O'Bryan, Joseph Benjamin Fire Controlman, Third Class, Serial No: 287 25 29, US Navy. Joseph was born April 12, 1917 in New Hope, Kentucky, the son of John Raymond and Mary Lucy (Smith) O'Bryan. *He came from a large family of nine boys and two girls. Eight of the men and one of the women served in the military.* Joseph enlisted in the US Navy June 21, 1938 in Louisville, Kentucky and reported for duty on the USS Arizona November 10, 1938. He was killed in action on December 7, 1941 at Pearl Harbor, Hawaii. Joseph was awarded the American Defense Service Medal, World War II Victory Medal and Purple Heart Medal posthumously. He remains on duty on the USS Arizona with his brother, George. Joseph is commemorated on the USS Arizona Memorial and Memorial Tablets of the Missing, National Memorial Cemetery of the Pacific, Honolulu, Hawaii. He was survived by his Parents, Mr. and Mrs. John Raymond O'Bryan, Brothers: Paul Harold, Aloysius, Raymond, Samuel, Earl, John and Vincent and sisters, Elizabeth and Mabel O'Bryan, New Hope, Kentucky. His brother, George was also killed in action on the USS Arizona.[575]

Ochoski, Henry Francis Gunner's Mate, Second Class, Serial No: 385 79 32, US Navy. Henry was born November 30, 1919 in Gray's Harbor, Washington the youngest son of Frank Joseph and Sophie (Iwanyszyn) Ochoski. He enlisted in the US Navy October 4, 1938 in Seattle, Washington and completed his basic training at the Naval Training Station in San Diego, California. Henry reported for duty on the USS Arizona January 2, 1939. *He was set to get out of the Navy and in those days it was a requirement to go back to his first commissioned ship. So after just getting engaged, he flew out to Hawaii to complete his last week in the service. On Sunday morning the 7th, his friend asked him to go into Honolulu, but he turned him down to stay behind to write a letter to his finance. That was the last he was seen.* He was killed in action on December 7, 1941 at Pearl Harbor, Hawaii. Henry was awarded the American Defense Service Medal, World War II Victory Medal and Purple Heart Medal posthumously. He remains on duty on the USS Arizona. Henry is commemorated on the USS Arizona Memorial and the Memorial Tablets of the Missing, National Memorial Cemetery of the Pacific, Honolulu, Hawaii. He was survived by his Father, Mr. Frank Ochoski, 515 North H Street, Aberdeen, Washington.[576]

Off, Virgil Simon Seaman, First Class, Serial No: 372 12 29, US Navy. Virgil was born May 24, 1911 in Del Norte, Colorado, the son of Simon Christian Off and Mary Ann (Robran) Off. He enlisted in the US Navy December 13, 1939 in Denver, Colorado and completed his basic training at the Naval Training Station in San Diego, California. Virgil reported for duty on the USS Arizona February 24, 1940. He was killed in action on December 7, 1941 at Pearl Harbor, Hawaii. Virgil was awarded the American Defense Service Medal, World War II Victory Medal and Purple Heart Medal posthumously. He remains on duty on the USS Arizona. Virgil is commemorated on the USS Arizona Memorial and the Memorial Tablets of the Missing, National Memorial Cemetery of the Pacific, Honolulu, Hawaii. He was survived by his Father, Mr. Simon Off, Route No. 3, Alamosa, Colorado.

---

[575] Joseph Benjamin O'Bryan, Information and Photo provided by his nephew, David O'Bryan.
[576] Henry Francis Ochoski, Information provided by his nephew, Lawrence J. Perkins, Photo from 1938 Aberdeen/Weatherwax High School, Aberdeen, Washington.

Ogle, Victor Willard   Seaman, Second Class, Serial No: 356 39 05, US Navy. Victor was born August 15, 1917 in Cardell, Oklahoma, the son of George B. Ogle and India Harriett (Campbell) Ogle. He enlisted in the US Navy October 22, 1940 in Dallas, Texas and completed his basic training at the Naval Training Station in San Diego, California. Victor reported for duty on the USS Arizona March 20, 1941. He was killed in action on December 7, 1941 at Pearl Harbor, Hawaii. Victor was awarded the American Defense Service Medal, World War II Victory Medal and Purple Heart Medal posthumously. He remains on duty on the USS Arizona. Victor is commemorated on the USS Arizona Memorial and the Memorial Tablets of the Missing, National Memorial Cemetery of the Pacific, Honolulu, Hawaii. He was survived by his Mother, Mrs. India Ogle, Route 3, Clinton, Oklahoma. The American Legion Post 41 in Clinton, Oklahoma was named in his and another, Private, Abner Franklin Power who also died on the Arizona, in their honor.

Oglesby, Lonnie Harris   Seaman, Second Class, Serial No: 644 00 81, US Naval Reserve. Lonnie was born January 4, 1919 in Jackson, Mississippi, the son of Alexander Stephens Oglesby and Annie Estelle (Marion) Oglesby. He enlisted in the US Navy June 20, 1941 in New Orleans, Louisiana and completed his basic training at the Naval Training Station in San Diego, California. Lonnie reported for duty on the USS Arizona August 29, 1941. He was killed in action on December 7, 1941 at Pearl Harbor, Hawaii. Lonnie was awarded the American Defense Service Medal, World War II Victory Medal and Purple Heart Medal posthumously. He remains on duty on the USS Arizona. Lonnie is commemorated on the USS Arizona Memorial and the Memorial Tablets of the Missing, National Memorial Cemetery of the Pacific, Honolulu, Hawaii. He was survived by his Father, Mr. Alexander S. Oglesby, Route 1, Box 34-A, Jackson, Mississippi.[577]

Oliphant, Harold Eugene   Gunner's Mate, Third Class, Serial No. 263 30 02, US Navy. Harold was born November 2, 1920 in Youngstown, Ohio, the son of Samuel H. and Mary E. Welsh Oliiphant. He enlisted in the US Navy November 8, 1939 in Cleveland, Ohio and completed his basic training at the Naval Training Station in Great Lakes, Illinois. He reported for duty on the USS Arizona January 27, 1940. He was serving on the USS Arizona on December 7, 1941 when the Japanese attacked Pearl Harbor. He served until March 30, 1944. Harold passed away October 24, 1989 in Youngstown, Ohio. His ashes were interred on the USS Arizona on August 1, 1990.[578]

Oliver, Raymond Brown   Seaman, First Class, Serial No: 382 29 18, US Navy. Raymond was born in about 1914 in West Los Angeles, California the son of Charles Oscar and Hazel B. Oliver. He enlisted in the US Navy October 29, 1940 in Los Angeles, California and completed his basic training at the Naval Training Station in San Diego, California. He reported for duty on the USS Arizona December 30, 1940. Raymond was killed in action on December 7, 1941 at Pearl Harbor, Hawaii. He was awarded the American Defense Service Medal, World War II Victory Medal and Purple Heart Medal posthumously. Raymond remains on duty on the

---

[577] Lonnie Harris Oglesby, Photo from Mississippi Honor States.
[578] Harold Eugene Oliphant, Photo provided by family member, Mary Weese.

USS Arizona. He is commemorated on the USS Arizona Memorial and the Memorial Tablets of the Missing, National Memorial Cemetery of the Pacific, Honolulu, Hawaii. Raymond was survived by his Father, Mr. Charles Oscar Oliver, 11684 Goshen Avenue, West Los Angeles, California.

Olsen, Edward Kern   Ensign, Serial No: 0-095892, US Navy Reserve. Edward was born September 12, 1913 in Bonner Springs, Kansas, the son of Frank Edward and Florence Etta (Kern) Olsen. *Before joining the Navy, he graduated from the University of Kansas with a business degree in 1937 and worked at Woolf Brothers clothing company as a salesman until 1940. He had been a member of the Delta Tau Delta fraternity at Kansas University.* Edward was serving on the Arizona as Junior Watch and Division 5 Officer. His battle station was AA Battery. Edward was killed in action on December 7, 1941 at Pearl Harbor, Hawaii. He was awarded the American Defense Service Medal, World War II Victory Medal and Purple Heart Medal posthumously. Edward remains on duty on the USS Arizona. He is commemorated on the USS Arizona Memorial and the Memorial Tablets of the Missing, National Memorial Cemetery of the Pacific, Honolulu, Hawaii and the Bonner Springs Cemetery, Bonner Springs, Kansas. Edward was survived by his Father, Mr. Frank Edward Olsen, 158 Clark Street, Bonner Springs, Kansas. The Olsen-McGraw-Thompson-Goins VFW 6402 in Bonner Springs, Kansas was named in his honor.[579]

Olsen, Vernon James   Seaman, First Class, Serial No. 300 19 05, US Navy. Vernon was born in Rockford, Illinois on March 1, 1920 the youngest of 14 children born to Oscar and Frances Olsen. He enlisted in the US Navy October 8, 1940 in Chicago, Illinois and completed his basic training at the Naval Training Station in Great Lakes, Illinois. Vernon reported for duty on the USS Arizona December 9, 1940. He was serving on the USS Arizona on December 7, 1941 when the Japanese attacked Pearl Harbor. Vern was assigned to mess duty for 5th Division when general quarters was sounded, his battle station was in the gun tubs on the after mast where he manned a 50 caliber water-cooled machine gun. Unable to access the ready-locker he did not have any ammunition or water needed to operate the machine gun. Shortly after reporting to his battle station, there was a huge explosion and he was ordered to abandon ship. During his attempt to abandon ship, he was severely burned on his arms. He found himself floundering in the harbor but was rescued and transported to Ford Island. Vernon went on to serve on the USS Lexington reporting for duty December 13, 1941 and served until she was sunk May 7, 1942 during the Battle of the Coral Sea. On July 8, 1942 after having survived the sinking of the Lexington, he was transferred to the USS Nassau (CVE-16) where he served until the end of the war. After the war he was assigned to the USS Fulton (AS-11) where he participated in the atomic testing at Bikini Atol in July 1946. He was honorably discharged December 9, 1946 with the rank of Electrician's Mate, First Class (Acting Chief). Vern died on April 22, 2011 in Port Charlotte, Florida. He was survived by his wife, Jo Ann (Castelles) Olsen.

---

[579] Edward Kern Olsen, Photo from Kansas Honor States.

Olson, Glen Martin   Seaman, Second Class, Serial No: 386 01 56, US Navy. Glen was born in 1924 in Montana, the son of Martin and Anna Olson. He enlisted in the US Navy June 19, 1941 in Seattle, Washington and completed his basic training at the Naval Training Station in San Diego, California. Glen reported for duty on the USS Arizona August 29, 1941. He was killed in action on December 7, 1941 at Pearl Harbor, Hawaii. Glen was awarded the American Defense Service Medal, World War II Victory Medal and Purple Heart Medal posthumously. He remains on duty on the USS Arizona. Glen is commemorated on the USS Arizona Memorial and the Memorial Tablets of the Missing, National Memorial Cemetery of the Pacific, Honolulu, Hawaii. He was survived by his Father, Mr. Martin Olson, Box 427, Arlington, Washington.

O'Neall, Rex Eugene   Seaman, First Class, Serial No: 372 19 81, US Navy. Rex was born May 22, 1922 in Seward, Nebraska, the son of Chester Scheon and Alma M. (Mercer) O'Neall. He enlisted in the US Navy October 25, 1940 in Denver, Colorado and completed his basic training at the Naval Training Station in San Diego, California. Rex reported for duty on the USS Arizona December 30, 1940. He was killed in action on December 7, 1941 at Pearl Harbor, Hawaii. Rex was awarded the American Defense Service Medal, World War II Victory Medal and Purple Heart Medal posthumously. He remains on duty on the USS Arizona. Rex is commemorated on the USS Arizona Memorial and the Memorial Tablets of the Missing, National Memorial Cemetery of the Pacific, Honolulu, Hawaii. He was survived by his Mother, Mrs. Alma Lawshe, 623 West 11th Avenue, Denver, Colorado.

O'Neill, William Thomas, Jr.   Ensign, Serial No: 0-095975, US Navy Reserve. William was born on November 28, 1914 in Stamford, Connecticut, the son of William Thomas and Lillian Ross O'Neill. He enlisted in the US Naval Reserve on July 17, 1940 as an Apprentice Seaman, performing his training aboard the USS New York (BB-34). On September 16, 1940 he was appointed midshipman in the Naval Reserve and completed training at Abbott Hall, Northwestern University, Chicago, Illinois. William was commissioned Ensign on December 12, 1940 and reported for duty on the USS Arizona on December 29, 1940. He was serving on the Arizona as Junior Watch and Division F Officer. His battle station was Plot. William was killed in action on December 7, 1941 at Pearl Harbor, Hawaii. He was awarded the American Defense Service Medal, World War II Victory Medal and Purple Heart Medal posthumously. Thomas remains on duty on the USS Arizona. He is commemorated on the USS Arizona Memorial and the Memorial Tablets of the Missing, National Memorial Cemetery of the Pacific, Honolulu, Hawaii. William was survived by his Mother, Mrs. Lillian Ross O'Neill, Stanley Road, Glenbrook, Connecticut. The destroyer escort USS O'Neill (DE-188) was named in his honor.[580]

Orr, Dwight Jerome   Seaman, First Class, Serial No: 382 23 88, US Navy. Dwight was born April 17, 1922 in Los Angeles County, California, the son of George Whitefield and Alice M. Orr. He enlisted in the US Navy August 6, 1940 in Los Angeles, California and completed his basic training at the Naval Training Station in San Diego, California. Dwight reported for duty on the USS Arizona October 14, 1940. He was killed in action on December 7, 1941 at Pearl Harbor, Hawaii. Dwight was awarded the American Defense Service Medal, World War II Victory Medal and Purple Heart Medal posthumously. He remains on duty on the USS Arizona. Dwight is commemorated on the USS Arizona Memorial and the Memorial Tablets of the

---

[580] William Thomas O'Neill, Jr., Photo from1942 Stamford High School, Stamford, Connecticut, Dedication page.

Missing, National Memorial Cemetery of the Pacific, Honolulu, Hawaii. He was survived by his Father, Mr. George Whitefield Orr, 1829 Arcadia Avenue, San Gabriel, California.

Orzech, Stanislaus Joseph   Seaman, Second Class, Serial No: 207 29 61, US Navy. Stanislaus was born in about 1921 in Meriden, Connecticut. He enlisted in the US Navy October 15, 1940 in New Haven, Connecticut and completed his basic training at the Naval Training Station in Newport, Rhode Island. He reported for duty on the USS Arizona December 10, 1940. Stanislaus was killed in action on December 7, 1941 at Pearl Harbor, Hawaii. He was awarded the American Defense Service Medal, World War II Victory Medal and Purple Heart Medal posthumously. Stanislaus remains on duty on the USS Arizona. He is commemorated on the USS Arizona Memorial and the Memorial Tablets of the Missing, National Memorial Cemetery of the Pacific, Honolulu, Hawaii. Stanislaus was survived by his Father, Mr. Ludwick Orzech, 256 Pratt Street, Meriden, Connecticut.[581]

Osborne, Mervin Eugene   Fireman, First Class, Serial No: 279 54 15, US Navy. Mervin was born in about 1922 to Alexander B. and Lula (Sewell) Osborne. He enlisted in the US Navy February 1, 1938 in Cincinnati, Ohio and reported for duty on the USS Arizona June 4, 1938. Mervin was killed in action on December 7, 1941 at Pearl Harbor, Hawaii. He was awarded the American Defense Service Medal, World War II Victory Medal and Purple Heart Medal posthumously. Mervin remains on duty on the USS Arizona. He is commemorated on the USS Arizona Memorial and the Memorial Tablets of the Missing, National Memorial Cemetery of the Pacific, Honolulu, Hawaii. Mervin was survived by his Father, Mr. Alexander Osborne, Keck, Kentucky.

Osborne, William Daniel, Jr.   Seaman, First Class, Serial No. 236 69 58, US Navy. William was born April 11, 1922 to William Daniel and Myrtle Veronica (Webb) Osborne. He enlisted in the US Navy October 15, 1940 in Albany, New York and completed his basic training at the Naval Training Station, Newport, Rhode Island. He reported for duty on the USS Arizona December 10, 1940. William was serving on the USS Arizona on December 7, 1941 when the Japanese attacked Pearl Harbor. After the attack, William was transferred to the USS Zane (DMS-14) for duty. William died March 22, 1982 in Syracuse, New York.

---

[581] Stanislaus Joseph Orzech, Photo and information from "Relatives Remember Meriden's Only Pearl Harbor Casualty" by Laurie Rich Salerno in the Meriden Patch, Meriden, Connecticut, December 7, 2010.

Osmond, Robert Hugh Fire Controlman, Third Class, Serial No. 356 21 48, US Navy. Robert was born September 11, 1921 in Texas, the son of Charles Hugh and Bessie Mae (McCormick) Osmond. He enlisted in the US Navy December 6, 1939 in Dallas, Texas and completed his basic training at the Naval Training Station in San Diego, California. He reported for duty on the USS Arizona February 24, 1940. He was serving on the USS Arizona on December 7, 1941 when the Japanese attacked Pearl Harbor. He went on to serve on the USS Argonne (AG-31) reporting on board August 5, 1941. On May 2, 1942 he was transferred from the USS Medusa to the USS California (BB-44). Robert died March 7, 1975 in Los Angeles, California.

Osterberg, Vernon Magnus Ensign, Serial No. 0-79951, US Navy Reserve. Vernon was born on August 1, 1914 in Kitsap, Washington, the only son of Gustave M. Osterberg and Christina W. (Magnus) Osterberg. He was commissioned August 12, 1928 in the US Navy and was serving as Watch and Division Officer on the USS Arizona where he was serving on December 7, 1941 when the Japanese attacked Pearl Harbor. His battle station was Starboard AA Con. Station. Vernon died on September 8, 1973 in Oregon and is buried in Section L, Site 3329, Willamette National Cemetery, Portland, Oregon.[582]

Ostrander, Leland Grimstead Pharmacist's Mate, Third Class, Serial No: 393 18 73, US Navy. Leland was born September 26, 1917 in Grant County, Minnesota, the son of Dr. Arley John Ostrander and Mable Louise (Grimstead) Ostrander. He enlisted in the US Navy in October of 1935 and reported for duty on the USS Arizona January 9, 1941. Leland was killed in action on December 7, 1941 at Pearl Harbor, Hawaii. He was awarded the American Defense Service Medal, World War II Victory Medal and Purple Heart Medal posthumously. Leland remains on duty on the USS Arizona. He is commemorated on the USS Arizona Memorial and the Memorial Tablets of the Missing, National Memorial Cemetery of the Pacific, Honolulu, Hawaii. Leland was survived by his Mother, Mrs. Mable Louise Ostrander, P.O. Box 74, Kensington, Minnesota.

Ott, Peter Dean Seaman, First Class, Serial No: 283 39 05, US Navy. Peter was born July 23, 1922 in Summit County, Ohio, the son of Harry Eden Ott and Hannah F. (Troutman) Ott. He enlisted in the US Navy September 9, 1940 in Cleveland, Ohio and completed his basic training at the Naval Training Station in Norfolk, Virginia. He reported for duty on the USS Arizona December 4, 1940. Peter was killed in action on December 7, 1941 at Pearl Harbor, Hawaii. He was awarded the American Defense Service Medal, World War II Victory Medal and Purple Heart Medal posthumously. Peter remains on duty on the USS Arizona. He is commemorated on the USS Arizona Memorial and the Memorial Tablets of the Missing, National Memorial Cemetery of the Pacific, Honolulu, Hawaii.

---

[582] Vernon Magnus Osterberg, Photo from the "Rare Books on U.S. Navy Given to ROTC Library" Seattle Daily Times, Seattle, Washington, Monday, March 2, 1936, Second Main News Section.

Peter was survived by his Father, Mr. Harry Eden Ott, Box 97, Lakemore, Ohio.[583]

Otterman, Clarence "Chuck" Wayne Gunner's Mate, Second Class, Serial No. 321 35 34, US Navy. Clarence was born October 17, 1919 in Carroll, Iowa, the son of Clarence Otterman and Lois (Ross) Otterman. He enlisted in the US Navy October 4, 1939 in Des Moines, Iowa and completed his training at the Naval Training Station, Great Lakes, Illinois. He reported for duty on the USS Arizona December 31, 1939. He was serving on the USS Arizona on December 7, 1941 when the Japanese attacked Pearl Harbor. His Official Statement:

"At about 7:30 or 15 to eight, I had just gone out on the quarter deck to my cleaning station on No. II catapult. As I was about to start cleaning, I heard some planes and stepped from under the awning and looked up; about that time I heard an explosion over on the air field and several machine gun reports. Then a plane came over rather close and I could see the red dots on the wings and told the boys on the catapult to seek shelter in turret four. By this time the air raid signal had gone. Just as we were going in the turret we saw a bomb hit just forward of the ARIZONA into the water. When I got into the turret I called down to the men below that it's the real thing and general quarters just went. Every one came to their general quarters stations and preparations had began to fire main battery; just then there was a terrific explosion and the main lighting system went out but auxiliary lights were still on. Then came another which hit the corner of turret four and the lights were completely out. We remained in the turret for awhile till the gas fumes were so bad we started out of the turret, and under the overhang of the turret. We were under there for a few minutes and Earl Pecotte went back in with a flash light and helped a few men that were left in the turret, on to the outside. We could see men lying around on deck and helped them under the overhang of the turret. Then Lt. Comdr. Fuqua who was on the quarter deck gave the word to abandon ship. Pacitti, Peil and more of us got down a life raft, but was not benefit to us. Then Bruns, Y2c and I got a motor boat to the beach. There was a motor launch tied up to the pier which Bruns and I jumped into and brought it back to the ship and helped pick up men swimming in the water and on the key, then came to the ship and got Mr. Fuqua and Ensign Fields and Ensign Miller and a wounded sailor on the key and returned to the beach with them and carried the injured to trucks to take them to the hospital."[584]

After the attack, Clarence was transferred to the USS Whitney for duty. After the war, Chuck finished out his enlistment time and got out of the Navy. He was a civilian for two years then decided to re-enlist. He wanted to go back into the Navy, but could not get his Chief Gunner's Mate rank because the need was not there. The Army offered him a good deal, so he joined the Army where he served until he retired as a Stg. Major after a total of 20 years in the service. He settled in East Texas where his wife was from and was hired as a policeman with the Center, Texas Police Department where he later held the position of Chief of Police. Clarence died November 17, 2003 in Center, Texas and is buried at the Clever Creek Cemetery, Center, Texas.

---

[583] Peter Dean Ott, photo from the Akron Beacon Journal, Akron, Ohio, December 22, 1941, page 27.
[584] Confidential Statement of C. W. Otterman, GM2c, U.S. Navy Concerning Action Against Enemy on December 7, 1941.

Owen, Fredrick Halden Seaman, Second Class, Serial No: 356 56 59, US Navy. Frederick was born March 11, 1921 in Konawa, Oklahoma, the son of Leonidas Leander Owen and Winnie Davis (Saunders) Owen. He enlisted in the US Navy April 19, 1941 in Dallas, Texas and completed his basic training at the Naval Training Station in San Diego, California. Fredrick reported for duty on the USS Arizona July 13, 1941. He was killed in action on December 7, 1941 at Pearl Harbor, Hawaii. Fredrick was awarded the American Defense Service Medal, World War II Victory Medal and Purple Heart Medal posthumously. He remains on duty on the USS Arizona. Fredrick is commemorated on the USS Arizona Memorial and the Memorial Tablets of the Missing, National Memorial Cemetery of the Pacific, Honolulu, Hawaii and the Collinsville Cemetery, Collinsville, Texas. He was survived by his Father, Mr. Lonnie L. Owen, Box 94, Collinsville, Texas.[585]

Owen, Paul Ralph Seaman, First Class, Serial No. 382 24 20, US Navy. Paul was born January 4, 1921 in Tennessee. He enlisted in the US Navy August 13, 1940 at Los Angeles, California and completed his training at the Naval Training Station, San Diego, California. He reported for duty on the USS Arizona October 14, 1940. He was serving on the USS Arizona on December 7, 1941 when the Japanese attacked Pearl Harbor. After the attack, Paul was transferred to the USS Pelias (AS-14) for duty. He died January 23, 1978 in Stanislaus, California.

Owens, Richard Allen Storekeeper, Second Class, Serial No: 371 98 29, US Navy. Richard was born March 3, 1917, the son of Roy Earl Owens and Emma Mae (Jonas) Owens. He enlisted in the US Navy June 13, 1936 in Denver, Colorado and completed his basic training at the Naval Training Station in San Diego, California. Richard reported for duty on the USS Arizona October 13, 1939. He was killed in action on December 7, 1941 at Pearl Harbor, Hawaii. Richard was awarded the American Defense Service Medal, World War II Victory Medal and Purple Heart Medal posthumously. He remains on duty on the USS Arizona. Richard is commemorated on the USS Arizona Memorial and the Memorial Tablets of the Missing, National Memorial Cemetery of the Pacific, Honolulu, Hawaii. He was survived by his Parents, Mr. and Mrs. Roy Earl Owens, Holyoke, Colorado, four sisters and one brother. The Holyoke Colorado VFW #6482 was named in honor of Zeiler-Owens-Lindsay, the three youths who lost their lives from Holyoke.

Owsley, Thomas Lea Ship's Cook, Second Class, Serial No: 368 42 37, US Navy. Thomas was born June 23, 1919 in Hageman, Idaho to Nathaniel Stine and Elizabeth Ann (Gourley) Owsley. He enlisted in the US Navy November 14, 1938 in Salt Lake City, Utah and completed his basic training at the Naval Training Station in San Diego, California. He reported for duty on the USS Arizona March 11, 1939. Thomas was killed in action on December 7, 1941 at Pearl Harbor, Hawaii. He was awarded the American Defense Service Medal, World War II Victory Medal and Purple Heart Medal posthumously. Thomas remains on duty on the USS Arizona. He is commemorated on the USS Arizona Memorial and the Memorial Tablets of the Missing, National Memorial Cemetery of the Pacific, Honolulu, Hawaii. Thomas was survived by his Mother, Mrs. Lizzle Owsley Ellis, Hagerman, Idaho.

---

[585] Fredrick Halden Owen, Photo provided by family member, Kathy Belcher.

Pablo, Patrocinio Officer's Steward, First Class, Serial No. 497 52 90, US Navy. Patrocinio was born July 21, 1899 in Cabiao, Philippine Islands. He immigrated to the United States from Manila, Philippine Islands arriving on the US Army Transport Sheridan on May 21, 1919. He enlisted in the US Navy in 1931 serving on the USS Medusa. Patrocino served on the USS Arizona from April 29, 1933 until December 7, 1941 when the Japanese attacked Pearl Harbor. After the attack, Patrocinio was transferred to the Submarine Base at Pearl Harbor for duty.

Pace, Amos Paul Boatswain's Mate, First Class, Serial No: 274 22 50, US Navy. Amos was born January 14, 1916 in Simsboro, Louisiana, the son of Amos Gideon Pace and Effie C. (Formby) Pace. Amos enlisted in the US Navy September 10, 1935 in New Orleans, Louisiana and reported for duty on the USS Arizona February 24, 1936. He was killed in action on December 7, 1941 at Pearl Harbor, Hawaii. Amos was awarded the American Defense Service Medal, World War II Victory Medal and Purple Heart Medal posthumously. He remains on duty on the USS Arizona. Amos is commemorated on the USS Arizona Memorial and the Memorial Tablets of the Missing, National Memorial Cemetery of the Pacific, Honolulu, Hawaii. He was survived by his Wife, Mrs. Connie Eldene Pace, 340-1/2 North Douglas Street, Los Angeles, California.[586]

Pacitti, Louis John Gunner's Mate, Third Class, Serial No. 337 16 50, US Navy. Louis was born January 17, 1919. He enlisted in the US Navy August 7, 1939 in St. Louis, Missouri and completed his training at the Naval Training Station, San Diego, California. He reported for duty on the USS Arizona October 20, 1939. Louis was serving on the USS Arizona on December 7, 1941 when the Japanese attacked Pearl Harbor. After the attack, Louis was transferred to the Navy Shipyard, Pearl Harbor, Hawaii. He served until September 5, 1945, having attained the rank of Chief Gunner's Mate. Louis died February 6, 1986 and is buried in Section A, Lot 7, Grave 1, Glades Cemetery, Cumberland Township, Pennsylvania.

Parker, William Whiteford Seaman, First Class, Serial No. 274 48 49, US Navy. William was born November 2, 1916 in Bannethburn, Georgia. He enlisted in the US Navy July 30, 1940 in New Orleans, Louisiana and completed his training at the Naval Training Station, San Diego, California. He reported for duty on the USS Arizona October 8, 1940. He was serving on the USS Arizona on December 7, 1941 when the Japanese attacked Pearl Harbor. His Official Statement:

"On December 7, 1941, at about 7:50 a.m. I was on the blister top of the U.S.S. ARIZONA when a squadron of Japanese dive bombers began to bomb the airdrome on Ford Island. I stood there a few minutes and watched, thinking it was a bombing practice. Air raid sirens began to blow. I went up to the battery on double time and manned gun. After firing one

---

[586] Amos Paul Pace, Photo from 1934 Quachita Parish High School Yearbook, Monroe, Louisiana.

round, the gun captain ordered us to take cover when they began strafing us with machine gun fire. All took cover with the exception of three of us who kept on firing. We still didn't understand what was taking place. Then we saw the West Virginia torpedoed. Next, we saw a flight of horizontal bombers that began to drop their bombs. One bomb hit in front of the forward turret. We think it went down in the magazine, for the whole forward part of the ship blew up and caught fire. Myself, and one of the other men must have gotten blown over the side, on the galley deck. About that time a bomb went down the stack. That's all I remembered until I was on the quarter deck and aware that they were taking men from the key over to Ford Island in whaleboats. About that time all the ships were getting organized and were putting up a heavy barrage of fire. The Jap planes were not doing so good then for they were being driven off. I saw four or five planes shot down. There were two planes shot down by our machine gunners who were on security watch on the ARIZONA. None of the ammunition we fired exploded in the air; why I don't know, unless it was because of the fuse not being set. This is all I can actually say that I saw."[587]

William received the Navy Cross for his actions that day:

The Navy Cross is presented to William Whiteford Parker, Seaman First Class, U.S. Navy, for exceptional courage, presence of mind, and devotion to duty and disregard for his personal safety while serving on board the U.S.S. ARIZONA (BB-39) during the Japanese attack on the United States Pacific Fleet in Pearl Harbor, Territory of Hawaii, 7 December 1941. Despite orders from his gun captain to take cover, Seaman First Class Parker remained at his station on antiaircraft gun No. 1 with two other members of his gun crew until he was blown overboard by an explosion. The conduct of Seaman First Class Parker throughout this action reflects great credit upon himself, and was in keeping with the highest traditions of the United States Naval Service.

After the attack, William was transferred to the USS Lexington (Sunk May 7, 1942 during the Battle of the Coral Sea). He passed away February 21, 1989 in Mojave, California.

Parkes, Harry Edward Boatswain's Mate, First Class, Serial No: 375 50 09, US Navy. Harry was born September 27, 1911. He enlisted in the US Navy December 9, 1938 in San Diego, California and completed his basic training at the Naval Training Station in San Diego, California. He reported for duty on the USS Arizona December 14, 1938. Harry was killed in action on December 7, 1941 at Pearl Harbor, Hawaii. He was awarded the American Defense Service Medal, World War II Victory Medal and Purple Heart Medal posthumously. Harry remains on duty on the USS Arizona. He is commemorated on the USS Arizona Memorial and the Memorial Tablets of the Missing, National Memorial Cemetery of the Pacific, Honolulu, Hawaii. Harry was survived by his Wife, Mrs. Lillian Rose Parkes, 585 Turk Street, San Francisco, California.

Paroli, Peter John Baker, Third Class, Serial No: 376 09 44, US Navy. Peter was born in about 1915 in California, the son of Pietro Paroli and Jaira (Martinelli) Paroli. His father died in 1923 and his Mother died in 1928 in Coloma, California. He enlisted in the US Navy August 6, 1940 in San Francisco, California and completed his basic training at the Naval Training Station in San Diego, California. He reported for duty on the USS Arizona October 14, 1940. Peter was killed in action on December 7, 1941 at Pearl Harbor, Hawaii. He was awarded the American Defense Service Medal, World War II Victory Medal and Purple Heart Medal posthumously. Peter remains on duty on the USS Arizona. He is commemorated on the USS Arizona Memorial and the Memorial Tablets of the Missing, National Memorial Cemetery of the

---

[587] Confidential Statement of William W. Parker, S1c, USN, December 31, 1941, Pearl Harbor, T. H.

Pacific, Honolulu, Hawaii. Peter was survived by his Brother, Mr. Albert Andrew Paroli, 1861 23rd Avenue, San Francisco, California.

Patterson, Harold Lemuel   Seaman, First Class, Serial No: 356 48 36, US Navy. Harold was born April 9, 1922 in Caddo County, Oklahoma, the fourth of seven children born to John W. Patterson and Zenia N. (Clemmons) Patterson. *The family moved to Ridgeway, Texas when Harold was six. Caught up in the height of the Great Depression, his father became physically unable to work. In 1938, Harold quit high school and joined the Civilian Conservation Corp as a way to help support his family, serving in different campsites in Arizona. He returned home to Ridgeway in September, 1940.* With no employment available, Harold enlisted in the US Navy January 18, 1941 in Dallas, Texas and completed his basic training at the Naval Training Station in San Diego, California. He reported for duty on the USS Arizona April 26, 1941 and was assigned to the 2nd Division, becoming one of the powder men for Turret No. 2. *On the morning of December 7th, Harold was serving as mess cook for his division when General Quarters was sounded.* He was killed in action on December 7, 1941 at Pearl Harbor. Harold was awarded the Air Medal with Gold Star, American Defense Service Medal, World War II Victory Medal and Purple Heart Medal posthumously. He remains on duty on the USS Arizona. Harold is commemorated on the USS Arizona Memorial and the Memorial Tablets of the Missing, National Memorial Cemetery of the Pacific, Honolulu, Hawaii. He was survived by his Parents, Mr. and Mrs. John W. Patterson, P. O. Box 37, Ridgeway, Texas and siblings; Alice Kennedy, Bonny Lockett, Ruby Briggs, Bob Patterson, Dorothy Head and Anjunell Bloss.[588]

Patterson, Richard, Jr.   Shipfitter, Third Class, Serial No: 207 29 54, US Navy. Richard was born February 15, 1920 in Newburyport, Massachusetts, the son of Richard Patterson and Pauline C. Patterson. Richard graduated from Berlin High School in Berlin, Connecticut. While there he was the captain of the football team and the intramural basketball and baseball teams during his senior year. He also was on the student council. He enlisted in the US Navy October 14, 1940 in New Haven, Connecticut and completed his basic training at the Naval Training Station in Newport, Rhode Island. Richard reported for duty on the USS Arizona December 10, 1940. He was killed in action on December 7, 1941 at Pearl Harbor, Hawaii. Richard was awarded the American Defense Service Medal, World War II Victory Medal and Purple Heart Medal posthumously. He remains on duty on the USS Arizona. Richard is commemorated on the USS Arizona Memorial and the Memorial Tablets of the Missing, National Memorial Cemetery of the Pacific, Honolulu, Hawaii. He was survived by his Father, Mr. Richard Patterson, Sr., Lower Lane, Berlin, Connecticut.[589]

Paulmand, Hilery   Officer's Steward, Serial No: 497 98 16, US Navy. Hilery re-enlisted in the US Navy on February 12, 1936 in Bremerton, Washington. He and reported for duty on the USS Arizona on March 7, 1930 where he served until he was killed in action on

---

[588] Harold Lemuel Patterson, Photo and information provided by family member, David Kennedy.
[589] Richard Patterson, Jr., Photo from Remembering Richard Patterson, The Newbury Port News, Newburyport, MA, December 7, 2011, by Dyke Hendrickson, Staff Writer and the Berlin High School Athletic Hall of Fame.

December 7, 1941 at Pearl Harbor, Hawaii. Hilery was awarded the American Defense Service Medal, World War II Victory Medal and Purple Heart Medal posthumously. He remains on duty on the USS Arizona. Hilery is commemorated on the USS Arizona Memorial and the Memorial Tablets of the Missing, National Memorial Cemetery of the Pacific, Honolulu, Hawaii. He was survived by his Mother, Mrs. Rufina Eladio Baguio, Mount Province, Philippine Islands.

Pavini, Bruno   Seaman, First Class, Serial No: 376 09 43, US Navy. Bruno was born July 23, 1922 in San Diego, California, the son of Anthony J. Pavini and Gina Pavini. He enlisted in the US Navy August 6, 1940 in San Francisco, California and completed his basic training at the Naval Training Station in San Diego, California. Bruno reported for duty on the USS Arizona October 14, 1940. He was killed in action on December 7, 1941 at Pearl Harbor, Hawaii. Bruno was awarded the Purple Heart Medal, American Campaign Medal and the Asiatic Pacific Campaign Medal posthumously. He remains on duty on the USS Arizona. Bruno is commemorated on the USS Arizona Memorial and the Memorial Tablets of the Missing, National Memorial Cemetery of the Pacific, Honolulu, Hawaii and the Golden Gate National Cemetery, San Bruno, California. He was survived by his Mother, Mrs. Gina Pavini, 647 Lisbon Street, San Francisco, California.

Pawlowski, Raymond Paul   Seaman, First Class, Serial No: 234 28 38, US Navy. Raymond was born August 29, 1922 in Buffalo, New York, the son of Robert Pawlowski and Agnes M. (Wroblewska) Pawlowski. He left Kensington High School to enlist in the US Navy October 15, 1940 in Buffalo, New York and completed his basic training at the Naval Training Station in Newport, Rhode Island. Raymond reported for duty on the USS Arizona December 10, 1940. He was killed in action on December 7, 1941 at Pearl Harbor, Hawaii. Raymond was awarded the American Defense Service Medal, World War II Victory Medal and Purple Heart Medal posthumously. He remains on duty on the USS Arizona. Raymond is commemorated on the USS Arizona Memorial and the Memorial Tablets of the Missing, National Memorial Cemetery of the Pacific, Honolulu, Hawaii. He was survived by his Father, Mr. Robert Pawlowski, 73 Peace Street, Buffalo, New York.[590]

Pearce, Alonzo, Jr.   Seaman, First Class, Serial No: 360 19 62, US Navy. Alonzo was born November 5, 1920 in Cushing, Oklahoma the son of Alonzo Pearce and Gertrude Maxine (Allen) Pearce. *He attended Muskogee High School and Oklahoma A & M College, Stillwater, Oklahoma. While in school, Alonzo was a member of both his high school and college bands.* He enlisted in the US Navy August 2, 1940 in Houston, Texas and completed his basic training at the Naval Training Station in San Diego, California. Alonzo reported for duty on board the USS Arizona on October 8, 1940. He was killed in action on December 7, 1941 at Pearl Harbor, Hawaii. Alonzo was awarded the American Defense Service Medal, World War II Victory Medal and Purple Heart Medal posthumously. He

---

[590] Raymond Paul Pawlowski, Photo from the Kensington High School Yearbook, Buffalo, New York, 1945, Page 11.

remains on duty on the USS Arizona. Alonzo is commemorated on the USS Arizona Memorial and the Memorial Tablets of the Missing, National Memorial Cemetery of the Pacific, Honolulu, Hawaii. He was survived by his Father, Mr. Alonzo Pearce, Sr., 315 West Henriettia, Kingsville, Texas.[591]

Pearson, Norman Cecil Seaman, Second Class, Serial No: 382 31 80, US Navy. Norman was born in about 1921 in New York, the son of Lawrence V. Pearson and Nellie Pearson. He enlisted in the US Navy November 26, 1940 and completed his basic training at the Naval Training Station in San Diego, California. Norman reported for duty on the USS Arizona June 25, 1941. He was killed in action on December 7, 1941 at Pearl Harbor, Hawaii. Norman was awarded the American Defense Service Medal, World War II Victory Medal and Purple Heart Medal posthumously. He remains on duty on the USS Arizona. Norman is commemorated on the USS Arizona Memorial and the Memorial Tablets of the Missing, National Memorial Cemetery of the Pacific, Honolulu, Hawaii. He was survived by his Mother, Mrs. Nellie M. Pearson, Route 1, Box 145, Riverside, California.[592]

Pearson, Robert "Bob" Stanley Fireman, First Class, Serial No: 368 53 36, US Navy. Robert was born October 30-31st, 1922 at home in Barber, Montana to Ernest Erie and Amelia Pearson. *The family moved to the Jocko Valley in a Model T Ford along with railroad cars loaded with cattle, machinery and household furnishings. He started school in Arlee, Montana when he was four years old. As a child, he was mischievous. He always had a twinkle in his eye. Bob played basketball and was on the high school debate team. He graduated from Arlee High School in 1938 at the age of sixteen.* Bob enlisted in the US Navy on November 6, 1940 in Salt Lake City, Utah and completed his basic training at the Naval Training Station in San Diego, California. He reported for duty on the USS Arizona January 11, 1941. Robert was killed in action on December 7, 1941 at Pearl Harbor, Hawaii. He was awarded the American Defense Service Medal, World War II Victory Medal and Purple Heart Medal posthumously. Robert remains on duty on the USS Arizona. He is commemorated on the USS Arizona Memorial and the Memorial Tablets of the Missing, National Memorial Cemetery of the Pacific, Honolulu, Hawaii and the Missoula Cemetery, Missoula, Montana. Robert was survived by his Parents, Mr. and Mrs. Ernest Erie Pearson, Arlee, Montana; brother, Dan; and sisters, Virginia, June and Mary.[593]

---

[591] Alonzo Pearce, Jr., Photo and information provided by his brother, Robert Pearce and niece, Valerie Pearce.
[592] Norman Cecil Pearson, Photo from California Honor States.
[593] Robert "Bob" Stanley Pearson, Information and photo provided by, Alvaretta Morin, Arlee, Montana Historical Society with permission from his sister.

Peavey, William "Billy" Howard Quartermaster, Second Class, Serial No: 382 07 74, US Navy. William was born October 10, 1919 in Centerville, Iowa, the son of Harry Bertrum Peavey and Mary Edna (Holland) Peavey. *He was a talented artist and could draw anything. Walt Disney offered him a job drawing their cartoon figures, but he decided to go into the US Navy instead.* Billy enlisted in the Navy October 5, 1938 in Los Angeles, California and completed his basic training at the Naval Training Station in San Diego, California. William reported for duty on the USS Arizona January 2, 1939. He was killed in action on December 7, 1941 at Pearl Harbor, Hawaii. William was awarded the American Defense Service Medal, World War II Victory Medal and Purple Heart Medal posthumously. He remains on duty on the USS Arizona. William is commemorated on the USS Arizona Memorial and the Memorial Tablets of the Missing, National Memorial Cemetery of the Pacific, Honolulu, Hawaii. He was survived by his Father, Mr. Harry Bertrum Peavey, 718 Iowa Street, Iowa Falls, Iowa, brother, Robert of Los Angeles, California and a sister, Bonnie Jeanne of Alhambra, California. In June 1955 the Hyman-Peavey American Legion Post No. 188 in Iowa Falls, Iowa was named in honor of the first two Iowa Falls men killed in the First and Second World Wars; W. Paul Hyman, who died in France in 1918, and William Howard Peavey, who died aboard the USS Arizona in Pearl Harbor December 7, 1941.[594]

Peckham, Howard William Fireman, Second Class, Serial No: 337 18 67, US Navy. Howard was born March 1,1920, the son of Leonard G. Peckham and Magdelona B. (Hermie) Peckham. He enlisted in the US Navy September 11, 1939 in St. Louis, Missouri and completed his basic training at the Naval Training Station in San Diego, California. Howard reported for duty on the USS Arizona November 10, 1939. He was killed in action on December 7, 1941 at Pearl Harbor, Hawaii. Howard was awarded the American Defense Service Medal, World War II Victory Medal and Purple Heart Medal posthumously. He remains on duty on the USS Arizona. Howard is commemorated on the USS Arizona Memorial and the Memorial Tablets of the Missing, National Memorial Cemetery of the Pacific, Honolulu, Hawaii. He was survived by his Father, Mr. Leonard G. Peckham, 6218 Julian Avenue, Wellston, Missouri.[595]

Pecotte, Earl Henry Gunner's Mate, Second Class, Serial No. 299 78 03, US Navy. Earl was born August 28, 1915. He enlisted in the US Navy July 30, 1935 in Chicago, Illinois and reported for duty on the USS Arizona November 23, 1935. He was serving on the USS Arizona on December 7, 1941 when the Japanese attacked Pearl Harbor. His official statement:

On Sunday Morning, December 7, 1941, I was on the second deck on "Security Watch: when the air raid alarm sounded. I ordered all hands to seek shelter on the third deck. General Quarters was sounded immediately after the air raid. I started for my battle station, in the Pointer Group of Turret Four, and passed the word as I went, "All hands man their stations on the double – this is a real attack". While I reached the Radio compartment I heard a violent explosion in the vicinity of the Officer's quarters which knocked the men in the radio compartment off their feet. On reaching the powder handling room of Turret Four, another explosion seemed to come from the third deck with water entering the lower room of the turret immediately after the explosion.

---

[594] William Howard Peavey, Photo and information from family member, Susan Peavey Cole.
[595] Howard William Peckham, Photo from Missouri Honor States.

As I climbed up inside of the turret I looked to see if the power was on in the electric deck, seeing it was not, I went on to my battle station and asked if Mr. Schafer was present, and he was not, so George K. Campbell, Chief turret captain, took charge of the men.

In a very short time the turret was starting to fill with gas that may have come from the batteries in the electric deck, the only lights we had were a flash light which come one handed me from the tool box. As the gas became mixed with smoke it was difficult to breathe and I asked Campbell for permission to have all men come up in the chambers of the turret, he ordered every one up and sent me outside to see if I could call for power on the turret and to see if there was gas on topside.

When I stepped out, the first person I noticed was Lieutenant Commander S. G. Fuqua, in charge of the topside. He was exposing himself to machine gun fire while directing the removal of the wounded. A motor launch from the U.S.S. Solace was alongside and he was directing the removal of some thirty or forty wounded men to the Solace boat. Through his presence of mind and quick thinking, all wounded men in sight, about the decks, were safely placed in the boat and it shoved off. When the Solace boat left there were only a few or us left on the ship and Mr. Fuqua was still looking for more wounded men when I asked him if the ship was being abandoned. He answered, "Yes". That is when I reported to Campbell in the turret and he ordered all men to the topside. I went to the gun pits and Peil, Boatswain's mate second class, and I made a search for wounded men in the upper part of the turret. We left after all hands were removed, and closed the hatch from the shell deck. When we left, water was knee deep in the gun pits. On the way out, we did not see anyone left in the turret.

As I reached the topside, Mr. Fuqua was the only person I noticed. I asked where everyone was and he answered, "Over the side and on to Ford Island and follow them". Just before I jumped in the water I asked him if he was going to swim for it, and he said he was not going to leave until the Japs left. As I jumped I caught on the life lines and some one posted me into the water. I am sure that it was Mr. Fuqua who helped me over the side. The last thing I saw was Mr. Fuqua alone on the quarterdeck and the ship was ablaze from Turret three forward. [596]

He was wounded in action and his wife, Mrs. Frances Ruth Pecotte of Stephenson, Michigan was notified. Earl passed away October 24, 2000 in Pocahontas, Arkansas. His ashes were interred on the USS Arizona June 8, 2001.

Peery, Max Valdyne Seaman, Second Class, Serial No: 376 33 59, US Navy. Max was born December 30, 1923 near Nelson, Nebraska, the son of Chancey Stephan Peery and Verna Lucille (Lee) Peery. *He was the second born of six children. Max was a diligent young man, when told to weed the garden he would start down the row and never lift his head until he reached the end of the row. He walked into town early to chop wood before going to school to help with expenses.* Max enlisted in the US Navy June 3, 1941 in San Francisco, California and completed his basic training at the Naval Training Station in San Diego, California. He reported for duty on the USS Arizona August 13, 1941. Max was killed in action on December 7, 1941 at Pearl Harbor, Hawaii 23 days short of his 18th birthday. He was awarded the American Defense Service Medal, World War II Victory Medal and Purple Heart Medal posthumously. Max remains on duty on the USS Arizona. He is commemorated on the USS Arizona Memorial and the Memorial Tablets of the

---

[596] Confidential Statement of Earl H. Pecotte, Gunner's Mate Second Class, U.S. Navy on January 5, 1942.

Missing, National Memorial Cemetery of the Pacific, Honolulu, Hawaii. Max was survived by his Mother, Mrs. Verna L. Peery, Nelson, Nebraska.[597]

Peil, William John Boatswain's Mate, Second Class, Serial No. 328 61 09, US Navy. William was born September 23, 1921 in Minnesota to William Jacob and Alberta Rae (Kitto) Peil. He enlisted in the US Navy October 3, 1939 in Minneapolis, Minnesota and completed his training at the Naval Training Station, Great Lakes, Illinois. He reported for duty on the USS Arizona December 31, 1939. William was serving on the USS Arizona on December 7, 1941 when the Japanese attacked Pearl Harbor. His official statement:

On the morning of December 7, 1941, I was prepared for Shore Patrol and was to leave the ship at 0800 to report to the Senior Patrol Officer.

At about 0755 a seaman from the Third Division spread the word of a Japanese air raid. The first thing I saw was smoke pouring out of a hangar on Ford Island. Then a Jap dive bomber, flying low over the houses on the island, strafed the upper decks of the Arizona. I didn't notice any casualties at that time.

General Quarters was sounded and all hands went to their battle stations. Those who couldn't reach their respective stations, went below the armored deck.

When "general quarters" was sounded, I proceeded first to my part of the ship (Fourth Division). There I helped close battle ports under the direction of Haerling, Boatswain's mate first class. To the best of my knowledge, all the air and battle ports in the fourth division part of the ship were dogged down tight. Then all the men in my division proceeded to Turret Four, via the A. A. ammunition passageway and lower handling rooms.

My battle station is in the officers' booth of Turret Four. My duty was that of turret talker. Neither of the turret officers were there. G. K. Campbell, Chief Turret Captain was in the gun chambers. The other men with me were the two range finder operators.

Shortly after I had reached my battle station, all the lights went out in the turret. The auxiliary lighting system refused to work. All telephone communications (battle phones, ship's service phones, and sound powered phones) were dead.

We were in the turret about twenty minutes. During that time all men were brought to the upper decks of turrets three and four. Water was rising from the lower room and shell deck into the gun pits. Gas of some nature was in the turret, probably formed by the action of salt water on the batteries.

One of the men, Earl H. Pecotte, Gunner's mate second class, had procured a flash light from some place. This he used to get around and help men into the safer parts of the turret. He closed the hatch in the gun pits to check water and gas coming from below. Pecotte then got permission from Campbell to leave the turret to get gas masks or receive any orders from Lieutenant Commander S. G. Fuqua, who was on deck at the time. He gave instruction to Pecotte for all men to leave the turret and try to make Ford Island, which was the nearest land. Every body left the turret in an orderly manner. Some grasped life-rings and life-rafts to use while going through the oil.

I was one of the last men out. Pecotte then went back into the turret to see that no one was trapped in the turret.

When I stepped out on deck, everyone was abandoning ship. I took off all my clothes except underwear in case I had to swim ashore. I went down the port side of the quarterdeck and crossed to the starboard side. The ship was on fire from frame 88 forward. Mutilated and burned bodies were scattered about the deck. Mr. Fuqua was on the starboard side of the quarterdeck, directing the removal of wounded men into Solace motor launches. He was the most calm and collected man I had seen all day. Somebody near me asked him if he wasn't going to leave. He reply was, "Not until the Japs leave". During this time the survivors were strafed mercilessly by

---

[597] Max Valdyne Peery, Photo and information provided by his sister, Helen Peery Miller.

the Japs. Splinters could be seen flying about where machine gun bullets had hit the deck. Mr. Fuqua worked calmly throughout this entire attack.

The Admiral's barge was alongside so I climbed in with a number of other sailors. Some of the men were wounded. Others were burned so badly that all the outer layer of skin was loose, their hair gone, and their eyes burned closed. We proceeded to Ford Island and unloaded. I helped carry two men to a truck and thence to the dispensary. I rode with the truck all day, picking up wounded men and taking to the dispensary. I stayed on Ford Island until Wednesday, December 10, 1941, while I was transferred to the Receiving Station, Pearl Harbor, T. H., my present location.

During this entire onslaught, all hands were calm and collected. They worked smoothly as a unit. There was no sign of confusion or terror.[598]

William passed away March 6, 1988 in Norcross, Georgia. His ashes were interred on the USS Arizona November 22, 1988.

Peleschak, Michael Seaman, First Class, Serial No: 223 89 68, US Navy. Michael was born March 7, 1919 in Shenandoah, Pennsylvania the son of Andrew and Mary Peleschak. He enlisted in the US Navy October 15, 1940 in New York, New York and completed his basic training at the Naval Training Station in Newport, Rhode Island. He reported for duty on the USS Arizona December 10, 1940. Michael was killed in action on December 7, 1941 at Pearl Harbor, Hawaii. He was awarded the American Defense Service Medal, World War II Victory Medal and Purple Heart Medal posthumously. Michael remains on duty on the USS Arizona. He is commemorated on the USS Arizona Memorial and the Memorial Tablets of the Missing, National Memorial Cemetery of the Pacific, Honolulu, Hawaii. Michael was survived by his Father, Mr. Andrew Peleschak, 952 Hillside Boulevard, New Hyde Park, New York.

Peltier, John Arthur Electrician's Mate, Third Class, Serial No: 279 72 90, US Navy. John was born February 28, 1918 in Delphos, Ohio, the only child of Frank Guy Peltier and Margaret (Davis) Peltier. He graduated from Delphos High School and enlisted in the Navy September 9, 1940 in Cincinnati, Ohio. John completed his basic training at the Naval Training Station in Norfolk, Virginia. He reported for duty on the USS Arizona December 4, 1940. John was killed in action on December 7, 1941 at Pearl Harbor, Hawaii. *His parents were notified that he was missing on December 22, 1941, two days before Christmas.* He was awarded the American Defense Service Medal, World War II Victory Medal and Purple Heart Medal posthumously. John remains on duty on the USS Arizona. He is commemorated on the USS Arizona Memorial and the Memorial Tablets of the Missing, National Memorial Cemetery of the Pacific, Honolulu, Hawaii. John was survived by his Parents, Mr. and Mrs. Frank Guy Peltier, Delphos, Ohio.[599]

Penton, Howard Lee Seaman, First Class, Serial No: 272 40 13, US Navy. Howard was born April 30, 1914 in Rockford, Alabama, the son of Julius Lee Penton and Sarah Emily (Waites) Penton. He enlisted in the US Navy September 23, 1940 in Birmingham, Alabama and completed his basic training at the Naval Training Station in Norfolk, Virginia. Howard reported for duty on the USS Arizona December 4, 1940. He was killed in action on December 7, 1941 at

[598] Confidential Statement of William John Peil, Boatswain's Mate Second Class, U. S. Navy, Pearl Harbor, T. H., January 5, 1942.
[599] John Arthur Peltier, Photo from the Pearl Harbor A day that has lived in Infamy, The Lima News, Wednesday, December 7, 2005, Page D3.

Pearl Harbor, Hawaii. Howard was awarded the American Defense Service Medal, World War II Victory Medal and Purple Heart Medal posthumously. He remains on duty on the USS Arizona. Howard is commemorated on the USS Arizona Memorial and the Memorial Tablets of the Missing, National Memorial Cemetery of the Pacific, Honolulu, Hawaii. He was survived by his Parents, Mr. and Mrs. Julius Lee Penton, 3 brothers and 11 sisters, Route 3, Clanton, Alabama.

Perkins, George Ernest Fireman, First Class, Serial No: 201 54 95, US Navy. George was born October 23, 1916, the son of Ernest Perkins and Gladys M. Perkins. He enlisted in the US Navy February 5, 1936 in Boston, Massachusetts and reported for duty on the USS Arizona October 14, 1939. George was killed in action on December 7, 1941 at Pearl Harbor, Hawaii. He was awarded the American Defense Service Medal, World War II Victory Medal and Purple Heart Medal posthumously. George remains on duty on the USS Arizona. He is commemorated on the USS Arizona Memorial and the Memorial Tablets of the Missing, National Memorial Cemetery of the Pacific, Honolulu, Hawaii. George was survived by his Father, Mr. Ernest Perkins, 40 Riverfarm Road, Cranston, Providence, Rhode Island.

Perry, Seth Harold Seaman, Second Class, Serial No. 346 98 67, US Navy. Seth was born August 18, 1922 in England, Arkansas the son of John Thomas Perry and Vertie Van Dola Smith. He enlisted in the US Navy April 18, 1941 in Little Rock, Arkansas and completed his training at the Naval Training Station, San Diego, California. He reported for duty on the USS Arizona July 13, 1941. He was serving on the USS Arizona on December 7, 1941 when the Japanese attacked Pearl Harbor. Seth died December 29, 2001 in Tidioute, Pennsylvania and is buried in the Warren County Memorial Park, Starbrick, Pennsylvania.[600]

Peterson, Albert Hendrix, Jr. Fire Controlman, Third Class, Serial No: 223 89 69, US Navy. Albert was born in about 1922 in New York, the son of Albert Hendrix and Ethel Peterson. Albert enlisted in the US Navy October 15, 1940 New York, New York and completed his basic training at the Naval Training Station in Norfolk, Virginia. He reported for duty on the USS Arizona December 30, 1940. Albert was killed in action on December 7, 1941 at Pearl Harbor, Hawaii. He was awarded the American Defense Service Medal, World War II Victory Medal and Purple Heart Medal posthumously. Albert remains on duty on the USS Arizona. He is commemorated on the USS Arizona Memorial and the Memorial Tablets of the Missing, National Memorial Cemetery of the Pacific, Honolulu, Hawaii. Albert was survived by his Father, Mr. Albert Hendrix Peterson, Sr., 109-06 210th Street, Bellaire, Jamaica, New York.[601]

---

[600] Seth Harold Perry, Photo provided by family member on Ancestry.com.
[601] Albert Hendrix Peterson, Jr., Photo from the 1939 Andrew Jackson High School Yearbook, Canbria Heights, New York.

Peterson, Elroy Vernon Fire Controlman, Second Class, Serial No: 328 39 09, US Navy. Elroy was born in 1918 in North Dakota, the son of Marcus C. Peterson and Julia A. Peterson. He enlisted in the US Navy July 12, 1935 in Minneapolis, Minnesota and reported for duty on the USS Arizona February 20, 1936. Elroy was killed in action on December 7, 1941 at Pearl Harbor, Hawaii. He was awarded the American Defense Service Medal, World War II Victory Medal and Purple Heart Medal posthumously. Elroy remains on duty on the USS Arizona. He is commemorated on the USS Arizona Memorial and the Memorial Tablets of the Missing, National Memorial Cemetery of the Pacific, Honolulu, Hawaii. Elroy was survived by his Wife, Mrs. Clara Edith (Stai) Peterson, 1012 South Palos Verdes Street, San Pedro, California and his son, Richard.[602]

Peterson, Hardy Wilbur Fire Controlman, Third Class, Serial No: 385 79 39, US Navy. Hardy was born in 1920 in Montana, the son of Fritz F. Peterson and Hildur Peterson. He enlisted in the US Navy November 14, 1938 in Seattle, Washington and completed his basic training at the Naval Training Station in San Diego, California. He reported for duty on the USS Arizona March 11, 1939. Hardy was killed in action on December 7, 1941 at Pearl Harbor, Hawaii. He was awarded the American Defense Service Medal, World War II Victory Medal and Purple Heart Medal posthumously. Hardy remains on duty on the USS Arizona. He is commemorated on the USS Arizona Memorial and the Memorial Tablets of the Missing, National Memorial Cemetery of the Pacific, Honolulu, Hawaii. Hardy was survived by his Father, Mr. Fritz Peterson, 4008 Letitia Street, Seattle, Washington.[603]

Peterson, Roscoe "Rocky" Earl Seaman, Second Class, Serial No: 376 14 72, US Navy. Roscoe was born in 1919 in Oregon, the son of Arthur Peterson and Gladys Fredrica (Richardson) Peterson. *He was a former Del Norte High School athlete who was a standout in both basketball and baseball. At the age of 14 when most youths were hoping to be good enough to play on a youth baseball team, Rocky became the starting outfielder for the Merchants. Rocky's baseball talents were such that between his junior and senior years in high school he signed a contract and started his professional baseball career. This made him ineligible to play for the Warriors during his senior year. Rocky was having a successful career in the Minor Leagues and was making big steps toward the Major Leagues. With the threat of war coming, Rocky joined the Navy.* He enlisted in the US Navy October 31, 1940 in San Francisco, California and completed his basic training at the Naval Training Station in San Diego, California. Roscoe reported for duty on the USS Arizona December 30, 1940. He was killed in action on December 7, 1941 at Pearl Harbor, Hawaii. Roscoe was awarded the American Defense Service Medal, World War II Victory Medal and Purple Heart Medal posthumously. He remains on duty on the USS Arizona. Roscoe is commemorated on the USS

---

[602] Elroy Vernon Peterson, Photo and information provided by his son, Rich Peterson.
[603] Hardy Wilbur Peterson, Photo from Franklin High School Yearbook, Seattle Washington, 1937, Page 32.

Arizona Memorial and the Memorial Tablets of the Missing, National Memorial Cemetery of the Pacific, Honolulu, Hawaii. He was survived by his Mother, Mrs. Gladys Fredrica Peterson, 742 2nd Street, Crescent City, California one sister and three brothers. Peterson Park in Crescent City, California was named in honor of Roscoe "Rocky" Peterson.[604]

Pettit, Charles Ross   Chief Radioman, Serial No: 290 69 49, US Navy. Charles was born July 8, 1902 in South Bend, Indiana, the son of James R. Pettit and Laura Gertrude (Keltner) Pettit. He enlisted in the US Navy July of 1919 in Indianapolis, Indiana and completed his basic training at the Naval Training Station in Great Lakes, Illinois. Charles reported for duty on the USS Arizona June 10, 1936. Charles was killed in action on December 7, 1941 at Pearl Harbor, Hawaii. He was awarded the American Defense Service Medal, World War II Victory Medal and Purple Heart Medal posthumously. Charles remains on duty on the USS Arizona. He is commemorated on the USS Arizona Memorial and the Memorial Tablets of the Missing, National Memorial Cemetery of the Pacific, Honolulu, Hawaii. Charles was survived by his Wife, Mrs. Evelyn Pettit, 623-B East 6th Street, Long Beach, California.

Petyak, John Joseph   Seaman, First Class, Serial No: 223 86 76, US Navy. John was born May 3, 1920 in Wilkes-Barre, Pennsylvania, the son of John Petyak and Anna (Djorda) Petyak. He enlisted in the US Navy October 1, 1940 in New York, New York and completed his basic training at the Naval Training Station in Newport, Rhode Island. John reported for duty on the USS Arizona December 10, 1940. He was killed in action on December 7, 1941 at Pearl Harbor, Hawaii. John was awarded the American Defense Service Medal, World War II Victory Medal and Purple Heart Medal posthumously. He remains on duty on the USS Arizona. John is commemorated on the USS Arizona Memorial and the Memorial Tablets of the Missing, National Memorial Cemetery of the Pacific, Honolulu, Hawaii. He was survived by his Father, Mr. John Petyak, 78 Anthracite Street, Wilkes-Barre, Pennsylvania.[605]

Phelps, George Edward   Seaman, First Class, Serial No: 238 69 45, US Navy. George was born May 26, 1922 in New York to Ross Brayton and Gertrude (Johnson) Phelps. His father passed away in 1940 in Watertown, New York. George enlisted in the US Navy October 15, 1940 in Albany, New York and completed his basic training at the Naval Training Station in Newport, Rhode Island. He reported for duty on the USS Arizona December 10, 1940. George was killed in action on December 7, 1941 at Pearl Harbor, Hawaii. He was awarded the American Defense Service Medal, World War II Victory Medal and Purple Heart Medal posthumously. George's remains were recovered and he was buried in Plot Q, Row 0, Grave 1017, National Memorial Cemetery of the Pacific, Honolulu, Hawaii. He is commemorated on the USS Arizona Memorial. George was survived by his Mother, Mrs. Gertrude J. Phelps, Henderson, New York.

Philbin, James Richard   Seaman, First Class, Serial No: 372 17 12, US Navy. James was born in 1916, the son of John J. Philbin and Geneveive Philbin. He enlisted in the US Navy on August 12, 1940 in Denver Colorado and completed his basic training at the Naval Training Station in San Diego, California. James reported for duty on the USS Arizona October 14, 1940.

---

[604] Roscoe "Rocky" Earl Peterson, Information from Warrior Memories: Remembering Rocky, lost at Pearl Harbor by Dick Trone, December 10, 2012, The Del Norte Triplicate, Crescent City California News, Sports & Weather, Crescent City, California.
[605] John Joseph Petyak, Photo from Pennsylvania Honor States.

He was killed in action on December 7, 1941 at Pearl Harbor, Hawaii. James was awarded the American Defense Service Medal, World War II Victory Medal and Purple Heart Medal posthumously. He remains on duty on the USS Arizona. James is commemorated on the USS Arizona Memorial and the Memorial Tablets of the Missing, National Memorial Cemetery of the Pacific, Honolulu, Hawaii. He was survived by his Mother, Mrs. Genevieve Philbin, 1205 East 7th Street, Pueblo, Colorado.

Phipps, Berwyn Robert Shipfitter, Second Class, Serial No. 299 79 94, US Navy. Berwyn was born July 21, 1916 in Peoria, Illinois the son of Robert William Phipps and Ina Estelle Stookey Phipps. He enlisted in the US Navy December 17, 1935 in Chicago, Illinois. Berwyn served on the USS Arizona from April 20, 1936 until December 7, 1941 when the Japanese attacked Pearl Harbor. He was on the tanker Neosho preparing to board the Arizona when the attack began. After the attack, Berwyn was transferred to the USS Neosho (AO-23) for duty. He survived the sinking of the Neosho and went on to serve on the USS Maddox (DD-622), surviving it's sinking on July 20, 1943. Berwyn died February 15, 1992 in Fairview, Illinois.

Phraner, George Dewey Seaman, Second Class, Serial No. 243 79 05, US Navy. George was born on October 5, 1922 in Philadelphia, Pennsylvania. He enlisted in the US Navy on October 16, 1940 in Philadelphia, Pennsylvania and completed his training at the Naval Training Station, Newport, Rhode Island. He reported for duty on the USS Arizona December 10, 1940. He was serving on the USS Arizona on December 7, 1941 when the Japanese attacked Pearl Harbor. George had just finished breakfast and drifted out of the compartment to get a little air. This was our normal routine on weekends as we had no work station to report to. It was fortunate for us that we were able to sleep in until 6:30 as many of us had been out the night before. Just as we left the mess area we heard this noise. We went outside to take a look because it's usually very quiet. When we arrived we could hear and see there were airplanes. I looked across the bow of the ship and could see large plumes of smoke coming up from Ford Island. At first, we didn't realize it was a bombing. It didn't mean anything to us until a large group of planes came near the ship and we could see for the first time the rising sun emblem on the plane wings. The bombing was becoming heavier all around us and we knew this was REALLY IT!

At first there was a rush of fear, the blood started to flow real fast. It was then that general quarters sounded over the speaker and everything became automatic. My battle station was on a forward 5 inch gun and it was standard practice to keep only a limited amount of ammunition at the guns. There was only one ready gun crew on each side and mine wasn't one of them. There we were, the Japanese dropping bombs over us and we had no ammo. All the training and practicing for a year and when the real thing came we had no ammunition where we needed it. As unfortunate as this was, that simple fact was to save my life. Somehow the gun captain pointed at me and said, "you go aft and start bringing up the ammunition out of the magazines". The aft magazines were five decks below.

A few moments later I found myself deep below the water line in a part of the ship I normally would never be in. I remember getting these cases of ammo powder and shells weighing about 90 pounds each. I had begun lifting shells into the hoist when a deafening roar filled the room and the entire ship shuttered. It was the forward magazine. One and half million pounds of gun powder exploding in a massive fireball disintegrating the whole forward part of the ship. Only moments before I stood with my gun crew just a few feet from the center of the explosion. Admiral Kidd, Captain. Van Valkenburg, my whole gun crew was killed. Everyone on top.

Seconds after the explosion the lights went out and it was pitch black. Almost immediately a thick acrid smoke filled the magazine locker and the metal walls began to get hot. In the dark and not being able to breath, we made our way to the door hatch, only to find it shut and locked. Somehow we were able to open the hatch and start to make our way up the ladder. I was nauseated by the smell of burning flesh, which turned out to be my own as I climbed up the hot ladder. A quick glance around revealed nothing in the darkness, but the moaning and sounds of falling bodies told me that some of my shipmates had succumbed to defeat and had died in their attempt to survive.

Getting through that choking kind of smoke was a real ordeal, the kind of smoke that really hurt your lungs. After awhile I began to get weak and lightheaded. I could feel myself losing the battle to save my own life. I hung to the ladder, feeling good. I felt that it was all right for me to let go. At that moment I looked up and could see a small point of light thru the smoke. It gave me the strength to go on. After what seemed to me like an eternity, I reached the deck gasping and choking. I laid down for a few moments. The warm Hawaiian air filled my lungs and cleared my head. I glanced over to the forward end of the ship to see nothing but a giant wall of flame and smoke.

Behind me, a marine lay dead on the deck, his body split in two. I began to realize there were dead men all around me. Some men were burning, wandering aimlessly. The sound of someone shouting "put out the fire" cut through the sound of the battle, but it was obvious the ship was doomed. I made my way to the side of the ship, which by this time was sinking fast and jumped off the fantail. The shoreline of Ford Island was only a short distance. There was burning oil all around the ship, but the aft was clear. After swimming to shore, I was taken to the naval air station. Every table in the mess hall had a man on it. After the attack was over, many of the battleship sailors, myself included, were taken to the USS TENNESSEE. I was there for one week and then transferred to the USS LEXINGTON and an appointment with a place called the Coral Sea.

George was badly burned during the attack and his parents, Mr. and Mrs. George D. and Mary Phraner were notified. George died on September 7, 2001 in Preston, Washington and his ashes were interred in turret #4 aboard the USS Arizona on December 7, 2001.[606]

Pike, Harvey Lee Electrician's Mate, Third Class, Serial No: 268 39 95, US Navy. Harvey was born November 3, 1921 in Georgia, the son of John Arthur and Lotice Mae (Abner) Pike. He enlisted in the US Navy November 28, 1939 in Macon, Georgia and reported for duty on the USS Arizona March 29, 1940. Harvey was killed in action on December 7, 1941 at Pearl Harbor, Hawaii. He was awarded the American Defense Service Medal, World War II Victory Medal and Purple Heart Medal posthumously. Harvey remains on duty on the USS Arizona. He is commemorated on the USS Arizona Memorial and the Memorial Tablets of the Missing, National Memorial Cemetery of the Pacific, Honolulu, Hawaii. Harvey was survived by his Father, Mr. John Arthur Pike, Concord, Florida.

---

[606] Information, story and photo of George D. Phraner provided by his son, Mark Phraner, 9/4/2008.

Pike, Lewis Jackson   Seaman, First Class, Serial No: 268 39 96, US Navy. Lewis was born April 16, 1919, the son of Albert Pike and Lilla Ora (Johnson) Pike. He enlisted in the US Navy November 28, 1939 in Macon, Georgia and reported for duty on the USS Arizona March 8, 1940.   Lewis was killed in action on December 7, 1941 at Pearl Harbor, Hawaii. He was awarded the American Defense Service Medal, World War II Victory Medal and Purple Heart Medal posthumously. Lewis remains on duty on the USS Arizona. He is commemorated on the USS Arizona Memorial, the Memorial Tablets of the Missing, National Memorial Cemetery of the Pacific, Honolulu, Hawaii and Campground Church Cemetery, Morven, Georgia. Lewis was survived by his Father, Mr. Albert Pike, R.F.D. 1, Barney, Florida.[607]

Pinkham, Albert Wesley   Seaman, Second Class, Serial No: 262 43 05, US Navy. Albert was born September 1, 1921 in Beaufort, North Carolina, the son of Benjamin Brady Pinkham and Arthilla Virginia (Waters) Pinkham. He enlisted in the US Navy November 8, 1939 in Raleigh, North Carolina and reported for duty on the USS Arizona September 30, 1940. Albert was killed in action on December 7, 1941 at Pearl Harbor, Hawaii. He was awarded the American Defense Service Medal, World War II Victory Medal and Purple Heart Medal posthumously. Albert remains on duty on the USS Arizona. He is commemorated on the USS Arizona Memorial and the Memorial Tablets of the Missing, National Memorial Cemetery of the Pacific, Honolulu, Hawaii. Albert was survived by his Father, Mr. Benjamin Brady Pinkham, Route 1, Pinetown, North Carolina.

Pitcher, Walter Giles   Gunner's Mate, First Class, Serial No: 257 97 55, US Navy. Walter was born July 1885 the son of Joseph and Katherine Pitcher. He enlisted in the US Navy August 16, 1934 in Baltimore, Maryland and reported for duty on the USS Arizona August 24, 1934. He was killed in action on December 7, 1941 at Pearl Harbor, Hawaii. Walter was awarded the American Defense Service Medal, World War II Victory Medal and Purple Heart Medal posthumously. He remains on duty on the USS Arizona. Walter is commemorated on the USS Arizona Memorial and the Memorial Tablets of the Missing, National Memorial Cemetery of the Pacific, Honolulu, Hawaii. He was survived by his Wife, Mrs. LaVon Marie Pitcher, 914 Loma Vista Avenue, Long Beach, California.

Pittard, George Franklin   Lieutenant, Serial No. 0-04903, US Navy. George was born July 28, 1911 in Winterville, Georgia the son of Harry Franklin Pittard and Estelle Murrell Pittard. He was appointed to the US Naval Academy on June 27, 1930 and was commissioned in May, 1934 in US Navy, serving on the USS Arizona as Assistant Air Defense Officer. He was serving on December 7, 1941 when the Japanese attacked Pearl Harbor. His battle station was Sky control. After the attack he was assigned temporary duty on the USS Tennessee. George later became the Commanding Officer of the USS San Diego (CL-53) and of the USS Kenneth D. Bailey (DD-713/DDR-713). He retired after 36 years service in November 1966 as a Rear Admiral. George passed away on May 9, 1991 in Escambia County, Florida.[608]

---

[607] Lewis Jackson Pike, Information and photo provided by family member, John R. Hancock.

Pitz, Robert Leo   Seaman, First Class, Aviation Unit (VO-1), Serial No. 328 67 20, US Navy. Robert was born December 21, 1915 in St. Paul, Minnesota, the son of Albert Joseph and Goldie Mae (McMillen) Pitz. He enlisted in the US Navy April 17, 1940 in Minneapolis, Minnesota and completed his training at the Naval Aviation Station, San Diego, California. He reported for duty on the USS Arizona November 27, 1940. Robert was serving on the Arizona on December 7, 1941 when the Japanese attacked Pearl Harbor. His Official Statement:

"The attack began as we were returning from special liberty and we arrived at the Fleet Landing during the first wave of attack. There was considerable confusion at the landing and although boats were available they were not immediately utilized due to the danger of strafing.

Finally one boat crew decided to chance it and endeavoring to reach our ship we entered the launch along with four other men. As we left the landing an enemy plane flew over at an altitude of less than 200 feet, but did not strafe us.

All battleships were being heavily bombed by high altitude and dive bombers coming out of the sun. When we got out in the harbor the Arizona blew up with a terrific explosion and was burning fiercely. Knowing it was impossible to get aboard our ship, we were at a loss as to just what to do. An officer came alongside in a whale boat (we were then about 100 yards off the Arizona) and told us to go to Ford Island. Enroute to Ford Island we picked up several men who were struggling in the water. They were burned and coated with oil. A motor launch ahead of us was strafed by an enemy plane just before we reached the air station.

After the injured were taken to the sick bay we remembered that our planes were on the air station. Shortly before we reached Ford Island the Nevada got underway and was going up the channel and was subject to extremely heavy fire by the second wave of attack.

We proceeded to the base force hangar to get our planes in condition to fly. One plane was damaged beyond repair and we prepared the other two for flight."[609]

Robert passed away on March 22, 1989 in Hennepin County, Minnesota and his ashes were interred on the USS Arizona on December 7, 1989.

Pollack, Francis Lee   Ship's Cook, Third Class, Serial No. 212 60 18, US Navy. Francis was born August 18, 1921. He enlisted in the US Navy October 14, 1940 in Springfield, Massachusetts and completed his training at the Naval Training Station, Newport, Rhode Island. He reported for duty on the USS Arizona December 10, 1940. Francis was serving on the USS Arizona on December 7, 1941 when the Japanese attacked Pearl Harbor. After the attack, Francis was transferred to Machine Gun School at Pucolo Point, Hawaii. He then served on the USS Medusa in 1942, USS West Virginia in 1943 thru the end of the war. Francis died August 20, 1976.

---

[608] George Franklin Pittard, Photo from Lucky Bag Yearbook, United States Naval Academy, Annapolis, MD, Class of 1934. Information provided by family member, David Coile.

[609] Confidential Statement of Robert Leo Pitz, Seaman First Class, Aviation Unit (VO-1), U.S. Navy, U.S.S. Arizona, regarding the attack on Pearl Harbor, T.H., December 7, 1941.

Pool, Elmer Leo Seaman, First Class, Serial No: 291 65 68, US Navy. Elmer was born on June 22, 1918 in Indiana the son of James E. and Matilda (Baker) Pool. He enlisted in the US Navy October 8, 1940 in Indianapolis, Indiana and completed his basic training at the Naval Training Station in Great Lakes, Illinois. Elmer reported for duty on the USS Arizona December 9, 1940. Assigned death #153, Elmer died as a result of wounds received in action on December 7, 1941 at Pearl Harbor, Hawaii[610]. He was awarded the American Defense Service Medal, World War II Victory Medal and Purple Heart Medal posthumously. Elmer's remains were recovered and he was returned home for burial in Section F, Site 3573, New Albany National Cemetery, New Albany, Indiana. He is commemorated on the USS Arizona Memorial, Pearl Harbor, Honolulu, Hawaii. Elmer was survived by his Mother, Mrs. Matilda Pool, 731 Colescotte Street, Shelbyville, Indiana, two brothers, James and Robert Pool and a sister, Mrs. Edith Jeffries all of Shelbyville, Indiana.[611]

Poole, Ralph Ernest Seaman, First Class, Serial No: 279 72 83, US Navy. Ralph was born November 14, 1921 in Scioto County, Ohio to Franklin Rufus Poole and Sarah A. (Lair) Poole. He enlisted in the US Navy September 9, 1940 in Cincinnati, Ohio and completed his basic training at the Naval Training Station in Norfolk, Virginia. Ralph reported for duty on the USS Arizona December 4, 1940. He was killed in action on December 7, 1941 at Pearl Harbor, Hawaii. Ralph was awarded the American Defense Service Medal, World War II Victory Medal and Purple Heart Medal posthumously. He remains on duty on the USS Arizona. Ralph is commemorated on the USS Arizona Memorial and the Memorial Tablets of the Missing, National Memorial Cemetery of the Pacific, Honolulu, Hawaii. He was survived by his Parents, Mr. and Mrs. Frank Poole, 1409 Mount Street, Portsmouth, Ohio a brother, Bernard Poole, serving in the US Army and three sisters, Alice and Caroljean Poole and Mrs. Carl Osmeyer, all of Portsmouth, Ohio.[612]

Port, Stanley Harrison, Jr. Coxswain, Serial No. 375 92 07, US Navy. Stanley was born on September 9, 1921 in Mill Valley, California the son of Stanley Harrison Port, Sr. and Grace Cleone (Wiser) Port. He enlisted in the US Navy November 15, 1938 in San Francisco, California and completed his training at the Naval Training Station, San Diego, California. He reported for duty on the USS Arizona March 11, 1939. He was serving on the USS Arizona on December 7, 1941 when the Japanese attacked Pearl Harbor. After the attack, Stanley was transferred to the USS Aylwin for duty. He served until August 1959. Stanley died on January 8, 1992 and was buried in Section 2B, Site 3108, Golden Gate National Cemetery, San Bruno, California.

Posey, Ernest Mendum Machinist's Mate, First Class, Serial No. 153 64 67, US Navy. Ernest was born March 2, 1896 in Eufaula, Oklahoma a native Eufaula Creek Indian. He was a veteran of World War 1. Ernest re-enlisted in the US Navy April 9, 1935 in San Francisco, California. Ernest was called up from the Fleet Naval Reserve August 1, 1940 and reported for duty on the USS Arizona January 2, 1941. He was serving on December 7, 1941 when the

---

[610] Elmer Leo Pool, Report of Changes of the USS Arizona for the month ending 31st day of December, 1941, Page 91, line 12.

[611] Elmer Leo Pool, Photo and information provided by family member, Susan Ingle.

[612] Ralph Ernest Poole, Photo from Ohio Honor States.

Japanese attacked Pearl Harbor. After the attack, Ernest was transferred to the USS Reid (DD-369). He also served on board the USS Radford (DD-446). In active combat in several major campaigns, he survived the sinking of two battleships. Ernest was listed as injured during the Port Chicago Naval Magazine Explosion on July 17, 1944. Ernest died September 1948 in the Veterans Hospital in Little Rock, Arkansas after a brief illness and was buried in the Posey Cemetery.

Post, Darrell Albert Chief Machinist's Mate, Serial No: 320 87 31, US Navy. Darrell was born August 10, 1912 in Nevada, Iowa, the son of Clarence Nathaniel Post and Dora May (Stahlman) Post. He enlisted in the US Navy February 21, 1933 in Des Moines, Iowa and reported for duty on the USS Arizona August 11, 1933. Darrell was killed in action on December 7, 1941 at Pearl Harbor, Hawaii. He was awarded the American Defense Service Medal, World War II Victory Medal and Purple Heart Medal posthumously. Darrell remains on duty on the USS Arizona. He is commemorated on the USS Arizona Memorial and the Memorial Tablets of the Missing, National Memorial Cemetery of the Pacific, Honolulu, Hawaii. Darrell was survived by his Wife, Mrs. Winifred Lel Post, 140 East Del Amo, North Long Beach, California.[613]

Potts, Howard Kenton Coxswain, Serial No. 337 20 51, US Navy. Howard enlisted in the US Navy October 4, 1939 in St. Louis, Missouri and completed his training at the Naval Training Station, Great Lakes, Illinois. He reported for duty on the USS Arizona December 31, 1939. Howard was serving on the USS Arizona on December 7, 1941 when the Japanese attacked Pearl Harbor. After the attack, Howard was transferred to the Naval Shipyard at Pearl Harbor for duty.

Pousson, Alfred Andrew Seaman, Second Class, Serial No. 274 51 74, US Navy. Alfred was born April 1, 1922 in Iota, Louisiana, son of John Durel Pousson and Ida (Bourgeois) Pousson. He enlisted in the US Navy October 1, 1940 in New Orleans, Louisiana and completed his training at the Naval Training Station, San Diego, California. He reported for duty on the USS Arizona January 25, 1941. According to the Pearl Harbor Muster Rolls, Alfred was sent to the Receiving Station at Pearl Harbor from the Naval Hospital in Pearl Harbor December 4, 1941. Alfred was serving on December 7, 1941 when the Japanese attacked Pearl Harbor. "I was blown into the air so high I didn't think I would ever hit the water, and when I did I had to fight the fire and oil." He was picked up by a rescue craft after swimming, presumably under water for long periods of time, in order to escape the burning oil fires and probably witnessing hundreds of his shipmates perish. He continued to serve on two more ships and participate in several enemy raids before being honorably discharged on September 30, 1948 after serving eight years in the US Navy. He received the Asiatic Pacific Campaign Medal, Navy Occupation Service Medal, Good Conduct Medal, American Defense SVC Medal, Honorable Service Lapel Pin, Honorable Discharge Button, Philippine Liberation Ribbon and the Philippine Presidential Unit Citation. Alfred died September 29, 1986 in Alexandria, Louisiana.

---

[613] Darrell Albert Post, Photo from California Honor States.

Povesko, George   Seaman, First Class, Serial No: 207 29 63, US Navy. George was born in 1922 in Bridgeport, Connecticut, son of George and Elizabeth Povesko. He enlisted in the US Navy October 15, 1940 in New Haven, Connecticut and completed his basic training at the Naval Training Station in Newport, Rhode Island. George reported for duty on the USS Arizona December 10, 1940. He was killed in action on December 7, 1941 at Pearl Harbor, Hawaii. George was awarded the American Defense Service Medal, World War II Victory Medal and Purple Heart Medal posthumously. He remains on duty on the USS Arizona. George is commemorated on the USS Arizona Memorial and the Memorial Tablets of the Missing, National Memorial Cemetery of the Pacific, Honolulu, Hawaii. He was survived by his Mother, Mrs. Elizabeth Povesko, 117 Grant Street, Bridgeport, Connecticut.

Powell, Thomas George   Seaman, First Class, Serial No: 300 18 98, US Navy. Thomas was born July 17, 1922 in Illinois. *His mother died when he was young and he was raised by his sister, Lucy Powell.* He enlisted in the US Navy October 8, 1940 in Chicago, Illinois and completed his basic training at the Naval Training Station in Great Lakes, Illinois. Thomas reported for duty on the USS Arizona December 9, 1940. He was killed in action on December 7, 1941 at Pearl Harbor, Hawaii. Thomas was awarded the American Defense Service Medal, World War II Victory Medal and Purple Heart Medal posthumously. He remains on duty on the USS Arizona. Thomas is commemorated on the USS Arizona Memorial and the Memorial Tablets of the Missing, National Memorial Cemetery of the Pacific, Honolulu, Hawaii. He was survived by his Father, Mr. Thomas H. Powell, 623 North Dixon Avenue, Dixon, Illinois.[614]

Presson, Wayne Harold   Seaman, First Class, Serial No: 283 39 03, US Navy. Wayne was born in 1918 in Ohio, the son of Samuel Craton Presson and Brooxie M. (Wilson) Presson. He enlisted in the US Navy September 9, 1940 in Cleveland, Ohio and completed his basic training at the Naval Training Station in Norfolk, Virginia. Wayne reported for duty on the USS Arizona December 4, 1940. He was killed in action on December 7, 1941 at Pearl Harbor, Hawaii. Wayne was awarded the American Defense Service Medal, World War II Victory Medal and Purple Heart Medal posthumously. He remains on duty on the USS Arizona. Wayne is commemorated on the USS Arizona Memorial and the Memorial Tablets of the Missing, National Memorial Cemetery of the Pacific, Honolulu, Hawaii. He was survived by his Father, Mr. Samuel Craton Presson, 574 Crouse Street, Akron, Ohio.[615]

---

[614] Thomas George Powell, Information and photo provided by family member, Linda Moll.
[615] Wayne Harold Presson, Photo and information from The Akron Beacon Journal, Akron, Ohio, July 16, 1942, Page 15.

Price, Arland Earl Radioman, Second Class, Serial No: 393 27 34, US Navy. Arland was born in 1918, the son of Thomas Price and Martha Florence Price. He enlisted in the US Navy August 16, 1938 in Portland, Oregon and completed his basic training at the Naval Training Station in San Diego, California. Arland reported for duty on the USS Arizona July 1, 1939. He was killed in action on December 7, 1941 at Pearl Harbor, Hawaii. Arland was awarded the American Defense Service Medal, World War II Victory Medal and Purple Heart Medal posthumously. He remains on duty on the USS Arizona. Arland is commemorated on the USS Arizona Memorial and the Memorial Tablets of the Missing, National Memorial Cemetery of the Pacific, Honolulu, Hawaii. He was survived by his Mother, Mrs. Martha Florence Price, 3435 Southeast Grant Street, Portland, Oregon.[616]

Pritchett, Robert Leo, Jr. Seaman, First Class, Serial No: 274 49 27, US Navy. Robert was born October 1, 1921 in Louisiana to Robert Lee Pritchett and Rose Pritchett. He enlisted in the US Navy August 10, 1940 in New Orleans, Louisiana and completed his basic training at the Naval Training Station in San Diego, California. Robert reported for duty on the USS Arizona October 8, 1940. He was killed in action on December 7, 1941 at Pearl Harbor, Hawaii. Robert was awarded the American Defense Service Medal, World War II Victory Medal and Purple Heart Medal posthumously. He remains on duty on the USS Arizona. Robert is commemorated on the USS Arizona Memorial and the Memorial Tablets of the Missing, National Memorial Cemetery of the Pacific, Honolulu, Hawaii. He was survived by his Father, Mr. Robert Lee Pritchett, Sr., 2412 Cleveland Avenue, New Orleans, Louisiana.[617]

Probst, Richard William Seaman, First Class, Serial No. 300 19 47, US Navy. Richard was born April 6, 1921 in Illinois. He enlisted in the US Navy October 8, 1940 in Chicago, Illinois and completed his training at the Naval Training Station, Great Lakes, Illinois. He reported for duty on the USS Arizona December 9, 1940. Richard was serving on the USS Arizona on December 7, 1941 when the Japanese attacked Pearl Harbor. After the attack, Richard was transferred to the USS Lexington for duty. (Sunk May 7, 1942 during the Battle of the Coral Sea.) Richard died April 15, 1989 in Spring Valley, California.

Puckett, Edwin Lester Storekeeper, Third Class, Serial No: 287 41 12, US Navy. Edwin was born November 10, 1919 in Hardin County, Kentucky to Galvin Puckett and Sarah Anna (Gerald) Puckett. He enlisted in the US Navy June 18, 1940 in Louisville, Kentucky and completed his basic training at the Naval Training Station in Great Lakes, Illinois. Edwin reported for duty on the USS Arizona October 25, 1940. He was killed in action on December 7, 1941 at Pearl Harbor, Hawaii. Edwin was awarded the American Defense Service Medal, World War II Victory Medal and Purple Heart Medal posthumously. He remains on duty on the USS Arizona. Edwin is commemorated on the USS Arizona Memorial and the Memorial Tablets of the Missing, National Memorial Cemetery of the Pacific, Honolulu, Hawaii. He was survived by his Father, Mr. Galvin Puckett, Glendale, Kentucky.

---

[616] Arland Earl Price, Photo from Oregon Honor States.
[617] Robert Leo Pritchett, Jr., Photo from the Times-Picayune Newspaper, New Orleans, LA, Tuesday, May 5, 1942, Page 4.

Puckett, Louis Alfred   Commander, Serial No. 0-08810, US Navy. Louis was the son of A. Y. and Johnie O. Puckett of Gainesville, TX. When he was not quite 17 and without waiting until he had finished high school, he enlisted in the Navy and by the time the United States entered the World War (World War I) he had worked himself up to where he was offered a chance to take the examinations for a commission and passed them. During WWI, he made more than a dozen round trips to Europe and back on the transport Susquehanna through mine and submarine-infested waters. In 1940, he had just completed a three-year hitch in the Orient on board the USS Beaver, a submarine tender. He was serving on the USS Arizona as Supply Officer. He was serving on December 7, 1941 when the Japanese attacked Pearl Harbor. His battle station was Coding Board.[618]

Pugh, John, Jr.   Shipfitter, Third Class, Serial No: 360 15 35, US Navy. John was born in about 1919 in Oklahoma to John and Pearl Pugh. He enlisted in the US Navy June 7, 1940 in Houston, Texas and completed his basic training at the Naval Training Station in San Diego, California. He reported for duty on the USS Arizona September 8, 1940. John was killed in action on December 7, 1941 at Pearl Harbor, Hawaii. He was awarded the American Defense Service Medal, World War II Victory Medal and Purple Heart Medal posthumously. John remains on duty on the USS Arizona. He is commemorated on the USS Arizona Memorial and the Memorial Tablets of the Missing, National Memorial Cemetery of the Pacific, Honolulu, Hawaii. John was survived by his Mother, Mrs. Pearl Carter, Alma, Arkansas.

Purvis, William Robinson   Fireman, Third Class, "M" Division, Serial No. 223 89 70, US Navy. William was born February 25, 1918 in Beyonne, New Jersey, the son of William Robinson and Lillian Purvis. He enlisted in the US Navy October 14, 1940 in New York, New York and completed his training at the Naval Training Station, Newport, Rhode Island. He reported for duty on the USS Arizona December 10, 1940. William was wounded in action on December 7, 1941 when the Japanese attacked Pearl Harbor. His Official statement:

"When General Quarters sounded on December 7, 1941, approximately 0753, I left the engine room to man #4 shaft alley. On arriving there I found the hatch to #4 locked.

There was with me at the time a man from Repair 5 who was to secure the hatch after I entered. His name was Dupree. On finding the alley locked we started to go back to the engine room. At that instant men burst out of the A. A. magazine which is situated above #4 shaft alley. Smoke and flames came out with them. The ship seemed to lurch and all lights went out. The smoke was very thick making breathing difficult. The opening of the magazine door knocked me off my feet. I followed the men up the ladder to the 3rd deck but before I reached the third deck a terrific explosion occurred blowing me back down. I picked myself up and went up again and finally arrived on the port side of the quarter deck. At the time the only officer in sight was Lieutenant Commander Fuqua. With a party of wounded men I went down the Admirals ladder and was taken to Landing C on Ford Island, by barge. The ship was sinking by the bow. The bottom step of the Admiral's ladder was already under water. The forecastle was on fire and so were parts of the 2nd and 3rd decks, approximately frames 105." [619]

---

[618] Louis Alfred Puckett, Information and photo from the Dallas Morning News, Dallas, TX, Section I, Page two, "Enlisting as GOB, Texan Wins Lieutenant Commander Rank".

[619] Confidential Statement of Purvis, William Robinson, F3c, U.S. Navy concerning attack on U.S.S. Arizona December 7, 1941. U.S.S. Arizona Office, Receiving Barracks, Pearl Harbor, T.H., December 17, 1941.

After the attack, William was transferred to the USS Salt Lake City for duty. He served until December 7, 1946. William died April 6, 1988 in Teaneck, New Jersey.

Putnam, Avis Boyd Ship's Cook, Third Class, Serial No: 360 19 02, US Navy. Avis was born July 22, 1922 in Morgan County, Alabama, the son of Nomer Marion Putnam and Zilphia Octavia (Briscoe) Putnam. He enlisted in the US Navy August 1, 1940 in Houston, Texas and completed his basic training at the Naval Training Station in San Diego, California. He reported for duty on the USS Arizona October 14, 1940. Avis was killed in action on December 7, 1941 at Pearl Harbor, Hawaii. He was awarded the American Defense Service Medal, World War II Victory Medal and Purple Heart Medal posthumously. Avis remains on duty on the USS Arizona. He is commemorated on the USS Arizona Memorial and the Memorial Tablets of the Missing, National Memorial Cemetery of the Pacific, Honolulu, Hawaii. Avis was survived by his Parents, Mr. and Mrs. Nomer Putnam, Childersburg, Alabama.[620]

Puzio, Edward Seaman, First Class, Serial No: 233 75 23, US Navy. Edward was born August 27, 1918 in East Stroudsburg, Pennsylvania, the third son of Joseph John Puzio and Anna Puzio. He enlisted in the US Navy September 4, 1940 in Philadelphia, Pennsylvania and completed his basic training at the Naval Training Station in Newport, Rhode Island. He reported for duty on the USS Arizona December 10, 1940. Edward was killed in action on December 7, 1941 at Pearl Harbor, Hawaii. He was awarded the American Defense Service Medal, World War II Victory Medal and Purple Heart Medal posthumously. Edward remains on duty on the USS Arizona. He is commemorated on the USS Arizona Memorial and the Memorial Tablets of the Missing, National Memorial Cemetery of the Pacific, Honolulu, Hawaii. Edward was survived by his Father, Mr. John Puzio, Route 3, East Stroudsburg, Pennsylvania.[621]

Quarto, Michael Joseph Seaman, First Class, Serial No: 207 29 55, US Navy. Mike was born in about 1920 in Connecticut to Joseph and Rosa Quarto. He enlisted in the US Navy October 15, 1940 in New Haven, Connecticut and completed his basic training at the Naval Training Station in Newport, Rhode Island. He reported for duty on the USS Arizona December 10, 1940. Mike was killed in action on December 7, 1941 at Pearl Harbor, Hawaii. He was awarded the American Defense Service Medal, World War II Victory Medal and Purple Heart Medal posthumously. Mike remains on duty on the USS Arizona. He is commemorated on the USS Arizona Memorial and the Memorial Tablets of the Missing, National Memorial Cemetery of the Pacific, Honolulu, Hawaii. Mike was survived by his Father, Mr. Joseph Quarto, 72 Boswell Avenue, Norwich, Connecticut. The Italian American Veterans Post 20 in Norwich, Connecticut was named in his honor. Quarto Road, Norwich, Connecticut was named in his honor.[622]

---

[620] Avis Boyd Putnam, photo provided by his niece, Christy Applegate.
[621] Edward Puzio, Photo from The Morning Call, Allentown, Pennsylvania, December 23, 1941, Page 23.
[622] Michael Joseph Quarto, Photo from Connecticut Honor States.

Quillin, Wallace "Frank" Franklin Seaman, First Class, Serial No. 272 41 72, US Navy. Wallace was born February 6, 1922 in Okolona, Mississippi. He enlisted in the US Navy October 5, 1940 in Birmingham, Alabama and completed his basic training at the Naval Training Station in Newport, Rhode Island. He reported for duty on the USS Arizona December 4, 1940. He was serving on the USS Arizona on December 7, 1941 when the Japanese attacked Pearl Harbor. After the attack, Wallace was transferred to the USS Neosho (AO-23) for duty. In June 1942 he was transferred to New Construction in San Francisco. He died December 6, 2006. On December 7, 2012, he joined his fellow shipmates on board the USS Arizona.

Quinata, Jose Sanchez Mess Attendant, Second Class, Serial No: 421 07 28, US Navy. Jose was born in 1920 in Umatac, Merizo, Guam. He enlisted in the US Navy December 2, 1940 at the Naval Station in Guam and reported for duty on the USS Arizona April 8, 1941. Jose was killed in action on December 7, 1941 at Pearl Harbor, Hawaii. He died as a result of wounds received in action. Assigned death #70. He was awarded the American Defense Service Medal, World War II Victory Medal and Purple Heart Medal posthumously. Jose's remains were recovered and he was buried in a Private Cemetery on Guam. He is commemorated on the USS Arizona Memorial and the Sons of Guam Pearl Harbor Memorial, Guam. Jose was survived by his Father, Mr. Vincente Aguon Quinata, Umatac, Guam.

Radford, Neal Jason Musician, Second Class, Serial No: 316 69 33, US Navy. Neal was born February 16, 1915 in Newark, Nebraska the son of Boyd Clyde Radford and Edna Meluzena (Gormly) Radford. *He attended Kearny High School in Kearny, Nebraska where he played the Baritone in the High School Band and was a member of the Future Farmers of America.* Neal enlisted in the US Navy October 14, 1940 and attended the Navy School of Music in Washington, DC graduating on May 23, 1941 as a member of the USS Arizona Band. He reported for duty on the USS Arizona June 17, 1941. *The battle station for all of the band members was in the black powder room passing ammunition to the Arizona's gunners during the attack. None of the band members survived the explosion.* Neal was killed in action on December 7, 1941 at Pearl Harbor, Hawaii. He was awarded the American Defense Service Medal, World War II Victory Medal and Purple Heart Medal posthumously. Neal remains on duty on the USS Arizona. He is commemorated on the USS Arizona Memorial and the Memorial Tablets of the Missing, National Memorial Cemetery of the Pacific, Honolulu, Hawaii. Neal was survived by his Father, Mr. Boyd Clyde Radford, Newark, Nebraska.[623]

Rahn, Carl Frederick, Jr. Seaman, First Class, Serial No. 238 69 46, US Navy. Carl was born January 27, 1922, son of Amelia Rahn. He enlisted in the US Navy October 15, 1940 in Albany, New York and completed his training at the Naval Training Station, Newport, Rhode Island. Carl reported for duty on the USS Arizona December 10, 1940. He was serving on the USS Arizona on December 7, 1941 when the Japanese attacked Pearl Harbor. After the attack,

---

[623] Neal Jason Radford, Photo from USS Arizona's Last Band by Molly Kent by permission of the author. For more information about this book, go to www.USSARIZONASLASTBAND.com.

Carl was transferred to the USS Mac Donough (DD-351) for duty. He died March 14, 2004 in San Diego, California.

Rampley, John Watson Gunner's Mate, Third Class, Serial No. 262 45 45, US Navy. John was born on August 27, 1917 in Inman, South Carolina. He enlisted in the US Navy November 29, 1939 in Raleigh, North Carolina and reported for duty on the USS Arizona March 8, 1940. He was serving on the USS Arizona on December 7, 1941 when the Japanese attacked Pearl Harbor. John went on to serve on the USS Mugford (DD-389), USS Whitney (AD-4), USS Drayton (DD-366) and the USS Stokes (AKA-68). During his service, John was awarded the Navy Good Conduct Medal, American Defense Service Medal with Gold Star, American Area Campaign Medal, Asiatic Pacific Campaign Medal with 7 Gold Stars and the World Ware II Victory Medal. John died on August 24, 1997 in Arizona and was buried in Section A, Row G, Site 78, Prescott National Cemetery, Prescott, Arizona.

Ramsdell, Millard Arthur Ensign, US Navy Reserve. Millard was born March 29, 1915 in Northport, Nebraska, son of Clyde Chester Ramsdell and Nona (Thompson) Ramsdell. He enlisted in the US Navy on May 1, 1939. Millard was commissioned Ensign in the US Navy May 26, 1940 and was serving as an Aviator on the USS Arizona. He was serving on December 7, 1941 when the Japanese attacked Pearl Harbor. The day of the attack, Millard was recovering from having his appendix removed. But he was a pilot and was needed. He reported for duty and continued to fight even after pulling his incision open. Millard was one of the few Americans to actually get his plane in the air that day. Mechanical problems finally grounded him. Millard passed away January 14, 1997 in Springfield, Oregon and his ashes were interred in Gun Turret No. 4 on the Arizona December 7, 2007.[624]

Rasmussen, Arthur Severin Carpenter's Mate, First Class, Serial No: 222 66 43, US Navy. Arthur was born February 2, 1902 in Brooklyn, New York. He enlisted in the US Navy in November of 1928 at Lakehurst, New Jersey. He served on the USS Arizona from July 10, 1939 until he was killed in action on December 7, 1941 at Pearl Harbor, Hawaii. Arthur was awarded the American Defense Service Medal, World War II Victory Medal and Purple Heart Medal posthumously. He remains on duty on the USS Arizona. Arthur is commemorated on the USS Arizona Memorial and the Memorial Tablets of the Missing, National Memorial Cemetery of the Pacific, Honolulu, Hawaii. He was survived by his Wife, Mrs. Helen Rasmussen, 3734 Hemlock Street, San Diego, California.

Rasmusson, George Vernon Fireman, Third Class, Serial No: 328 75 78, US Navy. George was born about 1916 in Minnesota, the son of Adolph Rasmusson, Perham, Minnesota. He enlisted in the US Navy October 8, 1940 in Minneapolis, Minnesota and completed his basic training at the Naval Training Station in Great Lakes, Illinois. He reported for duty on the USS Arizona December 9, 1940. George was killed in action on December 7, 1941 at Pearl Harbor, Hawaii. He was awarded the American Defense Service Medal, World War II Victory Medal and

---

[624] Millard Ramsdell, Photo from The Silver Spruce Yearbook, Colorado State University, Fort Collins, Colorado, 1937.

Purple Heart Medal posthumously. George remains on duty on the USS Arizona. He is commemorated on the USS Arizona Memorial and the Memorial Tablets of the Missing, National Memorial Cemetery of the Pacific, Honolulu, Hawaii. George was survived by his Wife, Mrs. Signe Rasmusson, 727 West 41st Drive, Los Angeles, California.

Ratkovich, William   Watertender, First Class, Serial No: 375 57 55, US Navy. William was born September 24, 1909 in Colorado to Max and Annie Ratkovich. He enlisted in the US Navy January 30, 1940 in San Diego, California and completed his basic training at the Naval Training Station in San Diego, California. He reported for duty on the USS Arizona February 3, 1940. William was killed in action on December 7, 1941 at Pearl Harbor, Hawaii. He was awarded the American Defense Service Medal, World War II Victory Medal and Purple Heart Medal posthumously. William's remains were recovered and he was buried in Plot A, Row 0, Grave 919, National Memorial Cemetery of the Pacific, Honolulu, Hawaii. He is commemorated on the USS Arizona Memorial. William was survived by his Brother, Mr. Nick Ratkovich, 2312-1/2 Curson Street, Los Angeles, California.

Rawhouser, Glen Donald   Fireman, Third Class, Serial No: 368 56 85, US Navy. Glen was born in about 1923 in Wyoming to Glen D. and Pearl R. Rawhouser. He enlisted in the US Navy December 27, 1940 in Salt Lake City, Utah and completed his basic training at the Naval Training Station in San Diego, California. He reported for duty on the USS Arizona April 26, 1941. Glen was killed in action on December 7, 1941 at Pearl Harbor, Hawaii. He was awarded the American Defense Service Medal, World War II Victory Medal and Purple Heart Medal posthumously. Glen remains on duty on the USS Arizona. He is commemorated on the USS Arizona Memorial and the Memorial Tablets of the Missing, National Memorial Cemetery of the Pacific, Honolulu, Hawaii. Glen was survived by his Mother, Mrs. J. B. Faubion, 1506 SE Woodward, Portland, Oregon.

Rawson, Clyde Jackson   Boatswain's Mate, First Class, Serial No: 257 97 68, US Navy. Clyde was born April 15, 1914 the son of Harry and Alice N. (Lewis) Rawson. He served in the US Navy from March 16, 1931 until he was killed in action on December 7, 1941 at Pearl Harbor, Hawaii. Clyde was transferred from the USS West Virginia on January 24, 1941 to the USS Arizona. He was awarded the American Defense Service Medal, World War II Victory Medal and Purple Heart Medal posthumously. Clyde's remains were identified by his name on his trousers and he was buried in Plot C, Row 0, Grave 787, National Memorial Cemetery of the Pacific, Honolulu, Hawaii.[625] He is commemorated on the USS Arizona Memorial. Clyde was survived by his Father, Mr. Harry Frank Rawson, Whaleyville, Maryland.[626]

---

[625] Report of Changes of the USS Arizona Flag Allowance (CBD-1) Commander Battleship Division One for the period ending 7th day of December, 1941, page 2, line29, Clyde Jackson Rawson.
[626] Clyde Jackson Rawson, Photo and information provided by family member, Richard Smith.

Ray, Harry Joseph Boatswain's Mate, Second Class, Serial No: 286 95 58, US Navy. Harry was born April 11, 1910 in Pennsylvania, the son of Harry V. and Anna (Weaver) Ray. He enlisted in the US Navy January 1926 in Louisville, Kentucky. He served on the USS Arizona from March 23, 1931 until he was killed in action on December 7, 1941 at Pearl Harbor, Hawaii. Harry was awarded the American Defense Service Medal, World War II Victory Medal and Purple Heart Medal posthumously. He remains on duty on the USS Arizona. Harry is commemorated on the USS Arizona Memorial and the Memorial Tablets of the Missing, National Memorial Cemetery of the Pacific, Honolulu, Hawaii. He was survived by his Wife, Mrs. Dorothy Agnes Ray, 2214 West Hill Street, Long Beach, California and daughter, Barbara Helen Ray.

Reaves, Casbie Seaman, First Class, Serial No: 346 87 52, US Navy. Casbie was born in February 7, 1917 in Jeff Davis Township, Little River, Arkansas, son of Joseph Allen and Bertha (Boren) Reaves. He enlisted in the US Navy November 7, 1940 in San Diego, California and completed his basic training at the Naval Training Station in San Diego, California. Casbie reported for duty on the USS Arizona January 11, 1941. He was killed in action on December 7, 1941 at Pearl Harbor, Hawaii. Casbie was awarded the American Defense Service Medal, World War II Victory Medal and Purple Heart Medal posthumously. He remains on duty on the USS Arizona. Casbie is commemorated on the USS Arizona Memorial and the Memorial Tablets of the Missing, National Memorial Cemetery of the Pacific, Honolulu, Hawaii. He was survived by his Father, Mr. Joseph Allen Reaves, Route 1, Box 77, Arkinda, Arkansas.[627]

Rector, Clay Cooper Storekeeper, Third Class, Serial No: 287 34 52, US Navy. Clay was born June 27, 1920 in Kentucky, son of Wendell Wesley Rector and Lela Florence (Cooper) Rector. He enlisted in the US Navy December 5, 1939 in Louisville, Kentucky and completed his basic training at the Naval Training Station in Great Lakes, Illinois. Clay reported for duty on the USS Arizona March 9, 1940 and was in charge of the storeroom. *The last family member to see him may have been his cousin Clay who met him in the Pacific in 1940. His cousin Clay left Pearl Harbor two days before the attack on the USS Arizona.* He was killed in action on December 7, 1941 at Pearl Harbor, Hawaii. Clay was awarded the American Defense Service Medal, World War II Victory Medal and Purple Heart Medal posthumously. He remains on duty on the USS Arizona. Clay is commemorated on the USS Arizona Memorial and the Memorial Tablets of the Missing, National Memorial Cemetery of the Pacific, Honolulu, Hawaii. He was survived by his Father, Mr. Wendell Rector, Albany, Kentucky.[628]

---

[627] Casbie Reaves, Photo from Arkansas Honor States.
[628] Clay Cooper Rector, Photo and information from family member, Colette Walls.

Reece, John Jeffris Seaman, Second Class, Serial No: 372 21 75, US Navy. John was born October 14, 1923 in Texas. He enlisted in the US Navy November 27, 1940 in Denver, Colorado and completed his basic training at the Naval Training Station in San Diego, California and reported for duty on the USS Arizona January 25, 1941. John was killed in action on December 7, 1941 at Pearl Harbor, Hawaii. He was awarded the American Defense Service Medal, World War II Victory Medal and Purple Heart Medal posthumously. John remains on duty on the USS Arizona. He is commemorated on the USS Arizona Memorial and the Memorial Tablets of the Missing, National Memorial Cemetery of the Pacific, Honolulu, Hawaii and the Brush Memorial Cemetery, Brush, Colorado. John was survived by his Aunt, Mrs. Nettie Blanch Reece, 500 Cameron Street, Brush, Colorado.

Reed, James Buchanan, Jr. Storekeeper, First Class, Serial No: 355 99 58, US Navy. James was born February 5, 1915 in Titus County, Texas, the son of James Buchanan Reed and Ethel Mae Reed. He enlisted in the US Navy September 11, 1936 in Dallas, Texas and completed his basic training at the Naval Training Station in San Diego, California. He reported for duty on the USS Arizona April 15, 1937. James was killed in action on December 7, 1941 at Pearl Harbor, Hawaii. He was awarded the American Defense Service Medal, World War II Victory Medal and Purple Heart Medal posthumously. James remains on duty on the USS Arizona. He is commemorated on the USS Arizona Memorial and the Memorial Tablets of the Missing, National Memorial Cemetery of the Pacific, Honolulu, Hawaii and Nevill's Chapel Cemetery, Mount Pleasant, Texas. James was survived by his Wife, Mrs. Hanna Ingrid Reed, 215 South Eldorado, San Mateo, California.[629]

Reed, Ray Ellison Seaman, Second Class, Serial No: 356 49 53, US Navy. Ray was born in about 1922 in Oklahoma to John E. and Cortie Reed. He enlisted in the US Navy January 25, 1941 in Dallas, Texas and reported for duty on the USS Arizona April 27, 1941. Ray was killed in action on December 7, 1941 at Pearl Harbor, Hawaii. He was awarded the American Defense Service Medal, World War II Victory Medal and Purple Heart Medal posthumously. Ray remains on duty on the USS Arizona. He is commemorated on the USS Arizona Memorial and the Memorial Tablets of the Missing, National Memorial Cemetery of the Pacific, Honolulu, Hawaii. Ray was survived by his Father, Mr. J. E. Reed, Route 4, Box 175, Okmulgee, Oklahoma.

Register, Paul James "Cash" Lieutenant Commander, Serial No: 0-056904, US Navy. Paul was born on November 5, 1899 in Bismarck, North Dakota the son of Francis Henry Register and Helen Marie (Donaldson) Register. *He was raised in the Methodist Church in Bismarck and attended school in Bismarck, North Dakota.* Paul was appointed to the United States Naval Academy, Annapolis, MD on June 12, 1917 as a Midshipman. He graduated from the Naval Academy and was commissioned Ensign on June 5, 1920. Assigned to duties on shore and at sea, with both the Battle and Scouting Fleets, during the interwar period, he was promoted to Lieutenant Commander July 1, 1939. *Paul studied law at night school when he was stationed in New York. He lacked one course of finishing his law studies and wanted to be a maritime lawyer in Charleston or Savannah when he retired. Paul had*

---

[629] James Buchanan Reed, Jr., Photo and information provided by family member, Shelby Beard.

enough service to retire but thought it was his duty to stay in the Navy with a war approaching. He was good at writing poetry. Paul reported for duty on the USS Arizona on March 20, 1941 and was serving as Communication Officer when he was killed in action on December 7, 1941 at Pearl Harbor, Hawaii. He was awarded the American Defense Service Medal, World War II Victory Medal and Purple Heart Medal posthumously. Paul remains buried on the USS Arizona. His battle station was the Conning Tower. He is commemorated on the USS Arizona Memorial and the Memorial Tablets of the Missing, National Memorial Cemetery of the Pacific, Honolulu, Hawaii. Paul was survived by his Wife, Mrs. Mary Ethel (Lohman) Register, 1402 8th Street, Coronado, San Diego, California, son Paul James Register, Jr. and daughter Nancy Steele Register. The High Speed Transport, USS Register (DE-92), was named in his honor. Launched on January 20, 1944 as a destroyer escort at the Navy Yard, Charleston, South Carolina and later commissioned as a high speed transport (APD-92) on January 11, 1945. The Register earned one battle star for her service during World War II (kamikaze attack).[630]

Reid, Everett Owen Machinist's Mate, First Class, Serial No. 342 01 16, US Navy. Everett was born December 6, 1917. He enlisted in the US Navy March 16, 1937 in Kansas City, Missouri. He reported for duty on the USS Arizona July 24, 1937. He was serving on the USS Arizona on December 7, 1941 when the Japanese attacked Pearl Harbor. After the attack, Everett was transferred to the USS Nevada for duty. Everett passed away July 8, 2004. He was cremated and interred at Evergreen Cemetery in Seattle, Washington.

Reifert, Eldon Ray Coxswain, Serial No. 291 48 83, US Navy. Eldon was born March 11, 1918 in Huntington County, Indiana, son of Otto Reifert and Effie (Shelly) Reid. He enlisted in the US Navy October 28, 1936 in Indianapolis, Indiana and completed his basic training at the Naval Training Station in Great Lakes, Illinois. He reported for duty on the USS Arizona July 6, 1937. He was serving on the USS Arizona on December 7, 1941 when the Japanese attacked Pearl Harbor. Eldon passed away May 27, 1988 in Concord, California.

---

[630] Paul James Register, Graduation photo, The Lucky Bag, US Naval Academy, Annapolis, Maryland 1920, Information and photo provided by his son, Paul James Register, Jr.

Restivo, Jack Martin Yeoman, Second Class, Serial No: 258 20 61, US Navy. Jack was born in 1918 in Maryland son of Jacob and Josephine Restivo. He enlisted in the US Navy June 28, 1938 in Baltimore, Maryland and reported for duty on the USS Arizona September 22, 1938. Jack was killed in action on December 7, 1941 at Pearl Harbor. He was awarded the American Defense Service Medal, World War II Victory Medal and Purple Heart Medal posthumously. Jack remains on duty on the USS Arizona. He is commemorated on the USS Arizona Memorial and the Memorial Tablets of the Missing, National Memorial Cemetery of the Pacific, Honolulu, Hawaii. Jack was survived by his Father, Mr. Jacob Restivo, 1813 Frederick Avenue, Baltimore, Maryland.[631]

Reynolds, Earl Arthur Seaman, Second Class, Serial No: 372 18 12, US Navy. Earl was born in 1922, son of Charles Waite Reynolds and Lucille May (Stout) Reynolds. He enlisted in the US Navy on September 17, 1940 in Denver, Colorado and completed his basic training at the Naval Training Station in San Diego, California. Earl reported for duty on the USS Arizona January 4, 1941. He was killed in action on December 7, 1941 at Pearl Harbor, Hawaii. Earl was awarded the American Defense Service Medal, World War II Victory Medal and Purple Heart Medal posthumously. He remains on duty on the USS Arizona. Earl is commemorated on the USS Arizona Memorial and the Memorial Tablets of the Missing, National Memorial Cemetery of the Pacific, Honolulu, Hawaii. He was survived by his Father, Mr. Charles Waite Reynolds, New Castle, Colorado.

Reynolds, Jack Franklyn Seaman, First Class, Serial No: 234 28 46, US Navy. Jack was born in 1919, son of Arnold Lewis Reynolds and Edythe E. Reynolds. He enlisted in the US Navy October 16, 1940 in Buffalo, New York and completed his basic training at the Naval Training Station in Newport, Rhode Island. Jack reported for duty on the USS Arizona December 40, 1940. He was killed in action on December 7, 1941 at Pearl Harbor, Hawaii. Jack was awarded the American Defense Service Medal, World War II Victory Medal and Purple Heart Medal posthumously. He remains on duty on the USS Arizona. Jack is commemorated on the USS Arizona Memorial and the Memorial Tablets of the Missing, National Memorial Cemetery of the Pacific, Honolulu, Hawaii. He was survived by his Father, Mr. Arnold Lewis Reynolds, 61 Coolidge Road, Rochester, New York.[632]

Rhodes, Birb Richard Fireman, Second Class, Serial No: 295 51 59, US Navy. Birb was born in February 1920 in Henderson County, Tennessee to Birb Richard Rhodes and Sarah Elizabeth (Lewis) Rhodes. He enlisted in the US Navy November 10, 1939 in Nashville, Tennessee and reported for duty on the USS Arizona January 8, 1941. He was killed in action on December 7, 1941 at Pearl Harbor, Hawaii. Birb was awarded the American Defense Service Medal, World War II Victory Medal and Purple Heart Medal posthumously. He remains on duty on the USS Arizona. Birb is commemorated on the USS Arizona Memorial and the Memorial Tablets of the Missing, National Memorial Cemetery of the Pacific, Honolulu, Hawaii and Oakwood Cemetery, Gibson County, Tennessee. He was survived by his Mother, Mrs. Sarah Elizabeth Rhodes, Cades, Tennessee.

---

[631] Jack Martin Restivo, Photo from the Baltimore Sun Newspaper, Baltimore Maryland, May 9, 1942.
[632] Jack Franklyn Reynolds, Photo from New York Honor States.

Rhodes, Mark Alexander Seaman, First Class, Serial No: 262 44 66, US Navy. Mark was born March 7, 1920 in Henderson County, North Carolina to Arthur and Stella Louetta (Lyda) Rhodes. He enlisted in the US Navy November 22, 1939 in Raleigh, North Carolina and reported for duty on the USS Arizona March 8, 1940. Assigned death #34, Mark died from wounds received in action on December 7, 1941 at Pearl Harbor, Hawaii.[633] He was awarded the American Defense Service Medal, World War II Victory Medal and Purple Heart Medal posthumously. Mark's remains were recovered and he was buried in Plot C, Row 0, Grave 767, National Memorial Cemetery of the Pacific, Honolulu, Hawaii. He is commemorated on the USS Arizona Memorial. Mark was survived by his Mother, Mrs. Stella Ruff, Route 2, Hendersonville, North Carolina. The Veterans of Foreign Wars Post 5206 in Hendersonville, North Carolina is named for Mark Alexander Rhodes and Paul Hedrick.[634]

Rice, William Albert Seaman, Second Class, Serial No: 385 96 62, US Navy. William was the only son born April 26, 1918 in Walla Walla, Washington to Thomas Harrison and Olive May (Marquis) Rice. *The family moved shortly after to Ellensburg, Washington. His mother, Olive died in a house fire when he was 16 months old. William lived with his grandparents in La Grande, Oregon and later in Portland until he finished grade school. He then returned to Ellensburg to live with his father until graduation from High School.* He enlisted in the US Navy January 28, 1941 in Seattle, Washington and completed his basic training at the Naval Training Station in San Diego, California. William reported for duty on the USS Arizona September 11, 1941. Assigned death #113, William died on December 10, 1941 from wounds received in action on December 7, 1941 at Pearl Harbor, Hawaii.[635] He was awarded the American Defense Service Medal, World War II Victory Medal and Purple Heart Medal posthumously. His body was buried in one of the "Unknown" graves in the Punchbowl. In 2001, his body was exhumed, identified and shipped home for burial in Plot A-251-06, IOOF Cemetery, Ellensburg, Washington. He is commemorated on the USS Arizona Memorial and the Memorial Tablets of the Missing, National Memorial Cemetery of the Pacific, Honolulu, Hawaii. Wilson was survived by his Father, Mr. Thomas Harrison Rice, 112 South Main Street, Ellensburg, Washington; his grandparents, Mr. and Mrs. Marquis and three aunts, Lucille, Lorna and Ruth Marquis of Portland, Oregon.[636]

---

[633] Mark Alexander Rhodes, Report of Changes of the USS Arizona for the month ending 31st day of December, 1941, Page 94, line 16.
[634] Mark Alexander Rhodes, Photo provided by the Hedrick-Rhodes VFW Post 5206, Hendersonville, NC.
[635] William Albert Rice, Report of Changes of the USS Arizona for the month ending 31st day of December, 1941, Page 94, Line 17.
[636] William Albert Rice, Information and photo provided by a local researcher, Alecia Dixon.

Rich, Claude Edward   Seaman, First Class, Serial No: 268 53 70, US Navy. Claude was born in 1922 in Volusia County, Florida, the son of Jesse Rockford and Lulu Viola (Baxter) Rich. *He dropped out of high school as a way out of the depression and enlisted in the US Navy. His father signed papers for him to enter the Navy even though his mother pleaded that he remain in school.* Claude enlisted on September 24, 1940 in Macon, Georgia and completed his basic training at the Naval Training Station in Norfolk, Virginia. He reported for duty on the USS Arizona December 4, 1940. Claude was killed in action on December 7, 1941 at Pearl Harbor, Hawaii. He was awarded the American Defense Service Medal, World War II Victory Medal and Purple Heart Medal posthumously. Claude remains on duty on the USS Arizona. He is commemorated on the USS Arizona Memorial and the Memorial Tablets of the Missing, National Memorial Cemetery of the Pacific, Honolulu, Hawaii. Claude was survived by his Father, Mr. Jesse Rockford Rich, 623 46th Street, West Palm Beach, Florida.[637]

Richar, Raymond Lyle   Seaman, First Class, Serial No: 234 28 33, US Navy. Raymond was born May 5, 1921 in Galeton, Pennsylvania, the first born son of Truman E. Richar and Grace (Campbell) Richar. *His younger brother, Ronald Eugene drowned on his mother's birthday in Pine Creek while sledding with Raymond. He attended Galeton Schools with his best friend Bill Gill. They enlisted in the US Navy October 15, 1940 in Elmira, New York and they completed his basic training at the Naval Training Station in Newport, Rhode Island. They traveled by train to the west coast and went to different ships in the Pacific fleet.* Bill was assigned to the USS Hovey (DMS-71) that operated along with the USS Arizona. *His friend, Bill, had left Pearl Harbor two weeks before Japan attacked Pearl Harbor in order to attend radio school.* Raymond reported for duty on the USS Arizona December 10, 1940. He was killed in action on December 7, 1941 at Pearl Harbor. Hawaii. Raymond was awarded the American Defense Service Medal, World War II Victory Medal and Purple Heart Medal posthumously. He remains on duty on the USS Arizona. He is commemorated on the USS Arizona Memorial and the Memorial Tablets of the Missing, National Memorial Cemetery of the Pacific, Honolulu, Hawaii. Raymond was survived by his Parents, Mr. Truman Richar and Mrs. Grace (Campbell) Richar, 157 Germania Street, Galeton, Pennsylvania. The Raymond Richar VFW Post 6611 in Galeton, Pennsylvania was named in his honor.[638]

---

[637] Claude Edward Rich, Information and photo from the Palm Beach Post obituaries provided by family member, Terri Overton.

[638] Raymond Lyle Richar, Photo from the portrait at Raymond Lyle Richar VFW Post 6611, Galeton, PA taken by the High School Art students under the direction of Alyson Leach, Galeton High School, Galeton, Pennsylvania. Additional information provided by family member, Thomas Richar.

Richardson, Warren John Coxswain, Serial No: 279 54 25, US Navy. Warren was born May 11, 1918 in Columbus, Ohio, son of Charles N. Richardson and Freda Rose (Kocher) Richardson. He enlisted in the Navy February 1, 1938 in Cincinnati, Ohio and in late 1941 re-enlisted for two years. Warren reported for duty on the USS Arizona June 4, 1938. He was killed in action on December 7, 1941 at Pearl Harbor, Hawaii. Warren was awarded the American Defense Service Medal, World War II Victory Medal and Purple Heart Medal posthumously. He remains on duty on the USS Arizona. Warren is commemorated on the USS Arizona Memorial and the Memorial Tablets of the Missing, National Memorial Cemetery of the Pacific, Honolulu, Hawaii. He was survived by his Mother, Mrs. Freda Rose Richardson, 4513 Clifton Avenue, Covington, Kentucky. Besides his mother, he leaves three brothers, James and Charles, of Covington, and Everett Richardson of Miami, Florida and two sisters, Mrs. Hazel Conley of Coshocten and Mrs. Ruth Myers of Latonia.[639]

Richison, Fred Louis Gunner's Mate, Third Class, Serial No: 375 97 26, US Navy. Fred was born August 31, 1921 in California, the son of Louise Richison and Emma Richison. He enlisted in the US Navy October 7, 1939 in San Francisco, California and completed his basic training at the Naval Training Station in San Diego, California. Fred reported for duty on the USS Arizona December 20, 1939. He was killed in action on December 7, 1941 at Pearl Harbor, Hawaii. Fred was awarded the American Defense Service Medal, World War II Victory Medal and Purple Heart Medal posthumously. He remains on duty on the USS Arizona. Fred is commemorated on the USS Arizona Memorial and the Memorial Tablets of the Missing, National Memorial Cemetery of the Pacific, Honolulu, Hawaii. He was survived by his Mother, Mrs. Emma Richison, 159 West St. James Street, San Jose, California.

Richter, Albert Wallace Coxswain, Serial No: 385 86 55, US Navy. Albert was born in 1920, son of Charles Richter and Ida Marie Richter. He enlisted in the US Navy April 9, 1940 in Seattle, Washington and completed his basic training at the Naval Training Station in San Diego, California. Albert reported for duty on the USS Arizona July 2, 1940. He was killed in action on December 7, 1941 at Pearl Harbor, Hawaii. Albert was awarded the American Defense Service Medal, World War II Victory Medal and Purple Heart Medal posthumously. He remains on duty on the USS Arizona. Albert is commemorated on the USS Arizona Memorial and the Memorial Tablets of the Missing, National Memorial Cemetery of the Pacific, Honolulu, Hawaii. He was survived by his Mother, Mrs. Ida Marie Richter, 411 North K Street, Tacoma, Washington.

Rico, Guadalupe "Gus" Augustine Seaman, First Class, Serial No: 376 14 85, US Navy. Guadalupe was born December 24, 1919 in Santa Clara, California, the son of Guadalupe Pilar Rico and Isabell (Azevedo) Rico. *He attended the San Jose High School completing 3 years and then went on to work as a farm laborer prior to enlisting.* Guadalupe enlisted in the US Navy October 31, 1940 in San Francisco, California and completed his basic training at the Naval Training Station in San Francisco, California. He reported for duty on the USS Arizona December 30, 1940. Guadalupe was killed in action on December 7, 1941 at Pearl Harbor, Hawaii. He was awarded the American Defense Service Medal, World War II Victory Medal and

---

[639] Warren John Richardson, Photo and information provided by family member, Tammy Kroger.

Purple Heart Medal posthumously. Guadalupe remains on duty on the USS Arizona. He is commemorated on the USS Arizona Memorial and the Memorial Tablets of the Missing, National Memorial Cemetery of the Pacific, Honolulu, Hawaii. Guadalupe was survived by his Parents, Mr. and Mrs. Guadalupe Pilar Rico, 1023 East Lincoln Court, San Jose, California and three sisters, Mary, Sarrah and Agnes.[640]

Riddell, Eugene Edward Seaman, First Class, Serial No: 279 73 51, US Navy. Eugene was born January 14, 1917 and grew up in rural Estill County, Kentucky, the second oldest of six children of Forest Lee Riddell and Dora Gertrude (Taylor) Riddell. *He grew up in a loving environment and was happy living in the Appalachian foothills, until jobs became very hard to find. As a result of the job situation, Eugene joined the navy with the plan being that he would return when things were better and he would go into the carpentry business with his father, who was a master carpenter. His parents, Forest and Dora Riddell, along with his two younger sisters, moved to Flint, Michigan where Forest was promised employment.* He enlisted in the US Navy October 7, 1940 in Cincinnati, Ohio and completed his basic training at the Naval Training Station in Great Lakes, Illinois. Eugene reported for duty on the USS Arizona December 9, 1940. He was killed in action on December 7, 1941 at Pearl Harbor, Hawaii. *His brother, Bill, was able to speak with one of Eugene's friends, who was also a shipmate, sometime after the attack on Pearl Harbor and it was from him that the family learned how Eugene died. He had been off of the ship when the Japanese started their surprise attack and he had raced to the harbor as soon as he became aware of the situation. Bill was told that the friend saw Eugene climbing a ladder to get to his duty station when the main explosion occurred and that the explosion killed him. His parents, Forest and Dora, and two young daughters were in Flint on December 7, 1941. They were at the home of one of Dora's sisters, about to share a lazy Sunday dinner as they listened to the radio. The programming was interrupted for an announcement of the attack on Pearl Harbor and, according to the youngest daughter, Jo, Eugene's mother, stricken with fear, suddenly stood straight up and exclaimed, "That's where Eugene is!" It wasn't long before the telegram arrived telling them that their son was missing in action. When the Christmas present they had sent to him (a watch) was returned to them, it signaled the end of all hope for them that Eugene was alive. His younger brother, Bill, upon hearing of the attack and the death of his brother, went immediately to Flint and after spending a short time with his parents, joined the Army Air Corps. He became a pilot and flew P-47's across Europe as a member of the 388th Squadron, 365th Fighter Bomber Group of the 9th Air Force, otherwise known as the Hellhawks.* Eugene was awarded the American Defense Service Medal, World War II Victory Medal and Purple Heart Medal posthumously. He remains on duty on the USS Arizona. Eugene is commemorated on the USS Arizona Memorial and the Memorial Tablets of the Missing, National Memorial Cemetery of the Pacific, Honolulu, Hawaii. He was survived by his Parents, Mr. and Mrs. Forest Riddell, 805 Rankin Street, Flint, Michigan; three sisters, Pauline, Jessie and Jo and one brother, Roland "Bill" Willard Riddell.[641]

---

[640] Guadalupe Augustine Rico, Photo from California Honor States.
[641] Eugene Edward Riddell, Information and photo provided by his nephew, Rob Mitchell.

Rider, Maurice David   Boatswain's Mate, First Class, Serial No. 212 27 77, US Navy. Maurice was born on September 14, 1911 in East Windsor, Connecticut, son of Isaac David Rider and Ines Emma (Parsons) Rider. He enlisted in the US Navy October 18, 1934 at age 17. He reported for duty on the USS Panay which was sunk by Japanese bombers 27 miles above Nanking on the Yangtze River. Maurice received the Navy Cross for his heroic action during this attack. He reported for duty on the USS Arizona April 15, 1939. Maurice was on reenlistment leave in the Continental U.S. when the USS Arizona was sunk on December 7, 1941 when the Japanese attacked Pearl Harbor. After the attack, Maurice was transferred to the USS Sacramento for duty. He also served during the Korean War. Maurice died on August 25, 1965 in California while undergoing open heart surgery and is buried in Section A-B, Site 474, Fort Rosencrans National Cemetery, San Diego, California. He is survived by his wife, Elizabeth (Slobaskaia) Rider and three children.

Ridley, William Hull   Radioman, Third Class (V-3), Serial No. 413 52 54, US Navy. William enlisted in the US Navy October 3, 1940 in Denver, Colorado and reported for duty on the USS Arizona April 27, 1941. He was serving on the USS Arizona on December 7, 1941 when the Japanese attacked Pearl Harbor. After the attack, William was transferred to the USS Salt Lake City for temporary duty and then onto the USS Dobbin (AD-3).

Riganti, Fred   Shipfitter, Third Class, Serial No: 382 12 64, US Navy. Fred was born February 12, 1919 in New York to Pietro and Clara Riganti. He enlisted in the US Navy October 12, 1939 in Los Angeles, California and completed his basic training at the Naval Training Station in San Diego, California. He reported for duty on the USS Arizona December 20, 1939. Fred was killed in action on December 7, 1941 at Pearl Harbor, Hawaii. He was awarded the American Defense Service Medal, World War II Victory Medal and Purple Heart Medal posthumously. Fred remains on duty on the USS Arizona. He is commemorated on the USS Arizona Memorial and the Memorial Tablets of the Missing, National Memorial Cemetery of the Pacific, Honolulu, Hawaii. Fred was survived by his Father, Mr. Pietro Riganti, 114 South Pacific, Redondo Beach, California.[642]

Riggins, Gerald Herald   Seaman, First Class, Serial No: 316 64 05, US Navy. Gerald was born October 16, 1918, son of Bernard Zelotus Riggins and Bell Height (Moore) Riggins. He enlisted in the US Navy March 27, 1940 in Omaha, Nebraska and completed his basic training at the Naval Training Station in Great Lakes, Illinois. Gerald reported for duty on the USS Arizona July 12, 1940. He was killed in action on December 7, 1941 at Pearl Harbor, Hawaii. Gerald was awarded the American Defense Service Medal, World War II Victory Medal and Purple Heart Medal posthumously. He remains on duty on the USS Arizona. Gerald is commemorated on the USS Arizona Memorial and the Memorial Tablets of the Missing, National Memorial Cemetery of the Pacific, Honolulu, Hawaii and Brule Cemetery, Brule, Nebraska. He was survived by his Mother, Mrs. Belle Height Riggins, 1503 Corinth Avenue, West Los Angeles, California.

---

[642] Fred Riganti, Photo provided by his brother, T. Riganti.

Riner, Earl William   Gunner's Mate, Third Class, Division 5, Serial No. 356 26 80, US Navy. Earle was born December 5, 1921 in Atoka, Oklahoma the son of Thomas Eldin Riner and Estelle Barrett Riner. He enlisted in the US Navy May 24, 1940 in Dallas, Texas and completed his training at the Naval Training Station, San Diego, California. He reported for duty on the USS Arizona August 24, 1940. He was wounded in action while serving on the USS Arizona on December 7, 1941 when the Japanese attacked Pearl Harbor. His uniform and much of his flesh were flash burned from his body. After the attack, Earle was taken to the Naval Hospital at Pearl Harbor, Hawaii for treatment. He was transferred on December 18th to the US Naval Hospital at Mare Island, California for further treatment. His Mother, Mrs. Estelle Riner, General Delivery, Lehigh, Oklahoma was notified. On June 3, 1945 Earl began serving on board the USS Lake Champlain (CV-39) in late 1944 where he served until June of 1946. He died on Friday, March 9, 2012 in Paradise Cove, Texas.[643]

Rivera, Francisco Unpingco   Mess Attendant, Second Class, Serial No: 421 07 16, US Navy. Francisco was born June 4, 1918 in Guahan, Las Islas Marianas, Guam the son of Juan Guzman Aguon and Maria Unpingco Castro. He enlisted in the US Navy November 1, 1940 and reported for duty on the USS Arizona April 8, 1941. *Francisco was supposed to be on leave December 7th but had traded his leave with another shipmate. He died December 11, 1941 from a fracture and gunshot wound received during the attack on Pearl Harbor December 7, 1941.* Assigned death no. 428 his body was sent home for burial.[644] He was awarded the American Defense Service Medal, World War II Victory Medal and Purple Heart Medal posthumously. Francisco is buried in Row C, Agana Cemetery, the US Naval Cemetery, Guam. He is commemorated on the USS Arizona Memorial and the Sons of Guam Pearl Harbor Memorial, Guam. Francisco was survived by his Sister, Miss Manuela Unpingco Rivera, Lot 321, Sumay, Guam.[645]

Roberts, Dwight Fisk   Fireman, First Class, Serial No: 342 08 54, US Navy. Dwight was born in 1919 in Cimarron, Kansas, the son of George L. Roberts and Cecil G. Roberts. He enlisted in the US Navy September 9, 1938 in Kansas City, Missouri and completed his basic training at the Naval Training Station, San Diego, California. He reported for duty on the USS Arizona March 11, 1939. Dwight was killed in action on December 7, 1941 at Pearl Harbor, Hawaii. He was awarded the American Defense Service Medal, World War II Victory Medal and Purple Heart Medal posthumously. Dwight remains on duty on the USS Arizona. He is commemorated on the USS Arizona Memorial and the Memorial Tablets of the Missing, National Memorial Cemetery of the Pacific, Honolulu, Hawaii. Dwight was survived by his Father, Mr. George L. Roberts, Cimarron, Kansas.

---

[643] Earl William Riner, Information and photo from his obituary in The Herald Democrat, March 15, 2012.
[644] Report of Changes of the USS Arizona Flag Allowance (CBD-1) Commander Battleship Division One for the period ending 7th day of December, 1941, Page 3, line 1, Rivera, Francisco Unpingco.
[645] Francisco Unpingco Rivera, Information and photo provided by his niece, Carmelita Edwards.

Roberts, Kenneth Franklin Boatswain's Mate, Second Class, Serial No: 385 79 47, US Navy. Kenneth was born October 20, 1919 in Thurston County, Washington, the son of Clarence John Roberts and Lena (Sturgis) Roberts. He enlisted in the US Navy November 14, 1938 in Seattle, Washington and completed his basic training at the Naval Training Station in San Diego, California. Kenneth reported for duty on the USS Arizona March 11, 1939. He was killed in action on December 7, 1941 at Pearl Harbor, Hawaii. Kenneth was awarded the American Defense Service Medal, World War II Victory Medal and Purple Heart Medal posthumously. He remains on duty on the USS Arizona. Kenneth is commemorated on the USS Arizona Memorial and the Memorial Tablets of the Missing, National Memorial Cemetery of the Pacific, Honolulu, Hawaii. He was survived by his Father, Mr. Clarence John Roberts, 3726 South Fawcett Avenue, Tacoma, Washington.

Roberts, McClellan Taylor Chief Pharmacist's Mate, Serial No: 371 32 58, US Navy. McClellan was born March 11, 1901 in Owsley County, Kentucky, son of Lazarus Lawson Roberts and Pauline (Baker) Roberts. He enlisted in the US Navy December 5, 1936 in Pearl Harbor, Hawaii. *McClellan was honored by being selected for a key role in the "Crossing the Line" ceremony on July 24, 1940. He signed the certificates as Davey Jones, His Majesty's Scribe.* McClellan served on the USS Arizona from March 2, 1940 until he was killed in action on December 7, 1941 at Pearl Harbor, Hawaii. His battle station would have been sick bay. He was awarded the American Defense Service Medal, World War II Victory Medal and Purple Heart Medal posthumously. McClellan remains on duty on the USS Arizona. He is commemorated on the USS Arizona Memorial and the Memorial Tablets of the Missing, National Memorial Cemetery of the Pacific, Honolulu, Hawaii. McClellan was survived by his Wife, Mrs. Marvel Veak Roberts, 2434 Chestnut Avenue, Long Beach, California.[646]

Roberts, Walter Scott, Jr. Radioman, First Class, Serial No: 341 96 17, US Navy. Walter was born in about 1919 in Kansas to Walter Scott and Edith O. Roberts. He enlisted in the US Navy March 10, 1936 in Kansas City, Missouri and reported for duty on the USS Arizona March 28, 1940. He was killed in action on December 7, 1941 at Pearl Harbor, Hawaii. Walter was awarded the American Defense Service Medal, World War II Victory Medal and Purple Heart Medal posthumously. He remains on duty on the USS Arizona. Walter is commemorated on the USS Arizona Memorial and the Memorial Tablets of the Missing, National Memorial Cemetery of the Pacific, Honolulu, Hawaii. He was survived by his Mother, Mrs. Edith Orran England, 3101 Pearl Avenue, Joplin, Missouri.[647]

---

[646] McClellan Taylor Roberts, Information and photo provided by his grandson, Dale S. Roberts.
[647] Walter Scott Roberts, Jr. Photo from Missouri Honor States.

Roberts, Wilburn Carle Baker, Third Class, Serial No: 274 48 17, US Navy. Wilburn was born July 20, 1920, one of eight children of William Elisha Roberts and Cora Martha (Rush) Roberts. He enlisted in the US Navy July 17, 1940 in New Orleans, Louisiana and completed his basic training at the Naval Training Station in San Diego, California. Wilburn reported for duty on the USS Arizona October 1, 1940. He was killed in action on December 7, 1941 at Pearl Harbor, Hawaii. Wilburn was awarded the American Defense Service Medal, World War II Victory Medal and Purple Heart Medal posthumously. He remains on duty on the USS Arizona. Wilburn is commemorated on the USS Arizona Memorial and the Memorial Tablets of the Missing, National Memorial Cemetery of the Pacific, Honolulu, Hawaii. When Wilburn was killed, the other three sons that were of age, joined the service. Wilburn's brother, ML was killed on a bomber plane in the Pacific. His mother, to her dying day, looked down the road praying to see her two sons (Wilburn and ML) walking up the road. Of course neither of their bodies were returned to her. He was survived by his Parents, Mr. William Elisha Roberts Mrs. Cora Martha Roberts, Pollock, Louisiana.[648]

Roberts, William Francis Seaman, Second Class, Serial No: 272 41 85, US Navy. William was born August 10, 1917 in Alabama to George Wyatt and Annie Pearl (Cleckler) Roberts. He enlisted in the US Navy October 5, 1940 in Birmingham, Alabama and completed his basic training at the Naval Training Station in Norfolk, Virginia. He reported for duty on the USS Arizona December 4, 1940. William was killed in action on December 7, 1941 at Pearl Harbor, Hawaii. He was awarded the American Defense Service Medal, World War II Victory Medal and Purple Heart Medal posthumously. William remains on duty on the USS Arizona. He is commemorated on the USS Arizona Memorial and the Memorial Tablets of the Missing, National Memorial Cemetery of the Pacific, Honolulu, Hawaii. William is survived by his Father, Mr. George Wyatt Roberts, 103 West 8th Street, Oxford, Alabama.[649]

Robertson, Edgar, Jr. Mess Attendant, Third Class, Serial No: 266 12 58, US Navy. Edgar was born in 1913, son of Edgar Robertson and Myrtle Robertson. He enlisted in the US Navy June 12, 1940 in Richmond, Virginia. Edgar transferred from the USS Pennsylvania to the USS Arizona August 22, 1941. He was killed in action on December 7, 1941 at Pearl Harbor, Hawaii. Edgar was awarded the American Defense Service Medal, World War II Victory Medal and Purple Heart Medal posthumously. He remains on duty on the USS Arizona. Edgar is commemorated on the USS Arizona Memorial and the Memorial Tablets of the Missing, National Memorial Cemetery of the Pacific, Honolulu, Hawaii. He was survived by his Father, Mr. Edgar Robertson, 210 2nd Avenue, Richmond, Virginia.

---

[648] Wilburn Carle Roberts, Photo and information provided by family member, Marinell Roberts Hollingsworth.
[649] William Francis Roberts, Photo from Alabama Honor States.

Robertson, James Milton   Machinist's Mate, First Class, Serial No: 295 33 32, US Navy. James was born August 24, 1918 in Tennessee to Rufus K. and Lenora "Linnie" (McCoy) Robertson. He enlisted in the US Navy October 26, 1936 in Nashville, Tennessee and reported for duty on the USS Arizona July 6, 1937. He was killed in action on December 7, 1941 at Pearl Harbor. James was awarded the American Defense Service Medal, World War II Victory Medal and Purple Heart Medal posthumously. He remains on duty on the USS Arizona. James is commemorated on the USS Arizona Memorial and the Memorial Tablets of the Missing, National Memorial Cemetery of the Pacific, Honolulu, Hawaii. He was survived by his Father, Mr. Rufus K. Robertson, Route 2, Morristown, Tennessee. The James Milton Robertson VFW Post No. 5266 in Morristown, Tennessee was named in his honor. A memorial marker is located in Liberty Hill United Methodist Church in Morristown, Tennessee and every year on Memorial Day the VFW 5266 Honor Guard places a wreath and honors his memory with a 21 gun salute and taps.[650]

Robinson, Harold Thomas   Seaman, Second Class, Serial No: 382 36 96, US Navy. Harold was born May 2, 1923 in Pasadena, California, the son of Harold Thomas and Hazel Mildred (Nott) Robinson. He enlisted in the US Navy January 23, 1941 in Los Angeles, California and completed his basic training at the Naval Training Station in San Diego, California. He reported for duty on the USS Arizona April 26, 1941. Harold was killed in action on December 7, 1941 at Pearl Harbor, Hawaii. He was awarded the American Defense Service Medal, World War II Victory Medal and Purple Heart Medal posthumously. Harold remains on duty on the USS Arizona. He is commemorated on the USS Arizona Memorial and the Memorial Tablets of the Missing, National Memorial Cemetery of the Pacific, Honolulu, Hawaii. Harold was survived by his Parents, Mr. and Mrs. Harold Thomas Robinson, 505 Ladera Street, Pasadena, California, one brother and one sister.[651]

Robinson, James Williams   Seaman, Second Class, Serial No: 382 36 47, US Navy. James was born October 10, 1923 in Texas. He enlisted in the US Navy January 18, 1941 in Los Angeles, California and completed his basic training at the Naval Training Station in San Diego, California. He reported for duty on the USS Arizona April 26, 1941. Assigned death #554, James was killed in action on December 7, 1941 at Pearl Harbor, Hawaii. His remains were identified by his waist band.[652] He was awarded the American Defense Service Medal, World War II Victory Medal and Purple Heart Medal posthumously. James' remains were recovered and he was buried in Plot C, Row 0, Grave 1189, National Memorial Cemetery of the Pacific, Honolulu, Hawaii. He is commemorated on the USS Arizona Memorial. James was survived by his Mother, Mrs. Beemie Rita Robinson, 11243 South Berendo Street, Los Angeles, California.

---

[650] James Milton Robertson, Information and Photo provided by the James Milton Robertson VFW Post No. 5266, Morristown, Tennessee.

[651] Harold Thomas Robinson, Photo and information from his nephew, Tom Marilyn Bruner.

[652] Report of Changes of the USS Arizona for the month ending 31st day of December, 1941, Page 95, line 8, James William Robinson.

Robinson, John James Electrician's Mate, First Class, Serial No: 393 25 82, US Navy. John was born August 1, 1919 in Montana to Loy H. and Ida V. Robinson. He enlisted in the US Navy February 14, 1938 and reported for duty on the USS Arizona October 6, 1938. John was killed in action on December 7, 1941 at Pearl Harbor, Hawaii. He was awarded the American Defense Service Medal, World War II Victory Medal and Purple Heart Medal posthumously. John remains on duty on the USS Arizona. He is commemorated on the USS Arizona Memorial and the Memorial Tablets of the Missing, National Memorial Cemetery of the Pacific, Honolulu, Hawaii. John was survived by his Mother, Mrs. Ida V. Robinson, 4835 S.I. 61st Street, Portland, Oregon.[653]

Robinson, Lewis Perrin Seaman, First Class, 5th Division, Serial No. 381 26 98, US Navy. Lewis was born September 9, 1919 in Delaware. He enlisted in the US Navy November 16, 1938 in San Diego, California and completed his training at the Naval Training Station, San Diego, California. He reported for duty on the USS Arizona March 11, 1939. He was serving on the USS Arizona on December 7, 1941 when the Japanese attacked Pearl Harbor. That morning he stood on a dock at Pearl Harbor waiting for a boat to return him to the USS Arizona after an overnight shore leave. After the attack, Lewis was transferred to the USS Argonne (AG-31) for duty. Lewis served four more years and was discharged in 1945. He died September 17, 1997 in Solona Beach, California. His ashes were interred in Turret IV on the USS Arizona December 7, 2001.

Robinson, Robert Warren Pharmacist's Mate, Third Class, Serial No: 258 28 64, US Navy. Robert was born April 22, 1922 in West Virginia, son of Willis O. Robinson and Virginia Grace Robinson. He enlisted in the US Navy June 12, 1940 in Baltimore, Maryland and reported for duty on the USS Arizona June 7, 1941. Robert was killed in action on December 7, 1941 at Pearl Harbor, Hawaii. He was awarded the American Defense Service Medal, World War II Victory Medal and Purple Heart Medal posthumously. Robert's remains were recovered and he was buried in Plot A, Row 0, Grave 880, National Memorial Cemetery of the Pacific, Honolulu, Hawaii. He is commemorated on the USS Arizona Memorial. Robert was survived by his Mother, Mrs. Virginia Grace Robinson, Fisher Building, Sistersville, West Virginia.

Roby, Raymond Arthur Seaman, First Class, Serial No: 250 54 03, US Navy. Raymond was born June 30, 1921, the only son of George H. Roby and Elsie Iona (Danser) Roby. He graduated from North Union High school and enlisted in the US Navy January 10, 1940 in Uniontown, Pennsylvania and reported for duty on the USS Arizona March 29, 1940. Raymond was killed in action on December 7, 1941 at Pearl Harbor, Hawaii. He was awarded the American Defense Service Medal, World War II Victory Medal and Purple Heart Medal posthumously. Raymond remains on duty on the USS Arizona. He is commemorated on the USS Arizona Memorial and the Memorial Tablets of the Missing, National Memorial Cemetery of the Pacific, Honolulu, Hawaii. Raymond

---

[653] John James Robinson, Photo from Oregon Honor States.

was survived by his Parents, Mr. and Mrs. George Roby, 34 Mill Street, Uniontown, Pennsylvania; four sisters, Beverly, Laura Jo, Lois and Anne and his grand-parents, Josephine and Guy Dancer of Uniontown, PA and Perry Roby of Johnstown, PA.[654]

Rodgers, John Dayton Seaman, First Class, Serial No: 250 54 60. US Navy. John was born in about 1920 in Pennsylvania the son of George M. Rodgers. He enlisted in the US Navy January 10, 1940 in Pittsburgh, Pennsylvania and completed his basic training at the Naval Training Station in Newport, Rhode Island. John reported for duty on the USS Arizona March 29, 1940. He was killed in action on December 7, 1941 at Pearl Harbor, Hawaii. John was awarded the American Defense Service Medal, World War II Victory Medal and Purple Heart Medal posthumously. He remains on duty on the USS Arizona. John is commemorated on the USS Arizona Memorial and the Memorial Tablets of the Missing, National Memorial Cemetery of the Pacific, Honolulu, Hawaii. He was survived by his Brother, Mr. George Rodgers, 148 Wallace Street, East Pittsburgh, Pennsylvania. The John Dayton Rodgers VFW Post 6681 in East Pittsburgh, Pennsylvania was named in his honor.[655]

Roehm, Harry "Turner" Turner Machinist's Mate, Second Class, Serial No: 337 00 14, US Navy. Harry was born March 26, 1918 in Belle Rive, Illinois, the eldest son of Harry Love Roehm and Minnie J. (Toppings) Roehm. He enlisted in the US Navy September 9, 1937 in St. Louis, Missouri and reported for duty on the USS Arizona January 7, 1938. Harry was killed in action on December 7, 1941 at Pearl Harbor, Hawaii. He was awarded the American Defense Service Medal, World War II Victory Medal and Purple Heart Medal posthumously. Harry remains on duty on the USS Arizona. He is commemorated on the USS Arizona Memorial and the Memorial Tablets of the Missing, National Memorial Cemetery of the Pacific, Honolulu, Hawaii. Harry was survived by his Parents, Mr. and Mrs. Harry Love Roehm, Belle Rive, Illinois.[656]

Rogers, Thomas Spurgeon Chief Water Tender, Serial No: 184 03 73, US Navy. Thomas was born September 2, 1892 in Alabama to John Wesley and Loretta (Armstrong) Rogers. He was recalled from the Feet Reserve and reported for duty on the USS Arizona September 30, 1940. Thomas was killed in action on December 7, 1941 at Pearl Harbor, Hawaii. He was awarded the American Defense Service Medal, World War II Victory Medal and Purple Heart Medal posthumously. Thomas remains on duty on the USS Arizona. He is commemorated on the USS Arizona Memorial and the Memorial Tablets of the Missing, National Memorial Cemetery of the Pacific, Honolulu, Hawaii. Thomas was survived by his Wife, Mrs. Thomas Spurgeon Rogers, 1530 46th Street, Belview Heights, Birmingham, Alabama.[657]

---

[654] Raymond Arthur Roby, Photo provided by family member, Lynn Chapdelaine, from newspaper article in the Evening Standard, Uniontown, Pennsylvania, February 6, 1942.
[655] John Dayton Rodgers, Photo provided by the John Dayton Rodgers VFW Post 6681, East Pittsburg, PA.
[656] Harry Turner Roehm, Photo from Missouri Honor States.
[657] Thomas Spurgeon Rogers, Photo from Alabama Honor States.

Romano, Simon Chief Carpenter's Mate, Serial No: 497 87 94, US Navy. Simon was born on October 28, 1897 in Dumaguite, Philippine Islands. He enlisted in the US Navy March 9, 1927 in the Philippines and reported for duty on the USS Arizona December 3, 1938. Simon was killed in action on December 7, 1941 at Pearl Harbor, Hawaii. He was awarded the American Defense Service Medal, World War II Victory Medal and Purple Heart Medal posthumously. Simon remains on duty on the USS Arizona. He is commemorated on the USS Arizona Memorial and the Memorial Tablets of the Missing, National Memorial Cemetery of the Pacific, Honolulu, Hawaii. Simon was survived by his Wife, Mrs. Ella Mae Romano, 2233 Keller Avenue, Norfolk, Virginia.[658]

Rombalski, Donald Roger Seaman, Second Class, Serial No: 385 99 96, US Navy. Donald was born April 22, 1924 in Washington, son of Sylvester Rombalski and Emma Rombalski. He enlisted in the US Navy April 25, 1941 in Seattle, Washington and completed his basic training at the Naval Training Station in San Diego, California. Donald reported for duty on the USS Arizona August 13, 1941. He was killed in action on December 7, 1941 at Pearl Harbor, Hawaii. Donald was awarded the American Defense Service Medal, World War II Victory Medal and Purple Heart Medal posthumously. He remains buried on the USS Arizona. Donald is commemorated on the USS Arizona Memorial and the Memorial Tablets of the Missing, National Memorial Cemetery of the Pacific, Honolulu, Hawaii. He was survived by his Father, Mr. Sylvester Antone Rombalski, Route 2, Box 35A, Centralia, Washington.[659]

Romero, Vladimir "Vlady" Mendoza Seaman, First Class, Serial No: 223 89 73, US Navy. Vladimir was born in about 1922 in Tampa, Florida the youngest child to Rafael Feliciano De La Trinidad Romero and Francisca Perales (Mendoza) Romero. *His father had a stroke in the 1930's and returned to Mexico while his mother, a union organizer, was in jail in Tampa, Florida leaving the children with their Grandmother. The family moved to New York City in about 1931 to look for work after trouble in the tobacco industry in Tampa.* Vlady enlisted in the US Navy October 15, 1940 in New York, New York and completed his basic training at the Naval Training Station in Newport, Rhode Island. He reported for duty on the USS Arizona December 10, 1940. Vladimir was killed in action on December 7, 1941 at Pearl Harbor, Hawaii. He was awarded the American Defense Service Medal, World War II Victory Medal and Purple Heart Medal posthumously. Vladimir remains on duty on the USS Arizona. He is commemorated on the USS Arizona Memorial and the Memorial Tablets of the Missing, National Memorial Cemetery of the Pacific, Honolulu, Hawaii. Vladimir was survived by his

---

[658] Simon Romano, Photo and information taken from his Petition for Naturalization, Southern District, Central Division, Los Angeles, California, District Court, November 20, 1933.
[659] Donald Roger Rombalski, Photo from the Daily Chronicle, Centralia, Washington, May 7, 1945.

Mother, Mrs. Frances Mendoza Romero, 224 East 112th Street, New York, New York, brother, Vesper and sisters Yorkina and Henrietta.[660]

Root, Melvin Lenord Seaman, First Class, Serial No: 283 41 34, US Navy. Melvin was born December 30, 1916, son of Virgil Riley Root and Frances C. Root. He enlisted in the US Navy October 9, 1940 in Cleveland, Ohio and completed his basic training at the Naval Training Station in Great Lakes, Illinois. Melvin reported for duty on the USS Arizona December 2, 1940. He was killed in action on December 7, 1941 at Pearl Harbor, Hawaii. Melvin was awarded the American Defense Service Medal, World War II Victory Medal and Purple Heart Medal posthumously. Melvin is commemorated on the USS Arizona Memorial and the Memorial Tablets of the Missing, National Memorial Cemetery of the Pacific, Honolulu, Hawaii and the World War II Monument Canfield, Ohio. He was survived by his Parents, Mr. and Mrs. Virgil Riley Root, Route 1, Canfield, Ohio.[661]

Rose, Chester "Chet" Clay Boatswain's Mate, First Class, Serial No: 287 11 64, US Navy. Chester was born February 29, 1916 in Clark County, Kentucky, son of Joseph Dailey Rose and Golden Katherine (Byrd) Rose. He enlisted in the US Navy July 12, 1934 in Louisville, Kentucky and completed his basic training at the Naval Training Station in Newport News, Virginia where he received an award for his Academic ability. *In 1939, Chester and shipmate Jim Vlach were on Shore Patrol in Seattle, Washington. Their job was to go into the bars to break up fights among the serviceman. On one particular occasion, Chet took on 2 big burly guys and booted them out of ton of these dives and into the street single handedly. Jim Vlatch said he knew he definitely wanted Chet with him if he should ever have a problem with big rowdies like those two again. Chester was a member of the Arizona Football Team. He weighed about 190 lbs. and was approximately 6 foot tall.* Chester served on the USS Arizona from December 22, 1934 until he was killed in action on December 7, 1941 at Pearl Harbor. *He survived the first attack. Chester and John Delmar Anderson, BM2c, made it to Ford Island and headed back to the ship to rescue others. While in a lifeboat pulling injured crew members out of the water their boat was hit and all were killed with the exception of Delmar.* Chester was awarded the American Defense Service Medal, World War II Victory Medal and Purple Heart Medal posthumously. It is unclear whether his remains were recovered; it is possible that he was buried in one of the "unknown" graves in the punchbowl. He is commemorated on the USS Arizona Memorial and the Memorial Tablets of the Missing, National Memorial Cemetery of the Pacific, Honolulu, Hawaii. Chester was survived by his Father, Mr. Joseph D. Rose, Route 1, Winchester, Kentucky and daughter, Margie Anne Rose of Los Angeles, California.[662]

---

[660] Vladimir Mendoza Romero, Picture and information provided by family member, Rebekah Tomlinson Mendoza.

[661] Melvin Lenord Root, Picture and information from World War II Young American Patriots, 1941-1945, Mahoning County, Ohio, Page 681.

[662] Chester Clay Rose, Photo and stories provided by his daughter, Margie Rose-Chirrick.

Rosenbery, Orval A.   Shipfitter, Second Class, Serial No: 299 92 68, US Navy. *Orval was born in August 1920 and reared on a farm two miles from a small town in north central Illinois called Chadwick. He graduated from a very small high school in 1938. At that time, recovering from the Depression, farming wasn't a very good life and his parents worked very hard to make ends meet. However, we always had plenty to eat and his very hard working mother was an excellent cook. His Dad, who was born and raised in the mountains of Pennsylvania, was also a very hard worker and served in the Army in WWI in France.*

Oval's idol was his Uncle Albert from Pennsylvania. He spent some time in the Navy in the early 1920's and became a welder. Orval, not caring for farming at all, decided he wanted to do what Uncle Albert did and became a U.S. Navy welder. We got a new tractor in 1936 and he could care less about learning how to run it and as well didn't ever learn to drive a car. His parents didn't promote his driving a car either.

Orval enlisted in the Navy November 15, 1938 in Chicago, Illinois and completed his basic training at the Naval Training Station at Great Lakes, Illinois. He reported for duty on the USS Arizona in Bremerton, Washington March 25, 1939.

As my mother and I were taking him to the train in Chadwick, March 1939, he started sobbing. His mother asked "what's wrong?" He replied, "I don't think I'll ever make it back home again!" His mother replied, "Oh! Don't feel that way!" As it turned out he never did make it home again, even though he had some "leave" he couldn't drive, he couldn't come back like some did in taking a car and sharing the driving time so they could sort of drive straight through. Apparently, I assume my parents couldn't afford to buy his train ticket.

Orval had a premonition that he would be killed. In some of his last letters he said "I'm spending all my money and having a good time 'cuz eventually we're all going to be lying down on the bottom of the Ocean floor anyway." He also mentioned that if a bomb ever hits the Arizona, I will be blown "sky high" as I'm assigned to the boiler room right near all the heavy munitions, explosives, etc. And that is exactly what happened. Orval was killed in action on December 7, 1941 at Pearl Harbor, Hawaii on board the USS Arizona. He was awarded the American Defense Service Medal, World War II Victory Medal and Purple Heart Medal posthumously. Orval remains on duty on the USS Arizona. He is commemorated on the USS Arizona Memorial and the Memorial Tablets of the Missing, National Memorial Cemetery of the Pacific, Honolulu, Hawaii. Orval was survived by his Parents, Mr. Benjamin Luther Rosenbery & Lucille Rosenbery, and his brother Vernon Rosenbery of Chadwick, Illinois.[663]

Ross, Deane Lundy   Seaman, Second Class, Serial No: 223 89 74, US Navy. Deane was born in about 1923 in South Dakota the son of Archie O. and Anna J. Ross. He enlisted in the US Navy October 15, 1940 in New York, New York and completed his basic training at the Naval Training Station in Newport, Rhode Island. He reported for duty on the USS Arizona December 10, 1940. Deane was killed in action on December 7, 1941 at Pearl Harbor, Hawaii. He was awarded the American Defense Service Medal, World War II Victory Medal and Purple Heart Medal posthumously. Deane remains on duty on the USS Arizona. He is commemorated on the USS Arizona Memorial and the Memorial Tablets of the Missing, National Memorial Cemetery of the Pacific, Honolulu, Hawaii. Deane was survived by his Father, Mr. Archie O. Ross, Shadyside Avenue, South Nyack, New York.

---

[663] Orval A. Rosenbery, Information and photo provided by his brother, Vernon C. Rosenbery.

Ross, William Fraser Gunner's Mate, Third Class, Serial No: 223 82 64, US Navy. William was born in about 1918 in Canada to Donald and Annie C. Ross. He enlisted in the US Navy September 5, 1940 in New York, New York and completed his basic training at the Naval Training Station in Newport, Rhode Island. He reported for duty on the USS Arizona October 10, 1940. William was killed in action on December 7, 1941 at Pearl Harbor, Hawaii. He was awarded the American Defense Service Medal, World War II Victory Medal and Purple Heart Medal posthumously. William remains on duty on the USS Arizona. He is commemorated on the USS Arizona Memorial and the Memorial Tablets of the Missing, National Memorial Cemetery of the Pacific, Honolulu, Hawaii. William was survived by his Father, Mr. Donald Ross, 97-10 125th Street, Richmond Hill, New York.[664]

Rourke, John Paul Seaman, First Class, Serial No. 223 89 75, US Navy. John was born May 5, 1921 in New Haven, Connecticut to Michael and Theresa (Gallogley) Rourke. He enlisted in the US Navy October 15, 1940 in New York, New York and completed his training at the Naval Training Station, Newport, Rhode Island. He reported for duty on the USS Arizona December 10, 1940. He was serving on the USS Arizona on December 7, 1941 when the Japanese attacked Pearl Harbor. After the attack, John was transferred to the USS Salt Lake City for duty. John died November 22, 1981 in Monterey, California.

Rowe, Eugene "Gene" Joseph Seaman, First Class, Serial No: 404 91 98, US Navy. Eugene was born in 1921, son of Eugene Rand Rowe and Agnes M. Rowe. *He attended Collingswood (NJ) High School prior to entering the Navy but did not graduate. After leaving High School, he attended Camden County Vocational School in Pennsauken, NJ and spent six months in a Civilian Conservation Corps camp. He also worked for a spell for the Radio Corporation of America in Camden, NJ. He enlisted with his classmate from high school, Walter Hamilton Simon, in the US Navy October 16, 1940 in Philadelphia, Pennsylvania and completed his basic training at the Naval Training Station in Newport, Rhode Island. Eugene reported for duty on the USS Arizona December 10, 1940. He was initially assigned as a cook, and later* transferred to a gun crew. Gene was killed in action on December 7, 1941 at Pearl Harbor, Hawaii. He was awarded the American Defense Service Medal, World War II Victory Medal and Purple Heart Medal posthumously. Gene remains on duty on the USS Arizona. He is commemorated on the USS Arizona Memorial and the Memorial Tablets of the Missing, National Memorial Cemetery of the Pacific, Honolulu, Hawaii. Gene was survived by his Parents, Mr. and Mrs. Eugene Ronda Rowe, 11 East Collingswood Avenue, Oaklyn, New Jersey.[665]

---

[664] William Fraser Ross, Photo from The Brooklyn Daily Eagle, Brooklyn, New York, Saturday, February 14, 1942, Page 7.
[665] Eugene Joseph Rowe, Information provided by the Camden County Historical Society, Photo from the 1942 Collingswood High School Yearbook, Collingswood, New Jersey.

Rowell, Frank Malcom   Seaman, Second Class, Serial No: 360 38 91, US Navy. Frank was born in 1924 in Liberty, Texas, the son of Jess Malcolm Rowell and Irene Melba (Walker) Rowell. He enlisted in the US Navy May 27, 1941 in Houston, Texas and completed his basic training at the Naval Training Station in San Diego, California. Frank reported for duty on the USS Arizona August 13, 1941. He was killed in action on December 7, 1941 at Pearl Harbor, Hawaii. Frank was awarded the American Defense Service Medal, World War II Victory Medal and Purple Heart Medal posthumously. He remains on duty on the USS Arizona. Frank is commemorated on the USS Arizona Memorial and the Memorial Tablets of the Missing, National Memorial Cemetery of the Pacific, Honolulu, Hawaii. He was survived by his Father, Mr. Jess Malcom Rowell, Hull, Texas.[666]

Rowley, Welton Dana   Lieutenant Commander, Serial No. 0-03099, US Navy. Welton was born on November 13, 1905 in Sioux Falls, South Dakota, eldest son of Clarence D. Rowley and Blanche Rowley. He was commissioned in the US Navy June 2, 1927 and reported for duty on the USS Arizona where he was serving Commanding VO1, technical Aviation Adv. To CBD-1 on December 7, 1941 when the Japanese attacked Pearl Harbor. Welton also served in the Korean War. Welton retired from the Navy attaining the rank of Captain in December 1957. He died on April 28, 1987 in California and is buried in Section 19A, Site 2567, Riverside National Cemetery, Riverside, California.[667]

Royals, William Nicholas   Fireman, First Class, Serial No: 265 93 20, US Navy. William was born January 1, 1921 in Norfolk County, Virginia, the son of Ira C. Royals and Mary Ann Royals. He enlisted in the US Navy September 11, 1939 in Norfolk, Virginia and reported for duty on the USS Arizona January 4, 1941. William was killed in action on December 7, 1941 at Pearl Harbor, Hawaii. He was awarded the American Defense Service Medal, World War II Victory Medal and Purple Heart Medal posthumously. William remains on duty on the USS Arizona. He is commemorated on the USS Arizona Memorial and the Memorial Tablets of the Missing, National Memorial Cemetery of the Pacific, Honolulu, Hawaii and Section E, Olive Branch Cemetery, Portsmouth, Virginia. William was survived by his Mother, Mrs. Mary Ann Royals, Route 3, Box 22, Portsmouth, Virginia.

---

[666] Frank Malcom Rowell, Photo from the Liberty Vindicator Newspaper, Liberty, Texas, Thursday, February 10, 1944, Page 1.

[667] Welton Dana Rowley, Photo from Lucky Bag Yearbook, United States Naval Academy, Annapolis, MD, class of 1927.

Royer, Howard Dale   Gunner's Mate, Third Class, Serial No: 283 39 09, US Navy. Howard was born November 8, 1918 in Suffield, Ohio the oldest of three boys born to Charles E. and Anna M. Royer. *The Royer family were farmers, hard-working, devoted to family, friends and neighbors. Howard played football and basketball.* He enlisted in the US Navy September 9, 1940 in Cleveland, Ohio and completed his basic training at the Naval Training Station in Norfolk, Virginia. He reported for duty on the USS Arizona December 4, 1940. Howard was killed in action on December 7, 1941 at Pearl Harbor, Hawaii. He was awarded the American Defense Service Medal, World War II Victory Medal and Purple Heart Medal posthumously. Howard remains on duty on the USS Arizona. He is commemorated on the USS Arizona Memorial and the Memorial Tablets of the Missing, National Memorial Cemetery of the Pacific, Honolulu, Hawaii. Howard was survived by his Wife, Mrs. Esther Royer, Route 1, Clinton, Ohio.[668]

Rozar, John Frank   Watertender, Second Class, Serial No: 372 02 46, US Navy. John was born in 1917 in Colorado Springs, Colorado, the son of Joseph and Mary Elizabeth (Rogula) Rozar. He enlisted in the US Navy July 10, 1937 in Denver Colorado and reported for duty on the USS Arizona January 7, 1938. He was killed in action on December 7, 1941 at Pearl Harbor, Hawaii. John was awarded the American Defense Service Medal, World War II Victory Medal and Purple Heart Medal posthumously. He remains on duty on the USS Arizona. John is commemorated on the USS Arizona Memorial and the Memorial Tablets of the Missing, National Memorial Cemetery of the Pacific, Honolulu, Hawaii. He was survived by his Mother, Mrs. Mary Elizabeth Rozar, 529 Redondo Street, Long Beach, California.[669]

Rozmus, Joseph Stanley   Seaman, First Class, Serial No: 201 78 68, US Navy. Joseph was born in about 1919 in Manchester, New Hampshire to Frank and Maria A. (Potoczna) Rozmus. He enlisted in the US Navy October 15, 1940 in Boston, Massachusetts and completed his basic training at the Naval Training Station in Newport, Rhode Island. He reported for duty on the USS Arizona December 10, 1940. Joseph was killed in action on December 7, 1941 at Pearl Harbor, Hawaii. He was awarded the American Defense Service Medal, World War II Victory Medal and Purple Heart Medal posthumously. Joseph remains on duty on the USS Arizona. He is commemorated on the USS Arizona Memorial and the Memorial Tablets of the Missing, National Memorial Cemetery of the Pacific, Honolulu, Hawaii. Joseph was survived by his Father, Mr. Frank Rozmus, 253 Cedar Street, Manchester, New Hampshire.[670]

---

[668] Howard Dale Royer, Information and photo provided by his niece, Diana Palma.

[669] John Frank Rozar, Photo from Colorado Springs High School Yearbook 1935, Colorado Springs, Colorado, Page 32.

[670] Joseph Stanley Rozmus, Photo from "Pearl Harbor USS Arizona Casualty: Manchester NY's Sea1c Joseph S. Rozmus (1919-1941) by Janice Brown, New Hampshire History Blog, June 20, 2013,

Ruddock, Cecil Roy Seaman, First Class, Serial No: 274 48 81, US Navy. Cecil was born August 24, 1919 in Mississippi, son of Thomas Jefferson Ruddock and Evylin Ruddock. He enlisted in the US Navy August 5, 1940 in New Orleans, Louisiana and completed his basic training at the Naval Training Station in San Diego, California. Cecil reported for duty on the USS Arizona October 8, 1940. He was killed in action on December 7, 1941 at Pearl Harbor, Hawaii. Cecil was awarded the American Defense Service Medal, World War II Victory Medal and Purple Heart Medal posthumously. He remains on duty on the USS Arizona. Cecil is commemorated on the USS Arizona Memorial and the Memorial Tablets of the Missing, National Memorial Cemetery of the Pacific, Honolulu, Hawaii and the Live Oak Cemetery, Pass Christian, Mississippi. He was survived by his Father, Mr. Thomas Jefferson Ruddock, 435 East 2nd Street, Pass Christian, Mississippi. The Cecil R. Ruddock VFW Post 5931 in Pass Christian, Mississippi was named in his honor.[671]

Ruggerio, William Fire Controlman, Third Class, Serial No: 223 88 24, US Navy. William was born in 1919 in New York, the son of Alphonse and Frances (Gambardella) Ruggerio. He enlisted in the US Navy October 8, 1940 in New York, New York and completed his basic training at the Naval Training Station in Newport, Rhode Island. He reported for duty on the USS Arizona December 10, 1940. William was killed in action on December 7, 1941 at Pearl Harbor, Hawaii. He was awarded the American Defense Service Medal, World War II Victory Medal and Purple Heart Medal posthumously. William remains on duty on the USS Arizona. He is commemorated on the USS Arizona Memorial and the Memorial Tablets of the Missing, National Memorial Cemetery of the Pacific, Honolulu, Hawaii. William was survived by his Sister, Mrs. Camille Mancari, 240 Court Street, Brooklyn, New York.

Ruhlman, Frederick Lee Lieutenant, Serial No. 0-04323, US Navy, Division A. Fred was born March 4, 1909, son of Joseph Florent E. Ruhlman and Addie (Yanson) Ruhlman. He was appointed from Nebraska and admitted to the Naval Academy June 14, 1928. He accepted the appointment as a way to get a college education. Fred never planned on making the military his life's profession. His plan was to fulfill his commitment to the military and then move on in a profession. However, it was during that "required time of service" that he found himself in the middle of World War II, and by the time it was over, it was a better move to stay on and retire from the Navy. Commissioned an officer in the US Navy August 1, 1939, he reported for duty on the USS Arizona where he was serving on December 7, 1941 when the Japanese attacked Pearl Harbor. Fred lived with his wife Peggy in the officers' residences and on that fateful morning Peggy was volunteering at the base hospital. Fred was off duty and was driving her to the hospital site when the bombing began. This spared his life. By the time he got to the ship, it was too late. Fred died from of a heart attack in April 18, 1980 in Escambia, Florida. [672]

---

[671] Cecil Roy Ruddock, Photo curtsey or the Cecil R. Ruddock VFW Post 5931, Pass Christian, Mississippi.
[672] Frederick Lee Ruhlman, Information from his Neice, Suzanne Ruhlman Fraley-Prigohzy. Photo from the Lucky Bag Yearbook, United States Naval Academy, Annapolis, MD, Class of 1939.

Runckel, Robert Gleason Buglemaster, First Class, Serial No: 376 15 09, US Navy. Robert was born March 14, 1916 in Siskiyou County, California to George Henry Runckel and Elizabeth Charlotte (Gleason) Runckel. He enlisted in the US Navy October 31, 1940 in San Francisco, California and reported for duty on the USS Arizona May 6, 1941. Robert was killed in action on December 7, 1941 at Pearl Harbor, Hawaii. He was awarded the American Defense Service Medal, World War II Victory Medal and Purple Heart Medal posthumously. Robert remains on duty on the USS Arizona. He is commemorated on the USS Arizona Memorial and the Memorial Tablets of the Missing, National Memorial Cemetery of the Pacific, Honolulu, Hawaii. Robert was survived by his Father, Mr. George Henry Runckel, Box 428, McCloud, California.[673]

Runiak, Nicholas Seaman, First Class, Serial No: 223 89 76, US Navy. Nicholas was born December 31, 1919. He enlisted in the US Navy October 15, 1940 in New York, New York and completed his basic training at the Naval Training Station in Newport, Rhode Island. He reported for duty on the USS Arizona December 10, 1940. Assigned death #527, Nicholas died December 27, 1941 from burns and a wound in the abdomen received in action on December 7, 1941 at Pearl Harbor, Hawaii.[674] He was awarded the American Defense Service Medal, World War II Victory Medal and Purple Heart Medal posthumously. Nicholas remains were recovered and he was buried in Plot B, Row 0, Grave 836, National Memorial Cemetery of the Pacific, Honolulu, Hawaii. He is commemorated on the USS Arizona Memorial. Nicholas was survived by his Father, Mr. Daniel Runiak, 246 Dayton Street, Newark, New Jersey. Runiak Avenue on the Newark-Elizabeth City line, adjacent to Mount Olivet Cemetery in New Jersey was named after Nicholas Runiak.[675]

Rush, Richard Perry Seaman, First Class, Serial No: 356 46 54, US Navy. Richard was born in 1922 in McKinney, Texas the son of James Richard and Mary Retha (Crouch) Rush. He enlisted in the US Navy January 14, 1941 in Dallas, Texas and completed his basic training at the Naval Training Station, San Diego, California. Richard reported for duty on the USS Arizona April 27, 1941. He was killed in action on December 7, 1941 at Pearl Harbor, Hawaii. Richard was awarded the American Defense Service Medal, World War II Victory Medal and Purple Heart Medal posthumously. He remains buried on the USS Arizona. Richard is commemorated on the USS Arizona Memorial and the Memorial Tablets of the Missing, National Memorial Cemetery of the Pacific, Honolulu, Hawaii. He was survived by his Father, Mr. James Richard Rush, Route 5, Box 305, Dallas, Texas.[676]

---

[673] Robert Gleason Runckel, Photo from the White and Gold Yearbook, Siskiyou Joint Union High School District, Mount Shasta, California 1942, Memorial Page.
[674] Report of Changes of the USS Arizona for the month ending 31st day of December, 1941, Page 97, line 3, Nicholas Runiak.
[675] Nicholas Runiak, Photo provided by family member, Frank Runiak.
[676] Richard Perry Rush, photo from Texas Honor States.

Rusher, Orville Lester Machinist's Mate, First Class, Serial No: 342 04 03, US Navy. Orville was born August 13, 1920 in Missouri, son of Otto Rusher and Eva (Teters) Rusher. He enlisted in the US Navy December 14, 1937 in Kansas City, Missouri and reported for duty on the USS Arizona March 12, 1938. Orville was killed in action on December 7, 1941 at Pearl Harbor, Hawaii. His battle station was in the boiler room. He was awarded the American Defense Service Medal, World War II Victory Medal and Purple Heart Medal posthumously. Orville remains on duty on the USS Arizona. He is commemorated on the USS Arizona Memorial and the Memorial Tablets of the Missing, National Memorial Cemetery of the Pacific, Honolulu, Hawaii. Orville was survived by his Mother, Mrs. Eva Dorrell, Marceline, Missouri.[677]

Ruskey, Joseph John Chief Boatswain's Mate, Serial No: 233 70 99, US Navy. Joseph was born February 2, 1901 in Pittston, Pennsylvania, son of Juozas J. Ruszkis and Agatha (Rakauskiute) Ruszkis. He re-enlisted in the US Navy September 9, 1936. Joseph served on the USS Arizona from June 30, 1932 until he was killed in action on December 7, 1941 at Pearl Harbor, Hawaii. He was awarded the American Defense Service Medal, World War II Victory Medal and Purple Heart Medal posthumously. Joseph's remains were recovered and he was buried in Plot P, Row 0, Grave 616, National Memorial Cemetery of the Pacific, Honolulu, Hawaii. He is commemorated on the USS Arizona Memorial. Joseph was survived by his Daughter, Miss Virginia Lee Ruskey, c/o Mrs. S. C. Allen, 319 North Montgomery Street, Bremerton, Washington.[678]

Rutkowski, John Peter Seaman, First Class, Serial No: 243 78 84, US Navy. John was born in about 1920, son of Frank Rutkowski and Anna Rutkowski. He enlisted in the US Navy October 16, 1940 in Philadelphia, Pennsylvania and completed his basic training at the Naval Training Station in Newport, Rhode Island. John reported for duty on the USS Arizona December 10, 1940. He was killed in action on December 7, 1941 at Pearl Harbor, Hawaii. His mother never recovered from his death and died a premature death at age 50. John was awarded the American Defense Service Medal, World War II Victory Medal and Purple Heart Medal posthumously. He remains on duty on the USS Arizona. John is commemorated on the USS Arizona Memorial and the Memorial Tablets of the Missing, National Memorial Cemetery of the Pacific, Honolulu, Hawaii. He was survived by his Mother, Mrs. Anna Rutkowski, 1210 Hanover Street, Nanticoke, Pennsylvania.

---

[677] Orville Lester Rusher, Photo and information provided by family member, Steven Shields.
[678] Joseph John Ruskey, Photo from Washington Honor States.

Ruttan, Dale Andrew Electrician's Mate, Third Class, Serial No: 268 53 49, US Navy. Dale was born June 22, 1922 in Michigan, the son of James Gordon and Olive F. (Davis) Ruttan. He enlisted in the US Navy September 23, 1940 in Macon, Georgia and completed his basic training at the Naval Training Station in Norfolk, Virginia. He reported for duty on the USS Arizona December 4, 1940. Dale was killed in action on December 7, 1941 at Pearl Harbor, Hawaii. He was awarded the American Defense Service Medal, World War II Victory Medal and Purple Heart Medal posthumously. Dale remains on duty on the USS Arizona. He is commemorated on the USS Arizona Memorial and the Memorial Tablets of the Missing, National Memorial Cemetery of the Pacific, Honolulu, Hawaii. Dale was survived by his Father, Mr. James Gordon Ruttan, 4437 Burlington Avenue, Saint Petersburg, Florida and two brothers; Fordham and Don. A third brother, Gordon J. Ruttan was serving in the U.S. Army Air Corps.[679]

Sadler, Jack Ivan Seaman, Second Class, Serial No. 632 01 91, US Navy. Jack was born April 30, 1922 in Los Angeles, California, the son of John Noel and Opha (McConnell) Sadler. He enlisted in the US Navy June 27, 1941 in Los Angeles, California and completed his training at the Naval Training Station, San Diego, California. He reported for duty on the USS Arizona August 29, 1941. He was serving on December 7, 1941 when the Japanese attacked Pearl Harbor. After the attack, Jack was transferred to the USS Patterson for duty. Jack passed away from cancer November 24, 1997 in Redondo Beach, California. His ashes were scattered near the USS Arizona October 6, 1998.

Sadowski, Joseph Stephen Seaman, First Class, Serial No. 201 78 92, US Navy. Joseph enlisted in the US Navy October 15, 1940 in Boston, Massachusetts and completed his basic training at the Naval Training Station in Newport, Rhode Island. He reported for duty on the USS Arizona December 10, 1940. He was serving on the USS Arizona on December 7, 1941 when the Japanese attacked Pearl Harbor. After the attack, Joseph was transferred to the USS Lexington (Sunk May 7, 1942 during the Battle of the Coral Sea.)

Sampson, Sherley Rolland Radioman, Third Class, Serial No: 410 34 40, US Navy. Sherley was born February 22, 1917 in Minnesota, the oldest of three children of Ernest R. Sampson and Inez Sampson. Their youngest child, a daughter named Mary Lou, drowned in 1933 in the Red Lake River. She was 10. Less than 15 months after Sherley died on the Arizona, his younger brother, Russell, was killed at the Del Valle Air Field base in Austin, Texas. None of the three children lived long enough to see their 25th birthday. He enlisted in the US Navy December 19, 1940 in Grand Forks, North Dakota and completed his basic training at the Naval Training Station in San Diego, California. Sherley reported for duty on the USS Arizona March 5, 1941. He was killed in action on December 7, 1941 at Pearl Harbor, Hawaii. Sherley was awarded the American Defense Service Medal, World War II Victory Medal and Purple Heart Medal posthumously. He remains on duty on the USS Arizona. Sherley is commemorated on the USS Arizona Memorial and the Memorial Tablets of the Missing, National Memorial Cemetery of the Pacific, Honolulu, Hawaii. He was survived by his

---

[679] Dale Andrew Ruttan, Photo from the St. Petersburg Tiimes, St. Petersburg, Florida, February 11, 1942, Page 8.

Wife, Mrs. Fern Vivian (Hole) Sampson, Erskine, Minnesota and his son, Sheldon Rene Sampson.[680]

Sandall, Merrill Keith   Shipfitter, Third Class, Serial No: 300 09 89, US Navy. Merrill was born January 28, 1922 in Maquon, Illinois, son of Henry Lee Sandall and Emma Mable (Bitner) Sandall. He enlisted in the US Navy June 11, 1940 in Chicago, Illinois and completed his basic training at the Naval Training Station in Great Lakes, Illinois. Merrill reported for duty on the USS Arizona October 25, 1940. He was killed in action on December 7, 1941 at Pearl Harbor, Hawaii. Merrill was awarded the American Defense Service Medal, World War II Victory Medal and Purple Heart Medal posthumously. He remains on duty on the USS Arizona. Merrill is commemorated on the USS Arizona Memorial and the Memorial Tablets of the Missing, National Memorial Cemetery of the Pacific, Honolulu, Hawaii and the Yates City Cemetery, Yates City, Illinois. He was survived by his Father, Mr. Henry Lee Sandall, Yates City, Illinois.

Sanders, Elmer Larimore   Gunner's Mate, First Class, Serial No. 295 18 90, US Navy. Elmer was born on September 19, 1905, in Warren, Tennessee, the son of Lavander Pope and Martha Ida (Turner) Sanders. He re-enlisted in the US Navy December 2, 1936. Elmer served on the USS Arizona from November 28, 1932 until December 7, 1941 when the Japanese attacked Pearl Harbor. Elmer was wounded in action during the attack. He was treated at Waipahu Hospital and then transferred the US Naval Hospital at Pearl Harbor, Hawaii. His wife, Mrs. Elmer Larimore Sanders, 1933 Harvard North, Seattle, Washington was notified. Elmer later served in the Korean War. He died on April 26, 1959 in Tennessee and was buried in Section MM, Site 254, Nashville National Cemetery, South Madison, Tennessee.

Sanders, Eugene Thomas   Ensign, Serial No: 0-071819, US Navy. Eugene was born on March 15, 1889 in Hubbard, Oregon. He enlisted in the Army on June 16, 1917 and was discharged on February 13, 1919. On September 18, 1919 he enlisted in the Navy and subsequently served on the USS Brant (AM-24) from December 4, 1932 to June 1, 1934. He then served on the USS Finch (AM-9) from August 30, 1934 to January 28, 1936. He also served at the Naval Station at Olongapo, Luzon, Philippine Islands and on submarine tender USS Canopus (AS-9). On May 7, 1940 he reported for duty on the USS Arizona. He was appointed Ensign on November 3, 1941. His battle station was Repair I. Eugene was killed in action on December 7, 1941 at Pearl Harbor, Hawaii. He was awarded the American Defense Service Medal, World War II Victory Medal and Purple Heart Medal posthumously. Eugene remains on duty on the USS Arizona. He is commemorated on the USS Arizona Memorial and the Memorial Tablets of the Missing, National Memorial Cemetery of the Pacific, Honolulu, Hawaii. Eugene was survived by his Wife, Mrs. Eugene T. Sanders, 319 East 17th Street, New York, New York. The destroyer escort USS Sanders (DE-40) was named in his honor. The USS Sanders received four battle stars for her World War II service[681]

---

[680] Sherley Rolland Sampson, Photo and information provided by family member, Debbie Joseph.
[681] Eugene Thomas Sanders, Dictionary of American Naval Fighting Ships, Naval Historical Center, USS Sanders (DE-40).

Sanderson, James Harvey Musician, Second Class, Serial No: 376 15 83, US Navy. James was born February 13, 1920 in Lindsay, California, son of James A. Sanderson and Anna Isabella (Dowling) Sanderson. James graduated from Lindsay High School. He enlisted in the US Navy November 18, 1940 and attended the Navy School of Music in Washington, DC graduating on May 23, 1941. James reported for duty on the USS Arizona June 17, 1941. H*e played Saxophone in the USS Arizona Band. His battle station was in the black powder room passing ammunition to the Arizona's Gunners during the attack.* James was killed in action on December 7, 1941 at Pearl Harbor, Hawaii. He was awarded the American Defense Service Medal, World War II Victory Medal and Purple Heart Medal posthumously. James remains on duty on the USS Arizona. He is commemorated on the USS Arizona Memorial and the Memorial Tablets of the Missing, National Memorial Cemetery of the Pacific, Honolulu, Hawaii. James was survived by his Mother, Mrs. James Sanderson, Route 2, Bix 775, Lindsay, California.[682]

Sanford, Thomas Steger Fireman, Third Class, Serial No: 272 41 70, US Navy. Thomas was born November 15, 1918 in Alabama, the son of R. M. Sanford and Susan Letitia (Steger) Sanford. He enlisted in the US Navy October 5, 1940 in Birmingham, Alabama and completed his basic training at the Naval Training Station in Norfolk, Virginia. He reported for duty on the USS Arizona December 4, 1940. Thomas was killed in action on December 7, 1941 at Pearl Harbor, Hawaii. He was awarded the American Defense Service Medal, World War II Victory Medal and Purple Heart Medal posthumously. Thomas remains on duty on the USS Arizona. He is commemorated on the USS Arizona Memorial and the Memorial Tablets of the Missing, National Memorial Cemetery of the Pacific, Honolulu, Hawaii and the Oakwood Cemetery, Tuscumbia, Alabama. Thomas was survived by his Mother, Mrs. Mary Lou Sherrod, 757 Ponce Avenue, St. Louis, Missouri. (Later address: 509 East 7th Street, Tuscumbia, Alabama.) The Thomas Steger Sanford American Legion Post 149 in Tuscumbia, Alabama was named in his honor.[683]

Santos, Filomeno Cook, Second Class, Serial No: 497 87 54, US Navy. Filomeno was born November 25, 1906 in Iloilo, Philippine Islands. He immigrated to the United States in July 1927 on board the President Jackson. He enlisted in the US Navy on February 6, 1937 in Bremerton, Washington initially serving on board the USS Idaho. Filomeno began serving on the USS Arizona on March 17, 1938. He was killed in action on December 7, 1941 at Pearl Harbor, Hawaii. Filomeno was awarded the American Defense Service Medal, World War II Victory Medal and Purple Heart Medal posthumously. He remains on duty on the USS Arizona. Filomeno is commemorated on the USS Arizona Memorial and the Memorial Tablets of the Missing, National Memorial Cemetery of the Pacific, Honolulu, Hawaii. He was survived by his Wife, Mrs. Flacida Santos, 207 East Bay Avenue, Balboa, California.[684]

---

[682] James Harvey Sanderson, Photo from USS Arizona's Last Band by Molly Kent. By permission of the author. For more information about this book, go to www.USSARIZONASLASTBAND.com.
[683] Thomas Steger Sanfor, Photo from Missouri Honor States.
[684] Filomento Santos, Information obtained from United States Department of Labor Immigration and Naturalization Service, Declaration of Intention No 80651, March 22, 1937.

Sargent, Robert Isaac, Jr.   Seaman, Second Class, Serial No. 381 32 56, US Navy. Robert was born July 13, 1921 in Mesa, Arizona to Robert Isaac and Nina Bell (Baker) Sargent. He enlisted in the US Navy March 8, 1940 in San Diego, California and completed his basic training at the Naval Training Station in San Diego, California. He reported for duty on the USS Arizona June 16, 1940. He was serving on December 7, 1941 when the Japanese attacked Pearl Harbor. After the attack on the 7th he was transferred to the USS Chester for duty. Robert died November 22, 1975 at age 54 in Norfolk, Virginia.

Sather, William "Bill" Ford   Patternmaker, First Class, Serial No: 321 02 36, US Navy. William was born March 30, 1915 in Humboldt, Iowa, son of Thomas O. Sather and Amelia Sather. He enlisted in the US Navy February 11, 1936 in Des Moines, Iowa and reported for duty on the USS Arizona June 6, 1936. William was killed in action on December 7, 1941 at Pearl Harbor. He was awarded the American Defense Service Medal, World War II Victory Medal and Purple Heart Medal posthumously. William remains on duty on the USS Arizona. He is commemorated on the USS Arizona Memorial and the Memorial Tablets of the Missing, National Memorial Cemetery of the Pacific, Honolulu, Hawaii and Indian Mound Cemetery, Humboldt, Iowa. William was survived by his Wife, Mrs. Zela Alberta (Williams) Sather, 3701 Ransom Street, Long Beach, California. The Sather Odgaard VFW Post 5240 in Dakota City, Humboldt County, Iowa is named for William and another Humboldt County native, Edwin Odegaard.[685]

Savage, Walter Samuel, Jr.   Ensign, Serial No: 0-109088, US Navy Reserve. Walter was born on April 26, 1919 in New Orleans, Louisiana, son of Walter Samuel Savage, Sr. and Gloria D. Savage. *He received a Naval Reserve commission as an Ensign on June 10, 1941. After attending the Navy Supply Corps School at Harvard University, he was assigned to the USS Arizona as Assistant Paymaster.* He was killed in action on December 7, 1941 at Pearl Harbor, Hawaii. Walter was awarded the American Defense Service Medal, World War II Victory Medal and Purple Heart Medal posthumously. He remains on duty on the USS Arizona. Walter is commemorated on the USS Arizona Memorial and Memorial Tablets of the Missing, National Memorial Cemetery of the Pacific, Honolulu, Hawaii. Walter was survived by his Father, Mr. Walter S. Savage, Sr., 1408 Emerson Avenue, Monroe, Louisiana. The escort ship USS Savage (DE-386, later DER-386), 1943-1975 was named in honor of Ensign Savage. The USS Savage earned one battle star for her World War II service and six for her service in Vietnam.[686]

---

[685] William "Bill" Ford Sather, Photo provided by David Lee, Post Commander, Sather-Odgaard VFW Post 5240, Dakota City, Iowa.
[686] Walter Samuel Savage, Jr., Dictionary of American Naval Fighting Ships, Naval Historical Center, USS Savage (DE-386).

Savin, Tom Radioman, Second Class, Serial No: 316 53 59, US Navy. Tom was born in about 1916 in Nebraska to George R. and Lillian E. Savin. He enlisted in the US Navy February 16, 1938 in Omaha, Nebraska and reported for duty on the USS Arizona on December 6, 1940 transferring from the USS Mississippi. He was killed in action on December 7, 1941 at Pearl Harbor, Hawaii. Tom was awarded the American Defense Service Medal, World War II Victory Medal and Purple Heart Medal posthumously. He remains on duty on the USS Arizona. Tom is commemorated on the USS Arizona Memorial and the Memorial Tablets of the Missing, National Memorial Cemetery of the Pacific, Honolulu, Hawaii. He was survived by his Wife, Mrs. Mildred May Savin, 6005 South 20th Avenue, Omaha, Nebraska, Parents, Mr. and Mrs. George R. Savin; Brother, Jerry; Sisters, Ruth Savin and Mrs. Mary Shutt of Omaha and Elinor of Los Angeles.[687]

Savinski, Michael Seaman, First Class, Serial No: 243 78 45, US Navy. Michael was born in 1918, son of Stephanus Savinski and Annie Savinski. He enlisted in the US Navy October 16, 1940 in Philadelphia, Pennsylvania and completed his basic training at the Naval Training Station in Newport, Rhode Island. Michael reported for duty on the USS Arizona December 10, 1940. He was killed in action on December 7, 1941 at Pearl Harbor, Hawaii. Michael was awarded the American Defense Service Medal, World War II Victory Medal and Purple Heart Medal posthumously. He remains on duty on the USS Arizona. Michael is commemorated on the USS Arizona Memorial and the Memorial Tablets of the Missing, National Memorial Cemetery of the Pacific, Honolulu, Hawaii. He was survived by his Father, Mr. Stephanus Savinski, 14th and Townsend Street, Chester, Pennsylvania.[688]

Schafer, Herman "Bud" Leroy, Jr. Ensign, Serial No. 0-07130, US Navy. Herman was born on December 23, 1916. He graduated from the United States Naval Academy at Annapolis, Maryland on June 6, 1940 and was serving as Watch and Division 4 Officer. His battle station was Turret IV. Bud was serving on board the USS Arizona (BB-39) on December 7, 1941 when the Japanese attacked Pearl Harbor. Herman was on shore leave when the attack occurred. He was later assigned duty on the USS Alabama where he saw action in every campaign up to Okinawa. Bud attained the rank of LCDR by the end of the war. He resigned because of unsatisfactory vision. He returned home to Manasquan, New Jersey, a seashore resort town where he started a lumber business. Bud passed away on August 1, 2009 in Brunswick, Maine. He was survived by his Wife, Ruth.[689]

---

[687] Tom Savin, Photo from the Nebraska, Iowa War Dead, World-Herald, Omaha, Nebraska, Sunday, July 4, 1943.

[688] Michael Savinski, Photo from "Philadelphia Naval Heroes Who Gave Lives for their Country", The Philadelphia Inquirer, Tuesday Morning, May 5, 1942.

[689] Herman Leroy Schafer, Jr., Photo, Lucky Bag, United States Naval Academy, Annapolis, Maryland, USA, 1940.

Schdowski, Joseph Seaman, First Class, Serial No: 328 75 74, US Navy. Joseph was born in 1918 in Minnesota to Michael and Pauline (Dulski) Schdowski. He enlisted in the US Navy October 8, 1940 in Minneapolis, Minnesota and completed his basic training at the Naval Training Station in Great Lakes, Illinois. He reported for duty on the USS Arizona December 9, 1940. Joseph was killed in action on December 7, 1941 at Pearl Harbor, Hawaii. He was awarded the American Defense Service Medal, World War II Victory Medal and Purple Heart Medal posthumously. Joseph remains on duty on the USS Arizona. He is commemorated on the USS Arizona Memorial and the Memorial Tablets of the Missing, National Memorial Cemetery of the Pacific, Honolulu, Hawaii. Joseph was survived by his Sister, Celia Fakler, 1605 12th Street North, Fargo, North Dakota.

Scheuerlein, George Albert Gunner's Mate, Third Class, Serial No: 243 79 06, US Navy. George was born in 1921 in Pennsylvania, the son of Martin John and Gladys (Hager) Scheuerlein. He enlisted in the US Navy October 16, 1940 in Philadelphia, Pennsylvania and completed his basic training at the Naval Training Station in Newport, Rhode Island. He reported for duty on the USS Arizona December 10, 1940. George was killed in action on December 7, 1941 at Pearl Harbor, Hawaii. He was awarded the American Defense Service Medal, World War II Victory Medal and Purple Heart Medal posthumously. George remains on duty on the USS Arizona. He is commemorated on the USS Arizona Memorial and the Memorial Tablets of the Missing, National Memorial Cemetery of the Pacific, Honolulu, Hawaii. George was survived by his Father, Mr. Martin John Scheuerlein, 3745 North Percy Street, Philadelphia, Pennsylvania.

Schiller, Ernest Seaman, Second Class, Serial No: 360 32 03, US Navy. Ernest was born in about 1922 in Milam County, Texas to Otto H. and Betsy Jane (Simmons) Schiller. At age 18, he enrolled in a CCC Camp in Texas. He enlisted in the US Navy January 21, 1941 in Houston, Texas and completed his basic training at the Naval Training Station in San Diego, California. Ernest reported for duty on the USS Arizona April 27, 1941. He was killed in action on December 7, 1941 at Pearl Harbor, Hawaii. Ernest was awarded the American Defense Service Medal, World War II Victory Medal and Purple Heart Medal posthumously. He remains on duty on the USS Arizona. Ernest is commemorated on the USS Arizona Memorial and the Memorial Tablets of the Missing, National Memorial Cemetery of the Pacific, Honolulu, Hawaii. He was survived by his Father, Mr. Otto Schiller, Hutto, Texas.[690]

---

[690] Ernest Schiller, Photo from Texas Honor States

Schlund, Elmer "Benny" Pershing Machinist's Mate, First Class, Serial No: 316 47 88, US Navy. Elmer was born in November of 1918, son of Harry Fidel Schlund and Maude E. Schlund. He enlisted in the US Navy November 17, 1936 in Omaha, Nebraska and reported for duty on the USS Arizona April 3, 1937. Elmer was killed in action on December 7, 1941 at Pearl Harbor, Hawaii. He was awarded the American Defense Service Medal, World War II Victory Medal and Purple Heart Medal posthumously. Elmer remains on duty on the USS Arizona. He is commemorated on the USS Arizona Memorial and the Memorial Tablets of the Missing, National Memorial Cemetery of the Pacific, Honolulu, Hawaii and Mount Pleasant Cemetery, Cairo, Nebraska. Elmer was survived by his Father, Mr. Harry F. Schlund, St. Michael, Nebraska.[691]

Schmidt, Vernon Joseph Seaman, First Class, Serial No: 328 75 81, US Navy. Vernon was born November 16, 1921 in Minnesota, son of Joseph A. Schmidt and E. Melita Schmidt. Vernon graduated from Roosevelt High School, Minneapolis, Minnesota where he was in the marching band and orchestra. He enlisted in the US Navy October 8, 1940 in Minneapolis, Minnesota and completed his basic training at the Naval Training Station in Great Lakes, Illinois. Vernon reported for duty on the USS Arizona December 9, 1940. He was killed in action on December 7, 1941 at Pearl Harbor, Hawaii. Vernon was awarded the American Defense Service Medal, World War II Victory Medal and Purple Heart Medal posthumously. He remains on duty on the USS Arizona. Vernon is commemorated on the USS Arizona Memorial and the Memorial Tablets of the Missing, National Memorial Cemetery of the Pacific, Honolulu, Hawaii and Fort Snelling National Cemetery, Minneapolis, Minnesota. He was survived by his Father, Mr. Joseph A. Schmidt, 4521 44th Avenue South, Minneapolis, Minnesota.[692]

Schrank, Harold Arthur Baker, First Class, Serial No: 355 94 48, US Navy. Harold was born January 10, 1917 in Hamilton County, Texas, son of Arthur Paul Schrank and Emma Marie (Kelm) Schrank. He enlisted in the US Navy November 15, 1935. Harold served on the USS Arizona from February 26, 1936 until he was killed in action on December 7, 1941 at Pearl Harbor, Hawaii. A memorial service was held at Hamilton High School Auditorium on February 22, 1942. He was awarded the American Defense Service Medal, World War II Victory Medal and Purple Heart Medal posthumously. Harold remains on duty on the USS Arizona. He is commemorated on the USS Arizona Memorial and the Memorial Tablets of the Missing, National Memorial Cemetery of the Pacific, Honolulu, Hawaii. Harold was survived by his Wife, Mrs. Jewel (Hyde) Schrank, 108 North 3rd Street, Temple, Texas and a daughter, Jo Lynda Schrank.

---

[691] Elmer Pershing Schlund, Photo from Nebraska Honor States.
[692] Vernon Joseph Schmidt, Photo from The Minneapolis Star, Minneapolis, Minnesota, May 5, 1942, page 12.

Schroeder, Henry Boatswain's Mate, First Class, Serial No: 228 12 43, US Navy. Henry was born in 1905 in Brooklyn, New York the oldest of six children born to Henry Christian and Margareta Elisa Schroeder (Henry, Anna, Margaret, Fredrick, Herman and John). His brothers Fredrick and Herman died of the 1916 influenza. Henry's father died in 1918. After his father's death, the family moved to Linden, New Jersey and his mother re-married. Henry enlisted in the US Navy May 13, 1924 in Newark, New Jersey and completed his boot training at the Naval Training Station in Newport, Rhode Island. He served on the battleship, USS New Mexico; the destroyer, USS Gilmer; the collier, USS Hannibal; the destroyer, USS Tillman; the destroyer, USS Selfridge; and the destroyer, USS Warrington. Henry reported for duty on the USS Arizona August 30, 1940. On June 7, 1941 an entry was made in his service certificate record by his commanding officer, E.H. Geiselman. The entry read as follows: *"Recommended for advancement to CBM. Eligible in all respects to take 1941 exams. Completed all practical factors required for advancement to CBM."* In a letter to his sister Anna, Henry wrote" The next time you see me, I'll be wearing brass buttons." Henry was killed in action on December 7, 1941 at Pearl Harbor, Hawaii. He was awarded the American Defense Service Medal, World War II Victory Medal and Purple Heart Medal posthumously. Henry remains on duty on the USS Arizona. He is commemorated on the USS Arizona Memorial and the Memorial Tablets of the Missing, National Memorial Cemetery of the Pacific, Honolulu, Hawaii. Henry was survived by his Mother, Mrs. Margaret Schroeder Stahnke, 816 Elizabeth Avenue, Linden, New Jersey.[693]

Schubert, Anthony Robert Ensign, Serial No. 0-06820, US Navy. Anthony was born October 24, 1918. He was a graduate of the US Naval Academy and received his commission on June 6, 1940, reporting for duty on the USS Arizona shortly thereafter. Anthony was serving as C Division Officer. He was wounded in action, suffering burns on December 7, 1941 during the Japanese attack on Pearl Harbor.[694] Anthony's story:

"At about 0755 Sunday, December 7, I was shaving in the wardroom head of the U.S.S. Arizona. I heard the air raid siren sound over the announcing system for about one second's duration, followed by the Passed word, "Air Raid". At the same time I could hear scattered gunfire. I went to the my room and looked out the port, where I saw several low-winged monoplanes at low altitude flying away from the line of moored battleships, apparently having finished a bombing or torpedo attack. I then heard the general alarm sound and the word passed for general quarters, and put on a pair of dungarees and slippers to go to my general quarters station, secondary Conn.

There were during this time one or more explosions which filled the air with fumes and vented out the port. The worst explosion filled the inboard end of the room with flame and left a residue of orange smoke which continued to vent out the port. By this time the ship was down by the bow and sinking so rapidly that the lines from the ship to the after key were snapping. I took a breath of air from out the port and went into the passageway, aft and up through a stores hatch which had been blown open.

[693] Henry Schroeder, Photo and information provided by his nephew, Ted Fussell.
[694] Anthony Robert Schubert, Photo, Lucky Bag, United States Naval Academy, Annapolis, Maryland, USA, 1940.

Lt. Comdr. Fuqua was directing operations on the quarter deck. I assisted in opening the hatches and in getting the wounded, chiefly burn cases, into the launches sent from the U.S.S. Solace. The ship was still sinking rapidly and oil was burning on the water and spreading aft. Because of the damage received there was no pressure on the fire main with which to fight the fire. I left the ship in the gig and returned in a motor boat with which we make two trips to the Ford Island landing removing men from the ship. We picked up Ensign Lennig, U.S.N.R. from the water, and I had the boat crew leave me off at the U.S.S. Solace to have a cut on head and burns on my hand and arm dressed.[695]

His Mother, Mrs. Nora Henrietta Schubert, 120 West Fifth Street, Hutchinson, Kansas was notified of his injuries. After Pearl Harbor, Anthony went on to serve on the USS South Dakota. He retired from the Navy with a rank of Lieutenant Commander after 13 years of service. After the service, he went to work in the oil fields of Saudi Arabia. He retired in the 1970's and moved back home to Hutchinson, Kansas. Anthony had resided in a nursing home in Hutchinson at the time of his death. A broken hip had caused a chain reaction of health problems that ultimately claimed his life before he reached his one goal of living to be 100. He died at the age of 90 on August 16, 2009 and was buried at Penwell-Gabel Cemetery in Hutchinson, Kansas.

Schumacher, William James Watertender, First Class, Serial No. 234 00 95, US Navy. William enlisted in the US Navy March 2, 1940 in Cadiz, Spain. He served on the USS Trenton before reporting for duty on the USS Arizona April 30, 1941. William was serving on the USS Arizona on December 7, 1941 when the Japanese attacked Pearl Harbor. He went on to serve on the USS Enterprise.

Schuman, Herman Lincoln Storekeeper, First Class, Serial No: 375 50 94, US Navy. Herman was born in about 1912 in Connecticut the son of Otto and Elizabeth Schuman. He enlisted in the US Navy in February 1931. Herman served on the USS Arizona from March 23, 1931 until he was killed in action on December 7, 1941 at Pearl Harbor, Hawaii. He was awarded the American Defense Service Medal, World War II Victory Medal and Purple Heart Medal posthumously. Herman remains on duty on the USS Arizona. He is commemorated on the USS Arizona Memorial and the Memorial Tablets of the Missing, National Memorial Cemetery of the Pacific, Honolulu, Hawaii. Herman was survived by his Wife, Mrs. Marjorie Lois (Ogle) Schuman, 119 East 12th Street, Long Beach, California.

Schurr, John Electrician's Mate, Second Class, Serial No: 342 10 64, US Navy. John was born February 17, 1919 in Kansas to Martin and Barbara (Lovenstein) Schurr. He enlisted in the US Navy February 23, 1939 in Kansas City, Missouri and completed his basic training at the Naval Training Station, Great Lakes, Illinois. John reported for duty on the USS Arizona June 10, 1939. He was killed in action on December 7, 1941 at Pearl Harbor, Hawaii. John was awarded the American Defense Service Medal, World War II Victory Medal and Purple Heart Medal posthumously. He remains on duty on the USS Arizona. John is commemorated on the USS Arizona Memorial and the Memorial Tablets of the Missing, National Memorial Cemetery of the Pacific, Honolulu, Hawaii. He was survived by his Father, Mr. Martin Schurr, Route 3, Oakley, Kansas.

---

[695] Statement of Ensign, A. R. Schubert, U.S.S. Arizona, Last Action Report.

Scilley, Harold Hugh Shipfitter, Second Class, Serial No: 368 34 11, US Navy. Harold was born April 3, 1917 in Fromberg, Montana the first son of Hugh Scilley and Alice Winifred (Nerlin) Scilley. *In January 1918, Harold and his parents moved to Young, Saskatchewan, Canada to farm with Hugh's father. They came back to the US in 1919 to live on a ranch near Luther, Montana. Harold went to elementary and high school in Butte, MT where his father worked as a miner.* He enlisted in the US Navy May 18, 1936 in Salt Lake City, Utah and reported for duty on the USS Arizona September 2, 1936. *Harold's pride in being in the military was an inspiration to his brother and cousin. His younger brother, James enlisted in the US Army in June 1941 and his cousin, William Smith, enlisted in the Navy on his 17th birthday in 1943.* Harold was killed in action on December 7, 1941 at Pearl Harbor, Hawaii. *For many days after the Pearl Harbor attack, Harold's mother, Alice held onto hope that Harold had somehow survived.* He was awarded the American Defense Service Medal, World War II Victory Medal and Purple Heart Medal posthumously. Harold remains on duty on the USS Arizona. He is commemorated on the USS Arizona Memorial and the Memorial Tablets of the Missing, National Memorial Cemetery of the Pacific, Honolulu, Hawaii. Harold was survived by his Parents, Mr. and Mrs. Hugh Scilley, Joliet, Montana and one brother, James N. Scilley. *His mother, Alice attended the dedication of the USS Arizona memorial in 1963. Viewing the monument was a haunting experience for Alice because it was a compelling reminder of those sorrowful days in 1941. Harold's parents mourned his death the rest of their lives. Even those in the family that were too young to have known Harold felt a great sadness at the loss of the family member, undoubtedly because the older family members had so much grief from his death.*[696]

Scott, A. J. Seaman, Second Class, Serial No: 356 59 53, US Navy. A.J. was born October 11, 1921 in Texas. Seaman Scott enlisted in the US Navy June 5, 1941 in Dallas, Texas and completed his basic training at the Naval Training Station in San Diego, California. He reported for duty on the USS Arizona August 13, 1941. A.J. was killed in action on December 7, 1941 at Pearl Harbor, Hawaii. He was awarded the American Defense Service Medal, World War II Victory Medal and Purple Heart Medal posthumously. A.J. remains on duty on the USS Arizona. He is commemorated on the USS Arizona Memorial and the Memorial Tablets of the Missing, National Memorial Cemetery of the Pacific, Honolulu, Hawaii. A. J. was survived by his Mother, Mrs. Anna Scott, Route 1, Boyd, Texas.

Scruggs, Jack Leo Musician, Second Class, Serial No: 382 34 07, US Navy. Jack was born on March 9, 1919 in Hanford, California. He enlisted in the US Navy December 30, 1940 and attended the Navy School of Music in Washington, DC graduating on May 23, 1941. Jack reported for duty on the USS Arizona June 17, 1941. His battle station was the black powder room passing ammunition to the Arizona's gunners during the attack. He was killed in action on December 7, 1941 at Pearl Harbor, Hawaii. Jack was awarded the Purple Heart Medal, American Defense Service Medal, Asiatic Pacific Campaign Medal with Bronze Star, World War II Victory Medal and Pearl Harbor Commemorative Medal posthumously. Jack's remains were recovered from the water and after identification; he was interred in Long Beach, California in 1947. He is

---

[696] Harold Hugh Scilley, Photo and information provided by Family members, Val Nerlin Hillers with assistance of Maripat Nerlin Hagen and other family members.

405

commemorated on the USS Arizona Memorial and the Memorial Tablets of the Missing, National Memorial Cemetery of the Pacific, Honolulu, Hawaii. Jack was survived by his Father, Mr. Henry Paul Scruggs, 919 Junipero Avenue, Long Beach, California.[697]

Seaman, Russell Otto Fireman, First Class, Serial No: 321 35 89, US Navy. Russell was born in 1918 on the family farm in Missouri to G. W. Seaman and Lillian May (Johnson) Seaman the second child of 8 siblings (3 boys and 5 girls). He graduated in 1936 from Fairfield High School. Russell was on the Honor Roll and played in the Senior Class Play. He enlisted in the US Navy October 18, 1939 in Des Moines, Iowa and completed his basic training at the Naval Training Station in Great Lakes, Illinois. He reported for duty on the USS Arizona January 27, 1940. Russell was killed in action on December 7, 1941 at Pearl Harbor, Hawaii. He was awarded the American Defense Service Medal, World War II Victory Medal and Purple Heart Medal posthumously. Russell remains on duty on the USS Arizona. He is commemorated on the USS Arizona Memorial and the Memorial Tablets of the Missing, National Memorial Cemetery of the Pacific, Honolulu, Hawaii and the Memorial Lawn Cemetery, Fairfield, Iowa. Russell was survived by his Mother, Mrs. Lillian May Seaman, 112-1/2 West Broadway, Fairfield, Iowa.[698]

Seeley, Robert Fox Seaman, Second Class, Serial No. 414 48 26, US Navy. Robert was born June 2, 1921 in Oregon to William Hansel and Lucile F. (Fox) Seeley. He enlisted in the US Navy January 18, 1941 in Seattle, Washington and completed his training at the Naval Training Station, San Diego, California. He reported for duty on the USS Arizona April 26, 1941. Robert was serving on the USS Arizona on December 7, 1941 when the Japanese attacked Pearl Harbor. After the attack, Robert was transferred to the USS Dorsey for duty. He died October 10, 1986 in San Francisco, California.

Seeley, William Eugene Seaman, First Class, Serial No: 207 29 56, US Navy. William was born October 8, 1922 in Groton, Connecticut to Paul and Frances Seeley. He enlisted in the US Navy October 15, 1940 in New Haven, Connecticut and completed his basic training at the Naval Training Station in Newport, Rhode Island. He reported for duty on the USS Arizona December 10, 1940. William was killed in action on December 7, 1941 at Pearl Harbor, Hawaii. He was awarded the American Defense Service Medal, World War II Victory Medal and Purple Heart Medal posthumously. William remains on duty on the USS Arizona. He is commemorated on the USS Arizona Memorial and the Memorial Tablets of the Missing, National Memorial Cemetery of the Pacific, Honolulu, Hawaii. William was survived by his Mother, Mrs. Frances D. Seeley, Fairview Avenue, Groton, New London, Connecticut.[699]

---

[697] Jack Leo Scruggs, Photo from USS Arizona's Last Band by Molly Kent. By permission of the author. For more information about this book, go to www.USSARIZONASLASTBAND.com.

[698] Russell Otto Seaman, Photo from the front page of the Memorial Service Program held Sunday, March 8, 1942 in the Fairfield High School Auditorium, Fairfield, Iowa.

[699] William Eugene Seeley, Photo and information from the Groton Times Newspaper, December 9, 2005, William Eugene Seeley by Jim Streeter. Article provided by Evelyn Bayna.

Sevier, Charles Clifton Seaman, First Class, Serial No: 382 29 93, US Navy. Charles was born September 19, 1915 in San Bernardino, California, son of John Pitman Sevier and Minnie Nancy Jane (Corbett) Sevier. He enlisted in the US Navy November 2, 1940 in Los Angeles, California and completed his basic training at the Naval Training Station in San Diego, California. Charles reported for duty on the USS Arizona January 11, 1941. He was killed in action on December 7, 1941 at Pearl Harbor, Hawaii. Charles was awarded the American Defense Service Medal, World War II Victory Medal and Purple Heart Medal posthumously. He remains buried on the USS Arizona. Charles is commemorated on the USS Arizona Memorial and the Memorial Tablets of the Missing, National Memorial Cemetery of the Pacific, Honolulu, Hawaii. He was survived by his Mother, Mrs. Minnie Jackson, Route 1, Thermal, California.[700]

Shaffer, John Jackson, III Lieutenant, Serial No. 0-03801, US Navy. John was born September 6, 1912 in Houma, Louisiana. He enlisted in the US Navy in June 1930 and was commissioned June 2, 1938. John was serving on board the USS Arizona (BB-39) as Aide & Flag Lieutenant on December 7, 1941, when the Japanese attacked Pearl Harbor. His battle station was the Flag Bridge. John was killed in action April 8, 1944 while commander of the USS Champlin (DD-601) and was buried at sea on April 9, 1944. The USS Champlin was ordered out on a submarine hunt, joining an all-day operation 7 April. At 1632, she made contact and dropped deep-set depth charges, driving the submarine to the surface. Immediately, her guns opened fire scoring several hits, including one on the conning tower, which started a furious fire. Champlin dashed in for the kill, ramming the stern of the submarine, and U-856 sank in 40 18' N., 62 18' W. The cost, however, included Champlin's commanding officer, Commander John J. Shaffer III, wounded by shrapnel during the attack, who died the next morning despite emergency surgery. The crew and officers of the USS Champlin assembled on the forecastle in dress blues to render honor to their deceased Commanding Officer, John Jackson Shaffer, III, Commander, US Navy.[701]

Shannon, William "Billy" Alfred Seaman, First Class, Serial No: 368 48 76, US Navy. William was born October 17, 1921 in Red Cloud, Nebraska, the second son in a family of six boys born to William Bacon Shannon and Ruth Isabel (Pegg) Shannon. Shortly after he graduated from High School at Red Cloud, Nebraska, his family moved to Idaho hoping to find work during the depression. Billy's older brother, Charles was already in the Navy. At age 17, his parents signed for him to enlist in the US Navy May 31, 1940 in Salt Lake City, Utah and completed his basic training at the Naval Training Station in San Diego, California. Billy reported for duty on the USS Arizona September 8, 1940. He was killed in action on December 7, 1941 at Pearl Harbor, Hawaii. William was awarded the American Defense Service Medal, World War II Victory Medal and Purple Heart Medal posthumously. He

---

[700] Charles Clifton Sevier, Photo from the 1931 Gardena High School Yearbook, Gardena, California.
[701] John Jackson Shaffer III, Photo from Lucky Bag Yearbook, United States Naval Academy, Annapolis, MD, Class of 1930.

remains on duty on the USS Arizona. William is commemorated on the USS Arizona Memorial and the Memorial Tablets of the Missing, National Memorial Cemetery of the Pacific, Honolulu, Hawaii. He was survived by his Mother, Mrs. Ruth Isabel Shannon, Route 1, Red Cloud, Nebraska. His father, William Bacon Shannon died on April 6, 1941. All six brothers served in the US Navy.[702]

Sharbaugh, Harry Robert Gunner's Mate, Third Class, Serial No: 243 78 40, US Navy. Harry was born February 8, 1919 in Pennsylvania, the son of Harry Sharbaugh and Ella M. (Repsher) Sharbaugh. His mother, Ella died shortly after his birth and it appears he went to live with his Grandmother, Caroline Repsher. He enlisted in the US Navy October 16, 1940 in Philadelphia, Pennsylvania and completed his basic training at the Naval Training Station in Newport, Rhode Island. Harry reported for duty on the USS Arizona December 10, 1940. Assigned death #404, Harry died December 11, 1941 from wounds received in action on December 7, 1941 at Pearl Harbor, Hawaii.[703] He was awarded the American Defense Service Medal, World War II Victory Medal and Purple Heart Medal posthumously. Harry was buried in Plot C, Row 0, Grave 1179, National Memorial Cemetery of the Pacific, Honolulu, Hawaii. He is commemorated on the USS Arizona Memorial. Harry was survived by his Father, Mr. Harry Sharbaugh, Easton, Pennsylvania.[704]

Sharon, Lewis Purdie Machinist's Mate, Second Class, Serial No: 382 07 92, US Navy. Lewis was born January 5, 1915 in Orange County, California to Lewis Lester and Elizabeth (Purdy) Sharon. He enlisted in the US Navy November 15, 1938 at Los Angeles, California and reported for duty on the USS Arizona March 11, 1939. He was killed in action on December 7, 1941 at Pearl Harbor, Hawaii. Lewis was awarded the American Defense Service Medal, World War II Victory Medal and Purple Heart Medal posthumously. He remains on duty on the USS Arizona. Lewis is commemorated on the USS Arizona Memorial and the Memorial Tablets of the Missing, National Memorial Cemetery of the Pacific, Honolulu, Hawaii. He was survived by his Father, Mr. Lewis Lester Sharon, 507 South Ross Street, Santa Ana, California.[705]

---

[702] William "Billy" Alfred Shannon, Information and photo provided by family members, Helen & Richard Shannon.

[703] Report of Changes of the USS Arizona for the month ending 31st day of December, 1941, Page 99, line 8, Harry Robert Sharbaugh.

[704] Harry Sharbaugh, photo from the Morning Call, Allentown, Pennsylvania, December 23, 1941, page 23.

[705] Lewis Purdie Sharon, Photo from the Santa Ana Register, Santa Ana, California, Tuesday, May 5, 1942, Page 1.

Shaw, Clyde Donald   Seaman, First Class, Serial No: 279 73 63, US Navy. Clyde was born in about 1917 in Ohio to Nannie E. Shaw. He enlisted in the US Navy October 7, 1940 in Cincinnati, Ohio and completed his basic training at the Naval Training Station in Great Lakes, Illinois. Clyde reported for duty on the USS Arizona December 9, 1940. He was killed in action on December 7, 1941 at Pearl Harbor, Hawaii. Clyde was awarded the American Defense Service Medal, World War II Victory Medal and Purple Heart Medal posthumously. He remains buried on the USS Arizona. Clyde is commemorated on the USS Arizona Memorial and the Memorial Tablets of the Missing, National Memorial Cemetery of the Pacific, Honolulu, Hawaii. He was survived by his Mother, Mrs. Nannie Sellers Shaw, Berryman Addition, Lima, Ohio.[706]

Shaw, Robert "Bobby" Kar   Musician, Second Class, Serial No: 160 26 62, US Navy. Robert was born October 3, 1922 in Harris County, Texas, son of Thomas Thuel Shaw and Edna E. (Killough) Shaw. He enlisted in the US Navy December 2, 1940 and attended the Navy School of Music in Washington, DC graduating on May 23, 1941 as a member of the USS Arizona Band. Robert reported for duty on the USS Arizona on June 17, 1941. His battle station was in the black powder room passing ammunition to the Arizona's gunners during the attack. None of the band members survived the explosion. Robert was killed in action on December 7, 1941 at Pearl Harbor, Hawaii. He was awarded the American Defense Service Medal, World War II Victory Medal and Purple Heart Medal posthumously. Robert's remains were recovered and he was buried in Grave 236 13 116, Nuuanu (US Naval Cemetery) Nuuanu, Hawaii. He is commemorated on the USS Arizona Memorial. Robert was survived by his Father, Mr. Thomas Shaw, Box 283, Pasadena, Texas.[707]

Shawn, Ernest Maurice   Gunner's Mate, Third Class, Serial No. 356 34 27, US Navy. Ernest was born on March 4, 1919 in Saratoga, Texas, the son of Arthur Milford and Mattie Lee (Morgan) Shawn. He enlisted in the US Navy August 10, 1940 in Dallas, Texas and completed his training at the Naval Training Station, San Diego, California. Ernest reported for duty on the USS Arizona October 14, 1940. He was serving on the USS Arizona on December 7, 1941 when the Japanese attacked Pearl Harbor. After the attack, Ernest was transferred to the USS Ralph Talbot for duty. Ernest died on January 28, 1998 and was buried in Belvedere Memorial Park, San Angelo, Texas.

Shebak, Joseph   Seaman, First Class, Serial No. 212 60 10, US Navy. Joseph was born on August 2, 1915 in Massachusetts the son of Egnace and Christina Shebak. He enlisted in the US Navy October 14, 1940 in Springfield, Massachusetts and completed his basic training at the Naval Training Station in Newport, Rhode Island. Joseph reported for duty on the USS Arizona December 10, 1940. He was serving on the USS Arizona on December 7, 1941 when the Japanese attacked Pearl Harbor. Joseph was wounded in action during the attack and his Father,

---

[706] Clyde Donald Shaw, Photo from Pearl Harbor, A day that has lived in infamy, by Kim Kincaid, The Lima News, Wednesday, December 7, 2005, page D3.
[707] Robert "Bobby" Kar Shaw, Photo provided by family members, Connie and Kathy Kircher.

Mr. Ignats Shebak, 157 Holyoke Street, Florence, Massachusetts was notified. He was later transferred to the USS Louisville (CA-28) for duty. Joseph died at 62 years old on June 9, 1978 in Cleveland, Ohio. He was never married.

Sheffer, George Robert Seaman, First Class, Serial No: 311 40 04, US Navy. George was born in 1915 in Indiana, son of George C. Sheffer and Minnie Sheffer. He enlisted in the US Navy January 10, 1940 in Detroit, Michigan and completed his basic training at the Naval Training Station in Newport, Rhode Island. He reported for duty on the USS Arizona March 29, 1940. George was killed in action on December 7, 1941 at Pearl Harbor, Hawaii. He was awarded the American Defense Service Medal, World War II Victory Medal and Purple Heart Medal posthumously. George remains buried on the USS Arizona. He is commemorated on the USS Arizona Memorial and the Memorial Tablets of the Missing, National Memorial Cemetery of the Pacific, Honolulu, Hawaii. George was survived by his Father, Mr. George Sheffer, 603 Olive Street, Goshen, Indiana.[708]

Sherrill, Warren Joseph Yeoman, Second Class, Serial No: 360 01 30, US Navy. Warren was born September 29, 1921 in Republic Kansas. Warren enlisted in the US Navy October 4, 1938 in Houston, Texas with his twin brother John and completed his basic training at the Naval Training Station in San Diego, California. They both reported for duty on the USS Arizona January 2, 1939 but his brother transferred to another ship. Warren was killed in action on December 7, 1941 at Pearl Harbor, Hawaii. His battle station was in the conning tower located within the foremast. The Captain ordered him to relay a message to the officer of the deck who was still on the quarterdeck. He got as far as the boat deck before being killed. He was awarded the American Defense Service Medal, World War II Victory Medal and Purple Heart Medal posthumously. Warren's remains were identified and were shipped home to Corpus Christi, Texas and buried in Holy Cross Cemetery, Corpus Christi, Texas. He is commemorated on the USS Arizona Memorial and the Memorial Tablets of the Missing, National Memorial Cemetery of the Pacific, Honolulu, Hawaii. Warren was survived by his Mother, Mrs. Lora Mary Sherrill, 1206 3rd Street, Corpus Christi, Texas; three sisters, Mrs. Bonnie Andrews of El Cajon, California, Mrs. Alice Goode of Compton, California and Lorcills Sherrill; a brother, John B. of Corpus Christi; three half brothers Pickney and Armond Sherrill of St Louis and Hardee Sherrill of Sweetwater. The American Legion Post 248 was named in honor of Warren J. Sherrill. Additionally, Sherrill Park in Corpus Christi, TX was named in his honor.[709]

---

[708] George Robert Sheffer, Photo from 1939 Butler University Yearbook, Indianapolis, Indiana.
[709] Warren Joseph Sherrill, Photo provided by the Corpus Christi Public Library, Corpus Christi, TX.

Sherven, Richard Stanton   Electrician's Mate, Third Class, Serial No: 328 75 65, US Navy. Richard was born on October 29, 1921 son of Mr. & Mrs. Helge Sherven. He was the middle son having two older brothers and two younger brothers. Richard grew up on the family farm. He attended and graduated high school in Sanish, North Dakota in 1940. He enlisted in the Navy October 8, 1940 in Minneapolis, Minnesota and completed his basic training at the Naval Training Station in Great Lakes, Illinois. Richard's first assignment was the USS Arizona where he reported for duty on December 9, 1940. Richard was killed in action on December 7, 1941 at Pearl Harbor, Hawaii. He was awarded the American Defense Service Medal, World War II Victory Medal and Purple Heart Medal posthumously. Richard remains buried on the USS Arizona. He is commemorated on the USS Arizona Memorial and the Memorial Tablets of the Missing, National Memorial Cemetery of the Pacific, Honolulu, Hawaii. Richard was survived by his Father, Mr. Helge Sherven, Charlson, North Dakota.[710]

Shew, Martin Luther   Machinist's Mate, Second Class, Serial No. 359 96 46, US Navy. Martin was born in 1919 in Texas the son of Thomas J and Georgia Shew. He enlisted in the US Navy October 8, 1937 in Houston, Texas and reported for duty on the USS Arizona January 25, 1938. Martin was serving on the USS Arizona on December 7, 1941 when the Japanese attacked Pearl Harbor. He went on to serve on the USS Neosho and other ships during the war. Martin passed away on April 15, 2013.

Shiffman, Harold Ely   Radioman, Third Class, Serial No: 410 96 63, US Navy. Harold was the youngest of five children born April 15, 1914 in Detroit to Morris Shiffman and Ida Shiffman. He enlisted in the US Navy August 27, 1940 and reported for duty on the USS Arizona January 25, 1941. Harold was about to be married to a very pretty, young woman by the name of Pat when he came back to the US on his next furlough. His Aunt Goldie and Uncle Harold Sobel were planning to go to his wedding in New York when the news came of the bombing. Harold was killed in action on December 7, 1941 at Pearl Harbor, Hawaii. He was awarded the American Defense Service Medal, World War II Victory Medal and Purple Heart Medal posthumously. Harold remains on duty on the USS Arizona. He is commemorated on the USS Arizona Memorial and the Memorial Tablets of the Missing, National Memorial Cemetery of the Pacific, Honolulu, Hawaii. Harold was survived by his Father, Mr. Morris Shiffman, 1751 Lee Place, Detroit, Michigan.[711]

---

[710] Richard Stanton Sherven, Information and photo provided by his brother, Vern H. Sherven.
[711] Harold Ely Shiffman, Photo provided by his great nephew, David Green, information provided by his Niece, Beverly Forman.

Shiley, Paul Eugene   Seaman, First Class, Serial No: 243 78 47, US Navy. Paul was born in 1922 in Wiconisco, Pennsylvania, the son of Lester Ruben Shiley and Minnie Gertrude (Paul) Shiley. He enlisted in the US Navy October 16, 1940 in Philadelphia, Pennsylvania and completed his basic training at the Naval Training Station in Newport, Rhode Island. Paul reported for duty on the USS Arizona December 10, 1940. He was killed in action on December 7, 1941 at Pearl Harbor, Hawaii. Paul was awarded the American Defense Service Medal, World War II Victory Medal and Purple Heart Medal posthumously. He remains on duty on the USS Arizona. Paul is commemorated on the USS Arizona Memorial and the Memorial Tablets of the Missing, National Memorial Cemetery of the Pacific, Honolulu, Hawaii. He was survived by his Father, Mr. Lester Ruben Shiley, his Mother, Minnie and his siblings, Clyde, June, Donald, Robert, Dorothy and Lawrence, Center Street, Wisconisco, Pennsylvania.[712]

Shimer, Melvin Irvin   Seaman, First Class, Serial No: 243 78 48, US Navy. Melvin was born in about 1923 in Bedford County, Pennsylvania to William and Alice (Guthridge) Shimer. In the 1930 census, Melvin was living in the Tressler Orphans' Home in Tyrone, Perry County Pennsylvania with his brother Gilbert and his sister Esther. He enlisted in the US Navy October 16, 1940 in Philadelphia, Pennsylvania and completed his basic training at the Naval Training Station in Newport, Rhode Island. Melvin reported for duty on the USS Arizona December 10, 1940. He was killed in action on December 7, 1941 at Pearl Harbor, Hawaii. Melvin was awarded the American Defense Service Medal, World War II Victory Medal and Purple Heart Medal posthumously. He remains buried on the USS Arizona. Melvin is commemorated on the USS Arizona Memorial and the Memorial Tablets of the Missing, National Memorial Cemetery of the Pacific, Honolulu, Hawaii. He was survived by his Mother, Mrs. Alice Shimer, General Delivery, Lewiston, Pennsylvania.

Shive, Malcolm Holman   Radioman, Third Class, Serial No: 412 11 12, US Navy Reserve. Malcolm was born October 30, 1923, son of Grover L. Shive and Lois Elizabeth (Eshom) Shive. He grew up in Laguna Beach, a small town back in those years. A place where folks let their children go to school barefooted. Malcolm's mother, Lois worked as a laundress. She did washing and ironing for Orange County Cleaners. Malcolm's father, Gordon was a gardener who developed a brain tumor in the early 1930's and sometime in 1935 he passed away. Soon after, his mother married a man that, in later years, would just be called "The Mean SOB". Malcolm spent eight months in radio school before enlisting in the Navy November 18, 1940, requesting that he be assigned to the USS Arizona where his brother, Gordon was serving. He reported for duty on the USS Arizona October 27, 1941, only 41 days prior to the Pearl Harbor Attack. Radiomen such as Malcolm, were bunked five decks below the main deck.[713] Malcolm was killed in action on December 7, 1941 at Pearl Harbor, Hawaii. He was awarded the American Defense Service Medal, World War II Victory Medal and Purple Heart Medal posthumously. Malcolm remains on duty on the USS Arizona. He is commemorated on the USS Arizona Memorial and the Memorial Tablets of the Missing, National

---

[712] Paul Eugene Shiley, Photo provided by his niece, Denise (Shiley) Carl.
[713] The Brothers by Andy Alison and Amy Wilson, The Orange County Register, Accent Section, Sunday, May 20, 2001.

Memorial Cemetery of the Pacific, Honolulu, Hawaii. Malcolm was survived by his Mother, Mrs. Lois Shive Westgate, 478 Jasmine, Laguna Beach, California and a younger brother, Robert Pendleton Shive. His brother, Gordon was also killed in action while serving on the Arizona.[714]

Shively, Benjamin Franklin Fireman, First Class, Serial No: 311 51 60, US Navy. Benjamin was born December 14, 1919 in Kalamazoo, Michigan to Harry Wilbur Shively and Agnes Shively. He enlisted in the US Navy October 8, 1940 in Detroit, Michigan and completed his basic training at the Naval Training Station in Great Lakes, Illinois. Benjamin reported for duty on the USS Arizona December 9, 1940. He was killed in action on December 7, 1941 at Pearl Harbor, Hawaii. Benjamin was awarded the American Defense Service Medal, World War II Victory Medal and Purple Heart Medal posthumously. He remains on duty on the USS Arizona. Benjamin is commemorated on the USS Arizona Memorial and the Memorial Tablets of the Missing, National Memorial Cemetery of the Pacific, Honolulu, Hawaii and Riverside Cemetery, Three Rivers, Michigan. He was survived by his Father, Mr. Harry Wilbur Shively, Route 2, Three Rivers, Michigan.[715]

Shores, Irland, Jr. Seaman, First Class, Serial No: 272 41 56, US Navy. Irland was born August 26, 1922 in Alabama. He enlisted in the US Navy October 5, 1940 in Birmingham, Alabama and completed his basic training at the Naval Training Station in Norfolk, Virginia. He reported for duty on the USS Arizona December 4, 1940. Assigned death #139, Irland died December 12, 1941 from wounds received in action on December 7, 1941 at Pearl Harbor, Hawaii.[716]. He was awarded the American Defense Service Medal, World War II Victory Medal and Purple Heart Medal posthumously. Irland's remains were recovered and he was buried in Plot A, Row 0, Grave 529, National Memorial Cemetery of the Pacific, Honolulu, Hawaii. He is commemorated on the USS Arizona Memorial. Irland was survived by his Father, Mr. Irland Shores, Sr., Route 1, Grant, Alabama.

Shugart, Marvin John Seaman, First Class, Serial No: 372 21 62, US Navy. Marvin was born February 18, 1917 in Fort Morgan, Colorado, the son of Elmer Arthur and Susan Beatrice (Lee) Shugart. He enlisted in the US Navy November 26, 1940 in Denver, Colorado and completed his basic training at the Naval Training Station in San Diego, California. He reported for duty on the USS Arizona July 8, 1941. Marvin was killed in action on December 7, 1941 at Pearl Harbor, Hawaii. He was awarded the American Defense Service Medal, World War II Victory Medal and Purple Heart Medal posthumously. Marvin remains on duty on the USS Arizona. He is commemorated on the USS Arizona Memorial and the Memorial Tablets of the Missing, National Memorial Cemetery of the Pacific, Honolulu, Hawaii. Marvin was survived by his Father, Mr. Elmer Arthur Shugart, 233 West Catlin Street, Cannon City, Colorado.[717]

---

[714] Malcolm Holman Shive, Information and photo provided by his nephew, Gary Shive.

[715] Benjamin Franklin Shively, Photo provided by James D. Holds.

[716] Report of Changes of the USS Arizona for the month ending 31st day of December, 1941, Page 100, line 22, Irland Shores, Jr.

[717] Marvin John Shugart, Photo from Colorado Honor States.

Sibley, Delmar Dale Seaman, First Class, Serial No: 238 69 49, US Navy. Delmar was born December 30, 1917 in Aurora, South Dakota the son of Harry and Ethel Sibley. When he was about a year old, his mother died and he was sent to live with relatives in Mitchell, SD. He worked building roads to Mount Rushmore for the Civilian Conservation Corps. At the time he enlisted he was living with his aunt and uncle, Lucie and Earl Sibley in Oswego, New York. He enlisted in the US Navy October 15, 1940 in Albany, New York and completed his basic training at the Naval Training Station in Newport, Rhode Island. He reported for duty on the USS Arizona December 10, 1940. Delmar was killed in action on December 7, 1941 at Pearl Harbor, Hawaii. He was awarded the American Defense Service Medal, World War II Victory Medal and Purple Heart Medal posthumously. Delmar remains on duty on the USS Arizona. He is commemorated on the USS Arizona Memorial and the Memorial Tablets of the Missing, National Memorial Cemetery of the Pacific, Honolulu, Hawaii. Delmar was survived by his Uncle, Mr. Earl Sibley, 502 Main Street, Oswego, New York. The Glenn A. Warner VFW Post 1371, Owego, Tioga County, New York has named the post's downstairs as Delmar Dale Sibley Memorial Dining Hall.[718]

Sidders, Russell Lewis Seaman, First Class, Serial No: 279 64 66, US Navy. Russell was born August 13, 1919, the first of 5 children born to Harry Elsworth Sidders and Elizabeth Euphemia (Barger) Sidders. They lived on a large farm with a large herd of dairy cattle that they milked by hand. Russell was allergic to the dust on the farm. So helping his parents on the farm was difficult for him. He enlisted in the US Navy November 27, 1939 in Cincinnati, Ohio and completed his basic training at the Naval Training Station in Great Lakes, Illinois. Russell reported for duty on the USS Arizona March 26, 1940. He was killed in action on December 7, 1941 at Pearl Harbor, Hawaii. Russell was awarded the American Defense Service Medal, World War II Victory Medal and Purple Heart Medal posthumously. He remains on duty on the USS Arizona. Russell is commemorated on the USS Arizona Memorial and the Memorial Tablets of the Missing, National Memorial Cemetery of the Pacific, Honolulu, Hawaii. He was survived by his Parents, Mr. and Mrs. Harry Sidders, Route 2, St. Paris, Ohio, one brother, William and three sisters, Nellie, Sara and Margery.[719]

Sidell, John Henry Gunner's Mate, Second Class, Serial No: 337 14 43, US Navy. John was born August 23, 1918 in Genoa, Colorado the eldest of six children born to Arthur James and Pearl Effie (Templeton) Sidell. He was named after his grandfather, John Henry Sidell. John enlisted in the US Navy May 15, 1939 in St. Louis, Missouri and completed his basic training at the Naval Training Station in San Diego, California. He reported for duty on the USS Arizona October 20, 1939. John was killed in action on December 7, 1941 at Pearl Harbor, Hawaii. He was awarded the American Defense Service Medal, World War II Victory Medal and Purple Heart Medal posthumously. John remains on duty on the

---

[718] Delmar Dale Sibley, Photo provided by the Glenn A. Warner VFW Post 1371, Owego, Tioga County, New York.

[719] Russell Lewis Sidders, Information and photo provided by family member, Becky Sidders Smith.

USS Arizona. He is commemorated on the USS Arizona Memorial and the Memorial Tablets of the Missing, National Memorial Cemetery of the Pacific, Honolulu, Hawaii. John was survived by his Father, Mr. Arthur Sidell, 5 South Pine Street, Villa Grove, Illinois.[720]

Silvey, Jesse   Machinist's Mate, Second Class, Serial No: 359 96 13, US Navy. Jesse was born January 12, 1918 in Velasco, Texas, son of William Jesse Silvey and Bertha Alice (Mitchell) Silvey. He enlisted in the US Navy September 10, 1937 in Houston, Texas and reported for duty on the USS Arizona January 7, 1938. Jesse was killed in action on December 7, 1941 at Pearl Harbor, Hawaii. He was awarded the American Defense Service Medal, World War II Victory Medal and Purple Heart Medal posthumously. Jesse remains on duty on the USS Arizona. He is commemorated on the USS Arizona Memorial and the Memorial Tablets of the Missing, National Memorial Cemetery of the Pacific, Honolulu, Hawaii. Jesse was survived by his Parents, Mr. and Mrs. William Jesse Silvey, Box 197, Alvin, Texas, three sisters and two brothers.[721]

   Simmons, Claude William, Jr.   Seaman, First Class, Serial No. 372 20 14, US Navy. Claude was born July 24, 1921. He enlisted in the US Navy November 1, 1940 in Denver, Colorado and completed his basic training at the Naval Training Station in San Diego, California. He reported for duty on the USS Arizona January 11, 1941. He was injured while serving on the USS Arizona on December 7, 1941 when the Japanese attacked Pearl Harbor. After spending a month and a half at the Naval Hospital in Pearl Harbor, Claude was transferred on January 21, 1942 to Naval Hospital on the mainland. He died August 20, 1972.

Simon, Walter "Billy" Hamilton   Seaman, First Class, Serial No: 243 78 94, US Navy. Walter was born July 24, 1918 in Collingswood, New Jersey to Dr. William Peltz Simon and Laura Estella (Down) Simon. After Billy's graduation from high school in 1938, the family moved to a rented farm about 15 miles away in Barnsboro, NJ. It was there that his mother, Stella, died just a year later from a blood clot caused by a fall. The farm was not a success and within another year, the Simons moved back to Collingswood. Walter enlisted in the US Navy on October 16, 1940 in Philadelphia, Pennsylvania and completed his basic training at the Naval Training Station in Newport, Rhode Island. He reported for duty on the USS Arizona December 10, 1940. Walter was killed in action on December 7, 1941 at Pearl Harbor, Hawaii. He was awarded the American Defense Service Medal, World War II Victory Medal and Purple Heart Medal posthumously. Walter remains on duty on the USS Arizona. He is commemorated on the USS Arizona Memorial and the Memorial Tablets of the Missing, National Memorial Cemetery of the Pacific, Honolulu, Hawaii. Walter was survived by his Father, Dr. William Peltz Simon, 574 Haddon Avenue, Collingswood, Camden, New Jersey and Sister Louise.[722]

---

[720] John Henry Sidell, Information provided by his cousin, June Riccio, photo provided by his great niece, Carrie Lumley.

[721] Jesse Silvey, Photo and information taken from, First Casualty For County Is Reported Here, The Freeport Facts, Freeport, Texas, Thursday, January 1, 1942, Front Page.

[722] Walter Hamilton Simon, Photo and information provided by his niece, Nancy Maack.

Simpson, Albert "Bucky" Eugene   Seaman, First Class, Serial No: 234 28 34, US Navy. Albert was born in 1922 in Elmira, New York, son of Vern A. Simpson and Beatrice G. Simpson. He enlisted in the US Navy October 15, 1940 in Buffalo, New York and completed his basic training at the Naval Training Station in Newport, Rhode Island. Albert reported for duty on the USS Arizona December 10, 1940. He was killed in action on December 7, 1941 at Pearl Harbor, Hawaii. Albert was awarded the American Defense Service Medal, World War II Victory Medal and Purple Heart Medal posthumously. He remains on duty on the USS Arizona. Albert is commemorated on the USS Arizona Memorial and the Memorial Tablets of the Missing, National Memorial Cemetery of the Pacific, Honolulu, Hawaii. He was survived by his Father, Mr. Vern Albert Simpson, Route 2, Watkins Glenn, New York.

Skeen, Harvey Leroy   Seaman, Second Class, Serial No: 381 42 97, US Navy. Harvey was born January 26, 1924 in Lassen, California to William D. and Laura Agatha (Holden) Skeen. He enlisted in the US Navy June 13, 1941 in San Diego, California and completed his basic training at the Naval Training Station in San Diego, California. He reported for duty on the USS Arizona August 13, 1941. Harvey was killed in action on December 7, 1941 at Pearl Harbor, Hawaii. He was awarded the American Defense Service Medal, World War II Victory Medal and Purple Heart Medal posthumously. Harvey remains on duty on the USS Arizona. He is commemorated on the USS Arizona Memorial and the Memorial Tablets of the Missing, National Memorial Cemetery of the Pacific, Honolulu, Hawaii and Pinal Cemetery, Gila County, Arizona. Harvey was survived by his Mother, Mrs. Laura Skeen, Route 1, Miami, Arizona.

Skiles, Charles Jackson, Jr.   Seaman, Second Class, Serial No: 242 44 39, US Navy. Charles was born February 8, 1923, son of Charles Jackson Skiles and Christina (Zuklin) Skiles. He enlisted in the US Navy April 14, 1941 in Kansas City, Missouri and completed his basic training at the Naval Training Station in San Diego, California. Charles reported for duty on the USS Arizona July 13, 1941. He was killed in action on December 7, 1941 at Pearl Harbor, Hawaii. Charles was awarded the American Defense Service Medal, World War II Victory Medal and Purple Heart Medal posthumously. He remains on duty on the USS Arizona. Charles is commemorated on the USS Arizona Memorial, the Memorial Tablets of the Missing, National Memorial Cemetery of the Pacific, Honolulu, Hawaii and Sunny Slope Cemetery, Richmond, Missouri. Charles was survived by his Father, Mr. Charley J. Skiles, Sr., Richmond, Missouri. His brother Eugene was killed in action while serving on the USS Arizona and his cousin, Garrold Skiles was killed in action on board the USS Oklahoma. The American Legion Post in Ray County, Missouri is named in honor of the three Skiles men.[723]

---

[723] Charles Jackson Skiles, Jr., Photo provided by Donald B. Louks, Post Commander, Griffith – Skiles American Legion Post 237, Richmond, MO.

Skiles, Eugene Seaman, Second Class, Serial No: 342 44 71, US Navy. Eugene was born February 20, 1917, son of Charles Jackson Skiles and Christina (Zuklin) Skiles. He served in the CCC before enlisting in the Navy. Eugene enlisted in the US Navy April 22, 1941 in Kansas City, Missouri and completed his basic training at the Naval Training Station in San Diego, California. He reported for duty on the USS Arizona July 13, 1941. Eugene was killed in action on December 7, 1941 at Pearl Harbor, Hawaii. He was awarded the American Defense Service Medal, World War II Victory Medal and Purple Heart Medal posthumously. Eugene remains on duty on the USS Arizona. He is commemorated on the USS Arizona Memorial, the Memorial Tablets of the Missing, National Memorial Cemetery of the Pacific, Honolulu, Hawaii and Sunny Slope Cemetery, Richmond, Missouri. Eugene was survived by his Father, Mr. Charley J. Skiles, Sr., Richmond, Missouri. His brother Charles was killed in action while serving on the USS Arizona and his cousin, Garrold Skiles was killed in action on board the USS Oklahoma. The American Legion Post in Ray County, Missouri is named in honor of the three Skiles men.[724]

Sletto, Earl Clifton Machinist's Mate, First Class, Serial No: 328 43 84, US Navy. Earl was born March 20, 1917 in Moe, Minnesota, son of Emil E. and Sarah Caroline (Lea) Sletto. He enlisted in the US Navy July 10, 1936 in Minneapolis, Minnesota and reported for duty on the USS Arizona April 29, 1940. Earl was killed in action on December 7, 1941 at Pearl Harbor, Hawaii. He was awarded the American Defense Service Medal, World War II Victory Medal and Purple Heart Medal posthumously. Earl remains on duty on the USS Arizona. He is commemorated on the USS Arizona Memorial and the Memorial Tablets of the Missing, National Memorial Cemetery of the Pacific, Honolulu, Hawaii. Earl was survived by his Father, Mr. Emil E. Sletto, Evansville, Minnesota.

Smalley, Jack G. Seaman, First Class, Serial No: 311 43 33, US Navy. Jack was born April 22, 1922, son of Vern Smalley and Gladys (Broderson) Smalley. He enlisted in the US Navy April 2, 1940 in Detroit, Michigan and reported for duty on the USS Arizona August 6, 1940. Jack was killed in action on December 7, 1941 at Pearl Harbor, Hawaii. He was awarded the American Defense Service Medal, World War II Victory Medal and Purple Heart Medal posthumously. Jack died from wounds received while at his portside anti-aircraft battle station during the attack and he was buried in Plot B, Row 0, Grave 201, National Memorial Cemetery of the Pacific, Honolulu, Hawaii. He is commemorated on the USS Arizona Memorial. Jack was survived by his Father, Mr. Vern Smalley, 2532 Cherry Street, Toledo, Ohio.[725]

---

[724] Eugene Skiles, Photo provided by Donald B. Louks, Post Commander, Griffith – Skiles American Legion Post 237, Richmond, MO.
[725] Jack G. Smalley, Photo provided by family member, Jeff London.

Smart, George David Coxswain, Serial No: 368 46 87, US Navy. George was born in 1920, son of George Wright and Julia L. Smart. He enlisted in the US Navy December 14, 1939 in Salt Lake City, Utah and completed his basic training at the Naval Training Station in San Diego, California. George reported for duty on the USS Arizona February 24, 1940. He was killed in action on December 7, 1941 at Pearl Harbor, Hawaii. The family was notified of his loss on February 4, 1942. A letter was received from Bernard Theena, who served with George from basic training until just before the attack. He wrote "George was very well liked by everyone aboard and held the goodwill of all the officers." George was awarded the American Defense Service Medal, World War II Victory Medal and Purple Heart Medal posthumously. He remains on duty on the USS Arizona. George is commemorated on the USS Arizona Memorial and the Memorial Tablets of the Missing, National Memorial Cemetery of the Pacific, Honolulu, Hawaii and the Miracle of America Museum, Polson, Montana. He was survived by his Parents, Mr. and Mrs. George Wright Smart, Box 683, Polson, Montana and one brother, Don.[726]

Smestad, Halge Hojen Radioman, Second Class, Serial No: 328 53 64, US Navy. Halge was born May 19, 1919 in Dovray, Minnesota, son of Halge Smestad and Matilda (Hojen) Smestad. He enlisted in the US Navy July 20, 1938 in Minneapolis, Minnesota and reported for duty on the USS Arizona May 29, 1940. Halge was killed in action on December 7, 1941 at Pearl Harbor, Hawaii. He was awarded the American Defense Service Medal, World War II Victory Medal and Purple Heart Medal posthumously. Halge remains on duty on the USS Arizona. He is commemorated on the USS Arizona Memorial and the Memorial Tablets of the Missing, National Memorial Cemetery of the Pacific, Honolulu, Hawaii. Halge was survived by his Father, Mr. Halge Smestad, Sr., Dovray, Minnesota.

Smith, Albert Joseph Lieutenant, Junior Grade, Serial No: 0-058441, US Navy. Albert was born November 20, 1895 in Dallas, Texas. He was killed in action on December 7, 1941 at Pearl Harbor, Hawaii. Albert was awarded the American Defense Service Medal, World War II Victory Medal and Purple Heart Medal posthumously. He remains on duty on the USS Arizona. Albert is commemorated on the USS Arizona Memorial and the Memorial Tablets of the Missing, National Memorial Cemetery of the Pacific, Honolulu, Hawaii. He was survived by his Wife, Mrs. Clydia Lee (Ash) Smith, 324 Prospect Avenue, Long Beach, California.

Smith, Clyde Crockett Chief Electrician's Mate, Serial No. 355 43 52, US Navy. Clyde was born June 9, 1904 in Texas to Benjamin Francis Smith, Sr., and Myrtle Julia (Crockett) Smith. He enlisted in the US Navy January 29, 1937 in San Diego, California. He served on the USS Arizona from July 29, 1939 until December 7, 1941 when the Japanese attacked Pearl Harbor. After the attack, Clyde was transferred to the USS Reid for duty. Clyde died December 2, 1987 and is buried in Section 35, Site 1418, Barrancas National Cemetery, Pensacola, Florida.

Smith, Earl "Smitty" Walter Fire Controlman, Third Class, Serial No: 268 29 38, US Navy. Earl was born November 13, 1916. He enlisted in the US Navy August 25, 1937 in Macon, Georgia and reported for duty on the USS Arizona March 8, 1938. Earl was killed in

---

[726] George David Smart, Information and photo graciously provided by Gil Mangels, Founder of the Miracle of America Museum, Polson, Montana.

action on December 7, 1941 at Pearl Harbor, Hawaii. He was awarded the American Defense Service Medal, World War II Victory Medal and Purple Heart Medal posthumously. Earl's remains were recovered and he was sent home for burial in Section 12, Site 3971, Arlington National Cemetery, Fort Myer, Virginia. Earl was survived by his Brother, Mr. Arthur Daniel Smith, P. O. Box 654, Homestead, Florida.

Smith, Earl, Jr. Seaman, First Class, Serial No: 337 12 19, US Navy. Earl enlisted in the US Navy February 2, 1939 in St. Louis, Missouri and completed his basic training at the Naval Training Station in Great Lakes, Illinois. He reported for duty on the USS Arizona July 8, 1939. Earl was killed in action on December 7, 1941 at Pearl Harbor, Hawaii. He was awarded the American Defense Service Medal, World War II Victory Medal and Purple Heart Medal posthumously. Earl remains on duty on the USS Arizona. He is commemorated on the USS Arizona Memorial and the Memorial Tablets of the Missing, National Memorial Cemetery of the Pacific, Honolulu, Hawaii. Earl was survived by his Mother, Mrs. Elva Smith, 1455 South 18th Street, St. Louis, Missouri.[727]

Smith, Edward A. Gunner's Mate, Third Class, Serial No: 337 23 78, US Navy. Edward was born May 26, 1917 in Greene County, Illinois to Charles Franklin Smith and Vallie (Coy) Smith. He enlisted in the US Navy December 5, 1939 in St. Louis, Missouri and reported for duty on the USS Arizona June 16, 1940. Edward was killed in action on December 7, 1941 at Pearl Harbor, Hawaii. He was awarded the American Defense Service Medal, World War II Victory Medal and Purple Heart Medal posthumously. Edward remains on duty on the USS Arizona. He is commemorated on the USS Arizona Memorial and the Memorial Tablets of the Missing, National Memorial Cemetery of the Pacific, Honolulu, Hawaii. Edward was survived by his Father, Mr. Frank Smith, 125 East Lincoln Street, White Hall, Illinois.[728]

Smith, Harold Francis Boatswain's Mate, Second Class, Serial No. 263 19 78, US Navy. Harold enlisted in the US Navy February 9, 1937 in Cleveland, Ohio. Harold served on the USS Arizona from June 19, 1937 until December 7, 1941 when the Japanese attacked Pearl Harbor. After the attack, Harold was transferred to the Naval Shipyard at Pearl Harbor. He served in the Navy until August 1963.

---

[727] Earl Smith, Jr., Photo from the St. Louis Post-Dispatch, St. Louis, Missouri, December 23, 1941, Page 3.
[728] Edward A. Smith, Photo provided by family member, Becky Scroggins Terpening.

Smith, Harry   Seaman, Second Class, Serial No: 412 19 86, US Navy Reserve. Harry was born October 1918 in Los Angeles, California to Samuel and Rosa (Novack) Smith. He enlisted in the US Navy October 4, 1940 in Los Angeles, California and completed his basic training at the Naval Training Station in San Diego, California. Harry reported for duty on the USS Arizona August 1, 1941. He was killed in action on December 7, 1941 at Pearl Harbor, Hawaii. Harry was awarded the Purple Heart Medal posthumously and the Asiatic Pacific Campaign Medal with Bronze Star. He remains on duty on the USS Arizona. Harry is commemorated on the USS Arizona Memorial and the Memorial Tablets of the Missing, National Memorial Cemetery of the Pacific, Honolulu, Hawaii. He was survived by his Father, Mr. Sam Smith, 127 South St. Andrews Place, Los Angeles, California.

Smith, John A.   Shipfitter, Third Class, Serial No: 279 72 51, US Navy. John was born in about 1921 in Greenfield, Ohio to Clarence Eugene and Elma (Ladd) Smith. He enlisted in the US Navy September 3, 1940 in Cincinnati, Ohio and completed his basic training at the Naval Training Station in Norfolk, Virginia. He reported for duty on the USS Arizona December 4, 1940. John was killed in action on December 7, 1941 at Pearl Harbor, Hawaii. He was awarded the American Defense Service Medal, World War II Victory Medal and Purple Heart Medal posthumously. John remains on duty on the USS Arizona. He is commemorated on the USS Arizona Memorial and the Memorial Tablets of the Missing, National Memorial Cemetery of the Pacific, Honolulu, Hawaii. John was survived by his Wife, Mrs. Rosetta Leugers Smith, South Frankfort Street, Minister, Ohio.[729]

Smith, John Edward   Seaman, First Class, Serial No: 381 26 91, US Navy. John enlisted in the US Navy November 16, 1938 in San Diego, California and completed his basic training at the Naval Training Station in San Diego, California. He reported for duty on the USS Arizona March 11, 1939. John was killed in action on December 7, 1941 at Pearl Harbor, Hawaii. He was awarded the American Defense Service Medal, World War II Victory Medal and Purple Heart Medal posthumously. John remains on duty on the USS Arizona. He is commemorated on the USS Arizona Memorial and the Memorial Tablets of the Missing, National Memorial Cemetery of the Pacific, Honolulu, Hawaii. John was survived by his Father, Mr. Edward Oscar Smith, P.O. Box 557, National City, California.

Smith, Luther Kent   Seaman, First Class, Serial No: 295 76 74, US Navy. Luther enlisted in the US Navy October 4, 1940 in Nashville, Tennessee and completed his basic training at the Naval Training Station in Norfolk, Virginia. He reported for duty on the USS Arizona December 4, 1940. Luther was killed in action on December 7, 1941 at Pearl Harbor, Hawaii. He was awarded the American Defense Service Medal, World War II Victory Medal and Purple Heart Medal posthumously. Luther remains on duty on the USS Arizona. He is commemorated on the USS Arizona Memorial and the Memorial Tablets of the Missing, National Memorial Cemetery of the Pacific, Honolulu, Hawaii. Luther was survived by his Mother, Mrs. Lela French, Route 1, Big Sandy, Tennessee.[730]

---

[729] John A. Smith, Photo and information provided by family member, Robert Eakins.
[730] Luther Kent Smith, Photo provided by J. Hall, Find A Grave.

Smith, Macleod "Mack" Lawrence   Seaman, First Class, Serial No: 295 76 67, US Navy. Mack was born in November of 1916 in Adair County, Oklahoma to James A. Smith and Margaret Clementine (Mullinix) Smith. He enlisted in the US Navy October 4, 1940 in Nashville, Tennessee and completed his basic training at the Naval Training Station in Norfolk, Virginia. Mack reported for duty on the USS Arizona December 4, 1940. He was killed in action on December 7, 1941 at Pearl Harbor, Hawaii. Mack was awarded the American Defense Service Medal, World War II Victory Medal and Purple Heart Medal posthumously. He remains on duty on the USS Arizona. Mack is commemorated on the USS Arizona Memorial and the Memorial Tablets of the Missing, National Memorial Cemetery of the Pacific, Honolulu, Hawaii. He was survived by his Father, Mr. James A. Smith, Stillwell, Oklahoma.[731]

Smith, Marvin "Ray" Ray   Seaman, First Class, Serial No: 356 42 63, US Navy. Marvin was born September 22, 1922 in Cross Plains, Texas to William Earl and Martha Aletha Lillian (Swafford) Smith. He was a star athlete at Cross Plains High School and graduated in 1940. *"He played tackle on the football team and won wide recognition as an outstanding player, an inspirational leader and fiery competitor, however, he drew commendation from both opponents and team mates for the sportsmanlike manner in which he played the game."* Ray enlisted in the US Navy November 16, 1940 in Dallas, Texas and completed his basic training at the Naval Training Station in San Diego, California. He reported for duty on the USS Arizona January 11, 1941. Ray was killed in action on December 7, 1941 at Pearl Harbor, Hawaii. He was awarded the American Defense Service Medal, World War II Victory Medal and Purple Heart Medal posthumously. Ray remains on duty on the USS Arizona. He is commemorated on the USS Arizona Memorial and the Memorial Tablets of the Missing, National Memorial Cemetery of the Pacific, Honolulu, Hawaii. Ray was survived by his Parents, Mr. and Mrs. William Earl Smith, Route 1, Cross Plains, Texas.[732]

Smith, Orville Stanley   Ensign, Serial No: 0-085061, US Navy. Orville was born on June 13, 1916 in Verden, Oklahoma. He enlisted in the Navy on October 19, 1934. Orville served on the USS California until November 1935. He was honorably discharged on July 8, 1936 to enter the US Naval Academy at Annapolis, Maryland. He graduated from the academy and was commissioned Ensign on June 6, 1940 and reported for duty on the USS Arizona on June 29, 1940. Orville was serving as the Junior Watch and Division 7 Officer. His battle station was Sec. Battery Officer. Orville was killed in action on December 7, 1941 at Pearl Harbor, Hawaii. He was awarded the American Defense Service Medal, World War II Victory Medal and Purple Heart Medal posthumously. Orville remains on duty on the USS Arizona. He is

---

[731] Macleod "Mack" Lawrence Smith, Photo and information provided by his niece, Lynda Williams.
[732] Marvin Ray Smith, Photo and information from The Cross Plains Review, Cross Plains, Texas, Friday, December 26, 1941, Page 6.

commemorated on the USS Arizona Memorial and the Memorial Tablets of the Missing, National Memorial Cemetery of the Pacific, Honolulu, Hawaii. Orville was survived by his Mother, Mrs. Beulah Mae Smith, Box 16, Albert, Oklahoma.[733]

Smith, Roscoe Bryant Gunner's Mate, Third Class, Serial No. 346 71 03, US Navy. Roscoe enlisted in the US Navy October 1, 1938 in Little Rock, Arkansas and completed his basic training at the Naval Training Station in San Diego, California. He reported for duty on the USS Arizona January 2, 1939. He was serving on the USS Arizona on December 7, 1941 when the Japanese attacked Pearl Harbor. Roscoe was transferred to the USS Jarvis (DD-393) and reported for duty December 10, 1941. He was missing in action August 9, 1942. During the Battle of Guadalcanal, the USS Jarvis having taken on heavy bombardment at Tulagi, retired westward with little speed, no radio communications and few operative guns. 40 miles off Guadalcanal, the Japanese believing her to be an escaping cruiser, attacked the USS Jarvis, raking the ship with bullets and torpedoes. Jarvis "split and sank" taking her entire crew. Roscoe was declared dead July 12, 1945. He is commemorated on the Tablets of the Missing at Fort William McKinley American Cemetery, Manila, Philippines. He was survived by his Mother, Mrs. Lu Ella Whitley, 219 Senator Avenue, Texarkana, Arkansas.

Smith, Walter Tharnel Steward's Mate, First Class, Serial No: 295 39 56, US Navy. Walter was born in about 1919 in Tennessee the son of Walter T. and Rosa L. Smith. He enlisted in the US Navy November 6, 1937 in Nashville, Tennessee and completed his basic training at the Naval Training Station in San Diego, California. He reported for duty on the USS Arizona April 21, 1939. Walter was killed in action on December 7, 1941 at Pearl Harbor, Hawaii. He was awarded the American Defense Service Medal, World War II Victory Medal and Purple Heart Medal posthumously. Walter remains on duty on the USS Arizona. He is commemorated on the USS Arizona Memorial and the Memorial Tablets of the Missing, National Memorial Cemetery of the Pacific, Honolulu, Hawaii. Walter was survived by his Mother, Mrs. Rosa Lee Smith, Gunnison, Mississippi.

Smith, William Hansford, Jr. Coxswain, Serial No. 272 08 50, US Navy. William was born September 25, 1917 in Pennsylvania, the son of William Hansford and Clara Annie (Montague) Smith. He enlisted in the US Navy May 13, 1939 in Denver, Colorado. He was transferred from the USS California (BB-40) to the USS Arizona on October 20, 1939. He was serving on the USS Arizona on December 7, 1941 when the Japanese attacked Pearl Harbor. After the attack, William was transferred to Section Bas, Bishop's Point, Oahu, Hawaii for duty. William died December 24, 1976 in Pueblo, Colorado.

Snow, Rutherford Hayes Watertender, First Class, Serial No. 214 89 54, US Navy. Rutherford was born on January 1, 1915 in Hackensack, New Jersey the son of Francis Lockwood and Elizabeth Beatrice (Smith) Snow. He lied about his age and enlisted in the US Navy January 13, 1930 at age 15 and completed his training at the Naval Training Station, Newport, Rhode Island. Rutherford served on the USS Arizona from December 31, 1930 until December 7, 1941 when the Japanese attacked Pearl Harbor. Rutherford received a commendation for his actions on the days following the attack:

---

[733] Orville Stanley Smith, Photo from The Lucky Bag Yearbook, United States Naval Academy, Annapolis, Maryland, Class of 1940.

"For meritorious conduct and outstanding performances of duty while voluntarily engaged in diving operations and directing the efforts of a group of divers incident to the salvage of vessels damaged by enemy action at Pearl Harbor on December 7, 1941. By his leadership, courage and devotion to duty under arduous and frequently hazardous conditions, he contributed materially to the success of the diving phase of these operations. His conduct throughout was in keeping with the highest traditions of the naval service. Admiral C.W. Nimitz"

After the attack, Rutherford was transferred to the salvage work on the USS Utah sunk at Pearl Harbor. He retired from the Navy on September 30, 1952 with the rank of LT (jg) having served over 22 years. Rutherford died on March 20, 1953 and is buried in Section 286, Row C, Site 3, Los Angeles National Cemetery, Los Angeles, California.[734]

Soens, Harold Mathias Ship's Cook, First Class, Serial No: 328 30 79, US Navy. Harold was born January 1, 1912 in Stillwater, Minnesota, son of William M. Soens and Minnie (Leihmann) Soens. He enlisted in the US Navy August 12, 1935 in San Diego, California and reported for duty on the USS Arizona May 6, 1941. Assigned death # 384, Harold died December 10, 1941 from wounds received in action on December 7, 1941 at Pearl Harbor, Hawaii.[735] He was awarded the American Defense Service Medal, World War II Victory Medal and Purple Heart Medal posthumously. Harold's remains were recovered and he was buried in Plot A, Row 0, Grave 519, National Memorial Cemetery of the Pacific, Honolulu, Hawaii. He is commemorated on the USS Arizona Memorial. Harold was survived by his Wife, Mrs. Margaret Gustie (O'Brien) Soens, 4215 35th Street, San Diego, California.

Sooter, James "Freddie" Frederick Radioman, Third Class, Serial No: 360 15 37, US Navy. James was born in about 1922, the son of James Milton and Beulah (Edwards) Sooter. He enlisted in the US Navy June 7, 1940 in Houston, Texas and reported for duty on the USS Arizona on November 28, 1940. James was killed in action on December 7, 1941 at Pearl Harbor, Hawaii. He was awarded the American Defense Service Medal, World War II Victory Medal and Purple Heart Medal posthumously. James remains on duty on the USS Arizona. He is commemorated on the USS Arizona Memorial and the Memorial Tablets of the Missing, National Memorial Cemetery of the Pacific, Honolulu, Hawaii. James was survived by his Father, Mr. James Milton Sooter, 308 Iowa Avenue, Weslaco, Texas.[736]

Sorensen, Holger Earl Seaman, First Class, Serial No: 372 14 27, US Navy. Holger was born September 9, 1921. He enlisted in the US Navy April 3, 1940 in Denver, Colorado and completed his basic training at the Naval Training Station in San Diego, California. He reported for duty on the USS Arizona July 2, 1940. Assigned death # 158, Holger died on December 10, 1941 from wounds received in action on December 7, 1941 at Pearl Harbor, Hawaii. He was awarded the American Defense Service Medal, World War II Victory Medal and Purple Heart Medal posthumously. Holger's remains were recovered and he was buried in Plot C, Row 0, Grave 1307, National Memorial Cemetery of the Pacific, Honolulu, Hawaii. He is commemorated on the USS Arizona Memorial. Holger was survived by his Mother, Mrs. Avis Grace Sorenson, Espanola, New Mexico.

---

[734] Rutherford Hayes Snow, Photo and information provided by his son, Richard Snow.

[735] Report of Changes of the USS Arizona for the month ending 31st day of December, 1941, Page 102, line 20, Harold Mathias Soens.

[736] James Frederick Sooter, Photo from the Weslaco Museum, Weslaco, Texas.

South, Charles Braxton Seaman, First Class, Serial No: 272 41 74, US Navy. Charles was born November 9, 1922 in Fayette County, Alabama, son of Charles Manley South and Pearl Sarah (Maddox) South. He enlisted in the US Navy October 5, 1940 in Birmingham, Alabama and completed his basic training at the Naval Training Station in Norfolk, Virginia. Charles reported for duty on the USS Arizona December 4, 1940. He was killed in action on December 7, 1941 at Pearl Harbor, Hawaii. Charles was awarded the American Defense Service Medal, World War II Victory Medal and Purple Heart Medal posthumously. He remains on duty on the USS Arizona. Charles is commemorated on the USS Arizona Memorial and the Memorial Tablets of the Missing, National Memorial Cemetery of the Pacific, Honolulu, Hawaii. He was survived by his Guardian, Mr. Richard Hobson Corr, Box 165, Moundville, Alabama. Both of his parents preceded him in death.[737]

Spence, Merle Joe Seaman, First Class, Serial No: 295 76 72, US Navy. Merle was born August 19, 1919, son of Green Berry Spence and Vadie C. (Cole) Spence. He enlisted in the US Navy October 4, 1940 in Nashville, Tennessee and completed his basic training at the Naval Training Station in Norfolk, Virginia. Merle reported for duty on the USS Arizona December 4, 1940. He was killed in action on December 7, 1941 at Pearl Harbor, Hawaii. Merle was awarded the American Defense Service Medal, World War II Victory Medal and Purple Heart Medal posthumously. He remains on duty on the USS Arizona. Merle is commemorated on the USS Arizona Memorial and the Memorial Tablets of the Missing, National Memorial Cemetery of the Pacific, Honolulu, Hawaii. He was survived by his Parents, Mr. and Mrs. Green Berry Spence, Route 1, Bruceton, Tennessee and brothers and sisters, Edith Nell, Avis, Valgene and Sidney Joyce.[738]

Spotz, Maurice Edwin Fireman, First Class, Serial No: 300 19 40, US Navy. Maurice was born February 18, 1916 in Kankakee, Illinois the only child to Edward E. Spotz and Ida Mae (Nowack) Spotz. His father, who was a mechanic and railroad car inspector, died March 27, 1937 of pneumonia. He enlisted in the US Navy October 8, 1940 in Chicago, Illinois and completed his basic training at the Naval Training Station in Great Lakes, Illinois. Maurice reported for duty on the USS Arizona December 9, 1940. He was killed in action on December 7, 1941 at Pearl Harbor, Hawaii. Maurice was awarded the American Defense Service Medal, World War II Victory Medal and Purple Heart Medal posthumously. He remains on duty on the USS Arizona. Maurice is commemorated on the USS Arizona Memorial and the Memorial Tablets of the Missing, National Memorial Cemetery of the Pacific, Honolulu, Hawaii. He was survived by his Mother, Mrs. Ida Mae Spotz, 209 North Wildwood Avenue, Kankakee, Illinois.[739]

[737] Charles Braxton South, Photo from the Birmingham News, Saturday, January 3, 1942.

[738] Merle Joe Spence, Photo and information provided by his cousin, Jo C. Owen.

[739] Maurice Edwin Spotz, Information provided by family member, Diane Spatz Smith, Photo from the Republican News, Kankakee, Illinois, February 2, 1942, Page 1.

Spreeman, Robert Lawrence   Gunner's Mate, Third Class, Serial No: 299 99 18, US Navy. Robert was born September 18, 1920 in Michigan to Albert Charles and Ida May (Mathews) Spreeman. In 1937 Robert at age 17, joined the CCC at Crystal Falls, Michigan. He enlisted in the US Navy November 8, 1939 in Chicago, Illinois and completed his basic training at the Naval Training Station in Great Lakes, Illinois. Robert reported for duty on the USS Arizona January 27, 1940. He died February 12, 1942 from wounds he received on December 7, 1941 in Honolulu, Hawaii. Robert was awarded the American Defense Service Medal, World War II Victory Medal and Purple Heart posthumously. He was buried in Plot C, Row 0, Grave 309, National Memorial Cemetery of the Pacific, Honolulu, Hawaii. Robert is commemorated on the USS Arizona Memorial and at the Forest Home Cemetery, Newberry, Michigan. He was survived by his Mother, Mrs. Ida May Simmons, Route 1, Box 105, Newberry, Michigan.[740]

Springer, Charles Harold   Seaman, Second Class, Serial No: 376 35 39, US Navy. Charles was born January 1, 1922 in California to Earl Leroy and Mabel Springer. He enlisted in the US Navy June 26, 1941 in San Francisco, California and completed his basic training at the Naval Training Station in San Diego, California. He reported for duty on the USS Arizona August 29, 1941. Charles was killed in action on December 7, 1941 at Pearl Harbor, Hawaii. He was awarded the American Defense Service Medal, World War II Victory Medal and Purple Heart Medal posthumously. Charles remains on duty on the USS Arizona. He is commemorated on the USS Arizona Memorial and the Memorial Tablets of the Missing, National Memorial Cemetery of the Pacific, Honolulu, Hawaii. Charles was survived by his Father, Mr. Earl Leroy Springer, 2339 Clinton Avenue, Richmond, California.

Stallings, Kermit Braxton   Fireman, First Class, Serial No: 262 45 04, US Navy. Kermit was born December 14, 1919 in Johnston County, North Carolina, son of William Clem Stallings and Edith (Creech) Stallings. He enlisted in the US Navy November 28, 1939 in Raleigh, North Carolina and reported for duty on the USS Arizona March 8, 1940. Kermit was killed in action on December 7, 1941 at Pearl Harbor, Hawaii. He was awarded the American Defense Service Medal, World War II Victory Medal and Purple Heart Medal posthumously. Kermit remains on duty on the USS Arizona. He is commemorated on the USS Arizona Memorial and the Memorial Tablets of the Missing, National Memorial Cemetery of the Pacific, Honolulu, Hawaii. Kermit was survived by his Parents, Mr. and Mrs. William Clem Stallings, Route 1, Selma, North Carolina three brothers, J. E., Willie and Roger Stallings and four sisters, Mrs. J. B. Capps of Selma, Mrs. Elton E. Boykin of Kenly and Misses Mamie and Louise of Selma. The Kermit B. Stallings VFW Post 5955 in Selma, North Carolina was named in his honor.[741]

---

[740] Robert Lawrence Spreeman, Information and photo provided by family member, Terri L. Hollister.
[741] Kermit Braxton Stallings, Photo courtesy of the Kermit B. Stallings VFW Post 5955, Selma, North Carolina.

Stanborough, Thomas William, Jr. Seaman, First Class, Serial No. 274 48 39, US Navy. Thomas was born on July 22, 1922 in New Orleans, Louisiana. He enlisted in the US Navy July 22, 1940 in New Orleans, Louisiana and reported for duty on the USS Arizona October 1, 1940. He was serving on the USS Arizona on December 7, 1941 when the Japanese attacked Pearl Harbor. Thomas died on May 30, 1943 in the Solomon Sea, aboard the USS LCI(L) 69.

"At approximately 6:30 in the evening on 30 May 1943, the ship on which Tommy was a member of the crew noticed that a ship ahead in column had stopped, turned on a searchlight, and showed a man overboard. Tommy's ship was maneuvered into a position alongside the man overboard. The man overboard was a passenger soldier, who was found to have a broken arm, and was unable to utilize any of the life saving aids thrown to him. Then Tommy went over the side of the ship (held by three other enlisted men). During the endeavor to bring the soldier aboard, the heavy seas and strong current swept him from the grasp of his mates and both men were swept away from the ship. Stanborough had given his life jacket to the injured soldier. Although he did have hold of a life ring, he let that go in order to go to the aid of the soldier. After both men had been picked out again by the searchlight, Tommy drifted away before the ship could be maneuvered to pick him up. An extensive search was made to no avail, and it is presumed that Tommy's death occurred by drowning."[742]

Thomas was considered missing and is commemorated at Fort William McKinley Cemetery, Manila, Philippines.

Starkovich, Charles "Charlie" Electrician's Mate, Third Class, Serial No: 385 92 44, US Navy. Charles was born November 3, 1916 in Kittitas County, Washington, son of Joseph Starkovich and Annie Starkovich. The family moved from the Kittitas County Coalfields to dig black gold for the Bellingham Coal Co. and do a little commercial fishing. Charles enlisted with his brother, Joseph in the US Navy November 5, 1940 in Seattle, Washington and completed his basic training at the Naval Training Station in San Diego, California. They both joined to "See the world." Charles reported for duty on the USS Arizona January 11, 1941. He was killed in action on December 7, 1941 at Pearl Harbor, Hawaii.

Charles was awarded the American Defense Service Medal, World War II Victory Medal and Purple Heart Medal posthumously. He remains on duty on the USS Arizona. Charles is commemorated on the USS Arizona Memorial and the Memorial Tablets of the Missing, National Memorial Cemetery of the Pacific, Honolulu, Hawaii. He was survived by his Parents, Mr. and Mrs. Joseph Starkovich, 3600 Meridian Street, Bellingham, Washington and three brothers; Harry, Fred and John. His older brother, Joseph was also killed in action while serving on the USS Arizona.[743]

---

[742] Letter detailing Thomas W. Stanborough, Jr.'s death, by Rear Admiral Randall Jacobs.
[743] Charles Starkovich, Photo provided by his Nephew, Mark Starkovich.

Starkovich, Joseph "Joe", Jr.   Fireman, Second Class, Serial No: 385 92 45, US Navy. Joseph was born in 1915, son of Joseph Starkovich and Annie Starkovich. The family moved from the Kittitas County Coalfields to dig black gold for the Bellingham Coal Co. and do a little commercial fishing. Joseph enlisted with his brother, Charles in the US Navy November 5, 1940 in Seattle, Washington and completed his basic training at the Naval Training Station in San Diego, California. They both joined to "See the world." Joseph reported for duty on the USS Arizona January 11, 1941. He was killed in action on December 7, 1941 at Pearl Harbor, Hawaii. Joseph was awarded the American Defense Service Medal, World War II Victory Medal and Purple Heart Medal posthumously.

He remains on duty on the USS Arizona. Joseph is commemorated on the USS Arizona Memorial and the Memorial Tablets of the Missing, National Memorial Cemetery of the Pacific, Honolulu, Hawaii. He was survived by his Parents, Mr. and Mrs. Joseph Starkovich, 3600 Meridian Street, Bellingham, Washington and three brothers; Harry, Fred and John. His younger brother, Charles was also killed in action while serving on the USS Arizona.[744]

Starks, Don Harrison   Machinist's Mate, First Class, Serial No. 287 19 63, US Navy. Don was born March 5, 1918 in Marshall, Kentucky to Don C. and Dollie (Vandevalde) Starks. He enlisted in the US Navy January 19, 1937 in Louisville, Kentucky and reported for duty on the USS Arizona May 24, 1937. He was serving on the USS Arizona on December 7, 1941 when the Japanese attacked Pearl Harbor. Don passed away June 17, 1999 in Palm Harbor, Florida and his ashes were interred on the USS Arizona in 1999.

Staudt, Alfred Parker   Fireman, Third Class, Serial No: 376 09 03, US Navy. Alfred was born May 23, 1920 in Arizona, son of Alfred John Staudt and Ila (Breakfield) Staudt. He enlisted in the US Navy July 24, 1940 in San Francisco, California and completed his basic training at the Naval Training Station in San Diego, California. Alfred reported for duty on the USS Arizona October 14, 1940. He was killed in action on December 7, 1941 at Pearl Harbor, Hawaii. Alfred was awarded the American Defense Service Medal, World War II Victory Medal and Purple Heart Medal posthumously. He remains on duty on the USS Arizona. Alfred is commemorated on the USS Arizona Memorial and the Memorial Tablets of the Missing, National Memorial Cemetery of the Pacific, Honolulu, Hawaii. He was survived by his Mother, Mrs. Ila Light, 789 18th Street, Richmond, California.

---

[744] Joseph Starkovich, Photo provided by his Nephew, Mark Starkovich.

Steffan, Joseph Philip Boatswain's Mate, Second Class, Serial No: 299 81 48, US Navy. Joseph was born May 1, 1911 in Chicago, one of three sons and three daughters born to Joseph Steffan and Anna Steffan. He enlisted in the US Navy April 21, 1936 in Chicago, Illinois and reported for duty on the USS Arizona September 5, 1940. Joseph was the boxing champ of the fleet at the time. Joseph was killed in action on December 7, 1941 at Pearl Harbor, Hawaii. The family was notified of his death by the Navy. A few days later they received a letter from Joseph. He was awarded the American Defense Service Medal, World War II Victory Medal and Purple Heart Medal posthumously. Joseph remains on duty on the USS Arizona. He is commemorated on the USS Arizona Memorial and the Memorial Tablets of the Missing, National Memorial Cemetery of the Pacific, Honolulu, Hawaii. Joseph was survived by his Parents, Mr. and Mrs. Joseph Steffan, 1916 South 60th Court, Cicero, Illinois and sister, Ann, Albina and Mildred. His two brothers Jim and Francis preceded him in death.[745]

Steigleder, Lester Leroy Coxswain, Serial No: 279 54 77, US Navy. Lester was born March 5, 1921 in Cincinnati, Ohio, son of Andrew Steigleder and Nora (Heim) Steigleder. He enlisted in the US Navy March 7, 1938 in Cincinnati, Ohio and reported for duty on the USS Arizona July 9, 1938. Lester was killed in action on December 7, 1941 at Pearl Harbor, Hawaii. He was awarded the American Defense Service Medal, World War II Victory Medal and Purple Heart Medal posthumously. Lester remains on duty on the USS Arizona. He is commemorated on the USS Arizona Memorial and the Memorial Tablets of the Missing, National Memorial Cemetery of the Pacific, Honolulu, Hawaii. Lester was survived by his Parents, Mr. and Mrs. Andrew Steigleder, Route 3, Box 321-B, Cincinnati, Ohio, Brother, Andrew and Sisters, Elenora and Joyce Steigleder.[746]

Steinhoff, Lloyd Delroy Seaman, First Class, Serial No: 381 33 25, US Navy. Lloyd was born in 1922 in Colorado, son of Linden A. Steinhoff and Lily A. Steinhoff. He enlisted in the US Navy April 5, 1940 in San Diego, California and reported for duty on the USS Arizona December 6, 1940. Lloyd was killed in action on December 7, 1941 at Pearl Harbor, Hawaii. He was the Ship's Bugler and a trumpet player in Band 3. Lloyd's brother, Lindy was a gunner on one of the other battleships at Pearl and was on a party searching for bodies in the water, he said he was fearful of finding his brother's body. Lloyd was awarded the American Defense Service Medal, World War II Victory Medal and Purple Heart Medal posthumously. He remains on duty on the USS Arizona. Lloyd is commemorated on the USS Arizona Memorial and the Memorial Tablets of the Missing, National Memorial Cemetery of the Pacific, Honolulu, Hawaii. He was survived by his Father, Mr. Linden A. Steinhoff, 4860 Art Street, San Diego,

---

[745] Joseph Philip Steffan, Photo from the 1934 Northwestern University Yearbook, Evanston, Illinois.
[746] Lester Leroy Steigleder, Photo provided by his Great Nephew, Mike Anderson.

California. The American Legion in San Diego began the "Lloyd Steinhoff Musician's Post 695 in honor of Lloyd Steinhoff.[747]

Stephens, Woodrow Wilson Electrician's Mate, First Class, Serial No: 287 13 57, US Navy. Woodrow was born November 19, 1912 in Kentucky to Fountain T. Stephens and Ellen (Goodwin) Stephens. He enlisted in the US Navy July 29, 1935 in Louisville, Kentucky and reported for duty on the USS Arizona November 23, 1935. Woodrow was killed in action on December 7, 1941 at Pearl Harbor, Hawaii. He was awarded the American Defense Service Medal, World War II Victory Medal and Purple Heart Medal posthumously. Woodrow remains on duty on the USS Arizona. He is commemorated on the USS Arizona Memorial and the Memorial Tablets of the Missing, National Memorial Cemetery of the Pacific, Honolulu, Hawaii. Woodrow was survived by his Wife, Mrs. Gwen Margaret Stephens, Tillicum, Washington.

Stephenson, Hugh Donald Seaman, First Class, Serial No: 238 61 61, US Navy. Hugh was born April 2, 1921 in Sauquoit, New York, the son of Robert Worthy Stephenson and Nettie Elizabeth (Bunn) Stephenson. He enlisted in the US Navy September 9, 1939 in Albany, New York and reported for duty on the USS Arizona January 8, 1941. Hugh was killed in action on December 7, 1941 at Pearl Harbor, Hawaii. Badly injured, he was removed to the USS Solace motor launch and died shortly thereafter. He was awarded the American Defense Service Medal, World War II Victory Medal and Purple Heart Medal posthumously. Hugh is believed to have been buried in one of the "Unknown" graves. He is commemorated on the USS Arizona Memorial and the Memorial Tablets of the Missing, National Memorial Cemetery of the Pacific, Honolulu, Hawaii and the Sauquoit Valley Cemetery, Clayville, New York. Hugh was survived by his Father, Mr. Robert W. Stephenson, Sauquoit, New York.[748]

Stevens, Jack Hazelip Seaman, First Class, Serial No: 360 14 89, US Navy. Jack was born October 3, 1920 in Beaumont, Texas, son of Albert Theodore Stevens and Ella Jane (Hazelip) Stevens. He enlisted in the US Navy May 21, 1940 in Houston, Texas and completed his basic training at the Naval Training Station, San Diego, California. Jack reported for duty on the USS Arizona August 25, 1940. He was killed in action on December 7, 1941 at Pearl Harbor, Hawaii. Jack was awarded the American Defense Service Medal, World War II Victory Medal and Purple Heart Medal posthumously. He remains on duty on the USS Arizona. Jack is commemorated on the USS Arizona Memorial and the Memorial Tablets of the Missing, National Memorial Cemetery of the Pacific, Honolulu, Hawaii. He was survived by his Father, Mr. Albert Theodore Stevens, 3735 Ogden Street, Beaumont, Texas.

---

[747] Lloyd Delroy Steinhoff, Photo and information provided by family member, Judy Reeve.
[748] Hugh Donald Stephenson, Photo from the 1942 Sauquoit Valley Central High School Yearbook, Sauquoit, New York.

Stevens, Theadore Roosevelt Aviation Machinist's Mate, Second Class, Aviation Unit (VO-1), Serial No: 368 38 59, US Navy. Theadore was born July 7, 1919 at home in Howe, Idaho, the son of Frank and Effie Stevens. He enlisted in the US Navy September 14, 1937 in Salt Lake City, Utah and reported for duty on the USS Arizona January 7, 1938. Theadore was killed in action on December 7, 1941 at Pearl Harbor, Hawaii. He was awarded the American Defense Service Medal, World War II Victory Medal and Purple Heart Medal posthumously. Theadore remains on duty on the USS Arizona. He is commemorated on the USS Arizona Memorial and the Memorial Tablets of the Missing, National Memorial Cemetery of the Pacific, Honolulu, Hawaii. Theadore was survived by his Wife, Mrs. Vivian Eunice Stevens, 4469 Tweedy Boulevard, South Gate, California.[749]

Stewart, Thomas Lester Ship's Cook, Third Class, Serial No: 346 80 73, US Navy. Thomas was born November 21, 1921 in Desha, Arkansas the son of Vaud Lester Stewart and Bertha N. (Mills) Stewart. He enlisted in the US Navy June 4, 1940 in Little Rock, Arkansas and reported for duty on the USS Arizona September 8, 1940. Thomas was killed in action on December 7, 1941 at Pearl Harbor, Hawaii. He was awarded the American Defense Service Medal, World War II Victory Medal and Purple Heart Medal posthumously. Thomas remains on duty on the USS Arizona. He is commemorated on the USS Arizona Memorial and the Memorial Tablets of the Missing, National Memorial Cemetery of the Pacific, Honolulu, Hawaii. Thomas was survived by his Father, Mr. Vaud Lester Stewart, Desha, Arkansas.

Stillings, Gerald Fay Fireman, Second Class, Serial No: 385 92 62, US Navy. Gerald was born in September 23, 1914 in Minnesota to Everett William and Bertha (White) Stillings. He enlisted in the US Navy November 9, 1940 in Seattle, Washington and completed his basic training at the Naval Training Station in San Diego, California. He reported for duty on the USS Arizona January 11, 1941. Gerald was killed in action on December 7, 1941 at Pearl Harbor, Hawaii. He was awarded the American Defense Service Medal, World War II Victory Medal and Purple Heart Medal posthumously. Gerald remains on duty on the USS Arizona. He is commemorated on the USS Arizona Memorial and the Memorial Tablets of the Missing, National Memorial Cemetery of the Pacific, Honolulu, Hawaii. Gerald was survived by his Mother, Mrs. Bertha A. Hughes, Yelm, Washington.

Stockman, Harold William Fire Controlman, Third Class, Serial No: 393 36 00, US Navy. Harold was born June 5, 1921 in Curlew, Washington, son of Frederick Wilhelm Stockman and Gertrude (Robinson) Stockman. He enlisted in the US Navy May 20, 1940 in Spokane, Washington and completed his basic training at the Naval Training Station in San Diego, California. Harold reported for duty on the USS Arizona August 25, 1940. He was killed in action on December 7, 1941 at Pearl Harbor, Hawaii. Harold was awarded the American Defense Service Medal, World War II Victory Medal and Purple Heart Medal posthumously. He remains on duty on the USS Arizona. Harold is commemorated on the USS Arizona Memorial and the Memorial Tablets of the Missing, National Memorial Cemetery of the Pacific, Honolulu, Hawaii. He was survived by his Father, Mr. Fred William Stockman, Box 191, Kootenai, Idaho.

---

[749] Theadore Roosevelt Stevens, Photo and information provided by his niece, Teralene Foxx and her page, A Family Story: Pearl Harbor December 7, 1941.

Stockton, Louis Alton Seaman, Second Class, Serial No: 382 47 92, US Navy. Louis was born in 1924, son of Floyd T. Stockton and Violet J. (Tiffin) Stockton. He enlisted in the US Navy June 23, 1941 in Los Angeles, California and completed his basic training at the Naval Training Station in San Diego, California. Louis reported for duty on the USS Arizona August 29, 1941. He was killed in action on December 7, 1941 at Pearl Harbor, Hawaii. Louis was awarded the American Defense Service Medal, World War II Victory Medal and Purple Heart Medal posthumously. He remains on duty on the USS Arizona. Louis is commemorated on the USS Arizona Memorial and the Memorial Tablets of the Missing, National Memorial Cemetery of the Pacific, Honolulu, Hawaii. He was survived by his Mother, Mrs. Violet Henn, Box 247, Blythe, California.[750]

Stoddard, William "Bill" Edison Seaman, First Class, Serial No: 360 25 17, US Navy. William was born July 10, 1920 in Louisiana, son of William Vern Stoddard and Angelina Anna (Duhon) Stoddard. He enlisted in the US Navy November 2, 1940 in Houston, Texas and completed his basic training at the Naval Training Station in San Diego, California. William reported for duty on the USS Arizona December 30, 1940. He was killed in action on December 7, 1941 at Pearl Harbor, Hawaii. William was awarded the American Defense Service Medal, World War II Victory Medal and Purple Heart Medal posthumously. He remains on duty on the USS Arizona. William is commemorated on the USS Arizona Memorial and the Memorial Tablets of the Missing, National Memorial Cemetery of the Pacific, Honolulu, Hawaii. He was survived by his Mother, Mrs. Angelina Anna Stoddard, General Delivery, Vinton, Louisiana.

Stoffer, Bernald Henry Aviation Machinist's Mate, First Class, Aviation Unit (VO-1), Serial No. 371 97 03, US Navy. Bernard was born November 28, 1916. He enlisted in the US Navy March 14, 1936 in Denver, Colorado and reported for duty on the USS Arizona August 1, 1939. Bernard was serving on the USS Arizona on December 7, 1941 when the Japanese attacked Pearl Harbor. His Official Statement:

"The attack began as we were returning from special liberty and we arrived at the Fleet Landing during the first wave of attack. There was considerable confusion at the landing and although boats were available they were not immediately utilized due to the danger of strafing.

Finally one boat crew decided to chance it and endeavoring to reach our ship we entered the launch along with four other men. As we left the landing an enemy plane flew over at an altitude of less than 200 feet, but did not strafe us.

All battleships were being heavily bombed by high altitude and dive bombers coming out of the sun. When we got out in the harbor the Arizona blew up with a terrific explosion and was burning fiercely. Knowing it was impossible to get aboard our ship, we were at a loss as to just what to do. An officer came alongside in a whale boat (we were then about 100 yards off the Arizona) and told us to go to Ford Island. Enroute to Ford Island we picked up several men who were struggling in the water. They were burned and coated with oil. A motor launch ahead of us was strafed by an enemy plane just before we reached the air station.

After the injured were taken to the sick bay we remembered that our planes were on the air station. Shortly before we reached Ford Island the Nevada got underway and was going up the channel and was subject to extremely heavy fire by the second wave of attack.

---

[750] Louis Alton Stockton, Photo from the 1942 Echo Yearbook, Palo Verde Union High School, Blythe, California.

We proceeded to the base force hangar to get our planes in condition to fly. One plane was damaged beyond repair and we prepared the other two for flight."[751]

After the attack, Bernald was transferred to Observation Squadron One for duty. Bernald died April 8, 1969 and is buried in Section 29, Site 203, Barrancas National Cemetery, Pensacola, Florida.

Stopyra, Julian John Radioman, Third Class, Serial No: 201 72 38, US Navy. John enlisted in the US Navy March 25, 1940 in Boston, Massachusetts and reported for duty on the USS Arizona September 30, 1940. Julian was killed in action on December 7, 1941 at Pearl Harbor, Hawaii. He was awarded the American Defense Service Medal, World War II Victory Medal and Purple Heart Medal posthumously. Julian remains on duty on the USS Arizona. He is commemorated on the USS Arizona Memorial and the Memorial Tablets of the Missing, National Memorial Cemetery of the Pacific, Honolulu, Hawaii. Julian was survived by his Father, Mr. Agustine Stopyra, 74 Park Street, Lawrence, Massachusetts. In 1947 the polish community in Lawrence organized and opened The Julian Stopyra Post PLAV of Lawrence, Massachusetts in his honor.[752]

Storm, Laun Lee Yeoman, First Class, Serial No: 385 74 74, US Navy. Laun was born November 6, 1913 in King County, Washington, son of Cleveland Long Storm and Elva (Middlebusher) Storm. He enlisted in the US Navy September 13, 1937 in Seattle, Washington and completed his basic training at the Naval Training Station in San Diego, California. Laun reported for duty on the USS Arizona January 7, 1938. He was killed in action on December 7, 1941 at Pearl Harbor, Hawaii. Laun was awarded the American Defense Service Medal, World War II Victory Medal and Purple Heart Medal posthumously. He remains on duty on the USS Arizona. Laun is commemorated on the USS Arizona Memorial and the Memorial Tablets of the Missing, National Memorial Cemetery of the Pacific, Honolulu, Hawaii. He was survived by his Wife, Mrs. Jane Diane (Wallace) Storm, 4227 Cedar, Long Beach, California.

Strange, Charles Orval Fireman, Second Class, Serial No: 287 45 01, US Navy. Charles was the son of Monte and Edith Strange of Washington, Indiana. He enlisted in the US Navy September 25, 1940 in Louisville, Kentucky and completed his basic training at the Naval Training Station in Great Lakes, Illinois. Charles reported for duty on the USS Arizona December 9, 1940. He was killed in action on December 7, 1941 at Pearl Harbor, Hawaii. Charles was awarded the American Defense Service Medal, World War II Victory Medal and Purple Heart Medal posthumously. He remains on duty on the USS Arizona. Charles is commemorated on the USS Arizona Memorial and the Memorial Tablets of the Missing, National Memorial Cemetery of the Pacific, Honolulu, Hawaii. He was survived by his Father, Mr. Monte Strange, Rural Route 1, Washington, Indiana.

---

[751] Confidential Statement of Bernald Henry Stoffer, Aviation Machinist's Mate, First Class, Aviation Unit (VO-1), U. S. Navy, U.S.S. Arizona regarding the attack on Pearl Harbor, T. H., December 7, 1941.
[752] Julian John Stopyra, Photo and information provided by niece, Ruth Ann Robust.

Stratton, Donald Gay Seaman, First Class, Serial No. 316 69 70, US Navy. Donald was born on July 14, 1922 in Inavale, Nebraska. He enlisted in the US Navy in Omaha, Nebraska on October 16, 1940 after graduating from high school. He completed his basic training at the Naval Training Station in Great Lakes, Illinois and reported for duty on the USS Arizona at the Puget Sound Naval Shipyard December 9, 1940. Donald was assigned to the 6th Division, (a boat deck division on the port side). His battle station was in the port AA director on the foremast.

On December 7th he went for breakfast around 7 a.m. Most of the crew were wearing shorts and T-shirts, the uniform of the day. After breakfast I headed for sick bay to visit with my friend, Harl Nelson. I had just stepped out of the mess area near the casemate on the bow of the ship when I could hear sailors yelling and hollering. Looking out at Ford Island we could see all sorts of planes. They would peel off and we could see the Rising Sun insignia on their wings and bombs exploding. I remember asking myself "What the hell is going on?"

I made an about face and headed for my battle station, which was one deck above the bridge. First I went up the ladder to the radio shack and from there climbed another ladder to the signal bridge, a third ladder to the Bridge and finally a fourth ladder to the Sky Control Platform. I arrived at my battle station just before "general quarters" was sounded.

Everything was happening so quickly, I didn't have time to think. We fired on the high altitude bombers but we could not reach them. Our shells were bursting before they ever reached the bombers altitude. Shortly after 8 am we were hit aft on top of No. 3 turret and it bounced over the side. Another bomb went through the afterdeck and didn't explode. The third bomb hit up above on the starboard side, it was big. It shook the ship like an earthquake. Shortly thereafter, there was a huge explosion, raising the ship nearly out of the water followed by a ball of flame that went 500 to 600 feet in the air. It engulfed the whole foremast where we were and the entire bow of the ship. Meanwhile inside the director, we tried to shield ourselves from the blaze by hiding under some of the equipment.

We stayed at our battle station attempting to take cover from the fire. A couple of the men jumped out, never to be seen again. We waited until a little sea breeze blew the smoke away and went out onto the platform. The entire deck was red-hot. By then I knew that I had been burned and was in terrible pain. My legs were burnt from my ankles to my thighs. My T-shirt had caught on fire and my back and both my arms were burned. My face and all the hair on my head was burned off and a part of an ear was gone.

The Vestal was tied up alongside the Arizona and we got a sailor (Joe George) to throw us a heaving line and then attached another heavier line to it so we could pull ourselves across to safety. I was badly burned and when we got ready to leave I grabbed the skin on my arms and just pulled it off like a big long sock and threw it on the deck. We crossed 40 feet in the air; the water below us was on fire. It was about 60 to 70 feet across. There were 6 of us that crossed to the Vestal. Two of the others died of their wounds later that night. We huddled on the Vestal for a while waiting for a boat that could take us ashore and to the hospital.

I was burned over 70 percent of my body. Not long, at least 3 weeks after we had first been treated, someone came into the room and said "Some of you are going to go to the States." "I'll go," I called out and he told me "No, we don't think you can make it. You probably wouldn't survive the trip." I told the man that I could and he said "If you can stand up while we change the linen, we'll think about it." So I stood up while they changed the linens. I didn't get up for a long time after that but they sent me stateside. I arrived on Christmas Day and was taken to a burn unit at Mare Island Naval Hospital. I spent 9 months at Mare Island and then was transferred to Corona, California where the Navy had taken over a hotel for convalescence. I weighed 92 pounds when I was able to roll out of bed after a few months. On the morning of the attack I weighed 165 to 170 pounds. I was medically discharged in September 1942 and returned home. After about a year I had regained much of the use of my left side, so I decided to go back in the Navy. I went to boot camp in January 1944 and after graduation they sent me to Treasure Island and later I was assigned the USS Stack (DD-406) where I participated in the invasion landings at New Guinea, Hallamahara, Leyte, Luzon and Okinawa.

Donald was discharged from the Navy in December 1945 attaining a rank of Gunner's Mate, second class. In 2018, Donald wrote a book "All The Gallant Men" detailing his ordeal.[753]

Stratton, John Raymond Seaman, First Class, Serial No: 291 65 72, US Navy. John was born October 23, 1918 in Ripley County, Indiana, son of Frank Stratton and Amy Jane (Edens) Stratton. He enlisted in the Navy October 8, 1940 in Indianapolis, Indiana and completed his basic training at the Naval Training Station in Great Lakes, Illinois. John reported for duty on the USS Arizona December 9, 1940. He was killed in action on December 7, 1941 at Pearl Harbor, Hawaii. John was awarded the American Defense Service Medal, World War II Victory Medal and Purple Heart Medal posthumously. He remains on duty on the USS Arizona. John is commemorated on the USS Arizona Memorial and the Memorial Tablets of the Missing, National Memorial Cemetery of the Pacific, Honolulu, Hawaii and the Holton Cemetery, Holton, Indiana. He was survived by his Father, Mr. Frank Stratton, Rural Route 1, Holton, Indiana.

Strong, Herbert Ronald Coxswain, Serial No. 393 30 48, US Navy. Herbert was born September 5, 1921. He enlisted in the US Navy September 8, 1939 in Portland, Oregon and completed his basic training at the Naval Training Station in San Diego, California. Herbert reported for duty on the USS Arizona January 24, 1940. He was serving on the USS Arizona on December 7, 1941 when the Japanese attacked Pearl Harbor. After the attack, Herbert was transferred to the USS Gridley for duty. Herbert died February 6, 2005 in Portland, Oregon and his ashes were interred in turret 4 on the Arizona.

Stuart, Jean Marcelle Seaman, First Class, Serial No. 356 20 29, US Navy. Jean was born on July 12, 1921 in Oklahoma. He enlisted in the US Navy December 7, 1939 in Dallas, Texas and completed his basic training at the Naval Training Station in San Diego, California. He reported for duty on the USS Arizona February 24, 1940. He was serving on the USS Arizona on December 7, 1941 when the Japanese attacked Pearl Harbor. After the attack he was assigned to the USS Arizona salvage. In June 1942 he was transferred to the USS George Clymer where he served until July 1943 at which time he was transferred to the Lunga and Tulagi Boat Pools. Jean died August 30, 1981 in Orange County, California.

---

[753] Donald Gay Stratton, Information, story and photo provided by himself. His book, All The Gallant Men, is available on Amazon.com. A must read!

Suggs, William Alfred   Seaman, First Class, Serial No: 268 40 04, US Navy. William was born January 1, 1919 in Ebro, Washington County, Florida to General Lafatte Suggs and Annie Rebecca (Anderson) Suggs. He enlisted in the US Navy November 28, 1939 in Macon, Georgia and reported for duty on the USS Arizona March 8, 1940. William had chickenpox and was in sickbay when he was killed in action on December 7, 1941 at Pearl Harbor, Hawaii. He was awarded the American Defense Service Medal, World War II Victory Medal and Purple Heart Medal posthumously. William remains on duty on the USS Arizona. He is commemorated on the USS Arizona Memorial and the Memorial Tablets of the Missing, National Memorial Cemetery of the Pacific, Honolulu, Hawaii and the Cashwell Cemetery, Lake County, Florida. William was survived by his Father, Mr. General Lafatte Suggs, P. O. Box 121, Clermont, Florida. The William Alfred Suggs Memorial VFW Post 5277 in Clermont, Florida was named in his honor.[754]

Sullivan, Aubrey Randolph   Coxswain, Serial No. 266 01 53, US Navy. Aubry was born May 15, 1918 in Virginia to Arba Randall and Mamie Sullivan. He enlisted in the US Navy November 24, 1939 in Richmond, Virginia and reported for duty on the USS Arizona March 8, 1940. He was serving on the USS Arizona on December 7, 1941 when the Japanese attacked Pearl Harbor. After the attack, Aubry was transferred to the USS Farragut for duty. He later served during the Korean War. Aubry passed away July 3, 1997 in Maryville, Tennessee and is buried in Sherwood Memorial Gardens, Alcoa, Tennessee.

Sulser, Frederick Franklin   Gunner's Mate, Third Class, Serial No: 279 54 75, US Navy. Frederick was born January 11, 1918 in Galion, Ohio, son of Franklin Joseph Sulser and Della (Frank) Sulser. His mother, Della died when he was just two years old. He enlisted in the US Navy March 7, 1938 in Cincinnati, Ohio and reported for duty on the USS Arizona July 9, 1938. Frederick would have completed his enlistment in March 1942 but was killed in action on December 7, 1941 at Pearl Harbor, Hawaii. He was awarded the American Defense Service Medal, World War II Victory Medal and Purple Heart Medal posthumously. Frederick remains on duty on the USS Arizona. He is commemorated on the USS Arizona Memorial and the Memorial Tablets of the Missing, National Memorial Cemetery of the Pacific, Honolulu, Hawaii. Frederick was survived by his Father, Mr. Franklin Joseph Sulser, 238 Walker Street, Galion, Ohio.[755]

Summers, Glen Allen   Yeoman, First Class, Arizona Flag Allowance (CBD-1), Serial No: 328 38 44, US Navy. Glen enlisted in the US Navy May 14, 1935 at Minneapolis, Minnesota and reported for duty on the USS Arizona on April 19, 1937. He was killed in action on December 7, 1941 at Pearl Harbor, Hawaii. Glen was awarded the American Defense Service Medal, World War II Victory Medal and Purple Heart Medal posthumously. He remains on duty on the USS Arizona. Glen is commemorated on the USS Arizona Memorial and the Memorial

---

[754] William Alfred Suggs, Photo courtesy of the William Alfred Suggs Memorial VFW Post 5277, Clermont, Florida.

[755] Frederick Franklin Sulser, Photo taken from the Mansfield Journal, provided by family member, Phil Middleton.

Tablets of the Missing, National Memorial Cemetery of the Pacific, Honolulu, Hawaii. He was survived by his Wife, Mrs. Helen Marie Summers, 9535 Dayton Avenue, Seattle, Washington.

Summers, Harold Edgar Signalman, Second Class, Serial No: 283 22 83, US Navy. Harold was born February 18, 1919 to Orlie Edgar and Nellie May (Malin) Summers. His mother, Nellie died when he was 13 years old. He enlisted in the US Navy February 2, 1938 in Cleveland, Ohio and reported for duty on the USS Arizona on June 4, 1938. He was killed in action on December 7, 1941 at Pearl Harbor, Hawaii. Harold was awarded the American Defense Service Medal, World War II Victory Medal and Purple Heart Medal posthumously. He remains on duty on the USS Arizona. Harold is commemorated on the USS Arizona Memorial and the Memorial Tablets of the Missing, National Memorial Cemetery of the Pacific, Honolulu, Hawaii. He was survived by his Father, Mr. Orlie Edgar Summers, 166 Oak Park Drive, Akron, Ohio.[756]

Sumner, Oren Seaman, Second Class, Serial No: 372 33 21, US Navy. Oren was born March 12, 1924 the son of John Franklin and Ruth (Anderson) Sumner. He enlisted in the Navy June 21, 1941 in Denver Colorado after serving a term in the CCC camp in the Sandia Mountains. He attended Albuquerque High School for a year and a half before entering CCC. Oren completed his basic training at the Naval Training Station in San Diego, California. He reported for duty on the USS Arizona August 29, 1941. Oren was killed in action on December 7, 1941 at Pearl Harbor, Hawaii. He was awarded the American Defense Service Medal, World War II Victory Medal and Purple Heart Medal posthumously. Oren remains on duty on the USS Arizona. He is commemorated on the USS Arizona Memorial, the Memorial Tablets of the Missing, National Memorial Cemetery of the Pacific, Honolulu, Hawaii and Santa Fe National Cemetery, New Mexico. Oren was survived by his Parents, Mr. and Mrs. John Franklin Sumner, Route 3, Box 620, Albuquerque, New Mexico.[757]

Sutton, Clyde Westly Chief Commissary Steward, Serial No: 194 95 93, US Navy. Clyde was born in about 1897 in Washington State to Dave and Nettie Sutton. He enlisted in the US Navy in 1917 in Bremerton, Washington and reported for duty on the USS Arizona on September 4, 1937. Clyde was a career Navy man. He was killed in action on December 7, 1941 at Pearl Harbor, Hawaii. Clyde was awarded the American Defense Service Medal, World War II Victory Medal and Purple Heart Medal posthumously. He remains on duty on the USS Arizona. Clyde is commemorated on the USS Arizona Memorial and the Memorial Tablets of the Missing, National Memorial Cemetery of the Pacific, Honolulu, Hawaii. He was survived by his Wife, Mrs. Ruby Sutton, 307 Coronada Avenue, Long Beach, California and his Parents, Mr. Dave Sutton 7331 12th Avenue SW, Seattle, Washington and Mrs. Nettie Duty, 5965 Beacon Avenue, Seattle, Washington, four sisters, Mrs. Gladys Hitt and Mrs. Rae Haynes of Seattle, and Mrs. May Smith of Tacoma and Mrs. Daisy Boettcher of Bellingham.[758]

---

[756] Harold Edgar Summers, Photo from The Akron Beacon Journal, Akron, Ohio, July 16, 1942, Page 15.
[757] Oren Sumner, Photo from New Mexico Honor States.

Sutton, George Woodrow Storekeeper, First Class, Serial No: 287 06 83, US Navy. George was born March 22, 1913 in Russell, Kentucky the son of Russell Aubrey Sutton and Plascette "Settie" Cornahan Sutton. He was five when his father died and ten when his mother died. He reenlisted in the US Navy June 20, 1940 in San Diego, California after having served for ten years. George completed his basic training at the Naval Training Station, San Diego, California. He reported for duty on the USS Arizona August 20, 1940. George was killed in action on December 7, 1941 at Pearl Harbor, Hawaii. He was awarded the American Defense Service Medal, World War II Victory Medal and Purple Heart Medal posthumously. George remains on duty on the USS Arizona. He is commemorated on the USS Arizona Memorial and the Memorial Tablets of the Missing, National Memorial Cemetery of the Pacific, Honolulu, Hawaii. George was survived by his Sister, Mrs. R. E. Powell, Russell, Kentucky.[759]

Swisher, Charles Elijah Seaman, First Class, Serial No: 381 37 90, US Navy. Charles was born October 23, 1922 in Orange County, California, son of Leon William Swisher and Mary Henrietta (Ingraham) Swisher. He enlisted in the US Navy November 7, 1940 in San Diego, California and completed his basic training at the Naval Training Station in San Diego, California. Charles reported for duty on the USS Arizona January 11, 1941. He was killed in action on December 7, 1941 at Pearl Harbor, Hawaii. Charles was awarded the American Defense Service Medal, World War II Victory Medal and Purple Heart Medal posthumously. He remains on duty on the USS Arizona. Charles is commemorated on the USS Arizona Memorial and the Memorial Tablets of the Missing, National Memorial Cemetery of the Pacific, Honolulu, Hawaii and the Loma Vista Memorial Park, Fullerton, California. He was survived by his Father, Mr. Leon William Swisher, Fallbrook, California. The Charles E. Swisher VFW Post 1924 in Loma Vista, California was named in his honor.[760]

Symonette, Henry Cook, First Class, Serial No: 174 60 20, US Navy. He was born in the Bahamas. Henry re-enlisted in the US Navy August 17, 1935. Henry served on the USS Arizona from April 29, 1933 until he was killed in action on December 7, 1941 at Pearl Harbor, Hawaii. He was awarded the American Defense Service Medal, World War II Victory Medal and Purple Heart Medal posthumously. Henry remains on duty on the USS Arizona. He is commemorated on the USS Arizona Memorial and the Memorial Tablets of the Missing, National Memorial Cemetery of the Pacific, Honolulu, Hawaii. Henry was survived by his Wife, Mrs. Tommie May Symonette, 851 East 51st Street, Los Angeles, California.

---

[758] Clyde Westly Sutton, Information and photo from "Navy Man's Last Letter Tells Mother of War Uncertainty" Seattle Daily Times, Seattle, WA, Saturday, January 3, 1942, Page 7.

[759] George Woodrow Sutton, Photo from news clipping contributed by the Margaret Callon Gordon Cummins Family.

[760] Charles Elijah Swisher, Photo provided by family member, Lesa Pfrommer.

Tagtmeyer, Laurence Ernest   Chief Gunner's Mate, Serial No. 0-09938, US Navy. Laurence was born May 24, 1899 in Indiana to William C. and Jessie E. (Fox) Tagtmeyer. He enlisted in the US Navy on October 16, 1936 and reported for duty on the USS Arizona where he was serving as Assistant to Gunnery Officer. His battle station was Repair IV on December 7, 1941 when the Japanese attacked Pearl Harbor. After the attack, Laurence was assigned temporary duty on the USS Tennessee. Laurence died on October 26, 1976 in Broward, Florida.

Tambolleo, Victor Charles   Shipfitter, Third Class, Serial No: 258 25 74, US Navy. Victor was born June 22, 1920 in Minturno, Italy to Nicola and Concetta Tambolleo. His family immigrated to the United States when he was still an infant. He enlisted in the US Navy November 28, 1939 in Baltimore, Maryland and reported for duty on the USS Arizona March 8, 1940. He was killed in action on December 7, 1941 at Pearl Harbor, Hawaii. Victor was awarded the American Defense Service Medal, World War II Victory Medal and Purple Heart Medal posthumously. He remains on duty on the USS Arizona. Victor is commemorated on the USS Arizona Memorial and the Memorial Tablets of the Missing, National Memorial Cemetery of the Pacific, Honolulu, Hawaii and Rocky Gap Veterans Cemetery, Flintstone, Maryland. He was survived by his Father, Mr. Nicola Tambolleo, 1 Auburn Avenue, Cumberland, Maryland. The Riverside Park in Cumberland, Maryland was changed to Tambolleo Park in his name. The Victor Tambolleo Post 1712 Catholic War Veterans post of Cumberland, Maryland was named after Victor, the first Cumberland, Maryland casualty in World War II.[761]

Tanner, Russell Allen   Gunner's Mate, Third Class, Serial No: 385 82 38, US Navy. Russell was born April 28, 1920 in Menlo, Washington, son of Elbert Francis Tanner and Anna Milinda (Cornell) Tanner. He enlisted in the US Navy September 15, 1939 in Seattle, Washington and completed his basic training at the Naval Training Station, San Diego, California. Russell reported for duty on the USS Arizona November 18, 1939. Russell and a shipmate, Harvey Milhorn had planned to go to the Waikiki Theater in Honolulu on December 7th to see a Tyron Power movie, "A Yank in the R.A.F.". While standing on deck that morning, they heard guns and saw a plane drop a bomb. It was the start of the Japanese attack on Pearl Harbor. Both of them went to their battle stations. Harvey never saw Russ again. He was killed in action on December 7, 1941 at Pearl Harbor, Hawaii. Russell was awarded the American Defense Service Medal, World War II Victory Medal and Purple Heart Medal posthumously. He remains on duty on the USS Arizona. Russell is commemorated on the USS Arizona Memorial and the Memorial Tablets of the Missing, National Memorial Cemetery of the Pacific, Honolulu, Hawaii. He was survived by his Father, Mr. Elbert Francis Tanner, Willapa, Washington.[762]

---

[761] Victor Charles Tambolleo, Photo from Maryland Honor States.
[762] Russell Allen Tanner, Information from Pacific County Historical Society and Museum in South Bend, Washington; Los Angeles Times; The Evening Sun of Baltimore, Maryland.

Tapie, Edward Casamiro Machinist's Mate, Second Class, Serial No: 380 97 81, US Navy. Edward was born May 12, 1917 in California, the son of Dolores (Martinez) Tapie. He enlisted in the US Navy July 15, 1936 in Los Angeles, California and completed his basic training at the Naval Training Station in San Diego, California. He reported for duty on the USS Arizona February 23, 1937. Edward was killed in action on December 7, 1941 at Pearl Harbor, Hawaii. He was awarded the American Defense Service Medal, World War II Victory Medal and Purple Heart Medal posthumously. Edward remains on duty on the USS Arizona. He is commemorated on the USS Arizona Memorial and the Memorial Tablets of the Missing, National Memorial Cemetery of the Pacific, Honolulu, Hawaii. Edward was survived by his Wife, Mrs. Colleen June Tapie, 1175 East Pacific Coast Highway, Long Beach, California.[763]

Tapp, Lambert Ray Gunner's Mate, Third Class, VO-1 Aviation Detachment, Serial No: 287 37 74, US Navy. Lambert was born October 25, 1918 in Webster County, Kentucky, son of Leighman A. Tapp and Helen (Callis) Tapp. He enlisted in the US Navy March 6, 1940 in Louisville, Kentucky and completed his basic training at the Naval Training Station in Great Lakes, Illinois. Lambert reported for duty on the USS Arizona July 12, 1940. He was killed in action on December 7, 1941 at Pearl Harbor, Hawaii. Lambert was awarded the American Defense Service Medal, World War II Victory Medal and Purple Heart Medal posthumously. He remains on duty on the USS Arizona. Lambert is commemorated on the USS Arizona Memorial and the Memorial Tablets of the Missing, National Memorial Cemetery of the Pacific, Honolulu, Hawaii and Shady Grove Cemetery, Poole, Kentucky. He was survived by his Father, Mr. Leighman A. Tapp, Harrodsburg, Kentucky.

Targ, John Chief Water Tender, Serial No: 250 16 58, US Navy. John was born in 1897 in Massachusetts, son of Wladislaw (Walter) Targ and Maria (Niedoiadlo) Targ. He was recalled to active duty in the Fleet Reserve when he reported for duty on the USS Arizona November 7, 1940. John was killed in action on December 7, 1941 at Pearl Harbor, Hawaii. He was awarded the American Defense Service Medal, World War II Victory Medal and Purple Heart Medal posthumously. John remains on duty on the USS Arizona. He is commemorated on the USS Arizona Memorial and the Memorial Tablets of the Missing, National Memorial Cemetery of the Pacific, Honolulu, Hawaii. John was survived by his Wife, Mrs. Grace Ann Targ, 3419 Euclid Avenue, San Diego, California.

Taylor, Aaron Gust Steward's Mate, First Class, Serial No: 346 61 71, US Navy. Aaron enlisted in the US Navy January 6, 1936 in Little Rock, Arkansas and reported for duty on the USS Arizona on September 16, 1938. On October 23, 1941 it was reported that Aaron was charged with second degree murder in Honolulu Hawaii in connection with the fatal stabbing of James Edward Everett of the USS Ellet on Nuuanu Avenue on Oct. 11. He allegedly stabbed Everett in a fight which started after he and three other Caucasian sailors bumped into Taylor and two other sailors in passing on the narrow sidewalk. Taylor knocked against a car door window by Everett, suffered wrist injuries and was hospitalized until he was charged. The case will be tried by a Navy Court.[764] He was killed in action on December 7, 1941 at Pearl Harbor, Hawaii.

---

[763] Edward Casamiro Tapie, Photo from the 1935 Nathaniel Narbonne High School Yearbook, Harbor City, California.
[764] Aaron Gust Taylor, Information from The Honolulu Advertiser, Honolulu, Hawaii, October 23, 1941, Page 20.

Aaron was awarded the American Defense Service Medal, World War II Victory Medal and Purple Heart Medal posthumously. He remains on duty on the USS Arizona. Aaron is commemorated on the USS Arizona Memorial and the Memorial Tablets of the Missing, National Memorial Cemetery of the Pacific, Honolulu, Hawaii. He was survived by his Wife, Mrs. Luceille Taylor, 2200 Imperial Avenue, Los Angeles, California.

Taylor, Charles Benton Electrician's Mate, Third Class, Serial No: 321 36 45, US Navy. Charles was born June 9, 1921 in Kansas the youngest son of five boys to Charles Andrew and Aggie Catherine (Gregory) Taylor. He enlisted in the US Navy November 15, 1939 in Des Moines, Iowa and completed his basic training at the Naval Training Station in Great Lakes, Illinois. He reported for duty on the USS Arizona January 27, 1940. Charles was killed in action on December 7, 1941 at Pearl Harbor, Hawaii. He was awarded the American Defense Service Medal, World War II Victory Medal and Purple Heart Medal posthumously. Charles remains on duty on the USS Arizona. He is commemorated on the USS Arizona Memorial and the Memorial Tablets of the Missing, National Memorial Cemetery of the Pacific, Honolulu, Hawaii and Boone Creek Cemetery, Licking, Missouri. Charles was survived by his Father, Mr. Charles Andrew Taylor, 4506 8th Street, Rock Island, Illinois.[765]

Taylor, Harry Theadore Gunner's Mate, Second Class, Serial No: 291 52 31, US Navy. Harry was born November 24, 1918 in Nebraska to Etta L. (Fisher) Taylor. He enlisted in the US Navy November 4, 1937 in Indianapolis, Indiana and reported for duty on the USS Arizona February 26, 1938. He had just extended his enlistment for two years on November 4, 1941. Harry was killed in action on December 7, 1941 at Pearl Harbor, Hawaii. He was awarded the American Defense Service Medal, World War II Victory Medal and Purple Heart Medal posthumously. Harry remains on duty on the USS Arizona. He is commemorated on the USS Arizona Memorial and the Memorial Tablets of the Missing, National Memorial Cemetery of the Pacific, Honolulu, Hawaii and Danville South Cemetery, Danville, Indiana. Harry was survived by his Mother, Mrs. Etta Eggers, 657 South Kentucky Street, Danville, Indiana.

Taylor, Robert Denzil Coxswain, Serial No: 321 34 94, US Navy. Robert was born September 9, 1921 in Maquoketa, Iowa the son of Howard Verne and Alice Amelia (Mann) Taylor. He enlisted in the US Navy October 4, 1939 in Des Moines, Iowa and completed his basic training at the Naval Training Station in Great Lakes, Illinois. He reported for duty on the USS Arizona February 10, 1940. Robert was killed in action on December 7, 1941 at Pearl Harbor, Hawaii. He was awarded the American Defense Service Medal, World War II Victory Medal and Purple Heart Medal posthumously. Robert remains on duty on the USS Arizona. He is commemorated on the USS Arizona Memorial and the Memorial Tablets of the Missing, National Memorial Cemetery of the Pacific, Honolulu, Hawaii. Robert was survived by his Father, Mr. Howard V. Taylor, Box 60, Sabula, Iowa.

---

[765] Charles Benton Taylor, photo from the Quad-City Times, Davenport, Iowa, May 5, 1942, page 3.

Teeling, Charles Madison Chief Printer, Serial No: 103 68 99, US Navy Reserve. Charles was born in about 1901 in New York, to William and Mary C. Teeling. He enlisted in the US Navy March 1, 1938 in San Pedro, California and served on the USS West Virginia until September 1, 1941 when he was transferred to the USS Arizona. He reported for duty on the USS Arizona on September 11, 1941. Charles was killed in action on December 7, 1941 at Pearl Harbor. He was awarded the American Defense Service Medal, World War II Victory Medal and Purple Heart Medal posthumously. Charles remains on duty on the USS Arizona. He is commemorated on the USS Arizona Memorial and the Memorial Tablets of the Missing, National Memorial Cemetery of the Pacific, Honolulu, Hawaii. Charles was survived by his Wife, Mrs. Edith Bink Teeling, 1273 Rowland Avenue, El Monte, California.[766]

Teer, Allen Ray Electrician's Mate, First Class, Serial No: 286 91 75, US Navy. Allen was born May 16, 1903 in Kentucky, son of Alman Lee Teer and Mariah Weller (Hodge) Teer. He re-enlisted in the US Navy December 4, 1936 in San Pedro, California. Allen served on the USS Arizona from June 30, 1933 until he was killed in action on December 7, 1941 at Pearl Harbor, Hawaii. He was awarded the American Defense Service Medal, World War II Victory Medal and Purple Heart Medal posthumously. Allen remains on duty on the USS Arizona. He is commemorated on the USS Arizona Memorial and the Memorial Tablets of the Missing, National Memorial Cemetery of the Pacific, Honolulu, Hawaii and Tyners Chapel Cemetery, Crittenden County, Kentucky. Allen was survived by his Wife, Mrs. Una Estell Teer, 270 Newport Avenue, Long Beach, California.

Tennell, Raymond Clifford Seaman, First Class, Serial No: 356 42 42, US Navy. Raymond was born September 18, 1922 in Collin County, Texas, son of Henry Stith Tennell and Tiley (Davidson) Tennell. He enlisted in the US Navy November 13, 1940 in Dallas, Texas and completed his basic training at the Naval Training Station in San Diego, California. Raymond reported for duty on the USS Arizona January 11, 1941. He was killed in action on December 7, 1941 at Pearl Harbor, Hawaii. Raymond was awarded the American Defense Service Medal, World War II Victory Medal and Purple Heart Medal posthumously. He remains on duty on the USS Arizona. Raymond is commemorated on the USS Arizona Memorial and the Memorial Tablets of the Missing, National Memorial Cemetery of the Pacific, Honolulu, Hawaii and Restland Memorial Park, Dallas, Texas. He was survived by his Parents, Mr. and Mrs. Henry S. Tennell, Plano, Texas, Sister, Mrs. Charles K. Traphagan of Richardson, Texas; two brothers, Henry S. Tennell, Jr. of Abernathy, Texas and Sidney Tennell of Plano, Texas.

Terrell, John Raymond Fireman, Second Class, Serial No: 295 76 83, US Navy. John was born in about 1921 in Arkansas to Harry William and Delphia Terrell. He enlisted in the US Navy October 4, 1940 in Nashville, Tennessee and completed his basic training at the Naval Training Station in Norfolk, Virginia. He reported for duty on the USS Arizona December 4, 1940. John was killed in action on December 7, 1941 at Pearl Harbor, Hawaii. He was awarded the American Defense Service Medal, World War II Victory Medal and Purple Heart Medal posthumously. John remains on duty on the USS Arizona. He is commemorated on the USS Arizona Memorial and the Memorial Tablets of the Missing, National Memorial Cemetery of the Pacific, Honolulu, Hawaii. John was survived by his Father, Mr. Harry William Terrell, Harrisburg, Arkansas.

---

[766] Charles Madison Teeling, Photo from California Honor States.

441

Teslow, Stanley Merlin   Gunner's Mate, Second Class, Serial No. 321 23 74, US Navy. Stanley was born on March 14, 1917 in Waukon, Iowa, the son of Albert Andrias Teslow and Hilda Margrette (Lovstuen) Teslow. He enlisted in the US Navy March 9, 1938 in Des Moines, Iowa and reported for duty on the USS Arizona July 9, 1938. He was serving on the USS Arizona on December 7, 1941 when the Japanese attacked Pearl Harbor. After the attack, Stanley was transferred to the USS Bagley (DD-386) for duty. Stanley was awarded the Silver Star Medal:

"For distinguishing himself conspicuously by gallantry and intrepidity in action against the enemy on October 14, 1944 while serving as Turret Captain aboard the USS Reno operating in the Central Pacific waters. In spite of concussion, smoke and flames which entered the gun chamber, while the ship was under attack, he displayed leadership and coolness which calmed his mount crew and continued the fire of his mount. By thus maintaining the fire of his turret he contributed to the destruction of eleven enemy torpedo bombers. His coolness, courage and skill were an example to the men in his turret and were at all times in keeping with the highest traditions of the United States Naval Service."

Stanley married Esther Emma Maria Pansch on December 12, 1943. They had two children. He died on March 27, 1982 in Stanislaus, California and his ashes were interred on the USS Arizona on April 12, 1982.[767]

Theiller, Rudolph "Rudy" Franklin   Seaman, First Class, Serial No: 376 09 75, US Navy. Rudolph was born July 24, 1922 in Sonoma County, California the son of Rudolph J. Theiller and Martha M. (Block) Theiller. He grew up on the family's Gravenstein apple ranch. He lettered in football and basketball at Analy High School and went hunting with his father. He was outgoing with his many friends but was otherwise reserved. Rudy graduated at age 16. He enlisted in the US Navy August 6, 1940 in San Francisco, California and completed his basic training at the Naval Training Station in San Diego, California. Rudolph reported for duty on the USS Arizona October 14, 1940. He was killed in action on December 7, 1941 at Pearl Harbor, Hawaii. Rudolph was awarded the American Defense Service Medal, World War II Victory Medal and Purple Heart Medal posthumously. He remains on duty on the USS Arizona. Rudolph is commemorated on the USS Arizona Memorial and the Memorial Tablets of the Missing, National Memorial Cemetery of the Pacific, Honolulu, Hawaii. He was survived by his Father, Mr. Rudolph Julius Theiller, Route 3, Box 457, Sebastopol, California.[768]

Thoma, Steven Joseph   Electrician's Mate, Third Class, Serial No. 283 41 09, US Navy. Steven enlisted in the US Navy October 9, 1940 in Cleveland, Ohio and left Mansfield, Ohio for the Naval Training Station in Great Lakes, Illinois to begin his training. He reported for duty on the USS Arizona December 9, 1940. Steven was serving on the USS Arizona on December 7, 1941 when the Japanese attacked Pearl Harbor. After the attack, Steven was assigned salvage duty on the USS Utah. He was later assigned duty on the USS Half Moon (AVP-26) where he served from June 1943 until March 1945.

---

[767] Stanley Merlin Teslow, photo and information provided by his daughter, Judith Teslow Neff.

[768] Rudolph "Rudy" Franklin Theiller, Information and photo from "Pearl Harbor Sailor Given Final Honor" by Patricia M. Roth, Staff Writer, Sonoma West News, November 29, 2006.

Thomas, Houston O'Neal Coxswain, Serial No: 346 76 96, US Navy. Houston was born December 21, 1920 in Texas, son of Samuel Houston Thomas and Ethel Mae (Meadow) Thomas. He enlisted in the US Navy December 19, 1939 in Little Rock, Arkansas and completed his basic training at the Naval Training Station in Great Lakes, Illinois. Houston reported for duty on the USS Arizona March 23, 1940. He was killed in action on December 7, 1941 at Pearl Harbor, Hawaii. Houston was awarded the American Defense Service Medal, World War II Victory Medal and Purple Heart Medal posthumously. He remains on duty on the USS Arizona. Houston is commemorated on the USS Arizona Memorial, the Memorial Tablets of the Missing, National Memorial Cemetery of the Pacific, Honolulu, Hawaii and Redwater Cemetery, Redriver, Bowie, Texas. He was survived by his Father, Mr. Sam Houston Thomas, Route 2, Box 533, Texarkana, Texas.

Thomas, Randall James Seaman, First Class, Serial No: 266 00 64, US Navy. Randall was born March 24, 1921 in Erbacon, Webster County, West Virginia to William Ausburn and Florence Elmira (Davis) Thomas. He enlisted in the US Navy November 10, 1939 in Richmond, Virginia and reported for duty on the USS West Virginia March 29, 1940. He was transferred to the USS Arizona December 6, 1940. Randall was killed in action on December 7, 1941 at Pearl Harbor, Hawaii. He was awarded the American Defense Service Medal, World War II Victory Medal and Purple Heart Medal posthumously. Randall remains on duty on the USS Arizona. He is commemorated on the USS Arizona Memorial and the Memorial Tablets of the Missing, National Memorial Cemetery of the Pacific, Honolulu, Hawaii. Randall was survived by his Mother, Mrs. Ella Thomas, Box 52, Cowen, West Virginia.

Thomas, Stanley Horace Fireman, Third Class, Serial No: 212 55 17, US Navy. Stanley was born November 1, 1920 in Northbridge, Massachusetts. He was the son of Eugene E. Thomas and Alice L. (Wing) Thomas. Stanley enlisted in the US Navy April 2, 1940 in Springfield, Massachusetts and reported for duty on the USS Arizona September 30, 1940. He was killed in action on December 7, 1941 at Pearl Harbor, Hawaii. Stanley was awarded the Purple Heart Medal, American Defense Service Medal, Asiatic-Pacific Campaign Medal and the World War II Victory Medal posthumously. He remains on duty on the USS Arizona. Stanley is commemorated on the USS Arizona Memorial and the Memorial Tablets of the Missing, National Memorial Cemetery of the Pacific, Honolulu, Hawaii. He was survived by his Father, Mr. Eugene E. Thomas, 3 A Street, Whitinsville, Massachusetts.

Thomas, Vincent Duron Coxswain, Serial No: 337 20 54, US Navy. Vincent was born June 19, 1920, the son of Ernest and Carrie (Schutz) Thomas. He enlisted with his best friend, Lloyd Bryant on October 4, 1939 in St. Louis, Missouri and they completed their basic training at the Naval Training Station in Great Lakes, Illinois. Vincent reported for duty on the USS Arizona December 31, 1939. Vincent was killed in action on December 7, 1941 at Pearl Harbor, Hawaii. He was awarded the American Defense Service Medal, World War II Victory Medal and Purple Heart Medal posthumously. Vincent remains on duty on the USS Arizona. He is commemorated on the USS Arizona Memorial and the Memorial Tablets of the Missing, National Memorial Cemetery of the Pacific, Honolulu, Hawaii and Pine Tree Cemetery, Patterson, Illinois. Vincent was survived by his Wife, Mrs. Myrtle Elizabeth Thomas, 232 North Crescent Drive, Beverly Hills, California. The American Legion Hall in Hillview, Illinois was named in memory of Vincent and Lloyd Bryant.

Thompson, Charles Leroy Seaman, First Class, Serial No: 300 19 53, US Navy. Charles was born February 14, 1920 the son of Roy Thompson and Rose Vanous Thompson. His father died in 1928 and his mother in 1931. He lived for a short time at the Illinois Soldiers and Sailors Children's School in Norman. Illinois, an orphanage opened after the Civil War for children of veterans. He enlisted in the US Navy October 8, 1940 in Chicago, Illinois and completed his basic training at the Naval Training Station in Great Lakes, Illinois. He reported for duty on the USS Arizona December 9, 1940. Charles died on board the USS Solace from wounds received in action on December 7, 1941 at Pearl Harbor, Hawaii.[769] He was awarded the American Defense Service Medal, World War II Victory Medal and Purple Heart Medal posthumously. Charles remains were recovered and he was buried in Plot F, Row 0, Grave 679, National Memorial Cemetery of the Pacific, Honolulu, Hawaii. He is commemorated on the USS Arizona Memorial. Charles was survived by his Sister, Mrs. Catherine McCollom, 116 East Iron, Salina, Kansas.[770]

Thompson, Irven Edgar Seaman, First Class, Serial No: 311 42 45, US Navy. Irven was born November 27, 1921 in Toledo, Ohio the son of Ralph Alonzo and Mable Mae (Perry) Thompson. His father died of appendicitis when he was just nine years old. Irven lettered in Football playing half back while attending the North Baltimore High School. He enlisted in the US Navy March 13, 1940 in Detroit, Michigan and completed his basic training at the Naval Training Station in Great Lakes, Illinois. Irven reported for duty on the USS Arizona July 12, 1940. He was killed in action on December 7, 1941 at Pearl Harbor, Hawaii. He was awarded the American Defense Service Medal, World War II Victory Medal and Purple Heart Medal posthumously. Irven remains on duty on the USS Arizona. He is commemorated on the USS Arizona Memorial and the Memorial Tablets of the Missing, National Memorial Cemetery of the Pacific, Honolulu, Hawaii. Irven was survived by his Mother, Mrs. Mabel Thompson, 237-1/2 North Main Street, North Baltimore, Ohio.[771]

Thompson, Norman Machinist's Mate, US Navy. Norman enlisted in the US Navy and was serving on the USS Arizona as Assistant to Engineering Officer. His battle station was Repair V where he was serving on December 7, 1941 when the Japanese attacked Pearl Harbor. After the attack, he had temporary duty on the USS Tennessee, four days later, he was ordered to PacFlt Pooling Officer, Receiving Station at Pearl Harbor.

---

[769] Report of Changes of the USS Arizona for the month ending 31st day of December, 1941, page 105, line 14, Charles Leroy Thompson.
[770] Charles Leroy Thompson, Photo from "Lost and Presumed Dead" by Matt Hanley, The Beacon News, Chicago, Illinois, December 6, 2011.
[771] Irven Edgar Thompson, information from The Republican Courier of Findlay, Ohio, North Baltimore High School Yearbook.

Thompson, Robert Gary Ship's Cook, First Class, Serial No: 385 78 23, US Navy. Robert was born in Georgia. He enlisted in the US Navy June 11, 1938 in Seattle, Washington and completed his basic training at the Naval Training Station, San Diego, California. He reported for duty on the USS Arizona June 14, 1938. Robert was killed in action on December 7, 1941 at Pearl Harbor, Hawaii. He was awarded the American Defense Service Medal, World War II Victory Medal and Purple Heart Medal posthumously. Robert remains on duty on the USS Arizona. He is commemorated on the USS Arizona Memorial and the Memorial Tablets of the Missing, National Memorial Cemetery of the Pacific, Honolulu, Hawaii. Robert was survived by his Wife, Mrs. Ruby Susan Thompson, 1011 Stanley, Long Beach, California.

Thorman, John Christopher Electrician's Mate, Second Class, Serial No: 321 23 84, US Navy. John was born January 15, 1917 in Granville, Iowa, son of John Jacob Thorman and Dorthea Marie (Bussanmus) Thorman. He enlisted in the US Navy March 9, 1938 in Des Moines, Iowa and reported for duty on the USS Arizona July 9, 1938. John was killed in action on December 7, 1941 at Pearl Harbor, Hawaii. He was awarded the American Defense Service Medal, World War II Victory Medal and Purple Heart Medal posthumously. John remains on duty on the USS Arizona. He is commemorated on the USS Arizona Memorial and the Memorial Tablets of the Missing, National Memorial Cemetery of the Pacific, Honolulu, Hawaii. John was survived by his Father, Mr. John J. Thorman, Granville, Iowa.[772]

Thornton, George Hayward Gunner's Mate, Third Class, Serial No: 295 76 86, US Navy. George was born March 29, 1916 in New Harmony, Mississippi, son of George Madison Thornton and Callie Mae (Kennedy) Thornton. He enlisted in the US Navy October 4, 1940 in Nashville, Tennessee and completed his basic training at the Naval Training Station in Norfolk, Virginia. George reported for duty on the USS Arizona December 4, 1940. He was killed in action on December 7, 1941 at Pearl Harbor, Hawaii. George was awarded the American Defense Service Medal, World War II Victory Medal and Purple Heart Medal posthumously. He remains on duty on the USS Arizona. George is commemorated on the USS Arizona Memorial and the Memorial Tablets of the Missing, National Memorial Cemetery of the Pacific, Honolulu, Hawaii. He was survived by his Father, Mr. George Madison Thornton, Route 1, Blue Springs, Mississippi.[773]

Tiner, Robert Reaves Fireman, Second Class, Serial No: 356 33 43, US Navy. Robert was born April 5, 1916 in South Athens, Texas, son of Cad Reeves Tiner and Rosie Lee (McCool) Tiner. He enlisted in the US Navy July 30, 1940 in Dallas, Texas and completed his basic training at the Naval Training Station in San Diego, California. Robert reported for duty on the USS Arizona January 11, 1941. He was killed in action on December 7, 1941 at Pearl Harbor, Hawaii. Robert was awarded the American Defense Service Medal, World War II Victory Medal and Purple Heart Medal posthumously. He remains on duty on the USS Arizona. Robert is commemorated on the USS Arizona Memorial and the Memorial Tablets of the Missing, National Memorial Cemetery of the Pacific, Honolulu, Hawaii. He was survived by his Father, Mr. Cad R. Tiner, Route 2, Athens, Texas.

---

[772] John Christopher Thorman, Photo from Iowa Honor States.
[773] George Hayward Thorton, Information and photo provided by family member, Hayward Eugene "Gene" Thornton.

Tisdale, William Esley Chief Water Tender, Serial No: 271 47 35, US Navy. William was born September 3, 1905 in Shelby, North Carolina, son of William Esley Tisdale, Sr. and Harriett "Hattie" Ella (Smith) Tisdale. He enlisted in the US Navy in 1920 and reported for duty on the USS Arizona October 22, 1935. He was a career navy man. Three months before the attack he had applied for a transfer to the Fleet Reserve. His intentions were to retire. William was killed in action on December 7, 1941 at Pearl Harbor, Hawaii. He was awarded the American Defense Service Medal, World War II Victory Medal and Purple Heart Medal posthumously. William remains on duty on the USS Arizona. He is commemorated on the USS Arizona Memorial and the Memorial Tablets of the Missing, National Memorial Cemetery of the Pacific, Honolulu, Hawaii. William was survived by his Wife, Mrs. Barbara Naydean Tisdale, 820 Loma Vista Drive, Long Beach, California.[774]

Trantham, Glenwood Orris Boatswain's Mate, First Class, Serial No. 270 10 55, US Navy. Glenwood was born October 20, 1907 in Florida, the son of Melvin Moore and Florence Geneva (Jennings) Trantham. He re-enlisted in the US Navy December 8, 1934. He served on the USS Arizona from December 31, 1930 until December 7, 1941 when the Japanese attacked Pearl Harbor. Glenwood was missing/killed in action on November 24, 1943 while serving on board the USS Liscombe Bay (CVE-56). "The baby flat-top, Liscombe Bay was sunk by a torpedo from an enemy submarine on the day before Thanksgiving of 1943. The Liscombe Bay was on her first battle assignment covering the occupation of Makin in the Gilbert Islands. The Submarine attack was a complete surprise. It was the Liscombe Bay's third day of the invasion, and her crew had lost the tenseness that goes with the beginning of a landing operation. By this time they were relaxed, and only their standard occupational alertness remained. The scuttlebutt reported that the nearest enemy ships were two days away. The torpedo struck a half-hour before dawn and it was still dark when the Liscombe Bay sank. The torpedo struck near the stern on the port side, and the havoc was instant and complete. The whole after section broke quickly into flames, and most of the crew stationed there died instantly."[775] Chief Boatswain's Mate Trantham was among the 646 crew that were lost. He was awarded the Purple Heart Medal posthumously. He is commemorated on the Memorial Tablets of the Missing, National Memorial Cemetery of the Pacific, Honolulu, Hawaii. He was survived by his Wife, Mrs. Frances Fayne Trantham, 63 Elm Street, Montclair, New Jersey.

Travioli, Vernon Alva Seaman, Second Class, Serial No. 376 15 02, US Navy. Vernon was born on July 22, 1921 in California; he was the adopted son of Walter Dean and Mabel L. (Wharton) Travioli. He enlisted in the US Navy October 31, 1940 in San Francisco, California and completed his basic training at the Naval Training Station in San Diego, California. He reported for duty on the USS Arizona December 30, 1940. Vernon was serving on the USS Arizona on December 7, 1941 when the Japanese attacked Pearl Harbor. After the attack, Vernon was transferred to the USS Lexington for duty. Vernon died on June 4, 1988 in Merced, California.

---

[774] William Esley Tisdale, Information and photo provided by family member, Jennifer Babuca.
[775] Yank The Army Weekly, June 11, The Sinking of the Liscombe Bay by Robert L. Schwartz Y2c Navy Correspondent.

Triplett, Thomas Edgar   Seaman, First Class, Serial No: 381 33 98, US Navy.   Thomas was born June 21, 1921 in Frederick, Kansas, son of Thomas Hays Triplett and Lucy (Yarnell) Triplett. He enlisted in the US Navy May 22, 1940 at San Diego, California and reported for duty on the USS Arizona August 25, 1940. Thomas was killed in action on December 7, 1941 at Pearl Harbor, Hawaii. He was awarded the American Defense Service Medal, World War II Victory Medal and Purple Heart Medal posthumously. Thomas remains on duty on the USS Arizona. He is commemorated on the USS Arizona Memorial and the Memorial Tablets of the Missing, National Memorial Cemetery of the Pacific, Honolulu, Hawaii. Thomas was survived by his Father, Mr. Thomas Hays Triplett, 550 Broadway, Hoisington, Kansas. After his only son died in the attack, his father tried to enlist. He wrote to Navy Secretary Frank Knox asking to be assigned to a ship in the Pacific. The Navy agreed and enlisted him as a water tender first class. He was assigned to the USS Pecos. The Hoisington, Kansas VFW post was named in honor of Thomas and two other local men.[776]

Trovato, Tom   Seaman, First Class, Serial No: 375 97 22, US Navy. Tom was born July 29, 1922 in Monterey, California to Jean and Rosa (Criscuolo) Trovato. He enlisted in the US Navy October 7, 1939 in San Francisco, California and completed his basic training at the Naval Training Station in San Diego, California. He reported for duty on the USS Arizona December 20, 1939. Tom was killed in action on December 7, 1941 at Pearl Harbor, Hawaii. He was awarded the American Defense Service Medal, World War II Victory Medal and Purple Heart Medal posthumously. Tom remains on duty on the USS Arizona. He is commemorated on the USS Arizona Memorial and the Memorial Tablets of the Missing, National Memorial Cemetery of the Pacific, Honolulu, Hawaii. Tom was survived by his Mother, Mrs. Rosina Trovato, 1280 6th Street, Monterey, California.[777]

Tucker, Edward Daniel   Boatswain's Mate, Second Class, Serial No. 299 76 10, US Navy. Edward was born on August 8, 1916. He enlisted in the US Navy August 9, 1934 in Chicago, Illinois. He transferred from the USS Pensacola to the USS Arizona on April 29, 1940. Edward was serving on the USS Arizona on December 7, 1941 when the Japanese attacked Pearl Harbor. A bomb hit a hatch door and blew it away. All he saw was smoke so he walked off the edge of the boat into the water. That saved his life. He went back six months later to retrieve records because he was familiar with the ship. After the attack, Edward was transferred to the Mary Anne Salvage Detail duty. Edward died on November 29, 1959 and is buried in Section 28, Site 493, Arlington National Cemetery, Arlington, Virginia.[778]

---

[776] Thomas Edgar Triplett, Photo and information provided by family member, M. Ford.

[777] Photo from the Monterey County Herald, Monday, December 3, 2001, 3 Oak Grove Men Died on USS Arizona by Kevin Howe.

[778] Information and photo provided by Lynne Warren 11/16/2011.

Tucker, Raymond Edward Coxswain, Serial No: 291 52 05, US Navy. Raymond was born November 15, 1918, son of R. R. Tucker and Wella T. (Brock) Tucker. He enlisted in the US Navy October 12, 1937 in Indianapolis, Indiana and reported for duty on the USS Arizona February 5, 1938. Raymond was killed in action on December 7, 1941 at Pearl Harbor, Hawaii. He was awarded the American Defense Service Medal, World War II Victory Medal and Purple Heart Medal posthumously. Raymond remains on duty on the USS Arizona. He is commemorated on the USS Arizona Memorial and the Memorial Tablets of the Missing, National Memorial Cemetery of the Pacific, Honolulu, Hawaii. Raymond was survived by his Wife, Mrs. Enida Tucker, Winslow, Indiana.

Tuntland, Earl Eugene Seaman, First Class, Serial No: 328 75 72, US Navy. Earl was born September 23, 1919 in North Dakota, son of Andrew Tuntland and Gustie Tuntland. He enlisted in the US Navy October 8, 1940 in Minneapolis, Minnesota and completed his basic training at the Naval Training Station in Great Lakes, Illinois. Earl reported for duty on the USS Arizona December 9, 1940. Assigned death #460, Earl died on December 10, 1941 from 3rd degree burns received in action on December 7, 1941 at Pearl Harbor, Hawaii.[779] He was awarded the American Defense Service Medal, World War II Victory Medal and Purple Heart Medal posthumously. Earl was interred in a Navy Plot, Nuuanu Cemetery, Honolulu, Oahu, Hawaii. He is commemorated on the USS Arizona Memorial and the Memorial Tablets of the Missing, National Memorial Cemetery of the Pacific, Honolulu, Hawaii and Greenwood Cemetery, Mobridge, North Dakota. Earl was survived by his Father, Mr. Andrew Tuntland, Shields, North Dakota.

Turner, Richard Newton, Jr. Seaman, First Class, Serial No. 356 17 83, US Navy. Richard was born on November 24, 1918 in West Plains, Missouri, the son of Richard N. Turner, Sr. and Fannie M. Turner. He enlisted in the US Navy October 10, 1939 in Dallas, Texas and completed his basic training at the Naval Training Station in San Diego, California. He reported for duty on the USS Arizona January 24, 1940. Richard was serving on December 7, 1941 when the Japanese attacked Pearl Harbor. After the attack, Richard was transferred to the Submarine Base at Pearl Harbor for duty. He retired from the US Navy in September 1958 after serving for over 20 years. Richard died on March 14, 1997 in Mena, Arkansas.

Turnipseed, John Morgan Fireman, Third Class, Serial No: 346 83 07, US Navy. John enlisted in the US Navy August 2, 1940 in Little Rock, Arkansas and completed his basic training at the Naval Training Station in San Diego, California. He reported for duty on the USS Arizona January 11, 1941. John was killed in action on December 7, 1941 at Pearl Harbor, Hawaii. He was awarded the American Defense Service Medal, World War II Victory Medal and Purple Heart Medal posthumously. John remains on duty on the USS Arizona. He is commemorated on the USS Arizona Memorial and the Memorial Tablets of the Missing, National Memorial Cemetery of the Pacific, Honolulu, Hawaii. John was survived by his Mother, Mrs. Marie Adda Hill, Route 1, Houston, Arkansas.

Tussey, Lloyd Harold Electrician's Mate, Third Class, Serial No: 262 29 39, US Navy. Lloyd was born February 25, 1916 in Davidson County, North Carolina, the eldest son of Arthur David Tussey and Lona Day (Temple) Tussey. He enlisted in the US Navy June 14, 1938 in Raleigh, North Carolina and reported for duty on the USS Arizona May 15, 1940. Lloyd was killed in action on December 7, 1941 at Pearl Harbor, Hawaii. He was awarded the American Defense Service Medal, World War II Victory Medal and Purple Heart Medal posthumously.

---

[779] Report of Changes of the USS Arizona for the month ending 31st day of December, 1941, page 106, line 27, Earl Eugene Tuntland.

Lloyd remains on duty on the USS Arizona. He is commemorated on the USS Arizona Memorial and the Memorial Tablets of the Missing, National Memorial Cemetery of the Pacific, Honolulu, Hawaii and Beulah United Church of Christ Cemetery, Welcome, North Carolina. Lloyd was survived by his Parents, Mr. and Mrs. Arthur David Tussey, Route 4, Box 26, Lexington, North Carolina; Brothers, Harold, Holland, David and Clyde; Sisters, Ruby T. Walser, Donese T. Leonard and Clatie O. Nelson.

Tyson, Robert (Ray) Fire Controlman, Third Class, Serial No: 274 45 53, US Navy. Robert was born November 9, 1911 in West Carroll Parish, Louisiana to Emery and Elizabeth Tyson. He attended Forrest High School and was an outstanding football player on that time. Before joining the Navy on June 4, 1940 in New Orleans, Louisiana, he was employed by the Oak Grove Utilities Corporation and completed his basic training at the Naval Training Station in San Diego, California. He reported for duty on the USS Arizona October 14, 1940. Robert was killed in action on December 7, 1941 at Pearl Harbor, Hawaii. He was awarded the American Defense Service Medal, World War II Victory Medal and Purple Heart Medal posthumously. Robert remains on duty on the USS Arizona. He is commemorated on the USS Arizona Memorial and the Memorial Tablets of the Missing, National Memorial Cemetery of the Pacific, Honolulu, Hawaii. Robert was survived by his Brother, Mr. J. Carland Tyson, Box 432, Oak Grove, Louisiana, his Parents, Mr. and Mrs. Emory Tyson of Round Hill, his wife, Mrs. Wilmar (Pollard) Tyson and infant daughter, Katherine Rae Tyson, and three sisters, Mrs. B. Carroll, Mrs. B. McIntyre and Mrs C. McIntyre all of Oak Grove .[780]

Uhrenholdt, Andrew "Curtis" Ensign, Serial No: 0-096391, US Navy Reserve. Andrew was born August 8, 1920 in Seeley, Wisconsin, son of Jens Uhrenholdt and Blanche Ruth (McCombs) Uhrenholdt. He attended the junior college in Ely, Minnesota for two years, staying with his cousin's family. Andrew was commissioned Ensign in the US Navy February 28, 1941 and was serving as Communication Watch Officer. His battle station was Plot. Andrew was killed in action on December 7, 1941 at Pearl Harbor, Hawaii. He was awarded the American Defense Service Medal, World War II Victory Medal and Purple Heart Medal posthumously. Andrew remains on duty on the USS Arizona. He is commemorated on the USS Arizona Memorial and the Memorial Tablets of the Missing, National Memorial Cemetery of the Pacific, Honolulu, Hawaii and Riverside Cemetery, Seeley, Wisconsin. Andrew was survived by his Mother, Mrs. Jens Uhrenholdt, Hayward, Wisconsin, a brother, Russell Uhrenholdt and a sister, Betty Lou (Uhrenholdt) Raymond. [781]

Urbaniak, Edmund Leo Chief Carpenter's Mate, Serial No. 10813, US Navy. Edmund was born in 1907 in Michigan to Thomas and Martha Urbaniak. He re-enlisted in the US Navy September 14, 1937 and reported for duty on the USS Arizona serving as Assistant to 1st Lieutenant. His battle station was Repair II on December 7, 1941 when the Japanese attacked Pearl Harbor. He later attained the rank of Lieutenant and served on board the USS Whitley (AKA-94).

---

[780] Robert Tyson, photo and information from The Times, Shreveport, Louisiana, May 5, 1942, page 16.
[781] Andrew Curtis Uhrenholdt, Photo from Wisconsin Honor States.

Valente, Richard Dominic Gunner's Mate, Third Class, Serial No: 375 91 98, US Navy. Richard was born in 1922, son of Ernesto Valente and Anna Valente. He enlisted in the US Navy November 9, 1938 in San Francisco, California and completed his basic training at the Naval Training Station in San Diego, California. Richard reported for duty on the USS Arizona March 11, 1939. He was killed in action on December 7, 1941 at Pearl Harbor, Hawaii. Richard was awarded the American Defense Service Medal, World War II Victory Medal and Purple Heart Medal posthumously. He remains on duty on the USS Arizona. Richard is commemorated on the USS Arizona Memorial and the Memorial Tablets of the Missing, National Memorial Cemetery of the Pacific, Honolulu, Hawaii. He was survived by his Father, Mr. Ernesto Joseph Valente, 286 Grand Avenue, San Jose, California.

Van Atta, Garland Wade Machinist's Mate, First Class, Serial No: 279 30 51, US Navy. Garland was born August 18, 1910 in Union Township, Ohio, son of Allen Wade Van Atta and Blanche Mae (Gilmer) Van Atta. He enlisted at age 17 in 1927 and had re-enlisted in the US Navy July 9, 1938 at Bremerton, Washington. Garland served on the USS Arizona from August 15, 1935 until he was killed in action on December 7, 1941 at Pearl Harbor, Hawaii. He was awarded the American Defense Service Medal, World War II Victory Medal and Purple Heart Medal posthumously. Garland remains on duty on the USS Arizona. He is commemorated on the USS Arizona Memorial and the Memorial Tablets of the Missing, National Memorial Cemetery of the Pacific, Honolulu, Hawaii. Garland was survived by his Wife, Mrs. Alicia Dorothy Van Atta, 9 Ontario Avenue, Long Beach, California.[782]

Van Horn, James Randolf Seaman, Second Class, Serial No: 356 59 43, US Navy. James was born March 31, 1924 in Okmulgee, Oklahoma. In the spring of 1941, Jim, a sophomore at Tucson High had just turned 17. He heard a recruiting talk by Admiral Isaac Kidd and decided to quit school and join the Navy. Remembering the day in 1941 when her son, who had lived all his life in the desert decided to go to sea, his mother said, "James never said anything about the Navy until he heard the admiral talk. Then nothing would hold him. He was inspired. He wanted to go." He enlisted in the US Navy June 4, 1941 in Dallas, Texas and completed his basic training at the Naval Training Station in San Diego, California. James reported for duty on the USS Arizona August 13, 1941. He was killed in action on December 7, 1941 at Pearl Harbor, Hawaii. It was pure coincidence – and perhaps irony – that Admiral Kidd, then commander of Battleship Division 1, was on the Arizona when the Japanese struck. James and his idol went down together. James was awarded the American Defense Service Medal, World War II Victory Medal and Purple Heart Medal posthumously. He remains on duty on the USS Arizona. James is commemorated on the USS Arizona Memorial and the Memorial Tablets of the Missing, National Memorial Cemetery of the Pacific, Honolulu, Hawaii. He was survived by his Mother, Mrs. Bonnie F. Cope, 2574 Orchard Street, Tucson, Arizona. December 1st has been named the James Randolph Van Horn day in Tucson, Arizona.[783]

---

[782] Garland Wade Van Atta, Photo from California Honor States.

[783] James Randolf Van Horn, Information from "Tucson High Boy Died With Admiral" by Peter Starrett, Tucson Daily Citizen, Tucson, Arizona, Thursday Evening, November 27, 1958, Page 4.

Van Valkenburgh, Franklin Captain, Serial No: 0-007187, US Navy. Franklin was born on April 5, 1888 in Minneapolis, Minnesota. He was appointed a midshipman in 1905 and graduated from the US Naval Academy in June 1909. His initial service was in battleships, punctuated by a tour with the Asiatic Squadron in 1911-14. He received postgraduate education in the field of steam engineering and was Engineering Officer of the battleship Rhode Island during the First World War. Van Valkenburgh was twice an instructor at the Naval Academy during the late 'Teens and in the 'Twenties, and also served on the battleships Minnesota and Maryland during that time. Following promotion to the rank of Commander, he was assigned to the Office of the Chief of Naval Operations, in Washington, D.C., during 1928-31. In the early 1930s, Commander Van Valkenburgh commanded the destroyer Talbot and Destroyer Squadron Five. He was a student at the Naval War College and inspector of naval materiel at the New York Navy Yard before again serving at sea as Commanding Officer of the destroyer tender Melville in 1936-38. Captain Van Valkenburg then spent a tour ashore with the Third Naval District and, in February 1941 became Commanding Officer of the battleship Arizona. He was planning on retiring and remarked how thrilled he was to be in command of a battleship at the end of his naval career. Franklin was killed in action on December 7, 1941 at Pearl Harbor, Hawaii all that remained was his academy ring in a pile of ash. He was awarded the Congressional Medal of Honor, American Defense Service Medal, World War II Victory Medal and the Purple Heart Medal posthumously. Franklin remains on duty on the USS Arizona. He is commemorated on the USS Arizona Memorial and the Memorial Tablets of the Missing, National Memorial Cemetery of the Pacific, Honolulu, Hawaii. Franklin was survived by his Wife, Mrs. Franklin Van Valkenburgh, 1023 East Ocean Boulevard, Long Beach, California.

Medal of Honor Citation: For conspicuous devotion to duty, extraordinary courage and complete disregard of his own life, during the attack on the Fleet in Pearl Harbor, T.H., by Japanese forces on 7 December 1941. As Commanding Officer of the U.S.S. Arizona, Captain Van Valkenburgh gallantly fought his ship until the U.S.S. Arizona blew up from magazine explosions and a direct bomb hit on the bridge which resulted in the loss of his life.

The destroyer USS Van Valkenburgh (DD-656) was named in his honor. The USS Van Valkenburgh won the Navy Unit Commendation for her service off Okinawa, was awarded three battle stars for her World War II duty and received one battle star for her service during the Korean War Operations.[784]

Van Winkle, Edward Laverne Fireman, Second Class, Serial No. 316 72 18, US Navy. Edward was born May 31, 1921. He enlisted in the US Navy December 2, 1940 in Omaha, Nebraska and reported for duty on the USS Arizona February 21, 1941. I show he was transferred to the Sub Base, Pearl Harbor for instruction in MM School. I do not find him returning to the Arizona. However, the National Park Service shows him as a survivor of the USS Arizona. After the attack, Edward was transferred to the USS Pelias (AS-14) for duty. Edward died November 7, 2004 in Clifton, New Jersey.

---

[784] Franklin Van Valkenburg, Dictionary of American Naval Fighting Ships, Naval Historical Center, USS Van Valkenburgh (DD-656).

Varchol, Boleslaw Brinley Gunner's Mate, Second Class, Serial No: 243 54 13, US Navy. Brinley was born in 1917, son of John Varchol and Helen Varchol. *His actual first name was Beleswaft Warhol a good polish name. When he was a child a neighbor began calling him "Brin" and the name stuck. By the time he entered school, he was using Brindley as his first name and it carried with him through his life.* He enlisted in the US Navy September 3, 1936 in Philadelphia, Pennsylvania and reported for duty on the USS Arizona February 3, 1937. *Brinley and his best friend Al Konnick played on the USS Arizona baseball team. Brinley played 2nd base and Al played 1st base. Both were being scouted by the National Baseball League to play once their enlistments were up. Unfortunately, Pearl Harbor happened before their enlistments ran out. Brinley had about six months to go before his enlistment was up.* He was killed in action on December 7, 1941 at Pearl Harbor, Hawaii. Brinley was awarded the American Defense Service Medal, World War II Victory Medal and Purple Heart Medal posthumously. He remains on duty on the USS Arizona. Brinley is commemorated on the USS Arizona Memorial and the Memorial Tablets of the Missing, National Memorial Cemetery of the Pacific, Honolulu, Hawaii. He was survived by his Father, Mr. John Varchol, 19 Steele Street, Hanover Township, Wilkes-Barre, Pennsylvania. *Brinley did not take out the life insurance offered. The Navy decided to pay out $10,000 on him anyway to his parents. The money was not paid in a lump sum, it was paid out in monthly amounts and when his parents passed away, the payments stopped. They had only received a few thousand dollars over 4 to 5 years.*[785]

Vaughan, William Frank Pharmacist's Mate, Second Class, Serial No: 380 86 27, US Navy. William was born March 14, 1891. He enlisted in the US Navy on June 14, 1941 at the Naval Yard, Mare Island, California and reported for duty on the USS Arizona on November 8, 1941. William was killed in action on December 7, 1941 at Pearl Harbor, Hawaii. He was awarded the American Defense Service Medal, World War II Victory Medal and Purple Heart Medal posthumously. William remains on duty on the USS Arizona. He is commemorated on the USS Arizona Memorial and the Memorial Tablets of the Missing, National Memorial Cemetery of the Pacific, Honolulu, Hawaii. William was survived by his Wife, Mrs. Madeline Vaughn, 1218 South Menlo, Los Angeles, California.

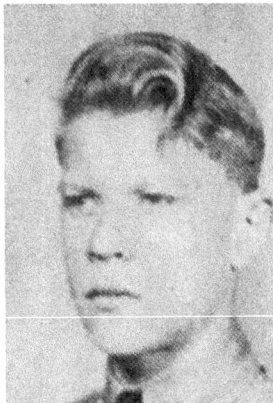

Veeder, Gordon Elliott Seaman, Second Class, Serial No: 368 53 34, US Navy. Gordon was born in 1923, son of Albert Leroy Veeder and Erma Mae (Elliott) Veeder. He enlisted in the US Navy November 5, 1940 in Salt Lake City, Utah and completed his basic training at the Naval Training Station in San Diego, California. Gordon reported for duty on the USS Arizona January 11, 1941. He was killed in action on December 7, 1941 at Pearl Harbor, Hawaii. Gordon was awarded the American Defense Service Medal, World War II Victory Medal and Purple Heart Medal posthumously. He remains on duty on the USS Arizona. Gordon is commemorated on the USS Arizona Memorial and the Memorial Tablets of the Missing, National Memorial Cemetery of the Pacific, Honolulu, Hawaii. He was survived by his Father, Mr. Albert L. Veeder, 1316 North 20th Street, Boise, Idaho.[786]

---

[785] Brinley Varchol, Information and photo provided by family members, Linda Messimer and brother, Daniel Varchol.
[786] Gordon Elliott Veeder, Photo from 1940 Boise High School Yearbook, Boise, Idaho.

Velia, Galen Steve Signalman, Third Class, Serial No: 411 09 23, US Navy. Galen was born in 1923, son of Stephen J. Velia and Josephine Fern (Robison) Velia. He enlisted in the US Navy October 5, 1940 in Kansas City, Missouri and completed his basic training at the Naval Training Station in San Diego, California. Galen reported for duty on the USS Arizona March 6, 1941. He was killed in action on December 7, 1941 at Pearl Harbor, Hawaii. Galen was awarded the American Defense Service Medal, World War II Victory Medal and Purple Heart Medal posthumously. He remains on duty on the USS Arizona. Galen is commemorated on the USS Arizona Memorial and the Memorial Tablets of the Missing, National Memorial Cemetery of the Pacific, Honolulu, Hawaii and the Highland Park Cemetery, Pittsburg, Kansas. He was survived by his Mother, Mrs. Josephine Fern Velia, 1209 North Grand, Pittsburg, Kansas. His older brother, Keith was serving on the USS Arizona and was among the survivors.[787]

Velia, Keith Lloyd Seaman, Second Class, Serial No. 142 43 07, US Navy. Keith was born on September 25, 1921 in Kansas, the son of Stevens and Josephine Fern Velia. He enlisted in the US Navy on March 18, 1941 in Kansas City, Missouri and completed his basic training at the Naval Training Station in Great Lakes, Illinois. He reported for duty on the USS Arizona June 25, 1941. He was serving on December 7, 1941 when the Japanese attacked Pearl Harbor. After the attack, Keith was transferred to the USS Chester for duty and later served on the USS Limon K. Swenson. Keith served in the US Navy until April 4, 1947. His younger brother, Galen Steve Velia was killed in action on board the USS Arizona. Keith died on February 13, 1991 in Wichita, Kansas and was buried in St. Mary's Cemetery, Pittsburg, Kansas. He was survived by his wife, Irma L. (Sannipoli) Velia and one brother, Jess Velia.

Vessels, James Allard Gunner's Mate, Third Class, Serial No. 287 33 35, US Navy. James was born March 17, 1920 in McCracken County, Kentucky to Walter and Anna (Hobbs) Vessels. He enlisted in the US Navy November 7, 1939 in Louisville, Kentucky and completed his basic training at the Naval Training Station in Great Lakes, Illinois. He reported for duty on the USS Arizona January 27, 1940. James was serving on the USS Arizona on December 7, 1941 when the Japanese attacked Pearl Harbor. After the Arizona was sunk, James was taken on board the USS Tennessee where he stayed until the 18th. From there he was sent to the Pooling Officer at Pearl Harbor for assignment. James died January 15, 1981 in McCracken County, Kentucky.

Vidal, Daniel Mess Attendant, First Class, Serial No. 498 50 47, US Navy. Daniel was born September 17, 1910 in the Philippines. He enlisted in the US Navy October 30, 1930. He served on the USS Arizona from September 17, 1938 until December 7, 1941 when the Japanese attacked Pearl Harbor. After the attack, Daniel was transferred to Comdt. 14th Naval District for duty with the Flag of Admiral Furlong. He was transferred to the Naval Shipyard at Pearl Harbor for duty on December 31, 1941. Daniel died December 9, 1990 in San Diego, California.

---

[787] Galen Steve Velia, Photo provided by the Reference Department, Pittsburg Public Library, taken from the Pittsburg Headlight Newspaper, Pittsburg, Kansas, December 25, 1941, Page 2.

Vieira, Alvaro Everett Seaman, Second Class, Serial No: 201 90 75, US Navy. Alvaro was born January 12, 1924 in Portsmouth, Newport, Rhode Island to Manuel and Lucinda (Leal) Vieira. He enlisted in the US Navy March 3, 1941 in Boston, Massachusetts and completed his basic training at the Naval Training Station in San Diego, California. He reported for duty on the USS Arizona July 13, 1941. Alvaro was killed in action on December 7, 1941 at Pearl Harbor, Hawaii. He was awarded the American Defense Service Medal, World War II Victory Medal and Purple Heart Medal posthumously. Alvaro remains on duty on the USS Arizona. He is commemorated on the USS Arizona Memorial and the Memorial Tablets of the Missing, National Memorial Cemetery of the Pacific, Honolulu, Hawaii. Alvaro was survived by his Father, Mr. Manuel V. Vieira, East Main Road, Portsmouth, Rhode Island. The Alvaro Everett Vieira VFW Post 5390 in Portsmouth, Rhode Island was named in his honor.[788]

Vlach, Vincent James, Jr. Yeoman, First Class, Serial No. 316 48 67, US Navy. Vincent was born on June 19, 1917 in St. Michael, Nebraska, son of Vincent J. and Myrtle Vlach. He enlisted in the US Navy June 12, 1937 in Omaha, Nebraska and reported for duty on the USS Arizona September 3, 1937. Vincent left the Navy in January 1941 but reenlisted February 6, 1941 and reported back on the USS Arizona April 4, 1941. He was serving on December 7, 1941 when the Japanese attacked Pearl Harbor. Jim was on shore leave the morning of the 7th. By the time he arrived at the Navy Yard, he was not permitted to return to the Arizona. Later he was stationed on the USS Gambler Bay. Vincent's wife was in Honolulu at the time and he was on shore leave visiting with her when the attack began. Vincent also served in the Korean War and retired from the Navy in 1960 with the rank of Lieutenant Commander. During his service Vincent was awarded the Navy Commendation Medal with Fleet Clasp, Navy Good Conduct Medal, American Campaign Medal, Asiatic Pacific Campaign Medal and the World War II Victory Medal. Vincent died on March 12, 2008 in Riverside, California and was buried with full military honors in Section 47, Site 4084, Riverside National Cemetery, Riverside, California. His wife Mrs. Jeanne Claire Vlach preceded him in death.

Vojta, Walter Arnold Seaman, First Class, Serial No: 328 77 96, US Navy. Walter was born November 1, 1921 in Hennepin County, Minnesota, son of Frank Vojta and Anne Vojta. He enlisted in the US Navy October 30, 1940 in Minneapolis, Minnesota and reported for duty on the USS Arizona June 7, 1941. Walter was killed in action on December 7, 1941 at Pearl Harbor, Hawaii. He was awarded the American Defense Service Medal, World War II Victory Medal and Purple Heart Medal posthumously. Walter remains on duty on the USS Arizona. He is commemorated on the USS Arizona Memorial and the Memorial Tablets of the Missing, National Memorial Cemetery of the Pacific, Honolulu, Hawaii. Walter was survived by his Mother, Mrs. Anne Vojta, 212 West 22nd Street, Minneapolis, Minnesota.[789]

---

[788] Alvaro Everett Vieira, Photo provided by Silvano Theunissen.
[789] Walter Arnold Vojta, Photo from the Star Tribune, Minneapolis, Minnesota, February 6, 1944.

Von Spreckelsen, Charles Albert. Painter, Second Class, R Division, Damage Control, Serial No. 291 45 21, US Navy. Charles was born on May 7, 1915 in Manchester, Tennessee. He enlisted in the US Navy July 31, 1935 and reported for duty on the USS Arizona November 23, 1935. He was serving on the USS Arizona on December 7, 1941 when the Japanese attacked Pearl Harbor. After the attack, Charles was transferred to Kingfisher-Meduaa Aviation repair unit for temporary duty. He was permanently transferred to Scouting Observation Service Unit until early 1943. Charles retired from the Navy in 1957. He died on January 1, 2004.

Vosti, Anthony August Gunner's Mate, Third Class, Serial No: 375 97 24, US Navy. Anthony was born in about 1921 in Santa Clara County, California to Basilio and Cora (Albertini) Vosti. He enlisted in the US Navy October 7, 1939 in San Francisco, California and completed his basic training at the Naval Training Station in San Diego, California. Anthony reported for duty on the USS Arizona December 20, 1939. He was killed in action on December 7, 1941 at Pearl Harbor, Hawaii. Anthony was awarded the American Defense Service Medal, World War II Victory Medal and Purple Heart Medal posthumously. He remains on duty on the USS Arizona. Anthony is commemorated on the USS Arizona Memorial and the Memorial Tablets of the Missing, National Memorial Cemetery of the Pacific, Honolulu, Hawaii. He was survived by his Sister, Miss Annette Vosti, 625 Market Street, San Francisco, California.

Arizona Football Team[790]

---

[790] Photo of Arizona Football Team provided by Margie Rose-Chirrick.

Wagner, Mearl James Frederick   Ship's Cook, Second Class, Serial No: 336 60 05, US Navy. Mearl was born August 10, 1910 in Collinsville, Illinois to William F. Wagner. He enlisted in the US Navy July 12, 1940 in Los Angeles, California and completed his basic training at the Naval Training Station in San Diego, California. Mearl reported for duty on the USS Arizona August 20, 1940. He was killed in action on December 7, 1941 at Pearl Harbor, Hawaii. Mearl was awarded the American Defense Service Medal, World War II Victory Medal and Purple Heart Medal posthumously. He remains on duty on the USS Arizona. Mearl is commemorated on the USS Arizona Memorial and the Memorial Tablets of the Missing, National Memorial Cemetery of the Pacific, Honolulu, Hawaii. He was survived by his Wife, Mrs. Georgia Harriet (Murphy) Wagner, 2784 Upshur Drive, San Diego, California and his parents, Mr. and Mrs. William F. Wagner, Sr., 214 South Center Street, Collinsville, Illinois.

Wagner, Robert Eugene   Seaman, First Class, Serial No. 328 75 75, US Navy. Robert was born March 29, 1916 in San Francisco, California. He enlisted in the US Navy October 8, 1940 in Minneapolis, Minnesota and completed his basic training at the Naval Training Station in Great Lakes, Illinois. He reported for duty on the USS Arizona December 9, 1940. He was serving on the USS Arizona on December 7, 1941 when the Japanese attacked Pearl Harbor. After the attack, Robert was transferred to the USS Medusa for duty. Robert died October 27, 2001 in Kaneohe, Honolulu, Hawaii.

Wagner, Rudolph Louis   Chief Boatswain's Mate, Serial No. 299 56 56, US Navy. Rudolph was born August 16, 1909. He re-enlisted in the US Navy May 10, 1940. He served on the USS Arizona from August 29, 1927 until December 7, 1941 when the Japanese attacked Pearl Harbor. After the attack, Rudolph was transferred to the US Naval Air Station, Pearl Harbor for duty. Ralph also served in the Korean War. He died November 25, 1977.

Wainwright, Silas Alonzo   Pharmacist's Mate, First Class, Serial No: 238 51 72, US Navy. Silas was born June 22, 1915 in Macomb, New York, the eldest son of Weldon Wainwright and Rachel Lucinda (Ingram) Wainwright. *He had ten brothers and sisters. Silas attended school in the Macomb area until entering the Dean High School in Gouverneur in September 1928. During his high school years, he was active in nearly every extra-curricular affair the school sponsored. He was outstanding in football, with that and the French Club being his favorites. After graduating from high school in 1932, he worked on the farm with his parents until October 8, 1935 when he was sworn into the U.S. Navy at Albany. His three month boot camp was at Newport N.T.S., in Newport, Rhode Island. He first wanted to become a doctor but later changed his goal to a lab tech specializing in x-ray work.* He reenlisted for four more years on October 7, 1939. Silas reported for duty on the USS Arizona January 25, 1941. He was killed in action on December 7, 1941 at Pearl Harbor, Hawaii. Silas was awarded the American Defense

---

[791] Silas Alonzo Wainwright, "Local VFW salutes Silas Wainwright, Post named in honor of native who died at Pearl Harbor in '41" by Dick Sterling, Gouveneur Tribune Press, Thursday, December 11, 2003, page 2.

Service Medal, World War II Victory Medal and Purple Heart Medal posthumously. He remains on duty on the USS Arizona. Silas is commemorated on the USS Arizona Memorial, the Memorial Tablets of the Missing, National Memorial Cemetery of the Pacific, Honolulu, Hawaii and Pleasant Lake Cemetery, Brasie Corners, Macomb, New York. He was survived by his Father, Mr. Weldon Wainwright, Route 1, Gouverneur, New York. The Gouverneur VFW Post 6338 was named the Silas Wainwright VFW in his honor.

Wait, Wayland Lemoyne Seaman, First Class, Serial No: 385 79 57, US Navy. Wayland was born in Washington State, the son of Wayland Douglas and Mary Bernice (Hershey) Wait. He enlisted in the US Navy November 15, 1938 in Seattle, Washington and completed his basic training at the Naval Training Station in San Diego, California. He reported for duty on the USS Arizona March 11, 1939. Wayland was killed in action on December 7, 1941 at Pearl Harbor, Hawaii. He was awarded the American Defense Service Medal, World War II Victory Medal and Purple Heart Medal posthumously. Wayland remains on duty on the USS Arizona. He is commemorated on the USS Arizona Memorial and the Memorial Tablets of the Missing, National Memorial Cemetery of the Pacific, Honolulu, Hawaii. Wayland was survived by his Father, Mr. Wayland Douglas Wait, General Delivery, Longview, Washington.

Walker, Bill Seaman, First Class, Serial No: 360 18 76, US Navy. Bill was born in 1923, son of John W. Walker and Agnes Walker. He enlisted in the US Navy July 15, 1940 in Houston, Texas and completed his basic training at the Naval Training Station in San Diego, California. Bill reported for duty on the USS Arizona October 1, 1940. He was killed in action on December 7, 1941 at Pearl Harbor, Hawaii. Bill was awarded the American Defense Service Medal, World War II Victory Medal and Purple Heart Medal posthumously. He remains on duty on the USS Arizona. Bill is commemorated on the USS Arizona Memorial and the Memorial Tablets of the Missing, National Memorial Cemetery of the Pacific, Honolulu, Hawaii. He was survived by his Older Brother, Mr. Latell Walker, 1719 Maury Street, Houston, Texas.

Walker, James Edward Quartermaster, Second Class, Serial No. 356 09 01, US Navy. James was born March 4, 1917 in Muskogee, Oklahoma, the son of James Edward and Mary Elizabeth (Rutledge) Walker. He enlisted in the US Navy January 21, 1938 in Dallas, Texas and completed his basic training at the Naval Training Station in San Diego, California. He reported for duty on the USS Arizona April 28, 1938. He was serving on the USS Arizona on December 7, 1941 when the Japanese attacked Pearl Harbor. James was a Naval Photographer. He took many of the photos of Pearl Harbor burning. After the attack, James was transferred to the USS Tern (AM-31) for duty. James died November 20, 1998 in Seattle, Washington.

Wallace, Houston Oliver Watertender, First Class, Serial No: 346 36 73, US Navy. Houston was born May 22, 1910 in Arkansas. He re-enlisted in the US Navy July 7, 1939 in San Diego, California and reported for duty on the USS Arizona August 12, 1939. Houston had been in the Navy for 14 ½ years. Houston was killed in action on December 7, 1941 at Pearl Harbor, Hawaii. He was awarded the American Defense Service Medal, World War II Victory Medal and Purple Heart Medal posthumously. Houston remains on duty on the USS Arizona. He is commemorated on the USS Arizona Memorial and the Memorial Tablets of the Missing, National Memorial Cemetery of the Pacific, Honolulu, Hawaii and Buckner Memorial Cemetery, Buckner,

Arkansas. Houston was survived by his Mother, Mrs. Mildred McCullain, Stamps, Arkansas, six sisters and two brothers.[792]

Wallace, James Frank Seaman, First Class, Serial No: 300 19 51, US Navy. James was born February 6, 1919 in New Haven, Wisconsin, son of James Michael Wallace and Clara Louisa (Cooper) Wallace. When he was a little boy, he and his brother, Chuck, used to entertain for Al Capone when he would come up to Wisconsin by playing the guitar and singing. He was a CCC enrollee at the Nepco Lake side camp in Wisconsin Rapids until his enlistment in the Navy October 15, 1940 in Chicago, Illinois. James completed his basic training at the Naval Training Station in Great Lakes, Illinois. He reported for duty on the USS Arizona December 9, 1940. James was killed in action on December 7, 1941 at Pearl Harbor, Hawaii. His family received notification of his death on his twenty-third birthday, February 6, 1942. James was awarded the American Defense Service Medal, World War II Victory Medal and Purple Heart Medal posthumously. James remains on duty on the USS Arizona. He is commemorated on the USS Arizona Memorial, the Memorial Tablets of the Missing, National Memorial Cemetery of the Pacific, Honolulu, Hawaii and Rock Gould Cemetery, Grand Marsh, Wisconsin. James was survived by his Parents, Mr. and Mrs. James M. Wallace, Route 1, Adams, Wisconsin and sisters, Mrs. Valetta Lovelace of Adams, WI, Mrs. Mary Johnson and Mrs. Violet Carlson both of Wisconsin Rapids, WI and Dolly Wallace of Adams, WI and brothers, Charles Wallace of Wisconsin Rapids, WI, Arthur and Michael Wallace of Adams, WI.[793]

Wallace, Ralph Leroy Fireman, Third Class, Serial No: 393 42 73, US Navy. Ralph was born March 29, 1920 in Coburg, Oregon, son of Kestner Harrison Wallace and Mabel Leona (Ingram) Wallace. He attended Monroe High School where he was a basketball star. Ralph enlisted in the US Navy November 6, 1940 in Portland, Oregon and completed his basic training at the Naval Training Station in San Diego, California. He reported for duty on the USS Arizona January 11, 1941. Ralph was killed in action on December 7, 1941 at Pearl Harbor, Hawaii. He was awarded the American Defense Service Medal, World War II Victory Medal and Purple Heart Medal posthumously. Ralph remains on duty on the USS Arizona. He is commemorated on the USS Arizona Memorial, the Memorial Tablets of the Missing, National Memorial Cemetery of the Pacific, Honolulu, Hawaii and Belfountain Cemetery, Belfountain, Oregon. Ralph was survived by his Parents, Mr. and Mrs. Kestner H. Wallace, Route 1, Monroe, Oregon, three brothers, Harrison, Louis, Harvey Wallace, and one sister, Patricia Ann.[794]

---

[792] Vernon Wesley Woods, information from The Times, Shreveport, Louisiana, May 5, 1942, Page 16.

[793] James Frank Wallace, Information and photo provided by family members, Nettie and Stephanie Smith.

[794] Ralph Leroy Wallace, Photo from The Eugene Guard Newspaper, Eugene, Oregon, Tuesday, May 5, 1942, Page 1.

Wallenstein, Richard Henry   Seaman, First Class, Serial No: 385 94 37, US Navy. Richard was born on November 17, 1923 in Chehalis, Washington, the son of Julius Cilas and Charlotte Nanna (Stevens) Wallenstein. He enlisted in the US Navy December 13, 1940 in Seattle, Washington and completed his basic training at the Naval Training Station in San Diego, California. Richard reported for duty on the USS Arizona April 26, 1941. He was killed in action on December 7, 1941 at Pearl Harbor, Hawaii. Richard was awarded the American Defense Service Medal, World War II Victory Medal and Purple Heart Medal posthumously. He remains on duty on the USS Arizona. Richard is commemorated on the USS Arizona Memorial and the Memorial Tablets of the Missing, National Memorial Cemetery of the Pacific, Honolulu, Hawaii. He was survived by his Father, Mr. Julius Cilas Wallenstein, 405 Davis Street, Rawlins, Wyoming.[795]

Walsh, Homan Leavell   Ensign, Serial No. 0-09266, US Navy. Homan was born August 20, 1914. He was commissioned in the US Navy January 18, 1940 and reported for duty on the USS Arizona where he was serving as S Division Officer on December 7, 1941 when the Japanese attacked Pearl Harbor. His battle station was Radio Central. Homan died in April of 1983 in Virginia Beach, Virginia. [796]

Walters, Clarence Arthur   Seaman, Second Class, Serial No: 376 35 05, US Navy. Clarence was born September 20, 1922 in Riverside, California to Phillip and Nora E. (Brown) Walters. He enlisted in the US Navy June 21, 1941 in San Francisco, California and completed his basic training at the Naval Training Station in San Diego, California. Clarence reported for duty on the USS Arizona August 29, 1941. He was killed in action on December 7, 1941 at Pearl Harbor, Hawaii. Clarence was awarded the American Defense Service Medal, World War II Victory Medal and Purple Heart Medal posthumously. He remains on duty on the USS Arizona. Clarence is commemorated on the USS Arizona Memorial and the Memorial Tablets of the Missing, National Memorial Cemetery of the Pacific, Honolulu, Hawaii. He was survived by his Father, Mr. Phillip Walters, Route 2, Box 144, Madera, California.

Walters, William "Billy" Spurgeon, Jr.   Fire Controlman, Third Class, Serial No: 372 16 24, US Navy. Billy was born December 16, 1921 in Tucumcari, New Mexico, the son of William Spurgeon and Nancy Louise (Tompkins) Walters. He attended Tucumcari High School for three years before enlisting in the US Navy August 3, 1940 in Denver, Colorado. Billy completed his basic training at the Naval Training Station in San Diego, California. He reported for duty on the USS Arizona October 14, 1940. Assigned death #520, Billy died on December 24, 1941 from wounds received in action on December 7,

---

[795] Richard Henry Wallenstein, Photo from the 1942 Rawlins High School Yearbook, Rawlins, Wyoming.
[796] Homan Leavell Walsh, Photo, Cornhusker Yearbook, University of Nebraska, Lincoln, Nebraska, 1934.

1941 at Pearl Harbor, Hawaii.[797] He was awarded the American Defense Service Medal, World War II Victory Medal and Purple Heart Medal posthumously. Billy's remains were recovered and he was buried in Plot C, Row 0, Grave 1630, National Memorial Cemetery of the Pacific, Honolulu, Hawaii. He is commemorated on the USS Arizona Memorial. Billy was survived by his Mother, Mrs. Nancy Louise Lasley, 323 Smith Street, Tucumcari, New Mexico four sisters, Louise, Betty Ann, Carolyn and Georgene and one brother, Dick Walters. For those mothers' who had sons serving in the Navy or Marines, a Mother's Club was organized. In memory of Billy, the club was called the Billy Walters Navy Mother's Club. On November 29, 2012, in Tucumcari, New Mexico, Mayor Curnutt proclaimed December 7, 2012 as William Spurgeon Walters, Jr. Day.[798]

Walther, Edward Alfred Fire Controlman, Third Class, Serial No: 279 72 61, US Navy. Edward was born September 5, 1922 in Kenton County, Kentucky, eldest son of Edward Joseph Walther and Helen (Miller) Walther. He enlisted in the US Navy September 5, 1940 in Cincinnati, Ohio and reported for duty on the USS Arizona December 4, 1940. Edward was killed in action on December 7, 1941 at Pearl Harbor, Hawaii. He was awarded the American Defense Service Medal, World War II Victory Medal and Purple Heart Medal posthumously. Edward remains on duty on the USS Arizona. He is commemorated on the USS Arizona Memorial and the Memorial Tablets of the Missing, National Memorial Cemetery of the Pacific, Honolulu, Hawaii. Edward was survived by his Mother, Mrs. Helen (Miller) Walther Leach, 115 West 33rd Street, Covington, Kentucky.

Walton, Alva Dowding Yeoman, Third Class, Serial No: 368 48 80, US Navy. Alva was born March 18, 1922 in Salt Lake City, Utah, son of Ephriam Ruben Walton and Henrietta (Dowding) Walton. His father died in 1930. Alva graduated from Granite High School eight days before he enlisted. He enlisted in the US Navy December 7, 1939 in Salt Lake City, Utah and completed his basic training at the Naval Training Station in San Diego, California. Alva reported for duty on the USS Arizona September 8, 1940. He was killed in action on December 7, 1941 at Pearl Harbor, Hawaii. Alva was awarded the American Defense Service Medal, World War II Victory Medal and Purple Heart Medal posthumously. He remains on duty on the USS Arizona. Alva is commemorated on the USS Arizona Memorial and the Memorial Tablets of the Missing, National Memorial Cemetery of the Pacific, Honolulu, Hawaii. He was survived by his Mother, Mrs. Henrietta Walton Bramble, 3052 South 3rd East Street, Salt Lake City, Utah, brother, Woodrow Walton and sisters Mrs. Donna Weiss and Mrs. Mae Crabbe.[799]

---

[797] Report of Changes of the USS Arizona for the month ending 31st day of December, 1941, Page 108, line 24, William Spurgeon Walters, Jr.
[798] William Spurgeon Walters, Jr, Photo provided by Linda Moore, City of Tucumcari Historical Museum, Tucumcari, New Mexico.
[799] Alva Dowding Walton, Photo from Granite High School, Salt Lake City, Utah Class of 1939, Information from "Navy Reveals S.L. Sailor Died in Action" The Salt Lake Tribune, February 6, 1942, Page 14.

Ward, Albert Lewis Seaman, First Class, Serial No: 356 21 73, US Navy. Albert was born January 26, 1921 in Florida. Upon the death of his mother, Albert became an orphan at the age of five and went to live with relations in Illinois. When he was 10, he was sent to live with his uncle Joe Gault in Sapulpa. He graduated Sapulpa High School in 1939. After graduation, he served in a print shop learning linotype. Albert enlisted in the US Navy December 7, 1939 in Dallas, Texas and completed his basic training at the Naval Training Station in San Diego, California. He reported for duty on the USS Arizona February 24, 1940. Albert was killed in action on December 7, 1941 at Pearl Harbor, Hawaii. Albert was awarded the American Defense Service Medal, World War II Victory Medal and Purple Heart Medal posthumously. He remains on duty on the USS Arizona. Albert is commemorated on the USS Arizona Memorial and the Memorial Tablets of the Missing, National Memorial Cemetery of the Pacific, Honolulu, Hawaii. He was survived by his Guardian, Mrs. Dora Gault, 200 South Mounds Street, Sapulpa, Oklahoma.[800]

Ward, James Robert Seaman, First Class, Serial No. 295 76 71, US Navy. James enlisted in the US Navy October 4, 1940 in Nashville, Tennessee and completed his basic training at the Naval Training Station in Norfolk, Virginia. He reported for duty on the USS Arizona December 4, 1940. He was serving on the USS Arizona on December 7, 1941 when the Japanese attacked Pearl Harbor. After the attack, James was transferred to the USS Neosho for duty.

Ward, William "Billy" Ernest Coxswain, Serial No: 337 14 22, US Navy. William was born January 27, 1919 in Christian County, Illinois, the son of Ernest and Ella Maronia (Renfro) Ward. He enlisted in the US Navy May 12, 1939 in St. Louis, Missouri and completed his basic training at the Naval Training Station in San Diego, California. He reported for duty on the USS Arizona September 8, 1939. William was killed in action on December 7, 1941 at Pearl Harbor, Hawaii. He was awarded the American Defense Service Medal, World War II Victory Medal and Purple Heart Medal posthumously. William remains on duty on the USS Arizona. He is commemorated on the USS Arizona Memorial and the Memorial Tablets of the Missing, National Memorial Cemetery of the Pacific, Honolulu, Hawaii. William was survived by his Father, Mr. Ernest Ward, General Delivery, Stonington, Illinois.[801]

Warriner, Kenneth Thomas Seaman, Second Class, Serial No. 300 30 98, US Navy. Kenneth was born on April 11, 1923 in Camp Douglas, Wisconsin, son of Sherman Warriner and Alma (Schmiedel) Warriner. He enlisted in the US Navy January 7, 1941 in Chicago, Illinois and completed his basic training at the Naval Training Station in Great Lakes, Illinois. He reported for duty on the USS Arizona April 29, 1941. Kenneth was at the Fleet Signal School in San Diego, California on December 7, 1941 when the Japanese attacked Pearl Harbor. Kenneth was on shore leave when the attack occurred. His brother, Russell Walter was on board the Arizona and was badly burned during the attack. This was the only set of brothers to survive the attack. Kenneth passed away January 29, 2001 in Beloit, Wisconsin.

---

[800] Albert Lewis Ward, Information and photo from "Students Remember Pearl Harbor, Ward" by John McCracken, Staff Writer, The Sapulpa Daily Herald, Sapulpa, OK, Wednesday, December 7, 2005.
[801] William Ernest Ward, Photo provided by family member, Holly Becker.

Warriner, Russell Walter   Seaman, First Class, Serial No. 300 18 83, US Navy. Russell was born January 20, 1916 in Camp Douglas, Wisconsin, son of Sherman Warriner and Alma (Schmiedl) Warriner. He enlisted in the US Navy October 8, 1940 in Chicago, Illinois and completed his basic training at the Naval Training Station in Great Lakes, Illinois. Russell reported for duty on the USS Arizona December 9, 1940. He was serving on the USS Arizona on December 7, 1941 when the Japanese attacked Pearl Harbor. Russell was badly burned during the attack and was transferred to the US Naval Hospital at Mare Island, California. His brother, Kenneth was on shore leave when the attack occurred. This was the only set of brothers to survive the attack. Russell died on November 30, 1998 in Beloit, Wisconsin. He was survived by his wife, Elsa P. (Schild) Warriner, daughter Suzanne, son Russell, four grandchildren; sister Arlene and brother Kenneth.

Washington, Joseph Henry   Mess Attendant, First Class, Serial No. 262 22 20, US Navy. Joseph was born on March 20, 1919. He enlisted in the US Navy August 9, 1937 in Raleigh, North Carolina and reported for duty on the USS Arizona December 18, 1937. Joseph was serving on the USS Arizona on December 7, 1941 when the Japanese attacked Pearl Harbor. After the attack, Joseph was transferred to the USS Dale (DD-353) for duty. He died on June 13, 2006 in South Carolina and is buried in Nazareth Re Church Cemetery, Pinopolis, South Carolina.

Watkins, Lenvil Leo   Fireman, Second Class, Serial No: 287 21 81, US Navy. Lenvil was born September 30, 1919 in Muhlenburg County, Kentucky, the son of Robert Albert Watkins and Mary (Pevelar) Watkins. He enlisted in the US Navy October 5, 1937 in Louisville, Kentucky and reported for duty on the USS Arizona February 5, 1938. Lenvil was killed in action on December 7, 1941 at Pearl Harbor, Hawaii. He was awarded the American Defense Service Medal, World War II Victory Medal and Purple Heart Medal posthumously. Lenvil remains on duty on the USS Arizona. He is commemorated on the USS Arizona Memorial and the Memorial Tablets of the Missing, National Memorial Cemetery of the Pacific, Honolulu, Hawaii. Lenvil was survived by his Father, Mr. Robert Albert Watkins, 725 East Jefferson Street, Louisville, Kentucky.

Watson, Howard Lincoln   Boatswain's Mate, First Class, Serial No. 336 96 31, US Navy. Howard was born February 12, 1919 in Illinois. He enlisted in the US Navy March 16, 1937 in St. Louis, Missouri and reported for duty on the USS Arizona July 24, 1937. He was serving on the USS Arizona on December 7, 1941 when the Japanese attacked Pearl Harbor. During the attack, he was taken on board the USS Tennessee. Afterward, Howard was transferred to salvage duty on the USS Utah. He died June 15, 1971 in Los Angeles, California.

Watson, William Lafayette   Fireman, Third Class, Serial No: 393 54 13, US Navy. William was born in March of 1920. He enlisted in the US Navy April 24, 1941 in Portland, Oregon and completed his basic training at the Naval Training Station in San Diego, California. He reported for duty on the USS Arizona on November 18, 1941. William was killed in action on December 7, 1941 at Pearl Harbor, Hawaii. He was awarded the American Defense Service Medal, World War II Victory Medal and Purple Heart Medal posthumously. William remains on duty on the USS Arizona. He is commemorated on the USS Arizona Memorial and the Memorial Tablets of the Missing, National Memorial Cemetery of the Pacific, Honolulu, Hawaii and

Shelfer Cemetery, Havana, Florida. William was survived by his Father, Mr. J. B. Watson, R.F.D. 1, Havana, Florida.

Watts, Sherman Maurice Hospital Apprentice, First Class, Serial No: 376 13 34, US Navy. Sherman was born in 1918 in Arkansas. He enlisted in the US Navy October 10, 1940 in San Francisco, California and completed his basic training at the Naval Training Station in San Diego, California. Sherman reported for duty on the USS Arizona October 11, 1941. He was killed in action on December 7, 1941 at Pearl Harbor, Hawaii. Sherman was awarded the American Defense Service Medal, World War II Victory Medal and Purple Heart Medal posthumously. He remains on duty on the USS Arizona. Sherman is commemorated on the USS Arizona Memorial and the Memorial Tablets of the Missing, National Memorial Cemetery of the Pacific, Honolulu, Hawaii. He was survived by his Father, Mr. William Edgar Watts, Pleasant Plains, Arkansas. The Watts & Aunspaugh VFW Post 10007 in Pleasant Plains, Arkansas was named in his honor.[802]

Watts, Victor Ed Gunner's Mate, Third Class, Serial No: 356 06 46, US Navy. Victor was born May 22, 1918 in Navarro, Texas, the son of Thad Tucker Watts and Mattie Lucy (Jordan) Watts. He enlisted in the US Navy November 14, 1938 in Dallas, Texas and completed his basic training at the Naval Training Station in San Diego, California. Victor reported for duty on board the USS Arizona March 11, 1939. He was killed in action on December 7, 1941 at Pearl Harbor, Hawaii. Victor was awarded the American Defense Service Medal, World War II Victory Medal and Purple Heart Medal posthumously. He remains on duty on the USS Arizona. Victor is commemorated on the USS Arizona Memorial and the Memorial Tablets of the Missing, National Memorial Cemetery of the Pacific, Honolulu, Hawaii. He was survived by his Father, Mr. Thad Tucker Watts, Route A, Box 285, Corsicana, Texas.[803]

Weaver, Richard Duncan Boatswain's Mate, First Class, Serial No. 291 52 37, US Navy. Richard was born July 5, 1918 in Dekalb County, Indiana to Daniel H. and Janette (Connors) Weaver. He enlisted in the US Navy November 4, 1937 in Indianapolis, Indiana and reported for duty on the USS Arizona February 26, 1938. Richard was serving on the USS Arizona on December 7, 1941 when the Japanese attacked Pearl Harbor. In January of 1942 he was transferred via the USS Tippecanoe to the Navy Yard, Puget Sound, Bremerton, Washington. On October 11, 1943 he was appointed to an Ensign while serving on board the USS Santa Fe. Richard died December 29, 1978 and is buried in Section 3, Site 1131 in the Santa Fe National Cemetery, Santa Fe, New Mexico.

---

[802] Sherman Maurice Watts, Photo provided by the Watts & Aunspaugh VFW Post 10007, Pleasant Plains, AR.

[803] Victor Ed Watts, Photo and information provided by family member, Ross Douglas Hines.

Weaver, Richard Walter Seaman, First Class, Serial No: 376 16 98, US Navy. Richard was born August 16, 1923 in Fallon, Nevada, the son of Ray Rhese Weaver and Margaret Lois (McCuistion) Weaver. *He was seventeen when he enlisted in the US Navy November 27, 1940 in San Francisco, California. He got his parents to give him permission to enlist. Years later his father, Ray, learned that Richard had gotten into an argument with a teacher and was thrown out of school. That's when he decided to enlist.* Richard completed his basic training at the Naval Training Station in San Diego, California. Richard reported for duty on the USS Arizona January 25, 1941. He was killed in action on December 7, 1941 at Pearl Harbor, Hawaii. He was awarded the American Defense Service Medal, World War II Victory Medal and Purple Heart Medal posthumously. Richard remains on duty on the USS Arizona. He is commemorated on the USS Arizona Memorial and the Memorial Tablets of the Missing, National Memorial Cemetery of the Pacific, Honolulu, Hawaii. Richard was survived by his Father, Mr. Ray Rhese Weaver, Route 1, Box 245, Fallon, Nevada. The Fallon, Nevada airport was named Weaver Field in honor of Richard.[804]

Webster, Harold Dwayne Seaman, Second Class, Serial No: 372 22 60, US Navy. Harold was born on October 21, 1923 in Loveland, Colorado to Bryan William Webster. He enlisted in the Navy December 7, 1940 in Denver, Colorado at the age of 17 and completed his basic training at the Naval Training Station in San Diego, California. Harold reported for duty on the USS Arizona June 25, 1941. He was killed in action on December 7, 1941 at Pearl Harbor, Hawaii. Harold was awarded the American Defense Service Medal, World War II Victory Medal and Purple Heart Medal posthumously and earned the American Defense Medal, World War II Victory Medal and The American Legion Gold Star Citation. He remains on duty on the USS Arizona. Harold is commemorated on the USS Arizona Memorial and the Memorial Tablets of the Missing, National Memorial Cemetery of the Pacific, Honolulu, Hawaii. He was survived by his Father, Mr. Bryan William Webster, Route 2, Box 115, Loveland, Colorado. The former Lakeside Park in Loveland, Colorado was renamed Dwayne Webster Veterans Park, in honor of Harold.

Weeden, Carl "Bud" Alfred Ensign, Serial No: 0-085062, US Navy. Carl was born on April 14, 1916 in Trinidad, Colorado. He was appointed a midshipman at the Naval Academy on June 22, 1936. Carl received his first commission on June 6, 1940 and reported for duty to the USS Arizona on June 9, 1940. Carl served as Assistant 1st Lt. Division R Officer. His battle station was Repair III. Carl was killed in action on December 7, 1941 when the Japanese attacked Pearl Harbor. He was posthumously awarded the American Defense Service Medal, Fleet Clasp, World War II Victory Medal and Purple Heart Medal and the Asiatic-Pacific Area Campaign Medal. Carl remains on duty on the USS Arizona. He is commemorated on the USS Arizona Memorial and the Memorial Tablets of the Missing, National Memorial Cemetery of

---

[804] Richard Walter Weaver, Photo from David Benson, information from The Reno Gazette-Journal.

the Pacific, Honolulu, Hawaii. Carl was survived by his Father, Mr. C. M. Weeden, 1952 Divisadero, San Francisco, California. The destroyer escort USS Weeden (DE-797) was named in his honor.[805]

Weidell, William "Bill" Peter Seaman, Second Class, Serial No: 328 83 69, US Navy. William was born December 14, 1922 in St. Paul, Minnesota, the oldest of four sons of William Wenzel Weidell and Lorinda Marie (Pluff) Weidell. He enlisted in the US Navy January 14, 1941 in Minneapolis, Minnesota and attended Naval Aviation School on Terminal Island, California. William reported for duty on the USS Arizona July 11, 1941. In a letter home, Billy was looking forward to a furlough home with his folks, anticipating being home for his birthday and Christmas. He was killed in action on December 7, 1941 at Pearl Harbor, Hawaii. The family received official news on February 5, 1942 that he was lost during the attack. William was awarded the American Defense Service Medal, World War II Victory Medal and Purple Heart Medal posthumously. He remains on duty on the USS Arizona. William is commemorated on the USS Arizona Memorial and the Memorial Tablets of the Missing, National Memorial Cemetery of the Pacific, Honolulu, Hawaii. He was survived by his Father, Mr. William Weidell, 1001 Marion Street, St. Paul, Minnesota.[806]

Welch, Frank, Jr. Ensign, US Navy. Frank was born in about 1919 in Louisiana to Frank and Emily L. Welch. Appointed from San Diego, California, he attended the United States Naval Academy in Annapolis, Maryland and was commissioned Ensign in the US Navy February 7, 1941. Frank was serving on the USS Arizona as Junior Watch and Division L Officer. His battle station was Aft Battle Lookout. He was serving on December 7, 1941 when the Japanese attacked Pearl Harbor.[807] Frank was assigned temporary duty on the USS Saratoga after the attack. He was detached from the Navy on September 14, 1942. His mother was listed as his next of kin, Mrs. Frank Welch, 3315 Second Avenue, San Diego, California.

---

[805] Carl "Bud" Alfred Weeden, Information and photo provided by his half brother, Ray Weeden. Additional information from USS Weeden, Dictionary of American Naval Fighting Ships.
[806] William "Bill" Peter Weidell, Information and photo provided by family member, Ruth Gensman.
[807] Frank Welch, Jr, Photo, Lucky Bag Yearbook, United States Naval Academy, Annapolis, Maryland, Class of 1941.

Weller, Ludwig Frederick Chief Storekeeper, Serial No: 242 90 59, US Navy. Ludwig was born in 1905 in Pennsylvania, the son of Ludwig and Anna C. Weller. He re-enlisted in the US Navy December 5, 1940. He served on the USS Arizona from December 19, 1934 until he was killed in action on December 7, 1941 at Pearl Harbor, Hawaii. Ludwig was awarded the American Defense Service Medal, World War II Victory Medal and Purple Heart Medal posthumously. He remains on duty on the USS Arizona. Ludwig is commemorated on the USS Arizona Memorial and the Memorial Tablets of the Missing, National Memorial Cemetery of the Pacific, Honolulu, Hawaii. He was survived by his Wife, Mrs. Hope Eva Weller, 122 East 52nd Street, Long Beach, California, son, William F. and daughter, Caroline S. Weller.[808]

Weller, Oree Cunningham Seaman, Second Class, Serial No. 360 37 30, US Navy. Oree was born on September 16, 1922 in Harris County, Texas, the son of Victor Charles and Evelyn (Cunningham) Weller. He enlisted in the US Navy April 18, 1941 in Houston, Texas and completed his basic training at the Naval Training Station in San Diego, California. He reported for duty on the USS Arizona July 13, 1941. He was serving on the USS Arizona on December 7, 1941 when the Japanese attacked Pearl Harbor. Oree was wounded in action during the attack and his parents, Mr. and Mrs. Victor C. and Evelyn Weller were notified. He later went on to serve on the USS Mugford. Oree died on September 7, 1993 in Bellevue, Washington.

Wells, Floyd Arthur Radioman, Second Class, Serial No: 328 52 11, US Navy. Floyd was born April 18, 1917, the son of Earl C. and Edna M. Wells of North Dakota. He enlisted in the US Navy April 5, 1938 in Minneapolis, Minnesota and reported for duty on the USS Arizona December 13, 1938. Floyd survived the attack on December 7, 1941 at Pearl Harbor, Hawaii. He was taken on board the USS Tennessee, badly wounded, he was sent to the Naval Hospital at Pearl Harbor. He did not survive the trip. Floyd was awarded the American Defense Service Medal, World War II Victory Medal and Purple Heart Medal posthumously. It is believed that he was buried in the Punchbowl cemetery marked as "unknown". Floyd is still listed as missing in action. He is commemorated on the USS Arizona Memorial and the Memorial Tablets of the Missing, National Memorial Cemetery of the Pacific, Honolulu, Hawaii and the Cavalier Cemetery, Cavalier, North Dakota. Floyd was survived by his Father, Mr. Earl Curtiss Wells, Fairdale, North Dakota.[809]

Wells, Harold Leroy Seaman, First Class, Serial No. 311 49 70, US Navy. Harold was born October 19, 1901. He enlisted in the US Navy September 9, 1940 in Detroit, Michigan and completed his basic training at the Naval Training Station in Norfolk, Virginia. He reported for duty on the USS Arizona December 4, 1940. He was serving on the USS Arizona on December 7, 1941 when the Japanese attacked Pearl Harbor. After the attack, Harold was transferred to the USS Lexington for duty. Harold served until September 30, 1970. He died June 28, 1986.

---

[808] Ludwig Frederick Weller, photo provided by family member, Bonnie Hopman Reyonlds.
[809] Floyd Arthur Wells, Photo provided by family member, Neal L. Martin.

Wells, Harvey Anthony   Shipfitter, Second Class, Serial No: 287 13 58, US Navy. Harvey was born June 30, 1917 in Grayson County, Kentucky, the son of Harvey W. Wells and Mattie Gertrude (Heaverin) Wells. He enlisted in the US Navy July 29, 1935 in Louisville, Kentucky and reported for duty on the USS Arizona November 23, 1935. Harvey died of drowning during the action on December 7, 1941 at Pearl Harbor, Hawaii[810] He was awarded the American Defense Service Medal, World War II Victory Medal and Purple Heart Medal posthumously. Harvey's remains were identified by his name on his shorts and he was buried in Plot B, Row 0, Grave 830, National Memorial Cemetery of the Pacific, Honolulu, Hawaii. He is commemorated on the USS Arizona Memorial. Harvey was survived by his Wife, Mrs. Jeanne Marie Wells, 749 Muscatel Avenue, San Gabriel, California, Mother, Mrs. Gertrude Wells Higdon, Clarkson, Kentucky, Brothers, Charles, Eugene, Wilbur and William Lee Wells and Sisters, Mrs. Floy Taylor and Mrs. Leslie Carman.[811]

Wells, Raymond Virgil, Jr.   Seaman, First Class, Serial No: 342 04 36, US Navy. Raymond was born in March 1919, the son of Raymond "Blackie" Virgil Wells, Sr. and Alice Wells. He enlisted in the US Navy on January 7, 1938 in Joplin, Missouri and completed his basic training at the Naval Training Station in Great Lakes, Illinois. Raymond reported for duty on the USS Arizona April 28, 1938. He was killed in action on December 7, 1941 at Pearl Harbor, Hawaii. Raymond was awarded the American Defense Service Medal, World War II Victory Medal and Purple Heart Medal posthumously. He remains on duty on the USS Arizona. Raymond is commemorated on the USS Arizona Memorial and the Memorial Tablets of the Missing, National Memorial Cemetery of the Pacific, Honolulu, Hawaii. Notification of his missing status was not received until January 1942. He was survived by his Mother, Mrs. Alice Wells, 1025 South Main Street, Nevada, Missouri, one sister, Joan and three brothers, Robert, Jack and Richard Wells. His younger brother, William was also killed in action while serving on the USS Arizona.[812]

Wells, William Bennett   Seaman, First Class, Serial No: 342 19 27, US Navy. William was born July 2, 1922 in Missouri, the son of Raymond "Blackie" Virgil Wells, Sr. and Alice Wells. In February 1934, his father, "Blackie" killed his lover in a suicide pact but he got away with it. Not long after the fatal affair, his father was arrested for armed robbery and went to prison. Because William was still a minor, he had to go before the local courts to have his mother named as his guardian. Five days later, he enlisted in the US Navy February 13, 1940 in Kansas City, Missouri and completed his basic training at the Naval Training Station, Great Lakes, Illinois. William reported for duty on the USS Arizona June 13, 1940. He was killed in action on December 7, 1941 at Pearl Harbor,

---

[810] Harvey Anthony Wells, Report of Changes of the USS Arizona for the month ending 31st day of December 1941, page 109, line 13.
[811] Harvey Anthony Wells, Photo from California Honor States.
[812] Raymond Virgil Wells, Photo and information provided by the Bushwhacker Museum, Vernon County Historical Society, Nevada, MO. They provided several articles from the Nevada Daily Mail Newspaper, Nevada, Missouri.

Hawaii. William was awarded the American Defense Service Medal, World War II Victory Medal and Purple Heart Medal posthumously. He remains on duty on the USS Arizona. William is commemorated on the USS Arizona Memorial and the Memorial Tablets of the Missing, National Memorial Cemetery of the Pacific, Honolulu, Hawaii. His mother was notified of his missing in action status two days before Christmas. He was survived by his Mother, Mrs. Alice Wells, 1025 South Main Street, Nevada, Missouri, one sister, Joan and three brothers, Robert, Jack and Richard. William's older brother, Raymond was also killed in action while serving on the USS Arizona.[813]

Welter, Edward "Eddie" Charles Seaman, First Class, Serial No. 382 30 56, US Navy. Eddie was born February 3, 1922 in Crookston, Minnesota the son of Fred and Elizabeth Edabarn Welter. He enlisted in the US Navy November 9, 1940 in Los Angeles, California and completed his basic training at the Naval Training Station in San Diego, California. He reported for duty on the USS Arizona January 11, 1941. He was serving on the USS Arizona on December 7, 1941 when the Japanese attacked Pearl Harbor. After the attack, Eddie was transferred to the Pearl Harbor Naval Shipyard for duty and served until 1946. Edward died Tuesday, February 12, 2013 in Iowa City, Iowa.[814]

Wentzlaff, Edward Louis Aviation Ordnanceman, Second Class, Aviation Unit (VO-1), Serial No. 328 49 91, US Navy. Edward was born on November 16, 1917 in Nicollet, Minnesota, the son of Henry and Leocadio Wentzlaff. He came from a big family. Times were hard due to the depression and there was hardly any work. Edward was working on a sugar beet farm for .15 cents an hour before he enlisted in the US Navy December 8, 1937 in Mankato, Minnesota. He wanted to see the world and the Navy paid much better. Edward went through training at Great Lakes and he was sent to ordnance electrical training school in San Diego for about 8 months. He liked torpedoes so much he asked for an assignment on a submarine but was sent for his first duty on the USS Arizona. Edward served on the USS Arizona, V Division from November 22, 1939 until December 7, 1941 when the Japanese attacked Pearl Harbor. December 7th 1941 was supposed to be his last day of his enlistment. After the attack, all enlistment dates were suspended.

On the Seventh of December a friend and I took an early morning shower because there was a shortage of hot water and if you went early you could get a hot water shower. After dressing, we went up to the foc'sle on the starboard side, about a dozen of us, to await the Sunday Morning services. While we were standing there waiting for church, at about 7:55 am, an airplane came in toward Merry Point and made a big turn. It had a big red ball on the wings and came right down along their side strafing us. There was a wood deck up there on top of the steel deck and you could see the wood splintering from the bullets hitting it. Someone hollered "Get below!" There was a theory that if you were below the second deck it was bomb proof. So we

---

[813] William Bennett Wells, Photo and information provided by the Bushwhacker Museum, Vernon County Historical Society, Nevada, MO. They provided several articles from the Nevada Daily Mail Newspaper, Nevada, MO in addition to a Minor Guardianship probate form from Vernon County, MO.
[814] Edward "Eddie" Charles Welter, Information and photo from WCF Courier, Cedar Valley, Iowa Obituary, February 14, 2013.

turned around and went down the ladder got onto the main deck and there was a ladder that went down to the next deck. I was the last one. Every one of those guys went down there.

Instead, I went to the back of the ship. There was a fire in the Marine compartment pretty near to the quarter deck. There was a fire in the exec compartment, but I got through there to our little cubicle where we hung out, we had 3 airplanes, the planes were on shore. But our crew was there, we had a little cubicle there I told these guys "Hey you better get going, we are being attacked, we are being bombed!" They shrugged and said that's the army. I said "take a look out the porthole over there." Hangers were on fire, airplanes were on fire. Our duty station during an emergency was repair one on the quarterdeck. Three or four of us got out on the quarterdeck and got the hose down. I told the guy don't turn the thing on until we get the nozzle on. "You grab the hose and I will turn it on." All of a sudden there was fire all over and smoke. It burned your hair and eyebrows off. You couldn't see anything for minutes. Turret 3 was ok; the guys came out of there and told us to abandon ship. One of the guys said to me, "Hey, lets go!" I was shaken out of my shock. You couldn't even see the smoke was so thick. It finally cleared and we went out on the deck. They were kicking guys over the side. The water was on fire from the fuel oil. That didn't look good to me so I didn't jump over.

Me and another guy went over to the officer's gangway. The Admiral had been ashore and he had just come aboard. Here was this beautiful barge of his tied to the side of the ship. I said "You get it started and I'll get it loose." It was being pulled under because it was tied to the Arizona which was sinking. I was pulling on a three inch rope, finally realizing I could not pull it apart, I located a flagstaff with a figurehead on it. I used this to chop away at the rope until I cut thru it. We then went over to the other gangway where the enlisted men came on and there stood a gang of them about 10 or 12 of them. They were frightful, all they had on was the band from their skivvies with their names stenciled on them. You couldn't recognize any of them they were burned so badly …. no hair, no eyebrows, and the bottom of their shoes were blown off. We managed to get them on the barge and took them over to the hospital ship, Solace which was about an eighth of a mile away. I can't believe any of them lived.

Then we were ordered to get into motor launches and go around the whole deal and pick up men in the water. The Arizona was the last one on the end. We came around the point there and we had a COX that was steering the boat, he had a twin brother that was on the Arizona. He wanted to go on that ship in the worst way to find his brother. I swore at him "If you go on that ship I'm going to kill ya!" We went around the whole group of ships. We came upon the ship service where they had a store and served meals and stuff. Well there was an overhang of about 15 to 20 feet, and it was just plum full of burned and injured guys. Then we were ordered to take them over the hospital. You know what they wanted? Every one of them asked for a cigarette. They couldn't hardly breathe, a lot of them died from inhaling the flames and smoke from the explosion, but they wanted a cigarette!

Then we went over to Ford Island and took our clothes off and used them to help clean the fuel oil off the other men. There were a bunch of ladies there, officer's wives; they were handing out gym shorts, where were we going to change? This was war! So right now in front of God and everybody, we threw our oil soaked clothes and put on the new ones. I can't believe yet, how much confusion there was.

After that, we went over to the landing. There they gave us rifles and stuff. It got to be dusk by then. The next day we had to go on work parties. We hauled dead out of the California. Then we went to the West Virginia but we couldn't do anything, they were still trying to keep it from going over. They did a good job of it too. It wasn't too long when an officer came along and told us to report up to a hanger. There were 6 hangers there, the one we were assigned had holes in the roof and we could look at the moon and stars above us. Everything was totally disorganized, we wandered around for about three days. We were drinking water out of swimming pools because the fresh water pipes from the main island had been severed when the Arizona went down.

Three days later, they got us together, marched us to the post office, handed out post cards to fill out stating "I'm ok, will write later" and that was all we were allowed to say. Then they took all of us orphans and made a squadron out of us. We cannibalized parts and picked up enough airplanes and stuff for an anti-submarine squadron so they could patrol around the Island. I was in that for about six months or so.

After that, I was assigned the USS Yorktown in time for the Battle of Midway in June 1942. Then I went back to another squadron. Then from there I went to a couple schools. Then finally after 47 months out there they sent me to Norfolk, VA. They kept telling me "we're not letting you go until we get a replacement; I was a warrant officer by then. You know I got back to the states and about every other guy I bumped into was a warrant officer. They were ducking it somehow. I got tired of sitting around so an officer said "Hey we need a warrant officer at Naval Air-station at Chincoteague Island. I said, "I'm going!" so I went over there. We trained the Franklin Roosevelt Carrier Group. I got out after 2 years at that. Excellent experience and the food was fantastic. It was a seafood port, oysters and lobsters. I never had so much shrimp in my life.

You know, I lost a lot of good friends on the Arizona. It's not like you knew everyone by their last name, but you would see a guy and you recognized him "I know you but I don't necessarily know your last name". We had an excellent crew, we were very competitive.

Edward retired from the Navy after 7-1/2 years with a rank of Chief Warrant Officer. He passed away on September 10, 2013 in Minnesota and was interred on the Arizona in December 2013.[815]

West, Broadus Franklin Seaman, First Class, Serial No: 262 50 56, US Navy. Broadus was born in December 9, 1915 in Simpsonville, South Carolina to Marcus Franklin West and Effie Estelle (Wood) West. He enlisted in the US Navy February 8, 1940 in Raleigh, North Carolina and reported for duty on the USS Arizona January 8, 1941. Broadus was killed in action on December 7, 1941 at Pearl Harbor, Hawaii. He was awarded the American Defense Service Medal, World War II Victory Medal and Purple Heart Medal posthumously. Broadus remains on duty on the USS Arizona. He is commemorated on the USS Arizona Memorial and the Memorial Tablets of the Missing, National Memorial Cemetery of the Pacific, Honolulu, Hawaii. Broadus was survived by his Father, Mr. Marcus Franklin West, Box 134, Simpsonville, South Carolina. His cousin, Mark Austin West was also serving on board the USS Arizona on December 7, 1941 and survived the attack.[816]

West, Mark Austin Chief Machinist's Mate, Serial No. 262 18 91, US Navy. Mark was born December 31, 1897 in Simpsonville, South Carolina to Daniel Lafayette and Hattie Jane (Austin) West. He enlisted in the US Navy on December 15, 1920. Mark served on the USS Arizona from June 22, 1935 until December 7, 1941 when the Japanese attacked Pearl Harbor. Mark was on leave status when Pearl Harbor was attacked. After the attack, Mark was transferred to the Submarine Base in Pearl Harbor and later to the USS West Virginia for duty. He died March 28, 1952 in the US Naval Hospital in Bremerton, Washington and is buried in the Washelli Cemetery, Seattle,

---

[815] Edward Louis Wentzlaff, Photo and information provided by himself.
[816] Broadus Franklin West, Photo and information provided by his cousin, Mary Elizabeth West Hopkins.

Washington. His cousin, Broadus Franklin West was also serving on board the USS Arizona and was killed in action that day.[817]

West, Webster Paul   Seaman, First Class, Serial No: 346 87 73, US Navy. Webster was born September 17, 1917 in Searcy, Arkansas, the son of Benjamin Stewart West and Bessie Vituria (Horton) West. He enlisted in the US Navy November 14, 1940 in Little Rock, Arkansas and completed his basic training at the Naval Training Station in San Diego, California. Webster reported for duty on the USS Arizona January 11, 1941. He was killed in action on December 7, 1941 at Pearl Harbor, Hawaii. Webster was awarded the American Defense Service Medal, World War II Victory Medal and Purple Heart Medal posthumously. He remains on duty on the USS Arizona. Webster is commemorated on the USS Arizona Memorial and the Memorial Tablets of the Missing, National Memorial Cemetery of the Pacific, Honolulu, Hawaii and the Canaan Cemetery, Marshall, Arkansas. He was survived by his Father, Mr. Ben Stewart West, Star Route, Canaan, Arkansas.

Westbrook, Clinton Howard   Seaman, First Class, Serial No. 223 69 13, US Navy. Clinton was born on March 1, 1919 in Brooklyn, New York, son of Alfred and Daisy M Westbrook. He enlisted in the US Navy April 2, 1940 in New York, New York and reported for duty on the USS Arizona September 30, 1940. He was serving on the USS Arizona on December 7, 1941 when the Japanese attacked Pearl Harbor. Clinton was in a 50 foot motor launch at the time of the attack, running crew and officers to and from the ship for church services, meals on shore, etc. He was on his way back to the vessel when it blew up. They immediately began rescue work making 3 round trips from Ford Island to the Navy Hospital Landing. During this time, the Japanese planes were continually strafing. He was wounded twice during the rescue operations. He received the Bronze Star Medal for his actions that day. Clinton was transferred to the USS Cunningham for six months. He later served on the USS Taylor and participated in 23 campaigns during WWII including the African Invasion and the recovery of Wake Island survivors. Clinton later served in the Korean War and the Vietnam War and retired from the Navy in August 1969. Clinton passed away on November 30, 2008 and was buried at Arlington National Cemetery.

Westcott, William Percy, Jr.   Seaman, First Class, Serial No: 291 65 78, US Navy. William was born in 1923 in Texas, the eldest son of William Percy Westcott and Eleanor J. Westcott. He lost his mother at a very young age and moved to Peru, Indiana with his Father and step-mother. He enlisted in the US Navy October 8, 1940 in Indianapolis, Indiana and completed his basic training at the Naval Training Station in Great Lakes, Illinois. William reported for duty on the USS Arizona December 9, 1940. He was killed in action on December 7, 1941 at Pearl Harbor, Hawaii. William was awarded the American Defense Service Medal, World War II Victory Medal and Purple Heart Medal posthumously. He remains on duty on the USS Arizona. William is commemorated on the USS Arizona Memorial and the Memorial Tablets of the Missing, National Memorial Cemetery of the Pacific, Honolulu, Hawaii. He was survived by his Father, Mr. William P. Westcott, Sr., 317 East Main Street, Peru, Indiana.[818]

---

[817] Mark Austin West, Photo and information provided by Mark's sister, Mary Elizabeth West Hopkins.

Westerfield, Ivan Ayers Seaman, First Class, Serial No: 382 24 04, US Navy. Ivan was born March 4, 1920 in Knox County, Illinois, the son of Frank Edward and Sara Anna (Lightner) Westerfield. He graduated from Antelope Valley High School in 1938. Ivan enlisted in the US Navy August 6, 1940 in Los Angeles, California and completed his basic training at the Naval Training Station in San Diego, California. He reported for duty on the USS Arizona October 14, 1940. Ivan was killed in action on December 7, 1941 at Pearl Harbor, Hawaii. He was awarded the American Defense Service Medal, World War II Victory Medal and Purple Heart Medal posthumously. Ivan remains on duty on the USS Arizona. He is commemorated on the USS Arizona Memorial and the Memorial Tablets of the Missing, National Memorial Cemetery of the Pacific, Honolulu, Hawaii. Ivan was survived by his Mother, Mrs. Sarah Anna Daugherty, Route 2, Box 296-A, Lancaster, California. The Ivan Ayers Westerfield Veterans Memorial Walkway was dedicated on Veteran's Day at the Veteran's Court of Honor, Lancaster Cemetery District, Lancaster, California. This was brought about by an Antelope Valley High School fundraising project and was attended by over 400 people including family members.[819]

Westin, Donald Vern Fireman, Third Class, Serial No: 393 42 60, US Navy. Donald was born April 13, 1922 in Portland, Oregon, the son of Gust A. Westin and Asta L. Westin. He was attending Edison High School in 1939 when he enrolled in a civilian conservation corps camp near Reedsport. Donald enlisted in the US Navy November 5, 1940 in Portland, Oregon and completed his basic training at the Naval Training Station in San Diego, California. Donald reported for duty on the USS Arizona January 11, 1941. He was killed in action on December 7, 1941 at Pearl Harbor, Hawaii. Donald was awarded the American Defense Service Medal, World War II Victory Medal and Purple Heart Medal posthumously. He remains on duty on the USS Arizona. Donald is commemorated on the USS Arizona Memorial and the Memorial Tablets of the Missing, National Memorial Cemetery of the Pacific, Honolulu, Hawaii. He was survived by his Parents, Mr. and Mrs. Gust A. Westin, 3510 Southeast Taylor Street, Portland, Oregon.

Westlund, Fred Edwin Boatswain's Mate, Second Class, Serial No: 385 61 99, US Navy. Fred was born November 28, 1915 in Snohomish, Washington, the son of Carl Emanuel and Jenny E. Westlund. He re-enlisted in the US Navy July 20, 1938. He served on the USS Arizona from January 7, 1935 until he was killed in action on December 7, 1941 at Pearl Harbor, Hawaii. Fred was awarded the American Defense Service Medal, World War II Victory Medal and Purple Heart Medal posthumously. He remains on duty on the USS Arizona. Fred is commemorated on the USS Arizona Memorial and the Memorial Tablets of the Missing, National Memorial Cemetery of the Pacific, Honolulu, Hawaii. He was survived by his Wife, Mrs. Sue Ann Westlund, 242 Chestnut Avenue, Long Beach, California.[820]

---

[818] William Percy Westcott, Jr., Photo from Indiana Honor States.
[819] Ivan Ayers Westerfield, photo provided by Dayle DeBry, Manager, Lancaster Cemetery, Lancaster, CA.
[820] Fred Edwin Westlund, Photo provided by family member, Magnus Salgo.

Whitaker, John William, Jr. Seaman, First Class, Serial No: 274 45 59, US Navy. John was born on June 4, 1922 in Texas to John W. and Virginia Whitaker. He enlisted in the US Navy June 5, 1940 New Orleans, Louisiana and completed his basic training at the Naval Training Station, San Diego, California. John reported for duty on the USS Arizona September 8, 1940. Assigned death #128, John died on December 10, 1941 from 2nd degree burns received in action on December 7, 1941 at Pearl Harbor, Hawaii.[821] John was awarded the American Defense Service Medal, World War II Victory Medal and Purple Heart Medal posthumously. His remains were recovered and he was sent home for burial in Section R, Site 281, Alexandria National Cemetery, Pineville, Louisiana. He is commemorated on the USS Arizona Memorial. John was survived by his Father, Mr. John W. Whitaker, Sr., Route 2, Pollock, Louisiana.[822]

Whitcomb, Cecil Eugene Electrician's Mate, Third Class, Serial No: 311 49 72, US Navy. Cecil was born January 3, 1922 in Homer, Michigan, the son of Seth Whitcomb and Mary Florence (Mead) Whitcomb. He enlisted in the US Navy September 9, 1940 in Detroit, Michigan and completed his basic training at the Naval Training Station in Norfolk, Virginia. Cecil reported for duty on the USS Arizona December 4, 1940. He was killed in action on December 7, 1941 at Pearl Harbor, Hawaii. Cecil was awarded the American Defense Service Medal, World War II Victory Medal and Purple Heart Medal posthumously. He remains on duty on the USS Arizona. Cecil is commemorated on the USS Arizona Memorial and the Memorial Tablets of the Missing, National Memorial Cemetery of the Pacific, Honolulu, Hawaii. He was survived by his Father, Mr. Seth Whitcomb, 500 West Main Street, Homer, Michigan.

White, Charles William Musician, Second Class, Serial No: 368 62 78, US Navy. Charles was born on April 11, 1920 in Bountiful, Utah to Arthur Edward and Catherine Wanda (Henderson) White. He enlisted in the US Navy March 13, 1941 and graduated the Navy School of Music in Washington Navy Yard on May 23, 1941. He reported for duty on the USS Arizona June 17, 1941. His battle station was in the black powder room, passing ammunition to the Arizona's gunners during the attack. Charles was killed in action on December 7, 1941 at Pearl Harbor, Hawaii. He was awarded the American Defense Service Medal, World War II Victory Medal and Purple Heart Medal posthumously. Charles remains on duty on the USS Arizona. He is commemorated on the USS Arizona Memorial and the Memorial Tablets of the Missing, National Memorial Cemetery of the Pacific, Honolulu, Hawaii. Charles was survived by his Parents, Mr. and Mrs. Arthur E. White, General Delivery, Bountiful, Utah and his Wife, Mrs. Mary Myrlene (Richins) White of Idaho.[823]

---

[821] Report of Changes of the USS Arizona for the month ending 31st day of December, 1941, Page 110, line 25, John William Whitaker, Jr.

[822] John William Whitaker, Jr., Photo provided by his great niece, Sarah Crawford.

[823] Charles William White, Photo from USS Arizona's Last Band by Molly Kent. By permission of the author. For more information about this book, go to www.USSARIZONASLASTBAND.com.

White, James "JC" Clifton Fireman, First Class, Serial No: 356 11 34, US Navy. James was born June 1, 1921 in Rowlett, Texas, the only son of James C. Bryant White and Winnie Faye (McCallum) White. He had one younger sister, Mary that he was very protective of. James enlisted in the US Navy November 14, 1938 in Dallas, Texas and completed his basic training at the Naval Training Station in San Diego, California. He reported for duty on the USS Arizona March 11, 1939. JC was not supposed to be on board the morning of the 7th. He had switched shifts with another person so that he could take an earlier leave and get home to his fiancé and family sooner. He never made it home. James was killed in action on December 7, 1941 at Pearl Harbor, Hawaii. He was awarded the American Defense Service Medal, World War II Victory Medal and Purple Heart Medal posthumously. JC remains on duty on the USS Arizona. He is commemorated on the USS Arizona Memorial and the Memorial Tablets of the Missing, National Memorial Cemetery of the Pacific, Honolulu, Hawaii. JC was survived by his Mother, Mrs. Winnie Faye White, 8136 Diceman Street, Dallas, Texas. After repeated letters to the Navy Department, Bureau of Naval Personnel by his mother, she received a letter January 2, 1943 stating that he had been officially declared to have lost his life.[824]

White, Thomas Arthur Boatswain's Mate, Second Class, Serial No. 265 79 39, US Navy. Thomas enlisted in the US Navy July 6, 1938 in Norfolk, Virginia and completed his basic training at the Naval Training Station in Norfolk, Virginia. He reported for duty on the USS Arizona November 10, 1938. He was serving on the USS Arizona on December 7, 1941 when the Japanese attacked Pearl Harbor. His official statement:

"At 0755 on December 7th when the air raid siren was sounded, I cleared the quarterdeck of sightseers. Then I rounded up the third division men and closed all the starboard side quarterdeck hatches. As we were closing the last hatch, General Quarters was sounded. I went directly to my battle station, pits of #3 turret, and directed by crew to do likewise. As I was putting on the sound power phones there was a big explosion that seemed to be forward. As I got the phones on I received word from the booth to run all men out of the turret to fight fire on topside. As I reached the quarterdeck from the turret I grabbed a fire hose. I yelled for them to turn on the water, but as the explosion forward had put all water mains out of order, just a trickle of water came forth. Then I received orders to go to the engine room and aid them. As I entered the Marine compartment, I was faced by a wall of fire, which was caused by the oil burning on top of the water. As I returned to the quarterdeck the awning had begun to burn. I grabbed a knife from one of my crew and cut it down so it would not fall and burn anyone. I then reported back to my superior that I could not reach the engine room. Then I got orders to open hatches on the quarterdeck. I went down the Admiral's hatch to get fire extinguishers, as I couldn't breathe below I promptly returned to topside. As I got on topside, I never saw my Division Officer, who had gone down with me. So I turned around and went below to look for him. I found him in the Captain's Cabin looking for the Captain as we never knew whether or not he had got to the bridge, so we returned to the quarterdeck. The orders came to abandon ship. Then I manned the Captain's Gig, as the ship was rapidly settling. The gig was nearly pinned down by the starboard quarter boom, but finally managed to free it with the help of 2 or 3 of my shipmates. Then I took some able bodied men to landing B at Ford Island to man the boats which were secured there. I returned to the ship and fouled the screw

---

[824] James "JC" Clifton White, Photo and information provided by his Great Niece, Jessica Halsell.

with a piece of canvas. I then dived under the gig and tried to clear the screw. As I was unable to do it, I swam to an abandoned Nevada motor whaleboat and returned to the ship. Then I proceeded to pick up men who were attempting to swim to Ford Island. When I had picked all men who had not reached safety I took them to landing B at Ford Island. Then as I glanced back at the Arizona something appeared to be wrong. I then noticed the Colors had not yet been run up. I returned to the ship to run up the Colors. When I had completed running up the Colors I started looking for any dead or injured persons lying around on the quarterdeck who had not managed to escape, bur there were none. I left the Arizona in the whaleboat and headed for landing B. The attackers were attempting to strafe the landing so I decided to go to the Solace. As I was going by the pipe line I tried to pick up two yard workmen but they refused to come, and stuck to their job. Then I noticed that the Solace had got underway so I headed across the channel and was strafed on the crossing but luckily I was not hit. Then I reported to the Submarine Base Dispensary. I then took a bath in gasoline, then glycerin, and good hot soapy water to get the oil off my body. I had got when trying to clear the Gig's screw. Then I received orders to report to the Receiving Station which I did and reported in as an Arizona survivor."[825]

White, Vernon Russell Seaman, First Class, Serial No: 262 67 84, US Navy. Vernon was born in 1919, the son of Joseph Clarence White and Lena (Watson) White. He enlisted in the US Navy September 22, 1940 in Raleigh, North Carolina and completed his basic training at the Naval Training Station in Norfolk, Virginia. Vernon reported for duty on the USS Arizona December 4, 1940. He was killed in action on December 7, 1941 at Pearl Harbor, Hawaii. Vernon was awarded the American Defense Service Medal, World War II Victory Medal and Purple Heart Medal posthumously. He remains on duty on the USS Arizona. Vernon is commemorated on the USS Arizona Memorial and the Memorial Tablets of the Missing, National Memorial Cemetery of the Pacific, Honolulu, Hawaii. He was survived by his Father, Mr. Joseph Clarence White, 480 Tryon Street, Spartanburg, South Carolina.[826]

White, Volmer Dowin Seaman, First Class, Serial No: 274 48 44, US Navy. Volmer was born March 11, 1920 in Darbun, Mississippi, the son of George Gordon and Minnie Anna (Ballard) White. He enlisted in the US Navy July 30, 1940 in New Orleans, Louisiana and completed his basic training at the Naval Training Station in San Diego, California. He reported for duty on the USS Arizona October 8, 1940. Volmer was killed in action on December 7, 1941 at Pearl Harbor, Hawaii. He was awarded the American Defense Service Medal, World War II Victory Medal and Purple Heart Medal posthumously. Volmer remains on duty on the USS Arizona. He is commemorated on the USS Arizona Memorial and the Memorial Tablets of the Missing, National Memorial Cemetery of the Pacific, Honolulu, Hawaii and the Darbun Mormon Cemetery, Walthall County, Mississippi. Volmer was survived by his Father, Mr. George L. White, Route 1, Kokomo, Mississippi.

---

[825] Confidential Statement of Thomas Arthur White, Boatswain's Mate Second Class, U. S. Navy, U.S.S. Arizona regarding the attack at Pearl Harbor, T. H., December 7, 1941.

[826] Vernon Russell White, Photo from "Spartans Recall Attack By Japs at Pearl Harbor" by Roger Simmons, The Spartanburg Herald, Spartanburg, South Carolina, Tuesday, December 3, 1957, Page 5.

Whitehead, Ulmont "Monty" Irving, Jr. Ensign, Serial No: O-85063, US Navy. Ulmont was born April 13, 1915 in Hartford, Connecticut. He was the son of Ulmont Irving Whitehead, Sr. Ulmont attended the US Naval Academy in Annapolis, Maryland and was commissioned June 6, 1940. He and was surviving as Watch and Junior Division 6 Officer on the USS Arizona. Ulmont's battle station was Port AA RK Operator. He was killed in action on December 7, 1941 at Pearl Harbor, Hawaii. Ulmont was awarded the American Defense Service Medal, World War II Victory Medal and Purple Heart Medal posthumously. He remains on duty on the USS Arizona. Ulmont is commemorated on the USS Arizona Memorial and the Memorial Tablets of the Missing, National Memorial Cemetery of the Pacific, Honolulu, Hawaii. He was survived by his Father, Mr. Ulmont Irving Whitehead, 208 New Britain Avenue, Hartford, Connecticut. The Whitehead Highway, which extends from the Hudson Street traffic circle in Hartford, Connecticut to Interstate 91, honors Ensign Ulmont I. Whitehead Jr., the first Hartford resident to loose his life in World War II.[827]

Whitlock, Paul Morgan Seaman, Second Class, Serial No: 360 19 23, US Navy. Paul was born November 8, 1916 in Texas The youngest child, to William W. Whitlock and Jessie Marion (Edwards) Whitlock. Paul was very handsome and outgoing. The family was very poor "country" people. Paul enlisted in the US Navy July 31, 1940 in Houston, Texas and completed his basic training at the Naval Training Station in San Diego, California. Paul reported for duty on the USS Arizona October 8, 1940. He was killed in action on December 7, 1941 at Pearl Harbor, Hawaii. Paul was awarded the American Defense Service Medal, World War II Victory Medal and Purple Heart Medal posthumously. He remains on duty on the USS Arizona. Paul is commemorated on the USS Arizona Memorial and the Memorial Tablets of the Missing, National Memorial Cemetery of the Pacific, Honolulu, Hawaii and the Osage Cemetery, Osage, Texas. His death was the most devastating thing that ever happened to his mother and the tragedy was talked about whenever family got together. Paul was survived by his Mother, Mrs. Jessie Whitlock, Iredell, Texas.

Whitson, Ernest Hubert, Jr. Musician, Second Class, Serial No: 279 79 54, US Navy. Ernest was born August 10, 1918 in Jefferson County, Kentucky the son of Ernest Hubert and Christine (Tomey) Whitson. He enlisted in the US Navy February 28, 1941 and attended the Navy School of Music in Washington, DC graduating on May 23, 1941 as a member of the USS Arizona Band. He reported for duty on the USS Arizona June 17, 1941. Ernest was killed in action on December 7, 1941 at Pearl Harbor, Hawaii. His battle station was in the black powder room passing ammunition to the Arizona's gunners during the attack. None of the band members survived the explosion. He was awarded the American Defense Service Medal, World War II Victory Medal and Purple Heart Medal posthumously. Ernest remains on duty on the USS Arizona. He is commemorated on the USS Arizona Memorial and the Memorial Tablets of the Missing, National Memorial Cemetery of the

---

[827] Ulmont "Monty" Irving Whitehead, Jr., Photo from The Lucky Bag Yearbook, U.S. Naval Academy, Annapolis, Maryland, Class of 1940, page 185.

Pacific, Honolulu, Hawaii. Ernest was survived by his Parents, Mr. and Mrs. Ernest Hubert Whitson, Sr., 2627 Highland Avenue, Cincinnati, Ohio.[828]

Ernest Whitson, Jr. back row, third from left, no hat and smoking a pipe with his band and shipmates from the USS Arizona.

Whitt, William Byron Gunner's Mate, Third Class, Serial No: 287 33 79, US Navy. William was born March 27, 1919 in Royalton, Kentucky, the son of Ballard Whitt and Josephine (Lykins) Whitt. He enlisted in the US Navy November 20, 1939 in Louisville, Kentucky and completed his basic training at the Naval Training Station in Great Lakes, Illinois. William reported for duty on the USS Arizona February 10, 1940. He was killed in action on December 7, 1941 at Pearl Harbor, Hawaii. William was awarded the American Defense Service Medal, World War II Victory Medal and Purple Heart Medal posthumously. He remains on duty on the USS Arizona. William is commemorated on the USS Arizona Memorial and the Memorial Tablets of the Missing, National Memorial Cemetery of the Pacific, Honolulu, Hawaii and the Bal Whitt Cemetery, Magoffin County, Kentucky. His brother, Forrest G. Whitt served in the Marines and was killed in action at Okinawa. When the Navy offered to bring the remains of Forest home for burial, his parents declined on the basis that if they could not bring both Byron and Forest home, they would leave them where they had fallen. He was survived by his Father, Mr. Bal Whitt, Royalton, Kentucky.[829]

---

[828] Ernest Hubert Whitson, Jr., Photo from USS Arizona's Last Band by Molly Kent. By permission of the author. For more information about this book, go to www.USSARIZONASLASTBAND.com.
[829] William Byron Whitt, Photo provided by his neighbor, Bruce Stephens.

Whittemore, Andrew Tiny   Steward's Mate, Second Class, Serial No: 295 73 17, US Navy. Andrew was born in the spring of 1919 near Lake Providence, Tennessee the son of Isaac and Katharine Whittemore. His father died when he was about five months old leaving his mother with seven children to support on her own. Andrew enlisted in the US Navy August 20, 1940 in Nashville, Tennessee and completed his basic training at the Naval Training Station in Norfolk, Virginia. He reported for duty on the USS Arizona November 28, 1940. Andrew was killed in action on December 7, 1941 at Pearl Harbor, Hawaii. He was awarded the American Defense Service Medal, World War II Victory Medal and Purple Heart Medal posthumously. Andrew remains on duty on the USS Arizona. He is commemorated on the USS Arizona Memorial and the Memorial Tablets of the Missing, National Memorial Cemetery of the Pacific, Honolulu, Hawaii. Andrew was survived by his Mother, Mrs. Katherine Whittemore, 22-1/2 Claiborne Street, Nashville, Tennessee.[830]

Wick, Everett Morris   Fire Controlman, Third Class, Serial No: 393 35 11, US Navy. Everett was born August 3, 1920 in Oregon, the son of Arthur Morris and Vina Elizabeth (Brown) Wick. He enlisted in the US Navy April 9, 1940 in Portland, Oregon and completed his basic training at the Naval Training Station in San Diego, California. Everett transferred from the Naval Yard in Mare Island, California to the USS Arizona July 2, 1940. He was killed in action on December 7, 1941 at Pearl Harbor, Hawaii. Everett was awarded the American Defense Service Medal, World War II Victory Medal and Purple Heart Medal posthumously. He remains on duty on the USS Arizona. Everett is commemorated on the USS Arizona Memorial and the Memorial Tablets of the Missing, National Memorial Cemetery of the Pacific, Honolulu, Hawaii. He was survived by his Father, Mr. Arthur Morris Wick, 818 Northeast 93rd Avenue, Portland, Oregon.[831]

Wicklund, John Joseph   Seaman, First Class, Serial No: 328 61 84, US Navy. John was born in about 1920 in Minnesota, the son of Raymond Leonard and Josephine Victoria (Hanus) Wicklund. He enlisted in the US Navy November 14, 1939 in Minneapolis, Minnesota and completed his basic training at the Naval Training Station in Great Lakes, Illinois. He reported for duty on the USS Arizona January 27, 1940. John was killed in action on December 7, 1941 at Pearl Harbor, Hawaii. He was awarded the American Defense Service Medal, World War II Victory Medal and Purple Heart Medal posthumously. John remains on duty on the USS Arizona. He is commemorated on the USS Arizona Memorial and the Memorial Tablets of the Missing, National Memorial Cemetery of the Pacific, Honolulu, Hawaii. John was survived by his Father, Mr. Raymond Leonard Wicklund, 2726 30th Avenue South, Minneapolis, Minnesota.[832]

---

[830] Andrew Tiny Whittemore, Photo and information from Tennessee Honor States and The Tennessean of Nashville.

[831] Everett Morris Wick, Photo from 1939 Benson Polytechnic High School, Portland, Oregon.

[832] John Joseph Wicklund, Photo from The Minneapolis Star, Minneapolis, Minnesota, May 5, 1942, page 12.

Wilcox, Arnold Alfred   Quartermaster, Second Class, Serial No: 321 08 02, US Navy. Arnold was born January 16, 1918 in Dumont, Iowa, the only son of Alfred Wilson and Icea Belle (Keister) Wilcox. *His father died of pneumonia when he was an infant. When he was 15, he and a friend hitch hiked 300 miles from their home in Dumont to see the World's Fair in Chicago.* He enlisted in the US Navy August 18, 1936 in Des Moines, Iowa and reported for duty on the USS Arizona December 2, 1936. Arnold was killed in action on December 7, 1941 at Pearl Harbor, Hawaii. He was awarded the American Defense Service Medal, World War II Victory Medal and Purple Heart Medal posthumously. Arnold remains on duty on the USS Arizona. He is commemorated on the USS Arizona Memorial and the Memorial Tablets of the Missing, National Memorial Cemetery of the Pacific, Honolulu, Hawaii. Arnold was survived by his Mother, Mrs. Icea Belle Wilcox, 1503 Clark Street, Charles City, Iowa.[833]

Will, Joseph William   Seaman, Second Class, Serial No: 372 26 68, US Navy. Joseph was born in 1920, the son of James Ewing Will and Nellie E. Will. He enlisted in the US Navy February 1, 1941 in Denver, Colorado and completed his basic training at the Naval Training Station in San Diego, California. Joseph reported for duty on the USS Arizona September 18, 1941. He was killed in action on December 7, 1941 at Pearl Harbor, Hawaii. Joseph was awarded the American Defense Service Medal, World War II Victory Medal and Purple Heart Medal posthumously. He remains on duty on the USS Arizona. Joseph is commemorated on the USS Arizona Memorial and the Memorial Tablets of the Missing, National Memorial Cemetery of the Pacific, Honolulu, Hawaii. He was survived by his Father, Mr. James Ewing Will, Box 194, Hugo, Colorado.

Willette, Laddie James   Seaman, Second Class, Serial No: 311 49 75, US Navy. Laddie was born April 26, 1921 in Michigan to James Henry and Marguerite (Ponce) Willette. He enlisted in the US Navy September 9, 1940 in Detroit, Michigan and completed his basic training at the Naval Training Station in Norfolk, Virginia. Laddie reported for duty on the USS Arizona December 4, 1940. He was killed in action on December 7, 1941 at Pearl Harbor, Hawaii. Laddie was awarded the American Defense Service Medal, World War II Victory Medal and Purple Heart Medal posthumously. He remains on duty on the USS Arizona. Laddie is commemorated on the USS Arizona Memorial and the Memorial Tablets of the Missing, National Memorial Cemetery of the Pacific, Honolulu, Hawaii. He was survived by his Father, Mr. James Henry Willette, 533 Wheaton Avenue, Battle Creek, Michigan. On February 7, 1950, Laddie's remains were interred in Section N, Site 967, Golden Gate National Cemetery, San Bruno, California.[834]

---

[833] Arnold Alfred Wilcox, Photo from The Mason City Globe-Gazette, Mason City, Iowa, Saturday, December 27, 1941, Page 7.
[834] Laddie James Willette, Photo from Michigan Honor States.

Williams, Adrian Delton Seaman, First Class, Serial No: 274 41 85, US Navy. Adrian was born in about 1919 in Louisiana to William T. Williams. He enlisted in the US Navy December 13, 1939 in New Orleans, Louisiana and completed his basic training at the Naval Training Station in San Diego, California. He reported for duty on the USS Arizona March 29, 1940. Adrian was killed in action on December 7, 1941 at Pearl Harbor, Hawaii. He was awarded the American Defense Service Medal, World War II Victory Medal and Purple Heart Medal posthumously. Adrian remains on duty on the USS Arizona. He is commemorated on the USS Arizona Memorial and the Memorial Tablets of the Missing, National Memorial Cemetery of the Pacific, Honolulu, Hawaii. Adrian was survived by his Father, Mr. William Thomas Williams, Route 2, Gonzales, Louisiana. The American Legion Gautreau-Williams Post 81, Gonzales, Louisiana, was named in his honor.[835]

Williams, Clyde Richard Musician, Second Class, Serial No: 356 42 55, US Navy. Clyde was born September 25, 1922 in Henryette, Oklahoma, the son of Richard B. Williams, Jr. and Martha Jane (Fretwell) Williams. He enlisted in the US Navy November 27, 1940 and attended the Navy School of Music in Washington, DC graduating on May 23, 1941 as a member of the USS Arizona Band. Clyde reported for duty on the USS Arizona June 17, 1941. His battle station was in the black powder room passing ammunition to the Arizona's gunners during the attack. He was killed in action on December 7, 1941 at Pearl Harbor, Hawaii. Clyde was awarded the Purple Heart Medal, American Defense Service Medal, Asiatic Pacific Campaign Medal with Bronze Star and World War II Victory Medal posthumously. He remains on duty on the USS Arizona. Clyde is commemorated on the USS Arizona Memorial and the Memorial Tablets of the Missing, National Memorial Cemetery of the Pacific, Honolulu, Hawaii. He was survived by his Father, Mr. Richard B. Williams, Jr. 1006 Griffin Street, Okmulgee, Oklahoma.[836]

Williams, George Washington Seaman, First Class, Serial No: 258 27 64, US Navy. George was born in about 1922 in Virginia to Charles B. and Lillian G. Williams. He enlisted in the US Navy March 18, 1940 in Baltimore, Maryland and completed his basic training at the Naval Training Station in Norfolk, Virginia. He reported for duty on the USS Arizona September 30, 1940. George was killed in action on December 7, 1941 at Pearl Harbor, Hawaii. He was awarded the American Defense Service Medal, World War II Victory Medal and Purple Heart Medal posthumously. George remains on duty on the USS Arizona. He is commemorated on the USS Arizona Memorial and the Memorial Tablets of the Missing, National Memorial Cemetery of the Pacific, Honolulu, Hawaii. George was survived by his Father, Mr. Charles Benjamin Williams, Wheatfield, Virginia.

---

[835] Adrian Delton Williams, Information and photo provided by Stephen T. Henry, Commander of the American Legion Gautreau-Williams Post 81, Golzales, LA.
[836] Clyde Richard Williams, Photo from USS Arizona's Last Band by Molly Kent. By permission of the author. For more information about this book, go to www.USSARIZONASLASTBAND.com.

Williams, Jack Herman   Radioman, Third Class, Serial No: 406 22 32, US Navy Reserve. Jack was born in about 1919 in South Carolina to Ross O. and Annie Williams. He enlisted in the US Navy May 29, 1940 in Columbia, South Carolina. He attended US Naval Reserve Radio School in Norton Heights, Connecticut, completing the course in March 1941. Jack was transported via the USS Wharton in March and reported for duty on the USS Arizona April 4, 1941. He was killed in action on December 7, 1941 at Pearl Harbor, Hawaii. Jack was awarded the American Defense Service Medal, World War II Victory Medal and Purple Heart Medal posthumously. He remains on duty on the USS Arizona. Jack is commemorated on the USS Arizona Memorial and the Memorial Tablets of the Missing, National Memorial Cemetery of the Pacific, Honolulu, Hawaii. He was survived by his Mother, Mrs. Annie Williams, 1231 Tobacco Street, Columbia, South Carolina.

Williams, John Francis   Gunner's Mate, Third Class, Serial No. 337 20 73, US Navy. John was born on November 28, 1919 in Missouri to Lee Honest and Laura A. Williams. He enlisted in the US Navy October 6, 1939 in St. Louis, Missouri and completed his basic training at the Naval Training Station in San Diego, California. He reported for duty on the USS Arizona December 20, 1939. He was serving on the USS Arizona on December 7, 1941 when the Japanese attacked Pearl Harbor. John died on January 26, 1995 in Oceanside, California.

Williams, Lawrence A.   Ensign, Serial No: 0-085934, US Navy Reserve. Lawrence was born in 1915, the son of Lawrence Williams and Annette Ruth (Barnett) Williams. He enlisted in the Naval Air Corps in 1940. Commissioned Ensign April 21, 1941 he was assigned duty as an Aviator in Division V. As an observation and scouting pilot, he flew one of the fleet's catapult-launched planes. The two seat, tandem plane was returned to shipboard by a crane. Lawrence was killed in action on December 7, 1941 at Pearl Harbor, Hawaii. He was awarded the American Defense Service Medal, World War II Victory Medal and Purple Heart Medal posthumously. Lawrence remains on duty on the USS Arizona. He is commemorated on the USS Arizona Memorial and the Memorial Tablets of the Missing, National Memorial Cemetery of the Pacific, Honolulu, Hawaii. Lawrence was survived by his Mother, Mrs. Ruth B. Williams, 304 West Church Street, Oxford, Ohio and sister, Mrs. Clyde Stiner of Canton, Ohio.[837]

---

[837] Lawrence A. Williams, Information and photo from The Canton Repository, Canton, Ohio, Sunday, June 8, 1941, page 12

Lawrence A. Williams, in the pilot's seat. Photo# 80-G-66109 OS2U is recovered at sea by USS Arizona, 6 Sept 1941

Williamson, Randolph, Jr. Steward's Mate, First Class, Serial No: 262 31 45, US Navy. Randolph was born in 1919, the son of Randolph Williamson and Julia W. Williamson. He graduated from Washington High School, Raleigh's first black public high school. Randolph enlisted in the Navy so he could help support his family. There were no jobs for black men in Raleigh at that time. He enlisted in the US Navy October 11, 1938 in Raleigh, North Carolina and reported for duty on the USS Arizona April 28, 1941. Randolph was killed in action on December 7, 1941 at Pearl Harbor, Hawaii. He was awarded the American Defense Service Medal, World War II Victory Medal and Purple Heart Medal posthumously. Randolph remains on duty on the USS Arizona. He is commemorated on the USS Arizona Memorial and the Memorial Tablets of the Missing, National Memorial Cemetery of the Pacific, Honolulu, Hawaii. Randolph was survived by his Father, Mr. Randolph Williams, Sr., 211 East South Street, Raleigh, North Carolina.[838]

Williamson, William Dean Radioman, Second Class, Serial No: 414 33 62, US Navy Reserve. William enlisted in the US Navy January 6, 1939 in San Diego, California and completed his basic training at the Naval Training Station in San Diego, California. He reported for duty on the USS Arizona September 8, 1939. William was killed in action on December 7, 1941 at Pearl Harbor, Hawaii. He was awarded the American Defense Service Medal, World War II Victory Medal and Purple Heart Medal posthumously. William remains on duty on the USS Arizona. He is commemorated on the USS Arizona Memorial and the Memorial Tablets of the Missing, National Memorial Cemetery of the Pacific, Honolulu, Hawaii. William was survived by his Wife, Mrs. Athalone Levis Williamson, 1255-1/2 Loma Vista Avenue, Long Beach, California.

---

[838] Randolph Williamson, Jr., Information from "Remembering Randolph Williamson Jr., and all who served" by Sharon Powell, The Midtown Raleigh News, May 29, 2011.

Willis, Robert "Bobby" Kenneth, Jr. Seaman, First Class, Serial No: 274 48 64, US Navy. Robert was born on February 2, 1923 in Louisiana, the son of Robert Kenneth and Julia Mae (Johnson) Willis. He graduated from Natchitoches High School, Louisiana in 1939. His mother died when he was barely 11 years old. Robert enlisted in the US Navy July 31, 1940 in New Orleans, Louisiana and completed his basic training at the Naval Training Station in San Diego, California. He reported for duty on the USS Arizona October 8, 1940. Robert was killed in action on December 7, 1941 at Pearl Harbor, Hawaii. He was awarded the American Defense Service Medal, World War II Victory Medal and Purple Heart Medal posthumously. Robert remains on duty on the USS Arizona. He is commemorated on the USS Arizona Memorial and the Memorial Tablets of the Missing, National Memorial Cemetery of the Pacific, Honolulu, Hawaii. Robert was survived by his Father, Mr. Robert K. Willis, Sr., Box 31, Pineville, Louisiana. The American Legion Post in Pineville, Louisiana was named the Robert K. Willis Jr. Post in honor of his service and duty to his country.[839]

Wilson, Bernard Martin Radioman, Third Class, V-3, Serial No: 403 70 06, US Navy Reserve. Bernard was born May 15, 1921 in Massachusetts, the son of Edward Wilson and Rita Wilson. He enlisted in the US Navy October 7, 1940 in Brooklyn, New York and reported for duty on the USS Arizona April 4, 1941. Bernard was killed in action on December 7, 1941 at Pearl Harbor, Hawaii. He was awarded the American Defense Service Medal, World War II Victory Medal and Purple Heart Medal posthumously. Bernard remains on duty on the USS Arizona. He is commemorated on the USS Arizona Memorial and the Memorial Tablets of the Missing, National Memorial Cemetery of the Pacific, Honolulu, Hawaii and the Boston United Hand in Hand Cemetery, West Roxbury, Massachusetts. Bernard was survived by his Mother, Mrs. Rita Wilson, 860 Riverside Drive, New York, New York.[840]

Wilson, Charles Lee Seaman, First Class, Serial No. 300 20 72, US Navy. Charles enlisted in the US Navy October 15, 1940 in Chicago, Illinois and completed his basic training at the Naval Training Station in Great Lakes, Illinois. He reported for duty on the USS Arizona December 9, 1940. He was serving on the USS Arizona on December 7, 1941 when the Japanese attacked Pearl Harbor. He was wounded during the Japanese attack and was transferred to the U.S. Naval Hospital, Mare Island, California for treatment. Charles passed away in November 1999.

---

[839] Robert Kenneth Willis, Jr., Photo provided by the Robert K. Willis Jr American Legion Post in Pineville, Louisiana.
[840] Bernard Martin Wilson, Photo courtesy of The Theodore R. Reiner Family Trust.

Wilson, Comer Anderson Chief Boatswain's Mate, Serial No: 271 99 14, US Navy. Comer was born March 23, 1907 in Andalusia, Alabama to Paul Anderson Wilson and Hannah Docia (Moore) Anderson. His mother died when he was very young and his father spent a lot of time at work. Comer quickly became both mother and father to his two younger sisters. He would use tree logs to simulate their father coming home so he could get his sisters out of bed and going to school. Comer enlisted in the US Navy on April 2, 1930. He served on the USS Arizona from March 2, 1931 until he was killed in action on December 7, 1941 at Pearl Harbor, Hawaii. Comer was on board the ship the morning of the 7th. He was going to go to friends in the area, but because he wasn't feeling well, he decided to stay on the ship. Comer was on deck when the big explosion happened and he was thrown from the ship. Comer made it to the shore, but died on December 10th from severe burns. He was assigned death #122 by the US Naval Hospital, at Pearl.[841] His wife, Martha was 7 months pregnant when he died. It was many years before she remarried but she loved and mourned him until the day she died in 2002. He was awarded the American Defense Service Medal, World War II Victory Medal and Purple Heart Medal posthumously. Comer's remains were returned home for burial in the Magnolia Cemetery, Andalusia, Alabama. He is commemorated on the USS Arizona Memorial and the Memorial Tablets of the Missing, National Memorial Cemetery of the Pacific, Honolulu, Hawaii. Comer was survived by his Wife, Mrs. Martha Anne (Murphree) Wilson, Route 2, Box 12, Andalusia, Alabama.[842]

Wilson, Harold Green, Jr. Fireman, Second Class, Serial No. 382 30 81, US Navy. Harold was born March 6, 1921 in Barstow, California to Harold Green and Ethel Mae (Stark) Wilson. He enlisted in the US Navy November 13, 1940 in Los Angeles, California and completed his basic training at the Naval Training Station in San Diego, California. He reported for duty on the USS Arizona January 11, 1941. Harold was serving on the USS Arizona on December 7, 1941 when the Japanese attacked Pearl Harbor. After the attack, Harold was transferred to the USS Pelias (AS-14) for duty. Harold died on March 20, 1972 in Barstow, California.

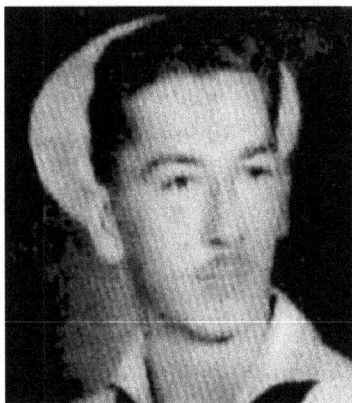

Wilson, Hurschel Woodrow Fireman, Second Class, Serial No: 279 72 46, US Navy. Hurschel was born in about 1922 in Greenfield, Ohio the son of Harry H. and Retta M. Wilson. He enlisted in the US Navy September 3, 1940 in Cincinnati, Ohio and completed his basic training at the Naval Training Station in Great Lakes, Illinois. He reported for duty on the USS Arizona December 4, 1940. Hurschel was killed in action on December 7, 1941 at Pearl Harbor, Hawaii. He was awarded the American Defense Service Medal, World War II Victory Medal and Purple Heart Medal posthumously. Hurschel remains on duty on the USS Arizona. He is commemorated on the USS Arizona Memorial and the Memorial Tablets of the Missing, National

---

[841] Comer Anderson Wilson, Report of Changes of the USS Arizona for the month ending 31st day of December, 1941, page 112, line 20.
[842] Comer Anderson Wilson, Photo provided by family member, Gloria Brady-Cross.

Memorial Cemetery of the Pacific, Honolulu, Hawaii. Hurschel was survived by his Father, Mr. Harry Hurschel Wilson, 738 South Street, Greenfield, Ohio.[843]

Wilson, John James Seaman, First Class, Serial No: 382 20 86, US Navy. John was born in 1922, the son of Duane Felshaw and Winifred L. (Wheatley) Wilson. John was one of seven children, 4 older and he was the oldest of 3 younger brothers. John enlisted in the US Navy June 11, 1940 in Los Angeles, California and completed his basic training at the Naval Training Station in San Diego, California. He reported for duty on the USS Arizona September 8, 1940. John was killed in action on December 7, 1941 at Pearl Harbor, Hawaii. He was awarded the American Defense Service Medal, World War II Victory Medal and Purple Heart Medal posthumously. John remains on duty on the USS Arizona. He is commemorated on the USS Arizona Memorial and the Memorial Tablets of the Missing, National Memorial Cemetery of the Pacific, Honolulu, Hawaii. John was survived by his Parents, Mr. and Mrs. Duane Felshaw Wilson, 1667 East 133rd Street, Willowbrook, California. Both of John's younger brothers enlisted as soon as they heard about their brother.[844]

Wilson, Neil "Willie" Mataweny Chief Metalsmith, Serial No: 72540, US Navy. Neil was born December 31, 1905 in Dicksonburg, Pennsylvania to Ned Davenport and Edna Agnes (Sloan) Wilson. He joined the Navy in 1923. After his enlistment was up, he sulked around the house without anything to do. Finally his wife got out his uniforms, ironed them, and laid them out on the bed. She then told "Willie" to "go re-enlist. There is a war coming and you are going to get yourself killed. But I'm not going to have you moping around the house every time a ship enters or leaves the harbor."[845] Neil was serving as Assistant to Eng. Officer. His battle station was Starboard Engine Room. Neil was killed in action on December 7, 1941 at Pearl Harbor, Hawaii. He was awarded the American Defense Service Medal, World War II Victory Medal and Purple Heart Medal posthumously. Neil remains on duty on the USS Arizona. He is commemorated on the USS Arizona Memorial and the Memorial Tablets of the Missing, National Memorial Cemetery of the Pacific, Honolulu, Hawaii. Neil was survived by his Wife, Mrs. Daisy Lawrence Wilson, 4721 Kansas Street, San Diego, California, two children, five Brothers, Allen E. of Andover, OH, Ned S. (WWI Army) of Greenville, PA, Arthur L. (Career Army) of Hardin, KY, Donald P. (WWII Navy) of Linesville, PA and James E. (Career Navy) of San Diego, CA and Sister, Agnes Durovey of Linesville, PA.

---

[843] Hurschel Woodrow Wilson, Photo from Ohio Honor States.
[844] John James Wilson, Photo and information provided by his niece, Georgia Ann (Wilson) Crain.
[845] Neil Mataweny Wilson, Family information and photo provided by his nephew, Dick Wilson.

Wilson, Ray Milo Radioman, Third Class, V-3, Serial No: 410 37 85, US Navy Reserve. Ray was born May 23, 1920 in Charles City, Iowa to Harry R. and Mona (Cole) Wilson. He enlisted in the US Navy May 13, 1938 in Charles City, Iowa and reported for duty on the USS Arizona November 12, 1941 from the Naval Air Station, Roosevelt Base, Terminal Island, California. Ray was killed in action on December 7, 1941 at Pearl Harbor, Hawaii. He was awarded the American Defense Service Medal, World War II Victory Medal and Purple Heart Medal posthumously. Ray remains on duty on the USS Arizona. He is commemorated on the USS Arizona Memorial and the Memorial Tablets of the Missing, National Memorial Cemetery of the Pacific, Honolulu, Hawaii and the Riverside Cemetery, Charles City, Iowa. Ray was survived by his Grandmother, Mrs. Reca S. Cole, 306 Brantingham Street, Charles City, Iowa.[846]

Wimberley, Paul Edwin Gunner's Mate, Third Class, Serial No: 295 54 94, US Navy. Paul was born in June 1918 in Henry County, Tennessee to Archie Isaac and Ruby A. Wimberley. He enlisted in the US Navy December 13, 1939 in Nashville, Tennessee and reported for duty on the USS Arizona March 29, 1940. Paul was killed in action on December 7, 1941 at Pearl Harbor, Hawaii. He was awarded the American Defense Service Medal, World War II Victory Medal and Purple Heart Medal posthumously. Paul remains on duty on the USS Arizona. He is commemorated on the USS Arizona Memorial and the Memorial Tablets of the Missing, National Memorial Cemetery of the Pacific, Honolulu, Hawaii. Paul was survived by his Father, Mr. Archie Isaac Wimberley, Route 1, Springville, Tennessee.

Winter, Edward Machinist's Mate, Serial No: 100905, US Navy Reserve. Edward was born in 1909 in Washington State, the son of Adolph and Julianna (Ziert) Winter. He was serving on the USS Arizona as Assistant to Engineering Officer. His battle station was Boiler Control. Edward was killed in action on December 7, 1941 at Pearl Harbor, Hawaii. He was awarded the American Defense Service Medal, World War II Victory Medal and Purple Heart Medal posthumously. Edward remains on duty on the USS Arizona. He is commemorated on the USS Arizona Memorial and the Memorial Tablets of the Missing, National Memorial Cemetery of the Pacific, Honolulu, Hawaii. Edward was survived by his Father, Mr. Adolph Winter, Winlock, Washington.[847]

Wise, James Louis Seaman, First Class, Serial No. 279 72 43, US Navy. James enlisted in the US Navy September 3, 1940 in Cleveland, Ohio and completed his basic training at the Naval Training Station in Great Lakes, Illinois. He reported for duty on the USS Arizona December 4, 1940. James was on launch boat duty that morning. He had just taken the launch over to shore around 7:00 am to pick up the chaplain for Sunday services and brought him to the ship. After securing the launch he boarded the USS Arizona and went to the galley and got himself a cup of coffee. He was drinking the coffee standing outside on the forecastle deck when he saw the first planes come over and bombs being dropped on Ford Island. He went running through the ship screaming "It's an attack, it's an attack". The other crewmen just stood there

---

[846] Ray Milo Wilson, Photo provided by the Charles City High School, Charles City, Iowa from their Yearbook, Class of 1938.
[847] Edward Winter, Photo from the Washington Honor States.

and looked 'stupefied'. He made his way to his gun mount near Turret #2 where he and his crew got off some frenzied rounds before a high altitude bomber dropped a bomb that ricocheted off the turret and penetrated through the deck 40-50 feet away from his gun mount. The bomb had a time delayed fuse and penetrated below deck to where the gun powder was stored and exploded. All the gun powder blew up and then ignited the aviation fuel tanks that were used for the scout planes. The blast seared off his uniform and blew him over the side. He hit the life rope that is attached around the sides of the ship on his way down to the water sending him cart wheeling into the water. He remembered swimming in the oil and fire covered water with the skin on his hands dripping off like candle was. A small launch boat happened to be nearby and saw that he had some life left in him so he navigated through the oil and fire and picked him up. He was badly burned on December 7, 1941 when the Japanese attacked Pearl Harbor. James was taken to the US Naval Hospital at Pearl Harbor for treatment. He was later transported to the Naval Hospital, Mare Island, California where he spent two years of treatment including 26 skin graph surgeries on his face and hands. James said at the time, if he had enough strength to walk to the window, he would have jumped out because the pain was unbearable. He never got completely over the experience.[848]

Wojtkiewicz, Frank Peter Chief Machinist's Mate, Serial No: 212 23 27, US Navy. Frank was born December 4, 1908 in Massachusetts the son of Joseph and Antonia (Wichrowski) Wojtkiewicz. He enlisted in the US Navy August 3, 1939 in Chefoo, China and reported for duty on the USS Arizona March 29, 1940. Frank was killed in action on December 7, 1941 at Pearl Harbor, Hawaii. He was awarded the Bronze Star, American Defense Service Medal, World War II Victory Medal and Purple Heart Medal posthumously. Frank remains on duty on the USS Arizona. He is commemorated on the USS Arizona Memorial and the Memorial Tablets of the Missing, National Memorial Cemetery of the Pacific, Honolulu, Hawaii. Frank is shown buried at Section M1, Row C, Site 32, Massachusetts Veteran Memorial Cemetery, Agawam, Massachusetts. He was survived by his Wife, Mrs. Agnia Wojtkiewicz, 1276 North Fairfax Avenue, West Hollywood, California. The Wojtkiewicz Park near the Great River Bridge near Boston, Massachusetts was named in his honor.[849]

Wolf, George Alexanderson, Jr. Ensign, E-V (G), Serial No: 0-097625, US Navy Reserve. George was born December 1, 1917 in Altoona, Pennsylvania, the son of George Alexanderson Wolf, Sr. and Maria (Pendergast) Wolf. In 1939 he graduated from Georgetown University then returned home to go into business with his father. His brother foresaw the war and the enactment of the draft law. He suggested to George that he enlist in the Navy V-7 program which enabled college grads to become officers with 90 days training at Annapolis. Rather than be drafted directly into the Army, George decided to do the V-7 program. He went to San Diego and was assigned to a seaplane tender in the Engineering Department. He was then transferred to the USS Arizona and sailed to Hawaii and Pearl Harbor. George was killed in action on December 7, 1941 at Pearl Harbor, Hawaii. All week following the attack, the family was apprehensive. There were no communications from George. Finally Western Union telegraph called Friday morning, five days

---

[848] James Louis Wise, Information and story provided by his son, James Louis Wise, Jr.
[849] Frank Peter Wojtkiewicz, Photo provided by Dave McCaffrey, Find a Grave.

after the attack telling them of the loss. His family was devastated, but his brother blamed himself for getting George to enlist and regretted it the rest of his life. George was awarded the American Defense Service Medal, World War II Victory Medal and Purple Heart Medal posthumously. He remains on duty on the USS Arizona. George is commemorated on the USS Arizona Memorial and the Memorial Tablets of the Missing, National Memorial Cemetery of the Pacific, Honolulu, Hawaii. He was survived by his Parents, Mr. and Mrs. George A. Wolf, Sr., Ant Hills, Hollidaysburg, Pennsylvania.[850]

Wood, Harold Baker Boatswain's Mate, Second Class, Serial No: 372 06 81, US Navy. Harold was born April 19, 1919 in Fargo, North Dakota. He enlisted in the US Navy September 9, 1938 in Denver, Colorado and completed his basic training at the Naval Training Station in San Diego, California. He reported for duty on the USS Arizona January 2, 1939. Harold was killed in action on December 7, 1941 at Pearl Harbor, Hawaii. He was awarded the American Defense Service Medal, World War II Victory Medal and Purple Heart Medal posthumously. Harold remains on duty on the USS Arizona. He is commemorated on the USS Arizona Memorial and the Memorial Tablets of the Missing, National Memorial Cemetery of the Pacific, Honolulu, Hawaii. Harold was survived by his Mother, Mrs. Grace Ellen Traynor, 860 1st Avenue, Grand Junction, Colorado.[851]

Wood, Horace Van Seaman, First Class, Serial No: 356 38 28, US Navy. Horace was born in May 1919 in Kaufman County, Texas to Robert Burton and Lousye E. Wood. His mother died in 1934. He enlisted in the US Navy October 12, 1940 in Dallas, Texas and completed his basic training at the Naval Training Station in San Diego, California. He reported for duty on the USS Arizona January 4, 1941. Horace was killed in action on December 7, 1941 at Pearl Harbor, Hawaii. He was awarded the American Defense Service Medal, World War II Victory Medal and Purple Heart Medal posthumously. Horace remains on duty on the USS Arizona. He is commemorated on the USS Arizona Memorial and the Memorial Tablets of the Missing, National Memorial Cemetery of the Pacific, Honolulu, Hawaii. Horace was survived by his Father, Mr. Robert Burton Wood, State Hospital, Terrell, Texas. His stepbrother, Dee Cumpie Ayers Jr. was also killed in action on the Arizona.[852]

Wood, Roy Eugene Fireman, First Class, Serial No: 356 17 58, US Navy. Roy enlisted in the US Navy October 3, 1939 in Dallas, Texas and completed his basic training at the Naval Training Station in San Diego, California. He reported for duty on the USS Arizona December 20, 1939. Roy was killed in action on December 7, 1941 at Pearl Harbor, Hawaii. He was awarded the American Defense Service Medal, World War II Victory Medal and Purple Heart Medal posthumously. Roy remains on duty on the USS Arizona. He is commemorated on the USS Arizona Memorial and the Memorial Tablets of the Missing, National Memorial Cemetery

---

[850] George Alexanderson Wolf, Jr., Information from his nephew, Chris Wolf, Photo from Pennsylvania Honor States.
[851] Harold Baker Wood, Photo from the Colorado Honor States.
[852] Horace Van Wood, Photo from his nephew, Terry W. Wood.

of the Pacific, Honolulu, Hawaii. Roy was survived by his Father, Mr. W. G. Wood, General Delivery, Healdton, Oklahoma.

Woods, Vernon Wesley Seaman, First Class, Serial No: 274 45 74, US Navy. Vernon was born in about 1919 in Mississippi to Thomas G. and Ruby J Woods. He enlisted in the US Navy June 8, 1940 in New Orleans, Louisiana and completed his basic training at the Naval Training Station in San Diego, California. He reported for duty on the USS Arizona October 8, 1940. Vernon was killed in action on December 7, 1941 at Pearl Harbor, Hawaii. He was awarded the American Defense Service Medal, World War II Victory Medal and Purple Heart Medal posthumously. Vernon remains on duty on the USS Arizona. He is commemorated on the USS Arizona Memorial and the Memorial Tablets of the Missing, National Memorial Cemetery of the Pacific, Honolulu, Hawaii. Vernon was survived by his Father, Mr. Thomas G. Woods, Springhill, Louisiana.[853]

Woods, William Anthony Seaman, Second Class, Serial No: 223 94 39, US Navy. William enlisted in the US Navy November 22, 1940 in New York, New York and reported for duty on the USS Arizona on October 26, 1941. He was killed in action on December 7, 1941 at Pearl Harbor, Hawaii. William was awarded the American Defense Service Medal, World War II Victory Medal and Purple Heart Medal posthumously. He remains on duty on the USS Arizona. William is commemorated on the USS Arizona Memorial and the Memorial Tablets of the Missing, National Memorial Cemetery of the Pacific, Honolulu, Hawaii. He was survived by his Father, Mr. Robert Emmet Woods, 87-22 56th Avenue, Elmhurst, Flushing, New York.

Woodward, Ardenne "Bill" Allen Machinist's Mate, Second Class, Serial No: 265 96 71, US Navy. Ardenne was born June 9, 1921 in Stafford County, Virginia to William Allen and Georgia Inez (Raines) Woodward. He enlisted in the US Navy July 11, 1938 in Richmond, Virginia and reported for duty on the USS Arizona November 10, 1938. He was killed in action on December 7, 1941 at Pearl Harbor, Hawaii. Ardenne was awarded the American Defense Service Medal, World War II Victory Medal and Purple Heart Medal posthumously. He remains on duty on the USS Arizona. Ardenne is commemorated on the USS Arizona Memorial and the Memorial Tablets of the Missing, National Memorial Cemetery of the Pacific, Honolulu, Hawaii and Maury Cemetery, Richmond, Virginia. He was survived by his Wife, Mrs. Virginia Opal (Greenwood) Woodward, 228 10th Drive, Berkeley, California, daughter, Karen Joan Woodward, Parents, William Allen and Georgia Inez Woodward of Petersburg Pike, Virginia and brother, William Alexander Woodward.[854]

---

[853] Vernon Wesley Woods, Photo from the Gumbo Yearbook, Louisiana State University, Baton Rough, Louisiana.
[854] Ardenne Allen Woodward, Information and picture provided by family member, Shelly Atalla.

Woody, Harlan Fred   Seaman, Second Class, Serial No: 382 41 50, US Navy. Harlan was born February 26, 1924 in Los Angeles County, California, the son of Helen Doris (Alley) Woody. He enlisted in the US Navy March 11, 1941 in Los Angeles, California and completed his basic training at the Naval Training Station in San Diego, California. He reported for duty on the USS Arizona July 13, 1941. Harlan was killed in action on December 7, 1941 at Pearl Harbor, Hawaii. He was awarded the American Defense Service Medal, World War II Victory Medal and Purple Heart Medal posthumously. Harlan remains on duty on the USS Arizona. He is commemorated on the USS Arizona Memorial and the Memorial Tablets of the Missing, National Memorial Cemetery of the Pacific, Honolulu, Hawaii. Harlan was survived by his Mother, Mrs. Helen Doris Woody, 214 South New Hampshire, Los Angeles, California.[855]

Woolf, Norman Bragg   Chief Water Tender, Serial No: 271 97 98, US Navy. Norman was born July 18, 1912 in Marengo, Alabama, the oldest son of Thomas Bragg Woolf and Mary Lois (Poellnitz) Woolf. He re-enlisted in the US Navy July 18, 1935. Norman served on the USS Arizona from March 1, 1931 until he was killed in action on December 7, 1941 at Pearl Harbor, Hawaii. He was awarded the American Defense Service Medal, World War II Victory Medal and Purple Heart Medal posthumously. Norman remains on duty on the USS Arizona. He is commemorated on the USS Arizona Memorial and the Memorial Tablets of the Missing, National Memorial Cemetery of the Pacific, Honolulu, Hawaii and the Campground Methodist Church Cemetery, Campground, Alabama. Norman was survived by his Mother, Mrs. Mary Poellnitz Woolf, Myrtlewood, Alabama and two Brothers, James Alfred and Charles P. Woolf.

Wright, Edward Henry   Seaman, Second Class, Serial No: 300 17 55, US Navy. Edward enlisted in the US Navy September 27, 1940 in Chicago, Illinois and completed his basic training at the Naval Training Station in Great Lakes, Illinois. He reported for duty on the USS Arizona December 9, 1940. Edward was killed in action on December 7, 1941 at Pearl Harbor, Hawaii. He was awarded the American Defense Service Medal, World War II Victory Medal and Purple Heart Medal posthumously. Edward remains on duty on the USS Arizona. He is commemorated on the USS Arizona Memorial and the Memorial Tablets of the Missing, National Memorial Cemetery of the Pacific, Honolulu, Hawaii. Edward was survived by his Father, Mr. Forrest Edward Wright, 1205 West Webster Avenue, Chicago, Illinois.[856]

Wyckoff, Robert Leroy   Fireman, First Class, Serial No: 223 71 86, US Navy. Robert was born June 12, 1913 in Newark, New Jersey, the youngest son of ten children born to Isaac Newton Wyckoff and Addie (Van Duyn) Wyckoff. Both of his parents died in the 1930's. He enlisted in the US Navy May 15, 1940 in New York, New York and reported for duty on the USS Arizona March 22, 1941. Robert was killed in action on December 7, 1941 at Pearl Harbor, Hawaii. He was awarded the American Defense Service Medal, World War II Victory Medal and Purple Heart Medal posthumously. Robert remains on duty on the USS Arizona. He is commemorated on the USS Arizona Memorial and the Memorial Tablets of the Missing, National Memorial Cemetery of the Pacific, Honolulu, Hawaii and Cedar Hill Cemetery, East Millstone,

---

[855] Harlan Fred Woody, photo provided by History Teacher and researcher, Thomas Clark.
[856] Edward Henry Wright, Photo from the Chicago Tribune, Chicago, Illinois, May 5, 1942, page 9.

490

New Jersey. Robert was survived by his Brother, Mr. Alfred Vanduyn Wyckoff, 75 Sheridan Street, Irvington, Newark, New Jersey.

Yates, Elmer Elias Ship's Cook, Third Class, Serial No: 382 23 20, US Navy. Elmer was born March 3, 1914 in Brigham City, Utah, the eldest child of a family of four brothers and two sisters to Elias Alvin Yates and Elizabeth Lizzie (Larsen) Yates. *A true son of the pioneers directly descended from early Mormon settlers of the state of Utah. He came from a family background of ranchers, farmers and railroad men. Elmer was raised in Brigham City, Utah, where he attended Box Elder High School. Many a boyhood day was spent on the farms and ranches of his numerous aunts and uncles in nearby Park Valley, Utah. He spent time in his late teens at Palisade, Eureka, Nevada. Where his father was employed as section foreman with the Southern Pacific Railroad and maintained a second family home. Growing up, Elmer was said to be a bright, adventurous and personable boy with a mischievous streak. As one or two tales of run ins with a truant officer do attest. As an adult he was well liked and had many friends. Among the attributes for which he was best known were a keen sense of humor and the love of practical jokes. He was held in particular awe and idolized by his youngest brother, some twenty hears his junior. Somewhere along the line, Elmer developed a great fondness for cooking. His recipe for "Pasta Shute" salad is something of a family legend. Elmer was a Mormon, perhaps a lapsed Mormon is a more apt description, and was more often seen enjoying a cold beer than in Sunday services. On September 29, 1933 he married Eva Johnson in Preston, Idaho. The marriage ended shortly after it began, unhappily and in divorce. As with most young men, Elmer tried to find his place in the world, this effort made all the harder by coming of age in the Great Depression. Like many others at this time, he went on the "bum" looking for a job. When he finally returned home, he was so disheveled that his won mother, literally, didn't recognize him. He had his first taste of military life when he saw service with the Utah National Guard during the 1930's. During the decade before his death, Elmer worked as a miner, ranch hand, cook and as a steam locomotive fireman on the Eureka-Nevada Railway. In 1940, Elmer visited his younger brother Tarvol in the Los Angeles area. While on this visit, he enlisted in the US Navy July 26, 1940 in Los Angeles, California and completed his basic training at the Naval Training Station in San Diego, California. Perhaps he was looking for some stability, maybe adventure or it could have been the opportunity to work in a field he liked as his rating of cook would suggest. He seemed to take to Navy life and joked about the day he would make Chief Petty Officer in his letters home. It is said that he had put in for and had been granted a transfer to a destroyer. He had hoped for Christmas leave en route to his new ship. An accident delayed the Arizona's departure from Hawaii and his planned homecoming. In a last letter home he told his family to look for him after the New Year and not to worry. He'd finished his Christmas shopping and had presents for one and all. Neither Elmer nor the presents would ever arrive in Utah.* Elmer reported for duty on the USS Arizona October 8, 1940. He was killed in action on December 7, 1941 at Pearl Harbor, Hawaii. *Whatever, Elmer was or wasn't, he was greatly loved by his family and his memory especially cherished by his youngest brother, Buzz. Always proud of Elmer, he carried the loss of his big brother and hero with him to his dying day.* Elmer was awarded the American Defense Service Medal, World War II Victory Medal and Purple Heart Medal posthumously. He remains on duty on the USS Arizona. Elmer is commemorated on the USS Arizona Memorial and the Memorial Tablets of the Missing, National Memorial Cemetery of the Pacific, Honolulu, Hawaii and the Brigham City Cemetery, Brigham, Utah. He was survived by his Parents, Mr. and Mrs. Elias Alvin Yates of Palisade, Nevada and Brigham City, Utah.[857]

---

[857] Elmer Elias Yates, Photo and story provided by his nephew, Mark Yates.

Yeats, Charles "Chuck", Jr. Coxswain, Serial No: 279 65 48, US Navy. Charles was born in about 1922, in Franklin, Ohio, the son of Charles Peter Yeats and Eva Laura (Gray) Yeats. He enlisted in the US Navy January 16, 1940 in Cincinnati, Ohio and completed his basic training at the Naval Training Station in Great Lakes, Illinois. He reported for duty on the USS Arizona March 26, 1940. Charles was killed in action on December 7, 1941 at Pearl Harbor, Hawaii. He was awarded the American Defense Service Medal, World War II Victory Medal and Purple Heart Medal posthumously. Charles remains buried on the USS Arizona. He is commemorated on the USS Arizona Memorial and the Memorial Tablets of the Missing, National Memorial Cemetery of the Pacific, Honolulu, Hawaii. Charles was survived by his Sister, Mrs. Irma Elizabeth Schueller, 2745 West 90th Street, Chicago, Illinois.[858]

Yomine, Frank Peter Fireman, Second Class, Serial No: 368 53 74, US Navy. Frank was born April 28, 1923 in Melrose Park, Illinois, the son of Nicholas Dominick and Josephine (Ciancio) Yomine. He enlisted in the US Navy November 13, 1940 in Salt Lake City, Utah and completed his basic training at the Naval Training Station in San Diego, California. Frank reported for duty on the USS Arizona January 11, 1941. He was killed in action on December 7, 1941 at Pearl Harbor, Hawaii. Frank was awarded the American Defense Service Medal, World War II Victory Medal and Purple Heart Medal posthumously. He remains on duty on the USS Arizona. Frank is commemorated on the USS Arizona Memorial and the Memorial Tablets of the Missing, National Memorial Cemetery of the Pacific, Honolulu, Hawaii. He was survived by his Father, Mr. Nickles Yomine, 161 North 23rd Avenue, Melrose Park, Illinois.

Young, Eric Reed Ensign, Serial No: 0-085064, US Navy. Eric was born September 6, 1916 in California, the son of James Reed and Ann Myrtle (Allen) Young. He graduated from the US Naval Academy and was commissioned in the US Navy June 6, 1940 and was serving as Watch and Junior Division 1 Officer. His battle station was Port AA control. Eric was killed in action on December 7, 1941 at Pearl Harbor, Hawaii. He was awarded the American Defense Service Medal, World War II Victory Medal and Purple Heart Medal posthumously. Eric remains on duty on the USS Arizona. He is commemorated on the USS Arizona Memorial and the Memorial Tablets of the Missing, National Memorial Cemetery of the Pacific, Honolulu, Hawaii. Eric was survived by his Father, Professor James Reed Young, 122 Maple Street, Reno, Nevada.[859]

---

[858] Charles Yeats, Jr., Photo and information provided by family member, Stephen E. Tobias.

[859] Eric Reed Young, Photo from the Lucky Bag Yearbook, United States Naval Academy, Annapolis, Maryland, Class of 1940.

Young, Glendale Rex   Seaman, First Class, Serial No: 393 42 71, US Navy. Glendale was born in 1920, the son of Elmer Vincent and Clara A. Young. He enlisted in the US Navy November 6, 1940 in Portland, Oregon and completed his basic training at the Naval Training Station in San Diego, California. Glendale reported for duty on the USS Arizona January 11, 1941. He was killed in action on December 7, 1941 at Pearl Harbor, Hawaii. Glendale was awarded the American Defense Service Medal, World War II Victory Medal and Purple Heart Medal posthumously. He remains on duty on the USS Arizona. Glendale is commemorated on the USS Arizona Memorial and the Memorial Tablets of the Missing, National Memorial Cemetery of the Pacific, Honolulu, Hawaii. He was survived by his Father, Mr. Elmer Vincent Young, Coburg, Oregon.[860]

Young, Jay Wesley   Seaman, First Class, Serial No: 368 53 06, US Navy. Jay was born October 29, 1912 in Tropic, Utah, the son of John Wesley and Minnie Irene (Wilden) Young. He enlisted in the US Navy October 28, 1940 in Salt Lake City, Utah and completed his basic training at the Naval Training Station in San Diego, California. Jay reported for duty on the USS Arizona December 30, 1940. He was killed in action on December 7, 1941 at Pearl Harbor, Hawaii. Jay was awarded the American Defense Service Medal, World War II Victory Medal and Purple Heart Medal posthumously. He remains on duty on the USS Arizona. Jay is commemorated on the USS Arizona Memorial and the Memorial Tablets of the Missing, National Memorial Cemetery of the Pacific, Honolulu, Hawaii. He was survived by his Parents, Mr. and Mrs. John Wesley Young, P.O. Box 58, Oakley, Utah, seven brothers and sisters; Mrs. Delsa Young of Woodland, Utah; Keith Young, serving in the US Army in California; Ida, Smith, Marion, Ted and Lynn Young all of Oakley, Utah.[861]

Young, Vivan Louis   Watertender, First Class, Serial No: 341 12 72, US Navy. Vivan was born in about 1897 in New Mexico. He enlisted in the US Navy March 2, 1935 in San Diego, California and completed his basic training at the Naval Training Station in San Diego, California. He reported for duty on the USS Arizona June 25, 1941. Vivan was killed in action on December 7, 1941 at Pearl Harbor, Hawaii. He was awarded the American Defense Service Medal, World War II Victory Medal and Purple Heart Medal posthumously. Vivan remains on duty on the USS Arizona. He is commemorated on the USS Arizona Memorial and the Memorial Tablets of the Missing, National Memorial Cemetery of the Pacific, Honolulu, Hawaii. Vivan was survived by his Sister, Mrs. G. W. Jacobs, 2101 Farragut Court, Alameda, California.

Zadik, Edward Albert   Seaman, Second Class, Serial No. 360 15 49, US Navy. Edward was born on April 13, 1918 in Texas, the son of Aaron King and Elizabeth Zadik. He enlisted in the US Navy June 7, 1940 in Houston, Texas and completed his basic training at the Naval Training Station in San Diego, California. He reported for duty on the USS Arizona September 8, 1940. He was serving on the USS Arizona on December 7, 1941 when the Japanese attacked Pearl Harbor. After the attack, Edward was transferred to the USS Mac Donough (DD-

---

[860] Glendale Rex Young, Photo from the Eugene Guard Newspaper, Eugene, Oregon, Tuesday, May 5, 1942, Page 1.
[861] Jay Wesley Young, Information and photo provided by family member, T. V. Young.

351) for duty. Edward died on December 16, 1991 and is buried in Section C, Site 545, Fort Sam Houston National Cemetery, San Antonio, Texas.

Zeiler, John Virgel Seaman, First Class, Serial No: 372 18 59, US Navy. John was born in about 1923 in Nebraska, the son of John Zeiler and Emma E. Zeiler. He enlisted in the US Navy October 1, 1940 in Denver, Colorado and reported for duty on the USS Arizona December 6, 1940. John was killed in action on December 7, 1941 at Pearl Harbor, Hawaii. He was awarded the American Defense Service Medal, World War II Victory Medal and Purple Heart Medal posthumously. John remains on duty on the USS Arizona. He is commemorated on the USS Arizona Memorial and the Memorial Tablets of the Missing, National Memorial Cemetery of the Pacific, Honolulu, Hawaii. John was survived by his Father, Mr. John Zeiler, Holyoke, Colorado. The Zeiler-Owens-Lindsay VFW Post #6482 in Holyoke, Colorado was name in his honor.

Ziembricke, Steve Anthony Seaman, First Class, Serial No: 223 62 89, US Navy. Steve enlisted in the US Navy January 2, 1940 in New York, New York and reported for duty on the USS Arizona March 22, 1940. Steve was killed in action on December 7, 1941 at Pearl Harbor, Hawaii. He was awarded the American Defense Service Medal, World War II Victory Medal and Purple Heart Medal posthumously. Steve remains on duty on the USS Arizona. He is commemorated on the USS Arizona Memorial and the Memorial Tablets of the Missing, National Memorial Cemetery of the Pacific, Honolulu, Hawaii. Steve was survived by his Father, Mr. Stanislaus Ziembricke, 216 Freeman Street, Brooklyn, New York.

Zimmerman, Fred Coxswain, Serial No: 328 65 05, US Navy. Fred was born May 10, 1921 in North Dakota, the oldest son of Frank George Zimmerman and Mary Edith (Burrows) Zimmerman. He attended the Cleveland, North Dakota School. At the time it was a 1st through 12th grade school. Fred enlisted in the US Navy January 24, 1940 in Minneapolis, Minnesota and completed his basic training at the Naval Training Station in Great Lakes, Illinois. He reported for duty on the USS Arizona March 26, 1940. Fred was killed in action on December 7, 1941 at Pearl Harbor, Hawaii. He was awarded the American Defense Service Medal, World War II Victory Medal and Purple Heart Medal posthumously. Fred remains on duty on the USS Arizona and is commemorated on the USS Arizona Memorial and the Memorial Tablets of the Missing, National Memorial Cemetery of the Pacific, Honolulu, Hawaii. He was survived by his Parents, Mr. Frank G. and Mrs. Mary E. Zimmerman, Cleveland, North Dakota one younger brother, Frank and 7 half brothers and sisters all much older than him.[862]

---

[862] Fred Zimmerman, Photo provided by family members Kenneth and Dianna Neukircher. Information provided by his younger brother, Frank Zimmerman.

Zimmerman, Lloyd McDonald   Seaman, Second Class, Serial No: 337 41 41, US Navy. Lloyd was born May 5, 1921 in Kennett, Missouri, the youngest son of Frank B. Zimmerman and Lucy Alice (Cornelison-Robbins) Zimmerman. He enlisted in the US Navy October 15, 1940 in St. Louis, Missouri and completed his basic training at the Naval Training Station in Great Lakes, Illinois. Lloyd reported for duty on the USS Arizona December 9, 1940. He was killed in action on December 7, 1941 at Pearl Harbor, Hawaii. Lloyd was awarded the American Defense Service Medal, World War II Victory Medal and Purple Heart Medal posthumously. He remains on duty on the USS Arizona. Lloyd is commemorated on the USS Arizona Memorial and the Memorial Tablets of the Missing, National Memorial Cemetery of the Pacific, Honolulu, Hawaii. He was survived by his Mother, Mrs. Lucy Alice Zimmerman, 207 Carey Street, Kennett, Missouri.

Zwarun, Michael, Jr.   Seaman, First Class, Serial No: 223 79 01, US Navy. Michael was born in about 1920 in New Jersey, the son of Michael Zwarun and Josephine Zwarun. He enlisted in the Navy on August 8, 1940 in New York, New York and reported for duty on the USS Ellet on October 26, 1940. Some days before the 7th of December, he went ashore from his own ship. While ashore, he got himself arrested by the shore patrol. His offences were drunkenness, disorderly conduct and swearing at the shore patrol. He was ordered to stand trial by general court martial and was confined under close arrest. His ship, the Ellet, did not have a brig, so he was sent to the USS Arizona's brig to serve his general court sentence on November 27, 1941. Michael was killed in action on December 7, 1941 at Pearl Harbor, Hawaii. He was awarded the American Defense Service Medal, World War II Victory Medal and Purple Heart Medal posthumously. Michael remains on duty on the USS Arizona. He is commemorated on the USS Arizona Memorial and the Memorial Tablets of the Missing, National Memorial Cemetery of the Pacific, Honolulu, Hawaii. Michael was survived by his Father, Mr. Michael Zwarun, Sr., 1305 Bower Street, Linden, New Jersey.[863]

---

[863] Michael Zwarun, Photo from New Jersey Honor States.

1940 A Division Softball Champions:

Back Row (Left to Right): Everett O. Reid, Elmer P. Schlund, Forrest N. Miller, Homer B. Powers, Clarence J. Hamilton, Edward S. Pawlowski
Front Row (Left to Right): William C. Shealy, Weldon V. Eskew, Charles W. Haislip, Vernon Matney, John F. Shea.

Radio Gang:

SHORE LEAVE U.S. NAVY
APRIL 1940 LAHAINA, MAUI

To THE BATTLESHIP ARIZONA

WE PUT her in commission down in Brooklyn long ago,
We knew her every bolt and nut for we had watched her grow,
For she was young, and we were young, the way it ought to be
When little fellows run away to serve a hitch at sea.

For fighting men are lonely men wherever they may roam
And when they love a battleship they tell you "It's a home!"
And such a home was my old ship—a source of endless pride—
A thing of thrilling beauty that enchanted every tide.

And now she sleeps beneath the waves, the ship we loved so well,
No more to thrill to bugler's "Taps". . . all silent is her bell.
Today the Fleet steamed up the bay—it was a sight to see—
But there's a lonely mooring where my old ship ought to be.

—NICK KENNY

Arizona Baseball Team:

Chapter Five: The Marines

Photo # NH 83062 USS Arizona sunk and burning at Pearl Harbor, 7 December 1941

The Marine contingent consisted of ninety-eight men. As the attack began in the early hours of Sunday, December 7, 1941, the Marines sprung into action. Corporal Soley had been on duty in the cupola on the mainmast and watched with horror as the attack began. Lieutenant Simensen led a group of men up the starboard mainmast ladder. This ladder was eighty feet and the men were totally exposed during their climb to their battle station. Lt. Simensen had just reached the first platform of the mainmast when he was struck down by shrapnel from a bomb hitting on the quarterdeck. The remaining ten Marines made for the cupola, bullets and shrapnel whistling by them during their climb. By this time, communications had gone out. Then at about 0813 a bomb penetrated the decks landing in the black powder room. The explosion sent the bow forty feet into the air. Flames rose hundreds of feet into the air and tore through the ship burning and killing hundreds of men in a flash. The Marines in the casemates were cut down where they stood. The Marines in the mainmast were shielded from the explosion by the bridge superstructure.

Of the ninety-eight men, seventy-three were killed in action during the attack on December 7, 1941. There were only fifteen Marines that survived the attack. The bodies of sixteen were identified and buried at Red Hill Cemetery. They were later exhumed and reburied at the National Memorial Cemetery of the Pacific. The remains of five Marines were later identified. Fifty-two Marines remain entombed in the Arizona.

Amundson, Leo DeVere Private, Serial No: 309872, US Marine Corps. Leo was born in 1924 in Wisconsin, the son of Alvin and Olga Amundson. He had just boarded the Arizona on December 6th and had not yet been assigned to a battle station. Leo was killed in action on December 7, 1941 in Pearl Harbor, Hawaii. He was last seen sitting on a bench just inside the Marines' area. Leo was awarded the American Defense Service Medal, World War II Victory Medal and Purple Heart Medal posthumously. He remains on duty on the USS Arizona. Leo is commemorated on the USS Arizona Memorial and the Memorial Tablets of the Missing, National Memorial Cemetery of the Pacific, Honolulu, Hawaii. He was survived by his Father, Mr. Alvin Amundson, 408 Cameron Avenue, La Crosse, Wisconsin.[864]

Arnold, Claude Duran, Jr. Fireman, Third Class, Serial No: 274 62 50, US Navy. Claude was born July 28, 1923 in Houston, Texas, the son of Claude Duran Arnold and Olga Francis (LaFaye) Arnold. He enlisted in the US Navy on April 25, 1941 in New Orleans, Louisiana and reported for duty on the USS Arizona on November 18, 1941. Claude was killed in action on December 7, 1941 in Pearl Harbor, Hawaii. He was awarded the American Defense Service Medal, World War II Victory Medal and Purple Heart Medal posthumously. Claude remains on duty on the USS Arizona. He is commemorated on the USS Arizona Memorial and the Memorial Tablets of the Missing, National Memorial Cemetery of the Pacific, Honolulu, Hawaii. Claude was survived by his Father, Mr. Claude Duran Arnold, Sr., 617 Mill Street, Lake Charles, Louisiana.[865] The VFW post in Lake Charles, Louisiana was named in honor of Claude and his brother Leslie Arnold and another local man that was killed during the War.

Atchison, John Calvin Private, Serial No: 291613, US Marine Corps. John was born in 1923 in Illinois. He enlisted in the Marine Corps on August 14, 1940 in Chicago, Illinois and completed his boot camp in San Diego, California. Two months later he was serving on board the USS Arizona where he was killed in action on December 7, 1941 in Pearl Harbor, Hawaii. He was awarded the American Defense Service Medal, World War II Victory Medal and Purple Heart Medal posthumously. John remains on duty on the USS Arizona. He is commemorated on the USS Arizona Memorial and the Memorial Tablets of the Missing, National Memorial Cemetery of the Pacific, Honolulu, Hawaii. John was survived by his Father, Mr. Earl Atchison, 2009 Oregon Avenue, St. Louis, Missouri.[866]

---

[864] Leo DeVere Amundson, Photo from the LaCrosse Tribune and Leader-Press, LaCrosse, Wisconsin, December 23, 1941.
[865] Claude Duran Arnold, Jr. Photo from Honor States, Louisiana.
[866] John Calvin Atchison, Photo from Missouri Honor States.

Bailey, George Richmond Private, First Class, Serial No: 289568, US Marine Corps. George was born June 14, 1921 in Los Angeles, California. He enlisted in the Marine Corps on July 24, 1940 in San Francisco, California and completed his boot camp in San Diego, California. He was killed in action on the signal bridge, December 7, 1941 in Pearl Harbor, Hawaii. He was awarded the American Defense Service Medal, World War II Victory Medal and Purple Heart Medal posthumously. George's remains were recovered and he was buried in Grave #403, Red Hill Cemetery, Oahu, Hawaii. His remains were later exhumed and reinterred in Plot B, Row 0, Grave 323, National Memorial Cemetery of the Pacific, Honolulu, Hawaii. He is commemorated on the USS Arizona Memorial. George was survived by his Mother, Mrs. Rose C. Bailey, 223 Bicknell Avenue, Santa Monica, California.[867]

Baker, John "Pop" McCray Sergeant, US Marine Corps. John was the whaleboat team coach on the USS Arizona. He was serving on board the USS Arizona (BB-39) on December 7, 1941 when the Japanese attacked Pearl Harbor. His official statement:

"On December 7, 1941 at approximately 0800 I was seated at the breakfast table in the marine compartment on the U.S.S. Arizona. The first thing I knew of the attack was when I heard the air raid alarm, some seconds later I heard an explosion in the distance and machine gun fire, our anti-aircraft guns came into action. I think, a little before general quarters sounded. I started up the starboard ladder and as there was considerable congestion there 2nd Lt. Simonsen, U.S.M.C. forced his way up the ladder which lead through the casemate #9. The gun was already manned and I heard Corporal Bond Yell train it out to 90. I followed Lt. Simonsen up the starboard ladder of the tripod mast under a hail of fragments and machine gun bullets. Just as the Lieutenant reached the first platform of the mainmast and stepped clear of the super structure there a bomb hit somewhere on the quarter-deck below, a fragment from which, or possibly a machine gun bullet struck him in the mid-section and he dropped in front of me; he was dead almost instantly. I made it to the control station, Secondary Aft, where I was range keeper operator, Group Three. Major Shapley, Corporal Nightingale, and several others were there. Less than a minute later what seemed to be a very large bomb went directly down our stack, a tremendous shock shook the ship and she seemed afire at once.

The Major shouted we might as well go below as we were no good there; I was the first, I think, to start down the ladder. When I reached the search light platform someone hollered "you can't use the ladder" whereupon K. D. Goodman who had been in the secondary aft, jumped for turret three and I found later that he had made it sustaining only slight injury to his ankle. The boat deck was a mass of wreckage and fire; several men who had been killed were lying there. I ran down the officer's ladder to the quarter deck. The first person I saw was Lt. Comdr. Fuqua; he was very calm and aiding men over the side—these men who had been burned severely were barely able to stand, and many apparently could not see, they would not have made shore if it had not been for the presence of mind of the Comdr. He was assisting two wounded men to the quay when I took off my clothes to swim for it. His calmness gave me courage and I looked around the deck to see if I could help. Lt. Comdr. Fuqua ordered me over the side and I saw Corp. Bond burned black on the ship as I looked back from the quay; he was still on his feet. I also saw Lt.

---

[867] George Richmond Bailey, Photo from California Honor States.

Comdr. Fuqua still on the quarter deck aiding men over the life line and directing others who were shocked too badly to more to abandon ship; there is no doubt in my mind that many men would never have reached safety except for the superb manner in which he (Comdr. Fuqua) kept control of the situation for there was a constant hail of splinters and the ship was being machine gunned continuously.

Lt. Comdr. Fuqua was exposed to all this and yet refused to leave the ship as long as he could help the men who were injured.

I swam for Ford Island and half way there I saw Major Alan Shaply struggling with Corporal Nightingale in the water; they were too far away for me to reach them, but I could see that the Major was very tired and was risking drowning by hanging on to Nightingale both of whom had on full clothing. I learned later they had been "blown" from the ship into the water. I reached Ford Island safely and made for shelter."

Wounded in Action, his wife Mrs. John M. Baker, 3801 South 52nd Street, Lincoln, Nebraska was notified. John received the Silver Star, Bronze Star and five Purple Hearts for his service during World War II and the Korean War. He retired from the Marine Corp in 1960 as a Captain and died in June 1974.

Baraga, Joseph Sergeant, Serial No: 269591, US Marine Corps. Joseph was born October 31, 1915 in Channing, Michigan to Karel Baraga and Josephine (Lavrie) Baraga. He enlisted in the Marine Corps on January 3, 1939 in San Diego, California completing his boot camp at San Diego. Joseph was assigned to the Marine detachment aboard the USS Arizona in April of 1939. He was serving on board the USS Arizona when he was killed in action on December 7, 1941 in Pearl Harbor, Hawaii Joseph was awarded the American Defense Service Medal, World War II Victory Medal and Purple Heart Medal posthumously. He remains on duty on the USS Arizona. Joseph is commemorated on the USS Arizona Memorial and the Memorial Tablets of the Missing, National Memorial Cemetery of the Pacific, Honolulu, Hawaii. Joseph was survived by his Mother, Mrs. Josephine Baraga, P.O. Box 72, Channing, Michigan.

Bartlett, David William Corporal, Serial No: 282720, US Marine Corps. David was born December 7, 1915 in Utah. He was assigned to the Marine detachment aboard the USS Arizona on July 13, 1941 after completing his Sea School training at the Naval Training Station, San Diego, California. He was serving on board the USS Arizona when he was killed in action on December 7, 1941 in Pearl Harbor, Hawaii while serving on board the USS Arizona. He was awarded the American Defense Service Medal, World War II Victory Medal and Purple Heart Medal posthumously. David's remains were recovered and he is buried in Plot C, Row 1, Grave 298, National Memorial Cemetery of the Pacific, Honolulu, Hawaii. He is commemorated on the USS Arizona Memorial. David was survived by his Wife, Mrs. Marjorie Ann Bartlett, 3570 Beck Street, Bell, California.[869]

---

[868] Confidential statement of John McCray Baker, Sergeant, U.S.M. C., of action against enemy December 7, 1941. Pearl Harbor, T.J., December 15, 1941.
[869] David William Bartlett, Photo from California Honor States.

Beaton, Freddie   Private, Serial No: 314538, US Marine Corps. Freddie was born on May 17, 1923 in Binger, Oklahoma. He enlisted in the US Marines on June 16, 1941 in Oklahoma City, Oklahoma and reported for duty on the USS Arizona on October 10, 1941. Freddie was killed in action on December 7, 1941 in Pearl Harbor, Hawaii. He was awarded the American Defense Service Medal with fleet clasp, World War II Victory Medal and Purple Heart Medal posthumously. Freddie remains on duty on the USS Arizona. He is commemorated on the USS Arizona Memorial and the Memorial Tablets of the Missing, National Memorial Cemetery of the Pacific, Honolulu, Hawaii. Freddie was survived by his Mother, Mrs. Edna Scott, General Delivery, Chickasha, Oklahoma.[870]

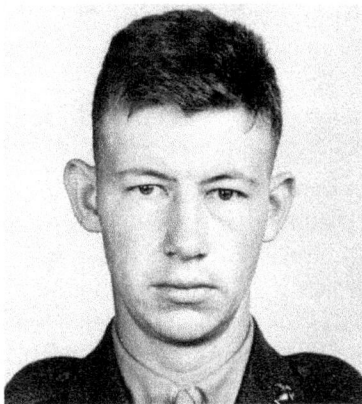

Belt, Everett Ray, Jr.   Private First Class, Serial No: 291740, US Marine Corps. Everett was born May 17, 1917 in Kansas the son of Everett R. Belt and Margaret Mae (Puckett) Belt. He enlisted in the Marine Corps on August 17, 1940 and completed his boot camp in San Diego. Two months later he was serving on board the USS Arizona where he was killed in action on December 7, 1941 in Pearl Harbor, Hawaii. Everett was awarded the American Defense Service Medal, World War II Victory Medal and Purple Heart Medal posthumously. He remains on duty on the USS Arizona. Everett is commemorated on the USS Arizona Memorial and the Memorial Tablets of the Missing, National Memorial Cemetery of the Pacific, Honolulu, Hawaii. He was survived by his Mother, Mrs. Margaret M. Belt, 842 Big Bend Road, Kirkwood, Missouri.[871]

Black, James Theron   Private, Serial No: 314626, US Marine Corps. James was born May 31, 1921 in Alabama to Ellis and Cora Geneva (Bynum) Black of Thompson, Alabama. He enlisted in the Marine Corps in 1941 and completed his boot camp in San Diego, California. James was killed in action while serving on board the USS Arizona on December 7, 1941 in Pearl Harbor, Hawaii. James was awarded the American Defense Service Medal, World War II Victory Medal and Purple Heart Medal posthumously. He remains on duty on the USS Arizona. James is commemorated on the USS Arizona Memorial and the Memorial Tablets of the Missing, National Memorial Cemetery of the Pacific, Honolulu, Hawaii and the Shady Grove Nazarene Church Cemetery, Bluff, Alabama. James was survived by his Mother, Mrs. Cora Geneva Black, Route 2, Covin, Alabama. The James Black-Nichols Brothers VFW Post 5406 in Fayette, Alabama was named in his honor.[872]

---

[870] Freddie Beaton, Photo provided by family member, Gerald Burr.

[871] Everett Ray Belt, Jr., Photo from Missouri Honor States.

[872] James Theron Black, Photo provided by SSGT Doc Doolittle, Black-Nichols Brothers VFW Post 5406, Fayette, Alabama.

Bond, Burnis Leroy Corporal, Serial No: 282672, US Marine Corps. Burnis was born on July 26, 1919 to John Lampkin Bond and Ellen (Sinclair) Bond of Mississippi. He enlisted on March 6, 1940 in New Orleans, Louisiana. *He was seen on the quarterdeck, starboard side. Burnis was the only man to make it out of number ten casemate, he was burned black, but still on his feet. Burnis was evacuated to the Naval Hospital where the staff did what they could to lessen his pain. He died shortly after.* Burnis died from his burns on December 7, 1941 in Pearl Harbor, Hawaii. Burnis was awarded the American Defense Service Medal, World War II Victory Medal and Purple Heart Medal posthumously. His remains were recovered and he was interred in grave #145 at Halawa Cemetery, Oahu, Hawaii his remains were shipped home for burial in Section Southside, Block 1, Lot 20, Grave 1, Woodlawn Park Cemetery, Wiggins, Colorado. Burnis is commemorated on the USS Arizona Memorial and the Memorial Tablets, National Memorial Cemetery of the Pacific, Honolulu, Hawaii. He was survived by his Mother, Mrs. Ellen S. Bond, Wiggins, Colorado.[873]

Borusky, Edwin Charles Corporal, Serial No: 275541, US Marine Corps. Edwin was born October 12, 1919 in Langdon, North Dakota to Fred and Flora Borusky of Langdon, North Dakota. After graduating from Landon High School he attended the University of North Dakota, where he was affiliated with Kappa Sigma fraternity. He enlisted in the Marine Corps on October 12, 1939 in Chicago, Illinois and completed his boot camp in San Diego, California. Edwin reported for duty on board the USS Arizona on December 23, 1939 and was serving on board when he was killed in action on December 7, 1941, in Pearl Harbor, Hawaii. Edwin was awarded the American Defense Service Medal, World War II Victory Medal and Purple Heart Medal posthumously. He remains on duty on the USS Arizona. Edwin is commemorated on the USS Arizona Memorial and the Memorial Tablets of the Missing, National Memorial Cemetery of the Pacific, Honolulu, Hawaii. He was survived by his Parents, Mr. and Mrs. Fred Borusky, Langdon, North Dakota, Brother, Rodney Borusky of Pearson, Wisconsin and Sister, Mrs. H. O. Reetz of Langdon, North Dakota.[874]

Braham, Edward James Private, First Class, US Marine Corps. Edward was born May 19, 1921 in Iowa to Edward and Jessie May (Brewer) Braham. He enlisted in the US Marine Corps on September 26, 1939 and completed his boot camp at the Marine Corps Base in San Diego, California. Edward was stationed with the Marine Detachment on the USS Arizona in June 1940. He was serving on board the USS Arizona (BB-39) December 7, 1941, when the Japanese attacked Pearl Harbor. He was awarded the Marine Good Conduct Medal and American Defense Medal with Fleet Bar. Edward served until September 25, 1945. On January 2, 1952, Edward joined the US Air Force retiring July 30, 1968 after having served in the Korean and Vietnam wars. Edward passed

---

[873] Burnis Leroy Bond, Photo from Mississippi Honor States.
[874] Edwin Charles Borusky, Information and photo from the Cavalier County Republican Newspaper, Langdon, North Dakota, December 18, 1941, front page.

away September 23, 1973 and is buried in the Garden of Memories Cemetery, Tampa, Florida.

Brickley, Eugene   Private, Serial No: 290538,   US Marine Corps. Eugene was born on May 28, 1922 to Keith Milo Brickley and Sylvia Opal (Finley) Brickley. He enlisted in the Marine Corps on July 31, 1940 and completed his boot camp in San Diego, California. Eugene was serving on board the USS Arizona when he was killed in action on December 7, 1941 in Pearl Harbor, Hawaii. Eugene was awarded the American Defense Service Medal, World War II Victory Medal and Purple Heart Medal posthumously. He remains on duty on the USS Arizona. Eugene is commemorated on the USS Arizona Memorial and the Memorial Tablets of the Missing, National Memorial Cemetery of the Pacific, Honolulu, Hawaii. He was survived by his Mother, Mrs. Silvia Brickley, Route 2, Grapevine, Texas. (Later address: Uniondale, Indiana).[875]

Cabiness, Frank R.   Private, First Class, US Marine Corps. Frank was born on December 3, 1916 in Texas the son of Tom and Maude Cabiness. He enlisted in the US Marine Corps September 13, 1940 in Dallas, Texas and completed his basic training at the Marine Corps Base in San Diego, California. He reported for duty on the USS Arizona in December 1940. Frank was serving on board the USS Arizona on December 7, 1941 when the Japanese attacked Pearl Harbor. *He was on the Marine color detail that morning. He narrowly avoided getting hit by machine gun fire, and luckily his only injury was from friction burns suffered when he slid down a ladder while rushing to abandon ship.* After the war, he worked for an oil pipeline company in Texas that later became Amoco Pipeline. Frank died on May 13, 2002 in Lewisville, Texas. His ashes were interred on the USS Arizona, December 23, 2011.

Carter, Edward J.   Platoon Sergeant, US Marine Corps. Edward was born on April 17, 1908. He enlisted in the US Marine Corps in 1925 and completed boot camp at Parris Island. Edward served in Quantico, Virginia, Mare Island, California and Shanghai, China from 1925 to 1940. He attended Sea School in San Diego in 1940 and reported for duty on the USS Arizona shortly thereafter. He was serving on December 7, 1941 when the Japanese attacked Pearl Harbor. *On the morning of the 7th Eddie was having coffee in the General Mess with a fellow marine and was thrown against the bulkhead by an explosion. He and the fellow Marine headed out the hatch and started to climb the maintop attempting to reach the machine gun anti-aircraft platform. The next thing that he remembers is being in the water surrounded by flames from burning fuel oil. He was picked up by a rescue boat.* Edward was awarded the Combat Action Ribbon, Navy Presidential Unit Citation, Navy Unit Commendation, Marine Corps Good Conduct Medal, China Service Medal, American Defense Service Medal, American Campaign Medal 1941-1946, Asiatic-Pacific Campaign Medal and the World War II Victory Medal. Edward died on August 18, 1989 in Maine and is buried in Section O, Row 12, Site 16, Maine Veteran's Memorial Cemetery, Augusta, Maine.

---

[875] Eugene Brickley, Photo from Indiana Honor States.

Chandler, Donald Ross Private, Serial No: 285467, US Marine Corps. Donald was born March 13, 1922 in Millport, Lamar County, Alabama to John Carlisle and Maude Pearl (Johnson) Chandler. He enlisted in the Marine Corps on June 14, 1940 and completed his basic training at Parris Island, South Carolina. He reported for duty on board the USS Arizona November 6, 1940 and was serving on board when he was killed in action on December 7, 1941 in Pearl Harbor, Hawaii. He was awarded the American Defense Service Medal, World War II Victory Medal and Purple Heart Medal posthumously. Donald remains on duty on the USS Arizona. He is commemorated on the USS Arizona Memorial and the Memorial Tablets of the Missing, National Memorial Cemetery of the Pacific, Honolulu, Hawaii. Donald was survived by his Father, Mr. John Carl Chandler, Box 264, Millport, Alabama. His brother, Edwin Ray, a Seaman, First Class in the Navy was also serving on the Arizona, but was on shore leave and survived.[876]

Cole, Charles Warren Sergeant, Serial No: 269595, US Marine Corps. Charles was born on March 5, 1920 in Snohomish, Washington to Ezra Ottis Cole and Martha E. (Knudson) Cole. He enlisted in the Marine Corps and arrived at the Marine Base on January 3, 1939. Charles was serving on board the USS Arizona when he was killed in action on December 7, 1941 in Pearl Harbor, Hawaii. Charles was awarded the American Defense Service Medal, World War II Victory Medal and Purple Heart Medal posthumously. He remains on duty on the USS Arizona. Charles is commemorated on the USS Arizona Memorial and the Memorial Tablets of the Missing, National Memorial Cemetery of the Pacific, Honolulu, Hawaii and the Grand Army of the Republic Cemetery, Snohomish, Washington. He was survived by his Father, Mr. Ezra Cole, Route 2, Arlington, Washington.[877]

Cory, James Evans Private, First Class, US Marine Corps, Combat Division 1. James was born on October 27, 1920 in Dallas, Texas. In his youth, Cory loved the ocean. He was infatuated with the stories of Horatio Hornblower. He read them all and longed for the romance of the sea. James attempted to join the Merchant Marines but was turned away because he wasn't old enough. He enlisted in the US Marine Corps on June 13, 1940 and reported for duty on the USS Arizona where he was serving on December 7, 1941 when the Japanese attacked Pearl Harbor. *He found the camaraderie he was looking for in his brothers in arms aboard the USS Arizona. On the day of the attack, PFC Cory was stationed in the secondary fire-control station located in the aft tripod mast of the Arizona. At 7:56 a.m., two explosions rocked the ship. The bridge shielded us from flames," Cory said. "Around the edges in these open windows came the heat and the sensation of the blast. We cringed there ... I think that at this moment I wanted to flee, but this was impossible. You're on station; you're in combat." The explosions caused the ship's midsection to open up, James and the men inside the compartment were ordered to head to the main deck below and then abandon ship. Heat from fires on the ship caused the magazine and forward oil storage to explode. Thousands of gallons of burning oil poured into the harbor. James was separated from the group but managed to make it to the quarter deck before diving into the flaming sea and swimming to nearby Ford Island. "Our own oil was bubbling up and*

---

[876] Donald Ross Chandler, Information and photo provided by his 1st Cousin, Dave Johnson.
[877] Charles Warren Cole, Photo from Washington Honor States.

congealing," said James. "People who have never seen this at sea cannot imagine what oil is like once it is exposed to cool seawater. It was catching fire slowly and was incinerating toward us." He survived the attack that day but he never forgot the memory of what he experienced. [878] James served in the Pacific theatre during the remainder of World War II and took part in the occupation of Japan. After the war, he attended Southern Methodist University. James passed away on July 9, 1978 in his hometown at age 56. His ashes were interred in the USS Arizona on May 11, 2008. He was the first Marine to be buried aboard the USS Arizona since World War II.

Coursey, John Paul First Lieutenant, Serial No. 0-13008, US Marine Corps. John was born December 20, 1914 in Lyons, Georgia. He transferred to the US Marine Corps from the Army and was commissioned June 3, 1940. He served on board the Arizona from May 1938 to 1939. He was on duty on the USS Arizona on December 7, 1941 when the Japanese attacked Pearl Harbor, serving as the Junior Marine Officer. *His battle station was Director Station No. 3. After the attack, he volunteered for flight training and was sent back to the mainland for training. After completion of his training in September 1944 he was ordered duty as commanding officer of VMR-152. He saw duty in the Philippines, Solomon Islands, Okinawa and the Palaus. John was called back to duty in the Korean conflict, serving as executive officer of Marine Air Group 33.* He received the Legion of Merit Medal with Combat "V" and the Distinguished Flying Cross for his actions during the Korean War:

Upon his return state-side in April 1953 he accepted duty at the U.S. Air Force Air University. He was promoted to Brigadier General in August 1962. John was awarded a second Legion of Merit for his actions during the Vietnam War. John died February 27, 1992 in Vidalia, Georgia.

Crawford, Lamar Smead Private, First Class, US Marine Corps. Lamar was born November 19, 1920 in Union County, Arkansas the son of Roy E and Zola Crawford. He enlisted in the Marine Corps on June 14, 1940. He was assigned duty on the USS Argonne in Pearl Harbor October 1940. In December 1940 he was stationed on the USS Arizona. *Lamar was serving on board the USS Arizona on December 7, 1941 when the Japanese attacked Pearl Harbor. "I awoke at reveille, 0600, had breakfast in the Marine's main deck living and sleeping quarters and got ready for Protestant Church service scheduled for 0900. In the meantime, I checked and cleaned my assigned firearm, a 1903 Springfield Army rifle. I then stepped outside the Marine compartment onto the portside Quarterdeck. As I came into the bright light, I heard the sound of airplane motors, several of them. Looking up I saw a Japanese dive bomber coming directly toward the Arizona. About that time, machine-gun bullets from the plane started bouncing off the tub-type gun mount immediately to my right. Realizing that we were being attacked, and that the bullets from the diving warplane were addressed "to whomever it may*

---

[878] James Evans Cory, Information and story taken from excerpts from "A Place of Honor" First Marine since World War II buried aboard USS Arizona by Cpl. Mark Fayloga, Press Chief, Hawaii Marine, Volume 38, Number 20, May 16, 2008.

concern," I did a quick dash back into the Marine Compartment. Within minutes of our arrival at our battle stations, we found that all communications lines were dead. Explosions and fires were raging uncontrolled throughout the ship. Suddenly, the forward magazines exploded with a deafening roar. The ship raised several feet in the harbor waters, then slowly began to sink to the bottom of the shallow harbor, a total loss. Major Shapley, the Senior Officer present, told us "Well, men, this is it. Abandon ship. It's every man for himself. Good luck and God Bless You All."[879] Lamar used the mooring lines to get off the ship. When he reached the quay, he sat down to remove his shoes when a motor whaleboat pulled alongside and pulled him into the boat. Once aboard, he helped pull men out of the water until the boat was full. He was taken to Ford Island. Lamar was involved in the preparation and submission of the December 1941 final muster roll for the Marine Detachment on the USS Arizona since he could type and had served as an active member of that detachment since September 1940.

In a letter from Lamar, he tells how the final report listing the Marines was done: "The payroll records were a different matter. Marine Units (Small Groups) were paid twice monthly. Once mid month on a Special Money Request and the end of the month payment was made on the consolidated format. Each man signing in the space evidencing payment to certify he had received the full amounts shown on the vouchers. Filing of Payroll records were the responsibility of the Disbursing Officer, in this case, Ensign H. B. "Bucky" Walsh, U.S. Navy Supply Corps, USS Arizona. His offices were located on the Zd deck (Below the main deck, directly underneath the US Marines living quarters). His safe equipment contained all payroll records of the ship's company plus allowable sums of cash, Treasurer's Checks, etc. (Officers were usually paid by issuance of US Treasurer checks, cash only if they specifically and individually requested). It was due to the integrity of the Safe equipment that we had any solid basis for the December reports later. US Navy Divers were able to open the safes using combinations furnished them by Walsh, after considerable trial and error. I was then called upon to examine the Marines Pay records and determine whether I could decipher them to prepare a December 1941 closing report. (From the November 1941 water soaked, oil streaked record recovered.) Fortunately, I could, and did this, preparing the reports necessary.

Things were far from routine or normal at the Marine Barracks, Pearl Harbor from December 7th 1941. Administrative functions had to be split up and "farmed out" to available space. I found an old L.C. Smith typewriter in a Supply Closet of the Base Paymaster. The Guard Company's Sergeant Major, Jackie Fine, furnished blank forms and provided guidance to me in preparing the reports for the Arizona's Marines that had to be made.

The Base Paymaster, Colonel W. W. Davidson, USMC noticed my labors, and recruited me to join his office staff – which had been then been re-designated "Paymaster, Marine Forces, 14th Naval District". I was then transferred to "Paymaster Personnel" and continued as such until the end of the War. At the time of the Japanese unconditional surrender, in August, 1945, I was serving as Deputy Paymaster, 34d Regiment, 3rd Marine Division, Fleet Marine Force on the Pacific Island of Guam.

Information concerning individual Marine's date and place of enlistment, home address and next of kin, educational background, social security Numbers, etc. were not obtainable from Muster Roll nor Payroll records. Each man had a Service Record Book in which such information was recorded. The Service Record Books of the Arizona's Marines were maintained in the offices of the First Sergeant, situated in a corner of the Marine living quarters on the Main Deck of the Ship. The First Sergeant on the Arizona was John Duveene. His assigned Company Clerk was Fredrick Eugene DeLong, Corporal, USMC. Both were killed in action December 7, 1941. (That's how I became involved in administrative duties, as a side line to my regular guard

---

[879] Observations from Lamar S. Crawford, USS Arizona Survivor, Pearl Harbor Visitor Center, Pearl Harbor, Honolulu, Hawaii.

and watch duties. All official records, including Personnel Jacket (Service Record Books) etc. as well as Personal clothing and other effects, were destroyed by fire."[880]

Lamar served with the 3rd Marine Air wing during the remainder of the war and was discharged on January 11, 1946. After the war he worked for the US Postal Service and retired after 36 years. Lamar passed away on Thursday, December 22, 2011 at The Hospice of East Texas, Tyler, Texas.

Davis, Virgil Denton Private, Serial No: 298403, US Marine Corps. Virgil was born in about 1922 in Peoria, Illinois. He enlisted in the Marine Corps on October 7, 1940 in Chicago, Illinois and completed his boot camp in San Diego, California. He was serving on board the USS Arizona when he was killed in action on December 7, 1941 in Pearl Harbor, Hawaii. He was awarded the American Defense Service Medal, Combat Action Ribbon, American Defense Medal, Pacific Campaign Medal with One Battle Star, World War II Victory Medal and Purple Heart Medal posthumously. Virgil remains on duty on the USS Arizona. He is commemorated on the USS Arizona Memorial and the Memorial Tablets of the Missing, National Memorial Cemetery of the Pacific, Honolulu, Hawaii. Virgil was survived by his Mother, Mrs. Georgia Davis, 608 Johnson Street, Peoria, Illinois.[881]

Dawson, James Berkley Private, Serial No: 305840, US Marine Corps. James was born January 27, 1922 in Nelson County, Kentucky to Allen and Ella (Truax) Dawson. He was serving on board the USS Arizona when he was killed in action on December 7, 1941 in Pearl Harbor, Hawaii. His sister tried to call the president and the commandant of the Marines to ask if her brother was alive. On December 17, the family was notified of his death. He had been blown off the ship and died of burns. His body was recovered from the water. James was interred in Grave #140, Red Hill Cemetery, Oahu, Hawaii. His remains were later exhumed and interred in Section A, Site 974, Zachary Taylor National Cemetery, Louisville, Kentucky. James was awarded the American Defense Service Medal, World War II Victory Medal and Purple Heart Medal posthumously. James is commemorated on the USS Arizona Memorial. He was survived by his Mother, Mrs. Ella R. Dawson, Theirman Apartments, Louisville, Kentucky, his Father, Allen A. Dawson, Kansas City; a sister, Mrs. Bernard Tilford, Louisville, Kentucky; grandfather, James Truax, four aunts and seven uncles.[882]

---

[880] Lamar Smead Crawford, Information, Marine Muster Roll, December 1941, story and picture provided in a letter from Lamar on February 10, 2010.

[881] Virgil Denton Davis, Photo from Illinois Honor States.

[882] James Berkley Dawson, Information and photo from The Courier-Journal, Louisville, Kentucky, December 18, 1941, Page 2.

De Long, Frederick Eugene Corporal, Serial No: 273229, US Marine Corps. Frederick was born May 12, 1912 in Cridersville, Ohio to Frank E. and Emma H. (Fryman) De Long. He enlisted in the US Marine Corps on July 17, 1939 and completed his boot camp and sea school at the Marine Corps Base in San Diego, California. Frederick was serving on board the USS Arizona when he was killed in action on December 7, 1941 in Pearl Harbor, Hawaii. Frederick was awarded the American Defense Service Medal, World War II Victory Medal and Purple Heart Medal posthumously. His remains were recovered and he was buried in Plot B, Row 1, Grave 275, National Memorial Cemetery of the Pacific, Honolulu, Hawaii. Frederick is commemorated on the USS Arizona Memorial. He was survived by his Mother, Mrs. Emma H. De Long, 113 West Main Street, Cridersville, Ohio.[883]

Dreesbach, Herbert Allen Private First Class, Serial No: 298404, US Marine Corps. Herbert was born on March 16, 1917 to Arthur and Elsie (Behrend) Dreesbach of Chicago, Illinois. *He was a tall, handsome young man with an easy going personality. After graduating from high school he went to work in a factory, Ilg Electric Ventilating Co that also employed his brother, Arthur and his grandfather, William.* Herbert enlisted in the Marine Corps on October 7, 1940 in Chicago, Illinois and completed his basic training in San Diego, California. He was serving on board the USS Arizona when he was killed in action on December 7, 1941 in Pearl Harbor, Hawaii. Herbert was awarded the American Defense Service Medal, World War II Victory Medal and Purple Heart Medal posthumously. He remains on duty on the USS Arizona. Herbert is commemorated on the USS Arizona Memorial and the Memorial Tablets of the Missing, National Memorial Cemetery of the Pacific, Honolulu, Hawaii. He was survived by his Mother, Mrs. Ella Dreesbach, 1820 North Lorel Avenue, Chicago, Illinois.[884]

Dunnam, Robert "Bob" Wesley Private, Serial No: 306243, US Marine Corps Reserve. Robert was born in November 23, 1921 in Harris County, Texas the son of Homer A. Dunnam and Allene W. Dunnam. He enlisted in the Marine Corps in 1941 and completed his boot camp and Sea School in San Diego, California. He was serving on board the USS Arizona when he was killed in action on December 7, 1941 in Pearl Harbor, Hawaii. Robert was awarded the American Defense Service Medal, World War II Victory Medal and Purple Heart Medal posthumously. He remains on duty on the USS Arizona. Robert is commemorated on the USS Arizona Memorial and the Memorial Tablets of the Missing, National Memorial Cemetery of the Pacific, Honolulu, Hawaii. He was survived by his Mother, Mrs. Allene Dunnam, 1302 West 22nd Street, Houston, Texas.[885]

---

[883] Frederick Eugene De Long, Photo from Ohio Honor States.
[884] Herbert Allen Dreesbach, Photo and information provided by his nephew, Don Dreesbach and his brother Arthur's wife, Aileen Dreesbach.
[885] Robert Wesley Dunnam, Photo provided by family member, Kara Sharits.

Durio, Russell Private First Class, Serial No: 299280, US Marine Corps. Russell born in 1922 in Louisiana to Simon and Marie Durio. *He graduated High School at age 15 and spent the next two years at college. At Age 17, Russell convinced his father to sign "the paperwork" so he could be on his way to serve his country ... after all, Russell said, "I'm going to sign up on my 18th birthday, with or without your permission!" His father was very worried Russell would end up going to war, but signed the papers anyway.* He enlisted in the Marine Corps on October 12, 1940 in New Orleans, Louisiana and completed his boot camp and Sea School in San Diego, California. Russell was assigned to the gun crew on board the USS Arizona. *He kept in touch by writing weekly letters to his family. His brother A. D. mailed the last letter he'd written back to Russell along* with a box of Christmas cookies on December 5, 1941. The ladies of the town had stayed up all night to make enough of the cookies so Russell could share with his shipmates. The Durio family and the small town of Sunset, Louisiana were shocked when they heard the news about the Pearl Harbor attack. Russell was serving on board the USS Arizona when he was killed in action on December 7, 1941 in Pearl Harbor, Hawaii. *One night in January, Russell's father answered the phone, fell against the wall and sank to the floor saying, "I should have never signed those papers."* Official letters arrived on January 27th 1942 saying that Russell Durio was listed among the missing and his body had not been recovered from the wrecked ship. Around the same time, the post office returned A.D.'s letter and the Christmas cookie box stamped, "Unclaimed." Russell's father took the box outside and buried it next to an old chimney – he knew his son would never be coming home. Russell was awarded the American Defense Service Medal, World War II Victory Medal and Purple Heart Medal posthumously. He remains on duty on the USS Arizona. Russell is commemorated on the USS Arizona Memorial and the Memorial Tablets of the Missing, National Memorial Cemetery of the Pacific, Honolulu, Hawaii. Russell was survived by his Parents, Mr. & Mrs. Simon Durio, Sunset, Louisiana, Brother, A. D. and Sister, Charlsey.[886]

Duveene, John First Sergeant, Serial No: 181999, US Marine Corps. John was born April 29, 1900. He enlisted in the US Marines June 23, 1922 in Massachusetts. He was serving on board the USS Arizona when he was killed in action on December 7, 1941 in Pearl Harbor, Hawaii. *He was standing near a ventilator shaft on the starboard side of the quarterdeck, burned beyond recognition. "I knew him by his voice. He called us Marine champions. John yelled out for us to 'Swim for it, champions.'" "Don't try to go back inside; everything in there is all burned up. I'm not going to make it. Get the hell out of here!"* He was awarded the American Defense Service Medal, World War II Victory Medal and Purple Heart Medal posthumously. John was buried in Grave #138, Red Hill Cemetery, Oahu, Hawaii. His remains were later exhumed and reburied in Plot E, Row 0, Grave 225, National Memorial Cemetery of the Pacific, Honolulu, Hawaii. He is commemorated on the USS Arizona Memorial. John was survived by his Wife, Mrs. Eleanor Duveene, 1230 Ridgely Drive, Los Angeles, California.

---

[886] Russell Durio, Information and picture provided by family members, Lorraine Justus and Dan Durio (Russell's grand-nephew).

Earle, John Horatio, Jr. Captain, Serial No. 0-12847, US Marine Corps. John was born on January 7, 1915 in Reading, Pennsylvania. He was the son of John Horatio Earle and Henrietta Grimm Earle. He was commissioned in the US Marine Corps in 1936, upon graduation from Virginia Military Institute. *John (Jack) had received orders to transfer to the USS Arizona from the USS Tennessee, where he had been stationed for about 2 years with the Marine Detachment. He could not carry out these orders until December 6, 1941, when both ships were at Pearl Harbor at the same time. He reported aboard the Arizona that day and relieved Alan Shapley, who had just been promoted to Major and thus "over-ranked" his position. Both officers then set about verifying the Marine Corps gear aboard. They were down in the bottom of the ship in sweltering heat when Alan suggested they go to the officer's club at Pearl Harbor for a beer. (Of course, no alcohol was allowed on the ship.)*

When they arrived at the club, Alan ran into a group of officers who were celebrating a birthday. They invited him to join them, so Alan told Jack to "Go home to your bride and we'll finish the job tomorrow morning." Jack happily complied and that was why he was not aboard the ship on December 7ᵗʰ when the attack occurred, although he made his way out to Pearl Harbor while the second wave of the attack was going on, only to find the Arizona burning. He gathered the men who remained from the Marine Detachment (about 15 of the original 85) and took them over to the Tennessee, by walking on the pipeline between the Arizona and the Tennessee nearby. His former shipmates were amazed to see him, but they promptly put these survivors to work on the Tennessee, which had been hit but, because it was wedged in by another ship, did not sink.

After the Pearl Harbor attack, he served in the Philippines as part of an air fighter group. He had been accepted into fighter training shortly after the Pearl Harbor attack and received his "wings" after 6 months training in Florida.

After the war, he went to the Pentagon, then later to become Chief of Staff for General Shell and later General Kier at the USMC Air station in Kanoehe, Hawaii.

He retired in 1962, studied at the University of Hawaii and received an MA degree in History. He later taught for the University.

He lived in Hawaii since 1958 until his death January 26, 2007 at the age of 92. John died of heart failure at the Queen's Medical Center and is buried in Section C10-K, Row 100, Site 173, National Memorial Cemetery of the Pacific, Honolulu, Hawaii. He left a wife, Barbara F. Earle, and 4 children, John, Sue, Tom and Jane. "We miss him terribly." (Barbara F. Earle, wife)[887]

Erskine, Robert "Bobbie" Charles Private, First Class, Serial No: 298406, US Marine Corps. Robert was born October 19, 1920 in Missouri to Leonard R. and Bertha A. Erskine. He enlisted in the US Marine Corps on October 7, 1940 in Chicago, Illinois and completed his basic training at the Marine Corps Base in San Diego, California. Robert was serving on board the USS Arizona when he was killed in action on December 7, 1941 in Pearl Harbor, Hawaii. He was awarded the American Defense Service Medal, World War II Victory Medal and Purple Heart Medal posthumously. Robert's remains were recovered and he was buried in Plot Q, Row 0, Grave 145, National Memorial Cemetery of the

---

[887] John Horatio Earle, Jr., Information, stories and Photo provided by his wife, Barbara F. Earle.

Pacific, Honolulu, Hawaii. He is commemorated on the USS Arizona Memorial. Robert was survived by his Parents, Mr. and Mrs. Leonard R. Erskine, Siloam Springs, Arkansas.[888]

Evans, David Delton   Private, Serial No: 250203, US Marine Corps. David enlisted in the Marine Corps on September 5, 1935 and attended weekly drills with Company B, Tenth Battalion, Fleet Marine Corps Reserve in New Orleans instead of attending boot camp. He re-enlisted on October 11, 1940 and completed his boot camp training and Sea School in San Diego, California. David was serving on board the USS Arizona when he was killed in action on December 7, 1941 in Pearl Harbor, Hawaii. He was awarded the American Defense Service Medal, World War II Victory Medal and Purple Heart Medal posthumously. David remains on duty on the USS Arizona. He is commemorated on the USS Arizona Memorial and the Memorial Tablets of the Missing, National Memorial Cemetery of the Pacific, Honolulu, Hawaii. David was survived by his Wife, Mrs. Faye R. Evans, 805 Alvar Street, New Orleans, Louisiana.[889]

Fincher, Allen Brady   Assistant Cook, Serial No: 292084, US Marine Corps. Allen was born in 1919, the oldest son of Allen and Clara Fincher of Van Zandt, Texas. He enlisted in the Marine Corps on August 15, 1940 and completed his boot camp at San Diego, California. After boot camp, he was assigned to Guard Company #1 at Puget Sound Navy Yard. He was assigned duty on the Arizona in November 1940. Allen was serving on board the USS Arizona when he was killed in action on December 7, 1941 in Pearl Harbor, Hawaii. He was awarded the American Defense Service Medal, World War II Victory Medal and Purple Heart Medal posthumously. Allen remains on duty on the USS Arizona. He is commemorated on the USS Arizona Memorial and the Memorial Tablets of the Missing, National Memorial Cemetery of the Pacific, Honolulu, Hawaii. Allen was survived by his Mother, Mrs. Clara Fincher, Route 3, Canton, Texas.[890]

Fincher, Dexter Wilson   Sergeant, Serial No: 273115, US Marine Corps. Dexter was born on February 23, 1917 in Prineville, Oregon to John Wilson and Grace Maud (Barney) Fincher. He enlisted in the US Marine Corps on July 10, 1939 in Portland, Oregon and completed his basic training at the Marine Corps Base in San Diego, California. He was serving on board the USS Arizona as a gun captain controlling the fire of one of the ship's secondary batteries when he was killed in action on December 7, 1941 in Pearl Harbor, Hawaii. Dexter was awarded the American Defense Service Medal, World War II Victory Medal and Purple Heart Medal posthumously. He remains on duty on the USS Arizona. Dexter is commemorated on the USS Arizona Memorial and the Memorial Tablets of the Missing, National Memorial

---

[888] Robert Charles Erskine, Photo from Arkansas Honor States.
[889] David Delton Evans, Photo from Louisiana Honor States.
[890] Allen Brady Fincher, Photo from Texas Honor States.

Cemetery of the Pacific, Honolulu, Hawaii and Juniper Haven Cemetery, Prineville, Oregon. He was survived by his Mother, Mrs. Grace M. Fincher, P.O. Box 35, Prineville, Oregon. The Dexter Fincher VFW Post No. 1412 of Prineville, Oregon was named in his honor.[891]

Finley, Woodrow Wilson   Private, First Class, Serial No: 299051, US Marine Corps. Woodrow was born January 23, 1916 in Selmer, Tennessee to James M. and Ada Finley. He enlisted in the US Marine Corps on October 10, 1940 in New Orleans, Louisiana and completed his basic training at the Marine Corps Base in San Diego, California. Woodrow was serving on board the USS Arizona when he was killed in action on December 7, 1941 in Pearl Harbor, Hawaii. He was awarded the American Defense Service Medal, World War II Victory Medal and Purple Heart Medal posthumously. Woodrow remains on duty on the USS Arizona. He is commemorated on the USS Arizona Memorial and Memorial Tablets of the Missing, National Memorial Cemetery of the Pacific, Honolulu, Hawaii. Woodrow was survived by his Parents, Mr. and Mrs. James M. Finley, Selmer, Tennessee.[892]

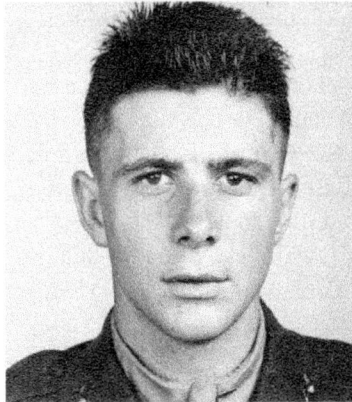

Fitzgerald, Kent Blake   Private, Serial No: 292824, US Marine Corps. Kent was born on March 1, 1922 in Richfield, Utah to Walter Day and Beatrice Mabel (Blake) Fitzgerald. He enlisted in the US Marine Corps on August 17, 1940 and completed his boot camp at the MCRD in San Diego, California. Kent reported for duty on the USS Arizona in October 1940. Kent was killed in action on December 7, 1941 in Pearl Harbor, Hawaii. He was awarded the American Defense Service Medal, World War II Victory Medal and Purple Heart Medal posthumously. Kent remains on duty on the USS Arizona. He is commemorated on the USS Arizona Memorial and the Memorial Tablets of the Missing, National Memorial Cemetery of the Pacific, Honolulu, Hawaii. Kent was survived by his Father, Mr. Walter D. Fitzgerald, 74 O Street, Salt Lake City, Utah.[893]

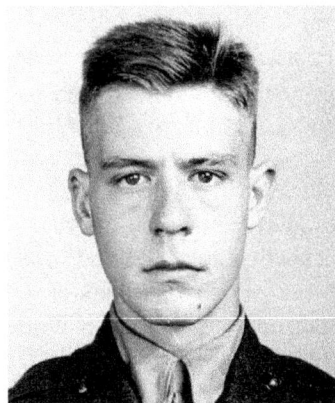

Fleetwood, Donald Eugene   Private, First Class, Serial No: 294438, US Marine Corps. Donald was born November 14, 1921 in Fort Dodge, Iowa to Claude A. and Elizabeth Fern (Dort) Fleetwood. He enlisted in the Marine Corps on September 9, 1940 in Chicago, Illinois and completed his boot camp and Sea School at San Diego, California. Donald was serving on board the USS Arizona when he was killed in action on December 7, 1941 in Pearl Harbor, Hawaii. He was awarded the American Defense Service Medal, World War II Victory Medal and Purple Heart Medal posthumously. Donald remains on duty on the USS Arizona. He is commemorated on the USS Arizona Memorial and the Memorial Tablets of the Missing, National Memorial

---

[891] Dexter Wilson Fincher, Photo from Oregon Honor States.
[892] Woodrow Wilson Finley, Photo from Tennessee Honor States.
[893] Kent Blake Fitzgerald Blake, Photo from Utah Honor States and information from the Salt Lake Telegram, Salt Lake City, Utah, December 17, 1941, Page 9.

Cemetery of the Pacific, Honolulu, Hawaii. Donald was survived by his Sister, Miss Dorothy Fleetwood, 1402 3rd Avenue North, Fort Dodge, Iowa.[894]

Fox, Daniel Russell Lieutenant Colonel, Serial No: 0-000307, US Marine Corps. Daniel was the Division Marine Officer, Intelligence Officer and Censor on the USS Arizona. Daniel was born at Shenkel, Pennsylvania on July 10, 1898 in Shenkel, Pennsylvania to William and Catherine Fox. He enlisted in the US Marine Corps on July 29, 1916 and completed his training in South Carolina. During World War I, in France on October 4, 1918, when he was a member of the 17th Company, Fifth Marines, he was awarded the Navy Cross. He also received the Army Distinguished Service Cross and the French Croix de Guerre during World War I. He was commissioned in 1921 and served in Nicaragua and China. Daniel was the most senior Marine officer to be killed in action on December 7, 1941 in Pearl Harbor, Hawaii, on the signal bridge of the USS Arizona. He was awarded the Navy Cross, Distinguished Service Cross, French Croix de Guerre during World War I and the American Defense Service Medal, World War II Victory Medal and Purple Heart Medal posthumously. Daniel was recommended for the Medal of Honor by Colonel Harry K. Pickett, the commanding officer of the Marine Forces of the Fourteenth Naval District. The recommendation was endorsed by the Commandant, Lieutenant General Thomas Holcomb. The recommendation was turned down. Daniel remains on duty on the USS Arizona. He is commemorated on the USS Arizona Memorial and the Memorial Tablets of the Missing, National Memorial Cemetery of the Pacific, Honolulu, Hawaii. Daniel was survived by his Wife, Mrs. Elsie B. Fox, 1811 East Ocean Boulevard, Long Beach, California.[895]

Goodman, Kenneth Dale Private, First Class, US Marine Corps. Kenneth was born in 1923 the son of Ernest and Opal Goodman of Bisbee, Arizona. He enlisted in the US Marine Corps on November 6, 1939 and completed his basic training at the Marine Corps base in San Diego, California. He reported for duty on board the USS Argonne for a time before reporting for duty on the USS Arizona in April of 1940. He was serving on board the USS Arizona on December 7, 1941 when the Japanese attacked Pearl Harbor.

Griffin, Lawrence John Private First Class, Serial No: 295032, US Marine Corps. Lawrence was born December 4, 1919 to Lawrence O. and Lydia M. Griffin in New Orleans, Louisiana. He enlisted in the Marine Corps on September 10, 1940 and completed his boot camp at San Diego, California. He was serving on board the USS Arizona when he was killed in action on December 7, 1941 at Pearl Harbor, Hawaii. Lawrence was awarded the American Defense Service Medal, World War II Victory Medal and Purple Heart Medal posthumously. He remains on duty on the USS Arizona. Lawrence is commemorated on the USS Arizona Memorial and the Memorial Tablets of the Missing, National Memorial Cemetery of the Pacific, Honolulu,

---

[894] Donald Eugene Fleetwood, Photo from Iowa Honor States.
[895] Daniel Russell Fox, Photo courtesy of the United States Marine Corps.

Hawaii and Westwego Cemetery, Westwego, Louisiana. He was survived by his Parents, Mr. and Mrs. Lawrence O. Griffin, 437 Celestine Street, Westwego, Louisiana. The Lawrence J. Griffin American Legion Post # 206, Westwego, Louisiana was named in his honor.[896]

Hamel, Don Edgar Field Musician, Serial No: 305354, US Marine Corps Reserve. Don was born around 1920 in Chicago, Illinois. He enlisted in the US Marine Corps on March 12, 1941 and completed his basic training at the Marine Corps Base in San Diego, California. *Don was the duty field music on December 7, 1941. As the first Japanese bullets bit into the* Arizona's *deck and ricocheted off her armor, Field Music Hamel brought his bugle to his mouth to sound the Air Defense call – "a strident series of short notes that were guaranteed to get everyone's attention." Minutes later, Hamel blew General Quarters, calling the battleship's sailors and Marines to action*[897]. He was serving on board the USS Arizona when he was killed in action on December 7, 1941 at Pearl Harbor, Hawaii. He was awarded the American Defense Service Medal, World War II Victory Medal and Purple Heart Medal posthumously. Don remains on duty on the USS Arizona. He is commemorated on the USS Arizona Memorial and the Memorial Tablets of the Missing, National Memorial Cemetery of the Pacific, Honolulu, Hawaii. Don was survived by his Mother, Mrs. Lucille Noval, 519 South St. Louis Street, Chicago, Illinois.[898]

Hardy, Charles L. Private, US Marine Corps. Charles enlisted in the US Marine Corps on May 27, 1941 and completed his boot training and sea training in San Diego, California. He reported for duty on the USS Arizona in October 1941 where he was serving on December 7, 1941 when the Japanese attacked Pearl Harbor. Charles crashed into the main deck suffering multiple leg fractures and was medically discharged. His mother, Mrs. Elda E. Hardy, Stratford Hotel, Los Angeles, California was notified. He died August 31, 1996.

Harmon, William Daniel Private, First Class, Serial No: 277834, US Marine Corps. William was born on October 28, 1920 in Vancouver, Washington to Daniel B. and Jane Janette (Elwell) Harmon. *His father died shortly after he was born. Danny grew up in Oregon, worked on the Big Muddy Ranch and was in the CCC before he enlisted in the Marine Corps on November 22, 1939 in Portland, Oregon shortly before his 19th birthday and completed his boot camp and Sea School in San Diego, California.* He was serving on board the USS Arizona when he was killed in action on December 7, 1941 at Pearl Harbor, Hawaii. William was awarded the American Defense Service Medal, World War II Victory Medal and Purple Heart Medal posthumously. He remains on duty on the USS Arizona. William is commemorated on the USS Arizona Memorial and the Memorial Tablets of the Missing, National Memorial Cemetery of the Pacific, Honolulu, Hawaii. He was survived by his Mother, Mrs. Jeanette F. Holt, 1805 S.W. 3rd Avenue, Portland, Oregon.[899]

---

[896] Lawrence John Griffin, Photo from Louisiana Honor States.
[897] Camp, Dick. "And The Band Played On: The Marine Detachment, USS Arizona." Leatherneck Magazine, December 2006, page 46.
[898] Don Edgar Hamel, Photo from Illinois Honor States.
[899] William Daniel Harmon, photo provided by his nephew, Chris Machnik.

Herrick, Paul Edward   Private, Serial No: 291621, US Marine Corps. Paul was born June 3, 1922 in Kenosha, Wisconsin, the son of Paul and Ruth L. Herrick. *His parents divorced in the 1930's and Paul went to live with his mother and sister, Teresa. Both children were employed at an early age; Paul started working at a local grocery store.* He enlisted in the Marine Corps on August 19, 1940 and completed boot camp at San Diego, California. Paul was serving on board the USS Arizona when he was killed in action on December 7, 1941 at Pearl Harbor, Hawaii. Paul was awarded the American Defense Service Medal, World War II Victory Medal and Purple Heart Medal posthumously. He remains on duty on the USS Arizona. Paul is commemorated on the USS Arizona Memorial and the Memorial Tablets of the Missing, National Memorial Cemetery of the Pacific, Honolulu, Hawaii. He was survived by his Mother, Mrs. Ruth L. Herrick, 7111 21st Avenue, Kenosha, Wisconsin. The American Legion Paul Herrick Post 21 in Kenosha, Wisconsin was named in his honor.[900]

Holzworth, Walter   Master Gunnery Sergeant, Serial No: 99523, US Marine Corps. Walter was born on October 12, 1892 in New Jersey, the son of William and Catherine Holzworth. He served in the 1st Aviation Company in World War I, China, Haiti and Guam. Walter was serving on board the USS Arizona when he was killed in action on December 7, 1941 at Pearl Harbor, Hawaii. He was awarded the American Defense Service Medal, World War II Victory Medal and Purple Heart Medal posthumously. Walter's remains were recovered and he was buried in Grave #272, Halawa Cemetery, Oahu, Hawaii. He was later exhumed and reburied in Plot A, Row 0, Grave 488, National Memorial Cemetery of the Pacific, Honolulu, Hawaii. Walter is commemorated on the USS Arizona Memorial. He was survived by his Wife, Mrs. Helen G. Holzworth, 112 East Clinton Avenue, Bergenfield, New Jersey[901]

Hope, Harold Wyatt   Private, Serial No: 314564, US Marine Corps. Harold was born on June 10, 1922 in Breckenridge, Texas, the son of Arthur Wesley and Dora Bryan (Harrison) Hope. *His father, Arthur worked in oil and gas production. Harold was a saxophone player in the marching band at Philips High School in Borger, Texas and was always trying to catch the eye of a pretty majorette. When his prank whistle calls fouled up her formation one too many times, he not only attracted her attention but the business end of her baton, which she broke over his head. Harold and his best friend, Dave Goldsmith had many adventures, including night time rat hunts, building their own apartment out of a disused auto shed, and an outhouse explosion that sent him flying through the door, burned and shaken but alive. Despite his shenanigans and poor grades, Harold graduated from Phillips High School in 1939, performing a saxophone solo at the commencement ceremony. He enlisted in the Marine Corps sometime in late December 1940 accompanied by several school friends who all piled into a car, drove across the state line*

---

[900] Paul Edward Herrick, photo and information provided by family member, Mary Moriarty.
[901] Walter Holzworth, Photo from California Honor States.

to Oklahoma and enlisted en masse. Harold was serving on board the USS Arizona when he was killed in action on December 7, 1941 at Pearl Harbor, Hawaii. Harold was awarded the American Defense Service Medal, World War II Victory Medal and Purple Heart Medal posthumously. He remains on duty on the USS Arizona. Harold is commemorated on the USS Arizona Memorial and the Memorial Tablets of the Missing, National Memorial Cemetery of the Pacific, Honolulu, Hawaii and Sweetwater Cemetery, Sweetwater, Texas. He was survived by his Mother, Mrs. Dora Bryan Hope, Box 287, Borger, Texas.[902]

Hudnall, Robert Chilton   Private First Class, Serial No: 287198, US Marine Corps. Robert was born on March 31, 1920, the son of Benjamin Napoleon and Elizabeth Leone (Dudley) Hudnall. He enlisted in the Marine Corps on July 3, 1940 and completed his boot camp at San Diego, California. Robert reported for duty on board the USS Arizona on October 5, 1940 and was serving on board when he was killed in action on December 7, 1941 at Pearl Harbor, Hawaii. Robert was awarded the American Defense Service Medal, World War II Victory Medal and Purple Heart Medal posthumously. He remains on duty on the USS Arizona. Robert is commemorated on the USS Arizona Memorial and the Memorial Tablets of the Missing, National Memorial Cemetery of the Pacific, Honolulu, Hawaii. He was survived by his Father, Mr. Ben Hudnall, Box 640, Pittsburg, Texas. His foster brother, Weldon Harvey Milligan was also killed in action on board the USS Arizona along with his first cousin, Royal Elwell.[903]

Huff, Robert Glenn   Private, Serial No: 311779, US Marine Corps. Robert was born July 2, 1923 in Texas to Clinton C. and Grayce M. Huff. He enlisted in the Marine Corps in 1941 in Fort Worth, Texas. Robert was serving on board the USS Arizona when he was killed in action on December 7, 1941 at Pearl Harbor, Hawaii. Robert was awarded the American Defense Service Medal, World War II Victory Medal and Purple Heart Medal posthumously. He remains on duty on the USS Arizona. Robert is commemorated on the USS Arizona Memorial and the Memorial Tablets of the Missing, National Memorial Cemetery of the Pacific, Honolulu, Hawaii. He was survived by his Mother, Mrs. Grayce Mary Huff, 2611 Columbus Street, Fort Worth, Texas.[904]

---

[902] Harold Wyatt Hope, Photo from Texas Honor States, information/story provided by his best friend, Dave Goldsmith.
[903] Robert Chilton Hudnall, Photo from Texas Honor States.
[904] Robert Glenn Huff, Photo from Texas Honor States.

Hughes, Marvin Austin   Private, Serial No: 306246, US Marine Corps Reserve. Marvin was born on September 14, 1921 in Houston, Texas, the son of Arthur Perry and Fannie (Hall) Hughes. He enlisted in the Marine Corps in early 1941 and completed boot camp and Sea School in San Diego, California. Marvin was serving on board the USS Arizona when he was killed in action on December 7, 1941 at Pearl Harbor, Hawaii. Marvin was awarded the American Defense Service Medal, World War II Victory Medal and Purple Heart Medal posthumously. He remains on duty on the USS Arizona. Marvin is commemorated on the USS Arizona Memorial and the Memorial Tablets of the Missing, National Memorial Cemetery of the Pacific, Honolulu, Hawaii. He was survived by his Mother, Mrs. Fannie Hughes, 2415 Jerrell Street, Houston, Texas.[905]

Hultman, Donald Standly   Private First Class, Serial No: 298688, US Marine Corps. Donald was born on April 11, 1922 in Dassel, Minnesota to Oscar Leonard and Ruth Irene (Olson) Hultman. He enlisted in the Marines on October 10, 1940 in Minneapolis, Minnesota and completed his boot camp at San Diego, California. Donald was serving on board the USS Arizona when he was killed in action on December 7, 1941 at Pearl Harbor, Hawaii. He was awarded the American Defense Service Medal, World War II Victory Medal and Purple Heart Medal posthumously. Donald remains on duty on the USS Arizona. He is commemorated on the USS Arizona Memorial and the Memorial Tablets of the Missing, National Memorial Cemetery of the Pacific, Honolulu, Hawaii. Donald was survived by his Mother, Mrs. Oscar Hultman, Dassel, Minnesota.[906]

Hux, Leslie Creade   Private First Class, Serial No: 291867, US Marine Corps. Leslie was born on December 10, 1913 in Dodson, Louisiana, the son of Johnnie Willington and Ara Adnie (Fowler) Hux. He enlisted in the Marine Corps on August 14, 1940 and completed boot camp at San Diego, California. *He was going through a hard time in life as most were during this period of history. He lost his job and was selling tomatoes on the side of the road. He was a very smart and ambitious person and wanted to make a difference in his life. He often said that he wanted to go down in history, so he enlisted into the Marine Corps. This was his first time out of the south, his first time in Hawaii and his name did go down in history, forever engraved in the memorial wall in Honolulu, Hawaii. His body was never recovered as most weren't. He was considered "Lost at Sea".* Leslie joined the Marine Detachment on the USS Arizona on December 6, 1940 and was serving on board when he was killed in action on December 7, 1941 at Pearl Harbor, Hawaii. Leslie was awarded the American Defense Service Medal, World War II Victory Medal and Purple Heart Medal posthumously. He remains on duty on the USS Arizona. Leslie is commemorated on the USS Arizona Memorial

---

[905] Marvin Austin Hughes, Photo from Texas Honor States.
[906] Donald Standly Hultman, Photo from the Minnesota Honor States.

and the Memorial Tablets of the Missing, National Memorial Cemetery of the Pacific, Honolulu, Hawaii. He was survived by his Parents, Mr. and Mrs. Johnnie W. Hux, Route 1, Dodson, Louisiana.[907]

Jerrison, Donald Dearborn Corporal, Serial No: 277521, US Marine Corps. Donald was born on January 29, 1920 in Des Moines, Iowa to Otto William and Ruby Louine (Dearborn) Jerrison. He enlisted in the Marine Corps on November 20, 1939 in Des Moines, Iowa and completed his basic training at the Marine Corps Base in San Diego, California. February 3, 1940 he was assigned to the Marine Detachment on the USS Arizona in Bremerton, Washington. Donald was killed in action on December 7, 1941 at Pearl Harbor, Hawaii. He was awarded the American Defense Service Medal, World War II Victory Medal and Purple Heart Medal posthumously. Donald's remains were recovered and he was initially interred in Grave #518, Halawa Cemetery, Oahu, Hawaii. He was later exhumed and was returned home for burial in Section D, Site 606, Golden Gate National Cemetery, San Bruno, California. Donald is commemorated on the USS Arizona Memorial. He was survived by his Parents, Mr. and Mrs. Otto W. Jerrison, 78th and College Avenue, Des Moines, Iowa.[908]

Jones, Quincy Eugene Private First Class, Serial No: 289396, US Marine Corps. Quincy was born on December 5, 1921 in Washington, Florida, the son of Lloyd L. and Laura Virginia (Everett) Jones. He was serving on board the USS Arizona when the Japanese attacked Pearl Harbor on December 7, 1941. *Quincy abandoned ship and made it to the shore. "He was burned to a crisp, even his eyelids were peeled off" stated fellow Marine Crawford. "He recognized my voice and said, "My God, Crawford! Is it that bad?" Crawford saw that he didn't have any dog tags and obviously would not live. He told a nearby navy corpsman to 'tag this man.' Quincy died before reaching the naval hospital.* He was awarded the American Defense Service Medal, World War II Victory Medal and Purple Heart Medal posthumously. Quincy's remains were interred in Grave #137, Red Hill Cemetery, Oahu, Hawaii. He was later re-interred at Section C, Site 938, in the National Memorial Cemetery of the Pacific, Honolulu, Hawaii. Quincy is commemorated on the USS Arizona Memorial and the Memorial Tablets of the Missing, National Memorial Cemetery of the Pacific, Honolulu, Hawaii. He was survived by his Father, Mr. Lloyd Jones, Perry, Florida.[909]

---

[907] Leslie Creade Hux, Information provided by his Niece, Diana Hux, Photo from Louisiana Honor States.
[908] Donald Dearborn Jerrison, Photo from Iowa Honor States.
[909] Quincy Eugene Jones, Photo provided by Jerry D. Rinkel, a close family friend to his brother, Myles Jones.

Kalinowski, Henry S. Private, Serial No: 307228, US Marine Corps Reserve. Henry was born May 13, 1920 in Ashtabula, Ohio the fourth child of eight to Adam and Anna K. Kalinowski. *The family farm faltered during the depression and was repossessed by the bank. Although their father managed to find work doing maintenance for JC Penney's, the children were sent to live with relatives from time to time. Henry was considered a family hero from an early age. While taking a ride in a Model A, his little cousin Dale decided to open one of the car doors. The rear-hinged door whipped backwards and Dale started to fall out of the moving car before Henry snatched him back inside, saving the two-year old from certain death. After graduating from high school in 1938, Henry worked for the Works Progress Administration earning ten dollars per week. He enlisted in the Marine Corps in March 1941. On December 6th he managed to get himself out of mess duty and was preparing to go ashore for a coveted spell of Saturday night liberty. Henry traded places with a friend that was supposed to go ashore to marry his sweetheart, but had pulled duty that night instead. On the morning of the 7th, Henry was at his battle station, manning the secondary five-inch batteries near the bow. When the armor-piercing bomb exploded, Henry was either killed instantly or horrendously burned.* Henry's body was never recovered. Henry was awarded the American Defense Service Medal, World War II Victory Medal and Purple Heart Medal posthumously. He remains on duty on the USS Arizona. Henry is commemorated on the USS Arizona Memorial and the Memorial Tablets of the Missing, National Memorial Cemetery of the Pacific, Honolulu, Hawaii. He was survived by his Father, Mr. Adam S. Kalinowski, 56 Jefferson Road, Ashtabula, Ohio.[910]

Keen, Billy Mack Private, Serial No: 311774, US Marine Corps. Billy was born November 29, 1922 in Rose City, Texas to Ernest and Mattie (Sanders) Keen of Newark, Texas. He enlisted in the Marine Corps in 1941 and completed his boot camp and Sea School in San Diego, California. Billy was serving on board the USS Arizona when he was killed in action on December 7, 1941 at Pearl Harbor, Hawaii. He was awarded the American Defense Service Medal, World War II Victory Medal and Purple Heart Medal posthumously. Billy remains on duty on the USS Arizona. He is commemorated on the USS Arizona Memorial and the Memorial Tablets of the Missing, National Memorial Cemetery of the Pacific, Honolulu, Hawaii. Billy was survived by his Mother, Mrs. Mattie Keen, Newark, Texas.[911]

---

[910] Henry S. Kalinowski, Information and photo derived from Together We Served and Hugh Hewitt.
[911] Billy Mack Keen, Photo from Texas Honor States.

Krahn, James Albert   Private, First Class, Serial No: 275556, US Marine Corps. James was born December 19, 1915 in Langdon, North Dakota to William and Mary Krahn. He enlisted in the Marine Corps on October 12, 1939 in Chicago, Illinois and completed his boot camp and Sea School at San Diego, California. James reported for duty on board the USS Arizona on December 23, 1939. He was serving on board the USS Arizona when he was killed in action on December 7, 1941 at Pearl Harbor, Hawaii. James was awarded the American Defense Service Medal, World War II Victory Medal and Purple Heart Medal posthumously. He remains on duty on the USS Arizona. James is commemorated on the USS Arizona Memorial and the Memorial Tablets of the Missing, National Memorial Cemetery of the Pacific, Honolulu, Hawaii. He was survived by his Parents, Mr. and Mrs. William Krahn, Langdon, North Dakota, five brothers, Peter of Langdon, Harry of Seattle and Clifford, Donald and Lawrence at home and three sisters, Hilda (Krahn) Olson of Puyallup, Washington, Annie of Minneapolis, Minnesota and Mildred Krahn at home.[912]

Lindsay, James Ernest, Jr.   Private, First Class, Serial No: 277912, US Marine Corps. James was born August 6, 1917 in Michigan. He enlisted in the US Marine Corps November 22, 1939 at the Western Recruiting Station, San Francisco, California and completed his boot camp and sea school at the Marine Corps Base, San Diego, California. James was serving on board the USS Arizona when he was killed in action on December 7, 1941 at Pearl Harbor, Hawaii. He was awarded the American Defense Service Medal, World War II Victory Medal and Purple Heart Medal posthumously. James remains were recovered and he was buried in Grave # 515, Red Hill Cemetery, Oahu, Hawaii. His remains were later exhumed and interred February 7, 1949 in Plot B, Row 0, Grave 1345, National Memorial Cemetery of the Pacific, Honolulu, Hawaii. He is commemorated on the USS Arizona Memorial. James was survived by his Mother, Mrs. Pearl Thomas, 3812 Ocean View, Montrose, California.[913]

Lovshin, William Joseph   Private, First Class, Serial No: 283661, US Marine Corps. William was born around 1923 in Minnesota. He enlisted in the US Marines on April 17, 1940 in Minneapolis, Minnesota and completed his boot camp and Sea School at the Marine Corps Base in San Diego, California. He was assigned duty in the Marine Detachment on the USS Arizona in December 1940. William was killed in action on December 7, 1941 at Pearl Harbor, Hawaii. He was awarded the American Defense Service Medal, World War II Victory Medal and Purple Heart Medal posthumously. William remains on duty on the USS Arizona. He is commemorated on the USS Arizona Memorial and the Memorial Tablets of the Missing, National Memorial Cemetery of the Pacific, Honolulu, Hawaii. William was survived by his Father, Mr. John Lovshin, Ely, Minnesota.[914]

---

[912] James Albert Krahn, Information and photo from the Cavalier County Republican Newspaper, Langdon, North Dakota, December 18, 1941, front page.
[913] James Ernest Lindsay, Jr., Photo from California Honor States.

McCarrens, James Francis Corporal, Serial No: 274786, US Marine Corps. James was born on March 5, 1916 in Ottawa, Illinois to George and Margaret Anna (Keller) McCarrens. He enlisted in the US Marine Corps on September 25, 1939 at Chicago, Illinois. After boot camp in San Diego, California he attended Sea School. His first assignment was Marine Detachment on the USS Mississippi. James was killed in action on December 7, 1941 at Pearl Harbor, Hawaii. He was awarded the American Defense Service Medal, World War II Victory Medal and Purple Heart Medal posthumously. James is buried in Section M1, Site 76 of Abraham Lincoln National Cemetery, Elwood, Illinois. He is commemorated on the USS Arizona Memorial and the Memorial Tablets of the Missing, National Memorial Cemetery of the Pacific, Honolulu, Hawaii. James was survived by his Mother, Mrs. Margaret McCarrens, 1105 Lafayette Street, Ottawa, Illinois. The Veterans of Foreign Wars Post 2470, Ottawa, Illinois was named in his honor along with his shipmate, Herman Koeppe.[915]

McCurdy, Russell James Private, US Marine Corps. Russell was born on July 14, 1917 in Chief, Michigan. He enlisted in the US Marine Corps and reported for duty on the USS Arizona where he was serving on December 7, 1941 when the Japanese attacked Pearl Harbor. *Russell was assigned as orderly to Rear Admiral Isaac C. Kidd. On that morning, he had just come off watch and was cleaning up to go on liberty. Hearing two loud thumps, he went outside on deck. Shortly thereafter, General Quarters was sounded and he reported to his battle station, the broadside fire control (guns) on top of the main mast. From there he watched the destruction of "Battleship Row". On the decks below, McCurdy saw charred bodies and sailors still alive whose clothes had been blown or burned off. They were in shock. "When I saw guys from the explosion dive into the water, it looked like they sizzled," he said. "They were done for. They didn't know what they were doing." When Arizona exploded, he was tossed to the deck. Realizing the ship was sinking he and his fellow Marines, abandoned their post and descended to the deck below. They were told to "Abandon Ship" and Russell made his way to Ford Island. "There was oil, fire, thick debris, plus you had to be sure your head was above water when a bomb or torpedo hit or it would concuss you and knock out your hearing."* After the attack, Russell was assigned to the 1st Marine Division. Russell retired from the Marine Corps February 1, 1965, attaining the rank of Lieutenant Colonel. During his service, Russell was awarded the Bronze Star medal with Combat "V" Purple Heart, Presidential Unit Citation – 1st Marine Division World War II, Marine Corps Good Conduct Medal, Asiatic Pacific Campaign Medal with 3 Gold Stars and the Pearl Harbor Survivor Medal. He worked in retail sales for fifteen years before retiring. Russell died on June 17, 2005 in Huntington, Indiana and was buried in Section CS-1, Site 123, Marion National Cemetery, Marion, Indiana.

---

[914] William Joseph Lovshin, Photo from Minnesota Honor States.

[915] James Francis McCarrens, Photo provided by his nephew, James McCarrens and the VFW Post 2470 in Ottawa, IL. Information provided by his son, Jim E. McCarrens.

Minear, Richard John, Jr.   Private, First Class, Serial No: 283919, US Marine Corps. Richard was born October 16, 1921 in Redding, California, the son of Richard John and Mary Elizabeth (Wood) Minear. Richard was raised in Shasta County and played tackle on the Sacramento Junior College football team. He enlisted in the Marine Corps and completed his boot camp training at the Marine Corps Base in San Diego, California. Richard reported for duty on the USS Arizona on August 2, 1940. He was killed in action on December 7, 1941 at Pearl Harbor, Hawaii. Richard was awarded the American Defense Service Medal, World War II Victory Medal and Purple Heart Medal posthumously. He remains on duty on the USS Arizona. Richard is commemorated on the USS Arizona Memorial and the Memorial Tablets of the Missing, National Memorial Cemetery of the Pacific, Honolulu, Hawaii. He was survived by his Father, Mr. Richard J. Minear, Sr., 1109 24th Street, Sacramento, California.[916]

Mostek, Francis Clayton   Private, First Class, Serial No: 282730, US Marine Corps. Francis was born October 17, 1919 in Spalding, Nebraska, the son of Stanislaus Charles and Sophia (Pier) Mostek. He enlisted in the Marine Corps on March 1, 1940 in San Francisco, California and completed boot camp and Sea School at San Diego, California. Francis joined the Marine Detachment on the Arizona on June 22, 1940. He was killed in action while serving on board the USS Arizona on December 7, 1941 at Pearl Harbor, Hawaii. Francis was awarded the American Defense Service Medal, World War II Victory Medal and Purple Heart Medal posthumously. He remains on duty on the USS Arizona. Francis is commemorated on the USS Arizona Memorial and the Memorial Tablets of the Missing, National Memorial Cemetery of the Pacific, Honolulu, Hawaii. He was survived by his Mother, Mrs. Sophia Mostek, Dover, Idaho.[917]

Nightingale, Earl C.   Corporal, US Marine Corps. Earl was born March 12, 1921 in Los Angeles, California. At age 11, his father left him, his mother and two brothers. It was the depression and many were out of work. He grew up in Tent City on the waterfront in Long Beach, California. Earl enlisted in the US Marine Corps at age 17 and reported for duty on the USS Arizona where he was serving on December 7, 1941 when the Japanese attacked Pearl Harbor. His official statement:

At approximately eight o'clock on the morning of December 7, 1941, I was leaving the breakfast table when the ship's siren for air defense sounded. Having no anti-aircraft battle station, I paid little attention to it. Suddenly I hear an explosion, I ran to the port door leading to the quarter deck and saw a bomb strike a barge of some sort alongside the USS Nevada, or in the vicinity. The Marine Color Guard came in at this point, saying we were being attacked. I could distinctly hear machine gun fire. I believe at this point our anti-aircraft battery opened up. We stood around awaiting orders of some kind. General quarters sounded and I started for my battle station in Secondary Aft. As I passed

---

[916] Richard John Minear, Photo from California Honor States.
[917] Francis Clayton Mostek, Photo from Idaho Honor States.

through casemate Nine I noted the gun was manned and being trained out. The men seemed extremely calm and collected. I reached the boat deck and our anti-aircraft guns were in full action firing very rapidly. I was about three quarters of the way to the first platform on the mast when it seemed as though a bomb struck our quarterdeck. I could hear shrapnel or fragments whistling past me. As soon as I reached the first platform, I saw Second Lieutenant Simonsen laying on his back with blood on his shirt front. I bent over him and taking him by the shoulders asked if there was anything I could do. He was dead, or so nearly so that speech was impossible. Seeing there was nothing I could do for the Lieutenant, I continued to my battle station. When I arrived in Secondary Aft I reported to Major Shapley that Mr. Simonsen had been hit and there was nothing to be done for him. There was a lot of talking going on and I shouted for silence, which came immediately. I had only been there a short time when a terrible explosion caused the ship to shake violently. I looked at the boat deck and every thing seemed aflame forward of the mainmast, I reported to the Major that the ship was aflame, which was rather needless, and after looking about, the Major ordered us to leave. I was the last man to leave Secondary Aft because I looked around and there was no one left. I followed the Major down the port side of the tripod mast. The railings, as we ascended, were very hot and as we reached the boat deck I noted that it was torn up and burned. The bodies of the dead were thick, and badly burned men were heading for the quarterdeck, only to fall apparently dead or badly wounded. The Major and I went between No. 3 and No. 4 turret to the starboard side and found Lieutenant Commander Fuqua ordering the men over the side, and assisting the wounded. He seemed exceptionally calm and the Major stopped and they talked for a moment. Charred bodies were everywhere. I made my way to the quay and started to remove my shoes, when I suddenly found myself in the water. I think the concussion of a bomb threw me in. I started swimming for the pipe line which was about one hundred and fifty feet away.

I was about half way when my strength gave out entirely, my clothes and shocked condition sapped my strength and I was about to go under when Major Shapley started to swim by, and seeing my distress, he grasped my shirt and told me to hang to his shoulders while he swam in. We were perhaps twenty-five feet from the pipe line when the Major's strength gave out and I saw he was floundering, so I loosed my grip on him and told him to make it alone. He stopped and grabbed me by the shirt and refused to let go. I would have drowned but for the Major. We finally reached the beach where a marine directed us to a bomb shelter, where I was given dry clothes and a place to rest.[918]

After the war, he played a character in the radio show Sky King. As host of his own daily network radio program, he became so successful that he retired in 1957 at age 35. His popularity as a radio and later, television personality continued to grow and he became the most highly syndicated radio program ever, heard across the US, Canada, Mexico, Australia, New Zealand, Fiji, South Africa, the Bahamas, 23 countries overseas as well as the Armed Forces Network. During his lifetime, Earl wrote and recorded over 7,000 radio programs and 250 audio programs.[919] Earl died in March 25, 1989 in Paradise Valley, Arizona.

---

[918] Confidential statement of Corporal Earl C. Nightingale, U.S. Marine Corps, Pearl Harbor, T.H., December 15, 1941.
[919] About Earl Nightingale, http://earlnightingale.com/store/index.

Nolatubby, Henry Ellis Private, First Class, Serial No: 286279, US Marine Corps. Henry was born January 11, 1922, the son of James Z. and Henrietta (Panick) Nolatubby. *He was raised in Maysville, Oklahoma by his mother, Henrietta. As a Choctaw Indian, he attended the Chilocco Indian School.* Henry enlisted in the US Marines June 22, 1940 in California and was assigned duty with the Marine Detachment, USS Arizona, Psnyd, Bremerton, Washington, December 1940. Henry was killed in action on December 7, 1941 at Pearl Harbor, Hawaii. *Henry was the first American Indian (Chickasaw) to give his live for his country in World War II.* He was awarded the American Defense Service Medal, World War II Victory Medal and Purple Heart Medal posthumously. Henry remains on duty on the USS Arizona. He is commemorated on the USS Arizona Memorial, the Memorial Tablets of the Missing, National Memorial Cemetery of the Pacific, Honolulu, Hawaii and Section MA, Site 15, Fort Bliss National Cemetery, Fort Bliss, Texas. Henry was survived by his Mother, Mrs. Henryetta Nolatubby, 2527 L Street, Bakersfield, California.[920]

O'Brien, Joseph Bernard Private, First Class, Serial No: 288408, US Marine Corps. Joseph was born in 1922 in Illinois to Patrick H. and Euphrena Effie (Wise) O'Brien. He enlisted in the Marine Corps on July 17, 1940 in Chicago, Illinois and completed his boot camp and Sea School at San Diego, California. Joseph was killed in action on December 7, 1941 at Pearl Harbor. Joseph was awarded the American Defense Service Medal, World War II Victory Medal and Purple Heart Medal posthumously. He remains buried on the USS Arizona. He is commemorated on the USS Arizona Memorial and the Memorial Tablets of the Missing, National Memorial Cemetery of the Pacific, Honolulu, Hawaii. Joseph was survived by his Mother, Mrs. Effie O'Brien, 5436 West Berteau Avenue, Chicago, Illinois and two brothers, William and Joseph.[921]

Patterson, Clarence Rankin Private, First Class, Serial No: 291894, US Marine Corps. Clarence was born April 9, 1920 in Plainview, Texas to Clarence Rankin Patterson and Lillian Edna (Beale) Patterson. He enlisted in the Marine Corps on August 15, 1940 in New Orleans, Louisiana and completed his boot camp at San Diego, California. Clarence was a member of the Marine Contingent serving on board the USS Arizona when he was killed in action on December 7, 1941 at Pearl Harbor, Hawaii. He was awarded the American Defense Service Medal, World War II Victory Medal and Purple Heart Medal posthumously. Clarence remains on duty on the USS Arizona. He is commemorated on the USS Arizona Memorial and the

---

[920] Henry Ellis Nolatubby, Information The Chilocco Annual, 1942, page 39 and family member, Francesca Shaw, Photo from the California Honor States.
[921] Joseph Bernard O'Brien, Photo from Illinois Honor States.

Memorial Tablets of the Missing, National Memorial Cemetery of the Pacific, Honolulu, Hawaii. Clarence was survived by his Wife, Mrs. Jadene L. Patterson, 1109 East 1st Street, Long Beach, California.[922]

Pedrotti, Francis James Private, Serial No: 296891, US Marine Corps. Francis was born in July of 1919, the son of Dennis Pedrotti and Mary Jane (Timlin) Pedrotti. He enlisted in the Marine Corps on September 26, 1940 in Chicago, Illinois. Francis was killed in action on December 7, 1941 at Pearl Harbor, Hawaii. He was awarded the American Defense Service Medal, World War II Victory Medal and Purple Heart Medal posthumously. Francis remains on duty on the USS Arizona. He is commemorated on the USS Arizona Memorial and the Memorial Tablets of the Missing, National Memorial Cemetery of the Pacific, Honolulu, Hawaii. Francis was survived by his Father, Mr. Dennis Pedrotti, 8024 Nola Avenue, St. Louis County, Missouri.[923]

Piasecki, Alexander Louis Corporal, Serial No: 274983, US Marine Corps. Alexander enlisted in the Marine Corps on September 23, 1939 in Colorado and completed his boot camp and Sea School in San Diego, California. He reported for duty on the USS Arizona on February 17, 1940. Alexander was serving in the Marine Contingent on the USS Arizona when he was killed in action on December 7, 1941 at Pearl Harbor, Hawaii. He was awarded the American Defense Service Medal, World War II Victory Medal and Purple Heart Medal posthumously. Alexander remains on duty on the USS Arizona. He is commemorated on the USS Arizona Memorial and the Memorial Tablets of the Missing, National Memorial Cemetery of the Pacific, Honolulu, Hawaii. Alexander was survived by his Sister, Mrs. Stella A. Romeo, General Delivery, Acme, Wyoming.[924]

Powell, Jack Newlin Speed Private, First Class, Serial No: 284047, US Marine Corps. Jack was born June 14, 1919 in Hobart, Oklahoma to Clement Sanford and Alta Anna (Newlin) Powell. He graduated from Belmont High School, Los Angeles, CA in 1938. Jack then followed his father into the barber profession becoming a licensed California Barber in 1939. He enlisted in the Marine Corps May 1, 1940 and completed his boot camp and Sea School in San Diego, California. Jack was assigned to the Marine detachment on the USS Arizona in August 1940. Jack was killed in action on December 7, 1941 at Pearl Harbor, Hawaii. He was awarded the American Defense Service Medal, Asiatic Pacific Campaign Medal, World War II Victory Medal and Purple Heart Medal posthumously. Jack remains on duty on the USS Arizona. He is commemorated on the USS Arizona Memorial and the Memorial Tablets of the Missing, National

---

[922] Clarence Rankin Patterson, Photo from California Honor States.
[923] Francis James Pedrotti, Photo from Missouri Honor States.
[924] Alexander Louis Piaseki, Photo from Wyoming Honor States.

Memorial Cemetery of the Pacific, Honolulu, Hawaii. Jack was survived by his Parents, Mr. and Mrs. Clem S. Powell, 1547 Sunset Boulevard, Los Angeles, California and a sister, Viola Geneva (Powell) Nolan of Lawton, Oklahoma.[925]

Power, Abner Franklin Private, Serial No: 314537, US Marine Corps. Abner was born in 1922 in Clinton, Oklahoma. He enlisted in 1941 and completed his boot camp and Sea School in San Diego, California. Abner was serving on board the USS Arizona in the Marine contingent when he was killed in action on December 7, 1941 at Pearl Harbor, Hawaii. He was awarded the American Defense Service Medal, World War II Victory Medal and Purple Heart Medal posthumously. Abner remains on duty on the USS Arizona. He is commemorated on the USS Arizona Memorial and the Memorial Tablets of the Missing, National Memorial Cemetery of the Pacific, Honolulu, Hawaii. Abner was survived by his Mother, Mrs. Louada Venamon, 508-1/2 Frisco Street, Clinton, Ohio. The American Legion Post 41 in Clinton, Oklahoma was named in his and another, Seaman 2c Victor W. Ogle who also died on the Arizona, in their honor.[926]

Reinhold, Rudolph Herbert Private, Serial No: 303326, US Marine Corps. Rudolph was born October 31, 1921 in Annaberg, Germany to Bernhardt Rudolph and Lina Martha (Grund) Reinhold. He immigrated to the United States in the 1920's and settled in Salt Lake City, Utah. Rudolph enlisted in the US Marine Corps on January 11, 1941 in Salt Lake City and completed his boot camp and Sea School in San Diego, California. Rudolph was killed in action on December 7, 1941 at Pearl Harbor, Hawaii. He was awarded the American Defense Service Medal, World War II Victory Medal and Purple Heart Medal posthumously. Rudolph remains on duty on the USS Arizona. He is commemorated on the USS Arizona Memorial and the Memorial Tablets of the Missing, National Memorial Cemetery of the Pacific, Honolulu, Hawaii. Rudolph was survived by his Mother, Mrs. Lina M. Reinhold, 210 Fruit Street, Salt Lake City, Utah.[927]

Schneider, William Jacob Private, First Class, Serial No: 283789, US Marine Corps. William was born in about 1920, the son of Arthur Baker and Anna Schneider. He enlisted in the Marine Corps on April 22, 1940 in Chicago, Illinois and completed his boot camp and Sea School at San Diego, California. He was killed in action on December 7, 1941 at Pearl Harbor, Hawaii. He was awarded the American Defense Service Medal, World War II Victory Medal and Purple Heart Medal posthumously. William remains on duty on the USS Arizona. He is commemorated on the USS Arizona Memorial and the Memorial Tablets of the Missing, National Memorial Cemetery of the Pacific, Honolulu, Hawaii. William was

---

[925] Jack Newlin Speed Powell, Information and photo provided by family member, Cary Glenn Nolan.
[926] Abner Franklin Power, Photo from the American Legion Post 41, Clinton, Oklahoma.
[927] Rudolph Herbert Reinhold, Photo provided by family member, Courtney Birkes.

survived by his Mother, Mrs. Anna Schneider, 2634 South Tripp Avenue, Chicago, Illinois.[928]

Scott, Crawford Edward   Private, First Class, Serial No: 298715, US Marine Corps. Crawford was born July 12, 1920 in Junction, Greene County, Iowa to John Edward Scott and Grace M. (Crawford) Scott. He enlisted in the Marine Corps on October 11, 1940 and completed his boot camp and Sea School in San Diego, California. Crawford was killed in action on December 7, 1941 at Pearl Harbor, Hawaii. He was awarded the American Defense Service Medal, World War II Victory Medal and Purple Heart Medal posthumously. Crawford remains on duty on the USS Arizona. He is commemorated on the USS Arizona Memorial and the Memorial Tablets of the Missing, National Memorial Cemetery of the Pacific, Honolulu, Hawaii. Crawford was survived by his Parents, Mr. and Mrs. John E. Scott, Route 4, North Kansas City, Missouri.[929]

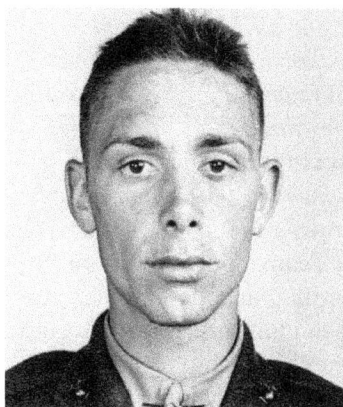

Scott, George Harrison   Private, First Class, Serial No: 290194, US Marine Corps. George was February 14, 1919 in Spokane, Washington to George Harrison and Ada I. (Mayenfeldt) Scott. He enlisted in the Marine Corps on July 25, 1940 in San Francisco, California and completed his boot camp and Sea School at San Diego, California. George was killed in action on December 7, 1941 at Pearl Harbor, Hawaii. He was awarded the American Defense Service Medal, World War II Victory Medal and Purple Heart Medal posthumously. George remains in duty on the USS Arizona. He is commemorated on the USS Arizona Memorial and the Memorial Tablets of the Missing, National Memorial Cemetery of the Pacific, Honolulu, Hawaii. George was survived by his Mother, Mrs. Ada I. Scott, West 2410 Sinto Avenue, Spokane, Washington.[930]

Shapley, Alan   Major, Serial No. 0-12489, US Marine Corps. Alan was born on February 9, 1903. He joined the US Marine Corps June 2, 1927 and reported for duty on the USS Arizona where he was serving when the Japanese attacked Pearl Harbor. Alan was up early on December 7th even though he didn't have any official duties. He was scheduled to play on the ship's baseball team against the USS Enterprise for the championship of the Pacific Fleet.

Alan was just finishing breakfast when the attack began. Hearing the sound of bombs, he went up top to see what all the noise was about. Everything happened so quickly, there was barely time to think. Alan received the Silver Star Medal for his actions that day:

The President of the United States takes pleasure in presenting the Silver Star
Medal to Major Alan Shapley, U.S. Marine Corps, for gallant and courageous conduct
during the attack on the United States Pacific Fleet by enemy Japanese forces in Pearl

[928] William Jacob Schneider, Photo from the Chicago Tribune, Chicago, Illinois, May 15, 1942, Page 10.
[929] Crawford Edward Scott, Photo from Missouri Honor States.
[930] George Harrison Scott, Photo from Washington Honor States.

Harbor, Territory of Hawaii, December 7, 1941. While swimming toward Ford Island after his ship had been bombed and set afire by the enemy, Major Shapley noticed a shipmate in distress in the water and about to go under. With no thought for his own safety, he braved the hazards of continuous enemy strafing and bombing to swim to the assistance of his helpless shipmate and, although exhausted himself, persisted in his efforts until he finally succeeded in b ring him safely ashore. His heroic action, performed at great peril to his own life, was in keeping with the highest traditions of the United States Naval Service.

Alan served in the Marine Corps throughout World War II and in the Korean War. He retired from the service in 1962. Alan died on May 13, 1973 at the National Naval Medical Center in Bethesda, Maryland.[931]

Shive, Gordon Eshom Private, First Class, Serial No: 283832, US Marine Corps. Gordon was born January 10, 1921, son of Grover L. Shive and Lois Elizabeth (Eshom) Shive. *He grew up in Laguna Beach, a small town back in those years. A place where folks let their children go to school barefooted. Gordon's mother, Lois worked as a laundress. She did washing and ironing for Orange County Cleaners. Gordon's father, Grover was a gardener who developed a brain tumor in the early 1930's and sometime in 1935 he passed away. Soon after, his mother married a man that, in later years, would just be called "The Mean SOB". Gordon joined the Marines in 1939 because the family needed the money and to get away from his stepfather.* He was a member of the Marine Rowing Team. Gordon was very strong and real competitive. He was killed in action on December 7, 1941 at Pearl Harbor, Hawaii. Gordon was at the five-inch guns, midship. His guns wouldn't have been usable that day, they weren't anti-aircraft guns, they were ship to ship guns. He was found floating in the bay, drowned. Nobody knows really if he was blown off the ship by the aerial bomb that hit the ship's magazine or if Gordon jumped in vain to save his life.[932] He was awarded the American Defense Service Medal, World War II Victory Medal and Purple Heart Medal posthumously. Gordon's remains were recovered and he was buried in Grave #517, Halawa Cemetery, Oahu, Hawaii. His remains were later exhumed and interred in Plot A, Row 0, Grave 464, National Memorial Cemetery of the Pacific, Honolulu, Hawaii. He is commemorated on the USS Arizona Memorial. Gordon was survived by his Mother, Mrs. Lois Westgate, 567 Through Street, Laguna Beach, California and a younger brother, Robert Shive. His brother, Malcolm was also killed in action while serving on the USS Arizona.[933]

---

[931] Alan Shapley, Photo from the Lucky Bag Yearbook, United States Naval Academy, Annapolis, MD, Class of 1927.
[932] The Brothers by Andy Alison and Amy Wilson, The Orange County Register, Accent Section, Sunday, May 20, 2001.
[933] Gordon Eshom Shive, Information and photo provided by his nephew, Gary Shive.

Simensen, Carleton Elliott Second Lieutenant, Serial No: 0-006679, US Marine Corps. Carleton was born January 25, 1919 in Grandin, North Dakota. Carleton attended the University of North Dakota where he was the top ROTC graduate. After he was commissioned, he spent his basic school in Philadelphia where he graduated in February 1941. He reported for duty on the Arizona in June 1941. Carleton was one of the most popular officers on the Arizona. Serving as the Junior Marine Officer, Division 8, his battle station was Director Station No. 1. He was killed in action on December 7, 1941 at Pearl Harbor. (Shortly after reaching the first platform of the mainmast and stepping clear of the superstructure, Carleton was struck in the midsection by shrapnel. Before dying, he ordered the men "Leave me, Go on!" Carleton was awarded the Bronze Star Medal, American Defense Service Medal, World War II Victory Medal and Purple Heart Medal posthumously.

"For heroic leadership and devotion to duty during the attack on the U.S. Pacific Fleet in Pearl Harbor, Territory of Hawaii, by Japanese forces on December 7, 1941. During the first few moments of the attack on the USS Arizona, he led the Marines up the exposed ladders of the mainmast in spite of the heavy bombing and strafing attack. Upon reaching the searchlight platform he was mortally wounded. He died almost instantly but not before he motioned to the Marine personnel not to assist him but to continue to their battle stations in secondary aft. His courage and gallant leadership are an inspiration to all."

Carleton's remains were recovered from the searchlight platform and he was buried in Red Hill Cemetery, Oahu, Hawaii. His remains were later exhumed and reburied in Plot C, Row 0, Grave 1158, National Memorial Cemetery of the Pacific, Honolulu, Hawaii. He is commemorated on the USS Arizona Memorial. Carleton was survived by his Father, Mr. C. O. Simensen, 703 5th Street, Devil's Lake, North Dakota.[934]

Sniff, Jack Bertrand Field Music Corporal, Serial No: 305320, US Marine Corps, Field Music. Jack was born February 22, 1922 in Valley, Illinois to Martin Leo Sniff and Martha E. (Hinman) Sniff. He enlisted in the Marine Corps in early 1941 and completed his boot camp at San Diego, California. Jack was then sent to Field Music School to learn bugle calls. On the morning of December 7th, Jack was at his battle station in one of the forward gun turrets. He was killed in action on December 7, 1941 at Pearl Harbor, Hawaii. Jack was awarded the American Defense Service Medal, World War II Victory Medal and Purple Heart Medal posthumously. He remains on duty on the USS Arizona. Jack is commemorated on the USS Arizona Memorial and the Memorial Tablets of the Missing, National Memorial Cemetery of the Pacific, Honolulu, Hawaii and Lawn Ridge Cemetery, Marshall County, Illinois. He was survived by his Parents, Mr. and Mrs. Martin Sniff, Speer, Illinois, Brother, Martin Ralph and Sister, Charlotte L. (Sniff) Tucker.

---

[934] Carleton Elliott Simensen, Photo and information provided by Russell McCurdy.

Soley, Michael Corporal, US Marine Corps. Michael was born on October 18, 1919 in Hammond, Indiana. He was the son of Andrew Soley and Julia (Gresmak) Soley. He came from a large family of 9 boys and 4 girls. He attended Wallace School, Maywood School and Hammond Tech High School. He graduated high school in 1938. The country was still experiencing an economic depression and Michael joined the Civilian Conservation Corp (CCC) in Panaca, Nevada. After 2 ½ terms at the camp he enlisted in the United States Marines in January 1940 and was sent to the Marine Base in San Diego, California. After several weeks of boot training he was selected to the Marine Sea School. On completion of his Sea School training he was assigned to the battleship USS Arizona. He was the captain and most valuable player of the Arizona basketball team and league. They were fleet champions in 1940 and 1941.

The morning of December 7th, Michael was high in the mainmast, watching the Nevada's band and color guard when his attention was drawn to an aircraft diving. As it roared overhead he could see red circles on the wings and fuselage. He watched as the Nevada's formation scattered as machine gun blasts hit the deck. This is when he realized that they were under attack from the Japanese. He shouted into his sound-powered headset, "Jap planes!" From the mainmast, he was able to see nearly all of battleship row, Ford Island and the surrounding area. He was overcome with emotion as he watched ship after ship take bomb and torpedo hits. He watched as a bomb hit the Arizona followed by a terrible explosion that tossed the ship up out of the water. The bridge of the ship shielded the men in the mainmast from the flames. Finally Major Shapely said, Well, men, this is it. Abandon ship. It's every man for himself. Good luck and God bless your all!" They descended the ladder while flames licked at them. Michael had gotten separated from the others and was burned. He had a pair of khaki shorts on and a skivvy shirt. But his hair had been scorched and burnt like those Indians that just had this row of hair down their head. That's the way he looked. He spotted the gangway that had been rigged between the ship and the quay. It was broken and turned up on its side, leaving only a two foot wide board to cross on. Seaman Musick and Michael made their way to the quay. Michael then said, "We'd better get down off the quay because if those things, the mooring lines, burst or break, they'll cut you in half!" The two of them slipped off the edge to a boat landing where they were picked up by a rescue boat. He served on the USS Tennessee for a period of time during the war. Michael was one of the fifteen survivors out of 88 Marines aboard the Arizona. Michael served his country through out World War II.

At the outbreak of the Korean War, Michael was assigned to the 1st Marine Division. He was at the Chosen Reservoir Campaign November and December 1950 and remained in Korea until the end of the conflict. He was awarded the Bronze Star for his action at Chosen.

"For meritorious service in connection with operations against the enemy while serving with a Marine weapons company in Korea from 15 September 1950 to 24 March 1951. Staff Sergeant Soley, section leader in a heavy machine gun platoon, showed excellent qualities of leadership and great professional ability throughout this period in the employment of his section. During the landing at Inchon, and again in the Chosin Reservoir operation, he maintained absolute control over his guns under most difficult conditions. His section was attached to a company which formed part of the division rearguard during the attack from Yudam-ni to Hagaru-ri. Despite sub-zero temperatures, extremely rugged terrain, and heavy enemy fire, he brought his men through with no battle casualties and a minimum of cases of injury from the cold. In the defense against the counterattack which followed, his section was assigned the mission of protecting the right flank of the company. In the face of enemy small arms fire and hand grenades, he continually exposed himself to direct the fire of his guns. Staff Sergeant

534

Soley's courage, skill and knowledge of his weapons contributed greatly to the success of the platoon in the accomplishment of its missions, and were in keeping with the highest traditions of the United States Naval Service."

After the end of the Korean War, Michael returned home and became a recruiting sergeant in the Chicago area. With failing health, he retired from the Marine Corp having served for 19 years 10 months and 16 days. After the loss of his wife, Ethel and daughter, Nancy, he lived with his mother and sister, Marie. In 1978 he moved to California because of his health and to be in a warmer climate. He liked to play golf with his friends. He was a member of the Hammond Tech basketball team.

Michael died on February 8, 2000 in Northridge, California.[935]

Stevenson, Frank Jake Private, First Class, Serial No: 298545, US Marine Corps. Frank was born November 16, 1921 in Waterville, Kansas to Roy James and Myrtle (Hubbard) Stevenson. He enlisted in the US Marine Corps on October 9, 1940 and completed his basic training in San Diego, California. He was killed in action on December 7, 1941 at Pearl Harbor, Hawaii. He was awarded the American Defense Service Medal, World War II Victory Medal and Purple Heart Medal posthumously. Frank remains were recovered and he was interred in Grave #509, Halawa Cemetery, Oahu, Hawaii he was shipped home for burial Riverside Cemetery, Waterville, Kansas. He is commemorated on the USS Arizona Memorial and the Memorial Tablets of the Missing, National Memorial Cemetery of the Pacific, Honolulu, Hawaii. Frank was survived by his Mother, Mrs. Myrtle Stevenson, 1441 Laramie Street, Manhattan, Kansas.[936]

Stovall, Richard Patt Private, First Class, Serial No: 298787, US Marine Corps. Richard was born November 27, 1917 in Ellis County, Texas, the son of Judson C. and Ebbie H. Stovall. He enlisted in the Marine Corps on October 9, 1940 and reported to San Diego, California for basic training. Richard was killed in action on December 7, 1941 at Pearl Harbor, Hawaii. He was awarded the American Defense Service Medal with Fleet clasp, Asiatic-Pacific Campaign Medal, World War II Victory Medal, Expert Rifle, pistol and bayonet and a special award for automatic rifleman of his company and Purple Heart Medal posthumously. Richard's remains were recovered and he was buried in Grave #301, Red Hill Cemetery, Oahu, Hawaii. His remains were later exhumed and interred in Plot B, Row 0, Grave 1261, National Memorial Cemetery of the Pacific, Honolulu, Hawaii. Richard is commemorated on the USS Arizona Memorial. He was survived by his Parents, Mr. J. C. Stovall and Mrs. Ebbie H. Stovall, Box 126, Hartley, Texas. The American Legion Post 494 in Dalhart, Texas was named in his honor.[937]

---

[935] Michael Soley, Photo and information provided by his brother, Nick Soley.

[936] Frank Jake Stevenson, Photo from "Kansas Snapshots," a blog by journalist Gloria Freeland U.S.M.C. photo.

[937] Richard Patt Stovall, Information from Heroes of World War II of the Dalhart, Texas Area by Molly Heard, Photo from Texas Honor States.

Swiontek, Stanley Stephen Field Cook, Serial No: 281279, US Marine Corps. Stanley was born November 2, 1918, son of John Swiontek and Victoria Swiontek. He enlisted in the Marine Corps January 20, 1940 in Chicago, Illinois and completed his boot camp and Sea School at San Diego, California. Stanley reported for duty on the USS Arizona on March 30, 1940. Stanley was killed in action on December 7, 1941 at Pearl Harbor, Hawaii. He was awarded the American Defense Service Medal, World War II Victory Medal and Purple Heart Medal posthumously. Stanley remains on duty on the USS Arizona. He is commemorated on the USS Arizona Memorial and the Memorial Tablets of the Missing, National Memorial Cemetery of the Pacific, Honolulu, Hawaii. Stanley was survived by his Mother, Mrs. Victoria Swiontek, 12025 Indiana Avenue, Chicago, Illinois.[938]

Szabo, Theodore Stephen Private, Serial No: 305655, US Marine Corps Reserve. Theodore was born February 11, 1922, eldest son of Steve Istvan Szabo and Laura Marie (Reisner) Szabo. He enlisted in March of 1941 and completed his boot training at the Marine Corps Base in San Diego, California. Theodore was first shown on board the USS Arizona in July of 1941. He was killed in action on December 7, 1941 at Pearl Harbor, Hawaii. Theodore was awarded the American Defense Service Medal, World War II Victory Medal and Purple Heart Medal posthumously. His remains were recovered and he was buried in Plot A, Row 0, Grave 724, National Memorial Cemetery of the Pacific, Honolulu, Hawaii. He is commemorated on the USS Arizona Memorial. Theodore was survived by his Parents, Mr. and Mrs. Steve Szabo, Castalia, Iowa, Seven brothers, William, Robert, Edward, Eugene, Dale, Victor and Leon Szabo and four sisters, Darlene, Agnes and Marilyn.[939]

Webb, Carl Edward Private, First Class, Serial No: 282719, US Marine Corps. Carl was born August 21, 1919 in Waco, McLennan County, Texas, the son of John Bryant and Hazel C. (Robinson) Frasier. He enlisted in the US Marines in March of 1940 in Dallas, Texas and completed his boot camp training and sea school in San Diego, California. Upon completion, he was assigned to the Marine detachment on the USS Arizona in June 1940. Carl was killed in action on December 7, 1941 at Pearl Harbor, Hawaii. He was awarded the American Defense Service Medal, World War II Victory Medal and Purple Heart Medal posthumously. Carl's remains were recovered and he was buried in Grave #364, Red Hill Cemetery, Oahu, Hawaii. His remains were later exhumed and interred in Plot C, Row 0, Grave 1076, National Memorial Cemetery of the Pacific, Honolulu, Hawaii. Carl is commemorated on the USS Arizona Memorial. He was survived by his Mother, Mrs. Hazel Frasier, 809 South 7th Street, Waco, Texas.[940]

---

[938] Stanley Stephen Swiontek, Photo from Illinois Honor States.

[939] Theodore Stephen Szabo, Information provided by his brother, Leon Szabo, Photo from Iowa Honor States.

[940] Carl Edward Webb, Photo from Texas Honor States.

Weier, Bernard Arthur Private, Serial No: 310339, US Marine Corps. Bernard was born February 18, 1917 in Chicago, Illinois to Bernhard Friedrich Wilhelm and Harriet Katherine (Herbold) Weier. He was killed in action on December 7, 1941 at Pearl Harbor, Hawaii. Bernard was awarded the American Defense Service Medal, World War II Victory Medal and Purple Heart Medal posthumously. His remains were recovered and he was buried in Grave #521, Halawa Naval Cemetery, Oahu, Hawaii. Bernard's remains were later exhumed and interred in Plot B, Row 0, Grave 984, National Memorial Cemetery of the Pacific, Honolulu, Hawaii. He is commemorated on the USS Arizona Memorial. Bernard was survived by his Parents, Mr. and Mrs. Friedrich Bernhard Weier, 5318 South Washington Street, Downers Grove, Illinois.[941]

Whisler, Gilbert Henry Private, First Class, Serial No: 294821, US Marine Corps. Gilbert was born May 22, 1911 in Iowa, the son of James Theodore Whisler and Edith Francis (Cox) Whisler. He enlisted in the US Marine Corps on September 11, 1940 in Des Moines, Iowa and completed his boot training at the Marine Corps Base in San Diego. He was a member of the Arizona's Golf Team. Gilbert was killed in action on December 7, 1941 at Pearl Harbor, Hawaii. He was awarded the American Defense Service Medal, World War II Victory Medal and Purple Heart Medal posthumously. Gilbert's remains were recovered and he was buried in Grave #519, Red Hill Cemetery, Oahu, Hawaii. His remains were later exhumed and interred in Plot C, Row 0, Grave 1013, National Memorial Cemetery of the Pacific, Honolulu, Hawaii. He is commemorated on the USS Arizona Memorial. Gilbert was survived by his Parents, Mr. and Mrs. James T. Whisler, General Delivery, Bloomfield, Iowa.[942]

Windish, Robert James Private, Serial No: 303079, US Marine Corps. Robert was born in 1921 in Missouri to John A. Windish and Anna Windish. He enlisted in the Marine Corps in 1941 and completed his boot camp and Sea School at San Diego, California. Robert was killed in action on December 7, 1941 at Pearl Harbor, Hawaii. Robert was awarded the American Defense Service Medal, World War II Victory Medal and Purple Heart Medal posthumously. He remains on duty on the USS Arizona. Robert is commemorated on the USS Arizona Memorial and the Memorial Tablets of the Missing, National Memorial Cemetery of the Pacific, Honolulu, Hawaii. He was survived by his Parents, Mr. and Mrs. John A. Windish, 4265 Blair Avenue, St. Louis, Missouri and his older brother, John A. Windish Junior.[943]

---

[941] Bernard Arthur Weir, Photo from Illinois Honor States.
[942] Gilbert Henry Whisler, Photo from Iowa Honor States.
[943] Robert James Windish, Photo from Missouri Honor States.

Windle, Robert England Private, First Class, Serial No: 285460, US Marine Corps. Robert was born in about 1922 in Arkansas the only son of W. B. and Carolyn (England) Windle. He was living with his grandfather, Ben C. England while he attended high school, graduating from the Jersey Township High School in June of 1940. Robert enlisted in the US Marine Corps on June 14, 1940 in Chicago, Illinois and completed his boot camp and Sea School at the Marine Training Center in San Diego, California. He reported for duty on board the USS Arizona on September 18, 1940 and was killed in action on December 7, 1941 at Pearl Harbor, Hawaii. He was awarded the American Defense Service Medal with Fleet Clasp, Asiatic Pacific Campaign Medal, World War II Victory Medal and Purple Heart Medal posthumously. Robert remains on duty on the USS Arizona. He is commemorated on the USS Arizona Memorial and the Memorial Tablets of the Missing, National Memorial Cemetery of the Pacific, Honolulu, Hawaii. Robert was survived by his Mother, Mrs. W. B. Windle, 1201 South Main Street, Jacksonville, Illinois. The Jersey County War Dads Chapter was named in memory of Robert Windle.[944]

Wittenberg, Russell Duane Private, Serial No: 298731, US Marine Corps. Russell was born June 22, 1920 in Iowa, the son of Gary C. and Matilda Wittenberg. He enlisted in the Marine Corps October 10, 1940 and reported to San Diego, California for Boot Camp, attending Sea School in December 1940. Russell was killed in action on December 7, 1941 at Pearl Harbor, Hawaii. He was awarded the American Defense Service Medal, World War II Victory Medal and Purple Heart Medal posthumously. Russell's remains were recovered and he was buried in Grave #512, Red Hill Cemetery, Oahu, Hawaii. His remains were later exhumed and interred in Plot A, Row 0, Grave 906, National Memorial Cemetery of the Pacific, Honolulu, Hawaii. He is commemorated on the USS Arizona Memorial. Russell was survived by his Father, Mr. Gary Wittenberg, Darwin, Minnesota.[945]

Young, Donald George Private, First Class, US Marine Corps. Donald enlisted in the US Marine Corps on June 12, 1940 and completed basic training and Sea School at the Marine Corps Base in San Diego, California. He reported for duty on the USS Arizona in December 1940 and was serving on December 7, 1941 when the Japanese attacked Pearl Harbor.

---

[944] Robert England Windle, Information provided by the Jersey County Historical Society, Jerseyville, Illinois, Photo from the Illinois Honor States.
[945] Russell Duane Wittenberg, Photo from Iowa Honor States.

Marine Whaleboat Rowing Team:

Back Row: (left to right) PFC Lawrence J. Griffin, PFC Herbert Allen Dreesbach, Pvt Marvin Austin Hughes, Sgt. John "Pop" McRay Baker, Pvt Eugene Brickley, Pvt Gordon Eshom Shive, Cpl Burnis Leroy Bond.
Front Row: (left to right) Pvt Francis James Pedrotti, Pvt Robert Charles Erskine, Pvt Robert Wesley Dunham, Pvt Donald Eugene Fleetwood, Cpl David William Bartlett, Pvt Russell James McCurdy.

Navy and Marine personnel waiting to return to their ship on Mala Wharf near Lahaina on Maui 1941.

Photo # 80-G-463589 USS Arizona pitching in heavy seas during the 1930s

Chapter Six: Crossing the Equator 1940

Subpoena and Summons Extraordinary

The Royal High Court of the Raging Main

Region of the South Seas
Domain of Neptune Rex } ss.

To All Who Shall See These Presents,

Greetings:

Whereas, The good ship ARIZONA, bound southward, is about to enter our domain; and whereas the aforesaid ship carries a large and loathsome cargo of landlubbers, beach-combers, guardo-rats, sea-lawyers, lounge-lizards, parlor-dunnigans, plow-deserters, chicken-chasers, four-flushers, dance-hall sheiks, drug-store cowboys, asphalt arabs, and other living creatures of the land, masquerading as seaman, of which low scum you are a member, having never appeared before us; and

Whereas, THE ROYAL HIGH COURT OF THE RAGING MAIN will convene on board the good ship ARIZONA, on the 24th day of July, 1940 in Latitude 0°0'00", and whereas, an inspection of our ROYAL ROSTER shows that it is high time your sad and wandering nautical soul appeared before Our August Presence;

Be it Known, That we hereby summon and command you

_____MATNEY, V.M., F3c_____ U. S. Navy,

to appear before the ROYAL HIGH COURT to be examined into your fitness to be taken into the citizenship of the deep and to hear your defense on the following charges:

CHARGE I: In that you have hitherto wilfully and maliciously failed to show reverence and allegiance to our ROYAL PERSON, and are therein and thereby a vile landlubber and pollywog.

CHARGE II: In that you desires to be "glamour boy" mess cook, also no consideration for loyal shellbacks on his particular mess.

Given under our hand and seal.

Davy Jones,
Scribe

Neptunus Rex,
Supreme Ruler

541

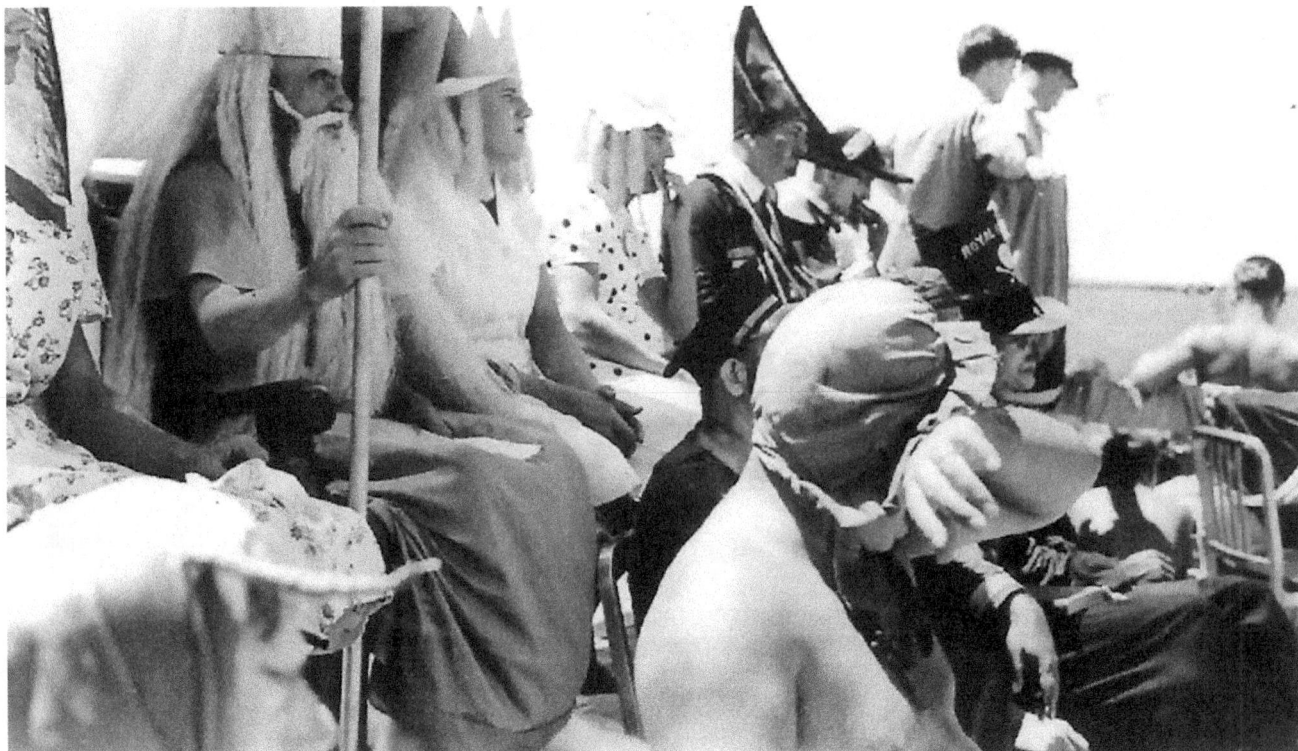

The oldest sailor (Walter Charles Ebel, Chief Turret Captain) who has crossed the equator becomes Neptunus Rex and presides over the ceremonies. Seated to his right, his queen, GM1c, Gordon E. Linbo.

The ceremony of Crossing the Equator commemorates a sailor's first crossing of the equator. The tradition was and is used to boost morale. It was also created as a test for seasoned sailors to ensure their new shipmates were capable of handling long rough times at sea. Sailors who have already crossed the Equator are referred to as *Shellbacks*. They are also referred to as *Sons of Neptune*. Those who have not crossed the Equator are called *Pollywogs*.

Equator-crossing ceremonies feature King Neptune. The two day event is a ritual in which previously indoctrinated crew members, Shellbacks are organized into a "Court of Neptune" to indoctrinate the Pollywogs into the Mysteries of the Deep".

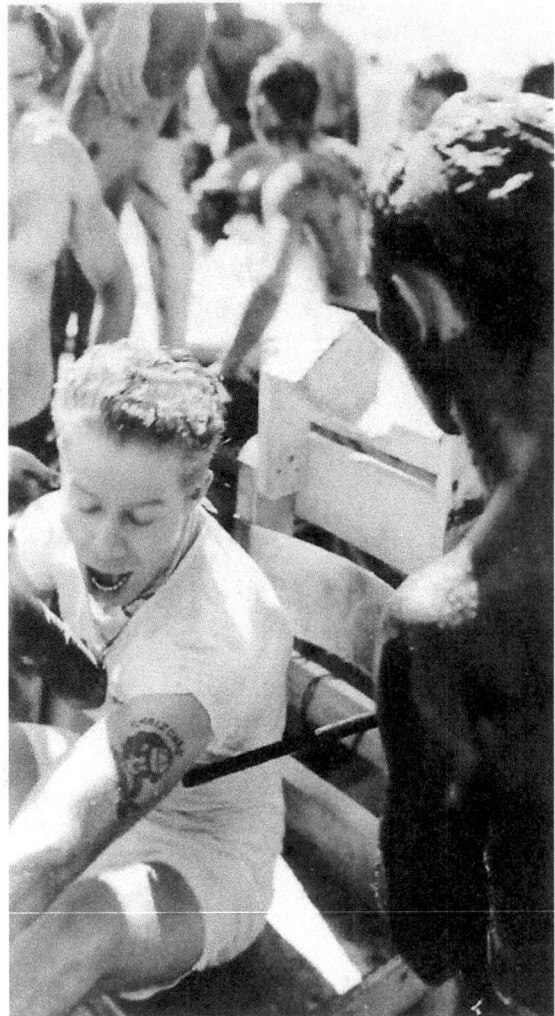

After crossing the equator, Pollywogs receive subpoenas to appear before King Neptune and his court, usually including his first assistant, Davy Jones, her Highness, Amphitrite and various other dignitaries who officiate at the ceremony. This is often preceded by a beauty contest of men dressing up as women. Each department on the ship is required to introduce one contestant in swimsuit drag. During the ceremony, the Pollywogs undergo a number of increasingly embarrassing ordeals. Once the ceremony is complete, the Pollywog receives a certificate declaring his new status as a Shellback.[946]

---

[946] Crossing the Equator photos provided by the daughter of Chester Clay Rose, Margie Rose-Chirrick.

544

Crossing the Equator Initiation

DOMAIN OF NEPTUNUS REX

To all Sailors wherever ye may be . . . and to all Mermaids, Sea Serpents, Whales,
Sharks, Porpoises, Dolphins, Skates, Eels, Suckers, Lobsters, Crabs, Pollywogs and other Living Things of the Sea.
Greeting: Know ye : That on this 24 day of July 1940 on Latitude 000°00" and Longitude 159°36' there appeared
within the limits of Our Royal Domain, the U.S.S. ARIZONA bound southward for South American Ports,

BE IT REMEMBERED

That the said Vessel and Officers and Crew thereof, have been inspected and passed on by Ourself and Our Royal Staff
And Be It Known : By all ye Sailors, Marines, Land Lubbers and others who may be honored by his presence, that

Walter C Ebel CTC

having been found worthy to be numbered as one of our trusty shellbacks has been gathered to our fold and duly initiated into the

Solemn Mysteries of the Ancient Order of the Deep

Be it further Understood : That by virtue of the power invested in me I do hereby command all my subjects to show due honor
and respect to him whenever he may enter Our Realm.

DISOBEY THIS ORDER UNDER PENALTY OF OUR ROYAL DISPLEASURE
Given under our hand and seal this 24th day of July 1940

Davy Jones
HIS MAJESTY'S SCRIBE

Walter S. Ebel
Neptunus Rex
RULER OF THE RAGING MAIN

545

Ships named in honor of members of the USS Arizona:

There were 24 ships named in honor of the men of the USS Arizona; Two Destroyers (DD), Two High Speed Transports (APD), 19 Destroyer Escorts (DE) and one Guided Missile Destroyer (DDG). They are listed here:

USS Bates (DE-68)   named after   Ensign Edward M. Bates
(The USS Bates (DE-68) was sunk on May 25, 1945 at Okinawa suffering 23 crew losses.)

USS Booth (DE-170)   named after   Ensign Robert Sinclair Booth, Jr.

USS Chung-Hoon (DDG-93)   named after   Rear Admiral Gordon Paiea Chung-Hoon

USS Cloues (DE-265)   named after   Ensign Edward Blanchard Cloues

USS Crowley (DE-303)   named after   Lieutenant Commander Thomas Ewing Crowley

USS Emery (DE-28)   named after   Ensign Jack Mandeville Emery

USS Gosselin (APD-126)   named after   Ensign Edward Webb Gosselin

USS Halloran (DE-305)   named after   Ensign William Ignatius Halloran

USS Haverfield (DE-393)   named after   Ensign James Wallace Haverfield

USS Hollis (DE-794)   named after   Ensign Ralph Hollis

USS Kidd (DD-661)   named after   Rear Admiral, Isaac Campbell Kidd

USS Kirkpatrick (DE-318)   named after   Captain Thomas Leroy Kirkpatrick

USS Lake (DE-301)   named after   Acting Payroll Clerk John Ervin Lake

USS Leopold (DE-319)   named after   Ensign Robert Lawrence Leopold
(The USS Leopold was sunk south of Iceland on March 9, 1944 suffering 171 officer and crew losses.)

USS Manlove (DE-36)   named after   Electrician Arthur C. Manlove

USS Marsh (DE-699)   named after   Ensign Benjamin Raymond Marsh, Jr.

USS Merrill (DE-392)   named after   Ensign Howard Deel Merrill

USS Moore (DE-240)   named after   Seaman 1st class Fred Kenneth Moore

USS O'Neill (DE-188)   named after   Ensign William Thomas O'Neill

USS Register (APD-92)   named after   Lt. Commander Paul James Register

USS Sanders (DE-40)   named after   Ensign Eugene Thomas Sanders

USS Savage (DE-386)   named after   Ensign Walter S. Savage, Jr.

USS Van Valkenburg (DD-656) named after   Captain Franklin Van Valkenburg

USS Weeden (DE-797)   named after   Ensign Carl Alfred Weeden

Bibliography

1) Dictionary of American Naval Fighting Ships. http://www.history.navy.mil/danfs/.
2) U. S. National Archives. http://www.archives.gov/.
3) American Battle Monuments Commission. http://www.abmc.gov/search/wwii.php.
4) American War Library. http://members.aol.com/veterans/.
5) State Summary of War Casualties from World War II for Navy, Marine Corps, and Coast Guard Personnel.
6) US Department of Veteran's Affairs, Nationwide Gravesite Locator. http://gravelocator.cem.va.gov/j2ee/servlet/NGL_v1
7) Arlington National Cemetery. http://www.arlingtoncemetery.net/.
8) Yeoman 2c, Navy Training Courses, Edition of 1945, US Government Printing Office.
9) USS Arizona Survivors Association. http://www.ussarizona.org
10) Pearl Harbor Survivors Association. http://www.pearlharborsurvivorsonline.org/.
11) Pearl Harbor Muster Rolls, National Archives.
12) National Personnel Records Center, St. Louis, Missouri.
13) United States Navy Memorial, Navy Logs http://www.navylog.org/.

Aaron, Hubert Charles Titus, 16
Abercrombie, Samuel Adolphus, 16
Adams, Robert Franklin, 16
Adkison, James Dillion, 17
Aguirre, Reyner Aceves, 17
Aguon, Gregorio San Nicholas, 17
Ahern, Richard James, 18
Alberovsky, Francis Severin, 18
Albright, Galen Winston, 18
Alexander, Elvis Author, 19
Allen, Robert Lee, 19
Allen, William Clayborn, 19
Allen, William Lewis, 19
Alley, Jay Edgar, 20
Allison, Andrew K., 20
Allison, J. T., 20
Alten, Ernest Mathew, 21
Amacher, Charles Andrew, 21
Amon, Frederick Purdy, 21
Amundson, Leo DeVere, 502
Anderson, Charles Titus, 22
Anderson, Delbert Jake, 22
Anderson, Donald William, 22
Anderson, Harry, 23
Anderson, Howard Taisey, 23
Anderson, Irwin Corinthis, 23
Anderson, James Pickins, Jr., 23
Anderson, John Delmar, 24
Anderson, Lawrence Donald, 24
Anderson, Robert Adair, 24
Andrews, Brainerd Wells, 25
Angle, Earnest Hersea, 25
Anthony, Glenn Samuel, 25
Aplin, James Raymon, 26
Apple, Robert William, 26
Aprea, Frank Anthony, 26
Arledge, Eston, 27
Arnaud, Achilles, 27
Arnold, Claude Duran, Jr., 502
Arnold, Thell, 27
Arrant, John Anderson, 28
Arvidson, Carl Harry, 28
Ashmore, Wilburn James, 28
Atchison, John Calvin, 502
Atkins, Gerald Arthur, 28
Austin, Laverne Alfred, 29
Autry, Eligah T., Jr., 29
Aves, Willard "Bill" Charles, 30
Aydell, Miller Xavier, 30
Ayers, Dee Cumpie, 30
Badilla, Manuel Domonic, 31

Bagby, Walter Franklin, 31
Bailey, George Richmond, 503
Baird, Billy Byron, 32
Bajorims, Joseph, 32
Baker, John "Pop" McCray, 503
Baker, Robert Dewey, 33
Ball, Masten A., 33
Ball, William V., 33
Ballard, Galen Owen, 33
Bandy, Wayne Lynn, 34
Bangert, John Henry, Jr., 35
Baraga, Joseph, 504
Bardon, Charles Thomas, 35
Barker, Loren Joe, 35
Barner, Walter Ray, 36
Barnes, Charles Edward, 36
Barnes, Delmar Hayes, 36
Barnett, William Thermon, 37
Barth, DeWayne, 37
Bartlett, David William, 504
Bartlett, Paul Clement, 38
Bass, Edward Forester, 38
Bates, Edward Monroe, Jr., 38
Bates, Robert Alvin, 38
Bator, Edward, 39
Bauer, Harold Walter, 39
Baumeister, William Nicolas, 39
Beaton, Freddie, 505
Beaumont, James Ammon, 40
Beck, George Richard, 40
Becker, Harvey Herman, 40
Becker, Marvin Otto, 41
Becker, Wesley Paulson, 41
Bedford, Purdy Renaker, 41
Beerman, Henry Carl, 42
Beggs, Harold Eugene, 42
Bell, Hershel Homer, 42
Bell, Richard Leroy, 42
Bellamy, James Curtis, 43
Belt, Everett Ray, Jr., 505
Bemis, Edwin Wallace, 43
Benford, Sam Austin, 43
Bennett, Earl Dean, 43
Bennett, William Edmond, Jr., 44
Benson, James Thomas, 44
Berdollt, George Anthony, Jr., 44
Bergin, Roger Joseph, 44
Berkanski, Albert Charles, 45
Bernard, Frank Peter, 45
Berry, Gordon Eugene, 45
Berry, James Winford, 46

Bersch, Arthur Anthony, 46
Bertie, George Allan, 46
Bibby, Charles Henry, 47
Bickel, Kenneth Robert, 47
Bicknell, Dale Deen, 47
Bircher, Frederick Robert, 47
Bird, Leroy Alexander, 48
Birdsell, Estelle, 48
Birdsell, Rayon Delois, 48
Birge, George Albert, 48
Birtwell, Daniel Thomas Jr., 49
Bishop, Grover Barron, 49
Bishop, Millard Charles, 49
Bishop, Wesley Horner, Jr., 50
Black, James Theron, 505
Blais, Albert Edward, 50
Blake, James Monroe, 50
Blanchard, Albert Richard, 51
Blankenship, Theron Andrew, 51
Blanton, Atticus Lee, 51
Blieffert, Richmond Frederick, 51
Block, Ivan Lee, 52
Blount, Wayman Boney, 52
Bodey, Edward Raymond, 52
Boggess, Roy Eugene, 52
Bohlender, Sam, 53
Bolling, Gerald Revese, 53
Bolling, Walter Karr, 53
Bond, Burnis Leroy, 506
Bonebrake, Buford Earl, 54
Bonfiglio, William John, 54
Booth, Robert Sinclair, Jr., 54
Booze, Asbury Legare, 55
Borger, Richard, 55
Borovich, Joseph John, 55
Borusky, Edwin Charles, 506
Bosley, Kenneth Leroy, 56
Boviall, Walter Robert, 56
Bowen, Andrew Jackson, Jr., 56
Bowman, Howard, 57
Boyd, Charles Andrew, 57
Boydstun, Don Jasper, 57
Boydstun, R. L., 58
Brabbzson, Oran "Buttercup" Merrill, 58
Bradley, Bruce Dean, 58
Bradshaw, Harry Frederick, 59
Braham, Edward James, 506
Brakke, Kenneth Gay, 59
Braydis, John, 59
Brickley, Eugene, 507
Bridges, James Leon, 60

Bridges, Paul Hyatt, 60
Bridie, Robert Maurice, 60
Brignole, Erminio Joseph, 60
Brittan, Charles Edward, 61
Broadhead, Johnnie Cecil, 61
Brock, Walter Pershing, 62
Bromley, George Edward, 62
Bromley, Jimmie, 62
Brooks, Robert Neal, 63
Broome, Loy Raymond, 63
Brooner, Allen Ottis, 63
Brophy, Myron Alonzo, 64
Brown, Charles Martin, 64
Brown, Elwyn LeRoy, 64
Brown, Frank George, 65
Brown, Gene Richard, 65
Brown, Richard Corbett, 65
Brown, William "Buzz" Howard, 66
Browne, Harry Lamont, 66
Browning, Robert James, 66
Browning, Tilmon David, 66
Bruce, John Franklin, 66
Brune, James William, 67
Bruner, Lauren Fay, 67
Bruns, Martin Benjamin, 68
Bryan, Leland Howard, 69
Bryant, Lloyd Glenn, 69
Buckley, Jack C., 70
Budd, Robert Emile, 70
Buehl, Herbert Vincent, 70
Buhr, Clarence Edward, 71
Burcham, Jimmie Charles, 71
Burden, Ralph Leon, 71
Burdette, Ralph Warren, 71
Burk, Leland Howard, 72
Burke, Frank Edmond, Jr., 73
Burnett, Charlie Leroy, 74
Burns, John Edward, 74
Bush, William Jack, 74
Busick, Dewey Olney, 75
Butcher, David Adrian, 75
Butler, John Dabney, 76
Byard, Ralph Duncan, 76
Byrd, Charles Dewitt, 76
Cabay, Louis Clarence, 77
Cabiness, Frank R., 507
Cade, Richard Esh, 77
Caldwell, Charles, Jr., 77
Callaghan, James Thomas, 77
Camden, Raymond Edward, 78
Camm, William Fielden, 78

Campa, Ralph, 78
Campbell, Burdette Charles, 79
Campbell, Frank Monroe, 79
Campbell, George Kilgore, 79
Caplinger, Donald William, 80
Carey, Francis Lloyd, 81
Carlisle, Robert Wayne, 81
Carlson, Harry Ludwig, 81
Carlson, Ray Christian, 82
Carmack, Harold Milton, 82
Carpenter, Robert Nelson, 82
Carroll, Robert Lewis, 82
Carson, Carl Malvin, 83
Carter, Burton Lowell, 84
Carter, Edward J., 507
Carter, Paxton Turner, 84
Casey, James Warren, 85
Casilan, Epifanio Miranda, 85
Caskey, Clarence Merton, 85
Castleberry, Claude William, Jr., 86
Catsos, George, 86
Chace, Raymond Vincent, 86
Chadwick, Charles Bruce, 86
Chadwick, Harold, 87
Chandler, Donald Ross, 508
Chandler, Edwin Ray, 87
Chapman, Naaman N., 87
Chapman, Noel B., 88
Chappell, William Robert, 88
Charlton, Charles Nicholas, 89
Chernucha, Harry Gregory, 89
Chester, Edward, 89
Christensen, Elmer Emil, 90
Christensen, Lloyd Raymond, 90
Christiansen, Edward Lee, 90
Christiansen, Harlan Carl, 91
Chung-Hoon, Gordon Paiea, 91
Cihlar, Lawrence John, 91
Clark, George Francis, 92
Clark, John Crawford Todd, 92
Clark, Malcolm, 92
Clark, Robert William, Jr., 92
Clarke, Robert Eugene, 93
Clash, Donald, 93
Clayton, Robert Roland, 93
Clemmens, Claude Albert, 93
Clift, Ray Emerson, 94
Cloues, Edward, 94
Clough, Edward Jay, 95
Clouser, Marion Howard, 95
Cobb, Ballard Burgher, 95

Coburn, George Wesley, 95
Coburn, Walter Overton, 96
Cockrum, Kenneth Earl, 96
Coffin, Robert, 96
Coffman, Marshal Herman, 96
Coker, Charles Walter, 97
Cole, Charles Warren, 508
Cole, David Lester, 97
Colegrove, Willett Stillman, Jr., 97
Collier, John, 98
Collier, Linald Long, Jr., 98
Collins, Austin, 98
Collins, Billy Murl, 98
Combs, Clyde Jefferson, 99
Condon, Daniel Jerome, 100
Conlin, Bernard Eugene, 100
Conlin, James Leo, 101
Connelly, Richard Earl, 101
Conrad, Homer Milton, Jr., 101
Conrad, Robert Frank, 102
Conrad, Walter Ralph, 102
Conter, Louis Anthony, 102
Cook, Lonnie David, 103
Coole, Lloyd Edward, 103
Cooper, Clarence Eugene, 103
Cooper, Kenneth Erven, 104
Coplin, Norman Walter, 104
Corbin, Ralph Victor Leon, 104
Corcoran, Gerard John, 104
Corey, Ernest Eugene, 105
Cornelius, Lyle Richard, 105
Cornelius, Phillip Wayne, 105
Corning, Russel Dale, 105
Cory, James Evans, 508
Cosby, Ray Charles, 106
Coulter, Arthur Lee, 106
Coursey, John Paul, 509
Cowan, William, 106
Cowden, Joel Beman, 106
Cox, Gerald Clinton, 107
Cox, John Madison, Jr., 107
Cox, William Milford, 107
Cozad, Francis Burnard G., 108
Craft, Harley Wade, 108
Crawford, Lamar Smead, 509
Crawley, Wallace Dewight, 108
Cremeens, Louis Edward, 108
Criscuolo, Michael, 109
Criswell, Wilfred John, 110
Crothers, Lee Raymond, 110
Crowe, Cecil Thomas, 110

Crowley, Thomas Ewing, 111
Cruz, Henry Mesa, 111
Culp, Donald Arthur, 111
Curry, William Joseph, 111
Curtis, Lloyd B., 112
Curtis, Lyle Carl, 112
Cybulski, Harold Bernard, 112
Cychosz, Francis Anton, 113
Czarnecki, Anthony Francis, 113
Czarnecki, Stanley, 113
Czekajski, Theophil, 114
Dahlheimer, Richard Norbert, 114
Daniel, Alfred Eugene, 114
Daniel, Lloyd Maxton, 115
Danik, Andrew Joseph, 115
Darch, Phillip Zane, 115
Dare, James Ashton, 116
Daugherty, Paul Eugene, 116
Davis, Carl Everette, 116
Davis, Elvin Clay, 117
Davis, John Quitman, 117
Davis, Milton Henry, 117
Davis, Murle Melvin, 118
Davis, Myrtle Clarence, 118
Davis, Thomas Ray, 118
Davis, Virgil Denton, 511
Davis, Walter Mindred, 119
Davison, Henry "Hank" Donald, 119
Dawson, James Berkley, 511
Day, William John, 120
De Armoun, Donald Edwin, 121
De Castro, Vicente, 121
De Long, Frederick Eugene, 512
De Witt, John James, 123
Dean, Lyle Bernard, 121
Dean, William Ernest, 122
Dearing, John Davis, 122
Decker, Deward, 122
Deritis, Russell Edwin, 122
Deserano, Joseph Charles, 123
Dial, John Buchanan, 123
Dick, Ralph R., 124
Dickerson, William Charles A., 124
Dickinson, Merle Edward, 124
Dine, John George, 124
Dineen, Robert Joseph, 125
Dobey, Milton Paul, Jr., 125
Dobson, Clarence Junior, 125
Doherty, George Walter, 125
Doherty, John Albert, 126
Doherty, John Andrew, 126

Donegan, Timothy Albert, 127
Donohue, Ned Burton, 127
Dority, John Monroe, 127
Doucett, John Walter, 127
Dougherty, Ralph Mc Clearn, 128
Doyle, Wand B., 128
Dreesbach, Herbert Allen, 512
Driver, Bill Lester, 128
Ducrest, Louis Felix, 129
Duke, Robert Edward, 129
Dullum, Jerald Fraser, 129
Dunaway, Kenneth Leroy, 130
Duncan, Henry Barnett, 130
Duncan, Tommie Wilson, 130
Dunham, Elmer Marvin, 131
Dunnam, Robert Wesley, 512
Dupree, Arthur Joseph, 131
Durham, William Teasdale, 132
Durio, Russell, 513
Duveene, John, 513
Dvorak, Alvin Albert, 132
Earle, John Horatio, Jr., 514
Eaton, Emory Lowell, 133
Ebel, Walter Charles, 133
Eberhart, Vincent Henry, 133
Echols, Charles Louis, Jr., 133
Echternkamp, Henry Clarence, 134
Edmonson, Kenneth Eugene, 134
Edmunds, Bruce Rosevelt, 134
Eernisse, William Frederick, 135
Egan, Paul Howard, 135
Egnew, Robert Ross, 136
Ehlert, Charles Casper, 136
Ehrmantraut, Frank, Jr., 136
Elkins, Merle, 137
Elliott, Lawrence Emitt, 137
Ellis, Francis Arnold, Jr., 137
Ellis, George William, 138
Ellis, Richard Everrett, 138
Ellis, Wilbur Danner, 138
Elwell, Royal, 139
Embrey, Bill Eugene, 139
Emery, Jack Mandeville, 139
Emery, John Marvin, 140
Emery, Wesley Vernon, 140
Enger, Stanley Gordon, 141
Enos, James Robert, 141
Erickson, Robert, 141
Erskine, Robert Charles, 514
Erwin, Stanley Joe, 142
Erwin, Walton Aluard, 142

Giovenazzo, Michael James, 171
Givens, Harold Reuben, 172
Glenn, Richard Clyde, 172
Gobbin, Angelo, 172
Goff, Wiley Coy, 172
Goldsberry, William Joseph, 173
Gomez, Edward, Jr., 173
Good, Leland, 173
Goodman, Kenneth Dale, 517
Goodwin, William Arthur, 174
Gordon, Donald Eugene, 174
Gordon, Peter Charles, Jr., 175
Goshen, William Eugene, 175
Gosselin, Edward Webb, 176
Gosselin, Joseph Adjutor, 176
Gould, Harry Lee, 177
Gove, Rupert Clair, 177
Grabowsky, Leon, 177
Graham, Donald Alexander, 178
Granger, Raymond Edward, 180
Grant, Lawrence Everett, 180
Gray, Albert James, 180
Gray, James Victor, 181
Gray, Lawrence Moore, 181
Gray, William James, 181
Green, Clay Douglas, Jr., 182
Green, Glen Hubert, 182
Green, James William, 182
Greenfield, Carroll Gale, 183
Griffin, Lawrence John, 517
Griffin, Reese Olin, 183
Griffiths, Robert Alfred, 183
Grim, George Edwin, 183
Grissinger, Robert Beryle, 183
Grosnickle, Warren Wilbert, 184
Gross, Milton Henry, 184
Grundstrom, Richard Gunner, 184
Guerin, Charles William, Jr., 185
Guna, Andrew, 185
Gurley, Jesse Herbert, 185
Haas, Curtis "Curt" Junior, 186
Haden, Samuel William, 187
Haerling, Howard Gustave, 187
Haerry, Raymond John, 188
Haffner, Floyd Bates, 188
Haines, Robert Wesley, 188
Hall, John Rudolph, 189
Halloran, William Ignatius, 189
Hamel, Don Edgar, 518
Hamilton, Clarence James, 190
Hamilton, Edwin Carrell, 190

Hamilton, Elsworth Fonzo, 190
Hamilton, James Edward, 190
Hamilton, William Holman, 191
Hammerud, George Winston, 191
Hampton, J. C., 191
Hampton, Ted W, Jr., 192
Hampton, Walter Lewis, 192
Hand, Vernon, 192
Hanna, David "Buster" Darling, 193
Hansen, Carlye B., 193
Hansen, Harvey Ralph, 193
Hanzel, Edward Joseph, 194
Hardin, Charles Eugene, 194
Hardy, Charles L., 518
Hargis, Paul Eugene, 195
Hargraves, Kenneth William, 195
Harmon, William Daniel, 518
Harr, Oliver Virgil, 195
Harrell, Allen Boyd, 195
Harrington, Keith Homer, 196
Harris, George Ellsworth, 196
Harris, Henry Sherman, 196
Harris, Hiram Dennis, 197
Harris, James William, 197
Harris, John David, 197
Harris, Noble Burnice, 198
Harris, Peter John, 198
Hart, James Willard, 198
Hartland, Alfred Jack, 199
Hartley, Alvin, 199
Hartsoe, Max June, 199
Hartson, Lonnie Moss, 199
Hasl, James Thomas, 200
Hauff, Richard, 200
Haverfield, James Wallace, 200
Havins, Harvey Linfille, 201
Hawkins, Russell Dean, 201
Hayes, John Doran, 201
Hayes, Kenneth Merle, 202
Haynes, Curtis James, 202
Hays, William Henry, 202
Hazdovac, Jack Claudius, 203
Head, Frank Bernard, 203
Heater, Verrell Roy, 203
Heath, Alfred Grant, 204
Hebel, Robert Lee, 204
Heckendorn, Warren Guy, 204
Hedger, Jess Laxton, 205
Hedrick, Paul Henry, 205
Heely, Leo Shinn, 205
Heidt, Edward Joseph, 205

Lawrence, Thomas Hurshel, 274
Lawson, James Lenox, 274
Lawson, Leonard George, 274
Lee, Carroll Volney, Jr., 274
Lee, Henry Lloyd, 275
Leedy, David Alonzo, 275
Leggett, John Goldie, 275
Legros, Joseph McNeil, 276
Leigh, Malcolm Hedrick, 276
Leight, James Webster, 276
Leighton, Lindsay Ray, 277
Lencses, Louis, 277
Lenning, George Birmingham, 277
Leopard, Curtis James, 278
Leopold, Robert Lawrence, 278
Lesmeister, Steve Louie, 279
Levar, Frank, 279
Lewis, Wayne Alman, 279
Lewis, William E., 280
Lewison, Neil Stanley, 280
Lightfoot, Worth "Tommy" Ross, 280
Linbo, Gordon Ellsworth, 281
Lincoln, John William, 281
Lindsay, James Ernest, 524
Lindsay, James Mitchell, 281
Lindsey, Jack Lawton, 281
Linton, George Edward, 282
Lipke, Clarence William, 282
Lipple, John Anthony, 282
Lisenby, Daniel Edward, 283
Livers, Raymond Edward, 283
Livers, Wayne Nicholas, 283
Lock, Douglas A., 284
Lohman, Earl Wynne, 284
Lomax, Frank Stuart, 284
Lomibao, Marciano, 285
Long, Benjamin Franklin, 285
Lott, Russell Ardell, 285
Lounsbury, Thomas William, 286
Loustanau, Charles Bernard, 286
Loveland, Frank Crook, 286
Lovshin, William Joseph, 524
Lucey, Neil Jermiah, 287
Lukasavitz, Steven Jerome, 287
Luna, James Edward, 288
Luzier, Ernest Burton, 288
Lynch, Emmett "Rusty" Isaac, 288
Lynch, James Robert, Jr., 289
Lynch, William Joseph, Jr., 289
MacQueen, Donald E., 289
Maddox, Raymond Dudley, 290

Madrid, Arthur John, 290
Mafnas, Francisco Reyes, 290
Magee, Gerald James, 291
Mainwaring, Billy Braun, 291
Malaski, John, 291
Malcolm, Everett Allen, 291
Malecki, Frank Edward, 292
Malinowski, John Stanley, 292
Malson, Harry Lynn, 292
Mancuso, Joseph, 293
Manion, Edward Paul, 293
Manlove, Arthur Cleon, 293
Mann, Charles Clark, 294
Mann, William Edward, 294
Manning, LeRoy, 294
Manske, Robert Francis, 295
Marcum, Harry Bedford, 295
Marinich, Steve Matt, 295
Maris, Elwood Henry, 296
Marks, Edward Joseph, 296
Marling, Joseph Henry, 296
Marlow, Urban Herschel, 297
Marsh, Benjamin Raymond, Jr., 297
Marsh, William Arthur, 297
Marshall, Thomas Donald, 298
Martin, Hugh Lee, 298
Martin, James Albert, 298
Martin, James Orrwell, 299
Martin, Luster Lee, 299
Mason, Byron Dalley, 299
Mastel, Clyde Harold, 299
Masters, Dayton Monroe, 300
Masterson, Cleburne Earl Carl, 300
Masterson, Kleber Sandlin, 300
Mathein, Harold Richard, 300
Mathison, Charles Harris, 301
Matney, Vernon Merferd, 301
Mattlage, Herbert, 301
Mattox, James Durant, 302
May, Louis Eugene, 302
Maybee, George Frederick, 302
Mayfield, Lester Ellsworth, 303
Mayo, Rex Haywood, 303
McCarrens, James Francis, 525
McCarron, John Harry, 303
McCary, William Moore, 303
McClafferty, John Charles, 304
McClung, Harvey Manford, 304
McCurdy, Russell James, 525
McDonald, Don Erwin, 304
McFaddin, Lawrence James, 305

O'Bryan, Joseph Benjamin, 339
Ochoski, Henry Francis, 339
Off, Virgil Simon, 339
Ogle, Victor Willard, 340
Oglesby, Lonnie Harris, 340
Oliphant, Harold Eugene, 340
Oliver, Raymond Brown, 340
Olsen, Edward Kern, 341
Olsen, Vernon James, 341
Olson, Glen Martin, 342
O'Neall, Rex Eugene, 342
O'Neill, William Thomas, Jr., 342
Orr, Dwight Jerome, 342
Orzech, Stanislaus Joseph, 343
Osborne, Mervin Eugene, 343
Osborne, William Daniel, Jr., 343
Osmond, Robert Hugh, 344
Osterberg, Vernon Magnus, 344
Ostrander, Leland Grimstead, 344
Ott, Peter Dean, 344
Otterman, Clarence Wayne, 345
Owen, Fredrick Halden, 346
Owen, Paul Ralph, 346
Owens, Richard Allen, 346
Owsley, Thomas Lea, 346
Pablo, Patrocinio, 347
Pace, Amos Paul, 347
Pacitti, Louis John, 347
Parker, William Whiteford, 347
Parkes, Harry Edward, 348
Paroli, Peter John, 348
Patterson, Clarence Rankin, 528
Patterson, Harold Lemuel, 349
Patterson, Richard, Jr., 349
Paulmand, Hilery, 349
Pavini, Bruno, 350
Pawlowski, Raymond Paul, 350
Pearce, Alonzo, Jr., 350
Pearson, Norman Cecil, 351
Pearson, Robert Stanley, 351
Peavey, William Howard, 352
Peckham, Howard William, 352
Pecotte, Earl Henry, 352
Pedrotti, Francis James, 529
Peery, Max Valdyn, 353
Peil, William John, 354
Peleschak, Michael, 355
Peltier, John Arthur, 355
Penton, Howard Lee, 355
Perkins, George Ernest, 356
Perry, Seth Harold, 356

Peterson, Albert Hendrix, Jr., 356
Peterson, Elroy Vernon, 357
Peterson, Hardy Wilbur, 357
Peterson, Roscoe Earl, 357
Pettit, Charles Ross, 358
Petyak, John Joseph, 358
Phelps, George Edward, 358
Philbin, James Richard, 358
Phipps, Berwyn Robert, 359
Phraner, George Dewey, 359
Piasecki, Alexander Louis, 529
Pike, Harvey Lee, 360
Pike, Lewis Jackson, 361
Pinkham, Albert Wesley, 361
Pitcher, Walter Giles, 361
Pittard, George Franklin, 361
Pitz, Robert Leo, 362
Pollack, Francis Lee, 362
Pool, Elmer Leo, 363
Poole, Ralph Ernest, 363
Port, Stanley Harrison, Jr., 363
Posey, Ernest Mendum, 363
Post, Darrell Albert, 364
Potts, Howard Kenton, 364
Pousson, Alfred Andrew, 364
Povesko, George, 365
Powell, Jack Newlin Speed, 529
Powell, Thomas George, 365
Power, Abner Franklin, 530
Presson, Wayne Harold, 365
Price, Arland Earl, 366
Pritchett, Robert Leo, Jr., 366
Probst, Richard William, 366
Puckett, Edwin Lester, 366
Puckett, Louis Alfred, 367
Pugh, John, Jr., 367
Purvis, William Robinson, 367
Putnam, Avis Boyd, 368
Puzio, Edward, 368
Quarto, Mike Joseph, 368
Quillin, Wallace Franklin, 369
Quinata, Jose Sanchez, 369
Radford, Neal Jason, 369
Rahn, Carl Frederick, Jr., 369
Rampley, John Watson, 370
Ramsdell, Millard Arthur, 370
Rasmussen, Arthur Severin, 370
Rasmusson, George Vernon, 370
Ratkovich, William, 371
Rawhouser, Glen Donald, 371
Rawson, Clyde Jackson, 371

Scott, George Harrison, 531
Scruggs, Jack Leo, 405
Seaman, Russell Otto, 406
Seeley, Robert Fox, 406
Seeley, William Eugene, 406
Sevier, Charles Clifton, 407
Shaffer, John Jackson, III, 407
Shannon, William Alfred, 407
Shapley, Alan, 531
Sharbaugh, Harry Robert, 408
Sharon, Lewis Purdie, 408
Shaw, Clyde Donald, 409
Shaw, Robert Kar, 409
Shawn, Ernest Maurice, 409
Shebak, Joseph, 409
Sheffer, George Robert, 410
Sherrill, Warren Joseph, 410
Sherven, Richard Stanton, 411
Shew, Martin Luther, 411
Shiffman, Harold Ely, 411
Shiley, Paul Eugene, 412
Shimer, Melvin Irvin, 412
Shive, Gordon Eshom, 532
Shive, Malcolm Holman, 412
Shively, Benjamin Franklin, 413
Shores, Irland, Jr., 413
Shugart, Marvin John, 413
Sibley, Delmar Dale, 414
Sidders, Russell Lewis, 414
Sidell, John Henry, 414
Silvey, Jesse, 415
Simensen, Carleton Elliott, 533
Simmons, Claude William, Jr., 415
Simon, Walter Hamilton, 415
Simpson, Albert Eugene, 416
Skeen, Harvey Leroy, 416
Skiles, Charles Jackson, Jr., 416
Skiles, Eugene, 417
Sletto, Earl Clifton, 417
Smalley, Jack G., 417
Smart, George David, 418
Smestad, Halge Hojen, 418
Smith, Albert Joseph, 418
Smith, Clyde Crockett, 418
Smith, Earl Walter, 418
Smith, Earl, Jr., 419
Smith, Edward, 419
Smith, Harold Francis, 419
Smith, Harry, 420
Smith, John A., 420
Smith, John Edward, 420

Smith, Luther Kent, 420
Smith, Mack Lawrence, 421
Smith, Marvin Ray, 421
Smith, Orville Stanley, 421
Smith, Roscoe Bryant, 422
Smith, Walter Tharnel, 422
Smith, William Hansford, Jr., 422
Sniff, Jack Bertrand, 533
Snow, Rutherford Hayes, 422
Soens, Harold Mathias, 423
Soley, Michael, 534
Sooter, James Frederick, 423
Sorensen, Holger Earl, 423
South, Charles Braxton, 424
Spence, Merle Joe, 424
Spotz, Maurice Edwin, 424
Spreeman, Robert Lawrence, 425
Springer, Charles Harold, 425
Stallings, Kermit Braxton, 425
Stanborough, Thomas William, Jr., 426
Starkovich, Charles, 426
Starkovich, Joseph, Jr., 427
Starks, Don Harrison, 427
Staudt, Alfred Parker, 427
Steffan, Joseph Philip, 428
Steigleder, Lester Leroy, 428
Steinhoff, Lloyd Delroy, 428
Stephens, Woodrow Wilson, 429
Stephenson, Hugh Donald, 429
Stevens, Jack Hazelip, 429
Stevens, Theodore Roosevelt, 430
Stevenson, Frank Jake, 535
Stewart, Thomas Lester, 430
Stillings, Gerald Fay, 430
Stockman, Harold William, 430
Stockton, Louis Alton, 431
Stoddard, William Edison, 431
Stoffer, Bernald Henry, 431
Stopyra, Julian John, 432
Storm, Laun Lee, 432
Stovall, Richard Patt, 535
Strange, Charles Orval, 432
Stratton, Donald Gay, 433
Stratton, John Raymond, 434
Strong, Herbert Ronald, 434
Stuart, Jean Marcelle, 434
Suggs, William Alfred, 435
Sullivan, Aubrey Randolph, 435
Sulser, Frederick Franklin, 435
Summers, Glen Allen, 435
Summers, Harold Edgar, 436

Weller, Oree Cunningham, 466
Wells, Floyd Arthur, 466
Wells, Harold Leroy, 466
Wells, Harvey Anthony, 467
Wells, Raymond Virgil, Jr., 467
Wells, William Bennett, 467
Welter, Eddie Charles, 468
Wentzlaff, Edward Louis, 468
West, Broadus Franklin, 470
West, Mark Austin, 470
West, Webster Paul, 471
Westbrook, Clinton Howard, 471
Westcott, William Percy, Jr., 471
Westerfield, Ivan Ayers, 472
Westin, Donald Vern, 472
Westlund, Fred Edwin, 472
Whisler, Gilbert Henry, 537
Whitaker, John William, Jr., 473
Whitcomb, Cecil Eugene, 473
White, Charles William, 473
White, James Clifton "JC", 474
White, Thomas Arthur, 474
White, Vernon Russell, 475
White, Volmer Dowin, 475
Whitehead, Ulmont Irving, Jr., 476
Whitlock, Paul Morgan, 476
Whitson, Ernest Hubert, Jr., 476
Whitt, William Byron, 477
Whittemore, Andrew Tiny, 478
Wick, Everett Morris, 478
Wicklund, John Joseph, 478
Wilcox, Arnold Alfred, 479
Will, Joseph William, 479
Willette, Laddie James, 479
Williams, Adrian Delton, 480
Williams, Clyde Richard, 480
Williams, George Washington, 480
Williams, Jack Herman, 481
Williams, John Francis, 481
Williams, Lawrence A., 481
Williamson, Randolph, Jr., 482
Williamson, William Dean, 482
Willis, Robert Kenneth, Jr., 483
Wilson, Bernard Martin, 483
Wilson, Charles Lee, 483
Wilson, Comer Anderson, 484
Wilson, Harold Green, Jr., 484
Wilson, Hurschel Woodrow, 484
Wilson, John James, 485
Wilson, Neil Mataweny, 485
Wilson, Ray Milo, 486

Wimberley, Paul Edwin, 486
Windish, Robert James, 537
Windle, Robert England, 538
Winter, Edward, 486
Wise, James Louis, 486
Wittenberg, Russell Duane, 538
Wojtkiewicz, Frank Peter, 487
Wolf, George Alexanderson, Jr., 487
Wood, Harold Baker, 488
Wood, Horace Van, 488
Wood, Roy Eugene, 488
Woods, Vernon Wesley, 489
Woods, William Anthony, 489
Woodward, Ardenne Allen, 489
Woody, Harlan Fred, 490
Woolf, Norman Bragg, 490
Wright, Edward Henry, 490
Wyckoff, Robert Leroy, 490
Yates, Elmer Elias, 491
Yeats, Charles, Jr., 492
Yomine, Frank Peter, 492
Young, Donald George, 538
Young, Eric Reed, 492
Young, Glendale Rex, 493
Young, Jay Wesley, 493
Young, Vivan Louis, 493
Zadik, Edward Albert, 493
Zeiler, John Virgel, 494
Ziembricke, Steve Anthony, 494
Zimmerman, Fred, 494
Zimmerman, Lloyd McDonald, 495
Zwarun, Michael, Jr., 495